Concise

Qu... W9-AXC-286

Susan Ratcliffe is an Associate Editor for Oxford
Quotations Dictionaries. Her previous publica-
tions include the *Little Oxford Dictionary of Quotations*, the *Oxford Dictionary of Phrase, Saying, and
Quotation*, and the *Oxford Dictionary of Quotations
by Subject*.

.OCT - - 2006

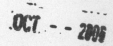

Concise
Oxford Dictionary of
Quotations

FIFTH EDITION

Edited by
SUSAN RATCLIFFE

OXFORD
UNIVERSITY PRESS

Great Clarendon Street, Oxford OX2 6DP

Oxford University Press is a department of the University of Oxford.
It furthers the University's objective of excellence in research, scholarship,
and education by publishing worldwide in

Oxford New York

Auckland Cape Town Dar es Salaam Hong Kong Karachi
Kuala Lumpur Madrid Melbourne Mexico City Nairobi
New Delhi Shanghai Taipei Toronto

With offices in

Argentina Austria Brazil Chile Czech Republic France Greece
Guatemala Hungary Italy Japan Poland Portugal Singapore
South Korea Switzerland Thailand Turkey Ukraine Vietnam

Oxford is a registered trade mark of Oxford University Press
in the UK and in certain other countries

Published in the United States
by Oxford University Press Inc., New York

First edition published 1964
Second edition published 1981
Third edition published 1993
Revised third edition published 1997
Fourth edition published 2001
Revised fourth edition published 2003
Fifth edition published 2006

British Library Cataloguing in Publication Data
Data available

Library of Congress Cataloging in Publication Data
Data available

ISBN-13: 978-0-19-861417-3
ISBN-10: 0-19-861417-9

1

Typeset by Interactive Sciences Ltd, Gloucester
Printed in Great Britain
on acid-free paper by
Clays Ltd, St Ives plc

CONTENTS

INTRODUCTION

This fifth edition of the *Concise Oxford Dictionary of Quotations* is based on the latest (sixth) edition of the *Oxford Dictionary of Quotations*, published in 2004. With yet more quotations from a wider range of sources to choose among, the task of abridging for the present text might seem to have been an even greater challenge than for previous editions.

Fortunately for this edition we have had the invaluable assistance of a new resource: the Oxford English Corpus, a database of examples of English speech and writing. The Corpus was set up as a tool for the OUP dictionaries programme, and while it was designed primarily to examine the frequency of single words and the contexts in which they are used, it has also proved possible to use it to establish a guide to the frequency of occurrence of individual quotations. For the first time, therefore, we have been able to identify on a more statistical and scientific basis those quotations which are most likely to be encountered. Since these quotations are those about which the reader is most likely to enquire, that information has been of great value in preparing this book.

Reassuringly, in many cases the frequency analysis has simply confirmed what was already received wisdom: Shakespeare and the Bible are indeed widely quoted. But it was particularly noticeable that while quotations from well-known plays such as *Macbeth* or *Hamlet* scored very highly, quotations from the minor plays were used much less. This reflected a general trend: that the words of famous people were more frequently quoted than those of obscure authors. Clearly people want to be able to say 'As Churchill said . . .', and expect their audience to identify the speaker without having to embark on further explanation. Traditional literary figures such as Jane Austen, Dickens, and Tennyson retain their place, and are joined by more quotations from major scientists, artists, and politicians. Areas which proved to be generally under-represented included songs and poetry, and, interestingly, North American culture. It is also clear that what might be described as inspirational and motivational quotations are particularly popular. Material from the seventeenth and eighteenth century (apart from the very famous authors), minor nineteenth-century poets, the earlier part of the twentieth century in general, and people of all periods who are no longer well-known had a much lower recognition factor. As a result, this book is very different from the previous edition, with more than 20% new material, and it should provide a closer guide to the quotations which are actually being used today than any other dictionary.

New quotations inherited from the latest sixth edition of the *Oxford Dictionary of Quotations* include 'Integrity has no need of rules' (Albert Camus), 'Courage is the price that Life exacts for granting peace' (Amelia Earhart), 'Nothing great was ever achieved without enthusiasm' (R. W. Emerson), and 'Trifles make perfection, and perfection is no trifle' (Michelangelo). New North American material ranges from the recent, such as the actor Michael J. Fox on his fight against Parkinson's disease 'It's all about losing your brain without losing your mind' and President George W. Bush on the 'axis of evil', to classic items such as William Lyon Mackenzie King's 'Not necessarily conscription, but conscription if necessary' and Mark Twain's 'Few things are harder to put up with than the annoyance of a good example'. Some newer quotations have come into prominence since the publication of the *Oxford Dictionary of Quotations*, and so you will find here amongst others John Prescott's comment on what happens when 'plates appear to be moving' and Donald Rumsfeld's remark on looting in Iraq: 'Stuff happens'.

Whether you believe with Thomas Carlyle that 'A good book is the purest essence of a human soul' or merely agree with Pliny that there is 'no book so bad that some good could not be got out of it' I hope you will find something here for you. It is true that the humorist Robert Benchley said that 'The surest way to make a monkey of a man is to quote him', but perhaps it is better to remember that the Czech dramatist Václav Havel celebrated inhabiting a system where 'words can prove mightier than ten military divisions'.

Acknowledgements

The book depends heavily on the work done for the *Oxford Dictionary of Quotations*, and thanks are due to all those who contributed to the sixth edition. I should like to thank especially Elizabeth Knowles, Publishing Manager for Oxford Quotations Dictionaries, for help and advice throughout the editing of this volume, and James McCracken, Project Manager, English Dictionaries, for setting up and advising on the Corpus software.

SUSAN RATCLIFFE
Oxford 2005

HOW TO USE THE DICTIONARY

The sequence of entries is by alphabetical order of author, usually by surname but with occasional exceptions such as members of royal families (e.g. **Diana, Princess of Wales** and **Elizabeth II**), or authors known by a pseudonym ('**Saki**') or nickname (**Caligula**). Authors' names are given in their most familiar form, so that we have **Harold Macmillan** (not Lord Stockton), **George Eliot** (not Mary Ann Evans), and **H. G. Wells** (not Herbert George Wells). Collections such as **Anonymous** and the **Bible** are included in the alphabetical author sequence.

Author names are followed by dates of birth and death (where known) and brief descriptions. Cross-references are made to other entries in which the author appears, e.g. '*see also* **Lennon and McCartney**'. Within each author entry, quotations are separated by literary form: novels, plays, poems, with the form for which the author is best known taking precedence. Quotations from diaries, letters, and speeches are given in chronological order, and usually follow the literary or published works quoted. Quotations from secondary sources which can be dated within the author's lifetime are arranged in sequence with diary entries and letters; undated and attributed quotations are arranged in alphabetical order of quotation text at the end of the entry.

Contextual information regarded as essential to a full appreciation of the quotation precedes the text in an italicized note; information providing amplification follows the text. Each quotation is accompanied by a bibliographical note of the source from which it is taken.

Cross-references to specific quotations are used to direct the reader to another related item. In each case a reference is given to the author's name, followed by the page number and then the unique quotation number on that page ('see **Tennyson** 311:22'). In some cases, the quotation may exist in two forms, or may depend on an earlier source not quoted in its own right; when this happens, the subordinate quotation is given directly below the quotation to which it relates. Authors who have their own entries are typographically distinguished by the use of bold ('*of William **Shakespeare***', '*by Mae **West***') in context or source notes.

Index
The most significant words from each quotation appear in the keyword index, allowing individual quotations to be traced. Both the keywords, and the context lines following each keyword, are

in strict alphabetical order. Singular and plural nouns (with their possessive forms) are grouped separately: for 'some old lover's ghost' see **lover**; for 'at lovers' perjuries' see **lovers**. Variant forms of common words (fresshe/fresh, luve/love) are grouped under a single heading: **fresh**, **love**. References are to the author's name (usually in abbreviated form, as AUST for Jane Austen) followed by the page number and the unique number of the quotation on the page. Thus AUST 19:18 means quotation number 18 on page 19, in the entry for Jane Austen.

Sayings and Slogans
The appendix 'Sayings and Slogans' covers an extensive range of sayings including advertising and political slogans, catchphrases, film lines, newspaper headlines, and misquotations. Quotations in these sections are arranged alphabetically, and are not indexed.

Diane Abbott 1953–
British Labour politician

1 Being an MP is the sort of job all working-class parents want for their children—clean, indoors and no heavy lifting.
   in *Independent* 18 January 1994

Peter Abelard 1079–1142
French scholar, theologian, and philosopher

2 *O quanta qualia sunt illa sabbata,*
Quae semper celebrat superna curia.
O what their joy and glory must be,
Those endless sabbaths the blessèd ones see!
   Hymnarius Paraclitensis bk. 1 (tr J. M. Neale, 1854)

Accius 170–*c*.86 BC
Roman poet and dramatist

3 *Oderint, dum metuant.*
Let them hate, so long as they fear.
   from *Atreus*, in Seneca *Dialogues* bks. 3–5

Goodman Ace 1899–1982
American humorist

4 TV—a clever contraction derived from the words Terrible Vaudeville . . . we call it a medium because nothing's well done.
   letter to Groucho Marx, in *The Groucho Letters* (1967)

Dean Acheson 1893–1971
American politician

5 I will undoubtedly have to seek what is happily known as gainful employment, which I am glad to say does not describe holding public office.
   in *Time* 22 December 1952

6 Great Britain has lost an empire and has not yet found a role.
   speech at the Military Academy, West Point, 5 December 1962

7 A memorandum is written not to inform the reader but to protect the writer.
   in *Wall Street Journal* 8 September 1977

Lord Acton 1834–1902
British historian

8 Liberty is not a means to a higher political end. It is itself the highest political end.
   The History of Freedom in Antiquity (1907), lecture delivered 26 February 1877

9 Power tends to corrupt and absolute power corrupts absolutely.
   letter to Bishop Mandell Creighton, 3 April 1887; see **Pitt** 264:4

Abigail Adams 1744–1818
American letter writer

10 In the new code of laws which I suppose it will be necessary for you to make I desire you would remember the ladies . . . Do not put such unlimited power into the hands of the husbands. Remember all men would be tyrants if they could.
   letter to John Adams, 31 March 1776; see **Defoe** 111:20

11 These are times in which a genius would wish to live. It is not in the still calm of life, or the repose of a pacific station, that great characters are formed . . . Great necessities call out great virtues.
   letter to John Quincy Adams, 19 January 1780

Charles Francis Adams 1807–86
American lawyer and diplomat

12 It would be superfluous in me to point out to your lordship that this is war.
   of the situation in the United States during the American Civil War
   dispatch to Earl Russell, 5 September 1863

Douglas Adams 1952–2001
English science fiction writer

13 The Answer to the Great Question Of . . . Life, the Universe and Everything . . . [is] Forty-two.
   The Hitch Hiker's Guide to the Galaxy (1979) ch. 27

Frank Adams
and **Will M. Hough**

14 I wonder who's kissing her now.
   title of song (1909)

Franklin P. Adams 1881–1960
American journalist and humorist

15 When the political columnists say 'Every thinking man' they mean themselves, and when candidates appeal to 'Every intelligent voter' they mean everybody who is going to vote for them.
   Nods and Becks (1944)

16 Middle age . . . occurs when you are too young to take up golf and too old to rush up to the net.
   Nods and Becks (1944)

17 Elections are won by men and women chiefly because most people vote against somebody rather than for somebody.
   Nods and Becks (1944); see **Fields** 135:21

Henry Brooks Adams 1838–1918
American historian

18 Politics, as a practice, whatever its professions, has always been the systematic organization of hatreds.
   The Education of Henry Adams (1907) ch. 1

19 All experience is an arch to build upon.
   The Education of Henry Adams (1907) ch. 6; see **Tennyson** 335:3

20 A friend in power is a friend lost.
   The Education of Henry Adams (1907) ch. 7

21 Chaos often breeds life, when order breeds habit.
   The Education of Henry Adams (1907) ch. 16

22 A teacher affects eternity; he can never tell where his influence stops.
   The Education of Henry Adams (1907) ch. 20

1 No one means all he says, and yet very few say all they mean, for words are slippery and thought is viscous.
   The Education of Henry Adams (1907) ch. 31

John Adams 1735–1826
American statesman, 2nd President of the US

2 The law, in all vicissitudes of government ... will preserve a steady undeviating course ... On the one hand it is inexorable to the cries of the prisoners; on the other it is deaf, deaf as an adder to the clamours of the populace.
   argument in defence of the British soldiers in the Boston Massacre Trials, 4 December 1770; see **Sidney** 316:10

3 There is danger from all men. The only maxim of a free government ought to be to trust no man living with power to endanger the public liberty.
   Notes for an Oration at Braintree (Spring 1772), in *Diary and Autobiography of John Adams* vol. 2 (1960)

4 A government of laws, and not of men.
   in *Boston Gazette* (1774) no. 7; later incorporated in the Massachusetts Constitution (1780); see **Ford** 139:7

5 In politics the middle way is none at all.
   letter to Horatio Gates, 23 March 1776

6 I must study politics and war that my sons may have liberty to study mathematics and philosophy. My sons ought to study mathematics and philosophy, geography, natural history, naval architecture, navigation, commerce, and agriculture, in order to give their children a right to study painting, poetry, music, architecture, statuary, tapestry, and porcelain.
   letter to Abigail Adams, 12 May 1780

7 My country has in its wisdom contrived for me the most insignificant office that ever the invention of man contrived or his imagination conceived.
   of the vice-presidency
   letter to Abigail Adams, 19 December 1793

8 Liberty cannot be preserved without a general knowledge among the people, who have a right ... and a desire to know; but besides this, they have a right, an indisputable, unalienable, indefeasible, divine right to that most dreaded and envied kind of knowledge, I mean of the characters and conduct of their rulers.
   A Dissertation on the Canon and Feudal Law (1765), in M. J. Kline (ed.) *Papers of John Adams* vol. 1 (1977)

9 The jaws of power are always opened to devour.
   A Dissertation on the Canon and the Feudal Law (1765)

10 The happiness of society is the end of government.
   Thoughts on Government (1776)

11 Fear is the foundation of most governments.
   Thoughts on Government (1776)

John Quincy Adams 1767–1848
American statesman, 6th President of the US

12 Think of your forefathers! Think of your posterity!
   Oration at Plymouth 22 December 1802

13 *Fiat justitia, pereat coelum* [Let justice be done, though heaven fall]. My toast would be, may our country be always successful, but whether successful or otherwise, always right.
   letter to John Adams, 1 August 1816; see **Decatur** 111:16, **Schurz** 286:18, **Watson** 351:15

14 Wherever the standard of freedom and Independence has been or shall be unfurled, there will her heart, her benedictions and her prayers be. But she [America] goes not abroad in search of monsters to destroy.
   speech to House of Representatives, 4 July 1821

Samuel Adams 1722–1803
American revolutionary leader

15 What a glorious morning is this.
   on hearing gunfire at Lexington, 19 April 1775; traditionally quoted as, 'What a glorious morning for America'
   J. K. Hosmer *Samuel Adams* (1886) ch. 19

16 A nation of shopkeepers are very seldom so disinterested.
   Oration in Philadelphia 1 August 1776 (the authenticity of this publication is doubtful); see **Napoleon** 248:7, **Smith** 318:5

Sarah Flower Adams 1805–48
English hymn-writer

17 Nearer, my God, to thee,
   Nearer to thee!
   'Nearer My God to Thee' in W. G. Fox *Hymns and Anthems* (1841)

Harold Adamson 1906–80
American songwriter

18 Comin' in on a wing and a pray'r.
   words derived from the contemporary comment of a war pilot, speaking from a disabled plane to ground control
   title of song (1943)

Joseph Addison 1672–1719
English poet, dramatist, and essayist

19 And, pleased th' Almighty's orders to perform,
   Rides in the whirlwind, and directs the storm.
   The Campaign (1705) l. 291

20 'Tis not in mortals to command success,
   But we'll do more, Sempronius; we'll deserve it.
   Cato (1713) act 1, sc. 2, l. 43

21 The woman that deliberates is lost.
   Cato (1713) act 4, sc. 1, l. 31

1 What pity is it
That we can die but once to serve our
country!
Cato (1713) act 4, sc. 1, l. 258

2 When vice prevails, and impious men bear
sway,
The post of honour is a private station.
Cato (1713) act 4, sc. 1, l. 320

3 From hence, let fierce contending nations
know
What dire effects from civil discord flow.
Cato (1713) act 5, sc. 1, closing lines

4 Music, the greatest good that mortals know,
And all of heaven we have below.
'A Song for St Cecilia's Day' (1694)

5 Sir Roger told them, with the air of a man
who would not give his judgement rashly,
that much might be said on both sides.
The Spectator no. 122 (20 July 1711)

6 I have often thought, says Sir Roger, it
happens very well that Christmas should
fall out in the Middle of Winter.
The Spectator no. 269 (8 January 1712)

7 The spacious firmament on high,
With all the blue ethereal sky,
And spangled heavens, a shining frame,
Their great Original proclaim.
The Spectator no. 465 (23 August 1712) 'Ode'

8 A woman seldom asks advice before she has
bought her wedding clothes.
The Spectator no. 475 (4 September 1712)

9 If we may believe our logicians, man is
distinguished from all other creatures by
the faculty of laughter.
The Spectator no. 494 (26 September 1712)

10 'We are always doing', says he, 'something
for Posterity, but I would fain see Posterity
do something for us.'
The Spectator no. 583 (20 August 1714)

11 See in what peace a Christian can die.
dying words to his stepson Lord Warwick
Edward Young *Conjectures on Original Composition*
(1759)

George Ade 1866–1944
American humorist and dramatist

12 After being turned down by numerous
publishers, he had decided to write for
posterity.
Fables in Slang (1900)

13 It is no time for mirth and laughter,
The cold, grey dawn of the morning after.
The Sultan of Sulu (1903) act 2

14 'Whom are you?' he asked, for he had
attended business college.
'The Steel Box' in *Chicago Record* 16 March 1898

Konrad Adenauer 1876–1967
German statesman

15 A thick skin is a gift from God.
in *New York Times* 30 December 1959

Adi Granth *see* Sikh Scriptures

Alfred Adler 1870–1937
Austrian psychologist and psychiatrist

16 The truth is often a terrible weapon of
aggression. It is possible to lie, and even to
murder, for the truth.
The Problems of Neurosis (1929) ch. 2

Polly Adler 1900–62
American writer

17 A house is not a home.
title of book (1954)

Theodor Adorno 1903–69
*German philosopher, sociologist, and
musicologist*

18 It is barbarous to write a poem after
Auschwitz.
I. Buruma *Wages of Guilt* (1994)

Aeschylus *c.*525–456 BC
Greek tragedian

19 Hell to ships, hell to men, hell to cities.
*of Helen (literally 'Ship-destroyer, man-destroyer,
city-destroyer')*
Agamemnon

20 Countless chuckles of the waves of the sea.
Prometheus Bound

21 Everyone's quick to blame the alien.
The Suppliant Maidens

Herbert Agar 1897–1980
American poet and writer

22 The truth which makes men free is for the
most part the truth which men prefer not to
hear.
A Time for Greatness (1942) ch. 7; see **Bible** 48:35

James Agate 1877–1947
British drama critic and novelist

23 My mind is not a bed to be made and remade.
diary, 9 June 1943

Agathon b. *c.*445–
Greek tragic poet

24 Even a god cannot change the past.
*literally, 'The one thing which even God cannot do
is to make undone what has been done'*
Aristotle *Nicomachaean Ethics* bk. 6

Spiro T. Agnew 1918–96
American Republican politician

25 I didn't say I wouldn't go into ghetto areas.
I've been in many of them and to some
extent I would have to say this: If you've
seen one city slum you've seen them all.
in *Detroit Free Press* 19 October 1968; see **Burton**
78:6

26 In the United States today, we have more
than our share of the nattering nabobs of
negativism.
speech in San Diego, 11 September 1970

Bertie Ahern 1951-
Irish Fianna Fáil statesman, Taoiseach since 1997

1 It is a day we should treasure. Today is about
the promise of a bright future, a day when
we hope a line will be drawn under the
bloody past.
on the Good Friday agreement
   in *Guardian* 11 April 1998

Arthur Campbell Ainger
1841-1919
English schoolmaster

2 God is working his purpose out as year
   succeeds to year;
God is working his purpose out and the time
   is drawing near;
Nearer and nearer draws the time, the time
   that shall surely be,
When the earth shall be filled with the glory
   of God as the waters cover the sea.
   'God is working his purpose out' (1894 hymn)

Jonathan Aitken 1942-
British Conservative politician

3 If it falls to me to start a fight to cut out the
cancer of bent and twisted journalism in our
country with the simple sword of truth and
the trusty shield of British fair play, so be it.
   statement, London, 10 April 1995, in *The Times*
   11 April 1995

Max Aitken *see* Lord Beaverbrook

Zoë Akins 1886-1958
American poet and dramatist

4 The Greeks had a word for it.
   title of play (1930)

Alain (Émile-Auguste Chartier)
1868-1951
French poet and philosopher

5 *Rien n'est plus dangereux qu'une idée, quand on
n'a qu'une idée.*
Nothing is more dangerous than an idea,
when you have only one idea.
   Propos sur la religion (1938) no. 74

Edward Albee 1928-
American dramatist

6 Who's afraid of Virginia Woolf?
   title of play (1962)

Alcuin c.735-804
English scholar and theologian

7 *Nec audiendi qui solent dicere, Vox populi, vox
Dei, quum tumultuositas vulgi semper insaniae
proxima sit.*
And those people should not be listened to
who keep saying the voice of the people is
the voice of God, since the riotousness of
the crowd is always very close to madness.
   letter 164 in *Works* (1863) vol. 1

Richard Aldington 1892-1962
English poet, novelist, and biographer

8 Patriotism is a lively sense of collective
responsibility. Nationalism is a silly cock
crowing on its own dunghill.
   The Colonel's Daughter (1931) pt. 1, ch. 6

Henry Aldrich 1647-1710
English scholar

9 If all be true that I do think,
There are five reasons we should drink;
Good wine—a friend—or being dry—
Or lest we should be by and by—
Or any other reason why.
   'Reasons for Drinking' (1689)

'Buzz' Aldrin 1930-
American astronaut

10 Beautiful! Beautiful! Magnificent desolation.
of the lunar landscape
   on the first moon walk, 20 July 1969

Alexander the Great 356-323 BC
Greek monarch, King of Macedon from 336 BC
see also **Diogenes** 116:19

11 If I were not Alexander, I would be
Diogenes.
   Plutarch *Parallel Lives* 'Alexander' ch. 14, sect. 3

12 Is it not worthy of tears that, when the
number of worlds is infinite, we have not
yet become lords of a single one?
*when asked why he wept on hearing from
Anaxarchus that there was an infinite number of
worlds*
   Plutarch *Moralia* 'On Tranquillity of the Mind'

Alexander II ('the Liberator')1818-81
Russian monarch, Tsar from 1855

13 Better to abolish serfdom from above than
to wait till it begins to abolish itself from
below.
   speech in Moscow, 30 March 1856

Cecil Frances Alexander 1818-95
Irish poet and hymn-writer

14 All things bright and beautiful,
All creatures great and small,
All things wise and wonderful,
The Lord God made them all.
   'All Things Bright and Beautiful' (1848)

15 The rich man in his castle,
The poor man at his gate,
God made them, high or lowly,
And ordered their estate.
   'All Things Bright and Beautiful' (1848)

16 Once in royal David's city
Stood a lowly cattle-shed.
   'Once in royal David's city' (1848)

17 I bind unto myself to-day
The strong name of the Trinity,
By invocation of the same
The Three in One and One in Three.
   'St Patrick's Breastplate' (1889); see **Patrick**
   260:12

18 There is a green hill far away,

Without a city wall.
'There is a green hill far away' (1848)

William Alexander, Lord Stirling c.1567–1640
Scottish poet and courtier

1 The weaker sex, to piety more prone.
'Doomsday' 5th Hour (1637)

Alfonso 'the Wise' 1221–84
Spanish monarch, King of Castile and León from 1252

2 Had I been present at the Creation, I would have given some useful hints for the better ordering of the universe.
on studying the Ptolemaic system
attributed

Nelson Algren 1909–
American novelist

3 A walk on the wild side.
title of novel (1956)

4 Never play cards with a man called Doc. Never eat at a place called Mom's. Never sleep with a woman whose troubles are worse than your own.
in *Newsweek* 2 July 1956

Ali ibn-Abi-Talib c.602–661
Arab ruler, fourth Islamic caliph

5 He who has a thousand friends has not a friend to spare,
And he who has one enemy will meet him everywhere.
A Hundred Sayings

Muhammad Ali (Cassius Clay) 1942–
American boxer

6 I'm the greatest.
adopted as his catchphrase from 1962, in *Louisville Times* 16 November 1962

7 Float like a butterfly, sting like a bee.
summary of his boxing strategy (probably originated by his aide Drew 'Bundini' Brown)
G. Sullivan *Cassius Clay Story* (1964) ch. 8

8 I ain't got no quarrel with the Viet Cong.
refusing to be drafted to fight in Vietnam
at a press conference in Miami, Florida, February 1966

Abbé d'Allainval 1700–53
French dramatist

9 *L'embarras des richesses.*
The embarrassment of riches.
title of comedy (1726)

Fred Allen (John Florence Sullivan) 1894–1956
American humorist

10 Committee—a group of men who individually can do nothing but as a group decide that nothing can be done.
attributed

Lewis Allen (Abel Meeropol)
American teacher

11 Southern trees bear strange fruit,
Blood on the leaves and blood at the root,
Black bodies swinging in the Southern breeze,
Strange fruit hanging from the poplar trees.
'Strange Fruit' (1939), adapted and sung by Billie **Holiday**

Woody Allen 1935–
American film director, writer, and actor

12 Don't knock masturbation. It's sex with someone I love.
Annie Hall (1977 film, with Marshall Brickman)

13 Is sex dirty? Only if it's done right.
Everything You Always Wanted to Know about Sex (1972 film)

14 A fast word about oral contraception. I asked a girl to go to bed with me and she said 'no'.
Woody Allen Volume Two (Colpix CP 488) side 4, band 6

15 It's not that I'm afraid to die. I just don't want to be there when it happens.
Death (1975)

16 If only God would give me some clear sign! Like making a large deposit in my name at a Swiss bank.
'Selections from the Allen Notebooks' in *New Yorker* 5 November 1973

17 On bisexuality: It immediately doubles your chances for a date on Saturday night.
in *New York Times* 1 December 1975

18 I don't want to achieve immortality through my work . . . I want to achieve it through not dying.
Eric Lax *Woody Allen and his Comedy* (1975) ch. 12

William Allingham 1824–89
Irish poet

19 Up the airy mountain,
Down the rushy glen,
We daren't go a-hunting,
For fear of little men.
'The Fairies' (1850)

Joseph Alsop 1910–89
American journalist

20 Gratitude, like love, is never a dependable international emotion.
in *Observer* 30 November 1952

Robert Altman 1922–
American film director

21 What's a cult? It just means not enough people to make a minority.
in *Guardian* 11 April 1981

St Ambrose c.339–397
French-born bishop of Milan

22 *Ubi Petrus, ibi ergo ecclesia.*
Where Peter is, there must be the Church.
'Explanatio psalmi 40' in *Corpus Scriptorum Ecclesiasticorum Latinorum* (1919) vol. 64

1 When I go to Rome, I fast on Saturday, but
here [Milan] I do not. Do you also follow the
custom of whatever church you attend, if
you do not want to give or receive scandal.
St Augustine: Letters vol. 1 (tr. Sister W. Parsons,
1951) 'Letter 54 to Januarius' (AD *c.*400)

Leo Amery 1873–1955
British Conservative politician

2 Speak for England.
to Arthur Greenwood in the House of
Commons, 2 September 1939

3 I will quote certain other words. I do it with
great reluctance, because I am speaking of
those who are old friends and associates of
mine, but they are words which, I think, are
applicable to the present situation. This is
what Cromwell said to the Long Parliament
when he thought it was no longer fit to
conduct the affairs of the nation: 'You have
sat too long here for any good you have
been doing. Depart, I say, and let us have
done with you. In the name of God, go.'
speech, House of Commons, 7 May 1940; see
Cromwell 107:11

Fisher Ames 1758–1808
American politician

4 A monarchy is a merchantman which sails
well, but will sometimes strike on a rock,
and go to the bottom; whilst a republic is a
raft which would never sink, but then your
feet are always in the water.
attributed to Ames, speaking in the House of
Representatives, 1795, but not traced in Ames's
speeches

Kingsley Amis 1922–95
English novelist and poet

5 His mouth had been used as a latrine by
some small creature of the night, and then
as its mausoleum.
Lucky Jim (1953) ch. 6

6 We men have got love well weighed up; our
stuff
Can get by without it.
Women don't seem to think that's good
enough;
They write about it.
'A Bookshop Idyll' (1956)

7 More will mean worse.
on expanding universities
in *Encounter* July 1960

8 If you can't annoy somebody with what you
write, I think there's little point in writing.
in *Radio Times* 1 May 1971

Anacharsis
Scythian prince of the 6th century BC

9 Written laws are like spiders' webs; they
will catch, it is true, the weak and poor, but
would be torn in pieces by the rich and
powerful.
Plutarch *Parallel Lives* 'Solon' bk. 5, sect. 2; see
Swift 328:8

Anatolius
8th-century hymn-writer

10 Fierce was the wild billow,
Dark was the night;
Oars laboured heavily,
Foam glimmered white;
Trembled the mariners,
Peril was nigh:
Then said the God of God,
'Peace! it is I.'
'Fierce was the wild billow' (tr. John Mason
Neale, 1862)

Hans Christian Andersen 1805–75
Danish novelist and writer of fairy stories

11 The Emperor's new clothes.
title of story in *Danish Fairy Legends and Tales*
(1846)

12 'But the Emperor has nothing on at all!'
cried a little child.
Danish Fairy Legends and Tales (1846) 'The
Emperor's New Clothes'

13 It doesn't matter about being born in a
duckyard, as long as you're hatched from a
swan's egg!
Danish Fairy Legends and Tales (1846) 'The Ugly
Duckling'

14 And so they could see she was a real
princess, because she had felt the pea
through twenty mattresses and twenty
eiderdowns.
Tales Told for Children (1835) 'The Princess and
the Pea'

Maxwell Anderson 1888–1959
American dramatist

15 But it's a long, long while
From May to December;
And the days grow short
When you reach September.
'September Song' (1938 song)

Maxwell Anderson 1888–1959
and **Lawrence Stallings** 1894–1968
American dramatists

16 What price glory?
title of play (1924)

Robert Anderson 1917–
American dramatist

17 Tea and sympathy.
title of play (1957)

Lancelot Andrewes 1555–1626
English preacher and writer of sermons

18 It was no summer progress. A cold coming
they had of it, at this time of the year; just,
the worst time of the year, to take a journey,
and specially a long journey, in. The ways
deep, the weather sharp, the days short, the
sun farthest off *in solstitio brumali*, the very
dead of Winter.
Of the Nativity (1622) Sermon 15; see **Eliot** 128:25

Norman Angell 1872–1967
English pacifist

1 The great illusion.
on the futility of war
title of book (1910), first published as 'Europe's optical illusion' (1909)

Maya Angelou 1928–
American writer

2 Children's talent to endure stems from their ignorance of alternatives.
I Know Why The Caged Bird Sings (1969) ch.17

3 You may shoot me with your words,
You may cut me with your eyes,
You may kill me with your hatefulness,
But still, like air, I'll rise.
'Still I Rise' (1978)

Paul Anka 1941–
Canadian singer and composer

4 I've lived a life that's full, I've travelled each and ev'ry highway
And more, much more than this. I did it my way.
'My Way' (1969 song)

Anonymous
English

5 An abomination unto the Lord, but a very present help in time of trouble.
definition of a lie
an amalgamation of Proverbs 12.22 and Psalms 46.1, often attributed to Adlai **Stevenson**; Bill Adler *The Stevenson Wit* (1966); see **Bible** 38:21, **Book of Common Prayer** 63:4

6 Action this day.
annotation as used by Winston Churchill at the Admiralty in 1940

7 All human beings are born free and equal in dignity and rights.
Universal Declaration of Human Rights (1948) article 1

8 All present and correct.
King's Regulations (Army) Report of the Orderly Sergeant to the Officer of the Day

9 And they lived happily ever after.
traditional ending to a fairy story
recorded (with slight variations) from the 1850s

10 Any officer who shall behave in a scandalous manner, unbecoming the character of an officer and a gentleman shall . . . be CASHIERED.
Articles of War (1872) 'Disgraceful Conduct' Article 79; the Naval Discipline Act, 10 August 1860, Article 24, uses the words 'conduct unbecoming the character of an Officer'

11 Appeal from Philip drunk to Philip sober.
paraphrase of the words of an unidentified woman in Valerius Maximus *Facta ac Dicta Memorabilia* (AD c.32) bk. 6, ch. 2

12 Are we downhearted? No!
expression much taken up by British soldiers during the First World War

13 Betwixt the stirrup and the ground
Mercy I asked, mercy I found.
epitaph for 'A gentleman falling off his horse [who] brake his neck'
William Camden *Remains Concerning Britain* (1605) 'Epitaphs'

14 Bigamy is having one husband too many. Monogamy is the same.
Erica Jong *Fear of Flying* (1973) ch. 1 (epigraph)

15 The cloud of unknowing.
title of mystical prose work (14th century)

16 A committee is a group of the unwilling, chosen from the unfit, to do the unnecessary.
various attributions (origin unknown)

17 A community in which power, wealth and opportunity are in the hands of the many not the few, where the rights we enjoy reflect the duties we owe . . . in which the enterprise of the market and the rigour of competition are joined with the forces of partnership and cooperation.
revised Clause Four of the Labour Party constitution, passed at a special conference 29 April 1995; see **Anonymous** 11:13

18 A Company for carrying on an undertaking of Great Advantage, but no one to know what it is.
The South Sea Company Prospectus (1711), in Virginia Cowles *The Great Swindle* (1963) ch. 5

19 Conduct . . . to the prejudice of good order and military discipline.
Army Discipline and Regulation Act (1879) Section 40

20 A contingency for the space shuttle has been declared.
Mission Control in Houston indicating that contact with the space shuttle Columbia had been lost
in *Sunday Times* 2 February 2003

21 Dalton McGuinty: He's an evil reptilian kitten-eater from another planet.
Canadian Conservative press release attacking the Liberal leader (later premier) during September 2003 Ontario election campaign
in *London Free Press News* 13 September 2003

22 [Death is] nature's way of telling you to slow down.
American life insurance proverb, in *Newsweek* 25 April 1960

23 The difficult we do immediately; the impossible takes a little longer.
US Armed Forces' slogan; see **Calonne** 82:20, **Nansen** 247:20

24 Do not fold, spindle or mutilate.
instruction on punched cards (found in this form in the 1950s, and in differing forms from the 1930s)

25 Early one morning, just as the sun was rising,
I heard a maid sing in the valley below:
'Oh, don't deceive me; Oh, never leave me!
How could you use a poor maiden so?'
'Early One Morning' (traditional song)

1 The eternal triangle.

book review title, in *Daily Chronicle* 5 December 1907

2 Everyman, I will go with thee, and be thy guide,
In thy most need to go by thy side.

spoken by Knowledge
Everyman (c.1509–19) l. 522

3 Expletive deleted.

in *Submission of Recorded Presidential Conversations to the Committee on the Judiciary of the House of Representatives by President Richard M. Nixon* 30 April 1974, appendix 1

4 Exterminate . . . the treacherous English, walk over General French's contemptible little army.

*allegedly a copy of Orders issued by the Kaiser **Wilhelm II** but most probably fabricated by the British*

annexe to BEF [British Expeditionary Force] Routine Orders of 24 September 1914, in Arthur Ponsonby *Falsehood in Wartime* (1928) ch. 10; see **Cromwell** 107:14

5 Faster than a speeding bullet! . . . Look! Up in the sky! It's a bird! It's a plane! It's Superman! Yes, it's Superman! Strange visitor from another planet . . . Who can change the course of mighty rivers, bend steel in his bare hands, and who—disguised as Clark Kent, mild-mannered reporter for a great metropolitan newspaper—fights a never ending battle for truth, justice and the American way!

Superman (US radio show, 1940 onwards) preamble

6 Fifty million Frenchmen can't be wrong.

saying popular with American servicemen during the First World War; later associated with Mae **West** and Texas Guinan (1884–1933), it was also the title of a 1927 song by Billy Rose and Willie Raskin

7 From ghoulies and ghosties and long-leggety beasties
And things that go bump in the night,
Good Lord, deliver us!

'The Cornish or West Country Litany', in Francis T. Nettleinghame *Polperro Proverbs and Others* (1926) 'Pokerwork Panels'

8 From Moses to Moses there was none like unto Moses.

later inscription on the tomb of the Jewish scholar Moses **Maimonides** (1135–1204)

9 From the halls of Montezuma,
To the shores of Tripoli.

'The Marines' Hymn' (1847)

10 God be in my head,
And in my understanding . . .
God be in my mouth,
And in my speaking . . .
God be at my end,
And at my departing.

Sarum Missal (11th century)

11 God save our gracious king!
Long live our noble king!
God save the king!
Send him victorious,
Happy, and glorious,
Long to reign over us:
God save the king!

'God save the King', attributed to various authors of the mid eighteenth century, including Henry **Carey**; Jacobite variants, such as James Hogg 'The King's Anthem' also exist

12 Go to jail. Go directly to jail. Do not pass go. Do not collect £200.

instructions on 'Community Chest' card in the game 'Monopoly'; invented by Charles Brace Darrow (1889–1967) in 1931

13 Greensleeves was all my joy,
Greensleeves was my delight,
Greensleeves was my heart of gold,
And who but Lady Greensleeves?

'A new Courtly Sonnet of the Lady Greensleeves, to the new tune of "Greensleeves" ', in *A Handful of Pleasant Delights* (1584)

14 Here lies Fred,
Who was alive and is dead:
Had it been his father,
I had much rather;
Had it been his brother,
Still better than another . . .
But since 'tis only Fred,
Who was alive and is dead,—
There's no more to be said.

*of Frederick Louis, Prince of Wales (1707–1751), son of **George II** and **Caroline** of Ansbach*
Horace Walpole *Memoirs of George II* (1847) vol. 1

15 Here's tae us; wha's like us?
Gey few, and they're a' deid.

Scottish toast, probably of 19th-century origin; the first line appears in T. W. H. Crosland *The Unspeakable Scot* (1902), and various versions of the second line are current

16 He was her man, but he done her wrong.

'Frankie and Albert', in John Huston *Frankie and Johnny* (1930) (St Louis ballad later better known as 'Frankie and Johnny')

17 How different, how very different from the home life of our own dear Queen!

comment overheard at a performance of Cleopatra by Sarah Bernhardt
Irvin S. Cobb *A Laugh a Day* (1924) (probably apocryphal)

18 Gode sir pray ich ye
for of saynte charite,
come ant daunce wyt me,
in irlaunde.

fourteenth century

19 If it moves, salute it; if it doesn't move, pick it up; and if you can't pick it up, paint it.

1940s saying, in Paul Dickson *The Official Rules* (1978)

20 If you really want to make a million . . . the quickest way is to start your own religion.

previously attributed to L. Ron Hubbard (1911–86) in B. Corydon and L. Ron Hubbard Jr. *L. Ron Hubbard* (1987), but attribution subsequently rejected by L. Ron Hubbard Jr., who also dissociated himself from this book

1 I'll go no more a-roving
With you fair maid.
   'A-roving' (traditional song)

2 I'll sing you twelve O.
Green grow the rushes O . . .
One is one and all alone
And ever more shall be so.
   'The Dilly Song'; see **Burns** 76:28

3 I'm armed with more than complete
steel—The justice of my quarrel.
   Lust's Dominion (1657) act 4, sc. 3 (attributed to
   Marlowe, though of doubtful authorship)

4 She's the most disthressful country that iver
yet was seen,
For they're hangin' men an' women for the
wearin' o' the Green.
   of Ireland
   'The Wearin' o' the Green' (*c.*1795 ballad)

5 It became necessary to destroy the town to
save it.
   statement by unidentified US Army Major,
   referring to Ben Tre in Vietnam
   in Associated Press Report, *New York Times* 8
   February 1968

6 Jacques Brel is alive and well and living in
Paris.
   title of musical entertainment (1968–72) which
   triggered numerous imitations

7 John Brown's body lies a mould'ring in the
grave,
His soul is marching on.
   inspired by the execution of the abolitionist John
   Brown, *after the raid on Harper's Ferry, on 2*
   December 1859
   song (1861), variously attributed to Charles
   Sprague Hall, Henry Howard Brownell, and
   Thomas Brigham Bishop

8 The King over the Water.
   Jacobite toast (18th-century)

9 Liberty is always unfinished business.
   title of 36th Annual Report of the American
   Civil Liberties Union, 1 July 1955–30 June 1956

10 Licensed to kill.
   popular description of the status of Secret
   Service agent James Bond, 007, in the novels of
   Ian **Fleming**

11 Lions led by donkeys.
   associated with British soldiers during the First
   World War
   attributed to Max Hoffman (1869–1927) in Alan
   Clark *The Donkeys* (1961); this attribution has not
   been traced elsewhere, and the phrase is of
   much earlier origin

12 Little Englanders.
   term applied to anti-imperialists
   in *Westminster Gazette* 1 August 1895; in *Pall Mall*
   Gazette 16 September 1884 the phrase 'believe
   in a little England' occurs

13 Lizzie Borden took an axe
And gave her mother forty whacks;

When she saw what she had done
She gave her father forty-one!
   after the acquittal of Lizzie Borden, in June 1893,
   from the charge of murdering her father and
   stepmother at Fall River, Massachusetts, on 4
   August 1892
   popular rhyme

14 Lloyd George knew my father,
My father knew Lloyd George.
   two-line comic song, sung to the tune of
   'Onward, Christian Soldiers' and possibly by
   Tommy Rhys Roberts (1910–75)

15 London, thou art the flower of cities all!
Gemme of all joy, jasper of jocunditie.
   'London' (poem of unknown authorship,
   previously attributed to William Dunbar,
   *c.*1465–*c.*1530) l. 16

16 Love me little, love me long,
Is the burden of my song.
   'Love me little, love me long' (1569–70)

17 Mademoiselle from Armenteers,
Hasn't been kissed for forty years,
Hinky, dinky, parley-voo.
   song of the First World War, variously
   attributed to Edward Rowland and to Harry
   Carlton

18 Matthew, Mark, Luke, and John,
The bed be blest that I lie on.
Four angels to my bed,
Four angels round my head,
One to watch, and one to pray,
And two to bear my soul away.
   traditional (the first two lines in Thomas Ady *A*
   Candle in the Dark, 1656)

19 Medicine for the soul.
   inscription on the library of Ramses II at Thebes
   (*c.*1292–1225 BC)
   Diodorus Siculus *Bibliotheca Historica* 60–30 BC

20 The ministry of all the talents.
   name given ironically to William Grenville's
   coalition of 1806, and also applied to later
   coalitions
   G. W. Cooke *The History of Party* (1837) vol. 3

21 My name is George Nathaniel Curzon,
I am a most superior person.
   of Lord **Curzon**
   The Masque of Balliol (*c.*1870), in W. G. Hiscock *The*
   Balliol Rhymes (1939); see **Beeching** 169:20

22 The nature of God is a circle of which the
centre is everywhere and the circumference
is nowhere.
   said to have been traced to a lost treatise of
   Empedocles; quoted in the *Roman de la Rose*, and
   by St Bonaventura in *Itinerarius Mentis in Deum*
   ch. 5, closing line

23 Now I lay me down to sleep;
I pray the Lord my soul to keep.
If I should die before I wake,
I pray the Lord my soul to take.
   first printed in a late edition of the *New England*
   Primer (1781)

24 O Death, where is thy sting-a-ling-a-ling,
O grave, thy victory?

The bells of Hell go ting-a-ling-a-ling
For you but not for me.
'For You But Not For Me', in S. Louis Guiraud (ed.) *Songs That Won the War* (1930); see **Bible** 51:4

1 O God, if there be a God, save my soul, if I have a soul!
prayer of a common soldier before the battle of Blenheim, 1704
in *Notes and Queries* vol. 173, no. 15 (9 October 1937); quoted in John Henry Newman *Apologia pro Vita Sua* (1864)

2 Oh, the comfort—the inexpressible comfort of feeling safe with a person, having neither to weigh thoughts, nor measure words, but pouring them all out, just as they are, chaff and grain together; knowing that a faithful hand will take and sift them—keep what is worth keeping— and with the breath of kindness blow the rest away.
19th century saying, often attributed to George **Eliot** or Dinah Mulock Craik (1826-87)

3 Once upon a time . . .
traditional opening to a story, especially a fairy story
Anonymous, recorded from 1595

4 It was resolved, That England was too pure an Air for Slaves to breathe in.
'In the 11th of Elizabeth' (17 November 1568-16 November 1569), in John Rushworth *Historical Collections* (1680-1722) vol. 2; see **Cowper** 105:24

5 O rare Ben Jonson.
inscription on the tomb of Ben **Jonson** in Westminster Abbey

6 O ye'll tak' the high road, and I'll tak' the low road,
And I'll be in Scotland afore ye,
But me and my true love will never meet again,
On the bonnie, bonnie banks o' Loch Lomon'.
'The Bonnie Banks of Loch Lomon'' (traditional song)

7 Peace, order, and good government.
British North America Act 1867 sect. 91, introduction

8 A place within the meaning of the Act.
usually taken to be a reference to the Betting Act 1853, sect. 2, which banned off-course betting on horse-races

9 Please do not shoot the pianist. He is doing his best.
printed notice in a dancing saloon
Oscar Wilde *Impressions of America* 'Leadville' (c.1882-3)

10 Please to remember the Fifth of November, Gunpowder Treason and Plot.
We know no reason why gunpowder treason
Should ever be forgot.
traditional rhyme on the Gunpowder Plot (1605)

11 Prudence is the other woman in Gordon's life.
of Gordon Brown as Chancellor
unidentified aide, quoted in BBC News online (Budget Briefing), 20 March 1998

12 Psychological flaws.
on which, according to an unnamed source, Gordon Brown needed to 'get a grip'
in *Observer* 18 January 1998; attributed to Alastair **Campbell** by Bernard **Ingham** in minutes of the Parliamentary Select Committee on Public Administration, 2 June 1998, but denied by Campbell in evidence to the Committee, 23 June 1998

13 The [*or* A] quick brown fox jumps over the lazy dog.
used by keyboarders to ensure that all letters of the alphabet are functioning
R. Hunter Middleton's introduction to *The Quick Brown Fox* (1945) by Richard H. Templeton Jr.

14 Raise the stone, and there thou shalt find me, cleave the wood and there am I.
Oxyrhynchus Papyri, in B. P. Grenfell and A. S. Hunt (eds.) *Sayings of Our Lord* (1897) Logion 5, l. 23

15 Rest in peace. The mistake shall not be repeated.
inscription on the cenotaph at Hiroshima, Japan

16 Say it ain't so, Joe.
'Shoeless' Joe Jackson and seven other Chicago players were charged with being bribed to lose the 1919 World Baseball Series
plea said to have been made by a boy as Jackson emerged from the hearing, September 1920

17 Science finds, industry applies, man conforms.
subtitle of guidebook to 1933 Chicago World's Fair

18 See the happy moron,
He doesn't give a damn,
I wish I were a moron,
My God! perhaps I am!
in *Eugenics Review* July 1929

19 Seven wealthy towns contend for HOMER dead
Through which the living HOMER begged his bread.
epilogue to *Aesop at Tunbridge; or, a Few Selected Fables in Verse* By No Person of Quality (1698); see **Heywood** 168:17

20 She was poor but she was honest . . .
Victim of a rich man's game . . .
It's the same the whole world over,
It's the poor wot gets the blame,
It's the rich wot gets the gravy.
Ain't it all a bleedin' shame?
'She was Poor but she was Honest' (sung by British soldiers in the First World War)

21 A soldier of the Great War known unto God.
standard epitaph for the unidentified dead of World War One
adopted by the War Graves Commission

22 So long as there shall but one hundred of us remain alive, we will never subject ourselves to the dominion of the English. For it is not glory, it is not riches, neither is it honour, but it is freedom alone that we fight and contend for, which no honest man will lose but with his life.

to the Pope, asserting the independence of Scotland

'Declaration of Arbroath', a letter sent by the Scottish Parliament, 6 April 1320

1 Some talk of Alexander, and some of Hercules;
Of Hector and Lysander, and such great names as these;
But of all the world's brave heroes, there's none that can compare
With a tow, row, row, row, row, row, for the British Grenadier.

'The British Grenadiers' (traditional song)

2 So much chewing gum for the eyes.

small boy's definition of certain television programmes

James Beasley Simpson *Best Quotes of '50, '55, '56* (1957)

3 So on the Twelfth I proudly wear the sash my father wore.

'The Sash My Father Wore', traditional Orange song

4 Sumer is icumen in,
Lhude sing cuccu!
Groweth sed, and bloweth med,
And springth the wude nu.

'Cuckoo Song' (c.1250), sung annually at Reading Abbey gateway and first recorded by John Fornset, a monk of Reading Abbey; see **Pound** 269:18

5 Swing low, sweet chariot—
Comin' for to carry me home.

Negro spiritual (c.1850)

6 Their name liveth for evermore.

*standard inscription on the Stone of Sacrifice in each military cemetery of World War One, proposed by Rudyard **Kipling** as a member of the War Graves Commission*

Charles Carrington *Rudyard Kipling* (rev. ed. 1978); see **Bible** 42:28, **Sassoon** 286:2

7 There is a lady sweet and kind,
Was never face so pleased my mind;
I did but see her passing by,
And yet I love her till I die.

found on the reverse of leaf 53 of 'Popish Kingdome or reigne of Antichrist', in Latin verse by Thomas Naogeorgus, and Englished by Barnabe Googe; printed in 1570; sometimes attributed to Thomas Forde

8 There is one thing stronger than all the armies in the world; and that is an idea whose time has come.

in *Nation* 15 April 1943; see **Hugo** 178:1

9 There is so much good in the worst of us, And so much bad in the best of us, That it hardly becomes any of us To talk about the rest of us.

attributed, among others, to Edward Wallis Hoch (1849–1945) on the grounds of it having appeared in his Kansas publication, the *Marion Record*, though in fact disclaimed by him

('behooves' sometimes substituted for 'becomes')

10 They haif said: Quhat say they? Lat thame say.

motto of the Earls Marischal of Scotland, inscribed at Marischal College, Aberdeen, 1593; a similarly defiant motto in Greek has been found engraved in remains from classical antiquity

11 Thirty days hath September,
April, June, and November;
All the rest have thirty-one,
Excepting February alone,
And that has twenty-eight days clear
And twenty-nine in each leap year.

Stevins MS (c.1555)

12 Though I yield to no one in my admiration for Mr Coolidge, I do wish he did not look as if he had been weaned on a pickle.

anonymous remark, in Alice Roosevelt Longworth *Crowded Hours* (1933) ch. 21

13 To secure for the workers by hand or by brain the full fruits of their industry and the most equitable distribution thereof that may be possible upon the basis of the common ownership of the means of production, distribution, and exchange.

Clause Four of the Labour Party's Constitution of 1918 (revised 1929); the commitment to common ownership of services was largely removed in 1995; see **Anonymous** 7:17

14 We hold these truths to be self-evident, that all men are created equal, that they are endowed by their Creator with certain unalienable rights, that among these are life, liberty and the pursuit of happiness.

The American Declaration of Independence, 4 July 1776; see **Jefferson** 183:18

15 We're here
Because
We're here.

sung to the tune of 'Auld Lang Syne', in John Brophy and Eric Partridge *Songs and Slang of the British Soldier 1914–18* (1930)

16 Were you there when they crucified my Lord?

title of Negro spiritual (1865)

17 We want eight, and we won't wait.

on the construction of Dreadnoughts

George Wyndham, speech in *The Times* 29 March 1909

18 Western wind, when will thou blow,
The small rain down can rain?
Christ, if my love were in my arms
And I in my bed again!

'Western Wind' (published 1790) in *New Oxford Book of Sixteenth-Century Verse* (1991)

19 What's the use of worrying?
It never was worth while,
So, pack up your troubles in your old kit-bag,
And smile, smile, smile.

'Pack up your Troubles' (1915 song), written by George Asaf (1880–1951)

20 When Israel was in Egypt land,

Let my people go,
Oppressed so hard they could not stand,
Let my people go.
Go down, Moses,
Way-down in Egypt land,
Tell old Pharaoh
To let my people go.
  'Go Down, Moses' (Negro spiritual); see **Bible**
  35:17

1 When war is declared, Truth is the first
casualty.
  attributed to Hiram Johnson, speaking in the
  US Senate, 1918, but not recorded in his speech;
  the first recorded use is as epigraph to Arthur
  Ponsonby's *Falsehood in Wartime* (1928); see
  Johnson 187:4

2 Who dares wins.
  motto of the British Special Air Service
  regiment, from 1942

3 The whole is more than the sum of the
parts.
  traditional saying, probably deriving from
  Aristotle; see **Aristotle** 15:11

4 A willing foe and sea room.
  naval toast in the time of **Nelson**
  W. N. T. Beckett *A Few Naval Customs, Expressions,*
  Traditions, and Superstitions (1931) 'Customs'

5 With a heart of furious fancies,
Whereof I am commander;
With a burning spear,
And a horse of air,
To the wilderness I wander.
  'Tom o' Bedlam'

6 Yankee Doodle came to town
Riding on a pony;
Stuck a feather in his cap
And called it Macaroni.
  'Yankee Doodle' (song, 1755 or earlier); Nicholas
  Smith *Stories of Great National Songs* (1899) ch. 2;
  see **Cohan** 99:10

7 Your King and Country need you.
  recruitment slogan for First World War, coined
  by Eric Field, July 1914; *Advertising* (1959)

8 You should make a point of trying every
experience once, excepting incest and folk-
dancing.
  Arnold Bax (1883–1953), quoting 'a sympathetic
  Scot' in *Farewell My Youth* (1943)

French

9 *Ça ira.*
Things will work out.
  refrain of 'Carillon national', popular song of
  the French Revolution (*c.*July 1790), tr. William
  Doyle; the phrase is believed to originate with
  Benjamin **Franklin**, who may have uttered it in
  1776 when asked for news of the American
  Revolution

10 *Cet animal est très méchant,*
Quand on l'attaque il se défend.
This animal is very bad; when attacked it
defends itself.
  'La Ménagerie' (1868 song) by 'Théodore P. K.'

11 *Chevalier sans peur et sans reproche.*
Fearless, blameless knight.

description in contemporary chronicles of
Pierre Bayard (1476–1524)

12 *Honi soit qui mal y pense.*
Evil be to him who evil thinks.
  motto of the Order of the Garter, originated by
  Edward III, probably on 23 April of 1348 or
  1349; see **Sellar and Yeatman** 00:00

13 *Il ne faut pas être plus royaliste que le roi.*
You mustn't be more of a royalist than the
king.
  saying from the time of Louis XVI; François
  René, Vicomte de Chateaubriand *De la monarchie*
  selon la charte (1816) ch. 81

14 *Ils ne passeront pas.*
They shall not pass.
  slogan used by the French army at the defence
  of Verdun in 1916; variously attributed to
  Marshal **Pétain** and to General Robert Nivelle,
  and taken up by the Republicans in the Spanish
  Civil War in the form '*No pasarán!*'; see **Ibarruri**
  180:3

15 *Je suis Marxiste—tendance Groucho.*
I am a Marxist—of the Groucho tendency.
  slogan used at Nanterre in Paris, 1968

16 *Laissez-nous-faire.*
Allow us to do [it].
  remark dating from *c.*1664, in *Journal*
  Oeconomique Paris, April 1751: 'Monsieur Colbert
  assembled several deputies of commerce at his
  house to ask what could be done for commerce;
  the most rational and the least flattering among
  them answered him in one word: "Laissez-nous-
  faire"'; see **Argenson** 15:2

17 *Nous n'irons plus aux bois, les lauriers sont*
coupés.
We'll to the woods no more,
The laurels all are cut.
  old nursery rhyme, quoted by Théodore de
  Banville in *Les Cariatides, les stalactites* (1842–6);
  tr. A. E. Housman in *Last Poems* (1922)
  introductory

18 *Revenons à ces moutons.*
Let us get back to these sheep [i.e. 'Let us get
back to the subject'].
  Maistre Pierre Pathelin l. 1191 (often quoted as
  '*Retournons à nos moutons* [Let us return to our
  sheep]')

19 *Tout passe, tout casse, tout lasse.*
Everything passes, everything perishes,
everything palls.
  Charles Cahier *Quelques six mille proverbes* (1856)
  no. 1718

German

20 *Arbeit macht frei.*
Work liberates.
  words inscribed on the gates of Dachau
  concentration camp, 1933, and subsequently on
  those of Auschwitz

21 *Jedem das Seine.*
To each his own.
  often quoted as 'Everyone gets what he deserves'
  inscription on the gate of Buchenwald
  concentration camp, *c.*1937

Greek

1 *Gnothi seauton.*
Know thyself.
inscribed on the temple of Apollo at Delphi
Plato, in Protagoras 343 b, ascribes the saying to
the Seven Wise Men; see **Goethe** 152:24

2 Let no one enter who does not know
geometry [mathematics].
inscription on **Plato's** *door, probably at the
Academy at Athens*
Elias Philosophus *In Aristotelis Categorias
Commentaria*; in A. Busse (ed.) *Commentaria in
Aristotelem Graeca* (1900) vol. 18, pt. 1

3 Nothing in excess.
inscribed on the temple of Apollo at Delphi
variously ascribed to the Seven Wise Men

4 Whenever God prepares evil for a man, He
first damages his mind, with which he
deliberates.
scholiastic annotation to Sophocles's *Antigone* l.
622

Latin

5 *Adeste, fideles.*
O come, all ye faithful.
French or German hymn (c.1743) in *Murray's
Hymnal* (1852); translation based on that of F.
Oakeley (1841)

6 *Ad majorem Dei gloriam.*
To the greater glory of God.
motto of the Society of Jesus

7 *Ave Caesar, morituri te salutant.*
Hail Caesar, those who are about to die
salute you.
gladiators saluting the Roman Emperor
Suetonius *Lives of the Caesars* 'Claudius' ch. 21

8 *Ave Maria, gratia plena, Dominus tecum:
Benedicta tu in mulieribus, et benedictus fructus
ventris tui, Jesus.*
Hail Mary, full of grace, the Lord is with
thee: Blessed art thou among women, and
blessed is the fruit of thy womb, Jesus.
'Ave Maria' or 'Hail Mary', also known as 'The
Angelic Salutation', dating from the 11th
century; see **Bible** 46:31

9 *Dominus illuminatio mea.*
The Lord is my light.
motto of the University of Oxford; see **Bible**
53:27

10 *Et in Arcadia ego.*
And I too in Arcadia.
tomb inscription, of disputed meaning, often
depicted in classical paintings, notably by
Poussin in 1655; E. Panofsky 'Et in Arcadia ego'
in R. K. Klibansky and H. J. Paton (eds.) *Philosophy
and History: Essays Presented to E. Cassirer* (1936)

11 *Gaudeamus igitur,
Juvenes dum sumus.*
Let us then rejoice,
While we are young.
medieval students' song, traced to 1267, but
revised in the 18th century

12 *Nemo me impune lacessit.*
No one provokes me with impunity.
motto of the Crown of Scotland and of all
Scottish regiments

13 *Nisi Dominus frustra.*
In vain without the Lord.
motto of the city of Edinburgh; see **Bible** 54:2

14 *Nullius in verba.*
In the word of none.
*emphasizing reliance on experiment rather than
authority*
motto of the Royal Society

15 *Per ardua ad astra.*
Through struggle to the stars.
motto of the Mulvany family, quoted and
translated by Rider **Haggard** in *The People of the
Mist* (1894) ch. 1; still in use as motto of the
R.A.F., having been proposed by J. S. Yule in
1912 and approved by King **George V** in 1913

16 *Post coitum omne animal triste.*
After coition every animal is sad.
post-classical saying

17 *Quidquid agis, prudenter agas, et respice finem.*
Whatever you do, do cautiously, and look to
the end.
Gesta Romanorum no. 103

18 *Semper eadem.*
Ever the same.
motto of **Elizabeth I**

19 *Sic semper tyrannis.*
Thus always to tyrants.
motto of the State of Virginia; see **Booth** 65:17

20 *Sic transit gloria mundi.*
Thus passes the glory of the world.
*said during the coronation of a new Pope, while
flax is burned to represent the transitoriness of
earthly glory*
used at the coronation of Alexander V in Pisa, 7
July 1409, but earlier in origin; see **Thomas à
Kempis** 337:8

21 *Similia similibus curantur.*
Like cures like.
motto of homeopathic medicine, although not
found in this form in the writings of C. F. S.
Hahnemann (1755–1843); the Latin appears as
an anonymous side-note in Paracelsus *Opera
Omnia* (c.1490–1541, ed. 1658) vol. 1

22 *Si monumentum requiris, circumspice.*
If you seek a monument, gaze around.
inscription in St Paul's Cathedral, London,
attributed to the son of Sir Christopher Wren
(1632–1723), its architect

23 *Vox et praeterea nihil.*
A voice and nothing more.
describing a nightingale
Plutarch *Moralia* sect. 233a, no. 15

Italian

24 *Se non è vero, è molto ben trovato.*
If it is not true, it is a happy invention.
common saying from the 16th century

Old English

1 Thought shall be the harder, heart the keener, courage the greater, as our might lessens.

   The Battle of Maldon (tr R. K. Gordon, 1926)

2 Men said openly that Christ slept and His saints.

   of England during the civil war between Stephen and Matilda

   Anglo-Saxon Chronicle for 1137

Old Norse

3 Cattle die, kinsmen die,
   the self must also die;
   but glory never dies,
   for the man who is able to achieve it.

   Hávamál ('Sayings of the High One'), *c.*10th century

Jean Anouilh 1910–87
French dramatist

4 There is love of course. And then there's life, its enemy.

   Ardèle (1949)

5 You know very well that love is, above all, the gift of oneself!

   Ardèle (1949)

Susan Brownell Anthony 1820–1906
American feminist and political activist

6 Join the union, girls, and together say, 'Equal Pay for Equal Work!'

   in *The Revolution* 8 October 1869

Guillaume Apollinaire 1880–1918
French poet

7 *Les souvenirs sont cors de chasse*
   Dont meurt le bruit parmi le vent.
   Memories are hunting horns
   Whose sound dies on the wind.

   · 'Cors de Chasse' (1912)

8 *Sous le pont Mirabeau coule la Seine.*
   Et nos amours, faut-il qu'il m'en souvienne?
   La joie venait toujours après la peine.
   Under Mirabeau Bridge flows the Seine.
   And our loves, must I remember them?
   Joy always came after pain.

   'Le Pont Mirabeau' (1912)

Edward Appleton 1892–1965
English physicist

9 I do not mind what language an opera is sung in so long as it is a language I don't understand.

   in *Observer* 28 August 1955

Thomas Gold Appleton 1812–84
American epigrammatist

10 Good Americans, when they die, go to Paris.

   Oliver Wendell Holmes *The Autocrat of the Breakfast Table* (1858) ch. 6; see **Wilde** 358:32

Arabian Nights Entertainments, or the Thousand and one Nights
a collection of stories written in Arabic

11 Who will change old lamps for new ones? . . . new lamps for old ones?

   'The History of Aladdin'

12 Open Sesame!

   'The History of Ali Baba'

Diane Arbus 1923–71
American photographer

13 A photograph is a secret about a secret. The more it tells you the less you know.

   Patricia Bosworth *Diane Arbus: a Biography* (1985)

John Arbuthnot 1667–1735
Scottish physician and pamphleteer

14 Law is a bottomless pit.

   The History of John Bull (1712) title of first pamphlet

Archilochus
Greek poet of the 7th century BC

15 The fox knows many things—the hedgehog one *big* one.

   E. Diehl (ed.) *Anthologia Lyrica Graeca* (3rd ed., 1949–52) vol. 1, no. 103; see **Berlin** 32:7

Archimedes *c.*287–212 BC
Greek mathematician and inventor

16 Eureka! [I've got it!]

   Vitruvius Pollio *De Architectura* bk. 9, preface, sect. 10

17 Give me but one firm spot on which to stand, and I will move the earth.

   on the action of a lever

   Pappus *Synagoge* bk. 8, proposition 10, sect. 11

Robert Ardrey 1908–80
American dramatist and evolutionist

18 Not in innocence, and not in Asia, was mankind born.

   African Genesis (1961)

Hannah Arendt 1906–75
American political philosopher

19 It was as though in those last minutes he was summing up the lessons that this long course in human wickedness had taught us—the lesson of the fearsome, word-and-thought-defying *banality of evil*.

   of Adolf Eichmann, responsible for the administration of the Nazi concentration camps

   Eichmann in Jerusalem (1963) ch. 15

20 Only crime and the criminal, it is true, confront us with the perplexity of radical evil; but only the hypocrite is really rotten to the core.

   On Revolution (1963) ch. 2, pt. 5

21 The most radical revolutionary will become a conservative on the day after the revolution.

   in *New Yorker* 12 September 1970

1 Under conditions of tyranny it is far easier to act than to think.
  W. H. Auden *A Certain World* (1970)

Marquis d'Argenson (René Louis de Voyer d'Argenson) 1694–1757
French politician and political essayist

2 *Laisser-faire.*
No interference.
  Mémoires et Journal Inédit du Marquis d'Argenson (1858 ed.) vol. 5; see **Anonymous** 12:16

Comte d'Argenson 1696–1764
French statesman

3 DESFONTAINES: I must live.
D'ARGENSON: I do not see the necessity.
  on Desfontaines having produced a pamphlet satirizing D'Argenson, his benefactor
  Voltaire *Alzire* (1736) 'Discours Préliminaire' footnote, in *Oeuvres Complètes Théâtre* (1877) vol. 2

Ludovico Ariosto 1474–1533
Italian poet and dramatist

4 *Natura il fece, e poi roppe la stampa.*
Nature made him, and then broke the mould.
  Orlando Furioso (1532) canto 10, st. 84

Aristophanes *c.*450–*c.*385 BC
Greek comic dramatist

5 How about 'Cloudcuckooland'?
naming the capital city of the Birds
  The Birds (414 BC) l. 819

6 This Second Logic then, I mean the Worse one,
They teach to talk unjustly, and—prevail.
  The Clouds (423 BC) l. 113; see **Milton** 238:3

7 Brekekekex koax koax.
cry of the Frogs
  The Frogs (405 BC) l. 209 and *passim*

8 You have all the characteristics of a popular politician: a horrible voice, bad breeding and a vulgar manner.
  The Knights (424 BC) l. 217

9 Under every stone lurks a politician.
  Thesmophoriazusae l. 530

Aristotle 384–322 BC
Greek philosopher
see also **Ascham** 17:15

10 All men by nature desire knowledge.
  Metaphysics bk. 1, ch. 1, 980a 22

11 Whenever anything which has several parts is such that the whole is something over and above its parts, and not just the sum of them all, like a heap, then it always has some cause.
  Metaphysics 1045a 10f; see **Anonymous** 12:3

12 Every art and every investigation, and likewise every practical pursuit or undertaking, seems to aim at some good:
hence it has been well said that the Good is That at which all things aim.
  Nicomachean Ethics bk. 1, 1094a 1–3

13 The Good of man is the active exercise of his soul's faculties in conformity with excellence or virtue . . . Moreover this activity must occupy a complete lifetime; for one swallow does not make spring, nor does one fine day; and similarly one day or a brief period of happiness does not make a man supremely blessed and happy.
  Nicomachean Ethics bk. 1, 1098a 16–20

14 We make war that we may live in peace.
  Nicomachean Ethics bk. 10, 1177b 5–6 (tr. M. Ostwald); see **Vegetius** 346:1

15 Tragedy is thus a representation of an action that is worth serious attention, complete in itself and of some amplitude . . . by means of pity and fear bringing about the purgation of such emotions.
  Poetics ch. 6, 1449b 24–8

16 A whole is that which has a beginning, a middle, and an end.
  Poetics ch. 7

17 So poetry is something more philosophical and more worthy of serious attention than history, for while poetry is concerned with universal truth, history treats of particular facts.
  Poetics ch. 9, 1451b 5–6

18 Probable impossibilities are to be preferred to improbable possibilities.
  Poetics ch. 24, 1460a 26–7

19 Man is by nature a political animal.
  Politics bk. 1, 1253a 2–3

20 He who is unable to live in society, or who has no need because he is sufficient for himself, must be either a beast or a god.
  Politics bk. 1, 1253a 27–9

21 Nature does nothing without purpose or uselessly.
  Politics bk. 1, 1256b 20–21

22 For if liberty and equality, as is thought by some, are chiefly to be found in democracy, they will be best attained when all persons alike share in the government to the utmost.
  Politics bk. 4, 1291b 35

23 *Amicus Plato, sed magis amica veritas.*
Plato is dear to me, but dearer still is truth.
  Latin translation of a Greek original ascribed to Aristotle

24 When he was asked 'What is a friend?' he said 'One soul inhabiting two bodies.'
  Diogenes Laertius *Lives of Philosophers* bk. 5, sect. 20

Lewis Addison Armistead
1817–63
American army officer

25 Give them the cold steel, boys!
during the American Civil War, 1863
  attributed

Harry Armstrong 1879–1951
American songwriter

1 There's an old mill by the stream, Nellie
Dean,
Where we used to sit and dream.
'Nellie Dean' (1905 song)

John Armstrong 1709–79
Scottish poet and physician

2 'Tis not for mortals always to be blest.
The Art of Preserving Health (1744) bk. 4, l. 260

3 'Tis not too late tomorrow to be brave.
The Art of Preserving Health (1744) bk. 4, l. 460

Lance Armstrong 1971–
American cyclist

4 This is a hard tour and hard work wins it.
Vive Le Tour.
on winning his seventh consecutive Tour de France
in *Independent* 25 July 2005

Louis Armstrong 1901–71
American singer and jazz musician

5 If you still have to ask . . . shame on you.
*when asked what jazz is; sometimes quoted as,
'Man, if you gotta ask you'll never know'*
Max Jones et al. *Salute to Satchmo* (1970)

6 All music is folk music, I ain't never heard
no horse sing a song.
in *New York Times* 7 July 1971

Neil Armstrong 1930–
American astronaut

7 Houston, Tranquillity Base here. The Eagle
has landed.
radio message as the lunar module touched down
in *The Times* 21 July 1969

8 That's one small step for a man, one giant
leap for mankind.
landing on the moon
in *New York Times* 21 July 1969; interference in
the transmission obliterated 'a'

Robert Armstrong 1927–
British civil servant

9 It contains a misleading impression, not a
lie. It was being economical with the truth.
during the 'Spycatcher' trial in New South Wales
in *Daily Telegraph* 19 November 1986; see **Burke**
76:1, **Clark** 97:3, **Twain** 343:10

Edwin Arnold 1832–1904
English poet and journalist

10 Nor ever once ashamed
So we be named
Press-men; Slaves of the Lamp; Servants of
Light.
'The Tenth Muse' (1895) st. 18

Matthew Arnold 1822–88
English poet and essayist

11 The Sea of Faith

Was once, too, at the full, and round earth's
shore
Lay like the folds of a bright girdle furled.
But now I only hear
Its melancholy, long, withdrawing roar.
'Dover Beach' (1867) l. 21

12 Ah, love, let us be true
To one another!
'Dover Beach' (1867) l. 29

13 And we are here as on a darkling plain
Swept with confused alarms of struggle and
flight,
Where ignorant armies clash by night.
'Dover Beach' (1867) l. 35

14 Come to me in my dreams, and then
By day I shall be well again!
For then the night will more than pay
The hopeless longing of the day.
'Faded Leaves' (1855) no. 5 (first published,
1852, as 'Longing')

15 Come, dear children, let us away;
Down and away below!
'The Forsaken Merman' (1849) l. 1

16 Now the wild white horses play,
Champ and chafe and toss in the spray.
'The Forsaken Merman' (1849) l. 4

17 Say, has some wet bird-haunted English
lawn
Lent it the music of its trees at dawn?
'Parting' (1852) l. 19

18 Eternal Passion!
Eternal Pain!
of the nightingale
'Philomela' (1853) l. 31

19 Cruel, but composed and bland,
Dumb, inscrutable and grand,
So Tiberius might have sat,
Had Tiberius been a cat.
'Poor Matthias' (1885) l. 40

20 Go, for they call you, Shepherd, from the
hill.
'The Scholar-Gipsy' (1853) l. 1

21 Resolve to be thyself: and know, that he
Who finds himself, loses his misery.
'Self-Dependence' (1852) l. 31

22 Others abide our question. Thou art free.
We ask and ask: Thou smilest and art still,
Out-topping knowledge.
'Shakespeare' (1849)

23 Truth sits upon the lips of dying men.
'Sohrab and Rustum' (1853) l. 656

24 Wandering between two worlds, one dead,
The other powerless to be born.
'Stanzas from the Grande Chartreuse' (1855)
l. 85

25 And that sweet City with her dreaming
spires.
of Oxford
'Thyrsis' (1866) l. 19

26 Who saw life steadily, and saw it whole:

The mellow glory of the Attic stage;
Singer of sweet Colonus, and its child.
of Sophocles
  'To a Friend' (1849)

1 And bade betwixt their shores to be
The unplumbed, salt, estranging sea.
  'To Marguerite—Continued' (1852) l. 24

2 The pursuit of perfection, then, is the
pursuit of sweetness and light . . . He who
works for sweetness and light united, works
to make reason and the will of God prevail.
  Culture and Anarchy (1869) ch. 1; see **Swift** 328:6

3 When I want to distinguish clearly the
aristocratic class from the Philistines proper,
or middle class, [I] name the former, in my
own mind *the Barbarians*.
  Culture and Anarchy (1869) ch. 3

4 Whispering from her towers the last
enchantments of the Middle Age . . . Home
of lost causes, and forsaken beliefs, and
unpopular names, and impossible loyalties!
of Oxford
  Essays in Criticism First Series (1865) preface; see
  Beerbohm 29:2

5 In poetry, no less than in life, he is 'a
beautiful and ineffectual angel, beating in
the void his luminous wings in vain'.
  Essays in Criticism Second Series (1888) 'Shelley'
  (quoting from his own essay on Byron in the
  same work)

6 Poetry is at bottom a criticism of life.
  Essays in Criticism Second Series (1888)
  'Wordsworth'

7 The true meaning of religion is thus not
simply morality, but morality touched by
emotion.
  Literature and Dogma (1873) ch. 1

8 The main effort, for now many years, has
been a *critical* effort; the endeavours, in all
branches of knowledge—theology,
philosophy, history, art, science—to see the
object as in itself it really is.
  On Translating Homer (1861) Lecture 2

9 Have something to say, and say it as clearly
as you can. That is the only secret of style.
  G. W. E. Russell *Collections and Recollections* (1898)
  ch. 13

Samuel James Arnold
English organist and composer

10 England, home and beauty.
  'The Death of Nelson' (1811 song)

Thomas Arnold 1795–1842
English historian and educator

11 My object will be, if possible, to form
Christian men, for Christian boys I can
scarcely hope to make.
*on appointment to the Headmastership of Rugby
School*
  letter to Revd John Tucker, 2 March 1828

12 What we must look for here is, 1st, religious
and moral principles: 2ndly, gentlemanly
conduct: 3rdly, intellectual ability.
*address to the praepostors [prefects] of Rugby
School*
  Arthur Penrhyn Stanley *The Life and
  Correspondence of Thomas Arnold* (1844) vol. 1,
  ch. 3

13 As for rioting, the old Roman way of dealing
with that is always the right one; flog the
rank and file, and fling the ringleaders from
the Tarpeian rock.
  from an unpublished letter written before 1828

Roger Ascham 1515–68
English scholar, writer, and courtier

14 There is no such whetstone, to sharpen a
good wit and encourage a will to learning,
as is praise.
  The Schoolmaster (1570) bk. 1

15 He that will write well in any tongue, must
follow this counsel of Aristotle, to speak as
the common people do, to think as wise
men do.
  Toxophilus (1545) 'To all gentlemen and yeomen
  of England'

Daisy Ashford 1881–1972
English child author

16 Mr Salteena was an elderly man of 42.
  The Young Visiters (1919) ch. 1

Isaac Asimov 1920–92
*Russian-born biochemist and science fiction
writer*

17 The three fundamental Rules of Robotics . . .
One, a robot may not injure a human being,
or, through inaction, allow a human being
to come to harm . . . Two . . . a robot must
obey the orders given it by human beings
except where such orders would conflict
with the First Law . . . three, a robot must
protect its own existence as long as such
protection does not conflict with the First or
Second Laws.
  I, Robot (1950) 'Runaround'

Cynthia Asquith 1887–1960
English writer

18 I am beginning to rub my eyes at the
prospect of peace . . . One will at last fully
recognize that the dead are not only dead
for the duration of the war.
  diary, 7 October 1918

Herbert Asquith 1852–1928
British Liberal statesman, Prime Minister 1908–16

19 We had better wait and see.
*phrase used repeatedly in speeches in 1910,
referring to the rumour that the House of Lords
was to be flooded with new Liberal peers to ensure
the passage of the Finance Bill*
  Roy Jenkins *Asquith* (1964)

20 Youth would be an ideal state if it came a
little later in life.
  in *Observer* 15 April 1923

1 [The War Office kept three sets of figures:] one to mislead the public, another to mislead the Cabinet, and the third to mislead itself.

Alistair Horne *Price of Glory* (1962) ch. 2

Margot Asquith 1864–1945
British political hostess

2 The *t* is silent, as in *Harlow*.

to Jean Harlow, who had been mispronouncing 'Margot'

T. S. Matthews *Great Tom* (1973) ch. 7

3 Lord Birkenhead is very clever but sometimes his brains go to his head.

in *Listener* 11 June 1953 'Margot Oxford' by Lady Violet Bonham Carter

4 He can't see a belt without hitting below it.

of *Lloyd George*

in *Listener* 11 June 1953 'Margot Oxford' by Lady Violet Bonham Carter

Jacob Astley 1579–1652
English soldier and royalist

5 O Lord! thou knowest how busy I must be this day: if I forget thee, do not thou forget me.

prayer before the Battle of Edgehill, 1642

Philip Warwick *Memoires* (1701)

Nancy Astor 1879–1964
American-born British Conservative politician
see also **Churchill** 96:10

6 I married beneath me, all women do.

in *Dictionary of National Biography 1961–1970* (1981)

Brooks Atkinson 1894–1984
American journalist and critic

7 After each war there is a little less democracy to save.

Once Around the Sun (1951) 7 January

Clement Attlee 1883–1967
British Labour statesman, Prime Minister 1945–51

8 Few thought he was even a starter
There were many who thought themselves smarter
But he ended PM
CH and OM
An earl and a knight of the garter.

describing himself in a letter to Tom Attlee, 8 April 1956

Kenneth Harris *Attlee* (1982)

9 Democracy means government by discussion, but it is only effective if you can stop people talking.

speech at Oxford, 14 June 1957

Margaret Atwood 1939–
Canadian novelist

10 Nobody dies from lack of sex. It's lack of love we die from.

The Handmaid's Tale (1986)

John Aubrey 1626–97
English antiquary and biographer

11 Anno 1670, not far from Cirencester, was an apparition; being demanded whether a good spirit or a bad? returned no answer, but disappeared with a curious perfume and most melodious twang. Mr W. Lilly believes it was a fairy.

Miscellanies (1696) 'Apparitions'

W. H. Auden 1907–73
English poet

12 Blessed Cecilia, appear in visions
To all musicians, appear and inspire:
Translated Daughter, come down and startle
Composing mortals with immortal fire.

Anthem for St Cecilia's Day (1941) pt. 1

13 I'll love you, dear, I'll love you
Till China and Africa meet
And the river jumps over the mountain
And the salmon sing in the street,
I'll love you till the ocean
Is folded and hung up to dry
And the seven stars go squawking
Like geese about the sky.

'As I Walked Out One Evening' (1940)

14 The glacier knocks in the cupboard,
The desert sighs in the bed,
And the crack in the teacup opens
A lane to the land of the dead.

'As I Walked Out One Evening' (1940)

15 The desires of the heart are as crooked as corkscrews
Not to be born is the best for man.

'Death's Echo' (1937); see **Sophocles** 320:16

16 To save your world you asked this man to die:
Would this man, could he see you now, ask why?

'Epitaph for the Unknown Soldier' (1955)

17 When he laughed, respectable senators burst with laughter,
And when he cried the little children died in the streets.

'Epitaph on a Tyrant' (1940)

18 Stop all the clocks, cut off the telephone,
Prevent the dog from barking with a juicy bone,
Silence the pianos and with muffled drum
Bring out the coffin, let the mourners come.

'Funeral Blues' (1936)

19 He was my North, my South, my East and West,
My working week and my Sunday rest,
My noon, my midnight, my talk, my song;
I thought that love would last for ever: I was wrong.

'Funeral Blues' (1936)

20 To us he is no more a person
now but a whole climate of opinion.

'In Memory of Sigmund Freud' (1940) st. 17

21 The mercury sank in the mouth of the dying day.
What instruments we have agree

The day of his death was a dark cold day.
'In Memory of W. B. Yeats' (1940) pt. 1

1 You were silly like us; your gift survived it
all:
The parish of rich women, physical decay,
Yourself. Mad Ireland hurt you into poetry.
'In Memory of W. B. Yeats' (1940) pt. 2

2 Poetry makes nothing happen.
'In Memory of W. B. Yeats' (1940) pt. 2

3 In the nightmare of the dark
All the dogs of Europe bark.
'In Memory of W. B. Yeats' (1940) pt. 3

4 Intellectual disgrace
Stares from every human face,
And the seas of pity lie
Locked and frozen in each eye.
'In Memory of W. B. Yeats' (1940) pt. 3

5 Time that with this strange excuse
Pardoned Kipling and his views,
And will pardon Paul Claudel,
Pardons him for writing well.
'In Memory of W. B. Yeats' (1940) pt. 3

6 In the deserts of the heart
Let the healing fountain start,
In the prison of his days
Teach the free man how to praise.
'In Memory of W. B. Yeats' (1940) pt. 3

7 Look, stranger, at this island now.
title of poem (1936)

8 Lay your sleeping head, my love,
Human on my faithless arm.
'Lullaby' (1940)

9 About suffering they were never wrong,
The Old Masters.
'Musée des Beaux Arts' (1940)

10 Even the dreadful martyrdom must run its
course
Anyhow in a corner, some untidy spot
Where the dogs go on with their doggy life
and the torturer's horse
Scratches its innocent behind on a tree.
'Musée des Beaux Arts' (1940)

11 This is the Night Mail crossing the Border,
Bringing the cheque and the postal order,
Letters for the rich, letters for the poor,
The shop at the corner, the girl next door.
'Night Mail' (1936) pt. 1

12 Private faces in public places
Are wiser and nicer
Than public faces in private places.
Orators (1932) dedication

13 Out on the lawn I lie in bed,
Vega conspicuous overhead.
'Out on the lawn I lie in bed' (1936)

14 O what is that sound which so thrills the ear
Down in the valley drumming, drumming?
Only the scarlet soldiers, dear,
The soldiers coming.
'O what is that sound' (1936)

15 Some thirty inches from my nose
The frontier of my Person goes,
And all the untilled air between
Is private *pagus* or demesne.

Stranger, unless with bedroom eyes
I beckon you to fraternize,
Beware of rudely crossing it:
I have no gun, but I can spit.
'Prologue: the Birth of Architecture' (1966)
postscript

16 I and the public know
What all schoolchildren learn,
Those to whom evil is done
Do evil in return.
'September 1, 1939' (1940)

17 But who can live for long
In an euphoric dream;
Out of the mirror they stare,
Imperialism's face
And the international wrong.
'September 1, 1939' (1940)

18 There is no such thing as the State
And no one exists alone;
Hunger allows no choice
To the citizen or the police;
We must love one another or die.
'September 1, 1939' (1940)

19 A shilling life will give you all the facts.
title of poem (1936)

20 A poet's hope: to be,
like some valley cheese,
local, but prized elsewhere.
'Shorts II' (1976)

21 History to the defeated
May say Alas but cannot help or pardon.
'Spain 1937' (1937) st. 23

22 Was he free? Was he happy? The question is
absurd:
Had anything been wrong, we should
certainly have heard.
'The Unknown Citizen' (1940)

23 Man is a history-making creature who can
neither repeat his past nor leave it behind.
The Dyer's Hand (1963) 'D. H. Lawrence'

24 When I find myself in the company of
scientists, I feel like a shabby curate who
has strayed by mistake into a drawing room
full of dukes.
The Dyer's Hand (1963) 'The Poet and the City'

25 Some books are undeservedly forgotten;
none are undeservedly remembered.
The Dyer's Hand (1963) 'Reading'

26 Art is born of humiliation.
Stephen Spender *World Within World* (1951) ch. 2

Émile Augier 1820–89
French poet and dramatist

27 *La nostalgie de la boue!*
Longing to be back in the mud!
Le Mariage d'Olympe (1855) act 1, sc. 1

St Augustine of Hippo AD 354–430
Roman Christian theologian

28 You have made us for yourself, and our
heart is restless until it rests in you.
Confessions (AD 397–8) bk. 1, ch. 1

1 Give me chastity and continency—but not yet!
Confessions (AD 397–8) bk. 8, ch. 7

2 When he was reading, he drew his eyes along over the leaves, and his heart searched into the sense, but his voice and tongue were silent.
of St Ambrose
Confessions (AD 397–8) bk. 6, ch. 3

3 *Tolle lege, tolle lege.*
Take up and read, take up and read.
Confessions (AD 397–8) bk. 8, ch. 12

4 Too late came I to love thee, O thou Beauty both so ancient and so fresh, yea too late came I to love thee. And behold, thou wert within me, and I out of myself, where I made search for thee.
Confessions (AD 397–8) bk. 10, ch. 27

5 You command continence; give what you command, and command what you will.
Confessions (AD 397–8) bk. 10, ch. 29

6 There is no salvation outside the church.
De Baptismo contra Donatistas bk. 4, ch. 17, sect. 24; see **Cyprian** 109:2, 109:4

7 *Audi partem alteram.*
Hear the other side.
De Duabus Animabus contra Manicheos ch. 14

8 *Dilige et quod vis fac.*
Love and do what you will.
often quoted as 'Ama et fac quod vis'
In Epistolam Joannis ad Parthos (AD 413) tractatus 7, sect. 8

9 To many, total abstinence is easier than perfect moderation.
On the Good of Marriage (AD 401) ch. 21

10 *Cum dilectione hominum et odio vitiorum.*
With love for mankind and hatred of sins.
often quoted as 'Love the sinner but hate the sin'
letter 211 in J.-P. Migne (ed.) *Patrologiae Latinae* (1845) vol. 33; see **Pope** 266:12

11 *Roma locuta est; causa finita est.*
Rome has spoken; the case is concluded.
traditional summary of words found in Sermons (Antwerp, 1702) no. 131, sect. 10

Augustus 63 BC–AD 14
first Roman emperor

12 Quintilius Varus, give me back my legions.
on Varus' loss of three legions in battle with Germanic tribes, AD 9
Suetonius *Lives of the Caesars* 'Divus Augustus' sect. 23

13 *Festina lente.*
Make haste slowly.
Suetonius *Lives of the Caesars* 'Divus Augustus' sect. 25

14 He could boast that he inherited it brick and left it marble.
referring to the city of Rome
Suetonius *Lives of the Caesars* 'Divus Augustus' sect. 28

Marcus Aurelius AD 121–180
Roman emperor from AD 161

15 Everything is fitting for me, my universe, which fits thy purpose. Nothing in its good time is too early or too late for me; everything is fruit for me which thy seasons, Nature, bear; from thee, in thee, to thee, are all things.
Meditations bk. 4, sect. 23

16 Nothing happens to anybody which he is not fitted by nature to bear.
Meditations bk. 5, sect. 18

17 Every instant of time is a pinprick of eternity.
Meditations bk. 6, sect. 36

18 To change your mind and to follow him who sets you right is to be nonetheless the free agent that you were before.
Meditations bk. 8, sect. 16

19 Mankind have been created for the sake of one another. Either instruct them, therefore, or endure them.
Meditations bk. 8, sect. 59

Jane Austen 1775–1817
English novelist

20 An egg boiled very soft is not unwholesome.
Emma (1816) ch. 3

21 One half of the world cannot understand the pleasures of the other.
Emma (1816) ch. 9

22 The sooner every party breaks up the better.
Emma (1816) ch. 25

23 One has no great hopes from Birmingham. I always say there is something direful in the sound.
Emma (1816) ch. 36

24 A large income is the best recipe for happiness I ever heard of. It certainly may secure all the myrtle and turkey part of it.
Mansfield Park (1814) ch. 22

25 Let other pens dwell on guilt and misery. I quit such odious subjects as soon as I can.
Mansfield Park (1814) ch. 48

26 'Oh! it is only a novel! . . . only Cecilia, or Camilla, or Belinda:' or, in short, only some work in which the most thorough knowledge of human nature, the happiest delineation of its varieties, the liveliest effusions of wit and humour are conveyed to the world in the best chosen language.
Northanger Abbey (1818) ch. 5

27 Oh! who can ever be tired of Bath?
Northanger Abbey (1818) ch. 10

28 Where people wish to attach, they should always be ignorant. To come with a well-informed mind, is to come with an inability of administering to the vanity of others, which a sensible person would always wish to avoid. A woman especially, if she have the misfortune of knowing any thing, should conceal it as well as she can.
Northanger Abbey (1818) ch. 14

1 From politics, it was an easy step to silence.
Northanger Abbey (1818) ch. 14

2 Every man is surrounded by a neighbourhood of voluntary spies, and where roads and newspapers lay every thing open.
Northanger Abbey (1818) ch. 34

3 'My idea of good company, Mr Elliot, is the company of clever, well-informed people, who have a great deal of conversation; that is what I call good company.' 'You are mistaken,' said he gently, 'that is not good company, that is the best.'
Persuasion (1818) ch. 16

4 Men have had every advantage of us in telling their own story. Education has been theirs in so much higher a degree; the pen has been in their hands.
Persuasion (1818) ch. 23

5 All the privilege I claim for my own sex . . . is that of loving longest, when existence or when hope is gone.
Persuasion (1818) ch. 23

6 It is a truth universally acknowledged, that a single man in possession of a good fortune, must be in want of a wife.
Pride and Prejudice (1813) ch. 1

7 She was a woman of mean understanding, little information, and uncertain temper.
Pride and Prejudice (1813) ch. 1

8 May I ask whether these pleasing attentions proceed from the impulse of the moment, or are the result of previous study?
Pride and Prejudice (1813) ch. 14

9 In his library he had been always sure of leisure and tranquillity; and though prepared . . . to meet with folly and conceit in every other room in the house, he was used to be free of them there.
Pride and Prejudice (1813) ch. 15

10 From this day you must be a stranger to one of your parents.—Your mother will never see you again if you do *not* marry Mr Collins, and I will never see you again if you *do*.
Pride and Prejudice (1813) ch. 20

11 For what do we live, but to make sport for our neighbours, and laugh at them in our turn?
Pride and Prejudice (1813) ch. 57

12 It is not time or opportunity that is to determine intimacy; it is disposition alone. Seven years would be insufficient to make some people acquainted with each other, and seven days are more than enough for others.
Sense and Sensibility (1811) vol. 2, ch. 12

13 3 or 4 families in a country village is the very thing to work on.
letter to Anna Austen, 9 September 1814

14 The little bit (two inches wide) of ivory on which I work with so fine a brush, as produces little effect after much labour?
letter to J. Edward Austen, 16 December 1816

15 Pictures of perfection as you know make me sick and wicked.
letter to Fanny Knight, 23 March 1817

16 I am going to take a heroine whom no-one but myself will much like.
on starting Emma
J. E. Austen-Leigh *A Memoir of Jane Austen* (1926 ed.)

Earl of Avon *see* Anthony Eden

Revd Awdry 1911–97
English writer of children's books

17 You've a lot to learn about trucks, little Thomas. They are silly things and must be kept in their place. After pushing them about here for a few weeks you'll know almost as much about them as Edward. Then you'll be a Really Useful Engine.
Thomas the Tank Engine (1946)

Alan Ayckbourn 1939–
English dramatist

18 This place, you tell them you're interested in the arts, you get messages of sympathy.
Chorus of Disapproval (1986) act 2

A. J. Ayer 1910–89
English philosopher

19 The criterion which we use to test the genuineness of apparent statements of fact is the criterion of verifiability. We say that a sentence is factually significant to any given person, if, and only if, he knows how to verify the proposition which it purports to express—that is, if he knows what observations would lead him, under certain conditions, to accept the proposition as being true, or reject it as being false.
Language, Truth, and Logic (1936) ch. 1

Charles Babbage 1792–1871
English mathematician and inventor

20 Every moment dies a man,
Every moment 1$\frac{1}{16}$ is born.
parody of **Tennyson**'s 'Vision of Sin', in an unpublished letter to the poet, in *New Scientist* 4 December 1958; see **Tennyson** 335:9

Lauren Bacall 1924–
American actress

21 I think your whole life shows in your face and you should be proud of that.
in *Daily Telegraph* 2 March 1988

Johann Sebastian Bach 1685–1750
German composer

22 There is nothing to it. You only have to hit the right notes at the right time and the instrument plays itself.
when complimented on his organ playing
K. Geiringer *The Bach Family* (1954)

Francis Bacon 1561–1626
English lawyer, courtier, philosopher, and essayist

1 If a man will begin with certainties, he shall end in doubts; but if he will be content to begin with doubts, he shall end in certainties.
The Advancement of Learning (1605) bk. 1, ch. 5, sect. 8

2 They are ill discoverers that think there is no land, when they can see nothing but sea.
The Advancement of Learning (1605) bk. 2, ch. 7, sect. 5

3 Words are the tokens current and accepted for conceits, as moneys are for values.
The Advancement of Learning (1605) bk. 2, ch. 16, sect. 3

4 A dance is a measured pace, as a verse is a measured speech.
The Advancement of Learning (1605) bk. 2, ch. 16, sect. 5

5 Age appears to be best in four things,—old wood best to burn, old wine to drink, old friends to trust, and old authors to read.
Apophthegms New and Old (1625) no. 97

6 Ancient times were the youth of the world.
De Dignitate et Augmentis Scientiarum (1623) bk. 1 (tr. Gilbert Watts, 1640)

7 Silence is the virtue of fools.
De Dignitate et Augmentis Scientiarum (1623) bk. 6, ch. 3, pt. 3 'The Antitheta of Things' no. 31 (tr. Gilbert Watts, 1640)

8 I hold every man a debtor to his profession.
The Elements of the Common Law (1596) preface

9 He is the fountain of honour.
An Essay of a King (1642); attribution doubtful

10 Prosperity doth best discover vice, but adversity doth best discover virtue.
Essays (1625) 'Of Adversity'

11 I had rather believe all the fables in the legend, and the Talmud, and the Alcoran, than that this universal frame is without a mind.
Essays (1625) 'Of Atheism'

12 A little philosophy inclineth man's mind to atheism, but depth in philosophy bringeth men's minds about to religion.
Essays (1625) 'Of Atheism'

13 Virtue is like a rich stone, best plain set.
Essays (1625) 'Of Beauty'

14 There is no excellent beauty that hath not some strangeness in the proportion.
Essays (1625) 'Of Beauty'

15 He said it that knew it best.
referring to **Demosthenes**
Essays (1625) 'Of Boldness'

16 In civil business; what first? boldness; what second and third? boldness: and yet boldness is a child of ignorance and baseness.
Essays (1625) 'Of Boldness'; see **Danton** 109:18, **Demosthenes** 112:21

17 Books will speak plain when counsellors blanch.
Essays (1625) 'Of Counsel'

18 I knew one that when he wrote a letter he would put that which was most material in the postscript, as if it had been a bymatter.
Essays (1625) 'Of Cunning'; see **Steele** 323:10

19 Nothing doth more hurt in a state than that cunning men pass for wise.
Essays (1625) 'Of Cunning'

20 Men fear death as children fear to go in the dark; and as that natural fear in children is increased with tales, so is the other.
Essays (1625) 'Of Death'

21 Revenge triumphs over death; love slights it; honour aspireth to it; grief flieth to it.
Essays (1625) 'Of Death'

22 Riches are for spending.
Essays (1625) 'Of Expense'

23 A crowd is not company, and faces are but a gallery of pictures, and talk but a tinkling cymbal, where there is no love.
Essays (1625) 'Of Friendship'

24 It redoubleth joys, and cutteth griefs in halves.
Essays (1625) 'Of Friendship'

25 Cure the disease and kill the patient.
Essays (1625) 'Of Friendship'

26 God Almighty first planted a garden; and, indeed, it is the purest of human pleasures.
Essays (1625) 'Of Gardens'

27 Nothing is more pleasant to the eye than green grass kept finely shorn.
Essays (1625) 'Of Gardens'

28 If a man be gracious and courteous to strangers, it shows he is a citizen of the world.
Essays (1625) 'Of Goodness, and Goodness of Nature'

29 All rising to great place is by a winding stair.
Essays (1625) 'Of Great Place'

30 As the births of living creatures at first are ill-shapen, so are all innovations, which are the births of time.
Essays (1625) 'Of Innovations'

31 He that will not apply new remedies must expect new evils; for time is the greatest innovator.
Essays (1625) 'Of Innovations'

32 He that hath wife and children hath given hostages to fortune; for they are impediments to great enterprises, either of virtue or mischief.
Essays (1625) 'Of Marriage and the Single Life'; see **Lucan** 220:9

33 Wives are young men's mistresses, companions for middle age, and old men's nurses.
Essays (1625) 'Of Marriage and the Single Life'

34 He was reputed one of the wise men that made answer to the question when a man

should marry? 'A young man not yet, an elder man not at all.'
Essays (1625) 'Of Marriage and the Single Life'; see **Punch** 271:17

1 The joys of parents are secret, and so are their griefs and fears.
Essays (1625) 'Of Parents and Children'

2 Children sweeten labours, but they make misfortunes more bitter.
Essays (1625) 'Of Parents and Children'

3 Fame is like a river, that beareth up things light and swollen, and drowns things weighty and solid.
Essays (1625) 'Of Praise'

4 Age will not be defied.
Essays (1625) 'Of Regimen of Health'

5 Revenge is a kind of wild justice.
Essays (1625) 'Of Revenge'

6 A man that studieth revenge keeps his own wounds green.
Essays (1625) 'Of Revenge'

7 Money is like muck, not good except it be spread.
Essays (1625) 'Of Seditions and Troubles'

8 The remedy is worse than the disease.
Essays (1625) 'Of Seditions and Troubles'

9 Studies serve for delight, for ornament, and for ability.
Essays (1625) 'Of Studies'

10 To spend too much time in studies is sloth.
Essays (1625) 'Of Studies'

11 Read not to contradict and confute, nor to believe and take for granted, nor to find talk and discourse, but to weigh and consider.
Essays (1625) 'Of Studies'

12 Some books are to be tasted, others to be swallowed, and some few to be chewed and digested.
Essays (1625) 'Of Studies'

13 Reading maketh a full man; conference a ready man; and writing an exact man.
Essays (1625) 'Of Studies'

14 There is nothing makes a man suspect much, more than to know little.
Essays (1625) 'Of Suspicion'

15 Travel, in the younger sort, is a part of education; in the elder, a part of experience. He that travelleth into a country before he hath some entrance into the language, goeth to school, and not to travel.
Essays (1625) 'Of Travel'

16 What is truth? said jesting Pilate; and would not stay for an answer.
Essays (1625) 'Of Truth'; see **Bible** 49:8

17 A mixture of a lie doth ever add pleasure.
Essays (1625) 'Of Truth'

18 All colours will agree in the dark.
Essays (1625) 'Of Unity in Religion'

19 It was prettily devised of Aesop, 'The fly sat upon the axle-tree of the chariot-wheel and said, what a dust do I raise.'
Essays (1625) 'Of Vain-Glory'

20 Be so true to thyself as thou be not false to others.
Essays (1625) 'Of Wisdom for a Man's Self'; see **Shakespeare** 291:31

21 It is the nature of extreme self-lovers, as they will set a house on fire, and it were but to roast their eggs.
Essays (1625) 'Of Wisdom for a Man's Self'

22 It is the wisdom of the crocodiles, that shed tears when they would devour.
Essays (1625) 'Of Wisdom for a Man's Self'

23 Young men are fitter to invent than to judge, fitter for execution than for counsel, and fitter for new projects than for settled business.
Essays (1625) 'Of Youth and Age'

24 God forbid that we should give out a dream of our own imagination for a pattern of the world.
The Great Instauration (1620) tr. J Spedding

25 Lucid intervals and happy pauses.
History of King Henry VII (1622) para. 3 in J. Spedding (ed.) *The Works of Francis Bacon* vol. 6 (1858)

26 The end of our foundation is the knowledge of causes, and secret motions of things; and the enlarging of the bounds of human Empire, to the effecting of all things possible.
New Atlantis (1627)

27 The subtlety of nature is greater many times over than the subtlety of the senses and understanding.
Novum Organum (1620) bk. 1, Aphorism 10 (tr. J. Spedding)

28 Nature cannot be ordered about, except by obeying her.
Novum Organum (1620) bk. 1, Aphorism 129 (tr. J. Spedding)

29 Books must follow sciences, and not sciences books.
Resuscitatio (1657) 'Proposition touching Amendment of Laws'

30 I have taken all knowledge to be my province.
'To My Lord Treasurer Burghley' (1592) in J. Spedding (ed.) *The Letters and Life of Francis Bacon* vol. 1 (1861)

31 *Nam et ipsa scientia potestas est.*
For also knowledge itself is power.
Meditationes Sacrae (1597) 'Of Heresies'

32 God's first Creature, which was Light.
New Atlantis (1627)

33 Printing, gunpowder, and the mariner's needle [compass] . . . these three have changed the whole face and state of things throughout the world.
Novum Organum (1620) bk. 1, Aphorism 129 (tr. J. Spedding); see **Carlyle** 85:8

34 Hope is a good breakfast, but it is a bad supper.
J. Spedding (ed.) *The Works of Francis Bacon* vol. 7 (1859) 'Apophthegms contained in *Resuscitatio*' no. 36

1 Anger makes dull men witty, but it keeps them poor.
*often attributed to Queen **Elizabeth** I from a misreading of the text*
J. Spedding (ed.) *The Works of Francis Bacon* vol. 7 (1859) 'Baconiana'

2 The world's a bubble; and the life of man
Less than a span.
The World (1629)

3 What then remains, but that we still should cry,
Not to be born, or being born, to die?
The World (1629)

Roger Bacon c.1220–c.92
English philosopher, scientist, Franciscan friar

4 If in other sciences we should arrive at certainty without doubt and truth without error, it behoves us to place the foundations of knowledge in mathematics.
Opus Majus bk. 1, ch. 4

Lord Baden-Powell 1857–1941
English soldier and founder of the Boy Scout movement

5 The scouts' motto is founded on my initials, it is: BE PREPARED.
Scouting for Boys (1908)

Joan Baez 1941–
American singer and songwriter

6 I've never had a humble opinion. If you've got an opinion, why be humble about it?
in *Observer* 29 February 2004

Walter Bagehot 1826–77
English economist and essayist

7 In such constitutions [as England's] there are two parts . . . first, those which excite and preserve the reverence of the population—the *dignified* parts . . . and next, the *efficient* parts—those by which it, in fact, works and rules.
The English Constitution (1867) 'The Cabinet'

8 *The Times* has made many ministries.
The English Constitution (1867) 'The Cabinet'

9 Our royalty is to be reverenced, and if you begin to poke about it you cannot reverence it . . . We must not let in daylight upon magic.
The English Constitution (1867) 'The Monarchy (continued)'

10 The Sovereign has, under a constitutional monarchy such as ours, three rights—the right to be consulted, the right to encourage, the right to warn.
The English Constitution (1867) 'The Monarchy (continued)'

11 Writers, like teeth, are divided into incisors and grinders.
Estimates of some Englishmen and Scotchmen (1858) 'The First Edinburgh Reviewers'

12 One of the greatest pains to human nature is the pain of a new idea.
Physics and Politics (1872) 'The Age of Discussion'

David Bailey 1938–
English photographer

13 It takes a lot of imagination to be a good photographer. You need less imagination to be a painter, because you can invent things. But in photography everything is so ordinary; it takes a lot of looking before you learn to see the ordinary.
interview in *The Face* December 1984

Philip James Bailey 1816–1902
English poet

14 We should count time by heart-throbs.
Festus (1839) sc. 5

15 America, thou half-brother of the world;
With something good and bad of every land.
Festus (1839) sc. 10

Bruce Bairnsfather 1888–1959
British cartoonist

16 Well, if you knows of a better 'ole, go to it.
Fragments from France (1915)

Henry Williams Baker 1821–77
English clergyman and hymn-writer

17 The King of love my shepherd is,
Whose goodness faileth never;
I nothing lack if I am his
And he is mine for ever . . .
'The King of love my shepherd is' (1868 hymn)

Michael Bakunin 1814–76
Russian revolutionary and anarchist

18 The urge for destruction is also a creative urge!
Jahrbuch für Wissenschaft und Kunst (1842) 'Die Reaktion in Deutschland' (under the pseudonym 'Jules Elysard')

James Baldwin 1924–87
American novelist and essayist

19 Children have never been very good at listening to their elders, but they have never failed to imitate them. They must, they have no other models.
Nobody Knows My Name (1961) 'Fifth Avenue, Uptown: a letter from Harlem'

20 Anyone who has ever struggled with poverty knows how extremely expensive it is to be poor.
Nobody Knows My Name (1961) 'Fifth Avenue, Uptown: a letter from Harlem'

21 Freedom is not something that anybody can be given; freedom is something people take and people are as free as they want to be.
Nobody Knows My Name (1961) 'Notes for a Hypothetical Novel'

22 Money, it turned out, was exactly like sex, you thought of nothing else if you didn't have it and thought of other things if you did.
in *Esquire* May 1961 'Black Boy looks at the White Boy'

1 If they take you in the morning, they will be coming for us that night.

in New York Review of Books 7 January 1971 'Open Letter to my Sister, Angela Davis'

Stanley Baldwin 1867–1947

British Conservative statesman, Prime Minister 1923–4, 1924–9, 1935–7

see also **Kipling** 203:25

2 A platitude is simply a truth repeated until people get tired of hearing it.

speech in the House of Commons, 29 May 1924

3 The bomber will always get through.

speech in the House of Commons, 10 November 1932

4 I shall be but a short time tonight. I have seldom spoken with greater regret, for my lips are not yet unsealed. Were these troubles over I would make a case, and I guarantee that not a man would go into the lobby against us.

on the Abyssinian crisis; popularly quoted as, 'My lips are sealed'

speech in the House of Commons, 10 December 1935

Arthur James Balfour 1848–1930

British Conservative statesman, Prime Minister 1902–5

5 His Majesty's Government view with favour the establishment in Palestine of a national home for the Jewish people, and will use their best endeavours to facilitate the achievement of this object, it being clearly understood that nothing shall be done which may prejudice the civil and religious rights of existing non-Jewish communities in Palestine, or the rights and political status enjoyed by Jews in any other country.

known as the 'Balfour Declaration'

letter to Lord Rothschild 2 November 1917

6 Zionism, be it right or wrong, good or bad, is rooted in age-long traditions, in present need, in future hopes, of far profounder import than the desires and prejudices of the seven hundred thousand Arabs who now inhabit that ancient land.

in August 1919; Max Egremont Balfour (1980)

7 I thought he was a young man of promise, but it appears he is a young man of promises.

of Winston **Churchill**

Winston Churchill *My Early Life* (1930) ch. 17

Ballads

8 All in the merry month of May, When green buds they were swellin', Young Jemmy Grove on his death-bed lay, For love of Barbara Allen.

'Barbara Allen's Cruelty'

9 I wish I were where Helen lies, Night and day on me she cries; O that I were where Helen lies, On fair Kirkconnell lea! Curst be the heart that thought the thought, And curst the hand that fired the shot, When in my arms burd Helen dropt, And died to succour me!

'Helen of Kirkconnell'

10 Och, Johnny, I hardly knew ye!

'Johnny, I hardly knew Ye'

11 'What gat ye to your dinner, Lord Randal, my Son? What gat ye to your dinner, my handsome young man?' 'I gat eels boil'd in broo'; mother, make my bed soon, For I'm weary wi' hunting, and fain wald lie down.'

'Lord Randal'

12 This ae nighte, this ae nighte, —*Every nighte and alle,* Fire and fleet and candle-lighte, *And Christe receive thy saule.*

'fleet' = corruption of 'flet', meaning house-room

'Lyke-Wake Dirge'

13 When captains courageous whom death could not daunt, Did march to the siege of the city of Gaunt, They mustered their soldiers by two and by three, And the foremost in battle was Mary Ambree.

'Mary Ambree'

14 Yestreen the Queen had four Maries, The night she'll hae but three; There was Marie Seaton, and Marie Beaton, And Marie Carmichael, and me.

'The Queen's Maries'

15 The king sits in Dunfermline town Drinking the blude-red wine.

'Sir Patrick Spens'

16 To Noroway, to Noroway, To Noroway o'er the faem; The king's daughter o' Noroway, 'Tis thou must bring her hame.

'Sir Patrick Spens'

17 I saw the new moon late yestreen Wi' the auld moon in her arm.

'Sir Patrick Spens'

18 Half-owre, half-owre to Aberdour, 'Tis fifty fathoms deep; And there lies good Sir Patrick Spens, Wi' the Scots lords at his feet!

'Sir Patrick Spens'

19 And see ye not yon braid, braid road, That lies across the lily leven? That is the Path of Wickedness, Though some call it the Road to Heaven.

'Thomas the Rhymer'

20 They waded thro' red blude to the knee; For a' the blude that's shed on the earth Rins through the springs o' that countrie.

'Thomas the Rhymer'

21 As I was walking all alane, I heard twa corbies making a mane: The tane unto the tither did say, 'Where sall we gang and dine the day?' '—In behint yon auld fail dyke

I wot there lies a new-slain knight;
And naebody kens that he lies there
But his hawk, his hound, and his lady fair.
'The Twa Corbies' (*corbies* ravens; *fail* turf)

1 The wind doth blow to-day, my love,
And a few small drops of rain;
I never had but one true love;
In cold grave she was lain.
I'll do as much for my true-love
As any young man may;
I'll sit and mourn all at her grave
For a twelvemonth and a day.
'The Unquiet Grave'

2 O waly, waly, up the bank,
And waly, waly, doun the brae,
And waly, waly, yon burn-side,
Where I and my Love wont to gae!
'Waly, Waly'

3 Tom Pearse, Tom Pearse, lend me your grey
mare,
All along, down along, out along, lee.
For I want for to go to Widdicombe Fair,
Wi' Bill Brewer, Jan Stewer, Peter Gurney,
Peter Davey, Dan'l Whiddon, Harry Hawk,
Old Uncle Tom Cobbleigh and all.
Old Uncle Tom Cobbleigh and all.
'Widdicombe Fair'

Whitney Balliett 1926–
American writer

4 A critic is a bundle of biases held loosely
together by a sense of taste.
Dinosaurs in the Morning (1962) introductory note

5 The sound of surprise.
title of book on jazz (1959)

Honoré de Balzac 1799–1850
French novelist

6 Man is neither good nor bad; he is born with
instincts and abilities.
La Comédie Humaine (1842) vol. 1, foreword

Tallulah Bankhead 1903–68
American actress

7 Cocaine habit-forming? Of course not. I
ought to know. I've been using it for years.
Tallulah (1952)

8 I'm as pure as the driven slush.
in *Saturday Evening Post* 12 April 1947

9 I read Shakespeare and the Bible and I can
shoot dice. That's what I call a liberal
education.
attributed

John Barbour c.1320–95
Scottish poet

10 A! fredome is a noble thing!
Fredome mayse man to haiff liking.
The Bruce (1375) bk. 1, l. 225

Alexander Barclay c.1475–1552
Scottish poet and priest

11 The lords will alway that people note and
see

Between them and servants some diversity,
Though it to them turn to no profit at all;
If they have pleasure, the servant shall have
small.
Eclogues (1514) no. 2, l. 790

R. H. Barham 1788–1845
English clergyman

12 Heedless of grammar, they all cried, 'That's
him!'
The Ingoldsby Legends (First Series, 1840) 'The
Jackdaw of Rheims'

Sabine Baring-Gould 1834–1924
English clergyman

13 Onward, Christian soldiers,
Marching as to war,
With the cross of Jesus
Going on before.
'Onward, Christian Soldiers' (1864 hymn)

14 Through the night of doubt and sorrow
Onward goes the pilgrim band.
'Through the night of doubt and sorrow' (1867
hymn); translated from the Danish of B. S.
Ingemann (1789–1862)

Frederick R. Barnard

15 One picture is worth ten thousand words.
in *Printers' Ink* 10 March 1927

Julian Barnes 1946–
English novelist

16 Books say: she did this because. Life says:
she did this. Books are where things are
explained to you; life is where things aren't.
Flaubert's Parrot (1984) ch. 13

17 Does history repeat itself, the first time as
tragedy, the second time as farce? No, that's
too grand, too considered a process. History
just burps, and we taste again that raw-
onion sandwich it swallowed centuries ago.
A History of the World in 10½ Chapters (1989)
'Parenthesis'; see **Marx** 230:7

18 Love is just a system for getting someone to
call you darling after sex.
Talking It Over (1991) ch. 16

Phineas T. Barnum 1810–91
American showman
see also **Lincoln** 215:8

19 There's a sucker born every minute.
attributed

Amelia E. Barr 1831–1919
American writer and journalist

20 The fate of love is that it always seems too
little or too much.
The Belle of Bolling Green (1904) ch. 4

J. M. Barrie 1860–1937
Scottish writer and dramatist

21 When the first baby laughed for the first
time, the laugh broke into a thousand
pieces and they all went skipping about, and
that was the beginning of fairies.
Peter Pan (1928) act 1

1 Every time a child says 'I don't believe in fairies' there is a little fairy somewhere that falls down dead.
  Peter Pan (1928) act 1

2 To die will be an awfully big adventure.
  Peter Pan (1928) act 3; see **Frohman** 143:3

3 Do you believe in fairies? Say quick that you believe! If you believe, clap your hands!
  Peter Pan (1928) act 4

4 There are few more impressive sights in the world than a Scotsman on the make.
  What Every Woman Knows (performed 1908, published 1918) act 2

Roland Barthes 1915–80
French writer and critic

5 What the public wants is the image of passion, not passion itself.
  Mythologies (1957) 'Le monde où l'on catche'

6 I think that cars today are almost the exact equivalent of the great Gothic cathedrals: I mean the supreme creation of an era, conceived with passion by unknown artists, and consumed in image if not in usage by a whole population which appropriates them as a purely magical object.
  Mythologies (1957) 'La nouvelle Citroën'

Bernard Baruch 1870–1965
American financier and presidential adviser

7 We are today in the midst of a cold war.
  'cold war' was suggested to him by H. B. Swope, former editor of the New York World
    speech to South Carolina Legislature, 16 April 1947

8 To me old age is always fifteen years older than I am.
  in *Newsweek* 29 August 1955

9 Vote for the man who promises least; he'll be the least disappointing.
  Meyer Berger *New York* (1960)

Jacques Barzun 1907–
American historian and educationist

10 If it were possible to talk to the unborn, one could never explain to them how it feels to be alive, for life is washed in the speechless real.
  The House of Intellect (1959) ch. 6

Matsuo Basho 1644–94
Japanese poet

11 Early autumn—
rice field, ocean,
one green.
  tr. Lucien Stryk

12 Old pond,
leap-splash—
a frog.
  tr. Lucien Stryk

13 Rainy days—
silkworms droop
on mulberries.
  tr. Lucien Stryk

14 Under the cherry—

blossom soup,
blossom salad.
  tr. Lucien Stryk

15 Days and months are travellers of eternity.
So are the years that pass by.
  The Narrow Road to the Deep North, tr. Nobuyuki Yuasa

Edgar Bateman
and George Le Brunn
British songwriters

16 Wiv a ladder and some glasses,
You could see to 'Ackney Marshes,
If it wasn't for the 'ouses in between.
  'If it wasn't for the 'Ouses in between' (1894 song)

Katherine Lee Bates 1859–1929
American writer and educationist

17 America! America!
God shed His grace on thee
And crown thy good with brotherhood
From sea to shining sea!
  'America the Beautiful' (1893)

Charles Baudelaire 1821–67
French poet and critic

18 *Hypocrite lecteur,—mon semblable,—mon frère.*
Hypocrite reader—my likeness—my brother.
  Les fleurs du mal (1857) 'Au Lecteur'

19 Nature is a temple, where, from living pillars, confused words are sometimes allowed to escape; here man passes, through forests of symbols, which watch him with looks of recognition.
  Les fleurs du mal (1857) 'Correspondances' no. 4

20 *Là, tout n'est qu'ordre et beauté,
Luxe, calme et volupté.*
Everything there is simply order and beauty, luxury, peace and sensual indulgence.
  Les fleurs du mal (1857) 'L'Invitation au voyage'—'Spleen et idéal' no. 56

21 *Il faut épater le bourgeois.*
One must astonish the bourgeois.
  attributed; also attributed to Privat d'Anglemont (*c.*1820–59) in the form *'Je les ai épatés, les bourgeois* [I flabbergasted them, the bourgeois]'

L. Frank Baum 1856–1919
American writer

22 The road to the City of Emeralds is paved with yellow brick.
  The Wonderful Wizard of Oz (1900) ch. 2; see **Harburg** 161:9

Beachcomber *see* J. B. Morton

David Beatty 1871–1936
British admiral

23 There's something wrong with our bloody ships today.
  at the Battle of Jutland, 1916
    Winston Churchill *The World Crisis 1916–1918* (1927) pt. 1

Pierre-Augustin Caron de Beaumarchais 1732–99
French dramatist

1 I hurry to laugh at everything, for fear of having to weep at it.
  Le Barbier de Séville (1775) act 1, sc. 2

2 Drinking when we are not thirsty and making love all year round, madam; that is all there is to distinguish us from other animals.
  Le Mariage de Figaro (1785) act 2, sc. 21

3 Because you are a great lord, you believe yourself to be a great genius! . . . You took the trouble to be born, but no more.
  Le Mariage de Figaro (1785) act 5, sc. 3

Francis Beaumont 1584–1616 and John Fletcher 1579–1625
English dramatists
see also **John Fletcher**

4 Those have most power to hurt us that we love.
  The Maid's Tragedy (written 1610–11) act 5

Lord Beaverbrook (Max Aitken, Lord Beaverbrook) 1879–1964
Canadian-born British newspaper proprietor and Conservative politician

5 Now who is responsible for this work of development on which so much depends? To whom must the praise be given? To the boys in the back rooms. They do not sit in the limelight. But they are the men who do the work.
  in *Listener* 27 March 1941

Kim Beazley Senior 1917–
Australian Labor politician

6 When I joined the Labor Party it was made up of the cream of the working-class. When I left it was made up of the dregs of the middle-class.
  quoted in the Legislative Assembly of New South Wales, 29 April 1992

Kim Beazley 1948–
Australian Labor politician

7 We have never pretended to be a small business party. The Labor Party has never pretended that.
  radio interview, 7 July 2000

Samuel Beckett 1906–89
Irish dramatist, novelist, and poet

8 Perhaps my best years are gone . . . but I wouldn't want them back. Not with the fire that's in me now.
  Krapp's Last Tape (1959)

9 To find a form that accommodates the mess, that is the task of the artist now.
  Proust (1961)

10 You must go on, I can't go on, I'll go on.
  The Unnamable (1959)

11 Nothing to be done.
  Waiting for Godot (1955) act 1

12 One of the thieves was saved. (*Pause*) It's a reasonable percentage.
  Waiting for Godot (1955) act 1

13 ESTRAGON: Charming spot. Inspiring prospects. Let's go.
  VLADIMIR: We can't.
  ESTRAGON: Why not?
  VLADIMIR: We're waiting for Godot.
  Waiting for Godot (1955) act 1

14 Nothing happens, nobody comes, nobody goes, it's awful!
  Waiting for Godot (1955) act 1

15 VLADIMIR: That passed the time.
  ESTRAGON: It would have passed in any case.
  VLADIMIR: Yes, but not so rapidly.
  Waiting for Godot (1955) act 1

16 They give birth astride of a grave, the light gleams an instant, then it's night once more.
  Waiting for Godot (1955) act 2

17 Habit is a great deadener.
  Waiting for Godot (1955) act 2

18 Ever tried. Ever failed. No matter. Try again. Fail again. Fail better.
  Worstward Ho (1983)

19 Even death is unreliable: instead of zero it may be some ghastly hallucination, such as the square root of minus one.
  attributed

Thomas Lovell Beddoes 1803–49
English poet and dramatist

20 If there were dreams to sell,
  What would you buy?
  'Dream-Pedlary' (written 1830, published 1851)

Barnard Elliott Bee 1823–61
American Confederate general

21 There is Jackson with his Virginians, standing like a stone wall. Let us determine to die here, and we will conquer.
  referring to General T. J. ('Stonewall') Jackson at the battle of Bull Run, 21 July, 1861 (in which Bee himself was killed)
  B. Perley Poore *Perley's Reminiscences* (1886) vol. 2, ch. 7

Thomas Beecham 1879–1961
English conductor

22 Like two skeletons copulating on a corrugated tin roof.
  describing the harpsichord
  Harold Atkins and Archie Newman *Beecham Stories* (1978)

23 There are two golden rules for an orchestra: start together and finish together. The public doesn't give a damn what goes on in between.
  Harold Atkins and Archie Newman *Beecham Stories* (1978)

1 Too much counterpoint; what is worse,
Protestant counterpoint.
of J. S. Bach
in *Guardian* 8 March 1971

Max Beerbohm 1872-1956
English critic, essayist, and caricaturist

2 The fading signals and grey eternal walls of
that antique station, which, familiar to
them and insignificant, does yet whisper to
the tourist the last enchantments of the
Middle Age.
Zuleika Dobson (1911) ch. 1; see **Arnold** 17:4

3 The dullard's envy of brilliant men is always
assuaged by the suspicion that they will
come to a bad end.
Zuleika Dobson (1911) ch. 4

Ethel Lynn Beers 1827-79
American poet

4 All quiet along the Potomac to-night,
No sound save the rush of the river,
While soft falls the dew on the face of the
dead—
The picket's off duty forever.
'The Picket Guard' (1861) st. 6; see **McClellan**
222:11

Ludwig van Beethoven 1770-1827
German composer

5 *Muss es sein? Es muss sein.*
Must it be? It must be.
String Quartet in F Major, Opus 135, epigraph

6 The immortal god of harmony.
of J. S. Bach
letter to Breitkopf und Härtel, 22 April 1801;
Michael Hamburger (ed.) *Beethoven: Letters,
Journals and Correspondence* (1951)

Brendan Behan 1923-64
Irish dramatist

7 When I came back to Dublin, I was
courtmartialled in my absence and
sentenced to death in my absence, so I said
they could shoot me in my absence.
Hostage (1958) act 1

8 There's no such thing as bad publicity
except your own obituary.
Dominic Behan *My Brother Brendan* (1965)

Aphra Behn 1640-89
English dramatist, poet, and novelist

9 Oh, what a dear ravishing thing is the
beginning of an Amour!
The Emperor of the Moon (1687) act 1, sc. 1

10 Love ceases to be a pleasure, when it ceases
to be a secret.
The Lover's Watch (1686) 'Four o' Clock. General
Conversation'

11 Variety is the soul of pleasure.
The Rover pt. 1 (1681) act 1; see **Cowper** 105:27

12 Come away; poverty's catching.
The Rover pt. 2 (1681) act 1

13 Money speaks sense in a language all
nations understand.
The Rover pt. 2 (1681) act 3

John Hay Beith *see* Ian Hay

Alexander Graham Bell 1847-1922
Scottish inventor

14 Mr Watson—come here—I want to see you.
*to his assistant, Thomas Watson; the first words
spoken on the telephone, 10 March 1876*
James Mackay *Sounds Out of Silence* (1997) ch. 6

Francis Bellamy 1856-1931
American clergyman and editor

15 I pledge allegiance to the flag of the United
States of America and to the republic for
which it stands, one nation under God,
indivisible, with liberty and justice for all.
The Pledge of Allegiance to the Flag (1892)

Hilaire Belloc 1870-1953
*British poet, essayist, historian, novelist, and
Liberal politician*

16 Child! do not throw this book about;
Refrain from the unholy pleasure
Of cutting all the pictures out!
Preserve it as your chiefest treasure.
A Bad Child's Book of Beasts (1896) dedication

17 I shoot the Hippopotamus
With bullets made of platinum,
Because if I use leaden ones
His hide is sure to flatten 'em.
A Bad Child's Book of Beasts (1896) 'The
Hippopotamus'

18 Physicians of the Utmost Fame
Were called at once; but when they came
They answered, as they took their Fees,
'There is no Cure for this Disease.'
Cautionary Tales (1907) 'Henry King'

19 And always keep a-hold of Nurse
For fear of finding something worse.
Cautionary Tales (1907) 'Jim'

20 Matilda told such Dreadful Lies,
It made one Gasp and Stretch one's Eyes.
Cautionary Tales (1907) 'Matilda'

21 For every time She shouted 'Fire!'
They only answered 'Little Liar!'
Cautionary Tales (1907) 'Matilda'

22 Here richly, with ridiculous display,
The Politician's corpse was laid away.
While all of his acquaintance sneered and
slanged
I wept: for I had longed to see him hanged.
'Epitaph on the Politician Himself' (1923)

23 I'm tired of Love: I'm still more tired of
Rhyme.
But Money gives me pleasure all the time.
'Fatigued' (1923)

24 Whatever happens we have got
The Maxim Gun, and they have not.
The Modern Traveller (1898) pt. 6

25 Oh! let us never, never doubt

What nobody is sure about!
More Beasts for Worse Children (1897) 'The Microbe'

1 Lord Finchley tried to mend the Electric Light
Himself. It struck him dead: And serve him right!
It is the business of the wealthy man
To give employment to the artisan.
More Peers (1911) 'Lord Finchley'

2 When I am dead, I hope it may be said:
'His sins were scarlet, but his books were read.'
'On His Books' (1923)

3 Pale Ebenezer thought it wrong to fight,
But Roaring Bill (who killed him) thought it right.
'The Pacifist' (1938)

4 Do you remember an Inn,
Miranda?
Do you remember an Inn?
'Tarantella' (1923)

5 There's nothing worth the wear of winning,
But laughter and the love of friends.
Verses (1910) 'Dedicatory Ode'

Saul Bellow 1915–2005
American novelist

6 If I am out of my mind, it's all right with me, thought Moses Herzog.
Herzog (1961)

7 Art has something to do with the achievement of stillness in the midst of chaos. A stillness which characterizes prayer, too, and the eye of the storm . . . an arrest of attention in the midst of distraction.
George Plimpton *Writers at Work* (1967) 3rd series

Robert Benchley 1889–1945
American humorist

8 The surest way to make a monkey of a man is to quote him.
My Ten Years in a Quandary (1936)

9 In America there are two classes of travel—first class, and with children.
Pluck and Luck (1925)

10 It took me fifteen years to discover that I had no talent for writing, but I couldn't give it up because by that time I was too famous.
Nathaniel Benchley *Robert Benchley* (1955) ch. 1

11 STREETS FLOODED. PLEASE ADVISE.
message sent on arriving in Venice
R. E. Drennan (ed.) *Wits End* (1973) 'Robert Benchley'

Julien Benda 1867–1956
French philosopher and novelist

12 *La trahison des clercs.*
The treachery of the intellectuals.
title of book (1927)

Peter Benenson 1921–2005
British founder of Amnesty International

13 Better to light a candle than curse the darkness.
at a Human Rights Day ceremony, 10 December 1961 (see also **Stevenson** 325:7)

Stephen Vincent Benét 1898–1943
American poet and novelist

14 I have fallen in love with American names,
The sharp, gaunt names that never get fat.
'American Names' (1927)

15 Bury my heart at Wounded Knee.
'American Names' (1927)

16 We thought we were done with these things but we were wrong.
We thought, because we had power, we had wisdom.
'Litany for Dictatorships' (1935)

Tony Benn 1925–
British Labour politician

17 *questions habitually asked on meeting somebody in a position of power:*
What power have you got? Where did you get it from? In whose interests do you exercise it? To whom are you accountable? How do we get rid of you?
'The Independent Mind', lecture at Nottingham, 18 June 1993

George Bennard 1873–1958
American Methodist minister and hymn-writer

18 I will cling to the old rugged cross,
And exchange it some day for a crown.
'The Old Rugged Cross' (1913 hymn)

Alan Bennett 1934–
English dramatist and actor

19 I have never understood this liking for war. It panders to instincts already catered for within the scope of any respectable domestic establishment.
Forty Years On (1969) act 1

20 Standards are always out of date. That is what makes them standards.
Forty Years On (1969) act 2

21 Sapper, Buchan, Dornford Yates, practitioners in that school of Snobbery with Violence that runs like a thread of good-class tweed through twentieth-century literature.
Forty Years On (1969) act 2

22 We started off trying to set up a small anarchist community, but people wouldn't obey the rules.
Getting On (1972) act 1

23 To be Prince of Wales is not a position. It is a predicament.
The Madness of King George (1995 film); in the 1992 play *The Madness of George III* the line was 'To be heir to the throne . . .'

Arnold Bennett 1867–1931
English novelist

1 'What great cause is he identified with?'
'He's identified . . . with the great cause of
cheering us all up.'
The Card (1911) ch. 12

2 The price of justice is eternal publicity.
Things that have Interested Me (2nd series, 1923)
'Secret Trials'

A. C. Benson 1862–1925
English writer

3 Land of Hope and Glory, Mother of the Free,
How shall we extol thee who are born of
thee?
Wider still and wider shall thy bounds be
set;
God who made thee mighty, make thee
mightier yet.
'Land of Hope and Glory' written to be sung as
the Finale to **Elgar**'s *Coronation Ode* (1902)

Stella Benson 1892–1933
English novelist

4 Call no man foe, but never love a stranger.
This is the End (1917)

Jeremy Bentham 1748–1832
English philosopher

5 Natural rights is simple nonsense: natural
and imprescriptible rights, rhetorical
nonsense—nonsense upon stilts.
Anarchical Fallacies in J. Bowring (ed.) *Works* vol. 2
(1843)

6 The greatest happiness of the greatest
number is the foundation of morals and
legislation.
*Bentham claimed to have acquired the 'sacred
truth' either from Joseph **Priestley** or Cesare
Beccaria (1738–94)*
The Commonplace Book in J. Bowring (ed.) *Works*
vol. 10 (1843); see **Hutcheson** 179:6

7 All punishment is mischief: all punishment
in itself is evil.
Principles of Morals and Legislation (1789) ch. 13,
para. 2

8 The question is not, Can they reason? nor,
Can they talk? but, Can they suffer?
Principles of Morals and Legislation (1789) ch. 17

Edmund Clerihew Bentley
1875–1956
English writer

9 The Art of Biography
Is different from Geography.
Geography is about Maps,
But Biography is about Chaps.
Biography for Beginners (1905) introduction

Lloyd Bentsen 1921–
American Democratic politician

10 *responding to Dan **Quayle**'s claim to have 'as
much experience in the Congress as Jack **Kennedy**
had when he sought the presidency':*

Senator, I served with Jack Kennedy. I knew
Jack Kennedy. Jack Kennedy was a friend of
mine. Senator, you're no Jack Kennedy.
in the vice-presidential debate, 5 October 1988

Henri Bergson 1859–1941
French philosopher

11 The present contains nothing more than the
past, and what is found in the effect was
already in the cause.
L'Évolution créatrice [Creative Evolution] (1907)
ch. 1

12 *L'élan vital.*
The vital spirit.
L'Évolution créatrice (1907) ch. 2 (section title)

George Berkeley 1685–1753
Irish philosopher and Anglican bishop

13 They are neither finite quantities, or
quantities infinitely small, nor yet nothing.
May we not call them the ghosts of departed
quantities?
*on **Newton**'s infinitesimals*
The Analyst (1734) sect. 35

14 [Tar water] is of a nature so mild and benign
and proportioned to the human
constitution, as to warm without heating, to
cheer but not inebriate.
Siris (1744) para. 217; see **Cowper** 105:29

15 Truth is the cry of all, but the game of the
few.
Siris (1744) para. 368

16 We have first raised a dust and then
complain we cannot see.
*A Treatise Concerning the Principles of Human
Knowledge* (1710) introduction, sect. 3

17 All the choir of heaven and furniture of
earth—in a word, all those bodies which
compose the mighty frame of the
world—have not any subsistence without a
mind.
*A Treatise Concerning the Principles of Human
Knowledge* (1710) pt. 1, sect. 6

18 Westward the course of empire takes its
way;
The first four acts already past,
A fifth shall close the drama with the day:
Time's noblest offspring is the last.
'On the Prospect of Planting Arts and Learning
in America' (1752) st. 6.

Irving Berlin 1888–1989
American songwriter

19 I seem to find the happiness I seek
When we're out together dancing cheek-to-
cheek.
'Cheek-to-Cheek' (1935 song) in *Top Hat*

20 God bless America,
Land that I love.
'God Bless America' (1939 song)

21 There may be trouble ahead,
But while there's moonlight and music and
love and romance,

Let's face the music and dance.
'Let's Face the Music and Dance' (1936 song) in *Follow the Fleet*

1 A pretty girl is like a melody
That haunts you night and day.
'A Pretty Girl is like a Melody' (1919 song)

2 The song is ended (but the melody lingers on).
title of song (1927)

3 There's no business like show business.
title of song in *Annie Get Your Gun* (1946)

4 I'm dreaming of a white Christmas,
Just like the ones I used to know.
'White Christmas' (1942 song) in *Holiday Inn*

5 Listen, kid, take my advice, never hate a song that has sold half a million copies.
*to Cole **Porter**, of the song 'Rosalie'*
Philip Furia *Poets of Tin Pan Alley* (1990)

Isaiah Berlin 1909–97
British philosopher

6 Men do not live only by fighting evils. They live by positive goals.
Four Essays on Liberty (1969) 'Political Ideas in the Twentieth Century'

7 There exists a great chasm between those, on one side, who relate everything to a single central vision . . . and, on the other side, those who pursue many ends, often unrelated and even contradictory . . . The first kind of intellectual and artistic personality belongs to the hedgehogs, the second to the foxes.
The Hedgehog and the Fox (1953) sect. 1; see **Archilochus** 14:15

8 Liberty is liberty, not equality or fairness or justice or human happiness or a quiet conscience.
Two Concepts of Liberty (1958)

Hector Berlioz 1803–69
French composer

9 Time is a great teacher but unfortunately it kills all its pupils.
attributed; in *Almanach des lettres françaises et étrangères* (1924) 11 May

Bernard of Chartres d. c.1130
French philosopher

10 We are like dwarfs on the shoulders of giants, so that we can see more than they, and things at a greater distance, not by virtue of any sharpness of sight on our part, or any physical distinction, but because we are carried high and raised up by their giant size.
John of Salisbury *The Metalogicon* (1159) bk. 3, ch. 4, quoted in R. K. Merton *On the Shoulders of Giants* (1965) ch. 9; see **Coleridge** 101:3, **Newton** 250:15

St Bernard of Clairvaux 1090–1153
French theologian, monastic reformer, and abbot

11 You will find something more in woods than in books. Trees and stones will teach you

that which you can never learn from masters.
Epistles no. 106; see **Shakespeare** 290:5; **Wordsworth** 366:9

Eric Berne 1910–70
American psychiatrist

12 Games people play: the psychology of human relationships.
title of book (1964)

Yogi Berra 1925–
American baseball player

13 The future ain't what it used to be.
attributed

14 If people don't want to come out to the ball park, nobody's going to stop 'em.
of baseball games
attributed

15 It ain't over till it's over.
comment on National League pennant race, 1973, quoted in many versions

16 It was déjà vu all over again.
attributed

Wendell Berry 1934–
American poet and novelist

17 I come into the peace of wild things
who do not tax their lives with forethought
of grief. I come into the presence of still
water.
And I feel above me the day-blind stars
waiting with their light.
'The Peace of Wild Things' (1968)

John Berryman 1914–72
American poet

18 We must travel in the direction of our fear.
'A Point of Age' (1942)

19 And moreover my mother told me as a boy (repeatedly) 'Ever to confess you're bored means you have no
Inner Resources.'
77 Dream Songs (1964) no. 14

Pierre Berton 1920–2004
Canadian writer

20 Somebody who knows how to make love in a canoe.
definition of a Canadian
in *Toronto Star, Canadian Magazine* 22 December 1973

Theobald von Bethmann Hollweg 1856–1921
German statesman, Chancellor 1909–17

21 Just for a word 'neutrality'—a word which in wartime has so often been disregarded—just for a scrap of paper, Great Britain is going to make war on a kindred nation who desires nothing better than to be friends with her.

summary of a report by Sir Edward Goschen to Sir Edward Grey

> British Documents on Origins of the War 1898–1914 (1926) vol. 11; *The Diary of Edward Goschen 1900–1914* (1980) Appendix B discusses the contentious origins of this statement

John Betjeman 1906–84
English poet

1 And girls in slacks remember Dad,
  And oafish louts remember Mum,
  And sleepless children's hearts are glad,
  And Christmas-morning bells say 'Come!'
    'Christmas' (1954)

2 And is it true? And is it true,
  This most tremendous tale of all,
  Seen in a stained-glass window's hue,
  A Baby in an ox's stall?
  The Maker of the stars and sea
  Become a Child on earth for me?
    'Christmas' (1954)

3 Old men who never cheated, never doubted,
  Communicated monthly, sit and stare
  At the new suburb stretched beyond the run-way
  Where a young man lands hatless from the air.
    'Death of King George V' (1937)

4 Come, friendly bombs, and fall on Slough!
  It isn't fit for humans now.
    'Slough' (1937)

5 Miss J. Hunter Dunn, Miss J. Hunter Dunn,
  Furnish'd and burnish'd by Aldershot sun.
    'A Subaltern's Love-Song' (1945)

6 Ghastly good taste, or a depressing story of the rise and fall of English architecture.
    title of book (1933)

Aneurin Bevan 1897–1960
British Labour politician

7 This island is made mainly of coal and surrounded by fish. Only an organizing genius could produce a shortage of coal and fish at the same time.
    speech at Blackpool, 24 May 1945

8 The Tory Party . . . So far as I am concerned they are lower than vermin.
    speech at Manchester, 4 July 1948

9 The language of priorities is the religion of Socialism.
    speech at Labour Party Conference in Blackpool, 8 June 1949, in *Report of the 48th Annual Conference* (1949)

10 We know what happens to people who stay in the middle of the road. They get run down.
    in *Observer* 6 December 1953

11 If you carry this resolution you will send Britain's Foreign Secretary naked into the conference chamber.
  speaking against a motion proposing unilateral nuclear disarmament by the UK at Labour Party Conference in Brighton, 3 October 1957
    in *Daily Herald* 4 October 1957

12 I read the newspapers avidly. It is my one form of continuous fiction.
    in *The Times* 29 March 1960

13 I stuffed their mouths with gold.
  of his handling of the consultants during the establishment of the National Health Service
    Brian Abel-Smith *The Hospitals 1800–1948* (1964) ch. 29

William Henry Beveridge
1879–1963
British economist

14 Ignorance is an evil weed, which dictators may cultivate among their dupes, but which no democracy can afford among its citizens.
    Full Employment in a Free Society (1944) pt. 7

15 Want is one only of five giants on the road of reconstruction . . . the others are Disease, Ignorance, Squalor and Idleness.
    Social Insurance and Allied Services (1942) pt. 7

Ernest Bevin 1881–1951
British Labour politician and trade unionist

16 My [foreign] policy is to be able to take a ticket at Victoria Station and go anywhere I damn well please.
    in *Spectator* 20 April 1951

17 If you open that Pandora's Box, you never know what Trojan 'orses will jump out.
  on the Council of Europe
    Roderick Barclay *Ernest Bevin and the Foreign Office* (1975)

18 *on the observation that Aneurin Bevan was sometimes his own worst enemy:*
  Not while I'm alive 'e ain't!
  also attributed to Bevin of Herbert Morrison
    Roderick Barclay *Ernest Bevin and the Foreign Office* (1975)

Bhagavadgita
Hindu poem composed between the 2nd century BC and the 2nd century AD and incorporated into the Mahabharata
textual translations are those of J. Mascaro, 1978

19 If any man thinks he slays, and if another thinks he is slain, neither knows the ways of truth. The Eternal in man cannot kill: the Eternal in man cannot die.
  He is never born, and he never dies. He is in Eternity, he is for evermore. Never-born and eternal, beyond times gone or to come, he does not die when the body dies.
    ch. 2, v. 19; see **Emerson** 131:18, **Upanishads** 344:15

20 I [Krishna] am all-powerful Time which destroys all things, and I have come here to

slay these men. Even if thou does not fight, all the warriors facing thee shall die.

ch. 11, v. 32; see **Oppenheimer** 253:17

1 Only by love can men see me, and know me, and come unto me.

ch. 11, v. 54

The Bible (Authorized Version, 1611)

many phrases derive from **Tyndale***'s translation of the early 16th century*

see also **Book of Common Prayer** *(Psalms)*

2 Upon the setting of that bright Occidental Star, Queen Elizabeth of most happy memory.

The Epistle Dedicatory

Old Testament: Genesis

3 In the beginning God created the heaven and the earth. And the earth was without form, and void; and darkness was upon the face of the deep. And the Spirit of God moved upon the face of the waters.
And God said, Let there be light: and there was light.

Genesis ch. 1, v. 1

4 And the evening and the morning were the first day.

Genesis ch. 1, v. 5

5 And God saw that it was good.

Genesis ch. 1, v. 10

6 Be fruitful, and multiply.

Genesis ch. 1, v. 28

7 And the Lord God planted a garden eastward in Eden.

Genesis ch. 2, v. 8

8 The tree of life also in the midst of the garden, and the tree of knowledge of good and evil.

Genesis ch. 2, v. 9

9 But of the tree of the knowledge of good and evil, thou shalt not eat of it: for in the day that thou eatest thereof thou shalt surely die.

Genesis ch. 2, v. 17

10 It is not good that the man should be alone; I will make him an help meet for him.

Genesis ch. 2, v. 18

11 And the rib, which the Lord God had taken from man, made he a woman.

Genesis ch. 2, v. 22

12 Bone of my bones, and flesh of my flesh.

Genesis ch. 2, v. 23; see **Milton** 239:8

13 Therefore shall a man leave his father and his mother, and shall cleave unto his wife: and they shall be one flesh.

Genesis ch. 2, v. 24

14 Now the serpent was more subtil than any beast of the field.

Genesis ch. 3, v. 1

15 Ye shall be as gods, knowing good and evil.

Genesis ch. 3, v. 5

16 And they sewed fig leaves together, and made themselves aprons.
And they heard the voice of the Lord God walking in the garden in the cool of the day.

'and made themselves breeches' in the Geneva Bible, 1560, known for that reason as the 'Breeches Bible'

Genesis ch. 3, v. 7

17 The woman whom thou gavest to be with me, she gave me of the tree, and I did eat.

Genesis ch. 3, v. 12

18 The serpent beguiled me, and I did eat.

Genesis ch. 3, v. 13

19 It shall bruise thy head, and thou shalt bruise his heel.

Genesis ch. 3, v. 15

20 In sorrow thou shalt bring forth children.

Genesis ch. 3, v. 16

21 In the sweat of thy face shalt thou eat bread.

Genesis ch. 3, v. 19

22 For dust thou art, and unto dust shalt thou return.

Genesis ch. 3, v. 19; see **Longfellow** 217:18

23 Am I my brother's keeper?

Genesis ch. 4, v. 9

24 And the Lord set a mark upon Cain.

Genesis ch. 4, v. 15

25 And Cain went out from the presence of the Lord, and dwelt in the land of Nod, on the east of Eden.

Genesis ch. 4, v. 16

26 And Enoch walked with God: and he was not; for God took him.

Genesis ch. 5, v. 24

27 There were giants in the earth in those days.

Genesis ch. 6, v. 4

28 There went in two and two unto Noah into the Ark, the male and the female.

Genesis ch. 7, v. 9

29 Whoso sheddeth man's blood, by man shall his blood be shed.

Genesis ch. 9, v. 6

30 Even as Nimrod the mighty hunter before the Lord.

Genesis ch. 10, v. 9

31 His [Ishmael's] hand will be against every man, and every man's hand against him.

Genesis ch. 16, v. 12

32 But his [Lot's] wife looked back from behind him, and she became a pillar of salt.

Genesis ch. 19, v. 26

33 A ram caught in a thicket.

Genesis ch. 22, v. 13

34 Esau selleth his birthright for a mess of pottage.

chapter heading in Geneva Bible, 1560

Genesis ch. 25

35 Behold, Esau my brother is a hairy man, and I am a smooth man.

Genesis ch. 27, v. 11

1 The voice is Jacob's voice, but the hands are the hands of Esau.
Genesis ch. 27, v. 22

2 And he dreamed, and behold a ladder set up on the earth, and the top of it reached to heaven: and behold the angels of God ascending and descending on it.
Genesis ch. 28, v. 12

3 Surely the Lord is in this place; and I knew it not.
Genesis ch. 28, v. 16

4 And Jacob served seven years for Rachel.
Genesis ch. 29, v. 20

5 The Lord watch between me and thee, when we are absent one from another.
Genesis ch. 31, v. 49

6 He made him a coat of many colours.
Genesis ch. 37, v. 3

7 Jacob saw that there was corn in Egypt.
Genesis ch. 42, v. 1

8 Then shall ye bring down my grey hairs with sorrow to the grave.
Genesis ch. 42, v. 38

9 Ye shall eat the fat of the land.
Genesis ch. 45, v. 18

10 Unstable as water, thou shalt not excel.
Genesis ch. 49, v. 4

Exodus

11 I have been a stranger in a strange land.
Exodus ch. 2, v. 22

12 Behold, the bush burned with fire, and the bush was not consumed.
Exodus ch. 3, v. 2

13 Put off thy shoes from off thy feet, for the place whereon thou standest is holy ground.
Exodus ch. 3, v. 5

14 A land flowing with milk and honey.
Exodus ch. 3, v. 8

15 I AM THAT I AM.
Exodus ch. 3, v. 14

16 And I will harden Pharaoh's heart, and multiply my signs and my wonders in the land of Egypt.
Exodus ch. 7, v. 3

17 Let my people go.
Exodus ch. 7, v. 16

18 And they shall eat the flesh in that night, roast with fire, and unleavened bread; and with bitter herbs they shall eat it.
Exodus ch. 12, v. 8

19 Ye shall eat it in haste; it is the Lord's passover.
Exodus ch. 12, v. 11

20 For I will pass through the land of Egypt this night, and will smite all the firstborn in the land of Egypt, both man and beast.
Exodus ch. 12, v. 12

21 And they spoiled the Egyptians.
Exodus ch. 12, v. 36

22 And the Lord went before them by day in a pillar of a cloud, to lead them the way; and by night in a pillar of fire, to give them light.
Exodus ch. 13, v. 21

23 Would to God we had died by the hand of the Lord in the land of Egypt, when we sat by the flesh pots, and when we did eat bread to the full.
Exodus ch. 16, v. 3

24 I am the Lord thy God, which have brought thee out of the land of Egypt, out of the house of bondage.
Thou shalt have no other gods before me.
Exodus ch. 20, v. 2

25 I the Lord thy God am a jealous God, visiting the iniquity of the fathers upon the children unto the third and fourth generation of them that hate me.
Exodus ch. 20, v. 5; see **Book of Common Prayer** 60:26

26 Thou shalt not take the name of the Lord thy God in vain.
Exodus ch. 20, v. 7

27 Remember the sabbath day, to keep it holy.
Exodus ch. 20, v. 8

28 Honour thy father and thy mother: that thy days may be long upon the land which the Lord thy God giveth thee.
Thou shalt not kill.
Thou shalt not commit adultery.
Thou shalt not steal.
Thou shalt not bear false witness against thy neighbour.
Thou shalt not covet thy neighbour's house, thou shalt not covet thy neighbour's wife, nor his manservant, nor his maidservant, nor his ox, nor his ass, nor any thing that is thy neighbour's.
Exodus ch. 20, v. 12; see **Book of Common Prayer** 61:2

29 Life for life,
Eye for eye, tooth for tooth.
Exodus ch. 21, v. 23

30 These be thy gods, O Israel.
Exodus ch. 32, v. 4

31 Thou art a stiffnecked people.
Exodus ch. 33, v. 3

Leviticus

32 Let him go for a scapegoat into the wilderness.
Leviticus ch. 16, v. 10

33 Ye shall therefore keep my statutes and my judgments: which if a man do, he shall live in them: I am the Lord.
Leviticus ch. 18, v. 5; see **Talmud** 330:16

34 Thou shalt love thy neighbour as thyself.
Leviticus ch. 19, v. 18; see **Bible** 45:28

Numbers

35 The Lord bless thee, and keep thee:
The Lord make his face shine upon thee, and be gracious unto thee:
The Lord lift up his countenance upon thee, and give thee peace.
Numbers ch. 6, v. 24

1 What hath God wrought!
quoted by Samuel **Morse** *in the first electric telegraph message, 24 May 1844*
Numbers ch. 23, v. 23

2 Be sure your sin will find you out.
Numbers ch. 32, v. 23

Deuteronomy

3 Hear, O Israel: The Lord our God is one Lord.
Deuteronomy ch. 6, v. 4; see **Siddur** 316:6

4 If there arise among you a prophet, or a dreamer of dreams . . . Thou shalt not hearken.
Deuteronomy ch. 13, v. 1

5 He found him in a desert land, and in the waste howling wilderness; he led him about, he instructed him, he kept him as the apple of his eye.
Deuteronomy ch. 32, v. 10

6 The eternal God is thy refuge, and underneath are the everlasting arms.
Deuteronomy ch. 33, v. 27

Joshua

7 When the people heard the sound of the trumpet, and the people shouted with a great shout, that the wall fell down flat.
Joshua ch. 6, v. 20

8 Let them live; but let them be hewers of wood and drawers of water unto all the congregation.
Joshua ch. 9, v. 21

9 I am going the way of all the earth.
Joshua ch. 23, v. 14

Judges

10 I arose a mother in Israel.
Judges ch. 5, v. 7

11 The stars in their courses fought against Sisera.
Judges ch. 5, v. 20

12 She brought forth butter in a lordly dish.
Judges ch. 5, v. 25

13 Why tarry the wheels of his chariots?
Judges ch. 5, v. 28

14 Faint, yet pursuing.
Judges ch. 8, v. 4

15 Then said they unto him, Say now Shibboleth: and he said Sibboleth: for he could not frame to pronounce it right.
Judges ch. 12, v. 6

16 Out of the eater came forth meat, and out of the strong came forth sweetness.
Judges ch. 14, v. 14

17 He smote them hip and thigh.
Judges ch. 15, v. 8

18 With the jawbone of an ass . . . have I slain a thousand men.
Judges ch. 15, v. 16

19 From Dan even to Beer-sheba.
Judges ch. 20, v. 1

20 The people arose as one man.
Judges ch. 20, v. 8

Ruth

21 Intreat me not to leave thee, or to return from following after thee: for whither thou goest, I will go; and where thou lodgest, I will lodge: thy people shall be my people, and thy God my God:
Ruth ch. 1, v. 16

I Samuel

22 Speak, Lord; for thy servant heareth.
I Samuel ch. 3, v. 9

23 And she named the child I-chabod, saying, The glory is departed from Israel.
I Samuel ch. 4, v. 21

24 And the asses of Kish Saul's father were lost. And Kish said to Saul his son, Take now one of the servants with thee, and arise, go seek the asses.
I Samuel ch. 9, v. 3; see **Milton** 239:17

25 Is Saul also among the prophets?
I Samuel ch. 10, v. 11

26 God save the king.
I Samuel ch. 10, v. 24

27 A man after his own heart.
I Samuel ch. 13, v. 14

28 For the Lord seeth not as man seeth: for man looketh on the outward appearance, but the Lord looketh on the heart.
I Samuel ch. 16, v. 7

29 Go, and the Lord be with thee.
I Samuel ch. 17, v. 37

30 Saul hath slain his thousands, and David his ten thousands.
I Samuel ch. 18, v. 7

31 And Saul said, God hath delivered him into mine hand.
I Samuel ch. 23, v. 7

II Samuel

32 The beauty of Israel is slain upon thy high places: how are the mighty fallen!
II Samuel ch. 1, v. 19

33 Tell it not in Gath, publish it not in the streets of Askelon; lest the daughters of the Philistines rejoice.
II Samuel ch. 1, v. 20

34 Saul and Jonathan were lovely and pleasant in their lives, and in their death they were not divided.
II Samuel ch. 1, v. 23

35 I am distressed for thee, my brother Jonathan: very pleasant hast thou been unto me: thy love to me was wonderful, passing the love of women.
How are the mighty fallen.
II Samuel ch. 1, v. 26

36 The poor man had nothing, save one little ewe lamb.
II Samuel ch. 12, v. 3

37 Thou art the man.
II Samuel ch. 12, v. 7

38 For we needs must die, and are as water

spilt on the ground, which cannot be gathered up again; neither doth God respect any person.
II Samuel ch. 14, v. 14

1 O my son Absalom, my son, my son Absalom! would God I had died for thee, O Absalom, my son, my son!
II Samuel ch. 18, v. 33

2 By my God have I leaped over a wall.
II Samuel ch. 22, v. 30

3 David . . . the sweet psalmist of Israel.
II Samuel ch. 23, v. 1

I Kings

4 And Zadok the priest took an horn of oil out of the tabernacle, and anointed Solomon. And they blew the trumpet; and all the people said, God save king Solomon.
I Kings ch. 1, v. 39

5 And when the queen of Sheba had seen all Solomon's wisdom . . . there was no more spirit in her.
I Kings ch. 10, v. 4

6 Behold, the half was not told me.
I Kings ch. 10, v. 7

7 Once in three years came the navy of Tharshish, bringing gold, and silver, ivory, and apes, and peacocks.
I Kings ch. 10, v. 22; see **Masefield** 230:16

8 My father hath chastised you with whips, but I will chastise you with scorpions.
I Kings ch. 12, v. 11

9 To your tents, O Israel.
I Kings ch. 12, v. 16

10 An handful of meal in a barrel, and a little oil in a cruse.
I Kings ch. 17, v. 12

11 How long halt ye between two opinions?
I Kings ch. 18, v. 21

12 There ariseth a little cloud out of the sea, like a man's hand.
I Kings ch. 18, v. 44

13 He girded up his loins.
I Kings ch. 18, v. 46

14 But the Lord was not in the wind: and after the wind an earthquake; but the Lord was not in the earthquake:
And after the earthquake a fire: but the Lord was not in the fire: and after the fire a still small voice.
I Kings ch. 19, v. 11

15 Elijah passed by him, and cast his mantle upon him.
I Kings ch. 19, v. 19

16 I saw all Israel scattered upon the hills, as sheep that have not a shepherd.
I Kings ch. 22, v. 17

17 Feed him with bread of affliction and with water of affliction, until I come in peace.
I Kings ch. 22, v. 27

18 And a certain man drew a bow at a venture, and smote the king of Israel between the joints of the harness.
I Kings ch. 22, v. 34

II Kings

19 Elijah went up by a whirlwind into heaven.
II Kings ch. 2, v. 11

20 The spirit of Elijah doth rest on Elisha.
II Kings ch. 2, v. 15

21 Go up, thou bald head.
II Kings ch. 2, v. 23

22 Is it well with the child? And she answered, It is well.
II Kings ch. 4, v. 26

23 There is death in the pot.
II Kings ch. 4, v. 40

24 I bow myself in the house of Rimmon.
II Kings ch. 5, v. 18

25 Whence comest thou, Gehazi?
II Kings ch. 5, v. 25

26 Is thy servant a dog, that he should do this great thing?
II Kings ch. 8, v. 13

27 The driving is like the driving of Jehu, the son of Nimshi; for he driveth furiously.
II Kings ch. 9, v. 20

28 She painted her face, and tired her head, and looked out at a window.
II Kings ch. 9, v. 30

29 Had Zimri peace, who slew his master?
II Kings ch. 9, v. 31

30 Who is on my side? who?
II Kings ch. 9, v. 32

Esther

31 And if I perish, I perish.
Esther ch. 4, v. 16

Job

32 And the Lord said unto Satan, Whence comest thou? Then Satan answered the Lord, and said, From going to and fro in the earth, and from walking up and down in it.
Job ch. 1, v. 7

33 The Lord gave, and the Lord hath taken away; blessed be the name of the Lord.
Job ch. 1, v. 21

34 All that a man hath will he give for his life.
Job ch. 2, v. 4

35 Curse God, and die.
Job ch. 2, v. 9

36 Let the day perish wherein I was born.
Job ch. 3, v. 3

37 There the wicked cease from troubling, and there the weary be at rest.
Job ch. 3, v. 17

38 Then a spirit passed before my face; the hair of my flesh stood up.
Job ch. 4, v. 15

39 Man is born unto trouble, as the sparks fly upward.
Job ch. 5, v. 7

1 Man that is born of a woman is of few days, and full of trouble.
He cometh forth like a flower, and is cut down: he fleeth also as a shadow, and continueth not.
> Job ch. 14, v. 1; see **Book of Common Prayer** 62:4

2 Miserable comforters are ye all.
> Job ch. 16, v. 2

3 I am escaped with the skin of my teeth.
> Job ch. 19, v. 20

4 I know that my redeemer liveth, and that he shall stand at the latter day upon the earth: And though after my skin worms destroy this body, yet in my flesh shall I see God.
> Job ch. 19, v. 25

5 The root of the matter is found in me.
> Job ch. 19, v. 28

6 The price of wisdom is above rubies.
> Job ch. 28, v. 18

7 Who is this that darkeneth counsel by words without knowledge?
> Job ch. 38, v. 2

8 Canst thou bind the sweet influences of Pleiades, or loose the bands of Orion?
> Job ch. 38, v. 31

9 He saith among the trumpets, Ha, ha; and he smelleth the battle afar off, the thunder of the captains, and the shouting.
> Job ch. 39, v. 25

10 Canst thou draw out leviathan with an hook?
> Job ch. 41, v. 1

Proverbs

11 Surely in vain the net is spread in the sight of any bird.
> Proverbs ch. 1, v. 17

12 For whom the Lord loveth he correcteth.
> Proverbs ch. 3, v. 12

13 Her ways are ways of pleasantness, and all her paths are peace.
> Proverbs ch. 3, v. 17

14 Wisdom is the principal thing; therefore get wisdom: and with all thy getting get understanding.
> Proverbs ch. 4, v. 7

15 Go to the ant thou sluggard; consider her ways, and be wise.
> Proverbs ch. 6, v. 6

16 Yet a little sleep, a little slumber, a little folding of the hands to sleep.
> Proverbs ch. 6, v. 10

17 Wisdom hath builded her house, she hath hewn out her seven pillars.
> Proverbs ch. 9, v. 1

18 Stolen waters are sweet.
> Proverbs ch. 9, v. 17

19 A wise son maketh a glad father: but a foolish son is the heaviness of his mother.
> Proverbs ch. 10, v. 1

20 A righteous man regardeth the life of his beast: but the tender mercies of the wicked are cruel.
> Proverbs ch. 12, v. 10

21 Lying lips are abomination to the Lord.
> Proverbs ch. 12, v. 22; see **Anonymous** 7:5

22 Hope deferred maketh the heart sick.
> Proverbs ch. 13, v. 12

23 The way of transgressors is hard.
> Proverbs ch. 13, v. 15

24 He that spareth his rod hateth his son.
> Proverbs ch. 13, v. 24

25 A soft answer turneth away wrath.
> Proverbs ch. 15, v. 1

26 A merry heart maketh a cheerful countenance.
> Proverbs ch. 15, v. 13

27 Better is a dinner of herbs where love is, than a stalled ox and hatred therewith.
> *'Better is a mess of pottage with love, than a fat ox with evil will' in Matthew's Bible (1535)*
> Proverbs ch. 15, v. 17

28 A word spoken in due season, how good is it!
> Proverbs ch. 15, v. 23

29 Pride goeth before destruction, and an haughty spirit before a fall.
> Proverbs ch. 16, v. 18

30 A merry heart doeth good like a medicine.
> Proverbs ch. 17, v. 22

31 There is a friend that sticketh closer than a brother.
> Proverbs ch. 18, v. 24; see **Kipling** 202:27

32 Wine is a mocker, strong drink is raging.
> Proverbs ch. 20, v. 1

33 Train up a child in the way he should go: and when he is old, he will not depart from it.
> Proverbs ch. 22, v. 6

34 Look not thou upon the wine when it is red.
> Proverbs ch. 23, v. 31

35 A word fitly spoken is like apples of gold in pictures of silver.
> Proverbs ch. 25, v. 11

36 If thine enemy be hungry, give him bread to eat; and if he be thirsty, give him water to drink.
For thou shalt heap coals of fire upon his head, and the Lord shall reward thee.
> Proverbs ch. 25, v. 21

37 As cold waters to a thirsty soul, so is good news from a far country.
> Proverbs ch. 25, v. 25

38 Answer not a fool according to his folly, lest thou also be like unto him.
Answer a fool according to his folly, lest he be wise in his own conceit.
> Proverbs ch. 26, v. 4

39 As a dog returneth to his vomit, so a fool returneth to his folly.
> Proverbs ch. 26, v. 11

1 The wicked flee when no man pursueth: but the righteous are bold as a lion.
Proverbs ch. 28, v. 1

2 He that maketh haste to be rich shall not be innocent.
Proverbs ch. 28, v. 20

3 Where there is no vision, the people perish.
Proverbs ch. 29, v. 18

4 There be three things which are too wonderful for me, yea, four which I know not:
The way of an eagle in the air; the way of a serpent upon a rock; the way of a ship in the midst of the sea; and the way of a man with a maid.
Proverbs ch. 30, v. 18

5 Who can find a virtuous woman? for her price is far above rubies.
Proverbs ch. 31, v. 10

Ecclesiastes

6 Vanity of vanities; all is vanity.
Ecclesiastes ch. 1, v. 2; see **Bible** 54:4

7 All the rivers run into the sea; yet the sea is not full.
Ecclesiastes ch. 1, v. 7

8 The thing that hath been, it is that which shall be; and that which is done is that which shall be done: and there is no new thing under the sun.
Ecclesiastes ch. 1, v. 9

9 He that increaseth knowledge increaseth sorrow.
Ecclesiastes ch. 1, v. 18

10 To every thing there is a season, and a time to every purpose under the heaven:
A time to be born, and a time to die; a time to plant, and a time to pluck up that which is planted.
Ecclesiastes ch. 3, v. 1

11 A time to weep, and a time to laugh; a time to mourn, and a time to dance.
Ecclesiastes ch. 3, v. 1

12 A time to love, and a time to hate; a time of war, and a time of peace.
Ecclesiastes ch. 3, v. 1

13 A threefold cord is not quickly broken.
Ecclesiastes ch. 4, v. 12

14 The sleep of a labouring man is sweet.
Ecclesiastes ch. 5, v. 12

15 As the crackling of thorns under a pot, so is the laughter of a fool.
Ecclesiastes ch. 7, v. 6

16 God hath made man upright; but they have sought out many inventions.
Ecclesiastes ch. 7, v. 29

17 There is no discharge in that war.
Ecclesiastes ch. 8, v. 8

18 A man hath no better thing under the sun, than to eat, and to drink, and to be merry.
Ecclesiastes ch. 8, v. 15; see **Bible** 40:21, **Bible** 47:20

19 A living dog is better than a dead lion.
Ecclesiastes ch. 9, v. 4

20 Whatsoever thy hand findeth to do, do it with thy might; for there is no work, nor device, nor knowledge, nor wisdom, in the grave, whither thou goest.
Ecclesiastes ch. 9, v. 10

21 The race is not to the swift, nor the battle to the strong.
Ecclesiastes ch. 9, v. 11; see **Davidson** 110:19

22 He that diggeth a pit shall fall into it.
Ecclesiastes ch. 10, v. 8

23 Woe to thee, O land, when thy king is a child.
Ecclesiastes ch. 10, v. 16; see **Shakespeare** 306:12

24 Wine maketh merry: but money answereth all things.
Ecclesiastes ch. 10, v. 19

25 Cast thy bread upon the waters: for thou shalt find it after many days.
Ecclesiastes ch. 11, v. 1

26 In the place where the tree falleth, there it shall be.
Ecclesiastes ch. 11, v. 3

27 Remember now thy Creator in the days of thy youth.
Ecclesiastes ch. 12, v. 1

28 And desire shall fail: because man goeth to his long home, and the mourners go about the streets:
Or ever the silver cord be loosed, or the golden bowl be broken, or the pitcher be broken at the fountain, or the wheel broken at the cistern.
Then shall the dust return to the earth as it was: and the spirit shall return unto God who gave it.
Ecclesiastes ch. 12, v. 5

29 Of making many books there is no end; and much study is a weariness of the flesh.
Ecclesiastes ch. 12, v. 12

30 Fear God, and keep his commandments: for this is the whole duty of man.
Ecclesiastes ch. 12, v. 13

Song of Solomon

31 I am black, but comely.
Song of Solomon ch. 1, v. 5

32 I am the rose of Sharon, and the lily of the valleys.
Song of Solomon ch. 2, v. 1

33 The time of the singing of birds is come, and the voice of the turtle is heard in our land.
Song of Solomon ch. 2, v. 12

34 My beloved is mine, and I am his: he feedeth among the lilies.
Until the day break, and the shadows flee away.
Song of Solomon ch. 2, v. 16

35 Behold, thou art fair, my love; behold, thou art fair.
Song of Solomon ch. 4, v. 1

1 A garden inclosed is my sister, my spouse; a spring shut up, a fountain sealed.
Song of Solomon ch. 4, v. 12

2 Love is strong as death; jealousy is cruel as the grave.
Song of Solomon ch. 8, v. 6

3 Many waters cannot quench love, neither can the floods drown it.
Song of Solomon ch. 8, v. 7

Isaiah

4 Though your sins be as scarlet, they shall be as white as snow.
Isaiah ch. 1, v. 18

5 They shall beat their swords into plowshares, and their spears into pruninghooks: nation shall not lift up sword against nation, neither shall they learn war any more.
Micah ch. 4, v. 3, Joel ch. 3, v. 10 have same image
Isaiah ch. 2, v. 4; see **Rendall** 275:5

6 What mean ye that ye beat my people to pieces, and grind the faces of the poor?
Isaiah ch. 3, v. 15

7 Woe unto them that join house to house, that lay field to field, till there be no place.
Isaiah ch. 5, v. 8

8 I saw also the Lord sitting upon a throne, high and lifted up, and his train filled the temple.
Above it stood the seraphims: each one had six wings; with twain he covered his face, and with twain he covered his feet, and with twain he did fly.
And one cried unto another, and said, Holy, holy, holy, is the Lord of hosts: the whole earth is full of his glory.
Isaiah ch. 6, v. 1

9 Woe is me! for I am undone; because I am a man of unclean lips, and I dwell in the midst of a people of unclean lips.
Isaiah ch. 6, v. 5

10 Whom shall I send, and who will go for us? Then said I, Here am I; send me.
Isaiah ch. 6, v. 8

11 Then said I, Lord, how long?
Isaiah ch. 6, v. 11

12 Behold, a virgin shall conceive, and bear a son, and shall call his name Immanuel.
Isaiah ch. 7, v. 14

13 The people that walked in darkness have seen a great light: they that dwell in the land of the shadow of death, upon them hath the light shined.
Isaiah ch. 9, v. 2

14 For unto us a child is born, unto us a son is given: and the government shall be upon his shoulder: and his name shall be called Wonderful, Counsellor, The mighty God, The everlasting Father, The Prince of Peace. Of the increase of his government and peace there shall be no end.
Isaiah ch. 9, v. 6

15 The zeal of the Lord of hosts will perform this.
Isaiah ch. 9, v. 7

16 And there shall come forth a rod out of the stem of Jesse, and a branch shall grow out of his roots.
And the spirit of the Lord shall rest upon him, the spirit of wisdom and understanding, the spirit of counsel and might, the spirit of knowledge and of the fear of the Lord.
Isaiah ch. 11, v. 1

17 The wolf also shall dwell with the lamb, and the leopard shall lie down with the kid; and the calf and the young lion and the fatling together; and a little child shall lead them.
Isaiah ch. 11, v. 6

18 They shall not hurt nor destroy in all my holy mountain: for the earth shall be full of the knowledge of the Lord, as the waters cover the sea.
Isaiah ch. 11, v. 9

19 How art thou fallen from heaven, O Lucifer, son of the morning!
Isaiah ch. 14, v. 12

20 Watchman, what of the night? Watchman, what of the night?
The watchman said, The morning cometh, and also the night.
Isaiah ch. 21, v. 11

21 Let us eat and drink; for to morrow we shall die.
Isaiah ch. 22, v. 13; see **Bible** 39:18, **Bible** 47:20

22 He will swallow up death in victory; and the Lord God will wipe away tears from off all faces.
Isaiah ch. 25, v. 8

23 For precept must be upon precept, precept upon precept; line upon line, line upon line; here a little, and there a little.
Isaiah ch. 28, v. 10

24 We have made a covenant with death, and with hell are we at agreement.
Isaiah ch. 28, v. 15; see **Garrison** 146:9

25 The bread of adversity, and the waters of affliction.
Isaiah ch. 30, v. 20

26 This is the way, walk ye in it.
Isaiah ch. 30, v. 21

27 The desert shall rejoice, and blossom as the rose.
Isaiah ch. 35, v. 1

28 Set thine house in order.
Isaiah ch. 38, v. 1

29 Comfort ye, comfort ye my people, saith your God.
Speak ye comfortably to Jerusalem, and cry unto her, that her warfare is accomplished.
Isaiah ch. 40, v. 1

30 The voice of him that crieth in the wilderness, Prepare ye the way of the Lord, make straight in the desert a highway for our God.

Every valley shall be exalted, and every mountain and hill shall be made low: and the crooked shall be made straight, and the rough places plain:
And the glory of the Lord shall be revealed, and all flesh shall see it together: for the mouth of the Lord hath spoken it.
Isaiah ch. 40, v. 3; see **Bible** 43:5

1 The voice said, Cry. And he said, What shall I cry? All flesh is grass, and all the goodliness thereof is as the flower of the field:
The grass withereth, the flower fadeth: because the spirit of the Lord bloweth upon it: surely the people is grass.
Isaiah ch. 40, v. 6; see **Bible** 52:25

2 He shall feed his flock like a shepherd: he shall gather the lambs with his arm, and carry them in his bosom, and shall gently lead those that are with young.
Isaiah ch. 40, v. 11

3 Have ye not known? have ye not heard? hath it not been told you from the beginning?
Isaiah ch. 40, v. 21

4 They shall mount up with wings as eagles; they shall run, and not be weary; and they shall walk, and not faint.
Isaiah ch. 40, v. 31

5 A bruised reed shall he not break, and the smoking flax shall he not quench.
Isaiah ch. 42, v. 3

6 There is no peace, saith the Lord, unto the wicked.
Isaiah ch. 48, v. 22

7 How beautiful upon the mountains are the feet of him that bringeth good tidings, that publisheth peace; that bringeth good tidings of good, that publisheth salvation.
Isaiah ch. 52, v. 7

8 For they shall see eye to eye, when the Lord shall bring again Zion.
Break forth into joy, sing together, ye waste places of Jerusalem: for the Lord hath comforted his people, he hath redeemed Jerusalem.
Isaiah ch. 52, v. 8

9 He is despised and rejected of men; a man of sorrows, and acquainted with grief.
Isaiah ch. 53, v. 3

10 But he was wounded for our transgressions, he was bruised for our iniquities: the chastisement of our peace was upon him; and with his stripes we are healed.
All we like sheep have gone astray; we have turned every one to his own way; and the Lord hath laid on him the iniquity of us all.
Isaiah ch. 53, v. 5

11 He is brought as a lamb to the slaughter, and as a sheep before her shearers is dumb, so he openeth not his mouth.
Isaiah ch. 53, v. 7

12 Yea, come, buy wine and milk without money and without price.
Isaiah ch. 55, v. 1

13 Seek ye the Lord while he may be found, call ye upon him while he is near.
Isaiah ch. 55, v. 6

14 For my thoughts are not your thoughts, neither are your ways my ways, saith the Lord.
Isaiah ch. 55, v. 8

15 Mine house shall be called an house of prayer for all people.
Isaiah ch. 56, v. 7; see **Bible** 45:24

16 Arise, shine; for thy light is come, and the glory of the Lord is risen upon thee.
Isaiah ch. 60, v. 1

17 The Spirit of the Lord God is upon me . . . To bind up the brokenhearted, to proclaim liberty to the captives, and the opening of the prison to them that are bound;
To proclaim the acceptable year of the Lord, and the day of vengeance of our God.
Isaiah ch. 61, v. 1

18 Stand by thyself, come not near to me; for I am holier than thou.
Isaiah ch. 65, v. 5

19 For, behold, I create new heavens and a new earth.
Isaiah ch. 65, v. 17

Jeremiah

20 The harvest is past, the summer is ended, and we are not saved.
Jeremiah ch. 8, v. 20

21 Is there no balm in Gilead?
Jeremiah ch. 8, v. 22

22 Can the Ethiopian change his skin, or the leopard his spots?
Jeremiah ch. 13, v. 23

23 The heart is deceitful above all things, and desperately wicked.
Jeremiah ch. 17, v. 9

Lamentations

24 Is it nothing to you, all ye that pass by? behold, and see if there be any sorrow like unto my sorrow.
Lamentations ch. 1, v. 12

25 Remembering mine affliction and my misery, the wormwood and the gall.
Lamentations ch. 3, v. 19

26 O Lord, thou hast seen my wrong: judge thou my cause.
Lamentations ch. 4, v. 59

Ezekiel

27 As is the mother, so is her daughter.
Ezekiel ch. 16, v. 44

28 The fathers have eaten sour grapes, and the children's teeth are set on edge.
Ezekiel ch. 18, v. 2

29 When the wicked man turneth away from his wickedness that he hath committed, and doeth that which is lawful and right, he shall save his soul alive.
Ezekiel ch. 18, v. 27

1 The king of Babylon stood at the parting of the ways.
   Ezekiel ch. 21, v. 21

2 The valley which was full of bones.
   Ezekiel ch. 37, v. 1

3 Can these bones live?
   Ezekiel ch. 37, v. 3

4 O ye dry bones, hear the word of the Lord.
   Ezekiel ch. 37, v. 4

Daniel

5 Cast into the midst of a burning fiery furnace.
   Daniel ch. 3, v. 4

6 And this is the writing that was written,
   MENE, MENE, TEKEL, UPHARSIN.
   This is the interpretation of the thing:
   MENE; God hath numbered thy kingdom, and finished it.
   TEKEL; Thou art weighed in the balances and art found wanting.
   PERES; Thy kingdom is divided, and given to the Medes and Persians.
   Daniel ch. 5, v. 25

7 Now, O king, establish the decree, and sign the writing, that it be not changed, according to the law of the Medes and Persians, which altereth not.
   Daniel ch. 6, v. 8

8 The Ancient of days did sit, whose garment was white as snow, and the hair of his head like the pure wool: his throne was like the fiery flame, and his wheels as burning fire. A fiery stream issued and came forth from before him: thousand thousands ministered unto him, and ten thousand times ten thousand stood before him: the judgement was set, and the books were opened.
   Daniel ch. 7, v. 9

9 O Daniel, a man greatly beloved.
   Daniel ch. 10, v. 11

Hosea

10 They have sown the wind, and they shall reap the whirlwind.
   Hosea ch. 8, v. 7

Joel

11 I will restore to you the years that the locust hath eaten.
   Joel ch. 2, v. 25

12 Your sons and your daughters shall prophesy, your old men shall dream dreams, your young men shall see visions.
   Joel ch. 2, v. 28

Amos

13 Ye were as a firebrand plucked out of the burning.
   Amos ch. 4, v. 11

Micah

14 But thou, Bethlehem Ephratah, though thou be little among the thousands of Judah, yet out of thee shall he come forth unto me that is to be ruler in Israel.
   Micah ch. 5, v. 2

15 What doth the Lord require of thee, but to do justly, and to love mercy, and to walk humbly with thy God?
   Micah ch. 6, v. 8

Habakkuk

16 Write the vision, and make it plain upon tables, that he may run that readeth it.
   Habakkuk ch. 2, v. 2

Malachi

17 But unto you that fear my name shall the Sun of righteousness arise with healing in his wings.
   Malachi ch. 4, v. 2

Apocrypha

18 Great is Truth, and mighty above all things.
   I Esdras ch. 4, v. 41; see **Bible** 54:14

19 I shall light a candle of understanding in thine heart, which shall not be put out.
   II Esdras ch. 14, v. 25; see **Latimer** 209:12

20 But the souls of the righteous are in the hand of God.
   Wisdom of Solomon ch. 3, v. 1

21 And in the time of their visitation they shall shine, and run to and fro like sparks among the stubble.
   Wisdom of Solomon ch. 3, v. 7

22 Laugh no man to scorn in the bitterness of his soul.
   Ecclesiasticus ch. 7, v. 11

23 Judge none blessed before his death.
   Ecclesiasticus ch. 11, v. 28; see **Solon** 320:5

24 He that toucheth pitch shall be defiled therewith.
   Ecclesiasticus ch. 13, v. 1

25 A merchant shall hardly keep himself from doing wrong.
   Ecclesiasticus ch. 26, v. 29

26 Honour a physician with the honour due unto him for the uses which ye may have of him: for the Lord hath created him.
   Ecclesiasticus ch. 38, v. 1

27 Let us now praise famous men, and our fathers that begat us.
   Ecclesiasticus ch. 44, v. 1

28 And some there be, which have no memorial . . . and are become as though they had never been born . . .
   But these were merciful men, whose righteousness hath not been forgotten . . .
   Their seed shall remain for ever, and their glory shall not be blotted out.
   Their bodies are buried in peace; but their name liveth for evermore.
   Ecclesiasticus ch. 44, v. 9

29 When he was at the last gasp.
   II Maccabees ch. 7, v. 9

New Testament: St Matthew

1 There came wise men from the east to Jerusalem,
Saying, Where is he that is born King of the Jews? for we have seen his star in the east, and are come to worship him.
St Matthew ch. 2, v. 1

2 They presented unto him gifts; gold, and frankincense, and myrrh.
St Matthew ch. 2, v. 11

3 In Rama was there a voice heard, lamentation, and weeping, and great mourning, Rachel weeping for her children, and would not be comforted, because they are not.
quoting Jeremiah ch. 31, v. 15
St Matthew ch. 2, v. 18

4 Repent ye: for the kingdom of heaven is at hand.
St Matthew ch. 3, v. 2

5 The voice of one crying in the wilderness, Prepare ye the way of the Lord, make his paths straight.
St Matthew ch. 3, v. 3; see **Bible** 40:30

6 John had his raiment of camel's hair, and a leathern girdle about his loins; and his meat was locusts and wild honey.
St Matthew ch. 3, v. 4

7 O generation of vipers, who hath warned you to flee from the wrath to come?
St Matthew ch. 3, v. 7

8 This is my beloved Son, in whom I am well pleased.
St Matthew ch. 3, v. 17

9 Man shall not live by bread alone, but by every word that proceedeth out of the mouth of God.
echoing Deuteronomy ch. 8, v. 3
St Matthew ch. 4, v. 4

10 Thou shalt not tempt the Lord thy God.
echoing Deuteronomy ch. 6, v. 16
St Matthew ch. 4, v. 7

11 The devil taketh him up into an exceeding high mountain, and sheweth him all the kingdoms of the world, and the glory of them.
St Matthew ch. 4, v. 8

12 Follow me, and I will make you fishers of men.
St Matthew ch. 4, v. 19

13 Blessed are the poor in spirit: for theirs is the kingdom of heaven.
Blessed are they that mourn: for they shall be comforted.
Blessed are the meek: for they shall inherit the earth.
Blessed are they which do hunger and thirst after righteousness: for they shall be filled.
Blessed are the merciful: for they shall obtain mercy.
Blessed are the pure in heart: for they shall see God.

Blessed are the peacemakers: for they shall be called the children of God.
St Matthew ch. 5, v. 3

14 Ye are the salt of the earth: but if the salt have lost his savour, wherewith shall it be salted?
St Matthew ch. 5, v. 13

15 Ye are the light of the world. A city that is set on an hill cannot be hid.
St Matthew ch. 5, v. 14

16 Let your light so shine before men, that they may see your good works.
St Matthew ch. 5, v. 16

17 Resist not evil: but whosoever shall smite thee on thy right cheek, turn to him the other also.
St Matthew ch. 5, v. 39

18 Whosoever shall compel thee to go a mile, go with him twain.
St Matthew ch. 5, v. 41

19 He maketh his sun to rise on the evil and on the good, and sendeth rain on the just and on the unjust.
St Matthew ch. 5, v. 45; see **Bowen** 66:17

20 Be ye therefore perfect, even as your Father which is in heaven is perfect.
St Matthew ch. 5, v. 48

21 When thou doest alms, let not thy left hand know what thy right hand doeth.
That thine alms may be in secret: and thy Father which seeth in secret himself shall reward you openly.
St Matthew ch. 6, v. 3

22 After this manner therefore pray ye: Our Father which art in heaven, Hallowed be thy name.
Thy kingdom come. Thy will be done in earth, as it is in heaven.
Give us this day our daily bread.
And forgive us our debts, as we forgive our debtors.
And lead us not into temptation, but deliver us from evil: For thine is the kingdom, and the power, and the glory, for ever. Amen.
St Matthew ch. 6, v. 9; see **Book of Common Prayer** 59:15, **Missal** 240:24

23 Lay not up for yourselves treasures upon earth, where moth and rust doth corrupt, and where thieves break through and steal:
But lay up for yourselves treasures in heaven.
St Matthew ch. 6, v. 19

24 Where your treasure is, there will your heart be also.
St Matthew ch. 6, v. 21

25 No man can serve two masters . . . Ye cannot serve God and mammon.
St Matthew ch. 6, v. 24

26 Consider the lilies of the field, how they grow; they toil not, neither do they spin:
And yet I say unto you, That even Solomon in all his glory was not arrayed like one of these.
St Matthew ch. 6, v. 28

1 Seek ye first the kingdom of God, and his righteousness; and all these things shall be added unto you.
St Matthew ch. 6, v. 33

2 Take therefore no thought for the morrow: for the morrow shall take thought for the things of itself. Sufficient unto the day is the evil thereof.
St Matthew ch. 6, v. 34

3 Judge not, that ye be not judged.
St Matthew ch. 7, v. 1

4 Why beholdest thou the mote that is in thy brother's eye, but considerest not the beam that is in thine own eye?
St Matthew ch. 7, v. 3

5 Neither cast ye your pearls before swine.
St Matthew ch. 7, v. 6

6 Ask, and it shall be given you; seek, and ye shall find; knock, and it shall be opened unto you.
St Matthew ch. 7, v. 7

7 Or what man is there of you, whom if his son ask bread, will he give him a stone?
St Matthew ch. 7, v. 9

8 Therefore all things whatsoever ye would that men should do to you, do ye even so to them: for this is the law and the prophets.
St Matthew ch. 7, v. 12

9 Wide is the gate, and broad is the way, that leadeth to destruction, and many there be that go in thereat.
St Matthew ch. 7, v. 13

10 Strait is the gate, and narrow is the way, which leadeth unto life, and few there be that find it.
St Matthew ch. 7, v. 14

11 Beware of false prophets, which come to you in sheep's clothing, but inwardly they are ravening wolves.
St Matthew ch. 7, v. 15

12 By their fruits ye shall know them.
St Matthew ch. 7, v. 20

13 The winds blew, and beat upon that house; and it fell not: for it was founded upon a rock.
St Matthew ch. 7, v. 25

14 Lord I am not worthy that thou shouldest come under my roof.
St Matthew ch. 8, v. 8; see **Missal** 241:1

15 But the children of the kingdom shall be cast out into outer darkness: there shall be weeping and gnashing of teeth.
St Matthew ch. 8, v. 12

16 The foxes have holes, and the birds of the air have nests; but the Son of man hath not where to lay his head.
St Matthew ch. 8, v. 20

17 Let the dead bury their dead.
St Matthew ch. 8, v. 22

18 Why eateth your Master with publicans and sinners?
St Matthew ch. 9, v. 11

19 They that be whole need not a physician, but they that are sick.
St Matthew ch. 9, v. 12

20 I am not come to call the righteous, but sinners to repentance.
St Matthew ch. 9, v. 13

21 Neither do men put new wine into old bottles.
St Matthew ch. 9, v. 17

22 Thy faith hath made thee whole.
St Matthew ch. 9, v. 22

23 The maid is not dead, but sleepeth.
St Matthew ch. 9, v. 24

24 The harvest truly is plenteous, but the labourers are few.
St Matthew ch. 9, v. 37

25 Freely ye have received, freely give.
St Matthew ch. 10, v. 8

26 When ye depart out of that house or city, shake off the dust of your feet.
St Matthew ch. 10, v. 14

27 Be ye therefore wise as serpents, and harmless as doves.
St Matthew ch. 10, v. 16

28 Are not two sparrows sold for a farthing? and one of them shall not fall on the ground without your Father.
The very hairs of your head are all numbered.
St Matthew ch. 10, v. 29; see **Bible** 47:19

29 I came not to send peace, but a sword.
St Matthew ch. 10, v. 34

30 He that findeth his life shall lose it: and he that loseth his life for my sake shall find it.
St Matthew ch. 10, v. 39

31 Art thou he that should come, or do we look for another?
St Matthew ch. 11, v. 3

32 What went ye out into the wilderness to see? A reed shaken with the wind?
St Matthew ch. 11, v. 7

33 Come unto me, all ye that labour and are heavy laden, and I will give you rest.
St Matthew ch. 11, v. 28

34 For my yoke is easy, and my burden is light.
St Matthew ch. 11, v. 28

35 He that is not with me is against me.
St Matthew ch. 12, v. 30 and St Luke ch. 11, v. 23

36 The blasphemy against the Holy Ghost shall not be forgiven unto men.
St Matthew ch. 12, v. 31

37 Out of the abundance of the heart the mouth speaketh.
St Matthew ch. 12, v. 34

38 Behold, a greater than Solomon is here.
St Matthew ch. 12, v. 42

39 And some fell among thorns; and the thorns sprang up and choked them:
But other fell into good ground, and brought forth fruit, some an hundredfold, some sixtyfold, some thirtyfold.
St Matthew ch. 13, v. 7

1 The kingdom of heaven is like to a grain of mustard seed.
St Matthew ch. 13, v. 31

2 The kingdom of heaven is like unto a merchant man, seeking goodly pearls: Who, when he had found one pearl of great price, went and sold all that he had, and bought it.
St Matthew ch. 13, v. 45

3 A prophet is not without honour, save in his own country, and in his own house.
St Matthew ch. 13, v. 57

4 Be of good cheer; it is I; be not afraid.
St Matthew ch. 14, v. 27

5 O thou of little faith, wherefore didst thou doubt?
St Matthew ch. 14, v. 31

6 If the blind lead the blind, both shall fall into the ditch.
St Matthew ch. 15, v. 14

7 The dogs eat of the crumbs which fall from their masters' table.
St Matthew ch. 15, v. 27

8 Can ye not discern the signs of the times?
St Matthew ch. 16, v. 3

9 Thou art Peter, and upon this rock I will build my church; and the gates of hell shall not prevail against it.
St Matthew ch. 16, v. 18

10 Get thee behind me, Satan.
St Matthew ch. 16, v. 23

11 If ye have faith as a grain of mustard seed, ye shall say unto this mountain, Remove hence to yonder place; and it shall remove.
St Matthew ch. 17, v. 20

12 Except ye be converted, and become as little children, ye shall not enter into the kingdom of heaven.
St Matthew ch. 18, v. 3

13 Whoso shall receive one such little child in my name receiveth me.
But whoso shall offend one of these little ones which believe in me, it were better for him that a millstone were hanged about his neck, and that he were drowned in the depth of the sea.
St Matthew ch. 18, v. 5

14 If thine eye offend thee, pluck it out, and cast it from thee.
St Matthew ch. 18, v. 9

15 For where two or three are gathered together in my name, there am I in the midst of them.
St Matthew ch. 18, v. 20

16 Lord, how oft shall my brother sin against me, and I forgive him? till seven times? Jesus saith unto him I say not unto thee, Until seven times: but Until seventy times seven.
St Matthew ch. 18, v. 21

17 What therefore God hath joined together, let not man put asunder.
St Matthew ch. 19, v. 6; see **Book of Common Prayer** 62:2

18 If thou wilt be perfect, go and sell that thou hast, and give to the poor, and thou shalt have treasure in heaven.
St Matthew ch. 19, v. 21

19 It is easier for a camel to go through the eye of a needle, than for a rich man to enter into the kingdom of God.
St Matthew ch. 19, v. 24. See also St Luke ch. 18, v. 24

20 With God all things are possible.
St Matthew ch. 19, v. 26

21 But many that are first shall be last; and the last shall be first.
St Matthew ch. 19, v. 30

22 The burden and heat of the day.
St Matthew ch. 20, v. 12

23 I will give unto this last, even as unto thee.
St Matthew ch. 20, v. 14

24 It is written, My house shall be called the house of prayer; but ye have made it a den of thieves.
St Matthew ch. 21, v. 13; see **Bible** 41:15

25 For many are called, but few are chosen.
St Matthew ch. 22, v. 14

26 Render therefore unto Caesar the things which are Caesar's; and unto God the things that are God's.
St Matthew ch. 22, v. 21

27 For in the resurrection they neither marry, nor are given in marriage.
St Matthew ch. 22, v. 30

28 Thou shalt love the Lord thy God with all thy heart, and with all thy soul, and with all thy mind.
This is the first and great commandment. And the second is like unto it, Thou shalt love thy neighbour as thyself.
St Matthew ch. 22, v. 38; see **Bible** 35:34

29 Woe unto you, scribes and Pharisees, hypocrites!
St Matthew ch. 23, v. 23

30 Ye blind guides, which strain at a gnat, and swallow a camel.
St Matthew ch. 23, v. 24

31 Ye are like unto whited sepulchres.
St Matthew ch. 23, v. 27

32 Ye shall hear of wars and rumours of wars.
St Matthew ch. 24, v. 6

33 For nation shall rise against nation, and kingdom against kingdom.
St Matthew ch. 24, v. 7

34 The abomination of desolation, spoken of by Daniel the prophet
referring to Daniel ch. 12, v. 11
St Matthew ch. 24, v. 15

35 Wheresoever the carcase is, there will the eagles be gathered together.
St Matthew ch. 24, v. 28

1 Heaven and earth shall pass away, but my words shall not pass away.
St Matthew ch. 24, v. 35

2 One shall be taken, and the other left.
St Matthew ch. 24, v. 40

3 Watch therefore: for ye know not what hour your Lord doth come.
St Matthew ch. 24, v. 42

4 Well done, thou good and faithful servant.
St Matthew ch. 25, v. 21

5 Unto every one that hath shall be given, and he shall have abundance: but from him that hath not shall be taken away even that which he hath.
St Matthew ch. 25, v. 29

6 And he shall set the sheep on his right hand, but the goats on the left.
St Matthew ch. 25, v. 33

7 I was a stranger, and ye took me in:
Naked, and ye clothed me: I was sick, and ye visited me: I was in prison, and ye came unto me.
St Matthew ch. 25, v. 35

8 Inasmuch as ye have done it unto one of the least of these my brethren, ye have done it unto me.
St Matthew ch. 25, v. 40

9 And they covenanted with him [Judas Iscariot] for thirty pieces of silver.
St Matthew ch. 26, v. 15

10 It had been good for that man if he had not been born.
St Matthew ch. 26, v. 24

11 Jesus took bread, and blessed it, and brake it, and gave it to the disciples, and said, Take, eat; this is my body.
St Matthew ch. 26, v. 26

12 This night, before the cock crow, thou shalt deny me thrice.
to St Peter
St Matthew ch. 26, v. 34

13 If it be possible, let this cup pass from me.
St Matthew ch. 26, v. 39

14 What, could ye not watch with me one hour?
St Matthew ch. 26, v. 40

15 Watch and pray, that ye enter not into temptation: the spirit indeed is willing but the flesh is weak.
St Matthew ch. 26, v. 41

16 All they that take the sword shall perish with the sword.
St Matthew ch. 26, v. 52

17 He [Pilate] took water, and washed his hands before the multitude, saying, I am innocent of the blood of this just person: see ye to it.
St Matthew ch. 27, v. 24

18 His blood be on us, and on our children.
St Matthew ch. 27, v. 25

19 He saved others; himself he cannot save.
St Matthew ch. 27, v. 42

20 Eli, Eli, lama sabachthani? . . . My God, my God, why hast thou forsaken me?
St Matthew ch. 27, v. 46

21 And, lo, I am with you alway, even unto the end of the world.
St Matthew ch. 28, v. 20

St Mark

22 The sabbath was made for man, and not man for the sabbath.
St Mark ch. 2, v. 27

23 How can Satan cast out Satan?
St Mark ch. 3, v. 23

24 If a house be divided against itself, that house cannot stand.
St Mark ch. 3, v. 25; see **Lincoln** 214:13

25 He that hath ears to hear, let him hear.
St Mark ch. 4, v. 9

26 My name is Legion: for we are many.
St Mark ch. 5, v. 9

27 For what shall it profit a man, if he shall gain the whole world, and lose his own soul?
St Mark ch. 8, v. 36; see **Bolt** 59:3

28 Lord, I believe; help thou mine unbelief.
St Mark ch. 9, v. 24

29 Suffer the little children to come unto me, and forbid them not: for of such is the kingdom of God.
St Mark ch. 10, v. 14

30 Go ye into all the world, and preach the gospel to every creature.
St Mark ch. 16, v. 15

St Luke

31 Hail, thou that art highly favoured, the Lord is with thee: blessed art thou among women.
the angel to the Virgin Mary
St Luke ch. 1, v. 28

32 And Mary said,
My soul doth magnify the Lord,
And my spirit hath rejoiced in God my Saviour.
For he hath regarded the low estate of his handmaiden: for, behold, from henceforth all generations shall call me blessed.
known as the Magnificat; beginning 'Tell out my soul, the greatness of the Lord' in New English Bible
St Luke ch. 1, v. 46; see **Bible** 54:7

33 He hath shewed strength with his arm; he hath scattered the proud in the imagination of their hearts.
He hath put down the mighty from their seats, and exalted them of low degree.
He hath filled the hungry with good things; and the rich he hath sent empty away.
the Magnificat
St Luke ch. 1, v. 51

34 To give light to them that sit in darkness and in the shadow of death, to guide our feet into the way of peace.
St Luke ch. 1, v. 79

1 And it came to pass in those days, that there went out a decree from Caesar Augustus, that all the world should be taxed.
St Luke ch. 2, v. 1

2 She brought forth her firstborn son, and wrapped him in swaddling clothes, and laid him in a manger; because there was no room for them in the inn.
And there were in the same country shepherds abiding in the field, keeping watch over their flock by night.
And, lo, the angel of the Lord came upon them, and the glory of the Lord shone round about them: and they were sore afraid.
St Luke ch. 2, v. 7

3 Behold, I bring you good tidings of great joy.
the angel to the shepherds
St Luke ch. 2, v. 10

4 Glory to God in the highest, and on earth peace, good will toward men.
the angels to the shepherds
St Luke ch. 2, v. 14; see **Missal** 240:18

5 But Mary kept all these things, and pondered them in her heart.
St Luke ch. 2, v. 19

6 Lord, now lettest thou thy servant depart in peace, according to thy word.
said by Simeon
St Luke ch. 2, v. 29; see **Bible** 54:8

7 Wist ye not that I must be about my Father's business?
St Luke ch. 2, v. 49

8 Physician, heal thyself.
St Luke ch. 4, v. 23

9 Love your enemies, do good to them which hate you.
St Luke ch. 6, v. 27

10 Give, and it shall be given unto you; good measure, pressed down, and shaken together, and running over, shall men give into your bosom.
St Luke ch. 6, v. 38

11 Her sins, which are many, are forgiven; for she loved much.
St Luke ch. 7, v. 47

12 No man, having put his hand to the plough, and looking back, is fit for the kingdom of God.
St Luke ch. 9, v. 62

13 For the labourer is worthy of his hire.
St Luke ch. 10, v. 7

14 A certain man went down from Jerusalem to Jericho, and fell among thieves.
St Luke ch. 10, v. 30

15 He passed by on the other side.
St Luke ch. 10, v. 31

16 Go, and do thou likewise.
St Luke ch. 10, v. 37

17 But Martha was cumbered about much serving.
St Luke ch. 10, v. 40

18 Mary hath chosen that good part.
St Luke ch. 10, v. 42

19 Are not five sparrows sold for two farthings, and not one of them is forgotten before God?
St Luke ch. 12, v. 6; see **Bible** 44:28

20 Soul, thou hast much goods laid up for many years; take thine ease, eat, drink, and be merry.
St Luke ch. 12, v. 19; see **Bible** 39:18, **Bible** 40:21

21 Thou fool, this night thy soul shall be required of thee.
St Luke ch. 12, v. 20

22 Friend, go up higher.
St Luke ch. 14, v. 10

23 For whosoever exalteth himself shall be abased; and he that humbleth himself shall be exalted.
St Matthew ch. 23, v. 12 is similar
St Luke ch. 14, v. 11

24 I have married a wife, and therefore I cannot come.
St Luke ch. 14, v. 20

25 Bring in hither the poor, and the maimed, and the halt, and the blind.
St Luke ch. 14, v. 21

26 Go out into the highways and hedges, and compel them to come in.
St Luke ch. 14, v. 23

27 Leave the ninety and nine in the wilderness.
St Luke ch. 15, v. 4

28 Rejoice with me; for I have found my sheep which was lost.
St Luke ch. 15, v. 6

29 Joy shall be in heaven over one sinner that repenteth, more than over ninety and nine just persons, which need no repentance.
St Luke ch. 15, v. 7

30 There wasted his substance with riotous living.
St Luke ch. 15, v. 13

31 I will arise and go to my father, and will say unto him, Father, I have sinned against heaven, and before thee,
And am no more worthy to be called thy son: make me as one of thy hired servants.
St Luke ch. 15, v. 18

32 Bring hither the fatted calf, and kill it.
St Luke ch. 15, v. 23

33 This my son was dead, and is alive again; he was lost, and is found.
St Luke ch. 15, v. 24

34 The children of this world are in their generation wiser than the children of light.
St Luke ch. 16, v. 8

35 Make to yourselves friends of the mammon of unrighteousness.
St Luke ch. 16, v. 9

36 He that is faithful in that which is least is faithful also in much.
St Luke ch. 16, v. 10

1 The crumbs which fell from the rich man's table.
St Luke ch. 16, v. 21

2 Between us and you there is a great gulf fixed.
St Luke ch. 16, v. 26

3 The kingdom of God is within you.
St Luke ch. 17, v. 21

4 Remember Lot's wife.
St Luke ch. 17, v. 32

5 God, I thank thee, that I am not as other men are.
St Luke ch. 18, v. 11

6 God be merciful to me a sinner.
St Luke ch. 18, v. 13

7 Not my will, but thine, be done.
St Luke ch. 22, v. 42

8 Father, forgive them: for they know not what they do.
St Luke ch. 23, v. 34

9 Lord, remember me when thou comest into thy kingdom.
said by the Penitent Thief
St Luke ch. 23, v. 42

10 To day shalt thou be with me in paradise.
to the Penitent Thief
St Luke ch. 23, v. 43

11 Father, into thy hands I commend my spirit.
St Luke ch. 23, v. 46; see **Book of Common Prayer** 62:20

12 He was known of them in breaking of bread.
St Luke ch. 24, v. 35

St John

13 In the beginning was the Word, and the Word was with God, and the Word was God.
St John ch. 1, v. 1

14 All things were made by him; and without him was not any thing made that was made.
St John ch. 1, v. 3

15 And the light shineth in darkness; and the darkness comprehended it not.
St John ch. 1, v. 5

16 There was a man sent from God, whose name was John.
St John ch. 1, v. 6

17 He was not that Light, but was sent to bear witness of that Light.
That was the true Light, which lighteth every man that cometh into the world.
St John ch. 1, v. 8

18 He was in the world, and the world was made by him, and the world knew him not.
He came unto his own, and his own received him not.
St John ch. 1, v. 10

19 And the Word was made flesh, and dwelt among us, (and we beheld his glory, the glory as of the only begotten of the Father), full of grace and truth.
St John ch. 1, v. 14; see **Missal** 241:3

20 He it is, who coming after me is preferred before me, whose shoe's latchet I am not worthy to unloose.
said by St John the Baptist
St John ch. 1, v. 27

21 Behold the Lamb of God, which taketh away the sin of the world.
St John ch. 1, v. 29; see **Missal** 240:25

22 Can there any good thing come out of Nazareth?
St John ch. 1, v. 46

23 Behold an Israelite indeed, in whom is no guile!
St John ch. 1, v. 47

24 Woman, what have I to do with thee? mine hour is not yet come.
St John ch. 2, v. 4

25 Verily, verily, I say unto thee, Except a man be born again, he cannot see the kingdom of God.
St John ch. 3, v. 3

26 The wind bloweth where it listeth, and thou hearest the sound thereof, but canst not tell whence it cometh, and whither it goeth.
St John ch. 3, v. 8

27 God so loved the world, that he gave his only begotten Son, that whosoever believeth in him should not perish, but have everlasting life.
St John ch. 3, v. 16

28 Except ye see signs and wonders, ye will not believe.
St John ch. 4, v. 48

29 Rise, take up thy bed, and walk.
St John ch. 5, v. 8

30 I am the bread of life: he that cometh to me shall never hunger; and he that believeth on me shall never thirst.
St John ch. 6, v. 35

31 Verily, verily, I say unto you, He that believeth on me hath everlasting life.
St John ch. 6, v. 47

32 And the scribes and the Pharisees brought unto him a woman taken in adultery.
St John ch. 8, v. 3

33 He that is without sin among you, let him first cast a stone at her.
St John ch. 8, v. 7

34 Neither do I condemn thee: go, and sin no more.
St John ch. 8, v. 11

35 And ye shall know the truth, and the truth shall make you free.
St John ch. 8, v. 32

36 I am the door.
St John ch. 10, v. 9

37 I am the good shepherd: the good shepherd giveth his life for the sheep.
St John ch. 10, v. 11

38 I am the resurrection, and the life.
St John ch. 11, v. 25

39 Jesus wept.
St John ch. 11, v. 35

1 It is expedient for us, that one man should die for the people.
said by Caiaphas
St John ch. 11, v. 50

2 The poor always ye have with you.
St John ch. 12, v. 8

3 Let not your heart be troubled.
St John ch. 14, v. 1

4 In my Father's house are many mansions . . . I go to prepare a place for you.
St John ch. 14, v. 2

5 I am the way, the truth, and the life: no man cometh unto the Father, but by me.
St John ch. 14, v. 6

6 Peace I leave with you, my peace I give unto you: not as the world giveth, give I unto you.
St John ch. 14, v. 27

7 Greater love hath no man than this, that a man lay down his life for his friends.
St John ch. 15, v. 13; see **Thorpe** 339:24

8 Pilate saith unto him, What is truth?
St John ch. 18, v. 38; see **Bacon** 23:16

9 Now Barabbas was a robber.
St John ch. 18, v. 40; see **Campbell** 83:13

10 A place called the place of a skull, which is called in the Hebrew Golgotha.
St John ch. 19, v. 17

11 What I have written I have written.
said by Pilate
St John ch. 19, v. 22

12 Woman, behold thy son! . . .
Behold thy mother!
to the Virgin Mary and, traditionally, St John
St John ch. 19, v. 26

13 I thirst.
St John ch. 19, v. 28

14 It is finished.
St John ch. 19, v. 30; see **Bible** 54:12

15 They have taken away my Lord, and I know not where they have laid him.
said by St Mary Magdalene
St John ch. 20, v. 13

16 Touch me not.
to St Mary Magdalene
St John ch. 20, v. 17; see **Bible** 54:13

17 Except I shall see in his hands the print of the nails, and put my finger into the print of the nails, and thrust my hand into his side, I will not believe.
said by St Thomas
St John ch. 20, v. 25

18 Blessed are they that have not seen, and yet have believed.
St John ch. 20, v. 29

19 Feed my sheep.
St John ch. 21, v. 16

Acts of the Apostles

20 Ye men of Galilee, why stand ye gazing up into heaven?
Acts of the Apostles ch. 1, v. 11

21 And suddenly there came a sound from heaven as of a rushing mighty wind, and it filled all the house where they were sitting. And there appeared unto them cloven tongues like as of fire.
Acts of the Apostles ch. 2, v. 2

22 Thy money perish with thee.
to Simon Magus
Acts of the Apostles ch. 8, v. 20

23 Saul, Saul, why persecutest thou me?
Acts of the Apostles ch. 9, v. 4

24 It is hard for thee to kick against the pricks.
Acts of the Apostles ch. 9, v. 5

25 The street which is called Straight.
Acts of the Apostles ch. 9, v. 11

26 God is no respecter of persons.
Acts of the Apostles ch. 10, v. 34

27 What must I do to be saved?
Acts of the Apostles ch. 16, v. 30

28 Certain lewd fellows of the baser sort.
Acts of the Apostles ch. 17, v. 5

29 Those that have turned the world upside down are come hither also.
Acts of the Apostles ch. 17, v. 6

30 I found an altar with this inscription, TO THE UNKNOWN GOD.
Acts of the Apostles ch. 17, v. 22

31 For in him we live, and move, and have our being.
Acts of the Apostles ch. 17, v. 28

32 Great is Diana of the Ephesians.
Acts of the Apostles ch. 19, v. 34

33 It is more blessed to give than to receive.
Acts of the Apostles ch. 20, v. 35

34 I appeal unto Caesar.
Acts of the Apostles ch. 25, v. 11

35 Hast thou appealed unto Caesar? unto Caesar shalt thou go.
Acts of the Apostles ch. 25, v. 12

36 Paul, thou art beside thyself; much learning doth make thee mad.
Acts of the Apostles ch. 26, v. 24

37 Almost thou persuadest me to be a Christian.
Acts of the Apostles ch. 26, v. 28

Romans

38 Patient continuance in well doing.
Romans ch. 2, v. 7

39 A law unto themselves.
Romans ch. 2, v. 14

40 Let us do evil, that good may come.
Romans ch. 3, v. 8

41 For where no law is, there is no transgression.
Romans ch. 4, v. 15

42 Who against hope believed in hope, that he might become the father of many nations.
of Abraham
Romans ch. 4, v. 18

1 Shall we continue in sin, that grace may
abound?
Romans ch. 6, v. 1

2 We also should walk in newness of life.
Romans ch. 6, v. 4

3 Christ being raised from the dead dieth no
more; death hath no more dominion over
him.
Romans ch. 6, v. 9; see **Thomas** 337:17

4 The wages of sin is death.
Romans ch. 6, v. 23

5 I had not known sin, but by the law.
Romans ch. 7, v. 7

6 For the good that I would I do not: but the
evil which I would not, that I do.
Romans ch. 7, v. 19; see **Ovid** 256:1

7 All things work together for good to them
that love God.
Romans ch. 8, v. 28

8 If God be for us, who can be against us?
Romans ch. 8, v. 31

9 For I am persuaded, that neither death, nor
life, nor angels, nor principalities, nor
powers, nor things present, nor things to
come,
Nor height, nor depth, nor any other
creature, shall be able to separate us from
the love of God, which is in Christ Jesus our
Lord.
Romans ch. 8, v. 38

10 Present your bodies a living sacrifice, holy,
acceptable unto God.
Romans ch. 12, v. 1

11 Vengeance is mine; I will repay, saith the
Lord.
Romans ch. 12, v. 19

12 The night is far spent, the day is at hand: let
us therefore cast off the works of darkness,
and let us put on the armour of light.
Romans ch. 13, v. 12

I Corinthians

13 The foolishness of preaching to save them
that believe.
I Corinthians ch. 1, v. 21

14 For the Jews require a sign, and the Greeks
seek after wisdom.
I Corinthians ch. 1, v. 22

15 We preach Christ crucified, unto the Jews a
stumbling-block, and unto the Greeks
foolishness.
I Corinthians ch. 1, v. 23

16 Absent in body, but present in spirit.
I Corinthians ch. 5, v. 3

17 Know ye not that a little leaven leaveneth
the whole lump?
I Corinthians ch. 5, v. 6

18 It is better to marry than to burn.
I Corinthians ch. 7, v. 9

19 I am made all things to all men.
I Corinthians ch. 9, v. 22

20 For the earth is the Lord's and the fulness
thereof.
I Corinthians ch. 10, v. 26; see **Book of
Common Prayer** 62:16

21 Doth not even nature itself teach you, that if
a man have long hair, it is a shame unto
him?
But if a woman have long hair, it is a glory
to her.
I Corinthians ch. 11, v. 14

22 Though I speak with the tongues of men
and of angels, and have not charity, I am
become as sounding brass, or a tinkling
cymbal.
And though I have the gift of prophecy, and
understand all mysteries, and all
knowledge; and though I have all faith; so
that I could remove mountains; and have
not charity, I am nothing.
I Corinthians ch. 13, v. 1

23 Charity suffereth long, and is kind; charity
envieth not; charity vaunteth not itself, is
not puffed up . . .
Beareth all things, believeth all things,
hopeth all things, endureth all things.
Charity never faileth
I Corinthians ch. 13, v. 4

24 For we know in part, and we prophesy in
part.
I Corinthians ch. 13, v. 9

25 When I was a child, I spake as a child, I
understood as a child, I thought as a child:
but when I became a man, I put away
childish things.
For now we see through a glass, darkly; but
then face to face: now I know in part; but
then shall I know even as also I am known.
And now abideth faith, hope, charity, these
three; but the greatest of these is charity.
I Corinthians ch. 13, v. 11

26 Let all things be done decently and in order.
I Corinthians ch. 14, v. 40

27 Last of all he was seen of me also, as of one
born out of due time.
For I am the least of the apostles, that am
not meet to be called an apostle, because I
persecuted the church of God.
But by the grace of God I am what I am.
I Corinthians ch. 15, v. 8

28 But now is Christ risen from the dead, and
become the first fruits of them that slept.
For since by man came death, by man came
also the resurrection of the dead.
For as in Adam all die, even so in Christ
shall all be made alive.
I Corinthians ch. 15, v. 20

29 The last enemy that shall be destroyed is
death.
I Corinthians ch. 15, v. 26

30 If after the manner of men I have fought
with beasts at Ephesus, what advantageth
me, if the dead rise not? let us eat and drink;
for to morrow we die.
I Corinthians ch. 15, v. 32; see **Bible** 39:18,
Bible 40:21, **Bible** 47:20

1 Evil communications corrupt good
manners.
  I Corinthians ch. 15, v. 33

2 The first man is of the earth, earthy.
  I Corinthians ch. 15, v. 47

3 Behold, I shew you a mystery; We shall not
all sleep, but we shall all be changed,
In a moment, in the twinkling of an eye, at
the last trump; for the trumpet shall sound,
and the dead shall be raised incorruptible,
and we shall be changed.
  I Corinthians ch. 15, v. 51

4 O death, where is thy sting? O grave, where
is thy victory?
  I Corinthians ch. 15, v. 55

II Corinthians

5 The letter killeth, but the spirit giveth life.
  II Corinthians ch. 3, v. 5

6 We have a building of God, an house not
made with hands, eternal in the heavens.
  II Corinthians ch. 5, v. 1; see **Browning** 71:24

7 God loveth a cheerful giver.
  II Corinthians ch. 9, v. 7

8 For ye suffer fools gladly, seeing ye
yourselves are wise.
  II Corinthians ch. 11, v. 19

9 I knew a man in Christ above fourteen years
ago (whether in the body, I cannot tell; or
whether out of the body, I cannot tell: God
knoweth).
  II Corinthians ch. 12, v. 2

10 There was given to me a thorn in the flesh,
the messenger of Satan to buffet me.
  II Corinthians ch. 12, v. 7

Galatians

11 Ye are fallen from grace.
  Galatians ch. 5, v. 4

12 But the fruit of the Spirit is love, joy, peace,
longsuffering, gentleness, goodness, faith,
Meekness, temperance.
  Galatians ch. 5, v. 22

13 Be not deceived; God is not mocked: for
whatsoever a man soweth, that shall he also
reap.
  Galatians ch. 6, v. 7

14 Let us not be weary in well doing: for in due
season we shall reap, if we faint not.
  *'Be not weary in well doing' in II Thessalonians ch.
  3, v. 13*
  Galatians ch. 6, v. 9

Ephesians

15 The unsearchable riches of Christ.
  Ephesians ch. 3, v. 8

16 We are members one of another.
  Ephesians ch. 4, v. 25

17 Be ye angry and sin not: let not the sun go
down upon your wrath.
  Ephesians ch. 4, v. 26

18 See then that ye walk circumspectly, not as
fools, but as wise,
Redeeming the time, because the days are
evil.
  Ephesians ch. 5, v. 15

19 Ye fathers, provoke not your children to
wrath.
  Ephesians ch. 6, v. 4

20 Put on the whole armour of God.
  Ephesians ch. 6, v. 11

21 For we wrestle not against flesh and blood,
but against principalities, against powers,
against the rulers of the darkness of this
world, against spiritual wickedness in high
places.
Wherefore take unto you the whole armour
of God, that ye may be able to withstand in
the evil day, and having done all, to stand.
Stand therefore, having your loins girt about
with truth, and having on the breastplate of
righteousness.
  Ephesians ch. 6, v. 12

Philippians

22 At the name of Jesus every knee should bow,
of things in heaven, and things in earth, and
things under the earth.
  Philippians ch. 2, v. 10; see **Noel** 251:20

23 Work out your own salvation with fear and
trembling.
  Philippians ch. 2, v. 12

24 Forgetting those things which are behind,
and reaching forth unto those things which
are before,
I press toward the mark.
  Philippians ch. 3, v. 13

25 Whose God is their belly, and whose glory is
in their shame.
  Philippians ch. 3, v. 19

26 Rejoice in the Lord alway: and again I say,
Rejoice.
  Philippians ch. 4, v. 4

27 The peace of God, which passeth all
understanding, shall keep your hearts and
minds through Christ Jesus.
  Philippians ch. 4, v. 7; see **James I** 182:13

28 Whatsoever things are true, whatsoever
things are honest, whatsoever things are
just, whatsoever things are pure,
whatsoever things are lovely, whatsoever
things are of good report; if there be any
virtue and if there be any praise, think on
these things.
  Philippians ch. 4, v. 8

29 I can do all things through Christ which
strengtheneth me.
  Philippians ch. 4, v. 13

Colossians

30 For by him were all things created, that are
in heaven, and that are in earth, visible and
invisible, whether they be thrones, or
dominions, or principalities, or powers.
  Colossians ch. 1, v. 16; see **Milton** 238:32

31 Husbands, love your wives, and be not bitter
against them.
  Colossians ch. 3, v. 19

1 Let your speech be alway with grace, seasoned with salt.
Colossians. 4, v. 6

I Thessalonians

2 Remembering without ceasing your work of faith and labour of love.
I Thessalonians ch. 1, v. 3

3 Prove all things; hold fast that which is good.
1 Thessalonians ch. 5, v. 21

II Thessalonians

4 If any would not work, neither should he eat.
II Thessalonians ch. 3, v. 10

I Timothy

5 Sinners; of whom I am chief.
I Timothy ch. 1, v. 15

6 Refuse profane and old wives' fables, and exercise thyself rather unto godliness.
I Timothy ch. 4, v. 7

7 Use a little wine for thy stomach's sake.
I Timothy ch. 5, v. 23

8 For we brought nothing into this world, and it is certain we can carry nothing out.
I Timothy ch. 6, v. 7

9 The love of money is the root of all evil.
I Timothy ch. 6, v. 10

10 Fight the good fight of faith, lay hold on eternal life.
I Timothy ch. 6, v. 12; see **Monsell** 242:11

II Timothy

11 I have fought a good fight, I have finished my course, I have kept the faith.
II Timothy ch. 4, v. 7

Titus

12 Unto the pure all things are pure.
Titus ch. 1, v. 15

Hebrews

13 It is a fearful thing to fall into the hands of the living God.
Hebrews ch. 10, v. 31

14 Faith is the substance of things hoped for, the evidence of things not seen.
Hebrews ch. 11, v. 1

15 Wherefore seeing we also are compassed about with so great a cloud of witnesses, let us lay aside every weight, and the sin which doth so easily beset us, and let us run with patience the race that is set before us,
Hebrews ch. 12, v. 1

16 Whom the Lord loveth he chasteneth.
Hebrews ch. 12, v. 6

17 Be not forgetful to entertain strangers: for thereby some have entertained angels unawares.
Hebrews ch. 13, v. 2

18 Jesus Christ the same yesterday, and to day, and for ever.
Hebrews ch. 13, v. 8

19 For here have we no continuing city, but we seek one to come.
Hebrews ch. 13, v. 14

James

20 But be ye doers of the word, and not hearers only, deceiving your own selves.
James ch. 1, v. 22

21 Faith without works is dead.
James ch. 2, v. 20

22 The tongue can no man tame; it is an unruly evil.
James ch. 3, v. 8

23 Ye have heard of the patience of Job.
James ch. 5, v. 11

24 Let your yea be yea; and your nay, nay.
James ch. 5, v. 12

I Peter

25 All flesh is as grass, and all the glory of man as the flower of grass. The grass withereth, and the flower thereof falleth away.
I Peter ch. 1, v. 24; see **Bible** 41:1

26 But ye are a chosen generation, a royal priesthood, an holy nation, a peculiar people.
I Peter ch. 2, v. 9

27 Honour all men. Love the brotherhood. Fear God. Honour the king.
I Peter ch. 2, v. 17

28 Giving honour unto the wife, as unto the weaker vessel.
I Peter ch. 3, v. 7

29 Charity shall cover the multitude of sins.
I Peter ch. 4, v. 8

30 Be sober, be vigilant; because your adversary the devil, as a roaring lion, walketh about, seeking whom he may devour.
I Peter ch. 5, v. 8

I John

31 If we say that we have no sin, we deceive ourselves, and the truth is not in us.
I John ch. 1, v. 8

32 He that loveth not knoweth not God; for God is love.
I John ch. 4, v. 8

33 There is no fear in love; but perfect love casteth out fear.
I John ch. 4, v. 18

34 If a man say, I love God, and hateth his brother, he is a liar: for he that loveth not his brother whom he hath seen, how can he love God whom he hath not seen?
I John ch. 4, v. 20

III John

35 He that doeth good is of God: but he that doeth evil hath not seen God.
III John v. 11

Revelation

36 The seven churches which are in Asia.
Revelation ch. 1, v. 4

1 I am Alpha and Omega, the beginning and the ending, saith the Lord.
Revelation ch. 1, v. 8

2 I have somewhat against thee, because thou hast left thy first love.
Revelation ch. 2, v. 4

3 Be thou faithful unto death, and I will give thee a crown of life.
Revelation ch. 2, v. 10

4 Because thou art lukewarm, and neither cold nor hot, I will spew thee out of my mouth.
Revelation ch. 3, v. 16

5 Behold, I stand at the door, and knock.
Revelation ch. 3, v. 20

6 Holy, holy, holy, Lord God Almighty, which was, and is, and is to come.
Revelation ch. 4, v. 8; see **Missal** 240:23

7 And I looked, and behold a pale horse: and his name that sat on him was Death.
Revelation ch. 6, v. 8

8 These are they which came out of great tribulation, and have washed their robes, and made them white in the blood of the Lamb.
Revelation ch. 7, v. 14; see **Lindsay** 215:9

9 God shall wipe away all tears from their eyes.
Revelation ch. 7, v. 17

10 And when he had opened the seventh seal, there was silence in heaven about the space of half an hour.
Revelation ch. 8, v. 1

11 And there appeared a great wonder in heaven; a woman clothed with the sun, and the moon under her feet, and upon her head a crown of twelve stars.
Revelation ch. 12, v. 1

12 And there was war in heaven: Michael and his angels fought against the dragon; and the dragon fought and his angels.
Revelation ch. 12, v. 7

13 And that no man might buy or sell, save he that had the mark, or the name of the beast, or the number of his name.
Revelation ch. 13, v. 17

14 Let him that hath understanding count the number of the beast: for it is the number of a man; and his number is Six hundred threescore and six.
Revelation ch. 13, v. 18

15 Babylon is fallen, is fallen, that great city.
Revelation ch. 14, v. 8

16 And the smoke of their torment ascendeth up for ever and ever: and they have no rest day or night, who worship the beast and his image.
Revelation ch. 14, v. 11

17 Behold, I come as a thief.
Revelation ch. 16, v. 15

18 And he gathered them together into a place called in the Hebrew tongue Armageddon.
Revelation ch. 16, v. 16

19 And upon her forehead was a name written, MYSTERY, BABYLON THE GREAT, THE MOTHER OF HARLOTS AND ABOMINATIONS OF THE EARTH.
Revelation ch. 17, v. 5

20 And I saw a great white throne.
Revelation ch. 20, v. 11

21 And the sea gave up the dead which were in it.
Revelation ch. 20, v. 13

22 And I saw a new heaven and a new earth: for the first heaven and the first earth were passed away; and there was no more sea. And I John saw the holy city, new Jerusalem, coming down from God out of heaven, prepared as a bride adorned for her husband.
Revelation ch. 21, v. 1

23 And God shall wipe away all tears from their eyes; and there shall be no more death, neither sorrow, nor crying, neither shall there be any more pain: for the former things are passed away.
And he that sat upon the throne said, Behold, I make all things new.
Revelation ch. 21, v. 4; see **Pound** 269:19

24 I will give unto him that is athirst of the fountain of the water of life freely.
Revelation ch. 21, v. 6

25 And the leaves of the tree were for the healing of the nations.
Revelation ch. 22, v. 2

26 Amen. Even so, come, Lord Jesus.
Revelation ch. 22, v. 20

Vulgate

27 *Dominus illuminatio mea, et salus mea, quem timebo?*
The Lord is the source of my light and my safety, so whom shall I fear?
Psalm 26, v. 1; see **Anonymous** 13:9

28 *Cantate Domino canticum novum, quia mirabilia fecit.*
Sing to the Lord a new song, because he has done marvellous things.
Psalm 97, v. 1 (Psalm 98, v. 1 in the Authorized Version); see **Book of Common Prayer** 64:1

29 *Jubilate Deo, omnis terra; servite Domino in laetitia.*
Sing joyfully to God, all the earth; serve the Lord with gladness.
Psalm 99, v. 2 (Psalm 100, v. 2 in the Authorized Version); see **Book of Common Prayer** 64:2

30 *Beatus vir qui timet Dominum, in mandatis ejus volet nimis!*
Happy is the man who fears the Lord, who is only too willing to follow his orders.
Psalm 111, v. 1 (Psalm 112, v. 1 in the Authorized Version)

1 *Non nobis, Domine, non nobis; sed nomini tuo da gloriam.*
Not unto us, Lord, not unto us; but to thy name give glory.
> Psalm 113 (second part), v. 1 (Psalm 115, v. 1 in the Authorized Version); see **Book of Common Prayer** 64:14

2 *Nisi Dominus aedificaverit domum, in vanum laboraverunt qui aedificant eam.*
Nisi Dominus custodierit civitatem, frustra vigilat qui custodit eam.
Unless the Lord has built the house, its builders have laboured in vain. Unless the Lord guards the city, the watchman watches in vain.
> Psalm 126, v. 1 (Psalm 127, v. 1 in the Authorized Version); see **Anonymous** 13:13, **Book of Common Prayer** 64:26

3 *De profundis clamavi ad te, Domine; Domine, exaudi vocem meam.*
Up from the depths I have cried to thee, Lord; Lord, hear my voice.
> Psalm 129, v. 1 (Psalm 130, v. 1 in the Authorized Version); see **Book of Common Prayer** 64:29

4 *Vanitas vanitatum, dixit Ecclesiastes; vanitas vanitatum, et omnia vanitas.*
Vanity of vanities, said the preacher; vanity of vanities, and everything is vanity.
> Ecclesiastes ch. 1, v. 2; see **Bible** 39:6

5 *Rorate, coeli, desuper, et nubes pluant Justum; aperiatur terra, et germinet Salvatorem.*
Drop down dew, heavens, from above, and let the clouds rain down righteousness; let the earth be opened, and a saviour spring to life.
> Isaiah ch. 45, v. 8

6 *Benedicite, omnia opera Domini, Domino; laudate et superexaltate eum in secula.*
Bless the Lord, all the works of the Lord; praise him and exalt him above all things for ever.
> Daniel ch. 3, v. 57; see **Book of Common Prayer** 59:22

7 *Magnificat anima mea Dominum; Et exsultavit spiritus meus in Deo salutari meo.*
My soul doth magnify the Lord: and my spirit hath rejoiced in God my Saviour.
> St Luke ch. 1, v. 46; see **Bible** 46:32

8 *Nunc dimittis servum tuum, Domine, secundum verbum tuum in pace.*
Lord, now lettest thou thy servant depart in peace: according to thy word.
> St Luke ch. 2, v. 29; see **Bible** 47:6

9 *Pax Vobis.*
Peace be unto you.
> St Luke ch. 24, v. 36

10 *Quo vadis?*
Where are you going?
> St John ch. 16, v. 5

11 *Ecce homo.*
Behold the man.
> St John ch. 19, v. 5

12 *Consummatum est.*
It is achieved.
> St John ch. 19, v. 30; see **Bible** 49:14

13 *Noli me tangere.*
Do not touch me.
> St John ch. 20, v. 17; see **Bible** 49:16

14 *Magna est veritas, et praevalet.*
Great is truth, and it prevails.
> III Esdras ch. 4, v. 41; see **Bible** 42:18, **Brooks** 70:8

E. H. Bickersteth 1825–1906
English clergyman

15 Peace, perfect peace, in this dark world of sin?
The Blood of Jesus whispers peace within.
> *Songs in the House of Pilgrimage* (1875) 'Peace, perfect peace'

Ambrose Bierce 1842–c.1914
American writer

16 ALLIANCE, *n.* In international politics, the union of two thieves who have their hands so deeply inserted in each other's pocket that they cannot separately plunder a third.
> *The Cynic's Word Book* (1906)

17 APPLAUSE, *n.* The echo of a platitude.
> *The Cynic's Word Book* (1906)

18 BATTLE, *n.* A method of untying with the teeth a political knot that would not yield to the tongue.
> *The Cynic's Word Book* (1906)

19 CONSERVATIVE, *n.* A statesman who is enamoured of existing evils, as distinguished from the Liberal, who wishes to replace them with others.
> *The Cynic's Word Book* (1906)

20 HISTORY, *n.* An account, mostly false, of events, mostly unimportant, which are brought about by rulers, mostly knaves, and soldiers, mostly fools.
> *The Cynic's Word Book* (1906)

21 PEACE, *n.* In international affairs, a period of cheating between two periods of fighting.
> *The Devil's Dictionary* (1911)

22 PREJUDICE, *n.* A vagrant opinion without visible means of support.
> *The Devil's Dictionary* (1911)

23 SAINT, *n.* A dead sinner revised and edited.
> *The Devil's Dictionary* (1911)

Laurence Binyon 1869–1943
English poet

24 They shall grow not old, as we that are left grow old.
Age shall not weary them, nor the years condemn.
At the going down of the sun and in the morning
We will remember them.
> *regularly recited as part of the ritual for Remembrance Day parades*
> 'For the Fallen' (1914)

1 Now is the time for the burning of the leaves.
  'The Ruins' (1942)

Lord Birkenhead *see* F. E. Smith

Augustine Birrell 1850–1933
British essayist

2 That great dust-heap called 'history'.
  Obiter Dicta (1884) 'Carlyle'; see **Trotsky** 342:6

Otto von Bismarck 1815–98
German statesman

3 The secret of politics? Make a good treaty with Russia.
  in 1863, when first in power
  A. J. P. Taylor *Bismarck* (1955) ch. 7

4 Politics is the art of the possible.
  in conversation with Meyer von Waldeck, 11 August 1867; see **Butler** 79:5, **Galbraith** 145:5, **Medawar** 232:1

5 We will not go to Canossa.
  during his quarrel with Pope Pius IX regarding papal authority over German subjects, in allusion to the Emperor Henry IV's submission to Pope Gregory VII at Canossa in Modena in 1077
  speech to the Reichstag, 14 May 1872

6 Not worth the healthy bones of a single Pomeranian grenadier.
  of possible German involvement in the Balkans; see **Harris** 162:16
  speech to the Reichstag, 5 December 1876

7 Whoever speaks of Europe is wrong, [it is] a geographical concept.
  marginal note on a letter from the Russian Chancellor Gorchakov, November 1876; see **Metternich** 233:17

8 I do not regard the procuring of peace as a matter in which we should play the role of arbiter between different opinions . . . more that of an honest broker who really wants to press the business forward.
  speech to the Reichstag, 19 February 1878

9 This policy cannot succeed through speeches, and shooting-matches, and songs; it can only be carried out through blood and iron.
  speech in the Prussian House of Deputies, 28 January 1886

10 If there is ever another war in Europe, it will come out of some damned silly thing in the Balkans.
  attributed by Herr Ballen and quoted by Winston S. **Churchill** in the House of Commons, 16 August 1945

James Black 1924–
British analytical pharmacologist

11 In the culture I grew up in you did your work and you did not put your arm around it to stop other people from looking—you took the earliest possible opportunity to make knowledge available.
  on modern scientific research
  in *Daily Telegraph* 11 December 1995

Valentine Blacker 1728–1823
Irish soldier

12 Put your trust in God, my boys, and keep your powder dry.
  often attributed to Oliver **Cromwell** *himself*
  'Oliver's Advice' in E. Hayes *Ballads of Ireland* (1856) vol. 1

William Blackstone 1723–80
English jurist

13 The king never dies.
  Commentaries on the Laws of England (1765) bk. 1, ch. 7

14 The royal navy of England hath ever been its greatest defence and ornament; it is its ancient and natural strength; the floating bulwark of the island.
  Commentaries on the Laws of England (1765) bk. 1, ch. 13; see **Coventry** 104:18

15 That the king can do no wrong, is a necessary and fundamental principle of the English constitution.
  Commentaries on the Laws of England (1765) bk. 3, ch. 17

16 It is better that ten guilty persons escape than one innocent suffer.
  Commentaries on the Laws of England (1765) bk. 4, ch. 27

Cherie Blair 1954–
British lawyer

17 I am not Superwoman. The reality of my daily life is that I'm juggling a lot of balls in the air . . . and sometimes some of the balls get dropped.
  personal statement, 10 December 2002; in *The Times* 11 December 2002

Tony Blair 1953–
British Labour statesman, Prime Minister since 1997

18 Labour is the party of law and order in Britain today. Tough on crime and tough on the causes of crime.
  as Shadow Home Secretary
  speech at the Labour Party Conference, 30 September 1993

19 Ask me my three main priorities for Government, and I tell you: education, education and education.
  speech at the Labour Party Conference, 1 October 1996

20 We are not the masters. The people are the masters. We are the servants of the people.
  addressing Labour MPs on the first day of the new Parliament, 7 May 1997; see **Burke** 76:6
  in *Guardian* 8 May 1997

21 She was the People's Princess, and that is how she will stay . . . in our hearts and in our memories forever.
  on hearing of the death of **Diana**, *Princess of Wales, 31 August 1997*
  in *The Times* 1 September 1997

22 We therefore here in Britain stand shoulder to shoulder with our American friends in

this hour of tragedy and we, like them, will not rest until this evil is driven from our world.

in Downing Street, London, 11 September 2001

1 The state of Africa is a scar on the conscience of the world.

speech to Labour Party Conference, 2 October 2001

2 PRESENTER: [Is Britain] prepared to send troops to commit themselves, to pay the blood price?

TONY BLAIR: Yes. What is important though is that at moments of crisis they [the USA] . . . need to know, 'Are you prepared to commit, are you prepared to be there when the shooting starts?'

interview on BBC2 *Hotline to the President* 8 September 2002

3 I believe we're at our best when we are boldest.

speech to the Labour Party Conference, 30 September 2002; see **Brown** 70:14

4 This is not the time to falter.

speech in the House of Commons, 18 March 2003

5 I can only go one way. I've not got a reverse gear.

speech, Labour Party Conference, Bournemouth, 30 September 2003

6 I've listened, and I've learned.

speech outside Downing Street, 6 May 2005

Eubie Blake 1883–1983
American ragtime pianist

7 If I'd known I was gonna live this long, I'd have taken better care of myself.

on reaching the age of 100

in *Observer* 13 February 1983 'Sayings of the Week'

William Blake 1757–1827
English poet

8 To see a world in a grain of sand
And a heaven in a wild flower,
Hold infinity in the palm of your hand
And eternity in an hour.

'Auguries of Innocence' (*c*.1803) l. 1

9 A robin red breast in a cage
Puts all Heaven in a rage.

'Auguries of Innocence' (*c*.1803) l. 5

10 A truth that's told with bad intent
Beats all the lies you can invent.

'Auguries of Innocence' (*c*.1803) l. 53

11 The strongest poison ever known
Came from Caesar's laurel crown.

'Auguries of Innocence' (*c*.1803) l. 97

12 If the Sun and Moon should doubt,
They'd immediately go out.
To be in a passion you good may do,
But no good if a passion is in you.

'Auguries of Innocence' (*c*.1803) l. 109

13 The whore and gambler, by the State
Licensed, build that nation's fate.
The harlot's cry from street to street
Shall weave old England's winding sheet.

'Auguries of Innocence' (*c*.1803) l. 113

14 Some are born to sweet delight,
Some are born to endless night.

'Auguries of Innocence' (*c*.1803) l. 123

15 Can wisdom be put in a silver rod?
Or love in a golden bowl?

The Book of Thel (1789) plate i 'Thel's Motto'

16 The Vision of Christ that thou dost see
Is my vision's greatest enemy.

The Everlasting Gospel (*c*.1818) (a) l. 1

17 This life's dim windows of the soul
Distorts the heavens from pole to pole
And leads you to believe a lie
When you see with, not through, the eye.

The Everlasting Gospel (*c*.1818) (d) l. 99

18 I must create a system, or be enslaved by another man's.
I will not reason and compare: my business is to create.

Jerusalem (1815) 'Chapter 1' (plate 10, l. 20)

19 He who would do good to another, must do it in minute particulars.

Jerusalem (1815) 'Chapter 3' (plate 55, l. 60)

20 I give you the end of a golden string;
Only wind it into a ball:
It will lead you in at Heaven's gate,
Built in Jerusalem's wall.

Jerusalem (1815) 'To the Christians' (plate 77) "I give you the end of a golden string"

21 Energy is Eternal Delight.

The Marriage of Heaven and Hell (1790–3) 'The voice of the Devil'

22 The reason Milton wrote in fetters when he wrote of Angels and God, and at liberty when of Devils and Hell, is because he was a true Poet, and of the Devil's party without knowing it.

The Marriage of Heaven and Hell (1790–3) 'The voice of the Devil' (note)

23 The road of excess leads to the palace of wisdom.

The Marriage of Heaven and Hell (1790–3) 'Proverbs of Hell'

24 Prudence is a rich, ugly, old maid courted by Incapacity.

The Marriage of Heaven and Hell (1790–3) 'Proverbs of Hell'

25 He who desires but acts not, breeds pestilence.

The Marriage of Heaven and Hell (1790–3) 'Proverbs of Hell'

26 A fool sees not the same tree that a wise man sees.

The Marriage of Heaven and Hell (1790–3) 'Proverbs of Hell'

27 Eternity is in love with the productions of time.

The Marriage of Heaven and Hell (1790–3) 'Proverbs of Hell'

28 If the fool would persist in his folly he would become wise.

The Marriage of Heaven and Hell (1790–3) 'Proverbs of Hell'

1 Prisons are built with stones of Law,
brothels with bricks of Religion.
The Marriage of Heaven and Hell (1790–3) 'Proverbs
of Hell'

2 The pride of the peacock is the glory of God.
The lust of the goat is the bounty of God.
The wrath of the lion is the wisdom of God.
The nakedness of woman is the work of
God.
The Marriage of Heaven and Hell (1790–3) 'Proverbs
of Hell'

3 The tygers of wrath are wiser than the
horses of instruction.
The Marriage of Heaven and Hell (1790–3) 'Proverbs
of Hell'

4 Damn braces: Bless relaxes.
The Marriage of Heaven and Hell (1790–3) 'Proverbs
of Hell'

5 Exuberance is beauty.
The Marriage of Heaven and Hell (1790–3) 'Proverbs
of Hell'

6 Sooner murder an infant in its cradle than
nurse unacted desires.
The Marriage of Heaven and Hell (1790–3) 'Proverbs
of Hell'

7 If the doors of perception were cleansed
everything would appear to man as it is,
infinite.
The Marriage of Heaven and Hell (1790–3) 'A
Memorable Fancy' plate 14

8 And did those feet in ancient time
Walk upon England's mountains green?
And was the holy Lamb of God
On England's pleasant pastures seen?
And did the Countenance Divine
Shine forth upon our clouded hills?
And was Jerusalem builded here
Among these dark Satanic mills?
Bring me my bow of burning gold:
Bring me my arrows of desire:
Bring me my spear: O clouds, unfold!
Bring me my chariot of fire.
I will not cease from mental fight,
Nor shall my sword sleep in my hand,
Till we have built Jerusalem,
In England's green and pleasant land.
Milton (1804–10) preface 'And did those feet in
ancient time'

9 Mock on, mock on Voltaire, Rousseau:
Mock on, mock on: tis all in vain!
You throw the sand against the wind,
And the wind blows it back again.
MS Note-Book

10 The atoms of Democritus
And Newton's particles of light
Are sands upon the Red sea shore,
Where Israel's tents do shine so bright.
MS Note-Book

11 Great things are done when men and
mountains meet;
This is not done by jostling in the street.
MS Note-Book

12 He who binds to himself a joy
Doth the winged life destroy;
But he who kisses the joy as it flies

Lives in Eternity's sunrise.
MS Note-Book 'Several Questions
Answered'—"He who binds to himself a joy"

13 What is it men in women do require?
The lineaments of gratified desire.
What is it women do in men require?
The lineaments of gratified desire.
MS Note-Book 'Several Questions
Answered'—"What is it men in women do
require"

14 Never pain to tell thy love
Love that never told can be;
For the gentle wind does move
Silently, invisibly.
MS Note-Book

15 Piping down the valleys wild,
Piping songs of pleasant glee,
On a cloud I saw a child.
Songs of Innocence (1789) introduction

16 Your chimneys I sweep, and in soot I sleep.
Songs of Innocence (1789) 'The Chimney Sweeper'

17 For Mercy has a human heart,
Pity a human face,
And Love, the human form divine,
And Peace, the human dress.
Songs of Innocence (1789) 'The Divine Image'

18 Then cherish pity, lest you drive an angel
from your door.
Songs of Innocence (1789) 'Holy Thursday'

19 Little Lamb who made thee?
Dost thou know who made thee?
Songs of Innocence (1789) 'The Lamb'

20 My mother bore me in the southern wild,
And I am black, but O! my soul is white;
White as an angel is the English child:
But I am black as if bereaved of light.
Songs of Innocence (1789) 'The Little Black Boy'

21 Hear the voice of the Bard!
Who present, past, and future, sees.
Songs of Experience (1794) introduction

22 Ah, Sun-flower! weary of time,
Who countest the steps of the Sun.
Songs of Experience (1794) 'Ah, Sun-flower!'

23 Love seeketh not itself to please,
Nor for itself hath any care;
But for another gives its ease,
And builds a Heaven in Hell's despair.
Songs of Experience (1794) 'The Clod and the
Pebble'

24 Love seeketh only Self to please,
To bind another to its delight,
Joys in another's loss of ease,
And builds a Hell in Heaven's despite.
Songs of Experience (1794) 'The Clod and the
Pebble'

25 My mother groaned! my father wept.
Into the dangerous world I leapt:
Helpless, naked, piping loud;
Like a fiend hid in a cloud.
Songs of Experience (1794) 'Infant Sorrow'

26 I was angry with my friend;
I told my wrath, my wrath did end.
I was angry with my foe:

I told it not, my wrath did grow.
Songs of Experience (1794) 'A Poison Tree'

1 In the morning glad I see,
My foe outstretched beneath the tree
Songs of Experience (1794) 'A Poison Tree'

2 O Rose, thou art sick!
The invisible worm
That flies in the night,
In the howling storm:
Has found out thy bed
Of crimson joy:
And his dark secret love
Does thy life destroy.
Songs of Experience (1794) 'The Sick Rose'

3 Tyger Tyger, burning bright,
In the forests of the night;
What immortal hand or eye,
Could frame thy fearful symmetry?
Songs of Experience (1794) 'The Tiger'

4 When the stars threw down their spears
And watered heaven with their tears:
Did he smile his work to see?
Did he who made the Lamb make thee?
Songs of Experience (1794) 'The Tiger'

5 Cruelty has a human heart,
And Jealousy a human face;
Terror the human form divine,
And Secrecy the human dress.
'A Divine Image'; etched but not included in
Songs of Experience (1794); see **Blake** 57:17

Jean Joseph Louis Blanc 1811–82
French utopian socialist

6 In the Saint-Simonian doctrine, the problem
of the distribution of benefits is resolved by
this famous saying: *To each according to his
ability; to each ability according to its fruits.*
*Blanc cites Saint-Simon in order to disagree with
his ideas*
Organisation du travail (1841 ed.); see **Marx** 230:6

Lesley Blanch 1907–
British writer

7 She was an Amazon. Her whole life was
spent riding at breakneck speed towards the
wilder shores of love.
of Jane Digby El Mezrab (1807–81)
The Wilder Shores of Love (1954) pt. 2, ch. 1

Danny Blanchflower 1926–93
English footballer

8 The game is about glory, it is about doing
things in style and with a flourish, about
going out and beating the lot, not waiting
for them to die of boredom.
attributed, 1972

Philip Paul Bliss 1838–76
American evangelist

9 Hold the fort, for I am coming.
suggested by a flag message from General
Sherman; *see* **Sherman** 315:23
Gospel Hymns and Sacred Songs (1875) no. 14

Hans Blix 1928–
Swedish diplomat

10 We have not found any smoking guns.
of weapons inspections in Iraq
in *Newsweek* 20 January 2003

11 You can put up a sign on the door, 'beware
of the dog', without having a dog.
in *Guardian* (online edition) 18 September 2003

Karen Blixen *see* Isak Dinesen

Judy Blume 1938–
American writer

12 Are you there God? It's me, Margaret.
title of book (1970)

John Ernest Bode 1816–74
English clergyman

13 O Jesus, I have promised
To serve thee to the end;
Be thou for ever near me,
My Master and my Friend.
'O Jesus, I have promised' (1869 hymn); written
for the confirmation of Bode's three children

Ivan F. Boesky 1937–
American businessman

14 Greed is all right . . . Greed is healthy. You
can be greedy and still feel good about
yourself.
commencement address, Berkeley, California,
18 May 1986

Boethius *c*.AD 476–524
Roman statesman and philosopher

15 For in every ill-turn of fortune the most
unhappy sort of unfortunate man is the one
who has been happy.
De Consolatione Philosophiae bk. 2, prose 4; see
Chaucer 92:3, **Dante** 109:12

John B. Bogart 1848–1921
American journalist

16 When a dog bites a man, that is not news,
because it happens so often. But if a man
bites a dog, that is news.
often attributed to Charles A. Dana
F. M. O'Brien *The Story of the* [New York] *Sun*
(1918) ch. 10

Niels Bohr 1885–1962
Danish physicist

17 Anybody who is not shocked by this subject
has failed to understand it.
of quantum mechanics
attributed; in *Nature* 23 August 1990

18 Never express yourself more clearly than
you think.
Abraham Pais *Einstein Lived Here* (1994)

Nicolas Boileau 1636–1711
French critic and poet

19 A fool can always find a greater fool to
admire him.
L'Art poétique (1674) canto 1, l. 232

Henry St John, Lord Bolingbroke 1678–1751
English politician

1 Truth lies within a little and certain compass, but error is immense.
   Reflections upon Exile (1716)

Robert Bolt 1924–95
English dramatist

2 This country's planted thick with laws from coast to coast—Man's laws, not God's—and if you cut them down—and you're just the man to do it—d'you really think you could stand upright in the winds that would blow then?
   A Man for All Seasons (1960) act 1

3 It profits a man nothing to give his soul for the whole world . . . But for Wales—!
   A Man for All Seasons (1960) act 2; see **Bible** 46:27

Andrew Bonar Law 1858–1923
Canadian-born British Conservative statesman, Prime Minister 1922–3

4 I can imagine no length of resistance to which Ulster will not go, in which I shall not be ready to support them.
   at a Unionist meeting at Blenheim in 1912
   Robert Blake *The Unknown Prime Minister* (1955)

Carrie Jacobs Bond 1862–1946
American songwriter

5 When you come to the end of a perfect day.
   'A Perfect Day' (1910 song)

David Bone 1874–1959
Scottish naval officer and writer

6 It's 'Damn you, Jack — I'm all right!' with you chaps.
   Brassbounder (1910) ch. 3

Violet Bonham Carter 1887–1969
British Liberal politician

7 HOW DARE YOU BECOME PRIME MINISTER WHEN I'M AWAY GREAT LOVE CONSTANT THOUGHT VIOLET.
   *telegram to her father, H. H. **Asquith**, 7 April 1908*
   Mark Bonham Carter and Mark Pottle (eds.) *Lantern Slides* (1996)

Dietrich Bonhoeffer 1906–45
German Lutheran theologian and martyr

8 I shall have no right to participate in the reconstruction of Christian life in Germany after the war if I do not share the trials of this time with my people.
   letter to Reinhold Niebuhr, July 1939

9 In me there is darkness, but with you there is light.
   prayer written for fellow-prisoners in a Nazi prison, 1943
   Letters and Papers from Prison (1971)

10 Jesus is there only for others . . . 'the man for others', and therefore the crucified.
   Widerstand und Ergebung (Resistance and Submission, 1951) 'Entwurf einer Arbeit'

The Book of Common Prayer
1662

11 Dearly beloved brethren, the Scripture moveth us in sundry places to acknowledge and confess our manifold sins and wickedness.
   Morning Prayer Sentences of the Scriptures

12 We have erred, and strayed from thy ways like lost sheep. We have followed too much the devices and desires of our own hearts.
   Morning Prayer General Confession

13 We have left undone those things which we ought to have done; And we have done those things which we ought not to have done; And there is no health in us.
   Morning Prayer General Confession

14 And grant, O most merciful Father, for his sake; That we may hereafter live a godly, righteous, and sober life.
   Morning Prayer General Confession

15 And forgive us our trespasses, As we forgive them that trespass against us.
   Morning Prayer The Lord's Prayer; see **Bible** 43:22, **Missal** 240:24

16 Glory be to the Father, and to the Son: and to the Holy Ghost; As it was in the beginning, is now, and ever shall be: world without end. Amen.
   Morning Prayer Gloria

17 We praise thee, O God: we acknowledge thee to be the Lord.
   All the earth doth worship thee: the Father everlasting.
   To thee all Angels cry aloud: the Heavens, and all the Powers therein.
   Morning Prayer Te Deum

18 The glorious company of the Apostles: praise thee.
   The goodly fellowship of the Prophets: praise thee.
   The noble army of Martyrs: praise thee.
   Morning Prayer Te Deum

19 When thou hadst overcome the sharpness of death: thou didst open the Kingdom of Heaven to all believers.
   Morning Prayer Te Deum

20 Day by day: we magnify thee;
   And we worship thy Name: ever world without end.
   Morning Prayer Te Deum

21 O Lord, in thee have I trusted: let me never be confounded.
   Morning Prayer Te Deum

22 O all ye Works of the Lord, bless ye the Lord.
   Morning Prayer Benedicite

23 I believe in God the Father Almighty, Maker of heaven and earth:
   And in Jesus Christ his only Son our Lord,
   Who was conceived by the Holy Ghost, Born

of the Virgin Mary, Suffered under Pontius Pilate, Was crucified, dead, and buried, He descended into hell; The third day he rose again from the dead, He ascended into heaven, And sitteth on the right hand of God the Father Almighty; From thence he shall come to judge the quick and the dead. I believe in the Holy Ghost; The holy Catholic Church; The Communion of Saints; The Forgiveness of sins; The Resurrection of the body, And the life everlasting. Amen.

Morning Prayer The Apostles' Creed; see **Book of Common Prayer** 61:3, **Missal** 240:20

1 Give peace in our time, O Lord.

Morning Prayer Versicle

2 O God, who art the author of peace and lover of concord, in knowledge of whom standeth our eternal life, whose service is perfect freedom; Defend us thy humble servants in all assaults of our enemies.

Morning Prayer The Second Collect, for Peace

3 Grant that this day we fall into no sin, neither run into any kind of danger.

Morning Prayer The Third Collect, for Grace

4 In Quires and Places where they sing, here followeth the Anthem.

Morning Prayer rubric following Third Collect

5 Almighty God, the fountain of all goodness.

Morning Prayer Prayer for the Royal Family

6 Almighty God, who hast given us grace at this time with one accord to make our common supplications unto thee; and dost promise, that when two or three are gathered together in thy Name thou wilt grant their requests: Fulfil now, O Lord, the desires and petitions of thy servants, as may be most expedient for them.

Morning Prayer Prayer of St Chrysostom

7 O God, from whom all holy desires, all good counsels, and all just works do proceed; Give unto thy servants that peace which the world cannot give.

Evening Prayer Second Collect

8 Lighten our darkness, we beseech thee, O Lord; and by thy great mercy defend us from all perils and dangers of this night.

Evening Prayer Third Collect

9 Whosoever will be saved: before all things it is necessary that he hold the Catholic Faith.

At Morning Prayer Athanasian Creed 'Quicunque vult'

10 Have mercy upon us miserable sinners.

The Litany

11 From envy, hatred, and malice, and from all uncharitableness,
Good Lord, deliver us.

The Litany

12 From all the deceits of the world, the flesh, and the devil,
Good Lord, deliver us.

The Litany

13 From battle and murder, and from sudden death,

Good Lord, deliver us.

The Litany

14 In the hour of death, and in the day of judgement,
Good Lord, deliver us.

The Litany

15 That it may please thee to preserve all that travel by land or by water, all women labouring of child, all sick persons, and young children; and to shew thy pity upon all prisoners and captives;
We beseech thee to hear us, good Lord.

The Litany

16 O God, the Creator and Preserver of all mankind, we humbly beseech thee for all sorts and conditions of men.

Prayers . . . upon Several Occasions 'Collect or Prayer for all Conditions of Men'

17 We commend to thy fatherly goodness all those, who are any ways afflicted, or distressed, in mind, body, or estate; that it may please thee to comfort and relieve them, according to their several necessities, giving them patience under their sufferings, and a happy issue out of all their afflictions.

Prayers . . . upon Several Occasions 'Collect or Prayer for all Conditions of Men'

18 O God our heavenly Father, who by thy gracious providence dost cause the former and the latter rain to descend upon the earth.

Thanksgivings For Rain

19 Almighty God, give us grace that we may cast away the works of darkness, and put upon us the armour of light.

Collects The first Sunday in Advent

20 Blessed Lord, who hast caused all holy Scriptures to be written for our learning; Grant that we may in such wise hear them, read, mark, learn, and inwardly digest them, that by patience, and comfort of thy holy Word.

Collects The second Sunday in Advent

21 O God, forasmuch as without thee we are not able to please thee; Mercifully grant, that thy Holy Spirit may in all things direct and rule our hearts.

Collects The nineteenth Sunday after Trinity

22 Stir up, we beseech thee, O Lord, the wills of thy faithful people.

Collects The five and twentieth Sunday after Trinity

23 An open and notorious evil liver.

Holy Communion introductory rubric

24 The Table, at the Communion-time having a fair white linen cloth upon it.

Holy Communion introductory rubric

25 Almighty God, unto whom all hearts be open, all desires known, and from whom no secrets are hid.

Holy Communion The Collect

26 I the Lord thy God am a jealous God, and visit the sins of the fathers upon the

children unto the third and fourth
generation of them that hate me.
*the phrase 'sins of the fathers' is also used in the
Douay/Rheims Bible (1609) in Numbers ch. 14, v.
18*

> *Holy Communion* The Ten Commandments; see
> **Bible** 35:25

1 Incline our hearts to keep this law.
> *Holy Communion* The Ten Commandments
> (response)

2 Thou shalt do no murder.
> *Holy Communion* The Ten Commandments; see
> **Bible** 35:28

3 I believe in one God the Father Almighty,
Maker of heaven and earth, And of all things
visible and invisible:
And in one Lord Jesus Christ, the only-
begotten Son of God, Begotten of his Father
before all worlds, God of God, Light of Light,
Very God of very God, Begotten, not made,
Being of one substance with the Father, By
whom all things were made.
> *Holy Communion* Nicene Creed; see **Book of
> Common Prayer** 59:23, **Missal** 240:20

4 And I believe one Catholick and Apostolick
Church.
> *Holy Communion* Nicene Creed, see **Missal** 240:20

5 Let us pray for the whole state of Christ's
Church militant here in earth.
> *Holy Communion* Prayer for the Church Militant

6 We humbly beseech thee most mercifully to
accept our alms and oblations.
> *Holy Communion* Prayer for the Church Militant

7 To inspire continually the universal Church
with the spirit of truth, unity, and concord.
> *Holy Communion* Prayer for the Church Militant

8 We do earnestly repent, And are heartily
sorry for these our misdoings; The
remembrance of them is grievous unto us;
The burden of them is intolerable.
> *Holy Communion* General Confession

9 Hear what comfortable words our Saviour
Christ saith unto all that truly turn to him.
> *Holy Communion* Comfortable Words (preamble)

10 Lift up your hearts.
> *Holy Communion* versicles and responses; see
> **Missal** 240:22

11 It is meet and right so to do.
> *Holy Communion* versicles and responses

12 It is very meet, right, and our bounden duty,
that we should at all times, and in all places,
give thanks unto thee.
> *Holy Communion* Hymn of Praise

13 Who made there (by his one oblation of
himself once offered) a full, perfect, and
sufficient sacrifice, oblation, and
satisfaction, for the sins of the whole world.
> *Holy Communion* Prayer of Consecration

14 Who, in the same night that he was
betrayed, took Bread; and, when he had
given thanks, he brake it, and gave it to his
disciples, saying, Take, eat, this is my Body
which is given for you: Do this in
remembrance of me.
> *Holy Communion* Prayer of Consecration

15 Among all the changes and chances of this
mortal life.
> *Holy Communion* Collects after the Offertory

16 O merciful God, grant that the old Adam in
this Child may be so buried, that the new
man may be raised up in him.
> *Public Baptism of Infants* Invocation of blessing on
> the child

17 QUESTION: Who gave you this Name?
ANSWER: My Godfathers and Godmothers in
my Baptism.
> *Catechism*

18 I should renounce the devil and all his
works, the pomps and vanity of this wicked
world, and all the sinful lusts of the flesh.
> *Catechism*

19 To keep my hands from picking and
stealing.
> *Catechism*

20 QUESTION: What meanest thou by this word
Sacrament?
ANSWER: I mean an outward and visible sign
of an inward and spiritual grace.
> *Catechism*

21 Lord, hear our prayers.
And let our cry come unto thee.
> *Order of Confirmation*

22 If any of you know cause, or just
impediment, why these two persons should
not be joined together in holy Matrimony,
ye are to declare it. This is the first [second, or
third] time of asking.
> *Solemnization of Matrimony* The Banns

23 Dearly beloved, we are gathered together
here in the sight of God, and in the face of
this congregation, to join together this Man
and this Woman in holy Matrimony.
> *Solemnization of Matrimony* Exhortation

24 Not by any to be enterprised, nor taken in
hand, unadvisedly, lightly, or wantonly, to
satisfy men's carnal lusts and appetites, like
brute beasts that have no understanding.
> *Solemnization of Matrimony* Exhortation

25 If any man can shew any just cause, why
they may not lawfully be joined together, let
him now speak, or else hereafter for ever
hold his peace.
> *Solemnization of Matrimony* Exhortation

26 Wilt thou love her, comfort her, honour,
and keep her in sickness and in health; and,
forsaking all other, keep thee only unto her,
so long as ye both shall live?
> *Solemnization of Matrimony* Betrothal

27 To have and to hold from this day forward,
for better for worse, for richer for poorer, in
sickness and in health, to love, cherish, and
to obey, till death us do part, according to

God's holy ordinance; and thereto I give thee my troth.

the man having used the words 'I plight thee my troth' and not having promised 'to obey'; the woman may also omit the promise 'to obey'
Solemnization of Matrimony Betrothal

1 With this Ring I thee wed, with my body I thee worship, and with all my worldly goods I thee endow.
Solemnization of Matrimony Wedding

2 Those whom God hath joined together let no man put asunder.
Solemnization of Matrimony Wedding; see **Bible** 45:17

3 Unto God's gracious mercy and protection we commit thee.
The Visitation of the Sick

4 Man that is born of a woman hath but a short time to live, and is full of misery.
The Burial of the Dead First Anthem; see **Bible** 38:1

5 In the midst of life we are in death.
The Burial of the Dead First Anthem

6 Forasmuch as it hath pleased Almighty God of his great mercy to take unto himself the soul of our dear brother here departed, we therefore commit his body to the ground; earth to earth, ashes to ashes, dust to dust; in sure and certain hope of the Resurrection to eternal life.
The Burial of the Dead Interment

7 Why do the heathen so furiously rage together: and why do the people imagine a vain thing?
Psalm 2, v. 1

8 Out of the mouth of very babes and sucklings hast thou ordained strength, because of thine enemies.
Psalm 8, v. 2

9 The fool hath said in his heart: There is no God.
Psalm 14, v. 1

10 The lot is fallen unto me in a fair ground: yea, I have a goodly heritage.
Psalm 16, v. 7; 'The lines are fallen unto me in pleasant places' as Psalm 16, v. 6 in Authorized Version of the Bible

11 The heavens declare the glory of God: and the firmament sheweth his handy-work.
Psalm 19, v. 1

12 The judgements of the Lord are true, and righteous altogether.
More to be desired are they than gold, yea, than much fine gold: sweeter also than honey, and the honey-comb.
Psalm 19, v. 10

13 They part my garments among them: and cast lots upon my vesture.
Psalm 22, v. 18

14 The Lord is my shepherd: therefore can I lack nothing.

He shall feed me in a green pasture: and lead me forth beside the waters of comfort.
Psalm 23, v. 1; see **Herbert** 167:23, **Scottish Metrical Psalms** 288:2; see also Psalm 23, v. 1, Authorized Version of the Bible, 'The Lord is my shepherd; I shall not want. He maketh me to lie down in green pastures: he leadeth me beside the still waters'

15 Yea, though I walk through the valley of the shadow of death, I will fear no evil: for thou art with me; thy rod and thy staff comfort me.
Thou shalt prepare a table before me against them that trouble me: thou hast anointed my head with oil, and my cup shall be full.
But thy loving-kindness and mercy shall follow me all the days of my life: and I will dwell in the house of the Lord for ever.
Psalm 23, v. 4; see **Scottish Metrical Psalms** 288:3

16 The earth is the Lord's, and all that therein is: the compass of the world, and they that dwell therein.
Psalm 24, v. 1

17 Lift up your heads, O ye gates, and be ye lift up, ye everlasting doors: and the King of glory shall come in.
Psalm 24, v. 7

18 I should utterly have fainted: but that I believe verily to see the goodness of the Lord in the land of the living.
Psalm 27, v. 15

19 Heaviness may endure for a night, but joy cometh in the morning.
Psalm 30, v. 5

20 Into thy hands I commend my spirit.
Psalm 31, v. 6; see **Bible** 48:11

21 Sing unto the Lord a new song: sing praises lustily unto him with a good courage.
Psalm 33, v. 3

22 O deliver my soul from the calamities which they bring on me, and my darling from the lions.
Psalm 35, v. 17

23 I have been young, and now am old: and yet saw I never the righteous forsaken, nor his seed begging their bread.
Psalm 37, v. 25

24 I myself have seen the ungodly in great power: and flourishing like a green bay-tree.
Psalm 37, v. 36

25 Lord, let me know mine end, and the number of my days: that I may be certified how long I have to live.
Psalm 39, v. 5

26 Yea, even mine own familiar friend, whom I trusted.
Psalm 41, v. 9

27 Like as the hart desireth the water-brooks: so longeth my soul after thee, O God.
My soul is a thirst for God, yea, even for the living God.
Psalm 42, v. 1; see **Tate** 330:19

As the hart panteth after the water brooks, so panteth my soul after thee, O God.
My soul thirsteth for God, the living God.
Psalm 42, v. 1 in the Authorized Version of the Bible

1 My heart is inditing of a good matter: I speak of the things which I have made unto the King.
My tongue is the pen: of a ready writer.
Psalm 45, v. 1

2 Thou hast loved righteousness, and hated iniquity: wherefore God, even thy God, hath anointed thee with the oil of gladness above thy fellows.
Psalm 45, v. 8

3 The King's daughter is all glorious within: her clothing is of wrought gold.
Psalm 45, v. 14

4 God is our hope and strength: a very present help in trouble.
Psalm 46, v. 1; see **Anonymous** 7:5

5 Be still then, and know that I am God.
Psalm 46, v. 10

6 Behold, I was shapen in wickedness: and in sin hath my mother conceived me.
Psalm 51, v. 5

7 Make me a clean heart, O God: and renew a right spirit within me.
Psalm 51, v. 10

8 Deliver me from blood-guiltiness, O God.
Psalm 51, v. 14

9 O that I had wings like a dove: for then would I flee away, and be at rest.
Psalm 55, v. 6

10 It was even thou, my companion: my guide, and mine own familiar friend.
We took sweet counsel together: and walked in the house of God as friends.
Psalm 55, v. 14

11 They have digged a pit before me, and are fallen into the midst of it themselves.
Psalm 57, v. 7

12 They are as venomous as the poison of a serpent: even like the deaf adder that stoppeth her ears;
Which refuseth to hear the voice of the charmer: charm he never so wisely.
Psalm 58, v. 4

13 Moab is my wash-pot; over Edom will I cast out my shoe.
Psalm 60, v. 8

14 Let God arise, and let his enemies be scattered: let them also that hate him flee before him.
Psalm 68, v. 1

15 The mountains also shall bring peace: and the little hills righteousness unto the people.
Psalm 72, v. 3

16 For promotion cometh neither from the east, nor from the west: nor yet from the south.
Psalm 75, v. 7

17 As one out of sleep: and like a giant refreshed with wine.
Psalm 78, v. 66

18 Yea, the sparrow hath found her an house, and the swallow a nest where she may lay her young: even thy altars, O Lord of hosts, my King and my God.
Psalm 84, v. 3

19 Blessed is the man whose strength is in thee: in whose heart are thy ways.
Who going through the vale of misery use it for a well: and the pools are filled with water.
They will go from strength to strength.
Psalm 84, v. 5

20 For one day in thy courts: is better than a thousand.
I had rather be a door-keeper in the house of my God: than to dwell in the tents of ungodliness.
Psalm 84, v. 10

21 Mercy and truth are met together: righteousness and peace have kissed each other.
Psalm 85, v. 10

22 For a thousand years in thy sight are but as yesterday: seeing that is past as a watch in the night.
Psalm 90, v. 4

23 The days of our age are threescore years and ten; and though men be so strong that they come to fourscore years: yet is their strength then but labour and sorrow; so soon passeth it away, and we are gone.
Psalm 90, v. 10

24 For he shall deliver thee from the snare of the hunter.
Psalm 91, v. 3

25 Thou shalt not be afraid for any terror by night: nor for the arrow that flieth by day;
For the pestilence that walketh in darkness: nor for the sickness that destroyeth in the noon-day.
Psalm 91, v. 5

26 O come, let us sing unto the Lord: let us heartily rejoice in the strength of our salvation.
Let us come before his presence with thanksgiving: and shew ourselves glad in him with psalms.
Psalm 95, v. 1

27 To-day if ye will hear his voice, harden not your hearts: as in the provocation, and as in the day of temptation in the wilderness.
Psalm 95, v. 8

28 O worship the Lord in the beauty of holiness: let the whole earth stand in awe of him.
Psalm 96, v. 9

1 O sing unto the Lord a new song: for he hath done marvellous things.
With his own right hand, and with his holy arm: hath he gotten himself the victory.
Psalm 98, v. 1; see **Bible** 53:28

2 O be joyful in the Lord, all ye lands: serve the Lord with gladness, and come before his presence with a song.
Be ye sure that the Lord he is God: it is he that hath made us, and not we ourselves; we are his people, and the sheep of his pasture.
Psalm 100, v. 1; see **Bible** 53:29

3 The days of man are but as grass: for he flourisheth as a flower of a field.
For as soon as the wind goeth over it, it is gone: and the place thereof shall know it no more.
Psalm 103, v. 15

4 Thou makest darkness that it may be night: wherein all the beasts of the forest do move.
The lions roaring after their prey: do seek their meat from God.
Psalm 104, v. 20

5 There go the ships, and there is that Leviathan: whom thou hast made to take his pastime therein.
Psalm 104, v. 26

6 The iron entered into his soul.
Psalm 105, v. 18

7 Thus were they stained with their own works: and went a whoring with their own inventions.
Psalm 106, v. 38

8 Such as sit in darkness, and in the shadow of death.
Psalm 107, v. 10

9 They that go down to the sea in ships: and occupy their business in great waters;
These men see the works of the Lord: and his wonders in the deep.
Psalm 107, v. 23

10 They reel to and fro, and stagger like a drunken man: and are at their wit's end.
Psalm 107, v. 27

11 Thou art a Priest for ever after the order of Melchisedech.
Psalm 110, v. 4

12 The fear of the Lord is the beginning of wisdom.
Psalm 111, v. 10

13 The mountains skipped like rams: and the little hills like young sheep.
Psalm 114, v. 4

14 Not unto us, O Lord, not unto us, but unto thy Name give the praise.
Psalm 115, v. 1; see **Bible** 54:1

15 They have mouths, and speak not: eyes have they, and see not.
They have ears, and hear not: noses have they, and smell not.
They have hands, and handle not: feet have

they, and walk not: neither speak they through their throat.
Psalm 115, v. 5

16 The snares of death compassed me round about: and the pains of hell gat hold upon me.
Psalm 116, v. 3

17 I said in my haste, All men are liars.
Psalm 116, v. 10

18 The same stone which the builders refused: is become the head-stone in the corner.
This is the Lord's doing: and it is marvellous in our eyes.
Psalm 118, v. 22

19 Blessed be he that cometh in the Name of the Lord.
Psalm 118, v. 26

20 I will lift up mine eyes unto the hills: from whence cometh my help.
Psalm 121, v. 1; see **Scottish Metrical Psalms** 288:4

21 So that the sun shall not burn thee by day: neither the moon by night.
Psalm 121, v. 6

22 The Lord shall preserve thy going out, and thy coming in: from this time forth for evermore.
Psalm 121, v. 8

23 O pray for the peace of Jerusalem: they shall prosper that love thee.
Psalm 122, v. 6

24 Our soul is escaped even as a bird out of the snare of the fowler: the snare is broken, and we are delivered.
Psalm 124, v. 6

25 They that sow in tears: shall reap in joy.
He that now goeth on his way weeping, and beareth forth good seed: shall doubtless come again with joy, and bring his sheaves with him.
Psalm 126, v. 6

26 Except the Lord build the house: their labour is but lost that build it.
Except the Lord keep the city: the watchman waketh but in vain.
Psalm 127, v. 1; see **Bible** 54:2

27 Like as the arrows in the hand of the giant: even so are the young children.
Happy is the man that hath his quiver full of them.
Psalm 127, v. 5

28 Thy wife shall be as the fruitful vine: upon the walls of thine house.
Thy children like the olive-branches: round about thy table.
Psalm 128, v. 3

29 Out of the deep have I called unto thee, O Lord: Lord, hear my voice.
Psalm 130, v. 1; see **Bible** 54:3

30 O give thanks unto the Lord, for he is gracious: and his mercy endureth for ever.
Psalm 136, v. 1; see **Milton** 236:26

1 By the waters of Babylon we sat down and wept: when we remembered thee, O Sion.
Psalm 137, v. 1

2 If I forget thee, O Jerusalem: let my right hand forget her cunning.
Psalm 137, v. 5

3 If I take the wings of the morning: and remain in the uttermost parts of the sea; Even there also shall thy hand lead me: and thy right hand shall hold me.
Psalm 139, v. 8

4 I will give thanks unto thee, for I am fearfully and wonderfully made.
Psalm 139, v. 13

5 O put not your trust in princes, nor in any child of man.
Psalm 146, v. 2

6 To bind their kings in chains: and their nobles with links of iron.
Psalm 149, v. 8

7 Praise him upon the well-tuned cymbals: praise him upon the loud cymbals. Let every thing that hath breath: praise the Lord.
Psalm 150, v. 5

8 Be pleased to receive into thy Almighty and most gracious protection the persons of us thy servants, and the Fleet in which we serve.
Forms of Prayer to be Used at Sea First Prayer

9 That we may be . . . a security for such as pass on the seas upon their lawful occasions.
Forms of Prayer to be Used at Sea First Prayer

10 We therefore commit his body to the deep, to be turned into corruption, looking for the resurrection of the body (when the Sea shall give up her dead).
Forms of Prayer to be Used at Sea At the Burial of their Dead at Sea

11 Holy Scripture containeth all things necessary to salvation.
Articles of Religion (1562) no. 6

12 Man is very far gone from original righteousness.
Articles of Religion (1562) no. 9

13 It is a thing plainly repugnant to the Word of God, and the custom of the Primitive Church, to have publick Prayer in the Church, or to minister the Sacraments in a tongue not understanded of the people.
Articles of Religion (1562) no. 24

14 The Bishop of Rome hath no jurisdiction in this Realm of England.
Articles of Religion (1562) no. 37

15 It is lawful for Christian men, at the commandment of the Magistrate, to wear weapons, and serve in the wars.
Articles of Religion (1562) no. 37

16 A Man may not marry his Mother.
A Table of Kindred and Affinity

John Wilkes Booth 1838–65
American actor and assassin

17 *Sic semper tyrannis!* The South is avenged.
having shot President **Lincoln**, *14 April 1865*
in *New York Times* 15 April 1865; the second part of the statement does not appear in any contemporary source, and is possibly apocryphal; see **Anonymous** 13:19

William Booth 1829–1912
British religious leader

18 The submerged tenth.
defined by Booth as 'three million men, women, and children, a vast despairing multitude in a condition nominally free, but really enslaved'
In Darkest England (1890) pt. 1, title of ch. 2

James H. Boren 1925–
American bureaucrat

19 Guidelines for bureaucrats: (1) When in charge, ponder. (2) When in trouble, delegate. (3) When in doubt, mumble.
in *New York Times* 8 November 1970

Jorge Luis Borges 1899–1986
Argentinian writer

20 On those remote pages [of the *Celestial Emporium of Benevolent Knowledge*] it is written that animals are divided into (a) those that belong to the Emperor, (b) embalmed ones, (c) those that are trained, (d) suckling pigs, (e) mermaids, (f) fabulous ones, (g) stray dogs, (h) those that are included in this classification, (i) those that tremble as if they were mad, (j) innumerable ones, (k) those drawn with a very fine camel's hair brush, (l) others, (m) those that have just broken a flower vase, (n) those that resemble flies from a distance.
Other Inquisitions (1966)

21 The original is unfaithful to the translation.
of Henley's translation of **Beckford**'s Vathek
Sobre el 'Vathek' de William Beckford (1943)

22 The Falklands thing was a fight between two bald men over a comb.
application of a proverbial phrase
in *Time* 14 February 1983

Cesare Borgia 1476–1507
Italian statesman, cardinal, and general

23 *Aut Caesar, aut nihil.*
Caesar or nothing.
motto inscribed on his sword

George Borrow 1803–81
English writer

24 Sun, moon, and stars, brother, all sweet things: there's likewise a wind on the heath.

Life is very sweet, brother; who would wish
to die?
Lavengro (1851) ch. 25

Pierre Bosquet 1810–61
French general

1 *C'est magnifique, mais ce n'est pas la guerre.*
It is magnificent, but it is not war.
*on the charge of the Light Brigade at Balaclava, 25
October 1854*
Cecil Woodham-Smith *The Reason Why* (1953) ch.
12

John Collins Bossidy 1860–1928
American oculist

2 And this is good old Boston,
The home of the bean and the cod,
Where the Lowells talk to the Cabots
And the Cabots talk only to God.
*verse spoken at Holy Cross College alumni
dinner in Boston, Massachusetts, 1910, in
Springfield Sunday Republican 14 December 1924*

Jacques-Bénigne Bossuet
1627–1704
French preacher

3 *L'Angleterre, ah, la perfide Angleterre, que le
rempart de ses mers rendait inaccessible aux
Romains, la foi du Sauveur y est abordée.*
England, ah, faithless England, which the
protection afforded by its seas rendered
inaccessible to the Romans, the faith of the
Saviour spread even there.
*first sermon on the feast of the Circumcision, in
Oeuvres de Bossuet (1816) vol. 11; see **Ximénèz**
367:8*

James Boswell 1740–95
Scottish lawyer; biographer of Samuel Johnson

4 I am, I flatter myself, completely a citizen of
the world. In my travels through Holland,
Germany, Switzerland, Italy, Corsica,
France, I never felt myself from home.
*Journal of a Tour to the Hebrides (ed. F. A. Pottle,
1936) 14 August 1773*

5 JOHNSON: Well, we had a good talk.
BOSWELL: Yes, Sir; you tossed and gored
several persons.
The Life of Samuel Johnson (1791) Summer 1768

Horatio Bottomley 1860–1933
British newspaper proprietor and financier

6 *reply to a prison visitor who asked if he were
sewing:*
No, reaping.
S. T. Felstead *Horatio Bottomley* (1936) ch. 16

Dion Boucicault 1820–90
Irish dramatist

7 Men talk of killing time, while time quietly
kills them.
London Assurance (1841) act 2, sc. 1

Antoine Boulay de la Meurthe
1761–1840
French statesman

8 It is worse than a crime, it is a blunder.
*on hearing of the execution of the Duc d'Enghien,
captured in Baden by Napoleon's forces, in 1804*
C.-A. Sainte-Beuve *Nouveaux Lundis* (1870) vol. 12

Harold Edwin Boulton 1859–1935
British songwriter

9 Speed, bonnie boat, like a bird on the wing,
'Onward,' the sailors cry;
Carry the lad that's born to be king,
Over the sea to Skye.
'Skye Boat Song' (1908)

Matthew Boulton 1728–1809
British engineer

10 I sell here, Sir, what all the world desires to
have—POWER.
*speaking to **Boswell** of his engineering works*
James Boswell *Life of Samuel Johnson* (1791) 22
March 1776

F. W. Bourdillon 1852–1921
English poet

11 The night has a thousand eyes,
And the day but one.
Among the Flowers (1878) 'Light'; see **Lyly** 220:23

E. E. Bowen 1836–1901
English schoolmaster

12 Forty years on, when afar and asunder
Parted are those who are singing to-day.
'Forty Years On' (Harrow School Song,
published 1886)

Elizabeth Bowen 1899–1973
*British novelist and short-story writer, born in
Ireland*

13 Fate is not an eagle, it creeps like a rat.
The House in Paris (1935) pt. 2, ch. 2

14 Jealousy is no more than feeling alone
against smiling enemies.
The House in Paris (1935) pt. 2, ch. 8

Lord Bowen 1835–94
English judge

15 The man on the Clapham omnibus.
the average man
in *Law Reports* (1903); attributed

16 When I hear of an 'equity' in a case like this,
I am reminded of a blind man in a dark
room—looking for a black hat—which isn't
there.
John Alderson Foote *Pie-Powder* (1911)

17 The rain, it raineth on the just
And also on the unjust fella:
But chiefly on the just, because
The unjust steals the just's umbrella.
Walter Sichel *Sands of Time* (1923) ch. 4: see
Bible 43:19

David Bowie (David Jones) 1947–
English rock musician

1 Ground control to Major Tom.
 'Space Oddity' (1969 song)

William Lisle Bowles 1762–1850
English clergyman and poet

2 The cause of Freedom is the cause of God!
 A Poetical Address to the Right Honourable Edmund Burke (1791) l. 78

Boy George 1961–
English pop singer and songwriter

3 She's a gay man trapped in a woman's body.
 of Madonna
 Take It Like a Man (1995)

4 Sex has never been an obsession with me. It's just like eating a bag of crisps. Quite nice, but nothing marvellous.
 in *Sun* 21 October 1982

John Bradford c.1510–55
English Protestant martyr

5 But for the grace of God there goes John Bradford.
 on seeing a group of criminals being led to their execution; usually quoted as, 'There but for the grace of God go I'
 in *Dictionary of National Biography* (1917–)

F. H. Bradley 1846–1924
English philosopher

6 Metaphysics is the finding of bad reasons for what we believe upon instinct; but to find these reasons is no less an instinct.
 Appearance and Reality (1893) preface

7 The world is the best of all possible worlds, and everything in it is a necessary evil.
 Appearance and Reality (1893) preface

Omar Bradley 1893–1981
American general

8 The way to win an atomic war is to make certain it never starts.
 speech on Armistice Day, 1948

9 We have grasped the mystery of the atom and rejected the Sermon on the Mount.
 speech on Armistice Day, 1948
 Collected Writings (1967) vol. 1

10 Ours is a world of nuclear giants and ethical infants.
 speech on Armistice Day, 1948
 Collected Writings (1967) vol. 1

Don Bradman 1908–2001
Australian cricketer

11 When you play Test cricket you don't give Englishmen an inch. Play it tough, all the way. Grind them into the dust.
 Jack Fingleton *Batting from Memory* (1981)

John Bradshaw 1602–59
English judge at the trial of Charles I

12 Rebellion to tyrants is obedience to God.
 supposititious epitaph

Anne Bradstreet c.1612–72
English-born American poet

13 I am obnoxious to each carping tongue, Who says my hand a needle better fits.
 'The Prologue' (1650)

14 Authority without wisdom is like a heavy axe without an edge, fitter to bruise than polish.
 The Tenth Muse (1650) 'Meditations Divine and Moral'

Louis D. Brandeis 1856–1941
American jurist

15 If we would guide by the light of reason, we must let our minds be bold.
 Jay Burns Baking Co. v. Bryan (1924) (dissenting)

16 Fear of serious injury alone cannot justify suppression of free speech and assembly. Men feared witches and burned women. It is the function of speech to free men from the bondage of irrational fears.
 in *Whitney v. California* (1927)

17 The greatest dangers to liberty lurk in insidious encroachment by men of zeal, well-meaning but without understanding.
 dissenting opinion in *Olmstead v. United States* (1928)

Joseph Brant (Thayendanegea) 1742–1807
American-born Canadian Mohawk leader

18 I bow to no man for I am considered a prince among my own people. But I will gladly shake your hand.
 on being presented to George III
 attributed

Georges Braque 1882–1963
French painter

19 Art is meant to disturb, science reassures.
 Le Jour et la nuit: Cahiers 1917–52

20 Truth exists; only lies are invented.
 Le Jour et la nuit: Cahiers 1917–52

John W. Bratton and James B. Kennedy
British songwriters

21 If you go down in the woods today
 You're sure of a big surprise
 If you go down in the woods today
 You'd better go in disguise
 For every Bear that ever there was
 Will gather there for certain because,
 Today's the day the Teddy Bears have their Picnic.
 'The Teddy Bear's Picnic' (1932 song)

Werner von Braun 1912–77
German-born American rocket engineer

1 Don't tell me that man doesn't belong out there. Man belongs wherever he wants to go—and he'll do plenty well when he gets there.
on space
  in *Time* 17 February 1958

2 Basic research is what I am doing when I don't know what I am doing.
  R. L. Weber *A Random Walk in Science* (1973)

Bertolt Brecht 1898–1956
German dramatist

3 The aim of science is not to open the door to infinite wisdom, but to set a limit to infinite error.
  The Life of Galileo (1939) sc. 9

4 ANDREA: Unhappy the land that has no heroes! . . .
  GALILEO: No. Unhappy the land that needs heroes.
  The Life of Galileo (1939) sc. 13

5 The resistible rise of Arturo Ui.
  title of play (1941)

6 Oh, the shark has pretty teeth, dear,
  And he shows them pearly white.
  Just a jackknife has Macheath, dear
  And he keeps it out of sight.
  The Threepenny Opera (1928) prologue

7 What is robbing a bank compared with founding a bank?
  The Threepenny Opera (1928) act 3, sc. 3

8 Who built Thebes of the seven gates?
  In the books you will find the names of kings.
  Did the kings haul up the lumps of rock?
  'Questions From A Worker Who Reads' (1935)

9 Would it not be easier
  In that case for the government
  To dissolve the people
  And elect another?
  on the uprising against the Soviet occupying forces in East Germany in 1953
  'The Solution' (1953)

L. Paul Bremer 1941–
American diplomat

10 Ladies and gentlemen, we got him.
  announcing the capture of Saddam Hussein, 14 December 2003
  in *Independent* 15 December 2003

Gerald Brenan 1894–1987
British travel writer and novelist

11 Those who have some means think that the most important thing in the world is love. The poor know that it is money.
  Thoughts in a Dry Season (1978)

Sydney Brenner 1927–
British scientist

12 A modern computer hovers between the obsolescent and the nonexistent.
  attributed in *Science* 5 January 1990

Nicholas Breton c.1545–1626
English writer and poet

13 I wish my deadly foe, no worse
  Than want of friends, and empty purse.
  'A Farewell to Town' (1577)

Aristide Briand 1862–1932
French statesman

14 The high contracting powers solemnly declare . . . that they condemn recourse to war and renounce it . . . as an instrument of their national policy towards each other . . . The settlement or the solution of all disputes or conflicts of whatever nature or of whatever origin they may be which may arise . . . shall never be sought by either side except by pacific means.
  draft, 20 June 1927, later incorporated into the Kellogg Pact, 1928

Edward Bridges 1892–1969
British civil servant

15 I confidently expect that we shall continue to be grouped with mothers-in-law and Wigan Pier as one of the recognized objects of ridicule.
  of civil servants
  Portrait of a Profession (1950)

Robert Bridges 1844–1930
English poet

16 All my hope on God is founded.
  'All my hope on God is founded' (1899 hymn)

17 When men were all asleep the snow came flying,
  In large white flakes falling on the city brown,
  Stealthily and perpetually settling and loosely lying,
  Hushing the latest traffic of the drowsy town.
  'London Snow' (1890)

John Bright 1811–89
English Liberal politician and reformer

18 The angel of death has been abroad throughout the land; you may almost hear the beating of his wings.
  on the effects of the war in the Crimea
  speech in the House of Commons, 23 February 1855

19 A gigantic system of outdoor relief for the aristocracy of Great Britain.
  of British foreign policy
  speech at Birmingham, 29 October 1858

20 I am for 'Peace, retrenchment, and reform', the watchword of the great Liberal party 30 years ago.
  speech at Birmingham, 28 April 1859

1 England is the mother of Parliaments.
  speech at Birmingham, 18 January 1865

Anthelme Brillat-Savarin
1755–1826
French jurist and gourmet

2 Tell me what you eat and I will tell you what you are.
  Physiologie du Goût (1825) aphorism no. 4; see **Feuerbach** 135:3

3 The discovery of a new dish does more for human happiness than the discovery of a star.
  Physiologie du Goût (1825) aphorism no. 9

Russell Brockbank 1913–
British cartoonist

4 Fog in Channel—Continent isolated.
  newspaper placard in cartoon, *Round the Bend with Brockbank* (1948); the phrase 'Continent isolated' was quoted as already current by John Gunther *Inside Europe* (1938)

Tom Brokaw 1940–
American journalist

5 We don't just have egg on our face. We have omelette all over our suits.
  on the networks' premature calls of a win in Florida in the presidential election, first to Al Gore and then to George W. Bush
  in *Atlanta Constitution-Journal* 9 November 2000 (online edition)

Jacob Bronowski 1908–74
Polish-born mathematician and humanist

6 The world can only be grasped by action, not by contemplation . . . The hand is the cutting edge of the mind.
  The Ascent of Man (1973) ch. 3

7 The essence of science: ask an impertinent question, and you are on the way to a pertinent answer.
  The Ascent of Man (1973) ch. 4

8 The wish to hurt, the momentary intoxication with pain, is the loophole through which the pervert climbs into the minds of ordinary men.
  The Face of Violence (1954) ch. 5

Charlotte Brontë 1816–55
English novelist

9 Conventionality is not morality. Self-righteousness is not religion. To attack the first is not to assail the last. To pluck the mask from the face of the Pharisee, is not to lift an impious hand to the Crown of Thorns.
  Jane Eyre (2nd ed., 1848) preface

10 There was no possibility of taking a walk that day.
  Jane Eyre (1847), opening words

11 Reader, I married him.
  Jane Eyre (1847) ch. 38

12 Be a governess! Better be a slave at once!
  Shirley (1849) ch. 13

Emily Brontë 1818–48
English novelist and poet

13 No coward soul is mine,
No trembler in the world's storm-troubled sphere:
I see Heaven's glories shine,
And faith shines equal, arming me from fear.
  'No coward soul is mine' (1846)

14 Cold in the earth—and fifteen wild Decembers,
From those brown hills, have melted into spring.
  'Remembrance' (1846)

15 My love for Heathcliff resembles the eternal rocks beneath:—a source of little visible delight, but necessary.
  Wuthering Heights (1847) ch. 9

16 I lingered round them, under that benign sky: watched the moths fluttering among the heath and hare-bells; listened to the soft wind breathing through the grass; and wondered how any one could ever imagine unquiet slumbers for the sleepers in that quiet earth.
  Wuthering Heights (1847), closing words

Patrick Brontë 1777–1861
Irish-born English clergyman

17 Charlotte has been writing a book, and it is much better than likely.
  to his younger daughters, on first reading Jane Eyre
  Elizabeth Gaskell *The Life of Charlotte Brontë* (1857)

Henry Brooke 1703–83
Irish poet and dramatist

18 For righteous monarchs,
Justly to judge, with their own eyes should see;
To rule o'er freemen, should themselves be free.
  Earl of Essex (performed 1750, published 1761) act 1; see **Johnson** 190:18

Rupert Brooke 1887–1915
English poet

19 Blow out, you bugles, over the rich Dead!
There's none of these so lonely and poor of old,
But, dying, has made us rarer gifts than gold.
These laid the world away; poured out the red
Sweet wine of youth.
  'The Dead' (1914)

20 Unkempt about those hedges blows
An English unofficial rose.
  'The Old Vicarage, Grantchester' (1915)

21 Stands the Church clock at ten to three?
And is there honey still for tea?
  'The Old Vicarage, Grantchester' (1915)

1 Now, God be thanked Who has matched us with His hour.
'Peace' (1914)

2 If I should die, think only this of me:
That there's some corner of a foreign field
That is for ever England.
'The Soldier' (1914)

3 History repeats itself; historians repeat one another.
letter to Geoffrey Keynes, 4 June 1906

Anita Brookner 1928–
British novelist and art historian

4 Good women always think it is their fault when someone else is being offensive. Bad women never take the blame for anything.
Hotel du Lac (1984) ch. 7

Gwendolyn Brooks 1917–2000
American poet

5 Abortions will not let you forget.
You remember the children you got that you did not get . . .
'The Mother' (1945)

J. Brooks

6 A four-legged friend, a four-legged friend,
He'll never let you down.
sung by Roy Rogers about his horse Trigger
'A Four Legged Friend' (1952)

Phillips Brooks 1835–93
American clergyman

7 O little town of Bethlehem,
How still we see thee lie!
Above thy deep and dreamless sleep
The silent stars go by.
Yet in thy dark streets shineth
The everlasting light;
The hopes and fears of all the years
Are met in thee to-night.
'O Little Town of Bethlehem' (1868 hymn)

Thomas Brooks 1608–80
English Puritan divine

8 For (*magna est veritas et praevalebit*) great is truth, and shall prevail.
The Crown and Glory of Christianity (1662); see **Bible** 54:14

Lord Brougham 1778–1868
Scottish lawyer and politician

9 The schoolmaster is abroad! and I trust more to the schoolmaster, armed with his primer, than I do to the soldier in full military array, for upholding and extending the liberties of his country.
sometimes quoted as 'Look out, gentlemen, the schoolmaster is abroad!'
in the House of Commons, 29 January 1828

10 Education makes a people easy to lead, but difficult to drive; easy to govern, but impossible to enslave.
attributed

Haywood Hale Broun 1918–
American actor

11 Sports do not build character. They reveal it.
attributed; James Michener *Sports in America* (1976)

Heywood Broun 1888–1939
American journalist

12 Everybody favours free speech in the slack moments when no axes are being ground.
in *New York World* 23 October 1926

Christy Brown 1932–81
Irish writer

13 Painting became everything to me . . .
Through it I made articulate all that I saw and felt, all that went on inside the mind that was housed within my useless body like a prisoner in a cell.
My Left Foot (1954)

Gordon Brown 1951–
British Labour politician

14 The Labour Party—best when we are boldest, best when we are united, best when we are Labour.
speech to the Labour Party Conference, 29 September 2003; see **Blair** 56:3

H. Rap Brown 1943–
American Black Power leader

15 I say violence is necessary. It is as American as cherry pie.
speech at Washington, 27 July 1967

John Brown 1800–59
American abolitionist

16 Now, if it is deemed necessary that I should forfeit my life for the furtherance of the ends of justice, and mingle my blood further with the blood of my children, and with the blood of millions in this slave country whose rights are disregarded by wicked, cruel, and unjust enactments, I say let it be done.
last speech to the court, 2 November 1859, in *The Life, Trial and Execution of Captain John Brown* (1859)

17 I, John Brown, am now quite certain that the crimes of this guilty land will never be purged away but with blood.
written on the day of his execution, 2 December 1859

Lew Brown 1893–1958
American songwriter

18 Life is just a bowl of cherries.
title of song (1931)

T. E. Brown 1830–97
Manx schoolmaster and poet

19 A garden is a lovesome thing, God wot!
'My Garden' (1893)

Thomas Brown 1663-1704
English satirist

1 A little before you made a leap into the
   dark.
   *Letters from the Dead to the Living (1702) 'Answer
   to Mr Joseph Haines'*

2 I do not love thee, Dr Fell.
   The reason why I cannot tell;
   But this I know, and know full well,
   I do not love thee, Dr Fell.
   *written while an undergraduate at Christ Church,
   Oxford, of which Dr Fell was Dean*
   A. L. Hayward (ed.) *Amusements Serious and
   Comical by Tom Brown* (1927); see **Martial** 229:8

Cecil Browne 1932–
American businessman

3 But not so odd
   As those who choose
   A Jewish God,
   But spurn the Jews.
   reply to verse by William Norman **Ewer**; see
   Ewer 133:11

Sir Thomas Browne 1605-82
English writer and physician

4 All things began in order, so shall they end,
   and so shall they begin again; according to
   the ordainer of order and mystical
   mathematics of the city of heaven.
   The Garden of Cyrus (1658) ch. 5

5 Old mortality, the ruins of forgotten times.
   *Hydriotaphia (Urn Burial, 1658) Epistle
   Dedicatory*

6 What song the Syrens sang, or what name
   Achilles assumed when he hid himself
   among women, though puzzling questions,
   are not beyond all conjecture.
   Hydriotaphia (Urn Burial, 1658) ch. 5

7 Generations pass while some trees stand,
   and old families last not three oaks.
   Hydriotaphia (Urn Burial, 1658) ch. 5

8 The iniquity of oblivion blindly scattereth
   her poppy, and deals with the memory of
   men without distinction to merit perpetuity.
   Hydriotaphia (Urn Burial, 1658) ch. 5

9 Man is a noble animal, splendid in ashes,
   and pompous in the grave.
   Hydriotaphia (Urn Burial, 1658) ch. 5

10 I have often admired the mystical way of
   Pythagoras, and the secret magic of
   numbers.
   Religio Medici (1643) pt. 1, sect. 12

11 We carry within us the wonders we seek
   without us: there is all Africa and her
   prodigies in us.
   Religio Medici (1643) pt. 1, sect. 15

12 All things are artificial, for nature is the art
   of God.
   Religio Medici (1643) pt. 1, sect. 16

13 We all labour against our own cure, for
   death is the cure of all diseases.
   Religio Medici (1643) pt. 2, sect. 9

Elizabeth Barrett Browning
1806-61
English poet

14 Earth's crammed with heaven,
   And every common bush afire with God.
   Aurora Leigh (1857) bk. 7, l. 821

15 And lips say, 'God be pitiful,'
   Who ne'er said, 'God be praised.'
   'The Cry of the Human' (1844) st. 1

16 What was he doing, the great god Pan,
   Down in the reeds by the river?
   'A Musical Instrument' (1862)

17 How do I love thee? Let me count the ways.
   I love thee to the depth and breadth and
   height
   My soul can reach.
   Sonnets from the Portuguese (1850) no. 43

18 I love thee with the breath,
   Smiles, tears, of all my life!—and if God
   choose,
   I shall but love thee better after death.
   Sonnets from the Portuguese (1850) no. 43

Frederick 'Boy' Browning
1896-1965
British soldier

19 I think we might be going a bridge too far.
   *expressing reservations about the Arnhem 'Market
   Garden' operation to Field Marshal **Montgomery**
   on 10 September 1944; R. E. Urquhart* Arnhem
   (1958)

Robert Browning 1812-89
English poet

20 Ah, but a man's reach should exceed his
   grasp,
   Or what's a heaven for?
   'Andrea del Sarto' (1855) l. 97

21 One who never turned his back but
   marched breast forward,
   Never doubted clouds would break.
   Asolando (1889) 'Epilogue'

22 The grand Perhaps!
   'Bishop Blougram's Apology' (1855) l. 190

23 Boot, saddle, to horse, and away!
   'Boot and Saddle' (1842)

24 When earth breaks up and heaven expands,
   How will the change strike me and you
   In the house not made with hands?
   *'By the Fireside' (1855) st. 27; see **Bible** 51:6*

25 Oh, the little more, and how much it is!
   And the little less, and what worlds away!
   'By the Fireside' (1855) st. 39

26 Dauntless the slug-horn to my lips I set,
   And blew. *'Childe Roland to the Dark Tower
   came.'*
   *'Childe Roland to the Dark Tower Came' (1855)
   st. 34; see **Shakespeare** 298:12*

27 How sad and bad and mad it was—
   But then, how it was sweet!
   'Confessions' (1864) st. 9

28 Stung by the splendour of a sudden thought.
   'A Death in the Desert' (1864) l. 59

1 ... Progress, man's distinctive mark alone,
Not God's, and not the beasts': God is, they
are,
Man partly is and wholly hopes to be.
'A Death in the Desert' (1864) l. 586

2 Open my heart and you will see
Graved inside of it, 'Italy'.
'De Gustibus' (1855) pt. 2, l. 43

3 If you get simple beauty and naught else,
You get about the best thing God invents.
'Fra Lippo Lippi' (1855) l. 217

4 That low man seeks a little thing to do,
Sees it and does it:
This high man, with a great thing to pursue,
Dies ere he knows it.
That low man goes on adding one to one,
His hundred's soon hit:
This high man, aiming at a million,
Misses an unit.
'A Grammarian's Funeral' (1855) l. 113

5 Oh, to be in England
Now that April's there.
'Home-Thoughts, from Abroad' (1845)

6 That's the wise thrush; he sings each song
twice over,
Lest you should think he never could
recapture
The first fine careless rapture!
'Home-Thoughts, from Abroad' (1845)

7 'With this same key
Shakespeare unlocked his heart,' once
more!
Did Shakespeare? If so, the less Shakespeare
he!
'House' (1876); see **Wordsworth** 365:25

8 How they brought the good news from
Ghent to Aix.
title of poem (1845)

9 I sprang to the stirrup, and Joris, and he;
I galloped, Dirck galloped, we galloped all
three.
'How they brought the Good News from Ghent
to Aix' (1845) l. 1

10 'You're wounded!' 'Nay,' the soldier's pride
Touched to the quick, he said:
'I'm killed, Sire!' And his chief beside,
Smiling the boy fell dead.
'Incident of the French Camp' (1842) st. 5

11 Ignorance is not innocence but sin.
The Inn Album (1875) canto 5

12 Just for a handful of silver he left us,
Just for a riband to stick in his coat.
of **Wordsworth**
'The Lost Leader' (1845)

13 We that had loved him so, followed him,
honoured him,
Lived in his mild and magnificent eye,
Learned his great language, caught his clear
accents,
Made him our pattern to live and to die!
Shakespeare was of us, Milton was for us,
Burns, Shelley, were with us—they watch
from their graves!
'The Lost Leader' (1845)

14 Never glad confident morning again!
'The Lost Leader' (1845)

15 A tap at the pane, the quick sharp scratch
And blue spurt of a lighted match,
And a voice less loud, through its joys and
fears,
Than the two hearts beating each to each!
'Meeting at Night' (1845)

16 Ah, did you once see Shelley plain.
'Memorabilia' (1855)

17 That's my last Duchess painted on the wall,
Looking as if she were alive.
'My Last Duchess' (1842) l. 1

18 She had
A heart—how shall I say?—too soon made
glad,
Too easily impressed; she liked whate'er
She looked on, and her looks went
everywhere.
'My Last Duchess' (1842) l. 21

19 Never the time and the place
And the loved one all together!
'Never the Time and the Place' (1883)

20 It was roses, roses, all the way.
'The Patriot' (1855)

21 Rats!
They fought the dogs and killed the cats,
And bit the babies in the cradles,
And ate the cheeses out of the vats,
And licked the soup from the cooks' own
ladles.
'The Pied Piper of Hamelin' (1842) st. 2

22 With shrieking and squeaking
In fifty different sharps and flats.
'The Pied Piper of Hamelin' (1842) st. 2

23 The year's at the spring
And day's at the morn;
Morning's at seven;
The hill-side's dew-pearled;
The lark's on the wing;
The snail's on the thorn:
God's in his heaven—
All's right with the world!
Pippa Passes (1841) pt. 1, l. 221

24 That moment she was mine, mine, fair,
Perfectly pure and good.
'Porphyria's Lover' (1842) l. 36

25 All her hair
In one long yellow string I wound
Three times her little throat around,
And strangled her. No pain felt she;
I am quite sure she felt no pain.
'Porphyria's Lover' (1842) l. 38

26 Fear death?—to feel the fog in my throat,
The mist in my face.
'Prospice' (1864)

27 I was ever a fighter, so—one fight more,
The best and the last!
I would hate that death bandaged my eyes,
and forbore,
And bade me creep past.
'Prospice' (1864)

28 Grow old along with me!
The best is yet to be,

The last of life, for which the first was made.
'Rabbi Ben Ezra' (1864) st. 1

1 O lyric Love, half-angel and half-bird.
The Ring and the Book (1868–9) bk. 1, l. 1391

2 Gr-r-r—there go, my heart's abhorrence!
Water your damned flowerpots, do!
If hate killed men, Brother Lawrence,
God's blood, would not mine kill you!
'Soliloquy of the Spanish Cloister' (1842) st. 1

3 There's a great text in Galatians,
Once you trip on it, entails
Twenty-nine distinct damnations,
One sure, if another fails.
'Soliloquy of the Spanish Cloister' (1842) st. 7

4 What of soul was left, I wonder, when the
kissing had to stop?
'A Toccata of Galuppi's' (1855) st. 14

5 Dear dead women, with such hair,
too—what's become of all the gold
Used to hang and brush their bosoms? I feel
chilly and grown old.
'A Toccata of Galuppi's' (1855) st. 15

6 When it was written, God and Robert
Browning knew what it meant; now only
God knows.
on Sordello
attributed; see **Klopstock** 204:6

Lenny Bruce 1925–66
American comedian

7 The liberals can understand everything but
people who don't understand them.
John Cohen (ed.) *The Essential Lenny Bruce* (1967)

8 I'll die young, but it's like kissing God.
on his drug addiction
attributed

Robert Bruce 1554–1631
Scottish minister

9 Now, God be with you, my children: I have
breakfasted with you and shall sup with my
Lord Jesus Christ this night.
Robert Fleming *The Fulfilling of the Scripture* (3rd
ed., 1693)

Beau Brummell 1778–1840
English dandy

10 Who's your fat friend?
referring to the Prince of Wales, later **George IV**
Capt. Jesse *Life of George Brummell* (1844) vol. 1

11 No perfumes, but very fine linen, plenty of
it, and country washing.
Memoirs of Harriette Wilson (1825) vol. 1

Frank Bruno 1961–
English boxer

12 Boxing's just show business with blood.
in *Guardian* 20 November 1991

13 Know what I mean, Harry?
supposed to have been said in interview with
sports commentator Harry Carpenter, possibly
apocryphal

William Jennings Bryan
1860–1925
American Democratic politician

14 You shall not press down upon the brow of
labour this crown of thorns, you shall not
crucify mankind upon a cross of gold.
opposing the gold standard
speech at the Democratic National Convention,
Chicago, 1896

John Buchan 1875–1940
Scottish novelist

15 An atheist is a man who has no invisible
means of support.
H. E. Fosdick *On Being a Real Person* (1943) ch. 10

Frank Buchman 1878–1961
American evangelist

16 There is enough in the world for everyone's
need, but not enough for everyone's greed.
Remaking the World (1947)

Gene Buck 1885–1957
and **Herman Ruby** 1891–1959

17 That Shakespearian rag,—
Most intelligent, very elegant.
'That Shakespearian Rag' (1912 song); see **Eliot**
129:25

George Villiers, 2nd Duke of Buckingham 1628–87
English courtier and writer

18 Ay, now the plot thickens very much upon
us.
The Rehearsal (1672) act 3, sc. 2

Comte de Buffon 1707–88
French naturalist

19 Style is the man himself.
Discours sur le style (address given to the
Académie Française, 25 August 1753)

20 Genius is only a greater aptitude for
patience.
Hérault de Séchelles *Voyage à Montbar* (1803);
see **Carlyle** 85:9

Arthur Buller 1874–1944
British botanist and mycologist

21 There was a young lady named Bright,
Whose speed was far faster than light;
She set out one day
In a relative way
And returned on the previous night.
'Relativity' in *Punch* 19 December 1923

Bernhard von Bülow 1849–1929
German statesman, Chancellor 1900–9

22 We desire to throw no one into the shade [in
East Asia], but we also demand our own
place in the sun.
in the Reichstag, 6 December 1897; see
Wilhelm II 359:25

Edward Robert Bulwer, Earl of Lytton *see* Owen Meredith

Edward George Bulwer-Lytton
1803–73
British novelist and politician

1 It was a dark and stormy night.
  Paul Clifford (1830), opening words

2 Beneath the rule of men entirely great
The pen is mightier than the sword.
  Richelieu (1839) act 2, sc. 2, l. 307; see **Burton** 78:5

3 In science, read, by preference, the newest works; in literature, the oldest.
  Caxtoniana (1863) 'Hints on Mental Culture'

Alfred 'Poet' Bunn *c.*1796–1860
English theatrical manager and librettist

4 I dreamed that I dwelt in marble halls
With vassals and serfs at my side.
  The Bohemian Girl (1843) act 2 'The Gipsy Girl's Dream'

Luis Buñuel 1900–83
Spanish film director

5 Thanks to God, I am still an atheist.
  in *Le Monde* 16 December 1959

John Bunyan 1628–88
English writer and Nonconformist preacher

6 As I walked through the wilderness of this world.
  The Pilgrim's Progress (1678) pt. 1, opening words

7 The name of the slough was Despond.
  The Pilgrim's Progress (1678) pt. 1

8 Down into the valley of Humiliation.
  The Pilgrim's Progress (1678) pt. 1

9 A foul Fiend coming over the field to meet him; his name is Apollyon.
  The Pilgrim's Progress (1678) pt. 1

10 It beareth the name of Vanity-Fair, because the town where 'tis kept, is lighter than vanity.
  The Pilgrim's Progress (1678) pt. 1

11 Hanging is too good for him, said Mr Cruelty.
  The Pilgrim's Progress (1678) pt. 1

12 Yet my great-grandfather was but a waterman, looking one way, and rowing another.
  The Pilgrim's Progress (1678) pt. 1; see **Burton** 78:3

13 Then I saw that there was a way to Hell, even from the gates of heaven.
  The Pilgrim's Progress (1678) pt. 1

14 So I awoke, and behold it was a dream.
  The Pilgrim's Progress (1678) pt. 1

15 A man that could look no way but downwards, with a muckrake in his hand.
  The Pilgrim's Progress (1684) pt. 2; see **Roosevelt** 280:2

16 He that is down needs fear no fall,
He that is low no pride.

He that is humble ever shall
Have God to be his guide.
  The Pilgrim's Progress (1684) pt. 2 'Shepherd Boy's Song'

17 Who would true valour see,
Let him come hither;
One here will constant be,
Come wind, come weather.
There's no discouragement
Shall make him once relent
His first avowed intent
To be a pilgrim.
  The Pilgrim's Progress (1684) pt. 2

18 I am going to my Fathers, and tho' with great difficulty I am got hither, yet now I do not repent me of all the trouble I have been at to arrive where I am. My sword, I give to him that shall succeed me in my pilgrimage, and my courage and skill to him that can get it. My marks and scars I carry with me, to be a witness for me, that I have fought his battles, who will now be my rewarder.
  Mr Valiant-for-Truth
  The Pilgrim's Progress (1684) pt. 2

19 So he passed over, and the trumpets sounded for him on the other side.
  Mr Valiant-for-Truth
  The Pilgrim's Progress (1684) pt. 2

Samuel Dickinson Burchard
1812–91
American Presbyterian minister

20 We are Republicans and don't propose to leave our party and identify ourselves with the party whose antecedents are rum, Romanism, and rebellion.
  speech at the Fifth Avenue Hotel, New York, 29 October 1884

Anthony Burgess 1917–93
English novelist and critic

21 A clockwork orange.
  title of novel (1962)

Gelett Burgess 1866–1951
American humorist and illustrator

22 I never saw a Purple Cow,
I never hope to see one;
But I can tell you, anyhow,
I'd rather see than be one!
  The Burgess Nonsense Book (1914) 'The Purple Cow'

23 Ah, yes! I wrote the 'Purple Cow'—
I'm sorry, now, I wrote it!
But I can tell you anyhow,
I'll kill you if you quote it!
  The Burgess Nonsense Book (1914) 'Confessional'

John William Burgon 1813–88
English clergyman

24 A rose-red city—half as old as Time!
  Petra (1845) l. 132

Edmund Burke 1729–97
Irish-born Whig politician and man of letters

1 Those who have been once intoxicated with power, and have derived any kind of emolument from it, even though for but one year, can never willingly abandon it.
Letter to a Member of the National Assembly (1791)

2 Liberty too must be limited in order to be possessed.
Letter to the Sheriffs of Bristol (1777)

3 Nothing in progression can rest on its original plan. We may as well think of rocking a grown man in the cradle of an infant.
Letter to the Sheriffs of Bristol (1777)

4 There is, however, a limit at which forbearance ceases to be a virtue.
Observations on a late Publication on the Present State of the Nation (2nd ed., 1769)

5 It is a general popular error to imagine the loudest complainers for the public to be the most anxious for its welfare.
Observations on a late Publication on the Present State of the Nation (2nd ed., 1769)

6 It is the nature of all greatness not to be exact; and great trade will always be attended with considerable abuses.
On American Taxation (1775)

7 To tax and to please, no more than to love and to be wise, is not given to men.
On American Taxation (1775)

8 It is not, what a lawyer tells me I *may* do; but what humanity, reason, and justice, tells me I ought to do.
On Conciliation with America (1775)

9 Every human benefit, every virtue and every prudent act, is founded on compromise.
On Conciliation with America (1775)

10 Slavery they can have anywhere. It is a weed that grows in every soil.
On Conciliation with America (1775)

11 Magnanimity in politics is not seldom the truest wisdom; and a great empire and little minds go ill together.
On Conciliation with America (1775)

12 No passion so effectually robs the mind of all its powers of acting and reasoning as fear.
On the Sublime and Beautiful (1757) pt. 2, sect. 2

13 Custom reconciles us to everything.
On the Sublime and Beautiful (1757) pt. 4, sect. 18

14 A state without the means of some change is without the means of its conservation.
Reflections on the Revolution in France (1790)

15 People will not look forward to posterity, who never look backward to their ancestors.
Reflections on the Revolution in France (1790)

16 Government is a contrivance of human wisdom to provide for human *wants*.
Reflections on the Revolution in France (1790)

17 I thought ten thousand swords must have leapt from their scabbards to avenge even a look that threatened her with insult.
of Marie-Antoinette
Reflections on the Revolution in France (1790)

18 The age of chivalry is gone.— That of sophisters, economists, and calculators, has succeeded; and the glory of Europe is extinguished for ever.
Reflections on the Revolution in France (1790)

19 This barbarous philosophy, which is the offspring of cold hearts and muddy understandings.
Reflections on the Revolution in France (1790)

20 In the groves of *their* academy, at the end of every vista, you see nothing but the gallows.
Reflections on the Revolution in France (1790)

21 Kings will be tyrants from policy when subjects are rebels from principle.
Reflections on the Revolution in France (1790)

22 Because half a dozen grasshoppers under a fern make the field ring with their importunate chink, whilst thousands of great cattle, reposed beneath the shadow of the British oak, chew the cud and are silent, pray do not imagine that those who make the noise are the only inhabitants of the field.
Reflections on the Revolution in France (1790)

23 Society is indeed a contract . . . it becomes a partnership not only between those who are living, but between those who are living, those who are dead, and those who are to be born.
Reflections on the Revolution in France (1790)

24 Superstition is the religion of feeble minds.
Reflections on the Revolution in France (1790)

25 He that wrestles with us strengthens our nerves, and sharpens our skill. Our antagonist is our helper.
Reflections on the Revolution in France (1790)

26 Our patience will achieve more than our force.
Reflections on the Revolution in France (1790)

27 We begin our public affections in our families. No cold relation is a zealous citizen.
Reflections on the Revolution in France (1790)

28 Ambition can creep as well as soar.
Third Letter . . . on the Proposals for Peace . . . (1797)

29 When bad men combine, the good must associate; else they will fall, one by one, an unpitied sacrifice in a contemptible struggle.
Thoughts on the Cause of the Present Discontents (1770); see **Burke** 76:10

30 Of this stamp is the cant of *Not men, but measures*; a sort of charm by which many people get loose from every honourable engagement.
Thoughts on the Cause of the Present Discontents (1770); see **Canning** 84:9, **Goldsmith** 153:21

31 Laws, like houses, lean on one another.
A Tract on the Popery Laws (planned *c.*1765) ch. 3

1 Falsehood and delusion are allowed in no case whatsoever: But, as in the exercise of all the virtues, there is an economy of truth.
Two Letters on the Proposals for Peace with the Regicide Directory (1796) pt. 1; see **Armstrong** 16:9

2 Example is the school of mankind, and they will learn at no other.
Two Letters on the Proposals for Peace with the Regicide Directory (9th ed., 1796)

3 The greater the power, the more dangerous the abuse.
speech on the Middlesex Election, 7 February 1771, in *The Speeches* (1854)

4 Your representative owes you, not his industry only, but his judgement; and he betrays, instead of serving you, if he sacrifices it to your opinion.
speech, 3 November 1774, in *Speeches at his Arrival at Bristol* (1774)

5 Bad laws are the worst sort of tyranny.
Speech at Bristol, previous to the Late Election (1780)

6 The people are the masters.
speech, House of Commons, 11 February 1780; see **Blair** 55:20

7 Not merely a chip of the old 'block', but the old block itself.
*on the younger **Pitt**'s maiden speech, February 1781*
N. W. Wraxall *Historical Memoirs of My Own Time* (1904 ed.) pt. 2

8 The people never give up their liberties but under some delusion.
speech at County Meeting of Buckinghamshire, 1784, attributed in E. Latham *Famous Sayings* (1904), with 'except' substituted for 'but'

9 An event has happened, upon which it is difficult to speak, and impossible to be silent.
speech, 5 May 1789, in E. A. Bond (ed.) *Speeches . . . in the Trial of Warren Hastings* (1859) vol. 2

10 It is necessary only for the good man to do nothing for evil to triumph.
attributed (in a number of forms) to Burke, but not found in his writings; see **Burke** 75:29

Johnny Burke 1908–64
American songwriter

11 Every time it rains, it rains
Pennies from heaven.
Don't you know each cloud contains
Pennies from heaven?
'Pennies from Heaven' (1936 song)

12 Like Webster's Dictionary, we're Morocco bound.
The Road to Morocco (1942 film) title song

Fanny Burney 1752–1840
English novelist and diarist

13 'The whole of this unfortunate business,' said Dr Lyster, 'has been the result of PRIDE AND PREJUDICE.'
Cecilia (1782) bk. 10, ch. 10

John Burns 1858–1943
British Liberal politician

14 The Thames is liquid history.
to an American who had compared the Thames disparagingly with the Mississippi
in *Daily Mail* 25 January 1943

Robert Burns 1759–96
Scottish poet

15 Address to the unco guid.
title of poem, 1787

16 Then gently scan your brother man,
Still gentler sister woman;
Tho' they may gang a kennin wrang,
To step aside is human.
'Address to the Unco Guid' (1787)

17 Ae fond kiss, and then we sever;
Ae fareweel, and then for ever!
'Ae fond Kiss' (1792)

18 Flow gently, sweet Afton, among thy green braes,
Flow gently, I'll sing thee a song in thy praise.
'Afton Water' (1792)

19 Should auld acquaintance be forgot
And never brought to mind?
'Auld Lang Syne' (1796)

20 We'll tak a cup o' kindness yet,
For auld lang syne.
'Auld Lang Syne' (1796)

21 Freedom and Whisky gang thegither!
'The Author's Earnest Cry and Prayer' (1786) l. 185

22 Ye banks and braes o' bonny Doon,
How can ye bloom sae fresh and fair;
How can ye chant, ye little birds,
And I sae weary fu' o' care!
'The Banks o' Doon' (1792)

23 O saw ye bonnie Lesley,
As she gaed o'er the border?
She's gane, like Alexander,
To spread her conquests farther.
To see her is to love her,
And love but her for ever.
'Bonnie Lesley' (1798)

24 Gin a body meet a body
Comin thro' the rye,
Gin a body kiss a body
Need a body cry?
'Comin thro' the rye' (1796)

25 Gie me ae spark o' Nature's fire,
That's a' the learning I desire.
'Epistle to J. L[apraik]' (1786) st. 13

26 The rank is but the guinea's stamp,
The man's the gowd for a' that!
'For a' that and a' that' (1790)

27 A man's a man for a' that.
'For a' that and a' that' (1790)

28 Green grow the rashes, O,
Green grow the rashes, O;
The sweetest hours that e'er I spend,
Are spent among the lasses, O.
'Green Grow the Rashes' (1787)

1 Corn rigs, an' barley rigs,
An' corn rigs are bonnie.
'It was upon a Lammas Night' (1796)

2 John Anderson my jo, John,
When we were first acquent,
Your locks were like the raven,
Your bonny brow was brent.
'John Anderson my Jo' (1790)

3 Some have meat and cannot eat,
Some cannot eat that want it:
But we have meat and we can eat,
Sae let the Lord be thankit.
'The Kirkudbright Grace' (1790), also known as
'The Selkirk Grace'

4 Man's inhumanity to man
Makes countless thousands mourn!
'Man was made to Mourn' (1786) st. 7

5 Go fetch to me a pint o' wine,
An' fill it in a silver tassie.
'My Bonnie Mary' (1790)

6 My heart's in the Highlands, my heart is not
here;
My heart's in the Highlands a-chasing the
deer.
'My Heart's in the Highlands' (1790)

7 My love she's but a lassie yet.
title of poem, 1787

8 O whistle, an' I'll come to you, my lad.
title of poem (1788); see **Fletcher** 138:14

9 O, my Luve's like a red, red rose
That's newly sprung in June;
O my Luve's like the melodie
That's sweetly play'd in tune.
'A Red Red Rose' (1796), derived from various
folk-songs

10 Scots, wha hae wi' Wallace bled,
Scots, wham Bruce has aften led,
Welcome to your gory bed,—
Or to victorie.
'Robert Bruce's March to Bannockburn' (1799),
also known as 'Scots, Wha Hae'

11 Liberty's in every blow!
Let us do—or die!!!
'Robert Bruce's March to Bannockburn' (1799)

12 But pleasures are like poppies spread,
You seize the flow'r, its bloom is shed.
'Tam o' Shanter' (1791) l. 59

13 Nae man can tether time or tide.
'Tam o' Shanter' (1791) l. 67

14 Inspiring, bold John Barleycorn,
What dangers thou canst make us scorn!
Wi' tippenny, we fear nae evil;
Wi' usquebae, we'll face the devil!
'Tam o' Shanter' (1791) l. 105

15 The mirth and fun grew fast and furious.
'Tam o' Shanter' (1791) l. 144

16 Tam tint his reason a' thegither,
And roars out—'Weel done, Cutty-sark!'
'Tam o' Shanter' (1791) l. 185

17 Fair fa' your honest, sonsie face,
Great chieftain o' the puddin'-race!
'To a Haggis' (1787)

18 O wad some Pow'r the giftie gie us

To see oursels as others see us!
'To a Louse' (1786)

19 Wee, sleekit, cow'rin', tim'rous beastie,
O what a panic's in thy breastie!
'To a Mouse' (1786)

20 I'm truly sorry Man's dominion
Has broken Nature's social union.
'To a Mouse' (1786)

21 The best laid schemes o' mice an' men
Gang aft a-gley.
'To a Mouse' (1786)

Aaron Burr 1756–1836
American politician

22 Law is whatever is boldly asserted and
plausibly maintained.
attributed

William S. Burroughs 1914–97
American novelist

23 Junk is the ideal product . . . the ultimate
merchandise. No sales talk necessary. The
client will crawl through a sewer and beg to
buy.
The Naked Lunch (1959) introduction

24 The face of 'evil' is always the face of total
need.
The Naked Lunch (1959) introduction

Benjamin Hapgood Burt
1880–1950
American songwriter

25 'You can tell a man who "boozes" by the
company he chooses'
And the pig got up and slowly walked away.
'The Pig Got Up and Slowly Walked Away' (1933
song)

26 When you're all dressed up and no place to
go.
title of song (1913)

Nat Burton

27 There'll be bluebirds over the white cliffs of
Dover,
Tomorrow, just you wait and see.
'The White Cliffs of Dover' (1941 song)

Richard Burton 1821–90
English explorer, anthropologist, and translator

28 Don't be frightened; I am recalled. Pay,
pack, and follow at convenience.
*note to his wife, 19 August 1871, on being
replaced as British Consul to Damascus*
Isabel Burton *Life of Captain Sir Richard F. Burton*
(1893) vol. 1, ch. 21

Robert Burton 1577–1640
English clergyman and scholar

29 All my joys to this are folly,
Naught so sweet as Melancholy.
The Anatomy of Melancholy (1621–51) 'The
Author's Abstract of Melancholy'

1 They lard their lean books with the fat of others' works.
   The Anatomy of Melancholy (1621–51) 'Democritus to the Reader'

2 A loose, plain, rude writer . . . I call a spade a spade.
   The Anatomy of Melancholy (1621–51) 'Democritus to the Reader'

3 Like watermen, that row one way and look another.
   The Anatomy of Melancholy (1621–51) 'Democritus to the Reader'; see **Bunyan** 74:12

4 All poets are mad.
   The Anatomy of Melancholy (1621–51) 'Democritus to the Reader'

5 From this it is clear how much the pen is worse than the sword.
   The Anatomy of Melancholy (1621–51) pt. 1; see **Bulwer-Lytton** 74:2

6 See one promontory (said Socrates of old), one mountain, one sea, one river, and see all.
   The Anatomy of Melancholy (1621–51) pt. 1

7 To enlarge or illustrate this power and effect of love is to set a candle in the sun.
   The Anatomy of Melancholy (1621–51) pt. 3; see **Sidney** 316:9, **Young** 369:25

8 Be not solitary, be not idle.
   The Anatomy of Melancholy (1621–51), closing words

Hermann Busenbaum 1600–68
German theologian

9 *Cum finis est licitus, etiam media sunt licita.*
   The end justifies the means.
   Medulla Theologiae Moralis (1650); literally 'When the end is allowed, the means also are allowed'

Barbara Bush 1925–
American First Lady, 1989–93

10 Somewhere out in this audience may even be someone who will one day follow in my footsteps, and preside over the White House as the President's spouse. I wish him well!
   remarks at Wellesley College Commencement, 1 June 1990

George Bush 1924–
American Republican statesman, 41st President of the US 1989–93

11 Oh, the vision thing.
   responding to the suggestion that he turn his attention from short-term campaign objectives and look to the longer term.
   in *Time* 26 January 1987

12 Read my lips: no new taxes.
   campaign pledge on taxation
   in *New York Times* 19 August 1988

13 I'm President of the United States, and I'm not going to eat any more broccoli!
   in *New York Times* 23 March 1990

14 And now, we can see a new world coming into view. A world in which there is the very real prospect of a new world order.
   speech, in *New York Times* 7 March 1991

15 [It is] time to turn our attention to pressing challenges like . . . how to make American families more like the Waltons and a little bit less like the Simpsons.
   speech, Neenah, Wisconsin, 27 July 1992

George W. Bush 1946–
American Republican statesman, 43rd President of the US since 2001

16 We will make no distinction between terrorists who committed these acts and those who harbour them.
   after the terrorist attacks of 11 September
   televised address, 12 September 2001

17 Today we feel what Franklin Roosevelt called the warm courage of national unity. This unity against terror is now extending across the world.
   address in Washington National Cathedral, 14 September 2001, at the day of mourning for those killed in the terrorist attacks of 11 September
   in *Times* 15 September 2001; see **Roosevelt** 279:9

18 This crusade, this war on terrorism is going to take a while.
   the President later retracted his use of the word 'crusade'
   at a White House press conference, 16 September 2001

19 States like these . . . constitute an axis of evil, arming to threaten the peace of this world.
   of Iraq, Iran, and North Korea
   State of the Union address, in *Newsweek* 11 February 2002

20 I earned capital in the campaign, political capital, and I intend to spend it.
   on his re-election as President
   in *New York Times* 5 November 2004 (online edition)

21 Brownie, you're doing a heck of a job.
   to FEMA director Michael Brown, after Hurricane Katrina
   comment in speech, Alabama, 2 September 2005

Comte de Bussy-Rabutin 1618–93
French soldier and poet

22 Love comes from blindness,
   Friendship from knowledge.
   Histoire Amoureuse des Gaules: Maximes d'Amour (1665) pt. 1

23 Absence is to love what wind is to fire;
   It extinguishes the small, it kindles the great.
   Histoire Amoureuse des Gaules: Maximes d'Amour (1665) pt. 2; see **Francis** 141:11, **La Rochefoucauld** 209:9

24 As you know, God is usually on the side of the big squadrons against the small.
   letter to the Comte de Limoges, 18 October 1677; see **Tacitus** 330:3, **Voltaire** 348:21

Joseph Butler 1692–1752
English bishop and theologian

1 But to us, probability is the very guide of life.
   The Analogy of Religion (1736) 'Introduction'

2 Everything is what it is, and not another thing.
   preface to *Fifteen Sermons preached at the Rolls Chapel* (ed. 2, 1729)

3 Sir, the pretending to extraordinary revelations and gifts of the Holy Ghost is a horrid thing—a very horrid thing.
   to John Wesley, 16 August 1739

Nicholas Murray Butler 1862–1947
American President of Columbia University, 1901–45

4 An expert is one who knows more and more about less and less.
   Commencement address at Columbia University (attributed)

R. A. ('Rab') Butler 1902–82
British Conservative politician

5 Politics is the Art of the Possible. That is what these pages show I have tried to achieve—not more—and that is what I have called my book.
   The Art of the Possible (1971); see Bismarck 55:4

6 In politics you must always keep running with the pack. The moment that you falter and they sense that you are injured, the rest will turn on you like wolves.
   Dennis Walters *Not Always with the Pack* (1989)

Samuel Butler 1612–80
English poet

7 Love is a boy, by poets styled,
   Then spare the rod, and spoil the child.
   Hudibras pt. 2 (1664), canto 1, l. 843

8 Doubtless the pleasure is as great
   Of being cheated, as to cheat.
   Hudibras pt. 2 (1664), canto 3, l. 1

9 He that complies against his will,
   Is of his own opinion still.
   Hudibras pt. 3 (1680), canto 3, l. 547

Samuel Butler 1835–1902
English novelist

10 It has been said that though God cannot alter the past, historians can; it is perhaps because they can be useful to Him in this respect that He tolerates their existence.
   Erewhon Revisited (1901) ch. 14; see Agathon 3:24

11 All animals, except man, know that the principal business of life is to enjoy it.
   The Way of All Flesh (1903) ch. 19

12 The best liar is he who makes the smallest amount of lying go the longest way.
   The Way of All Flesh (1903) ch. 39

13 It was very good of God to let Carlyle and Mrs Carlyle marry one another and so make only two people miserable instead of four.
   letter, 21 November 1884

14 All progress is based upon a universal innate desire on the part of every organism to live beyond its income.
   Notebooks (1912) ch. 1

15 An apology for the Devil: It must be remembered that we have only heard one side of the case. God has written all the books.
   Notebooks (1912) ch. 14

16 A definition is the enclosing a wilderness of idea within a wall of words.
   Notebooks (1912) ch. 14

17 To live is like to love — all reason is against it, and all healthy instinct for it.
   Notebooks (1912) ch. 14

18 You can do very little with faith, but you can do nothing without it.
   Notebooks (1912) ch. 20

William Butler 1535–1618
English physician

19 Doubtless God could have made a better berry, but doubtless God never did.
   of the strawberry
   Izaak Walton *The Compleat Angler* (3rd ed., 1661) pt. 1, ch. 5

A. S. Byatt 1936–
English novelist

20 Ms. Rowling's magic world has no place for the numinous.
   in *New York Times* 7 July 2003

William Byrd 1543–1623
English composer

21 The exercise of singing is delightful to Nature, and good to preserve the health of man. It doth strengthen all parts of the breast, and doth open the pipes.
   Psalms, Sonnets and Songs (1588)

John Byrom 1692–1763
English poet

22 Christians, awake! Salute the happy morn,
   Whereon the Saviour of the world was born.
   Hymn (c.1750)

23 Strange! that such high dispute should be
   'Twixt Tweedledum and Tweedledee.
   'On the Feuds between Handel and Bononcini' (1727)

24 God bless the King, I mean the Faith's Defender;
   God bless—no harm in blessing—the Pretender;
   But who Pretender is, or who is King,
   God bless us all—that's quite another thing.
   'To an Officer in the Army, Extempore, Intended to allay the Violence of Party-Spirit' (1773)

Lord Byron 1788–1824
English poet

1 Year after year they voted cent per cent
Blood, sweat, and tear-wrung
millions—why? for rent!
'The Age of Bronze' (1823) st. 14; see **Churchill**
95:6

2 Hereditary bondsmen! know ye not
Who would be free themselves must strike
the blow?
Childe Harold's Pilgrimage (1812–18) canto 2, st. 76

3 There was a sound of revelry by night.
Childe Harold's Pilgrimage (1812–18) canto 3, st. 21

4 But hush! hark! a deep sound strikes like a
rising knell!
Childe Harold's Pilgrimage (1812–18) canto 3, st. 22

5 On with the dance! let joy be unconfined;
No sleep till morn, when Youth and Pleasure
meet
To chase the glowing Hours with flying feet.
Childe Harold's Pilgrimage (1812–18) canto 3, st. 22

6 He rushed into the field, and, foremost
fighting, fell.
Childe Harold's Pilgrimage (1812–18) canto 3, st. 23

7 I stood
Among them, but not of them; in a shroud
Of thoughts which were not their thoughts.
Childe Harold's Pilgrimage (1812–18) canto 3, st.
113

8 I stood in Venice, on the Bridge of Sighs:
A palace and a prison on each hand.
Childe Harold's Pilgrimage (1812–18) canto 4, st. 1

9 Oh Rome! my country! city of the soul!
Childe Harold's Pilgrimage (1812–18) canto 4, st. 78

10 Of its own beauty is the mind diseased.
Childe Harold's Pilgrimage (1812–18) canto 4, st.
122

11 Time, the avenger! unto thee I lift
My hands, and eyes, and heart, and crave of
thee a gift.
Childe Harold's Pilgrimage (1812–18) canto 4, st.
130

12 *There* were his young barbarians all at play,
There was their Dacian mother— he, their
sire,
Butchered to make a Roman holiday.
Childe Harold's Pilgrimage (1812–18) canto 4, st.
141

13 While stands the Coliseum, Rome shall
stand;
When falls the Coliseum, Rome shall fall;
And when Rome falls—the World.
Childe Harold's Pilgrimage (1812–18) canto 4, st.
145

14 There is a pleasure in the pathless woods,
There is a rapture on the lonely shore,
There is society, where none intrudes,
By the deep sea, and music in its roar:
I love not man the less, but nature more.
Childe Harold's Pilgrimage (1812–18) canto 4, st.
178

15 Roll on, thou deep and dark blue
Ocean—roll!

Ten thousand fleets sweep over thee in vain;
Man marks the earth with ruin—his control
Stops with the shore.
Childe Harold's Pilgrimage (1812–18) canto 4, st.
179

16 The glory and the nothing of a name.
'Churchill's Grave' (1816)

17 There was a laughing devil in his sneer.
The Corsair (1814) canto 1, st. 9

18 The Assyrian came down like the wolf on
the fold,
And his cohorts were gleaming in purple
and gold;
And the sheen of their spears was like stars
on the sea,
When the blue wave rolls nightly on deep
Galilee.
'The Destruction of Sennacherib' (1815) st. 1

19 For the Angel of Death spread his wings on
the blast,
And breathed in the face of the foe as he
passed.
'The Destruction of Sennacherib' (1815) st. 3

20 And Coleridge, too, has lately taken wing,
But, like a hawk encumbered with his hood,
Explaining metaphysics to the nation—
I wish he would explain his explanation.
Don Juan (1819–24) canto 1, dedication st. 2

21 What men call gallantry, and gods adultery,
Is much more common where the climate's
sultry.
Don Juan (1819–24) canto 1, st. 63

22 A little still she strove, and much repented,
And whispering 'I will ne'er
consent'—consented.
Don Juan (1819–24) canto 1, st. 117

23 Pleasure's a sin, and sometimes sin's a
pleasure.
Don Juan (1819–24) canto 1, st. 133

24 Man's love is of man's life a thing apart,
'Tis woman's whole existence.
Don Juan (1819–24) canto 1, st. 194

25 There's nought, no doubt, so much the
spirit calms
As rum and true religion.
Don Juan (1819–24) canto 2, st. 34

26 Let us have wine and women, mirth and
laughter,
Sermons and soda-water the day after.
Don Juan (1819–24) canto 2, st. 178

27 In her first passion woman loves her lover,
In all the others all she loves is love.
Don Juan (1819–24) canto 3, st. 3

28 Think you, if Laura had been Petrarch's
wife,
He would have written sonnets all his life?
Don Juan (1819–24) canto 3, st. 8

29 The isles of Greece, the isles of Greece!
Where burning Sappho loved and sung,
Where grew the arts of war and peace,
Where Delos rose, and Phoebus sprung!
Eternal summer gilds them yet,
But all, except their sun, is set!
Don Juan (1819–24) canto 3, st. 86 (1)

1 The mountains look on Marathon—
And Marathon looks on the sea;
And musing there an hour alone,
I dreamed that Greece might still be free.
Don Juan (1819–24) canto 3, st. 86 (3)

2 And if I laugh at any mortal thing,
'Tis that I may not weep.
Don Juan (1819–24) canto 4, st. 4

3 . . . That all-softening, overpowering knell,
The tocsin of the soul—the dinner bell.
Don Juan (1819–24) canto 5, st. 49

4 A lady of a 'certain age', which means
Certainly aged.
Don Juan (1819–24) canto 6, st. 69

5 And, after all, what is a lie? 'Tis but
The truth in masquerade.
Don Juan (1819–24) canto 11, st. 37

6 Merely innocent flirtation,
Not quite adultery, but adulteration.
Don Juan (1819–24) canto 12, st. 63

7 Now hatred is by far the longest pleasure;
Men love in haste, but they detest at leisure.
Don Juan (1819–24) canto 13, st. 4

8 The English winter—ending in July,
To recommence in August.
Don Juan (1819–24) canto 13, st. 42

9 Society is now one polished horde,
Formed of two mighty tribes, the *Bores* and
Bored.
Don Juan (1819–24) canto 13, st. 95

10 'Tis strange—but true; for truth is always
strange;
Stranger than fiction.
Don Juan (1819–24) canto 14, st. 101

11 I'll publish, right or wrong:
Fools are my theme, let satire be my song.
English Bards and Scotch Reviewers (1809) l. 5

12 With just enough of learning to misquote.
English Bards and Scotch Reviewers (1809) l. 66

13 Friendship is Love without his wings!
'L'Amitié est l'amour sans ailes' (written 1806,
published 1831)

14 The Cincinnatus of the West.
*of George **Washington***
'Ode to Napoleon Bonaparte' (1814) st. 19

15 My days are in the yellow leaf;
The flowers and fruits of love are gone;
The worm, the canker, and the grief
Are mine alone!
'On This Day I Complete my Thirty-Sixth Year'
(1824); see **Shakespeare** 301:27

16 My hair is grey, but not with years,
Nor grew it white
In a single night,
As men's have grown from sudden fears.
The Prisoner of Chillon (1816) st. 1

17 She walks in beauty, like the night
Of cloudless climes and starry skies;
And all that's best of dark and bright

Meet in her aspect and her eyes.
'She Walks in Beauty' (1815) st. 1

18 A mind at peace with all below,
A heart whose love is innocent!
'She Walks in Beauty' (1815)

19 Eternal spirit of the chainless mind!
Brightest in dungeons, Liberty! thou art.
'Sonnet on Chillon' (1816)

20 So, we'll go no more a-roving
So late into the night,
Though the heart be still as loving,
And the moon be still as bright.
'So we'll go no more a-roving' (written 1817)

21 Oh, talk not to me of a name great in story;
The days of our youth are the days of our
glory.
'Stanzas Written on the Road between Florence
and Pisa, November 1821'

22 I knew it was love, and I felt it was glory.
'Stanzas Written on the Road between Florence
and Pisa, November 1821'

23 Still I can't contradict, what so oft has been
said,
'Though women are angels, yet wedlock's
the devil.'
'To Eliza' (1806)

24 And when we think we lead, we are most
led.
The Two Foscari (1821) act 2, sc. 1, l. 361

25 When we two parted
In silence and tears,
Half broken-hearted
To sever for years,
Pale grew thy cheek and cold,
Colder thy kiss.
'When we two parted' (1816)

26 If I should meet thee
After long years,
How should I greet thee?—
With silence and tears.
'When we two parted' (1816)

27 Near this spot are deposited the remains of
one who possessed beauty without vanity,
strength without insolence, courage
without ferocity, and all the virtues of Man,
without his vices.
'Inscription on the Monument of a
Newfoundland Dog' (1808)

28 My Princess of Parallelograms.
*of his future wife Annabella Milbanke, a keen
amateur mathematician; Byron explains: 'Her
proceedings are quite rectangular, or rather we
are two parallel lines prolonged to infinity side by
side but never to meet'*
letter to Lady Melbourne, 18 October 1812

29 Pure invention is but the talent of a liar.
letter to John Murray from Venice, 2 April 1817

30 I awoke one morning and found myself
famous.
on the instantaneous success of Childe Harold
Thomas Moore *Letters and Journals of Lord Byron*
(1830) vol. 1

James Branch Cabell 1879–1958
American novelist and essayist

1 The optimist proclaims that we live in the best of all possible worlds; and the pessimist fears this is true.
   The Silver Stallion (1926) bk. 4, ch. 26

Augustus Caesar *see* Augustus

Irving Caesar 1895–1996
American songwriter

2 Picture you upon my knee,
   Just tea for two and two for tea.
   'Tea for Two' (1925 song)

Julius Caesar 100–44 BC
Roman general and statesman

3 *Gallia est omnis divisa in partes tres.*
   Gaul as a whole is divided into three parts.
   De Bello Gallico bk. 1, sect. 1

4 Men are nearly always willing to believe what they wish.
   De Bello Gallico bk. 3, sect. 18

5 Caesar's wife must be above suspicion.
   divorcing his wife Pompeia after unfounded allegations were made against her
   oral tradition, based on Plutarch *Parallel Lives* 'Julius Caesar' ch. 10, sect. 9

6 Caesar had rather be first in a village than second at Rome.
   Francis Bacon *The Advancement of Learning* pt. 2, ch. 23, sect. 36; based on Plutarch

7 *Iacta alea est.*
   The die is cast.
   at the crossing of the Rubicon, the boundary beyond which he was forbidden to lead his army
   Suetonius *Lives of the Caesars* 'Divus Julius' sect. 32; originally spoken in Greek, Plutarch *Parallel Lives* 'Pompey' ch. 60, sect. 2

8 *Veni, vidi, vici.*
   I came, I saw, I conquered.
   inscription displayed in Caesar's Pontic triumph, according to Suetonius Lives of the Caesars 'Divus Julius' sect. 37; *or, according to Plutarch Parallel Lives* 'Julius Caesar' ch. 50, sect. 2, *written in a letter by Caesar, announcing the victory of Zela which concluded the Pontic campaign*

9 *Et tu, Brute?*
   You too, Brutus?
   traditional rendering of Suetonius

John Cage 1912–
American composer, pianist, and writer

10 I have nothing to say and I am saying it and that is poetry.
   'Lecture on nothing' (1961)

James M. Cain 1892–1977
American novelist

11 The postman always rings twice.
   title of novel (1934)

Caligula (Gaius Julius Caesar Germanicus) AD 12–41
Roman emperor from AD 37

12 Would that the Roman people had but one neck!
   Suetonius *Lives of the Caesars* 'Gaius Caligula' sect. 30

13 Strike him so that he can feel that he is dying.
   Suetonius *Lives of the Caesars* 'Gaius Caligula' sect. 30

James Callaghan 1912–2005
British Labour statesman, Prime Minister 1976–9

14 You cannot now, if you ever could, spend your way out of a recession.
   speech at Labour Party Conference, 28 September 1976

15 You never reach the promised land. You can march towards it.
   in a television interview, 20 July 1978

16 I had known it was going to be a 'winter of discontent'.
   television interview, 8 February 1979

17 It's the first time in recorded history that turkeys have been known to vote for an early Christmas.
   in the debate resulting in the fall of the Labour government, when the pact between Labour and the Liberals had collapsed, and the Scottish and Welsh Nationalists had also withdrawn their support
   in the House of Commons, 28 March 1979

Callimachus c.305–c.240 BC
Greek poet and scholar

18 Someone spoke of your death, Heraclitus. It brought me
   Tears, and I remembered how often together
   We ran the sun down with talk.
   R. Pfeiffer (ed) *Callimachus* (1949–53) Epigram 2; translated by Peter Jay; see **Cory** 104:13

19 A great book is like great evil.
   R. Pfeiffer (ed.) *Callimachus* (1949–53) Fragment 465

Charles Alexandre de Calonne 1734–1802
French statesman

20 *Madame, si c'est possible, c'est fait; impossible? cela se fera.*
   Madam, if a thing is possible, consider it done; the impossible? that will be done.
   in J. Michelet *Histoire de la Révolution Française* (1847) vol. 1; see **Nansen** 247:20

Helder Camara 1909–99
Brazilian priest

21 When I give food to the poor they call me a saint. When I ask why the poor have no food they call me a communist.
   attributed

Pierre, Baron de Cambronne
1770–1842
French general

1 *La Garde meurt, mais ne se rend pas.*
The Guards die but do not surrender.
attributed to Cambronne when called upon to surrender at Waterloo, 1815, but later denied by him

> H. Houssaye *La Garde meurt et ne se rend pas* (1907); an alternative version is that he replied, '*Merde!* [Shit!]', known in French as the '*mot de Cambronne*'

Lord Camden 1714–94
British Whig politician

2 Taxation and representation are inseparable . . . whatever is a man's own, is absolutely his own; no man hath a right to take it from him without his consent either expressed by himself or representative.
on the taxation of Americans by the British parliament
> speech in the House of Lords, 10 February 1766; see **Otis** 255:22

Julia Margaret Cameron 1815–79
English photographer

3 I longed to arrest all beauty that came before me.
> *Annals of my Glass House* (1874)

Alastair Campbell 1957–
British journalist

4 The day of the bog-standard comprehensive is over.
> press briefing, 12 February 2001

5 I'm sorry, we don't do God.
*when Tony **Blair** was asked about his Christian faith in an interview for* Vanity Fair *magazine*
> in *Daily Telegraph* 5 May 2003

Jane Montgomery Campbell
1817–78
English hymn-writer

6 We plough the fields, and scatter
The good seed on the land,
But it is fed and watered
By God's almighty hand.
> 'We plough the fields, and scatter' (1861 hymn); translated from the German of Matthias Claudius (1740–1815)

Mrs Patrick Campbell 1865–1940
English actress

7 The deep, deep peace of the double-bed after the hurly-burly of the chaise-longue.
on her recent marriage
> Alexander Woollcott *While Rome Burns* (1934) 'The First Mrs Tanqueray'

8 It doesn't matter what you do in the bedroom as long as you don't do it in the street and frighten the horses.
> Daphne Fielding *The Duchess of Jermyn Street* (1964) ch. 2

Roy Campbell 1901–57
South African poet

9 You praise the firm restraint with which they write—
I'm with you there, of course:
They use the snaffle and the curb all right,
But where's the bloody horse?
> 'On Some South African Novelists' (1930)

Thomas Campbell 1777–1844
Scottish poet

10 O leave this barren spot to me!
Spare, woodman, spare the beechen tree.
> 'The Beech-Tree's Petition' (1800); see **Morris** 245:9

11 Coming events cast their shadows before.
> *Lochiel's Warning* (1801)

12 'Tis distance lends enchantment to the view,
And robes the mountain in its azure hue.
> *Pleasures of Hope* (1799) pt. 1, l. 7

13 Now Barabbas was a publisher.
*also attributed, wrongly, to **Byron***
> attributed, in Samuel Smiles *A Publisher and his Friends: Memoir and Correspondence of the late John Murray* (1891) vol. 1, ch. 14; see **Bible** 49:9

Thomas Campion 1567–1620
English poet and musician

14 There is a garden in her face
Where roses and white lilies grow;
A heavenly paradise is that place,
Wherein all pleasant fruits do flow.
There cherries grow, which none may buy
Till 'Cherry ripe' themselves do cry.
> *The Fourth Book of Airs* (c.1617) no. 7; music by Richard Alison, who published the song in *An Hour's Recreation in Music* (1606)

Albert Camus 1913–60
French novelist, dramatist, and essayist

15 *Intellectuel = celui qui se dédouble.*
An intellectual is someone whose mind watches itself.
> *Carnets, 1935–42* (1962)

16 Politics and the fate of mankind are formed by men without ideals and without greatness.
> *Carnets, 1935–42* (1962)

17 You know what charm is: a way of getting the answer yes without having asked any clear question.
> *The Fall* (1956)

18 There is no fate that cannot be surmounted by scorn.
> *The Myth of Sisyphus* (1942) (tr. Justin O'Brien)

19 Integrity has no need of rules.
> *The Myth of Sisyphus* (1942)

20 The struggle itself towards the heights is enough to fill a human heart. One must imagine that Sisyphus is happy.
> *The Myth of Sisyphus* (1942)

21 What is a rebel? A man who says no.
> *The Rebel* (1951)

1 All modern revolutions have ended in a reinforcement of the State.
The Rebel (1951)

2 Every revolutionary ends as an oppressor or a heretic.
The Rebel (1951)

3 What I know most surely about morality and the duty of man I owe to sport.
often quoted as ' . . . I owe to football'
Herbert R. Lottman *Albert Camus* (1979)

4 Without work, all life goes rotten, but when work is soulless, life stifles and dies.
attributed; E. F. Schumacher *Good Work* (1979)

Elias Canetti 1905–94
Bulgarian-born writer and novelist

5 All the things one has forgotten scream for help in dreams.
Die Provinz der Menschen (1973)

George Canning 1770–1827
British Tory statesman, Prime Minister 1827

6 In matters of commerce the fault of the Dutch
Is offering too little and asking too much.
The French are with equal advantage content,
So we clap on Dutch bottoms just twenty per cent.
dispatch, in cipher, to the English ambassador at the Hague, 31 January 1826
Sir Harry Poland *Mr Canning's Rhyming 'Dispatch' to Sir Charles Bagot* (1905)

7 A steady patriot of the world alone,
The friend of every country but his own.
on the Jacobin
'New Morality' (1821) l. 113; see **Disraeli** 117:15

8 Give me the avowed, erect and manly foe;
Firm I can meet, perhaps return the blow;
But of all plagues, good Heaven, thy wrath can send,
Save me, oh, save me, from the candid friend.
'New Morality' (1821) l. 207

9 Away with the cant of 'Measures not men'!—the idle supposition that it is the harness and not the horses that draw the chariot along. If the comparison must be made, if the distinction must be taken, men are everything, measures comparatively nothing.
speech on the Army estimates, 8 December 1802, in *Speeches of . . . Canning* (1828) vol. 2; the phrase 'measures not men' may be found as early as 1742 (in a letter from Chesterfield to Dr Chevenix, 6 March); see **Burke** 75:30, **Goldsmith** 153:21

10 I called the New World into existence, to redress the balance of the Old.
speech on the affairs of Portugal, in House of Commons 12 December 1826

11 [The Whip's duty is] to make a House, and keep a House, and cheer the minister.
J. E. Ritchie *Modern Statesmen* (1861) ch. 7; attributed

Hughie Cannon 1877–1912
American songwriter

12 Won't you come home Bill Bailey, won't you come home?
'Bill Bailey, Won't You Please Come Home' (1902 song)

Eric Cantona 1966–
French footballer

13 When seagulls follow a trawler, it is because they think sardines will be thrown into the sea.
to the media at the end of a press conference, 31 March 1995

Robert Capa 1913–54
Hungarian-born American photojournalist

14 If your pictures aren't good enough, you aren't close enough.
Russell Miller *Magnum: Fifty years at the Front Line of History* (1997)

Truman Capote 1924–84
American writer and novelist

15 Other voices, other rooms.
title of novel (1948)

Al Capp 1907–79
American cartoonist

16 A product of the untalented, sold by the unprincipled to the utterly bewildered.
of abstract art
in *National Observer* 1 July 1963; see **Zappa** 370:10

Francesco Caracciolo 1752–99
Neapolitan diplomat

17 In England there are sixty different religions, and only one sauce.
attributed

Thomas Carew c.1595–1640
English poet and courtier

18 Here lies a king, that ruled as he thought fit
The universal monarchy of wit.
'An Elegy upon the Death of Dr John Donne' (1640)

19 Ask me no more where Jove bestows,
When June is past, the fading rose;
For in your beauty's orient deep
These flowers, as in their causes, sleep.
'A Song' (1640)

George Carey 1935–
English Anglican archbishop

20 We must recall that the Church is always 'one generation away from extinction.'
Working Party Report *Youth A Part: Young People and the Church* (1996) foreword

Henry Carey c.1687–1743
English comic dramatist and songwriter

21 Of all the girls that are so smart
There's none like pretty Sally,
She is the darling of my heart,

And she lives in our alley.
'Sally in our Alley' (1729)

Richard Carleton 1943–
Australian journalist

1 How does it feel to have blood on your hands?
to Bob Hawke, new leader of the Australian Labor Party, after the resignation of Bill Hayden as Opposition leader
television interview, 3 February 1983

Thomas Carlyle 1795–1881
Scottish historian and political philosopher

2 A witty statesman said, you might prove anything by figures.
Chartism (1839) ch. 2

3 In epochs when cash payment has become the sole nexus of man to man.
Chartism (1839) ch. 6

4 History is the essence of innumerable biographies.
Critical and Miscellaneous Essays (1838) 'On History'

5 A well-written Life is almost as rare as a well-spent one.
Critical and Miscellaneous Essays (1838) 'Jean Paul Friedrich Richter'

6 Silence is deep as Eternity; speech is shallow as Time.
Critical and Miscellaneous Essays (1838) 'Sir Walter Scott'

7 To the very last he [Napoleon] had a kind of idea; that, namely, of *La carrière ouverte aux talents*, The tools to him that can handle them.
Critical and Miscellaneous Essays (1838) 'Sir Walter Scott' (*La carrière . . .* Career open to the talents)

8 The three great elements of modern civilization, Gunpowder, Printing, and the Protestant Religion.
Critical and Miscellaneous Essays (1838) 'The State of German Literature'; see **Bacon** 23:33

9 'Genius' (which means transcendent capacity of taking trouble, first of all).
History of Frederick the Great (1858–65) bk. 4, ch. 3; see **Buffon** 73:20

10 A whiff of grapeshot.
History of the French Revolution (1837) vol. 1, bk. 5, ch. 3

11 History a distillation of rumour.
History of the French Revolution (1837) vol. 1, bk. 7, ch. 5

12 The seagreen Incorruptible.
describing **Robespierre**
History of the French Revolution (1837) vol. 2, bk. 4, ch. 4

13 France was long a despotism tempered by epigrams.
History of the French Revolution (1837) vol. 3, bk. 7, ch. 7

14 The true University of these days is a collection of books.
On Heroes, Hero-Worship, and the Heroic (1841) 'The Hero as Man of Letters'

15 A Parliament speaking through reporters to Buncombe and the twenty-seven millions mostly fools.
Latter-Day Pamphlets (1850) 'Parliaments'; see **Walker** 349:11

16 The Dismal Science.
on political economy
Latter-Day Pamphlets (1850) 'The Present Time'

17 Adversity is sometimes hard upon a man; but for one man who can stand prosperity, there are a hundred that will stand adversity.
On Heroes, Hero-Worship, and the Heroic (1841) 'The Hero as Man of Letters'

18 Captains of industry.
Past and Present (1843) bk. 4, ch. 4 (title)

19 Man is a tool-using animal . . . Without tools he is nothing, with tools he is all.
Sartor Resartus (1834) bk. 1, ch. 5

20 The everlasting No.
Sartor Resartus (1834) bk. 2, ch. 7 (title)

21 A good book is the purest essence of a human soul.
speech in support of the London Library, 24 June 1840, in F. Harrison Carlyle and the London Library *(1907)*

22 Gad! she'd better!
on hearing that Margaret Fuller 'accept[ed] the universe'
William James Varieties of Religious Experience *(1902) lecture 2*

23 If Jesus Christ were to come to-day, people would not even crucify him. They would ask him to dinner, and hear what he had to say, and make fun of it.
D. A. Wilson Carlyle at his Zenith *(1927)*

Stokely Carmichael 1941–98
American Black Power leader

24 The only position for women in SNCC is prone.
response to a question about the position of women
at a Student Nonviolent Coordinating Committee conference, November 1964

Andrew Carnegie 1835–1919
American industrialist and philanthropist

25 The man who dies . . . rich dies disgraced.
North American Review June 1889 'Wealth'

Dale Carnegie 1888–1955
American writer and lecturer

26 How to win friends and influence people.
title of book (1936)

Julia A. Carney 1823–1908

27 Little drops of water,
Little grains of sand,

Make the mighty ocean
And the beauteous land.
'Little Things' (1845)

Joseph Edwards Carpenter
1813–85
English poet and songwriter

1 What are the wild waves saying
Sister, the whole day long,
'What are the Wild Waves Saying?' (1850 song)

Emily Carr 1871–1945
Canadian artist

2 You come into the world alone and you go
out of the world alone yet it seems to me
you are more alone while living than even
going and coming.
Hundreds and Thousands: The Journals of Emily Carr
(1966) 16 July 1933

Lewis Carroll 1832–98
English writer and logician

3 'What is the use of a book', thought Alice,
'without pictures or conversations?'
Alice's Adventures in Wonderland (1865) ch. 1

4 'Curiouser and curiouser!' cried Alice.
Alice's Adventures in Wonderland (1865) ch. 2

5 How doth the little crocodile
Improve his shining tail,
And pour the waters of the Nile
On every golden scale!
Alice's Adventures in Wonderland (1865) ch. 2; see
Watts 351:18

6 EVERYBODY has won, and all must have
prizes.
Alice's Adventures in Wonderland (1865) ch. 3

7 'You are old, Father William,' the young
man said,
'And your hair has become very white;
And yet you incessantly stand on your
head—
Do you think, at your age, it is right?'
Alice's Adventures in Wonderland (1865) ch. 5; see
Southey 320:21

8 'If everybody minded their own business,'
said the Duchess in a hoarse growl, 'the
world would go round a good deal faster
than it does.'
Alice's Adventures in Wonderland (1865) ch. 6

9 He only does it to annoy,
Because he knows it teases.
Alice's Adventures in Wonderland (1865) ch. 6

10 This time it vanished quite slowly,
beginning with the end of the tail, and
ending with the grin, which remained some
time after the rest of it had gone.
the Cheshire Cat
Alice's Adventures in Wonderland (1865) ch. 6

11 'Then you should say what you mean,' the
March Hare went on. 'I do,' Alice hastily
replied; 'at least—at least I mean what I
say—that's the same thing, you know.' 'Not
the same thing a bit!' said the Hatter. 'Why,

you might just as well say that "I see what I
eat" is the same thing as "I eat what I see!" '
Alice's Adventures in Wonderland (1865) ch. 7

12 Twinkle, twinkle, little bat!
How I wonder what you're at!
Up above the world you fly!
Like a teatray in the sky.
Alice's Adventures in Wonderland (1865) ch. 7; see
Taylor 331:2

13 Off with her head!
the Queen of Hearts
Alice's Adventures in Wonderland (1865) ch. 8

14 Everything's got a moral, if you can only
find it.
Alice's Adventures in Wonderland (1865) ch. 9

15 Take care of the sense, and the sounds will
take care of themselves.
Alice's Adventures in Wonderland (1865) ch. 9

16 'That's the reason they're called lessons,' the
Gryphon remarked: 'because they lessen
from day to day.'
Alice's Adventures in Wonderland (1865) ch. 9

17 'Will you walk a little faster?' said a whiting
to a snail.
Alice's Adventures in Wonderland (1865) ch. 10

18 Will you, won't you, will you, won't you,
will you join the dance?
Alice's Adventures in Wonderland (1865) ch. 10

19 Soup of the evening, beautiful Soup!
Alice's Adventures in Wonderland (1865) ch. 10

20 Begin at the beginning,' the King said,
gravely, 'and go on till you come to the end:
then stop.
Alice's Adventures in Wonderland (1865) ch. 12

21 'It's the oldest rule in the book,' said the
King.
'Then it ought to be Number One,' said
Alice.
Alice's Adventures in Wonderland (1865) ch. 12

22 No! No! Sentence first—verdict afterwards.
Alice's Adventures in Wonderland (1865) ch. 12

23 'Twas brillig, and the slithy toves
Did gyre and gimble in the wabe;
All mimsy were the borogoves,
And the mome raths outgrabe.
'Beware the Jabberwock, my son!
The jaws that bite, the claws that catch!'
Through the Looking-Glass (1872) ch. 1

24 'And hast thou slain the Jabberwock?
Come to my arms, my beamish boy!
O frabjous day! Callooh! Callay!'
He chortled in his joy.
Through the Looking-Glass (1872) ch. 1

25 Curtsey while you're thinking what to say. It
saves time.
Through the Looking-Glass (1872) ch. 2

26 Now, *here*, you see, it takes all the running
you can do, to keep in the same place. If you
want to get somewhere else, you must run
at least twice as fast as that!
Through the Looking-Glass (1872) ch. 2

1 Speak in French when you can't think of the English for a thing.
Through the Looking-Glass (1872) ch. 2

2 'Contrariwise,' continued Tweedledee, 'if it was so, it might be; and if it were so, it would be: but as it isn't, it ain't. That's logic.'
Through the Looking-Glass (1872) ch. 4

3 'The time has come,' the Walrus said,
'To talk of many things:
Of shoes—and ships—and sealing wax—
Of cabbages—and kings—
And why the sea is boiling hot—
And whether pigs have wings.'
Through the Looking-Glass (1872) ch. 4

4 But answer came there none.
Through the Looking-Glass (1872) ch. 4; see **Scott** 287:7

5 The rule is, jam to-morrow and jam yesterday—but never jam today.
Through the Looking-Glass (1872) ch. 5

6 Why, sometimes I've believed as many as six impossible things before breakfast.
Through the Looking-Glass (1872) ch. 5

7 With a name like yours, you might be any shape, almost.
Through the Looking-Glass (1872) ch. 6

8 They gave it me,—for an un-birthday present.
Through the Looking-Glass (1872) ch. 6

9 There's glory for you!
Through the Looking-Glass (1872) ch. 6

10 'When *I* use a word,' Humpty Dumpty said in a rather scornful tone, 'it means just what I choose it to mean—neither more nor less.'
Through the Looking-Glass (1872) ch. 6

11 'The question is,' said Humpty Dumpty, 'which is to be master—that's all.'
Through the Looking-Glass (1872) ch. 6; see **Shawcross** 313:7

12 You see it's like a portmanteau—there are two meanings packed up into one word.
Through the Looking-Glass (1872) ch. 6

13 He's an Anglo-Saxon Messenger—and those are Anglo-Saxon attitudes.
Through the Looking-Glass (1872) ch. 7

14 It's as large as life, and twice as natural!
Through the Looking-Glass (1872) ch. 7

15 It's my own invention.
the White Knight
Through the Looking-Glass (1872) ch. 8

16 No admittance till the week after next!
Through the Looking-Glass (1872) ch. 9

17 What I tell you three times is true.
The Hunting of the Snark (1876) 'Fit the First: The Landing'

18 'What's the good of *Mercator's* North Poles and Equators,
Tropics, Zones and Meridian lines?'
So the Bellman would cry: and the crew would reply,

'They are merely conventional signs!'
The Hunting of the Snark (1876) 'Fit the Second: The Bellman's Speech'

19 But oh, beamish nephew, beware of the day,
If your Snark be a Boojum! For then
You will softly and suddenly vanish away,
And never be met with again!
The Hunting of the Snark (1876) 'Fit the Third: The Baker's Tale'

20 They sought it with thimbles, they sought it with care;
They pursued it with forks and hope;
They threatened its life with a railway-share;
They charmed it with smiles and soap.
The Hunting of the Snark (1876) 'Fit the Fifth: The Beaver's Lesson'

21 For the Snark *was* a Boojum, you see.
The Hunting of the Snark (1876) 'Fit the Eighth: The Vanishing'

22 If you want to inspire confidence, *give plenty of statistics.*
C. L. Dodgson *Three Years in a Curatorship by One Whom It Has Tried* (1886)

William Herbert Carruth
1859–1924

23 Some call it evolution,
And others call it God.
'Each In His Own Tongue' (1908)

Edward Carson 1854–1935
British lawyer and politician

24 We must be prepared . . . the morning Home Rule passes, ourselves to become responsible for the government of the Protestant Province of Ulster.
speech at Craigavon, 23 September 1911

Rachel Carson 1907–64
American zoologist

25 Over increasingly large areas of the United States, spring now comes unheralded by the return of the birds, and the early mornings are strangely silent where once they were filled with the beauty of bird song.
The Silent Spring (1962)

Angela Carter 1940–92
English novelist

26 Comedy is tragedy that happens to *other* people.
Wise Children (1991) ch. 4

Henry Carter d. 1806

27 True patriots we; for be it understood,
We left our country for our country's good.
prologue, written for, but not recited at, the opening of the Playhouse, Sydney, New South Wales, 16 January 1796, when the actors were principally convicts
previously attributed to George Barrington (b. 1755)

Howard Carter 1874–1939
English archaeologist

1 Yes, wonderful things.
when asked what he could see on first looking into the tomb of Tutankhamun, 26 November 1922; his notebook records the words as 'Yes, it is wonderful'
The Tomb of Tut-ankh-amen (1933)

James Earl 'Jimmy' Carter 1924–
American Democratic statesman, 39th President of the US 1977–81

2 I've looked on a lot of women with lust. I've committed adultery in my heart many times. This is something that God recognizes I will do—and I have done it—and God forgives me for it.
in Playboy November 1976

Sydney Carter 1915–2004
English folk-song writer

3 It's God they ought to crucify
Instead of you and me,
I said to the carpenter
A-hanging on the tree.
'Friday Morning' (1967)

4 Dance then wherever you may be,
I am the Lord of the Dance, said he,
And I'll lead you all, wherever you may be
And I'll lead you all in the dance, said he.
'Lord of the Dance' (1967)

5 One more step along the world I go.
'One More Step'

Jacques Cartier 1491–1557
French navigator and explorer

6 I am rather inclined to believe that this is the land God gave to Cain.
on discovering the northern shore of the Gulf of St Lawrence (now Labrador and Quebec) in 1534; after the murder of Abel, Cain was exiled to the desolate land of Nod (see Bible 34:25)
La Première Relation; H. P. Biggar (ed.) The Voyages of Jacques Cartier (1924)

Henri Cartier-Bresson 1908–2005
French photographer and artist

7 The decisive moment.
title of book (1952); see Retz 275:6

8 To me, photography is the simultaneous recognition, in a fraction of a second, of the significance of an event as well as of a precise organisation of forms which give that event its proper expression.
The Decisive Moment (1952)

Barbara Cartland 1901–2000
English writer

9 After forty a woman has to choose between losing her figure or her face. My advice is to keep your face, and stay sitting down.
Libby Purves 'Luncheon à la Cartland'; in The Times 6 October 1993; similar remarks have been attributed since c.1980

John Cartwright 1740–1824
English political reformer

10 One man shall have one vote.
The People's Barrier Against Undue Influence (1780) ch. 1 'Principles, maxims, and primary rules of politics' no. 68

Barbara Castle 1910–2002
British Labour politician

11 I will fight for what I believe in until I drop dead. And that's what keeps you alive.
in Guardian 14 January 1998

Ted Castle 1907–79
British journalist

12 In place of strife.
title of Government White Paper, 17 January 1969, suggested by Castle to his wife, Barbara Castle, then Secretary of State for Employment
Barbara Castle, diary, 15 January 1969

Fidel Castro 1927–
Cuban statesman

13 History will absolve me.
title of pamphlet (1953)

Edward Caswall 1814–78
English hymn-writer

14 Jesu, the very thought of Thee
With sweetness fills the breast.
translation of 'Jesu dulcis memoria, dans vera cordis gaudia', *usually attributed to St Bernard*
'Jesu, the very thought of Thee' (1849 hymn)

15 See, amid the winter's snow,
Born for us on earth below,
See, the Lamb of God appears,
Promised from eternal years!
'See, amid the winter's snow' (1858 hymn)

A Catechism of Christian Doctrine 1898
Popularly known as the 'Penny Catechism'

16 Who made you? God made me.
Why did God make you? God made me to know Him, love him, and serve Him in this world, and to be happy with Him for ever in the next.
ch. 1

Willa Cather 1873–1947
American novelist

17 Where there is great love there are always miracles.
Death Comes for the Archbishop (1927)

18 That is happiness: to be dissolved into something complete and great.
on her gravestone in Jaffrey, New Hampshire
My Ántonia (1918) bk 1, ch 2

19 I like trees because they seem more resigned to the way they have to live than other things do.
O Pioneers! (1913) pt. 2, ch. 4

Catherine the Great 1729–96
Russian monarch, empress from 1762

1 I shall be an autocrat: that's my trade. And the good Lord will forgive me: that's his.
   attributed

Cato the Elder (or 'the Censor') 234–149 BC
Roman statesman, orator, and writer

2 *Delenda est Carthago.*
   Carthage must be destroyed.
   words concluding every speech Cato made in the Senate
   Pliny the Elder *Naturalis Historia* bk. 15, ch. 74

3 *Rem tene; verba sequentur.*
   Grasp the subject, the words will follow.
   Caius Julius Victor *Ars Rhetorica* 'De inventione'

Carrie Chapman Catt 1859–1947
American feminist

4 No written law has ever been more binding than unwritten custom supported by popular opinion.
   speech at Senate hearing on woman's suffrage, 13 February 1900
   Why We Ask for the Submission of an Amendment (1900)

Catullus *c*.84–*c*.54 BC
Roman poet

5 *Lugete, O Veneres Cupidinesque,*
   Et quantum est hominum venustiorum.
   Passer mortuus est meae puellae,
   Passer, deliciae meae puellae.
   Mourn, you powers of Charm and Desire, and all you who are endowed with charm. My lady's sparrow is dead, the sparrow which was my lady's darling.
   Carmina no. 3

6 *Vivamus, mea Lesbia, atque amemus.*
   Let us live, my Lesbia, and let us love.
   Carmina no. 5; see **Jonson** 191:18

7 *Da mi basia mille.*
   Give me a thousand kisses.
   Carmina no. 5

8 *Odi et amo: quare id faciam, fortasse requiris.*
   Nescio, sed fieri sentio et excrucior.
   I hate and I love: why I do so you may well ask. I do not know, but I feel it happen and am in agony.
   Carmina no. 85

9 *Atque in perpetuum, frater, ave atque vale.*
   And so, my brother, hail, and farewell evermore!
   Carmina no. 101 (tr. Sir William Marris)

10 *At non effugies meos iambos.*
   But you shall not escape my iambics.
   R. A. B. Mynors (ed.) *Catulli Carmina* (1958) Fragment 3

Constantine Cavafy 1863–1933
Greek poet

11 When you set out for Ithaka

ask that your way be long.
   'Ithaka' (1911) (tr. E. Keeley and P. Sherrard)

12 What are we waiting for, gathered in the market-place?
   The barbarians are to arrive today.
   'Waiting for the Barbarians' (1904) (tr. E. Keeley and P. Sherrard)

13 And now, what will become of us without the barbarians?
   Those people were a kind of solution.
   'Waiting for the Barbarians' (1904)

Edith Cavell 1865–1915
English nurse

14 Standing, as I do, in view of God and eternity, I realize that patriotism is not enough. I must have no hatred or bitterness towards anyone.
   on the eve of her execution
   in *The Times* 23 October 1915

Count Cavour 1810–61
Italian statesman

15 We are ready to proclaim throughout Italy this great principle: a free church in a free state.
   speech, 27 March 1861

Paul Celan 1920–70
German poet

16 Your ashen hair Shulamith we shovel a grave in the air there you won't lie too cramped.
   'Deathfugue' (written 1944)

17 *Der Tod ist ein Meister aus Deutschland.*
   Death is a master from Germany.
   'Deathfugue' (written 1944)

Susannah Centlivre *c*.1669–1723
English actress and dramatist

18 The real Simon Pure.
   A Bold Stroke for a Wife (1718) act 5, sc. 1

Cervantes 1547–1616
Spanish novelist

19 The Knight of the Doleful Countenance.
   Don Quixote (1605) pt. 1, ch. 19

20 There are only two families in the world . . . the haves and the have-nots.
   Don Quixote (1605) pt. 2, ch. 20

21 What I say is, patience, and shuffle the cards.
   Don Quixote (1605) pt. 2, ch. 23

22 Diligence is the mother of good fortune, and idleness, its opposite, never led to good intention's goal.
   Don Quixote (1605) pt. 2, ch. 43

Paul Cézanne 1839–1906
French painter

23 Treat nature in terms of the cylinder, the sphere, the cone, all in perspective.
   letter to Emile Bernard, 1904; Emile Bernard *Paul Cézanne* (1925)

Joseph Chamberlain 1836–1914
British Liberal politician

1 Provided that the City of London remains, as it is at present, the clearing-house of the world, any other nation may be its workshop.
   speech at the Guildhall, 19 January 1904; see **Disraeli** 117:5

2 The day of small nations has long passed away. The day of Empires has come.
   speech at Birmingham, 12 May 1904

Neville Chamberlain 1869–1940
British Conservative statesman, Prime Minister 1937–40

3 In war, whichever side may call itself the victor, there are no winners, but all are losers.
   speech at Kettering, 3 July 1938, in *The Times* 4 July 1938

4 How horrible, fantastic, incredible it is that we should be digging trenches and trying on gas-masks here because of a quarrel in a far away country between people of whom we know nothing.
   on Germany's annexation of the Sudetenland
   radio broadcast, 27 September 1938

5 This is the second time in our history that there has come back from Germany to Downing Street peace with honour. I believe it is peace for our time.
   speech from 10 Downing Street, 30 September 1938; see **Disraeli** 117:16, **Russell** 283:16

6 This morning, the British Ambassador in Berlin handed the German government a final Note stating that, unless we heard from them by eleven o'clock that they were prepared at once to withdraw their troops from Poland, a state of war would exist between us. I have to tell you now that no such undertaking has been received, and that consequently this country is at war with Germany.
   radio broadcast, 3 September 1939

7 Whether it was that Hitler thought he might get away with what he had got without fighting for it, or whether it was that after all the preparations were not sufficiently complete—however, one thing is certain—he missed the bus.
   speech at Central Hall, Westminster, 4 April 1940

Haddon Chambers 1860–1921
English dramatist

8 The long arm of coincidence.
   Captain Swift (1888) act 2

Nicolas-Sébastien Chamfort 1741–94
French writer

9 Of all days, the one most surely wasted is the one on which one has not laughed.
   Maximes et Pensées (1796) ch. 1

Raymond Chandler 1888–1959
American writer of detective fiction

10 It was a blonde. A blonde to make a bishop kick a hole in a stained glass window.
   Farewell, My Lovely (1940) ch. 13

11 A big hard-boiled city with no more personality than a paper cup.
   of Los Angeles
   The Little Sister (1949) ch. 26

12 Down these mean streets a man must go who is not himself mean, who is neither tarnished nor afraid.
   in *Atlantic Monthly* December 1944 'The Simple Art of Murder'

13 When I split an infinitive, God damn it, I split it so it will stay split.
   letter to Edward Weeks, 18 January 1947

14 When in doubt have a man come through the door with a gun in his hand.
   attributed

Henry ('Chips') Channon 1897–1958
American-born British Conservative politician and diarist

15 What is more dull than a discreet diary? One might just as well have a discreet soul.
   diary, 26 July 1935

Charlie Chaplin 1889–1977
English film actor and director

16 All I need to make a comedy is a park, a policeman and a pretty girl.
   My Autobiography (1964) ch. 10

Arthur Chapman 1873–1935
American poet

17 Out where the handclasp's a little stronger, Out where the smile dwells a little longer, That's where the West begins.
   Out Where the West Begins (1916)

George Chapman c.1559–1634
English scholar, poet, and dramatist

18 Who to himself is law, no law doth need, Offends no law, and is a king indeed.
   Bussy D'Ambois (1607–8) act 2, sc. 1

19 I am ashamed the law is such an ass.
   Revenge for Honour (1654) act 3, sc. 2; see **Dickens** 115:16

Charles I 1600–49
British monarch, King of England, Scotland, and Ireland from 1625

20 I see all the birds are flown.
   *after attempting to arrest five members of the Long Parliament (**Pym**, Hampden, Haselrig, Holles, and Strode)*
   in the House of Commons, 4 January 1642

21 A subject and a sovereign are clean different things.
   speech on the scaffold, 30 January 1649

Charles II 1630–85
British monarch, King of England, Scotland, and Ireland from 1660

1 It is upon the navy under the good Providence of God that the safety, honour, and welfare of this realm do chiefly depend.
'Articles of War' preamble (probably a popular paraphrase); Geoffrey Callender *The Naval Side of British History* (1952) pt. 1, ch. 8

2 This is very true: for my words are my own, and my actions are my ministers'.
*reply to Lord **Rochester**'s epitaph on him*
Thomas Hearne: *Remarks and Collections* (1885–1921) 17 November 1706; see **Rochester** 278:4

3 He had been, he said, an unconscionable time dying; but he hoped that they would excuse it.
Lord Macaulay *History of England* (1849) vol. 1, ch. 4

4 Let not poor Nelly starve.
*referring to Nell **Gwyn**, his mistress*
Bishop Gilbert Burnet *History of My Own Time* (1724) vol. 1, bk. 3

Charles V 1500–58
Spanish monarch, Holy Roman Emperor, 1519–56; King of Spain from 1516

5 To God I speak Spanish, to women Italian, to men French, and to my horse—German.
attributed; Lord Chesterfield *Letters to his Son*

Charles, Prince of Wales 1948–
heir apparent to the British throne

6 *when asked if he was 'in love':*
Yes . . . whatever that may mean.
after the announcement of his engagement
interview, 24 February 1981

7 A monstrous carbuncle on the face of a much-loved and elegant friend.
on the proposed extension to the National Gallery
speech to the Royal Institute of British Architects, 30 May 1984; see **Spencer** 321:17

8 I just come and talk to the plants, really—very important to talk to them, they respond I find.
television interview, 21 September 1986

Pierre Charron 1541–1603
French philosopher and theologian

9 The true science and study of man is man.
De la Sagesse (1601) bk. 1, preface; see **Pope** 267:27

Salmon Portland Chase 1808–73
American lawyer and politician

10 The Constitution, in all its provisions, looks to an indestructible Union composed of indestructible States.
decision in Texas v. White, 1868, in *Cases Argued and Decided in the Supreme Court of the United States* (1926) bk. 19

Geoffrey Chaucer c.1343–1400
English poet

11 Whan that Aprill with his shoures soote
The droghte of March hath perced to the roote.
The Canterbury Tales 'The General Prologue' l. 1

12 And smale foweles maken melodye,
That slepen al the nyght with open ye
(So priketh hem nature in hir corages),
Thanne longen folk to goon on pilgrimages.
The Canterbury Tales 'The General Prologue' l. 9

13 He was a verray, parfit gentil knyght.
The Canterbury Tales 'The General Prologue' l. 72

14 He was as fressh as is the month of May.
The Canterbury Tales 'The General Prologue' l. 92

15 And Frenssh she spak ful faire and fetisly,
After the scole of Stratford atte Bowe,
For Frenssh of Parys was to hire unknowe.
The Canterbury Tales 'The General Prologue' l. 124

16 And theron heng a brooch of gold ful sheene,
On which ther was first write a crowned A,
And after *Amor vincit omnia*.
The Canterbury Tales 'The General Prologue' l. 160; see **Virgil** 347:25

17 A Clerk there was of Oxenford also.
The Canterbury Tales 'The General Prologue' l. 285

18 And gladly wolde he lerne and gladly teche.
The Canterbury Tales 'The General Prologue' l. 308

19 Nowher so bisy a man as he ther nas,
And yet he semed bisier than he was.
The Canterbury Tales 'The General Prologue' l. 321

20 Housbondes at chirche dore she hadde fyve.
The Canterbury Tales 'The General Prologue' l. 460

21 This noble ensample to his sheep he yaf,
That first he wroghte, and afterward he taughte.
The Canterbury Tales 'The General Prologue' l. 496

22 If gold ruste, what shall iren do?
The Canterbury Tales 'The General Prologue' l. 500

23 Love wol nat been constreyned by maistrye.
When maistrie comth, the God of Love anon
Beteth his wynges, and farewel, he is gon!
The Canterbury Tales 'The Franklin's Tale' l. 764

24 The bisy larke, messager of day.
The Canterbury Tales 'The Knight's Tale' l. 1491

25 For pitee renneth soone in gentil herte.
The Canterbury Tales 'The Knight's Tale' l. 1761

26 The smylere with the knyf under the cloke.
The Canterbury Tales 'The Knight's Tale' l. 1999

27 Mordre wol out; that se we day by day.
The Canterbury Tales 'The Nun's Priest's Tale' l. 3052

28 Yblessed be god that I have wedded fyve!
Welcome the sixte, whan that evere he shal.
The Canterbury Tales 'The Wife of Bath's Prologue' l. 44

29 A likerous mouth moste han a likerous tayl.
The Canterbury Tales 'The Wife of Bath's Prologue' l. 466

30 Wommen desiren to have sovereynetee

As wel over hir housbond as hir love.
The Canterbury Tales 'The Wife of Bath's Tale' l. 1038

1 And she was fayr as is the rose in May.
The Legend of Good Women 'Cleopatra' l. 613

2 That lyf so short,
the craft so long to lerne.
The Parliament of Fowls l. 1; see **Hippocrates** 169:15

3 For of fortunes sharpe adversitee
The worst kynde of infortune is this,
A man to han ben in prosperitee,
And it remembren, whan it passed is.
Troilus and Criseyde bk. 3, l. 1625; see **Boethius** 58:15

4 Go, litel bok, go, litel myn tragedye.
Troilus and Criseyde bk. 5, l. 1786; see **Stevenson** 326:4

5 And ther he saugh, with ful avysement
The erratik sterres, herkenyng armonye
With sownes ful of hevenyssh melodie.
Troilus and Criseyde bk. 5, l. 1815

6 O yonge, fresshe folkes, he or she,
In which that love up groweth with youre age.
Troilus and Criseyde bk. 5, l. 1835

7 O moral Gower, this book I directe
To the.
Troilus and Criseyde bk. 5, l. 1856

Anton Chekhov 1860–1904
Russian dramatist and short-story writer

8 MEDVEDENKO: Why do you wear black all the time?
MASHA: I'm in mourning for my life, I'm unhappy.
The Seagull (1896) act 1

9 Medicine is my lawful wife and literature is my mistress. When I get tired of one I spend the night with the other.
letter to A. S. Suvorin, 11 September 1888

10 Brevity is the sister of talent.
letter to Alexander Chekhov, 11 April 1889

11 Love, friendship, respect do not unite people as much as common hatred for something.
Notebooks (1921)

Cher 1946–
American singer and actress

12 If grass can grow through cement, love can find you at every time in your life.
in *The Times* 30 May 1998

Lord Chesterfield 1694–1773
English writer and politician

13 Religion is by no means a proper subject of conversation in a mixed company.
Letters . . . to his Godson and Successor (1890) Letter 142

14 The knowledge of the world is only to be acquired in the world, and not in a closet.
Letters to his Son (1774) 4 October 1746

15 An injury is much sooner forgotten than an insult.
Letters to his Son (1774) 9 October 1746

16 Take the tone of the company that you are in.
Letters to his Son (1774) 16 October 1747

17 I recommend to you to take care of minutes: for hours will take care of themselves.
Letters to his Son (1774) 6 November 1747; see **Lowndes** 220:6

18 Advice is seldom welcome; and those who want it the most always like it the least.
Letters to his Son (1774) 29 January 1748

19 Wear your learning, like your watch in a private pocket: and do not merely pull it out and strike it, merely to show that you have one.
Letters to his Son (1774) 22 February 1748

20 Women, then, are only children of a larger growth.
Letters to his Son (1774) 5 September 1748; see **Dryden** 121:28

21 Idleness is only the refuge of weak minds.
Letters to his Son (1774) 20 July 1749

22 It is commonly said, and more particularly by Lord Shaftesbury, that ridicule is the best test of truth.
Letters to his Son (1774) 6 February 1752

23 The chapter of knowledge is a very short, but the chapter of accidents is a very long one.
letter to Solomon Dayrolles, 16 February 1753

24 The pleasure is momentary, the position ridiculous, and the expense damnable.
of sex
attributed

G. K. Chesterton 1874–1936
English essayist, novelist, and poet

25 I tell you naught for your comfort,
Yea, naught for your desire,
Save that the sky grows darker yet
And the sea rises higher.
The Ballad of the White Horse (1911) bk. 1

26 For the great Gaels of Ireland
Are the men that God made mad,
For all their wars are merry,
And all their songs are sad.
The Ballad of the White Horse (1911) bk. 2

27 Fools! For I also had my hour;
One far fierce hour and sweet:
There was a shout about my ears,
And palms before my feet.
'The Donkey' (1900)

28 From all that terror teaches,
From lies of tongue and pen,
From all the easy speeches
That comfort cruel men,
From sale and profanation
Of honour and the sword,
From sleep and from damnation,
Deliver us, good Lord!
'A Hymn' (1915)

1 The cold queen of England is looking in the glass;
The shadow of the Valois is yawning at the Mass.
'Lepanto' (1915)

2 Strong gongs groaning as the guns boom far,
Don John of Austria is going to the war.
'Lepanto' (1915)

3 Before the Roman came to Rye or out to Severn strode,
The rolling English drunkard made the rolling English road.
'The Rolling English Road' (1914)

4 A merry road, a mazy road, and such as we did tread
The night we went to Birmingham by way of Beachy Head.
'The Rolling English Road' (1914)

5 For there is good news yet to hear and fine things to be seen,
Before we go to Paradise by way of Kensal Green.
'The Rolling English Road' (1914)

6 Smile at us, pay us, pass us; but do not quite forget.
For we are the people of England, that never have spoken yet.
'The Secret People' (1915)

7 And Noah he often said to his wife when he sat down to dine,
'I don't care where the water goes if it doesn't get into the wine.'
'Wine and Water' (1914)

8 An adventure is only an inconvenience rightly considered. An inconvenience is only an adventure wrongly considered.
All Things Considered (1908) 'On Running after one's Hat'

9 Literature is a luxury; fiction is a necessity.
The Defendant (1901) 'A Defence of Penny Dreadfuls'

10 The rich are the scum of the earth in every country.
The Flying Inn (1914) ch. 15

11 One sees great things from the valley; only small things from the peak.
The Innocence of Father Brown (1911)

12 Thieves respect property. They merely wish the property to become their property that they may more perfectly respect it.
The Man who was Thursday (1908) ch. 4

13 Tradition means giving votes to the most obscure of all classes, our ancestors. It is the democracy of the dead.
Orthodoxy (1908) ch. 4

14 All conservatism is based upon the idea that if you leave things alone you leave them as they are. But you do not. If you leave a thing alone you leave it to a torrent of change.
Orthodoxy (1908) ch. 7

15 Democrats object to men being disqualified by the accident of birth; tradition objects to their being disqualified by the accident of death.
Orthodoxy (1908) ch. 4

16 It isn't that they can't see the solution. It is that they can't see the problem.
The Scandal of Father Brown (1935)

17 They say travel broadens the mind; but you must have the mind.
'The Shadow of the Shark' (1921)

18 Lying in bed would be an altogether perfect and supreme experience if only one had a coloured pencil long enough to draw on the ceiling.
Tremendous Trifles (1909)

19 The Christian ideal has not been tried and found wanting. It has been found difficult; and left untried.
What's Wrong with the World (1910) pt. 1 'The Unfinished Temple'

20 If a thing is worth doing, it is worth doing badly.
What's Wrong with the World (1910) pt. 4 'Folly and Female Education'

21 To be clever enough to get all that money, one must be stupid enough to want it.
The Wisdom of Father Brown (1914)

22 Journalism largely consists in saying 'Lord Jones Dead' to people who never knew that Lord Jones was alive.
The Wisdom of Father Brown (1914)

23 Democracy means government by the uneducated, while aristocracy means government by the badly educated.
in New York Times 1 February 1931, pt. 5

24 AM IN MARKET HARBOROUGH. WHERE OUGHT I TO BE?
telegram to his wife in London
Autobiography (1936)

25 When men stop believing in God they don't believe in nothing; they believe in anything.
widely attributed, although not traced in his works; first recorded as 'The first effect of not believing in God is to believe in anything' in Emile Cammaerts Chesterton: The Laughing Prophet (1937)

Joseph Benedict 'Ben' Chifley
1885–1951
Australian Labor statesman

26 We have a great objective—the light on the hill—which we aim to reach by working for the betterment of mankind not only here but anywhere we may give a helping hand.
speech to the Annual Conference of the New South Wales branch of the Australian Labor Party, 12 June 1949

Erskine Childers 1870–1922
British writer and Irish nationalist

27 The riddle of the sands.
title of novel (1903)

William Chillingworth 1602–44
English scholar

1 The Bible and the Bible only is the religion of Protestants.
The Religion of Protestants (1637)

Charles Chilton *see* Joan Littlewood

Jacques Chirac 1932–
French statesman

2 You have been very rude, and I have never been spoken to like this before.
*to Tony **Blair** at the EU enlargement summit in Brussels*
in *Guardian* online 29 October 2002

3 It is not well-brought-up behaviour. They missed a good opportunity to keep quiet.
criticizing the support from Central and Eastern European states for the Anglo-American stance on Iraq
in *The Times* 19 February 2003

Thomas O. Chisholm 1866–1960

4 Great is thy faithfulness! Great is thy faithfulness!
Morning by morning new mercies I see.
'Great is thy faithfulness' (hymn)

Rufus Choate 1799–1859
American lawyer and politician

5 Its constitution the glittering and sounding generalities of natural right which make up the Declaration of Independence.
letter to the Maine Whig State Central Committee, 9 August 1856; see **Emerson** 132:21

Noam Chomsky 1928–
American linguistics scholar

6 Colourless green ideas sleep furiously.
Syntactic Structures (1957) ch. 2

7 As soon as questions of will or decision or reason or choice of action arise, human science is at a loss.
television interview, in *Listener* 6 April 1978

8 The Internet is an élite organization; most of the population of the world has never even made a phone call.
on the limitations of the World Wide Web
in *Observer* 18 February 1996

Jean Chrétien 1934–
Canadian Liberal statesman

9 Leadership means making people feel good.
in *Toronto Star* 7 June 1984

Agatha Christie 1890–1976
English writer of detective fiction

10 War settles *nothing* . . . to win a war is as disastrous as to lose one!
An Autobiography (1977) pt. 10

11 He [Hercule Poirot] tapped his forehead. 'These little grey cells. It is "up to them".'
The Mysterious Affair at Styles (1920) ch. 10

David Christy 1802–c.68

12 Cotton is King; or, the economical relations of slavery.
title of book, 1855

Chuang Tzu (Zhuangzi) c.369–286 BC
Chinese philosopher

13 I do not know whether it was Chou dreaming that he was a butterfly or the butterfly dreaming that it was Chou.
Chuang Tzu ch. 2

Francis Pharcellus Church 1839–1906

14 Yes, Virginia, there is a Santa Claus.
replying to a letter from eight-year-old Virginia O'Hanlon
editorial in New York *Sun*, 21 September 1897

Charles Churchill 1731–64
English poet

15 Be England what she will,
With all her faults, she is my country still.
The Farewell (1764) l. 27; see **Cowper** 105:26

16 Apt Alliteration's artful aid.
The Prophecy of Famine (1763) l. 86

Lord Randolph Churchill 1849–94
British Conservative politician

17 I decided some time ago that if the G. O. M. went for Home Rule, the Orange card would be the one to play. Please God it may turn out the ace of trumps and not the two.
*'G. O. M.' = Grand Old Man (**Gladstone**)*
letter to Lord Justice FitzGibbon, 16 February 1886; see **Shapiro** 311:5

18 Ulster will fight; Ulster will be right.
public letter, 7 May 1886

19 An old man in a hurry.
*on **Gladstone***
address to the electors of South Paddington, 19 June 1886

20 I never could make out what those damned dots [decimal points] meant.
W. S. Churchill *Lord Randolph Churchill* (1906) vol. 2

Winston Churchill 1874–1965
British Conservative statesman, Prime Minister 1940–5, 1951–5

21 It cannot in the opinion of His Majesty's Government be classified as slavery in the extreme acceptance of the word without some risk of terminological inexactitude.
speech in the House of Commons, 22 February 1906

22 The whole map of Europe has been changed . . . but as the deluge subsides and the waters fall short we see the dreary steeples of Fermanagh and Tyrone emerging once again.
speech in the House of Commons, 16 February 1922

1 Anyone can rat, but it takes a certain amount of ingenuity to re-rat.
on rejoining the Conservatives twenty years after leaving them for the Liberals, c.1924
  Kay Halle *Irrepressible Churchill* (1966)

2 I have waited 50 years to see the boneless wonder sitting on the Treasury Bench.
*of Ramsay **MacDonald***
  speech in the House of Commons, 28 January 1931

3 [The Government] go on in strange paradox, decided only to be undecided, resolved to be irresolute, adamant for drift, solid for fluidity, all-powerful to be impotent.
  speech in the House of Commons, 12 November 1936

4 Dictators ride to and fro upon tigers which they dare not dismount. And the tigers are getting hungry.
  letter, 11 November 1937

5 I cannot forecast to you the action of Russia. It is a riddle wrapped in a mystery inside an enigma.
  radio broadcast, 1 October 1939

6 I have nothing to offer but blood, toil, tears and sweat.
  speech in the House of Commons, 13 May 1940; see **Byron** 80:1

7 What is our policy? . . . to wage war against a monstrous tyranny, never surpassed in the dark, lamentable catalogue of human crime.
  speech in the House of Commons, 13 May 1940

8 What is our aim? . . . Victory, victory at all costs, victory in spite of all terror; victory, however long and hard the road may be; for without victory, there is no survival.
  speech in the House of Commons, 13 May 1940

9 We shall not flag or fail. We shall go on to the end. We shall fight in France, we shall fight on the seas and oceans, we shall fight with growing confidence and growing strength in the air, we shall defend our island, whatever the cost may be. We shall fight on the beaches, we shall fight on the landing grounds, we shall fight in the fields and in the streets, we shall fight in the hills; we shall never surrender.
  speech in the House of Commons, 4 June 1940

10 Let us therefore brace ourselves to our duty, and so bear ourselves that, if the British Empire and its Commonwealth lasts for a thousand years, men will still say, 'This was their finest hour.'
  speech in the House of Commons, 18 June 1940

11 Never in the field of human conflict was so much owed by so many to so few.
on the Battle of Britain
  speech in the House of Commons, 20 August 1940

12 Give us the tools and we will finish the job.
  radio broadcast, 9 February 1941

13 When I warned them [the French Government] that Britain would fight on alone whatever they did, their generals told their Prime Minister and his divided Cabinet, 'In three weeks England will have her neck wrung like a chicken.' Some chicken! Some neck!
  speech to Canadian Parliament, 30 December 1941

14 Now this is not the end. It is not even the beginning of the end. But it is, perhaps, the end of the beginning.
on the Battle of Egypt
  speech at the Mansion House, London, 10 November 1942

15 We make this wide encircling movement in the Mediterranean, having for its primary object the recovery of the command of that vital sea, but also having for its object the exposure of the underbelly of the Axis, especially Italy, to heavy attack.
often quoted as, 'The soft underbelly of Europe'
  speech in the House of Commons, 11 November 1942

16 National compulsory insurance for all classes for all purposes from the cradle to the grave.
  radio broadcast, 21 March 1943, in *Complete Speeches* (1974) vol. 7

17 There is no finer investment for any community than putting milk into babies.
  radio broadcast, 21 March 1943

18 The empires of the future are the empires of the mind.
  speech at Harvard, 6 September 1943, in *Onwards to Victory* (1944)

19 From Stettin in the Baltic to Trieste in the Adriatic an iron curtain has descended across the Continent.
*'iron curtain' previously had been applied by others to the Soviet Union or her sphere of influence, e.g. Ethel Snowden Through Bolshevik Russia (1920), Dr **Goebbels** Das Reich (25 February 1945), and by Churchill himself in a cable to President **Truman** (4 June 1945)*
  speech at Westminster College, Fulton, Missouri, 5 March 1946

20 Democracy is the worst form of Government except all those other forms that have been tried from time to time.
  speech in the House of Commons, 11 November 1947

21 This is the sort of English up with which I will not put.
  Ernest Gowers *Plain Words* (1948) 'Troubles with Prepositions'

22 Naval tradition?. Monstrous. Nothing but rum, sodomy, prayers, and the lash.
often quoted as 'rum, sodomy, and the lash', as in Peter Gretton Former Naval Person (1968)
  Harold Nicolson, diary, 17 August 1950

23 To jaw-jaw is always better than to war-war.
  speech at White House, 26 June 1954

24 It was the nation and the race dwelling all round the globe that had the lion's heart. I

had the luck to be called upon to give the roar.
speech at Westminster Hall, 30 November 1954

1 I have taken more out of alcohol than alcohol has taken out of me.
Quentin Reynolds *By Quentin Reynolds* (1964) ch. 11

2 In defeat unbeatable: in victory unbearable.
of Lord **Montgomery**
Edward Marsh *Ambrosia and Small Beer* (1964) ch. 5

3 Courage is rightly esteemed the first of human qualities because as has been said, it is the quality which guarantees all others.
Great Contemporaries (1937)

4 It is a good thing for an uneducated man to read books of quotations.
My Early Life (1930) ch. 9

5 In war: resolution. In defeat: defiance. In victory: magnanimity. In peace: goodwill.
The Second World War vol. 1 (1948) epigraph, which according to Edward Marsh in *A Number of People* (1939), occurred to Churchill shortly after the conclusion of the First World War

6 If Hitler invaded hell I would make at least a favourable reference to the devil in the House of Commons.
The Second World War (1950) vol. 3, ch. 20

7 Jellicoe was the only man on either side who could lose the war in an afternoon.
The World Crisis (1927) pt. 1, ch. 5

8 The ability to foretell what is going to happen tomorrow, next week, next month, and next year. And to have the ability afterwards to explain why it didn't happen.
describing the qualifications desirable in a prospective politician
B. Adler *Churchill Wit* (1965)

9 I am fond of pigs. Dogs look up to us. Cats look down on us. Pigs treat us as equals.
attributed, in M. Gilbert *Never Despair* (1988)

10 NANCY ASTOR: If I were your wife I would put poison in your coffee!
CHURCHILL: And if I were your husband I would drink it.
Consuelo Vanderbilt Balsan *Glitter and Gold* (1952)

11 A sheep in sheep's clothing.
of Clement **Attlee**
Lord Home *The Way the Wind Blows* (1976) ch. 6

Count Galeazzo Ciano 1903–44
Italian fascist politician

12 Victory has a hundred fathers, but defeat is an orphan.
literally 'no-one wants to recognise defeat as his own'
Diary (1946) vol. 2, 9 September 1942

Colley Cibber 1671–1757
English dramatist

13 Perish the thought!
Richard III (1700) act 5 (adapted from Shakespeare)

14 Conscience avaunt, Richard's himself again.
Richard III (1700) act 5 (adapted from Shakespeare)

Cicero (Marcus Tullius Cicero) 106–43
BC
Roman orator and statesman

15 There is nothing so absurd but some philosopher has said it.
De Divinatione bk. 2, ch. 119

16 *Salus populi suprema est lex.*
The good of the people is the chief law.
De Legibus bk. 3, ch. 8

17 *'Ipse dixit.' 'Ipse' autem erat Pythagoras.*
'He himself said', and this 'himself' was Pythagoras.
De Natura Deorum bk. 1, ch. 10

18 *Summum bonum.*
The highest good.
De Officiis bk. 1, ch. 5

19 How long will you abuse our patience, Catiline?
In Catilinam Speech 1, ch. 1

20 *O tempora, O mores!*
Oh, the times! Oh, the manners!
In Catilinam Speech 1, ch. 1

21 *Civis Romanus sum.*
I am a Roman citizen.
In Verrem Speech 5, ch. 147; see **Kennedy** 199:3, **Palmerston** 319:13

22 The sinews of war, unlimited money.
Fifth Philippic ch. 5

23 Laws are silent in time of war.
Pro Milone ch. 11

24 *Cui bono?*
To whose profit?
Pro Roscio Amerino ch. 84 and *Pro Milone* ch. 12, sect. 32, quoting L. Cassius Longinus Ravilla

25 *Cum dignitate otium.*
Leisure with honour.
Pro Sestio ch. 98

John Clare 1793–1864
English poet

26 I am—yet what I am, none cares or knows;
My friends forsake me like a memory lost:
I am the self-consumer of my woes.
'I Am' (1848)

27 There to abide with my Creator God
And sleep as I in childhood sweetly slept,
Untroubling and untroubled where I lie
The grass below, above, the vaulted sky.
'I Am' (1848)

Edward Hyde, Earl of Clarendon
1609–74
English statesman and historian

28 He had a head to contrive, a tongue to persuade, and a hand to execute any mischief.
of John Hampden
The History of the Rebellion (1703, ed. W. D. Macray, 1888) vol. 3; see **Gibbon** 148:18

1 He will be looked upon by posterity as a
brave bad man.
of **Cromwell**
The History of the Rebellion (1703, ed. W. D.
Macray, 1888) vol. 6

Alan Clark 1928–99
British Conservative politician

2 There are no true friends in politics. We are
all sharks circling, and waiting, for traces of
blood to appear in the water.
diary, 30 November 1990

3 Our old friend economical . . . with the
actualité.
*under cross-examination at the Old Bailey during
the Matrix Churchill case*
in *Independent* 10 November 1992; see
Armstrong 16:9

Arthur C. Clarke 1917–
English science fiction writer

4 When a distinguished but elderly scientist
states that something is possible, he is
almost certainly right. When he states that
something is impossible, he is very probably
wrong.
Profiles of the Future (1962) ch. 2

5 Any sufficiently advanced technology is
indistinguishable from magic.
Profiles of the Future (1962) ch. 2

6 How inappropriate to call this planet Earth
when it is clearly Ocean.
in *Nature* 8 March 1990

Austin Clarke 1896–1974
Irish poet, dramatist, and novelist

7 And O! She was the Sunday
In every week.
'The Planter's Daughter' (1929)

Grant Clarke 1891–1931
and **Edgar Leslie** 1885–1976

8 He'd have to get under, get out and get
under
And fix up his automobile.
He'd Have to Get Under—Get Out and Get Under
(1913 song)

Appius Claudius Caecus fl.
312–279 BC
Roman censor, orator, and prose writer

9 *Faber est suae quisque fortunae.*
Each man is the smith of his own fortune.
Sallust *Ad Caesarem Senem de Re Publica Oratio* ch.
1, sect. 2

Karl von Clausewitz 1780–1831
Prussian soldier and military theorist

10 The general unreliability of all information
presents a special problem in war: all action
takes place, so to speak, in a kind of
twilight, which, like fog or moonlight, often
tends to make things seem grotesque and
larger than they really are.
often alluded to by the phrase 'fog of war'
On War (1832–4) bk 2, ch. 2

11 Everything is very simple in war, but the
simplest thing is difficult. These difficulties
accumulate and produce a friction which no
man can imagine exactly who has not seen
war.
On War (1832–4) bk. 1, ch. 7, tr. J. J. Graham

12 War is nothing but a continuation of politics
with the admixture of other means.
*commonly rendered as 'War is the continuation of
politics by other means'*
On War (1832–4) bk. 8, ch. 6, sect. B

Henry Clay 1777–1852
American politician

13 The gentleman [Josiah Quincy] can not have
forgotten his own sentiment, uttered even
on the floor of this House, 'peaceably if we
can, forcibly if we must'.
speech in Congress, 8 January 1813; see **Quincy**
272:10

14 The arts of power and its minions are the
same in all countries and in all ages. It
marks its victim; denounces it; and excites
the public odium and the public hatred, to
conceal its own abuses and encroachments.
speech in the Senate, 14 March 1834, in C.
Colton (ed.) *The Works of Henry Clay* (1904) vol. 5

15 I had rather be right than be President.
to Senator Preston of South Carolina, 1839
attributed; S. W. McCall *Life of Thomas Brackett
Reed* (1914) ch. 14

Philip 'Tubby' Clayton 1885–1972
*Australian-born British clergyman, founder of
Toc H*

16 CHAIRMAN: What is service?
CANDIDATE: The rent we pay for our room
on earth.
*admission ceremony of Toc H, a society founded
after the First World War to provide Christian
fellowship and social service*
Tresham Lever *Clayton of Toc H* (1971)

Eldridge Cleaver 1935–98
American political activist

17 What we're saying today is that you're
either part of the solution or you're part of
the problem.
speech in San Francisco, 1968

John Cleese 1939–
and **Connie Booth**
*British comedy writer and actor; British comedy
actress*

18 They're Germans. Don't mention the war.
Fawlty Towers 'The Germans' (BBC TV
programme, 1975)

John Cleland 1710–89
English writer

1 Truth! stark naked truth, is the word.
   Memoirs of a Woman of Pleasure a.k.a. *Fanny Hill* (1749) vol. 1

Georges Clemenceau 1841–1929
French statesman, Prime Minister of France 1906–9, 1917–20

2 War is too serious a matter to entrust to military men.
   attributed to Clemenceau, but also to Briand and Talleyrand; see **de Gaulle** 112:4

3 It is easier to make war than to make peace.
   speech at Verdun, 20 July 1919

Clement XIII 1693–1769
Italian cleric; Pope 1758–69

4 *Sint ut sunt aut non sint.*
   Let them be as they are or not be at all.
   replying to a request for changes in the constitutions of the Society of Jesus
   J. A. M. Crétineau-Joly *Clément XIV et les Jésuites* (1847)

Grover Cleveland 1837–1908
American Democratic statesman, 22nd and 24th President of the US 1885–9 and 1893–7

5 I have considered the pension list of the republic a roll of honour.
   Veto of Dependent Pension Bill, 5 July 1888

6 The lessons of paternalism ought to be unlearned and the better lesson taught that, while the people should patriotically and cheerfully support their government, its functions do not include the support of the people.
   inaugural address, 4 March 1893, in *New York Times* 5 March 1893

Harlan Cleveland 1918–
American government official

7 The revolution of rising expectations.
   phrase coined 1950; Arthur Schlesinger *A Thousand Days* (1965) ch. 16

Hillary Rodham Clinton 1947–
American lawyer

8 I am not standing by my man, like Tammy Wynette. I am sitting here because I love him, I respect him, and I honour what he's been through and what we've been through together.
   interview on *60 Minutes*, CBS-TV, 27 January 1992

9 I could have stayed home and baked cookies and had teas. But what I decided was to fulfil my profession, which I entered before my husband was in public life.
   in *Albany Times-Union* 17 March 1992

William Jefferson ('Bill') Clinton 1946–
American Democratic statesman, 42nd President of the US 1993–2001

10 I experimented with marijuana a time or two. And I didn't like it, and I didn't inhale.
   in *Washington Post* 30 March 1992

11 The comeback kid!
   description of himself after coming second in the New Hampshire primary in the 1992 presidential election (since 1952, no presidential candidate had won the election without first winning in New Hampshire)
   Michael Barone and Grant Ujifusa *The Almanac of American Politics 1994*

12 I did not have sexual relations with that woman.
   television interview, in *Daily Telegraph* 27 January 1998

13 It depends on what the meaning of 'is' is.
   videotaped evidence to the grand jury; tapes broadcast 21 September 1998
   in *Guardian* 22 September 1998

Lord Clive 1725–74
British general; Governor of Bengal

14 By God, Mr Chairman, at this moment I stand astonished at my own moderation!
   reply during Parliamentary cross-examination, 1773
   G. R. Gleig *The Life of Robert, First Lord Clive* (1848) ch. 29

Arthur Hugh Clough 1819–61
English poet

15 How pleasant it is to have money, heigh ho!
   How pleasant it is to have money.
   Dipsychus (1865) sc. 5

16 Thou shalt have one God only; who
   Would be at the expense of two?
   'The Latest Decalogue' (1862); see **Bible** 35:24

17 Thou shalt not kill; but need'st not strive
   Officiously to keep alive.
   'The Latest Decalogue' (1862)

18 Do not adultery commit;
   Advantage rarely comes of it.
   'The Latest Decalogue' (1862)

19 Thou shalt not steal; an empty feat,
   When it's so lucrative to cheat.
   'The Latest Decalogue' (1862)

20 Thou shalt not covet; but tradition
   Approves all forms of competition.
   'The Latest Decalogue' (1862)

21 Say not the struggle naught availeth,
   The labour and the wounds are vain,
   The enemy faints not, nor faileth,
   And as things have been, things remain.
   'Say not the struggle naught availeth' (1855)

22 If hopes were dupes, fears may be liars.
   'Say not the struggle naught availeth' (1855)

23 In front the sun climbs slow, how slowly,
   But westward, look, the land is bright.
   'Say not the struggle naught availeth' (1855)

Kurt Cobain 1967-94
American rock singer, guitarist, and songwriter
see also **Young** 370:6

1 I'd rather be dead than cool.
   'Stay Away' (1991 song)

William Cobbett 1762-1835
English political reformer and radical journalist

2 The great wen of all.
   of London
   Rural Rides: The Kentish Journal in Cobbett's Weekly
   Political Register 5 January 1822, vol. 40

Alison Cockburn 1713-94
Scottish poet and songwriter

3 O fickle Fortune, why this cruel sporting?
   Why thus torment us poor sons of day?
   Nae mair your smiles can cheer me, nae
      mair your frowns can fear me,
   For the flowers of the forest are a' wade
      away.
   wade *weeded (often quoted as 'For the flowers of
   the forest are withered away')*
   'The Flowers of the Forest' (1765)

Bruce Cockburn 1945-
Canadian singer and songwriter

4 Got to kick at the darkness 'til it bleeds
   daylight.
   'Lovers in a Dangerous Time' (1984 song)

Claud Cockburn 1904-81
British writer and journalist

5 Small earthquake in Chile. Not many dead.
   *winning entry for a dullest headline competition
   at The Times*
   In Time of Trouble (1956) ch. 10

Jean Cocteau 1889-1963
French dramatist and film director

6 Life is a horizontal fall.
   Opium (1930)

7 Victor Hugo was a madman who thought he
   was Victor Hugo.
   Opium (1930)

8 If it has to choose who is to be crucified, the
   crowd will always save Barabbas.
   Le Rappel à l'ordre (1926) 'Le Coq et l'Arlequin'

George M. Cohan 1878-1942
American songwriter, dramatist, and producer

9 Over there, over there,
   Send the word, send the word over there
   That the Yanks are coming.
   The drums rum-tumming everywhere.
   'Over There' (1917 song)

10 I'm a Yankee Doodle Dandy,
   A Yankee Doodle, do or die;
   A real live nephew of my Uncle Sam's,
   Born on the fourth of July.
   'Yankee Doodle Boy' (1904 song); see
   Anonymous 12:6

Leonard Cohen 1934-
Canadian singer and writer

11 I don't consider myself a pessimist. I think
   of a pessimist as someone who is waiting for
   it to rain. And I feel soaked to the skin.
   in *Observer* 2 May 1993 'Sayings of the Week'

Desmond Coke 1879-1931
English writer and schoolmaster

12 His blade struck the water a full second
   before any other: the lad had started well.
   Nor did he flag as the race wore on . . . as the
   boats began to near the winning-post, his
   oar was dipping into the water nearly *twice*
   as often as any other.
   *often misquoted as, 'All rowed fast, but none so
   fast as stroke'*
   Sandford of Merton (1903) ch. 12

Edward Coke 1552-1634
English jurist

13 Reason is the life of the law, nay the
   common law itself is nothing else but
   reason.
   The First Part of the Institutes of the Laws of England
   (1628) bk. 2, ch. 6, sect. 138

14 For a man's house is his castle, *et domus sua
   cuique est tutissimum refugium* [and each man's
   home is his safest refuge].
   The Third Part of the Institutes of the Laws of England
   (1628) ch. 73

15 They [corporations] cannot commit treason,
   nor be outlawed, nor excommunicate, for
   they have no souls.
   The Reports of Sir Edward Coke (1658) vol. 5, pt. 10
   'The case of Sutton's Hospital'; see **Thurlow**
   340:8

16 Magna Charta is such a fellow, that he will
   have no sovereign.
   *on the Lords' Amendment to the Petition of Right,
   17 May 1628*
   J. Rushworth Historical Collections (1659) vol. 1

Jean-Baptiste Colbert 1619-83
French statesman

17 The art of taxation consists in so plucking
   the goose as to obtain the largest possible
   amount of feathers with the smallest
   possible amount of hissing.
   attributed

Hartley Coleridge 1796-1849
English poet

18 But what is Freedom? Rightly understood,
   A universal licence to be good.
   'Liberty' (1833)

19 She is not fair to outward view
   As many maidens be;
   Her loveliness I never knew
   Until she smiled on me.
   'She is not fair' (1833)

Samuel Taylor Coleridge
1772–1834
English poet, critic, and philosopher

1 O Lady! we receive but what we give,
And in our life alone does Nature live.
'Dejection: an Ode' (1802) st. 4

2 But oh! each visitation
Suspends what nature gave me at my birth,
My shaping spirit of imagination.
'Dejection: an Ode' (1802) st. 6

3 And the Devil did grin, for his darling sin
Is pride that apes humility.
'The Devil's Thoughts' (1799)

4 What is an Epigram? a dwarfish whole,
Its body brevity, and wit its soul.
'Epigram' (1809)

5 The frost performs its secret ministry,
Unhelped by any wind.
'Frost at Midnight' (1798) l. 1

6 At this moment he was unfortunately called
out by a person on business from Porlock.
'Kubla Khan' (1816) preliminary note

7 In Xanadu did Kubla Khan
A stately pleasure-dome decree:
Where Alph, the sacred river, ran
Through caverns measureless to man
Down to a sunless sea.
So twice five miles of fertile ground
With walls and towers were girdled round.
'Kubla Khan' (1816)

8 A savage place! as holy and enchanted
As e'er beneath a waning moon was
haunted
By woman wailing for her demon-lover!
And from this chasm, with ceaseless turmoil
seething,
As if this earth in fast thick pants were
breathing,
A mighty fountain momently was forced.
'Kubla Khan' (1816)

9 It was a miracle of rare device,
A sunny pleasure-dome with caves of ice.
'Kubla Khan' (1816)

10 And 'mid this tumult Kubla heard from far
Ancestral voices prophesying war!
'Kubla Khan' (1816)

11 A damsel with a dulcimer
In a vision once I saw:
It was an Abyssinian maid,
And on her dulcimer she played,
Singing of Mount Abora.
'Kubla Khan' (1816)

12 And all who heard should see them there,
And all should cry, Beware! Beware!
His flashing eyes, his floating hair!
Weave a circle round him thrice,
And close your eyes with holy dread,
For he on honey-dew hath fed,
And drunk the milk of Paradise.
'Kubla Khan' (1816)

13 All thoughts, all passions, all delights,
Whatever stirs this mortal frame,
All are but ministers of Love,

And feed his sacred flame.
'Love' (1800)

14 It is an ancient Mariner,
And he stoppeth one of three.
'The Rime of the Ancient Mariner' (1798) pt. 1

15 He holds him with his glittering eye—
The Wedding-Guest stood still.
'The Rime of the Ancient Mariner' (1798) pt. 1

16 And ice, mast-high, came floating by,
As green as emerald.
'The Rime of the Ancient Mariner' (1798) pt. 1

17 'Why look'st thou so?'—With my cross-bow
I shot the Albatross.
'The Rime of the Ancient Mariner' (1798) pt. 1

18 We were the first that ever burst
Into that silent sea.
'The Rime of the Ancient Mariner' (1798) pt. 2

19 As idle as a painted ship
Upon a painted ocean.
'The Rime of the Ancient Mariner' (1798) pt. 2

20 Water, water, everywhere,
And all the boards did shrink;
Water, water, everywhere,
Nor any drop to drink.
'The Rime of the Ancient Mariner' (1798) pt. 2

21 The Night-mare LIFE-IN-DEATH was she,
Who thicks man's blood with cold.
'The Rime of the Ancient Mariner' (1798) pt. 3

22 The Sun's rim dips; the stars rush out;
At one stride comes the dark.
'The Rime of the Ancient Mariner' (1798) pt. 3

23 The hornèd Moon, with one bright star
Within the nether tip.
'The Rime of the Ancient Mariner' (1798) pt. 3;
see **Wordsworth** 364:6

24 And a thousand thousand slimy things
Lived on; and so did I.
'The Rime of the Ancient Mariner' (1798) pt. 4

25 Oh Sleep! it is a gentle thing,
Beloved from pole to pole.
'The Rime of the Ancient Mariner' (1798) pt. 5

26 Like one, that on a lonesome road
Doth walk in fear and dread,
And having once turned round walks on,
And turns no more his head;
Because he knows, a frightful fiend
Doth close behind him tread.
'The Rime of the Ancient Mariner' (1798) pt. 6

27 He prayeth well, who loveth well
Both man and bird and beast.
He prayeth best, who loveth best
All things both great and small.
'The Rime of the Ancient Mariner' (1798) pt. 7

28 A sadder and a wiser man,
He rose the morrow morn.
'The Rime of the Ancient Mariner' (1798) pt. 7

29 Well, they are gone, and here must I
remain,
This lime-tree bower my prison!
'This Lime-Tree Bower my Prison' (1800) l. 1

30 He who begins by loving Christianity better
than Truth will proceed by loving his own

sect or church better than Christianity, and end by loving himself better than all.

Aids to Reflection (1825) 'Moral and Religious Aphorisms' no. 25

1 The primary imagination I hold to be the living Power and prime Agent of all human Perception, and as a repetition in the finite mind of the eternal act of creation in the infinite I AM.

Biographia Literaria (1817) ch. 13

2 That willing suspension of disbelief for the moment, which constitutes poetic faith.

Biographia Literaria (1817) ch. 14

3 The dwarf sees farther than the giant, when he has the giant's shoulder to mount on.

The Friend (1818) vol. 2 'On the Principles of Political Knowledge'; see **Bernard** 32:10, **Newton** 250:15

4 To see him act, is like reading Shakespeare by flashes of lightning.

of Edmund Kean

Table Talk (1835) 27 April 1823

5 Prose = words in their best order;—poetry = the *best* words in the best order.

Table Talk (1835) 12 July 1827

6 In politics, what begins in fear usually ends in folly.

Table Talk (1835) 5 October 1830

7 The light which experience gives is a lantern on the stern, which shines only on the waves behind us!

Table Talk (1835) 18 December 1831

William Collingbourne d. 1484
English landowner

8 The Cat, the Rat, and Lovell our dog Rule all England under a hog.

referring to Sir William Catesby (d. 1485), Sir Richard Ratcliffe (d. 1485), Lord Lovell (1454–c.1487), whose crest was a dog, and King Richard III, whose emblem was a wild boar

Robert Fabyan *The Concordance of Chronicles* (ed. H. Ellis, 1811)

Lord Collingwood 1748–1810
English admiral

9 Now, gentlemen, let us do something today which the world may talk of hereafter.

before the Battle of Trafalgar, 21 October 1805

G. L. Newnham Collingwood (ed.) *A Selection from the Correspondence of Lord Collingwood* (1828) vol. 1

R. G. Collingwood 1889–1943
English philosopher and archaeologist

10 Perfect freedom is reserved for the man who lives by his own work and in that work does what he wants to do.

Speculum Mentis (1924); see **Gill** 150:28

Charles Collins
English songwriter

11 Any old iron, any old iron, Any any old old iron? You look neat

Talk about a treat, You look dapper from your napper to your feet.

'Any Old Iron' (1911 song, with E. A. Sheppard and Fred Terry); the second line often sung 'Any any any old iron?'

12 My old man said, 'Follow the van, Don't dilly-dally on the way!'

'Don't Dilly-Dally on the Way' (1919 song, with Fred Leigh); popularized by Marie Lloyd

Michael Collins 1890–1922
Irish revolutionary

13 That volley which we have just heard is the only speech which it is proper to make over the grave of a dead Fenian.

at the funeral of Thomas Ashe, who had died in prison while on hunger strike

Glasnevin cemetery, 30th September 1917

Tim Collins 1960–
British soldier

14 I expect you to rock their world. Wipe them out if that is what they choose. But if you are ferocious in battle remember to be magnanimous in victory.

speech to the men under his command on arrival in Iraq, 20 March 2003

William Collins 1721–59
English poet

15 To fair Fidele's grassy tomb Soft maids and village hinds shall bring Each opening sweet of earliest bloom, And rifle all the breathing spring.

'Dirge' (1744); occasionally included in 18th-century performances of Shakespeare's *Cymbeline*

16 How sleep the brave, who sink to rest, By all their country's wishes blest! 'Ode Written in the Year 1746' (1748)

George Colman, the Elder 1732–94
and David Garrick 1717–79
English dramatists

17 Love and a cottage! Eh, Fanny! Ah, give me indifference and a coach and six!

The Clandestine Marriage (1766) act 1; see **Keats** 196:1

George Colman, the Younger 1762–1836
English dramatist

18 Says he, 'I am a handsome man, but I'm a gay deceiver.'

Love Laughs at Locksmiths (1808) act 2

Charles Caleb Colton c.1780–1832
English clergyman and writer

19 When you have nothing to say, say nothing.

Lacon (1820) vol. 1, no. 183

1 Examinations are formidable even to the best prepared, for the greatest fool may ask more than the wisest man can answer.
Lacon (1820) vol. 1, no. 322

St Colum Cille ?521–597
Irish cleric and missionary

2 To every cow her calf, to every book its copy.
traditionally attributed

Betty Comden 1919–
and Adolph Green 1915–

3 New York, New York,—a helluva town.
'New York, New York' (1945 song)

4 The party's over, it's time to call it a day.
'The Party's Over' (1956)

Confucius (K'ung Fu-tzu) 551–479 BC
Chinese philosopher
textual translations are those of Wing-Tsit Chan, 1963

5 A man who reviews the old so as to find out the new is qualified to teach others.
Analects ch. 2, v. 11

William Congreve 1670–1729
English dramatist

6 Music has charms to sooth a savage breast.
The Mourning Bride (1697) act 1, sc. 1

7 Heaven has no rage, like love to hatred turned,
Nor Hell a fury, like a woman scorned.
The Mourning Bride (1697) act 3, sc. 8

8 Courtship to marriage, as a very witty prologue to a very dull play.
The Old Bachelor (1693) act 5, sc. 10

9 They come together like the Coroner's Inquest, to sit upon the murdered reputations of the week.
The Way of the World (1700) act 1, sc. 1

10 Say what you will, 'tis better to be left than never to have been loved.
The Way of the World (1700) act 2, sc. 1; see **Tennyson** 332:29

11 These articles subscribed, if I continue to endure you a little longer, I may by degrees dwindle into a wife.
The Way of the World (1700) act 4, sc. 5

12 I confess freely to you, I could never look long upon a monkey, without very mortifying reflections.
letter to John Dennis, 10 July 1695

James M. Connell 1852–1929
Irish socialist songwriter

13 The people's flag is deepest red;
It shrouded oft our martyred dead.
'The Red Flag' (1889) in H. E. Piggott *Songs that made History* (1937) ch. 6

14 Then raise the scarlet standard high!
Within its shade we'll live or die.
Tho' cowards flinch and traitors sneer,

We'll keep the red flag flying here.
'The Red Flag' (1889) in H. E. Piggott *Songs that made History* (1937) ch. 6

Billy Connolly 1942–
Scottish comedian

15 Marriage is a wonderful invention; but, then again, so is a bicycle repair kit.
Duncan Campbell *Billy Connolly* (1976)

Cyril Connolly 1903–74
English writer

16 Whom the gods wish to destroy they first call promising.
Enemies of Promise (1938) ch. 13

17 There is no more sombre enemy of good art than the pram in the hall.
Enemies of Promise (1938) ch. 14

18 Imprisoned in every fat man a thin one is wildly signalling to be let out.
The Unquiet Grave (1944) pt. 2; see **Orwell** 254:13

19 Our memories are card-indexes consulted, and then put back in disorder by authorities whom we do not control.
The Unquiet Grave (1944) pt. 3

Joseph Conrad 1857–1924
Polish-born English novelist

20 The conquest of the earth, which mostly means the taking it away from those who have a different complexion or slightly flatter noses than ourselves, is not a pretty thing when you look into it.
Heart of Darkness (1902) ch. 1

21 We live, as we dream—alone.
Heart of Darkness (1902) ch. 1

22 Exterminate all the brutes!
Heart of Darkness (1902) ch. 2

23 The horror! The horror!
Heart of Darkness (1902) ch. 3

24 Mistah Kurtz—he dead.
Heart of Darkness (1902) ch. 3

25 My task which I am trying to achieve is by the power of the written word, to make you hear, to make you feel—it is, before all, to make you *see*. That—and no more, and it is everything.
The Nigger of the Narcissus (1897) preface

26 The terrorist and the policeman both come from the same basket.
The Secret Agent (1907) ch. 4

27 Imagination, not invention, is the supreme master of art, as of life.
Some Reminiscences (1912) ch. 1

28 A belief in a supernatural source of evil is not necessary; men alone are quite capable of every wickedness.
Under Western Eyes (1911) pt. 2, ch. 4

Shirley Conran 1932–
English writer

29 Life is too short to stuff a mushroom.
Superwoman (1975)

John Constable 1776–1837
English painter

1 The sound of water escaping from mill-dams, etc., willows, old rotten planks, slimy posts, and brickwork . . . those scenes made me a painter and I am grateful.
  letter to John Fisher, 23 October 1821

2 A gentleman's park—is my aversion. It is not beauty because it is not nature.
  of Fonthill
  letter to John Fisher, 7 October 1822

3 There is nothing ugly; *I never saw an ugly thing in my life*: for let the form of an object be what it may,—light, shade, and perspective will always make it beautiful.
  C. R. Leslie *Memoirs of the Life of John Constable* (1843) ch. 17

Benjamin Constant 1767–1834
French novelist, political philosopher, and politician

4 Art for art's sake, with no purpose, for any purpose perverts art. But art achieves a purpose which is not its own.
  describing a conversation with Crabb Robinson about the latter's work on **Kant**'s *aesthetics*
  Journal intime 11 February 1804; see **Cousin** 104:17

Constantine the Great c.AD 288–337
Roman emperor from AD 306

5 *In hoc signo vinces.*
  In this sign shalt thou conquer.
  traditional form of Constantine's vision (AD 312)

Constitution of the United States 1787
the first ten amendments are known as the Bill of Rights

6 Representatives and direct taxes shall be apportioned among the several States which may be included within this Union, according to their respective numbers, which shall be determined by adding to the whole number of free persons, including those bound to service for a term of years, and excluding Indians not taxed, three fifths of all other persons.
  article 1, sect. 2 (see also **Rice** 275:16)

7 Congress shall make no law respecting an establishment of religion, or prohibiting the free exercise thereof; or abridging the freedom of speech, or of the press; or the right of the people peaceably to assemble, and to petition the government for a redress of grievances.
  First Amendment (1791)

8 A well-regulated militia, being necessary to the security of a free State, the right of the people to keep and bear arms, shall not be infringed.
  Second Amendment (1791)

9 Excessive bail shall not be required, nor excessive fines imposed, nor cruel and unusual punishment inflicted.
  Eighth Amendment (1791)

A. J. Cook 1885–1931
English labour leader

10 Not a penny off the pay, not a second on the day.
  often quoted with 'minute' substituted for 'second'
  speech at York, 3 April 1926, in *The Times* 5 April 1926

Eliza Cook 1818–89
English poet

11 Better build schoolrooms for 'the boy', Than cells and gibbets for 'the man'.
  'A Song for the Ragged Schools' (1853)

Robin Cook 1946–2005
British Labour politician

12 Our foreign policy must have an ethical dimension and must support the demands of other people for the democratic rights on which we insist for ourselves.
  mission statement by the new Foreign Secretary, 12 May 1997
  in *The Times* 13 May 1997

Calvin Coolidge 1872–1933
American Republican statesman, 30th President of the US 1923–9

13 There is no right to strike against the public safety by anybody, anywhere, any time.
  telegram to Samuel Gompers, 14 September 1919

14 The chief business of the American people is business.
  speech in Washington, 17 January 1925

15 They hired the money, didn't they?
  on war debts incurred by England and others
  John H. McKee *Coolidge: Wit and Wisdom* (1933)

16 Nothing in the world can take the place of persistence. Talent will not; nothing is more common than unsuccessful men with talent. Genius will not; unrewarded genius is almost a proverb. Education will not; the world is full of educated derelicts. Persistence and determination are omnipotent. The slogan 'press on' has solved and always will solve the problems of the human race.
  attributed in the programme of a memorial service for Coolidge in 1933

Duff Cooper 1890–1954
British Conservative politician, diplomat, and writer

17 Your two stout lovers frowning at one another across the hearth rug, while your small, but perfectly formed one kept the party in a roar.
  letter to Lady Diana Manners, later his wife, October 1914

Wendy Cope 1945-
English poet

1 Making cocoa for Kingsley Amis.
  title of poem (1986)

Aaron Copland 1900-90
American composer, pianist, and conductor

2 The whole problem can be stated quite simply by asking, 'Is there a meaning to music?' My answer to that would be, 'Yes.' And 'Can you state in so many words what the meaning is?' My answer to that would be, 'No.'
  What to Listen for in Music (1939)

Richard Corbet 1582-1635
English poet and prelate

3 Farewell, rewards and Fairies,
  Good housewives now may say,
  For now foul sluts in dairies
  Do fare as well as they.
  'The Fairies' Farewell'

Pierre Corneille 1606-84
French dramatist

4 When there is no peril in the fight, there is no glory in the triumph.
  Le Cid (1637) act 2, sc. 2

5 Do your duty, and leave the outcome to the Gods.
  Horace (1640) act 2, sc. 8

6 A first impulse was never a crime.
  Horace (1640) act 5, sc. 3; see **Montrond** 243:10

Bernard Cornfeld 1927-
American businessman

7 Do you sincerely want to be rich?
  stock question to salesmen
  C. Raw et al. *Do You Sincerely Want to be Rich?* (1971)

Frances Cornford 1886-1960
English poet

8 O fat white woman whom nobody loves,
  Why do you walk through the fields in gloves . . .
  Missing so much and so much?
  'To a Fat Lady seen from the Train' (1910)

Francis M. Cornford 1874-1943
English academic

9 Every public action, which is not customary, either is wrong, or, if it is right, is a dangerous precedent. It follows that nothing should ever be done for the first time.
  Microcosmographia Academica (1908) ch. 7

10 That branch of the art of lying which consists in very nearly deceiving your friends without quite deceiving your enemies.
  of propaganda
  Microcosmographia Academica (1922 ed.)

Mme Cornuel 1605-94
French society hostess

11 No man is a hero to his valet.
  Lettres de Mlle Aïssé à Madame C (1787) Letter 13 'De Paris, 1728'

Coronation Service 1689

12 Here is wisdom; this is the royal Law; these are the lively Oracles of God.
  The Presenting of the Holy Bible; L. G. Wickham Legge *English Coronation Records* (1901)

William Cory (born Johnson) 1823-92
English poet and schoolmaster

13 They told me, Heraclitus, they told me you were dead,
  They brought me bitter news to hear and bitter tears to shed.
  I wept as I remembered how often you and I
  Had tired the sun with talking and sent him down the sky.
  'Heraclitus' (1858); see **Callimachus** 82:18

Baron Pierre de Coubertin
1863-1937
French sportsman and educationist

14 The important thing in life is not the victory but the contest; the essential thing is not to have won but to have fought well.
  speech at a government banquet in London, 24 July 1908

Émile Coué 1857-1926
French psychologist

15 Every day, in every way, I am getting better and better.
  to be said 15 to 20 times, morning and evening
  De la suggestion et de ses applications (1915)

Douglas Coupland 1961-
Canadian writer

16 Generation X: tales for an accelerated culture.
  title of book (1991)

Victor Cousin 1792-1867
French philosopher

17 We must have religion for religion's sake, morality for morality's sake, as with art for art's sake . . . the beautiful cannot be the way to what is useful, or to what is good, or to what is holy; it leads only to itself.
  Du Vrai, du beau, et du bien [Sorbonne lecture, 1818] (1853) pt. 2; see **Constant** 103:4

Thomas Coventry 1578-1640
English judge

18 The dominion of the sea, as it is an ancient and undoubted right of the crown of England, so it is the best security of the land . . . The wooden walls are the best walls of this kingdom.
  wooden walls = ships
  speech to the Judges, 17 June 1635; see **Blackstone** 55:13, **Themistocles** 337:6

Noël Coward 1899–1973
English dramatist, actor, and composer

1 Don't let's be beastly to the Germans
When our Victory is ultimately won.
'Don't Let's Be Beastly to the Germans' (1943 song)

2 The most I've had is just
A talent to amuse.
'If Love Were All' (1929 song)

3 Mad about the boy.
title of song (1932)

4 Mad dogs and Englishmen
Go out in the midday sun.
'Mad Dogs and Englishmen' (1931 song)

5 Don't put your daughter on the stage, Mrs Worthington,
Don't put your daughter on the stage.
'Mrs Worthington' (1935 song)

6 Poor little rich girl.
title of song (1925)

7 The Stately Homes of England,
How beautiful they stand,
To prove the upper classes
Have still the upper hand.
'The Stately Homes of England' (1938 song); see **Hemans** 166:1

8 Very flat, Norfolk.
Private Lives (1930) act 1

9 Extraordinary how potent cheap music is.
Private Lives (1930) act 1

10 Certain women should be struck regularly, like gongs.
Private Lives (1930) act 3

11 Just say the lines and don't trip over the furniture.
advice on acting
D. Richards *The Wit of Noël Coward* (1968)

12 Television is for appearing on, not looking at.
D. Richards *The Wit of Noël Coward* (1968)

Abraham Cowley 1618–67
English poet and essayist

13 God the first garden made, and the first city Cain.
Essays, in Verse and Prose (1668) 'The Garden'; see **Cowper** 105:24

14 Life is an incurable disease.
'To Dr Scarborough' (1656) st. 6

William Cowper 1731–1800
English poet

15 We perished, each alone:
But I beneath a rougher sea,
And whelmed in deeper gulfs than he.
'The Castaway' (written 1799) l. 61

16 John Gilpin was a citizen
Of credit and renown,
A train-band captain eke was he
Of famous London town.
'John Gilpin' (1785) l. 1

17 My sister and my sister's child,
Myself and children three,
Will fill the chaise; so you must ride
On horseback after we.
'John Gilpin' (1785) l. 13

18 God moves in a mysterious way
His wonders to perform;
He plants his footsteps in the sea,
And rides upon the storm.
Olney Hymns (1779) 'Light Shining out of Darkness'

19 Behind a frowning providence
He hides a smiling face.
Olney Hymns (1779) 'Light Shining out of Darkness'

20 Oh! for a closer walk with God.
Olney Hymns (1779) 'Walking with God'

21 Toll for the brave—
The brave! that are no more:
All sunk beneath the wave,
Fast by their native shore.
'On the Loss of the Royal George' (written 1782)

22 Remorse, the fatal egg by pleasure laid.
'The Progress of Error' (1782) l. 239

23 Philologists, who chase
A panting syllable through time and space,
Start it at home, and hunt it in the dark,
To Gaul, to Greece, and into Noah's ark.
'Retirement' (1782) l. 691

24 God made the country, and man made the town.
The Task (1785) bk. 1 'The Sofa' l. 749; see **Cowley** 105:13

25 Slaves cannot breathe in England, if their lungs
Receive our air, that moment they are free;
They touch our country, and their shackles fall.
The Task (1785) bk. 2 'The Timepiece' l. 40; see **Anonymous** 10:4

26 England, with all thy faults, I love thee still—
My country!
The Task (1785) bk. 2 'The Timepiece' l. 206; see **Churchill** 94:15

27 Variety's the very spice of life,
That gives it all its flavour.
The Task (1785) bk. 2 'The Timepiece' l. 606; see **Behn** 29:11

28 I was a stricken deer, that left the herd
Long since.
The Task (1785) bk. 3 'The Garden' l. 108; see **Shakespeare** 293:11

29 And, while the bubbling and loud-hissing urn
Throws up a steamy column, and the cups,
That cheer but not inebriate, wait on each,
So let us welcome peaceful evening in.
The Task (1785) bk. 4 'The Winter Evening' l. 34; see **Berkeley** 31:14

30 But war's a game, which, were their subjects wise,

Kings would not play at.
The Task (1785) bk. 5 'The Winter Morning Walk'
l. 187

1 Knowledge dwells
In heads replete with thoughts of other
men;
Wisdom in minds attentive to their own.
The Task (1785) bk. 6 'The Winter Walk at Noon'
l. 89

2 Knowledge is proud that he has learned so
much;
Wisdom is humble that he knows no more.
The Task (1785) bk. 6 'The Winter Walk at Noon'
l. 96

3 I would not enter on my list of friends
(Tho' graced with polished manners and
fine sense,
Yet wanting sensibility) the man
Who needlessly sets foot upon a worm.
The Task (1785) bk. 6 'The Winter Walk at Noon'
l. 560

4 I am monarch of all I survey,
My right there is none to dispute;
From the centre all round to the sea
I am lord of the foul and the brute.
'Verses Supposed to be Written by Alexander
Selkirk' (1782)

George Crabbe 1754–1832
English poet

5 Habit with him was all the test of truth,
'It must be right: I've done it from my
youth.'
The Borough (1810) Letter 3 'The Vicar' l. 138

6 A master passion is the love of news.
'The Newspaper' (1785) l. 279

Maurice James Craig 1919–
Irish poet and architectural historian

7 O the bricks they will bleed and the rain it
will weep
And the damp Lagan fog lull the city to
sleep;
It's to hell with the future and live on the
past:
May the Lord in His mercy be kind to Belfast.
*based on the traditional refrain 'May God in His
mercy look down on Belfast'*
'Ballad to a Traditional Refrain' (1974)

Hart Crane 1899–1932
American poet

8 Stars scribble on our eyes the frosty sagas,
The gleaming cantos of unvanquished
space.
'Cape Hatteras' (1930)

Stephen Crane 1871–1900
American writer

9 The red badge of courage.
title of novel (1895)

Thomas Cranmer 1489–1556
English Anglican prelate and martyr

10 This was the hand that wrote it [his
recantation], therefore it shall suffer first
punishment.
at the stake, Oxford, 21 March 1556
John Richard Green *A Short History of the English
People* (1874) ch. 7, sect. 2

Richard Crashaw c.1612–49
English poet

11 *Nympha pudica Deum vidit, et erubuit.*
The conscious water saw its God, and
blushed.
*literally, 'the chaste nymph saw . . .'; the
translation above is attributed to* **Dryden**, *when a
schoolboy*
Epigrammata Sacra (1634) 'Aquae in vinum
versae [Water changed into wine]'; the
translation is discussed in *Notes and Queries* 4th
series (1869) vol. 4

12 Welcome, all wonders in one sight!
Eternity shut in a span.
'Hymn of the Nativity' (1652)

Julia Crawford c.1800–c.55
Irish poet and composer

13 Kathleen Mavourneen! the grey dawn is
breaking,
The horn of the hunter is heard on the hill.
'Kathleen Mavourneen' in *Metropolitan Magazine*,
London (1835)

Crazy Horse c.1849–77
Sioux chief

14 One does not sell the earth upon which the
people walk.
Dee Brown *Bury My Heart at Wounded Knee* (1970)
ch. 12

Mandell Creighton 1843–1901
English prelate

15 No people do so much harm as those who
go about doing good.
in *The Life and Letters of Mandell Creighton* by his
wife (1904) vol. 2

Michel Guillaume Jean de Crèvecoeur 1735–1813
French-born immigrant to America

16 What then is the American, this new man?
He is either a European, or the descendant
of a European, hence that strange mixture
of blood, which you will find in no other
country . . . Here individuals of all nations
are melted into a new race of men, whose
labours and posterity will one day cause
great changes in the world.
Letters from an American Farmer (1782)

Francis Crick 1916–2004
English biophysicist

17 We have discovered the secret of life!
on the discovery of the structure of DNA, 1953
James D. Watson *The Double Helix* (1968)

1 'You' your joys and your sorrows, your memories and ambitions, your sense of personal identity and free will, are in fact no more than the behaviour of a vast assembly of nerve cells and their associated molecules.
The Astonishing Hypothesis: The Scientific Search for the Soul (1994) ch. 1

Francis Crick 1916–2004
and James D. Watson 1928–
English biophysicist; American biologist

2 It has not escaped our notice that the specific pairing we have postulated immediately suggests a possible copying mechanism for the genetic material.
proposing the double helix as the structure of DNA, and hence the chemical mechanism of heredity
in *Nature* 25 April 1953

Quentin Crisp 1908–99
English writer

3 There was no need to do any housework at all. After the first four years the dirt doesn't get any worse.
The Naked Civil Servant (1968) ch. 15

4 An autobiography is an obituary in serial form with the last instalment missing.
The Naked Civil Servant (1968) ch. 29

Julian Critchley 1930–2000
British Conservative politician and journalist

5 The only safe pleasure for a parliamentarian is a bag of boiled sweets.
in *Listener* 10 June 1982

Oliver Cromwell 1599–1658
English soldier and statesman; Lord Protector from 1653

6 A few honest men are better than numbers.
letter to William Spring, September 1643, in Thomas Carlyle *Oliver Cromwell's Letters and Speeches* (2nd ed., 1846)

7 I would rather have a plain russet-coated captain that knows what he fights for, and loves what he knows, than that which you call 'a gentleman' and is nothing else.
letter to William Spring, September 1643

8 Cruel necessity.
on the execution of Charles I
Joseph Spence *Anecdotes* (1820)

9 I beseech you, in the bowels of Christ, think it possible you may be mistaken.
letter to the General Assembly of the Kirk of Scotland, 3 August 1650

10 The dimensions of this mercy are above my thoughts. It is, for aught I know, a crowning mercy.
letter to William Lenthall, Speaker of the Parliament of England, 4 September 1651

11 You have sat too long here for any good you have been doing. Depart, I say, and let us have done with you. In the name of God, go!
addressing the Rump Parliament, 20 April 1653; oral tradition; see **Amery** 6:3

12 Take away that fool's bauble, the mace.
often quoted as, 'Take away these baubles'
at the dismissal of the Rump Parliament, 20 April 1653

13 Necessity hath no law.
speech to Parliament, 12 September 1654, in Thomas Carlyle *Oliver Cromwell's Letters and Speeches* (1845)

14 Your poor army, those poor contemptible men, came up hither.
speech to Parliament, 21 April 1657; see **Anonymous** 8:4

15 Hell or Connaught.
summary of the choice offered to the Catholic population of Ireland, transported to the western counties to make room for settlers
traditionally attributed

16 Mr Lely, I desire you would use all your skill to paint my picture truly like me, and not flatter me at all; but remark all these roughnesses, pimples, warts, and everything as you see me; otherwise I will never pay a farthing for it.
often summarized as, 'Warts and all'
Horace Walpole *Anecdotes of Painting in England* vol. 3 (1763) ch. 1

17 My design is to make what haste I can to be gone.
last words; John Morley *Oliver Cromwell* (1900) bk. 5, ch. 10

Bing Crosby 1903–77
American singer and film actor

18 Where the blue of the night meets the gold of the day.
title of song (1931), with Roy Turk and Fred Ahlert

Douglas Cross
American songwriter

19 I left my heart in San Francisco
High on a hill it calls to me.
To be where little cable cars climb half-way to the stars,
The morning fog may chill the air—
I don't care!
'I Left My Heart in San Francisco' (1954 song)

Richard Assheton, Lord Cross 1823–1914
British Conservative politician

20 I hear a smile.
when the House of Lords laughed at his speech in favour of Spiritual Peers
G. W. E. Russell *Collections and Recollections* (1898) ch. 29

Samuel Crossman 1624–83
English clergyman

21 My song is love unknown,

My saviour's love for me,
Love to the loveless shown,
That they might lovely be.
O, who am I,
That for my sake
My Lord should take
Frail flesh and die?

> 'My song is love unknown' (1664); set to music
> as a hymn from 1868, and by John Ireland in
> 1919

Crowfoot c.1830–90
Blackfoot chief

1 A little while and I will be gone from among
you, whither I cannot tell. From nowhere
we came, into nowhere we go. What is life?
It is a flash of a firefly in the night. It is a
breath of a buffalo in the winter time. It is
as the little shadow that runs across the
grass and loses itself in the sunset.

> attributed farewell to his people, 25 April 1890;
> see **Haggard** 159:2

Aleister Crowley 1875–1947
English diabolist

2 Do what thou wilt shall be the whole of the
Law.

> *Book of the Law* (1909) l. 40; see **Rabelais** 272:12

Richard Cumberland 1631–1718
English divine

3 It is better to wear out than to rust out.

> George Horne *The Duty of Contending for the Faith*
> (1786)

e. e. cummings (Edward Estlin
Cummings) 1894–1962
American poet

4 anyone lived in a pretty how town
(with up so floating many bells down)
spring summer autumn winter
he sang his didn't he danced his did.

> *50 Poems* (1949) no. 29

5 'next to of course god america i
love you land of the pilgrims' and so forth.

> *is 5* (1926) p. 62

6 a politician is an arse upon
which everyone has sat except a man.

> *1 x 1* (1944) no. 10

7 plato told

him: he couldn't
believe it (jesus

told him; he
wouldn't believe

it) lao

tsze
certainly told

him, and general
(yes

mam)
sherman.

> *1 x 1* (1944) no. 13

8 pity this busy monster, manunkind,
not. Progress is a comfortable disease.

> *1 x 1* (1944) no. 14

9 listen: there's a hell
of a good universe next door; let's go.

> *1 x 1* (1944) no. 14

10 i like my body when it is with your
body. It is so quite new a thing.
Muscles better and nerves more.

> 'Sonnets–Actualities' no. 8 (1925)

11 the Cambridge ladies who live in furnished
souls
are unbeautiful and have comfortable
minds.

> 'Sonnets–Realities' no. 1 (1923)

William Thomas Cummings
1903–45
American priest

12 There are no atheists in the foxholes.

> Carlos P. Romulo *I Saw the Fall of the Philippines*
> (1943) ch. 15

Allan Cunningham 1784–1842
Scottish poet

13 A wet sheet and a flowing sea,
A wind that follows fast
And fills the white and rustling sail
And bends the gallant mast.

> 'A Wet Sheet and a Flowing Sea' (1825)

Mario Cuomo 1932–
American Democratic politician

14 You campaign in poetry. You govern in
prose.

> in *New Republic*, Washington, DC, 8 April 1985

Marie Curie 1867–1934
Polish-born French physicist

15 In science, we must be interested in things,
not in persons.

> *to an American journalist, c.1904, after she and
> her husband Pierre had shared the Nobel Prize for
> Physics with A.-H. Becquerel*
> Eve Curie *Madame Curie* (1937)

John Philpot Curran 1750–1817
Irish judge

16 The condition upon which God hath given
liberty to man is eternal vigilance.

> speech on the right of election of the Lord
> Mayor of Dublin, 10 July 1790

17 Like the silver plate on a coffin.

> *describing Robert **Peel**'s smile*
> quoted by Daniel O'Connell, House of
> Commons, 26 February 1835

John Curtin 1885–1945
Australian Labor statesman

18 Australia looks to America, free of any pangs
as to our traditional links or kinship with
the United Kingdom.

> *of the threat from Japan, and British reluctance to
> recall Australian troops from the Middle East*
> in *Herald* (Melbourne) 27 December 1941

Michael Curtiz 1888–1962
Hungarian-born American film director

1 Bring on the empty horses!
while directing The Charge of the Light
Brigade *(1936 film)*
   David Niven *Bring on the Empty Horses* (1975)
   ch. 6

St Cyprian *c.*AD 200–258
Roman writer and martyr; Bishop of Carthage

2 He cannot have God for his father who has
not the church for his mother.
   De Ecclesiae Catholicae Unitate sect. 6; see
   Augustine 20:6

3 *Fratres nostros non esse lugendos arcessitione
dominica de saeculo liberatos, cum sciamus non
amitti sed praemitti.*
   Our brethren who have been freed from the
world by the summons of the Lord should
not be mourned, since we know that they
are not lost but sent before.
   De Mortalite ch. 20 (ed. M. L. Hannam, 1933); see
   Norton 252:5, **Rogers** 278:12

4 There cannot be salvation for any, except in
the Church.
   Epistle Ad Pomponium, De Virginibus sect. 4; see
   Augustine 20:6, **Cyprian** 109:2

Samuel Daniel 1563–1619
English poet and dramatist

5 Care-charmer Sleep, son of the sable Night,
Brother to Death, in silent darkness born.
   Delia (1592) Sonnet 54; see **Fletcher** 138:13,
   Shelley 314:17

6 Princes in this case
Do hate the traitor, though they love the
treason.
   The Tragedy of Cleopatra (1594) act 4, sc. 1; see
   Dryden 282:2

Dante Alighieri 1265–1321
Italian poet

7 *Nel mezzo del cammin di nostra vita.*
Midway along the path of our life.
   Divina Commedia 'Inferno' canto 1, l. 1

8 LASCIATE OGNI SPERANZA VOI CH'ENTRATE!
Abandon all hope, you who enter!
inscription at the entrance to Hell
   Divina Commedia 'Inferno' canto 3, l. 1

9 *Non ragioniam di lor, ma guarda, e passa.*
Let us not speak of them, but look, and pass
on.
   Divina Commedia 'Inferno' canto 3, l. 51

10 *Il gran rifiuto.*
The great refusal.
   Divina Commedia 'Inferno' canto 3, l. 60

11 *Il maestro di color che sanno.*
The master of those who know.
of **Aristotle**
   Divina Commedia 'Inferno' canto 4, l. 131

12 . . . *Nessun maggior dolore,
Che ricordarsi del tempo felice
Nella miseria.*

There is no greater pain than to remember a
happy time when one is in misery.
   Divina Commedia 'Inferno' canto 5, l. 121; see
   Boethius 58:15

13 *Considerate la vostra semenza:
Fatti non foste a viver come bruti,
Ma per seguir virtute e conoscenza.*
Consider your origins: you were not made to
live as brutes, but to follow virtue and
knowledge.
   Divina Commedia 'Inferno' canto 26, l. 118

14 *Men che dramma
Di sangue m'è rimaso, che no tremi;
Conosco i segni dell' antica fiamma.*
Less than a drop of blood remains in me that
does not tremble; I recognize the signals of
the ancient flame.
   Divina Commedia 'Purgatorio' canto 30, l. 46; see
   Virgil 347:7

15 *E'n la sua volontade è nostra pace.*
In His will is our peace.
   Divina Commedia 'Paradiso' canto 3, l. 85

16 *Tu proverai sì come sa di sale
Lo pane altrui, e com'è duro calle
Lo scendere e'l salir per l'altrui scale.*
You shall find out how salt is the taste of
another man's bread, and how hard is the
way up and down another man's stairs.
   Divina Commedia 'Paradiso' canto 17, l. 58

17 *L'amor che muove il sole e l'altre stelle.*
The love that moves the sun and the other
stars.
   Divina Commedia 'Paradiso' canto 33, l. 145

Georges Jacques Danton 1759–94
French revolutionary

18 *De l'audace, et encore de l'audace, et toujours de
l'audace!*
Boldness, and again boldness, and always
boldness!
   speech to the Legislative Committee of General
   Defence, 2 September 1792

19 Thou wilt show my head to the people: it is
worth showing.
to his executioner, 5 April 1794
   Thomas Carlyle *History of the French Revolution*
   (1837) vol. 3, bk. 6, ch. 2

Joe Darion 1917–2001
American songwriter

20 Dream the impossible dream.
   'The Impossible Dream' (1965 song)

Bill Darnell
Canadian environmentalist

21 Make it a *green* peace.
*at a meeting of the Don't Make a Wave
Committee, which preceded the formation of
Greenpeace*
   in Vancouver, 1970; Robert Hunter *The
   Greenpeace Chronicle* (1979)

Clarence Darrow 1857-1938
American lawyer

1 I do not pretend to know where many ignorant men are sure—that is all that agnosticism means.

speech at the trial of John Thomas Scopes for teaching Darwin's theory of evolution in school, 15 July 1925

2 When I was a boy I was told that anybody could become President. I'm beginning to believe it.

Irving Stone *Clarence Darrow for the Defence* (1941)

Charles Darwin 1809-82
English natural historian

3 The highest possible stage in moral culture is when we recognize that we ought to control our thoughts.

The Descent of Man (1871) ch. 4

4 False views, if supported by some evidence, do little harm, for everyone takes a salutary pleasure in proving their falseness.

The Descent of Man (1871) ch. 21

5 A hairy quadruped, furnished with a tail and pointed ears, probably arboreal in its habits.
on man's probable ancestors

The Descent of Man (1871) ch. 21

6 I have called this principle, by which each slight variation, if useful, is preserved, by the term of Natural Selection.

On the Origin of Species (1859) ch. 3

7 We will now discuss in a little more detail the Struggle for Existence.

On the Origin of Species (1859) ch. 3

8 The expression often used by Mr Herbert Spencer of the Survival of the Fittest is more accurate [than 'Struggle for Existence'], and is sometimes equally convenient.

On the Origin of Species (1869 ed.) ch. 3; see **Spencer** 321:9

9 From the war of nature, from famine and death, the most exalted object which we are capable of conceiving, namely, the production of the higher animals, directly follows.

On the Origin of Species (1859) ch. 3

10 There is grandeur in this view of life.

On the Origin of Species (1859) ch. 14

11 What a book a devil's chaplain might write on the clumsy, wasteful, blundering, low, and horridly cruel works of nature!

letter to J. D. Hooker, 13 July 1856, in *Correspondence of Charles Darwin* vol. 6 (1990)

12 Animals, whom we have made our slaves, we do not like to consider our equal.

Notebook B (1837-8) in P. H. Barrett et al. (eds.) *Charles Darwin's Notebooks 1836-1844* (1987)

13 With me the horrid doubt always arises whether the convictions of man's mind which has been developed from the mind of the lower animals, are of any value or at all trustworthy.

Francis Darwin (ed.) *The Life and Letters of Charles Darwin* (1887) ch. 3

Erasmus Darwin 1731-1802
English physician

14 A fool . . . is a man who never tried an experiment in his life.

F. V. Barry (ed.) *Maria Edgeworth: Chosen Letters* (1931) To Sophy Ruxton, 9 March 1792

Francis Darwin 1848-1925
English botanist

15 In science the credit goes to the man who convinces the world, not to the man to whom the idea first occurs.

in *Eugenics Review* April 1914 'Francis Galton'

William D'Avenant 1606-68
English dramatist and poet

16 The lark now leaves his wat'ry nest
And, climbing, shakes his dewy wings.

'Song: The Lark' (1638)

Elizabeth David 1913-92
British cook and writer

17 The cooking of the Mediterranean shores, endowed with all the natural resources, the colour and flavour of the South, is a blend of tradition and brilliant improvisation. The Latin genius flashes from the kitchen pans.

Mediterranean Food (1950) introduction

John Davidson 1857-1909
Scottish poet

18 A runnable stag, a kingly crop.

'A Runnable Stag' (1906)

19 The race is to the swift,
The battle to the strong.

'War Song' (1899) st. 1; see **Bible** 39:21

John Davies 1569-1626
English poet

20 This wondrous miracle did Love devise,
For dancing is love's proper exercise.

'Orchestra, or a Poem of Dancing' (1596) st. 18

Robertson Davies 1913-95
Canadian novelist

21 I see Canada as a country torn between a very northern, rather extraordinary, mystical spirit which it fears and its desire to present itself to the world as a Scotch banker.

The Enthusiasms of Robertson Davies (1990)

Ron Davies 1946-
British Labour politician

22 It was a moment of madness for which I have subsequently paid a very, very heavy price.
of the episode on Clapham Common leading to his resignation as Welsh Secretary

interview with BBC Wales and HTV, 30 October 1998

Scrope Davies c.1783–1852
English conversationalist

1 Babylon in all its desolation is a sight not so
  awful as that of the human mind in ruins.
  ***Addison**, in* The Spectator *no. 421 (3 July 1712),
  also remarked of 'a distracted person' that
  'Babylon in ruins is not so melancholy a spectacle'*
  letter to Thomas Raikes, May 1835, in *A Portion
  of the Journal kept by Thomas Raikes* (1856) vol. 2

W. H. Davies 1871–1940
Welsh poet

2 What is this life if, full of care,
  We have no time to stand and stare.
  'Leisure' (1911)

Sammy Davis Jnr. 1925–90
American entertainer

3 Being a star has made it possible for me to
  get insulted in places where the average
  Negro could never *hope* to go and get
  insulted.
  Yes I Can (1965) pt. 3, ch. 23

Thomas Davis 1814–45
Irish poet and nationalist

4 And then I prayed I yet might see
  Our fetters rent in twain,
  And Ireland, long a province, be
  A Nation once again.
  'A Nation Once Again' (1846)

5 But—hark!—some voice like thunder spake:
  The West's awake! the West's awake!
  'The West's Asleep' (1846)

Richard Dawkins
English biologist

6 [Natural selection] has no vision, no
  foresight, no sight at all. If it can be said to
  play the role of watchmaker in nature, it is
  the *blind* watchmaker.
  The Blind Watchmaker (1986) ch. 1; see **Paley**
  258:1

7 However many ways there may be of being
  alive, it is certain that there are vastly more
  ways of being dead.
  The Blind Watchmaker (1986) ch. 1

8 The essence of life is statistical
  improbability on a colossal scale.
  The Blind Watchmaker (1986) ch. 11

9 They go by the name of genes, and we are
  their survival machines.
  The Selfish Gene (1976) ch. 2

Christopher Dawson 1889–1970
English historian

10 As soon as men decide that all means are
   permitted to fight an evil, then their good
   becomes indistinguishable from the evil
   that they set out to destroy.
   The Judgement of the Nations (1942)

C. Day-Lewis 1904–72
English poet and critic

11 It is the logic of our times,

No subject for immortal verse—
That we who lived by honest dreams
Defend the bad against the worse.
'Where are the War Poets?' (1943)

John Dean 1938–
American lawyer

12 We have a cancer within, close to the
   Presidency, that is growing.
   [Nixon] Transcripts, 21 March 1973

Simone de Beauvoir 1908–86
French novelist and feminist

13 One is not born a woman: one becomes one.
   The Second Sex (1949) vol. 2, pt. 1, ch. 1

Eugene Victor Debs 1855–1926
American socialist

14 When great changes occur in history, when
   great principles are involved, as a rule the
   majority are wrong. The minority are right.
   speech at his trial for sedition in Cleveland,
   Ohio, 11 September 1918; in *Speeches* (1928); see
   Dillon 116:16

15 While there is a lower class, I am in it; while
   there is a criminal element, I am of it; while
   there is a soul in prison, I am not free.
   at his trial for sedition, 14 September 1918

Stephen Decatur 1779–1820
American naval officer

16 Our country! In her intercourse with foreign
   nations, may she always be in the right; but
   our country, right or wrong.
   Decatur's toast at Norfolk, Virginia, April 1816;
   see **Adams** 2:13, **Schurz** 286:18

Daniel Defoe 1660–1731
English novelist and journalist

17 Things as certain as death and taxes, can be
   more firmly believed.
   History of the Devil (1726) bk. 2, ch. 6; see
   Franklin 142:3

18 He told me . . . that mine was the middle
   state, or what might be called the upper
   station of low life, which he had found by
   long experience was the best state in the
   world, the most suited to human happiness.
   Robinson Crusoe (1719)

19 My man Friday.
   Robinson Crusoe (1719)

20 Nature has left this tincture in the blood,
   That all men would be tyrants if they could.
   The History of the Kentish Petition (1712–13)
   addenda, l. 11

21 From this amphibious ill-born mob began
   That vain, ill-natured thing, an Englishman.
   The True Born Englishman (1701) pt.1, l. 132

22 Your Roman-Saxon-Danish-Norman English.
   The True-Born Englishman (1701) pt. 1, l. 139

23 Titles are shadows, crowns are empty
   things,
   The good of subjects is the end of kings.
   The True-Born Englishman (1701) pt. 2, l. 313

Edgar Degas 1834–1917
French artist

1 Art is vice. You don't marry it legitimately, you rape it.
  Paul Lafond *Degas* (1918)

Charles de Gaulle 1890–1970
French soldier and statesman, President of France 1959–69

2 France has lost a battle. But France has not lost the war!
  proclamation, 18 June 1940

3 *Je vous ai compris.*
  I have understood you.
  speech to French colonists at Algiers, 4 June 1958, in *Discours et Messages* vol. 3 (1970); by 1962 Algeria had achieved independence

4 Politics are too serious a matter to be left to the politicians.
  replying to **Attlee**'s *remark that* '*De Gaulle is a very good soldier and a very bad politician*'
  Clement Attlee *A Prime Minister Remembers* (1961) ch. 4; see **Clemenceau** 98:2

5 *Europe des patries.*
  A Europe of nations.
  widely associated with De Gaulle, c.1962, and taken as encapsulating his views, although perhaps not coined by him
  J. Lacouture *De Gaulle: the Ruler* (1991)

6 How can you govern a country which has 246 varieties of cheese?
  Ernest Mignon *Les Mots du Général* (1962)

7 Since a politician never believes what he says, he is quite surprised to be taken at his word.
  Ernest Mignon *Les Mots du Général* (1962)

8 Treaties, you see, are like girls and roses: they last while they last.
  speech at Elysée Palace, 2 July 1963, in André Passeron *De Gaulle parle 1962–6* (1966)

9 *Vive Le Québec Libre.*
  Long Live Free Quebec.
  speech in Montreal, 24 July 1967, in *Discours et messages* (1970)

Thomas Dekker 1570–1641
English dramatist

10 Golden slumbers kiss your eyes,
  Smiles awake you when you rise.
  Patient Grissil (1603) act 4, sc. 2

Walter de la Mare 1873–1956
English poet and novelist

11 Ann, Ann!
  Come! quick as you can!
  There's a fish that *talks*
  In the frying-pan.
  'Alas, Alack' (1913)

12 Oh, no man knows
  Through what wild centuries
  Roves back the rose.
  'All That's Past' (1912)

13 Look thy last on all things lovely.
  'Fare Well' (1918)

14 'Is there anybody there?' said the Traveller,
  Knocking on the moonlit door.
  'The Listeners' (1912)

15 'Tell them I came, and no one answered,
  That I kept my word,' he said.
  'The Listeners' (1912)

16 What is the world, O soldiers?
  It is I:
  I, this incessant snow,
  This northern sky;
  Soldiers, this solitude
  Through which we go
  Is I.
  'Napoleon' (1906)

17 Slowly, silently, now the moon
  Walks the night in her silver shoon.
  'Silver' (1913)

Agnes de Mille 1908–93
American dancer and choreographer

18 The truest expression of a people is in its dances and its music. Bodies never lie.
  in *New York Times Magazine* 11 May 1975

Democritus *c.*460–*c.*370 BC
Greek philosopher

19 By convention there is colour, by convention sweetness, by convention bitterness, but in reality there are atoms and space.
  fragment 125

Demosthenes *c.*384–*c.*322 BC
Greek orator and Athenian statesman

20 There is one safeguard known generally to the wise, which is an advantage and security to all, but especially to democracies against despots—suspicion.
  Philippic

21 When asked what was first in oratory, [he] replied to his questioner, 'action,' what second, 'action,' and again third, 'action'.
  Cicero *Brutus* ch. 37, sect. 142

Jack Dempsey 1895–1983
American boxer

22 Honey, I just forgot to duck.
  to his wife, on losing the World Heavyweight title, 23 September 1926; after a failed attempt on his life in 1981, Ronald **Reagan** *quipped 'I forgot to duck'*
  J. and B. P. Dempsey *Dempsey* (1977)

Deng Xiaoping 1904–97
Chinese Communist statesman

23 It doesn't matter if a cat is black or white, as long as it catches mice.
  in the early 1960s; in *Daily Telegraph* 20 February 1997, obituary

Lord Denman 1779–1854
English politician and lawyer

1 Trial by jury itself, instead of being a
security to persons who are accused, will be
a delusion, a mockery, and a snare.
*on a case involving the fraudulent omission of
sixty names from the list of jurors in Dublin*
speech in the House of Lords, 4 September 1844

Lord Denning 1899–1999
British judge

2 To every subject of this land, however
powerful, I would use Thomas Fuller's
words over three hundred years ago, 'Be ye
never so high, the law is above you.'
in a High Court ruling against the Attorney-
General, January 1977

3 The keystone of the rule of law in England
has been the independence of judges. It is
the only respect in which we make any real
separation of powers.
The Family Story (1981)

John Dennis 1657–1734
English critic, poet, and dramatist

4 A man who could make so vile a pun would
not scruple to pick a pocket.
in *The Gentleman's Magazine* (1781) editorial note

5 Damn them! They will not let my play run,
but they steal my thunder!
*on hearing his new thunder effects used at a
performance of* Macbeth, *following the
withdrawal of one of his own plays after only a
short run*
William S. Walsh *A Handy-Book of Literary
Curiosities* (1893)

Thomas De Quincey 1785–1859
English essayist and critic

6 A duller spectacle this earth of ours has not
to show than a rainy Sunday in London.
Confessions of an English Opium Eater (1822, ed.
1856) pt. 2

7 Thou hast the keys of Paradise, oh just,
subtle, and mighty opium!
Confessions of an English Opium Eater (1822, ed.
1856) pt. 2

8 Murder considered as one of the fine arts.
title of essay in *Blackwood's Magazine* February
1827

9 If once a man indulges himself in murder,
very soon he comes to think little of
robbing; and from robbing he comes next to
drinking and sabbath-breaking, and from
that to incivility and procrastination.
'On Murder Considered as One of the Fine Arts'
(Supplementary Paper) in *Blackwood's Magazine*
November 1839

10 There is first the literature of *knowledge*, and
secondly, the literature of *power*.
review of the *Works of Pope* (1847 ed.) in *North
British Review* August 1848, vol. 9

Edward Stanley, 14th Earl of Derby 1799–1869
*British Conservative statesman, Prime Minister
1852, 1858–9, 1866–8*

11 The duty of an Opposition [is] very simple
... to oppose everything, and propose
nothing.
quoting 'Mr Tierney, a great Whig authority'
in the House of Commons, 4 June 1841

Jacques Derrida 1930–2004
Algerian-born French philosopher and critic

12 *Il n'y a pas de hors-texte.*
There is nothing outside of the text.
Of Grammatology (1967)

René Descartes 1596–1650
French philosopher and mathematician

13 Common sense is the best distributed
commodity in the world, for every man is
convinced that he is well supplied with it.
Le Discours de la méthode (1637) pt. 1

14 For it is not enough to have a good mind;
the main thing is to use it well.
Le Discours de la méthode (1637) pt. 1

15 *Je pense, donc je suis.*
I think, therefore I am.
*usually quoted as, 'Cogito, ergo sum', from the
1641 Latin edition*
Le Discours de la méthode (1637) pt. 4

16 It is contrary to reason to say that there is a
vacuum or space in which there is
absolutely nothing.
Principia Philosophiae (1644) pt. 2, sect. 16 (tr. E. S.
Haldane and G. R. T. Ross)

Philippe Néricault Destouches 1680–1754
French dramatist

17 The absent are always in the wrong.
L'Obstacle imprévu (1717) act 1, sc. 6

Buddy De Sylva 1895–1950 and Lew Brown 1893–1958

18 The moon belongs to everyone,
The best things in life are free.
'The Best Things in Life are Free' (1927 song)

Eamonn de Valera 1882–1975
American-born Irish statesman

19 That Ireland which we dreamed of would be
the home of a people who valued material
wealth only as a basis of right living, of a
people who were satisfied with frugal
comfort and devoted their leisure to the
things of the spirit; a land whose
countryside would be bright with cosy
homesteads, whose fields and villages would
be joyous with sounds of industry, the
romping of sturdy children, the contests of
athletic youths, the laughter of comely
maidens; whose firesides would be the
forums of the wisdom of serene old age.
St Patrick's Day broadcast, 17 March 1943

Robert Devereux, Earl of Essex
see **Essex**

Peter De Vries 1910–93
American novelist and humorist

1 Gluttony is an emotional escape, a sign
something is eating us.
   Comfort Me With Apples (1956)

2 It is the final proof of God's omnipotence
that he need not exist in order to save us.
   The Mackerel Plaza (1958) ch. 1

3 The value of marriage is not that adults
produce children but that children produce
adults.
   The Tunnel of Love (1954) ch. 8

James Dewar 1842–1923
Scottish physicist

4 Minds are like parachutes. They only
function when they are open.
   attributed

Lord Dewar 1864–1930
British industrialist

5 [There are] only two classes of pedestrians in
these days of reckless motor traffic—the
quick, and the dead.
   George Robey *Looking Back on Life* (1933) ch. 28

George Dewey 1837–1917
American naval officer

6 You may fire when you are ready, Gridley.
   to the captain of his flagship at Manila, 1 May
   1898, in *Autobiography* (1913) ch. 15

Sergei Diaghilev 1872–1929
Russian ballet impresario

7 *Étonne-moi.*
Astonish me.
   to Jean **Cocteau**
   Wallace Fowlie (ed.) *Journals of Jean Cocteau*
   (1956) ch. 1

Diana, Princess of Wales 1961–97
British princess

8 I'd like to be a queen in people's hearts but I
don't see myself being Queen of this
country.
   interview on *Panorama*, BBC1 TV, 20 November
   1995

9 There were three of us in this marriage, so it
was a bit crowded.
   interview on *Panorama*, BBC1 TV, 20 November
   1995

Porfirio Diaz 1830–1915
*Mexican revolutionary and statesman; President
of Mexico, 1877–80, 1884–1911*

10 Poor Mexico, so far from God and so close to
the United States.
   attributed

Thomas Dibdin 1771–1841
English songwriter

11 Oh! what a snug little Island,

A right little, tight little Island!
   'The Snug Little Island' (1833)

Charles Dickens 1812–70
English novelist

12 Jarndyce and Jarndyce still drags its dreary
length before the Court, perennially
hopeless.
   Bleak House (1853) ch. 1

13 The one great principle of the English law
is, to make business for itself.
   Bleak House (1853) ch. 39

14 'Bah,' said Scrooge. 'Humbug!'
   A Christmas Carol (1843) stave 1

15 I am the Ghost of Christmas Past.
   A Christmas Carol (1843) stave 2

16 'God bless us every one!' said Tiny Tim.
   A Christmas Carol (1843) stave 3

17 I am a lone lorn creetur . . . and everythink
goes contrairy with me.
   Mrs Gummidge
   David Copperfield (1850) ch. 3

18 Barkis is willin'.
   David Copperfield (1850) ch. 5

19 Annual income twenty pounds, annual
expenditure nineteen six, result
happiness. Annual income twenty pounds,
annual expenditure twenty pounds ought
and six, result misery.
   Mr Micawber
   David Copperfield (1850) ch. 12

20 We are so very 'umble.
   Uriah Heep
   David Copperfield (1850) ch. 17

21 I only ask for information.
   Miss Rosa Dartle
   David Copperfield (1850) ch. 20

22 It was as true . . . as taxes is. And nothing's
truer than them.
   Mr Barkis
   David Copperfield (1850) ch. 21

23 Accidents will occur in the best-regulated
families.
   David Copperfield (1850) ch. 28 (Mr Micawber)

24 When found, make a note of.
   Captain Cuttle
   Dombey and Son (1848) ch. 15

25 What the waves were always saying.
   Dombey and Son (1848) title of ch. 16

26 'He calls the knaves, Jacks, this boy,' said
Estella with disdain, before our first game
was out.
   Great Expectations (1861) ch. 8

27 What larks.
   message from Joe Gargery to Pip
   Great Expectations (1861) ch. 27

28 In the little world in which children have
their existence, whosoever brings them up,
there is nothing so finely perceived and so
finely felt, as injustice.
   Great Expectations (1861) ch. 8

1 It is a most miserable thing to feel ashamed of home.
Great Expectations (1861) ch. 14

2 Now, what I want is, Facts . . . Facts alone are wanted in life.
Mr Gradgrind
Hard Times (1854) bk. 1, ch. 1

3 Whatever was required to be done, the Circumlocution Office was beforehand with all the public departments in the art of perceiving—HOW NOT TO DO IT.
Little Dorrit (1857) bk. 1, ch. 10

4 There's milestones on the Dover Road!
Mr F.'s Aunt
Little Dorrit (1857) bk. 1, ch. 23

5 The word Papa, besides, gives a pretty form to the lips. Papa, potatoes, poultry, prunes, and prism, are all very good words for the lips: especially prunes and prism.
Mrs General
Little Dorrit (1857) bk. 2, ch. 5

6 Affection beaming in one eye, and calculation shining out of the other.
Mrs Todgers
Martin Chuzzlewit (1844) ch. 8

7 Here's the rule for bargains: 'Do other men, for they would do you.'
Jonas Chuzzlewit
Martin Chuzzlewit (1844) ch. 11

8 He'd make a lovely corpse.
Mrs Gamp
Martin Chuzzlewit (1844) ch. 25

9 He had but one eye, and the popular prejudice runs in favour of two.
Mr Squeers
Nicholas Nickleby (1839) ch. 4

10 Subdue your appetites my dears, and you've conquered human natur.
Mr Squeers
Nicholas Nickleby (1839) ch. 5

11 Language was not powerful enough to describe the infant phenomenon.
Nicholas Nickleby (1839) ch. 23

12 All is gas and gaiters.
The Gentleman in the Small-clothes
Nicholas Nickleby (1839) ch. 49

13 Please, sir, I want some more.
Oliver
Oliver Twist (1838) ch. 2

14 Known by the *sobriquet* of 'The artful Dodger'.
Oliver Twist (1838) ch. 8

15 There is a passion for hunting something deeply implanted in the human breast.
Oliver Twist (1838) ch. 10

16 'If the law supposes that,' said Mr Bumble . . . 'the law is a ass—a idiot.'
Bumble
Oliver Twist (1838) ch. 51; see **Chapman** 90:19

17 He had used the word in its Pickwickian sense . . . He had merely considered him a humbug in a Pickwickian point of view.
Mr Blotton
Pickwick Papers (1837) ch. 1

18 Kent, sir—everybody knows Kent—apples, cherries, hops, and women.
Jingle
Pickwick Papers (1837) ch. 2

19 I wants to make your flesh creep.
The Fat Boy
Pickwick Papers (1837) ch. 8

20 'It's always best on these occasions to do what the mob do.' 'But suppose there are two mobs?' suggested Mr Snodgrass. 'Shout with the largest,' replied Mr Pickwick.
Pickwick Papers (1837) ch. 13

21 Poverty and oysters always seem to go together.
Sam Weller
Pickwick Papers (1837) ch. 22

22 Minerva House . . . where some twenty girls . . . acquired a smattering of everything, and a knowledge of nothing.
Sketches by Boz (1839) Tales, ch. 3 'Sentiment'

23 It was the best of times, it was the worst of times.
A Tale of Two Cities (1859) bk. 1, ch. 1

24 It is a far, far better thing that I do, than I have ever done; it is a far, far better rest that I go to, than I have ever known.
Sydney Carton's thoughts on the scaffold
A Tale of Two Cities (1859) bk. 3, ch. 15

Emily Dickinson 1830–86
American poet

25 After great pain, a formal feeling comes.
'After great pain, a formal feeling comes' (1862)

26 Because I could not stop for Death—
He kindly stopped for me—
The Carriage held but just Ourselves—
And Immortality.
'Because I could not stop for Death' (c.1863)

27 Since then—'tis Centuries—and yet
Feels shorter than the Day
I first surmised the Horses Heads
Were toward Eternity.
'Because I could not stop for Death' (c.1863)

28 There is no Frigate like a Book
To take us Lands away
Nor any Coursers like a Page
Of prancing Poetry.
'A Book (2)' (c.1873)

29 The Bustle in a House
The Morning after Death
Is solemnest of industries
Enacted upon Earth—
The Sweeping up the Heart
And putting Love away
We shall not want to use again
Until Eternity.
'The Bustle in a House' (c.1866)

30 Heaven is what I cannot reach

The apple on the tree
'Forbidden Fruit' (c.1861)

1 There interposed a Fly—
With Blue—uncertain stumbling Buzz—
Between the light—and me—
And then the Windows failed—and then
I could not see to see.
'I heard a Fly buzz—when I died' (c.1862)

2 Parting is all we know of heaven,
And all we need of hell.
'My life closed twice before its close'

3 The Soul selects her own Society—
Then—shuts the Door—
To her divine Majority—
Present no more.
'The Soul selects her own Society' (c.1862)

4 Success is counted sweetest
By those who ne'er succeed.
To comprehend a nectar
Requires sorest need.
'Success is counted sweetest' (1859)

5 There's a certain Slant of light,
Winter Afternoons—
That oppresses like the Heft
Of Cathedral Tunes—
'There's a certain Slant of light' (c.1861)

6 They shut me up in prose—
As when a little girl
They put me in the closet—
Because they liked me 'still'.
'They shut me up in prose' (c.1862)

7 This is my letter to the world
That never wrote to me.
'This is my letter to the world' (c.1862)

John Dickinson 1732–1808
American politician

8 Our cause is just, our union is perfect.
declaration of reasons for taking up arms against England, presented to Congress, 8 July 1775
C. J. Stillé *The Life and Times of John Dickinson* (1891) ch. 5

9 Then join hand in hand, brave Americans all,—
By uniting we stand, by dividing we fall.
'The Liberty Song' (1768)

Paul Dickson 1939–
American writer

10 Rowe's Rule: the odds are five to six that the light at the end of the tunnel is the headlight of an oncoming train.
in *Washingtonian* November 1978; see **Lowell** 220:5

Denis Diderot 1713–84
French philosopher and man of letters

11 And [with] the guts of the last priest
Let's shake the neck of the last king.
Dithrambe sur fête de rois; see **Meslier** 233:15

12 *L'esprit de l'escalier.*
Staircase wit.
the witty riposte one thinks of only when one has left the drawing-room and is already on the way downstairs
Paradoxe sur le Comédien (written 1773–8, published 1830)

Joan Didion 1934–
American writer

13 When we start deceiving ourselves into thinking not that we want something or need something, not that it is a pragmatic necessity for us to have it, but that it is a *moral imperative* that we have it, then is when we join the fashionable madmen, and then is when the thin whine of hysteria is heard in the land, and then is when we are in bad trouble.
Slouching towards Bethlehem (1968) 'On Morality'

Wentworth Dillon, Lord Roscommon *c.*1633–85
Irish poet and critic

14 Choose an author as you choose a friend.
Essay on Translated Verse (1684) l. 96

15 Immodest words admit of no defence,
For want of decency is want of sense.
Essay on Translated Verse (1684) l. 113

16 The multitude is always in the wrong.
Essay on Translated Verse (1684) l. 183; see **Ibsen** 180:5

Ernest Dimnet
French priest, writer, and lecturer

17 Architecture, of all the arts, is the one which acts the most slowly, but the most surely, on the soul.
What We Live By (1932) pt. 2, ch. 12

Isak Dinesen 1885–1962
Danish novelist and short-story writer

18 What is man, when you come to think upon him, but a minutely set, ingenious machine for turning, with infinite artfulness, the red wine of Shiraz into urine?
Seven Gothic Tales (1934) 'The Dreamers'

Diogenes *c.*400–*c.*325 BC
Greek Cynic philosopher

19 Alexander . . . asked him if he lacked anything. 'Yes,' said he, 'that I do: that you stand out of my sun a little.'
Plutarch *Parallel Lives* 'Alexander' ch. 14, sect. 4 (tr. by T. North, 1579)

20 I am looking for a man.
on his reason for taking around a lamp in daylight; the context implies 'a good man', but often quoted as 'an honest man'
Diogenes Laertius *Lives of the Philosophers*

Dionysius of Halicarnassus fl.
30–7 BC
Greek historian

1 History is philosophy from examples.
Ars Rhetorica ch. 11, sect. 2

Paul Dirac 1902–84
British theoretical physicist

2 It is more important to have beauty in one's equations than to have them fit experiment.
in *Scientific American* May 1963

Walt Disney 1901–66
American animator and film producer

3 Fancy being remembered around the world for the invention of a mouse!
during his last illness
Leonard Mosley *Disney's World* (1985)

Benjamin Disraeli, Lord
Beaconsfield 1804–81
British Tory statesman and novelist; Prime Minister 1868, 1874–80

4 Though I sit down now, the time will come when you will hear me.
maiden speech in the House of Commons, 7 December 1837

5 The Continent will [not] suffer England to be the workshop of the world.
speech, House of Commons, 15 March 1838; see **Chamberlain** 90:1

6 A Conservative Government is an organized hypocrisy.
speech, House of Commons, 17 March 1845

7 Justice is truth in action.
speech, House of Commons, 11 February 1851

8 Is man an ape or an angel? Now I am on the side of the angels.
speech at Oxford, 25 November 1864

9 Assassination has never changed the history of the world.
speech, House of Commons, 1 May 1865

10 Change is inevitable in a progressive country. Change is constant.
speech at Edinburgh, 29 October 1867, in *The Times* 30 October 1867

11 You behold a range of exhausted volcanoes.
of the Treasury Bench
speech at Manchester, 3 April 1872

12 Increased means and increased leisure are the two civilizers of man.
speech at Manchester, 3 April 1872, in *The Times* 4 April 1872

13 A University should be a place of light, of liberty, and of learning.
speech, House of Commons, 11 March 1873

14 Upon the education of the people of this country the fate of this country depends.
speech, House of Commons, 15 June 1874

15 Cosmopolitan critics, men who are the friends of every country save their own.
speech at Guildhall, 9 November 1877; see **Canning** 84:7

16 Lord Salisbury and myself have brought you back peace—but a peace I hope with honour.
speech on returning from the Congress of Berlin, 16 July 1878; see **Chamberlain** 90:5, **Russell** 283:16

17 A sophistical rhetorician, inebriated with the exuberance of his own verbosity.
of Gladstone
in *The Times* 29 July 1878

18 I will not go down to posterity talking bad grammar.
while correcting proofs of his last Parliamentary speech, 31 March 1881
Robert Blake *Disraeli* (1966) ch. 32

19 No Government can be long secure without a formidable Opposition.
Coningsby (1844) bk. 2, ch. 1

20 'A sound Conservative government,' said Taper, musingly. 'I understand: Tory men and Whig measures.'
Coningsby (1844) bk. 2, ch. 6

21 Youth is a blunder; Manhood a struggle; Old Age a regret.
Coningsby (1844) bk. 3, ch. 1

22 It seems to me a barren thing this Conservatism—an unhappy cross-breed, the mule of politics that engenders nothing.
Coningsby (1844) bk. 3, ch. 5; see **Power** 270:17

23 With words we govern men.
Contarini Fleming (1832) pt. 1, ch. 21

24 Read no history: nothing but biography, for that is life without theory.
Contarini Fleming (1832) pt. 1, ch. 23; see **Emerson** 132:8

25 His Christianity was muscular.
Endymion (1880) ch. 14

26 As for our majority . . . one is enough.
Endymion (1880) ch. 64

27 'Sensible men are all of the same religion.' 'And pray what is that?' . . . 'Sensible men never tell.'
Endymion (1880) ch. 81; see **Shaftesbury** 289:6

28 You know who the critics are? The men who have failed in literature and art.
Lothair (1870) ch. 35

29 'Two nations; between whom there is no intercourse and no sympathy; who are as ignorant of each other's habits, thoughts, and feelings, as if they were dwellers in different zones, or inhabitants of different planets; who are formed by a different breeding, are fed by a different food, are ordered by different manners, and are not governed by the same laws.' 'You speak of—' said Egremont, hesitatingly, 'THE RICH AND THE POOR.'
Sybil (1845) bk. 2, ch. 5; see **Foster** 140:6

30 Mr Kremlin himself was distinguished for ignorance, for he had only one idea,—and that was wrong.
Sybil (1845) bk. 4, ch. 5; see **Johnson** 188:23

1 The Youth of a Nation are the trustees of Posterity.
Sybil (1845) bk. 6, ch. 13

2 The East is a career.
Tancred (1847) bk. 2, ch. 14

3 All power is a trust.
Vivian Grey (1826) bk. 6, ch. 7; see **Dryden** 121:19

4 Damn your principles! Stick to your party.
attributed to Disraeli and believed to have been said to Edward **Bulwer-Lytton**
E. Latham *Famous Sayings and their Authors* (1904)

5 Everyone likes flattery; and when you come to Royalty you should lay it on with a trowel.
to Matthew **Arnold**
G. W. E. Russell *Collections and Recollections* (1898) ch. 23

6 I have climbed to the top of the greasy pole.
on becoming Prime Minister
W. Monypenny and G. Buckle *Life of Benjamin Disraeli* vol. 4 (1916) ch. 16

7 I never deny; I never contradict; I sometimes forget.
said to Lord Esher of his relations with Queen **Victoria**
Elizabeth Longford *Victoria R. I* (1964) ch. 27

8 Never complain and never explain.
J. Morley *Life of William Ewart Gladstone* (1903) vol. 1; see **Fisher** 136:4

9 There are three kinds of lies: lies, damned lies and statistics.
attributed to Disraeli in Mark Twain Autobiography (1924) vol. 1

10 When I want to read a novel, I write one.
W. Monypenny and G. Buckle *Life of Benjamin Disraeli* vol. 6 (1920) ch. 17; see **Punch** 271:22

William Chatterton Dix 1837–98
English clergyman

11 As with gladness men of old
Did the guiding star behold.
'As with gladness men of old' (1861 hymn)

Henry Austin Dobson 1840–1921
English poet, biographer, and essayist

12 All passes. Art alone
Enduring stays to us;
The Bust outlasts the throne,—
The Coin, Tiberius.
'Ars Victrix' (1876); translation of Théophile Gautier's 'L'Art'

13 Time goes, you say? Ah no!
Alas, Time stays, *we* go.
'The Paradox of Time' (1877)

Ken Dodd 1931–
British comedian

14 Freud's theory was that when a joke opens a window and all those bats and bogeymen fly out, you get a marvellous feeling of relief and elation. The trouble with Freud is that

he never had to play the old Glasgow Empire on a Saturday night after Rangers and Celtic had both lost.
in Guardian *30 April 1991; quoted in many, usually much contracted, forms since the mid-1960s*

Philip Doddridge 1702–51
English Nonconformist divine

15 O God of Bethel, by whose hand
Thy people still are fed,
Who through this weary pilgrimage
Hast all our fathers led.
Hymns (1755) 'O God of Bethel'

Aelius Donatus
Roman grammarian of the 4th century AD

16 Confound those who have said our remarks before us.
St Jerome *Commentary on Ecclesiastes* bk 1

J. P. Donleavy 1926–
Irish-American novelist

17 When you don't have any money, the problem is food. When you have money, it's sex. When you have both it's health.
The Ginger Man (1955) ch. 5

John Donne 1572–1631
English poet and divine
Verse dates are those of composition

18 New philosophy calls all in doubt.
An Anatomy of the World: The First Anniversary (1611) l. 205

19 Love built on beauty, soon as beauty, dies.
Elegies 'The Anagram' (*c.*1595)

20 No spring, nor summer beauty hath such grace,
As I have seen in one autumnal face.
Elegies 'The Autumnal' (*c.*1600)

21 License my roving hands, and let them go,
Behind, before, above, between, below.
O my America, my new found land,
My kingdom, safeliest when with one man manned.
Elegies 'To His Mistress Going to Bed' (*c.*1595)

22 Death be not proud, though some have called thee
Mighty and dreadful, for thou art not so.
Holy Sonnets (1609) no. 6 (ed. J. Carey, 1990)

23 One short sleep past, we wake eternally,
And death shall be no more; Death thou shalt die.
Holy Sonnets (1609) no. 6 (ed. J. Carey, 1990)

24 Batter my heart, three-personed God; for, you
As yet but knock, breathe, shine, and seek to mend.
Holy Sonnets (after 1609) no. 10 (ed. J. Carey, 1990)

25 Take me to you, imprison me, for I
Except you enthral me, never shall be free,
Nor ever chaste, except you ravish me.
Holy Sonnets (after 1609) no. 10 (ed. J. Carey, 1990)

1 What if this present were the world's last
night?
Holy Sonnets (after 1609) no. 19 (ed. J. Carey,
1990)

2 Wilt thou forgive that sin where I begun,
Which is my sin, though it were done
before?
Wilt thou forgive those sins, through which
I run
And do them still: though still I do deplore?
When thou hast done, thou hast not done,
For, I have more.
'A Hymn to God the Father' (1623)

3 Nature's great masterpiece, an elephant,
The only harmless great thing.
'The Progress of the Soul' (1601) st. 39

4 On a huge hill,
Cragged, and steep, Truth stands, and he
that will
Reach her, about must, and about must go.
Satire no. 3 (1594–5) l. 79

5 Air and angels.
title of poem, *Songs and Sonnets*

6 All other things, to their destruction draw,
Only our love hath no decay;
This, no tomorrow hath, nor yesterday,
Running it never runs from us away,
But truly keeps his first, last, everlasting day.
Songs and Sonnets 'The Anniversary'

7 Come live with me, and be my love,
And we will some new pleasures prove
Of golden sands, and crystal brooks,
With silken lines, and silver hooks.
Songs and Sonnets 'The Bait'; see **Marlowe**
228:15, **Ralegh** 272:22

8 For God's sake hold your tongue, and let me
love.
Songs and Sonnets 'The Canonization'

9 I wonder by my troth, what thou, and I
Did, till we loved, were we not weaned till
then?
But sucked on country pleasures, childishly?
Or snorted we in the seven sleepers den?
Songs and Sonnets 'The Good-Morrow'

10 And now good morrow to our waking souls,
Which watch not one another out of fear.
Songs and Sonnets 'The Good-Morrow'

11 I long to talk with some old lover's ghost,
Who died before the god of love was born.
Songs and Sonnets 'Love's Deity'

12 'Tis the year's midnight, and it is the day's.
Songs and Sonnets 'A Nocturnal upon St Lucy's
Day'

13 A bracelet of bright hair about the bone.
Songs and Sonnets 'The Relic'

14 Go, and catch a falling star,
Get with child a mandrake root,
Tell me, where all past years are,
Or who cleft the Devil's foot,
Teach me to hear mermaids singing.
Songs and Sonnets 'Song: Go and catch a falling
star'

15 Busy old fool, unruly sun,
Why dost thou thus,

Through windows, and through curtains
call on us?
Must to thy motions lovers' seasons run?
Songs and Sonnets 'The Sun Rising'

16 Love, all alike, no season knows, nor clime,
Nor hours, days, months, which are the rags
of time.
Songs and Sonnets 'The Sun Rising'

17 This bed thy centre is, these walls thy
sphere.
Songs and Sonnets 'The Sun Rising'

18 I am two fools, I know,
For loving, and for saying so
In whining poetry.
Songs and Sonnets 'The Triple Fool'

19 I have done one braver thing
Than all the Worthies did,
And yet a braver thence doth spring,
Which is, to keep that hid.
Songs and Sonnets 'The Undertaking'

20 Sir, more than kisses, letters mingle souls.
'To Sir Henry Wotton' (1597–8)

21 But I do nothing upon my self, and yet I am
mine own Executioner.
Devotions upon Emergent Occasions (1624)
'Meditation XII'

22 No man is an Island, entire of it self.
Devotions upon Emergent Occasions (1624)
'Meditation XVII'

23 Any man's death diminishes me, because I
am involved in Mankind; And therefore
never send to know for whom the bell tolls;
it tolls for thee.
Devotions upon Emergent Occasions (1624)
'Meditation XVII'

24 I throw myself down in my Chamber, and I
call in, and invite God, and his Angels
thither, and when they are there, I neglect
God and his Angels, for the noise of a fly, for
the rattling of a coach, for the whining of a
door.
LXXX Sermons (1640) 12 December 1626 'At the
Funeral of Sir William Cokayne'

25 John Donne, Anne Donne, Un-done.
*in a letter to his wife, on being dismissed from the
service of his father-in-law, Sir George More*
Izaak Walton *The Life of Dr Donne* (first printed in
LXXX Sermons, 1640)

Fedor Dostoevsky 1821–81
Russian novelist

26 If you were to destroy in mankind the belief
in immortality, not only love but every
living force maintaining the life of the
world would at once be dried up.
The Brothers Karamazov (1879–80) bk. 2, ch. 6

27 Beauty is mysterious as well as terrible. God
and devil are fighting there, and the
battlefield is the heart of man.
The Brothers Karamazov (1879–80) bk. 3, ch. 3

28 If the devil doesn't exist, but man has
created him, he has created him in his own
image and likeness.
The Brothers Karamazov (1879–80) bk. 5, ch. 4

1 Imagine that you are creating a fabric of human destiny with the object of making men happy in the end, giving them peace and rest at last, but that it was essential and inevitable to death only one tiny creature . . . and to found that edifice on its unavenged tears, would you consent to be the architect on those conditions?
The Brothers Karamazov (1879–80) bk. 5, ch. 4

Lord Alfred Douglas 1870–1945
English poet

2 I am the Love that dare not speak its name.
'Two Loves' (1896)

Keith Douglas 1920–44
English poet

3 Remember me when I am dead
And simplify me when I'm dead.
'Simplify me when I'm Dead' (1941)

4 For here the lover and killer are mingled
who had one body and one heart.
And death, who had the soldier singled
has done the lover mortal hurt.
'Vergissmeinnicht, 1943'

Norman Douglas 1868–1952
Scottish-born novelist and essayist

5 To find a friend one must close one eye. To keep him—two.
Almanac (1941)

6 You can tell the ideals of a nation by its advertisements.
South Wind (1917) ch. 6

Alec Douglas-Home *see* Lord Home

Frederick Douglass *c.*1818–95
American former slave and civil rights campaigner

7 Every tone [of the songs of the slaves] was a testimony against slavery, and a prayer to God for deliverance from chains.
Narrative of the Life of Frederick Douglass (1845) ch. 2

8 The life of the nation is secure only while the nation is honest, truthful, and virtuous.
speech on the 23rd anniversary of Emancipation in the District of Columbia, Washington DC, April 1885

Lorenzo Dow 1777–1834
American divine

9 You will be damned if you do—And you will be damned if you don't.
on the Calvinist doctrine of 'Particular Election'
Reflections on the Love of God (1836) ch. 6

Ernest Dowson 1867–1900
English poet

10 I have forgot much, Cynara! gone with the wind,
Flung roses, roses, riotously, with the throng,
Dancing, to put thy pale, lost lilies out of mind;

But I was desolate and sick of an old passion,
Yea, all the time, because the dance was long:
I have been faithful to thee, Cynara! in my fashion.
'Non Sum Qualis Eram' (1896) (also known as 'Cynara'); see **Horace** 175:19

11 They are not long, the days of wine and roses.
'Vitae Summa Brevis' (1896)

Arthur Conan Doyle 1859–1930
Scottish-born writer of detective fiction

12 A man should keep his little brain attic stocked with all the furniture that he is likely to use, and the rest he can put away in the lumber room of his library, where he can get it if he wants it.
The Adventures of Sherlock Holmes (1892) 'The Five Orange Pips'

13 It is quite a three-pipe problem.
The Adventures of Sherlock Holmes (1892) 'The Red-Headed League'

14 You see, but you do not observe.
The Adventures of Sherlock Holmes (1892) 'Scandal in Bohemia'

15 The giant rat of Sumatra, a story for which the world is not yet prepared.
The Case-Book of Sherlock Homes (1927) 'The Sussex Vampire'

16 Good old Watson! You are the one fixed point in a changing age.
His Last Bow (1917) title story

17 'Excellent,' I cried. 'Elementary,' said he.
often misquoted as, 'Elementary, my dear Watson', a remark attributed to Sherlock Holmes, but not found in this form in any book by Arthur Conan Doyle, first found in P.G. **Wodehouse** *Psmith Journalist* (1915)
The Memoirs of Sherlock Holmes (1894) 'The Crooked Man'

18 Ex-Professor Moriarty of mathematical celebrity . . . is the Napoleon of crime, Watson.
The Memoirs of Sherlock Holmes (1894) 'The Final Problem'

19 'Is there any other point to which you would wish to draw my attention?'
'To the curious incident of the dog in the night-time.'
'The dog did nothing in the night-time.'
'That was the curious incident,' remarked Sherlock Holmes.
The Memoirs of Sherlock Holmes (1894) 'Silver Blaze'

20 What one man can invent another can discover.
The Return of Sherlock Holmes (1905) 'The Dancing Men'

21 When you have eliminated the impossible, whatever remains, *however improbable*, must be the truth?
The Sign of Four (1890) ch. 6

22 You know my methods. Apply them.
The Sign of Four (1890) ch. 6

1 It is the unofficial force—the Baker Street irregulars.
The Sign of Four (1890) ch. 8

2 London, that great cesspool into which all the loungers and idlers of the Empire are irresistibly drained.
A Study in Scarlet (1888) ch. 1

3 It is a capital mistake to theorize before you have all the evidence. It biases the judgement.
A Study in Scarlet (1888) ch. 3

4 Where there is no imagination there is no horror.
A Study in Scarlet (1888) ch. 5

5 Mediocrity knows nothing higher than itself, but talent instantly recognizes genius.
The Valley of Fear (1915) ch. 1

Francis Drake *c.*1540–96
English sailor and explorer

6 There must be a beginning of any great matter, but the continuing unto the end until it be thoroughly finished yields the true glory.
dispatch to Francis Walsingham, 17 May 1587, in *Navy Records Society* vol. 11 (1898)

7 The singeing of the King of Spain's Beard.
on the expedition to Cadiz, 1587
Francis Bacon *Considerations touching a War with Spain* (1629)

8 I must have the gentleman to haul and draw with the mariner, and the mariner with the gentleman ... I would know him, that would refuse to set his hand to a rope, but I know there is not any such here.
J. S. Corbett *Drake and the Tudor Navy* (1898) vol. 1, ch. 9

9 There is plenty of time to win this game, and to thrash the Spaniards too.
attributed, in *Dictionary of National Biography* (1917–)

Michael Drayton 1563–1631
English poet

10 Since there's no help, come let us kiss and part,
Nay, I have done: you get no more of me.
Idea (1619) Sonnet 61

11 That shire which we the Heart of England well may call.
of Warwickshire
Poly-Olbion (1612–22) Song 13, l. 2

12 Next these, learn'd Jonson, in this list I bring,
Who had drunk deep of the Pierian spring.
'To Henry Reynolds, of Poets and Poesy' (1627) l. 129; see **Pope** 267:6

13 Fair stood the wind for France
When we our sails advance,
Nor now to prove our chance
Longer will tarry.
To the Cambro-Britons (1619) 'Agincourt'

William Drennan 1754–1820
Irish writer

14 Nor one feeling of vengeance presume to defile
The cause, or the men, of the Emerald Isle.
Erin (1795) st. 3

William Driver 1803–86
American sailor

15 I name thee Old Glory.
saluting a new flag hoisted on his ship, the Charles Doggett
attributed

Thomas Drummond 1797–1840
British government official

16 Property has its duties as well as its rights.
letter to the Earl of Donoughmore, 22 May 1838

John Dryden 1631–1700
English poet, critic, and dramatist

17 Great wits are sure to madness near allied.
Absalom and Achitophel (1681) pt. 1, l. 163

18 In friendship false, implacable in hate:
Resolved to ruin or to rule the state.
Absalom and Achitophel (1681) pt. 1, l. 173

19 All empire is no more than power in trust.
Absalom and Achitophel (1681) pt. 1, l. 411; see **Disraeli** 118:3

20 But far more numerous was the herd of such
Who think too little and who talk too much.
Absalom and Achitophel (1681) pt. 1, l. 533

21 A man so various that he seemed to be
Not one, but all mankind's epitome.
Stiff in opinions, always in the wrong;
Was everything by starts, and nothing long.
Absalom and Achitophel (1681) pt. 1, l. 545

22 Nor is the people's judgement always true:
The most may err as grossly as the few.
Absalom and Achitophel (1681) pt. 1, l. 781

23 Beware the fury of a patient man.
Absalom and Achitophel (1681) pt. 1, l. 1005

24 None but the brave deserves the fair.
Alexander's Feast (1697) l. 7

25 Sweet is pleasure after pain.
Alexander's Feast (1697) l. 60

26 Revenge, revenge! Timotheus cries.
Alexander's Feast (1697) l. 131

27 Errors, like straws, upon the surface flow;
He who would search for pearls must dive below.
All for Love (1678) prologue

28 Men are but children of a larger growth;
Our appetites as apt to change as theirs,
And full as craving too, and full as vain.
All for Love (1678) act 4, sc. 1; see **Chesterfield** 92:20

1 By viewing nature, nature's handmaid art,
Makes mighty things from small beginnings
grow.
Annus Mirabilis (1667) st. 155

2 I am as free as nature first made man,
Ere the base laws of servitude began,
When wild in woods the noble savage ran.
The Conquest of Granada (1670) pt. 1, act 1, sc. 1

3 The wise, for cure, on exercise depend;
God never made his work, for man to mend.
Epistle 'To my honoured kinsman John Driden'
(1700) l. 92

4 And love's the noblest frailty of the mind.
The Indian Emperor (1665) act 2, sc. 2

5 War is the trade of kings.
King Arthur (1691) act 2, sc. 2

6 Fairest Isle, all isles excelling.
King Arthur (1691) act 5 'Song of Venus'; see
Wesley 354:22

7 All human things are subject to decay,
And, when fate summons, monarchs must
obey.
MacFlecknoe (1682) l. 1

8 The rest to some faint meaning make
pretence,
But Shadwell never deviates into sense.
MacFlecknoe (1682) l. 19

9 For secrets are edged tools,
And must be kept from children and from
fools.
Sir Martin Mar-All (1667) act 2, sc. 2

10 From harmony, from heavenly harmony
This universal frame began:
From harmony to harmony
Through all the compass of the notes it ran,
The diapason closing full in Man.
A Song for St Cecilia's Day (1687) st. 1

11 What passion cannot Music raise and quell?
A Song for St Cecilia's Day (1687) st. 2

12 The soft complaining flute.
A Song for St Cecilia's Day (1687) st. 4

13 The trumpet shall be heard on high,
The dead shall live, the living die,
And Music shall untune the sky.
A Song for St Cecilia's Day (1687) 'Grand Chorus'

14 There is a pleasure sure,
In being mad, which none but madmen
know!
The Spanish Friar (1681) act 1, sc. 1

15 Wit will shine
Through the harsh cadence of a rugged line.
'To the Memory of Mr Oldham' (1684)

16 Happy the man, and happy he alone,
He, who can call to-day his own:
He who, secure within, can say,
Tomorrow do thy worst, for I have lived
today.
translation of Horace *Odes* bk. 3, no. 29; see
Smith 319:13

17 Not Heaven itself upon the past has power;

But what has been, has been, and I have had
my hour.
translation of Horace *Odes* bk. 3, no. 29

18 She knows her man, and when you rant and
swear,
Can draw you to her *with a single hair*.
Translation of Persius *Satires* no. 5, l. 246

19 Arms, and the man I sing.
translation of Virgil *Aeneid* (*Aeneis*, 1697) bk. 1, l.
1; see **Virgil** 346:19

20 The famous rules, which the French call *Des
Trois Unitez*, or, the Three Unities, which
ought to be observed in every regular play;
namely, of Time, Place, and Action.
An Essay of Dramatic Poesy (1668)

21 He needed not the spectacles of books to
read Nature: he looked inwards, and found
her there.
on **Shakespeare**
An Essay of Dramatic Poesy (1668)

22 'Tis sufficient to say, according to the
proverb, that here is God's plenty.
of **Chaucer**
Fables Ancient and Modern (1700) preface

23 Cousin Swift, you will never be a poet.
Samuel Johnson *Lives of the English Poets*
(1779–81) 'Dryden'

Alexander Dubček 1921–92
Czechoslovak statesman

24 In the service of the people we followed
such a policy that socialism would not lose
its human face.
in *Rudé Právo* 19 July 1968

W. E. B. Du Bois 1868–1963
American social reformer and political activist

25 One thing alone I charge you. As you live,
believe in life!
last message, written 26 June, 1957, and read at
his funeral, 1963

26 The problem of the twentieth century is the
problem of the colour line—the relation of
the darker to the lighter races of men in
Asia and Africa, in America and the islands
of the sea.
The Souls of Black Folk (1905) ch. 2

Mme Du Deffand 1697–1780
French literary hostess

27 *La distance n'y fait rien; il n'y a que le premier
pas qui coûte.*
The distance is nothing; it is only the first
step that is difficult.
*commenting on the legend that St Denis, carrying
his head in his hands, walked two leagues*
letter to Jean Le Rond d'Alembert, 7 July 1763

George Duffield 1818–88
American Presbyterian minister

28 Stand up!—stand up for Jesus!

Ye soldiers of the Cross.
'Stand Up, Stand Up for Jesus' (1858 hymn); the opening line inspired by the dying words of the American evangelist, Dudley Atkins Tyng

Georges Duhamel 1884–1966
French novelist

1 I have too much respect for the idea of God to make it responsible for such an absurd world.
Le désert de Bièvres (1937)

John Foster Dulles 1888–1959
American international lawyer and politician

2 The ability to get to the verge without getting into the war is the necessary art . . . We walked to the brink and we looked it in the face.
in *Life* 16 January 1956; see **Stevenson** 325:6

Alexandre Dumas 1802–70
French novelist and dramatist

3 *Cherchons la femme.*
Let us look for the woman.
attributed to Joseph Fouché (1763–1820) in the form 'Cherchez la femme'
Les Mohicans de Paris (1854–5) *passim*

4 *Tous pour un, un pour tous.*
All for one, one for all.
Les Trois Mousquetaires (1844) ch. 9

Daphne Du Maurier 1907–89
English novelist

5 Last night I dreamt I went to Manderley again.
Rebecca (1938) ch. 1; opening words

Charles François du Périer Dumouriez 1739–1823
French general

6 The courtiers who surround him have forgotten nothing and learnt nothing.
of Louis XVIII, at the time of the Declaration of Verona, September 1795; quoted by **Napoleon** *in his Declaration to the French on his return from Elba, 1815*
Examen impartial d'un Écrit intitulé Déclaration de Louis XVIII (1795); see **Talleyrand** 330:9

Paul Lawrence Dunbar 1872–1906
American poet

7 I know why the caged bird sings!
adopted by Maya **Angelou** *as the title of her autobiography, 1969*
'Sympathy' st. 3; see **Webster** 353:3

William Dunbar *c.*1465–*c.*1513
Scottish poet and priest

8 *Timor mortis conturbat me.*
Fear of death troubles me.
'Lament for the Makaris [Makers]'

Isadora Duncan 1878–1927
American dancer

9 *Adieu, mes amis. Je vais à la gloire.*
Farewell, my friends. I go to glory.
before her scarf caught in a car wheel, breaking her neck
Mary Desti *Isadora Duncan's End* (1929) ch. 25

Ian Dunlop 1940–
British art historian

10 The shock of the new: seven historic exhibitions of modern art.
title of book (1972)

John Dunning 1731–83
English lawyer and politician

11 The influence of the Crown has increased, is increasing, and ought to be diminished.
resolution passed in the House of Commons, 6 April 1780

John George Lambton, Lord Durham 1792–1840
English Whig politician

12 £40,000 a year a moderate income—such a one as a man *might jog on with.*
Thomas Creevey, letter to Elizabeth Ord, 13 September 1821

13 I expected to find a contest between a government and a people: I found two nations warring in the bosom of a single state.
of Canada
Report of the Affairs of British North America (1839)

Leo Durocher 1906–91
American baseball coach

14 I called off his players' names as they came marching up the steps behind him . . . All nice guys. They'll finish last. Nice guys. Finish last.
casual remark at a practice ground in the presence of a number of journalists, July 1946, generally quoted as 'Nice guys finish last'
Nice Guys Finish Last (1975) pt. 1

Ian Dury 1942–2000
British rock singer and songwriter

15 Sex and drugs and rock and roll.
title of song (1977)

Andrea Dworkin 1946–2005
American feminist and writer

16 Seduction is often difficult to distinguish from rape. In seduction, the rapist bothers to buy a bottle of wine.
speech to women at Harper & Row, 1976

Edward Dyer d. 1607
English poet

17 My mind to me a kingdom is.
'In praise of a contented mind' (1588), attributed

John Dyer 1700–58
Welsh clergyman and poet

1   A little rule, a little sway,
    A sunbeam in a winter's day,
    Is all the proud and mighty have
    Between the cradle and the grave.
      Grongar Hill (1726) l. 88

John Dyer
English poet

2   And he that will this health deny,
    Down among the dead men let him lie.
      'Down among the Dead Men' (*c.*1700)

Bob Dylan 1941–
American singer and songwriter

3   How many roads must a man walk down
    Before you can call him a man? . . .
    The answer, my friend, is blowin' in the
      wind,
    The answer is blowin' in the wind.
      'Blowin' in the Wind' (1962 song)

4   And it's a hard rain's a gonna fall.
      'A Hard Rain's A Gonna Fall' (1963 song)

5   Money doesn't talk, it swears.
      'It's Alright, Ma (I'm Only Bleeding)' (1965 song)

6   She takes just like a woman, yes, she does
    She makes love just like a woman, yes, she
      does
    And she aches just like a woman
    But she breaks like a little girl.
      'Just Like a Woman' (1966 song)

7   How does it feel
    To be on your own
    With no direction home
    Like a complete unknown
    Like a rolling stone?
      'Like a Rolling Stone' (1965 song)

8   She knows there's no success like failure
    And that failure's no success at all.
      'Love Minus Zero / No Limit' (1965 song)

9   Hey! Mr Tambourine Man, play a song for
      me.
      'Mr Tambourine Man' (1965 song)

10 Ah, but I was so much older then,
    I'm younger than that now.
      'My Back Pages' (1964 song)

11 Señor, señor, do you know where we're
      headin'?
    Lincoln County Road or Armageddon?
      'Señor (Tale of Yankee Power)' (1978 song)

12 All that foreign oil controlling American
      soil.
      'Slow Train' (1979 song)

13 The times they are a-changin'.
      title of song (1964)

14 Come mothers and fathers,
    Throughout the land
    And don't criticize
    What you can't understand.
      'The Times They Are A-Changing' (1964 song)

15 But I can't think for you
    You'll have to decide,
    Whether Judas Iscariot
    Had God on his side.
      'With God on our Side' (1963 song)

Amelia Earhart 1898–1937
American aviator

16 Courage is the price that Life exacts for
      granting peace.
      'Courage' (1927)

Shirin Ebadi 1947–
Iranian lawyer

17 Judges and lawyers are each one wing of the
      angel of justice, but one of them has been
      amputated in Iran.
      in *Independent* 15 February 2005

Abba Eban 1915–2002
Israeli diplomat

18 History teaches us that men and nations
      behave wisely once they have exhausted all
      other alternatives.
      speech in London, 16 December 1970, in *The
      Times* 17 December 1970

Arthur Eddington 1882–1944
British astrophysicist

19 We do not argue with the critic who urges
      that the stars are not hot enough for this
      process; we tell him to go and find a hotter
      place.
      *on the formation of heavier elements by nuclear
      reactions*
      The Internal Constitution of the Stars (1926)

20 I shall use the phrase 'time's arrow' to
      express this one-way property of time which
      has no analogue in space.
      The Nature of the Physical World (1928) ch. 4

21 If an army of monkeys were strumming on
      typewriters they *might* write all the books in
      the British Museum.
      The Nature of the Physical World (1928); see
      Wilensky 359:24

22 If someone points out to you that your pet
      theory of the universe is in disagreement
      with Maxwell's equations—then so much
      the worse for Maxwell's equations. If it is
      found to be contradicted by
      observation—well, these experimentalists
      do bungle things sometimes. But if your
      theory is found to be against the second law
      of thermodynamics I can give you no hope;
      there is nothing for it but to collapse in
      deepest humiliation.
      The Nature of the Physical World (1928) ch. 14

23 Science is an edged tool, with which men
      play like children, and cut their own fingers.
      attributed in Robert L. Weber *More Random
      Walks in Science* (1982)

Mary Baker Eddy 1821–1910
American religious leader and founder of the Christian Science movement

1 Disease is an experience of so-called mortal mind. It is fear made manifest on the body.
  Science and Health with Key to the Scriptures (1875)

Anthony Eden, Earl of Avon 1897–1977
British Conservative statesman, Prime Minister 1955–7

2 We are in an armed conflict; that is the phrase I have used. There has been no declaration of war.
  on the Suez crisis
    speech in the House of Commons, 1 November 1956

Marriott Edgar 1880–1951
British actor and writer

3 There's a famous seaside place called Blackpool,
  That's noted for fresh air and fun,
  And Mr and Mrs Ramsbottom
  Went there with young Albert, their son.
  'The Lion and Albert' (1932)

Thomas Alva Edison 1847–1931
American inventor

4 For most of my life I refused to work at any problem unless its solution seemed to be capable of being put to commercial use.
  interview, in *New York Sun* February 1917

5 Genius is one per cent inspiration, ninety-nine per cent perspiration.
  said *c.*1903, in *Harper's Monthly Magazine* September 1932

James Edmeston 1791–1867
English architect and hymn-writer

6 Lead us, Heavenly Father, lead us
  O'er the world's tempestuous sea;
  Guard us, guide us, keep us, feed us,
  For we have no help but Thee.
  'Lead us, heavenly Father, lead us' (1821)

John Maxwell Edmonds 1875–1958
English classicist

7 When you go home, tell them of us and say,
  'For your tomorrows these gave their today.'
  second line often quoted as 'For your tomorrow we gave our today', as on the Kohima memorial to the Burma campaign of the Second World War
    Inscriptions Suggested for War Memorials (1919)

Edward III 1312–77
English monarch, King from 1327

8 Also say to them, that they suffre hym this day to wynne his spurres, for if god be

pleased, I woll this journey be his, and the honoure therof.
  speaking of the Black Prince at Crécy, 1346; commonly quoted 'Let the boy win his spurs'
    The Chronicle of Froissart (tr. Sir John Bourchier, Lord Berners, 1523–5) ch. 130

Edward VIII, afterwards Duke of Windsor 1894–1972
British monarch, King of the United Kingdom, 1936

9 These works brought all these people here. Something should be done to get them at work again.
  speaking at the derelict Dowlais Iron and Steel Works, 18 November 1936; often misquoted as, 'Something must be done'
    in *Western Mail* 19 November 1936

10 At long last I am able to say a few words of my own . . . you must believe me when I tell you that I have found it impossible to carry the heavy burden of responsibility and to discharge my duties as King as I would wish to do without the help and support of the woman I love.
  radio broadcast following his abdication, 11 December 1936

11 The thing that impresses me most about America is the way parents obey their children.
  in *Look* 5 March 1957

Jonathan Edwards 1703–58
American theologian

12 The bodies of those that made such a noise and tumult when alive, when dead, lie as quietly among the graves of their neighbours as any others.
  Sermon on procrastination in *Works* (1834) vol. 2

Oliver Edwards 1711–91
English lawyer

13 I have tried too in my time to be a philosopher; but, I don't know how, cheerfulness was always breaking in.
  James Boswell *Life of Samuel Johnson* (1791) 17 April 1778

Paul Ralph Ehrlich 1932–
American biologist

14 The first rule of intelligent tinkering is to save all the parts.
  in *Saturday Review* 5 June 1971

John Ehrlichman 1925–99
American Presidential assistant to Richard Nixon

15 I think we ought to let him hang there. Let him twist slowly, slowly in the wind.
  Richard Nixon had withdrawn his support for Patrick Gray, nominated as director of the FBI, although Gray himself had not been informed
    in a telephone conversation with John Dean; in *Washington Post* 27 July 1973

Max Ehrmann 1872–1945
American writer

1 Go placidly amid the noise and the haste,
and remember what peace there may be
in silence.
*often wrongly dated to 1692, the date of
foundation of a church in Baltimore whose vicar
circulated the poem in 1956*
'Desiderata' (1948)

Albert Einstein 1879–1955
German-born theoretical physicist

2 Science without religion is lame, religion
without science is blind.
Science, Philosophy and Religion: a Symposium (1941)
ch. 13

3 $E = mc^2$.
*the usual form of Einstein's original statement: 'If
a body releases the energy L in the form of
radiation, its mass is decreased by L/V^2'*
in *Annalen der Physik* 18 (1905)

4 God is subtle but he is not malicious.
*remark made during a week at Princeton
beginning 9 May 1921, later carved above the
fireplace of the Common Room of Fine Hall (the
Mathematical Institute), Princeton University*

5 I am convinced that *He* [God] does not play
dice.
often quoted as: 'God does not play dice'
letter to Max Born, 4 December 1926; in *Einstein
und Born Briefwechsel* (1969)

6 I never think of the future. It comes soon
enough.
in an interview, given on the *Belgenland*,
December 1930

7 The eternal mystery of the world is its
comprehensibility . . . The fact that it is
comprehensible is a miracle.
*usually quoted as 'The most incomprehensible fact
about the universe is that it is comprehensible'*
in *Franklin Institute Journal* March 1936 'Physics
and Reality'

8 Some recent work by E. Fermi and L. Szilard,
which has been communicated to me in
manuscript, leads me to expect that the
element uranium may be turned into a new
and important source of energy in the
immediate future. Certain aspects of the
situation which has arisen seem to call for
watchfulness and, if necessary, quick action
on the part of the Administration.
*warning of the possible development of an atomic
bomb, and leading to the setting up of the
Manhattan Project*
letter to Franklin **Roosevelt**, 2 August 1939,
drafted by Leo Szilard and signed by Einstein

9 The unleashed power of the atom has
changed everything save our modes of
thinking and we thus drift toward
unparalleled catastrophe.
telegram to prominent Americans, 24 May
1946, in *New York Times* 25 May 1946

10 If *A* is a success in life, then *A* equals *x* plus *y*
plus *z*. Work is *x*; *y* is play; and *z* is keeping
your mouth shut.
in *Observer* 15 January 1950

11 Common sense is nothing more than a
deposit of prejudices laid down in the mind
before you reach eighteen.
Lincoln Barnett *The Universe and Dr Einstein* (1950
ed.)

12 The grand aim of all science [is] to cover the
greatest number of empirical facts by logical
deduction from the smallest possible
number of hypotheses or axioms.
Lincoln Barnett *The Universe and Dr Einstein* (1950
ed.)

13 If I would be a young man again and had to
decide how to make my living, I would not
try to become a scientist or scholar or
teacher. I would rather choose to be a
plumber or a peddler in the hope to find
that modest degree of independence still
available under present circumstances.
in *Reporter* 18 November 1954

14 The distinction between past, present and
future is only an illusion, however
persistent.
letter to Michelangelo Besso, 21 March 1955

15 Nationalism is an infantile sickness. It is the
measles of the human race.
Helen Dukas and Banesh Hoffman *Albert
Einstein, the Human Side* (1979)

Dwight D. Eisenhower 1890–1969
*American Republican statesman, 34th President
of the US 1953–61*

16 This world in arms is not spending money
alone. It is spending the sweat of its
labourers, the genius of its scientists, the
hopes of its children.
speech in Washington, 16 April 1953, in *Public
Papers of Presidents 1953* (1960)

17 You have broader considerations that might
follow what you might call the 'falling
domino' principle. You have a row of
dominoes set up. You knock over the first
one, and what will happen to the last one is
that it will go over very quickly. So you have
the beginning of a disintegration that would
have the most profound influences.
speech at press conference, 7 April 1954

18 I think that people want peace so much that
one of these days governments had better
get out of the way and let them have it.
broadcast discussion, 31 August 1959

19 In preparing for battle I have always found
that plans are useless, but planning is
indispensable.
Richard Nixon *Six Crises* (1962); attributed

Alfred Eisenstaedt 1898–1995
*German-born American photographer and
photojournalist*

20 It's more important to click with people
than to click the shutter
in *Life* 24 August 1995 (electronic edition),
obituary

Eleazar of Worms 1176–1238
Jewish rabbi

1 The highest sacrifice is a broken and contrite heart; the highest wisdom is that which is found in the Torah; the noblest of all ornaments is modesty; and the most beautiful thing that man can do, is to forgive a wrong.
   Sefer Rokeah

Edward Elgar 1857–1934
English composer

2 To my friends pictured within.
   Enigma Variations (1899) dedication

3 There is music in the air.
   R. J. Buckley *Sir Edward Elgar* (1905) ch. 4

George Eliot 1819–80
English novelist

4 Our deeds determine us, as much as we determine our deeds.
   Adam Bede (1859) ch. 29

5 He was like a cock who thought the sun had risen to hear him crow.
   Adam Bede (1859) ch. 33

6 We hand folks over to God's mercy, and show none ourselves.
   Adam Bede (1859) ch. 42

7 A difference of taste in jokes is a great strain on the affections.
   Daniel Deronda (1876) bk. 2, ch. 15

8 There is a great deal of unmapped country within us which would have to be taken into account in an explanation of our gusts and storms.
   Daniel Deronda (1876) bk. 3, ch. 24

9 There is no private life which has not been determined by a wider public life.
   Felix Holt (1866) ch. 3

10 An election is coming. Universal peace is declared, and the foxes have a sincere interest in prolonging the lives of the poultry.
   Felix Holt (1866) ch. 5

11 A woman can hardly ever choose . . . she is dependent on what happens to her. She must take meaner things, because only meaner things are within her reach.
   Felix Holt (1866) ch. 27

12 Debasing the moral currency.
   The Impressions of Theophrastus Such (1879) essay title

13 Many Theresas have been born who found for themselves no epic life wherein there was a constant unfolding of far-resonant action; perhaps only a life of mistakes, the offspring of a certain spiritual grandeur ill-matched with the meanness of opportunity; perhaps a tragic failure which found no sacred poet and sank unwept into oblivion.
   Middlemarch (1871–2) Prelude

14 Pride helps us; and pride is not a bad thing when it only urges us to hide our own hurts, not to hurt others.
   Middlemarch (1871–2) bk. 1, ch. 6

15 Among all forms of mistake, prophecy is the most gratuitous.
   Middlemarch (1871–2) bk. 1, ch. 10

16 Fred's studies are not very deep . . . he is only reading a novel.
   Middlemarch (1871–2) bk 1, ch. 11

17 If we had a keen vision and feeling of all ordinary human life, it would be like hearing the grass grow and the squirrel's heart beat, and we should die of that roar which lies on the other side of silence.
   Middlemarch (1871–2) bk. 2, ch. 20

18 Anger and jealousy can no more bear to lose sight of their objects than love.
   The Mill on the Floss (1860) bk. 1, ch. 10

19 The dead level of provincial existence.
   The Mill on the Floss (1860) bk. 5, ch. 3

20 The happiest women, like the happiest nations, have no history.
   The Mill on the Floss (1860) bk. 6, ch. 3; see **Montesquieu** 243:7

21 'Character' says Novalis, in one of his questionable aphorisms—'character is destiny.'
   The Mill on the Floss (1860) bk. 6, ch. 6; see **Heraclitus** 167:4, **Novalis** 252:7

22 In every parting there is an image of death.
   Scenes of Clerical Life (1858) 'Amos Barton' ch. 10

23 Oh may I join the choir invisible
   Of those immortal dead who live again
   In minds made better by their presence.
   'Oh May I Join the Choir Invisible' (1867)

T. S. Eliot 1888–1965
American-born British poet, critic, and dramatist

24 Because I do not hope to turn again
   Because I do not hope
   Because I do not hope to turn.
   Ash-Wednesday (1930) pt. 1

25 Teach us to care and not to care
   Teach us to sit still.
   Ash-Wednesday (1930) pt. 1

26 Lady, three white leopards sat under a juniper-tree
   In the cool of the day.
   Ash-Wednesday (1930) pt. 2

27 What is hell?
   Hell is oneself,
   Hell is alone, the other figures in it
   Merely projections.
   The Cocktail Party (1950) act 1, sc. 3; see **Sartre** 285:23

28 Success is relative:
   It is what we can make of the mess we have made of things.
   The Family Reunion (1939) pt. 2, sc. 3

29 Time present and time past
   Are both perhaps present in time future,
   And time future contained in time past.
   Four Quartets 'Burnt Norton' (1936) pt. 1

1 Footfalls echo in the memory
Down the passage which we did not take
Towards the door we never opened
Into the rose-garden.
Four Quartets 'Burnt Norton' (1936) pt. 1

2 Human kind
Cannot bear very much reality.
Four Quartets 'Burnt Norton' (1936) pt. 1.

3 At the still point of the turning world.
Four Quartets 'Burnt Norton' (1936) pt. 2

4 Words strain,
Crack and sometimes break, under the
burden,
Under the tension, slip, slide, perish,
Decay with imprecision, will not stay in
place,
Will not stay still.
Four Quartets 'Burnt Norton' (1936) pt. 5

5 In my beginning is my end.
Four Quartets 'East Coker' (1940) pt. 1; see **Mary**
230:15

6 The intolerable wrestle
With words and meanings.
Four Quartets 'East Coker' (1940) pt. 2

7 The houses are all gone under the sea.
The dancers are all gone under the hill.
Four Quartets 'East Coker' (1940) pt. 2

8 O dark dark dark. They all go into the dark,
The vacant interstellar spaces, the vacant
into the vacant.
Four Quartets 'East Coker' (1940) pt. 3

9 The wounded surgeon plies the steel
That questions the distempered part;
Beneath the bleeding hands we feel
The sharp compassion of the healer's art
Resolving the enigma of the fever chart.
Four Quartets 'East Coker' (1940) pt. 4

10 I think that the river
Is a strong brown god—sullen, untamed and
intractable.
Four Quartets 'The Dry Salvages' (1941) pt. 1

11 The communication
Of the dead is tongued with fire beyond the
language of the living.
Four Quartets 'Little Gidding' (1942) pt. 1

12 Ash on an old man's sleeve
Is all the ash the burnt roses leave.
Four Quartets 'Little Gidding' (1942) pt. 2

13 This is the death of air.
Four Quartets 'Little Gidding' (1942) pt. 2

14 Speech impelled us
To purify the dialect of the tribe.
Four Quartets 'Little Gidding' (1942) pt. 2

15 We shall not cease from exploration
And the end of all our exploring
Will be to arrive where we started
And know the place for the first time.
Four Quartets 'Little Gidding' (1942) pt. 5

16 What we call the beginning is often the end
And to make an end is to make a beginning.
The end is where we start from.
Four Quartets 'Little Gidding' (1942) pt. 5

17 So, while the light fails
On a winter's afternoon, in a secluded
chapel
History is now and England.
Four Quartets 'Little Gidding' (1942) pt. 5

18 And all shall be well and
All manner of thing shall be well
When the tongues of flame are in-folded
Into the crowned knot of fire
And the fire and the rose are one.
Four Quartets 'Little Gidding' (1942) pt. 5; see
Julian 193:14

19 Here I am, an old man in a dry month
Being read to by a boy, waiting for rain.
'Gerontion' (1920)

20 After such knowledge, what forgiveness?
'Gerontion' (1920)

21 Tenants of the house,
Thoughts of a dry brain in a dry season.
'Gerontion' (1920)

22 We are the hollow men.
'The Hollow Men' (1925)

23 *Here we go round the prickly pear*
Prickly pear prickly pear.
Between the idea
And the reality
Between the motion
And the act
Falls the Shadow.
'The Hollow Men' (1925)

24 This is the way the world ends
Not with a bang but a whimper.
'The Hollow Men' (1925)

25 A cold coming we had of it,
Just the worst time of the year
For a journey, and such a long journey:
The ways deep and the weather sharp,
The very dead of winter.
'Journey of the Magi' (1927); see **Andrewes** 6:18

26 I had seen birth and death
But had thought they were different.
'Journey of the Magi' (1927)

27 An alien people clutching their gods.
'Journey of the Magi' (1927)

28 Let us go then, you and I,
When the evening is spread out against the
sky
Like a patient etherized upon a table.
'The Love Song of J. Alfred Prufrock' (1917)

29 In the room the women come and go
Talking of Michelangelo.
'The Love Song of J. Alfred Prufrock' (1917)

30 The yellow fog that rubs its back upon the
window-panes.
'The Love Song of J. Alfred Prufrock' (1917)

31 I have measured out my life with coffee
spoons.
'The Love Song of J. Alfred Prufrock' (1917)

32 I should have been a pair of ragged claws
Scuttling across the floors of silent seas.
'The Love Song of J. Alfred Prufrock' (1917)

1 I have seen the moment of my greatness
  flicker,
And I have seen the eternal Footman hold
  my coat, and snicker,
And in short, I was afraid.
  The Love Song of J. Alfred Prufrock (1917)

2 No! I am not Prince Hamlet, nor was meant
  to be;
Am an attendant lord, one that will do
To swell a progress.
  The Love Song of J. Alfred Prufrock (1917)

3 I grow old . . . I grow old . . .
I shall wear the bottoms of my trousers
  rolled.
  The Love Song of J. Alfred Prufrock (1917)

4 Shall I part my hair behind? Do I dare to eat
  a peach?
I shall wear white flannel trousers, and walk
  upon the beach.
I have heard the mermaids singing, each to
  each.
I do not think that they will sing to me.
  The Love Song of J. Alfred Prufrock (1917); see
  Donne 119:14

5 Yet we have gone on living,
Living and partly living.
  Murder in the Cathedral (1935) pt. 1

6 The last temptation is the greatest treason:
To do the right deed for the wrong reason.
  Murder in the Cathedral (1935) pt. 1

7 Clear the air! clean the sky! wash the wind!
  Murder in the Cathedral (1935) pt. 2

8 The Naming of Cats is a difficult matter,
It isn't just one of your holiday games;
You may think at first I'm as mad as a hatter
  when I tell you, a cat must have THREE
  DIFFERENT NAMES.
  Old Possum's Book of Practical Cats (1939) 'The
  Naming of Cats'

9 He always has an alibi, and one or two to
  spare:
At whatever time the deed took
  place—MACAVITY WASN'T THERE!
  Old Possum's Book of Practical Cats (1939)
  'Macavity: the Mystery Cat'

10 The burnt-out ends of smoky days.
  'Preludes' (1917)

11 Midnight shakes the memory
As a madman shakes a dead geranium.
  'Rhapsody on a Windy Night' (1917)

12 Where is the wisdom we have lost in
  knowledge?
Where is the knowledge we have lost in
  information?
  The Rock (1934) pt. 1

13 And the wind shall say: 'Here were decent
  godless people:
Their only monument the asphalt road
And a thousand lost golf balls.'
  The Rock (1934) pt. 1

14 Birth, and copulation, and death.
That's all the facts when you come to brass
  tacks.
  Sweeney Agonistes (1932) 'Fragment of an Agon'

15 I gotta use words when I talk to you.
  Sweeney Agonistes (1932) 'Fragment of an Agon'

16 The nightingales are singing near
The Convent of the Sacred Heart,
And sang within the bloody wood
When Agamemnon cried aloud
And let their liquid siftings fall
To stain the stiff dishonoured shroud.
  'Sweeney among the Nightingales' (1919)

17 April is the cruellest month, breeding
Lilacs out of the dead land.
  The Waste Land (1922) pt. 1

18 I read, much of the night, and go south in
  the winter.
  The Waste Land (1922) pt. 1

19 I will show you fear in a handful of dust.
  The Waste Land (1922) pt. 1

20 Madame Sosostris, famous clairvoyante,
Had a bad cold, nevertheless
Is known to be the wisest woman in Europe,
With a wicked pack of cards.
  The Waste Land (1922) pt. 1

21 A crowd flowed over London Bridge, so
  many,
I had not thought death had undone so
  many.
  The Waste Land (1922) pt. 1

22 The Chair she sat in, like a burnished
  throne,
Glowed on the marble.
  The Waste Land (1922) pt. 2; see **Shakespeare**
  289:17

23 And still she cried, and still the world
  pursues,
'Jug Jug' to dirty ears.
  The Waste Land (1922) pt. 2; see **Lyly** 220:22

24 I think we are in rats' alley
Where the dead men lost their bones.
  The Waste Land (1922) pt. 2

25 O O O O that Shakespeherian Rag—
It's so elegant
So intelligent.
  The Waste Land (1922) pt. 2; see **Buck** 73:17

26 But at my back from time to time I hear
The sound of horns and motors, which shall
  bring
Sweeney to Mrs Porter in the spring.
O the moon shone bright on Mrs Porter
And on her daughter
They wash their feet in soda water.
  The Waste Land (1922) pt. 3; see **Marvell** 229:21

27 I Tiresias, old man with wrinkled dugs.
  The Waste Land (1922) pt. 3

28 One of the low on whom assurance sits
As a silk hat on a Bradford millionaire.
  The Waste Land (1922) pt. 3

29 When lovely woman stoops to folly and
Paces about her room again, alone,
She smooths her hair with automatic hand,
And puts a record on the gramophone.
  The Waste Land (1922) pt. 3; see **Goldsmith**
  153:27

30 Phlebas the Phoenician, a fortnight dead,

Forgot the cry of gulls, and the deep sea
swell
And the profit and loss.
The Waste Land (1922) pt. 4

1 Who is the third who walks always beside
you?
When I count, there are only you and I
together
But when I look ahead up the white road
There is always another one walking beside
you.
The Waste Land (1922) pt. 5

2 These fragments I have shored against my
ruins.
The Waste Land (1922) pt. 5

3 Shantih, shantih, shantih.
The Waste Land (1922) closing words; see
Upanishads 344:13

4 Webster was much possessed by death
And saw the skull beneath the skin.
'Whispers of Immortality' (1919)

5 The only way of expressing emotion in the
form of art is by finding an 'objective
correlative'.
The Sacred Wood (1920) 'Hamlet and his
Problems'

6 Immature poets imitate; mature poets steal.
The Sacred Wood (1920) 'Philip Massinger'

7 Someone said: 'The dead writers are remote
from us because we *know* so much more
than they did.' Precisely, and they are that
which we know.
The Sacred Wood (1920) 'Tradition and Individual
Talent'

8 In the seventeenth century a dissociation of
sensibility set in, from which we have never
recovered.
Selected Essays (1932) 'The Metaphysical Poets'
(1921)

9 To me . . . [*The Waste Land*] was only the relief
of a personal and wholly insignificant
grouse against life; it is just a piece of
rhythmical grumbling.
The Waste Land (ed. Valerie Eliot, 1971) epigraph

Elizabeth I 1533–1603
*English monarch, Queen of England and Ireland
from 1558*

10 The queen of Scots is this day leichter of a
fair son, and I am but a barren stock.
to her ladies, June 1566

11 I know what it is to be a subject, what to be
a Sovereign, what to have good neighbours,
and sometimes meet evil-willers.
speech to a Parliamentary deputation at
Richmond, 12 November 1586, from a report
'which the Queen herself heavily amended in
her own hand'

12 In trust I have found treason.
traditional concluding words of the speech to a
Parliamentary deputation at Richmond, 12
November 1586

13 I will make you shorter by the head.
*to the leaders of her Council, who were opposing
her course towards **Mary** Queen of Scots*
F. Chamberlin *Sayings of Queen Elizabeth* (1923)

14 I know I have the body of a weak and feeble
woman, but I have the heart and stomach of
a king, and of a king of England too; and
think foul scorn that Parma or Spain, or any
prince of Europe, should dare to invade the
borders of my realm.
speech to the troops at Tilbury on the approach
of the Armada, 1588

15 The daughter of debate, that eke discord
doth sow.
*on **Mary** Queen of Scots*
George Puttenham (ed.) *The Art of English Poesie*
(1589) bk. 3, ch. 20

16 Though God hath raised me high, yet this I
count the glory of my crown: that I have
reigned with your loves.
The Golden Speech, 1601

17 Must! Is *must* a word to be addressed to
princes? Little man, little man! thy father, if
he had been alive, durst not have used that
word.
*to Robert **Cecil**, on his saying she must go to bed,
shortly before her death*
J. R. Green *A Short History of the English People*
(1874) ch. 7

18 If thy heart fails thee, climb not at all.
*lines after Sir Walter **Ralegh**, written on a
window-pane*
Thomas Fuller *Worthies of England* vol. 1; see
Ralegh 273:2

19 I would not open windows into men's souls.
oral tradition, in J. B. Black *Reign of Elizabeth
1558–1603* (1936)

20 My Lord, I had forgot the fart.
*to Edward de Vere, Earl of Oxford, on his return
from seven years self-imposed exile, occasioned by
the acute embarrassment to himself of breaking
wind in the presence of the Queen*
John Aubrey *Brief Lives* 'Edward de Vere'

21 'Twas God the word that spake it,
He took the bread and brake it;
And what the word did make it;
That I believe, and take it.
*answer on being asked her opinion of Christ's
presence in the Sacrament*
S. Clarke *The Marrow of Ecclesiastical History* (1675)
pt. 2, bk. 1 'The Life of Queen Elizabeth'

22 All my possessions for a moment of time.
last words; attributed, but almost certainly
apocryphal

Elizabeth II 1926–
*British monarch, Queen of the United Kingdom
from 1952*

23 I declare before you all that my whole life,
whether it be long or short, shall be devoted
to your service and the service of our great
Imperial family to which we all belong.
broadcast speech, as Princess Elizabeth, to the
Commonwealth from Cape Town, 21 April 1947

1 I think everybody really will concede that on this, of all days, I should begin my speech with the words 'My husband and I'.
speech at Guildhall, London, on her 25th wedding anniversary
in *The Times* 21 November 1972

2 In the words of one of my more sympathetic correspondents, it has turned out to be an 'annus horribilis'.
speech at Guildhall, London, 24 November 1992

3 I for one believe that there are lessons to be drawn from her life and from the extraordinary and moving reaction to her death.
broadcast from Buckingham Palace on the evening before the funeral of Diana, Princess of Wales, 5 September 1997
in *The Times* 6 September 1997

4 *Vive la différence, mais vive l'entente cordiale.*
Long live the difference, but long live the Entente Cordiale.
speech, Paris, 5 April 2004

Queen Elizabeth, the Queen Mother 1900–2002
British Queen Consort of George VI

5 I'm glad we've been bombed. It makes me feel I can look the East End in the face.
to a London policeman, 13 September 1940
John Wheeler-Bennett *King George VI* (1958) pt. 3, ch. 6

6 The Princesses would never leave without me and I couldn't leave without the King, and the King will never leave.
on the suggestion that the royal family be evacuated during the Blitz
Penelope Mortimer *Queen Elizabeth* (1986) ch. 25

John Ellerton 1826–93
English clergyman

7 The day Thou gavest, Lord, is ended, The darkness falls at Thy behest.
Hymn (1870), the first line borrowed from an earlier, anonymous hymn

Duke Ellington 1899–1974
American jazz pianist, composer, and band-leader

8 Playing 'Bop' is like scrabble with all the vowels missing.
in *Look* 10 August 1954

Jane Elliot 1727–1805
Scottish poet

9 The flowers of the forest are a' wede away.
'The Flowers of the Forest' (1769), the most popular version of the traditional lament for the Battle of Flodden in 1513; see **Cockburn** 99:3

Charlotte Elliott 1789–1871
English hymn-writer

10 Just as I am, without one plea.
Invalid's Hymn Book (1834) 'Just as I am'

Ebenezer Elliott 1781–1849
English poet

11 What is a communist? One who hath yearnings
For equal division of unequal earnings.
'Epigram' (1850)

12 When wilt thou save the people?
Oh, God of Mercy! when?
The people, Lord, the people!
Not thrones and crowns, but men!
'The People's Anthem' (1850)

George Ellis 1753–1815
English poet and journalist

13 Snowy, Flowy, Blowy,
Showery, Flowery, Bowery,
Hoppy, Croppy, Droppy,
Breezy, Sneezy, Freezy.
'The Twelve Months'

Havelock Ellis (Henry Havelock Ellis) 1859–1939
English sexologist

14 What we call 'progress' is the exchange of one nuisance for another nuisance.
Impressions and Comments (1914) 31 July 1912

15 All civilization has from time to time become a thin crust over a volcano of revolution.
Little Essays of Love and Virtue (1922) ch. 7

Friar Elstow
English Franciscan

16 With thanks to God we know the way to heaven, to be as ready by water as by land, and therefore we care not which way we go.
when threatened with drowning by Henry VIII
John Stow *The Annals of England* (1615); see **Gilbert** 149:14

Paul Éluard 1895–1952
French poet

17 *Adieu tristesse*
Bonjour tristesse
Farewell sadness
Good-day sadness.
'À peine défigurée' (1932)

Ralph Waldo Emerson 1803–82
American philosopher and poet

18 If the red slayer think he slays,
Or if the slain think he is slain,
They know not well the subtle ways
I keep, and pass, and turn again.
'Brahma' (1867); see **Upanishads** 344:15

19 I am the doubter and the doubt.
'Brahma' (1867)

20 Here once the embattled farmers stood,
And fired the shot heard round the world.
'Concord Hymn' (1837)

21 Things are in the saddle,
And ride mankind.
'Ode' inscribed to W. H. Channing (1847)

1 When Duty whispers low, *Thou must*,
The youth replies, *I can*.
'Voluntaries' no. 3 (1867)

2 Make yourself necessary to someone.
The Conduct of Life (1860) 'Considerations by the
way'

3 Art is a jealous mistress.
The Conduct of Life (1860) 'Wealth'

4 The louder he talked of his honour, the
faster we counted our spoons.
The Conduct of Life (1860) 'Worship'; see **Johnson**
188:15, **Shaw** 312:5

5 Nothing great was ever achieved without
enthusiasm.
Essays (1841) 'Circles'

6 The only reward of virtue is virtue; the only
way to have a friend is to be one.
Essays (1841) 'Friendship'

7 It was a high counsel that I once heard given
to a young person, 'Always do what you are
afraid to do.'
Essays (1841) 'Heroism'

8 There is properly no history; only biography.
Essays (1841) 'History'; see **Disraeli** 117:24

9 In skating over thin ice, our safety is in our
speed.
Essays (1841) 'Prudence'

10 Whoso would be a man must be a
nonconformist.
Essays (1841) 'Self-Reliance'

11 A foolish consistency is the hobgoblin of
little minds.
Essays (1841) 'Self-Reliance'

12 Is it so bad, then, to be misunderstood?
Pythagoras was misunderstood, and
Socrates, and Jesus, and Luther, and
Copernicus, and Galileo, and Newton, and
every pure and wise spirit that ever took
flesh. To be great is to be misunderstood.
Essays (1841) 'Self-Reliance'

13 To fill the hour—that is happiness.
Essays. Second Series (1844) 'Experience'

14 Language is fossil poetry.
Essays. Second Series (1844) 'The Poet'

15 What is a weed? A plant whose virtues have
not been discovered.
Fortune of the Republic (1878)

16 Every hero becomes a bore at last.
Representative Men (1850) 'Uses of Great Men'

17 Hitch your wagon to a star.
Society and Solitude (1870) 'Civilization'

18 We boil at different degrees.
Society and Solitude (1870) 'Eloquence'

19 There never was a child so lovely but his
mother was glad to get asleep.
Journal 1836

20 I hate quotations. Tell me what you know.
Journals and Miscellaneous Notebooks (1961) May
1849

21 Glittering generalities! They are blazing
ubiquities.
on Rufus **Choate**
attributed; see **Choate** 94:5

22 If a man write a better book, preach a better
sermon, or make a better mouse-trap than
his neighbour, tho' he build his house in the
woods, the world will make a beaten path to
his door.
attributed to Emerson in Sarah S. B. Yule
Borrowings (1889); the quotation was the
occasion of a long controversy owing to Elbert
Hubbard's claim to its authorship

Robert Emmet 1778–1803
Irish nationalist

23 Let no man write my epitaph . . . When my
country takes her place among the nations
of the earth, *then*, and *not till then*, let my
epitaph be written.
speech from the dock when condemned to
death, 19 September 1803

William Empson 1906–84
English poet and literary critic

24 Waiting for the end, boys, waiting for the
end.
'Just a smack at Auden' (1940)

25 Seven types of ambiguity.
title of book (1930)

Friedrich Engels 1820–95
German socialist

26 *Der Staat wird nicht 'abgeschafft', er stirbt ab.*
The State is not 'abolished', *it withers away*.
Anti-Dühring (1878) pt. 3, ch. 2

Epictetus *c.*AD 50–120
Phrygian Stoic philosopher

27 Everything has two handles, by one of
which it ought to be carried and by the
other not.
The Encheiridion sect. 43

Epicurus 341–271 BC
Greek philosopher

28 Death, therefore, the most awful of evils, is
nothing to us, seeing that, when we are
death is not come, and when death is come,
we are not.
Diogenes Laertius *Lives of Eminent Philosophers* bk.
10

Olaudah Equiano *c.*1745–*c.*97
African writer and former slave

29 We are . . . a nation of dancers, singers and
poets.
of the Ibo people
Narrative of the Life of Olaudah Equiano (1789) ch. 1

30 When I recovered a little I found some black
people about me . . . I asked them if we were
not to be eaten by those white men with
horrible looks, red faces, and loose hair.
Narrative of the Life of Olaudah Equiano (1789) ch. 3

Erasmus c.1469–1536
Dutch Christian humanist

1 *In regione caecorum rex est luscus.*
In the country of the blind the one-eyed
man is king.
  Adages bk. 3, century 4, no. 96

Susan Ertz 1894–1985
American writer

2 Millions long for immortality who don't
know what to do with themselves on a rainy
Sunday afternoon.
  Anger in the Sky (1943)

Henri Estienne 1531–98
French printer and publisher

3 *Si jeunesse savait; si vieillesse pouvait.*
If youth knew; if age could.
  Les Prémices (1594) bk. 4, epigram 4

Euclid fl. c.300 BC
Greek mathematician

4 *Quod erat demonstrandum.*
Which was to be proved.
  often abbreviated to QED
    Latin translation from the Greek of *Elementa* bk.
    1, proposition 5 and *passim*

5 A line is length without breadth.
  Elementa bk. 1, definition 2

6 There is no 'royal road' to geometry.
  addressed to Ptolemy I, in Proclus *Commentary
  on the First Book of Euclid's Elementa* prologue, pt. 2

Euripides c.485–c.406 BC
Greek dramatist

7 My tongue swore, but my mind's unsworn.
  Hippolytus lamenting his breaking of an oath
  Hippolytus l. 612

8 Man's best possession is a sympathetic wife.
  fragment no. 164; Augustus Nauck *Tragicorum
  Graecorum Fragmenta*

Abel Evans 1679–1737
English poet and divine

9 Under this stone, Reader, survey
Dead Sir John Vanbrugh's house of clay.
Lie heavy on him, Earth! for he
Laid many heavy loads on thee!
  'Epitaph on Sir John Vanbrugh, Architect of
  Blenheim Palace'

Lord Eversley *see* Charles Shaw-Lefevre

William Norman Ewer 1885–1976
British writer

10 I gave my life for freedom—This I know:
For those who bade me fight had told me so.
  'Five Souls' (1917)

11 How odd
Of God
To choose
The Jews.
  Week-End Book (1924); see **Browne** 71:3

Winifred Ewing 1929–
Scottish Nationalist politician

12 The Scottish Parliament which adjourned
on 25 March in the year 1707 is hereby
reconvened.
  *opening speech, as oldest member of the new
  Parliament*
    in *Scottish Parliament* 12 May 1999

Frederick William Faber 1814–63
English priest

13 Faith of our Fathers! living still
In spite of dungeon, fire, and sword:
Oh, how our hearts beat fast with joy
Whene'er they hear that glorious word.
Faith of our Fathers! Holy Faith!
We will be true to thee till death.
  'Faith of our Fathers'

14 My God, how wonderful Thou art!
Thy Majesty how bright!
  Oratory Hymns (1854) 'The Eternal Father'

15 There's a wideness in God's mercy
Like the wideness of the sea.
  Oratory Hymns (1854) 'Souls of men, why will ye
  scatter'

Robert Fabyan d. 1513
English chronicler

16 Ranulphe says he took a surfeit by eating of
a lamprey, and thereof died.
  The New Chronicles of England and France (1516)
  vol. 1, ch. 229

17 The Duke of Clarence . . . then being a
prisoner in the Tower, was secretly put to
death and drowned in a barrel of Malmesey
wine within the said Tower.
  The New Chronicles of England and France (1516)
  vol. 2 '1478'; 'malvesye' for 'malmesey' in early
  editions

Clifton Fadiman 1904–
American critic

18 Milk's leap toward immortality.
  of cheese
    Any Number Can Play (1957)

Lucius Cary, Lord Falkland
1610–43
English royalist politician

19 When it is not necessary to change, it is
necessary not to change.
  Discourses of Infallibility (1660) 'A Speech
  concerning Episcopacy' delivered in 1641

Frantz Fanon 1925–61
French West Indian psychoanalyst and writer

20 The shape of Africa resembles a revolver,
and the Congo is the trigger.
  attributed

Michael Faraday 1791–1867
English physicist and chemist

21 Nothing is too wonderful to be true, if it be
consistent with the laws of nature, and in

such things as these, experiment is the best test of such consistency.

diary, 19 March 1849

1 Why sir, there is every possibility that you will soon be able to tax it!

to Gladstone, when asked about the usefulness of electricity

W. E. H. Lecky *Democracy and Liberty* (1899 ed.)

Wallace Fard *c*.1891–1934
American religious leader

2 The blue-eyed devil white man.

Malcolm X with Alex Haley *The Autobiography of Malcolm X* (1965); see **Malcolm X** 226:1

Eleanor Farjeon 1881–1965
English writer for children

3 Morning has broken
Like the first morning,
Blackbird has spoken
Like the first bird.

Children's Bells (1957) 'A Morning Song (for the First Day of Spring)'

Herbert Farjeon 1887–1945
English writer and theatre critic

4 I've danced with a man who's danced with a girl
Who's danced with the Prince of Wales!

'I've danced with a man who's danced with a girl'; first written for Elsa Lanchester and sung at private parties; later sung on stage by Mimi Crawford (1928)

James Farley 1888–1976
American Democratic politician

5 As Maine goes, so goes Vermont.

after predicting correctly that Franklin Roosevelt would carry all but two states in the election of 1936

statement to the press, 4 November 1936

Farouk 1920–65
Egyptian monarch, King 1936–52

6 The whole world is in revolt. Soon there will be only five Kings left—the King of England, the King of Spades, the King of Clubs, the King of Hearts and the King of Diamonds.

said to Lord Boyd-Orr at a conference in Cairo, 1948

George Farquhar 1678–1707
Irish dramatist

7 My Lady Bountiful.

The Beaux' Stratagem (1707) act 1, sc. 1

8 Poetry's a mere drug, Sir.

Love and a Bottle (1698) act 3, sc. 2; see **Lowell** 219:17

David Glasgow Farragut 1801–70
American admiral

9 Damn the torpedoes! Full speed ahead.

at the battle of Mobile Bay, 5 August 1864 (torpedoes *mines*)

A. T. Mahan *Great Commanders: Admiral Farragut* (1892) ch. 10

Marie Fatayi-Williams
Nigerian mother

10 How much blood must be spilled? How many tears shall we cry? How many mothers' hearts must be maimed?

mother of Anthony Fatayi-Williams, killed in the London bombings of 7 July 2005

speech near Tavistock Square, London, 11 July 2005

William Faulkner 1897–1962
American novelist

11 The past is never dead. It's not even past.

Requiem for a Nun (1951) act 1

12 I believe man will not merely endure, he will prevail. He is immortal, not because he, alone among creatures, has an inexhaustible voice but because he has a soul, a spirit capable of compassion and sacrifice and endurance.

Nobel Prize acceptance speech, Stockholm, 10 December 1950

13 The writer's only responsibility is to his art. He will be completely ruthless if he is a good one . . . If a writer has to rob his mother, he will not hesitate; the *Ode on a Grecian Urn* is worth any number of old ladies.

in *Paris Review* Spring 1956

Guy Fawkes 1570–1606
English conspirator in the Gunpowder Plot, 1605

14 A desperate disease requires a dangerous remedy.

6 November 1605, in *Dictionary of National Biography* (1917–); see **Shakespeare** 293:25

Dianne Feinstein 1933–
American Democratic politician

15 Toughness doesn't have to come in a pinstripe suit.

in *Time* 4 June 1984

James Fenton 1949–
English poet

16 'The fact is
In soteriological terms
I'm a crude existential malpractice
And you are a diet of worms.'

'God, A Poem' (1983)

Edna Ferber 1887–1968
American writer

17 Roast Beef, Medium, is not only a food. It is a philosophy.

foreword to *Roast Beef, Medium* (1911)

Ferdinand I 1503–64
Holy Roman Emperor from 1558

18 *Fiat justitia et pereat mundus.*
Let justice be done, though the world perish.

motto of Ferdinand I (1503–64), Holy Roman Emperor; see **Watson** 351:15

Pierre de Fermat 1601–65
French mathematician

1 *Cuius rei demonstrationem mirabilem sane detexi hanc marginis exiguitas non caperet.*

I have a truly marvellous demonstration of this proposition which this margin is too narrow to contain.

of 'Fermat's last theorem', written in the margin of his copy of Diophantus' Arithmetica, *and subsequently published by his son in 1670 in an edition of the book containing Fermat's annotations*

Simon Singh *Fermat's Last Theorem* (1997)

Enrico Fermi 1901–54
Italian-born American atomic physicist

2 Whatever Nature has in store for mankind, unpleasant as it may be, men must accept, for ignorance is never better than knowledge.

Laura Fermi *Atoms in the Family* (1955)

Ludwig Feuerbach 1804–72
German philosopher

3 *Der Mensch ist, was er isst.*

Man is what he eats.

Jacob Moleschott *Lehre der Nahrungsmittel: Für das Volk* (1850) 'Advertisement'; see **Brillat-Savarin** 69:2

Richard Phillips Feynman 1918–88
American theoretical physicist

4 For a successful technology, reality must take precedence over public relations, for nature cannot be fooled.

appendix to the *Rogers Commission Report on the Space Shuttle Challenger Accident* 6 June 1986

5 What I cannot create, I do not understand.
attributed

Eugene Field 1850–95
American poet and journalist

6 Wynken, Blynken, and Nod one night
Sailed off in a wooden shoe—
Sailed on a river of crystal light,
Into a sea of dew.
'Wynken, Blynken, and Nod' (1889)

Helen Fielding 1958–
British writer

7 I will not . . . sulk about having no boyfriend, but develop inner poise and authority and sense of self as woman of substance, complete *without* boyfriend, as best way to obtain boyfriend.
Bridget Jones's Diary (1996)

Henry Fielding 1707–54
English novelist and dramatist

8 It hath been often said, that it is not death, but dying, which is terrible.
Amelia (1751) bk. 3, ch. 4

9 The dusky night rides down the sky,

And ushers in the morn;
The hounds all join in glorious cry,
The huntsman winds his horn:
And a-hunting we will go.
Don Quixote in England (1733) act 2, sc. 5 'A-Hunting We Will Go'

10 He in a few minutes ravished this fair creature, or at least would have ravished her, if she had not, by a timely compliance, prevented him.
Jonathan Wild (1743) bk. 3, ch. 7

11 Love and scandal are the best sweeteners of tea.
Love in Several Masques (1728) act 4, sc. 11

12 What is commonly called love, namely the desire of satisfying a voracious appetite with a certain quantity of delicate white human flesh.
Tom Jones (1749) bk. 6, ch. 1

13 His designs were strictly honourable, as the phrase is; that is, to rob a lady of her fortune by way of marriage.
Tom Jones (1749) bk. 11, ch. 4

14 All Nature wears one universal grin.
Tom Thumb the Great (1731) act 1, sc. 1

Dorothy Fields 1905–74
American songwriter

15 A fine romance with no kisses.
A fine romance, my friend, this is.
'A Fine Romance' (1936 song)

16 Leave your worry on the doorstep,
Just direct your feet
To the sunny side of the street.
'On the Sunny Side of the Street' (1930 song)

W. C. Fields 1880–1946
American humorist

17 Never give a sucker an even break.
title of a W. C. Fields film (1941); the catchphrase (Fields's own) is said to have originated in the musical comedy *Poppy* (1923)

18 Some weasel took the cork out of my lunch.
You Can't Cheat an Honest Man (1939 film)

19 It ain't a fit night out for man or beast.
adopted by Fields but claimed by him not to be original; letter, 8 February 1944

20 Fish fuck in it.
on being asked why he never drank water
attributed

21 Hell, I never vote *for* anybody. I always vote *against*.
Robert Lewis Taylor *W. C. Fields* (1950); see **Adams** 1:16

22 Here lies W. C. Fields. I would rather be living in Philadelphia.
suggested epitaph for himself, in *Vanity Fair* June 1925

Ronald Firbank 1886–1926
English novelist

23 There was a pause—just long enough for an angel to pass, flying slowly.
Vainglory (1915) ch. 6

Michael Fish 1944–
British weather forecaster

1 A woman rang to say she heard there was a hurricane on the way. Well don't worry, there isn't.

weather forecast on the night before serious gales in southern England
    BBC TV, 15 October 1987

H. A. L. Fisher 1856–1940
English historian

2 Europe is a continent of energetic mongrels.
    A History of Europe (1935) ch. 1

John Arbuthnot Fisher 1841–1920
British admiral

3 Sack the lot!
on government overmanning and overspending
    letter to *The Times*, 2 September 1919

4 Never contradict
Never explain
Never apologize.
    letter to *The Times*, 5 September 1919; see
    Disraeli 118:8, **Hubbard** 177:7

R. A. Fisher 1890–1962
English statistician and geneticist

5 It was Darwin's chief contribution, not only to Biology but to the whole of natural science, to have brought to light a process by which contingencies *a priori* improbable are given, in the process of time, an increasing probability, until it is their non-occurrence, rather than their occurrence, which becomes highly improbable.
sometimes quoted as 'Natural selection is a mechanism for generating an exceedingly high degree of improbability'
    'Retrospect of the criticisms of the Theory of Natural Selection' in Julian Huxley *Evolution as a Process* (1954)

Edward Fitzgerald 1809–83
English scholar and poet

6 Awake! for Morning in the bowl of night
Has flung the stone that puts the stars to flight:
And Lo! the Hunter of the East has caught
The Sultan's turret in a noose of light.
    The Rubáiyát of Omar Khayyám (1859) st. 1

7 Each morn a thousand roses brings, you say;
Yes, but where leaves the rose of yesterday?
    The Rubáiyát of Omar Khayyám (4th ed., 1879) st. 9

8 Here with a loaf of bread beneath the bough,
A flask of wine, a book of verse—and Thou
Beside me singing in the wilderness—
And wilderness is paradise enow.
    The Rubáiyát of Omar Khayyám (1859) st. 11
    A book of verses underneath the bough,
    A jug of wine, a loaf of bread—and Thou
    Beside me singing in the wilderness—
    Oh, wilderness were paradise enow!
    The Rubáiyát of Omar Khayyám (4th ed., 1879) st. 12

9 Ah, take the cash in hand and waive the rest;
Oh, the brave music of a *distant drum*!
    The Rubáiyát of Omar Khayyám (1859) st. 12
    Ah, take the cash and let the credit go,
    Nor heed the rumble of a distant drum!
    The Rubáiyát of Omar Khayyám (4th ed., 1879) st. 13

10 I sometimes think that never blows so red
The rose as where some buried Caesar bled.
    The Rubáiyát of Omar Khayyám (1859) st. 18

11 Dust into dust, and under dust, to lie,
Sans wine, sans song, sans singer, and—sans End!
    The Rubáiyát of Omar Khayyám (1859) st. 23

12 One thing is certain, and the rest is lies;
The flower that once hath blown for ever dies.
    The Rubáiyát of Omar Khayyám (1859) st. 26
    One thing is certain and the rest is lies;
    The flower that once has blown for ever dies.
    The Rubáiyát of Omar Khayyám (4th ed., 1879) st. 63

13 Ah, fill the cup:—what boots it to repeat
How time is slipping underneath our feet:
Unborn TOMORROW, and dead YESTERDAY,
Why fret about them if TODAY be sweet!
    The Rubáiyát of Omar Khayyám (1859) st. 37

14 'Tis all a chequer-board of nights and days
Where Destiny with Men for pieces plays:
Hither and thither moves, and mates, and slays,
And one by one back in the closet lays.
    The Rubáiyát of Omar Khayyám (1859) st. 49
    But helpless pieces of the game he plays
    Upon this chequerboard of nights and days;
    Hither and thither moves, and checks, and slays,
    And one by one back in the closet lays.
    The Rubáiyát of Omar Khayyám (4th ed., 1879) st. 69

15 The ball no question makes of Ayes and Noes,
But here or there as strikes the player goes;
And he that tossed you down into the field,
He knows about it all—HE knows—HE knows!
    The Rubáiyát of Omar Khayyám (4th ed., 1879) st. 70

16 The moving finger writes; and, having writ,
Moves on: nor all thy piety nor wit
Shall lure it back to cancel half a line,
Nor all thy tears wash out a word of it.
    The Rubáiyát of Omar Khayyám (1859) st. 51; 'all your tears' in 4th ed. (1879) st. 71

17 That inverted bowl we call The Sky.
    The Rubáiyát of Omar Khayyám (1859) st. 52; 'they call the Sky' in 4th ed. (1879) st. 72

18 They sneer at me for leaning all awry;
What! did the hand then of the potter shake?
    The Rubáiyát of Omar Khayyám (4th ed., 1879) st. 86

1 Who *is* the potter, pray, and who the pot?
   The Rubáiyát of Omar Khayyám (1859) st. 60

2 Indeed the idols I have loved so long
   Have done my credit in this world much
      wrong:
   Have drowned my glory in a shallow cup
   And sold my reputation for a song.
   The Rubáiyát of Omar Khayyám (4th ed., 1879) st.
   93

3 Alas, that spring should vanish with the
      rose!
   That youth's sweet-scented manuscript
      should close!
   The Rubáiyát of Omar Khayyám (1859) st. 72

4 And when Thyself with shining foot shall
      pass
   Among the guests star-scattered on the
      grass,
   And in thy joyous errand reach the spot
   Where I made one—turn down an empty
      glass!
   The Rubáiyát of Omar Khayyám (1859) st. 75
   And when like her, O Saki, you shall pass
   Among the guests star-scattered on the
      grass,
   And in your joyous errand reach the spot
   Where I made one—turn down an empty
      glass!
   The Rubáiyát of Omar Khayyám (4th ed., 1879) st.
   101

5 Taste is the feminine of genius.
   letter to J. R. Lowell, October 1877

F. Scott Fitzgerald 1896–1940
American novelist

6 Let me tell you about the very rich. They are
   different from you and me.
   *to which Ernest **Hemingway** replied, 'Yes, they
   have more money'*
   All the Sad Young Men (1926) 'Rich Boy'

7 The beautiful and damned.
   title of novel (1922)

8 At eighteen our convictions are hills from
   which we look; at forty-five they are caves in
   which we hide.
   'Bernice Bobs her Hair' (1920)

9 Show me a hero and I will write you a
   tragedy.
   Edmund Wilson (ed.) *The Crack-Up* (1945) 'Note-
   Books E'

10 I've been drunk for about a week now, and I
   thought it might sober me up to sit in a
   library.
   The Great Gatsby (1925) ch. 3

11 Her voice is full of money.
   The Great Gatsby (1925) ch. 7

12 They were careless people, Tom and
   Daisy—they smashed up things and
   creatures and then retreated back into their
   money or their vast carelessness, or
   whatever it was that kept them together,
   and let other people clean up the mess they
   had made.
   The Great Gatsby (1925) ch. 9

13 In a real dark night of the soul it is always
   three o'clock in the morning.
   'Handle with Care' in *Esquire* March 1936; see **St
   John of the Cross** 185:15

14 See that little stream—we could walk to it in
   two minutes. It took the British a month to
   walk it—a whole empire walking very
   slowly, dying in front and pushing forward
   behind. And another empire walked very
   slowly backward a few inches a day, leaving
   the dead like a million bloody rugs.
   Tender is the Night (1934)

15 There are no second acts in American lives.
   Edmund Wilson (ed.) *The Last Tycoon* (1941)
   'Hollywood, etc.'

16 An author ought to write for the youth of
   his own generation, the critics of the next,
   and the schoolmasters of ever after.
   letter to the Booksellers' Convention, April
   1920; Andrew Turnbull (ed.) *Selected Letters of F.
   Scott Fitzgerald* (1963)

17 All good writing is *swimming under water* and
   holding your breath.
   letter (undated) to his daughter, Frances Scott
   Fitzgerald; Andrew Turnbull (ed.) *Selected Letters
   of F. Scott Fitzgerald* (1963)

Robert Fitzsimmons 1862–1917
New Zealand boxer

18 The bigger they are, the further they have to
   fall.
   prior to a fight
   in *Brooklyn Daily Eagle* 11 August 1900

Bud Flanagan 1896–1968
British comedian

19 Underneath the Arches,
   I dream my dreams away,
   Underneath the Arches,
   On cobble-stones I lay.
   'Underneath the Arches' (1932 song)

Michael Flanders 1922–75
and Donald Swann 1923–94
English songwriters

20 Have Some Madeira, M'dear.
   title of song (*c.*1956)

21 Mud! Mud! Glorious mud!
   Nothing quite like it for cooling the blood.
   'The Hippopotamus' (1952)

22 Eating people is wrong!
   'The Reluctant Cannibal' (1956 song); adopted
   as the title of a novel (1959) by Malcolm
   Bradbury

Gustave Flaubert 1821–80
French novelist

23 Human speech is like a cracked kettle on
   which we tap crude rhythms for bears to
   dance to, while we long to make music that
   will melt the stars.
   Madame Bovary (1857) pt. 1, ch. 12 (tr. F.
   Steegmuller)

24 Poetry is a subject as precise as geometry.
   letter to Louise Colet, 14 August 1853

1 Books are made not like children but like
pyramids . . . and they're just as useless! and
they stay in the desert! . . . Jackals piss at
their foot and the bourgeois climb up on
them.
  letter to Ernest Feydeau, November/December
  1857

2 *Madame Bovary, c'est moi.*
Madame Bovary is myself.
  attributed

James Elroy Flecker 1884–1915
English poet

3 The dragon-green, the luminous, the dark,
the serpent-haunted sea.
  'The Gates of Damascus' (1913)

4 For lust of knowing what should not be
known,
We take the Golden Road to Samarkand.
  The Golden Journey to Samarkand (1913) pt. 1,
  'Epilogue'

5 We are the Pilgrims, master; we shall go
Always a little further.
  The Golden Journey to Samarkand (1913) pt. 1,
  'Epilogue'

Ari Fleischer 1960–
American government spokesman

6 The problem with guns that are hidden is
you can't see their smoke.
  on BBC News Online, 10 January 2003; see **Blix**
  58:10

Ian Fleming 1908–64
English thriller writer

7 A medium Vodka dry Martini—with a slice
of lemon peel. Shaken and not stirred.
  Dr No (1958) ch. 14

8 The licence to kill for the Secret Service, the
double-0 prefix, was a great honour.
  Dr No (1958); popularly quoted as 'Licensed to
  kill'

Robert, Marquis de Flers
1872–1927
and Arman de Caillavet 1869–1915
French dramatists

9 Democracy is the name we give the people
whenever we need them.
  L'habit vert act 1, sc. 12, in *La petite Illustration
  série théâtre* 31 May 1913

Andrew Fletcher of Saltoun
1655–1716
Scottish patriot and anti-Unionist

10 If a man were permitted to make all the
ballads, he need not care who should make
the laws of a nation.
  'An Account of a Conversation concerning a
  Right Regulation of Government for the Good
  of Mankind. In a Letter to the Marquis of
  Montrose' (1704)

John Fletcher 1579–1625
English dramatist

11 Death hath so many doors to let out life.
  The Custom of the Country (with Massinger) act 2,
  sc. 2; see **Massinger** 231:3, **Seneca** 288:23,
  Webster 352:23

12 Our acts our angels are, or good or ill,
Our fatal shadows that walk by us still.
  The Honest Man's Fortune epilogue

13 Care-charming Sleep, thou easer of all woes,
Brother to Death.
  Valentinian (performed *c.*1610–14) act 5, sc. 7
  'Song'; see **Daniel** 109:5, **Shelley** 314:17

14 Whistle and she'll come to you.
  Wit Without Money act 4, sc. 4; see **Burns** 77:8

Phineas Fletcher 1582–1650
English clergyman and poet

15 Drop, drop, slow tears,
And bathe those beauteous feet,
Which brought from Heaven
The news and Prince of Peace.
  Poetical Miscellanies (1633) 'An Hymn'

Jean-Pierre Claris de Florian
1755–94
French writer and poet

16 *Plaisir d'amour ne dure qu'un moment,
Chagrin d'amour dure toute la vie.*
Love's pleasure lasts but a moment;
Love's sorrow lasts all through life.
  Célestine (1784)

Dario Fo 1926–
Italian dramatist

17 *Non si paga, non si paga*
We won't pay, we won't pay.
  title of play (1975; translated by Lino Pertile in
  1978 as 'We Can't Pay? We Won't Pay!' and
  performed in London in 1981 as *'Can't Pay?
  Won't Pay!'*)

Ferdinand Foch 1851–1929
French Marshal

18 My centre is giving way, my right is
retreating, situation excellent, I am
attacking.
  *message during the first Battle of the Marne,
  September 1914*
  R. Recouly *Foch* (1919) ch. 6

19 This is not a peace treaty, it is an armistice
for twenty years.
  at the signing of the Treaty of Versailles, 1919
  Paul Reynaud *Mémoires* (1963) vol. 2

J. Foley 1906–70
British songwriter

20 Old soldiers never die,
They simply fade away.
  'Old Soldiers Never Die' (1920 song);
  copyrighted by Foley but possibly a 'folk-song'
  from the First World War

Jane Fonda 1937–
American actress

1 A man has every season, while a woman has only the right to spring.
   in *Daily Mail* 13 September 1989

Michael Foot 1913–
British Labour politician

2 Think of it! A second Chamber selected by the Whips. A seraglio of eunuchs.
   speech in the House of Commons, 3 February 1969

3 It is not necessary that every time he rises he should give his famous imitation of a semi-house-trained polecat.
   of Norman Tebbit
   speech in the House of Commons, 2 March 1978

Samuel Foote 1720–77
English actor and dramatist

4 So she went into the garden to cut a cabbage-leaf to make an apple-pie; and at the same time a great she-bear coming up the street, pops its head into the shop. 'What! no soap?' So he died, and she very imprudently married the barber; and there were present the Picninnies, and the Joblillies, and the Garyulies, and the grand Panjandrum himself, with the little round button at top; and they all fell to playing the game of catch as catch can, till the gun powder ran out at the heels of their boots.
   nonsense composed to test the vaunted memory of the actor Charles Macklin (1697?–1797)
   Maria Edgeworth *Harry and Lucy* (1825) vol. 2

Gerald Ford 1909–
American Republican statesman, 38th President of the US 1974–7

5 If the Government is big enough to give you everything you want, it is big enough to take away everything you have.
   John F. Parker *If Elected* (1960)

6 I am a Ford, not a Lincoln.
   on taking the vice-presidential oath, 6 December 1973
   in *Washington Post* 7 December 1973

7 Our long national nightmare is over. Our Constitution works; our great Republic is a Government of laws and not of men.
   on being sworn in as President, 9 August 1974
   G. J. Lankevich *Gerald R. Ford* (1977); see **Adams** 2:4

Henry Ford 1863–1947
American car manufacturer and businessman

8 Any customer can have a car painted any colour that he wants so long as it is black.
   on the Model T Ford, 1909
   Henry Ford with Samuel Crowther *My Life and Work* (1922) ch. 2

9 History is more or less bunk.
   in *Chicago Tribune* 25 May 1916

Lena Guilbert Ford 1870–1916
English songwriter

10 Keep the Home-fires burning,
   While your hearts are yearning,
   Though your lads are far away
   They dream of Home.
   There's a silver lining
   Through the dark cloud shining;
   Turn the dark cloud inside out,
   Till the boys come Home.
   'Till the Boys Come Home!' (1914 song); music by Ivor Novello

George Foreman 1948–
American boxer

11 The most horrifying thing in the world is to be without an adventure.
   considering a comeback at 55
   in *Independent* 29 December 2003

Howell Forgy 1908–83
American naval chaplain

12 Praise the Lord and pass the ammunition.
   at Pearl Harbor, 7 December 1941, while Forgy moved along a line of sailors passing ammunition by hand to the deck
   in *New York Times* 1 November 1942; later the title of a song by Frank **Loesser**, 1942

E. M. Forster 1879–1970
English novelist

13 Yes—oh dear yes—the novel tells a story.
   Aspects of the Novel (1927) ch. 2

14 It is a period between two wars—the long week-end it has been called.
   The Development of English Prose between 1918 and 1939 (1945)

15 Railway termini. They are our gates to the glorious and the unknown. Through them we pass out into adventure and sunshine, to them, alas! we return.
   Howards End (1910) ch. 2

16 Only connect! . . . Only connect the prose and the passion.
   Howards End (1910) ch. 22

17 Pathos, piety, courage—they exist, but are identical, and so is filth. Everything exists, nothing has value.
   A Passage to India (1924) ch. 14

18 If I had to choose between betraying my country and betraying my friend, I hope I should have the guts to betray my country.
   Two Cheers for Democracy (1951) 'What I Believe'

19 So Two cheers for Democracy: one because it admits variety and two because it permits criticism. Two cheers are quite enough: there is no occasion to give three. Only Love the Beloved Republic deserves that.
   Two Cheers for Democracy (1951) 'What I Believe'; see **Swinburne** 329:13

Venantius Fortunatus c.AD 530–c.610
Frankish poet and priest

20 Pange, lingua, gloriosi

Proelium certaminis.
Sing, my tongue, of the battle in the glorious struggle.
Passiontide hymn, most commonly sung as: 'Sing, my tongue, the glorious battle'
'Pange lingua gloriosi'; see **Thomas Aquinas** 337:12

1 *Vexilla regis prodeunt,*
Fulget crucis mysterium.
The banners of the king advance, the mystery of the cross shines bright.
hymn, usually sung as 'The royal banners forward go'
'Vexilla Regis'

2 *Regnavit a ligno Deus.*
God reigned from the wood.
'Vexilla Regis'

Harry Emerson Fosdick 1878–1969
American Baptist minister

3 I renounce war for its consequences, for the lies it lives on and propagates, for the undying hatred it arouses, for the dictatorships it puts in the place of democracy, for the starvation that stalks after it.
Armistice Day Sermon in New York, 1933

Charles Foster 1828–1904
American politician

4 Isn't this a billion dollar country?
responding to a Democratic gibe about a 'million dollar Congress'
at the 51st Congress; also attributed to Thomas B. Reed

George Foster 1847–1931
Canadian politician

5 In these somewhat troublesome days when the great Mother Empire stands splendidly isolated in Europe.
headlined as 'Splendid isolation' in The Times *22 January 1896*
in *Official Report of the Debates of the House of Commons of the Dominion of Canada* (1896) vol. 41, for 16 January 1896

John Foster 1770–1843
English Baptist minister

6 But the two classes [the educated and the uneducated] so beheld in contrast, might they not seem to belong to two different nations?
Essay on the Evils of Popular Ignorance (1820); see **Disraeli** 117:29

Stephen Collins Foster 1826–64
American songwriter

7 Beautiful dreamer, wake unto me,
Starlight and dewdrop are waiting for thee.
'Beautiful Dreamer' (1864 song)

8 I dream of Jeanie with the light brown hair,
Floating, like a vapour, on the soft summer air.
'Jeanie with the Light Brown Hair' (1854)

9 Way down upon the Swanee River,
Far, far, away,
There's where my heart is turning ever;
There's where the old folks stay.
'The Old Folks at Home' (1851)

10 All the world is sad and dreary
Everywhere I roam,
Oh! darkies, how my heart grows weary,
Far from the old folks at home.
'The Old Folks at Home' (1851) chorus

Charles Fourier 1772–1837
French social theorist

11 The extension of women's rights is the basic principle of all social progress.
Théorie des Quatre Mouvements (1808) vol. 2, ch. 4

H. W. Fowler 1858–1933
English lexicographer and grammarian

12 The English speaking world may be divided into (1) those who neither know nor care what a split infinitive is; (2) those who do not know, but care very much; (3) those who know and condemn; (4) those who know and approve; and (5) those who know and distinguish. Those who neither know nor care are the vast majority and are a happy folk, to be envied by most of the minority classes.
Modern English Usage (1926)

Norman Fowler 1938–
British Conservative politician

13 I have a young family and for the next few years I should like to devote more time to them.
often quoted as 'spend more time with my family'
resignation letter to the Prime Minister, in *Guardian* 4 January 1990; see **Thatcher** 337:1

Charles James Fox 1749–1806
English Whig politician

14 How much the greatest event it is that ever happened in the world! and how much the best!
on the fall of the Bastille
letter to Richard Fitzpatrick, 30 July 1789

George Fox 1624–91
English founder of the Society of Friends (Quakers)

15 I saw also that there was an ocean of darkness and death, but an infinite ocean of light and love, which flowed over the ocean of darkness.
Journal 1647

16 I told them I lived in the virtue of that life and power that took away the occasion of all wars.
on being offered a captaincy in the army of the Commonwealth, against the forces of the King
Journal 1651

17 I . . . espied three steeple-house spires, and they struck at my life.
on seeing the spires of Lichfield
Journal 1651

1 Walk cheerfully over the world, answering that of God in every one.
  Journal 1656

2 All bloody principles and practices, we, as to our own particulars, do utterly deny, with all outward wars and strife and fightings with outward weapons, for any end or under any pretence whatsoever. And this is our testimony to the whole world.
  Journal 1661

Henry Fox *see* Lord Holland

Michael J. Fox 1961–
Canadian actor

3 It's all about losing your brain without losing your mind.
  on his fight against Parkinson's disease
  in *The Times* 16 September 2000

Terry Fox 1958–81
Canadian runner

4 I'm not a dreamer . . . but I believe in miracles. I have to.
  planning a fund-raising run across Canada after his right leg was amputated because of cancer; he completed two thirds of his 'Marathon of Hope'
  letter to the Canadian Cancer Society, 15 October 1979

Janet Frame 1924–2004
New Zealand writer

5 For your own good is a persuasive argument that will eventually make a man agree to his own destruction.
  Faces in the Water (1961) ch. 4

Anatole France 1844–1924
French novelist and man of letters

6 In every well-governed state, wealth is a sacred thing; in democracies it is the only sacred thing.
  L'Île des pingouins (1908) pt. 6, ch. 2

7 Christianity has done a great deal for love by making a sin of it.
  Le Jardin d'Épicure (1895)

8 They [the poor] have to labour in the face of the majestic equality of the law, which forbids the rich as well as the poor to sleep under bridges, to beg in the streets, and to steal bread.
  Le Lys rouge (1894) ch. 7

9 You think you are dying for your country; you die for the industrialists.
  in *L'Humanité* 18 July 1922

Francis I 1494–1547
French monarch, King from 1515

10 De toutes choses ne m'est demeuré que l'honneur et la vie qui est saulve.

Of all I had, only honour and life have been spared.
  letter to his mother following his defeat at Pavia, 1525; usually quoted as 'Tout est perdu fors l'honneur [All is lost save honour]'
  in *Collection des Documents Inédits sur l'Histoire de France* (1847) vol. 1

St Francis de Sales 1567–1622
French bishop

11 Big fires flare up in a wind, but little ones are blown out unless they are carried in under cover.
  Introduction à la vie dévote (1609) pt. 3, ch. 34; see **Bussy-Rabutin** 78:23, **La Rochefoucauld** 209:9

12 It has been well said, that heart speaks to heart, whereas language only speaks to the ears.
  letter to the Archbishop of Bourges, 5 October 1604, in *Oeuvres de Saint François de Sales* (1834) vol. 3

St Francis of Assisi 1181–1226
Italian monk

13 Praised be You, my Lord, with all your creatures,
especially Sir Brother Sun,
Who is the day and through whom You give us light.
  'The Canticle of Brother Sun'

14 Lord, make me an instrument of Your peace!
Where there is hatred let me sow love;
Where there is injury, pardon;
Where there is doubt, faith;
Where there is despair, hope;
Where there is darkness, light;
Where there is sadness, joy.
  'Prayer of St Francis' (attributed)

Felix Frankfurter 1882–1965
American judge

15 It is a fair summary of history to say that the safeguards of liberty have been forged in controversies involving not very nice people.
  dissenting opinion in *United States v. Rabinowitz* (1950)

Benjamin Franklin 1706–90
American politician, inventor, and scientist

16 Remember that time is money.
  Advice to a Young Tradesman (1748)

17 Some are weather-wise, some are otherwise.
  Poor Richard's Almanac (1735) February

18 Necessity never made a good bargain.
  Poor Richard's Almanac (1735) April

19 At twenty years of age, the will reigns; at thirty, the wit; and at forty, the judgement.
  Poor Richard's Almanac (1741) June

20 He that lives upon hope will die fasting.
  Poor Richard's Almanac (1758) preface

1 We must indeed all hang together, or, most
assuredly, we shall all hang separately.
  at the signing of the Declaration of
  Independence, 4 July 1776 (possibly not
  original)

2 There never was a good war, or a bad peace.
  letter to Josiah Quincy, 11 September 1783

3 In this world nothing can be said to be
certain, except death and taxes.
  letter to Jean Baptiste Le Roy, 13 November
  1789; see **Defoe** 111:17

4 Man is a tool-making animal.
  James Boswell *Life of Samuel Johnson* (1791) 7
  April 1778

5 What is the use of a new-born child?
  when asked what was the use of a new invention
  J. Parton *Life and Times of Benjamin Franklin* (1864)
  pt. 4, ch. 17

Rosalind Franklin 1920–58
English physical chemist and molecular biologist

6 Science and everyday life cannot and should
not be separated.
  letter to her father, summer 1940; Brenda
  Maddox *Rosalind Franklin: the Dark Lady of DNA*
  (2002) ch. 4

Tommy Franks 1945–
American general

7 This will be a campaign unlike any other in
history. A campaign characterized by shock,
by surprise, by flexibility, by the
employment of precise munitions on a scale
never before seen, and by the application of
overwhelming force.
  briefing in Qatar, 22 March 2003; see **Ullman**
  344:9

Malcolm Fraser 1930–
Australian Liberal statesman

8 Life is not meant to be easy.
  5th Alfred Deakin Lecture, 20 July 1971; see
  Shaw 311:9

Frederick the Great 1712–86
Prussian monarch, King from 1740

9 My people and I have come to an agreement
which satisfies us both. They are to say what
they please, and I am to do what I please.
  his interpretation of benevolent despotism
  attributed

10 Rascals, would you live for ever?
  to hesitant Guards at Kolin, 18 June 1757
  attributed

Cathy Freeman 1973–
Australian athlete

11 I was so angry because they were denying
they had done anything wrong, denying
that a whole generation was stolen.
  *of official response to concerns about the 'stolen
  generation' of Aboriginal children forcibly
  removed from their families*
  interview in *Daily Telegraph* 16 July 2000

E. A. Freeman 1823–92
English historian

12 History is past politics, and politics is
present history.
  Methods of Historical Study (1886)

Marilyn French 1929–
American writer

13 Whatever they may be in public life,
whatever their relations with men, in their
relations with women, all men are rapists,
and that's all they are. They rape us with
their eyes, their laws, and their codes.
  The Women's Room (1977)

14 'I hate discussions of feminism that end up
with who does the dishes,' she said. So do I.
But at the end, there are always the damned
dishes.
  The Women's Room (1977)

Percy French 1854–1920
Irish songwriter

15 Where the Mountains of Mourne sweep
down to the sea.
  'The Mountains of Mourne'

Sigmund Freud 1856–1939
Austrian psychiatrist; originator of psychoanalysis

16 Anatomy is destiny.
  Collected Writings (1924) vol. 5

17 The interpretation of dreams is the royal
road to a knowledge of the unconscious
activities of the mind.
  *often misquoted as, 'Dreams are the royal road to
  the unconscious'*
  The Interpretation of Dreams (2nd ed., 1909) ch. 7,
  sect. E

18 The great question that has never been
answered and which I have not yet been
able to answer, despite my thirty years of
research into the feminine soul, is 'What
does a woman want?'
  *letter to Marie Bonaparte, in Ernest Jones
  Sigmund Freud: Life and Work* (1955) vol. 2, pt. 3,
  ch. 16

19 All that matters is love and work.
  attributed

Betty Friedan 1921–
American feminist

20 The problem that has no name.
  *being the fact that American women are kept from
  growing to their full human capacities*
  The Feminine Mystique (1963) ch. 14

21 It is easier to live through someone else
than to become complete yourself.
  The Feminine Mystique (1963) ch. 14

Milton Friedman 1912–
American economist

22 There is an invisible hand in politics that
operates in the opposite direction to the
invisible hand in the market. In politics,
individuals who seek to promote only the

public good are led by an invisible hand to promote special interests that it was no part of their intention to promote.

Bright Promises, Dismal Performance: An Economist's Protest (1983); see **Smith** 318:4

1 Inflation is the one form of taxation that can be imposed without legislation.

in *Observer* 22 September 1974

Max Frisch 1911–91
Swiss novelist and dramatist

2 Technology . . . the knack of so arranging the world that we need not experience it.

Homo Faber (1957) pt. 2

Charles Frohman 1860–1915
American theatrical manager

3 Why fear death? It is the most beautiful adventure in life.

before drowning in the Lusitania, *7 May 1915*
I. F. Marcosson and D. Frohman *Charles Frohman* (1916); see **Barrie** 27:2

Erich Fromm 1900–80
American philosopher and psychologist

4 Immature love says: 'I love you because I need you.' Mature love says: 'I need you because I love you.'

The Art of Loving (1956) ch. 2

5 In the nineteenth century the problem was that *God is dead*; in the twentieth century the problem is that *man is dead*.

The Sane Society (1955) ch. 9

David Frost 1939–
English broadcaster and writer

6 Having one child makes you a parent; having two you are a referee.

in *Independent* 16 September 1989

Robert Frost 1874–1963
American poet

7 I have been one acquainted with the night.

'Acquainted with the Night' (1928)

8 . . . Life is too much like a pathless wood
Where your face burns and tickles with the cobwebs
Broken across it, and one eye is weeping
From a twig's having lashed across it open.

'Birches' (1916)

9 I'd like to get away from earth awhile
And then come back to it and begin over.
May no fate wilfully misunderstand me
And half grant what I wish and snatch me away
Not to return. Earth's the right place for love:
I don't know where it's likely to go better.

'Birches' (1916)

10 Most of the change we think we see in life
Is due to truths being in and out of favour.

'The Black Cottage' (1914)

11 Forgive, O Lord, my little jokes on Thee
And I'll forgive Thy great big one on me.

'Cluster of Faith' (1962)

12 And nothing to look backward to with pride,
And nothing to look forward to with hope.

'The Death of the Hired Man' (1914)

13 'Home is the place where, when you have to go there,
They have to take you in.'

'The Death of the Hired Man' (1914)

14 They cannot scare me with their empty spaces
Between stars—on stars where no human race is.
I have it in me so much nearer home
To scare myself with my own desert places.

'Desert Places' (1936)

15 Some say the world will end in fire,
Some say in ice.

'Fire and Ice' (1923)

16 The land was ours before we were the land's.
She was our land more than a hundred years
Before we were her people.

'The Gift Outright' (1942)

17 Happiness makes up in height for what it lacks in length.

title of poem (1942)

18 I had a lover's quarrel with the world.

'The Lesson for Today' (1942)

19 Something there is that doesn't love a wall,
That sends the frozen-ground-swell under it.

'Mending Wall' (1914)

20 My apple trees will never get across
And eat the cones under his pines, I tell him.
He only says, 'Good fences make good neighbours.'

'Mending Wall' (1914)

21 Before I built a wall I'd ask to know
What I was walling in or walling out,
And to whom I was like to give offence.

'Mending Wall' (1914)

22 I never dared be radical when young
For fear it would make me conservative when old.

'Precaution' (1936)

23 No memory of having starred
Atones for later disregard,
Or keeps the end from being hard.

'Provide Provide' (1936)

24 Two roads diverged in a wood, and I—
I took the one less travelled by,
And that has made all the difference.

'The Road Not Taken' (1916)

25 We dance round in a ring and suppose,
But the Secret sits in the middle and knows.

'The Secret Sits' (1942)

26 Pressed into service means pressed out of shape.

'The Self-Seeker' (1914)

27 The woods are lovely, dark and deep.
But I have promises to keep,
And miles to go before I sleep,

And miles to go before I sleep.
'Stopping by Woods on a Snowy Evening' (1923)

1 No tears in the writer, no tears in the reader.
No surprise for the writer, no surprise for
the reader.
Collected Poems (1939) 'The Figure a Poem Makes'

2 Poetry is a way of taking life by the throat.
Elizabeth S. Sergeant Robert Frost (1960) ch. 18

3 I'd as soon write free verse as play tennis
with the net down.
Edward Lathem Interviews with Robert Frost (1966)

4 Poetry is what is lost in translation. It is also
what is lost in interpretation.
Louis Untermeyer Robert Frost (1964)

Christopher Fry 1907–2005
English dramatist

5 The dark is light enough.
title of play (1954)

6 The lady's not for burning.
title of play (1949); see Thatcher 336:15

7 What after all
Is a halo? It's only one more thing to keep
clean.
The Lady's not for Burning (1949) act 1

Elizabeth Fry 1780–1845
English Quaker prison reformer

8 Punishment is not for revenge, but to lessen
crime and reform the criminal.
note found among her papers; Rachel È.
Cresswell and Katharine Fry Memoir of the Life of
Elizabeth Fry (1848)

Roger Fry 1866–1934
English art critic

9 Art is significant deformity.
Virginia Woolf Roger Fry (1940) ch. 8

Mary E. Frye 1905–2004
American housewife and poet

10 Do not stand at my grave and weep:
I am not there. I do not sleep.
I am a thousand winds that blow.
I am the diamond glints on snow.
I am the sunlight on ripened grain.
I am the gentle autumn's rain.
When you awaken in the morning's hush,
I am the swift uplifting rush
Of quiet birds in circled flight.
I am the soft stars that shine at night.
Do not stand at my grave and cry;
I am not there, I did not die.
quoted in letter left by British soldier Stephen
Cummins when killed by the IRA, March 1989
originally circulated privately from 1932 on

Francis Fukuyama 1952–
American historian

11 What we may be witnessing is not just the
end of the Cold War but the end of history
as such: that is, the end point of man's
ideological evolution and the universalism
of Western liberal democracy.
in Independent 20 September 1989

R. Buckminster Fuller 1895–1983
American designer and architect

12 Either war is obsolete or men are.
in New Yorker 8 January 1966

13 God, to me, it seems,
is a verb
not a noun,
proper or improper.
No More Secondhand God (1963) (untitled poem
written in 1940)

14 Now there is one outstandingly important
fact regarding Spaceship Earth, and that is
that no instruction book came with it.
Operating Manual for Spaceship Earth (1969) ch. 4

Thomas Fuller 1608–61
English preacher and historian

15 Anger is one of the sinews of the soul.
The Holy State and the Profane State bk. 3 'Of
Anger'

16 Light (God's eldest daughter) is a principal
beauty in building.
The Holy State and the Profane State bk. 3 'Of
Building'

Thomas Fuller 1654–1734
English writer and physician

17 He that plants trees loves others beside
himself.
Gnomologia (1732) no. 2247

18 We are all Adam's children but silk makes
the difference.
Gnomologia (1732) no. 5425

Alfred Funke 1869–1941
German writer

19 Gott strafe England!
God punish England!
Schwert und Myrte (1914)

David Maxwell Fyfe see Lord
Kilmuir

Rose Fyleman 1877–1957
English writer for children

20 There are fairies at the bottom of our
garden!
Fairies and Chimneys (1918) 'The Fairies' (first
published in Punch 23 May 1917)

Hugh Gaitskell 1906–63
British Labour politician

21 There are some of us . . . who will fight and
fight and fight again to save the Party we
love.
speech at Labour Party Conference, 5 October
1960

22 It means the end of a thousand years of
history.
on a European federation
speech at Labour Party Conference, 3 October
1962

Gaius (or Caius) *c.*AD 110–*c.*180
Roman jurist

1 *Damnosa hereditas.*
Ruinous inheritance.
The Institutes bk. 2, ch. 163

J. K. Galbraith 1908–
Canadian-born American economist

2 The affluent society.
title of book (1958)

3 The salary of the chief executive of the large
corporation is not a market reward for
achievement. It is frequently in the nature
of a warm personal gesture by the
individual to himself.
Annals of an Abiding Liberal (1979)

4 Trickle-down theory—the less than elegant
metaphor that if one feeds the horse
enough oats, some will pass through to the
road for the sparrows.
The Culture of Contentment (1992)

5 Politics is not the art of the possible. It
consists in choosing between the disastrous
and the unpalatable.
speech to President Kennedy, 2 March 1962; see
Bismarck 55:4

Galen AD 129–199
Greek physician

6 The chief merit of language is clearness, and
we know that nothing detracts so much
from this as do unfamiliar terms.
On the Natural Faculties bk. 1, sect. 1

Galileo Galilei 1564–1642
Italian astronomer and physicist

7 Philosophy is written in that great book
which ever lies before our eyes—I mean the
universe . . . This book is written in
mathematical language and its characters
are triangles, circles and other geometrical
figures, without whose help . . . one wanders
in vain through a dark labyrinth.
often quoted as 'The book of nature is written . . . '
The Assayer (1623)

8 *Eppur si muove.*
But it does move.
after his recantation, that the earth moves around
the sun, in 1632
attributed; Baretti *Italian Library* (1757) is
possibly the earliest appearance of the phrase

George Galloway 1954–
Scottish politician

9 Sir, I salute your courage, your strength,
your indefatigability
to Saddam **Hussein**
in Baghdad, 1994; quoted in *The Scotsman* 20
October 2003 (online edition)

10 I met Saddam Hussein exactly the same
number of times as Donald Rumsfeld met

him. The difference is that Donald Rumsfeld
met him to sell him guns.
appearing before the US Senate Permanent
Subcommittee on Investigations, 17 May 2005
in *Times* 23 May 2005 (online edition)

John Galsworthy 1867–1933
English novelist

11 A man of action forced into a state of
thought is unhappy until he can get out of
it.
Maid in Waiting (1931) ch. 3

John Galt 1779–1839
Scottish writer

12 From the lone shieling of the misty island
Mountains divide us, and the waste of seas—
Yet still the blood is strong, the heart is
Highland,
And we in dreams behold the Hebrides!
'Canadian Boat Song' translated from the Gaelic
in *Blackwoods Edinburgh Magazine* September
1829, and later attributed to Galt

Ray Galton 1930–
and **Alan Simpson** 1929–
English scriptwriters

13 I came in here in all good faith to help my
country. I don't mind giving a reasonable
amount [of blood], but a pint . . . why that's
very nearly an armful.
Hancock's Half Hour 'The Blood Donor' (1961
television programme); words spoken by Tony
Hancock

Mahatma Gandhi 1869–1948
Indian statesman

14 What difference does it make to the dead,
the orphans and the homeless, whether the
mad destruction is wrought under the name
of totalitarianism or the holy name of
liberty or democracy?
Non-Violence in Peace and War (1942) vol. 1, ch.
142

15 The moment the slave resolves that he will
no longer be a slave, his fetters fall. He frees
himself and shows the way to others.
Freedom and slavery are mental states.
Non-Violence in Peace and War (1949) vol. 2, ch. 5

16 Non-violence is the first article of my faith.
It is also the last article of my creed.
speech at Shahi Bag, 18 March 1922, on a
charge of sedition

17 Non-cooperation with evil is as much a duty
as is cooperation with good.
speech in Ahmadabad, 23 March 1922

18 *on being asked what he thought of modern*
civilization:
That would be a good idea.
while visiting England in 1930
E. F. Schumacher *Good Work* (1979)

Greta Garbo (Greta Lovisa Gustafsson) 1905–90
Swedish film actress

1 I want to be alone.
> *Grand Hotel* (1932 film), the phrase already being associated with Garbo

Frederico García Lorca *see* **Lorca**

Ed Gardner 1901–63
American radio comedian

2 Opera is when a guy gets stabbed in the back and, instead of bleeding, he sings.
> in *Duffy's Tavern* (US radio programme, 1940s)

James A. Garfield 1831–81
American Republican statesman; 20th President of the US 1881

3 Fellow-citizens: God reigns, and the Government at Washington lives!
> speech on the assassination of President Lincoln, 17 April 1865

Giuseppe Garibaldi 1807–82
Italian patriot and military leader

4 Men, I'm getting out of Rome. Anyone who wants to carry on the war against the outsiders, come with me. I can offer you neither honours nor wages; I offer you hunger, thirst, forced marches, battles and death. Anyone who loves his country, follow me.
> Giuseppe Guerzoni *Garibaldi* (1882) vol. 1 (not a verbatim record)

John Nance Garner 1868–1967
American Democratic politician

5 The vice-presidency isn't worth a pitcher of warm piss.
> O. C. Fisher *Cactus Jack* (1978) ch. 11

David Garrick 1717–79
English actor-manager

6 Heart of oak are our ships,
Heart of oak are our men:
We always are ready;
Steady, boys, steady;
We'll fight and we'll conquer again and again.
> *Harlequin's Invasion* (1759) 'Heart of Oak' (song)

7 Here lies Nolly Goldsmith, for shortness called Noll,
Who wrote like an angel, but talked like poor Poll.
> 'Impromptu Epitaph' (written 1773/4); see **Johnson** 190:5

8 Heaven sends us good meat, but the Devil sends cooks.
> 'On Doctor Goldsmith's Characteristical Cookery' (1777)

William Lloyd Garrison 1805–79
American anti-slavery campaigner

9 I am in earnest—I will not equivocate—I will not excuse—I will not retreat a single inch—and I will be heard!
> in *The Liberator* 1 January 1831 'Salutatory Address'

10 Our country is the world—our countrymen are all mankind.
> *The Liberator* 15 December 1837 'Prospectus'

11 The compact which exists between the North and the South is 'a covenant with death and an agreement with hell'.
> resolution adopted by the Massachusetts Anti-Slavery Society, 27 January 1843; see **Bible** 40:24

Samuel Garth 1661–1719
English poet and physician

12 A barren superfluity of words.
> *The Dispensary* (1699) canto 2, l. 82

Elizabeth Gaskell 1810–65
English novelist

13 A man . . . is *so* in the way in the house!
> *Cranford* (1853) ch. 1

14 I'll not listen to reason . . . Reason always means what someone else has got to say.
> *Cranford* (1853) ch. 14

15 That kind of patriotism which consists in hating all other nations.
> *Sylvia's Lovers* (1863) ch. 1

Paul Gauguin 1848–1903
French painter

16 A hint—don't paint too much direct from nature. Art is an abstraction! study nature then brood on it and treasure the creation which will result, which is the only way to ascend towards God—to create like our Divine Master.
> letter to Emile Schuffenecker, 14 August 1888

Gavarni (Guillaume Sulpice Chevalier) 1804–66
French lithographer

17 Les enfants terribles.
The little terrors.
> title of a series of prints (1842)

John Gay 1685–1732
English poet and dramatist

18 Our Polly is a sad slut! nor heeds what we have taught her.
I wonder any man alive will ever rear a daughter!
> *The Beggar's Opera* (1728) act 1, sc. 8, air 7

19 Do you think your mother and I should have lived comfortably so long together, if ever we had been married?
> *The Beggar's Opera* (1728) act 1, sc. 8

20 The comfortable estate of widowhood, is the only hope that keeps up a wife's spirits.
> *The Beggar's Opera* (1728) act 1, sc. 10

1 If with me you'd fondly stray.
Over the hills and far away.
The Beggar's Opera (1728) act 1, sc. 13, air 16

2 How happy could I be with either,
Were t'other dear charmer away!
The Beggar's Opera (1728) act 2, sc. 13, air 35

3 And when a lady's in the case,
You know, all other things give place.
Fables (1727) 'The Hare and Many Friends' l. 41

4 Those who in quarrels interpose,
Must often wipe a bloody nose.
Fables (1727) 'The Mastiffs' l. 1

5 An open foe may prove a curse,
But a pretended friend is worse.
Fables (1727) 'The Shepherd's Dog and the Wolf'
l. 33

6 An inconstant woman, tho' she has no
chance to be very happy, can never be very
unhappy.
'Polly' (1729) act 1, sc. 14

7 All in the Downs the fleet was moored,
The streamers waving in the wind,
When black-eyed Susan came aboard.
'Sweet William's Farewell to Black-Eyed Susan'
(1720)

8 They'll tell thee, sailors, when away,
In ev'ry port a mistress find.
'Sweet William's Farewell to Black-Eyed Susan'
(1720)

Noel Gay 1898–1954
British songwriter

9 I'm leaning on a lamp post at the corner of
the street,
In case a certain little lady comes by.
'Leaning on a Lamp Post' (1937); sung by George
Formby in the film *Father Knew Best*

Eric Geddes 1875–1937
British politician and administrator

10 The Germans, if this Government is
returned, are going to pay every penny; they
are going to be squeezed as a lemon is
squeezed—until the pips squeak.
speech at Cambridge, 10 December 1918

Bob Geldof 1954–
and Midge Ure 1953–
Irish rock musician; Scottish rock musician

11 Do they know it's Christmas?
title of song (1984)

Jean Genet 1910–86
French novelist, poet, and dramatist

12 What we need is hatred. From it our ideas
are born.
The Blacks (1959); epigraph

Genghis Khan (Temujin) 1162–1227
Mongol ruler

13 Happiness lies in conquering one's enemies,
in driving them in front of oneself, in taking
their property, in savouring their despair, in
outraging their wives and daughters.
Witold Rodzinski *The Walled Kingdom: A History of
China* (1979)

George I 1660–1727
*British monarch, King of Great Britain and Ireland
from 1714*

14 I hate all Boets and Bainters.
John Campbell *Lives of the Chief Justices* (1849)
'Lord Mansfield'

George II 1683–1760
*British monarch, King of Great Britain and Ireland
from 1727*

15 *Non, j'aurai des maîtresses.*
No, I shall have mistresses.
*when Queen **Caroline**, on her deathbed in 1737,
urged him to marry again; the Queen replied, 'Ah!
mon dieu! cela n'empêche pas [Oh, my God!
That won't make any difference]'*
John Hervey *Memoirs of the Reign of George II*
(1848) vol. 2.

16 Mad, is he? Then I hope he will *bite* some of
my other generals.
*replying to the Duke of Newcastle, who had
complained that General **Wolfe** was a madman*
Henry Beckles Willson *Life and Letters of James
Wolfe* (1909) ch. 17

George III 1738–1820
*British monarch, King of Great Britain and Ireland
from 1760*

17 Born and educated in this country, I glory in
the name of Briton.
The King's Speech on Opening the Session House of
Lords, 18 November 1760

George IV 1762–1830
*British monarch, King of Great Britain and Ireland
from 1820*

18 Harris, I am not well; pray get me a glass of
brandy.
*on first seeing Caroline of Brunswick, his future
wife*
Earl of Malmesbury *Diaries and Correspondence*
(1844), 5 April 1795

George V 1865–1936
*British monarch, King of Great Britain and Ireland
from 1910*

19 I venture to allude to the impression which
seemed generally to prevail among their
brethren across the seas, that the Old
Country must wake up if she intends to
maintain her old position of pre-eminence
in her Colonial trade against foreign
competitors.
speech at Guildhall, 5 December 1901,
reprinted in 1911 under the title 'Wake up,
England'

20 I have many times asked myself whether
there can be more potent advocates of peace
upon earth through the years to come than

this massed multitude of silent witnesses to the desolation of war.

> message read at Terlincthun Cemetery, Boulogne, 13 May 1922

1 After I am dead, the boy will ruin himself in twelve months.

of his son, the future **Edward VIII**

> Keith Middlemas and John Barnes *Baldwin* (1969) ch. 34

2 *on H. G.* **Wells's** *comment on 'an alien and uninspiring court':*
I may be uninspiring, but I'll be damned if I'm an alien!

> Sarah Bradford *George VI* (1989); attributed

3 Bugger Bognor.

on his deathbed in 1936, when someone remarked 'Cheer up, your Majesty, you will soon be at Bognor again'; alternatively, a comment made in 1929, when it was proposed that the town be named Bognor Regis on account of the king's convalescence there after a serious illness

> probably apocryphal; Kenneth Rose *King George V* (1983) ch. 9

George VI 1895–1952
British monarch, King of Great Britain and Northern Ireland from 1936

4 The family firm.

description of the British monarchy
attributed

Dan George 1899–1981
Canadian native chief and actor

5 When the white man came we had the land and they had the bibles; now they have the land and we have the bibles.

> Gerald Walsh *Indians in Transition: An Inquiry Approach* (1971)

Lloyd George *see* David Lloyd George

Geronimo *c.*1829–1909
Apache chief

6 Once I moved about like the wind. Now I surrender to you and that is all.

> surrendering to General Crook, 25 March 1886

Ira Gershwin 1896–1983
American songwriter

7 I don't think I'll fall in love today.

> title of song (1928, from *Treasure Girl*)

8 I got rhythm.

> title of song (1930, from *Girl Crazy*)

9 In time the Rockies may crumble,
Gibraltar may tumble,
They're only made of clay,
But our love is here to stay.

> 'Love is Here to Stay' (1938 song) in *The Goldwyn Follies*

10 Holding hands at midnight
'Neath a starry sky,
Nice work if you can get it,
And you can get it if you try.

> 'Nice Work If You Can Get It' (1937 song) in *Damsel in Distress*

J. Paul Getty 1892–1976
American industrialist

11 If you can actually count your money, then you are not really a rich man.

> in *Observer* 3 November 1957

Giuseppe Giacosa 1847–1906 and Luigi Illica 1857–1919
Italian librettists

12 Che gelida manina.
Your tiny hand is frozen.

Rodolfo to Mimi

> *La Bohème* (1896) act 1; music by Puccini

Edward Gibbon 1737–94
English historian

13 The various modes of worship, which prevailed in the Roman world, were all considered by the people as equally true; by the philosopher, as equally false; and by the magistrate, as equally useful.

> *The Decline and Fall of the Roman Empire* (1776–88) ch. 2

14 History . . . is, indeed, little more than the register of the crimes, follies, and misfortunes of mankind.

> *The Decline and Fall of the Roman Empire* (1776–88) ch. 3; see **Voltaire** 348:20

15 Twenty-two acknowledged concubines, and a library of sixty-two thousand volumes, attested the variety of his inclinations, and from the productions which he left behind him, it appears that the former as well as the latter were designed for use rather than ostentation. [Footnote] By each of his concubines the younger Gordian left three or four children. His literary productions were by no means contemptible.

> *The Decline and Fall of the Roman Empire* (1776–88) ch. 7

16 Whenever the offence inspires less horror than the punishment, the rigour of penal law is obliged to give way to the common feelings of mankind.

> *The Decline and Fall of the Roman Empire* (1776–88) ch. 14

17 Corruption, the most infallible symptom of constitutional liberty.

> *The Decline and Fall of the Roman Empire* (1776–88) ch. 21

18 In every deed of mischief he had a heart to resolve, a head to contrive, and a hand to execute.

of Comnenus

> *The Decline and Fall of the Roman Empire* (1776–88) ch. 48; see **Clarendon** 96:28

19 Our sympathy is cold to the relation of distant misery.

> *The Decline and Fall of the Roman Empire* (1776–88) ch. 49

1 All that is human must retrograde if it does
not advance.
The Decline and Fall of the Roman Empire (1776–88)
ch. 71

2 I sighed as a lover, I obeyed as a son.
Memoirs of My Life (1796) ch. 4 n.

3 It was at Rome, on the fifteenth of October,
1764, as I sat musing amidst the ruins of the
Capitol, while the barefoot friars were
singing vespers in the Temple of Jupiter,
that the idea of writing the decline and fall
of the city first started to my mind.
Memoirs of My Life (1796) ch. 6 n.

4 My English text is chaste, and all licentious
passages are left in the obscurity of a
learned language.
parodied as 'decent obscurity' in the Anti-
Jacobin, 1797–8
Memoirs of My Life (1796) ch. 8

Orlando Gibbons 1583–1625
English organist and composer

5 The silver swan, who, living had no note,
When death approached unlocked her
silent throat.
The First Set of Madrigals and Motets of Five Parts
(1612) 'The Silver Swan'

Stella Gibbons 1902–89
English novelist

6 Something nasty in the woodshed.
Cold Comfort Farm (1932) ch. 10

Wolcott Gibbs 1902–58
American critic

7 Backward ran sentences until reeled the
mind.
satirizing the style of Time *magazine*
in New Yorker 28 November 1936 'Time . . .
Fortune . . . Life . . . Luce'

Kahlil Gibran 1883–1931
Syrian writer and painter

8 Are you a politician who says to himself: 'I
will use my country for my own benefit'? . . .
Or are you a devoted patriot, who whispers
in the ear of his inner self: 'I love to serve
my country as a faithful servant.'
The New Frontier (1931), tr. Anthony R. Ferris in
The Voice of the Master (1958); see **Kennedy** 199:1

9 Your children are not your children.
They are the sons and daughters of Life's
longing for itself.
They came through you but not from you
And though they are with you yet they
belong not to you.
The Prophet (1923) 'On Children'

10 You shall be together when the white wings
of death scatter your days.
Ay, you shall be together even in the silent
memory of God.
But let there be spaces in your togetherness,
And let the winds of the heavens dance
between you.
The Prophet (1923) 'On Marriage'

11 Work is love made visible.
The Prophet (1923) 'On Work'

12 An exaggeration is a truth that has lost its
temper.
Sand and Foam (1926)

André Gide 1869–1951
French novelist and critic

13 Hugo—alas!
*when asked who was the greatest 19th-century
poet*
Claude Martin *La Maturité d'André Gide* (1977)

Humphrey Gilbert c.1537–83
English explorer

14 We are as near to heaven by sea as by land!
Richard Hakluyt *Third and Last Volume of the
Voyages . . . of the English Nation* (1600); see **Elstow**
131:16

W. S. Gilbert 1836–1911
English writer of comic and satirical verse

15 Of that there is no manner of doubt—
No probable, possible shadow of doubt—
No possible doubt whatever.
The Gondoliers (1889) act 1

16 When every one is somebodee.
Then no one's anybody.
The Gondoliers (1889) act 2

17 The Law is the true embodiment
Of everything that's excellent.
It has no kind of fault or flaw,
And I, my Lords, embody the Law.
Iolanthe (1882) act 1

18 I often think it's comical
How Nature always does contrive
That every boy and every gal,
That's born into the world alive,
Is either a little Liberal,
Or else a little Conservative!
Iolanthe (1882) act 2

19 The House of Peers, throughout the war,
Did nothing in particular,
And did it very well.
Iolanthe (1882) act 2

20 When you're lying awake with a dismal
headache, and repose is taboo'd by
anxiety,
I conceive you may use any language you
choose to indulge in, without impropriety.
Iolanthe (1882) act 2

21 A wandering minstrel I—
A thing of shreds and patches.
Of ballads, songs and snatches,
And dreamy lullaby!
The Mikado (1885) act 1; see **Shakespeare** 293:20

22 I can trace my ancestry back to a
protoplasmal primordial atomic globule.
Consequently, my family pride is something
in-conceivable. I can't help it. I was born
sneering.
The Mikado (1885) act 1

23 As some day it may happen that a victim
must be found,

I've got a little list—I've got a little list
Of society offenders who might well be
under ground
And who never would be missed—who
never would be missed!
The Mikado (1885) act 1

1 The idiot who praises, with enthusiastic
tone,
All centuries but this, and every country but
his own.
The Mikado (1885) act 1

2 Three little maids from school are we.
The Mikado (1885) act 1

3 Modified rapture!
The Mikado (1885) act 1

4 Awaiting the sensation of a short, sharp
shock,
From a cheap and chippy chopper on a big
black block.
The Mikado (1885) act 1

5 Here's a how-de-doo!
The Mikado (1885) act 2

6 My object all sublime
I shall achieve in time—
To let the punishment fit the crime—
The punishment fit the crime.
The Mikado (1885) act 2

7 Something lingering, with boiling oil in it, I
fancy.
The Mikado (1885) act 2

8 Merely corroborative detail, intended to give
artistic verisimilitude to an otherwise bald
and unconvincing narrative.
The Mikado (1885) act 2

9 The flowers that bloom in the spring,
Tra la,
Have nothing to do with the case.
The Mikado (1885) act 2

10 On a tree by a river a little tom-tit
Sang 'Willow, titwillow, titwillow!'
The Mikado (1885) act 2

11 There's a fascination frantic
In a ruin that's romantic;
Do you think you are sufficiently decayed?
The Mikado (1885) act 2

12 If you're anxious for to shine in the high
aesthetic line as a man of culture rare.
Patience (1881) act 1

13 The meaning doesn't matter if it's only idle
chatter of a transcendental kind.
Patience (1881) act 1

14 An attachment à la Plato for a bashful young
potato, or a not too French French bean!
Patience (1881) act 1

15 If you walk down Piccadilly with a poppy or
a lily in your medieval hand.
Patience (1881) act 1

16 A greenery-yallery, Grosvenor Gallery,
Foot-in-the-grave young man!
Patience (1881) act 2

17 And so do his sisters, and his cousins and his
aunts!
HMS Pinafore (1878) act 1

18 I always voted at my party's call,
And I never thought of thinking for myself
at all.
HMS Pinafore (1878) act 1

19 Stick close to your desks and never go to
sea,
And you all may be Rulers of the Queen's
Navee!
HMS Pinafore (1878) act 1

20 For he himself has said it,
And it's greatly to his credit,
That he is an Englishman!
HMS Pinafore (1878) act 2

21 For he might have been a Roosian,
A French, or Turk, or Proosian,
Or perhaps Ital-ian!
But in spite of all temptations
To belong to other nations,
He remains an Englishman!
HMS Pinafore (1878) act 2

22 It is, it is a glorious thing
To be a Pirate King.
The Pirates of Penzance (1879) act 1

23 I'm very good at integral and differential
calculus,
I know the scientific names of beings
animalculous;
In short, in matters vegetable, animal, and
mineral,
I am the very model of a modern Major-
General.
The Pirates of Penzance (1879) act 1

24 When constabulary duty's to be done,
A policeman's lot is not a happy one.
The Pirates of Penzance (1879) act 2

25 Man is Nature's sole mistake!
Princess Ida (1884) act 2

26 This particularly rapid, unintelligible patter
Isn't generally heard, and if it is it doesn't
matter.
Ruddigore (1887) act 2

27 She may very well pass for forty-three
In the dusk with a light behind her!
Trial by Jury (1875)

Eric Gill 1882–1940
English sculptor, engraver, and typographer

28 That state is a state of slavery in which a
man does what he likes to do in his spare
time and in his working time that which is
required of him.
Art-nonsense and Other Essays (1929) 'Slavery and
Freedom'; see **Collingwood** 101:10

Andrew Gilligan 1968–
British journalist

29 I have spoken to a British official who was
involved in the preparation of the dossier
. . . He said: [Voiceover]: 'It was

transformed in the week before it was published, to make it sexier'.
  BBC Radio 4 *Today* programme, 29 May 2003; in *Guardian* 27 June 2003

Charlotte Perkins Gilman
1860–1935
American writer and feminist

1 There is no female mind. The brain is not an organ of sex. As well speak of a female liver.
  Women and Economics (1898) ch. 8

Allen Ginsberg 1926–97
American poet and novelist

2 What if someone gave a war & Nobody came?
  Life would ring the bells of Ecstasy and Forever be Itself again.
  'Graffiti' (1972); see **Sandburg** 285:7

3 I saw the best minds of my generation destroyed by madness, starving hysterical naked,
  dragging themselves through the negro streets at dawn looking for an angry fix,
  angelheaded hipsters burning for the ancient heavenly connection to the starry dynamo in the machinery of the night.
  Howl (1956)

4 What thoughts I have of you tonight, Walt Whitman, for I walked
  down the sidestreets under the trees with a headache self-
  conscious looking at the full moon.
  'A Supermarket in California' (1956)

5 What peaches and what penumbras! Whole families shopping at night! Aisles full of husbands! Wives in the avocados, babies in the tomatoes!—and you, Garcia Lorca what were you doing down by the watermelons?
  'A Supermarket in California' (1956)

6 Ah, dear father, graybeard, lonely old courage-teacher, what
  America did you have when Charon quit poling his ferry and you
  got out on a smoking bank and stood watching the boat
  disappear on the black waters of Lethe?
  on Walt **Whitman**
  'A Supermarket in California' (1956)

George Gipp 1895–1920
American footballer

7 Tell them to go in there with all they've got and win just one for the Gipper.
  the catchphrase 'Win one for the Gipper' was later used by Ronald **Reagan***, who played Gipp in the 1940 film* Knute Rockne, All American
  Knut Rockne 'Gipp the Great' in *Collier's* 22 November 1930

Jean Giraudoux 1882–1944
French dramatist

8 No poet ever interpreted nature as freely as a lawyer interprets the truth.
  La Guerre de Troie n'aura pas lieu (1935) act 2, sc. 5

Rudolph Giuliani 1944–
American Republican politician

9 The number of casualties will be more than any of us can bear.
  in the aftermath of the terrorist attacks which destroyed the World Trade Center in New York, and damaged the Pentagon, 11 September 2001
  in *The Times* 12 September 2001

Edna Gladney
American philanthropist

10 There are no illegitimate children, only illegitimate parents.
  MGM paid her a large sum for the line for the 1941 film based on her life, 'Blossoms in the Dust'
  A. Loos *Kiss Hollywood Good-Bye* (1978)

W. E. Gladstone 1809–98
British Liberal statesman, Prime Minister 1868–74, 1880–5, 1886, 1892–4

11 Ireland, Ireland! that cloud in the west, that coming storm.
  letter to his wife, 12 October 1845

12 You cannot fight against the future. Time is on our side.
  speech on the Reform Bill, in House of Commons, 27 April 1866

13 My mission is to pacify Ireland.
  on receiving news that he was to form his first cabinet, 1st December 1868
  H. C. G. Matthew *Gladstone 1809–1874* (1986) ch. 5

14 Let the Turks now carry away their abuses in the only possible manner, namely by carrying off themselves . . . one and all, bag and baggage, shall I hope clear out from the province they have desolated and profaned.
  Bulgarian Horrors and the Question of the East (1876)

15 All the world over, I will back the masses against the classes.
  speech in Liverpool, 28 June 1886

16 [Money should] fructify in the pockets of the people.
  H. G. C. Matthew *Gladstone 1809–1874* (1986)

Hannah Glasse fl. 1747
English cook

17 Take your hare when it is cased.
  'cased' = skinned
  The Art of Cookery Made Plain and Easy (1747) ch. 1

William Henry, Duke of Gloucester 1743–1805

18 Another damned, thick, square book! Always scribble, scribble, scribble! Eh! Mr Gibbon?
  Henry Best *Personal and Literary Memorials* (1829); alternatively attributed to the Duke of Cumberland and King George III

Jean-Luc Godard 1930–
French film director

1 Photography is truth. The cinema is truth 24 times per second.
  Le Petit Soldat (1960 film)

2 *Ce n'est pas une image juste, c'est juste une image.*
  This is not a just image, it is just an image.
  Colin MacCabe *Godard: Images, Sounds, Politics* (1980)

3 GEORGES FRANJU: Movies should have a beginning, a middle and an end.
  JEAN-LUC GODARD: Certainly, but not necessarily in that order.
  in *Time* 14 September 1981; see **Aristotle** 15:16

A. D. Godley 1856–1925
English classicist

4 What is this that roareth thus?
  Can it be a Motor Bus?
  Yes, the smell and hideous hum
  Indicat Motorem Bum!
  letter to C. R. L. Fletcher, 10 January 1914, in *Reliquiae* (1926) vol. 1

Joseph Goebbels 1897–1945
German Nazi leader

5 We can manage without butter but not, for example, without guns. If we are attacked we can only defend ourselves with guns not with butter.
  speech in Berlin, 17 January 1936; see **Goering** 152:6

Hermann Goering 1893–1946
German Nazi leader
see also **Johst** 191:6

6 We have no butter . . . but I ask you—would you rather have butter or guns? . . . preparedness makes us powerful. Butter merely makes us fat.
  speech at Hamburg, 1936, in W. Frischauer *Goering* (1951) ch. 10; see **Goebbels** 152:5

7 I herewith commission you to carry out all preparations with regard to . . . a *total solution* of the Jewish question in those territories of Europe which are under German influence.
  instructions to Heydrich, 31 July 1941; see **Heydrich** 168:12

Johann Wolfgang von Goethe
1749–1832
German poet, novelist, and dramatist

8 Man will err while yet he strives.
  Faust pt. 1 (1808) 'Prolog im Himmel'

9 Deny yourself! You must deny yourself! That is the song that never ends.
  Faust pt. 1 (1808) 'Studierzimmer'

10 All theory, dear friend, is grey, but the golden tree of actual life springs ever green.
  Faust pt. 1 (1808) 'Studierzimmer'

11 Just trust yourself and you'll learn the art of living.
  Faust pt. 1 (1808) 'Studierzimmer'

12 *Meine Ruh' ist hin,*
  Mein Herz ist schwer.
  My peace is gone,
  My heart is heavy.
  Faust pt. 1 (1808) 'Gretchen am Spinnrad'

13 *Die Tat ist alles, nichts der Ruhm.*
  The deed is all, the glory nothing.
  Faust pt. 2 (1832) 'Hochgebirg'

14 *Das Ewig-Weibliche zieht uns hinan.*
  Eternal Woman draws us upward.
  Faust pt. 2 (1832) 'Hochgebirg' closing words

15 In art the best is good enough.
  Italienische Reise (1816–17) 3 March 1787

16 Talent develops in quiet places, character in the full current of human life.
  Torquato Tasso (1790) act 1, sc. 2

17 *Die Wahlverwandtschaften.*
  Elective affinities.
  title of novel (1809)

18 *Über allen Gipfeln*
  Ist Ruh'.
  Over all the mountain tops is peace.
  Wanderers Nachtlied (1821)

19 *Kennst du das Land, wo die Zitronen blühn?*
  Im dunkeln Laub die Gold-Orangen glühn.
  Know you the land where the lemon-trees bloom? In the dark foliage the gold oranges glow.
  Wilhelm Meisters Lehrjahre (1795–6) bk. 3, ch. 1

20 If I love you, what does that matter to you!
  Wilhelm Meisters Lehrjahre (1795–6) bk. 4, ch. 9

21 None but the lonely heart
  Knows what I suffer!
  Wilhelm Meisters Lehrjahre (1795–6) bk. 4, ch. 11 'Mignons Lied'

22 When we take people, thou wouldst say, merely as they are, we make them worse; when we treat them as if they were what they should be, we improve them as far as they can be improved.
  sometimes quoted as 'Treat a man as he is, and that is what he remains. Treat a man as he can be, and that is what he becomes'
  Wilhelm Meisters Lehrjare (1795–6) bk. 8, ch. 4, translated by Carlyle

23 *Ohne Hast, aber ohne Rast.*
  Without haste, but without rest.
  Zahme Xenien (with Schiller, 1796) sect. 2, no. 6, l. 281

24 I do not know myself, and God forbid that I should.
  J. P. Eckermann *Conversations with Goethe in the Last Years of his Life* (1836–48) 10 April 1829; see **Anonymous** 13:1

25 *Mehr Licht!*
  More light!
  abbreviated version of his last words: 'Macht doch den zweiten Fensterladen auch auf, damit mehr Licht hereinkomme [Open the second shutter, so that more light can come in]'
  K. W. Müller *Goethes letze literarische Thätigkeit* (1832)

Isaac Goldberg 1887-1938

1 Diplomacy is to do and say
The nastiest thing in the nicest way.
   in *The Reflex* October 1927

Whoopi Goldberg 1949-
American actress

2 I dislike this idea that if you're a black
person in America then you must be called
an African-American. I'm not an African. I'm
an American. Just call me black, if you want
to call me anything.
   in *Irish Times* 25 April 1998 'Quotes of the Week'

Emma Goldman 1869-1940
American anarchist

3 Anarchism, then, really, stands for the
liberation of the human mind from the
dominion of religion; the liberation of the
human body from the dominion of
property; liberation from the shackles and
restraints of government.
   Anarchism and Other Essays (1910)

Oliver Goldsmith 1728-74
Irish writer, poet, and dramatist

4 Sweet Auburn, loveliest village of the plain.
   The Deserted Village (1770) l. 1

5 Ill fares the land, to hast'ning ills a prey,
Where wealth accumulates, and men decay;
Princes and lords may flourish, or may fade;
A breath can make them, as a breath has
made;
But a bold peasantry, their country's pride,
When once destroyed, can never be
supplied.
   The Deserted Village (1770) l. 51

6 How happy he who crowns in shades like
these,
A youth of labour with an age of ease.
   The Deserted Village (1770) l. 99

7 And the loud laugh that spoke the vacant
mind.
   The Deserted Village (1770) l. 122

8 A man he was to all the country dear,
And passing rich with forty pounds a year.
   The Deserted Village (1770) l. 141

9 Truth from his lips prevailed with double
sway,
And fools, who came to scoff, remained to
pray.
   The Deserted Village (1770) l. 179

10 And still they gazed, and still the wonder
grew,
That one small head could carry all he knew.
   The Deserted Village (1770) l. 215

11 How wide the limits stand
Between a splendid and a happy land.
   The Deserted Village (1770) l. 267

12 Man wants but little here below,
Nor wants that little long.
   'Edwin and Angelina, or the Hermit' (1766); see
   Young 370:1

13 The doctor found, when she was dead,—
Her last disorder mortal.
   'Elegy on Mrs Mary Blaize' (1759)

14 The man recovered of the bite,
The dog it was that died.
   'Elegy on the Death of a Mad Dog' (1766)

15 Such is the patriot's boast, where'er we
roam,
His first, best country ever is, at home.
   The Traveller (1764) l. 73

16 And honour sinks where commerce long
prevails.
   The Traveller (1764) l. 92

17 Laws grind the poor, and rich men rule the
law.
   The Traveller (1764) l. 386

18 How small, of all that human hearts endure,
That part which laws or kings can cause or
cure!
   The Traveller (1764) l. 429; see **Johnson** 187:23

19 The true use of speech is not so much to
express our wants as to conceal them.
   The Bee no. 3 (20 October 1759) 'On the Use of
   Language'

20 Don't let us make imaginary evils, when you
know we have so many real ones to
encounter.
   The Good-Natured Man (1768) act 1

21 Measures not men, have always been my
mark.
   The Good Natured Man (1768) act 2; see **Burke**
   75:30, **Canning** 84:9

22 Let schoolmasters puzzle their brain,
With grammar, and nonsense, and learning,
Good liquor, I stoutly maintain,
Gives genius a better discerning.
   She Stoops to Conquer (1773) act 1, sc. 1 'Song'

23 The very pink of perfection.
   She Stoops to Conquer (1773) act 1

24 This is Liberty-Hall, gentlemen.
   She Stoops to Conquer (1773) act 2

25 The first blow is half the battle.
   She Stoops to Conquer (1773) act 2

26 I . . . chose my wife, as she did her wedding
gown, not for a fine glossy surface, but such
qualities as would wear well.
   The Vicar of Wakefield (1766) ch. 1

27 When lovely woman stoops to folly
And finds too late that men betray,
What charm can soothe her melancholy,
What art can wash her guilt away?
   The Vicar of Wakefield (1766) ch. 29; see **Eliot**
   129:29

28 There is no arguing with Johnson; for when
his pistol misses fire, he knocks you down
with the butt end of it.
   James Boswell *Life of Samuel Johnson* (1791) 26
   October 1769

Barry Goldwater 1909-98
American Republican politician

29 I would remind you that extremism in the
defence of liberty is no vice! And let me

remind you also that moderation in the pursuit of justice is no virtue!

accepting the presidential nomination, 16 July 1964

Sam Goldwyn 1882–1974
American film producer

1 Gentlemen, include me out.

resigning from the Motion Picture Producers and Distributors of America, October 1933

Michael Freedland *The Goldwyn Touch* (1986) ch. 10

2 That's the way with these directors, they're always biting the hand that lays the golden egg.

Alva Johnston *The Great Goldwyn* (1937) ch. 1

3 A verbal contract isn't worth the paper it is written on.

Alva Johnston *The Great Goldwyn* (1937) ch. 1

4 Any man who goes to a psychiatrist should have his head examined.

Norman Zierold *Moguls* (1969) ch. 3

5 Pictures are for entertainment, messages should be delivered by Western Union.

Arthur Marx *Goldwyn* (1976) ch. 15

Amy Goodman 1957–
American journalist

6 Go to where the silence is and say something.

accepting an award from Columbia University for her coverage of the 1991 massacre in East Timor by Indonesian troops

in *Columbia Journalism Review* March/April 1994

Mikhail Sergeevich Gorbachev 1931–
Soviet statesman; General Secretary of the Communist Party of the USSR 1985–91 and President 1988–91

7 The idea of restructuring [perestroika] . . . combines continuity and innovation, the historical experience of Bolshevism and the contemporaneity of socialism.

speech on the seventieth anniversary of the Russian Revolution, 2 November 1987

Adam Lindsay Gordon 1833–70
Australian poet

8 Life is mostly froth and bubble,
Two things stand like stone,
Kindness in another's trouble,
Courage in your own.

Ye Wearie Wayfarer (1866) 'Fytte 8'

Mack Gordon 1904–59
American songwriter

9 Pardon me boy is that the Chattanooga Choo-choo,
Track twenty nine,
Boy you can gimme a shine.

'Chattanooga Choo-choo' (1941 song)

Albert Gore Jr. 1948–
American Democratic politician

10 I am Al Gore, and I used to be the next president of the United States of America.

addressing Bocconi University in Milan

in *Newsweek* 19 March 2001

Maxim Gorky 1868–1936
Russian writer and revolutionary

11 The proletarian state must bring up thousands of excellent 'mechanics of culture', 'engineers of the soul'.

speech at the Writers' Congress 1934; see **Kennedy** 199:4, **Stalin** 322:23

Stuart Gorrell 1902–63
American songwriter

12 Georgia, Georgia, no peace I find,
Just an old sweet song keeps Georgia on my mind.

'Georgia on my Mind' (1930 song)

Glenn Gould 1932–82
Canadian pianist and composer

13 The purpose of art is the lifelong construction of a state of wonder.

commencement address, York University, Toronto, 6 November 1982

Stephen Jay Gould 1941–2002
American palaeontologist

14 A man does not attain the status of Galileo merely because he is persecuted; he must also be right.

Ever since Darwin (1977)

15 Science is an integral part of culture. It's not this foreign thing, done by an arcane priesthood. It's one of the glories of human intellectual tradition.

in *Independent* 24 January 1990

Goya 1746–1828
Spanish painter

16 One cannot look at this.

The Disasters of War (1863) title of etching, no. 26

17 The dream of reason produces monsters.

Los Caprichos (1799) plate 43 (title)

Baltasar Gracián 1601–58
Spanish philosopher

18 Never open the door to the least of evils, for many other, greater ones lurk outside.

The Art of Worldly Wisdom (tr. Christopher Maurer, 1994)

D. M. Graham 1911–99
British broadcaster

19 That this House will in no circumstances fight for its King and Country.

motion worded by Graham for a debate at the Oxford Union, of which he was Librarian, 9 February 1933 (passed by 275 votes to 153)

Harry Graham 1874–1936
British writer and journalist

20 'There's been an accident,' they said,

'Your servant's cut in half; he's dead!'
'Indeed!' said Mr Jones, 'and please,
Send me the half that's got my keys.'
> *Ruthless Rhymes for Heartless Homes* (1899) 'Mr Jones' (attributed to 'G.W.')

1 Billy, in one of his nice new sashes,
Fell in the fire and was burnt to ashes;
Now, although the room grows chilly,
I haven't the heart to poke poor Billy.
> *Ruthless Rhymes for Heartless Homes* (1899) 'Tender-Heartedness'

James Graham *see* Marquess of Montrose

Martha Graham 1894–1991
American dancer, teacher, and choreographer

2 Dance is the hidden language of the soul.
> *Blood Memory* (1991)

Kenneth Grahame 1859–1932
Scottish-born writer

3 There is *nothing*—absolutely nothing—half so much worth doing as simply messing about in boats.
> *The Wind in the Willows* (1908) ch. 1

4 The poetry of motion! The *real* way to travel! The *only* way to travel! Here today—in next week tomorrow! Villages skipped, towns and cities jumped—always somebody else's horizon!
> *The Wind in the Willows* (1908) ch. 2; see Kaufman and Anthony 195:6

5 O bliss! O poop-poop! O my!
> *The Wind in the Willows* (1908) ch. 2

6 The clever men at Oxford
Know all that there is to be knowed.
But they none of them know one half as much
As intelligent Mr Toad!
> *The Wind in the Willows* (1908) ch. 10

Bernie Grant 1944–2000
British Labour politician

7 The police were to blame for what happened on Sunday night and what they got was a bloody good hiding.
> *after a riot in which a policeman was killed*
> speech as leader of Haringey Council outside Tottenham Town Hall, 8 October 1985

Robert Grant 1785–1838
British lawyer and politician

8 O worship the King, all-glorious above;
O gratefully sing his power and his love:
Our Shield and Defender, the Ancient of Days,
Pavilioned in splendour, and girded with praise.
> 'O worship the King, all glorious above' (1833 hymn)

Ulysses S. Grant 1822–85
American Unionist general and statesman, 18th President of the US 1869–77

9 No terms except unconditional and immediate surrender can be accepted. I propose to move immediately upon your works.
> to Simon Bolivar Buckner, under siege at Fort Donelson, 16 February 1862

10 I purpose to fight it out on this line, if it takes all summer.
> dispatch to Washington, from head-quarters in the field, 11 May 1864

11 The war is over—the rebels are our countrymen again.
> *preventing his men from cheering after Lee's surrender at Appomattox*
> on 9 April, 1865

12 Let us have peace.
> letter to General Joseph R. Hawkey, 29 May 1868, accepting the presidential nomination, in P. C. Headley *The Life and Campaigns of General U. S. Grant* (1869) ch. 29

13 I know no method to secure the repeal of bad or obnoxious laws so effective as their stringent execution.
> inaugural address, 4 March 1869

14 Let no guilty man escape, if it can be avoided . . . No personal consideration should stand in the way of performing a public duty.
> *on the implication of his private secretary in a tax fraud*
> endorsement of a letter relating to the Whiskey Ring received 29 July 1875, in E. P. Oberholtzer *History of the United States Since the Civil War* (1937) vol. 3, ch. 19

John Woodcock Graves 1795–1886
British huntsman and songwriter

15 D'ye ken John Peel with his coat so grey?
D'ye ken John Peel at the break of the day?
D'ye ken John Peel when he's far far away
With his hounds and his horn in the morning?
> *an alternative version 'coat so gay' is often sung*
> 'John Peel' (1820)

Robert Graves 1895–1985
English poet

16 There's a cool web of language winds us in,
Retreat from too much joy or too much fear.
> 'The Cool Web' (1927)

17 Truth-loving Persians do not dwell upon
The trivial skirmish fought near Marathon.
> 'The Persian Version' (1945)

18 Love is a universal migraine.
A bright stain on the vision
Blotting out reason.
> 'Symptoms of Love'

19 Goodbye to all that.
> title of autobiography (1929)

1 If there's no money in poetry, neither is there poetry in money.

speech at London School of Economics, 6 December 1963

John Gray 1951–

2 Men are from Mars, women are from Venus.

title of book (1992)

John Chipman Gray 1839–1915
American lawyer

3 Dirt is only matter out of place; and what is a blot on the escutcheon of the Common Law may be a jewel in the crown of the Social Republic.

Restraints on the Alienation of Property (2nd ed., 1895) preface

Patrick, Lord Gray d. 1612

4 A dead woman bites not.

pressing for the execution of **Mary** *Queen of Scots in 1587*

oral tradition

Thomas Gray 1716–71
English poet

5 Ruin seize thee, ruthless King!
Confusion on thy banners wait.

The Bard (1757) l. 1

6 In gallant trim the gilded vessel goes;
Youth on the prow, and Pleasure at the helm.

'The Bard' (1757) l. 73

7 The curfew tolls the knell of parting day,
The lowing herd wind slowly o'er the lea,
The ploughman homeward plods his weary way,
And leaves the world to darkness and to me.

Elegy Written in a Country Churchyard (1751) l. 1

8 Beneath those rugged elms, that yew-tree's shade,
Where heaves the turf in many a mouldering heap,
Each in his narrow cell for ever laid,
The rude forefathers of the hamlet sleep.

Elegy Written in a Country Churchyard (1751) l. 13

9 The paths of glory lead but to the grave.

Elegy Written in a Country Churchyard (1751) l. 36

10 Can storied urn or animated bust
Back to its mansion call the fleeting breath?

Elegy Written in a Country Churchyard (1751) l. 41

11 Full many a gem of purest ray serene,
The dark unfathomed caves of ocean bear:
Full many a flower is born to blush unseen,
And waste its sweetness on the desert air.

Elegy Written in a Country Churchyard (1751) l. 53

12 Some mute inglorious Milton here may rest.

Elegy Written in a Country Churchyard (1751) l. 59

13 Forbad to wade through slaughter to a throne,
And shut the gates of mercy on mankind.

Elegy Written in a Country Churchyard (1751) l. 67

14 Far from the madding crowd's ignoble strife,

Their sober wishes never learned to stray.

Elegy Written in a Country Churchyard (1751) l. 73

15 Here rests his head upon the lap of Earth
A youth to fortune and to fame unknown.

Elegy Written in a Country Churchyard (1751) l. 117

16 Alas, regardless of their doom,
The little victims play!
No sense have they of ills to come,
Nor care beyond to-day.

Ode on a Distant Prospect of Eton College (1747) l. 51

17 To each his suff'rings, all are men,
Condemned alike to groan;
The tender for another's pain,
Th' unfeeling for his own.

Ode on a Distant Prospect of Eton College (1747) l. 91

18 Where ignorance is bliss,
'Tis folly to be wise.

Ode on a Distant Prospect of Eton College (1747) l. 99

19 What female heart can gold despise?
What cat's averse to fish?

'Ode on the Death of a Favourite Cat' (1748)

20 Not all that tempts your wand'ring eyes
And heedless hearts, is lawful prize;
Nor all, that glisters, gold.

'Ode on the Death of a Favourite Cat' (1748)

21 He saw; but blasted with excess of light,
Closed his eyes in endless night.

of **Milton**

The Progress of Poesy (1757) l. 101

Horace Greeley 1811–72
American founder and editor of the New York Tribune

22 Go West, young man, and grow up with the country.

Hints toward Reforms (1850)

Graham Greene 1904–91
English novelist

23 Catholics and Communists have committed great crimes, but at least they have not stood aside, like an established society, and been indifferent. I would rather have blood on my hands than water like Pilate.

The Comedians (1966) pt. 3, ch. 4

24 In human relations kindness and lies are worth a thousand truths.

The Heart of the Matter (1948) bk. 1, pt. 2, ch. 4

25 What do we ever get nowadays from reading to equal the excitement and the revelation in those first fourteen years?

The Lost Childhood and Other Essays (1951) title essay

26 There is always one moment in childhood when the door opens and lets the future in.

The Power and the Glory (1940) pt. 1, ch. 1

27 Innocence always calls mutely for protection, when we would be so much wiser to guard ourselves against it: innocence is like a dumb leper who has lost his bell, wandering the world meaning no harm.

The Quiet American (1955) pt. 1, ch. 3

1 I never knew a man who had better motives for all the trouble he caused.

The Quiet American (1955) pt. 1, ch. 4

Robert Greene *c.*1560–92
English poet and dramatist

2 For there is an upstart crow, beautified with our feathers, that with his tiger's heart wrapped in a player's hide, supposes he is as well able to bumbast out a blank verse as the best of you; and being an absolute *Johannes fac totum*, is in his own conceit the only Shake-scene in a country.

Groatsworth of Wit Bought with a Million of Repentance (1592); see **Shakespeare** 296:6

Alan Greenspan 1926–
American economist

3 How do we know when irrational exuberance has unduly escalated asset values?

speech in Washington, 5 December 1996

4 An infectious greed seemed to grip much of our business community.

of the late 1990s

in *New York Times* 17 July 2002 (online edition)

Germaine Greer 1939–
Australian feminist

5 The female eunuch.

title of book (1970)

6 Women have very little idea of how much men hate them.

The Female Eunuch (1970)

Pope Gregory the Great *c.*AD 540–604
Roman cleric, Pope from 590

7 *Non Angli sed Angeli.*
Not Angles but Angels.

on seeing English slaves in Rome

oral tradition, based on 'Responsum est, quod Angli vocarentur. At ille: 'Bene', inquit; 'nam et angelicam habent faciem, et tales angelorum in caelis decet esse coheredes [It is well,' he said, 'for they have the faces of angels, and such should be the co-heirs of the angels of heaven]'; Bede *Historia Ecclesiastica* bk. 2

Pope Gregory VII *c.*1020–85
Italian cleric, Pope from 1073

8 I have loved justice and hated iniquity: therefore I die in exile.

last words, at Salerno, following his conflict with the Emperor Henry IV

J. W. Bowden *The Life and Pontificate of Gregory VII* (1840) vol. 2

Stephen Grellet 1773–1855
French Quaker and missionary

9 I expect to pass through this world but once; any good thing therefore that I can do, or any kindness that I can show to any fellow-creature, let me do it now; let me not defer or neglect it, for I shall not pass this way again.

attributed; some of the many other claimants to authorship are given in John o' London *Treasure Trove* (1925)

Joyce Grenfell 1910–79
English comedy actress and writer

10 George—don't do that.

recurring line in monologues about a nursery school, from the 1950s, in *George—Don't Do That* (1977)

Julian Grenfell 1888–1915
English soldier and poet

11 And Life is Colour and Warmth and Light
And a striving evermore for these;
And he is dead, who will not fight;
And who dies fighting has increase.

'Into Battle' in *The Times* 28 May 1915

Wayne Gretzky 1961–
Canadian ice-hockey player

12 I skate to where the puck is going to be, not where it's been.

attributed, 1985; John Robert Colombo *Colombo's New Canadian Quotations* (1987)

Lord Grey of Fallodon 1862–1933
British Liberal politician

13 The lamps are going out all over Europe; we shall not see them lit again in our lifetime.

on the eve of the First World War

25 Years (1925) vol. 2, ch. 18

John Grigg 1924–2001
British writer and journalist

14 The personality conveyed by the utterances which are put into her mouth is that of a priggish schoolgirl, captain of the hockey team, a prefect, and a recent candidate for confirmation. It is not thus that she will be able to come into her own as an independent and distinctive character.

of Queen Elizabeth II

in *National and English Review* August 1958

Jacob Grimm 1785–1863
and Wilhelm Grimm 1786–1859
German philologists and folklorists

15 Mirror, mirror on the wall,
Who is the fairest of them all?

Kinder- und Hausmärchen [Fairytales and Household Stories] (1812–14) 'Snow White'

16 Rapunzel, Rapunzel, let down your hair.

Kinder- und Hausmärchen [Fairytales and Household Stories] (1812–14) 'Rapunzel'

Jo Grimond 1913–93
British Liberal politician

17 In bygone days, commanders were taught that when in doubt, they should march their troops towards the sound of gunfire. I

intend to march my troops towards the
sound of gunfire.

speech to the Liberal Party Assembly, 14
September 1963

Andrei Gromyko 1909–89
Soviet statesman; President of the USSR 1985–8

1 Comrades, this man has a nice smile, but
he's got iron teeth.

of Mikhail Gorbachev

speech to Soviet Communist Party Central
Committee, 11 March 1985

George Grossmith 1847–1912
English actor, singer, and writer

2 You should see me dance the Polka,
You should see me cover the ground,
You should see my coat-tails flying,
As I jump my partner round.

'See me Dance the Polka' (*c.*1887 song)

George Grossmith 1847–1912
and **Weedon Grossmith** 1854–1919
English writers

3 What's the good of a home if you are never
in it?

The Diary of a Nobody (1894) ch. 1

4 I left the room with silent dignity, but
caught my foot in the mat.

The Diary of a Nobody (1894) ch. 12

5 I am a poor man, but I would gladly give ten
shillings to find out who sent me the
insulting Christmas card I received this
morning.

The Diary of a Nobody (1894) ch. 13

Andrew Grove 1936–
Hungarian-born American businessman

6 Only the paranoid survive.

*dictum on which he has long run his company, the
Intel Corporation*

in *New York Times* 18 December 1994

Edgar A. Guest 1881–1959
American writer, journalist, and poet

7 The best of all the preachers are the men
who live their creeds.

'Sermons we See' (1926)

Che Guevara 1928–67
Argentinian revolutionary and guerrilla leader

8 The Revolution is made by man, but man
must forge his revolutionary spirit from day
to day.

Socialism and Man in Cuba (1968)

Nubar Gulbenkian 1896–1972
British industrialist and philanthropist

9 The best number for a dinner party is
two—myself and a dam' good head waiter.

in *Daily Telegraph* 14 January 1965

Dorothy Frances Gurney
1858–1932
English poet

10 The kiss of the sun for pardon,
The song of the birds for mirth,
One is nearer God's Heart in a garden
Than anywhere else on earth.

'God's Garden' (1913)

Woody Guthrie 1912–67
American folk singer and songwriter

11 This land is your land, this land is my land,
From California to the New York Island.
From the redwood forest to the Gulf Stream
waters
This land was made for you and me.

'This Land is Your Land' (1956 song)

Nell Gwyn 1650–87
English actress and courtesan

12 Pray, good people, be civil. I am the
Protestant whore.

at Oxford, during the Popish Terror, 1681

Hadrian AD 76–138
Roman emperor from 117

13 *Animula vagula blandula,
Hospes comesque corporis.*
Ah! gentle, fleeting, wav'ring sprite,
Friend and associate of this clay!

J. W. Duff (ed.) *Minor Latin Poets* (1934); tr. Byron
as 'Adrian's Address to His Soul When Dying';
see **Pope** 266:10

Ernst Haeckel 1834–1919
German biologist and philosopher

14 Ontogenesis, or the development of the
individual, is a short and quick
recapitulation of phylogenesis, or the
development of the tribe to which it
belongs, determined by the laws of
inheritance and adaptation.

*this discredited theory is often summarized as,
'ontogeny recapitulates phylogeny'*

The History of Creation (1868)

Haggadah
*the text recited at the Seder on the first two
nights of the Jewish Passover*

15 Let all who are hungry come and eat; let all
who are in need come to our Passover feast.

The narration

16 Now we are slaves; next year may we be
free!

The narration

17 In every generation men have risen up
against us to destroy us, but the Holy One,
blessed be he, has saved us from their
hands.

In every generation

18 Rabban Gamaliel says: 'Whoever does not
mention the following three things at
Passover has not fulfilled his duty—the

Passover sacrifice, unleavened bread, and bitter herbs.'
The three essentials of the Seder

1 Next year in Jerusalem!
Accepted

H. Rider Haggard 1856–1925
English writer

2 Out of the dark we came, into the dark we go . . . Life is nothing. Life is all. It is the hand with which we hold off death. It is the glow-worm that shines in the night-time and is black in the morning; it is the white breath of the oxen in winter; it is the little shadow that runs across the grass and loses itself at sunset.
King Solomon's Mines (1886) ch. 5; see **Crowfoot** 108:1

3 She who must be obeyed.
She (1887) ch. 6 and *passim*

Earl Haig 1861–1928
British general

4 A very weak-minded fellow I am afraid, and, like the feather pillow, bears the marks of the last person who has sat on him!
describing Lord Derby
letter to Lady Haig, 14 January 1918

5 With our backs to the wall, and believing in the justice of our cause, each one of us must fight on to the end.
order to British troops, 12 April 1918

Quintin Hogg, Lord Hailsham 1907–2001
British Conservative politician

6 The elective dictatorship.
title of the Dimbleby Lecture, 19 October 1976

Hakuin 1686–1769
Japanese monk, writer, and artist

7 If someone claps his hand a sound arises. Listen to the sound of the single hand!
often quoted as 'What is the sound of one hand clapping?'
attributed

J. B. S. Haldane 1892–1964
Scottish mathematical biologist

8 Now, my own suspicion is that the universe is not only queerer than we suppose, but queerer than we *can* suppose.
Possible Worlds and Other Essays (1927) 'Possible Worlds'

9 If my mental processes are determined wholly by the motions of atoms in my brain, I have no reason for supposing that my beliefs are true. They may be sound chemically, but that does not make them sound logically. And hence I have no reason

for supposing my brain to be composed of atoms.
Possible Worlds (1927) 'When I am Dead'

10 The Creator, if He exists, has a special preference for beetles.
on observing that there are 400,000 species of beetle on this planet, but only 8,000 species of mammals
report of lecture, 7 April 1951, in *Journal of the British Interplanetary Society* (1951) vol. 10

H. R. Haldeman 1929–93
American Presidential assistant to Richard Nixon

11 Once the toothpaste is out of the tube, it is awfully hard to get it back in.
on the Watergate affair
to John Dean, 8 April 1973

Edward Everett Hale 1822–1909
American Unitarian clergyman

12 'Do you pray for the senators, Dr Hale?' 'No, I look at the senators and I pray for the country.'
Van Wyck Brooks *New England Indian Summer* (1940)

Matthew Hale 1609–76
English judge

13 Christianity is part of the laws of England.
William Blackstone's summary of Hale's words (Taylor's case, 1676) in *Commentaries* (1769); the origin of the expression has been traced to Sir John Prisot (d. 1460)

Nathan Hale 1755–76
American revolutionary

14 Every kind of service necessary to the public good becomes honourable by being necessary.
letter to William Hull, 10 September 1776

15 I only regret that I have but one life to lose for my country.
prior to his execution by the British for spying, 22 September 1776
Henry Phelps Johnston *Nathan Hale, 1776* (1914) ch. 7; see **Addison** 3:1

Sarah Josepha Hale 1788–1879
American writer

16 Mary had a little lamb,
Its fleece was white as snow,
And everywhere that Mary went
The lamb was sure to go.
Poems for Our Children (1830) 'Mary's Little Lamb'

Judah Ha-Levi c.1075–1141
Jewish poet and philosopher, born in Spain

17 I understand the difference between the God and the Lord and I see how great is the difference between the God of Abraham and the God of Aristotle.
The Kuzari 4.16

George Savile, Lord Halifax ('the Trimmer') 1633–95
English politician and essayist

1 A known liar should be outlawed in a well-ordered government.
> *Political, Moral, and Miscellaneous Thoughts and Reflections* (1750) 'Miscellaneous: Lying'

2 Men are not hanged for stealing horses, but that horses may not be stolen.
> *Political, Moral, and Miscellaneous Thoughts and Reflections* (1750) 'Of Punishment'

3 Wherever a knave is not punished, an honest man is laughed at.
> *Political, Moral, and Miscellaneous Thoughts and Reflections* (1750) 'Of Punishment'

4 State business is a cruel trade; good nature is a bungler in it.
> *Political, Moral, and Miscellaneous Thoughts and Reflections* (1750) 'Wicked Ministers'

5 [Halifax] had heard of many kicked down stairs, but never of any that was kicked up stairs before.
> Gilbert Burnet *History of My Own Time* (written 1683–6) vol. 1 (1724)

Joseph Hall 1574–1656
English bishop

6 Perfection is the child of Time.
> *Works* (1625)

Radclyffe Hall 1883–1943
English novelist

7 The well of loneliness
> title of novel (1928)

8 You're neither unnatural, nor abominable, nor mad; you're as much a part of what people call nature as anyone else; only you're unexplained as yet—you've not got your niche in creation.
> *of lesbianism*
> *The Well of Loneliness* (1928) bk. 2, ch. 20, sect. 3

Fitz-Greene Halleck 1790–1867
American poet

9 Green be the turf above thee,
Friend of my better days!
None knew thee but to love thee,
Nor named thee but to praise.
> 'On the Death of Joseph Rodman Drake' (1820)

Friedrich Halm 1806–71
German dramatist

10 *Zwei Seelen und ein Gedanke,*
Zwei Herzen und ein Schlag!
Two souls with but a single thought,
Two hearts that beat as one.
> *Der Sohn der Wildnis* (1842) act 2

Alexander Hamilton *c.*1755–1804
American politician

11 A national debt, if it is not excessive, will be to us a national blessing.
> letter to Robert Morris, 30 April 1781

William Hamilton 1788–1856
Scottish metaphysician

12 Truth, like a torch, the more it's shook it shines.
> *Discussions on Philosophy* (1852) title page (epigram)

13 On earth there is nothing great but man; in man there is nothing great but mind.
> *Lectures on Metaphysics and Logic* (1859); attributed in a Latin form to Favorinus in Pico di Mirandola (1463–94) *Disputationes Adversus Astrologiam Divinatricem*

Oscar Hammerstein II 1895–1960
American songwriter

14 Fish got to swim and birds got to fly
I got to love one man till I die,
Can't help lovin' dat man of mine.
> 'Can't Help Lovin' Dat Man of Mine' (1927 song) in *Showboat*

15 Climb ev'ry mountain, ford ev'ry stream
Follow ev'ry rainbow, till you find your dream.
> 'Climb Ev'ry Mountain' (1959 song) in *The Sound of Music*

16 I'm gonna wash that man right outa my hair.
> title of song (1949) from *South Pacific*

17 June is bustin' out all over.
> title of song (1945) in *Carousel*

18 The corn is as high as an elephant's eye.
> 'Oh, What a Beautiful Mornin' ' (1943 song) in *Oklahoma!*

19 Ol' man river, dat ol' man river,
He must know sumpin', but don't say nothin',
He jus' keeps rollin',
He jus' keeps rollin' along.
> 'Ol' Man River' (1927 song) in *Showboat*

20 Some enchanted evening,
You may see a stranger,
You may see a stranger,
Across a crowded room.
> 'Some Enchanted Evening' (1949 song) in *South Pacific*

21 The hills are alive with the sound of music,
With songs they have sung for a thousand years.
The hills fill my heart with the sound of music,
My heart wants to sing ev'ry song it hears.
> 'The Sound of Music' (1959 title-song in show)

22 There is nothin' like a dame.
> title of song (1949) in *South Pacific*

23 I'm as corny as Kansas in August,
High as a flag on the Fourth of July!
> 'A Wonderful Guy' (1949 song) in *South Pacific*

24 You'll never walk alone.
> title of song (1945) in *Carousel*

25 You've got to be taught to be afraid
Of people whose eyes are oddly made,
Of people whose skin is a different shade.

You've got to be carefully taught.
'You've Got to be Carefully Taught' (1949 song)
in *South Pacific*

George Frederick Handel
1685–1759
German-born composer and organist

1 Whether I was in my body or out of my
body as I wrote it I know not. God knows.
of the 'Hallelujah Chorus' in his Messiah; *echoing
St Paul*
   Romain Rolland *A Musical Tour Through the Land
   of the Past* (1922); see **Bible** 51:9

Kate Hankey 1834–1911
English evangelist

2 Tell me the old, old story.
Title of hymn (1867)

Brian Hanrahan 1949–
British journalist

3 I counted them all out and I counted them
all back.
*on the number of British aeroplanes joining the
raid on Port Stanley in the Falkland Islands*
   BBC broadcast report, 1 May 1982

Lorraine Hansberry 1930–65
American dramatist

4 Though it be a thrilling and marvellous
thing to be merely young and gifted in such
times, it is doubly so, doubly dynamic—to
be young, gifted and *black.*
   *To be young, gifted and black: Lorraine Hansberry in
   her own words* (1969) adapted by Robert
   Nemiroff; see **Irvine** 181:1

Otto Harbach 1873–1963
American songwriter

5 Now laughing friends deride tears I cannot
hide,
So I smile and say 'When a lovely flame dies,
Smoke gets in your eyes.'
   'Smoke Gets in your Eyes' (1933 song)

E. Y. ('Yip') Harburg 1898–1981
American songwriter

6 Brother can you spare a dime?
title of song (1932)

7 Say, it's only a paper moon,
Sailing over a cardboard sea.
   'It's Only a Paper Moon' (1933 song, with Billy
   Rose)

8 Somewhere over the rainbow
Way up high,
There's a land that I heard of
Once in a lullaby.
   'Over the Rainbow' (1939 song) in *The Wizard of
   Oz*

9 Follow the yellow brick road.
   'We're Off to See the Wizard' (1939 song); see
   Baum 27:22, **John** 186:2

William Harcourt 1827–1904
British Liberal politician

10 We are all socialists now.
*during the passage of Lord **Goschen**'s 1888
budget, noted for the reduction of the national
debt*
   attributed; Hubert Bland 'The Outlook' in G. B.
   Shaw (ed.) *Fabian Essays in Socialism* (1889)

D. W. Harding 1906–
British psychologist and critic

11 Regulated hatred.
*title of an article on the novels of Jane **Austen***
in *Scrutiny* March 1940

Warren G. Harding 1865–1923
*American Republican statesman, 29th President
of the US 1921–3*

12 America's present need is not heroics, but
healing; not nostrums but normalcy; not
revolution, but restoration.
   speech at Boston, 14 May 1920, in Frederick E.
   Schortemeier *Rededicating America* (1920) ch. 17

Godfrey Harold Hardy 1877–1947
English mathematician

13 Beauty is the first test: there is no
permanent place in the world for ugly
mathematics.
   A Mathematician's Apology (1940)

Thomas Hardy 1840–1928
English novelist and poet

14 War makes rattling good history; but Peace
is poor reading.
   The Dynasts (1904) pt. 1, act 2, sc. 5

15 Done because we are too menny.
   Jude the Obscure (1896) pt. 6, ch. 2

16 Dialect words—those terrible marks of the
beast to the truly genteel.
   The Mayor of Casterbridge (1886) ch. 20

17 Happiness was but the occasional episode in
a general drama of pain.
   The Mayor of Casterbridge (1886) ch. 45, closing
   words

18 'Justice' was done, and the President of the
Immortals (in Aeschylean phrase) had ended
his sport with Tess.
   Tess of the D'Urbervilles (1891) ch. 59

19 After two thousand years of mass
We've got as far as poison-gas.
   'Christmas: 1924' (1928)

20 In a solitude of the sea
Deep from human vanity,
And the Pride of Life that planned her, stilly
couches she.
   'Convergence of the Twain' (1914)

21 The Immanent Will that stirs and urges
everything.
   'Convergence of the Twain' (1914)

22 An aged thrush, frail, gaunt, and small,
In blast-beruffled plume.
   'The Darkling Thrush' (1902)

1 There trembled through
His happy good-night air
Some blessed Hope, whereof he knew
And I was unaware.
'The Darkling Thrush' (1902)

2 If way to the Better there be, it exacts a full
look at the worst.
'De Profundis' (1902)

3 I am the family face;
Flesh perishes, I live on,
Projecting trait and trace
Through time to times anon,
And leaping from place to place
Over oblivion.
'Heredity' (1917)

4 Yes; quaint and curious war is!
You shoot a fellow down
You'd treat if met where any bar is,
Or help to half-a-crown.
'The Man he Killed' (1909)

5 What of the faith and fire within us
Men who march away.
'Men Who March Away' (1914)

6 In the third-class seat sat the journeying boy
And the roof-lamp's oily flame
Played down on his listless form and face,
Bewrapt past knowing to what he was
going,
Or whence he came.
'Midnight on the Great Western' (1917)

7 Woman much missed, how you call to me,
call to me.
'The Voice' (1914)

8 This is the weather the cuckoo likes,
And so do I.
'Weathers' (1922)

9 When I set out for Lyonnesse,
A hundred miles away,
The rime was on the spray,
And starlight lit my lonesomeness
When I set out for Lyonnesse
A hundred miles away.
'When I set out for Lyonnesse' (1914)

10 If this sort of thing continues no more
novel-writing for me. A man must be a fool
to deliberately stand up and be shot at.
of a hostile review of Tess of the D'Urbervilles,
1891
Florence Hardy The Early Life of Thomas Hardy
(1928)

Maurice Evan Hare 1886–1967
English limerick writer

11 There once was an old man who said,
'Damn!
It is borne in upon me I am
An engine that moves
In determinate grooves,
I'm not even a bus, I'm a tram.'
'Limerick' (1905)

W. F. Hargreaves 1846–1919
British songwriter

12 I'm Burlington Bertie

I rise at ten thirty and saunter along like a
toff,
I walk down the Strand with my gloves on
my hand,
Then I walk down again with them off.
'Burlington Bertie from Bow' (1915 song)

John Harington 1561–1612
English writer and courtier

13 Treason doth never prosper, what's the
reason?
For if it prosper, none dare call it treason.
Epigrams (1618) bk. 4, no. 5

Harold II *c.*1019–66
English monarch, King 1066

14 He will give him seven feet of English
ground, or as much more as he may be
taller than other men.
*his offer to Harald Hardrada of Norway, invading
England, before the battle of Stamford Bridge*
King Harald's Saga 1, in Snorri Sturluson
*Heimskringla (c.*1260)

Jimmy Harper, Will E. Haines, and Tommy Connor

15 The biggest aspidistra in the world.
title of song (1938); popularized by Gracie Fields

Arthur Harris 1892–1984
British Air Force Marshal

16 I would not regard the whole of the
remaining cities of Germany as worth the
bones of one British Grenadier.
*supporting the continued strategic bombing of
German cities*
letter to Norman Bottomley, deputy Chief of Air
Staff, 29 March 1945; see **Bismarck** 55:6

Joel Chandler Harris 1848–1908
American writer

17 Bred en bawn in a brier-patch!
Uncle Remus and His Legends of the Old Plantation
(1881) 'How Mr Rabbit was too Sharp for Mr
Fox'

Josephine Hart 1942–
Irish novelist

18 Damaged people are dangerous. They know
they can survive.
Damage (1991) ch. 12

Lorenz Hart 1895–1943
American songwriter

19 Bewitched, bothered, and bewildered am I.
'Bewitched' (1941 song) in *Pal Joey* (1941)

20 When love congeals
It soon reveals
The faint aroma of performing seals.
'I Wish I Were in Love Again' (1937 song) in
Babes in Arms

21 I get too hungry for dinner at eight.
I like the theatre, but never come late.
I never bother with people I hate.

That's why the lady is a tramp.
'The Lady is a Tramp' (1937 song) in *Babes in Arms*

1 Thou swell! Thou witty!
Thou sweet! Thou grand!
Wouldst kiss me pretty?
Wouldst hold my hand?
'Thou Swell' (1927 song)

Bret Harte 1836–1902
American poet

2 If, of all words of tongue and pen,
The saddest are, 'It might have been,'
More sad are these we daily see:
'It is, but hadn't ought to be!'
'Mrs Judge Jenkins' (1867); see **Whittier** 357:15

L. P. Hartley 1895–1972
English novelist

3 The past is a foreign country: they do things
differently there.
The Go-Between (1953) prologue; see **Morley** 245:2

F. W. Harvey b. 1888
English poet

4 From troubles of the world
I turn to ducks
Beautiful comical things.
'Ducks' (1919)

Minnie Louise Haskins 1875–1957
English teacher and writer

5 And I said to the man who stood at the gate
of the year: 'Give me a light that I may tread
safely into the unknown.'
And he replied:
'Go out into the darkness and put your
hand into the Hand of God. That shall be to
you better than light and safer than a
known way.'
*quoted by George VI in his Christmas broadcast,
1939*
Desert (1908) 'God Knows'

Edwin Hatch 1835–89
English clergyman and scholar

6 Breathe on me, Breath of God,
Fill me with life anew.
'Breathe on me, Breath of God' (1878 hymn)

Helen Hathaway 1893–1932
American writer

7 More tears have been shed over men's lack
of manners than their lack of morals.
Manners for Men (1928)

Václav Havel 1936–
Czech dramatist and statesman

8 I really do inhabit a system in which words
are capable of shaking the entire structure
of government, where words can prove
mightier than ten military divisions.
speech in Germany accepting a peace prize,
October 1989, in *Independent* 9 December 1989

Bob Hawke 1929–
Australian Labor statesman

9 No longer content to be just the lucky
country, Australia must now become the
clever country.
speech, *c.*1990; attributed

R. S. Hawker 1803–75
English clergyman and poet

10 And have they fixed the where and when?
And shall Trelawny die?
Here's twenty thousand Cornish men
Will know the reason why!
*the last three lines have been in existence since the
imprisonment by James II, in 1688, of seven
bishops, including Trelawny, Bishop of Bristol*
'The Song of the Western Men'

Jacquetta Hawkes 1910–96
English archaeologist and writer

11 Every age has the Stonehenge it
deserves—or desires.
in *Antiquity* no. 41, 1967

Stephen Hawking 1942–
English theoretical physicist

12 What is it that breathes fire into the
equations and makes a universe for them to
describe . . . Why does the universe go to all
the bother of existing?
A Brief History of Time (1988)

13 If we find the answer to that [why it is that
we and the universe exist], it would be the
ultimate triumph of human reason—for
then we would know the mind of God.
A Brief History of Time (1988) ch. 11

Nathaniel Hawthorne 1804–64
American novelist

14 The scarlet letter.
title of novel (1850)

15 America is now given over to a damned mob
of scribbling women.
letter, 1855; Caroline Ticknor *Hawthorne and his
Publisher* (1913)

Ian Hay 1876–1952
Scottish novelist and dramatist

16 War is hell, and all that, but it has a good
deal to recommend it. It wipes out all the
small nuisances of peace-time.
The First Hundred Thousand (1915)

17 What do you mean, funny? Funny-peculiar
or funny ha-ha?
The Housemaster (1938) act 3

Franz Joseph Haydn 1732–1809
Austrian composer

18 But all the world understands my language.
*on being advised by Mozart, in 1790, not to visit
England because he knew too little of the world
and too few languages*
Rosemary Hughes *Haydn* (1950) ch. 6

Alfred Hayes 1911–85
American songwriter

1 I dreamed I saw Joe Hill last night
Alive as you and me.
Says I, 'But Joe, you're ten years dead.'
'I never died,' says he.
'I Dreamed I Saw Joe Hill Last Night' (1936 song)

J. Milton Hayes 1884–1940
British writer

2 There's a one-eyed yellow idol to the north
of Khatmandu,
There's a little marble cross below the town,
There's a broken-hearted woman tends the
grave of Mad Carew,
And the Yellow God forever gazes down.
The Green Eye of the Yellow God (1911)

William Hazlitt 1778–1830
English essayist

3 He talked on for ever; and you wished him
to talk on for ever.
of Coleridge
Lectures on the English Poets (1818) 'On the Living
Poets'

4 The love of liberty is the love of others; the
love of power is the love of ourselves.
Political Essays (1819) 'The Times Newspaper'

5 Rules and models destroy genius and art.
Sketches and Essays (1839) 'On Taste'

6 We can scarcely hate any one that we know.
Table Talk vol. 2 (1822) 'On Criticism'

7 Well, I've had a happy life.
W. C. Hazlitt Memoirs of William Hazlitt (1867)

Denis Healey 1917–
British Labour politician

8 Like being savaged by a dead sheep.
*on being criticized by Geoffrey Howe in the House
of Commons*
in the House of Commons, 14 June 1978

Timothy Michael Healy 1855–1931
Irish nationalist politician

9 REDMOND: Gladstone is now master of the
Party!
HEALY: Who is to be mistress of the Party?
*at the meeting of the Irish Parliamentary Party on
6 December 1890, when the Party split over
Parnell's involvement in the O'Shea divorce;
Healy's reference to Katherine O'Shea was
particularly damaging to Parnell*
Robert Kee The Laurel and the Ivy (1993)

Seamus Heaney 1939–
Irish poet

10 But then, once in a lifetime
The longed-for tidal wave
Of justice can rise up
And hope and history rhyme.
The Cure at Troy (version of Sophocles' *Philoctetes*,
1990)

11 Between my finger and my thumb

The squat pen rests.
I'll dig with it.
'Digging' (1966)

12 Don't be surprised
If I demur, for, be advised
My passport's green.
No glass of ours was ever raised
To toast *The Queen*.
rebuking the editors of The Penguin Book of
Contemporary British Poetry *for including him
among its authors*
Open Letter (Field Day pamphlet no. 2, 1983)

13 The famous
Northern reticence, the tight gag of place
And times: yes, yes. Of the 'wee six' I sing
Where to be saved you only must save face
And whatever you say, you say nothing.
'Whatever You Say Say Nothing' (1975)

William Randolph Hearst
1863–1951
American newspaper publisher and tycoon

14 You furnish the pictures and I'll furnish the
war.
*message to the artist Frederic Remington in
Havana, Cuba, during the Spanish-American War
of 1898*
attributed

Edward Heath 1916–2005
*British Conservative statesman; Prime Minister,
1970–4*

15 The unpleasant and unacceptable face of
capitalism.
on the Lonrho affair
in the House of Commons, 15 May 1973

Reginald Heber 1783–1826
English clergyman

16 Brightest and best of the sons of the
morning,
Dawn on our darkness and lend us thine aid.
'Brightest and best of the sons of the morning'
(1827 hymn)

17 From Greenland's icy mountains,
From India's coral strand.
'From Greenland's icy mountains' (1821 hymn)

18 What though the spicy breezes
Blow soft o'er Ceylon's isle;
Though every prospect pleases,
And only man is vile:
In vain with lavish kindness
The gifts of God are strown;
The heathen in his blindness
Bows down to wood and stone.
'From Greenland's icy mountains' (1821 hymn);
Heber later altered 'Ceylon's isle' to 'Java's isle';
see Kipling 201:22

19 Holy, Holy, Holy! all the saints adore thee,
Casting down their golden crowns around
the glassy sea,
Cherubim and Seraphim falling down
before thee,

Which wert, and art, and evermore shalt be.
'Holy, Holy, Holy! Lord God Almighty!' (1826 hymn)

G. W. F. Hegel 1770–1831
German idealist philosopher
see also Marx 230:7

1 What experience and history teach is this—that nations and governments have never learned anything from history, or acted upon any lessons they might have drawn from it.
Lectures on the Philosophy of World History: Introduction (1830, tr. H. B. Nisbet, 1975) introduction

2 Only in the state does man have a rational existence . . . Man owes his entire existence to the state, and has his being within it alone.
Lectures on the Philosophy of World History: Introduction (1830, tr. H. B. Nisbet, 1975)

3 What is rational is actual and what is actual is rational.
Philosophy of Right (1821, tr. T. M. Knox, 1952)

4 When philosophy paints its grey on grey, then has a shape of life grown old. By philosophy's grey on grey it cannot be rejuvenated but only understood. The owl of Minerva spreads its wings only with the falling of the dusk.
Philosophy of Right (1821, tr. T. M. Knox, 1952)

Piet Hein 1905–96
Danish poet and cartoonist

5 Problems worthy
of attack
prove their worth
by hitting back.
'Problems' (1969)

Heinrich Heine 1797–1856
German poet

6 *Dort, wo man Bücher*
Verbrennt, verbrennt man auch am Ende Menschen.
Wherever books will be burned, men also, in the end, are burned.
Almansor (1823) l. 245

7 *Auf Flügeln des Gesanges.*
On wings of song.
title of song (1823)

8 What then is music? . . . It exists between thought and phenomenon, like a twilight medium, it stands between spirit and matter, related to and yet different from both; it is spirit, but spirit governed by time; it is matter, but matter that can manage without space.
On the French Stage: Intimate letters to August Lewald (1857)

9 Maximilien Robespierre was nothing but the hand of Jean Jacques Rousseau, the bloody hand that drew from the womb of time the body whose soul Rousseau had created.
Zur Geschichte der Religion und Philosophie in Deutschland (1834) bk. 3, para. 3

10 *Dieu me pardonnera, c'est son métier.*
God will pardon me, it is His trade.
on his deathbed
Alfred Meissner *Heinrich Heine. Erinnerungen* (1856) ch. 5; see **Catherine** 89:1

Werner Heisenberg 1901–76
German mathematical physicist

11 An expert is someone who knows some of the worst mistakes that can be made in his subject and who manages to avoid them.
Der Teil und das Ganze (1969) ch. 17 (tr. A. J. Pomerans as *Physics and Beyond*, 1971)

12 *on Felix Bloch's stating that space was the field of linear operations:*
Nonsense. Space is blue and birds fly through it.
Felix Bloch 'Heisenberg and the early days of quantum mechanics' in *Physics Today* December 1976

Joseph Heller 1923–99
American novelist

13 There was only one catch and that was Catch-22, which specified that a concern for one's own safety in the face of dangers that were real and immediate was the process of a rational mind . . . Orr would be crazy to fly more missions and sane if he didn't, but if he was sane he had to fly them. If he flew them he was crazy and didn't have to; but if he didn't want to he was sane and had to.
Catch-22 (1961) ch. 5

14 Some men are born mediocre, some men achieve mediocrity, and some men have mediocrity thrust upon them. With Major Major it had been all three.
Catch-22 (1961) ch. 9; see **Shakespeare** 309:2

15 When I read something saying I've not done anything as good as *Catch-22* I'm tempted to reply, 'Who has?'
in *The Times* 9 June 1993

Lillian Hellman 1905–84
American dramatist

16 I cannot and will not cut my conscience to fit this year's fashions.
letter to John S. Wood, 19 May 1952, in *US Congress Committee Hearing on Un-American Activities* (1952) pt. 8

Leona Helmsley c.1920–
American hotelier

17 Only the little people pay taxes.
comment made to her housekeeper in 1983, and reported at her trial for tax evasion
in *New York Times* 12 July 1989

Felicia Hemans 1793–1835
English poet

18 The boy stood on the burning deck

Whence all but he had fled.
'Casabianca' (1849)

1 The stately homes of England,
How beautiful they stand!
'The Homes of England' (1849); see **Coward** 105:7

Ernest Hemingway 1899–1961
American novelist
see also **Fitzgerald** *137:6,* **Stein** *323:18*

2 But did thee feel the earth move?
For Whom the Bell Tolls (1940) ch. 13

3 Paris is a movable feast.
A Movable Feast (1964) epigraph

4 The sun also rises.
title of novel (1926)

5 Grace under pressure.
when asked what he meant by 'guts' in an interview with Dorothy **Parker**
in *New Yorker* 30 November 1929

6 The most essential gift for a good writer is a built-in, shock-proof shit detector.
in *Paris Review* Spring 1958

Arthur W. D. Henley

7 Nobody loves a fairy when she's forty.
title of song (1934)

W. E. Henley 1849–1903
English poet and dramatist

8 Out of the night that covers me,
Black as the Pit from pole to pole,
I thank whatever gods may be
For my unconquerable soul.
In the fell clutch of circumstance,
I have not winced nor cried aloud:
Under the bludgeonings of chance
My head is bloody, but unbowed.
'Invictus. In Memoriam R.T.H.B.' (1888)

9 It matters not how strait the gate,
How charged with punishments the scroll,
I am the master of my fate:
I am the captain of my soul.
'Invictus. In Memoriam R.T.H.B.' (1888)

10 What have I done for you,
England, my England?
'Pro Rege Nostro' (1900); see **MacDonell** 223:1

11 I was a King in Babylon
And you were a Christian slave.
'To W. A.' (1888)

Henri IV 1553–1610
French monarch, King from 1589

12 I want there to be no peasant in my kingdom so poor that he is unable to have a chicken in his pot every Sunday.
Hardouin de Péréfixe *Histoire de Henry le Grand* (1681); see **Hoover** 173:5

13 Paris is well worth a mass.
attributed to Henri IV; alternatively to his minister Sully, in conversation with Henri

14 The wisest fool in Christendom.
of **James I** *of England*
attributed both to Henri IV and Sully

Henry I 1068–1135
English monarch, King from 1100

15 An illiterate king is a crowned ass.
described as a proverbial usage on the part of Henry by William of Malmesbury in *De Gestis Regum Anglorum*, and probably first coined by Count Foulques II of Anjou, *c.*950

Henry II 1133–89
English monarch, King from 1154

16 Will no one rid me of this turbulent priest?
of Thomas Becket, Archbishop of Canterbury, murdered in Canterbury Cathedral, December 1170
oral tradition, conflating a number of variant forms

Henry VIII 1491–1547
English monarch, King from 1509

17 That man hath the sow by the right ear.
of Thomas **Cranmer***, June 1529*
Acts and Monuments of John Foxe ['Fox's Book of Martyrs'] (1570)

18 The King found her so different from her picture . . . that . . . he swore they had brought him a Flanders mare.
of Anne of Cleves
Tobias Smollett *A Complete History of England* (3rd ed., 1759) vol. 6

Matthew Henry 1662–1714
English divine

19 They that die by famine die by inches.
An Exposition on the Old and New Testament (1710) Psalm 59, v. 15, gloss 5 (referring incorrectly to v. 13)

O. Henry 1862–1910
American short-story writer

20 It was beautiful and simple as all truly great swindles are.
Gentle Grafter (1908) 'Octopus Marooned'

21 Turn up the lights; I don't want to go home in the dark.
last words, quoting a song; Charles Alphonso Smith *O. Henry Biography* (1916) ch. 9
I'm afraid to come home in the dark.
Harry Williams (1874–1924) title of song (1907)

Patrick Henry 1736–99
American statesman

22 Caesar had his Brutus—Charles the First, his Cromwell—and George the Third—('Treason,' cried the Speaker) . . . *may profit by their example. If this* be treason, make the most of it.
speech in the Virginia assembly, May 1765

23 I am not a Virginian, but an American.
in [John Adams's] Notes of Debates in the Continental Congress, Philadelphia, 6 September 1774

24 I know not what course others may take; but as for me, give me liberty, or give me death!
speech in Virginia Convention, 23 March 1775

Philip Henry 1631–96
English clergyman

1 All this, and heaven too!
  in Matthew Henry *Life of Mr Philip Henry* (1698)
  ch. 5

Heraclitus *c*.540–*c*.480 BC
Greek philosopher

2 Everything flows and nothing stays.
  Plato *Cratylus* 402a

3 You can't step twice into the same river.
  Plato *Cratylus* 402a

4 A man's character is his fate.
  On the Universe fragment 121 (tr. W. H. S. Jones);
  see **Eliot** 127:21, **Novalis** 252:7

5 The road up and the road down are one and
  the same.
  H. Diels and W. Kranz *Die Fragmente der
  Vorsokratiker* (7th ed., 1954) fragment 60

A. P. Herbert 1890–1971
English writer and humorist

6 This high official, all allow,
  Is grossly overpaid;
  There wasn't any Board, and now
  There isn't any Trade.
  'The President of the Board of Trade' (1922)

7 Holy deadlock.
  title of novel (1934)

8 People must not do things for fun. We are
  not here for fun. There is no reference to
  fun in any Act of Parliament.
  Uncommon Law (1935) 'Is it a Free Country?'

9 The critical period in matrimony is
  breakfast-time.
  Uncommon Law (1935) 'Is Marriage Lawful?'

George Herbert 1593–1633
English poet and clergyman

10 Let all the world in ev'ry corner sing
  My God and King.
  'Antiphon: Let all the world in ev'ry corner sing'
  (1633)

11 I struck the board, and cried, 'No more.
  I will abroad.'
  'The Collar' (1633)

12 Away; take heed:
  I will abroad.
  Call in thy death's-head there: tie up thy
  fears.
  'The Collar' (1633)

13 But as I raved and grew more fierce and wild
  At every word,
  Methought I heard one calling, 'Child';
  And I replied, 'My Lord.'
  'The Collar' (1633)

14 Teach me, my God and King,
  In all things Thee to see,
  And what I do in any thing
  To do it as for Thee.
  'The Elixir' (1633)

15 A servant with this clause
  Makes drudgery divine:

Who sweeps a room as for Thy laws
Makes that and th' action fine.
  'The Elixir' (1633)

16 Who says that fictions only and false hair
  Become a verse? Is there in truth no beauty?
  Is all good structure in a winding stair?
  'Jordan (1)' (1633)

17 Love bade me welcome: yet my soul drew
  back,
  Guilty of dust and sin.
  But quick-eyed Love, observing me grow
  slack
  From my first entrance in,
  Drew nearer to me, sweetly questioning,
  If I lacked any thing.
  'Love: Love bade me welcome' (1633)

18 'You must sit down,' says Love, 'and taste my
  meat.'
  So I did sit and eat.
  'Love: Love bade me welcome' (1633)

19 The land of spices; something understood.
  'Prayer: Prayer the Church's banquet' (1633)

20 When God at first made man,
  Having a glass of blessings standing by;
  Let us (said he) pour on him all we can:
  Let the world's riches, which dispersed lie,
  Contract into a span.
  'The Pulley' (1633)

21 If goodness lead him not, yet weariness
  May toss him to My breast.
  'The Pulley' (1633)

22 Fine nets and stratagems to catch us in,
  Bibles laid open, millions of surprises.
  'Sin: Lord, with what care Thou hast begirt us
  round!' (1633)

23 The God of love my Shepherd is,
  And He that doth me feed:
  While He is mine, and I am His,
  What can I want or need?
  'The 23rd Psalm' (1633); see **Book of Common
  Prayer** 62:14

24 Sweet day, so cool, so calm, so bright,
  The bridal of the earth and sky.
  'Virtue' (1633)

25 Sweet spring, full of sweet days and roses,
  A box where sweets compacted lie.
  'Virtue' (1633)

26 Only a sweet and virtuous soul,
  Like seasoned timber, never gives.
  'Virtue' (1633)

27 He that lives in hope danceth without
  music.
  Outlandish Proverbs (1640) no. 1006

Herodotus *c*.485–*c*.425 BC
Greek historian

28 In peace, children inter their parents; war
  violates the order of nature and causes
  parents to inter their children.
  Histories bk. 1 sect. 87

Robert Herrick 1591–1674
English poet and clergyman

29 Here a little child I stand,

Heaving up my either hand;
Cold as paddocks though they be,
Here I lift them up to Thee,
For a benison to fall
On our meat, and on us all. Amen.
'Another Grace for a Child' (1647)

1 I sing of brooks, of blossoms, birds, and
    bowers:
Of April, May, of June, and July-flowers.
I sing of May-poles, Hock-carts, wassails,
    wakes,
Of bride-grooms, brides, and of their bridal-
    cakes.
'The Argument of his Book' from *Hesperides*
(1648)

2 Cherry-ripe, ripe, ripe, I cry,
Full and fair ones; come and buy:
If so be, you ask me where
They do grow? I answer, there,
Where my Julia's lips do smile;
There's the land, or cherry-isle.
'Cherry-Ripe' (1648)

3 A sweet disorder in the dress
Kindles in clothes a wantonness:
'Delight in Disorder' (1648)

4 Fair daffodils, we weep to see
You haste away so soon.
'To Daffodils' (1648)

5 Gather ye rosebuds while ye may,
Old Time is still a-flying:
And this same flower that smiles to-day,
To-morrow will be dying.
'To the Virgins, to Make Much of Time' (1648)

6 Then be not coy, but use your time;
And while ye may, go marry:
For having lost but once your prime,
You may for ever tarry.
'To the Virgins, to Make Much of Time' (1648)

7 Whenas in silks my Julia goes,
Then, then (methinks) how sweetly flows
That liquefaction of her clothes.
Next, when I cast mine eyes and see
That brave vibration each way free;
O how that glittering taketh me!
'Upon Julia's Clothes' (1648)

Theodor Herzl 1860–1904
*Hungarian-born journalist, dramatist, and Zionist
leader*

8 At Basle I founded the Jewish state.
of the first Zionist congress, held in Basle in 1897
diary, 3 September 1897

Hesiod
Greek poet of c.700 BC

9 The half is greater than the whole.
Works and Days l. 40

Hermann Hesse 1877–1962
German novelist and poet

10 If you hate a person, you hate something in
him that is part of yourself. What isn't part
of ourselves doesn't disturb us.
Demian (1919) ch. 6

Gordon Hewart 1870–1943
British lawyer and politician

11 A long line of cases shows that it is not
merely of some importance, but is of
fundamental importance that justice should
not only be done, but should manifestly and
undoubtedly be seen to be done.
Rex v Sussex Justices, 9 November 1923

Reinhard Heydrich 1904–42
German Nazi leader

12 Now the rough work has been done we
begin the period of finer work. We need to
work in harmony with the civil
administration. We count on you gentlemen
as far as the final solution is concerned.
*on the planned mass murder of all European Jews;
see* **Goering** 152:7
speech in Wannsee, 20 January 1942

Du Bose Heyward 1885–1940
and **Ira Gershwin** 1896–1983
American songwriters

13 It ain't necessarily so,
It ain't necessarily so,
De t'ings dat yo' li'ble
To read in de Bible
It ain't necessarily so.
'It ain't necessarily so' (1935 song) in *Porgy and
Bess*

14 Summer time an' the livin' is easy,
Fish are jumpin' an' the cotton is high.
'Summertime' (1935 song) in *Porgy and Bess*

15 A woman is a sometime thing.
title of song (1935) in *Porgy and Bess*

John Heywood c.1497–c.1580
English dramatist

16 All a green willow, willow;
All a green willow is my garland.
'The Green Willow'; see **Shakespeare** 305:10

Thomas Heywood c.1574–1641
English dramatist

17 Seven cities warred for Homer, being dead,
Who, living, had no roof to shroud his head.
'The Hierarchy of the Blessed Angels' (1635); see
Anonymous 10:19

J. R. Hicks 1904–89
British economist

18 The best of all monopoly profits is a quiet
life.
Econometrica (1935) 'The Theory of Monopoly'

David Hilbert 1862–1943
German mathematician

19 We must know,
We will know.
epitaph on his tombstone, Göttingen;
Constance Reid *Hilbert* (1970) ch. 25

Hildegard of Bingen 1098–1179
German abbess, scholar, composer, and mystic

1 A feather does not fly of its own accord, it is borne up by the air. So too I am not imbued with human doctrine or strong powers . . . Rather, I depend entirely on God's help.
often summarized 'Thus am I a feather on the breath of God'
letter to Odo of Soissons, 1148, in *Selected Writings* (2001, tr. M. Atherton)

Aaron Hill 1685–1750
English poet and dramatist

2 Tender-handed stroke a nettle,
And it stings you for your pains;
Grasp it like a man of mettle,
And it soft as silk remains.
'Verses Written on a Window in Scotland'

Damon Hill 1960–
English motor-racing driver

3 Winning is everything. The only ones who remember you when you come second are your wife and your dog.
in *Sunday Times* 18 December 1994 'Quotes of the Year'

Joe Hill 1879–1915
Swedish-born American labour leader and songwriter

4 You will eat, bye and bye,
In that glorious land above the sky;
Work and pray, live on hay,
You'll get pie in the sky when you die.
'Preacher and the Slave' in *Songs of the Workers* (Industrial Workers of the World, 1911)

5 I will die like a true-blue rebel. Don't waste any time in mourning—organize.
before his death by firing squad
farewell telegram to Bill Haywood, 18 November 1915

Pattie S. Hill 1868–1946
American educationist

6 Happy birthday to you.
title of song (1935)

Rowland Hill 1744–1833
English clergyman

7 He did not see any reason why the devil should have all the good tunes.
E. W. Broome *The Rev. Rowland Hill* (1881) ch. 7

Edmund Hillary 1919–
New Zealand mountaineer

8 Well, we knocked the bastard off!
on conquering Mount Everest, 1953
Nothing Venture, Nothing Win (1975) ch. 10

Fred Hillebrand 1893–1963

9 Home James, and don't spare the horses.
title of song (1934)

Hillel 'The Elder' *c*.60 BC–*c*.AD 9
Jewish scholar and teacher

10 What is hateful to you do not do to your neighbour: that is the whole Torah.
in *Talmud* Shabbat 31a

11 Be of the disciples of Aaron, loving peace and pursuing peace.
in *Talmud* Mishnah 'Pirqei Avot' 1:12

12 If I am not for myself who is for me? and being for my own self what am I? If not now when?
in *Talmud* Mishnah 'Pirqei Avot' 1:14

13 Say not, When I have leisure I will study; perchance thou wilt never have leisure.
in *Talmud* Mishnah 'Pirqei Avot' 2:5

Hippocleides
Greek aristocrat of 6th century BC Athens

14 Hippocleides doesn't care.
on being told that he had ruined his marriage chances with the daughter of a tyrant, concluding a dance by standing on his head and gesticulating with his legs
Herodotus *Histories* bk. 6, sect. 129

Hippocrates *c*.460–357 BC
Greek physician

15 Life is short, the art long.
often quoted as 'Ars longa, vita brevis', after Seneca's *rendering in De Brevitate Vitae sect. 1*
Aphorisms sect. 1, para. 1 (tr. W. H. S. Jones); see **Chaucer** 92:2

16 Extreme remedies are most appropriate for extreme diseases.
Aphorisms sect. 1, para. 6 (tr. W. H. S. Jones)

17 I swear by Apollo the physician, by Asclepius, by Health, by Panacea and by all the gods and goddesses, making them my witnesses, that I will carry out, according to my ability and judgement, this oath and this indenture.
The Hippocratic Oath (tr. W. H. S. Jones)

18 I will use treatment to help the sick according to my ability and judgement, but never with a view to injury or wrong-doing. Neither will I administer a poison to anybody when asked to do so, nor will I suggest such a course.
The Hippocratic Oath (tr. W. H. S. Jones)

19 I will not use the knife, not even, verily, on sufferers from stone but I will give place to such as are craftsmen therein.
The Hippocratic Oath (tr. W. H. S. Jones)

20 And whatsoever I shall see or hear in the course of my profession, as well as outside my profession in my intercourse with men, if it be what should not be published abroad, I will never divulge holding such things to be holy secrets.
The Hippocratic Oath (tr. W. H. S. Jones)

21 Healing is a matter of time, but it is sometimes also a matter of opportunity.
Precepts ch. 1 (tr. W. H. S. Jones, 1923)

Emperor Hirohito 1901–89
Japanese monarch, Emperor from 1926

1 The war situation has developed not
necessarily to Japan's advantage.
*announcing Japan's surrender, in a broadcast to
his people after atom bombs had destroyed
Hiroshima and Nagasaki*
    on 15 August 1945

Damien Hirst 1965–
English artist

2 It's amazing what you can do with an E in
A-level art, twisted imagination and a
chainsaw.
after winning the 1995 Turner Prize
    in *Observer* 3 December 1995 'Sayings of the
    Week'

Alfred Hitchcock 1899–1980
British-born film director

3 Actors are cattle.
    in *Saturday Evening Post* 22 May 1943

4 Television has brought back murder into the
home—where it belongs.
    in *Observer* 19 December 1965

5 There is no terror in a bang, only in the
anticipation of it.
    Leslie Halliwell (ed.) *Halliwell's Filmgoer's
    Companion* (1984); attributed

Adolf Hitler 1889–1945
German dictator

6 The broad mass of a nation . . . will more
easily fall victim to a big lie than to a small
one.
    Mein Kampf (1925) vol. 1, ch. 10

7 The night of the long knives.
*referring to the massacre of Ernst Roehm and his
associates by Hitler on 29–30 June 1934
(subsequently associated with Harold **Macmillan's**
Cabinet dismissals of 13 July 1962)*
    S. H. Roberts *The House Hitler Built* (1937) pt. 2,
    ch. 3

8 I go the way that Providence dictates with
the assurance of a sleepwalker.
    speech in Munich, 15 March 1936,

9 It is the last territorial claim which I have to
make in Europe, but it is the claim from
which I will not recede and which, God-
willing, I will make good.
on the Sudetenland
    speech at Berlin Sportpalast, 26 September
    1938

10 My patience is now at an end!
    speech at Berlin Sportpalast, 26 September
    1938,

11 Is Paris burning?
    on 25 August 1944, in Larry Collins and
    Dominique Lapierre *Is Paris Burning?* (1965) ch. 5

Thomas Hobbes 1588–1679
English philosopher

12 Laughter is nothing else but sudden glory
arising from some sudden conception of
some eminency in ourselves, by comparison
with the infirmity of others, or with our
own formerly.
    Human Nature (1650) ch. 9, sect. 13

13 By art is created that great Leviathan, called
a commonwealth or state, (in Latin *civitas*)
which is but an artificial man . . . and in
which, the sovereignty is an artificial soul.
    Leviathan (1651); introduction

14 Words are wise men's counters, they do but
reckon by them: but they are the money of
fools, that value them by the authority of an
Aristotle, a Cicero, or a Thomas, or any
other doctor whatsoever, if but a man.
    Leviathan (1651) pt. 1, ch. 4

15 I put for a general inclination of all
mankind, a perpetual and restless desire of
power after power, that ceaseth only in
death.
    Leviathan (1651) pt. 1, ch. 11

16 They that approve a private opinion, call it
opinion; but they that mislike it, heresy:
and yet heresy signifies no more than
private opinion.
    Leviathan (1651) pt. 1, ch. 11

17 During the time men live without a
common power to keep them all in awe,
they are in that condition which is called
war; and such a war as is of every man
against every man.
    Leviathan (1651) pt. 1, ch. 13

18 For as the nature of foul weather, lieth not
in a shower or two of rain; but in an
inclination thereto of many days together:
so the nature of war consisteth not in actual
fighting, but in the known disposition
thereto during all the time there is no
assurance to the contrary.
    Leviathan (1651) pt. 1, ch. 13

19 No arts; no letters; no society; and which is
worst of all, continual fear and danger of
violent death; and the life of man, solitary,
poor, nasty, brutish, and short.
    Leviathan (1651) pt. 1, ch. 13

20 Force, and fraud, are in war the two cardinal
virtues.
    Leviathan (1651) pt. 1, ch. 13

21 Liberties . . . depend on the silence of the
law.
    Leviathan (1651) pt. 2, ch. 16

22 The papacy is not other than the ghost of
the deceased Roman Empire, sitting
crowned upon the grave thereof.
    Leviathan (1651) pt. 4, ch. 47

23 I am about to take my last voyage, a great
leap in the dark.
    last words; attributed (see **Vanbrugh** 345:4), but
    with no authoritative source

John Cam Hobhouse, Lord Broughton 1786–1869
English politician

1 When I invented the phrase 'His Majesty's Opposition' [Canning] paid me a compliment on the fortunate hit.
   Recollections of a Long Life (1865) vol. 2, ch. 12; also recorded by Bagehot a few years later

David Hockney 1937–
British artist

2 Art has to move you and design does not, unless it's a good design for a bus.
   in *Guardian* 26 October 1988

3 The thing with high-tech is that you always end up using scissors.
   in *Observer* 10 July 1994 'Sayings of the Week'

Ralph Hodgson 1871–1962
English poet

4 'Twould ring the bells of Heaven
   The wildest peal for years,
   If Parson lost his senses
   And people came to theirs,
   And he and they together
   Knelt down with angry prayers
   For tamed and shabby tigers
   And dancing dogs and bears,
   And wretched, blind, pit ponies,
   And little hunted hares.
   'Bells of Heaven' (1917)

Al Hoffman 1902–60
and **Dick Manning** 1912–

5 Takes two to tango.
   title of song (1952)

August Heinrich Hoffman
(Hoffman von Fallersleben) 1798–1874
German poet

6 *Deutschland über alles.*
   Germany above all.
   title of poem (1841)

Heinrich Hoffmann 1809–94
German writer for children

7 Look at little Johnny there,
   Little Johnny Head-In-Air!
   Struwwelpeter (1848) 'Johnny Head-In-Air'; see also **Pudney** 271:14

8 The door flew open, in he ran,
   The great, long, red-legged scissor-man.
   Struwwelpeter (1848) 'The Little Suck-a-Thumb'

9 Snip! Snap! Snip! They go so fast.
   That both his thumbs are off at last.
   Struwwelpeter (1848) 'The Little Suck-a-Thumb'

10 Anything to me is sweeter
   Than to see Shock-headed Peter.
   Struwwelpeter (1848) 'Shock-Headed Peter' (title poem)

Gerard Hoffnung 1925–59
English humorist

11 Standing among savage scenery, the hotel offers stupendous revelations. There is a French widow in every bedroom, affording delightful prospects.
   supposedly quoting a letter from a Tyrolean landlord
      speech at the Oxford Union, 4 December 1958

Lancelot Hogben 1895–1975
English scientist

12 This is not the age of pamphleteers. It is the age of the engineers. The spark-gap is mightier than the pen.
   Science for the Citizen (1938) epilogue

James Hogg 1770–1835
Scottish poet

13 Where the pools are bright and deep
   Where the gray trout lies asleep,
   Up the river and o'er the lea
   That's the way for Billy and me.
   'A Boy's Song' (1838)

14 The private memoirs and confessions of a justified sinner.
   title of novel (1824)

Paul Henri, Baron d'Holbach
1723–89
French philosopher

15 If ignorance of nature gave birth to the Gods, knowledge of nature is destined to destroy them.
   Système de la Nature (1770) pt. 2, ch. 1

Billie Holiday 1915–59
American singer

16 Mama may have, papa may have,
   But God bless the child that's got his own!
   That's got his own.
   'God Bless the Child' (1941 song, with Arthur Herzog Jnr)

17 Mom and Pop were just a couple of kids when they got married. He was eighteen, she was sixteen, and I was three.
   Lady Sings the Blues (1956)

Henry Scott Holland 1847–1918
English theologian and preacher

18 Death is nothing at all; it does not count. I have only slipped away into the next room.
   sermon preached on Whitsunday 1910

John H. Holmes 1879–1964
American Unitarian minister

19 This, now, is the judgement of our scientific age—the third reaction of man upon the universe! This universe is not hostile, nor yet is it friendly. It is simply indifferent.
   The Sensible Man's View of Religion (1932) ch. 4

Oliver Wendell Holmes 1809–94
American physician, poet, and essayist

1 It is the province of knowledge to speak and it is the privilege of wisdom to listen.
The Poet at the Breakfast-Table (1872) ch. 10

2 Blank cheques of intellectual bankruptcy.
definition of catchphrases
attributed

Oliver Wendell Holmes Jr.
1841–1935
American lawyer

3 We pause to . . . recall what our country has done for each of us and to ask ourselves what we can do for our country in return.
speech, Keene, New Hampshire, 30 May 1884; see **Kennedy** 199:1

4 It is better to be seventy years young than forty years old!
reply to invitation from Julia Ward **Howe** *to her seventieth birthday party, 27 May 1889*
Laura Richards and Maud Howe Elliott *Julia Ward Howe* (1916) vol. 2

5 Certitude is not the test of certainty. We have been cocksure of many things that were not so.
'Natural Law' (1918)

6 The most stringent protection of free speech would not protect a man falsely shouting fire in a theatre and causing a panic.
sometimes quoted as, 'shouting fire in a crowded theatre'
in *Schenck v. United States* (1919)

John Home 1722–1808
Scottish dramatist

7 My name is Norval; on the Grampian hills My father feeds his flocks.
Douglas (1756) act 2, sc. 1

Homer
Greek poet of the 8th century BC

8 Achilles' cursed anger sing, O goddess, that son of Peleus, which started a myriad sufferings for the Achaeans.
The Iliad bk. 1, l. 1; see **Pope** 268:4

9 Winged words.
The Iliad bk. 1, l. 201

10 Very like leaves
upon this earth are the generations of men—
old leaves, cast on the ground by wind, young leaves
the greening forest bears when spring comes in.
The Iliad bk. 6, l. 146

11 Smiling through her tears.
The Iliad bk. 6, l. 484

12 Hateful to me as the gates of Hades is that man who hides one thing in his heart and speaks another.
The Iliad bk. 9, l. 312

13 It lies in the lap of the gods.
The Iliad bk. 17, l. 514 and elsewhere

14 Tell me, Muse, of the man of many devices, who wandered far and wide after he had sacked Troy's sacred city, and saw the towns of many men and knew their mind.
of Odysseus
The Odyssey bk. 1, l. 1

15 Rosy-fingered dawn.
The Odyssey bk. 2, l. 1 and *passim*

16 Athene sent them a following breeze, a strong west wind that whistled over the wine-dark sea.
The Odyssey bk. 2, l. 420

Arthur Honegger 1892–1955
Swiss composer

17 The first requirement for a composer is to be dead.
Je suis compositeur (1951)

Thomas Hood 1799–1845
English poet and humorist

18 Take her up tenderly,
Lift her with care;
Fashioned so slenderly,
Young, and so fair!
'The Bridge of Sighs' (1844)

19 The bleak wind of March
Made her tremble and shiver;
But not the dark arch,
Or the black flowing river.
'The Bridge of Sighs' (1844)

20 Mad from life's history,
Glad to death's mystery,
Swift to be hurled.
'The Bridge of Sighs' (1844)

21 And Eugene Aram walked between,
With gyves upon his wrist.
'The Dream of Eugene Aram' (1829)

22 They went and told the sexton, and
The sexton tolled the bell.
'Faithless Sally Brown' (1826)

23 I remember, I remember,
The house where I was born,
The little window where the sun
Came peeping in at morn.
'I Remember' (1826)

24 But evil is wrought by want of thought,
As well as want of heart!
'The Lady's Dream' (1844)

25 No fruits, no flowers, no leaves, no birds,—
November!
'No!' (1844)

26 Stitch! stitch! stitch!
In poverty, hunger, and dirt.
And still with a voice of dolorous pitch
She sang the 'Song of the Shirt'.
'The Song of the Shirt' (1843)

27 Oh! God! that bread should be so dear,
And flesh and blood so cheap!
'The Song of the Shirt' (1843)

Richard Hooker c.1554–1600
English theologian

1 Alteration though it be from worse to better hath in it inconveniences, and those weighty.
   Of the Laws of Ecclesiastical Polity (1593) bk. 4; see **Johnson** 186:16

Ellen Sturgis Hooper 1816–41
American poet

2 I slept, and dreamed that life was beauty; I woke, and found that life was duty.
   'Beauty and Duty' (1840)

Herbert Hoover 1874–1964
American Republican statesman, 31st President of the US, 1929–33

3 Our country has deliberately undertaken a great social and economic experiment, noble in motive and far-reaching in purpose.
   on the Eighteenth Amendment enacting Prohibition
   letter to Senator W. H. Borah, 23 February 1928

4 The American system of rugged individualism.
   speech in New York City, 22 October 1928

5 The slogan of progress is changing from the full dinner pail to the full garage.
   sometimes paraphrased as, 'a car in every garage and a chicken in every pot'
   speech, 22 October 1928; see **Henri IV** 166:12

6 The grass will grow in the streets of a hundred cities, a thousand towns.
   on proposals 'to reduce the protective tariff to a competitive tariff for revenue'
   speech, 31 October 1932

7 Older men declare war. But it is youth who must fight and die.
   speech at the Republican National Convention, Chicago, 27 June 1944, in *Addresses upon the American Road* (1946)

Anthony Hope 1863–1933
English novelist

8 Economy is going without something you do want in case you should, some day, want something you probably won't want.
   The Dolly Dialogues (1894) no. 12

9 Oh, for an hour of Herod!
   *at the first night of J. M. **Barrie's** Peter Pan in 1904*
   Denis Mackail *The Story of JMB* (1941) ch. 17

Bob Hope 1903–2003
American comedian

10 A bank is a place that will lend you money if you can prove that you don't need it.
   In Alan Harrington *Life in the Crystal Palace* (1959) 'The Tyranny of Farms'

11 Well, I'm still here.
   after erroneous reports of his death, marked by tributes paid to him in Congress
   in *Mail on Sunday* 7 June 1998 'Quotes of the Week'

Laurence Hope 1865–1904
English-born Indian poet

12 Pale hands I loved beside the Shalimar, Where are you now? Who lies beneath your spell?
   The Garden of Kama (1901) 'Kashmiri Song'

13 Less than the dust, beneath thy Chariot wheel.
   The Garden of Kama (1901) 'Less than the Dust'

Gerard Manley Hopkins 1844–89
English poet and priest

14 Not, I'll not, carrion comfort, Despair, not feast on thee;
   Not untwist—slack they may be—these last strands of man
   In me or, most weary, cry *I can no more*. I can;
   Can something, hope, wish day come, not choose not to be.
   'Carrion Comfort' (written 1885)

15 Towery city and branchy between towers;
   Cuckoo-echoing, bell-swarmèd, lark-charmèd, rook-racked, river-rounded.
   'Duns Scotus's Oxford' (written 1879)

16 The world is charged with the grandeur of God.
   It will flame out like shining from shook foil
   . . .
   Generations have trod, have trod, have trod;
   And all is seared with trade; bleared, smeared with toil;
   And wears man's smudge and shares man's smell: the soil
   Is bare now, nor can foot feel, being shod.
   'God's Grandeur' (written 1877)

17 Because the Holy Ghost over the bent World broods with warm breast and with ah! bright wings.
   'God's Grandeur' (written 1877)

18 Elected Silence, sing to me
   And beat upon my whorlèd ear.
   'The Habit of Perfection' (written 1866)

19 I have desired to go
   Where springs not fail,
   To fields where flies no sharp and sided hail
   And a few lilies blow.
   'Heaven-Haven' (written 1864)

20 What would the world be, once bereft
   Of wet and wildness? Let them be left,
   O let them be left, wildness and wet;
   Long live the weeds and the wilderness yet.
   'Inversnaid' (written 1881)

21 No worst, there is none. Pitched past pitch of grief,
   More pangs will, schooled at forepangs, wilder wring.
   'No worst, there is none' (written 1885)

22 O the mind, mind has mountains; cliffs of fall
   Frightful, sheer, no-man-fathomed. Hold them cheap
   May who ne'er hung there.
   'No worst, there is none' (written 1885)

1 Glory be to God for dappled things.
'Pied Beauty' (written 1877)

2 All things counter, original, spare, strange;
Whatever is fickle, freckled (who knows how?)
With swift, slow; sweet, sour; adazzle, dim;
He fathers-forth whose beauty is past change:
Praise him.
'Pied Beauty' (written 1877)

3 Márgarét, áre you grieving
Over Goldengrove unleaving?
'Spring and Fall: to a young child' (written 1880)

4 Áh! ás the heart grows older
It will come to such sights colder
By and by, nor spare a sigh
Though worlds of wanwood leafmeal lie;
And yet you *will* weep and know why.
'Spring and Fall: to a young child' (written 1880)

5 It ís the blight man was born for,
It is Margaret you mourn for.
'Spring and Fall: to a young child' (written 1880)

6 I am all at once what Christ is, since he was what I am, and
This Jack, joke, poor potsherd, patch, matchwood, immortal diamond,
Is immortal diamond.
'That Nature is a Heraclitean Fire' (written 1888)

7 Thou art indeed just, Lord, if I contend
With thee; but, sir, so what I plead is just.
Why do sinners' ways prosper? and why must
Disappointment all I endeavour end?
'Thou art indeed just, Lord' (written 1889)

8 Birds build—but not I build; no, but strain,
Time's eunuch, and not breed one work that wakes.
Mine, O thou lord of life, send my roots rain.
'Thou art indeed just, Lord' (written 1889)

9 I caught this morning morning's minion,
kingdom of daylight's dauphin, dapple-dawn-drawn Falcon.
'The Windhover' (written 1877)

10 My heart in hiding
Stirred for a bird,—the achieve of, the mastery of the thing!
'The Windhover' (written 1877)

11 To lift up the hands in prayer gives God glory, but a man with a dungfork in his hand, a woman with a slop-pail, give him glory too. He is so great that all things give him glory if you mean they should.
'The Principle or Foundation' (1882)

Horace 65–8 BC
Roman poet

12 *Inceptis gravibus plerumque et magna professis*
Purpureus, late qui splendeat, unus et alter
Adsuitur pannus.
Works of serious purpose and grand promises often have a purple patch or two stitched on, to shine far and wide.
Ars Poetica l. 14

13 *Brevis esse laboro,*
Obscurus fio.
I strive to be brief, and I become obscure.
Ars Poetica l. 25

14 *Grammatici certant et adhuc sub iudice lis est.*
Scholars dispute, and the case is still before the courts.
Ars Poetica l. 78

15 *Proicit ampullas et sesquipedalia verba.*
He throws aside his paint-pots and his words a foot and a half long.
Ars Poetica l. 97

16 *Parturient montes, nascetur ridiculus mus.*
Mountains will go into labour, and a silly little mouse will be born.
Ars Poetica l. 139

17 *Semper ad eventum festinat et in medias res*
Non secus ac notas auditorem rapit.
He always hurries to the main event and whisks his audience into the middle of things as though they knew already.
Ars Poetica l. 148

18 *Difficilis, querulus, laudator temporis acti*
Se puero, castigator censorque minorum.
Tiresome, complaining, a praiser of past times, when he was a boy, a castigator and censor of the young generation.
Ars Poetica l. 173

19 *Indignor quandoque bonus dormitat Homerus.*
I'm aggrieved when sometimes even excellent Homer nods.
Ars Poetica l. 359

20 *Ut pictura poesis.*
A poem is like a painting.
Ars Poetica l. 361

21 *Si possis recte, si non, quocumque modo rem.*
If possible honestly, if not, somehow, make money.
Epistles bk. 1, no. 1, l. 66; see **Pope** 268:8

22 *Nos numerus sumus et fruges consumere nati.*
We are just statistics, born to consume resources.
Epistles bk. 1, no. 2, l. 27

23 *Dimidium facti qui coepit habet: sapere aude.*
To have begun is half the job: dare to know.
Epistles bk. 1, no. 2, l. 40

24 *Ira furor brevis est.*
Anger is a short madness.
Epistles bk. 1, no. 2, l. 62

25 *Nil admirari prope res est una, Numici,*
Solaque quae possit facere et servare beatum.
To marvel at nothing is just about the one and only thing, Numicius, that can make a man happy and keep him that way.
Epistles bk. 1, no. 6, l. 1; see **Pope** 268:9

26 *Naturam expelles furca, tamen usque recurret.*
You may drive out nature with a pitchfork, yet she'll be constantly running back.
Epistles bk. 1, no. 10, l. 24

27 *Caelum non animum mutant qui trans mare currunt.*

They change their clime, not their frame of mind, who rush across the sea.
Epistles bk. 1, no. 11, l. 27

1 *Concordia discors.*
Discordant harmony.
Epistles bk. 1, no. 12, l. 19

2 *Et semel emissum volat irrevocabile verbum.*
And once sent out a word takes wing beyond recall.
Epistles bk. 1, no. 18, l. 71

3 *Nam tua res agitur, paries cum proximus ardet.*
For it is your business, when the wall next door catches fire.
Epistles bk. 1, no. 18, l. 84

4 *O imitatores, servum pecus.*
O imitators, you slavish herd.
Epistles bk. 1, no. 19, l. 19

5 *Atque inter silvas Academi quaerere verum.*
And seek for truth in the groves of Academe.
Epistles bk. 2, no. 2, l. 45

6 *Nil desperandum.*
Never despair.
Odes bk. 1, no. 7, l. 27

7 *Dum loquimur, fugerit invida Aetas: carpe diem, quam minimum credula postero.*
While we're talking, envious time is fleeing: seize the day, put no trust in the future.
Odes bk. 1, no. 11, l. 7

8 *Integer vitae scelerisque purus.*
Wholesome of life and free of crimes.
Odes bk. 1, no. 22, l. 1

9 *Nunc est bibendum, nunc pede libero Pulsanda tellus.*
Now for drinking, now the Earth must shake beneath a lively foot.
Odes bk. 1, no. 37, l. 1

10 *Auream quisquis mediocritatem Diligit.*
Someone who loves the golden mean.
Odes bk. 2, no. 10, l. 5

11 *Eheu fugaces, Postume, Postume, Labuntur anni.*
Ah me, Postumus, Postumus, the fleeting years are slipping by.
Odes bk. 2, no. 14, l. 1

12 *Nihil est ab omni Parte beatum.*
Nothing is an unmixed blessing.
Odes bk. 2, no. 16, l. 27

13 *Post equitem sedet atra Cura.*
Black Care sits behind the horseman.
Odes bk. 3, no. 1, l. 40

14 *Dulce et decorum est pro patria mori.*
Lovely and honourable it is to die for one's country.
Odes bk. 3, no. 2, l. 13; see **Owen** 256:11, **Pound** 269:23

15 *Opaco Pelion imposuisse Olympo.*

To pile Pelion on top of shady Olympus.
Odes bk. 3, no. 4, l. 52

16 *O fons Bandusiae, splendidior vitro.*
O spring of Bandusia, brighter than glass.
Odes bk. 3, no. 13, l. 1

17 *Exegi monumentum aere perennius.*
I have erected a monument more lasting than bronze.
Odes bk. 3, no. 30, l. 1

18 *Non omnis moriar.*
I shall not altogether die.
Odes bk. 3, no. 30, l. 6

19 *Non sum qualis eram bonae Sub regno Cinarae.*
I am not as I was when good Cinara was my queen.
Odes bk. 4, no. 1, l. 3; see **Dowson** 120:10

20 *Misce stultitiam consiliis brevem: Dulce est desipere in loco.*
Mix a little foolishness with your prudence: it's good to be silly at the right moment.
Odes bk. 4, no. 12, l. 27

21 . . . *Mutato nomine de te Fabula narratur.*
Change the name and it's about you, that story.
Satires bk. 1, no. 1, l. 69

22 *Est modus in rebus.*
There is moderation in everything.
Satires bk. 1, no. 1, l. 106

23 . . . *Ab ovo Usque ad mala.*
From the egg right through to the apples.
from the start to the finish of a meal
Satires bk. 1, no. 3, l. 6

24 *Etiam disiecti membra poetae.*
Even though broken up, the limbs of a poet.
of Ennius
Satires bk. 1, no. 4, l. 62

25 *Hoc erat in votis: modus agri non ita magnus, Hortus ubi et tecto vicinus iugis aquae fons Et paulum silvae super his foret.*
This was among my prayers: a piece of land not so very large, where a garden should be and a spring of ever-flowing water near the house, and a bit of woodland as well as these.
Satires bk. 2, no. 6, l. 1

Nick Hornby 1957–
British writer

26 The natural state of the football fan is bitter disappointment, no matter what the score.
Fever Pitch (1992)

Samuel Horsley 1733–1806
English bishop

27 In this country . . . the individual subject . . . 'has nothing to do with the laws but to obey them.'
defending a maxim he had used earlier in committee
speech, House of Lords, 13 November 1795

A. E. Housman 1859–1936
English poet

1 Oh who is that young sinner with the
handcuffs on his wrists?
And what has he been after that they groan
and shake their fists?
And wherefore is he wearing such a
conscience-stricken air?
Oh they're taking him to prison for the
colour of his hair.

*first drafted in summer 1895, following the trial
and imprisonment of Oscar Wilde*
Collected Poems (1939) 'Additional Poems' no. 18

2 The Grizzly Bear is huge and wild;
He has devoured the infant child.
The infant child is not aware
He has been eaten by the bear.
'Infant Innocence' (1938)

3 I, a stranger and afraid
In a world I never made.
Last Poems (1922) no. 12

4 Their shoulders held the sky suspended;
They stood, and earth's foundations stay;
What God abandoned, these defended,
And saved the sum of things for pay.
Last Poems (1922) no. 37 'Epitaph on an Army of
Mercenaries'

5 Life, to be sure, is nothing much to lose;
But young men think it is, and we were
young.
More Poems (1936) no. 36

6 Loveliest of trees, the cherry now
Is hung with bloom along the bough,
And stands about the woodland ride
Wearing white for Eastertide.
A Shropshire Lad (1896) no. 2

7 And since to look at things in bloom
Fifty springs are little room,
About the woodlands I will go
To see the cherry hung with snow.
A Shropshire Lad (1896) no. 2

8 When I was one-and-twenty
I heard a wise man say,
'Give crowns and pounds and guineas
But not your heart away;
Give pearls away and rubies,
But keep your fancy free.'
But I was one-and-twenty,
No use to talk to me.
A Shropshire Lad (1896) no. 13

9 In summertime on Bredon
The bells they sound so clear;
Round both the shires they ring them
In steeples far and near,
A happy noise to hear.
Here of a Sunday morning
My love and I would lie,
And see the coloured counties,
And hear the larks so high
About us in the sky.
A Shropshire Lad (1896) no. 21

10 On Wenlock Edge the wood's in trouble;
His forest fleece the Wrekin heaves.
A Shropshire Lad (1896) no. 31

11 To-day the Roman and his trouble
Are ashes under Uricon.
A Shropshire Lad (1896) no. 31

12 From far, from eve and morning
And yon twelve-winded sky,
The stuff of life to knit me
Blew hither: here am I.
A Shropshire Lad (1896) no. 32

13 What are those blue remembered hills,
What spires, what farms are those?
That is the land of lost content,
I see it shining plain,
The happy highways where I went
And cannot come again.
A Shropshire Lad (1896) no. 40

14 Clunton and Clunbury,
Clungunford and Clun,
Are the quietest places
Under the sun.
A Shropshire Lad (1896) no. 50 (epigraph)

15 By brooks too broad for leaping
The lightfoot boys are laid.
A Shropshire Lad (1896) no. 54

16 And malt does more than Milton can
To justify God's ways to man.
A Shropshire Lad (1896) no. 62; see **Milton** 237:17

17 Mithridates, he died old.
A Shropshire Lad (1896) no. 62

Samuel Houston 1793–1863
American politician and military leader

18 The North is determined to preserve this
Union. They are not a fiery, impulsive
people as you are, for they live in colder
climates. But when they begin to move in a
given direction . . . they move with the
steady momentum and perseverance of a
mighty avalanche.
*in 1861, warning the people of Texas against
secession*
Geoffrey C. Ward *The Civil War* (1991) ch. 1

John Howard 1939–
Australian statesman

19 That's Lazarus with a triple bypass.
*asked if he thought he could regain leadership of
his party*
at a press conference, 9 May 1989; David
Barnett *John Howard: Prime Minister* (1997)

20 I want people to reflect on the loss of life. I
want them to reflect on what it means in
terms of the loss of innocence . . . in relation
to this country's dealings with different
parts of the world.
on the Bali bombing, 12 October 2002
interview on Australian television (Channel Ten
News), 14 October 2002

Geoffrey Howe 1926–
British Conservative politician

21 It is rather like sending your opening
batsmen to the crease only for them to find
the moment that the first balls are bowled

that their bats have been broken before the game by the team captain.

on the difficulties caused him as Foreign Secretary by Margaret **Thatcher***'s anti-European views*
resignation speech as Deputy Prime Minister, in the House of Commons, 13 November 1990

Gordie Howe 1928–
Canadian ice-hockey player

1 All pro athletes are bilingual. They speak English and profanity.
in *Toronto Star* 27 May 1975

Julia Ward Howe 1819–1910
American Unitarian lay preacher

2 Mine eyes have seen the glory of the coming of the Lord:
He is trampling out the vintage where the grapes of wrath are stored;
He hath loosed the fateful lightning of his terrible swift sword:
His truth is marching on.
'Battle Hymn of the Republic' (1862)

Mary Howitt 1799–1888
English writer for children

3 Buttercups and daisies,
Oh, the pretty flowers;
Coming ere the springtime,
To tell of sunny hours.
'Buttercups and Daisies' (1838)

4 'Will you walk into my parlour?' said a spider to a fly:
''Tis the prettiest little parlour that ever you did spy.'
'The Spider and the Fly' (1834)

Edmond Hoyle 1672–1769
English writer on card-games

5 When in doubt, win the trick.
Hoyle's Games Improved (ed. Charles Jones, 1790) 'Twenty-four Short Rules for Learners'; though attributed to Hoyle, it is not found in earlier editions

Fred Hoyle 1915–2001
English astrophysicist

6 Space isn't remote at all. It's only an hour's drive away if your car could go straight upwards.
in *Observer* 9 September 1979 'Sayings of the Week'

Elbert Hubbard 1859–1915
American writer

7 Never explain—your friends do not need it and your enemies will not believe you anyway.
The Motto Book (1907); see **Disraeli** 118:8; **Wodehouse** 362:20

8 Life is just one damned thing after another.
Philistine December 1909; often attributed to Frank Ward O'Malley

9 Editor: a person employed by a newspaper, whose business it is to separate the wheat from the chaff, and to see that the chaff is printed.
The Roycroft Dictionary (1914)

Frank McKinney ('Kin') Hubbard 1868–1930
American humorist

10 It's no disgrace t'be poor, but it might as well be.
Short Furrows (1911)

Howard Hughes Jr. 1905–76
American industrialist, aviator, and film producer

11 That man's ears make him look like a taxi-cab with both doors open.
of Clark Gable
Charles Higham and Joel Greenberg *Celluloid Muse* (1969)

Jimmy Hughes
and **Frank Lake**

12 You'll get no promotion this side of the ocean,
So cheer up, my lads, Bless 'em all!
Bless 'em all! Bless 'em all! The long and the short and the tall.
'Bless 'Em All' (1940 song)

Langston Hughes 1902–67
American writer and poet

13 I, too, sing America.
I am the darker brother.
They send me to eat in the kitchen
When company comes.
'I, Too' in *Survey Graphic* March 1925

14 I've known rivers:
I've known rivers ancient as the world and older than the flow of human blood in human veins.
'The Negro Speaks of Rivers' (1921)

15 I got the Weary Blues
And I can't be satisfied.
'Weary Blues' (1926)

Ted Hughes 1930–98
English poet

16 It took the whole of Creation
To produce my foot, my each feather:
Now I hold Creation in my foot.
'Hawk Roosting' (1960)

17 . . . With a sudden sharp hot stink of fox,
It enters the dark hole of the head.
'The Thought-Fox' (1957)

Thomas Hughes 1822–96
English lawyer, politician, and writer

18 It's more than a game. It's an institution.
of cricket
Tom Brown's Schooldays (1857) pt. 2, ch. 7

Victor Hugo 1802–85
French poet, novelist, and dramatist

1 A stand can be made against invasion by an army; no stand can be made against invasion by an idea.
  Histoire d'un Crime (written 1851–2, published 1877) pt. 5, sect. 10

2 Take away *time is money*, and what is left of England? take away *cotton is king*, and what is left of America?
  Les Misérables (1862) 'Marius' bk. 4 ch. 4

Hui-neng 638–713
Chinese philosopher, 6th Zen Patriarch

3 Since all is void,
  Where can the dust alight?
  Platform Scripture ch. 1, tr. Wong Mou-Lam

David Hume 1711–76
Scottish philosopher

4 Custom, then, is the great guide of human life.
  An Enquiry Concerning Human Understanding (1748) sect. 5, pt. 1

5 If we take in our hand any volume; of divinity or school metaphysics, for instance; let us ask, *Does it contain any abstract reasoning concerning quantity or number?* No. *Does it contain any experimental reasoning, concerning matter of fact and existence?* No. Commit it then to the flames: for it can contain nothing but sophistry and illusion.
  An Enquiry Concerning Human Understanding (1748) sect. 12, pt. 3

6 The Christian religion not only was at first attended with miracles, but even at this day cannot be believed by any reasonable person without one.
  An Enquiry Concerning Human Understanding (1748) 'Of Miracles' pt. 2

7 Avarice, the spur of industry.
  Essays: Moral and Political (1741–2) 'Of Civil Liberty'

8 Money . . . is none of the wheels of trade: it is the oil which renders the motion of the wheels more smooth and easy.
  Essays: Moral and Political (1741–2) 'Of Money'

9 The heart of man is made to reconcile the most glaring contradictions.
  Essays, Moral, Political, and Literary (ed. T. H. Green and T. H. Grose, 1875) 'Of the Parties of Great Britain' (1741–2)

10 Beauty is no quality in things themselves. It exists merely in the mind which contemplates them.
  Essays, Moral, Political, and Literary (ed. T. H. Green and T. H. Grose, 1875) 'Of the Standard of Taste' (1757)

11 Never literary attempt was more unfortunate than my Treatise of Human Nature. It fell *dead-born from the press.*
  My Own Life (1777) ch. 1

12 Reason is, and ought only to be the slave of the passions, and can never pretend to any other office than to serve and obey them.
  A Treatise upon Human Nature (1739) bk. 2, pt. 3

13 It is not contrary to reason to prefer the destruction of the whole world to the scratching of my finger.
  A Treatise upon Human Nature (1739) bk. 2, pt. 3

Hubert Humphrey 1911–78
American Democratic politician

14 Here we are the way politics ought to be in America, the politics of happiness, the politics of purpose and the politics of joy.
  speech in Washington, 27 April 1968, in *New York Times* 28 April 1968

G. W. Hunt *c.*1829–1904
English composer of music-hall songs

15 We don't want to fight, but, by jingo if we do,
  We've got the ships, we've got the men, we've got the money too.
  'We Don't Want to Fight' (1878 music hall song)

Leigh Hunt 1784–1859
English poet and essayist

16 Abou Ben Adhem (may his tribe increase!) Awoke one night from a deep dream of peace.
  'Abou Ben Adhem' (1838)

17 Write me as one that loves his fellow-men.
  'Abou Ben Adhem' (1838)

18 The laughing queen that caught the world's great hands.
  referring to Cleopatra
  'The Nile' (1818)

19 Jenny kissed me when we met,
  Jumping from the chair she sat in.
  'Rondeau' (1838)

Anne Hunter 1742–1821
Scottish poet

20 My mother bids me bind my hair
  With bands of rosy hue,
  Tie up my sleeves with ribbons rare,
  And lace my bodice blue.
  'A Pastoral Song' (1794)

Herman Hupfeld 1894–1951
American songwriter

21 You must remember this, a kiss is still a kiss,
  A sigh is just a sigh;
  The fundamental things apply,
  As time goes by.
  'As Time Goes By' (1931 song)

Zora Neale Hurston *c.*1901–60
American writer

22 I do not weep at the world—I am too busy sharpening my oyster knife.
  How It Feels to Be Colored Me (1928)

John Huss c.1372–1415
Bohemian preacher and reformer

1 *O sancta simplicitas!*
O holy simplicity!
*at the stake, seeing an aged peasant bringing a
bundle of twigs to throw on the pile*
J. W. Zincgreff and J. L. Weidner *Apophthegmata*
(Amsterdam, 1653) pt. 3; see **Jerome** 185:3

Saddam Hussein 1937–
Iraqi statesman; President 1979–2003

2 The mother of battles.
*popular interpretation of his description of the
approaching Gulf War*
speech in Baghdad, 6 January 1991

3 Baghdad is determined to force the Mongols
of our age to commit suicide at its gates.
in *Independent* 18 January 2003

4 I am Saddam Hussein, the president of Iraq.
*response when asked who he was at the beginning
of his trial; the judge ordered the clerk to 'put
down "former" in brackets'*
in *Guardian* 2 July 2004

Francis Hutcheson 1694–1746
Scottish philosopher

5 Wisdom denotes the pursuing of the best
ends by the best means.
*An Inquiry into the Original of our Ideas of Beauty
and Virtue* (1725) Treatise 1

6 That action is best, which procures the
greatest happiness for the greatest numbers.
*An Inquiry into the Original of our Ideas of Beauty
and Virtue* (1725) Treatise 2; see **Bentham** 31:6

Lord Hutton 1931–
British judge

7 I make it clear that it will be for me to
decide as I think right within my terms of
reference the matters which will be the
subject of my investigation.
statement on the terms of the inquiry into the
death of Dr David **Kelly**, 21 July 2003

Aldous Huxley 1894–1963
English novelist

8 The proper study of mankind is books.
Crome Yellow (1921) ch. 28; see **Pope** 267:27

9 Consistency is contrary to nature, contrary
to life. The only completely consistent
people are the dead.
Do What You Will (1929) 'Wordsworth in the
Tropics'

10 The end cannot justify the means, for the
simple and obvious reason that the means
employed determine the nature of the ends
produced.
Ends and Means (1937) ch. 1

11 So long as men worship the Caesars and
Napoleons, Caesars and Napoleons will duly
arise and make them miserable.
Ends and Means (1937) ch. 8

12 Chastity—the most unnatural of all the
sexual perversions.
Eyeless in Gaza (1936) ch. 27

13 Several excuses are always less convincing
than one.
Point Counter Point (1928) ch. 1

Julian Huxley 1887–1975
English biologist

14 Operationally, God is beginning to resemble
not a ruler but the last fading smile of a
cosmic Cheshire cat.
Religion without Revelation (1957 ed.) ch. 3; see
Carroll 86:10

T. H. Huxley 1825–95
English biologist

15 I, the man without a rag of a label to cover
himself with . . . took thought, and invented
what I conceived to be the appropriate title
of 'agnostic'.
Collected Essays (1893–4) 'Agnosticism'

16 The great tragedy of Science—the slaying of
a beautiful hypothesis by an ugly fact.
Collected Essays (1893–4) 'Biogenesis and
Abiogenesis'

17 If a little knowledge is dangerous, where is
the man who has so much as to be out of
danger?
Collected Essays vol. 3 (1895) 'On Elementary
Instruction in Physiology' (written 1877)

18 The chessboard is the world; the pieces are
the phenomena of the universe; the rules of
the game are what we call the laws of
Nature. The player on the other side is
hidden from us. We know that his play is
always fair, just, and patient. But also we
know, to our cost, that he never overlooks a
mistake, or makes the smallest allowance
for ignorance.
Lay Sermons, Addresses, and Reviews (1870) 'A
Liberal Education'

19 It is the customary fate of new truths to
begin as heresies and to end as
superstitions.
Science and Culture and Other Essays (1881) 'The
Coming of Age of the Origin of Species'

20 Irrationally held truths may be more
harmful than reasoned errors.
Science and Culture and Other Essays (1881) 'The
Coming of Age of the Origin of Species'

21 Logical consequences are the scarecrows of
fools and the beacons of wise men.
Science and Culture and Other Essays (1881) 'On the
Hypothesis that Animals are Automata'

22 A man has no reason to be ashamed of
having an ape for his grandfather. If there
were an ancestor whom I should feel shame
in recalling it would rather be a *man*—a man
of restless and versatile intellect—who, not
content with an equivocal success in his
own sphere of activity, plunges into
scientific questions with which he has no
real acquaintance, only to obscure them by
an aimless rhetoric, and distract the

attention of his hearers from the real point at issue by eloquent digressions and skilled appeals to religious prejudice.

replying to Bishop Samuel **Wilberforce** *in the debate on* **Darwin***'s theory of evolution; see* **Wilberforce** *357:24*

meeting of the British Association in Oxford, 30 June 1860

1 I am too much of a sceptic to deny the possibility of anything.

letter to Herbert Spencer, 22 March 1886

Edward Hyde *see* Earl of Clarendon

Dolores Ibarruri ('La Pasionaria') 1895–1989
Spanish Communist leader

2 It is better to die on your feet than to live on your knees.

also attributed to Emiliano **Zapata**
speech in Paris, 3 September 1936

3 *No pasarán.*
They shall not pass.

radio broadcast, Madrid, 19 July 1936

Henrik Ibsen 1828–1906
Norwegian dramatist

4 The worst enemy of truth and freedom in our society is the compact majority. Yes, the damned, compact, liberal majority.

An Enemy of the People (1882) act 4

5 The majority never has right on its side.

An Enemy of the People (1882) act 4; see **Dillon** 116:16

6 You should never have your best trousers on when you go out to fight for freedom and truth.

An Enemy of the People (1882) act 5

7 Mother, give me the sun.

Ghosts (1881) act 3

8 But good God, people don't do such things!

Hedda Gabler (1890) act 4

9 Castles in the air—they are so easy to take refuge in. And easy to build, too.

The Master Builder (1892) act 3

10 On the contrary.

last words, after a nurse had said that he 'seemed to be a little better'
Michael Meyer *Ibsen* (1967)

Ice-T 1958–
American rap musician

11 Passion makes the world go round. Love just makes it a safer place.

The Ice Opinion (as told to Heidi Sigmund, 1994) ch. 4

St Ignatius Loyola 1491–1556
Spanish theologian, founder of the Jesuits

12 Teach us, good Lord, to serve Thee as Thou deservest:
To give and not to count the cost;
To fight and not to heed the wounds;

To toil and not to seek for rest;
To labour and not to ask for any reward
Save that of knowing that we do Thy will.

'Prayer for Generosity' (1548)

Ivan Illich 1926–
American sociologist

13 In a consumer society there are inevitably two kinds of slaves: the prisoners of addiction and the prisoners of envy.

Tools for Conviviality (1973) ch. 3

William Ralph Inge 1860–1954
English writer; Dean of St. Paul's, 1911–34

14 To become a popular religion, it is only necessary for a superstition to enslave a philosophy.

Idea of Progress (Romanes Lecture delivered at Oxford, 27 May 1920)

15 It takes in reality only one to make a quarrel. It is useless for the sheep to pass resolutions in favour of vegetarianism, while the wolf remains of a different opinion.

Outspoken Essays: First Series (1919) 'Patriotism'

16 A man may build himself a throne of bayonets, but he cannot sit on it.

a similar image was used by Boris **Yeltsin** *at the time of the failed military coup in Russia, August 1991*
Philosophy of Plotinus (1923) vol. 2, Lecture 22

Robert G. Ingersoll 1833–99
American agnostic

17 An honest God is the noblest work of man.

The Gods (1876) pt. 1; see **Pope** 268:2

18 In nature there are neither rewards nor punishments—there are consequences.

Some Reasons Why (1881) pt. 8 'The New Testament'

John Kells Ingram 1823–1907
Irish social philosopher and songwriter

19 They rose in dark and evil days.

'The Memory of the Dead' (1843)

20 Who fears to speak of Ninety-Eight?
Who blushes at the name?

'The Memory of the Dead' (1843)

J. A. D. Ingres 1780–1867
French painter

21 Drawing is the true test of art.

Pensées d'Ingres (1922)

22 Make copies, young man, many copies. You can only become a good artist by copying the masters.

to Degas; A. Vollard Souvenirs d'un marchand de tableaux (1937)

St Irenaeus *c.*AD 130–*c.*200
Greek theologian

23 The glory of God is a man fully alive.

attributed

Weldon J. Irvine
American songwriter

1 Young, gifted and black.
   title of song (1969); see **Hansberry** 161:4

Washington Irving 1783–1859
American writer

2 A sharp tongue is the only edged tool that
   grows keener with constant use.
   The Sketch Book (1820) 'Rip Van Winkle'

3 There is a certain relief in change, even
   though it be from bad to worse . . . it is often
   a comfort to shift one's position and be
   bruised in a new place.
   Tales of a Traveller (1824) 'To the Reader'

4 The almighty dollar, that great object of
   universal devotion.
   Wolfert's Roost (1855) 'The Creole Village'

Christopher Isherwood 1904–86
English novelist

5 The common cormorant (or shag)
   Lays eggs inside a paper bag,
   You follow the idea, no doubt?
   It's to keep the lightning out.
   But what these unobservant birds
   Have never thought of, is that herds
   Of wandering bears might come with buns
   And steal the bags to hold the crumbs.
   'The Common Cormorant' (written *c.*1925)

6 I am a camera with its shutter open, quite
   passive, recording, not thinking.
   Goodbye to Berlin (1939) 'Berlin Diary' Autumn
   1930

Alec Issigonis 1906–88
British engineer

7 A camel is a horse designed by a committee.
   on his dislike of working in teams
   in *Guardian* 14 January 1991 'Notes and
   Queries'; attributed

Charles Ives 1874–1954
American composer

8 Beauty in music is too often confused with
   something that lets the ears lie back in an
   easy chair.
   Joseph Machlis *Introduction to Contemporary Music*
   (1963)

Alija Izetbegović 1925–2003
Bosnian statesman

9 And to my people I say, this may not be a
   just peace, but it is more just than a
   continuation of war.
   *after signing the Dayton accord with
   representatives of Serbia and Croatia*
   in Dayton, Ohio, 21 November 1995

Eddie Izzard 1962–
British comedian

10 'Cake or death?' 'Cake, please.'
   *imagining how a Church of England Inquisition
   might have worked*
   Dress to Kill (stage show, San Francisco, 1998)

Andrew Jackson 1767–1845
*American Democratic statesman; 7th President of
the US, 1829–37*

11 Our Federal Union: it must be preserved.
   toast given on the Jefferson Birthday
   Celebration, 13 April 1830

12 Each public officer who takes an oath to
   support the constitution swears that he will
   support it as he understands it, and not as it
   is understood by others.
   *vetoing the bill to re-charter the Bank of the
   United States*
   Presidential message, 10 July 1832, in H. S.
   Commager (ed.) *Documents of American History*
   vol. 1 (1963)

Jesse Jackson 1941–
American Democratic politician and clergyman

13 When I look out at this convention, I see the
   face of America, red, yellow, brown, black,
   and white. We are all precious in God's
   sight—the real rainbow coalition.
   speech at Democratic National Convention,
   Atlanta, 19 July 1988

Mahalia Jackson 1911–72
American singer

14 It's easy to be independent when you've got
   money. But to be independent when you
   haven't got a thing—that's the Lord's test.
   Movin' On Up (with Evan McLoud Wylie 1966)
   ch.1

Michael Jackson 1958–
American pop singer

15 Before you judge me, try hard to love me,
   look within your heart
   Then ask,—have you seen my childhood?
   'Childhood' (1995 song)

Robert H. Jackson 1892–1954
American lawyer and judge

16 That four great nations, flushed with victory
   and stung with injury, stay the hands of
   vengeance and voluntarily submit their
   captive enemies to the judgement of the
   law, is one of the most significant tributes
   that Power has ever paid to Reason.
   *opening statement for the prosecution at
   Nuremberg*
   before the International Military Tribunal in
   Nuremberg, 21 November 1945

Thomas Jonathan 'Stonewall' Jackson 1824–63
American Confederate general

17 Always mystify, mislead, and surprise the
   enemy, if possible.
   his strategic motto during the Civil War
   M. Miner and H. Rawson *American Heritage
   Dictionary of American Quotations* (1997)

18 Let us cross over the river and rest under the
   shade of the trees.
   last words; M. Miner and H. Rawson *American
   Heritage Dictionary of American Quotations* (1997)

Joe Jacobs 1896–1940
American boxing manager

1 We was robbed!

after Jack Sharkey beat Max Schmeling (of whom Jacobs was manager) in the heavyweight title fight, 21 June 1932
> Peter Heller *In This Corner* (1975)

Jacopone da Todi c.1230–1306
Italian Franciscan lay brother

2 Stabat Mater dolorosa,
Iuxta crucem lacrimosa.

At the cross her station keeping,
Stood the mournful Mother weeping.
> 'Stabat Mater dolorosa', ascribed also to Pope Innocent III and others (translation based on that of E. Caswall in *Lyra Catholica*, 1849)

Mick Jagger 1943–
and Keith Richards 1943–
English rock musicians

3 Get off of my cloud.
> title of song (1966)

4 And though she's not really ill,
There's a little yellow pill:
She goes running for the shelter
Of a mother's little helper.
> 'Mother's Little Helper' (1966 song)

5 I can't get no satisfaction
I can't get no girl reaction.
> '(I Can't Get No) Satisfaction' (1965 song)

6 Ev'rywhere I hear the sound of marching,
charging feet, boy.
> 'Street Fighting Man' (1968 song)

7 Please allow me to introduce myself
I'm a man of wealth and taste.
> 'Sympathy for the Devil' (1968 song)

Jaina Sutras
Indian tradition, founded in the 6th century BC

8 This is the quintessence of wisdom: not to kill anything. Know this to be the legitimate conclusion from the principle of the reciprocity with regard to non-killing.
> *Sūtrakritāṅga* bk. 1, lecture 1, ch. 4, v. 10, tr. H. Jacobi

James I (James VI of Scotland) 1566–1625
British monarch, King of Scotland from 1567 and of England from 1603

9 A custom loathsome to the eye, hateful to the nose, harmful to the brain, dangerous to the lungs, and in the black, stinking fume thereof, nearest resembling the horrible Stygian smoke of the pit that is bottomless.
> *A Counterblast to Tobacco* (1604)

10 No bishop, no King.
> *to a deputation of Presbyterians from the Church of Scotland, seeking religious tolerance in England*
> W. Barlow *Sum and Substance of the Conference* (1604)

11 The state of monarchy is the supremest thing upon earth; for kings are not only God's lieutenants upon earth, and sit upon God's throne, but even by God himself they are called gods.
> speech to Parliament, 21 March 1610, in *Works* (1616)

12 The king is truly *parens patriae*, the politique father of his people.
> speech to Parliament, 21 March 1610

13 Dr Donne's verses are like the peace of God; they pass all understanding.
> remark recorded by Archdeacon Plume (1630–1704); see **Bible** 51:27

James V 1512–42
Scottish monarch, King from 1513

14 It came with a lass, and it will pass with a lass.
> *of the crown of Scotland, on learning of the birth of* **Mary** Queen of Scots, December 1542
> Robert Lindsay of Pitscottie (c.1500–65) *History of Scotland* (1728)

Evan James
Welsh bard

15 The land of my fathers, how fair is thy fame.
> 'Land of My Fathers' (1856), translated by W. G. Rothery

Henry James 1843–1916
American novelist

16 Live all you can; it's a mistake not to. It doesn't so much matter what you do in particular, so long as you have your life. If you haven't had that, what *have* you had?
> *The Ambassadors* (1903) bk. 5, ch. 11

17 Cats and monkeys—monkeys and cats—all human life is there!
> *The Madonna of the Future* (1879) vol. 1

18 We work in the dark—we do what we can—we give what we have. Our doubt is our passion and our passion is our task. The rest is the madness of art.
> 'The Middle Years' (short story, 1893)

19 Experience is never limited, and it is never complete; it is an immense sensibility, a kind of huge spider-web of the finest silken threads suspended in the chamber of consciousness, and catching every air-borne particle in its tissue.
> *Partial Portraits* (1888) 'The Art of Fiction'

20 What is character but the determination of incident? What is incident but the illustration of character?
> *Partial Portraits* (1888) 'The Art of Fiction'

21 The house of fiction has in short not one window, but a million ... but they are, singly or together, as nothing without the posted presence of the watcher.
> *The Portrait of a Lady* (1908 ed.) preface

22 The note I wanted; that of the strange and sinister embroidered on the very type of the normal and easy.
> *Prefaces* (1909) 'The Altar of the Dead'

23 The turn of the screw
> title of novel (1898)

1 We were alone with the quiet day, and his little heart, dispossessed, had stopped.
  The Turn of the Screw (1898)

2 Of course, of course.
  on hearing that Rupert **Brooke** *had died on a Greek island*
  C. Hassall *Rupert Brooke* (1964) ch. 14

3 Summer afternoon—summer afternoon . . . the two most beautiful words in the English language.
  Edith Wharton *A Backward Glance* (1934) ch. 10

4 So here it is at last, the distinguished thing!
  on experiencing his first stroke
  Edith Wharton *A Backward Glance* (1934) ch. 14

P. D. James 1920–
English writer of detective stories

5 What the detective story is about is not murder but the restoration of order.
  in *Face* December 1986

William James 1842–1910
American philosopher

6 There is no more miserable human being than one in whom nothing is habitual but indecision.
  The Principles of Psychology (1890) vol. 1, ch. 4

7 The art of being wise is the art of knowing what to overlook.
  The Principles of Psychology (1890) vol. 2, ch. 22

8 There is no worse lie than a truth misunderstood by those who hear it.
  The Varieties of Religious Experience (1902)

9 The moral flabbiness born of the exclusive worship of the bitch-goddess *success*.
  letter to H. G. Wells, 11 September 1906

10 Hogamus, higamous
   Man is polygamous
   Higamus, hogamous
   Woman monogamous.
   in *Oxford Book of Marriage* (1990)

Randall Jarrell 1914–65
American poet

11 When I died they washed me out of the turret with a hose.
   'The Death of the Ball Turret Gunner' (1945)

12 In bombers named for girls, we burned
   The cities we had learned about in school—
   Till our lives wore out; our bodies lay among
   The people we had killed and never seen.
   When we lasted long enough they gave us medals;
   When we died they said, 'Our casualties were low.'
   'Losses' (1963)

Douglas Jay 1907–96
British Labour politician

13 In the case of nutrition and health, just as in the case of education, the gentleman in Whitehall really does know better what is good for people than the people know themselves.
   The Socialist Case (1939) ch. 30

James Jeans 1877–1946
English astronomer, physicist, and mathematician

14 If we assume that the last breath of, say, Julius Caesar has by now become thoroughly scattered through the atmosphere, then the chances are that each of us inhales one molecule of it with every breath we take.
   now usually quoted as the 'dying breath of Socrates'
   An Introduction to the Kinetic Theory of Gases (1940)

15 Life exists in the universe only because the carbon atom possesses certain exceptional properties.
   The Mysterious Universe (1930) ch. 1

16 From the intrinsic evidence of his creation, the Great Architect of the Universe now begins to appear as a pure mathematician.
   The Mysterious Universe (1930) ch. 5

Thomas Jefferson 1743–1826
American Democratic Republican statesman; 3rd President of the US, 1801–9

17 When in the course of human events, it becomes necessary for one people to dissolve the political bonds which have connected them with another, and to assume among the powers of the earth the separate and equal station to which the laws of nature and of Nature's God entitle them, a decent respect to the opinions of mankind requires that they should declare the causes which impel them to the separation.
   American Declaration of Independence, 4 July 1776, preamble

18 We hold these truths to be sacred and undeniable; that all men are created equal and independent, that from that equal creation they derive rights inherent and inalienable, among which are the preservation of life, and liberty, and the pursuit of happiness.
   'Rough Draft' of the American Declaration of Independence, in J. P. Boyd et al. *Papers of Thomas Jefferson* (1950) vol. 1; see **Anonymous** 11:14

19 Our liberty depends on freedom of the press, and that cannot be limited without being lost.
   letter to James Currie, 28 January 1786, in *Papers of Thomas Jefferson* (1954) vol. 9

20 Experience declares that man is the only animal which devours its own kind, for I can apply no milder term to the governments of Europe, and to the general prey of the rich on the poor.
   letter to Colonel Edward Carrington, 16 January 1787, in *Papers of Thomas Jefferson* (1955) vol. 11

21 A little rebellion now and then is a good thing.
   letter to James Madison, 30 January 1787, in *Papers of Thomas Jefferson* (1955) vol. 11

1 State a moral case to a ploughman and a professor. The former will decide it as well, and often better than the latter, because he has not been led astray by artificial rules.
   letter to Peter Carr, 10 August 1787, in *Papers of Thomas Jefferson* (1955) vol. 12

2 The tree of liberty must be refreshed from time to time with the blood of patriots and tyrants. It is its natural manure.
   letter to W. S. Smith, 13 November 1787

3 I think our governments will remain virtuous for many centuries; as long as they are chiefly agricultural; and this will be as long as there shall be vacant lands in any part of America. When they get piled upon one another in large cities, as in Europe, they will become corrupt as in Europe.
   letter to James Madison, 20 December 1787, in *Papers of Thomas Jefferson* (1955) vol. 12

4 Whenever a man has cast a longing eye on them [official positions], a rottenness begins in his conduct.
   letter to Tench Coxe, 21 May 1799, in P. L. Ford (ed.) *Writings of Thomas Jefferson* (1896) vol. 7

5 Though the will of the majority is in all cases to prevail, that will to be rightful must be reasonable; . . . the minority possess their equal rights, which equal law must protect, and to violate would be oppression.
   first inaugural address, 4 March 1801

6 Would the honest patriot, in the full tide of successful experiment, abandon a government which has so far kept us free and firm?
   first inaugural address, 4 March 1801

7 Peace, commerce, and honest friendship with all nations—entangling alliances with none.
   first inaugural address, 4 March 1801

8 Freedom of religion; freedom of the press, and freedom of person under the protection of *habeas corpus*, and trial by juries impartially selected. These principles form the bright constellation which has gone before us, and guided our steps through an age of revolution and reformation.
   first inaugural address, 4 March 1801

9 I have learned to expect that it will rarely fall to the lot of imperfect man to retire from this station with the reputation and the favour which bring him into it.
   first inaugural address, 4 March 1801

10 If a due participation of office is a matter of right, how are vacancies to be obtained? Those by death are few; by resignation none.
   often quoted as, 'Few die and none resign'
   letter to E. Shipman and others, 12 July 1801

11 When a man assumes a public trust, he should consider himself as public property.
   to Baron von Humboldt, 1807

12 Nothing can now be believed which is seen in a newspaper. Truth itself becomes suspicious by being put into that polluted vehicle.
   letter to John Norvell, 14 June 1807, in *The Portable Thomas Jefferson* (1977)

13 But though an old man, I am but a young gardener.
   letter to Charles Willson Peale, 20 August 1811, in *Thomas Jefferson's Garden Book* (1944)

14 I agree with you that there is a natural aristocracy among men. The grounds of this are virtue and talents.
   letter to John Adams, 28 October 1813, in P. L. Ford (ed.) *Writings of Thomas Jefferson* (1898) vol. 9

15 If a nation expects to be ignorant and free, in a state of civilization, it expects what never was and never will be.
   letter to Colonel Charles Yancey, 6 January 1816, in P. L. Ford (ed.) *Writings of Thomas Jefferson* (1899) vol. 10

16 We have the wolf by the ears; and we can neither hold him, nor safely let him go. Justice is in one scale, and self-preservation in the other.
   on slavery
   letter to John Holmes, 22 April 1820

17 I know no safe depository of the ultimate powers of the society but the people themselves; and if we think them not enlightened enough to exercise their control with a wholesome discretion, the remedy is not to take it from them, but to inform their discretion by education.
   letter to William Charles Jarvis, 28 September 1820, in P. L. Ford (ed.) *Writings of Thomas Jefferson* (1899) vol. 10

18 To attain all this [universal republicanism], however, rivers of blood must yet flow, and years of desolation pass over; yet the object is worth rivers of blood, and years of desolation.
   letter to John Adams, 4 September 1823; see **Powell** 270:12, **Virgil** 347:10

19 Millions of innocent men, women, and children, since the introduction of Christianity, have been burnt, tortured, fined, imprisoned; yet we have not advanced one inch towards uniformity [of opinion]. What has been the effect of coercion? To make one half the world fools, and the other half hypocrites.
   Notes on the State of Virginia (1781–5) Query 17

20 Indeed I tremble for my country when I reflect that God is just.
   Notes on the State of Virginia (1781–5) Query 18

21 No duty the Executive had to perform was so trying as to put the right man in the right place.
   J. B. MacMaster *History of the People of the United States* (1883–1913) vol. 2, ch. 13

Francis, Lord Jeffrey 1773–1850
Scottish critic

22 This will never do.
   *on **Wordsworth's** The Excursion (1814)*
   in *Edinburgh Review* November 1814

David Jenkins 1925-
English theologian and bishop

1 I am not clear that God manoeuvres physical things . . . After all, a conjuring trick with bones only proves that it is as clever as a conjuring trick with bones.
on the Resurrection
  in 'Poles Apart' (BBC radio, 4 October 1984)

Roy Jenkins 1920-2003
British politician; co-founder of the Social Democratic Party, 1981

2 The politics of the left and centre of this country are frozen in an out-of-date mould which is bad for the political and economic health of Britain and increasingly inhibiting for those who live within the mould. Can it be broken?
  speech to Parliamentary Press Gallery, 9 June 1980, in *The Times* 10 June 1980

St Jerome *c.*AD 342-420
Roman Christian monk and scholar

3 *Venerationi mihi semper fuit non verbosa rusticitas, sed sancta simplicitas.*
I have revered always not crude verbosity, but holy simplicity.
  letter 57, To Pammachius; see Huss 179:1

Jerome K. Jerome 1859-1927
English writer

4 It is impossible to enjoy idling thoroughly unless one has plenty of work to do.
  Idle Thoughts of an Idle Fellow (1886) 'On Being Idle'

5 It is a most extraordinary thing, but I never read a patent medicine advertisement without being impelled to the conclusion that I am suffering from the particular disease therein dealt with in its most virulent form.
  Three Men in a Boat (1889) ch. 1

6 I like work: it fascinates me. I can sit and look at it for hours. I love to keep it by me: the idea of getting rid of it nearly breaks my heart.
  Three Men in a Boat (1889) ch. 15

William Jerome 1865-1932
American songwriter

7 Any old place I can hang my hat is home sweet home to me.
  title of song (1901)

Douglas Jerrold 1803-57
English dramatist and journalist

8 The best thing I know between France and England is—the sea.
  The Wit and Opinions of Douglas Jerrold (1859) 'The Anglo-French Alliance'

9 Earth is here so kind, that just tickle her with a hoe and she laughs with a harvest.
of Australia
  The Wit and Opinions of Douglas Jerrold (1859) 'A Land of Plenty'

John Jewel 1522-71
English bishop

10 In old time we had treen chalices and golden priests, but now we have treen priests and golden chalices.
  Certain Sermons Preached Before the Queen's Majesty (1609)

Steve Jobs 1955-
American computer executive

11 It turns out people want keyboards. When Apple first started out, people couldn't type. We realized: Death would eventually take care of this.
  interview, 28 May 2003

Pope John XXIII 1881-1963
Italian cleric, Pope from 1958

12 If civil authorities legislate for or allow anything that is contrary to that order and therefore contrary to the will of God, neither the laws made or the authorizations granted can be binding on the consciences of the citizens, since God has more right to be obeyed than man.
  Pacem in Terris (1963)

13 I want to throw open the windows of the Church so that we can see out and the people can see in.
  attributed

St John of the Cross 1542-91
Spanish mystic and poet

14 *Muero porque no muero.*
I die because I do not die.
  *the same words occur in St **Teresa** of Ávila 'Versos nacidos del fuego del amor de Dios' (c.1571-3)*
    'Coplas del alma que pena por ver a Dios' (c.1578)

15 *Noche oscura.*
Dark night.
  often quoted as, 'Faith, the dark night of the soul'; the phrase appears in the chapter heading for the poem in Complete Works *(1864), translated by David Lewis*
    title of poem, St John of the Cross (1542-91) *The Ascent of Mount Carmel* (1578-80)

Elton John 1947-
and Bernie Taupin 1950-
English pop singer and songwriter; songwriter

16 Goodbye Norma Jean . . .
It seems to me you lived your life
Like a candle in the wind.
Never knowing who to cling to
When the rain set in.
*of Marilyn **Monroe***
  'Candle in the Wind' (song, 1973)

17 The candle burned out long before
Your legend ever did.
  'Candle in the Wind' (song, 1973)

18 Goodbye England's rose;

May you ever grow in our hearts.
*rewritten for and sung at the funeral of **Diana**, Princess of Wales, 7 September 1997*
   'Candle in the Wind' (song, revised version, 1997)

1 And it seems to me you lived your life
Like a candle in the wind:
Never fading with the sunset
When the rain set in.
And your footsteps will always fall here
On England's greenest hills;
Your candle's burned out long before
Your legend ever will.
   'Candle in the Wind' (song, revised version, 1997)

2 Goodbye yellow brick road.
   title of song (1973); see **Harburg** 161:9

Pope John Paul II 1920–2005
Polish cleric, Pope since 1978

3 It would be simplistic to say that Divine Providence caused the fall of communism. It fell by itself as a consequence of its own mistakes and abuses. It fell by itself because of its own inherent weaknesses.
when asked if the fall of the USSR could be ascribed to God
   Carl Bernstein and Marco Politi *His Holiness: John Paul II and the Hidden History of our Time* (1996)

Linton Kwesi Johnson 1952–
Jamaican-born poet

4 Fire in the head and a dread beat bleeding, beating fire: dread.
   'Dread Beat an Blood' (1975)

Lyndon Baines Johnson 1908–73
American Democratic statesman; 36th President of the US 1963–9

5 I am a free man, an American, a United States Senator, and a Democrat, in that order.
   in *Texas Quarterly* Winter 1958

6 All I have I would have given gladly not to be standing here today.
*following the assassination of J. F. **Kennedy***
   first speech to Congress as President, 27 November 1963

7 In your time we have the opportunity to move not only toward the rich society and the powerful society, but upward to the Great Society.
   speech at University of Michigan, 22 May 1964

8 We still seek no wider war.
   speech on radio and television, 4 August 1964, in *Public Papers of . . . Lyndon B. Johnson 1963–64* vol. 2

9 We are not about to send American boys 9 or 10,000 miles away from home to do what Asian boys ought to be doing for themselves.
   speech at Akron University, 21 October 1964; see **Roosevelt** 279:13

10 I don't want loyalty. I want *loyalty*. I want him to kiss my ass in Macy's window at high noon and tell me it smells like roses. I want his pecker in my pocket.
discussing a prospective assistant
   David Halberstam *The Best and the Brightest* (1972) ch. 20

11 Better to have him inside the tent pissing out, than outside pissing in.
of J. Edgar Hoover, head of the FBI
   David Halberstam *The Best and the Brightest* (1972) ch. 20

12 So dumb he can't fart and chew gum at the same time.
*of Gerald **Ford***
   Richard Reeves *A Ford, not a Lincoln* (1975) ch. 2

Pauline Johnson (Tekahionwake) 1861–1913
Canadian poet

13 For soft is the song my paddle sings.
   'The Song My Paddle Sings'

Philander Chase Johnson 1866–1939

14 Cheer up! the worst is yet to come!
   in *Everybody's Magazine* May 1920

Philip Johnson 1906–
American architect

15 Architecture is the art of how to waste space.
   New York Times 27 December 1964

Samuel Johnson 1709–84
English poet, critic, and lexicographer

16 Change is not made without inconvenience, even from worse to better.
   A Dictionary of the English Language (1755) preface; see **Hooker** 173:1

17 I am not yet so lost in lexicography as to forget that words are the daughters of earth, and that things are the sons of heaven. Language is only the instrument of science, and words are but the signs of ideas: I wish, however, that the instrument might be less apt to decay, and that signs might be permanent, like the things which they denote.
   A Dictionary of the English Language (1755) preface; see **Madden** 224:16

18 Every quotation contributes something to the stability or enlargement of the language.
on citations of usage in a dictionary
   A Dictionary of the English Language (1755) preface

19 *Lexicographer.* A writer of dictionaries, a harmless drudge.
   A Dictionary of the English Language (1755)

20 *Network.* Anything reticulated or decussated at equal distances, with interstices between the intersections.
   A Dictionary of the English Language (1755)

1 *Oats.* A grain, which in England is generally given to horses, but in Scotland supports the people.
A Dictionary of the English Language (1755)

2 *Patron.* Commonly a wretch who supports with insolence, and is paid with flattery.
A Dictionary of the English Language (1755)

3 When two Englishmen meet, their first talk is of the weather.
in *The Idler* no. 11 (24 June 1758)

4 Among the calamities of war may be jointly numbered the diminution of the love of truth, by the falsehoods which interest dictates and credulity encourages.
in *The Idler* no. 30 (11 November 1758)

5 Promise, large promise, is the soul of an advertisement.
The Idler no. 40 (20 January 1759)

6 At seventy-seven it is time to be in earnest.
A Journey to the Western Islands of Scotland (1775) 'Col'

7 A hardened and shameless tea-drinker, who has for twenty years diluted his meals with only the infusion of this fascinating plant; whose kettle has scarcely time to cool; who with tea amuses the evening, with tea solaces the midnight, and with tea welcomes the morning.
review in the *Literary Magazine* vol. 2, no. 13 (1757)

8 Language is the dress of thought.
Lives of the English Poets (1779–81) 'Cowley'; see **Pope** 267:10, **Wesley** 355:5

9 The father of English criticism.
Lives of the English Poets (1779–81) 'Dryden'

10 I rejoice to concur with the common reader.
Lives of the English Poets (1779–81) 'Gray'

11 An exotic and irrational entertainment, which has been always combated, and always has prevailed.
of Italian opera
Lives of the English Poets (1779–81) 'Hughes'

12 I am disappointed by that stroke of death, which has eclipsed the gaiety of nations and impoverished the public stock of harmless pleasure.
on the death of **Garrick**
Lives of the English Poets (1779–81) 'Edmund Smith'

13 Nothing can please many, and please long, but just representations of general nature.
Plays of William Shakespeare . . . (1765) preface

14 I have always suspected that the reading is right, which requires many words to prove it wrong; and the emendation wrong, that cannot without so much labour appear to be right.
Plays of William Shakespeare . . . (1765) preface

15 It is better to suffer wrong than to do it, and happier to be sometimes cheated than not to trust.
in *Rambler* no. 79 (18 December 1750)

16 No place affords a more striking conviction of the vanity of human hopes, than a public library.
in *The Rambler* no. 106 (23 March 1751)

17 He [the poet] must write as the interpreter of nature, and the legislator of mankind.
Rasselas (1759) ch. 10; see **Shelley** 315:6

18 Human life is everywhere a state in which much is to be endured, and little to be enjoyed.
Rasselas (1759) ch. 11

19 Marriage has many pains, but celibacy has no pleasures.
Rasselas (1759) ch. 26

20 Example is always more efficacious than precept.
Rasselas (1759) ch. 30

21 Integrity without knowledge is weak and useless, and knowledge without integrity is dangerous and dreadful.
Rasselas (1759) ch. 41

22 How is it that we hear the loudest yelps for liberty among the drivers of negroes?
Taxation No Tyranny (1775)

23 How small of all that human hearts endure,
That part which laws or kings can cause or cure.
lines added to Oliver Goldsmith's *The Traveller* (1764) l. 429; see **Goldsmith** 153:18

24 Let observation with extensive view,
Survey mankind, from China to Peru.
The Vanity of Human Wishes (1749) l. 1

25 A frame of adamant, a soul of fire,
No dangers fright him, and no labours tire.
of Charles XII of Sweden
The Vanity of Human Wishes (1749) l. 193

26 He left the name, at which the world grew pale,
To point a moral, or adorn a tale.
of Charles XII of Sweden
The Vanity of Human Wishes (1749) l. 221

27 Hides from himself his state, and shuns to know,
That life protracted is protracted woe.
The Vanity of Human Wishes (1749) l. 257

28 Still raise for good the supplicating voice,
But leave to heaven the measure and the choice.
The Vanity of Human Wishes (1749) l. 351

29 A lawyer has no business with the justice or injustice of the cause which he undertakes, unless his client asks his opinion, and then he is bound to give it honestly. The justice or injustice of the cause is to be decided by the judge.
James Boswell *Journal of a Tour to the Hebrides* (1785) 15 August 1773

30 I am always sorry when any language is lost, because languages are the pedigree of nations.
James Boswell *Tour to the Hebrides* (1785) 18 September 1773

1 A cucumber should be well sliced, and dressed with pepper and vinegar, and then thrown out, as good for nothing.
James Boswell *Tour to the Hebrides* (1785) 5 October 1773

2 I am sorry I have not learned to play at cards. It is very useful in life: it generates kindness and consolidates society.
James Boswell *Tour to the Hebrides* (1785) 21 November 1773

3 Sir, we are a nest of singing birds.
of Pembroke College, Oxford
James Boswell *Life of Samuel Johnson* (1791) 1730

4 I'll come no more behind your scenes, David; for the silk stockings and white bosoms of your actresses excite my amorous propensities.
to Garrick
James Boswell *Life of Samuel Johnson* (1791) 1750

5 A man may write at any time, if he will set himself doggedly to it.
James Boswell *Life of Samuel Johnson* (1791) March 1750

6 This man I thought had been a Lord among wits; but, I find, he is only a wit among Lords.
of Lord Chesterfield
James Boswell *Life of Samuel Johnson* (1791) 1754

7 They teach the morals of a whore, and the manners of a dancing master.
of the Letters of Lord Chesterfield
James Boswell *Life of Samuel Johnson* (1791) 1754

8 Is not a Patron, my Lord, one who looks with unconcern on a man struggling for life in the water, and, when he has reached ground, encumbers him with help? The notice which you have been pleased to take of my labours, had it been early, had been kind; but it has been delayed till I am indifferent, and cannot enjoy it; till I am solitary, and cannot impart it; till I am known, and do not want it.
James Boswell *Life of Samuel Johnson* (1791) letter to Lord Chesterfield, 7 February 1755

9 Ignorance, madam, pure ignorance.
on being asked why he had defined pastern *as the 'knee' of a horse*
James Boswell *Life of Samuel Johnson* (1791) 1755

10 If a man does not make new acquaintance as he advances through life, he will soon find himself left alone. A man, Sir, should keep his friendship in constant repair.
James Boswell *Life of Samuel Johnson* (1791) 1755

11 No man will be a sailor who has contrivance enough to get himself into a jail; for being in a ship is being in a jail, with the chance of being drowned.
James Boswell *Life of Samuel Johnson* (1791) 16 March 1759

12 BOSWELL: I do indeed come from Scotland, but I cannot help it . . .
JOHNSON: That, Sir, I find, is what a very great many of your countrymen cannot help.
James Boswell *Life of Samuel Johnson* (1791) 16 May 1763

13 The noblest prospect which a Scotchman ever sees, is the high road that leads him to England!
James Boswell *Life of Samuel Johnson* (1791) 6 July 1763

14 A man ought to read just as inclination leads him; for what he reads as a task will do him little good.
James Boswell *Life of Samuel Johnson* (1791) 14 July 1763

15 But if he does really think that there is no distinction between virtue and vice, why, Sir, when he leaves our houses, let us count our spoons.
James Boswell *Life of Samuel Johnson* (1791) 14 July 1763; see **Emerson** 132:4

16 Truth, Sir, is a cow, that will yield such people [sceptics] no more milk, and so they are gone to milk the bull.
James Boswell *Life of Samuel Johnson* (1791) 21 July 1763

17 Why, Sir, Sherry is dull, naturally dull; but it must have taken him a great deal of pains to become what we now see him. Such an excess of stupidity, Sir, is not in Nature.
of Thomas Sheridan
James Boswell *Life of Samuel Johnson* (1791) 28 July 1763

18 A woman's preaching is like a dog's walking on his hinder legs. It is not done well; but you are surprised to find it done at all.
James Boswell *Life of Samuel Johnson* (1791) 31 July 1763

19 Don't, Sir, accustom yourself to use big words for little matters.
James Boswell *Life of Samuel Johnson* (1791) 6 August 1763

20 I refute it *thus*.
on Boswell observing of Bishop Berkeley's theory of the non-existence of matter that though they were satisfied it was not true, they were unable to refute it, Johnson struck his foot against a large stone, till he rebounded from it, with these words
James Boswell *Life of Samuel Johnson* (1791) 6 August 1763

21 Most schemes of political improvement are very laughable things.
James Boswell *Life of Samuel Johnson* (1791) 26 October 1769

22 It matters not how a man dies, but how he lives. The act of dying is not of importance, it lasts so short a time.
James Boswell *Life of Samuel Johnson* (1791) 26 October 1769

23 That fellow seems to me to possess but one idea, and that is a wrong one.
of a chance-met acquaintance
James Boswell *Life of Samuel Johnson* (1791) 1770; see **Disraeli** 117:30

1 The triumph of hope over experience.
*of a man who remarried immediately after the
death of a wife with whom he had been unhappy*
James Boswell *Life of Samuel Johnson* (1791) 1770

2 Every man has a lurking wish to appear
considerable in his native place.
letter to Sir Joshua Reynolds, 17 July 1771

3 ELPHINSTON: What, have you not read it
through?
JOHNSON: No, Sir, do *you* read books *through*?
James Boswell *Life of Samuel Johnson* (1791) 19
April 1773

4 Read over your compositions, and where
ever you meet with a passage which you
think is particularly fine, strike it out.
quoting a college tutor
James Boswell *Life of Samuel Johnson* (1791) 30
April 1773

5 There are few ways in which a man can be
more innocently employed than in getting
money.
James Boswell *Life of Samuel Johnson* (1791) 27
March 1775

6 He was dull in a new way, and that made
many people think him *great*.
of Thomas **Gray**
James Boswell *Life of Samuel Johnson* (1791) 28
March 1775

7 Fleet-street has a very animated appearance;
but I think the full tide of human existence
is at Charing-Cross.
James Boswell *Life of Samuel Johnson* (1791) 2
April 1775

8 A man will turn over half a library to make
one book.
James Boswell *Life of Samuel Johnson* (1791) 6
April 1775

9 Patriotism is the last refuge of a scoundrel.
James Boswell *Life of Samuel Johnson* (1791) 7
April 1775

10 Knowledge is of two kinds. We know a
subject ourselves, or we know where we can
find information upon it.
James Boswell *Life of Samuel Johnson* (1791) 18
April 1775

11 Politics are now nothing more than means
of rising in the world.
James Boswell *Life of Samuel Johnson* (1791) 18
April 1775

12 In lapidary inscriptions a man is not upon
oath.
James Boswell *Life of Samuel Johnson* (1791) 1775

13 There is nothing which has yet been
contrived by man, by which so much
happiness is produced as by a good tavern or
inn.
James Boswell *Life of Samuel Johnson* (1791) 21
March 1776; see **Shenstone** 315:7

14 No man but a blockhead ever wrote, except
for money.
James Boswell *Life of Samuel Johnson* (1791) 5
April 1776

15 A man who has not been in Italy, is always
conscious of an inferiority, from his not
having seen what it is expected a man
should see.
James Boswell *Life of Samuel Johnson* (1791) 11
April 1776

16 BOSWELL: Sir, what is poetry?
JOHNSON: Why Sir, it is much easier to say
what it is not. We all *know* what light is; but
it is not easy to *tell* what it is.
James Boswell *Life of Samuel Johnson* (1791) 12
April 1776

17 If I had no duties, and no reference to
futurity, I would spend my life in driving
briskly in a post-chaise with a pretty
woman.
James Boswell *Life of Samuel Johnson* (1791) 19
September 1777

18 Depend upon it, Sir, when a man knows he
is to be hanged in a fortnight, it
concentrates his mind wonderfully.
*on the execution of Dr Dodd for forgery, 27 June
1777*
James Boswell *Life of Samuel Johnson* (1791) 19
September 1777

19 When a man is tired of London, he is tired
of life.
James Boswell *Life of Samuel Johnson* (1791) 20
September 1777

20 All argument is against it; but all belief is for
it.
of the existence of ghosts
James Boswell *Life of Samuel Johnson* (1791) 31
March 1778

21 Every man thinks meanly of himself for not
having been a soldier, or not having been at
sea.
James Boswell *Life of Samuel Johnson* (1791) 10
April 1778

22 Johnson had said that he could repeat a
complete chapter of 'The Natural History of
Iceland', from the Danish of Horrebow, the
whole of which was exactly thus:—'CHAP.
LXXII. *Concerning snakes*. There are no snakes
to be met with throughout the whole
island.'
James Boswell *Life of Samuel Johnson* (1791) 13
April 1778

23 A country governed by a despot is an
inverted cone.
James Boswell *Life of Samuel Johnson* (1791) 14
April 1778

24 So it is in travelling; a man must carry
knowledge with him, if he would bring
home knowledge.
James Boswell *Life of Samuel Johnson* (1791) 17
April 1778

25 Sir, the insolence of wealth will creep out.
James Boswell *Life of Samuel Johnson* (1791) 18
April 1778

26 Were it not for imagination, Sir, a man
would be as happy in the arms of a
chambermaid as of a Duchess.
James Boswell *Life of Samuel Johnson* (1791) 9 May
1778

1 Claret is the liquor for boys; port, for men; but he who aspires to be a hero (smiling) must drink brandy.

> James Boswell *Life of Samuel Johnson* (1791) 7 April 1779

2 Worth seeing, yes; but not worth going to see.

> *on the Giant's Causeway*
> James Boswell *Life of Samuel Johnson* (1791) 12 October 1779

3 Every man has a right to utter what he thinks truth, and every other man has a right to knock him down for it. Martyrdom is the test.

> James Boswell *Life of Samuel Johnson* (1791) 1780

4 They are forced plants, raised in a hot-bed; and they are poor plants; they are but cucumbers after all.

> *of Thomas **Gray's** Odes*
> James Boswell *Life of Samuel Johnson* (1791) 1780

5 No man was more foolish when he had not a pen in his hand, or more wise when he had.

> *of Oliver **Goldsmith***
> James Boswell *Life of Samuel Johnson* (1791) 1780; see **Garrick** 146:7

6 This merriment of parsons is mighty offensive.

> James Boswell *Life of Samuel Johnson* (1791) March 1781

7 We are not here to sell a parcel of boilers and vats, but the potentiality of growing rich, beyond the dreams of avarice.

> *at the sale of Thrale's brewery*
> James Boswell *Life of Samuel Johnson* (1791) 6 April 1781; see **Moore** 243:18

8 Classical quotation is the *parole* of literary men all over the world.

> James Boswell *Life of Samuel Johnson* (1791) 8 May 1781

9 Always, Sir, set a high value on spontaneous kindness. He whose inclination prompts him to cultivate your friendship of his own accord, will love you more than one whom you have been at pains to attach to you.

> James Boswell *Life of Samuel Johnson* (1791) May 1781

10 Resolve not to be poor: whatever you have, spend less. Poverty is a great enemy to human happiness; it certainly destroys liberty, and it makes some virtues impracticable, and others extremely difficult.

> James Boswell *Life of Samuel Johnson* (1791) letter to Boswell, 7 December 1782

11 How few of his friends' houses would a man choose to be at when he is sick.

> James Boswell *Life of Samuel Johnson* (1791) 1783

12 There is a wicked inclination in most people to suppose an old man decayed in his intellects. If a young or middle-aged man, when leaving a company, does not recollect where he laid his hat, it is nothing; but if

the same inattention is discovered in an old man, people will shrug up their shoulders, and say, 'His memory is going.'

> James Boswell *Life of Samuel Johnson* (1791) 1783

13 Sir, there is no settling the point of precedency between a louse and a flea.

> *on the relative merits of two minor poets*
> James Boswell *Life of Samuel Johnson* (1791) 1783

14 When I observed he was a fine cat, saying, 'Why yes, Sir, but I have had cats whom I liked better than this'; and then as if perceiving Hodge to be out of countenance, adding, 'but he is a very fine cat, a very fine cat indeed.'

> James Boswell *Life of Samuel Johnson* (1791) 1783

15 Clear your mind of cant.

> James Boswell *Life of Samuel Johnson* (1791) 15 May 1783

16 The black dog I hope always to resist, and in time to drive, though I am deprived of almost all those that used to help me.

> *on his attacks of melancholia; more recently associated with Winston **Churchill**, who used the phrase 'black dog' when alluding to his own periodic bouts of depression*
> letter to Mrs Thrale, 28 June 1783

17 If a man were to go by chance at the same time with Burke under a shed, to shun a shower, he would say—'this is an extraordinary man.'

> *on Edmund **Burke***
> James Boswell *Life of Samuel Johnson* (1791) 15 May 1784

18 It might as well be said 'Who drives fat oxen should himself be fat.'

> *parodying Henry **Brooke***
> James Boswell *Life of Samuel Johnson* (1791) June 1784; see **Brooke** 69:18

19 Sir, I have found you an argument; but I am not obliged to find you an understanding.

> James Boswell *Life of Samuel Johnson* (1791) June 1784

20 No man is a hypocrite in his pleasures.

> James Boswell *Life of Samuel Johnson* (1791) June 1784

21 Dictionaries are like watches, the worst is better than none, and the best cannot be expected to go quite true.

> letter to Francesco Sastres, 21 August 1784

22 Sir, I look upon every day to be lost, in which I do not make a new acquaintance.

> James Boswell *Life of Samuel Johnson* (1791) November 1784

23 Difficult do you call it, Sir? I wish it were impossible.

> *on the performance of a celebrated violinist*
> William Seward *Supplement to the Anecdotes of Distinguished Persons* (1797)

24 Love is the wisdom of the fool and the folly of the wise.

> William Cooke *Life of Samuel Foote* (1805) vol. 2

1 A man is in general better pleased when he has a good dinner upon his table, than when his wife talks Greek.

> John Hawkins (ed.) *The Works of Samuel Johnson* (1787) 'Apophthegms, Sentiments, Opinions, etc.' vol. 11

2 Of music Dr Johnson used to say that it was the only sensual pleasure without vice.

> in *European Magazine* (1795)

3 What is written without effort is in general read without pleasure.

> William Seward *Biographia* (1799)

Samuel Johnson 1822-82
American nonconformist minister

4 City of God, how broad and far.

> title of hymn (1864)

John Benn Johnstone 1803-91
English dramatist

5 I want you to assist me in forcing her on board the lugger; once there, I'll frighten her into marriage.

> *often quoted as, 'Once aboard the lugger and the maid is mine'*
> The Gipsy Farmer (performed 1845)

Hanns Johst 1890-1978
German dramatist

6 Whenever I hear the word culture . . . I release the safety-catch of my Browning!

> *often attributed to Hermann **Goering**, and quoted as 'Whenever I hear the word culture, I reach for my pistol!'*
> Schlageter (1933) act 1, sc. 1

Al Jolson 1886-1950
American singer

7 You think that's noise—you ain't heard nuttin' yet!

> *in a café, competing with the din from a neighbouring building site, in 1906; subsequently an aside in the 1927 film* The Jazz Singer
> Martin Abramson *The Real Story of Al Jolson* (1950) (later the title of a Jolson song, 1919, in the form 'You Ain't Heard Nothing Yet')

Henry Arthur Jones 1851-1929 and Henry Herman 1832-94
English dramatists

8 O God! Put back Thy universe and give me yesterday.

> The Silver King (1907) act 2, sc. 4

John Paul Jones 1747-92
American admiral

9 I have not yet begun to fight.

> *when asked whether he had lowered his flag, as his ship was sinking, 23 September 1779*
> Mrs Reginald De Koven *Life and Letters of John Paul Jones* (1914) vol. 1

Mary Harris 'Mother' Jones
*c.*1837-1930
Irish-born American labour activist

10 Pray for the dead and fight like hell for the living!

> The Autobiography of Mother Jones (1925)

Steve Jones 1944–
English geneticist

11 Sex and taxes are in many ways the same. Tax does to cash what males do to genes. It dispenses assets among the population as a whole. Sex, not death, is the great leveller.

> speech to the Royal Society; in *Independent* 25 January 1997

Erica Jong 1942–
American novelist

12 The zipless fuck is the purest thing there is.

> Fear of Flying (1973) ch. 1

13 Jealousy is all the fun you *think* they had.

> How to Save Your Own Life (1977)

Ben Jonson *c.*1573-1637
English dramatist and poet

14 Queen and huntress, chaste and fair,
Now the sun is laid to sleep,
Seated in thy silver chair,
State in wonted manner keep:
Hesperus entreats thy light,
Goddess, excellently bright.

> Cynthia's Revels (1600) act 5, sc. 3

15 Still to be neat, still to be drest,
As you were going to a feast;
Still to be powdered, still perfumed,
Lady, it is to be presumed,
Though art's hid causes are not found,
All is not sweet, all is not sound.

> Epicene (1609) act 1, sc. 1

16 Such sweet neglect more taketh me,
Than all the adulteries of art;
They strike mine eyes, but not my heart.

> Epicene (1609) act 1, sc. 1

17 Suns, that set, may rise again;
But if once we lose this light,
'Tis with us perpetual night.

> Volpone (1606) act 3, sc. 5

18 Come, my Celia, let us prove,
While we can, the sports of love.

> Volpone (1606) act 3, sc. 5; see **Catullus** 89:6

19 You have a gift, sir, (thank your education),
Will never let you want, while there are men,
And malice, to breed causes.

> *to a lawyer*
> Volpone (1606) act 5, sc. 1

20 Rest in soft peace, and, asked, say here doth lie
Ben Jonson his best piece of poetry.

> 'On My First Son' (1616)

21 This figure that thou here seest put,
It was for gentle Shakespeare cut,
Wherein the graver had a strife

With Nature, to out-do the life.
on the portrait of **Shakespeare**
    First Folio Shakespeare (1623) 'To the Reader'

1 Reader, look
Not on his picture, but his book.
on the portrait of **Shakespeare**
    First Folio Shakespeare (1623) 'To the Reader'

2 Drink to me only with thine eyes,
And I will pledge with mine;
Or leave a kiss but in the cup,
And I'll not look for wine.
    'To Celia' (1616)

3 In small proportions we just beauty see,
And in short measures life may perfect be.
    'To the Immortal Memory . . . of . . . Sir Lucius
    Carey and Sir H. Morison' (1640)

4 Soul of the Age!
The applause, delight, the wonder of our
stage!
    'To the Memory of My Beloved, the Author, Mr
    William Shakespeare' (1623)

5 How far thou didst our Lyly outshine,
Or sporting Kyd, or Marlowe's mighty line.
    'To the Memory of . . . Shakespeare' (1623)

6 Thou hadst small Latin, and less Greek.
    'To the Memory of . . . Shakespeare' (1623)

7 He was not of an age, but for all time!
    'To the Memory of . . . Shakespeare' (1623)

8 Sweet Swan of Avon!
    'To the Memory of . . . Shakespeare' (1623)

9 Donne, for not keeping of accent, deserved
hanging . . . Shakespeare wanted art.
    in *Conversations with William Drummond of
    Hawthornden* (written 1619) no. 3

10 Whatsoever he [Shakespeare] penned, he
never blotted out a line. My answer hath
been 'Would he had blotted a thousand'.
    Timber, or Discoveries made upon Men and Matter
    (1641) l. 658 'De Shakespeare Nostrati'; see
    Pope 268:10

Janis Joplin 1943–70
American singer

11 Fourteen heart attacks and he had to die in
my week. In MY week.
    when ex-President **Eisenhower's** *death prevented
    her photograph appearing on the cover of*
    Newsweek
    in *New Musical Express* 12 April 1969

12 Onstage I make love to twenty-five thousand
people, then I go home alone.
    in *New Yorker* 14 August 1971

Joseph II 1741–90
Austrian monarch, Holy Roman Emperor

13 Too beautiful for our ears, and much too
many notes, dear Mozart.
    of The Abduction from the Seraglio (1782)
    attributed; Franz Xaver Niemetschek *Life of
    Mozart* (1798)

Chief Joseph *c.*1840–1904
Nez Percé chief

14 From where the sun now stands I will fight
no more forever.
    speech at the end of the Nez Percé war in 1877

Jenny Joseph 1932–
English poet

15 When I am an old woman I shall wear
purple
With a red hat which doesn't go, and
doesn't suit me.
And I shall spend my pension on brandy and
summer gloves
And satin sandals, and say we've got no
money for butter.
    'Warning' (1974)

Benjamin Jowett 1817–93
English classicist

16 One man is as good as another until he has
written a book.
    Evelyn Abbott and Lewis Campbell (eds.) *Life and
    Letters of Benjamin Jowett* (1897) vol. 1

James Joyce 1882–1941
Irish novelist

17 His soul swooned slowly as he heard the
snow falling faintly through the universe
and faintly falling, like the descent of their
last end, upon all the living and the dead.
    Dubliners (1914) 'The Dead'

18 Dear, dirty Dublin.
    Dubliners (1914) 'A Little Cloud'

19 riverrun, past Eve and Adam's, from swerve
of shore to bend of bay, brings us by a
commodious vicus of recirculation back to
Howth Castle and Environs.
    Finnegans Wake (1939) pt. 1

20 All moanday, tearsday, wailsday, thumpsday,
frightday, shatterday till the fear of the Law.
    Finnegans Wake (1939) pt. 2

21 Three quarks for Muster Mark!
    Finnegans Wake (1939) pt. 2

22 A portrait of the artist as a young man.
    title of book (1916)

23 Once upon a time and a very good time it
was there was a moocow coming down
along the road and this moocow that was
down along the road met a nicens little boy
named baby tuckoo.
    A Portrait of the Artist as a Young Man (1916);
    opening words

24 Poor Parnell! he cried loudly. My dead king!
    A Portrait of the Artist as a Young Man (1916) ch. 1

25 When the soul of a man is born in this
country, there are nets flung at it to hold it
back from flight. You talk to me of
nationality, language, religion. I shall try to
fly by those nets.
    A Portrait of the Artist as a Young Man (1916) ch. 5

26 Ireland is the old sow that eats her farrow.
    A Portrait of the Artist as a Young Man (1916) ch. 5

1 The artist, like the God of the creation, remains within or behind or beyond or above his handiwork, invisible, refined out of existence, indifferent, paring his fingernails.
  A Portrait of the Artist as a Young Man (1916) ch. 5

2 The only arms I allow myself to use, silence, exile, and cunning.
  A Portrait of the Artist as a Young Man (1916) ch. 5

3 Stately, plump Buck Mulligan came from the stairhead, bearing a bowl of lather on which a mirror and a razor lay crossed.
  Ulysses (1922); opening words

4 The snotgreen sea. The scrotumtightening sea.
  Ulysses (1922)

5 It is a symbol of Irish art. The cracked lookingglass of a servant.
  Ulysses (1922)

6 I fear those big words, Stephen said, which make us so unhappy.
  Ulysses (1922)

7 History, Stephen said, is a nightmare from which I am trying to awake.
  Ulysses (1922)

8 The heaventree of stars hung with humid nightblue fruit.
  Ulysses (1922)

9 O, father forsaken,
  Forgive your son!
  'Ecce Puer'

William Joyce (Lord Haw-Haw) 1906–46
American-born wartime broadcaster from Nazi Germany, executed for treason

10 Germany calling! Germany calling!
  habitual introduction to propaganda broadcasts to Britain during the Second World War

Juan Carlos I 1938–
Spanish monarch, King from 1975

11 I will neither abdicate the Crown nor leave Spain. Whoever rebels will provoke a new civil war and will be responsible.
  on the occasion of the attempted coup in 1981
  television broadcast at 1.15 a.m., 24 February 1981

Jack Judge 1878–1938 and Harry Williams 1874–1924
British songwriters

12 It's a long way to Tipperary,
  It's a long way to go;
  It's a long way to Tipperary,
  To the sweetest girl I know!
  Goodbye, Piccadilly,
  Farewell, Leicester Square,
  It's a long, long way to Tipperary,
  But my heart's right there!
  'It's a Long Way to Tipperary' (1912 song)

Julian of Norwich 1343–after 1416
English anchoress

13 He showed me something small, no bigger than a hazelnut, lying in the palm of my hand, as it seemed to me, and it was as round as a ball. I looked at it with the eye of my understanding, and thought: What can this be? I was amazed that it could last, for I thought that because of its littleness it would suddenly have fallen into nothing. And I was answered in my understanding: It lasts and always will, because God loves it; and thus every thing has being through the love of God.
  Revelations of Divine Love (the long text) ch. 5

14 Sin is behovely, but all shall be well and all shall be well and all manner of thing shall be well.
  Revelations of Divine Love (the long text) ch. 27, Revelation 13; see **Eliot** 128:18

Julian the Apostate c.AD 332–363
Roman emperor from AD 360

15 Vicisti, Galilaee.
  You have won, Galilean.
  supposed dying words
  a late embellishment of Theodoret *Ecclesiastical History* (AD c.450); see **Swinburne** 329:14

Carl Gustav Jung 1875–1961
Swiss psychologist

16 The contents of the personal unconscious are chiefly the *feeling-toned complexes* . . . The contents of the collective unconscious, on the other hand, are known as *archetypes*.
  Eranos Jahrbuch (1934)

17 A man who has not passed through the inferno of his passions has never overcome them.
  Memories, Dreams, Reflections (1962) ch. 9

18 As far as we can discern, the sole purpose of human existence is to kindle a light in the darkness of mere being.
  Memories, Dreams, Reflections (1962) ch. 11

19 Every form of addiction is bad, no matter whether the narcotic be alcohol or morphine or idealism.
  Memories, Dreams, Reflections (1962) ch. 12

20 The meeting of two personalities is like the contact of two chemical substances: if there is any reaction, both are transformed.
  Modern Man in Search of a Soul (1933)

21 If there is anything that we wish to change in the child, we should first examine it and see whether it is not something that could better be changed in ourselves.
  'Vom Werden der Persönlichkeit' (1932)

Jung Chang 1952–
Chinese writer

22 At the age of fifteen my grandmother became the concubine of a warlord general.
  Wild Swans (1991)

'Junius'
English 18th-century pseudonymous writer

1 The liberty of the press is the *Palladium* of all the civil, political, and religious rights of an Englishman.
> *The Letters of Junius* (1772 ed.) 'Dedication to the English Nation'

2 There is a holy mistaken zeal in politics as well as in religion. By persuading others, we convince ourselves.
> in *Public Advertiser* 19 December 1769, letter 35

Donald Justice 1925–2004
American poet

3 Men at forty
Learn to close softly
The doors to rooms they will not be
Coming back to.
> 'Men at Forty' (1967)

Juvenal *c.*AD 60–*c.*130
Roman satirist

4 It's hard not to write satire.
> *Satires* no. 1, l. 30

5 Honesty is praised and left to shiver.
> *Satires* no. 1, l. 74 (translation by G. G. Ramsay)

6 *Nemo repente fuit turpissimus.*
No one ever suddenly became depraved.
> *Satires* no. 2, l. 83

7 *Rara avis in terris nigroque simillima cycno.*
A rare bird on this earth, like nothing so much as a black swan.
> *Satires* no. 6, l. 165

8 *Sed quis custodiet ipsos
Custodes?*
But who is to guard the guards themselves?
> *Satires* no. 6, l. 347

9 *Tenet insanabile multos
Scribendi cacoethes et aegro in corde senescit.*
Many suffer from the incurable disease of writing, and it becomes chronic in their sick minds.
> *Satires* no. 7, l. 51

10 Travel light and you can sing in the robber's face.
> *Satires* no. 10, l. 22

11 . . . *Duas tantum res anxius optat,
Panem et circenses.*
Only two things does he [the modern citizen] anxiously wish for—bread and circuses.
> *Satires* no. 10, l. 80

12 *Mens sana in corpore sano.*
A sound mind in a sound body.
> *Satires* no. 10, l. 356

Pauline Kael 1919–
American film critic

13 The words 'Kiss Kiss Bang Bang' which I saw on an Italian movie poster, are perhaps the briefest statement imaginable of the basic appeal of movies.
> *Kiss Kiss Bang Bang* (1968) 'Note on the Title'

Franz Kafka 1883–1924
Czech novelist

14 When Gregor Samsa awoke one morning from uneasy dreams he found himself transformed in his bed into a gigantic insect.
> *The Metamorphosis* (1915) ch. 1

15 Someone must have traduced Joseph K., for without having done anything wrong he was arrested one fine morning.
> *The Trial* (1925) ch. 1

16 It's often better to be in chains than to be free.
> *The Trial* (1925) ch. 8

Frida Kahlo 1907–54
Mexican painter

17 I paint my own reality.
> Hayden Herrera *Frida* (1983)

Gus Kahn 1886–1941
and **Raymond B. Egan** 1890–1952
American songwriters

18 There's nothing surer,
The rich get rich and the poor get children.
> 'Ain't We Got Fun' (1921 song)

Immanuel Kant 1724–1804
German philosopher

19 Two things fill the mind with ever new and increasing wonder and awe, the more often and the more seriously reflection concentrates upon them: the starry heaven above me and the moral law within me.
> *Critique of Practical Reason* (1788)

20 Nothing in the world—indeed nothing even beyond the world—can possibly be conceived which could be called good without qualification except a *good will*.
> *Foundation of the Metaphysics of Morals* (1785) sect. 1

21 I am never to act otherwise than so that I could also will that my maxim should become a universal law.
> *Fundamental Principles of the Metaphysics of Ethics* (1785) sect. 1 (tr. T. K. Abbott)

22 There is an imperative which commands a certain conduct immediately, without having as its condition any other purpose to be attained by it. This imperative is Categorical . . . This imperative may be called that of Morality.
> *Fundamental Principles of the Metaphysics of Ethics* (1785) sect. 2 (tr. T. K. Abbott)

23 Happiness is not an ideal of reason but of imagination.
> *Fundamental Principles of the Metaphysics of Ethics* (1785) sect. 2 (tr. T. K. Abbott)

24 So act as to treat humanity, whether in thine own person or in that of any other, in every case as an end withal, never as means only.
> *Fundamental Principles of the Metaphysics of Ethics* (1785) sect. 2 (tr. T. K. Abbott)

1 Out of the crooked timber of humanity no straight thing can ever be made.
Idee zu einer allgemeinen Geschichte in weltbürgerlicher Absicht (1784) proposition 6

Alphonse Karr 1808–90
French novelist and journalist

2 If we are to abolish the death penalty, let the murderers take the first step.
Les Guêpes January 1849 (6th series, 1859)

3 *Plus ça change, plus c'est la même chose.*
The more things change, the more they are the same.
Les Guêpes January 1849 (6th series, 1859)

George S. Kaufman 1889–1961
American dramatist

4 Satire is what closes Saturday night.
Scott Meredith *George S. Kaufman and his Friends* (1974) ch. 6

Gerald Kaufman 1930–
British Labour politician

5 The longest suicide note in history.
on the Labour Party manifesto New Hope for Britain (1983)
Denis Healey *The Time of My Life* (1989) ch. 20

Paul Kaufman
and **Mike Anthony**
American songwriters

6 Poetry in motion.
title of song (1960); see **Grahame** 155:4

Christoph Kaufmann 1753–95
German man of letters

7 *Sturm und Drang.*
Storm and stress.
title suggested by Kaufmann for a romantic drama of the American War of Independence by the German dramatist, F. M. Klinger (1775), and thereafter given to a period of literary ferment which prevailed in Germany during the latter part of the 18th century

Paul Keating 1944–
Australian Labor statesman

8 You look like an Easter Island statue with an arse full of razor blades.
in the Australian Parliament to the then Prime Minister, Malcolm **Fraser**
in 1983; Michael Gordon *A Question of Leadership* (1993)

John Keats 1795–1821
English poet

9 Bright star, would I were steadfast as thou art.
first line of sonnet (written 1819)

10 A thing of beauty is a joy for ever.
Endymion (1818) bk. 1, l. 1

11 St Agnes' Eve—Ah, bitter chill it was!
The owl, for all his feathers, was a-cold.
'The Eve of St Agnes' (1820) st. 1

12 The silver, snarling trumpets 'gan to chide.
'The Eve of St Agnes' (1820) st. 4

13 By degrees
Her rich attire creeps rustling to her knees.
'The Eve of St Agnes' (1820) st. 26

14 Trembling in her soft and chilly nest.
'The Eve of St Agnes' (1820) st. 27

15 As though a rose should shut, and be a bud again.
'The Eve of St Agnes' (1820) st. 27

16 And still she slept an azure-lidded sleep,
In blanchèd linen, smooth, and lavendered,
While he from forth the closet brought a heap
Of candied apple, quince, and plum, and gourd;
With jellies soother than the creamy curd,
And lucent syrops, tinct with cinnamon.
'The Eve of St Agnes' (1820) st. 30

17 And they are gone: aye, ages long ago
These lovers fled away into the storm.
'The Eve of St Agnes' (1820) st. 42

18 Fanatics have their dreams, wherewith they weave
A paradise for a sect.
'The Fall of Hyperion' (written 1819) l. 1

19 Ever let the fancy roam,
Pleasure never is at home.
'Fancy' (1820) l. 1

20 In drear nighted December
Too happy, happy tree
Thy branches ne'er remember
Their green felicity.
'In drear nighted December' (written 1817)

21 'For cruel 'tis,' said she,
'To steal my Basil-pot away from me.'
'Isabella; or, The Pot of Basil' (1820) st. 62

22 Here are sweet peas, on tip-toe for a flight.
'I stood tip-toe upon a little hill' (1817) l. 57

23 Oh, what can ail thee knight at arms
Alone and palely loitering?
The sedge has withered from the lake
And no birds sing!
'La belle dame sans merci' (1820) st. 1

24 I see a lily on thy brow
With anguish moist and fever dew,
And on thy cheeks a fading rose
Fast withereth too.
'La belle dame sans merci' (1820) st. 3

25 I met a lady in the meads
Full beautiful, a faery's child
Her hair was long, her foot was light
And her eyes were wild.
'La belle dame sans merci' (1820) st. 4

26 . . . La belle dame sans merci
Thee hath in thrall.
'La belle dame sans merci' (1820) st. 10

27 I saw their starved lips in the gloam
With horrid warning gapèd wide
And I awoke and found me here
On the cold hill's side.
'La belle dame sans merci' (1820) st. 11

28 She was a gordian shape of dazzling hue,

Vermilion-spotted, golden, green, and blue;
Striped like a zebra, freckled like a pard,
Eyed like a peacock, and all crimson barred.
'Lamia' (1820) pt. 1, l. 47

1 Love in a hut, with water and a crust,
Is—Love, forgive us!—cinders, ashes, dust.
'Lamia' (1820) pt. 2, l. 1; see **Colman** 101:17

2 Do not all charms fly
At the mere touch of cold philosophy?
'Lamia' (1820) pt. 2, l. 229

3 Philosophy will clip an Angel's wings.
'Lamia' (1820) pt. 2, l. 234

4 Souls of poets dead and gone,
What Elysium have ye known,
Happy field or mossy cavern,
Choicer than the Mermaid Tavern?
'Lines on the Mermaid Tavern' (1820)

5 Thou still unravished bride of quietness,
Thou foster-child of silence and slow time.
'Ode on a Grecian Urn' (1820) st. 1

6 What men or gods are these? What maidens
loth?
What mad pursuit? What struggle to
escape?
'Ode on a Grecian Urn' (1820) st. 1

7 Heard melodies are sweet, but those
unheard
Are sweeter.
'Ode on a Grecian Urn' (1820) st. 2

8 For ever wilt thou love, and she be fair!
'Ode on a Grecian Urn' (1820) st. 2

9 For ever piping songs for ever new.
'Ode on a Grecian Urn' (1820) st. 3

10 For ever warm and still to be enjoyed,
For ever panting, and for ever young.
'Ode on a Grecian Urn' (1820) st. 3

11 O Attic shape! Fair attitude!
'Ode on a Grecian Urn' (1820) st. 5

12 'Beauty is truth, truth beauty,'—that is all
Ye know on earth, and all ye need to know.
'Ode on a Grecian Urn' (1820) st. 5

13 No, no, go not to Lethe, neither twist
Wolf's-bane, tight-rooted, for its poisonous
wine.
'Ode on Melancholy' (1820) st. 1

14 Then glut thy sorrow on a morning rose,
Or on the rainbow of the salt sand-wave,
Or on the wealth of globèd peonies.
'Ode on Melancholy' (1820) st. 1

15 She dwells with Beauty—Beauty that must
die;
And Joy, whose hand is ever at his lips
Bidding adieu.
'Ode on Melancholy' (1820) st. 3

16 My heart aches, and a drowsy numbness
pains
My sense, as though of hemlock I had
drunk,
Or emptied some dull opiate to the drains.
'Ode to a Nightingale' (1820) st. 1

17 O, for a draught of vintage! that hath been
Cooled a long age in the deep-delvèd earth,

Tasting of Flora and the country green.
'Ode to a Nightingale' (1820) st. 2

18 O for a beaker full of the warm South,
Full of the true, the blushful Hippocrene,
With beaded bubbles winking at the brim,
And purple-stainèd mouth.
'Ode to a Nightingale' (1820) st. 2

19 Away! away! for I will fly to thee,
Not charioted by Bacchus and his pards,
But on the viewless wings of Poesy,
Though the dull brain perplexes and
retards:
Already with thee! tender is the night.
'Ode to a Nightingale' (1820) st. 4

20 Darkling I listen; and, for many a time
I have been half in love with easeful Death.
'Ode to a Nightingale' (1820) st. 6

21 Now more than ever seems it rich to die,
To cease upon the midnight with no pain.
'Ode to a Nightingale' (1820) st. 6

22 Thou wast not born for death, immortal
bird!
No hungry generations tread thee down;
'Ode to a Nightingale' (1820) st. 7

23 Perhaps the self-same song that found a
path
Through the sad heart of Ruth, when, sick
for home,
She stood in tears amid the alien corn;
The same that oft-times hath
Charmed magic casements, opening on the
foam
Of perilous seas, in faery lands forlorn.
'Ode to a Nightingale' (1820) st. 7

24 Forlorn! the very word is like a bell
To toll me back from thee to my sole self!
Adieu! the fancy cannot cheat so well
As she is famed to do, deceiving elf.
'Ode to a Nightingale' (1820) st. 8

25 Was it a vision, or a waking dream?
Fled is that music:—do I wake or sleep?
'Ode to a Nightingale' (1820) st. 8

26 'Mid hushed, cool-rooted flowers, fragrant-
eyed,
Blue, silver-white, and budded Tyrian.
'Ode to Psyche' (1820) st. 1

27 Much have I travelled in the realms of gold,
And many goodly states and kingdoms seen.
'On First Looking into Chapman's Homer'
(1817)

28 Then felt I like some watcher of the skies
When a new planet swims into his ken;
Or like stout Cortez when with eagle eyes
He stared at the Pacific—and all his men
Looked at each other with a wild surmise—
Silent, upon a peak in Darien.
'On First Looking into Chapman's Homer'
(1817)

29 The poetry of earth is never dead.
'On the Grasshopper and Cricket' (1817)

30 Turn the key deftly in the oilèd wards,

And seal the hushèd casket of my soul.
'Sonnet to Sleep' (written 1819)

1 Season of mists and mellow fruitfulness,
Close bosom-friend of the maturing sun;
Conspiring with him how to load and bless
With fruit the vines that round the thatch-
eaves run.
'To Autumn' (1820) st. 1

2 Who hath not seen thee oft amid thy store?
'To Autumn' (1820) st. 2

3 Where are the songs of Spring? Ay, where
are they?
Think not of them, thou hast thy music too.
'To Autumn' (1820) st. 3

4 Then in a wailful choir the small gnats
mourn
Among the river sallows, borne aloft
Or sinking as the light wind lives or dies.
'To Autumn' (1820) st. 3

5 To one who has been long in city pent,
'Tis very sweet to look into the fair
And open face of heaven.
'To one who has been long in city pent' (1817);
see Milton 239:5

6 When I have fears that I may cease to be
Before my pen has gleaned my teeming
brain.
'When I have fears that I may cease to be'
(written 1818)

7 When I behold, upon the night's starred
face
Huge cloudy symbols of a high romance.
'When I have fears that I may cease to be'
(written 1818)

8 Then on the shore
Of the wide world I stand alone and think
Till love and fame to nothingness do sink.
'When I have fears that I may cease to be'
(written 1818)

9 I am certain of nothing but the holiness of
the heart's affections and the truth of
imagination—what the imagination seizes
as beauty must be truth—whether it existed
before or not.
letter to Benjamin Bailey, 22 November 1817;
see Keats 196:12

10 O for a life of sensations rather than of
thoughts!
letter to Benjamin Bailey, 22 November 1817

11 Negative Capability, that is when man is
capable of being in uncertainties, mysteries,
doubts, without any irritable reaching after
fact and reason.
letter to George and Thomas Keats, 21
December 1817

12 There is nothing stable in the
world—uproar's your only music.
letter to George and Thomas Keats, 13 January
1818, in H. E. Rollins (ed.) Letters of John Keats
(1958) vol. 1

13 If poetry comes not as naturally as the
leaves to a tree it had better not come at all.
letter to John Taylor, 27 February 1818

14 It is impossible to live in a country which is
continually under hatches . . . Rain! Rain!
Rain!
letter to J. H. Reynolds from Devon, 10 April
1818

15 I am in that temper that if I were under
water I would scarcely kick to come to the
top.
letter to Benjamin Bailey, 25 May 1818

16 The Wordsworthian or egotistical sublime.
letter to Richard Woodhouse, 27 October 1818

17 Call the world if you please 'The vale of soul-
making'.
letter to George and Georgiana Keats, 21 April
1819, in H. E. Rollins (ed.) Letters of John Keats
(1958) vol. 2

18 Fine writing is next to fine doing the top
thing in the world.
letter to J. H. Reynolds, 24 August 1819

19 The only means of strengthening one's
intellect is to make up one's mind about
nothing—to let the mind be a thoroughfare
for all thoughts. Not a select party.
letter to George and Georgiana Keats, 24
September 1819, in H. E. Rollins (ed.) Letters of
John Keats (1958) vol. 2

20 'Load every rift' of your subject with ore.
letter to Shelley, August 1820; see Spenser
322:1

21 Here lies one whose name was writ in water.
epitaph for himself
Richard Monckton Milnes Life, Letters and Literary
Remains of John Keats (1848) vol. 2; see
Shakespeare 296:16

John Keble 1792–1866
English clergyman

22 Blessed are the pure in heart,
For they shall see our God,
The secret of the Lord is theirs,
Their soul is Christ's abode.
The Christian Year (1827) 'Blessed are the pure in
heart'

23 New every morning is the love
Our wakening and uprising prove.
The Christian Year (1827) 'Morning'

24 The trivial round, the common task,
Would furnish all we ought to ask.
The Christian Year (1827) 'Morning'

25 The voice that breathed o'er Eden,
That earliest wedding-day.
'Holy Matrimony' (1857 hymn)

Garrison Keillor 1942–
American humorous writer and broadcaster

26 Years ago, manhood was an opportunity for
achievement, and now it is a problem to be
overcome.
The Book of Guys (1994)

Helen Keller 1880–1968
*American writer and social reformer, blind and
deaf from the age of 19 months*

27 The mystery of language was revealed to
me. I knew then that 'w-a-t-e-r' meant the

wonderful cool something that was flowing over my hand. That living word awakened my soul, gave it light, joy, set it free!
The Story of My Life (1902) ch. 4

1 Everything has its wonders, even darkness and silence, and I learn, whatever state I may be in, therein to be content.
The Story of My Life (1902) ch. 22

Frank B. Kellogg *see* Aristide Briand

David Kelly 1944–2003
British scientist

2 I will probably be found dead in the woods.
remark made in February 2003 on what would happen if Iraq was invaded
evidence from David Broucher to the Hutton Inquiry, 21 August 2003

Thomas Kelly 1769–1855
Irish clergyman and hymn-writer

3 The head that once was crowned with thorns
Is crowned with glory now.
'The head that once was crowned with thorns' (1820 hymn)

Lord Kelvin 1824–1907
British scientist

4 When you can measure what you are speaking about, and express it in numbers, you know something about it; but when you cannot measure it, when you cannot express it in numbers, your knowledge is of a meagre and unsatisfactory kind: it may be the beginning of knowledge, but you have scarcely, in your thoughts, advanced to the stage of *science*, whatever the matter may be.
often quoted as 'If you cannot measure it, then it is not science'
Popular Lectures and Addresses vol. 1 (1889) 'Electrical Units of Measurement', delivered 3 May 1883

Thomas à Kempis *see* Thomas

Thomas Ken 1637–1711
English divine

5 Awake, my soul, and with the sun
Thy daily stage of duty run.
Shake off dull sloth, and joyful rise
To pay thy morning sacrifice.
'Morning Hymn' in Winchester College *Manual of Prayers* (1695) but already in use by 1674

6 Teach me to live, that I may dread
The grave as little as my bed.
'Evening Hymn' (1695) v. 3

Jaan Kenbrovin
and **William Kellette**

7 I'm forever blowing bubbles.
title of song (1919)

Charles Kennedy 1959–
British Liberal Democrat politician, Party Leader 1999–2006

8 War is not the word; nor is crusade. Resolve is.
*of the appropriate response to terrorism; see **Bush** 78:18*
speech to the Liberal Democrat Party Conference, 24 December 2001

9 The era of three-party politics right across the UK is now with us.
speech, 6 May 2005

Florynce Kennedy 1916–2000
American lawyer

10 If men could get pregnant, abortion would be a sacrament.
in *Ms.* March 1973

Jimmy Kennedy
and **Michael Carr**
British songwriters

11 We're gonna hang out the washing on the Siegfried Line.
title of song (1939)

John F. Kennedy 1917–63
American Democratic statesman, 35th President of the US, 1961–3

12 Don't buy a single vote more than necessary. I'll be damned if I'm going to pay for a landslide.
telegraphed message from his father, read at a Gridiron dinner in Washington, 15 March 1958, and almost certainly JFK's invention; J. F. Cutler *Honey Fitz* (1962)

13 We stand today on the edge of a new frontier.
speech accepting the Democratic nomination in Los Angeles, 15 July 1960

14 Let the word go forth from this time and place, to friend and foe alike, that the torch has been passed to a new generation of Americans—born in this century, tempered by war, disciplined by a hard and bitter peace.
inaugural address, 20 January 1961, in *Vital Speeches* 1 February 1961

15 We shall pay any price, bear any burden, meet any hardship, support any friend, oppose any foe to assure the survival and the success of liberty.
inaugural address, 20 January 1961

16 If a free society cannot help the many who are poor, it cannot save the few who are rich.
inaugural address, 20 January 1961

17 Let us never negotiate out of fear. But let us never fear to negotiate.
inaugural address, 20 January 1961

18 All this will not be finished in the first 100 days. Nor will it be finished in the first 1,000 days, nor in the life of this Administration,

nor even perhaps in our lifetime on this planet. But let us begin.
  inaugural address, 20 January 1961

1 And so, my fellow Americans: ask not what your country can do for you—ask what you can do for your country.
  inaugural address, 20 January 1961; see **Gibran** 149:8, **Holmes** 172:3

2 Mankind must put an end to war or war will put an end to mankind.
  speech to United Nations General Assembly, 25 September 1961, in *New York Times* 26 September 1961

3 *Ich bin ein Berliner.*
I am a Berliner.
  speech in West Berlin, 26 June 1963; see **Cicero** 96:21

4 In free society art is not a weapon . . . Artists are not engineers of the soul.
  speech at Amherst College, Mass., 26 October 1963; see **Gorky** 154:11, **Stalin** 322:23

5 It was involuntary. They sank my boat.
  on being asked how he became a war hero
  Arthur M. Schlesinger Jr. *A Thousand Days* (1965) ch. 4

Joseph P. Kennedy 1888–1969
American financier and diplomat

6 When the going gets tough, the tough get going.
  also attributed to Knute Rockne
  J. H. Cutler *Honey Fitz* (1962)

Robert Kennedy 1925–68
American Democratic politician

7 One-fifth of the people are against everything all the time.
  speech, University of Pennsylvania, 6 May 1964; in *Philadelphia Inquirer* 7 May 1964

8 Moral courage is a rarer commodity than bravery in battle or great intelligence.
  speech in Cape Town, 7 June 1966

Jack Kerouac 1922–69
American novelist

9 The beat generation.
  phrase coined in the course of a conversation; in *Playboy* June 1959

Jean Kerr 1923–2003
American writer

10 As someone pointed out recently, if you can keep your head when all about you are losing theirs, it's just possible you haven't grasped the situation.
  Please Don't Eat the Daisies (1957) introduction; see **Kipling** 202:9

11 I feel about airplanes the way I feel about diets. It seems to me that they are wonderful things for other people to go on.
  The Snake Has All the Lines (1958)

12 I'm tired of all this nonsense about beauty being only skin-deep. That's deep enough. What do you want—an adorable pancreas?
  The Snake has all the Lines (1958)

John Kerry 1943–
American Democratic politician

13 How do you ask a man to be the last man to die in Vietnam? How do you ask a man to be the last man to die for a mistake?
  to Senate Committee, 23 April 1971

14 It's one thing to be certain, but you can be certain and you can be wrong.
  televised presidential debate with George W. Bush, 30 September 2004; in *New York Times* 1 October 2004 (electronic edition)

William Kethe d. 1594
Scottish Calvinist

15 All people that on earth do dwell,
  Sing to the Lord with cheerful voice.
  'All people that on earth do dwell' in *Fourscore and Seven Psalms of David* (Geneva, 1561; later known as the Geneva Psalter); usually sung to the tune 'Old Hundredth', and often known by that name

16 O enter then his gates with praise,
  Approach with joy his courts unto.
  'All people that on earth do dwell' in *Fourscore and Seven Psalms of David* (Geneva, 1561; later known as the Geneva Psalter)

Francis Scott Key 1779–1843
American lawyer and verse-writer

17 'Tis the star-spangled banner; O long may it wave
  O'er the land of the free, and the home of the brave!
  'The Star-Spangled Banner' (1814)

John Maynard Keynes 1883–1946
English economist

18 I work for a Government I despise for ends I think criminal.
  letter to Duncan Grant, 15 December 1917

19 Lenin was right. There is no subtler, no surer means of overturning the existing basis of society than to debauch the currency.
  The Economic Consequences of the Peace (1919) ch. 6

20 I do not know which makes a man more conservative—to know nothing but the present, or nothing but the past.
  The End of Laissez-Faire (1926) pt. 1

21 Madmen in authority, who hear voices in the air, are distilling their frenzy from some academic scribbler of a few years back.
  General Theory (1947 ed.) ch. 24

22 *In the long run we are all dead.*
  A Tract on Monetary Reform (1923) ch. 3

Ruhollah Khomeini 1900–89
Iranian Shiite Muslim leader

23 I would like to inform all the intrepid Muslims in the world that the author of the book entitled *The Satanic Verses*, which has been compiled, printed and published in opposition to Islam, the Prophet and the Qur'an, as well as those publishers who

were aware of its contents, have been declared *madhur el dam* [those whose blood must be shed]. I call on all zealous Muslims to execute them quickly, wherever they find them, so that no-one will dare to insult Islam again. Whoever is killed in this path will be regarded as a martyr.

fatwa against Salman **Rushdie**, issued 14 February 1989

Nikita Khrushchev 1894–1971
Soviet statesman; Premier, 1958–64

1 If anyone believes that our smiles involve abandonment of the teaching of Marx, Engels and Lenin he deceives himself. Those who wait for that must wait until a shrimp learns to whistle.

speech in Moscow, 17 September 1955

2 Whether you like it or not, history is on our side. We will bury you.

speech to Western diplomats at reception in Moscow for Polish leader Mr Gomulka, 18 November 1956

3 If one cannot catch the bird of paradise, better take a wet hen.

in *Time* 6 January 1958

Joyce Kilmer 1886–1918
American poet

4 I think that I shall never see
A poem lovely as a tree.
'Trees' (1914); see **Nash** 248:15

5 Poems are made by fools like me,
But only God can make a tree.
'Trees' (1914)

David Maxwell Fyfe, Lord Kilmuir 1900–67
British Conservative politician and lawyer

6 Loyalty is the Tory's secret weapon.
Anthony Sampson *Anatomy of Britain* (1962) ch. 6

Francis Kilvert 1840–79
English clergyman and diarist

7 Of all noxious animals, too, the most noxious is a tourist. And of all tourists the most vulgar, ill-bred, offensive and loathsome is the British tourist.

diary, 5 April 1870

Benjamin Franklin King 1857–94
American poet

8 Nothing to do but work,
Nothing to eat but food,
Nothing to wear but clothes
To keep one from going nude.
'The Pessimist'

Henry King 1592–1669
English poet and bishop

9 Sleep on (my Love!) in thy cold bed
Never to be disquieted.
My last Good-night! Thou wilt not wake
Till I thy fate shall overtake.
'An Exequy' (1657) l. 81 (written for his wife Anne, d. 1624)

10 Stay for me there: I will not fail
To meet thee in that hollow vale.
'An Exequy' (1657) l. 81 (written for his wife Anne, d. 1624)

11 But hark! My pulse, like a soft drum
Beats my approach, tells thee I come.
'An Exequy' (1657) l. 111

Martin Luther King 1929–68
American civil rights leader

12 I want to be the white man's brother, not his brother-in-law.
in *New York Journal-American* 10 September 1962

13 Judicial decrees may not change the heart; but they can restrain the heartless.

speech in Nashville, Tennessee, 27 December 1962, in James Melvin Washington (ed.) *A Testament of Hope: The Essential Writings of Martin Luther King, Jr.* (1986) ch. 22

14 Injustice anywhere is a threat to justice everywhere.

letter from Birmingham Jail, Alabama, 16 April 1963

15 The Negro's great stumbling block in the stride toward freedom is not the White Citizens Councillor or the Ku Klux Klanner but the white moderate who is more devoted to order than to justice; who prefers a negative peace which is the absence of tension to a positive peace which is the presence of justice.

letter from Birmingham Jail, Alabama, 16 April 1963, in *Atlantic Monthly* August 1963

16 If a man hasn't discovered something he will die for, he isn't fit to live.

speech in Detroit, 23 June 1963

17 I have a dream that one day on the red hills of Georgia the sons of former slaves and the sons of former slave owners will be able to sit down together at the table of brotherhood . . .
I have a dream that my four little children will one day live in a nation where they will not be judged by the colour of their skin but by the content of their character.

speech at Civil Rights March in Washington, 28 August 1963

18 We must learn to live together as brothers or perish together as fools.

speech at St Louis, 22 March 1964, in *St Louis Post-Dispatch* 23 March 1964

19 Cowardice asks the question, 'Is it safe?' Expediency asks the question, 'Is it politic?' Vanity asks the question, 'Is it popular?' But Conscience asks the question, 'Is it right?'

c.1967; in *Autobiography of Martin Luther King Jr.* (1999)

20 I just want to do God's will. And he's allowed me to go up to the mountain. And I've looked over, and I've seen the promised land . . . So I'm happy tonight. I'm not worried about anything. I'm not fearing any man.

on the day before his assassination
speech in Memphis, 3 April 1968

1 Our scientific power has outrun our
spiritual power. We have guided missiles
and misguided men.
Strength to Love (1963) ch. 7

2 A riot is at bottom the language of the
unheard.
Where Do We Go From Here? (1967) ch. 4

Stoddard King 1889–1933
British songwriter

3 There's a long, long trail awinding
Into the land of my dreams.
'There's a Long, Long Trail' (1913 song)

William Lyon Mackenzie King
1874–1950
*Canadian Liberal statesman, Prime Minister
1921–6, 1926–30, and 1935–48*

4 If some countries have too much history, we
have too much geography.
speech, Canadian House of Commons, 18 June
1936

5 Not necessarily conscription, but
conscription if necessary.
speech, Canadian House of Commons, 7 July
1942

Charles Kingsley 1819–75
English writer and clergyman

6 Be good, sweet maid, and let who will be
clever;
Do noble things, not dream them, all day
long.
'A Farewell' (1858)

7 O Mary, go and call the cattle home,
And call the cattle home,
And call the cattle home,
Across the sands of Dee.
'The Sands of Dee' (1858)

8 For men must work, and women must
weep,
And there's little to earn, and many to keep,
'The Three Fishers' (1858)

9 When all the world is young, lad,
And all the trees are green;
And every goose a swan, lad,
And every lass a queen;
Then hey for boot and horse, lad,
And round the world away:
Young blood must have its course, lad,
And every dog his day.
'Young and Old' (from *The Water Babies*, 1863)

10 We have used the Bible as if it was a
constable's handbook—an opium-dose for
keeping beasts of burden patient while they
are being overloaded.
Letters to the Chartists no. 2; see **Marx** 230:5

Hugh Kingsmill (Hugh Kingsmill
Lunn) 1889–1949
English man of letters

11 What still alive at twenty-two,
A clean upstanding chap like you?
Sure, if your throat 'tis hard to slit,
Slit your girl's, and swing for it.
'Two Poems, after A. E. Housman' (1933) no. 1

12 But bacon's not the only thing
That's cured by hanging from a string.
'Two Poems, after A. E. Housman' (1933) no. 1

Neil Kinnock 1942–
British Labour politician

13 If Margaret Thatcher wins on Thursday, I
warn you not to be ordinary, I warn you not
to be young, I warn you not to fall ill, and I
warn you not to grow old.
on the prospect of a Conservative re-election
speech at Bridgend, 7 June 1983

14 Why am I the first Kinnock in a thousand
generations to be able to get to a university?
*later plagiarized by the American politician Joe
Biden*
speech in party political broadcast, 21 May 1987

Alfred Kinsey 1894–1956
American zoologist and sex researcher

15 The only unnatural sex act is that which you
cannot perform.
in *Time* 21 January 1966

Rudyard Kipling 1865–1936
English writer and poet

16 He's an absent-minded beggar and his
weaknesses are great.
'The Absent-Minded Beggar' (1899) st. 1

17 Oh, East is East, and West is West, and never
the twain shall meet,
Till Earth and Sky stand presently at God's
great Judgement Seat;
But there is neither East nor West, Border,
nor Breed, nor Birth,
When two strong men stand face to face,
tho' they come from the ends of earth!
'The Ballad of East and West' (1892)

18 Foot—foot—foot—foot—sloggin' over
Africa—
(Boots—boots—boots—boots—movin' up
and down again!)
'Boots' (1903)

19 If any question why we died,
Tell them, because our fathers lied.
'Common Form' (1919)

20 It's clever, but is it Art?
'The Conundrum of the Workshops' (1892)

21 They've taken of his buttons off an' cut his
stripes away,
An' they're hangin' Danny Deever in the
mornin'.
'Danny Deever' (1892)

22 The 'eathen in 'is blindness bows down to
wood an' stone;
'E don't obey no orders unless they is 'is
own.
'The 'Eathen' (1896); see **Heber** 164:18

23 And what should they know of England who
only England know?
'The English Flag' (1892)

1 I could not dig: I dared not rob:
  Therefore I lied to please the mob.
  Now all my lies are proved untrue
  And I must face the men I slew.
  What tale shall serve me here among
  Mine angry and defrauded young?
    'Epitaphs of the War: A Dead Statesman' (1919)

2 The female of the species is more deadly
  than the male.
    'The Female of the Species' (1919)

3 So 'ere's to you, Fuzzy-Wuzzy, at your 'ome
  in the Soudan;
  You're a pore benighted 'eathen but a first-
  class fightin' man.
    'Fuzzy-Wuzzy' (1892)

4 Gentlemen-rankers out on the spree,
  Damned from here to Eternity,
  God ha' mercy on such as we,
  Baa! Yah! Bah!
    'Gentlemen-Rankers' (1892)

5 God help us, for we knew the worst too
  young!
    'Gentlemen-Rankers' (1892)

6 Our England is a garden, and such gardens
  are not made
  By singing:—'Oh, how beautiful!' and sitting
  in the shade.
    'The Glory of the Garden' (1911)

7 As it will be in the future, it was at the birth
  of Man—
  There are only four things certain since
  Social Progress began:—
  That the Dog returns to his Vomit and the
  Sow returns to her Mire,
  And the burnt Fool's bandaged finger goes
  wabbling back to the Fire.
    'The Gods of the Copybook Headings' (1927)

8 You're a better man than I am, Gunga Din!
    'Gunga Din' (1892)

9 If you can keep your head when all about
  you
  Are losing theirs and blaming it on you . . .
  If you can meet with triumph and disaster
  And treat those two impostors just the
  same.
    'If—' (1910)

10 If you can talk with crowds and keep your
  virtue,
  Or walk with Kings—nor lose the common
  touch . . .
  Yours is the Earth and everything that's in
  it,
  And—which is more—you'll be a Man, my
  son!
    'If—' (1910)

11 There are nine and sixty ways of
  constructing tribal lays,
  And—every—single—one—of—them—is—
  right!
    'In the Neolithic Age' (1893)

12 Then ye returned to your trinkets; then ye
  contented your souls

With the flannelled fools at the wicket or
the muddied oafs at the goals.
  'The Islanders' (1903)

13 For the Colonel's Lady an' Judy O'Grady
  Are sisters under their skins!
    'The Ladies' (1896)

14 Down to Gehenna or up to the Throne,
  He travels the fastest who travels alone.
    L'Envoi to The Story of the Gadsbys (1890), 'The
    Winners'

15 On the road to Mandalay,
  Where the flyin'-fishes play,
  An' the dawn comes up like thunder outer
  China 'crost the Bay!
    'Mandalay' (1892)

16 Ship me somewheres east of Suez, where
  the best is like the worst.
    'Mandalay' (1892)

17 And the end of the fight is a tombstone
  white, with the name of the late deceased,
  And the epitaph drear: 'A fool lies here who
  tried to hustle the East.'
    The Naulahka (1892) ch. 5

18 Brothers and Sisters, I bid you beware
  Of giving your heart to a dog to tear.
    'The Power of the Dog' (1909)

19 The tumult and the shouting dies—
  The captains and the kings depart—
  Still stands Thine ancient Sacrifice,
  An humble and a contrite heart.
  Lord God of Hosts, be with us yet,
  Lest we forget—lest we forget!
    'Recessional' (1897)

20 Lo, all our pomp of yesterday
  Is one with Nineveh, and Tyre!
    'Recessional' (1897)

21 Such boasting as the Gentiles use,
  Or lesser breeds without the Law.
    'Recessional' (1897)

22 For frantic boast and foolish word—
  Thy mercy on Thy People, Lord.
    'Recessional' (1897)

23 How far is St. Helena from the field of
  Austerlitz?
    'A St. Helena Lullaby' (1910)

24 Five and twenty ponies,
  Trotting through the dark—
  Brandy for the Parson,
  'Baccy for the Clerk;
  Laces for a lady, letters for a spy,
  Watch the wall, my darling, while the
  Gentlemen go by!
    'A Smuggler's Song' (1906)

25 Them that asks no questions isn't told a lie.
  Watch the wall, my darling, while the
  Gentlemen go by!
    'A Smuggler's Song' (1906)

26 If blood be the price of admiralty,
  Lord God, we ha' paid in full!
    'The Song of the Dead' (1896)

27 One man in a thousand, Solomon says,
  Will stick more close than a brother.
    'The Thousandth Man' (1910); see Bible 38:31

1 Then it's Tommy this, an' Tommy that, an'
'Tommy 'ow's yer soul?'
But it's 'Thin red line of 'eroes' when the
drums begin to roll.
'Tommy' (1892); see **Russell** 283:17

2 Of all the trees that grow so fair,
Old England to adorn,
Greater are none beneath the Sun,
Than Oak, and Ash, and Thorn.
'A Tree Song' (1906)

3 A fool there was and he made his prayer
(Even as you and I!)
To a rag and a bone and a hank of hair
(We called her the woman who did not care)
But the fool he called her his lady fair—
(Even as you and I!)
'The Vampire' (1897) st. 1

4 They shut the road through the woods
Seventy years ago.
Weather and rain have undone it again,
And now you would never know
There was once a road through the woods.
'The Way through the Woods' (1910)

5 And that is called paying the Dane-geld;
But we've proved it again and again,
That if once you have paid him the Dane-
geld
You never get rid of the Dane.
'What Dane-geld means' (1911)

6 And only the Master shall praise us, and
only the Master shall blame;
And no one shall work for money, and no
one shall work for fame,
But each for the joy of the working, and
each, in his separate star,
Shall draw the Thing as he sees It for the
God of Things as They are!
'When Earth's Last Picture is Painted' (1896)

7 When 'Omer smote 'is bloomin' lyre,
He'd 'eard men sing by land an' sea;
An' what he thought 'e might require,
'E went an' took—the same as me!
'When 'Omer smote 'is bloomin' lyre' (1896)

8 Take up the White Man's burden—
Send forth the best ye breed—
Go, bind your sons to exile
To serve your captives' need.
'The White Man's Burden' (1899)

9 When you're wounded and left on
Afghanistan's plains
And the women come out to cut up what
remains
Just roll to your rifle and blow out your
brains
An' go to your Gawd like a soldier.
'The Young British Soldier' (1892)

10 They settled things by making up a saying,
'What the Bandar-log think now the Jungle
will think later': and that comforted them a
great deal.
The Jungle Book (1894) 'Kaa's Hunting'

11 We be of one blood, thou and I.
The Jungle Book (1894) 'Kaa's Hunting'

12 The motto of all the mongoose family is,
'Run and find out.'
The Jungle Book (1894) 'Rikki-Tikki-Tavi'

13 He walked by himself, and all places were
alike to him.
Just So Stories (1902) 'The Cat that Walked by
Himself'

14 And he went back through the Wet Wild
Woods, waving his wild tail and walking by
his wild lone.
Just So Stories (1902) 'The Cat that Walked by
Himself'

15 An Elephant's Child—who was full of
'satiable curtiosity.
Just So Stories (1902) 'The Elephant's Child'

16 The great grey-green, greasy, Limpopo River,
all set about with fever trees.
Just So Stories (1902) 'The Elephant's Child'

17 I keep six honest serving-men
(They taught me all I knew);
Their names are What and Why and When
And How and Where and Who.
Just So Stories (1902) 'The Elephant's Child'

18 He was a man of infinite-resource-and-
sagacity.
Just So Stories (1902) 'How the Whale got his
Throat'

19 Little Friend of all the World.
Kim's nickname
Kim (1901) ch. 1

20 The man who would be king.
title of short story (1888)

21 He swathed himself in quotations—as a
beggar would enfold himself in the purple
of Emperors.
Many Inventions (1893) 'The Finest Story in the
World'

22 The silliest woman can manage a clever
man; but it takes a very clever woman to
manage a fool.
Plain Tales from the Hills (1888) 'Three and—an
Extra'

23 Now this is the Law of the Jungle—as old
and as true as the sky;
And the Wolf that shall keep it may prosper,
but the Wolf that shall break it must die.
The Second Jungle Book (1895) 'The Law of the
Jungle'

24 'Tisn't beauty, so to speak, nor good talk
necessarily. It's just It. Some women'll stay
in a man's memory if they once walked
down a street.
Traffics and Discoveries (1904) 'Mrs Bathurst'

25 Power without responsibility: the
prerogative of the harlot throughout the
ages.
summing up Lord **Beaverbrook**'s political
standpoint vis-à-vis the Daily Express, and
quoted by Stanley **Baldwin**, 18 March 1931
in Kipling Journal vol. 38, no. 180, December
1971

Henry Kissinger 1923–
American politician

1 The conventional army loses if it does not win. The guerrilla wins if he does not lose.
   in *Foreign Affairs* January 1969

2 Power is the great aphrodisiac.
   in *New York Times* 19 January 1971

Paul Klee 1879–1940
German-Swiss painter

3 Art does not reproduce the visible; rather, it makes visible.
   Inward Vision (1958) 'Creative Credo' (1920)

4 An active line on a walk, moving freely without a goal. A walk for walk's sake.
   Pedagogical Sketchbook (1925)

5 Colour has taken hold of me; no longer do I have to chase after it. I know that it has hold of me for ever.
   on a visit to Tunis in 1914
   Herbert Read *A Concise History of Modern Painting* (1968)

Friedrich Klopstock 1724–1803
German poet

6 God and I both knew what it meant once; now God alone knows.
   C. Lombroso *The Man of Genius* (1891) pt. 1, ch. 2;
   see **Browning** 73:6

Charles Knight
and **Kenneth Lyle**
British songwriters

7 When there's trouble brewing,
   When there's something doing,
   Are we downhearted?
   No! Let 'em all come!
   'Here we are! Here we are again!!' (1914 song)

L. C. Knights 1906–97
English critic and academic

8 How many children had Lady Macbeth?
   satirizing an over-realistic approach to criticism
   title of essay (1933)

John Knox c.1505–72
Scottish Protestant reformer

9 The first blast of the trumpet against the monstrous regiment of women.
   'regiment' = rule
   title of pamphlet (1558)

10 A man with God is always in the majority.
   inscription on the Reformation Monument, Geneva

Ronald Knox 1888–1957
English writer and Roman Catholic priest

11 There once was a man who said, 'God
   Must think it exceedingly odd
   If he finds that this tree
   Continues to be
   When there's no one about in the Quad.'
   Langford Reed *Complete Limerick Book* (1924), to which came the anonymous reply:

Dear Sir,
Your astonishment's odd:
I am always about in the Quad.
And that's why the tree
Will continue to be,
Since observed by
Yours faithfully,
God.

12 A loud noise at one end and no sense of responsibility at the other.
   definition of a baby
   attributed

Vicesimus Knox 1752–1821
English writer

13 Can anything be more absurd than keeping women in a state of ignorance, and yet so vehemently to insist on their resisting temptation?
   Mary Wollstonecraft *A Vindication of the Rights of Woman* (1792) ch. 7

Ted Koehler
American songwriter

14 Stormy weather,
   Since my man and I ain't together.
   'Stormy Weather' (1933 song)

Arthur Koestler 1905–83
Hungarian-born writer

15 God seems to have left the receiver off the hook, and time is running out.
   The Ghost in the Machine (1967) ch. 18

Helmut Kohl 1930–
German statesman, Chancellor of West Germany (1982–90), Chancellor of Germany (1990–8)

16 The policy of European integration is in reality a question of war and peace in the 21st century.
   speech at Louvain University, 2 February 1996

The Koran
textual translations are those of A. J. Arberry, 1964

17 In the Name of God, the Merciful, the Compassionate.
   sura 1

18 Praise belongs to God, the Lord of all Being.
   sura 1

19 Guide us in the straight path,
   the path of those whom Thou hast blessed,
   not of those against whom Thou art wrathful,
   nor of those who are astray.
   sura 1

20 The month of Ramadan, wherein the Koran was sent down to be a guidance
   to the people, and as clear signs
   of the Guidance and the Salvation
   So let those of you, who are present
   at the month, fast it.
   sura 2

21 And fight in the way of God with those

who fight with you, but aggress not: God
loves
not the aggressors.
> sura 2

1 No compulsion is there in religion.
> sura 2

2 God has
permitted trafficking, and forbidden usury.
> sura 2

3 Say to the unbelievers: 'You shall be
overthrown, and mustered into Gehenna—
an evil cradling!'
> sura 3

4 The true religion with God is Islam.
> sura 3

5 Whoso desires another religion than Islam,
it shall
not be accepted of him; in the next world he
shall
be among the losers.
> sura 3

6 Every soul shall taste of death; you shall
surely
be paid in full your wages on the Day
of Resurrection.
> sura 3

7 Men are the managers of the affairs of
women.
> sura 4

8 Righteous women are therefore obedient,
guarding the secret for God's guarding.
And those you fear may be rebellious
admonish; banish them to their couches,
and beat them.
> sura 4

9 So let them fight in the way of God who
sell the present life for the world to come;
and whosoever fights in the way of God
and is slain, or conquers, We shall bring him
a mighty wage.
> sura 4

10 The Messiah, Jesus son of Mary,
was only the Messenger of God.
> sura 4

11 Today I have perfected your religion
for you, and I have completed My blessing
upon you and I have approved Islam for
your religion.
> sura 5

12 Whoso slays a soul not to retaliate for a soul
slain, nor for corruption done in the land,
shall be as if he had slain mankind
altogether.
> sura 5

13 And we have sent down to thee the Book
with the truth, confirming the Book
that was before it, and assuring it.
> sura 5

14 Glory be to Him, who carried His servant by
night
from the Holy Mosque to the Further
Mosque.
> sura 17

15 He
named you Muslims
aforetime and in this, that the Messenger
might be a witness against you, and that
you might be witnesses against mankind.
> sura 22

16 God is the Light of the heavens and the
earth.
> sura 24

17 Muhammad is not the father of any one
of your men, but the Messenger of God,
and the Seal of the Prophets
> sura 33

18 Not equal are the good deed and the evil
deed.
Repel with that which is fairer
and behold, he between whom and thee
there is enmity shall be as if he were
a loyal friend.
> sura 41;

Good and evil shall not be held equal.
Turn away evil with that which is better;
and behold the man between whom and
thyself there was enmity, shall become, as
it were, thy warmest friend.
> in George Sale's translation, 1734

19 It belongs not to any mortal that
God should speak to him, except
by revelation, or from behind
a veil.
> sura 42

20 And those who are slain in the way of God,
He
will not send their works astray.
> sura 47

21 It is He who has sent his Messenger with
the guidance and the religion of truth, that
He may uplift it above every religion.
> sura 48

22 Muhammed is the Messenger of God,
and those who are with him are hard
against the unbelievers, merciful
one to another.
> sura 48

23 We indeed created man; and We know
what his soul whispers within him,
and We are nearer to him than the
jugular vein.
> sura 50

24 He [God] is the First and the Last, the
Outward and the Inward.
> sura 57

25 Recite: In the Name of thy Lord who created
created Man of a blood-clot.
> sura 96

Karl Kraus 1874–1936
Austrian satirist

26 How is the world ruled and how do wars
start? Diplomats tell lies to journalists and
then believe what they read.
> *Aphorisms and More Aphorisms* (1909)

Jiddu Krishnamurti d. 1986
Indian spiritual philosopher

1 Truth is a pathless land, and you cannot approach it by any path whatsoever, by any religion, by any sect.
   speech in Holland, 3 August 1929

Kris Kristofferson 1936–
American actor

2 Freedom's just another word for nothin' left to lose,
   Nothin' ain't worth nothin', but it's free.
   'Me and Bobby McGee' (1969 song, with Fred Foster)

Leopold Kronecker 1823–91
German mathematician

3 God made the integers, all the rest is the work of man.
   Jahrsberichte der Deutschen Mathematiker Vereinigung

Stanley Kubrick 1928–99
American film director

4 The great nations have always acted like gangsters, and the small nations like prostitutes.
   in Guardian 5 June 1963

Satish Kumar 1937–
Indian writer

5 Lead me from death to life, from falsehood to truth.
   Lead me from despair to hope, from fear to trust.
   Lead me from hate to love, from war to peace.
   Let peace fill our heart, our world, our universe.
   'Prayer for Peace' (1981); adapted from the **Upanishads**; see **Upanishads** 344:12

Milan Kundera 1929–
Czech novelist

6 The struggle of man against power is the struggle of memory against forgetting.
   The Book of Laughter and Forgetting (1979) pt. 1, ch. 2

7 The unbearable lightness of being.
   title of novel (1984)

8 Mankind's true moral test, its fundamental test (which lies deeply buried from view) consists of its attitudes towards those who are at its mercy: animals.
   The Unbearable Lightness of Being (1984)

Thomas Kyd 1558–94
English dramatist

9 Hieronimo is mad again.
   alternative title given to *The Spanish Tragedy* in 1615

Jean de la Bruyère 1645–96
French satiric moralist

10 *Il faut rire avant que d'être heureux, de peur de mourir sans avoir ri.*
   We must laugh before we are happy, for fear of dying without having laughed at all.
   Les Caractères ou les moeurs de ce siècle (1688) 'Du Coeur'

11 *Le commencement et le déclin de l'amour se font sentir par l'embarras où l'on est de se trouver seuls.*
   The onset and the waning of love make themselves felt in the uneasiness experienced at being alone together.
   Les Caractères ou les moeurs de ce siècle (1688) 'Du Coeur'

Jean de la Fontaine 1621–95
French poet

12 Death never takes the wise man by surprise; he is always ready to go.
   Fables bk. 8 (1678–9) 'La Mort et le Mourant'; see **Montaigne** 242:16

Jules Laforgue 1860–87
French poet

13 *Ah! que la vie est quotidienne.*
   Oh, what a day-to-day business life is.
   Complainte sur certains ennuis (1885)

Fiorello La Guardia 1882–1947
American politician

14 When I make a mistake, it's a beaut!
   on the appointment of Herbert O'Brien as a judge in 1936
   William Manners *Patience and Fortitude* (1976)

John Lahr 1941–
American critic

15 Society drives people crazy with lust and calls it advertising.
   in Guardian 2 August 1989

R. D. Laing 1927–89
Scottish psychiatrist

16 The divided self.
   title of book (1960) on schizophrenia

17 Madness need not be all breakdown. It may also be break-through.
   The Politics of Experience (1967) ch. 6

Lady Caroline Lamb 1785–1828
English wife of William Lamb, Lord Melbourne

18 Mad, bad, and dangerous to know.
   of Byron, after their first meeting at a ball
   diary, March 1812; in Elizabeth Jenkins *Lady Caroline Lamb* (1932)

Charles Lamb 1775–1834
English writer

19 Presents, I often say, endear Absents.
   Essays of Elia (1823) 'A Dissertation upon Roast Pig'

20 The human species, according to the best theory I can form of it, is composed of two

distinct races, *the men who borrow*, and *the men who lend.*
Essays of Elia (1823) 'The Two Races of Men'

1 Your *borrowers of books*—those mutilators of collections, spoilers of the symmetry of shelves, and creators of odd volumes.
Essays of Elia (1823) 'The Two Races of Men'

2 Not many sounds in life . . . exceed in interest a knock at the door.
Essays of Elia (1823) 'Valentine's Day'

3 Books think for me.
Last Essays of Elia (1833) 'Detached Thoughts on Books and Reading'

4 [A pun] is a pistol let off at the ear; not a feather to tickle the intellect.
Last Essays of Elia (1833) 'Popular Fallacies' no. 9

5 I have had playmates, I have had companions,
In my days of childhood, in my joyful school-days,—
All, all are gone, the old familiar faces.
'The Old Familiar Faces'

6 Nothing puzzles me more than time and space; and yet nothing troubles me less, as I never think about them.
letter to Thomas Manning, 2 January 1810, in E. W. Marrs (ed.) *Letters of Charles and Mary Lamb* (1978) vol. 3

7 When my sonnet was rejected, I exclaimed, 'Damn the age; I will write for Antiquity!'
letter to B. W. Proctor, 22 January 1829

8 The greatest pleasure I know, is to do a good action by stealth, and to have it found out by accident.
'Table Talk by the late Elia' in *The Athenaeum* 4 January 1834

John George Lambton *see* Lord Durham

George Lamming 1927–
Barbados-born novelist and poet

9 In the castle of my skin.
title of novel (1953)

Norman Lamont 1942–
British Conservative politician

10 Rising unemployment and the recession have been the price that we've had to pay to get inflation down. [Labour shouts] That is a price well worth paying.
speech in the House of Commons, 16 May 1991

11 The green shoots of economic spring are appearing once again.
often misquoted as, 'the green shoots of recovery'
speech at Conservative Party Conference, 9 October 1991

12 We give the impression of being in office but not in power.
as a backbencher
speech in the House of Commons, 9 June 1993

Giuseppe di Lampedusa
1896–1957
Italian writer

13 If we want things to stay as they are, things will have to change.
The Leopard (1957)

Walter Savage Landor 1775–1864
English poet

14 I strove with none; for none was worth my strife;
Nature I loved, and, next to Nature, Art.
'Dying Speech of an Old Philosopher' (1853)

Andrew Lang 1844–1912
Scottish man of letters

15 They hear like ocean on a western beach
The surge and thunder of the Odyssey.
'The Odyssey' (1881)

16 He uses statistics as a drunken man uses lamp posts—for support rather than illumination.
Alan L. Mackay *Harvest of a Quiet Eye* (1977); attributed

Susanne Langer 1895–1985
American philosopher

17 Art is the objectification of feeling, and the subjectification of nature.
Mind (1967) vol. 1

William Langland *c.*1330–*c.*1400
English poet

18 In a somer seson, whan softe was the sonne.
The Vision of Piers Plowman B text (ed. A. V. C. Schmidt, 1987) prologue l. 1

Stephen Langton d. 1228
English cleric, Archbishop of Canterbury

19 *Veni, Sancte Spiritus,*
Et emitte coelitus
Lucis tuae radium.
Come, Holy Spirit, and send out from heaven the beam of your light.
The 'Golden Sequence' for Whit Sunday (also attributed to several others, notably Pope Innocent III)

Lao Tzu *c.*604–*c.*531 BC
Chinese philosopher; founder of Taoism
textual translations are those of Wing-Tsit Chan, 1963

20 The Tao [Way] that can be told of is not the eternal Tao;
The name that can be named is not the eternal name.
The Nameless is the origin of Heaven and Earth;
The Named is the mother of all things.
Tao-te Ching ch. 1

21 Front and back follow each other.
Therefore the sage manages affairs without action
And spreads doctrines without words.
Tao-te Ching ch. 2

1 Heaven and earth are not humane
They regard all things as straw dogs.
The sage is not humane.
He regards all people as straw dogs.
   Tao-te Ching ch. 5

2 The best [rulers] are those whose existence
is [merely] known by the people.
The next best are those who are loved and
praised.
The next are those who are feared.
And the next are those who are reviled . . .
[The great rulers] accomplish their task;
they complete their work.
Nevertheless their people say that they
simply follow Nature.
   Tao-te Ching ch. 17

3 Let people hold on to these:
Manifest plainness,
Embrace simplicity,
Reduce selfishness,
Have few desires.
   Tao-te Ching ch. 19

4 All things in the world come from being.
And being comes from non-being.
   Tao-te Ching ch. 40

5 Tao produced the One.
The One produced the two.
The two produced the three.
And the three produced the ten thousand
things.
The ten thousand things carry the yin and
embrace the yang,
and through the blending of the material
force they achieve harmony.
   Tao-te Ching ch. 42

6 One may know the world without going out
of doors.
One may see the Way of Heaven without
looking through windows.
The further one goes, the less one knows.
   Tao-te Ching ch. 47

7 The pursuit of learning is to increase day
after day.
The pursuit of Tao is to decrease day after
day.
It is to decrease and further decrease until
one reaches the point of taking no action.
No action is undertaken, and yet nothing is
left undone.
   Tao-te Ching ch. 48

8 He who knows does not speak.
He who speaks does not know.
   Tao-te Ching ch. 56

9 The more laws and orders are made
prominent,
The more thieves and bandits there will be.
   Tao-te Ching ch. 57

10 There is nothing softer and weaker than
water,
And yet there is nothing better for attacking
hard and strong things.
For this reason there is no substitute for it.
All the world knows that the weak
overcomes the strong and the soft
overcomes the hard.

But none can practice it.
   Tao-te Ching ch. 78

Dionysius Lardner 1793–1859
Irish scientific writer

11 Men might as well project a voyage to the
moon as attempt to employ steam
navigation against the stormy North
Atlantic Ocean.
   speech to the British Association for the
   Advancement of Science, 1838

Ring Lardner 1885–1933
American writer

12 Are you lost daddy I arsked tenderly.
Shut up he explained.
   The Young Immigrunts (1920) ch. 10

James Larkin 1867–1947
Irish labour leader

13 Hell has no terror for me. I have lived there.
Thirty six years of hunger and poverty have
been my portion. They cannot terrify me
with hell. Better to be in hell with Dante
and Davitt than to be in heaven with Carson
and Murphy.
*in 1913, during the 'Dublin lockout' labour
dispute*
   Ulick O'Connor *The Troubles* (rev. ed., 1996)

Philip Larkin 1922–85
English poet

14 Sexual intercourse began
In nineteen sixty-three
(Which was rather late for me) —
Between the end of the *Chatterley* ban
And the Beatles' first LP.
   'Annus Mirabilis' (1974)

15 What will survive of us is love.
   'An Arundel Tomb' (1964)

16 What are days for?
Days are where we live.
   'Days' (1964)

17 Life is first boredom, then fear.
   'Dockery & Son' (1964)

18 And that will be England gone,
The shadows, the meadows, the lanes,
The guildhalls, the carved choirs.
There'll be books; it will linger on
In galleries; but all that remains
For us will be concrete and tyres.
   'Going, Going' (1974)

19 Nothing, like something, happens
anywhere.
   'I Remember, I Remember' (1955)

20 Never such innocence again.
   'MCMXIV' (1964)

21 They fuck you up, your mum and dad.
They may not mean to, but they do.
They fill you with the faults they had
And add some extra, just for you.
   'This Be The Verse' (1974)

22 Man hands on misery to man.
It deepens like a coastal shelf.

Get out as early as you can,
And don't have any kids yourself.
'This Be The Verse' (1974)

1 Why should I let the toad *work*
Squat on my life?
Can't I use my wit as a pitchfork
And drive the brute off?
'Toads' (1955)

2 A beginning, a muddle, and an end.
on the 'classic formula' for a novel
in *New Fiction* no. 15, January 1978; see **Aristotle**
15:16

3 Deprivation is for me what daffodils were
for Wordsworth.
Required Writing (1983); see **Wordsworth** 364:18

Duc de la Rochefoucauld 1613–80
French moralist

4 We are all strong enough to bear the
misfortunes of others.
Maximes (1678) no. 19

5 There is no disguise which can hide love for
long where it exists, or feign it where it does
not.
Maximes (1678) no. 70

6 Everyone complains of his memory, and no
one complains of his judgement.
Maximes (1678) no. 89

7 Hypocrisy is a tribute which vice pays to
virtue.
Maximes (1678) no. 218

8 The height of cleverness is to be able to
conceal it.
Maximes (1678) no. 245

9 Absence diminishes commonplace passions
and increases great ones, as the wind
extinguishes candles and kindles fire.
Maximes (1678) no. 276; see **Bussy-Rabutin**
78:23, **Francis de Sales** 141:11

10 In the misfortune of our best friends, we
always find something which is not
displeasing to us.
Réflexions ou Maximes Morales (1665) maxim 99

Hugh Latimer *c*.1485–1555
English Protestant martyr

11 *Gutta cavat lapidem, non vi sed saepe cadendo.*
The drop of rain maketh a hole in the stone,
not by violence, but by oft falling.
The Second Sermon preached before the King's Majesty
(19 April 1549); see **Ovid** 255:25

12 Be of good comfort Master Ridley, and play
the man. We shall this day light such a
candle by God's grace in England, as (I trust)
shall never be put out.
prior to being burned for heresy, 16 October 1555
John Foxe *Actes and Monuments* (1570 ed.); see
Bible 42:19

Harry Lauder 1870–1950
Scottish music-hall entertainer

13 Keep right on to the end of the road,
Keep right on to the end.

Tho' the way be long, let your heart be
strong,
Keep right on round the bend.
'The End of the Road' (1924 song)

14 I love a lassie, a bonnie, bonnie lassie,
She's as pure as the lily in the dell.
She's as sweet as the heather, the bonnie
bloomin' heather—
Mary, ma Scotch Bluebell.
'I Love a Lassie' (1905 song)

15 Roamin' in the gloamin'.
'Roamin' in the Gloamin'' (1911 song)

Stan Laurel 1890–1965
American film comedian, born in Britain

16 Another nice mess you've gotten me into.
often 'another fine mess'
Another Fine Mess (1930 film) and many other
Laurel and Hardy films; spoken by Oliver Hardy

Wilfrid Laurier 1841–1919
*Canadian Liberal statesman, Prime Minister
1896–1911*

17 The nineteenth century was the century of
the United States. I think we can claim that
it is Canada that shall fill the twentieth
century.
speech in Ottawa, 18 January 1904

D. H. Lawrence 1885–1930
English novelist and poet

18 Pornography is the attempt to insult sex, to
do dirt on it.
Phoenix (1936) 'Pornography and Obscenity'
ch. 3

19 Never trust the artist. Trust the tale. The
proper function of a critic is to save the tale
from the artist who created it.
Studies in Classic American Literature (1923) ch. 1

20 Be a good animal, true to your instincts.
The White Peacock (1911) pt. 2, ch. 2

21 Don't you find it a beautiful clean thought, a
world empty of people, just uninterrupted
grass, and a hare sitting up?
Women in Love (1920) ch. 11

22 How beastly the bourgeois is
Especially the male of the species.
'How Beastly the Bourgeois Is' (1929)

23 I never saw a wild thing
Sorry for itself.
'Self-Pity' (1929)

24 Now it is autumn and the falling fruit
And the long journey towards oblivion . . .
Have you built your ship of death, O have
you?
O build your ship of death, for you will need
it.
'Ship of Death' (1932)

25 Not I, not I, but the wind that blows through
me!
'Song of a Man who has Come Through' (1917)

26 When I read Shakespeare I am struck with
wonder

That such trivial people should muse and
thunder
In such lovely language.
'When I Read Shakespeare' (1929)

1 The dead don't die. They look on and help.
letter to J. Middleton Murry, 2 February 1923

T. E. Lawrence 1888–1935
English soldier and writer

2 I loved you, so I drew these tides of men into
my hands and wrote my will across the
sky in stars.
The Seven Pillars of Wisdom (1926) dedication

Kenneth L. Lay 1942–
American businessman, former CEO of Enron

3 I am deeply troubled about asserting these
rights, because it may be perceived by some
that I have something to hide.
*invoking his Fifth Amendment protection and
declining to answer Congress's questions on the
Enron collapse*
in *Newsweek* 25 February 2002

Irving Layton 1912–
Canadian poet

4 We love in another's soul
whatever of ourselves
we can deposit in it;
the greater the deposit,
the greater the love.
The Whole Bloody Bird (1969) 'Aphs'

Emma Lazarus 1849–87
American poet

5 Give me your tired, your poor,
Your huddled masses yearning to breathe
free.
inscription on the Statue of Liberty, New York
'The New Colossus' (1883)

Stephen Leacock 1869–1944
Canadian humorist

6 Advertising may be described as the science
of arresting human intelligence long
enough to get money from it.
Garden of Folly (1924) 'The Perfect Salesman'

7 Lord Ronald said nothing; he flung himself
from the room, flung himself upon his
horse and rode madly off in all directions.
Nonsense Novels (1911) 'Gertrude the Governess'

Edward Lear 1812–88
English artist and writer of humorous verse

8 Who, or why, or which, or what,
Is the Akond of Swat?
'The Akond of Swat' (1888)

9 There was an Old Man with a beard,
Who said, 'It is just as I feared!—
Two Owls and a Hen,
Four Larks and a Wren,
Have all built their nests in my beard!'
A Book of Nonsense (1846)

10 On the coast of Coromandel

Where the early pumpkins blow,
In the middle of the woods,
Lived the Yonghy-Bonghy-Bó.
'The Courtship of the Yonghy-Bonghy-Bó' (1871)

11 The Dong with a luminous nose.
title of poem (1871)

12 Far and few, far and few,
Are the lands where the Jumblies live;
Their heads are green, and their hands are
blue,
And they went to sea in a Sieve.
'The Jumblies' (1871)

13 There was an old man of Thermopylae,
Who never did anything properly.
More Nonsense (1872) 'One Hundred Nonsense
Pictures and Rhymes'

14 'How pleasant to know Mr Lear!'
Who has written such volumes of stuff!
Some think him ill-tempered and queer,
But a few think him pleasant enough.
Nonsense Songs (1871) preface

15 The Owl and the Pussy-Cat went to sea
In a beautiful pea-green boat.
They took some honey, and plenty of
money,
Wrapped up in a five-pound note.
'The Owl and the Pussy-Cat' (1871)

16 Pussy said to the Owl, 'You elegant fowl!
How charmingly sweet you sing!
O let us be married! too long we have
tarried:
But what shall we do for a ring?'
They sailed away for a year and a day,
To the land where the Bong-tree grows,
And there in a wood a Piggy-wig stood
With a ring at the end of his nose.
'The Owl and the Pussy-Cat' (1871)

17 They dined on mince, and slices of quince,
Which they ate with a runcible spoon;
And hand in hand, on the edge of the sand,
They danced by the light of the moon.
'The Owl and the Pussy-Cat' (1871)

18 The Pobble who has no toes
Had once as many as we;
When they said, 'Some day you may lose
them all';—
He replied,—'Fish fiddle de-dee!'
'The Pobble Who Has No Toes' (1871)

19 He has gone to fish, for his Aunt Jobiska's
Runcible Cat with crimson whiskers!
'The Pobble Who Has No Toes' (1871)

Timothy Leary 1920–96
American psychologist

20 If you take the game of life seriously, if you
take your nervous system seriously, if you
take your sense organs seriously, if you take
the energy process seriously, you must turn
on, tune in and drop out.
lecture, June 1966, in *The Politics of Ecstasy* (1968)
ch. 21

21 The PC is the LSD of the '90s.
remark made in the early 1990s; in *Guardian* 1
June 1996

1 Why not? Why not? Why not? Yeah.
last words; in *Independent* 1 June 1996

Mary Elizabeth Lease 1853–1933
American writer and lecturer

2 Kansas had better stop raising corn and begin raising hell.
E. J. James et al. *Notable American Women 1607–1950* (1971) vol. 2

F. R. Leavis 1895–1978
English literary critic

3 The common pursuit.
title of book (1952)

Fran Lebowitz 1946–
American writer

4 There is no such thing as inner peace. There is only nervousness or death.
Metropolitan Life (1978)

5 The best fame is a writer's fame: it's enough to get a table at a good restaurant, but not enough that you get interrupted when you eat.
in *Observer* 30 May 1993 'Sayings of the Week'

Stanislaw Lec 1909–66
Polish writer

6 Is it progress if a cannibal uses knife and fork?
Unkempt Thoughts (1962)

John le Carré 1931–
English thriller writer

7 The spy who came in from the cold.
title of novel (1963)

Le Corbusier 1887–1965
French architect

8 A house is a machine for living in.
Vers une architecture (1923); see **Tolstoy** 341:4

9 A hundred times I have thought: New York is a catastrophe, and fifty times: it is a beautiful catastrophe.
When the Cathedrals were White (1947) 'The Fairy Catastrophe'

Alexandre Auguste Ledru-Rollin 1807–74
French politician

10 Ah well! I am their leader, I really had to follow them!
E. de Mirecourt *Les Contemporains* vol. 14 (1857) 'Ledru-Rollin'

Gypsy Rose Lee 1914–70
American striptease artiste

11 God is love, but get it in writing.
attributed

Harper Lee 1926–
American novelist

12 Shoot all the bluejays you want, if you can hit 'em, but remember it's a sin to kill a mockingbird.
To Kill a Mockingbird (1960) ch. 10

Henry Lee ('Light-Horse Harry') 1756–1818
American soldier and politician

13 A citizen, first in war, first in peace, and first in the hearts of his countrymen.
Funeral Oration on the death of General Washington (1800)

Laurie Lee 1914–97
English writer

14 I was set down from the carrier's cart at the age of three; and there with a sense of bewilderment and terror my life in the village began.
Cider with Rosie (1959)

Nathaniel Lee *c.*1653–92
English dramatist

15 They called me mad, and I called them mad, and damn them, they outvoted me.
attributed

Robert E. Lee 1807–70
American Confederate general

16 It is well that war is so terrible. We should grow too fond of it.
after the battle of Fredericksburg, December 1862
attributed

17 *refusing an offer to write his memoirs:*
I should be trading on the blood of my men.
attributed, perhaps apocryphal

Ursula K. Le Guin 1929–
American writer

18 Love doesn't just sit there, like a stone, it has to be made, like bread; remade all the time, made new.
The Lathe of Heaven (1971) ch. 10

Tom Lehrer 1928–
American humorist

19 Plagiarize! Let no one else's work evade your eyes,
Remember why the good Lord made your eyes.
'Lobachevski' (1953 song)

20 Poisoning pigeons in the park.
song title, 1953

21 It is sobering to consider that when Mozart was my age he had already been dead for a year.
N. Shapiro (ed.) *An Encyclopedia of Quotations about Music* (1978)

Gottfried Wilhelm Leibniz
1646–1716
German philosopher

1 *Nihil est sine ratione.*
There is nothing without a reason.
  Studies in Physics and the Nature of Body (1671)

2 *Eadem sunt quorum unum potest substitui alteri salva veritate.*
Two things are identical if one can be substituted for the other without affecting the truth.
  'Table de définitions' (1704) in L. Coutourat (ed.) *Opuscules et fragments inédits de Leibniz* (1903)

Fred W. Leigh d. 1924
British songwriter

3 Can't get away to marry you today,
My wife won't let me!
  'Waiting at the Church (My Wife Won't Let Me)' (1906 song)

4 Why am I always the bridesmaid,
Never the blushing bride?
  'Why Am I Always the Bridesmaid?' (1917 song, with Charles Collins and Lily Morris)

Curtis E. LeMay 1906–90
American Air Force officer

5 They've got to draw in their horns and stop their aggression, or we're going to bomb them back into the Stone Age.
on the North Vietnamese
  Mission with LeMay (1965)

Lenin 1870–1924
Russian revolutionary

6 Imperialism is the monopoly stage of capitalism.
  Imperialism as the Last Stage of Capitalism (1916) ch. 7 'Briefest possible definition of imperialism'

7 While the State exists, there can be no freedom. When there is freedom there will be no State.
  State and Revolution (1919) ch. 5

8 What is to be done?
  title of pamphlet (1902); originally the title of a novel (1863) by N. G. Chernyshevsky

9 Communism is Soviet power plus the electrification of the whole country.
  Report to 8th Congress, 1920

10 Who? Whom? [i.e. Who masters whom?]
definition of political science, meaning 'Who will outstrip whom?'
  in *Polnoe Sobranie Sochinenii* vol. 44 (1970) 17 October 1921 and elsewhere

11 A good man fallen among Fabians.
of George Bernard Shaw
  Arthur Ransome *Six Weeks in Russia in 1919* (1919) 'Notes of Conversations with Lenin'

12 Liberty is precious—so precious that it must be rationed.
  Sidney and Beatrice Webb *Soviet Communism* (1936)

John Lennon 1940–80
English pop singer and songwriter
see also **Lennon and McCartney**

13 Happiness is a warm gun.
  title of song (1968)

14 Imagine there's no heaven,
It's easy if you try.
  'Imagine' (1971 song)

15 Will the people in the cheaper seats clap your hands? All the rest of you, if you'll just rattle your jewellery.
  at the Royal Variety Performance, 4 November 1963

16 We're more popular than Jesus now; I don't know which will go first—rock 'n' roll or Christianity.
of The Beatles
  interview in *Evening Standard* 4 March 1966

John Lennon 1940–80
and Paul McCartney 1942–
English pop singers and songwriters
see also **Lennon**

17 For I don't care too much for money,
For money can't buy me love.
  'Can't Buy Me Love' (1964 song)

18 All the lonely people, where do they all come from?
  'Eleanor Rigby' (1966 song)

19 Give peace a chance.
  title of song (1969)

20 It's been a hard day's night,
And I've been working like a dog.
  'A Hard Day's Night' (1964 song)

21 Strawberry fields forever.
  title of song (1967)

22 She's got a ticket to ride, but she don't care.
  'Ticket to Ride' (1965 song)

23 Will you still need me, will you still feed me,
When I'm sixty four?
  'When I'm Sixty Four' (1967 song)

24 Oh I get by with a little help from my friends,
Mm, I get high with a little help from my friends.
  'With a Little Help From My Friends' (1967 song)

Dan Leno (George Galvin) 1860–1904
English entertainer

25 Ah! what is man? Wherefore does he why? Whence did he whence? Whither is he withering?
  Dan Leno Hys Booke (1901) ch. 1

William Lenthall 1591–1662
English politician, Speaker of the House of Commons

1 I have neither eye to see, nor tongue to speak here, but as the House is pleased to direct me.
to **Charles I**, *on being asked if he had seen any of the five MPs whom the King had ordered to be arrested, 4 January 1642*
John Rushworth *Historical Collections. The Third Part* vol. 2 (1692)

Leonardo da Vinci 1452–1519
Italian painter and designer

2 In her [Nature's] inventions nothing is lacking, and nothing is superfluous.
Edward McCurdy (ed. and trans.) *Leonardo da Vinci's Notebooks* (1906) bk. 1

3 The span of a man's outspread arms is equal to his height.
Irma Richter (ed.) *Selections from the Notebooks of Leonardo da Vinci* (World's Classics, 1952)

4 The poet ranks far below the painter in the representation of visible things, and far below the musician in that of invisible things.
Irma A. Richter (ed.) *Selections from the Notebooks of Leonardo da Vinci* (1952)

Alan Jay Lerner 1918–86
American songwriter

5 Don't let it be forgot
That once there was a spot
For one brief shining moment that was known
As Camelot.
now particularly associated with the White House of John Fitzgerald **Kennedy**
'Camelot' (1960 song)

6 Why can't a woman be more like a man? Men are so honest, so thoroughly square.
'A Hymn to Him' (1956 song) in *My Fair Lady*

7 I've grown accustomed to her face.
title of song (1956) in *My Fair Lady*

8 The rain in Spain stays mainly in the plain.
'The Rain in Spain' (1956 song) in *My Fair Lady*

Doris Lessing 1919–
English writer

9 What of October, that ambiguous month, the month of tension, the unendurable month?
Martha Quest (1952) pt. 4, sect. 1

G. E. Lessing 1729–81
German dramatist and critic

10 One single grateful thought raised to heaven is the most perfect prayer.
Minna von Barnhelm (1767) act 2, sc. 7

Lord Leverhulme 1851–1925
English industrialist and philanthropist

11 Half the money I spend on advertising is wasted, and the trouble is I don't know which half.
David Ogilvy *Confessions of an Advertising Man* (1963)

Primo Levi 1919–87
Italian novelist and poet

12 Our language lacks words to express this offence, the demolition of a man.
of a year spent in Auschwitz
If This is a Man (1958)

Bernard Levin 1928–2004
British journalist

13 Whom the mad would destroy, they first make gods.
of **Mao** *Zedong in 1967*
Levin quoting himself in *The Times* 21 September 1987

Duc de Lévis 1764–1830
French soldier and writer

14 *Noblesse oblige.*
Nobility has its obligations.
Maximes et Réflexions (1812 ed.) 'Morale: Maximes et Préceptes' no. 73

15 *Gouverner, c'est choisir.*
To govern is to choose.
Maximes et Réflexions (1812 ed.) 'Politique: Maximes de Politique' no. 19

C. S. Lewis 1898–1963
English literary scholar

16 No one ever told me that grief felt so like fear.
A Grief Observed (1961)

17 Every one says forgiveness is a lovely idea, until they have something to forgive.
Mere Christianity (1952) bk. 3, ch. 7

18 We have trained them [men] to think of the Future as a promised land which favoured heroes attain—not as something which everyone reaches at the rate of sixty minutes an hour, whatever he does, whoever he is.
The Screwtape Letters (1942) no. 25

19 She's the sort of woman who lives for others—you can always tell the others by their hunted expression.
The Screwtape Letters (1942) no. 26

20 A young man who wishes to remain a sound atheist cannot be too careful of his reading.
Surprised by Joy (1955)

21 Often when I pray I wonder if I am not posting letters to a non-existent address.
letter to Arthur Greeves, 24 December 1930

22 He that but looketh on a plate of ham and eggs to lust after it, hath already committed breakfast with it in his heart.
letter, 10 March 1954

1 Courage is not simply *one* of the virtues but
the form of every virtue at the testing point.
  Cyril Connolly *The Unquiet Grave* (1944) ch. 3

David Lewis 1909–81
Canadian politician

2 Louder voices: the corporate welfare bums.
  title of book, 1972

George Cornewall Lewis 1806–63
British Liberal politician and writer

3 Life would be tolerable but for its
amusements.
  in *The Times* 18 September 1872; see **Surtees**
  328:1

Sam M. Lewis 1885–1959
and Joe Young 1889–1939
American songwriters

4 How 'ya gonna keep 'em down on the farm
(after they've seen Paree)?
  title of song (1919)

Sinclair Lewis 1885–1951
American novelist

5 Our American professors like their
literature clear and cold and pure and very
dead.
  The American Fear of Literature (Nobel Prize
  Address, 12 December 1930)

6 It can't happen here.
  title of novel (1935)

George Leybourne d. 1884
English songwriter

7 He'd fly through the air with the greatest of
ease,
A daring young man on the flying trapeze.
  'The Flying Trapeze' (1868 song)

Liberace 1919–87
American showman

8 When the reviews are bad I tell my staff that
they can join me as I cry all the way to the
bank.
  Autobiography (1973) ch. 2

A. J. Liebling 1904–63
American writer

9 Freedom of the press is guaranteed only to
those who own one.
  'The Wayward Press: Do you belong in
  Journalism?' (1960)

Gordon Lightfoot 1938–
Canadian singer and songwriter

10 Does any one know where the love of God
goes
When the waves turn the minutes to hours?
  'The Wreck of the Edmund Fitzgerald' (1976
  song)

Charles-Joseph, Prince de Ligne
1735–1814
Belgian soldier

11 *Le congrès ne marche pas, il danse.*
The Congress makes no progress; it dances.
  Auguste de la Garde-Chambonas *Souvenirs du
  Congrès de Vienne* (1820) ch. 1

Abraham Lincoln 1809–65
American statesman, 16th President of the US

12 To give victory to the right, not bloody
bullets, but peaceful ballots only, are
necessary.
  *often quoted as, 'The ballot is stronger than the
  bullet'*
  speech, 18 May 1858

13 'A house divided against itself cannot stand.'
I believe this government cannot endure
permanently, half slave and half free.
  speech, 16 June 1858; see **Bible** 46:24

14 What is conservatism? Is it not adherence to
the old and tried, against the new and
untried?
  speech, 27 February 1860, in R. P. Basler (ed.)
  Collected Works . . . (1953) vol. 3

15 Let us have faith that right makes might,
and in that faith, let us, to the end, dare to
do our duty as we understand it.
  speech, 27 February 1860, in R. P. Basler (ed.)
  Collected Works . . . (1953) vol. 3

16 The mystic chords of memory, stretching
from every battlefield and patriot grave to
every living heart and heartstone all over
this broad land, will yet swell the chorus of
the Union when again touched, as surely
they will be, by the better angels of our
nature.
  first inaugural address, 4 March 1861

17 I think the necessity of being *ready*
increases. Look to it.
  the whole of a letter to Governor Andrew
  Curtin of Pennsylvania, 8 April 1861, in R. P.
  Basler (ed.) *Collected Works . . .* (1953) vol. 4

18 My paramount object in this struggle is to
save the Union . . . If I could save the Union
without freeing any slave, I would do it; and
if I could save it by freeing all the slaves, I
would do it; and if I could save it by freeing
some and leaving others alone, I would also
do that.
  letter to Horace Greeley, 22 August 1862, in R. P.
  Basler (ed.) *Collected Works . . .* (1953) vol. 5

19 In giving freedom to the slave, we assure
freedom to the free—honourable alike in
what we give and what we preserve. We
shall nobly save, or meanly lose, the last,
best hope of earth.
  Annual Message to Congress, 1 December 1862

20 Fourscore and seven years ago our fathers
brought forth upon this continent a new
nation, conceived in liberty, and dedicated
to the proposition that all men are created

equal . . . In a larger sense we cannot dedicate, we cannot consecrate, we cannot hallow this ground. The brave men, living and these dead, who struggled here, have consecrated it far above our power to add or detract. The world will little note, nor long remember, what we say here, but it can never forget what they did here. It is for us, the living, rather to be dedicated here to the unfinished work which they who fought here have thus far so nobly advanced . . . we here highly resolve that the dead shall not have died in vain, that this nation, under God, shall have a new birth of freedom; and that government of the people, by the people, and for the people, shall not perish from the earth.

the Lincoln Memorial inscription reads 'by the people, for the people'

> address at the dedication of the National Cemetery at Gettysburg, 19 November 1863, as reported the following day, in R. P. Basler (ed.) *Collected Works . . .* (1953) vol. 7; see **Webster** 352:18

1 The Lord prefers common-looking people. That is the reason he makes so many of them.

> John Hay *Letters of John Hay and Extracts from Diary* (1908) vol 1, 23 December 1863

2 I claim not to have controlled events, but confess plainly that events have controlled me.

> letter to A. G. Hodges, 4 April 1864

3 It is not best to swap horses when crossing streams.

> reply to National Union League, 9 June 1864

4 Fondly do we hope, fervently do we pray, that this mighty scourge of war may speedily pass away. Yet, if God wills that it continue until all the wealth piled by the bond-man's two hundred and fifty years of unrequited toil shall be sunk, and until every drop of blood drawn with the lash shall be paid by another drawn with the sword, as was said three thousand years ago, so still it must be said, 'The judgements of the Lord are true and righteous altogether.'

> second inaugural address, 4 March 1865, in R. P. Basler (ed.) *Collected Works . . .* (1953) vol. 8; see **Book of Common Prayer** 62:12

5 With malice toward none; with charity for all; with firmness in the right, as God gives us to see the right, let us strive on to finish the work we are in: to bind up the nation's wounds; to care for him who shall have borne the battle, and for his widow and his orphan, to do all which may achieve and cherish a just and lasting peace among ourselves, and with all nations.

> second inaugural address, 4 March 1865

6 People who like this sort of thing will find this the sort of thing they like.

> *judgement of a book*
> G. W. E. Russell *Collections and Recollections* (1898) ch. 30

7 So you're the little woman who wrote the book that made this great war!

> *on meeting Harriet Beecher* **Stowe**, *author of* Uncle Tom's Cabin
> Carl Sandburg *Abraham Lincoln: The War Years* (1936) vol. 2, ch. 39

8 You may fool all the people some of the time; you can even fool some of the people all the time; but you can't fool all of the people all the time.

> *also attributed to Phineas* **Barnum**
> Alexander K. McClure *Lincoln's Yarns and Stories* (1904)

Vachel Lindsay 1879–1931
American poet

9 Booth led boldly with his big bass drum—
(Are you washed in the blood of the Lamb?)

> 'General William Booth Enters into Heaven' (1913); see **Bible** 53:8

Graham Linehan
and Arthur Mathews
Irish writers

10 Careful now!

> *placard alerting Craggy Island to a banned film*
> 'The Passion of St Tibulus' (1994), episode from *Father Ted* (Channel 4 TV, 1994–8)

Art Linkletter 1912–
American broadcaster and humorist

11 The four stages of man are infancy, childhood, adolescence and obsolescence.

> *A Child's Garden of Misinformation* (1965) ch. 8

George Linley 1798–1865
English songwriter

12 Among our ancient mountains,
And from our lovely vales,
Oh, let the prayer re-echo:
'God bless the Prince of Wales!'

> 'God Bless the Prince of Wales' (1862 song); translated from the Welsh original by J. C. Hughes (1837–87)

Lin Yutang 1895–1976
Chinese writer and philologist

13 A good traveller is one who does not know where he is going to, and a perfect traveller does not know where he came from.

> *The Importance of Living* (1938) ch. 11

Walter Lippmann 1889–1974
American journalist

14 The final test of a leader is that he leaves behind him in other men the conviction and the will to carry on.

> in *New York Herald Tribune* 14 April 1945

Joan Littlewood 1914–2002
and Charles Chilton 1914–

15 Oh what a lovely war.

> title of stage show (1963)

Maxim Litvinov 1876–1951
Soviet diplomat

1 Peace is indivisible.
note to the Allies, 25 February 1920; A. U. Pope
Maxim Litvinoff (1943)

Penelope Lively 1933–
English novelist

2 We are walking lexicons. In a single
sentence of idle chatter we preserve Latin,
Anglo-Saxon, Norse; we carry a museum
inside our heads, each day we
commemorate peoples of whom we have
never heard.
Moon Tiger (1987)

Ken Livingstone 1945–
British Labour politician

3 If voting changed anything, they'd abolish it.
title of book, 1987

Livy 59 BC–AD 17
Roman historian

4 *Vae victis.*
Down with the defeated!
*cry (already proverbial) of the Gallic King,
Brennus, on capturing Rome in 390 BC*
Ab Urbe Condita bk. 5, ch. 48, sect. 9

Richard Llewellyn (Richard
Llewellyn Lloyd) 1907–83
Welsh novelist and dramatist

5 How green was my valley.
title of book (1939)

Robert Lloyd
English poet

6 While all the art of Imitation,
Is pilf'ring from the first creation.
'Shakespeare' (1762)

David Lloyd George 1863–1945
British Liberal statesman; Prime Minister, 1916–22

7 The leal and trusty mastiff which is to watch
over our interests, but which runs away at
the first snarl of the trade unions . . . A
mastiff? It is the right hon. Gentleman's
poodle.
*on the House of Lords and A. J. Balfour
respectively*
in the House of Commons, 26 June 1907

8 A fully-equipped duke costs as much to keep
up as two Dreadnoughts; and dukes are just
as great a terror and they last longer.
speech at Newcastle, 9 October 1909, in *The
Times* 11 October 1909

9 At eleven o'clock this morning came to an
end the cruellest and most terrible war that
has ever scourged mankind. I hope we may

say that thus, this fateful morning, came to
an end all wars.
speech in the House of Commons, 11 November
1918; see Wells 354:13

10 What is our task? To make Britain a fit
country for heroes to live in.
speech at Wolverhampton, 23 November 1918

11 Unless I am mistaken, by the steps we have
taken [in Ireland] we have murder by the
throat.
speech at the Mansion House, 9 November 1920

12 Negotiating with de Valera . . . is like trying
to pick up mercury with a fork.
*to which de Valera replied, 'Why doesn't he use a
spoon?'*
M. J. MacManus *Eamon de Valera* (1944) ch. 6

John Locke 1632–1704
English philosopher

13 New opinions are always suspected, and
usually opposed, without any other reason
but because they are not already common.
An Essay concerning Human Understanding (1690)
'Dedicatory Epistle'

14 No man's knowledge here can go beyond his
experience.
An Essay concerning Human Understanding (1690)
bk. 2, ch. 1, sect. 19

15 It is one thing to show a man that he is in
error, and another to put him in possession
of truth.
An Essay concerning Human Understanding (1690)
bk. 4, ch. 7, sect. 11

16 All men are liable to error; and most men
are, in many points, by passion or interest,
under temptation to it.
An Essay concerning Human Understanding (1690)
bk. 4, ch. 20, sect. 17

17 Whatsoever . . . [man] removes out of the
state that nature hath provided and left it
in, he hath mixed his labour with, and
joined to it something that is his own, and
thereby makes it his property.
Second Treatise of Civil Government (1690) ch. 5,
sect. 27

18 The end of law is, not to abolish or restrain,
but to preserve and enlarge freedom.
Second Treatise of Civil Government (1690) ch. 6,
sect. 57

19 Man being . . . by nature all free, equal, and
independent, no one can be put out of this
estate, and subjected to the political power
of another, without his own consent.
Second Treatise of Civil Government (1690) ch. 8,
sect. 95

20 The only way by which any one divests
himself of his natural liberty and puts on
the bonds of civil society is by agreeing with
other men to join and unite into a
community.
Second Treatise of Civil Government (1690) ch. 8,
sect. 95

21 The great and chief end, therefore, of men's
uniting into commonwealths, and putting

themselves under government, is the preservation of their property.
Second Treatise of Civil Government (1690) ch. 9, sect. 124

John Gibson Lockhart 1794–1854
Scottish writer and critic

1 It is a better and a wiser thing to be a starved apothecary than a starved poet; so back to the shop Mr John, back to 'plasters, pills, and ointment boxes.'
reviewing Keats's Endymion
in *Blackwood's Edinburgh Magazine* August 1818

David Lodge 1935–
English novelist

2 Literature is mostly about having sex and not much about having children. Life is the other way round.
The British Museum is Falling Down (1965) ch. 4

Frank Loesser 1910–69
American songwriter

3 See what the boys in the back room will have
And tell them I'm having the same.
'Boys in the Back Room' (1939 song)

Christopher Logue 1926–
English poet

4 Come to the edge.
We might fall.
Come to the edge.
It's too high!
COME TO THE EDGE!
And they came
and he pushed
and they flew . . .
on Apollinaire
'Come to the edge' (1969)

Jack London 1876–1916
American novelist

5 The call of the wild.
title of novel (1903)

Henry Wadsworth Longfellow 1807–82
American poet

6 I shot an arrow into the air,
It fell to earth, I knew not where.
'The Arrow and the Song' (1845)

7 Thou, too, sail on, O Ship of State!
Sail on, O Union, strong and great!
'The Building of the Ship' (1849)

8 Between the dark and the daylight,
When the night is beginning to lower,
Comes a pause in the day's occupations,
That is known as the Children's Hour.
'The Children's Hour' (1859)

9 The cares that infest the day

Shall fold their tents, like the Arabs,
And as silently steal away.
'The Day is Done' (1844)

10 If you would hit the mark, you must aim a little above it;
Every arrow that flies feels the attraction of earth.
'Elegiac Verse' (1880)

11 This is the forest primeval.
Evangeline (1847) introduction

12 The shades of night were falling fast,
As through an Alpine village passed
A youth, who bore, 'mid snow and ice,
A banner with the strange device,
Excelsior!
'Excelsior' (1841)

13 I like that ancient Saxon phrase, which calls
The burial-ground God's-Acre!
'God's-Acre' (1841)

14 The holiest of all holidays are those
Kept by ourselves in silence and apart;
The secret anniversaries of the heart.
'Holidays' (1877)

15 The heights by great men reached and kept
Were not attained by sudden flight,
But they, while their companions slept,
Were toiling upward in the night.
'The Ladder of Saint Augustine' (1850)

16 A boy's will is the wind's will
And the thoughts of youth are long, long thoughts.
'My Lost Youth' (1858)

17 Not in the clamour of the crowded street,
Not in the shouts and plaudits of the throng,
But in ourselves, are triumph and defeat.
'The Poets' (1876)

18 Life is real! Life is earnest!
And the grave is not its goal;
Dust thou art, to dust returnest,
Was not spoken of the soul.
'A Psalm of Life' (1838); see **Bible** 34:22

19 Art is long, and Time is fleeting,
And our hearts, though stout and brave,
Still, like muffled drums, are beating
Funeral marches to the grave.
'A Psalm of Life' (1838); see **Hippocrates** 169:15

20 Trust no Future, howe'er pleasant!
Let the dead Past bury its dead!
Act,—act in the living Present!
Heart within, and God o'erhead!
'A Psalm of Life' (1838); see **Bible** 44:17

21 Lives of great men all remind us
We can make our lives sublime,
And, departing, leave behind us
Footprints on the sands of time.
'A Psalm of Life' (1838)

22 Let us, then, be up and doing,
With a heart for any fate;
Still achieving, still pursuing,
Learn to labour and to wait.
'A Psalm of Life' (1838)

1 Though the mills of God grind slowly, yet
  they grind exceeding small;
  Though with patience He stands waiting,
  with exactness grinds He all.
    'Retribution' (1870), translation of Friedrich von
    Logau (1604–55) *Sinnegedichte* (1654) no. 3224

2 A Lady with a Lamp shall stand
  In the great history of the land,
  A noble type of good,
  Heroic womanhood.
    *on Florence **Nightingale***
    'Santa Filomena' (1857)

3 By the shore of Gitche Gumee,
  By the shining Big-Sea-Water,
  Stood the wigwam of Nokomis.
    The Song of Hiawatha (1855) 'Hiawatha's
    Childhood'

4 Dark behind it rose the forest,
  Rose the black and gloomy pine-trees,
  Rose the firs with cones upon them;
  Bright before it beat the water,
  Beat the clear and sunny water,
  Beat the shining Big-Sea-Water.
    The Song of Hiawatha (1855) 'Hiawatha's
    Childhood'

5 Listen, my children, and you shall hear
  Of the midnight ride of Paul Revere,
  On the eighteenth of April in Seventy-five.
    Tales of a Wayside Inn pt. 1 (1863) 'The Landlord's
    Tale: Paul Revere's Ride'

6 One if by land and two if by sea;
  And I on the opposite shore will be,
  Ready to ride and sound the alarm.
    Tales of a Wayside Inn pt. 1 (1863) 'The Landlord's
    Tale: Paul Revere's Ride'; see **Revere** 275:8

7 The fate of a nation was riding that night.
    Tales of a Wayside Inn pt. 1 (1863) 'The Landlord's
    Tale: Paul Revere's Ride'

8 Ships that pass in the night, and speak each
  other in passing;
  Only a signal shown and a distant voice in
  the darkness.
    Tales of a Wayside Inn pt. 3 (1874) 'The
    Theologian's Tale: Elizabeth' pt. 4

9 Under a spreading chestnut tree
  The village smithy stands;
  The smith, a mighty man is he,
  With large and sinewy hands.
    'The Village Blacksmith' (1839)

10 Something attempted, something done,
  Has earned a night's repose.
    'The Village Blacksmith' (1839)

11 It was the schooner Hesperus,
  That sailed the wintry sea;
  And the skipper had taken his little
  daughter,
  To bear him company.
    'The Wreck of the Hesperus' (1839)

12 There was a little girl
  Who had a little curl
  Right in the middle of her forehead,
  When she was good
  She was very, very good,

But when she was bad she was horrid.
  *composed for, and sung to, his second daughter
  while a babe in arms, c.1850*
    B. R. Tucker-Macchetta *The Home Life of Henry W.
    Longfellow* (1882) ch. 5

Alice Roosevelt Longworth
1884–1980
American daughter of Theodore Roosevelt

13 If you haven't got anything good to say
  about anyone come and sit by me.
    maxim embroidered on a cushion in her home
    Michael Teague *Mrs L: Conversations with Alice
    Roosevelt Longworth* (1981)

Anita Loos 1893–1981
American writer

14 Gentlemen prefer blondes.
    title of book (1925)

15 So I really think that American gentlemen
  are the best after all, because kissing your
  hand may make you feel very very good but
  a diamond and safire bracelet lasts forever.
    Gentlemen Prefer Blondes (1925) ch. 4; see **Robin**
    277:13

Federico García Lorca 1899–1936
Spanish poet and dramatist

16 *A las cinco de la tarde.*
  Eran las cinco en punto de la tarde.
  Un niño trajo la blanca sábana
  a las cinco de la tarde.
  At five in the afternoon.
  It was exactly five in the afternoon.
  A boy brought the white sheet
  at five in the afternoon.
    Llanto por Ignacio Sánchez Mejías (1935) 'La Cogida
    y la muerte'

17 *Verde que te quiero verde.*
  Verde viento. Verdes ramas.
  El barco sobre la mar
  y el caballo en la montaña.
  Green how I love you green.
  Green wind.
  Green boughs.
  The ship on the sea
  and the horse on the mountain.
    Romance sonámbulo (1924–7)

Edward N. Lorenz 1917–
American meteorologist

18 Predictability: Does the flap of a butterfly's
  wings in Brazil set off a tornado in Texas?
    title of paper given to the American Association
    for the Advancement of Science, Washington,
    29 December 1979; James Gleick *Chaos* (1988)

Konrad Lorenz 1903–89
Austro-German zoologist

19 It is a good morning exercise for a research
  scientist to discard a pet hypothesis every
  day before breakfast. It keeps him young.
    Das Sogenannte Böse (1963; tr. Marjorie Latzke as
    On Aggression, 1966) ch. 2

Louis XIV (the 'Sun King') 1638–1715
French monarch, King from 1643

1 *L'État c'est moi.*
I am the State.
before the Parlement de Paris, 13 April 1655
   probably apocryphal; J. A. Dulaure *Histoire de Paris* (1834) vol. 6

2 *Il n'y a plus de Pyrénées.*
The Pyrenees are no more.
on the accession of his grandson to the throne of Spain, 1700
   attributed to Louis by Voltaire in *Siècle de Louis XIV* (1753) ch. 26, but to the Spanish Ambassador to France in the *Mercure Galant* (Paris) November 1700

Louis XVI 1754–93
French monarch, King from 1774; deposed in 1789

3 *diary entry for 14 July 1789, the day of the storming of the Bastille:*
Rien.
Nothing.
   Simon Schama *Citizens* (1989) ch. 10

Louis XVIII 1755–1824
French monarch, King from 1814

4 Remember that there is not one of you who does not carry in his cartridge-pouch the marshal's baton of the duke of Reggio; it is up to you to bring it forth.
   speech to Saint-Cyr cadets, 9 August 1819

5 *L'exactitude est la politesse des rois.*
Punctuality is the politeness of kings.
   attributed in *Souvenirs de J. Lafitte* (1844) bk. 1, ch. 3

Joe Louis 1914–81
American boxer

6 He can run. But he can't hide.
of Billy Conn, his opponent, before a heavyweight title fight, 19 June 1946
   Louis: *My Life Story* (1947)

Louis Philippe 1773–1850
French monarch, King 1830–48

7 Died, has he? Now I wonder what he meant by that?
of Talleyrand
   attributed, perhaps apocryphal

Ada Lovelace 1815–52
English mathematican

8 The Analytical Engine weaves algebraic patterns just as the Jacquard loom weaves flowers and leaves.
of Babbage's mechanical computer
   Luigi Menabrea *Sketch of the Analytical Engine invented by Charles Babbage* (1843), translated and annotated by Ada Lovelace, Note A

Richard Lovelace 1618–58
English poet

9 Stone walls do not a prison make,
Nor iron bars a cage;
Minds innocent and quiet take
That for an hermitage.
   'To Althea, From Prison' (1649)

10 I could not love thee, Dear, so much,
Loved I not honour more.
   'To Lucasta, Going to the Wars' (1649)

James Lovell 1928–
American astronaut

11 Houston, we've had a problem.
on Apollo 13 space mission, 14 April 1970
   in *The Times* 15 April 1970

Samuel Lover 1797–1868
Irish writer

12 When once the itch of literature comes over a man, nothing can cure it but the scratching of a pen.
   Handy Andy (1842) ch. 36

13 Young Rory O'More courted Kathaleen bawn,
He was bold as a hawk, and she soft as the dawn.
   'Rory O'More' (1837 song)

David Low 1891–1963
British political cartoonist

14 Colonel Blimp.
   Cartoon creation, proponent of reactionary establishment opinions

Robert Lowe, Lord Sherbrooke 1811–92
British Liberal politician

15 The Chancellor of the Exchequer is a man whose duties make him more or less of a taxing machine. He is intrusted with a certain amount of misery which it is his duty to distribute as fairly as he can.
   speech, House of Commons, 11 April 1870

Amy Lowell 1874–1925
American poet

16 And the softness of my body will be guarded by embrace
By each button, hook, and lace.
For the man who should loose me is dead,
Fighting with the Duke in Flanders,
In a pattern called a war.
Christ! What are patterns for?
   'Patterns' (1916)

17 All books are either dreams or swords,
You can cut, or you can drug, with words.
   'Sword Blades and Poppy Seed' (1914); see **Farquhar** 134:8

James Russell Lowell 1819–91
American poet

18 There comes Poe with his raven like Barnaby Rudge,
Three-fifths of him genius, and two-fifths sheer fudge.
   'A Fable for Critics' (1848) l. 1215; see **Poe** 265:19

1 Blessèd are the horny hands of toil!
'A Glance Behind the Curtain' (1844); see
Salisbury 284:21

2 Once to every man and nation comes the
moment to decide,
In the strife of Truth with Falsehood, for the
good or evil side.
'The Present Crisis' (1845)

3 Truth forever on the scaffold, Wrong forever
on the throne.
'The Present Crisis' (1845)

Robert Lowell 1917–77
American poet

4 Their monument sticks like a fishbone
in the city's throat.
'For the Union Dead' (1964)

5 If we see light at the end of the tunnel,
It's the light of the oncoming train.
'Since 1939' (1977); see **Dickson** 116:10

William Lowndes 1652–1724
English politician

6 Take care of the pence, and the pounds will
take care of themselves.
Lord Chesterfield *Letters to his Son* (1774) 5
February 1750; see **Carroll** 86:15, **Chesterfield**
92:17

Malcolm Lowry 1909–57
English novelist

7 How alike are the groans of love to those of
the dying.
Under the Volcano (1947) ch. 12

Lucan AD 39–65
Roman poet

8 Thinking nothing done while anything
remained to be done.
Pharsalia bk. 2, l. 657; see **Rogers** 278:11

9 I have a wife, I have sons: we have given so
many hostages to the fates.
Pharsalia bk. 6, l. 661; see **Bacon** 22:32

Clare Booth Luce 1903–87
American diplomat, politician, and writer

10 Much of . . . his global thinking is, no matter
how you slice it, still globaloney.
speech to the House of Representatives,
February 1943

Lucilius c.180–102 BC
Roman poet

11 *Maior erat natu; non omnia possumus omnes.*
He was greater in years; we cannot all do
everything.
Macrobius *Saturnalia* bk. 6, ch. 1, sect. 35; see
Virgil 347:24

Lucretius c.94–55 BC
Roman poet

12 *Tantum religio potuit suadere malorum.*
So much wrong could religion induce.
De Rerum Natura bk. 1, l. 101

13 . . . *Nil posse creari*
De nilo.
Nothing can be created out of nothing.
De Rerum Natura bk. 1, l. 155

14 *Inque brevi spatio mutantur saecla animantum*
Et quasi cursores vitai lampada tradunt.
Some races increase, others are reduced,
and in a short while the generations of
living creatures are changed and like
runners relay the torch of life.
De Rerum Natura bk. 2, l. 8

Fray Luis de León c.1527–91
Spanish poet and religious writer

15 We were saying yesterday . . .
*on resuming a lecture at Salamanca University in
1577, after five years' imprisonment*
attributed, among others, by A. F. G. Bell in *Luis
de León* (1925) ch. 8

Luiz Inácio Lula da Silva 1945–
Brazilian statesman

16 A war can perhaps be won single-handedly.
But peace—lasting peace—cannot be
secured without the support of all.
speech, United Nations, 23 September 2003; in
Guardian (online edition) 24 September 2003

Martin Luther 1483–1546
German Protestant theologian

17 Here stand I. I can do no other. God help me.
Amen.
speech at the Diet of Worms, 18 April 1521;
attributed

18 For, where God built a church, there the
devil would also build a chapel . . . In such
sort is the devil always God's ape.
Colloquia Mensalia (1566) ch. 2 (tr. H. Bell as
Martin Luther's Divine Discourses, 1652)

19 A safe stronghold our God is still,
A trusty shield and weapon.
'Eine feste Burg ist unser Gott' (1529); tr.
Thomas Carlyle

20 Who loves not woman, wine, and song
Remains a fool his whole life long.
attributed (later inscribed in the Luther room in
the Wartburg, but with no proof of authorship)

Rosa Luxemburg 1871–1919
German revolutionary

21 Freedom is always and exclusively freedom
for the one who thinks differently.
Die Russische Revolution (1918) sect. 4

John Lyly c.1554–1606
English poet and dramatist

22 What bird so sings, yet so does wail?
O 'tis the ravished nightingale.
Jug, jug, jug, jug, tereu, she cries,
And still her woes at midnight rise.
Campaspe (1584) act 5, sc. 1; see **Eliot** 129:23

23 Night hath a thousand eyes.
The Maydes Metamorphosis (1600) act 3, sc. 1

Jonathan Lynn 1943–
and Antony Jay 1930–
English writers

1 I think it will be a clash between the political will and the administrative won't.
  Yes Prime Minister (1987) vol. 2

Henry Francis Lyte 1793–1847
English hymn-writer

2 Abide with me: fast falls the eventide;
  The darkness deepens; Lord, with me abide.
  'Abide with Me' (probably written in 1847)

3 Change and decay in all around I see;
  O Thou, who changest not, abide with me.
  'Abide with Me' (probably written in 1847)

4 Praise my soul, the King of heaven;
  To his feet thy tribute bring.
  Ransomed, healed, restored, forgiven,
  Who like me his praise should sing?
  'Praise, my soul, the King of heaven' (1834 hymn)

5 Father-like, he tends and spares us.
  'Praise, my soul, the King of heaven' (1834 hymn)

E. R. Bulwer, Lord Lytton *see* Owen Meredith

Douglas MacArthur 1880–1964
American general

6 I came through and I shall return.
  on reaching Australia, 20 March 1942, having broken through Japanese lines en route from Corregidor
  in *New York Times* 21 March 1942

7 In war, indeed, there can be no substitute for victory.
  in *Congressional Record* 19 April 1951, vol. 97, pt. 3

Rose Macaulay 1881–1958
English novelist

8 'Take my camel, dear,' said my aunt Dot, as she climbed down from this animal on her return from High Mass.
  The Towers of Trebizond (1956)

Thomas Babington Macaulay
1800–59
English politician and historian

9 The gallery in which the reporters sit has become a fourth estate of the realm.
  Essays Contributed to the Edinburgh Review (1843) vol. 1 'Hallam'

10 The gigantic body, the huge massy face, seamed with the scars of disease, the brown coat, the black worsted stockings, the grey wig with the scorched foretop, the dirty hands, the nails bitten and pared to the quick.
  Essays Contributed to the Edinburgh Review (1843) vol. 1 'Samuel Johnson'

11 If men are to wait for liberty till they become wise and good in slavery, they may indeed wait for ever.
  Essays Contributed to the Edinburgh Review (1843) vol. 1 'Milton'

12 We know no spectacle so ridiculous as the British public in one of its periodical fits of morality.
  Essays Contributed to the Edinburgh Review (1843) vol. 1 'Moore's *Life of Lord Byron*'

13 Every schoolboy knows who imprisoned Montezuma, and who strangled Atahualpa.
  Essays Contributed to the Edinburgh Review (1843) vol. 3 'Lord Clive'; see **Taylor** 331:4

14 She [the Roman Catholic Church] may still exist in undiminished vigour when some traveller from New Zealand shall, in the midst of a vast solitude, take his stand on a broken arch of London Bridge to sketch the ruins of St Paul's.
  Essays Contributed to the Edinburgh Review (1843) vol. 3 'Von Ranke'; see **Walpole** 350:2

15 The Puritan hated bear-baiting, not because it gave pain to the bear, but because it gave pleasure to the spectators.
  History of England vol. 1 (1849) ch. 2

16 The English Bible, a book which, if everything else in our language should perish, would alone suffice to show the whole extent of its beauty and power.
  T. F. Ellis (ed.) *Miscellaneous Writings of Lord Macaulay* (1860) 'John Dryden' (1828)

17 His imagination resembled the wings of an ostrich. It enabled him to run, though not to soar.
  T. F. Ellis (ed.) *Miscellaneous Writings of Lord Macaulay* (1860) 'John Dryden' (1828)

18 This province of literature is a debatable line. It lies on the confines of two distinct territories . . . It is sometimes fiction. It is sometimes theory.
  of history
  T. F. Ellis (ed.) *Miscellaneous Writings of Lord Macaulay* (1860) vol. 1 'History' (1828)

19 And the Man of Blood was there, with his long essenced hair,
  And Astley, and Sir Marmaduke, and Rupert of the Rhine.
  'The Battle of Naseby' (1824)

20 Lars Porsena of Clusium
  By the nine gods he swore
  That the great house of Tarquin
  Should suffer wrong no more.
  Lays of Ancient Rome (1842) 'Horatius' st. 1

21 And how can man die better
  Than facing fearful odds,
  For the ashes of his fathers,
  And the temples of his Gods?
  Lays of Ancient Rome (1842) 'Horatius' st. 27

22 Now who will stand on either hand,
  And keep the bridge with me?
  Lays of Ancient Rome (1842) 'Horatius' st. 29

23 Then none was for a party;

Then all were for the state.
Lays of Ancient Rome (1842) 'Horatius' st. 32

1 Was none who would be foremost
To lead such dire attack;
But those behind cried 'Forward!'
And those before cried 'Back!'
Lays of Ancient Rome (1842) 'Horatius' st. 50

2 Oh, Tiber! father Tiber
To whom the Romans pray,
A Roman's life, a Roman's arms,
Take thou in charge this day!
Lays of Ancient Rome (1842) 'Horatius' st. 59

3 And even the ranks of Tuscany
Could scarce forbear to cheer.
Lays of Ancient Rome (1842) 'Horatius' st. 60

4 Thank you, madam, the agony is abated.
aged four, having had hot coffee spilt over his legs
G. O. Trevelyan *Life and Letters of Lord Macaulay* (1876) ch. 1

5 We must at present do our best to form a
class who may be interpreters between us
and the millions whom we govern; a class of
persons, Indian in blood and colour, but
English in taste, in opinions, in morals, and
in intellect.
minute, as Member of Supreme Council of
India, 2 February 1835, in W. Nassan Lees *Indian Musalmāns* (1871)

Anthony McAuliffe 1898–1975
American general

6 Nuts!
*replying to the German demand for surrender at
Bastogne, Belgium, 22 December 1944*
in *New York Times* 28 December 1944

Joseph McCarthy 1908–57
American politician and anti-Communist agitator

7 I have here in my hand a list of two hundred
and five [people] that were known to the
Secretary of State as being members of the
Communist Party and who nevertheless are
still working and shaping the policy of the
State Department.
speech at Wheeling, West Virginia, 9 February
1950

8 McCarthyism is Americanism with its
sleeves rolled.
speech in Wisconsin, 1952

Mary McCarthy 1912–89
American novelist

9 If someone tells you he is going to make a
'realistic decision', you immediately
understand that he has resolved to do
something bad.
On the Contrary (1961) 'American Realist
Playwrights'

10 Every word she writes is a lie, including
'and' and 'the'.
on Lillian Hellman
in *New York Times* 16 February 1980

George B. McClellan 1826–85
American soldier and politician

11 All quiet along the Potomac.
said at the time of the American Civil War
attributed; see **Beers** 29:4

Ewan MacColl 1915–89
English folk singer and songwriter

12 And I used to sleep standing on my feet
As we hunted for the shoals of herring.
'The Shoals of Herring' (1960 song, from the
BBC Radio broadcast *Singing the Fishing*)

David McCord 1897–
13 By and by
God caught his eye.
'Remainders' (1935); epitaph for a waiter

P. D. McCormick c.1834–1916
Australian musician

14 In joyful strains then let us sing
Advance Australia fair.
the national anthem of Australia, from 1984
'Advance Australia Fair' (c.1878 song)

Horace McCoy 1897–1955
American novelist

15 They shoot horses don't they.
title of novel (1935)

John McCrae 1872–1918
Canadian poet and military physician

16 In Flanders fields the poppies blow
Between the crosses, row on row.
'In Flanders Fields' (1915)

Hugh MacDiarmid 1892–1978
Scottish poet and nationalist

17 The rose of all the world is not for me.
I want for my part
Only the little white rose of Scotland
That smells sharp and sweet—and breaks
the heart.
'The Little White Rose' (1934)

George MacDonald 1824–1905
Scottish writer and poet

18 Where did you come from, baby dear?
Out of the everywhere into here.
At the Back of the North Wind (1871) ch. 33 'Song'

John A. Macdonald 1815–91
*Scottish-born Canadian Liberal-Conservative
statesman*

19 A British subject I was born, and a British
subject I will die.
speech, 17 February 1891, in Toronto *Empire* 18
February 1891

Ramsay MacDonald 1866–1937
*British Labour statesman; Prime Minister, 1924,
1931–5*

20 We hear war called murder. It is not: it is
suicide.
in *Observer* 4 May 1930

A. G. MacDonell 1889–1941
Scottish writer

1 England, their England.
   title of novel (1933); see **Henley** 166:10

Ian McEwan 1948–
English novelist

2 I love you . . . That is what they were all
   saying down their phones, from the
   hijacked planes and the burning towers.
   There is only love, and then oblivion. Love
   was all they had to set against the hatred of
   their murderers.
   *of the last messages received from those trapped
   by terrorist attack in buildings and planes, 11
   September 2001*
   in *Guardian* 15 September 2001

William McGonagall *c.*1825–1902
Scottish writer of doggerel

3 Beautiful Railway Bridge of the Silv'ry Tay!
   Alas, I am very sorry to say
   That ninety lives have been taken away
   On the last Sabbath day of 1879,
   Which will be remembered for a very long
   time.
   'The Tay Bridge Disaster'

Patrick McGoohan 1928– ,
George Markstein, and David
Tomblin
American actor; scriptwriters

4 I am not a number, I am a free man!
   Number Six, in *The Prisoner* (TV series 1967–68);
   additional title sequence from the second
   episode onwards

Roger McGough 1937–
English poet

5 Let me die a youngman's death
   Not a clean & in-between-
   The-sheets, holy-water death.
   'Let Me Die a Youngman's Death' (1967)

Martin McGuinness 1950–
Northern Irish politician

6 My war is over. My job as a political leader is
   to prevent war.
   in *Daily Telegraph* 30 October 2002

Niccolò Machiavelli 1469–1527
*Italian political philosopher and Florentine
statesman*

7 Men should be either treated generously or
   destroyed, because they take revenge for
   slight injuries—for heavy ones they cannot.
   The Prince (written 1513) ch. 3 (tr. Allan Gilbert)

8 It is much safer for a prince to be feared
   than loved, if he is to fail in one of the two.
   The Prince (written 1513) ch. 8 (tr. Allan Gilbert)

9 The prince must be a fox, therefore, to
   recognize the traps and a lion to frighten
   the wolves.
   The Prince (written 1513) ch. 18 (tr. Allan Gilbert)

Claude McKay 1890–1948
American poet and novelist

10 If we must die, let it not be like hogs
   Hunted and penned in an inglorious spot,
   While round us bark the mad and hungry
   dogs,
   Making their mock at our accursed lot.
   'If We Must Die' (1953)

Peter MacKay 1965–
Canadian Conservative politician

11 My head's clear. My heart's a little banged
   up, but that will heal
   *after the decision by his former Conservative
   colleague Belinda Stronach, with whom he had
   had a romantic relationship, to join the Liberal
   Party just before a key budget vote*
   in an interview with CBC News, 18 May 2005

Kelvin Mackenzie 1946–
British journalist and media executive

12 We are surfing food.
   of cable television
   in *Trouble at the Top* (BBC2) 12 February 1997

James Mackintosh 1765–1832
Scottish philosopher and historian

13 The Commons, faithful to their system,
   remained in a wise and masterly inactivity.
   Vindiciae Gallicae (1791) sect. 1

Don McLean 1945–
American songwriter

14 Something touched me deep inside
   The day the music died.
   on the death of Buddy Holly
   'American Pie' (1972 song)

15 So, bye, bye, Miss American Pie,
   Drove my Chevy to the levee
   But the levee was dry.
   Them good old boys was drinkin' whiskey
   and rye
   Singin' 'This'll be the day that I die.'
   'American Pie' (1972 song)

Archibald MacLeish 1892–1982
American poet and public official

16 A poem should not mean
   But be.
   'Ars Poetica' (1926)

Marshall McLuhan 1911–80
Canadian communications scholar

17 The new electronic interdependence
   recreates the world in the image of a global
   village.
   The Gutenberg Galaxy (1962)

18 The medium is the message.
   Understanding Media (1964) ch. 1 (title)

19 Television brought the brutality of war into
   the comfort of the living room. Vietnam was
   lost in the living rooms of America—not the
   battlefields of Vietnam.
   in *Montreal Gazette* 16 May 1975

1 Advertising is the greatest art form of the twentieth century.

in *Advertising Age* 3 September 1976

2 Gutenberg made everybody a reader. Xerox makes everybody a publisher.

in *Guardian Weekly* 12 June 1977

Comte de MacMahon 1808–93
French soldier and statesman; President of the Third Republic, 1873–9

3 J'y suis, j'y reste.

Here I am, and here I stay.

at the taking of the Malakoff fortress during the Crimean War, 8 September 1855

G. Hanotaux *Histoire de la France Contemporaine* (1903–8) vol. 2

Harold Macmillan 1894–1986
British Conservative statesman; Prime Minister, 1957–63

4 Let us be frank about it: most of our people have never had it so good.

'You Never Had It So Good' was the Democratic Party slogan during the 1952 US election campaign

speech at Bedford, 20 July 1957

5 The wind of change is blowing through this continent, and, whether we like it or not, this growth of [African] national consciousness is a political fact.

speech at Cape Town, 3 February 1960

6 First of all the Georgian silver goes, and then all that nice furniture that used to be in the saloon. Then the Canalettos go.

on privatization; often quoted as, 'Selling off the family silver'

speech to the Tory Reform Group, 8 November 1985

7 The opposition of events.

on his biggest problem; popularly quoted as, 'Events, dear boy. Events'

David Dilks *The Office of Prime Minister in Twentieth Century Britain* (1993)

Robert McNamara 1916–
American Democratic politician

8 I don't object to it's being called 'McNamara's War' . . . It is a very important war and I am pleased to be identified with it and do whatever I can to win it.

in *New York Times* 25 April 1964

9 We . . . acted according to what we thought were the principles and traditions of this nation. We were wrong. We were terribly wrong.

of the conduct of the Vietnam War by the Kennedy and Johnson administrations

in *Daily Telegraph* (electronic edition) 10 April 1995

Louis MacNeice 1907–63
British poet, born in Belfast

10 The glass is falling hour by hour, the glass will fall for ever,

But if you break the bloody glass you won't hold up the weather.

'Bagpipe Music' (1938)

11 I am not yet born; O fill me

With strength against those who would freeze my

humanity.

'Prayer Before Birth' (1944)

12 Let them not make me a stone and let them not spill me,

Otherwise kill me.

'Prayer Before Birth' (1944)

Robert MacNeil 1931–
Canadian writer

13 Parents can plant magic in a child's mind through certain words spoken with some thrilling quality of voice, some uplift of the heart and spirit.

Wordstruck (1989)

William Macpherson of Cluny 1926–
Scottish lawyer

14 For the purposes of our Inquiry the concept of institutional racism which we apply consists of:

The collective failure of an organisation to provide an appropriate and professional service to people because of their colour, culture, or ethnic origin.

The Stephen Lawrence Inquiry: Report (February 1999) ch. 6

Geoffrey Madan 1895–1947
English bibliophile

15 The dust of exploded beliefs may make a fine sunset.

Livre sans nom: Twelve Reflections (privately printed 1934) no. 12

Samuel Madden 1686–1765
Irish poet

16 Words are men's daughters, but God's sons are things.

Boulter's Monument (1745) l. 377; see **Johnson** 186:17

Winnie Madikizela-Mandela 1934–
South African political activist

17 With that stick of matches, with our necklace, we shall liberate this country.

speech in black townships, 14 April 1986, in *Guardian* 15 April 1986

18 Maybe there is no rainbow nation after all because it does not have the colour black.

at the funeral of a black child reportedly shot dead by a white farmer

in *Irish Times* 25 April 1998 'Quotes of the Week'

James Madison 1751–1836
American Democratic Republican statesman, 4th President of the US 1809–17

19 Liberty is to faction what air is to fire, an aliment without which it instantly expires.

But it could not be less folly to abolish liberty, which is essential to political life, because it nourishes faction than it would be to wish the annihilation of air, which is essential to animal life, because it imparts to fire its destructive agency.
The Federalist (1787) no. 10

1 The diversity in the faculties of men, from which the rights of property originate, is not less an insuperable obstacle to a uniformity of interests. The protection of these faculties is the first object of government. From the protection of different and unequal faculties of acquiring property, the possession of different degrees and kinds of property immediately results.
The Federalist (1787) no. 10

John Gillespie Magee 1922–41
American airman, member of the Royal Canadian Airforce

2 Oh! I have slipped the surly bonds of earth And danced the skies on laughter-silvered wings.
'High Flight' (1943); see **Reagan** 274:8

3 And, while with silent lifting mind I've trod The high, untrespassed sanctity of space, Put out my hand and touched the face of God.
'High Flight' (1943); see **Reagan** 274:8

Magna Carta
political charter signed by King John at Runnymede, 1215

4 That the English Church shall be free.
Clause 1

5 No free man shall be taken or imprisoned or dispossessed, or outlawed or exiled, or in any way destroyed, nor will we go upon him, nor will we send against him except by the lawful judgement of his peers or by the law of the land.
Clause 39

6 To no man will we sell, or deny, or delay, right or justice.
Clause 40

Mahāyāna Buddhist texts
a tradition which emerged in India around the 1st century AD, which later spread to China, Japan, and elsewhere

7 Where there is no perception, appellation, conception, or conventional expression, there one speaks of 'perfect wisdom'.
Perfect Wisdom in 8,000 Lines (c.100 BC–100 AD) ch. 7, v. 177

8 A Bodhisattva who is full of pity and concerned with the welfare of all beings, who dwells in friendliness, compassion, sympathetic joy and even mindedness.
Perfect Wisdom in 8,000 Lines (c.100 BC–100 AD) ch. 20, v. 373

9 Form is emptiness and the very emptiness is form; emptiness does not differ from form, nor does form differ from emptiness;

whatever is form, that is emptiness, whatever is emptiness, that is form.
Heart Sutra (4th century AD) v. 3

10 The spell of great knowledge, the utmost spell, the unequalled spell, allayer of all suffering, in truth,—for what could go wrong?
Heart Sutra (4th century AD) v. 8

11 Gone, gone, gone beyond, gone altogether beyond, O what an awakening, all hail!
Heart Sutra (4th century AD) v. 8

Gustav Mahler 1860–1911
Austrian composer

12 Fortissimo at last!
on seeing Niagara Falls
K. Blaukopf *Gustav Mahler* (1973) ch. 8

13 The symphony must be like the world. It must embrace everything.
remark to Sibelius, Helsinki, 1907

Maimonides (Moses ben Maimon) 1135–1204
Jewish philosopher and Rabbinic scholar, born in Spain

14 *The first fundamental principle* is the existence of the Creator.
Commentary on the Mishnah Sanhedrin 10 (Heleq)

Henry Maine 1822–88
English jurist

15 The movement of the progressive societies has hitherto been a movement *from Status to Contract*.
Ancient Law (1861) ch. 5

Joseph de Maistre 1753–1821
French writer and diplomat

16 *Toute nation a le gouvernement qu'elle mérite.*
Every country has the government it deserves.
Lettres et Opuscules Inédits (1851) vol. 1, letter 53 (15 August 1811)

John Major 1943–
British Conservative statesman; Prime Minister, 1990–7

17 If the policy isn't hurting, it isn't working.
on controlling inflation
speech in Northampton, 27 October 1989

18 Society needs to condemn a little more and understand a little less.
interview with *Mail on Sunday* 21 February 1993

19 Fifty years on from now, Britain will still be the country of long shadows on county [cricket] grounds, warm beer, invincible green suburbs, dog lovers, and—as George Orwell said—old maids bicycling to Holy Communion through the morning mist.
speech to the Conservative Group for Europe, 22 April 1993; see **Orwell** 254:18

20 It is time to get back to basics: to self-discipline and respect for the law, to

consideration for others, to accepting responsibility for yourself and your family, and not shuffling it off on the state.

speech to the Conservative Party Conference, 8 October 1993

Malcolm X 1925–65
American civil rights campaigner

1 The white man was *created* a devil, to bring chaos upon this earth.

speech, *c.*1953; Malcolm X with Alex Haley *The Autobiography of Malcolm X* (1965); see **Fard** 134:2

2 If you're born in America with a black skin, you're born in prison.

in an interview, June 1963

3 You can't separate peace from freedom because no one can be at peace unless he has his freedom.

speech in New York, 7 January 1965, *Malcolm X Speaks* (1965)

Stéphane Mallarmé 1842–98
French poet

4 La chair est triste, hélas! et j'ai lu tous les livres.

The flesh, alas, is wearied; and I have read all the books there are.

'Brise Marin' (1887)

5 Prélude à l'après-midi d'un faune.

Prelude to the afternoon of a faun.

title of poem (*c.*1865)

George Leigh Mallory 1886–1924
British mountaineer

6 Because it's there.

on being asked why he wanted to climb Mount Everest (Mallory was lost on Everest in the following year)

in *New York Times* 18 March 1923

Thomas Malory d. 1471
English writer

7 Whoso pulleth out this sword of this stone and anvil is rightwise King born of all England.

Le Morte D'Arthur (finished 1470, printed by Caxton 1485) bk. 1, ch. 4

8 The questing beast . . . had in shape like a serpent's head and a body like a leopard, buttocked like a lion and footed like a hart. And in his body there was such a noise as it had been twenty couple of hounds questing.

'questing' = yelping

Le Morte d'Arthur (1485) bk. 9, ch. 12

9 And many men say that there is written upon his tomb this verse: *Hic iacet Arthurus, rex quondam rexque futurus* [Here lies Arthur, the once and future king].

Le Morte d'Arthur (1485) bk. 31, ch. 7

André Malraux 1901–76
French novelist, essayist, and art critic

10 La condition humaine.

The human condition.

title of book (1933)

11 L'art est un anti-destin.

Art is a revolt against fate.

Les Voix du silence (1951) pt. 4, ch. 7

Thomas Robert Malthus
1766–1834
English political economist

12 Population, when unchecked, increases in a geometrical ratio. Subsistence only increases in an arithmetical ratio.

Essay on the Principle of Population (1798) ch. 1

13 The perpetual struggle for room and food.

Essay on the Principle of Population (1798) ch. 3

Lord Mancroft 1914–87
British Conservative politician

14 Cricket—a game which the English, not being a spiritual people, have invented in order to give themselves some conception of eternity.

Bees in Some Bonnets (1979)

W. R. Mandale

15 Up and down the City Road,
In and out the Eagle,
That's the way the money goes—
Pop goes the weasel!

'Pop Goes the Weasel' (1853 song); also attributed to Charles Twiggs

Nelson Mandela 1918–
South African statesman

16 I have dedicated my life to this struggle of the African people. I have fought against white domination, and I have fought against black domination. I have cherished the ideal of a democratic and free society in which all persons live together in harmony with equal opportunities. It is an ideal which I hope to live for, and to see realized. But if needs be, it is an ideal for which I am prepared to die.

speech at his trial in Pretoria, 20 April 1964

17 No one is born hating another person because of the colour of his skin, or his background, or his religion. People must learn to hate, and if they can learn to hate, they can be taught to love, for love comes more naturally to the human heart than its opposite.

Long Walk to Freedom (1994)

18 True reconciliation does not consist in merely forgetting the past.

speech, 7 January 1996

19 Overcoming poverty is not a gesture of charity. It is an act of justice.

speech in Trafalgar Square, London, 3 February 2005

Peter Mandelson 1953–
British Labour politician

20 They underestimated me, because I am a fighter and not a quitter.

on winning back his Hartlepool seat in the General Election

speech, 8 June 2001

Manilius (Marcus Manilius)
Roman poet of the 1st century AD

1 *Eripuitque Jovi fulmen viresque tonandi,*
et sonitum ventis concessit, nubibus ignem.
And snatched from Jove the lightning shaft
and power to thunder, and attributed the
noise to the winds, the flame to the clouds.
of human intelligence
   Astronomica bk. 1, l. 104; see **Turgot** 343:3

Mrs Manley 1663–1724
English novelist and dramatist

2 No time like the present.
   The Lost Lover (1696) act 4, sc. 1

Horace Mann 1796–1859
American educationist

3 Lost, yesterday, somewhere between Sunrise
and Sunset, two golden hours, each set with
sixty diamond minutes. No reward is
offered, for they are gone forever.
   'Lost, Two Golden Hours'

Thomas Mann 1875–1955
German novelist

4 Time has no divisions to mark its passage,
there is never a thunderstorm or blare of
trumpets to announce the beginning of a
new month or year. Even when a new
century begins it is only we mortals who
ring bells and fire off pistols.
   The Magic Mountain (1924) ch. 4, sect. 4 (tr. H. T.
   Lowe-Porter)

5 Speech is civilisation itself. The word, even
the most contradictory word, preserves
contact—it is silence which isolates.
   The Magic Mountain (1924) ch. 6 (tr. H. T. Lowe-
   Porter)

6 We come out of the dark and go into the
dark again, and in between lie the
experiences of our life.
   The Magic Mountain (1924) ch. 6, sect. 8 (tr. H. T.
   Lowe-Porter)

7 A man's dying is more the survivors' affair
than his own.
   The Magic Mountain (1924) ch. 6, sect. 8 (tr. H. T.
   Lowe-Porter)

John Manners, Duke of Rutland
1818–1906
English Tory politician and writer

8 Let wealth and commerce, laws and
learning die,
But leave us still our old nobility!
   England's Trust (1841) pt. 3, l. 227

Katherine Mansfield 1888–1923
New Zealand-born short-story writer

9 Whenever I prepare for a journey I prepare
as though for death. Should I never return,
all is in order.
   Journal (1927) 29 January 1922

Richard Mant 1776–1848
Irish divine and ecclesiastical historian

10 Bright the vision that delighted
Once the sight of Judah's seer;
Sweet the countless tongues united
To entrance the prophet's ear.
   'Bright the vision that delighted' (1837 hymn)

Mao Zedong 1893–1976
*Chinese statesman; de facto leader of the
Communist Party*

11 Politics is war without bloodshed while war
is politics with bloodshed.
   lecture, 1938

12 Every Communist must grasp the truth,
'Political power grows out of the barrel of a
gun'.
   speech, 6 November 1938

13 The atom bomb is a paper tiger which the
United States reactionaries use to scare
people. It looks terrible, but in fact it isn't
. . . All reactionaries are paper tigers.
   interview, 1946

14 Letting a hundred flowers blossom and a
hundred schools of thought contend is the
policy for promoting progress in the arts
and the sciences and a flourishing socialist
culture in our land.
   speech in Peking, 27 February 1957,

Diego Maradona 1960–
Argentinian football player

15 The goal was scored a little bit by the hand
of God, another bit by head of Maradona.
*on his controversial goal against England in the
1986 World Cup*
   in *Guardian* 1 July 1986

William Learned Marcy 1786–1857
American politician

16 The politicians of New York . . . see nothing
wrong in the rule, that to the victor belong
the spoils of the enemy.
   speech to the Senate, 25 January 1832

Lynn Margulis 1938–
American biologist

17 Gaia is a tough bitch. People think the earth
is going to die and they have to save it,
that's ridiculous . . . There's no doubt that
Gaia can compensate for our output of
greenhouse gases, but the environment
that's left will not be happy for any people.
   in *New York Times Biographical Service* January
   1996

Marie-Antoinette 1755–93
French Queen consort of Louis XVI

18 *Qu'ils mangent de la brioche.*
Let them eat cake.
on being told that her people had no bread
   attributed, but much older; in his *Confessions*
   (1740) Rousseau refers to a similar remark
   being a well-known saying; another version is

'*Que ne mangent-ils de la croûte de pâté?* [Why don't they eat pastry?]', attributed to Marie-Thérèse (1638–83), wife of Louis XIV

Edwin Markham 1852–1940
American poet

1 A thing that grieves not and that never hopes,
Stolid and stunned, a brother to the ox?
'The Man with the Hoe' (1899)

Johnny Marks 1909–85
American songwriter

2 Rudolph, the Red-Nosed Reindeer
Had a very shiny nose.
'Rudolph, the Red-Nosed Reindeer' (1949 song)

Leo Marks 1920–2001
English cryptographer and screenwriter

3 The life that I have
Is all that I have
And the life that I have
Is yours.
The love that I have
Of the life that I have
Is yours and yours and yours.
given to the British secret agent Violette Szabo (1921–45), for use with the Special Operations Executive
'The Life that I Have' (written 1943)

Bob Marley 1945–81
Jamaican reggae musician and songwriter

4 Get up, stand up
Stand up for your rights
Get up, stand up
Never give up the fight.
'Get up, Stand up' (1973 song)

5 I shot the sheriff
But I swear it was in self-defence
I shot the sheriff
And they say it is a capital offence.
'I Shot the Sheriff' (1974 song)

Christopher Marlowe 1564–93
English dramatist and poet

6 Why, this is hell, nor am I out of it.
Doctor Faustus (1604) act 1, sc. 3

7 Was this the face that launched a thousand ships,
And burnt the topless towers of Ilium?
Doctor Faustus (1604) act 5, sc. 1

8 Stand still, you ever-moving spheres of heaven,
That time may cease, and midnight never come.
Doctor Faustus (1604) act 5, sc. 2

9 *O lente lente currite noctis equi.*
The stars move still, time runs, the clock will strike,
The devil will come, and Faustus must be damned.
O I'll leap up to my God: who pulls me down?
See, see, where Christ's blood streams in the firmament.

One drop would save my soul, half a drop, ah my Christ.
Doctor Faustus (1604) act 5, sc. 2; see **Ovid** 255:23

10 My men, like satyrs grazing on the lawns,
Shall with their goat feet dance an antic hay.
Edward II (1593) act 1, sc. 1

11 Where both deliberate, the love is slight;
Who ever loved that loved not at first sight?
Hero and Leander (1598) First Sestiad, l. 175

12 I count religion but a childish toy,
And hold there is no sin but ignorance.
The Jew of Malta (*c.*1592) prologue

13 Thus methinks should men of judgement frame
Their means of traffic from the vulgar trade,
And, as their wealth increaseth, so enclose
Infinite riches in a little room.
The Jew of Malta (*c.*1592) act 1, sc. 1

14 BARNARDINE: Thou hast committed—
BARABAS: Fornication? But that was in another country: and besides, the wench is dead.
The Jew of Malta (*c.*1592) act 4, sc. 1

15 Come live with me, and be my love,
And we will all the pleasures prove,
That valleys, groves, hills and fields,
Woods or steepy mountain yields.
'The Passionate Shepherd to his Love'; see **Donne** 119:7, **Ralegh** 272:22

16 Our swords shall play the orators for us.
Tamburlaine the Great (1590) pt. 1, act 1, sc. 2

17 Is it not passing brave to be a king,
And ride in triumph through Persepolis?
Tamburlaine the Great (1590) pt. 1, act 2, sc. 5

18 The ripest fruit of all,
That perfect bliss and sole felicity,
The sweet fruition of an earthly crown.
Tamburlaine the Great (1590) pt. 1, act 2, sc. 7

19 Virtue is the fount whence honour springs.
Tamburlaine the Great (1590) pt. 1, act 4, sc. 4

Don Marquis 1878–1937
American poet and journalist

20 procrastination is the
art of keeping
up with yesterday.
archy and mehitabel (1927) 'certain maxims of archy'

21 an optimist is a guy
that has never had
much experience.
archy and mehitabel (1927) 'certain maxims of archy'

22 it s cheerio
my deario that
pulls a lady through.
archy and mehitabel (1927) 'cheerio, my deario'

23 Writing a book of poetry is like dropping a rose petal down the Grand Canyon and waiting for the echo.
E. Anthony *O Rare Don Marquis* (1962)

John Marriot 1780–1825
English clergyman

1 Thou, whose eternal Word
Chaos and darkness heard,
And took their flight,
Hear us, we humbly pray,
And, where the Gospel-day
Sheds not its glorious ray,
Let there be light!
'almighty' substituted for 'eternal' from 1861
   'Thou, whose eternal Word' (hymn written
   c.1813)

Arthur Marshall 1910–89
British journalist and former schoolmaster

2 What, knocked a tooth out? Never mind,
dear, laugh it off, laugh it off; it's all part of
life's rich pageant.
   The Games Mistress (recorded monologue, 1937)

John Marshall 1755–1835
American jurist

3 The power to tax involves the power to
destroy.
   in *McCulloch v. Maryland* (1819)

4 The people made the Constitution, and the
people can unmake it. It is the creature of
their own will, and lives only by their will.
   in *Cohens v. Virginia* (1821)

Thomas R. Marshall 1854–1925
American politician

5 What this country needs is a really good
5-cent cigar.
   in *New York Tribune* 4 January 1920, pt. 7

Thurgood Marshall 1908–93
American Supreme Court judge

6 We must never forget that the only real
source of power that we as judges can tap is
the respect of the people.
   in *Chicago Tribune* 15 August 1981

Martial c.AD 40–c.104
Roman epigrammatist, born in Spain

7 *Non est, crede mihi, sapientis dicere 'Vivam':*
Sera nimis vita est crastina: vive hodie.
Believe me, wise men don't say 'I shall live
to do that', tomorrow's life's too late; live
today.
   Epigrammata bk. 1, no. 15

8 *Non amo te, Sabidi, nec possum dicere quare:*
Hoc tantum possum dicere, non amo te.
I don't love you, Sabidius, and I can't tell
you why; all I can tell you is this, that I don't
love you.
   Epigrammata bk. 1, no. 32; see **Brown** 71:2

9 *Laudant illa sed ista legunt.*
They praise those works, but read these.
   Epigrammata bk. 4, no. 49

10 *Non est vivere, sed valere vita est.*
Life's not just being alive, but being well.
   Epigrammata bk. 6, no. 70

11 *Difficilis facilis, iucundus acerbus es idem:*

Nec tecum possum vivere nec sine te.
Difficult or easy, pleasant or bitter, you are
the same you: I cannot live with you—or
without you.
   Epigrammata bk. 12, no. 46(47)

12 *Rus in urbe.*
Country in the town.
   Epigrammata bk. 12, no. 57

Andrew Marvell 1621–78
English poet

13 Where the remote Bermudas ride
In the ocean's bosom unespied.
   'Bermudas' (c.1653)

14 My love is of a birth as rare
As 'tis for object strange and high:
It was begotten by Despair
Upon Impossibility.
   'The Definition of Love' (1681)

15 How vainly men themselves amaze
To win the palm, the oak, or bays.
   'The Garden' (1681) st. 1

16 What wondrous life is this I lead!
Ripe apples drop about my head;
The luscious clusters of the vine
Upon my mouth do crush their wine;
The nectarine, and curious peach,
Into my hands themselves do reach;
Stumbling on melons, as I pass,
Ensnared with flowers, I fall on grass.
   'The Garden' (1681) st. 5

17 Annihilating all that's made
To a green thought in a green shade.
   'The Garden' (1681) st. 6

18 *He* nothing common did or mean
Upon that memorable scene:
But with his keener eye
The axe's edge did try.
   on the execution of **Charles I**
   'An Horatian Ode upon Cromwell's Return from
   Ireland' (written 1650) l. 57

19 Had we but world enough, and time,
This coyness, lady, were no crime.
   'To His coy Mistress' (1681) l. 1

20 I would
Love you ten years before the flood:
And you should, if you please, refuse
Till the conversion of the Jews.
My vegetable love should grow
Vaster than empires, and more slow.
   'To His coy Mistress' (1681) l. 7

21 But at my back I always hear
Time's wingèd chariot hurrying near:
And yonder all before us lie
Deserts of vast eternity.
   'To His Coy Mistress' (1681) l. 21; see **Eliot**
   129:26

22 The grave's a fine and private place,
But none, I think, do there embrace.
   'To His Coy Mistress' (1681) l. 27

23 Let us roll all our strength, and all
Our sweetness, up into one ball:
And tear our pleasures with rough strife,
Thorough the iron gates of life.

Thus, though we cannot make our sun
Stand still, yet we will make him run.
'To His Coy Mistress' (1681) l. 41

Holt Marvell
English songwriter

1 A cigarette that bears a lipstick's traces,
An airline ticket to romantic places;
And still my heart has wings
These foolish things
Remind me of you.
'These Foolish Things Remind Me of You' (1935 song)

Chico Marx 1891–1961
American film comedian

2 I wasn't kissing her, I was just whispering in her mouth.
on being discovered by his wife with a chorus girl
Groucho Marx and Richard J. Anobile *Marx Brothers Scrapbook* (1973) ch. 24

Groucho Marx 1890–1977
American film comedian

3 PLEASE ACCEPT MY RESIGNATION. I DON'T WANT TO BELONG TO ANY CLUB THAT WILL ACCEPT ME AS A MEMBER.
Groucho and Me (1959) ch. 26

4 I never forget a face, but in your case I'll be glad to make an exception.
Leo Rosten *People I have Loved, Known or Admired* (1970) 'Groucho'

Karl Marx 1818–83
German political philosopher

5 Religion is . . . the opium of the people.
A Contribution to the Critique of Hegel's Philosophy of Right (1843–4) introduction; see **Kingsley** 201:10

6 From each according to his abilities, to each according to his needs.
Critique of the Gotha Programme (written 1875, but of earlier origin); see **Blanc** 58:6, **Morelly** 244:22, and 'The formula of Communism, as propounded by Cabet, may be expressed thus:—"the duty of each is according to his faculties; his right according to his wants" ' in *North British Review* (1849) vol 10

7 Hegel says somewhere that all great events and personalities in world history reappear in one fashion or another. He forgot to add: the first time as tragedy, the second as farce.
The Eighteenth Brumaire of Louis Bonaparte (1852) sect. 1; see **Hegel**165:1

8 The philosophers have only interpreted the world in various ways; the point is to change it.
Theses on Feuerbach (written 1845, published 1888) no. 11

9 The class struggle necessarily leads to the dictatorship of the proletariat.
the phrase 'dictatorship of the proletariat' had been used earlier in the Constitution of the World Society of Revolutionary Communists (1850), signed by Marx and others
letter to Georg Weydemeyer 5 March 1852; Marx claimed that the phrase had been coined by Auguste Blanqui (1805–81), but it has not been found in this form in Blanqui's work

10 All I know is that I am not a Marxist.
attributed in a letter from Friedrich Engels to Conrad Schmidt, 5 August 1890; in Karl Marx and Friedrich Engels Correspondence (1934)

Karl Marx 1818–83
and Friedrich Engels 1820–95
German political philosopher and German socialist

11 A spectre is haunting Europe—the spectre of Communism.
The Communist Manifesto (1848) opening words

12 The history of all hitherto existing society is the history of class struggles.
The Communist Manifesto (1848) pt. 1

13 The proletarians have nothing to lose but their chains. They have a world to win.
WORKING MEN OF ALL COUNTRIES, UNITE!
commonly rendered as 'Workers of the world, unite!'
The Communist Manifesto (1848) closing words (from the 1888 translation by Samuel Moore, edited by Engels)

Mary I (Mary Tudor) 1516–58
English monarch, Queen from 1553

14 When I am dead and opened, you shall find 'Calais' lying in my heart.
Holinshed's Chronicles vol. 4 (1808)

Mary, Queen of Scots 1542–87
Scottish monarch, Queen 1542–67

15 *En ma fin git mon commencement.*
In my end is my beginning.
motto embroidered with an emblem of her mother, Mary of Guise, and quoted in a letter from William Drummond of Hawthornden to Ben Jonson in 1619; see **Eliot** 128:5

John Masefield 1878–1967
English poet

16 Quinquireme of Nineveh from distant Ophir
Rowing home to haven in sunny Palestine,
With a cargo of ivory,
And apes and peacocks,
Sandalwood, cedarwood, and sweet white wine.
'Cargoes' (1903); see **Bible** 37:7

17 Dirty British coaster with a salt-caked smoke stack,
Butting through the Channel in the mad March days,
With a cargo of Tyne coal,
Road-rails, pig lead,
Firewood, ironware, and cheap tin trays.
'Cargoes' (1903)

18 I must go down to the sea again, to the lonely sea and the sky,
And all I ask is a tall ship and a star to steer her by.
'I must down to the seas' in the original of 1902, possibly a misprint
'Sea Fever' (1902)

1 I must go down to the sea again, for the call
of the running tide
Is a wild call and a clear call that may not be
denied.
  'Sea Fever' (1902)

Donald Mason 1913–
American naval officer

2 Sighted sub, sank same.
  *on sinking a Japanese submarine in the Atlantic
  region (the first US naval success in the war)*
    radio message, 28 January 1942

Philip Massinger 1583–1640
English dramatist

3 Death has a thousand doors to let out life:
I shall find one.
  A Very Woman (licensed 1634, published 1655)
  act 5, sc. 4; see **Fletcher** 138:11, **Seneca** 288:23,
  Webster 352:23

Cotton Mather 1662–1728
American puritan preacher and divine

4 I write the wonders of the Christian
religion, flying from the depravations of
Europe, to the American strand: and,
assisted by the Holy Author of that religion,
I do . . . report the wonderful displays of His
infinite power, wisdom, goodness, and
faithfulness, wherewith His Divine
Providence hath irradiated an Indian
wilderness.
  introduction to *Magnalia Christi Americana* (1702),
  opening line

5 That there is a Devil is a thing doubted by
none but such as are under the influences of
the Devil. For any to deny the being of a
Devil must be from an ignorance or
profaneness worse than diabolical.
  The Wonders of the Invisible World (1693)

Henri Matisse 1869–1954
French painter

6 What I dream of is an art of balance, of
purity and serenity devoid of troubling or
depressing subject matter . . . a soothing,
calming influence on the mind, rather like a
good armchair which provides relaxation
from physical fatigue.
  Notes d'un peintre (1908)

Leonard Matlovich d. 1988
American Air Force Sergeant

7 When I was in the military, they gave me a
medal for killing two men and a discharge
for loving one.
  attributed

W. Somerset Maugham 1874–1965
English novelist

8 The most useful thing about a principle is
that it can always be sacrificed to
expediency.
  The Circle (1921) act 3

9 People ask you for criticism, but they only
want praise.
  Of Human Bondage (1915) ch. 50

10 Money is like a sixth sense without which
you cannot make a complete use of the
other five.
  Of Human Bondage (1915) ch. 51

11 I [Death] was astonished to see him in
Baghdad, for I had an appointment with
him tonight in Samarra.
  Sheppey (1933) act 3

12 Dying is a very dull, dreary affair. And my
advice to you is to have nothing whatever to
do with it.
  to his nephew Robin, in 1965
    Robin Maugham *Conversations with Willie* (1978)

Bill Mauldin 1921–
American cartoonist

13 I feel like a fugitive from th' law of averages.
  cartoon caption in *Up Front* (1945)

André Maurois 1885–1967
French writer

14 Growing old is no more than a bad habit
which a busy man has no time to form.
  The Art of Living (1940) ch. 8

James Clerk Maxwell 1831–79
Scottish physicist

15 Scientific truth should be presented in
different forms, and should be regarded as
equally scientific whether it appears in the
robust form and the vivid colouring of a
physical illustration, or in the tenuity and
paleness of a symbolic expression.
  attributed

Theresa May 1956–
British Conservative politician

16 You know what some people call us: the
nasty party.
  speech to the Conservative Conference, 7
  October 2002

Vladimir Mayakovsky 1893–1930
Russian poet

17 If you wish—
. . . I'll be irreproachably tender;
not a man, but—a cloud in trousers!
  'The Cloud in Trousers' (1915) (tr. Samuel
  Charteris)

Shepherd Mead 1914–
American advertising executive

18 How to succeed in business without really
trying.
  title of book (1952)

Hughes Mearns 1875–1965
American writer

19 As I was walking up the stair
I met a man who wasn't there.
He wasn't there again today.

I wish, I wish he'd stay away.

lines written for *The Psycho-ed*, an amateur play,
in Philadelphia, 1910 (set to music in 1939 as
'The Little Man Who Wasn't There')

Peter Medawar 1915–87
English immunologist and writer

1 If politics is the art of the possible, research
is surely the art of the soluble. Both are
immensely practical-minded affairs.
in *New Statesman* 19 June 1964; see **Bismarck**
55:4

Cosimo de' Medici 1389–1464
Italian statesman and patron of the arts

2 We read that we ought to forgive our
enemies; but we do not read that we ought
to forgive our friends.
*speaking of what **Bacon** refers to as 'perfidious
friends'*
Francis Bacon *Apophthegms* (1625) no. 206

Golda Meir 1898–1978
Israeli stateswoman, Prime Minister 1969–74

3 Those that perished in Hitler's gas chambers
were the last Jews to die without standing
up to defend themselves.
speech to United Jewish Appeal Rally, New
York, 11 June 1967

4 Pessimism is a luxury that a Jew can never
allow himself.
in *Observer* 29 December 1974

Nellie Melba 1861–1931
Australian operatic soprano

5 Sing 'em muck! It's all they can understand!
*advice prior to Dame Clara Butt's departure for
Australia*
W. H. Ponder *Clara Butt* (1928) ch. 12

William Lamb, Lord Melbourne
1779–1848
*British Whig statesman; Prime Minister 1834,
1835–41*

6 God help the Minister that meddles with
art!
Lord David Cecil *Lord M* (1954) ch. 3

7 I wish I was as cocksure of anything as Tom
Macaulay is of everything.
Lord Cowper's preface to *Lord Melbourne's Papers*
(1889)

8 Now, is it to lower the price of corn, or isn't
it? It is not much matter which we say, but
mind, we must all say *the same.*
attributed; Walter Bagehot *The English
Constitution* (1867) ch. 1

9 Things have come to a pretty pass when
religion is allowed to invade the sphere of
private life.
on hearing an evangelical sermon
G. W. E. Russell *Collections and Recollections* (1898)
ch. 6

10 What all the wise men promised has not
happened, and what all the d—d fools said
would happen has come to pass.
of the Catholic Emancipation Act (1829)
H. Dunckley *Lord Melbourne* (1890) ch. 9

11 What I want is men who will support me
when I am in the wrong.
*replying to a politician who said 'I will support
you as long as you are in the right'*
Lord David Cecil *Lord M* (1954) ch. 4

David Mellor 1949–
British Conservative politician and broadcaster

12 I do believe the popular press is drinking in
the last chance saloon.
interview on *Hard News* (Channel 4), 21
December 1989

Herman Melville 1819–91
American novelist and poet

13 Call me Ishmael.
Moby Dick (1851), opening words

14 A whaleship was my Yale College and my
Harvard.
Moby Dick (1851) ch. 24

15 Towards thee I roll, thou all-destroying but
unconquering whale . . . from hell's heart I
stab at thee.
Moby Dick (1851) ch. 135

Menander 342–*c*.292 BC
Greek comic dramatist

16 Whom the gods love dies young.
Dis Exapaton fragment 4, in F. H. Sandbach (ed.)
Menandri Reliquiae Selectae (1990)

17 We live, not as we wish to, but as we can.
The Lady of Andros in *Menander: the Principal
Fragments* (tr. F. G. Allinson, 1951)

Mencius *see* **Meng-tzu**

H. L. Mencken 1880–1956
American journalist and literary critic

18 Love is the delusion that one woman differs
from another.
Chrestomathy (1949) ch. 30; see **Shaw** 311:29

19 Puritanism. The haunting fear that
someone, somewhere, may be happy.
Chrestomathy (1949) ch. 30

20 Democracy is the theory that the common
people know what they want, and deserve
to get it good and hard.
A Little Book in C major (1916)

21 Conscience: the inner voice which warns us
that someone may be looking.
A Little Book in C major (1916)

22 It is now quite lawful for a Catholic woman
to avoid pregnancy by a resort to
mathematics, though she is still forbidden
to resort to physics and chemistry.
Notebooks (1956) 'Minority Report'

23 There is always a well-known solution to
every human problem—neat, plausible, and
wrong.
Prejudices 2nd series (1920)

Meng-tzu (Mencius) 371–289 BC
Chinese philosopher

1 All men have the mind which cannot bear
[to see the suffering of] others.
The Book of Mencius bk. 2, pt. A, v. 6

David Mercer 1928–80
English dramatist

2 A suitable case for treatment.
title of television play (1962); later filmed as
Morgan—A Suitable Case for Treatment (1966)

Johnny Mercer 1909–76
American songwriter

3 You've got to ac-cent-tchu-ate the positive
Elim-my-nate the negative
Latch on to the affirmative
Don't mess with Mister In-between.
'Ac-cent-tchu-ate the Positive' (1944 song)

4 Jeepers Creepers—where you get them
peepers?
'Jeepers Creepers' (1938 song)

5 Make it one for my baby
And one more for the road.
'One For My Baby' (1943 song)

6 That old black magic.
title of song (1942)

George Meredith 1828–1909
English novelist and poet

7 Kissing don't last: cookery do!
The Ordeal of Richard Feverel (1859) ch. 28

8 The lark ascending.
title of poem (1881)

9 Ah, what a dusty answer gets the soul
When hot for certainties in this our life!
Modern Love (1862) st. 50

10 Enter these enchanted woods,
You who dare.
'The Woods of Westermain' (1883)

Owen Meredith (Lord Lytton)
1831–91
English poet and statesman

11 Genius does what it must, and Talent does
what it can.
'Last Words of a Sensitive Second-Rate Poet'
(1868)

Bob Merrill 1921–98
American songwriter and composer

12 How much is that doggie in the window?
title of song (1953)

13 People who need people are the luckiest
people in the world.
'People who Need People' (1964 song)

Dixon Lanier Merritt 1879–1972
American editor

14 Oh, a wondrous bird is the pelican!
His beak holds more than his belican.
He takes in his beak

Food enough for a week.
But I'll be darned if I know how the helican.
in *Nashville Banner* 22 April 1913

Jean Meslier c.1664–1733
French priest

15 An ignorant, uneducated man . . . said he
wished . . . that all the great men in the
world and all the nobility could be hanged,
and strangled with the guts of priests.
*often quoted 'I should like . . . the last of the kings
to be strangled with the guts of the last priest'*
Testament (ed. R. Charles, 1864) vol. 1, ch. 2; see
Diderot 116:11

Methodist Service Book 1975

16 I am no longer my own, but yours. Put me to
what you will, rank me with whom you will;
put me to doing, put me to suffering.
The Covenant Prayer (based on the words of
Richard Alleine in the First Covenant Service,
1782)

Prince Metternich 1773–1859
Austrian statesman

17 Italy is a geographical expression.
discussing the Italian question with **Palmerston** *in
1847*
*Mémoires, Documents, etc. de Metternich publiés par
son fils* (1883) vol. 7

Michelangelo 1475–1564
Italian sculptor, painter, architect, and poet

18 The marble not yet carved can hold the
form
Of every thought the greatest artist has.
Sonnet 15, tr. Elizabeth Jennings

19 Trifles make perfection, and perfection is no
trifle.
attributed; Samuel Smiles *Self-Help* (1859) ch. 5

Thomas Middleton c.1580–1627
English dramatist

20 Anything for a quiet life.
title of play (written c.1620, possibly with John
Webster)

21 Nine coaches waiting—hurry, hurry, hurry.
The Revenger's Tragedy (1607) act 2, sc. 1

Bette Midler 1945–
American actress

22 When it's three o'clock in New York, it's still
1938 in London.
attributed

Ludwig Mies van der Rohe
1886–1969
German-born architect and designer

23 God is in the details.
in *New York Times* 19 August 1969

George Mikes 1912–
Hungarian-born writer

24 On the Continent people have good food; in
England people have good table manners.
How to be an Alien (1946)

1 An Englishman, even if he is alone, forms
   an orderly queue of one.
   How to be an Alien (1946) p. 44

William Porcher Miles 1822–96

2 'Vote early and vote often,' the advice
   openly displayed on the election banners in
   one of our northern cities.
   in the House of Representatives, 31 March 1858

John Stuart Mill 1806–73
English philosopher and economist

3 Ask yourself whether you are happy, and
   you cease to be so.
   Autobiography (1873) ch. 5

4 No great improvements in the lot of
   mankind are possible, until a great change
   takes place in the fundamental constitution
   of their modes of thought.
   Autobiography (1873) ch. 7

5 The Conservatives . . . being by the law of
   their existence the stupidest party.
   Considerations on Representative Government (1861)
   ch. 7 n.

6 I will call no being good, who is not what I
   mean when I apply that epithet to my
   fellow-creatures; and if such a being can
   sentence me to hell for not so calling him,
   to hell I will go.
   Examination of Sir William Hamilton's Philosophy
   (1865) ch. 7

7 The only purpose for which power can be
   rightfully exercised over any member of a
   civilized community, against his will, is to
   prevent harm to others. His own good,
   either physical or moral, is not a sufficient
   warrant.
   On Liberty (1859) ch. 1

8 If all mankind minus one were of one
   opinion, and only one person were of the
   contrary opinion, mankind would be no
   more justified in silencing that one person,
   than he, if he had the power, would be
   justified in silencing mankind.
   On Liberty (1859) ch. 2

9 The liberty of the individual must be thus
   far limited; he must not make himself a
   nuisance to other people.
   On Liberty (1859) ch. 3

10 Liberty consists in doing what one desires.
   On Liberty (1859) ch. 5

11 A State which dwarfs its men, in order that
   they may be more docile instruments in its
   hands even for beneficial purposes, will find
   that with small men no great thing can
   really be accomplished.
   On Liberty (1859) ch. 5

12 The principle which regulates the existing
   social relations between the two sexes—the
   legal subordination of one sex to the
   other—is wrong in itself, and now one of
   the chief hindrances to human
   improvement.
   The Subjection of Women (1869) ch. 1

13 What is now called the nature of women is
   an eminently artificial thing—the result of
   forced repression in some directions,
   unnatural stimulation in others.
   The Subjection of Women (1869) ch. 1

14 No slave is a slave to the same lengths, and
   in so full a sense of the word, as a wife is.
   The Subjection of Women (1869) ch. 2

15 It is better to be a human being dissatisfied
   than a pig satisfied; better to be Socrates
   dissatisfied than a fool satisfied.
   Utilitarianism (1863) ch. 2

Edna St Vincent Millay 1892–1950
American poet

16 Childhood is the kingdom where nobody
   dies.
   Nobody that matters, that is.
   'Childhood is the Kingdom where Nobody dies'
   (1934)

17 Down, down, down into the darkness of the
   grave
   Gently they go, the beautiful, the tender,
   the kind;
   Quietly they go, the intelligent, the witty,
   the brave.
   I know. But I do not approve. And I am not
   resigned.
   'Dirge Without Music' (1928)

18 My candle burns at both ends;
   It will not last the night;
   But ah, my foes, and oh, my friends—
   It gives a lovely light.
   A Few Figs From Thistles (1920) 'First Fig'

19 Euclid alone
   Has looked on Beauty bare.
   The Harp-Weaver and Other Poems (1923) sonnet
   22

20 Justice denied in Massachusetts.
   *relating to the trial of Sacco and Vanzetti and
   their execution on 22 August 1927*
   title of poem (1928)

Alice Duer Miller 1874–1942
American writer

21 I am American bred,
   I have seen much to hate here—much to
   forgive,
   But in a world where England is finished
   and dead,
   I do not wish to live.
   The White Cliffs (1940)

Arthur Miller 1915–2005
American dramatist

22 Death of a salesman.
   title of play (1949)

23 He's a human being, and a terrible thing is
   happening to him. So attention must be
   paid.
   Death of a Salesman (1949) act 1

24 He's a man way out there in the blue, riding
   on a smile and a shoeshine. And when they
   start not smiling back—that's an

earthquake . . . A salesman is got to dream, boy. It comes with the territory.
Death of a Salesman (1949) 'Requiem'

1 This is Red Hook, not Sicily . . . This is the gullet of New York swallowing the tonnage of the world.
A View from the Bridge (1955) act 1

2 A good newspaper, I suppose, is a nation talking to itself.
in *Observer* 26 November 1961

Henry Miller 1891–1980
American novelist

3 Every man with a bellyful of the classics is an enemy to the human race.
Tropic of Cancer (1934)

Jonathan Miller 1934–
English writer and director

4 In fact, I'm not really a *Jew*. Just Jew-*ish*. Not the whole hog, you know.
Beyond the Fringe (1960 review) 'Real Class'

Spike Milligan 1918–2002
Irish comedian

5 Money couldn't buy friends but you got a better class of enemy.
Puckoon (1963) ch. 6

A. J. Mills, Fred Godfrey, and Bennett Scott
British songwriters

6 Take me back to dear old Blighty.
title of song (1916)

Irving Mills 1894–1985

7 It don't mean a thing
If it ain't got that swing.
'It Don't Mean a Thing' (1932 song; music by Duke **Ellington**)

Henry Hart Milman 1791–1868
English clergyman

8 Ride on! ride on in majesty!
The wingèd squadrons of the sky
Look down with sad and wond'ring eyes
To see the approaching sacrifice.
'Ride on! ride on in majesty!' (1827 hymn)

A. A. Milne 1882–1956
English writer for children

9 The more he looked inside the more Piglet wasn't there.
The House at Pooh Corner (1928) ch. 1

10 'I don't *want* him,' said Rabbit. 'But it's always useful to know where a friend-and-relation *is*, whether you want him or whether you don't.'
The House at Pooh Corner (1928) ch. 3

11 He respects Owl, because you can't help respecting anybody who can spell TUESDAY, even if he doesn't spell it right; but spelling isn't everything. There are days when spelling Tuesday simply doesn't count.
The House at Pooh Corner (1928) ch. 5

12 When you are a Bear of Very Little Brain, and you Think of Things, you find sometimes that a Thing which seemed very Thingish inside you is quite different when it gets out into the open and has other people looking at it.
The House at Pooh Corner (1928) ch. 6

13 They're changing guard at Buckingham Palace—
Christopher Robin went down with Alice.
Alice is marrying one of the guard.
'A soldier's life is terrible hard,'
Says Alice.
When We Were Very Young (1924) 'Buckingham Palace'

14 James James
Morrison Morrison
Weatherby George Dupree
Took great
Care of his Mother,
Though he was only three.
James James
Said to his Mother,
'Mother,' he said, said he;
'You must never go down to the end of the town, if you don't go down with me.'
When We Were Very Young (1924) 'Disobedience'

15 The King asked
The Queen, and
The Queen asked
The Dairymaid:
'Could we have some butter for
The Royal slice of bread?'
When We Were Very Young (1924) 'The King's Breakfast'

16 Hush! Hush! Whisper who dares!
Christopher Robin is saying his prayers.
When We Were Very Young (1924) 'Vespers'; see **Morton** 246:6

17 Isn't it funny
How a bear likes honey?
Buzz! Buzz! Buzz!
I wonder why he does?
Winnie-the-Pooh (1926) ch. 1

18 'Pathetic,' he [Eeyore] said. 'That's what it is. Pathetic.'
Winnie-the-Pooh (1926) ch. 6

19 Time for a little something.
Winnie-the-Pooh (1926) ch. 6

20 My spelling is Wobbly. It's good spelling but it Wobbles, and the letters get in the wrong places.
Winnie-the-Pooh (1926) ch. 6

Lord Milner 1854–1925
British colonial administrator

21 If we believe a thing to be bad, and if we have a right to prevent it, it is our duty to try to prevent it and to damn the consequences.
speech in Glasgow, 26 November 1909

John Milton 1608–74

English poet

1 Such sweet compulsion doth in music lie.
  'Arcades' (1645) l. 68

2 Blest pair of Sirens, pledges of heaven's joy,
  Sphere-born harmonious sisters, Voice, and
  Verse.
  'At a Solemn Music' (1645)

3 An old and haughty nation proud in arms.
  Comus (1637) l. 33

4 Come, knit hands, and beat the ground,
  In a light fantastic round.
  Comus (1637) l. 143

5 He that has light within his own clear breast
  May sit i' the centre, and enjoy bright day,
  But he that hides a dark soul, and foul
  thoughts
  Benighted walks under the midday sun;
  Himself is his own dungeon.
  Comus (1637) l. 381

6 'Tis chastity, my brother, chastity:
  She that has that, is clad in complete steel.
  Comus (1637) l. 420

7 How charming is divine philosophy!
  Not harsh and crabbèd, as dull fools
  suppose,
  But musical as is Apollo's lute.
  Comus (1637) l. 475

8 And filled the air with barbarous
  dissonance.
  Comus (1637) l. 550

9 Against the threats
  Of malice or of sorcery, or that power
  Which erring men call chance, this I hold
  firm,
  Virtue may be assailed, but never hurt,
  Surprised by unjust force, but not
  enthralled.
  Comus (1637) l. 586

10 Sabrina fair,
   Listen where thou art sitting
   Under the glassy, cool, translucent wave,
   In twisted braids of lilies knitting
   The loose train of thy amber-dropping hair.
   Comus (1637) l. 859 'Song'

11 Hence, vain deluding joys,
   The brood of folly without father bred.
   'Il Penseroso' (1645) l. 1

12 Come, pensive nun, devout and pure,
   Sober, steadfast, and demure.
   'Il Penseroso' (1645) l. 31

13 Far from all resort of mirth,
   Save the cricket on the hearth.
   'Il Penseroso' (1645) l. 81

14 Where more is meant than meets the ear.
   'Il Penseroso' (1645) l. 120

15 Hide me from day's garish eye.
   'Il Penseroso' (1645) l. 141

16 And storied windows richly dight,
   Casting a dim religious light.
   'Il Penseroso' (1645) l. 159

17 Hence, loathèd Melancholy,

Of Cerberus, and blackest Midnight born,
   In Stygian cave forlorn
   'Mongst horrid shapes, and shrieks, and
   sights unholy.
   'L'Allegro' (1645) l. 1

18 So buxom, blithe, and debonair.
   of Euphrosyne [Mirth], *one of the three Graces*
   'L'Allegro' (1645) l. 24

19 Nods, and becks, and wreathèd smiles.
   'L'Allegro' (1645) l. 28

20 Come, and trip it as ye go
   On the light fantastic toe.
   'L'Allegro' (1645) l. 33

21 Meadows trim with daisies pied,
   Shallow brooks, and rivers wide.
   'L'Allegro' (1645) l. 75

22 Where perhaps some beauty lies,
   The cynosure of neighbouring eyes.
   'L'Allegro' (1645) l. 79

23 Then to the spicy nut-brown ale.
   'L'Allegro' (1645) l. 100

24 Towered cities please us then,
   And the busy hum of men.
   'L'Allegro' (1645) l. 117

25 Such sights as youthful poets dream
   On summer eves by haunted stream.
   Then to the well-trod stage anon,
   If Jonson's learnèd sock be on,
   Or sweetest Shakespeare fancy's child,
   Warble his native wood-notes wild.
   'L'Allegro' (1645) l. 129

26 Let us with a gladsome mind
   Praise the Lord, for he is kind,
   For his mercies ay endure,
   Ever faithful, ever sure.
   'Let us with a gladsome mind' (1645);
   paraphrase of Psalm 136; see **Book of Common
   Prayer** 64:30

27 Yet once more, O ye laurels, and once more
   Ye myrtles brown, with ivy never sere.
   'Lycidas' (1638) l. 1

28 For Lycidas is dead, dead ere his prime,
   Young Lycidas, and hath not left his peer.
   'Lycidas' (1638) l. 8

29 To sport with Amaryllis in the shade,
   Or with the tangles of Neaera's hair.
   'Lycidas' (1638) l. 68

30 Fame is the spur that the clear spirit doth
   raise
   (That last infirmity of noble mind).
   'Lycidas' (1638) l. 70

31 Comes the blind Fury with th' abhorrèd
   shears,
   And slits the thin-spun life.
   'Lycidas' (1638) l. 75

32 The hungry sheep look up, and are not fed.
   'Lycidas' (1638) l. 125

33 But that two-handed engine at the door
   Stands ready to smite once, and smite no
   more.
   'Lycidas' (1638) l. 130

34 Bring the rathe primrose that forsaken dies,

The tufted crow-toe, and pale jessamine.
'Lycidas' (1638) l. 142

1 Look homeward angel now, and melt with ruth.
'Lycidas' (1638) l. 163

2 So sinks the day-star in the ocean bed,
And yet anon repairs his drooping head,
And tricks his beams, and with new spangled ore,
Flames in the forehead of the morning sky.
'Lycidas' (1638) l. 168

3 Through the dear might of Him that walked the waves.
'Lycidas' (1638) l. 173

4 At last he rose, and twitched his mantle blue:
Tomorrow to fresh woods, and pastures new.
'Lycidas' (1638) l. 192

5 For what can war, but endless war still breed?
'On the Lord General Fairfax at the Siege of Colchester' (written 1648)

6 The star-led wizards haste with odours sweet.
'On the Morning of Christ's Nativity' (1645) st. 4

7 It was the winter wild,
While the heaven-born child
All meanly wrapped in the rude manger lies;
Nature in awe to him
Had doffed her gaudy trim,
With her great master so to sympathize.
'On the Morning of Christ's Nativity' (1645) 'The Hymn' st. 1

8 Time will run back, and fetch the age of gold.
'On the Morning of Christ's Nativity' (1645) 'The Hymn' st. 14

9 So when the sun in bed,
Curtained with cloudy red,
Pillows his chin upon an orient wave.
'On the Morning of Christ's Nativity' (1645) 'The Hymn' st. 26

10 Time is our tedious song should here have ending.
'On the Morning of Christ's Nativity' (1645) 'The Hymn' st. 27

11 New *Presbyter* is but old *Priest* writ large.
'On the New Forcers of Conscience under the Long Parliament' (1646)

12 Fly envious Time, till thou run out thy race,
Call on the lazy leaden-stepping hours.
'On Time' (1645)

13 Rhyme being . . . but the invention of a barbarous age, to set off wretched matter and lame metre.
Paradise Lost (1667) 'The Verse' (preface, added 1668)

14 The troublesome and modern bondage of rhyming.
Paradise Lost (1667) 'The Verse' (preface, added 1668)

15 Of man's first disobedience, and the fruit
Of that forbidden tree, whose mortal taste
Brought death into the world, and all our woe,
With loss of Eden.
Paradise Lost (1667) bk. 1, l. 1

16 Things unattempted yet in prose or rhyme.
Paradise Lost (1667) bk. 1, l. 16

17 What in me is dark
Illumine, what is low raise and support;
That to the height of this great argument
I may assert eternal providence,
And justify the ways of God to men.
Paradise Lost (1667) bk. 1, l. 22; see **Housman** 176:16, **Pope** 267:19

18 The infernal serpent; he it was, whose guile
Stirred up with envy and revenge, deceived
The mother of mankind.
Paradise Lost (1667) bk. 1, l. 34

19 No light, but rather darkness visible
Served only to discover sights of woe.
Paradise Lost (1667) bk. 1, l. 63

20 What though the field be lost?
All is not lost; the unconquerable will,
And study of revenge, immortal hate,
And courage never to submit or yield.
Paradise Lost (1667) bk. 1, l. 105

21 And out of good still to find means of evil.
Paradise Lost (1667) bk. 1, l. 165

22 The mind is its own place, and in itself
Can make a heaven of hell, a hell of heaven.
Paradise Lost (1667) bk. 1, l. 254

23 Better to reign in hell, than serve in heaven.
Paradise Lost (1667) bk. 1, l. 263

24 A wand,
He walked with to support uneasy steps
Over the burning marl.
Paradise Lost (1667) bk. 1, l. 292

25 Thick as autumnal leaves that strew the brooks
In Vallombrosa, where the Etrurian shades
High overarched imbower.
Paradise Lost (1667) bk. 1, l. 302

26 First Moloch, horrid king besmeared with blood
Of human sacrifice, and parents' tears.
Paradise Lost (1667) bk. 1, l. 392

27 And when night
Darkens the streets, then wander forth the sons
Of Belial, flown with insolence and wine.
Paradise Lost (1667) bk. 1, l. 500

28 A shout that tore hell's concave, and beyond
Frighted the reign of Chaos and old Night.
Paradise Lost (1667) bk. 1, l. 542

29 Who overcomes
By force, hath overcome but half his foe.
Paradise Lost (1667) bk. 1, l. 648

30 Mammon led them on,
Mammon, the least erected spirit that fell
From heaven.
Paradise Lost (1667) bk. 1, l. 678

31 Let none admire
That riches grow in hell; that soil may best

Deserve the precious bane.
Paradise Lost (1667) bk. 1, l. 690

1   From morn
To noon he fell, from noon to dewy eve,
A summer's day; and with the setting sun
Dropped from the zenith like a falling star.
Paradise Lost (1667) bk. 1, l. 742

2   Pandemonium, the high capital
Of Satan and his peers.
Paradise Lost (1667) bk. 1, l. 756

3   But all was false and hollow; though his
tongue
Dropped manna, and could make the worse
appear
The better reason.
Paradise Lost (1667) bk. 2, l. 112; see
Aristophanes 15:6

4   To perish rather, swallowed up and lost
In the wide womb of uncreated night,
Devoid of sense and motion?
Paradise Lost (1667) bk. 2, l. 149

5   With grave
Aspect he rose, and in his rising seemed
A pillar of state; deep on his front engraven
Deliberation sat and public care;
And princely counsel in his face yet shone,
Majestic though in ruin.
Paradise Lost (1667) bk. 2, l. 300

6   To sit in darkness here
Hatching vain empires.
Paradise Lost (1667) bk. 2, l. 377

7   Long is the way
And hard, that out of hell leads up to light.
Paradise Lost (1667) bk. 2, l. 432

8   For eloquence the soul, song charms the
sense.
Paradise Lost (1667) bk. 2, l. 556

9   Vain wisdom all, and false philosophy.
Paradise Lost (1667) bk. 2, l. 565

10 Black it stood as night,
Fierce as ten Furies, terrible as hell,
And shook a dreadful dart.
Paradise Lost (1667) bk. 2, l. 670

11 Incensed with indignation Satan stood
Unterrified, and like a comet burned
That fires the length of Ophiuchus huge
In the Arctic sky, and from his horrid hair
Shakes pestilence and war.
Paradise Lost (1667) bk. 2, l. 707

12 Chaos umpire sits,
And by decision more embroils the fray.
Paradise Lost (1667) bk. 2, l. 907

13 Sable-vested Night, eldest of things.
Paradise Lost (1667) bk. 2, l. 962

14 With ruin upon ruin, rout on rout,
Confusion worse confounded.
Paradise Lost (1667) bk. 2, l. 995

15 Die he or justice must.
Paradise Lost (1667) bk. 3, l. 210

16 Dark with excessive bright.
Paradise Lost (1667) bk. 3, l. 380

17 Hypocrisy, the only evil that walks

Invisible, except to God alone.
Paradise Lost (1667) bk. 3, l. 683

18 Me miserable! which way shall I fly
Infinite wrath, and infinite despair?
Which way I fly is hell; myself am hell.
Paradise Lost (1667) bk. 4, l. 73

19 Evil, be thou my good.
Paradise Lost (1667) bk. 4, l. 110

20 Flowers of all hue, and without thorn the
rose.
Paradise Lost (1667) bk. 4, l. 256

21 Not that fair field
Of Enna, where Proserpine gathering
flowers
Herself a fairer flower by gloomy Dis
Was gathered, which cost Ceres all that
pain.
Paradise Lost (1667) bk. 4, l. 268

22 He for God only, she for God in him.
Paradise Lost (1667) bk. 4, l. 299

23 Adam, the goodliest man of men since born
His sons, the fairest of her daughters Eve.
Paradise Lost (1667) bk. 4, l. 323

24 These two
Emparadised in one another's arms
The happier Eden, shall enjoy their fill
Of bliss on bliss.
Paradise Lost (1667) bk. 4, l. 505

25 With thee conversing I forget all time.
Paradise Lost (1667) bk. 4, l. 639

26 Millions of spiritual creatures walk the earth
Unseen, both when we wake, and when we
sleep.
Paradise Lost (1667) bk. 4, l. 677

27 Sleep on
Blest pair; and O yet happiest if ye seek
No happier state, and know to know no
more.
Paradise Lost (1667) bk. 4, l. 773

28 Him there they found
Squat like a toad, close at the ear of Eve.
Paradise Lost (1667) bk. 4, l. 799

29 But wherefore thou alone? Wherefore with
thee
Came not all hell broke loose?
Paradise Lost (1667) bk. 4, l. 917

30 My fairest, my espoused, my latest found,
Heaven's last best gift, my ever new delight.
Paradise Lost (1667) bk. 5, l. 18

31 What if earth
Be but the shadow of heaven, and things
therein
Each to other like, more than on earth is
thought?
Paradise Lost (1667) bk. 5, l. 574

32 Hear all ye angels, progeny of light,
Thrones, dominations, princedoms, virtues,
powers.
Paradise Lost (1667) bk. 5, l. 600; see **Bible** 51:30

33 Still govern thou my song,
Urania, and fit audience find, though few.
Paradise Lost (1667) bk. 7, l. 30

1   There Leviathan
Hugest of living creatures, on the deep
Stretched like a promontory sleeps or
swims.
Paradise Lost (1667) bk. 7, l. 412

2   So absolute she seems
And in herself complete.
Paradise Lost (1667) bk. 8, l. 547

3   Oft-times nothing profits more
Than self esteem, grounded on just and
right
Well managed.
Paradise Lost (1667) bk. 8, l. 571

4   The serpent subtlest beast of all the field.
Paradise Lost (1667) bk. 9, l. 86

5   As one who long in populous city pent,
Where houses thick and sewers annoy the
air,
Forth issuing on a summer's morn to
breathe
Among the pleasant villages and farms
Adjoined, from each thing met conceives
delight.
Paradise Lost (1667) bk. 9, l. 445; see **Keats** 197:5

6   Earth felt the wound, and Nature from her
seat
Sighing through all her works gave signs of
woe
That all was lost.
Paradise Lost (1667) bk. 9, l. 782

7   O fairest of creation, last and best
Of all God's works.
Paradise Lost (1667) bk. 9, l. 896

8   Flesh of flesh,
Bone of my bone thou art, and from thy
state
Mine never shall be parted, bliss or woe.
Paradise Lost (1667) bk. 9, l. 914; see **Bible** 34:12

9   . . . Yet I shall temper so
Justice with mercy.
Paradise Lost (1667) bk. 10, l. 77

10   He hears
On all sides, from innumerable tongues
A dismal universal hiss, the sound
Of public scorn.
Paradise Lost (1667) bk. 10, l. 506

11   Demoniac frenzy, moping melancholy
And moon-struck madness.
Paradise Lost (1667) bk. 11, l. 485

12   The evening star,
Love's harbinger.
Paradise Lost (1667) bk. 11, l. 588

13   A paradise within thee, happier far.
Paradise Lost (1667) bk. 12, l. 587

14   The world was all before them, where to
choose
Their place of rest, and Providence their
guide:
They hand in hand, with wandering steps
and slow,
Through Eden took their solitary way.
Paradise Lost (1667) bk. 12, l. 646

15   But on occasion's forelock watchful wait.
Paradise Regained (1671) bk. 3, l. 173

16   The childhood shows the man,
As morning shows the day.
Paradise Regained (1671) bk. 4, l. 220; see
Wordsworth 365:1

17   He who seeking asses found a kingdom.
of Saul
Paradise Regained (1671) bk. 3, l. 242; see **Bible**
36:24

18   Athens, the eye of Greece, mother of arts
And eloquence . . .
See there the olive grove of Academe,
Plato's retirement, where the Attic bird
Trills her thick-warbled notes the summer
long.
Paradise Regained (1671) bk. 4, l. 240

19   The first and wisest of them all professed
To know this only, that he nothing knew.
Paradise Regained (1671) bk. 4, l. 293; see
Socrates 319:23

20   Deep-versed in books and shallow in
himself.
Paradise Regained (1671) bk. 4, l. 327

21   Ask for this great deliverer now, and find
him
Eyeless in Gaza at the mill with slaves.
Samson Agonistes (1671) l. 40

22   O dark, dark, dark, amid the blaze of noon,
Irrecoverably dark, total eclipse
Without all hope of day!
Samson Agonistes (1671) l. 80

23   The sun to me is dark
And silent as the moon,
When she deserts the night
Hid in her vacant interlunar cave.
Samson Agonistes (1671) l. 86

24   To live a life half dead, a living death.
Samson Agonistes (1671) l. 100

25   Just are the ways of God,
And justifiable to men;
Unless there be who think not God at all.
Samson Agonistes (1671) l. 293

26   Nothing is here for tears, nothing to wail.
Samson Agonistes (1671) l. 1721

27   And calm of mind, all passion spent.
Samson Agonistes (1671) l. 1758

28   Time the subtle thief of youth.
Sonnet 7 'How soon hath time' (1645)

29   Licence they mean when they cry liberty;
For who loves that, must first be wise and
good.
Sonnet 12 'I did but prompt the age' (1673)

30   When I consider how my light is spent,
E're half my days, in this dark world and
wide,
And that one talent which is death to hide
Lodged with me useless.
*Sonnet 16 'When I consider how my light is
spent' (1673)*

31   They also serve who only stand and wait.
*Sonnet 16 'When I consider how my light is
spent' (1673)*

32   Methought I saw my late espousèd saint

Brought to me like Alcestis from the grave.
Sonnet 19 'Methought I saw my late espousèd saint' (1673)

1 Cromwell, our chief of men.
'To the Lord General Cromwell' (written 1652)

2   Peace hath her victories
No less renowned than war.
'To the Lord General Cromwell' (written 1652)

3 As good almost kill a man as kill a good book: who kills a man kills a reasonable creature, God's image; but he who destroys a good book, kills reason itself, kills the image of God, as it were in the eye.
Areopagitica (1644)

4 A good book is the precious life-blood of a master spirit, embalmed and treasured up on purpose to a life beyond life.
Areopagitica (1644)

5 I cannot praise a fugitive and cloistered virtue, unexercised and unbreathed, that never sallies out and sees her adversary, but slinks out of the race, where that immortal garland is to be run for, not without dust and heat.
Areopagitica (1644)

6 If we think to regulate printing, thereby to rectify manners, we must regulate all recreations and pastimes, all that is delightful to man.
Areopagitica (1644)

7 What does he [God] then but reveal Himself to his servants, and as his manner is, first to his Englishmen?
Areopagitica (1644)

8 Opinion in good men is but knowledge in the making.
Areopagitica (1644)

9 Give me the liberty to know, to utter, and to argue freely according to conscience, above all liberties.
Areopagitica (1644)

10 Though all the winds of doctrine were let loose to play upon the earth, so Truth be in the field, we do injuriously by licensing and prohibiting to misdoubt her strength. Let her and Falsehood grapple; who ever knew Truth put to the worse, in a free and open encounter?
Areopagitica (1644)

11 Let not England forget her precedence of teaching nations how to live.
The Doctrine and Discipline of Divorce (1643) 'To the Parliament of England'

12 What I have spoken, is the language of that which is not called amiss *The good old Cause.*
The Ready and Easy Way to Establish a Free Commonwealth (2nd ed., 1660); see **Wordsworth** 365:12

Comte de Mirabeau 1749–91
French revolutionary

13 War is the national industry of Prussia.
attributed to Mirabeau by Albert Sorel (1842–1906), based on Mirabeau's introduction

to *De la monarchie prussienne sous Frédéric le Grand* (1788)

The Missal
the Latin Eucharistic liturgy used by the Roman Catholic Church up to 1964

14 *Dominus vobiscum.*
Et cum spiritu tuo.
The Lord be with you.
And with thy spirit.
The Ordinary of the Mass

15 *In Nomine Patris, et Filii, et Spiritus Sancti.*
In the Name of the Father, and of the Son, and of the Holy Ghost.
The Ordinary of the Mass

16 *Quia peccavi nimis cogitatione, verbo, et opere, mea culpa, mea culpa, mea maxima culpa.*
I have sinned exceedingly in thought, word, and deed, through my fault, through my fault, through my most grievous fault.
The Ordinary of the Mass

17 *Kyrie eleison . . . Christe eleison.*
Lord, have mercy upon us . . . Christ, have mercy upon us.
The Ordinary of the Mass

18 *Gloria in excelsis Deo, et in terra pax hominibus bonae voluntatis.*
Glory be to God on high, and on earth peace to men of good will.
The Ordinary of the Mass; see **Bible** 47:4

19 *Deo gratias.*
Thanks be to God.
The Ordinary of the Mass

20 *Credo in unum Deum.*
I believe in one God.
The Ordinary of the Mass 'The Nicene Creed'; see **Book of Common Prayer** 59:23

21 *Et homo factus est.*
And was made man.
The Ordinary of the Mass 'The Nicene Creed'

22 *Sursum corda.*
Lift up your hearts.
The Ordinary of the Mass; see **Book of Common Prayer** 61:10

23 *Sanctus, sanctus, sanctus, Dominus Deus Sabaoth. Pleni sunt coeli et terra gloria tua. Hosanna in excelsis. Benedictus qui venit in nomine Domini.*
Holy, holy, holy, Lord God of Hosts. Heaven and earth are full of thy glory. Hosanna in the highest. Blessed is he that cometh in the name of the Lord.
The Ordinary of the Mass; see **Bible** 53:6

24 *Pater noster, qui es in coelis, sanctificetur nomen tuum; adveniat regnum tuum; fiat voluntas tua sicut in coelo, et in terra . . . sed libera nos a malo.*
Our Father, who art in heaven, hallowed be thy name; thy kingdom come; thy will be done on earth, as it is in heaven . . . but deliver us from evil.
The Ordinary of the Mass; see **Bible** 43:22

25 *Agnus Dei, qui tollis peccata mundi, miserere nobis.*

Lamb of God, who takest away the sins of the world, have mercy on us.
The Ordinary of the Mass; see **Bible** 48:21

1 *Domine, non sum dignus ut intres sub tectum meum; sed tantum dic verbo, et sanabitur anima mea.*
Lord, I am not worthy that thou shouldst enter under my roof; but say only the word, and my soul shall be healed.
The Ordinary of the Mass; see **Bible** 44:14

2 *Ite missa est.*
Go, you are dismissed.
commonly interpreted as 'Go, the Mass is ended'
The Ordinary of the Mass

3 *Verbum caro factum est.*
The word was made flesh.
The Ordinary of the Mass; see **Bible** 48:19

4 *Requiem aeternam dona eis, Domine: et lux perpetua luceat eis.*
Grant them eternal rest, O Lord; and let perpetual light shine on them.
Order of Mass for the Dead

5 *Dies irae, dies illa,*
Solvet saeclum in favilla.
That day, the day of wrath, will turn the universe to ashes.
Order of Mass for the Dead 'Sequentia' l. 1; commonly known as *Dies Irae* and sometimes attributed to Thomas of Celano (*c.*1190–1260)

6 *Requiescant in pace.*
May they rest in peace.
Order of Mass for the Dead

7 *O felix culpa, quae talem ac tantum meruit habere Redemptorem.*
O happy fault, which has earned such a mighty Redeemer.
'Exsultet' on Holy Saturday

Mistinguett 1875–1956
French actress

8 A kiss can be a comma, a question mark or an exclamation point. That's basic spelling that every woman ought to know.
in *Theatre Arts* December 1955

Adrian Mitchell 1932–
English poet, novelist, and dramatist

9 Most people ignore most poetry because
most poetry ignores most people.
Poems (1964)

Joni Mitchell (Roberta Joan Anderson) 1945–
Canadian singer and songwriter

10 They paved paradise
And put up a parking lot,
With a pink hotel,
A boutique, and a swinging hot spot.
'Big Yellow Taxi' (1970 song)

11 I've looked at life from both sides now,
From win and lose and still somehow
It's life's illusions I recall;

I really don't know life at all.
'Both Sides Now' (1967 song)

12 We are stardust,
We are golden,
And we got to get ourselves
Back to the garden.
'Woodstock' (1969 song)

Margaret Mitchell 1900–49
American novelist

13 Death and taxes and childbirth! There's never any convenient time for any of them.
Gone with the Wind (1936) ch. 38

14 I wish I could care what you do or where you go but I can't . . . My dear, I don't give a damn.
Gone with the Wind (1936) ch. 57

15 After all, tomorrow is another day.
Gone with the Wind (1936), closing words

Nancy Mitford 1904–73
English writer

16 Love in a cold climate.
title of book (1949); see **Southey** 320:23

17 Frogs . . . are slightly better than Huns or Wops, but abroad is unutterably bloody and foreigners are fiends.
The Pursuit of Love (1945) ch. 15

François Mitterrand 1916–96
French socialist statesman; President of France 1981–95

18 She has the eyes of Caligula, but the mouth of Marilyn Monroe.
of Margaret **Thatcher***, briefing his new European Minister Roland Dumas*
in *Observer* 25 November 1990

Wilson Mizner 1876–1933
American dramatist

19 Be nice to people on your way up because you'll meet 'em on your way down.
Alva Johnston *The Legendary Mizners* (1953) ch. 4

20 If you steal from one author, it's plagiarism; if you steal from many, it's research.
Alva Johnston *The Legendary Mizners* (1953) ch. 4

Ariane Mnouchkine 1934–
French theatre director

21 A cultural Chernobyl.
of Euro Disney
in *Harper's Magazine* July 1992

Emilio Mola 1887–1937
Spanish nationalist general

22 Fifth column.
an extra body of supporters claimed by General Mola in a broadcast as being within Madrid when he besieged the city with four columns of Nationalist forces
in *New York Times* 16 and 17 October 1936

Molière 1622–73
French comic dramatist

1 One should eat to live, and not live to eat.
  L'Avare (1669) act 3, sc. 1

2 Good heavens! For more than forty years I
  have been speaking prose without knowing
  it.
  Le Bourgeois Gentilhomme (1671) act 2, sc. 4

3 One dies only once, and it's for such a long
  time!
  Le Dépit amoureux (performed 1656, published
  1662) act 5, sc. 3

Helmuth von Moltke 1800–91
Prussian military commander

4 No plan of operations reaches with any
  certainty beyond the first encounter with
  the enemy's main force.
  Kriegsgechichtiche Einzelschriften (1880); often
  quotes as, 'No plan survives first contact with
  the enemy'

5 Everlasting peace is a dream, and not even a
  pleasant one; and war is a necessary part of
  God's arrangement of the world . . . Without
  war the world would deteriorate into
  materialism.
  letter to Dr J. K. Bluntschli, 11 December 1880

Walter Mondale 1928–
American Democratic politician

6 When I hear your new ideas I'm reminded
  of that ad, 'Where's the beef?'
  in a televised debate with Gary Hart, 11 March
  1984

James, Duke of Monmouth
1649–85
English illegitimate son of Charles II

7 Do not hack me as you did my Lord Russell.
  to his executioner
  T. B. Macaulay *History of England* vol. 1 (1849)
  ch. 5

James Monroe 1758–1831
*American Democratic Republican statesman, 5th
President of the US 1817–25*

8 We owe it . . . to the amicable relations
  existing between the United States and
  those [European] powers to declare that we
  should consider any attempt on their part to
  extend their system to any portion of this
  hemisphere as dangerous to our peace and
  safety.
  *principle that became known as the 'Monroe
  Doctrine'*
  annual message to Congress, 2 December 1823

Marilyn Monroe 1926–62
American actress

9 *when asked if she really had nothing on in a
  calendar photograph:*
  I had the radio on.
  in *Time* 11 August 1952

10 *on being asked what she wore in bed:*
   Chanel No. 5.
   Pete Martin *Marilyn Monroe* (1956)

John Samuel Bewley Monsell
1811–75
Irish-born clergyman

11 Fight the good fight with all thy might.
   'The Fight for Faith' (1863 hymn); see **Bible**
   52:10

12 O worship the Lord in the beauty of
   holiness,
   Bow down before him, his glory proclaim.
   'O Worship the Lord' (1863 hymn)

Lady Mary Wortley Montagu
1689–1762
English writer

13 General notions are generally wrong.
   letter to her husband Edward Wortley Montagu,
   28 March 1710

14 Civility costs nothing and buys everything.
   letter to her daughter Lady Bute, 30 May 1756

C. E. Montague 1867–1928
British writer

15 War hath no fury like a non-combatant.
   Disenchantment (1922) ch. 16

Montaigne 1533–92
French moralist and essayist

16 One should always have one's boots on, and
   be ready to leave.
   Essais (1580, ed. M. Rat, 1958) bk. 1, ch. 20; see
   La Fontaine 206:12

17 I want death to find me planting my
   cabbages, but caring little for it, and even
   less about the imperfections of my garden.
   Essais (1580, ed. M. Rat, 1958) bk. 1, ch. 20

18 The value of life lies not in the length of
   days but in the use you make of them; he
   has lived for a long time who has little lived.
   Whether you have lived enough depends
   not on the number of your years but on
   your will.
   Essais (1580, ed. M. Rat, 1958) bk. 1, ch. 20

19 It should be noted that children at play are
   not playing about; their games should be
   seen as their most serious-minded activity.
   Essais (1580, ed. M. Rat, 1958) bk. 1, ch. 23

20 If I am pressed to say why I loved him, I feel
   it can only be explained by replying:
   'Because it was he; because it was me.'
   of his friend Étienne de la Boétie
   Essais (1580, ed. M. Rat, 1958) bk. 1, ch. 28

21 There is scarcely any less bother in the
   running of a family than in that of an entire
   state. And domestic business is no less
   importunate for being less important.
   Essais (1580, ed. M. Rat, 1958) bk. 1, ch. 39

22 The greatest thing in the world is to know
   how to be oneself.
   Essais (1580, ed. M. Rat, 1958) bk. 1, ch. 39

1 When I play with my cat, who knows whether she isn't amusing herself with me more than I am with her?
Essais (1580, ed. M. Rat, 1958) bk. 2, ch. 12

2 *Que sais-je?*
What do I know?
on the position of the sceptic
Essais (1580, ed. M. Rat, 1958) bk. 2, ch. 12

3 Man is quite insane. He wouldn't know how to create a maggot, and he creates gods by the dozen.
Essais (1580, ed. M. Rat, 1958) bk. 2, ch. 12

4 It could be said of me that in this book I have only made up a bunch of other men's flowers, providing of my own only the string that ties them together.
Essais (1580, ed. M. Rat, 1958) bk. 3, ch. 12

Montesquieu 1689–1755
French political philosopher

5 If the triangles were to make a God they would give him three sides.
Lettres Persanes (1721) no. 59 (tr. J. Ozell, 1722)

6 In most things success depends on knowing how long it takes to succeed.
Pensées et fragments inédits . . . vol. 1 (1901) no. 630

7 Happy the people whose annals are blank in history-books!
attributed to Montesquieu by Thomas Carlyle in *History of Frederick the Great* bk. 16, ch. 1

Lord Montgomery of Alamein
1887–1976
British field marshal

8 *Here* we will stand and fight; there will be no further withdrawal. I have ordered that all plans and instructions dealing with further withdrawal are to be burnt, and at once. We will stand and fight *here*. If we can't stay here alive, then let us stay here dead.
speech in Cairo, 13 August 1942

Robert Montgomery 1807–55
English clergyman and poet

9 The solitary monk who shook the world.
Luther: a Poem (1842) ch. 3 'Man's Need and God's Supply'

Casimir, Comte de Montrond
1768–1843
French diplomat

10 Have no truck with first impulses for they are always generous ones.
attributed; see **Corneille** 104:6

James Graham, Marquess of Montrose 1612–50
Scottish royalist general and poet

11 He either fears his fate too much,
Or his deserts are small,
That puts it not unto the touch
To win or lose it all.
'My Dear and Only Love' (written *c.*1642)

Percy Montrose
American songwriter

12 In a cavern, in a canyon,
Excavating for a mine,
Dwelt a miner, Forty-niner,
And his daughter, Clementine.
Oh, my darling, oh my darling, oh my darling Clementine!
Thou art lost and gone for ever, dreadful sorry, Clementine.
'Clementine' (1884 song)

Monty Python's Flying Circus
1969–74
BBC TV programme, written by Graham Chapman (1941–89), John Cleese (1939–), Terry Gilliam (1940–), Eric Idle (1943–), Terry Jones (1942–), and Michael Palin (1943–)

13 Your wife interested in . . . *photographs*? Eh? Know what I mean—*photographs*? He asked him knowingly . . . nudge nudge, snap snap, grin grin, wink wink, say no more.
Monty Python's Flying Circus (1969)

14 It's *not* pining—it's passed on! This parrot is no more! It has ceased to be! It's expired and gone to meet its maker! This is a late parrot! It's a stiff! Bereft of life it rests in peace—if you hadn't nailed it to the perch it would be pushing up the daisies! It's rung down the curtain and joined the choir invisible! THIS IS AN EX-PARROT!
Monty Python's Flying Circus (1969)

15 Nobody expects the Spanish Inquisition!
Monty Python's Flying Circus (1970)

Clement C. Moore 1779–1863
American writer

16 'Twas the night before Christmas, when all through the house
Not a creature was stirring, not even a mouse.
'A Visit from St Nicholas' (December 1823)

Edward Moore 1712–57
English dramatist

17 This is adding insult to injuries.
The Foundling (1748) act 5, sc. 5

18 I am rich beyond the dreams of avarice.
The Gamester (1753) act 2, sc. 2; see **Johnson** 190:7

George Moore 1852–1933
Irish novelist

19 A man travels the world in search of what he needs and returns home to find it.
The Brook Kerith (1916) ch. 11

Jo Moore
British government adviser

20 It is now a very good day to get out anything we want to bury.
email sent in the aftermath of the terrorist action in America, 11 September 2001; commonly quoted as 'a good day to bury bad news'
in *Daily Telegraph* 10 October 2001

Marianne Moore 1887–1972
American poet

1   O to be a dragon,
a symbol of the power of Heaven—of
  silkworm
size or immense; at times invisible.
Felicitous phenomenon!
  'O To Be a Dragon' (1959)

2 I, too, dislike it: there are things that are
  important beyond all this fiddle.
Reading it, however, with a perfect
  contempt for it, one discovers in it, after
  all, a place for the genuine.
  'Poetry' (1935)

3 Imaginary gardens with real toads in them.
  'Poetry' (1935)

4 My father used to say,
  'Superior people never make long visits,
have to be shown Longfellow's grave
or the glass flowers at Harvard.'
  'Silence' (1935)

5 I am troubled, I'm dissatisfied, I'm Irish.
  'Spenser's Ireland' (1941)

Thomas Moore 1779–1852
Irish musician and songwriter

6 Believe me, if all those endearing young
  charms,
Which I gaze on so fondly today,
Were to change by tomorrow, and fleet in
  my arms,
Like fairy gifts fading away!
  Irish Melodies (1807) 'Believe me, if all those
  endearing young charms'

7 You may break, you may shatter the vase, if
  you will,
But the scent of the roses will hang round it
  still.
  Irish Melodies (1807) 'Farewell!—but whenever'

8 The harp that once through Tara's halls
The soul of music shed,
Now hangs as mute on Tara's walls
As if that soul were fled.
  Irish Melodies (1807) 'The harp that once through
  Tara's halls'

9 No, there's nothing half so sweet in life
As love's young dream.
  Irish Melodies (1807) 'Love's Young Dream'

10 The Minstrel Boy to the war is gone,
In the ranks of death you'll find him;
His father's sword he has girded on,
And his wild harp slung behind him.
  Irish Melodies (1807) 'The Minstrel Boy'

11 'Tis the last rose of summer
Left blooming alone;
All her lovely companions
Are faded and gone.
  Irish Melodies (1807) ''Tis the last rose of summer'

12 I never nursed a dear gazelle,
To glad me with its soft black eye,
But when it came to know me well,
And love me, it was sure to die!
  Lalla Rookh (1817) 'The Fire-Worshippers' pt. 1, l.
  283; see **Payn** 260:18

13 Oft, in the stilly night,
Ere Slumber's chain has bound me,
Fond Memory brings the light
Of other days around me.
  National Airs (1815) 'Oft in the Stilly Night'

Thomas Osbert Mordaunt
1730–1809
British soldier

14 One crowded hour of glorious life
Is worth an age without a name.
  'A Poem, said to be written by Major Mordaunt
  during the last German War', in *The Bee, or
  Literary Weekly Intelligencer* 12 October 1791

Thomas More 1478–1535
English scholar and saint

15 Your sheep, that were wont to be so meek
and tame, and so small eaters, now, as I hear
say, be become so great devourers, and so
wild, that they eat up and swallow down the
very men themselves.
  Utopia (1516) bk. 1

16 Anyone who campaigns for public office
becomes disqualified for holding any office
at all.
  Utopia (1516) bk. 2

17 Is not this house as nigh heaven as my own?
  of the Tower of London
  William Roper *Life of Sir Thomas More*

18 Fare well my dear child and pray for me,
and I shall for you and all your friends that
we may merrily meet in heaven.
  last letter to his daughter Margaret Roper, 5 July
  1535, on the eve of his execution

19 I pray you, master Lieutenant, see me safe
up, and my coming down let me shift for
my self.
  of mounting the scaffold
  William Roper *Life of Sir Thomas More*

20 This hath not offended the king.
  *lifting his beard aside after laying his head on the
  block*
  Francis Bacon *Apophthegms New and Old* (1625)
  no. 22

Thomas Morell 1703–84
English librettist

21 See, the conquering hero comes!
Sound the trumpets, beat the drums!
  Judas Maccabeus (1747) 'A chorus of youths' and
  Joshua (1748) pt. 3 (to music by Handel)

Morelly
French writer

22 Every citizen will make his own
contribution to the activities of the
community according to his strength, his
talent, and his age: it is on this basis that his
duties will be determined, conforming with
the distributive laws.
  Code de la Nature (1755) pt. 4; see **Blanc** 58:6,
  Marx 230:6

Robin Morgan 1941-
American feminist

1 Sisterhood is powerful.
  title of book (1970)

Christopher Morley 1890-1957
American writer

2 Life is a foreign language: all men
  mispronounce it.
  Thunder on the Left (1925) ch. 14; see **Hartley**
  163:3

Lord Morley 1838-1923
British Liberal politician and writer

3 You have not converted a man, because you
  have silenced him.
  On Compromise (1874) ch. 5

Countess Morphy (Marcelle Azra
Forbes) fl. 1930-50

4 The tragedy of English cooking is that
  'plain' cooking cannot be entrusted to
  'plain' cooks.
  English Recipes (1935)

Charles Morris 1745-1838
English songwriter

5 But a house is much more to my mind than
  a tree,
  And for groves, O! a good grove of chimneys
  for me.
  'Country and Town' (1840)

Desmond Morris 1928-
English anthropologist

6 The city is not a concrete jungle, it is a
  human zoo.
  The Human Zoo (1969) introduction

7 There are one hundred and ninety-three
  living species of monkeys and apes. One
  hundred and ninety-two of them are
  covered with hair. The exception is a naked
  ape self-named *Homo sapiens.*
  The Naked Ape (1967) introduction

Estelle Morris 1952-
British Labour politician

8 I am not good at dealing with the modern
  media . . . I have not felt I have been as
  effective as I should be, or as effective as you
  need me to be.
  resignation letter to Tony Blair, 23 October
  2002; in *Guardian* 24 October 2002 (electronic
  edition)

George Pope Morris 1802-64
American poet

9 Woodman, spare that tree!
  Touch not a single bough!
  In youth it sheltered me,
  And I'll protect it now.
  'Woodman, Spare That Tree' (1830); see
  Campbell 83:10

William Morris 1834-96
English writer, artist, and designer

10 The idle singer of an empty day.
  The Earthly Paradise (1868-70) 'An Apology'

11 Dreamer of dreams, born out of my due
  time,
  Why should I strive to set the crooked
  straight?
  The Earthly Paradise (1868-70) 'An Apology'

12 Forget the spreading of the hideous town;
  Think rather of the pack-horse on the down,
  And dream of London, small and white and
  clean,
  The clear Thames bordered by its gardens
  green.
  The Earthly Paradise (1868-70) 'Prologue: The
  Wanderers' l. 3

13 Fellowship is heaven, and lack of fellowship
  is hell.
  A Dream of John Ball (1888) ch. 4

14 Have nothing in your houses that you do not
  know to be useful, or believe to be beautiful.
  Hopes and Fears for Art (1882) 'Making the Best of
  It'

15 I spend my life ministering to the swinish
  luxury of the rich.
  reported by Sir Lowthian Bell to Alfred Powell,
  c.1877; W.R. Lethaby *Philip Webb* (1935)

Herbert 'Herb' Morrison d. 1989
American radio announcer

16 It's bursting into flames . . . Oh, the
  humanity, and all the passengers!
  *eyewitness account of the Hindenburg airship
  bursting into flames*
  recorded broadcast, 6 May 1937

Jim Morrison 1943-71
American rock singer and songwriter

17 Five to one, baby, one in five,
  No one here gets out alive . . .
  They got the guns but we got the numbers
  Gonna win, yeah, we're takin' over.
  'Five to One' (1968 song)

18 C'mon, baby, light my fire.
  'Light My Fire' (1967 song, with Robby Krieger)

19 We want the world and we want it now!
  'When the Music's Over' (1967 song)

20 I'm interested in anything about revolt,
  disorder, chaos, especially activity that
  appears to have no meaning. It seems to me
  to be the road toward freedom.
  in *Time* 24 January 1968

21 When you make your peace with authority,
  you become an authority.
  Andrew Doe and John Tobler *In Their Own Words:
  The Doors* (1988)

Van Morrison 1945-
Irish singer, songwriter, and musician

22 Music is spiritual. The music business is not.
  in *The Times* 6 July 1990

Dwight Morrow 1873–1931
American lawyer, banker, and diplomat

1 The world is divided into people who do things and people who get the credit. Try, if you can, to belong to the first class. There's far less competition.

   letter to his son, in Harold Nicolson *Dwight Morrow* (1935) ch. 3

Samuel Morse 1791–1872
American inventor

2 What hath God wrought.

   Samuel Morse, in the first electric telegraph message, 24 May 1844; see **Bible** 36:1

Wayne Lyman Morse 1900–74
American Democratic politician

3 I believe that history will record that we have made a great mistake.

   in the Senate debate on the Tonkin Gulf Resolution, which committed the United States to intervention in Vietnam; Morse was the only Senator to vote against the resolution
   in *Congressional Record* 6–7 August 1964

John Mortimer 1923–
English novelist, barrister, and dramatist

4 No brilliance is needed in the law. Nothing but common sense, and relatively clean fingernails.

   A Voyage Round My Father (1971) act 1

J. B. Morton ('Beachcomber') 1893–1975
British journalist

5 One disadvantage of being a hog is that at any moment some blundering fool may try to make a silk purse out of your wife's ear.

   By the Way (1931)

6 Hush, hush,
Nobody cares!
Christopher Robin
Has
Fallen
Down-
Stairs.

   By the Way (1931); see **Milne** 235:16

Jelly Roll Morton 1885–1941
American jazz pianist, composer, and bandleader

7 Jazz music is to be played sweet, soft, plenty rhythm.

   Mister Jelly Roll (1950)

Thomas Morton *c.*1764–1838
English dramatist

8 Approbation from Sir Hubert Stanley is praise indeed.

   A Cure for the Heartache (1797) act 5, sc. 2

9 Always ding, dinging Dame Grundy into my ears—what will Mrs Grundy zay? What will Mrs Grundy think?

   Speed the Plough (1798) act 1, sc. 1

John Lothrop Motley 1814–77
American historian

10 Give us the luxuries of life, and we will dispense with its necessities.

   Oliver Wendell Holmes *Autocrat of the Breakfast-Table* (1857–8) ch. 6

Lord Mountbatten 1900–79
British sailor, soldier, and statesman

11 Right, now I understand people think you're the Forgotten Army on the Forgotten Front. I've come here to tell you you're quite wrong. You're not the Forgotten Army on the Forgotten Front. No, make no mistake about it. Nobody's ever *heard* of you.

   encouragement to troops when taking over as Supreme Allied Commander South-East Asia in late 1943
   R. Hough *Mountbatten* (1980)

Wolfgang Amadeus Mozart 1756–91
Austrian composer

12 Melody is the essence of music. I compare a good melodist to a fine racer, and counterpoints to hack post-horses.

   remark to Michael Kelly, 1786

13 The whole, though it be long, stands almost complete and finished in my mind, so that I can survey it, like a fine picture or a beautiful statue, at a glance. Nor do I hear in my imagination the parts *successively*, but I hear them, as it were, all at once.

   on his method of composition
   letter, Edward Holmes *The Life of Mozart* (1845)

Hosni Mubarak 1928–
Egyptian statesman

14 Instead of having one [Osama] bin Laden, we will have 100 bin Ladens.

   on the probable result of a western invasion of Iraq
   in *Newsweek* 14 April 2003

Robert Mugabe 1924–
African statesman

15 Cricket civilizes people and creates good gentlemen. I want everyone to play cricket in Zimbabwe; I want ours to be a nation of gentlemen.

   in *Sunday Times* 26 February 1984

16 Blair, keep your England and let me keep my Zimbabwe.

   at the Earth Summit in Johannesburg, 2 September 2002

Malcolm Muggeridge 1903–90
British journalist

17 Something beautiful for God.

   title of book (1971); see **Teresa** 335:17

18 The orgasm has replaced the Cross as the focus of longing and the image of fulfilment.

   Tread Softly (1966)

1 Good taste and humour . . . are a
contradiction in terms, like a chaste whore.
  in Time *14 September 1953*

Frank Muir 1920-98
English writer and broadcaster

2 The thinking man's crumpet.
  of Joan Bakewell
  attributed

Ethel Watts Mumford et al.
1878-1940
American writer and humorist

3 In the midst of life we are in debt.
  Altogether New Cynic's Calendar *(1907); see* **Book
  of Common Prayer** 62:5

Lewis Mumford 1895-1990
American sociologist

4 Our national flower is the concrete
cloverleaf.
  in Quote Magazine *8 October 1961*

Mumonkan *c.*1228
a Japanese Zen textbook

5 A monk asked Tōzan, 'What is the Buddha?'
He replied 'Three pounds of flax.'
  case 18

Iris Murdoch 1919-99
English novelist

6 Dora Greenfield left her husband because
she was afraid of him. She decided six
months later to return to him for the same
reason.
  The Bell *(1958) ch. 1*

7 We live in a fantasy world, a world of
illusion. The great task in life is to find
reality.
  in The Times *15 April 1983 'Profile'*

C. W. Murphy
and Will Letters

8 Has anybody here seen Kelly?
Kelly from the Isle of Man?
  'Has Anybody Here Seen Kelly?' *(1909 song)*

Les A. Murray 1938-
Australian poet

9 Nothing's said till it's dreamed out in words
And nothing's true that figures in words
only.
  'Poetry and Religion' *(1987)*

Ed Murrow 1908-65
American broadcaster and journalist

10 No one can terrorize a whole nation, unless
we are all his accomplices.
  of Joseph McCarthy
  'See It Now', *broadcast, 7 March 1954*

11 He mobilized the English language and sent
it into battle to steady his fellow
countrymen and hearten those Europeans
upon whom the long dark night of tyranny
had descended.
  of Winston Churchill
  broadcast, 30 November 1954, in In Search of
  Light *(1967)*

12 Anyone who isn't confused doesn't really
understand the situation.
  on the Vietnam War
  Walter Bryan The Improbable Irish *(1969) ch. 1*

A. J. Muste 1885-1967
American pacifist

13 There is no way to peace. Peace is the way.
  in New York Times *16 November 1967*

Vladimir Nabokov 1899-1977
Russian novelist

14 Lolita, light of my life, fire of my loins. My
sin, my soul. Lo-lee-ta: the tip of the tongue
taking a trip of three steps down the palate
to tap, at three, on the teeth. Lo. Lee. Ta.
  Lolita *(1955) ch. 1*

15 You can always count on a murderer for a
fancy prose style.
  Lolita *(1955) ch. 1*

16 Life is a great surprise. I do not see why
death should not be an even greater one.
  Pale Fire *(1962)*

17 The cradle rocks above an abyss, and
common sense tells us that our existence is
but a brief crack of light between two
eternities of darkness.
  Speak, Memory *(1951) ch. 1*

Ralph Nader 1934-
American consumer protectionist

18 Unsafe at any speed.
  title of book (1965)

Nagarjuna *c.*2nd century AD
Indian philosopher

19 The doctrine of the Buddha is taught with
reference to two truths—conventional truth
and ultimate truth.
  Root Verses of the Middle Way *ch. 24, v. 8*

Fridtjof Nansen 1861-1930
Norwegian polar explorer

20 Never stop because you are afraid—you are
never so likely to be wrong. Never keep a
line of retreat: it is a wretched invention.
The difficult is what takes a little time; the
impossible is what takes a little longer.
  in Listener *14 December 1939; see* **Anonymous**
  7:23, **Calonne** 82:20

Napoleon I 1769-1821
French monarch, emperor 1804-15

21 Think of it, soldiers; from the summit of
these pyramids, forty centuries look down
upon you.
  before the Battle of the Pyramids
  speech to the Army of Egypt on 21 July 1798

1 I want the whole of Europe to have one currency; it will make trading much easier.
  letter to his brother Louis, 6 May 1807

2 There is only one step from the sublime to the ridiculous.
  to De Pradt, Polish ambassador, after the retreat from Moscow in 1812
  D. G. De Pradt *Histoire de l'Ambassade dans le grand-duché de Varsovie en 1812* (1815); see **Paine** 257:4

3 As to moral courage, I have very rarely met with two o'clock in the morning courage: I mean instantaneous courage.
  E. A. de Las Cases *Mémorial de Ste-Hélène* (1823) vol. 1, pt. 2, 4–5 December 1815; see **Thoreau** 339:15

4 An army marches on its stomach.
  attributed, but probably condensed from a long passage in E. A. de Las Cases *Mémorial de Ste-Hélène* (1823) vol. 4, 14 November 1816; also attributed to **Frederick the Great**

5 As though he had 200,000 men.
  when asked how to deal with the Pope
  J. M. Robinson *Cardinal Consalvi* (1987); see **Stalin** 322:24

6 *La carrière ouverte aux talents.*
  The career open to the talents.
  Barry E. O'Meara *Napoleon in Exile* (1822) vol. 1

7 England is a nation of shopkeepers.
  Barry E. O'Meara *Napoleon in Exile* (1822) vol. 2; see **Adams** 2:16, **Smith** 318:5

8 Not tonight, Josephine.
  attributed, but probably apocryphal; the phrase does not appear in contemporary sources, but was current by the early twentieth century

9 *of Talleyrand:*
  A pile of shit in a silk stocking.
  attributed

Ogden Nash 1902–71
American humorist

10 The turtle lives 'twixt plated decks
Which practically conceal its sex.
I think it clever of the turtle
In such a fix to be so fertile.
  'Autres Bêtes, Autres Moeurs' (1931)

11 The camel has a single hump;
The dromedary, two;
Or else the other way around,
I'm never sure. Are you?
  'The Camel' (1936)

12 The cow is of the bovine ilk;
One end is moo, the other, milk.
  'The Cow' (1931)

13 Any kiddie in school can love like a fool,
But hating, my boy, is an art.
  'Plea for Less Malice Toward None' (1933)

14 Candy
Is dandy
But liquor
Is quicker.
  'Reflections on Ice-breaking' (1931)

15 I think that I shall never see
A billboard lovely as a tree.

Perhaps, unless the billboards fall,
I'll never see a tree at all.
  'Song of the Open Road' (1933); see **Kilmer** 200:4

16 Sure, deck your lower limbs in pants;
Yours are the limbs, my sweeting.
You look divine as you advance—
Have you seen yourself retreating?
  'What's the Use?' (1940)

Thomas Nashe 1567–1601
English pamphleteer and dramatist

17 O, tis a precious apothegmatical Pedant, who will find matter enough to dilate a whole day of the first invention of *Fy, fa, fum,* I smell the blood of an English-man.
  Have with you to Saffron-walden (1596); see **Shakespeare** 298:12

18 Brightness falls from the air;
Queens have died young and fair;
Dust hath closed Helen's eye.
I am sick, I must die.
Lord have mercy on us.
  Summer's Last Will and Testament (1600) l. 1590

19 From winter, plague and pestilence, good lord, deliver us!
  Summer's Last Will and Testament (1600) l. 1878

Martina Navratilova 1956–
Czech-born American tennis player

20 Do what you love and love what you do and everything else is detail.
  in *The Times* 3 July 2004

James Ball Naylor 1860–1945

21 King David and King Solomon
Led merry, merry lives,
With many, many lady friends,
And many, many wives;
But when old age crept over them—
With many, many qualms!—
King Solomon wrote the Proverbs
And King David wrote the Psalms.
  'King David and King Solomon' (1935)

John Mason Neale 1818–66
English clergyman

22 All glory, laud, and honour
To thee, Redeemer, King,
To whom the lips of children
Made sweet hosannas ring.
  'All glory, laud, and honour' (1851 hymn)

23 Good King Wenceslas looked out,
On the feast of Stephen;
When the snow lay round about,
Deep and crisp and even.
  'Good King Wenceslas'

24 Jerusalem the golden,
With milk and honey blessed.
  'Jerusalem the golden' (1858 hymn); translated from the Latin of St Bernard of Cluny (b. *c.*1100)

Jawaharlal Nehru 1889-1964
Indian statesman

1 At the stroke of the midnight hour, while the world sleeps, India will awake to life and freedom.
immediately prior to Independence
speech to the Indian Constituent Assembly, 14 August 1947

2 The light has gone out of our lives and there is darkness everywhere.
*following **Gandhi**'s assassination*
broadcast, 30 January 1948; Richard J. Walsh *Nehru on Gandhi* (1948) ch. 6

3 There is no easy walk-over to freedom anywhere, and many of us will have to pass through the valley of the shadow again and again before we reach the mountain-tops of our desire.
'From Lucknow to Tripuri' (1939)

Horatio, Lord Nelson 1758-1805
British admiral

4 You must consider every man your enemy who speaks ill of your king: and . . . you must hate a Frenchman as you hate the devil.
Robert Southey *Life of Nelson* (1813) ch. 3

5 I have only one eye,—I have a right to be blind sometimes . . . I really do not see the signal!
at the battle of Copenhagen, 1801
Robert Southey *Life of Nelson* (1813) ch. 7

6 When I came to explain to them the '*Nelson touch*', it was like an electric shock.
letter to Lady Hamilton, 1 October 1805

7 May humanity after Victory be the predominant feature of the British Fleet.
diary entry, on the eve of the battle of Trafalgar, 21 October 1805
Nicholas Harris Nicolas (ed.) *Dispatches and Letters of . . . Nelson* (1846) vol. 7, p. 139

8 England expects that every man will do his duty.
at the battle of Trafalgar, 21 October 1805
Robert Southey *Life of Nelson* (1813) ch. 9

9 Thank God, I have done my duty.
at the battle of Trafalgar, 21 October 1805
Robert Southey *Life of Nelson* (1813) ch. 9

10 Kiss me, Hardy.
at the battle of Trafalgar, 21 October 1805
Robert Southey *Life of Nelson* (1813) ch. 9

Nero AD 37-68
Roman emperor from AD 54

11 *Qualis artifex pereo!*
What an artist dies with me!
Suetonius *Lives of the Caesars* 'Nero'

Pablo Neruda 1904-73
Chilean poet

12 *Es tan corto el amor, y es tan largo el olvido.*
Love is so short, forgetting is so long.
'Tonight I Can Write' (1924)

Gérard de Nerval 1808-55
French poet

13 *Je suis le ténébreux,—le veuf,—l'inconsolé,*
Le prince d'Aquitaine à la tour abolie.
I am the darkly shaded, the bereaved, the inconsolate, the prince of Aquitaine, with the blasted tower.
Les Chimères (1854) 'El Desdichado'

John von Neumann 1903-57
Hungarian-born American mathematician and computer pioneer

14 In mathematics you don't understand things. You just get used to them.
Gary Zukav *The Dancing Wu Li Masters* (1979)

Henry Newbolt 1862-1938
English lawyer, poet, and man of letters

15 'Take my drum to England, hang et by the shore,
Strike et when your powder's runnin' low;
If the Dons sight Devon, I'll quit the port o' Heaven,
An' drum them up the Channel as we drummed them long ago.'
'Drake's Drum' (1897)

16 Drake he's in his hammock till the great Armadas come.
(Capten, art tha sleepin' there below?)
'Drake's Drum' (1897)

17 Now the sunset breezes shiver,
And she's fading down the river,
But in England's song for ever
She's the Fighting Téméraire.
'The Fighting Téméraire' (1897)

18 There's a breathless hush in the Close to-night—
Ten to make and the match to win—
A bumping pitch and a blinding light,
An hour to play and the last man in.
And it's not for the sake of a ribboned coat,
Or the selfish hope of a season's fame,
But his Captain's hand on his shoulder smote—
'Play up! play up! and play the game!'
'Vitaï Lampada' (1897)

Anthony Newley 1931-
and Leslie Bricusse 1931-

19 Stop the world, I want to get off.
title of musical (1961)

John Henry Newman 1801-90
English theologian and leader of the Oxford Movement; later Cardinal

20 Two and two only supreme and luminously self-evident beings, myself and my Creator.
Apologia pro Vita Sua (1864) 'History of My Religious Opinions to the Year 1833'

21 Ten thousand difficulties do not make one doubt.
Apologia pro Vita Sua (1864) 'Position of my Mind since 1845'

1 It is almost a definition of a gentleman to say that he is one who never inflicts pain.
   The Idea of a University (1852) 'Knowledge and Religious Duty'

2 She [the Catholic Church] holds that it were better for sun and moon to drop from heaven, for the earth to fail, and for all the many millions who are upon it to die of starvation in extremest agony, as far as temporal affliction goes, than that one soul, I will not say, should be lost, but should commit one single venial sin.
   Lectures on Anglican Difficulties (1852) Lecture 8

3 If I am obliged to bring religion into after-dinner toasts (which indeed does not seem quite the thing) I shall drink—to the Pope, if you please—still, to Conscience first, and to the Pope afterwards.
   A Letter Addressed to the Duke of Norfolk . . . (1875) sect. 5

4 May He support us all the day long, till the shades lengthen, and the evening comes, and the busy world is hushed, and the fever of life is over, and our work is done! Then in His mercy may He give us a safe lodging, and a holy rest, and peace at the last.
   'Wisdom and Innocence' (19 February 1843)

5 Firmly I believe and truly
   God is Three, and God is One;
   And I next acknowledge duly
   Manhood taken by the Son.
   The Dream of Gerontius (1865)

6 Praise to the Holiest in the height,
   And in the depth be praise;
   In all his words most wonderful,
   Most sure in all His ways.
   The Dream of Gerontius (1865)

7 Lead, kindly Light, amid the encircling gloom,
   Lead thou me on.
   'Lead, kindly Light' (1834)

8 *We can believe what we choose*. We are answerable for what we choose to believe.
   letter to Mrs William Froude, 27 June 1848

9 *Cor ad cor loquitur.*
   Heart speaks to heart.
   motto of Newman; see **Francis** 141:12

Huey Newton 1942-
American political activist

10 I suggested [in 1966] that we use the panther as our symbol and call our political vehicle the Black Panther Party. The panther is a fierce animal, but he will not attack until he is backed into a corner; then he will strike out.
   Revolutionary Suicide (1973) ch. 16

Isaac Newton 1642-1727
English mathematician and physicist

11 Every body continues in its state of rest, or of uniform motion in a right line, unless it is compelled to change that state by forces impressed upon it.
   Principia Mathematica (1687) Laws of Motion 1 (tr. Andrew Motte, 1729)

12 The alteration of motion is ever proportional to the motive force impressed; and is made in the direction of the right line in which that force is impressed.
   Principia Mathematica (1687) Laws of Motion 2 (tr. Andrew Motte, 1729)

13 To every action there is always opposed an equal reaction: or, the mutual actions of two bodies upon each other are always equal, and directed to contrary parts.
   Principia Mathematica (1687) Laws of Motion 3 (tr. Andrew Motte, 1729)

14 *Hypotheses non fingo.*
   I do not feign hypotheses.
   Principia Mathematica (1713 ed.) 'Scholium Generale'

15 If I have seen further it is by standing on the shoulders of giants.
   letter to Robert Hooke, 5 February 1676; see **Bernard** 32:10, **Coleridge** 101:3

16 I don't know what I may seem to the world, but as to myself, I seem to have been only like a boy playing on the sea-shore and diverting myself in now and then finding a smoother pebble or a prettier shell than ordinary, whilst the great ocean of truth lay all undiscovered before me.
   Joseph Spence *Anecdotes* (ed. J. Osborn, 1966) no. 1259

17 O Diamond! Diamond! thou little knowest the mischief done!
   to a dog, who knocked over a candle which set fire to some papers and thereby 'destroyed the almost finished labours of some years'
   Thomas Maude *Wensley-Dale . . . a Poem* (1772) st. 23 n.; probably apocryphal

John Newton 1725-1807
English clergyman

18 Amazing grace! how sweet the sound
   That saved a wretch like me!
   Olney Hymns (1779) 'Amazing grace'

19 Glorious things of thee are spoken,
   Zion, city of our God!
   Olney Hymns (1779) 'Glorious things of thee are spoken'

20 How sweet the name of Jesus sounds
   In a believer's ear!
   Olney Hymns (1779) 'How sweet the name of Jesus sounds'

Nicholas I 1796-1855
Russian monarch, emperor from 1825

21 Turkey is a dying man. We may endeavour to keep him alive, but we shall not succeed. He will, he must die.
   F. Max Müller (ed.) *Memoirs of Baron Stockmar* (tr. G. A. M. Müller, 1873) vol. 2

1 Russia has two generals in whom she can confide—Generals Janvier [January] and Février [February].
attributed; in *Punch* 10 March 1855

Reinhold Niebuhr 1892–1971
American theologian

2 Man's capacity for justice makes democracy possible, but man's inclination to injustice makes democracy necessary.
Children of Light and Children of Darkness (1944) foreword

Martin Niemöller 1892–1984
German theologian

3 When Hitler attacked the Jews I was not a Jew, therefore, I was not concerned. And when Hitler attacked the Catholics, I was not a Catholic, and therefore, I was not concerned. And when Hitler attacked the unions and the industrialists, I was not a member of the unions and I was not concerned. Then, Hitler attacked me and the Protestant church—and there was nobody left to be concerned.
often quoted in the form 'In Germany they came first for the Communists, and I didn't speak up because I wasn't a Communist . . . ' and so on
in *Congressional Record* 14 October 1968

Friedrich Nietzsche 1844–1900
German philosopher and writer

4 I teach you the superman. Man is something to be surpassed.
Also Sprach Zarathustra (1883) prologue, sect. 3

5 You are going to women? Do not forget the whip!
Also Sprach Zarathustra (1883) bk. 1 'Von Alten und jungen Weiblein'

6 God is dead: but considering the state the species Man is in, there will perhaps be caves, for ages yet, in which his shadow will be shown.
Die fröhliche Wissenschaft (1882) bk. 3, sect. 108; see **Plato** 265:1

7 Morality is the herd-instinct in the individual.
Die fröhliche Wissenschaft (1882) bk. 3, sect. 116

8 The secret of reaping the greatest fruitfulness and the greatest enjoyment from life is to *live dangerously!*
Die fröhliche Wissenschaft (1882) bk. 4, sect. 283

9 He who fights with monsters might take care lest he thereby become a monster.
Jenseits von Gut und Böse (1886) ch. 4, no. 146

10 The thought of suicide is a great source of comfort: with it a calm passage is to be made across many a bad night.
Jenseits von Gut und Böse (1886) ch. 4, no. 157

11 Master-morality and slave-morality.
Jenseits von Gut und Böse (1886) ch. 9, no. 260

12 At the base of all these aristocratic races the predator is not to be mistaken, the splendorous *blond beast*, avidly rampant for plunder and victory.
Zur Genealogie der Moral (1887) 1st treatise, no. 11

Florence Nightingale 1820–1910
English nurse

13 It may seem a strange principle to enunciate as the very first requirement in a Hospital that it should do the sick no harm.
Notes on Hospitals (1863 ed.) preface

Anaïs Nin 1903–77
French-born American writer

14 Anxiety is love's greatest killer. It creates the failures. It makes others feel as you might when a drowning man holds on to you. You want to save him, but you know he will strangle you with his panic.
diary, February 1947; *The Diary of Anaïs Nin* vol. 4 (1944–7)

Richard Milhous Nixon 1913–94
American Republican statesman, 37th President of the US 1969–74

15 The great silent majority.
broadcast, 3 November 1969, in *New York Times* 4 November 1969

16 There can be no whitewash at the White House.
on Watergate
television speech, 30 April 1973

17 I welcome this kind of examination because people have got to know whether or not their President is a crook. Well, I'm not a crook.
speech at press conference, 17 November 1973, in *New York Times* 18 November 1973

18 I brought myself down. I gave them a sword. And they stuck it in.
television interview, 19 May 1977

19 When the President does it, that means that it is not illegal.
David Frost *I Gave Them a Sword* (1978) ch. 8

Caroline Maria Noel 1817–77
English hymn-writer

20 At the name of Jesus
Every knee shall bow,
Every tongue confess him
King of glory now.
'At the name of Jesus' (1861 hymn); see **Bible** 51:22

Thomas Noel 1799–1861
English poet

21 Rattle his bones over the stones;
He's only a pauper, whom nobody owns!
'The Pauper's Drive' (1841)

Christopher North 1785–1854
Scottish literary critic

22 His Majesty's dominions, on which the sun never sets.
Blackwood's Magazine (April 1829) 'Noctes Ambrosianae' no. 42; see **Schiller** 286:9

1 Laws were made to be broken.
   Blackwood's Magazine (May 1830) 'Noctes
   Ambrosianae' no. 49

Lord North 1732–92
British statesman, Prime Minister 1770–82

2 Oh God! It is all over!
   *on receiving the news of Cornwallis's surrender at
   Yorktown, 19 October 1781*
   in *Dictionary of National Biography* (1917–)

Alfred Harmsworth, Lord Northcliffe 1865–1922
British newspaper proprietor

3 The power of the press is very great, but not
   so great as the power of suppress.
   office message, *Daily Mail* 1918

4 When I want a peerage, I shall buy it like an
   honest man.
   Tom Driberg *Swaff* (1974) ch. 2

Caroline Norton 1808–77
English poet and songwriter

5 And all our calm is in that balm—
   Not lost but gone before.
   'Not Lost but Gone Before'; see **Cyprian** 109:3,
   Rogers 278:12

Jack Norworth 1879–1959
American songwriter

6 Oh, shine on, shine on, harvest moon
   Up in the sky.
   I ain't had no lovin'
   Since April, January, June, or July.
   'Shine On, Harvest Moon' (1908 song)

Novalis 1772–1801
German poet and novelist

7 I often feel, and ever more deeply I realize,
   that Fate and character are the same
   conception.
   *often quoted as 'Character is destiny' or
   'Character is fate'*
   Heinrich von Ofterdingen (1802) bk. 2; see **Eliot**
   127:21, **Heraclitus** 167:4

8 A God-intoxicated man.
   of **Spinoza**
   attributed

Alfred Noyes 1880–1958
English poet

9 Go down to Kew in lilac-time, in lilac-time,
   in lilac-time,
   Go down to Kew in lilac-time (it isn't far
   from London!).
   'The Barrel-Organ' (1904)

10 The road was a ribbon of moonlight over the
   purple moor,
   And the highwayman came riding—
   Riding—riding—
   The highwayman came riding, up to the old
   inn-door.
   'The Highwayman' (1907)

11 Look for me by moonlight;

Watch for me by moonlight;
I'll come to thee by moonlight, though hell
   should bar the way!
   'The Highwayman' (1907)

Sam Nunn 1938–
American Democratic politician

12 Don't ask, don't tell.
   summary of the **Clinton** administration's
   compromise policy on homosexuals serving in
   the armed forces, in *New York Times* 12 May 1993

Bill Nye 1850–96
American humorist

13 I have been told that Wagner's music is
   better than it sounds.
   Mark Twain *Autobiography* (1924) vol. 1

Charles Edward Oakley 1832–65
English clergyman

14 Hills of the North, rejoice:
   Rivers and mountain-spring,
   Hark to the advent voice!
   Valley and lowland, sing!
   'Hills of the North, rejoice' (1870 hymn)

Lawrence Oates 1880–1912
English polar explorer

15 I am just going outside and may be some
   time.
   Robert Falcon Scott diary entry, 16–17 March
   1912

Barack Obama 1959–
American Democratic politician

16 There is not a black America and a white
   America and Latino American and Asian
   America; there's the United States of
   America . . . We worship an awesome God in
   the blue states, and we don't like federal
   agents poking round our libraries in the red
   states.
   *on the view of a red and blue America divided by
   party*
   in *New York Times* 28 July 2004 (online edition)

Edna O'Brien 1932–
Irish novelist and short-story writer

17 August is a wicked month.
   title of novel (1965)

Flann O'Brien 1911–66
Irish novelist and journalist

18 A pint of plain is your only man.
   At Swim-Two-Birds (1939) 'The Workman's
   Friend'

Sean O'Casey 1880–1964
Irish dramatist

19 English literature's performing flea.
   of P. G. **Wodehouse**
   P. G. Wodehouse *Performing Flea* (1953)

William of Occam *c.1285–1349*
English Franciscan friar and philosopher

1 *Entia non sunt multiplicanda praeter necessitatem.*
No more things should be presumed to exist than are absolutely necessary.
'Occam's Razor', an ancient philosophical principle often attributed to Occam but earlier in origin
  not found in this form in his writings, although he frequently used similar expressions.

David Ogilvy *1911–99*
British-born advertising executive

2 The consumer isn't a moron; she is your wife.
  Confessions of an Advertising Man (1963) ch. 5

John O'Hara *1905–70*
American writer

3 An artist is his own fault.
  The Portable F. Scott Fitzgerald (1945) introduction

Theodore O'Hara *1820–67*
American poet

4 The bivouac of the dead.
  title of poem (1847)

5 Sons of the dark and bloody ground.
  'The Bivouac of the Dead' (1847) st. 1

Georgia O'Keefe *1887–1986*
American painter

6 Filling a space in a beautiful way. That's what art means to me.
  in Art News December 1977

Dennis O'Kelly *c.1720–87*
Irish racehorse-owner

7 Eclipse first, the rest nowhere.
  comment at Epsom on the occasion of the horse Eclipse's first race, 3 May 1769; the Dictionary of National Biography gives the occasion as the Queen's Plate at Winchester, 1769
  in Annals of Sporting vol. 2 (1822)

Laurence Olivier *1907–89*
English actor and director

8 The tragedy of a man who could not make up his mind.
  introduction to his 1948 screen adaptation of Hamlet

9 Shakespeare—the nearest thing in incarnation to the eye of God.
  in Kenneth Harris Talking To (1971) 'Sir Laurence Olivier'

10 Acting is a masochistic form of exhibitionism. It is not quite the occupation of an adult.
  in Time 3 July 1978

Frank Ward O'Malley *see* **Elbert Hubbard**

Omar *c.581–644*
Arab caliph, conqueror of Syria, Palestine, and Egypt

11 If these writings of the Greeks agree with the book of God, they are useless and need not be preserved; if they disagree, they are pernicious and ought to be destroyed.
  on burning the library of Alexandria, AD c.641
  Edward Gibbon *The Decline and Fall of the Roman Empire (1776–88) ch. 51*

Jacqueline Kennedy Onassis *1929–94*
American First Lady 1961–3

12 If you bungle raising your children I don't think whatever else you do well matters very much.
  Theodore C. Sorenson *Kennedy (1965)*

Eugene O'Neill *1888–1953*
American dramatist

13 The iceman cometh.
  title of play (1946)

14 A long day's journey into night.
  title of play (written 1940–1)

15 Mourning becomes Electra
  title of play (1931)

Yoko Ono *1933–*
Japanese poet and songwriter

16 Woman is the nigger of the world.
  remark made in a 1968 interview for Nova magazine and adopted by her husband John **Lennon** *as the title of a song (1972)*

Brian O'Nolan *see* **Flann O'Brien**

J. Robert Oppenheimer *1904–67*
American physicist

17 I remembered the line from the Hindu scripture, the *Bhagavad Gita* . . . 'I am become death, the destroyer of worlds.'
  on the explosion of the first atomic bomb near Alamogordo, New Mexico, 16 July 1945
  Len Giovannitti and Fred Freed *The Decision to Drop the Bomb (1965); see* **Bhagavadgita** 33:20

18 The physicists have known sin; and this is a knowledge which they cannot lose.
  lecture at Massachusetts Institute of Technology, 25 November 1947

19 When you see something that is technically sweet, you go ahead and do it and you argue about what to do about it only after you have had your technical success. That is the way it was with the atomic bomb.
  in In the Matter of J. Robert Oppenheimer, USAEC Transcript of Hearing Before Personnel Security Board (1954)

Susie Orbach 1946–
American psychotherapist

1 Fat is a feminist issue.
   title of book (1978)

Roy Orbison 1936–88
and Joe Melson
American singer and songwriter

2 Only the lonely (know the way I feel).
   title of song (1960)

Baroness Orczy 1865–1947
Hungarian-born novelist

3 We seek him here, we seek him there,
   Those Frenchies seek him everywhere.
   Is he in heaven?—Is he in hell?
   That demmed, elusive Pimpernel?
   The Scarlet Pimpernel (1905) ch. 12

Meta Orred
Scottish 19th-century writer and poet

4 In the gloaming, Oh my darling!
   When the lights are dim and low,
   And the quiet shadows falling
   Softly come and softly go.
   'In the Gloaming' (1877 song)

José Ortega y Gasset 1883–1955
Spanish writer and philosopher

5 I am I plus my surroundings, and if I do not
   preserve the latter I do not preserve myself.
   Meditaciones del Quijote (1914)

Joe Orton 1933–67
English dramatist

6 I'd the upbringing a nun would envy . . .
   Until I was fifteen I was more familiar with
   Africa than my own body.
   Entertaining Mr Sloane (1964) act 1

7 It's all any reasonable child can expect if the
   dad is present at the conception.
   Entertaining Mr Sloane (1964) act 3

George Orwell 1903–50
English novelist

8 Man is the only creature that consumes
   without producing.
   Animal Farm (1945) ch. 1

9 Four legs good, two legs bad.
   Animal Farm (1945) ch. 3

10 All animals are equal but some animals are
   more equal than others.
   Animal Farm (1945) ch. 10

11 The creatures outside looked from pig to
   man, and from man to pig, and from pig to
   man again, but already it was impossible to
   say which was which.
   Animal Farm (1945); closing words

12 Good prose is like a window-pane.
   Collected Essays (1968) vol. 1 'Why I Write'

13 I'm fat, but I'm thin inside. Has it ever
   struck you that there's a thin man inside

every fat man, just as they say there's a
statue inside every block of stone?
   Coming up For Air (1939) pt. 1, ch. 3; see
   Connolly 102:18

14 Down and out in Paris and London.
   title of book (1933)

15 He was an embittered atheist (the sort of
   atheist who does not so much disbelieve in
   God as personally dislike Him).
   Down and Out in Paris and London (1933) ch. 30

16 Keep the aspidistra flying.
   title of novel (1936)

17 Advertising is the rattling of a stick inside a
   swill bucket.
   Keep the Aspidistra Flying (1936) ch. 3

18 Old maids biking to Holy Communion
   through the mists of the autumn mornings
   . . . these are not only fragments, but
   characteristic fragments, of the English scene.
   The Lion and the Unicorn (1941) pt. 1 'England
   Your England'; see **Major** 225:19

19 Probably the battle of Waterloo *was* won on
   the playing-fields of Eton, but the opening
   battles of all subsequent wars have been lost
   there.
   The Lion and the Unicorn (1941) pt. 1 'England
   Your England'; see **Wellington** 354:8

20 It was a bright cold day in April, and the
   clocks were striking thirteen.
   Nineteen Eighty-Four (1949) pt. 1, ch. 1

21 BIG BROTHER IS WATCHING YOU.
   Nineteen Eighty-Four (1949) pt. 1, ch. 1

22 War is peace. Freedom is slavery. Ignorance
   is strength.
   Nineteen Eighty-Four (1949) pt. 1, ch. 1

23 Who controls the past controls the future:
   who controls the present controls the past.
   Nineteen Eighty-Four (1949) pt. 1, ch. 3

24 Don't you see that the whole aim of
   Newspeak is to narrow the range of
   thought? In the end we shall make
   thoughtcrime literally impossible, because
   there will be no words in which to express
   it.
   Nineteen Eighty-Four (1949) pt. 1, ch. 5

25 Freedom is the freedom to say that two plus
   two make four. If that is granted, all else
   follows.
   Nineteen Eighty-Four (1949) pt. 1, ch. 7

26 The Lottery, with its weekly pay-out of
   enormous prizes, was the one public event
   to which the proles paid serious attention
   . . . It was their delight, their folly, their
   anodyne, their intellectual stimulant . . . the
   prizes were largely imaginary. Only small
   sums were actually paid out, the winners of
   the big prizes being non-existent persons.
   Nineteen Eighty-Four (1949) pt. 1, ch. 8

27 *Doublethink* means the power of holding two
   contradictory beliefs in one's mind
   simultaneously, and accepting both of them.
   Nineteen Eighty-Four (1949) pt. 2, ch. 9

28 Power is not a means, it is an end. One does
   not establish a dictatorship in order to

safeguard a revolution; one makes the revolution in order to establish the dictatorship.
Nineteen Eighty-Four (1949) pt. 3, ch. 3

1 If you want a picture of the future, imagine a boot stamping on a human face—for ever.
Nineteen Eighty-Four (1949) pt. 3, ch. 3

2 Serious sport . . . is war minus the shooting.
Shooting an Elephant (1950) 'I Write as I Please'

3 The great enemy of clear language is insincerity. When there is a gap between one's real and one's declared aims, one turns as it were instinctively to long words and exhausted idioms, like a cuttlefish squirting out ink.
Shooting an Elephant (1950) 'Politics and the English Language'

4 In our time, political speech and writing are largely the defence of the indefensible.
Shooting an Elephant (1950) 'Politics and the English Language'

5 Political language . . . is designed to make lies sound truthful and murder respectable, and to give an appearance of solidity to pure wind.
Shooting an Elephant (1950) 'Politics and the English Language'

6 Saints should always be judged guilty until they are proved innocent.
Shooting an Elephant (1950) 'Reflections on Gandhi'

7 Whatever is funny is subversive, every joke is ultimately a custard pie . . . A dirty joke is a sort of mental rebellion.
in *Horizon* September 1941 'The Art of Donald McGill'

8 The quickest way of ending a war is to lose it.
in *Polemic* May 1946 'Second Thoughts on James Burnham'

9 At 50, everyone has the face he deserves.
last words in his notebook, 17 April 1949

John Osborne 1929–94
English dramatist

10 Don't clap too hard—it's a very old building.
The Entertainer (1957) no. 7

11 But I have a go, lady, don't I? I 'ave a go. I do.
The Entertainer (1957) no. 7

12 Look back in anger.
title of play (1956); see **Paul** 260:14

13 They spend their time mostly looking forward to the past.
Look Back in Anger (1956) act 2, sc. 1

14 This is a letter of hate. It is for you my countrymen, I mean those men of my country who have defiled it. The men with manic fingers leading the sightless, feeble, betrayed body of my country to its death . . . damn you England.
in *Tribune* 18 August 1961

Arthur O'Shaughnessy 1844–81
English poet

15 We are the music makers,
We are the dreamers of dreams . . .
We are the movers and shakers
Of the world for ever, it seems.
'Ode' (1874)

16 For each age is a dream that is dying,
Or one that is coming to birth.
'Ode' (1874)

William Osler 1849–1919
Canadian-born physician

17 One finger in the throat and one in the rectum makes a good diagnostician.
Aphorisms from his Bedside Teachings (1961)

18 The desire to take medicine is perhaps the greatest feature which distinguishes man from animals.
H. Cushing *Life of Sir William Osler* (1925) vol. 1, ch. 14

John L. O'Sullivan 1813–95
American journalist and diplomat

19 The best government is that which governs least.
in *United States Magazine and Democratic Review* (1837) introduction; see **Thoreau** 339:5

20 A spirit of hostile interference against us . . . checking the fulfilment of our manifest destiny to overspread the continent allotted by Providence for the free development of our yearly multiplying millions.
on opposition to the annexation of Texas
in *United States Magazine and Democratic Review* (1845) vol. 17

21 A torchlight procession marching down your throat.
describing certain kinds of whisky
G. W. E. Russell *Collections and Recollections* (1898) ch. 19

James Otis 1725–83
American politician

22 Taxation without representation is tyranny.
associated with his attack on writs of assistance, 1761, and later a watchword of the American Revolution; see **Camden** 83:2

Ovid 43 BC–c.AD 17
Roman poet

23 *Lente currite noctis equi.*
Run slowly, horses of the night.
Amores bk. 1, no. 13, l. 40; see **Marlowe** 228:9

24 *Expedit esse deos, et, ut expedit, esse putemus.*
It is convenient that there be gods, and, as it is convenient, let us believe that there are.
Ars Amatoria bk. 1, l. 637; see **Voltaire** 348:16

25 *Gutta cavat lapidem, consumitur anulus usu.*
Dripping water hollows out a stone, a ring is worn away by use.
Epistulae Ex Ponto bk. 4, no. 10, l. 5; see **Latimer** 209:11

26 *Medio tutissimus ibis.*

You will go most safely by the middle way.
Metamorphoses bk. 2, l. 137

1 *Video meliora, proboque;*
Deteriora sequor.
I see the better things, and approve; I follow the worse.
Metamorphoses bk. 7, l. 20; see **Bible** 50:6

2 *Tempus edax rerum.*
Time the devourer of everything.
Metamorphoses bk. 15, l. 234

3 *Qui finem quaeris amoris,*
Cedet amor rebus; res age, tutus eris.
You who seek an end of love, love will yield to business: be busy, and you will be safe.
Remedia Amoris l. 143

John Owen *c.*1563–1622
Welsh epigrammatist

4 God and the doctor we alike adore
But only when in danger, not before;
The danger o'er, both are alike requited,
God is forgotten, and the Doctor slighted.
Epigrams; see **Quarles** 272:8

Robert Owen 1771–1858
Welsh-born socialist and philanthropist

5 All the world is queer save thee and me, and even thou art a little queer.
to his partner W. Allen, on severing business relations at New Lanark, 1828
attributed

Wilfred Owen 1893–1918
English poet

6 My subject is War, and the pity of War.
The Poetry is in the pity.
Preface (written 1918) in *Poems* (1963)

7 All a poet can do today is warn.
Preface (written 1918) in *Poems* (1963)

8 What passing-bells for these who die as cattle?
Only the monstrous anger of the guns.
'Anthem for Doomed Youth' (written 1917)

9 The shrill, demented choirs of wailing shells;
And bugles calling for them from sad shires.
'Anthem for Doomed Youth' (written 1917)

10 The pallor of girls' brows shall be their pall;
Their flowers the tenderness of patient minds,
And each slow dusk a drawing-down of blinds.
'Anthem for Doomed Youth' (written 1917)

11 If you could hear, at every jolt, the blood
Come gargling from the froth-corrupted lungs,
Obscene as cancer, bitter as the cud
Of vile, incurable sores on innocent tongues,—
My friend, you would not tell with such high zest
To children ardent for some desperate glory,
The old Lie: Dulce et decorum est

Pro patria mori.
'Dulce et Decorum Est' (1963 ed.); see **Horace** 175:14

12 Was it for this the clay grew tall?
'Futility' (written 1918)

13 It seemed that out of battle I escaped
Down some profound dull tunnel, long since scooped
Through granites which titanic wars had groined.
'Strange Meeting' (written 1918)

14 Whatever hope is yours,
Was my life also.
'Strange Meeting' (written 1918)

15 I am the enemy you killed, my friend.
'Strange Meeting' (written 1918)

16 Let us sleep now.
'Strange Meeting' (written 1918)

Count Oxenstierna 1583–1654
Swedish statesman

17 Dost thou not know, my son, with how little wisdom the world is governed?
letter to his son, 1648, in J. F. af Lundblad *Svensk Plutark* (1826) pt. 2; an alternative attribution quotes 'a certain Pope' (possibly Julius III, 1487–1555) saying, 'Thou little thinkest what *a little foolery governs the whole world!*'

Vance Packard 1914–97
American writer and journalist

18 The hidden persuaders.
title of a study of the advertising industry (1957)

John Page 1743–1808
American politician

19 We know the race is not to the swift nor the battle to the strong. Do you not think an angel rides in the whirlwind and directs this storm.
*quoted by George W. **Bush** in his first inaugural address, 20 January 2001*
letter to Thomas Jefferson, 20 July 1776; see **Addison** 2:19, **Bible** 39:21

William Tyler Page 1868–1942

20 I believe in the United States of America as a government of the people, by the people, for the people, whose just powers are derived from the consent of the governed; a democracy in a republic; a sovereign Nation of many sovereign States; a perfect Union, one and inseparable, established upon those principles of freedom, equality, justice, and humanity for which American patriots sacrificed their lives and fortunes. I therefore believe it is my duty to my country to love it, to support its Constitution, to obey its laws, to respect its flag, and to defend it against all enemies.
American's Creed (prize-winning competition entry, 1918) in *Congressional Record* vol. 56; see **Lincoln** 214:20

Camille Paglia 1947–
American writer and critic

1 There is no female Mozart because there is no female Jack the Ripper.
   in *International Herald Tribune* 26 April 1991

Thomas Paine 1737–1809
English political theorist

2 It is necessary to the happiness of man that he be mentally faithful to himself. Infidelity does not consist in believing, or in disbelieving, it consists in professing to believe what one does not believe.
   The Age of Reason pt. 1 (1794)

3 Any system of religion that has any thing in it that shocks the mind of a child cannot be a true system.
   The Age of Reason pt. 1 (1794)

4 The sublime and the ridiculous are often so nearly related, that it is difficult to class them separately. One step above the sublime, makes the ridiculous; and one step above the ridiculous, makes the sublime again.
   The Age of Reason pt. 2 (1795); see **Napoleon** 248:2

5 Government, even in its best state, is but a necessary evil; in its worst state, an intolerable one. Government, like dress, is the badge of lost innocence; the palaces of kings are built upon the ruins of the bowers of paradise.
   Common Sense (1776) ch. 1

6 Though we have been wise enough to shut and lock a door against absolute Monarchy, we at the same time have been foolish enough to put the crown in possession of the key.
   Common Sense (1776) ch. 1

7 Monarchy and succession have laid . . . the world in blood and ashes.
   Common Sense (1776) ch. 2

8 Freedom hath been hunted round the globe. Asia and Africa have long expelled her. Europe regards her like a stranger, and England hath given her warning to depart. O! receive the fugitive, and prepare in time an asylum for mankind.
   to America
   Common Sense (1776) ch. 3

9 As to religion, I hold it to be the indispensable duty of government to protect all conscientious professors thereof, and I know of no other business which government hath to do therewith.
   Common Sense (1776) ch. 4

10 These are the times that try men's souls. The summer soldier and the sunshine patriot will, in this crisis, shrink from the service of their country; but he that stands it *now*, deserves the love and thanks of men and women.
   The Crisis (December 1776) introduction

11 The religion of humanity.
   The Crisis (November 1778)

12 As he rose like a rocket, he fell like the stick.
   on Edmund **Burke**'s *losing the debate on the French Revolution to Charles James* **Fox**, *in the House of Commons*
   Letter to the Addressers on the late Proclamation (1792)

13 [He] is not affected by the reality of distress touching his heart, but by the showy resemblance of it striking his imagination. He pities the plumage, but forgets the dying bird.
   on Edmund **Burke**'s *Reflections on the Revolution in France, 1790*
   The Rights of Man (1791)

14 Lay then the axe to the root, and teach governments humanity. It is their sanguinary punishments which corrupt mankind.
   The Rights of Man (1791)

15 The idea of hereditary legislators is as inconsistent as that of hereditary judges, or hereditary juries; and as absurd as an hereditary mathematician, or an hereditary wise man; and as ridiculous as an hereditary poet laureate.
   The Rights of Man (1791)

16 Persecution is not an original feature of *any* religion; but it is always the strongly marked feature of all law-religions, or religions established by law.
   The Rights of Man (1791)

17 I compare it to something kept behind a curtain, about which there is a great deal of bustle and fuss, and a wonderful air of seeming solemnity; but when, by any accident, the curtain happens to be open, and the company see what it is, they burst into laughter.
   of monarchy
   The Rights of Man pt. 2 (1792)

18 My country is the world, and my religion is to do good.
   The Rights of Man pt. 2 (1792)

19 I do not believe that any two men, on what are called doctrinal points, think alike who think at all. It is only those who have not thought that appear to agree.
   The Rights of Man pt. 2 (1792)

20 A share in two revolutions is living to some purpose.
   Eric Foner *Tom Paine and Revolutionary America* (1976) ch. 7

José de Palafox 1780–1847
Spanish general

21 *Guerra a cuchillo.*
   War to the knife.
   on 4 August 1808, at the siege of Saragossa, the French general Verdier sent a one-word suggestion: 'Capitulation'. Palafox replied 'Guerra y cuchillo [War and the knife]', *later*

reported as above; it subsequently appeared, at
the behest of Palafox himself, on survivors' medals
  José Gòmez de Arteche y Moro *Guerra de la*
  Indopondoncia (1875) vol. ?. ch. 4

William Paley 1743–1805
English theologian and philosopher

1 Suppose I had found a *watch* upon the
  ground, and it should be enquired how the
  watch happened to be in that place . . . the
  inference, we think, is inevitable; that the
  watch must have had a maker, that there
  must have existed, at some time and at
  some place or other, an artificer or
  artificers, who formed it for the purpose
  which we find it actually to answer; who
  comprehended its construction, and
  designed its use.
    Natural Theology (1802) ch. 1; see **Dawkins** 111:6

2 Who can refute a sneer?
    Principles of Moral and Political Philosophy (1785)
    bk. 5, ch. 9

Pali Tripitaka
the earliest collection of Buddhist sacred texts,
c.2nd century BC

3 The Noble Truth of the Path leading to the
  Cessation of suffering is this: It is simply the
  Noble Eightfold Path, namely right view;
  right thought; right speech; right action;
  right livelihood; right effort; right
  mindfulness; right concentration.
    First Sermon of the Buddha
    Samyutta-nikāya [Kindred Sayings] pt. 56, p. 11

Lord Palmerston 1784–1865
British statesman; Prime Minister, 1855–8,
1859–65

4 We have no eternal allies and we have no
  perpetual enemies. Our interests are eternal
  and perpetual, and those interests it is our
  duty to follow.
    speech, House of Commons, 1 March 1848

5 As the Roman, in days of old, held himself
  free from indignity, when he could say *Civis
  Romanus sum*; so also a British subject, in
  whatever land he may be, shall feel
  confident that the watchful eye and the
  strong arm of England will protect him
  against injustice and wrong.
    in the debate on the protection afforded to the
    Greek trader David Pacifico (1784–1854) who had
    been born a British subject at Gibraltar
    speech, House of Commons, 25 June 1850; see
    Cicero 96:21

6 Lord Palmerston, with characteristic levity
  had once said that only three men in Europe
  had ever understood [the Schleswig-Holstein
  question], and of these the Prince Consort
  was dead, a Danish statesman (unnamed)
  was in an asylum, and he himself had
  forgotten it.
    R. W. Seton-Watson *Britain in Europe 1789–1914*
    (1937) ch. 11

7 Die, my dear Doctor, that's the last thing I
  shall do!
    last words; E. Latham *Famous Sayings and their*
    Authors (1904)

Emmeline Pankhurst 1858–1928
English suffragette leader

8 The argument of the broken window pane is
  the most valuable argument in modern
  politics.
    George Dangerfield *The Strange Death of Liberal*
    England (1936)

Mitchell Parish
American songwriter

9 When the deep purple falls over sleepy
  garden walls.
    'Deep Purple' (1939); words added to music
    (1934) by Peter de Rose

Charlie Parker 1920–55
American jazz saxophonist

10 Music is your own experience, your
   thoughts, your wisdom. If you don't live it,
   it won't come out of your horn.
     Nat Shapiro and Nat Hentoff *Hear Me Talkin' to Ya*
     (1955)

Dorothy Parker 1893–1967
American critic and humorist

11 Oh, life is a glorious cycle of song,
   A medley of extemporanea;
   And love is a thing that can never go wrong;
   And I am Marie of Roumania.
     'Comment' (1937)

12 Four be the things I'd been better without:
   Love, curiosity, freckles, and doubt.
     'Inventory' (1937)

13 Men seldom make passes
   At girls who wear glasses.
     'News Item' (1937)

14 Why is it no one ever sent me yet
   One perfect limousine, do you suppose?
   Ah no, it's always just my luck to get
   One perfect rose.
     'One Perfect Rose' (1937)

15 If, with the literate, I am
   Impelled to try an epigram,
   I never seek to take the credit;
   We all assume that Oscar said it.
     'A Pig's-Eye View of Literature' (1937)

16 Guns aren't lawful;
   Nooses give;
   Gas smells awful;
   You might as well live.
     'Résumé' (1937)

17 Where's the man could ease a heart like a
   satin gown?
     'The Satin Dress' (1937)

18 By the time you say you're his,
   Shivering and sighing
   And he vows his passion is
   Infinite, undying—
   Lady, make a note of this:

One of you is lying.
'Unfortunate Coincidence' (1937)

1 Excuse my dust.
suggested epitaph for herself (1925)
Alexander Woollcott *While Rome Burns* (1934)
'Our Mrs Parker'

2 She ran the whole gamut of the emotions from A to B.
of Katharine Hepburn at a Broadway first night, 1933
attributed

3 Wit has truth in it; wise-cracking is simply callisthenics with words.
in *Paris Review* Summer 1956

4 Hollywood money isn't money. It's congealed snow, melts in your hand, and there you are.
Malcolm Cowley *Writers at Work* 1st Series (1958)

5 You can lead a horticulture, but you can't make her think.
John Keats *You Might as well Live* (1970)

6 It serves me right for putting all my eggs in one bastard.
on her abortion
John Keats *You Might as well Live* (1970) pt. 2, ch. 3

Martin Parker d. *c.*1656
English balladmonger

7 You gentlemen of England
Who live at home at ease,
How little do you think
On the dangers of the seas.
'The Valiant Sailors'

8 The times will not mend
Till the King enjoys his own again.
'Upon Defacing of Whitehall' (1671)

Ross Parker 1914–74
and **Hugh Charles** 1907–95
British songwriters

9 There'll always be an England
While there's a country lane.
'There'll always be an England' (1939 song)

Henry Parkes 1815–95
English-born Australian statesman

10 The crimson thread of kinship runs through us all.
on Australian federation
speech at banquet in Melbourne 6 February 1890; *The Federal Government of Australasia* (1890)

C. Northcote Parkinson 1909–93
English writer

11 Expenditure rises to meet income.
The Law and the Profits (1960) ch. 1

12 Work expands so as to fill the time available for its completion.
Parkinson's Law (1958) ch. 1

13 Time spent on any item of the agenda will be in inverse proportion to the sum involved.
Parkinson's Law (1958) ch. 3

14 The man who is denied the opportunity of taking decisions of importance begins to regard as important the decisions he is allowed to take.
Parkinson's Law (1958) ch. 10

Charles Stewart Parnell 1846–91
Irish nationalist leader

15 No man has a right to fix the boundary of the march of a nation; no man has a right to say to his country—thus far shalt thou go and no further.
speech at Cork, 21 January 1885

Blaise Pascal 1623–62
French mathematician, physicist, and moralist

16 I have made this [letter] longer than usual, only because I have not had the time to make it shorter.
Lettres Provinciales (1657) no. 16; see **Thoreau** 339:9

17 The last thing one knows in constructing a work is what to put first.
Pensées (1670, ed. L. Brunschvicg, 1909) sect. 1, no. 19

18 When we see a natural style, we are quite surprised and delighted, for we expected to see an author and we find a man.
Pensées (1670, ed. L. Brunschvicg, 1909) sect. 1, no. 29

19 Had Cleopatra's nose been shorter, the whole face of the world would have changed.
Pensées (1670, ed. L. Brunschvicg, 1909) sect. 2, no. 162

20 The eternal silence of these infinite spaces [the heavens] terrifies me.
Pensées (1670, ed. L. Brunschvicg, 1909) sect. 2, no. 206

21 'God is or he is not.' But to which side shall we incline?... Let us weigh the gain and the loss in wagering that God is. Let us estimate the two chances. If you gain, you gain all; if you lose, you lose nothing. Wager then without hesitation that he is.
known as Pascal's wager
Pensées (1670, ed. L. Brunschvicg, 1909) sect. 3, no. 233

22 The heart has its reasons which reason knows nothing of.
Pensées (1670, ed. L. Brunschvicg, 1909) sect. 4, no. 277

23 Man is only a reed, the weakest thing in nature; but he is a thinking reed.
Pensées (1670, ed. L. Brunschvicg, 1909) sect. 6, no. 347

24 FIRE. God of Abraham, God of Isaac, God of Jacob, not of the philosophers and scholars. Certainty. Certainty. Feeling. Joy. Peace.
on a paper, dated 23 November 1654, stitched into the lining of his coat and found after his death

Boris Pasternak 1890–1960
Russian novelist and poet

1 Man is born to live, not to prepare for life.
   Doctor Zhivago (1958) pt. 2, ch. 9, sect. 14 (tr. Max Hayward and Manya Harari)

2 I am alone; all drowns in the Pharisees' hypocrisy.
   To live your life is not as simple as to cross a field.
   Doctor Zhivago (1958) 'Zhivago's Poems: Hamlet'

Louis Pasteur 1822–95
French chemist and bacteriologist

3 Where observation is concerned, chance favours only the prepared mind.
   address given on the inauguration of the Faculty of Science, University of Lille, 7 December 1854

4 There are no such things as applied sciences, only applications of science.
   address, 11 September 1872

5 Wine may well be considered the most healthful and most hygienic of beverages.
   Études sur le vin (1873) pt. 1, ch. 2

Walter Pater 1839–94
English essayist and critic

6 She is older than the rocks among which she sits.
   of the Mona Lisa
   Studies in the History of the Renaissance (1873) 'Leonardo da Vinci'

7 All art constantly aspires towards the condition of music.
   Studies in the History of the Renaissance (1873) 'The School of Giorgione'

8 To burn always with this hard, gemlike flame, to maintain this ecstasy, is success in life.
   Studies in the History of the Renaissance (1873) 'Conclusion'

'Banjo' Paterson 1864–1941
Australian poet

9 Once a jolly swagman camped by a billabong,
   Under the shade of a coolibah tree;
   And he sang as he watched and waited till his 'Billy' boiled:
   'You'll come a-waltzing, Matilda, with me.'
   'Waltzing Matilda' (1903 song)

Coventry Patmore 1823–96
English poet

10 The angel in the house.
   title of poem (1854–62)

Alan Paton 1903–88
South African writer

11 Cry, the beloved country.
   title of novel (1948)

St Patrick fl. 5th cent.
patron saint and Apostle of Ireland, of Romano-British parentage

12 Today I put on
   a terrible strength
   invoking the Trinity,
   confessing the Three
   with faith in the one.
   'St Patrick's Breastplate', traditionally attributed to St Patrick; see **Alexander** 13:5

13 Christ beside me,
   Christ before me,
   Christ behind me,
   Christ within me,
   Christ beneath me,
   Christ above me.
   'St Patrick's Breastplate'

Leslie Paul 1905–85
Irish writer

14 Angry young man.
   the phrase was later associated with John Osborne's play Look Back in Anger (1956)
   title of book (1951)

Wolfgang Pauli 1900–58
Austrian-born American physicist who worked chiefly in Switzerland

15 I don't mind your thinking slowly: I mind your publishing faster than you think.
   attributed

Jeremy Paxman 1950–
British journalist and broadcaster

16 Did you threaten to overrule him?
   question asked 14 times of Michael Howard, referring to the sacking of a prison governor by Derek Lewis, Director of the Prison Service
   interview, BBC2 *Newsnight* 13 May 1997

17 Labour's attack dog.
   description of the Labour politician John Reid, to which Reid took great exception (see **Reid** 275:2)
   on BBC2 *Newsnight*, 8 March 2005

James Payn 1830–98
English writer

18 I had never had a piece of toast
   Particularly long and wide,
   But fell upon the sanded floor,
   And always on the buttered side.
   in *Chambers's Journal* 2 February 1884; see **Moore** 244:12

J. H. Payne 1791–1852
American actor, dramatist, and songwriter

19 Home, sweet home.
   title of song, from *Clari, or, The Maid of Milan* (1823 opera)

20 Mid pleasures and palaces though we may roam,
   Be it ever so humble, there's no place like home.
   Clari, or, The Maid of Milan (1823 opera) 'Home, Sweet Home'

Norman Vincent Peale 1898–1993
American religious broadcaster and writer

21 The power of positive thinking.
   title of book (1952)

Patrick Pearse 1879–1916
Irish nationalist leader

1 The fools, the fools, the fools, they have left us our Fenian dead, and while Ireland holds these graves Ireland unfree shall never be at peace.
    oration over the grave of the Fenian Jeremiah O'Donovan Rossa, 1 August 1915

Hesketh Pearson 1887–1964
English actor and biographer

2 Misquotation is, in fact, the pride and privilege of the learned.
    Common Misquotations (1934) introduction

Lester Pearson 1897–1972
Canadian Liberal statesman, Prime Minister 1963–8

3 The grim fact is that we prepare for war like precocious giants and for peace like retarded pygmies.
    speech in Toronto, 14 March 1955

Robert Peel 1788–1850
British Conservative statesman; Prime Minister, 1834–5, 1841–6

4 All my experience in public life is in favour of the employment of what the world would call young men instead of old ones.
    to Wellington in 1829

George Peele c.1556–96
English dramatist and poet

5 His golden locks time hath to silver turned;
O time too swift, O swiftness never ceasing!
    Polyhymnia (1590) 'Sonnet'

6 Goddess, allow this aged man his right,
To be your beadsman now that was your knight.
    Polyhymnia (1590) 'Sonnet'

Charles Péguy 1873–1914
French poet and essayist

7 Tyranny is always better organised than freedom.
    Basic Verities (1943) 'War and Peace'

Pelé 1940–
Brazilian footballer

8 Football? It's the beautiful game.
    attributed

Lord Pembroke c.1534–1601

9 A parliament can do any thing but make a man a woman, and a woman a man.
    quoted by his son, the 4th Earl, in a speech on 11 April 1648, proving himself Chancellor of Oxford in *Harleian Miscellany* (1745) vol. 5

Henry Herbert, Lord Pembroke 1734–94

10 Dr Johnson's sayings would not appear so extraordinary, were it not for his bow-wow way.
    James Boswell *Life of Samuel Johnson* (1791) 27 March 1775; see **Scott** 287:27

William Penn 1644–1718
English Quaker; founder of Pennsylvania

11 No pain, no palm; no thorns, no throne; no gall, no glory; no cross, no crown.
    No Cross, No Crown (1669 pamphlet)

12 It is a reproach to religion and government to suffer so much poverty and excess.
    Some Fruits of Solitude (1693) pt. 1, no. 52

13 Men are generally more careful of the breed of their horses and dogs than of their children.
    Some Fruits of Solitude (1693) pt. 1, no. 85

Roger Penrose 1931–
British mathematician and theoretical physicist

14 Consciousness . . . is the phenomenon whereby the universe's very existence is made known.
    The Emperor's New Mind (1989) ch. 10 'Conclusion'

Samuel Pepys 1633–1703
English diarist

15 And so to bed.
    Diary 20 April 1660

16 I went out to Charing Cross, to see Major-general Harrison hanged, drawn, and quartered; which was done there, he looking as cheerful as any man could do in that condition.
    Diary 13 October 1660

17 Pretty witty Nell.
    of Nell **Gwyn**
    Diary 3 April 1665

18 Strange to see how a good dinner and feasting reconciles everybody.
    Diary 9 November 1665

19 Music and women I cannot but give way to, whatever my business is.
    Diary 9 March 1666

20 And so I betake myself to that course, which is almost as much as to see myself go into my grave—for which, and all the discomforts that will accompany my being blind, the good God prepare me!
    Diary 31 May 1669 closing lines

S. J. Perelman 1904–79
American humorist

21 Crazy like a fox.
    title of book (1944)

Shimon Peres 1923–
Israeli statesman

22 Television has made dictatorship impossible, but democracy unbearable.
    at a Davos meeting, in *Financial Times* 31 January 1995

Pericles c.495–429 BC
Greek statesman and Athenian general

1 Taking everything together then, I declare
that our city is an education to Greece.
of Athens
> Thucydides *History of the Peloponnesian War* bk. 2
> ch. 41

2 For famous men have the whole earth as
their memorial.
> Thucydides *History of the Peloponnesian War* bk. 2

3 Your great glory is not to be inferior to what
God has made you, and the greatest glory of
a woman is to be least talked about by men,
whether they are praising you or criticizing
you.
> Thucydides *History of the Peloponnesian War* bk. 2

Eva Perón 1919–52
Argentinian wife of Juan Perón

4 Keeping books on charity is capitalist
nonsense! I just use the money for the poor.
I can't stop to count it.
> Fleur Cowles *Bloody Precedent: the Peron Story*
> (1952)

5 I will return. And I will be millions.
> inscription on the tomb of Eva Perón, Buenos
> Aires

Charles Perrault 1628–1703
French poet and critic

6 *Anne, ma sœur Anne, ne vois-tu rien venir?*
Anne, sister Anne, do you see nothing
coming?
> *Histoires et contes du temps passé* [Stories and Tales
> of Past Times] (1697) 'La barbe bleue'

7 'Oh Grandmother! What big ears you have!'
'All the better to hear you with.'
> *Histoires et contes du temps passé* [Stories and Tales
> of Past Times] (1697) 'Little Red Riding Hood'

Edward Perronet 1726–92
English clergyman

8 All hail the power of Jesus' Name;
Let Angels prostrate fall;
Bring forth the royal diadem
To crown Him Lord of all.
> 'All hail the power of Jesus' Name' (1780 hymn)

Oliver Hazard Perry 1785–1819
American naval officer

9 We have met the enemy and they are ours.
> reporting his victory over the British in the
> battle of Lake Erie, 10 September 1813

Persius (Aulus Persius Flaccus) AD
34–62
Roman poet

10 *Venienti occurrite morbo.*
Confront disease at its onset.
> *often quoted as,* 'Meet the misfortune when it
> comes'
> *Satires* no. 3, l. 64; see **Ovid** 263:7

Ted Persons

11 Things ain't what they used to be.
> title of song (1941)

Laurence J. Peter 1919–90
Canadian writer

12 In a hierarchy every employee tends to rise
to his level of incompetence.
> *The Peter Principle* (1969) ch. 1

Petrarch (Francesco Petrarca) 1304–74
Italian poet

13 O you who hear within these scattered
verses
the sound of sighs with which I fed my
heart
in my first errant youthful days when I
in part was not the man I am today.
> *Canzoniere* no. 1 (c.1352) tr. Mark Musa

14 I find no peace, and I am not at war,
I fear and hope, and burn and I am ice.
> *Canzoniere* no. 134 (c.1352) tr. Mark Musa

Jamie Petrie
and **Peter Cunnah**
British singers and songwriters

15 Things can only get better.
> title of song (1994); used as a Labour campaign
> slogan, 1997

Petronius Arbiter d. AD 65
Roman satirist

16 *Cave canem.*
Beware of the dog.
> *Satyricon* 'Cena Trimalchionis' ch. 29

17 *Abiit ad plures.*
He's gone to join the majority.
> *meaning the dead*
> *Satyricon* 'Cena Trimalchionis' ch. 42; see **Young**
> 370:4

18 *Nam Sibyllam quidem Cumis ego ipse oculis meis
vidi in ampulla pendere, et cum illi pueri dicerent:*
Sibylla, ti theleis; *respondebat illa:* apothanein
thelo.
I myself with my own eyes saw the Sibyl at
Cumae hanging in a flask; and when the
boys cried at her: ' Sibyl, Sibyl, what do you
want?' 'I would that I were dead,' she used
to answer.
> *Satyricon* 'Cena Trimalchionis' ch. 48, sect. 8

Edward John Phelps 1822–1900
American lawyer and diplomat

19 The man who makes no mistakes does not
usually make anything.
> speech at the Mansion House, London, 24
> January 1889

Kim Philby 1912–88
British intelligence officer and Soviet spy

20 To betray, you must first belong.
> in *Sunday Times* 17 December 1967

Prince Philip, Duke of Edinburgh 1921–
husband of Elizabeth II

1 If you stay here much longer you'll all be slitty-eyed.
    remark to Edinburgh University students in Peking, 16 October 1986

Jack Philip 1840–1900
American naval captain

2 Don't cheer, men; those poor devils are dying.
    at the Battle of Santiago, 4 July 1898
    in *Dictionary of American Biography* vol. 14 (1934) 'John Woodward Philip'

Ambrose Philips *c.*1675–1749
English poet

3 The flowers anew, returning seasons bring;
    But beauty faded has no second spring.
    The First Pastoral (1708) 'Lobbin' l. 47

Arthur Angell Phillips 1900–85
Australian critic and editor

4 Above our writers—and other artists—looms the intimidating mass of Anglo-Saxon culture. Such a situation almost inevitably produces the characteristic Australian Cultural Cringe.
    Meanjin (1950) 'The Cultural Cringe'

Pablo Picasso 1881–1973
Spanish painter

5 No, painting is not made to decorate apartments. It's an offensive and defensive weapon against the enemy.
    interview with Simone Téry, 24 March 1945, in Alfred H. Barr *Picasso* (1946)

6 The artist is a receptacle for emotions that come from all over the place: from the sky, from the earth, from a scrap of paper, from a passing shape, from a spider's web.
    Alfred H. Barr Jr. *Picasso: Fifty Years of his Art* (1946)

7 When I was the age of these children I could draw like Raphael: it took me many years to learn how to draw like these children.
    *to Herbert **Read**, when visiting an exhibition of childen's drawings*
    quoted in letter from Read to *The Times* 27 October 1956

8 I paint objects as I think them, not as I see them.
    John Golding *Cubism* (1959)

9 God is really only another artist. He invented the giraffe, the elephant, and the cat. He has no real style. He just goes on trying other things.
    F. Gilot and C. Lake *Life With Picasso* (1964) pt. 1

10 Every positive value has its price in negative terms . . . The genius of Einstein leads to Hiroshima.
    F. Gilot and C. Lake *Life With Picasso* (1964) pt. 2

11 We all know that Art is not truth. Art is a lie that makes us realize truth.
    Dore Ashton *Picasso on Art* (1972) 'Two statements by Picasso'

Pindar 518–438 BC
Greek lyric poet

12 Water is best. But gold shines like fire blazing in the night, supreme of lordly wealth.
    Olympian Odes bk. 1, l. 1

13 Mankind is a dream of a shadow.
    Pythian Odes bk. 8, l. 135

Harold Pinter 1930–
English dramatist

14 Apart from the known and the unknown, what else is there?
    The Homecoming (1965) act 2, sc. 1

15 The weasel under the cocktail cabinet.
    on being asked what his plays were about
    J. Russell Taylor *Anger and After* (1962)

Luigi Pirandello 1867–1936
Italian dramatist and novelist

16 Six characters in search of an author.
    title of play (1921)

Robert M. Pirsig 1928–
American writer

17 Zen and the art of motorcycle maintenance.
    title of book (1974)

18 That's the classical mind at work, runs fine inside but looks dingy on the surface.
    Zen and the Art of Motorcycle Maintenance (1974) pt. 3, ch. 26

Walter B. Pitkin 1878–1953

19 Life begins at forty.
    title of book (1932)

William Pitt 1759–1806
British Tory statesman; Prime Minister, 1783–1801, 1804–6

20 Necessity is the plea for every infringement of human freedom: it is the argument of tyrants; it is the creed of slaves.
    speech, House of Commons, 18 November 1783

21 England has saved herself by her exertions, and will, as I trust, save Europe by her example.
    replying to a toast in which he had been described as the saviour of his country in the wars with France
    R. Coupland *War Speeches of William Pitt* (1915)

22 Roll up that map; it will not be wanted these ten years.
    of a map of Europe, on hearing of Napoleon's victory at Austerlitz, December 1805
    Earl Stanhope *Life of the Rt. Hon. William Pitt* vol. 4 (1862) ch. 43

1 Oh, my country! how I leave my country!

also variously reported as 'How I love my country';
and 'My country! oh, my country!'

Earl Stanhope *Life of the Rt. Hon. William Pitt* vol.
3 (1879) ch. 43; Earl Stanhope *Life of the Rt. Hon.*
William Pitt (1st ed.), vol. 4 (1862) ch. 43; and G.
Rose *Diaries and Correspondence* (1860) vol. 2, 23
January 1806; oral tradition reports, 'I think I
could eat one of Bellamy's veal pies'

William Pitt, Earl of Chatham
1708–78
British Whig statesman; Prime Minister, 1766–8

2 The atrocious crime of being a young man
. . . I shall neither attempt to palliate nor
deny.

speech, House of Commons, 2 March 1741

3 The poorest man may in his cottage bid
defiance to all the forces of the Crown. It
may be frail—its roof may shake—the wind
may blow through it—the storm may
enter—the rain may enter—but the King of
England cannot enter!

speech, *c.*March 1763, in Lord Brougham
Historical Sketches of Statesmen in the Time of George
III First Series (1845) vol. 1

4 Unlimited power is apt to corrupt the minds
of those who possess it.

speech, House of Lords, 9 January 1770; see
Acton 1:9

5 You cannot conquer America.

speech, House of Lords, 18 November 1777

6 I invoke the genius of the Constitution!

speech, House of Lords, 18 November 1777

7 The parks are the lungs of London.

quoted by William Windham in the House of
Commons, 30 June 1808

Pius VII 1742–1823
Italian cleric, Pope from 1800

8 We are prepared to go to the gates of
Hell—but no further.

attempting to reach an agreement with
Napoleon, *c.1800–1*

J. M. Robinson *Cardinal Consalvi* (1987)

Pius XII 1876–1958
Italian cleric, Pope from 1939

9 One Galileo in two thousand years is
enough.

*on being asked to proscribe the works of **Teilhard***
de Chardin

attributed; Stafford Beer *Platform for Change*
(1975)

Max Planck 1858–1947
German physicist

10 A new scientific truth does not triumph by
convincing its opponents and making them
see the light, but rather because its
opponents eventually die, and a new
generation grows up that is familiar with it.

A Scientific Autobiography (1949, tr. F. Gaynor)

Sylvia Plath 1932–63
American poet

11 Is there no way out of the mind?

'Apprehensions' (1971)

12 I have always been scared of *you*,
With your Luftwaffe, your gobbledygoo.
And your neat moustache
And your Aryan eye, bright blue.
Panzer-man, panzer-man, O You—

'Daddy' (1963)

13 Every woman adores a Fascist,
The boot in the face, the brute
Brute heart of a brute like you.

'Daddy' (1963)

14 The woman is perfected
Her dead
Body wears the smile of accomplishment.

opening lines of her last poem, written a week
before her suicide
'Edge'

15 Dying,
Is an art, like everything else.

'Lady Lazarus' (1963)

16 Out of the ash
I rise with my red hair
And I eat men like air.

'Lady Lazarus' (1963)

17 Love set you going like a fat gold watch.

'Morning Song' (1965)

Plato 429–347 BC
Greek philosopher

18 Socrates, he says, breaks the law by
corrupting young men and not recognizing
the gods that the city recognizes, but some
other new deities.

Apologia 24b

19 Is that which is holy loved by the gods
because it is holy, or is it holy because it is
loved by the gods?

Euthyphro 10

20 This was the end, Echekrates, of our friend;
a man of whom we may say that of all
whom we met at that time he was the
wisest and justest and best.

*on the death of **Socrates***
Phaedo 118a

21 What I say is that 'just' or 'right' means
nothing but what is in the interest of the
stronger party.

spoken by Thrasymachus
The Republic bk. 1, 338c (tr. F. M. Cornford)

22 Can we devise one of those lies—the kind
which crop up as the occasion demands,
which we were talking about not so long
ago—so that with a single noble lie we can
indoctrinate the rulers themselves,
preferably, but at least the rest of the
community?

The Republic bk. 3, 414b (tr. Robin Waterfield)

23 And so with the objects of knowledge: these
derive from the Good not only their power
of being known, but their very being and

reality; and Goodness is not the same thing
as being, but even beyond being, surpassing
it in dignity and power.

The Republic bk. 6, 509b (tr. F. M. Cornford)

1 Behold! human beings living in a
underground den . . . Like ourselves . . . they
see only their own shadows, or the shadows
of one another, which the fire throws on the
opposite wall of the cave.

The Republic bk. 7, 515b; see **Nietzsche** 251:6

2 The blame is his who chooses: God is
blameless.

The Republic bk. 10, 617e

3 But if we are guided by me we shall believe
that the soul is immortal and capable of
enduring all extremes of good and evil, and
so we shall hold ever to the upward way and
pursue righteousness with wisdom always
and ever.

The Republic bk. 10, 621c

4 God is always doing geometry.

Plutarch Moralia

Plautus c.250–184 BC
Roman comic dramatist

5 *Dictum sapienti sat est.*
A sentence is enough for a sensible man.

proverbially: 'Verbum sapienti sat est [A word
is enough for the wise]', *and abbreviated to*
'verb. sap.'

Persa l. 729

Pliny the Elder AD 23–79
Roman statesman and scholar

6 *Semper aliquid novi Africam adferre.*
Africa always brings [us] something new.

often quoted as 'Ex Africa semper aliquid novi
[Always something new out of Africa]'

Historia Naturalis bk. 8, sect. 42

7 *Addito salis grano.*
With the addition of a grain of salt.

commonly quoted as 'Cum grano salis [With a
grain of salt]'

Historia Naturalis bk. 23, sect. 149

8 [Pliny] always said that there was no book so
bad that some good could not be got out of
it.

Pliny the Younger Letters bk. 3, no. 5

George Washington Plunkitt
1842–1924
American Tammany politician

9 The politician who steals is worse than a
thief. He is a fool. With the grand
opportunities all around for a man with a
political pull, there's no excuse for stealin' a
cent.

'On the Shame of Cities' in William L. Riordon
Plunkitt of Tammany Hall (1905)

Plutarch c.AD 46–c.120
Greek philosopher and biographer

10 For the mind does not require filling like a
bottle, but rather, like wood, it only requires
kindling to create in it an impulse to think
independently and an ardent desire for the
truth.

Moralia sect. 48c 'On Listening to Lectures'; see
Rabelais 272:13

11 For we are told that when a certain man was
accusing both of them to him, he [Caesar]
said that he had no fear of those fat and
long-haired fellows, but rather of those pale
and thin ones.

Parallel Lives 'Anthony' sect. 11; see **Shakespeare**
296:20

12 He who cheats with an oath acknowledges
that he is afraid of his enemy, but that he
thinks little of God.

Parallel Lives 'Lysander' ch. 8

Edgar Allan Poe 1809–49
American writer

13 I was a child and she was a child,
In this kingdom by the sea;
But we loved with a love which was more
than love—
I and my Annabel Lee.

'Annabel Lee' (1849)

14 To the tintinnabulation that so musically
wells
From the bells, bells, bells, bells.

'The Bells' (1849) st. 1

15 All that we see or seem
Is but a dream within a dream.

'A Dream within a Dream' (1849)

16 The fever called 'Living'
Is conquered at last.

'For Annie' (1849)

17 Once upon a midnight dreary, while I
pondered, weak and weary,
Over many a quaint and curious volume of
forgotten lore,
While I nodded, nearly napping, suddenly
there came a tapping,
As of some one gently rapping, rapping at
my chamber door.

'The Raven' (1845) st. 1

18 For the rare and radiant maiden whom the
angels name Lenore—
Nameless here for evermore.

'The Raven' (1845) st. 2

19 Ghastly, grim and ancient raven wandering
from the Nightly shore—
Tell me what thy lordly name is on the
Night's Plutonian shore!

'The Raven' (1845) st. 8

20 Take thy beak from out my heart, and take
thy form from off my door!
Quoth the Raven, 'Nevermore'.

'The Raven' (1845) st. 17

21 And his eyes have all the seeming of a
demon's that is dreaming.

'The Raven' (1845) st. 18

22 The glory that was Greece
And the grandeur that was Rome.

'To Helen' (1831)

Henri Poincaré 1854–1912
French mathematician and philosopher of science

1 Science is built up of facts, as a house is
built of stones; but an accumulation of facts
is no more a science than a heap of stones is
a house.
  Science and Hypothesis (1905) ch. 9

Polybius *c.*200–*c.*118 BC
Greek historian

2 Those who know how to win are much
more numerous than those who know how
to make proper use of their victories.
  History bk. 10

John Pomfret 1667–1702
English clergyman

3 We live and learn, but not the wiser grow.
  'Reason' (1700) l. 112

Madame de Pompadour 1721–64
French favourite of Louis XV of France

4 *Après nous le déluge.*
  After us the deluge.
  Madame du Hausset *Mémoires* (1824)

Alexander Pope 1688–1744
English poet

5 Poetic Justice, with her lifted scale.
  The Dunciad (1742) bk. 1, l. 52

6 All crowd, who foremost shall be damned to
Fame.
  The Dunciad (1742) bk. 3, l. 158

7 A wit with dunces, and a dunce with wits.
  The Dunciad (1742) bk. 4, l. 90

8 The Right Divine of Kings to govern wrong.
  The Dunciad (1742) bk. 4, l. 187

9 Lo! thy dread empire, Chaos! is restored;
Light dies before thy uncreating word:
Thy hand, great Anarch! lets the curtain fall;
And universal darkness buries all.
  The Dunciad (1742) bk. 4, l. 653

10 Vital spark of heav'nly flame!
Quit, oh quit this mortal frame:
Trembling, hoping, ling'ring, flying,
Oh the pain, the bliss of dying!
  'The Dying Christian to his Soul' (1730); see
  Hadrian 158:13

11 On all the line a sudden vengeance waits,
And frequent hearses shall besiege your
gates.
  'Elegy to the Memory of an Unfortunate Lady'
  (1717) l. 37

12 How shall I lose the sin, yet keep the sense,
And love th'offender, yet detest th'offence?
  'Eloisa to Abelard' (1717) l. 191; see **Augustine**
  20:10

13 How happy is the blameless Vestal's lot!
The world forgetting, by the world forgot.
  'Eloisa to Abelard' (1717) l. 207

14 I am his Highness' dog at Kew;
Pray, tell me sir, whose dog are you?
  'Epigram Engraved on the Collar of a Dog
  which I gave to his Royal Highness' (1738)

15 Sir, I admit your gen'ral rule
That every poet is a fool:
But you yourself may serve to show it,
That every fool is not a poet.
  'Epigram from the French' (1732)

16 You think this cruel? take it for a rule,
No creature smarts so little as a fool.
  'An Epistle to Dr Arbuthnot' (1735) l. 83

17 As yet a child, nor yet a fool to fame,
I lisped in numbers, for the numbers came.
  'An Epistle to Dr Arbuthnot' (1735) l. 127

18 The Muse but served to ease some friend,
not wife,
To help me through this long disease, my
life.
  'An Epistle to Dr Arbuthnot' (1735) l. 131

19 Pretty! in amber to observe the forms
Of hairs, or straws, or dirt, or grubs, or
worms;
The things, we know, are neither rich nor
rare,
But wonder how the devil they got there?
  'An Epistle to Dr Arbuthnot' (1735) l. 169

20 And he, whose fustian's so sublimely bad,
It is not poetry, but prose run mad.
  'An Epistle to Dr Arbuthnot' (1735) l. 187

21 Damn with faint praise, assent with civil
leer,
And without sneering, teach the rest to
sneer;
Willing to wound, and yet afraid to strike.
  of **Addison**
  'An Epistle to Dr Arbuthnot' (1735) l. 201; see
  Wycherley 367:5

22 'Satire or sense, alas! can Sporus feel?
Who breaks a butterfly upon a wheel?'
  of Lord **Hervey**
  'An Epistle to Dr Arbuthnot' (1735) l. 307

23 Unlearn'd, he knew no schoolman's subtle
art,
No language, but the language of the heart.
  of his own father
  'An Epistle to Dr Arbuthnot' (1735) l. 398

24 And mistress of herself, though china fall.
  Epistles to Several Persons 'To a Lady' (1735) l. 268

25 Who shall decide, when doctors disagree?
  Epistles to Several Persons 'To Lord Bathurst' (1733)
  l. 1

26 Die, and endow a college, or a cat.
  Epistles to Several Persons 'To Lord Bathurst' (1733)
  l. 98

27 The ruling passion, be it what it will,
The ruling passion conquers reason still.
  Epistles to Several Persons 'To Lord Bathurst' (1733)
  l. 155; see **Pope** 267:1

28 Consult the genius of the place in all.
  Epistles to Several Persons 'To Lord Burlington'
  (1731) l. 57; see **Virgil** 347:15

29 'Tis use alone that sanctifies expense.
  Epistles to Several Persons 'To Lord Burlington'
  (1731) l. 179

30 'Tis education forms the common mind,

Just as the twig is bent, the tree's inclined.
Epistles to Several Persons 'To Lord Cobham' (1734)
l. 101

1 Search then the Ruling Passion: There,
alone,
The wild are constant, and the cunning
known;
The fool consistent, and the false sincere.
Epistles to Several Persons 'To Lord Cobham' (1734)
l. 174; see **Pope** 266:27

2 Odious! in woollen! 'twould a saint provoke!
Epistles to Several Persons 'To Lord Cobham' (1734)
l. 242

3 Old politicians chew on wisdom past,
And totter on in business to the last.
Epistles to Several Persons 'To Lord Cobham' (1734)
l. 248

4 Nature, and Nature's laws lay hid in night.
God said, *Let Newton be!* and all was light.
'Epitaph: Intended for Sir Isaac Newton' (1730);
see **Squire** 322:21

5 Great wits sometimes may gloriously
offend,
And rise to faults true critics dare not mend.
From vulgar bounds with brave disorder
part
And snatch a grace beyond the reach of art.
An Essay on Criticism (1711) l. 152

6 A little learning is a dangerous thing;
Drink deep, or taste not the Pierian spring:
There shallow draughts intoxicate the brain,
And drinking largely sobers us again.
An Essay on Criticism (1711) l. 215; see **Drayton**
121:12

7 Hills peep o'er hills, and Alps on Alps arise!
An Essay on Criticism (1711) l. 232

8 Whoever thinks a faultless piece to see,
Thinks what ne'er was, nor is, nor e'er shall
be.
An Essay on Criticism (1711) l. 253

9 True wit is Nature to advantage dressed,
What oft was thought, but ne'er so well
expressed.
An Essay on Criticism (1711) l. 297

10 Expression is the dress of thought.
An Essay on Criticism (1711) l. 318; see **Johnson**
187:8, **Wesley** 355:5

11 As some to church repair,
Not for the doctrine, but the music there.
An Essay on Criticism (1711) l. 342

12 A needless Alexandrine ends the song,
That, like a wounded snake, drags its slow
length along.
An Essay on Criticism (1711) l. 356

13 True ease in writing comes from art, not
chance.
An Essay on Criticism (1711) l. 362

14 The sound must seem an echo to the sense.
An Essay on Criticism (1711) l. 365

15 Some praise at morning what they blame at
night;
But always think the last opinion right.
An Essay on Criticism (1711) l. 430

16 To err is human; to forgive, divine.
An Essay on Criticism (1711) l. 525

17 Men must be taught as if you taught them
not,
And things unknown proposed as things
forgot.
An Essay on Criticism (1711) l. 574

18 For fools rush in where angels fear to tread.
An Essay on Criticism (1711) l. 625

19 Eye Nature's walks, shoot Folly as it flies,
And catch the Manners living as they rise.
Laugh where we must, be candid where we
can;
But vindicate the ways of God to man.
An Essay on Man Epistle 1 (1733) l. 13; see **Milton**
237:17

20 Hope springs eternal in the human breast:
Man never Is, but always To be blest.
An Essay on Man Epistle 1 (1733) l. 95

21 Lo! the poor Indian, whose untutored mind
Sees God in clouds, or hears him in the
wind.
An Essay on Man Epistle 1 (1733) l. 99

22 Why has not man a microscopic eye?
For this plain reason, man is not a fly.
An Essay on Man Epistle 1 (1733) l. 193

23 The spider's touch, how exquisitely fine!
Feels at each thread, and lives along the line.
An Essay on Man Epistle 1 (1733) l. 217

24 All are but parts of one stupendous whole,
Whose body, Nature is, and God the soul.
An Essay on Man Epistle 1 (1733) l. 267

25 All nature is but art, unknown to thee;
All chance, direction, which thou canst not
see;
All discord, harmony, not understood;
All partial evil, universal good.
An Essay on Man Epistle 1 (1733) l. 289

26 And, spite of Pride, in erring Reason's spite,
One truth is clear, 'Whatever IS, is RIGHT.'
An Essay on Man Epistle 1 (1733) l. 293

27 Know then thyself, presume not God to
scan;
The proper study of mankind is man.
An Essay on Man Epistle 2 (1733) l. 1; see **Charron**
91:9, **Huxley** 179:8

28 Created half to rise, and half to fall;
Great lord of all things, yet a prey to all;
Sole judge of truth, in endless error hurled;
The glory, jest, and riddle of the world!
An Essay on Man Epistle 2 (1733) l. 15

29 Vice is a monster of so frightful mien,
As, to be hated, needs but to be seen;
Yet seen too oft, familiar with her face,
We first endure, then pity, then embrace.
An Essay on Man Epistle 2 (1733) l. 217

30 The learn'd is happy nature to explore,
The fool is happy that he knows no more.
An Essay on Man Epistle 2 (1733) l. 263

31 Behold the child, by Nature's kindly law
Pleased with a rattle, tickled with a straw.
An Essay on Man Epistle 2 (1733) l. 275

32 For forms of government let fools contest;

Whate'er is best administered is best.
An Essay on Man Epistle 3 (1733) l. 303

1 Thus God and nature linked the gen'ral frame,
And bade self-love and social be the same.
An Essay on Man Epistle 3 (1733) l. 317; *An Essay on Man* Epistle 4 (1734) l. 396 is similar

2 An honest man's the noblest work of God.
An Essay on Man Epistle 4 (1734) l. 248; see **Ingersoll** 180:17

3 All our knowledge is, ourselves to know.
An Essay on Man Epistle 4 (1734) l. 398

4 Achilles' wrath, to Greece the direful spring
Of woes unnumbered, heavenly goddess, sing!
translation of *The Iliad* (1715) bk. 1, l. 1; see **Homer** 172:8

5 The feast of reason and the flow of soul.
Imitations of Horace Horace bk. 2, Satire 1 (1734) l. 128

6 For I, who hold sage Homer's rule the best,
Welcome the coming, speed the going guest.
Imitations of Horace Horace bk. 2, Satire 2 (1734) l. 159; Pope's translation of *The Odyssey* (1725–6) bk. 15, l. 84, has 'Speed the parting guest'

7 Not to go back, is somewhat to advance,
And men must walk at least before they dance.
Imitations of Horace Horace bk. 1, Epistle 1 (1738) l. 53

8 Get place and wealth, if possible, with grace;
If not, by any means get wealth and place.
Imitations of Horace Horace bk. 1, Epistle 1 (1738) l. 103; see **Horace** 174:21

9 Not to admire, is all the art I know,
To make men happy, and to keep them so.
Imitations of Horace Horace bk. 1, Epistle 6 (1738) l. 1; see **Horace** 174:25

10 Ev'n copious Dryden, wanted, or forgot,
The last and greatest art, the art to blot.
Imitations of Horace Horace bk. 2, Epistle 1 (1737) l. 280; see **Jonson** 192:10

11 There still remains, to mortify a wit,
The many-headed monster of the pit.
Imitations of Horace Horace bk. 2, Epistle 1 (1737) l. 304

12 Let humble Allen, with an awkward shame,
Do good by stealth, and blush to find it fame.
Imitations of Horace Epilogue to the Satires (1738) Dialogue 1, l. 135

13 Thus let me live, unseen, unknown;
Thus unlamented let me die;
Steal from the world, and not a stone
Tell where I lie.
'Ode on Solitude' (written *c.*1700)

14 Where'er you walk, cool gales shall fan the glade,
Trees, where you sit, shall crowd into a shade.
Pastorals (1709) 'Summer' l. 73

15 They shift the moving toyshop of their heart.
The Rape of the Lock (1714) canto 1, l. 100

16 Fair tresses man's imperial race insnare,
And beauty draws us with a single hair.
The Rape of the Lock (1714) canto 2, l. 27

17 Belinda smiled, and all the world was gay.
The Rape of the Lock (1714) canto 2, l. 52

18 Here thou, great Anna! whom three realms obey,
Dost sometimes counsel take—and sometimes tea.
The Rape of the Lock (1714) canto 3, l. 7

19 At ev'ry word a reputation dies.
The Rape of the Lock (1714) canto 3, l. 16; see **Sheridan** 315:15

20 The hungry judges soon the sentence sign,
And wretches hang that jury-men may dine.
The Rape of the Lock (1714) canto 3, l. 21

21 Coffee, (which makes the politician wise,
And see thro' all things with his half-shut eyes).
The Rape of the Lock (1714) canto 3, l. 117

22 Party-spirit, which at best is but the madness of many for the gain of a few.
letter to Edward Blount, 27 August 1714

23 A man should never be ashamed to own he has been in the wrong, which is but saying, in other words, that he is wiser to-day than he was yesterday.
Miscellanies (1727) vol. 2 'Thoughts on Various Subjects'

24 All gardening is landscape-painting.
Joseph Spence *Anecdotes* (ed. J. Osborn, 1966) no. 606

25 Here am I, dying of a hundred good symptoms.
to George, Lord Lyttelton, 15 May 1744

Karl Popper 1902–94
Austrian-born philosopher

26 It must be possible for an empirical scientific system to be refuted by experience.
The Logic of Scientific Discovery (1934) ch. 1, sect. 6

27 Science must begin with myths, and with the criticism of myths.
'The Philosophy of Science' in C. A. Mace (ed.) *British Philosophy in the Mid-Century* (1957)

Cole Porter 1891–1964
American songwriter

28 But I'm always true to you, darlin', in my fashion.
Yes I'm always true to you, darlin', in my way.
'Always True to You in my Fashion' (1949 song)

29 In olden days a glimpse of stocking
Was looked on as something shocking
Now, heaven knows,
Anything goes.
'Anything Goes' (1934 song)

30 When they begin the Beguine.
'Begin the Beguine' (1935 song)

1 Oh, give me land, lots of land under starry
skies above,
Don't fence me in.
Let me ride through the wide open country
that I love,
Don't fence me in.
'Don't Fence Me In' (1944 song)

2 I get no kick from champagne,
Mere alcohol doesn't thrill me at all,
So tell me why should it be true
That I get a kick out of you?
'I Get a Kick Out of You' (1934 song) in *Anything
Goes*

3 Birds do it, bees do it,
Even educated fleas do it.
Let's do it, let's fall in love.
'Let's Do It' (1954 song; words added to the 1928
original)

4 Miss Otis regrets (she's unable to lunch
today).
title of song (1934)

5 What a swell party this is.
'Well, Did You Evah?' (1940 song; revived for
the film *High Society*, 1956)

6 You're the top! You're the Coliseum,
You're the top! You're the Louvre Museum,
'You're the Top' (1934 song) in *Anything Goes*

Beilby Porteus 1731–1808
English poet and prelate

7 . . . One murder made a villain,
Millions a hero.
Death (1759) l. 154; see **Rostand** 281:3

Michael Portillo 1953–
British Conservative politician

8 You don't look tall if you surround yourself
by short grasses.
*on Iain Duncan **Smith***
in *Independent* 22 February 2003

Francis Pott 1832–1909
English clergyman

9 The strife is o'er, the battle done;
Now is the Victor's triumph won;
O let the song of praise be sung:
Alleluia!
'The strife is o'er, the battle done' (1861 hymn);
translation of 'Finita iam sunt praelia' (*c.*1695)

Beatrix Potter 1866–1943
English writer for children

10 I have NO MORE TWIST.
The Tailor of Gloucester (1903)

11 It is said that the effect of eating too much
lettuce is 'soporific'.
The Tale of the Flopsy Bunnies (1909)

12 Don't go into Mr McGregor's garden: your
father had an accident there, he was put
into a pie by Mrs McGregor.
The Tale of Peter Rabbit (1902)

Dennis Potter 1935–94
English television dramatist

13 Below my window . . . the blossom is out in
full now . . . I *see* it is the whitest, frothiest,
blossomiest blossom that there ever could
be, and I can see it . . . The nowness of
everything is absolutely wondrous.
*on his heightened awareness of things, in the face
of his imminent death*
interview with Melvyn Bragg on Channel 4,
March 1994

14 Religion to me has always been the wound,
not the bandage.
interview with Melvyn Bragg on Channel 4,
March 1994

Stephen Potter 1900–69
British writer

15 *How to be one up*—how to make the other
man feel that something has gone wrong,
however slightly.
Lifemanship (1950)

16 A good general rule is to state that the
bouquet is better than the taste, and vice
versa.
on wine-tasting
One-Upmanship (1952) ch. 14

17 The theory and practice of gamesmanship
or The art of winning games without
actually cheating.
title of book (1947)

Ezra Pound 1885–1972
American poet

18 Winter is icummen in,
Lhude sing Goddamm,
Raineth drop and staineth slop,
And how the wind doth ramm!
Sing: Goddamm.
'Ancient Music' (1917); see **Anonymous** 11:4

19 Tching prayed on the mountain and
wrote MAKE IT NEW
on his bath tub.
Cantos (1954) no. 53; see **Bible** 53:23

20 And even I can remember
A day when the historians left blanks in
their writings,
I mean for things they didn't know.
Draft of XXX Cantos (1930) no. 13

21 For three years, out of key with his time,
He strove to resuscitate the dead art
Of poetry; to maintain 'the sublime'
In the old sense. Wrong from the start.
Hugh Selwyn Mauberley (1920) 'E. P. Ode pour
l'élection de son sépulcre' pt. 1

22 The age demanded an image
Of its accelerated grimace.
Hugh Selwyn Mauberley (1920) 'E. P. Ode . . . ' pt. 2

23 Died some, pro patria,
non 'dulce' non 'et decor' . . .
walked eye-deep in hell
believing in old men's lies, the unbelieving

came home, home to a lie.
Hugh Selwyn Mauberley (1920) 'E. P. *Ode* . . . ' pt. 4; see **Horace** 175:14

1 There died a myriad,
And of the best, among them,
For an old bitch gone in the teeth,
For a botched civilization.
Hugh Selwyn Mauberley (1920) 'E. P. *Ode* . . . ' pt. 5

2 The ant's a centaur in his dragon world.
Pisan Cantos (1948) no. 81

3 Pull down thy VANITY
Thou art a beaten dog beneath the hail,
A swollen magpie in a fitful sun,
Half black half white
Nor knowst'ou wing from tail.
Pisan Cantos (1948) no. 81

4 Music begins to atrophy when it departs too far from the dance; that poetry begins to atrophy when it gets too far from music.
The ABC of Reading (1934) 'Warning'

5 Literature is news that STAYS news.
The ABC of Reading (1934) ch. 2

6 Real education must ultimately be limited to one who INSISTS on knowing, the rest is mere sheep-herding.
The ABC of Reading (1934) ch. 8

7 Poetry must be *as well written as prose*.
letter to Harriet Monroe, January 1915

Anthony Powell 1905–2000
English novelist

8 Books do furnish a room.
title of novel (1971); see **Smith** 319:8

9 A dance to the music of time.
title of novel sequence (1951–75), after '*Le 4 stagioni che ballano al suono del tempo* [The four seasons dancing to the sound of time]', title given by Giovanni Pietro Bellori to a painting by Nicolas Poussin

10 Growing old is like being increasingly penalized for a crime you haven't committed.
Temporary Kings (1973) ch. 1

Colin Powell 1937–
American general and Republican politician

11 First, we are going to cut it off, and then, we are going to kill it.
strategy for dealing with the Iraqi Army in the Gulf War
at a press conference, 23 January 1991

Enoch Powell 1912–98
British Conservative politician

12 As I look ahead, I am filled with foreboding. Like the Roman, I seem to see 'the River Tiber foaming with much blood'.
speech in Birmingham, 20 April 1968; see **Virgil** 347:10

13 To write a diary every day is like returning to one's own vomit.
interview in *Sunday Times* 6 November 1977

14 For a politician to complain about the press is like a ship's captain complaining about the sea.
in *Guardian* 3 December 1984

15 All political lives, unless they are cut off in midstream at a happy juncture, end in failure, because that is the nature of politics and of human affairs.
Joseph Chamberlain (1977)

John Powell 1645–1713
English judge

16 Nothing is law that is not reason.
Lord Raymond's *Reports* (1765) vol. 2

John O'Connor Power 1848–1919
Irish lawyer and politician

17 The mules of politics: without pride of ancestry, or hope of posterity.
of the Liberal Unionists
H. H. Asquith *Memories and Reflections* (1928) vol. 1, ch. 16; see **Disraeli** 117:22

Terry Pratchett 1948–
English science fiction writer

18 Personal isn't the same as important.
Men at Arms (1993)

19 Most modern fantasy just rearranges the furniture in Tolkien's attic.
Stan Nicholls (ed.) *Wordsmiths of Wonder* (1993)

John Prescott 1938–
British Labour politician

20 When plates appear to be moving, everyone positions themselves for it.
in *The Times* 15 May 2004

Richard Price 1723–91
English nonconformist minister

21 Now, methinks, I see the ardour for liberty catching and spreading; a general amendment beginning in human affairs; the dominion of kings changed for the dominion of laws, and the dominion of priests giving way to the dominion of reason and conscience.
A Discourse on the Love of our Country (1790)

J. B. Priestley 1894–1984
English novelist, dramatist, and critic

22 Our great-grand-children, when they learn how we began this war by snatching glory out of defeat, and then swept on to victory, may also learn how the little holiday steamers made an excursion to hell and came back glorious.
radio broadcast, 5 June 1940

Matthew Prior 1664–1721
English poet

23 Be to her virtues very kind;
Be to her faults a little blind;
Let all her ways be unconfined;
And clap your padlock—on her mind.
'An English Padlock' (1705) l. 79

1 Cured yesterday of my disease,
I died last night of my physician.
  'The Remedy Worse than the Disease' (1727)

2 No, no; for my virginity,
When I lose that, says Rose, I'll die:
Behind the elms last night, cried Dick,
Rose, were you not extremely sick?
  'A True Maid' (1718)

3 They never taste who always drink;
They always talk, who never think.
  'Upon this Passage in Scaligerana' (1740)

Adelaide Ann Procter 1825–64
English writer of popular verse

4 A lost chord.
  title of poem (1858)

5 It may be that Death's bright Angel
Will speak in that chord again
It may be that only in Heaven
I shall hear that grand Amen.
  'A Lost Chord' (1858)

Romano Prodi 1939–
Italian statesman

6 I know very well that the stability pact is
stupid, like all decisions that are rigid.
  on the rules underpinning the single currency
  interview in *Le Monde* (electronic edition) 17
  October 2002

Protagoras b. *c.*485 BC
Greek sophist

7 That man is the measure of all things.
  Plato *Theaetetus* 160d

Pierre-Joseph Proudhon 1809–65
French social reformer

8 *La propriété c'est le vol.*
Property is theft.
  Qu'est-ce que la propriété? (1840) ch. 1

Marcel Proust 1871–1922
French novelist
Textual translations are those of C. K. Scott-
Moncrieff and S. Hudson, revised by T. Kilmartin,
1981

9 And suddenly the memory revealed itself.
The taste was that of the little piece of
madeleine which on Sunday mornings at
Combray . . . my aunt Léonie used to give
me, dipping it first in her own cup of tea or
tisane.
  Du côté de chez Swann (Swann's Way, 1913) vol. 1

10 We are healed of a suffering only by
experiencing it to the full.
  Albertine disparue (The Sweet Cheat Gone, 1925)
  ch. 1

11 The true paradises are the paradises that we
have lost.
  Le Temps retrouvé (Time Regained, 1926) ch. 3

Publilius Syrus
Roman freedman and writer of mimes of the 1st
century BC

12 *Inopi beneficium bis dat qui dat celeriter.*
He gives the poor man twice as much good
who gives quickly.
  proverbially 'Bis dat qui cito dat [He gives
  twice who gives soon]'
    Sententiae no. 274, in J. and A. Duff *Minor Latin*
    Poets

13 *Necessitas dat legem non ipsa accipit.*
Necessity gives the law without itself
acknowledging one.
  proverbially 'Necessitas non habet legem
  [Necessity has no law]'
    Sententiae no. 444, in J. and A. Duff *Minor Latin*
    Poets

John Pudney 1909–77
English poet and writer

14 Do not despair
For Johnny-head-in-air;
He sleeps as sound
As Johnny underground.
  'For Johnny' (1942); see **Hoffmann** 171:7

Joseph Pulitzer 1847–1911
Hungarian-born American newspaper proprietor
and editor

15 Our Republic and its press will rise or fall
together.
  referring to the importance of media
  independence
    in *North American Review* May 1904

16 A cynical, mercenary, demagogic, corrupt
press will produce in time a people as base
as itself.
  inscribed on the gateway to the Columbia School
  of Journalism in New York
    W. J. Granberg *The World of Joseph Pulitzer* (1965)

Punch 1841–1992
English humorous weekly periodical

17 Advice to persons about to marry.—'Don't.'
  4 January 1845; see **Bacon** 22:34

18 You pays your money and you takes your
choice.
  3 January 1846

19 Never do to-day what you can put off till to-
morrow.
  22 December 1849

20 What is Matter?—Never mind.
What is Mind?—No matter.
  14 July 1855

21 Go directly—see what she's doing, and tell
her she mustn't.
  16 November 1872

22 I never read books—I *write* them.
  11 May 1878; see **Disraeli** 118:10

23 I'm afraid you've got a bad egg, Mr Jones.
Oh no, my Lord, I assure you! Parts of it are
excellent!
  11 May 1895

1 Look here, Steward, if this is coffee, I want tea; but if this is tea, then I wish for coffee.
   23 July 1902

2 Sometimes I sits and thinks, and then again I just sits.
   24 October 1906

Alexander Pushkin 1799–1837
Russian poet

3 Moscow: those syllables can start
A tumult in the Russian heart.
   Eugene Onegin (1833) ch. 7, st. 36 (tr. Babette Deutsch)

Israel Putnam 1718–90
American general

4 Don't one of you fire until you see the white of their eyes.
   also attributed to William Prescott (1726–95)
   at Bunker Hill, 1775, in R. Frothingham *History of the Siege of Boston* (1873) ch. 5

Mario Puzo 1920–99
American novelist

5 I'll make him an offer he can't refuse.
   The Godfather (1969) ch. 1

6 A lawyer with his briefcase can steal more than a hundred men with guns.
   The Godfather (1969) ch. 1

Pyrrhus 319–272 BC
Greek monarch, King of Epirus from 306 BC

7 One more such victory and we are lost.
   on defeating the Romans at Asculum, 279 BC
   Plutarch *Parallel Lives* 'Pyrrhus' ch. 21, sect. 9

Francis Quarles 1592–1644
English poet

8 Our God and soldiers we alike adore
Ev'n at the brink of danger; not before:
After deliverance, both alike requited,
Our God's forgotten, and our soldiers slighted.
   Divine Fancies (1632) 'Of Common Devotion'; see **Owen** 256:4

9 We spend our midday sweat, our midnight oil;
We tire the night in thought, the day in toil.
   Emblems (1635) bk. 2, no. 2, l. 33

Josiah Quincy 1772–1864
American Federalist politician

10 As it will be the right of all, so it will be the duty of some, definitely to prepare for a separation, amicably if they can, violently if they must.
   speech, 14 January 1811; see **Clay** 97:13

The Qur'an *see* The Koran

François Rabelais *c.*1494–*c.*1553
French humanist, satirist, and physician

11 Nature abhors a vacuum.
   quoting, in Latin, an article of ancient wisdom
   Gargantua (1534) bk. 1, ch. 5

12 *Fay ce que vouldras.*
Do what you like.
   Gargantua (1534) bk. 1, ch. 57; see **Crowley** 108:2

13 A child is not a vase to be filled, but a fire to be lit.
   attributed; see **Plutarch** 265:10

14 I am going to seek a great perhaps . . . Bring down the curtain, the farce is played out.
   last words; attributed, but probably apocryphal

Yitzhak Rabin 1922–95
Israeli statesman and military leader, Prime Minister 1974–7 and 1992–5

15 We say to you today in a loud and a clear voice: enough of blood and tears. Enough.
   to the Palestinians, at the signing of the Israel–Palestine Declaration
   in Washington, 13 September, 1993

Jean Racine 1639–99
French tragedian

16 She floats, she hesitates; in a word, she's a woman.
   Athalie (1691) act 3, sc. 3

17 *C'est Vénus tout entière à sa proie attachée.*
It's Venus entire latched onto her prey.
   Phèdre (1677) act 1, sc. 3

18 *Dans le fond des forêts votre image me suit.*
Deep in the forest glade your picture chases me.
   Phèdre (1677) act 2, sc. 2

James Rado 1939–
and Gerome Ragni 1942–
American songwriters

19 When the moon is in the seventh house,
And Jupiter aligns with Mars . . .
This is the dawning of the age of Aquarius.
   'Aquarius' (1967 song) in *Hair*

Thomas Rainborowe d. 1648
English soldier and parliamentarian

20 The poorest he that is in England hath a life to live as the greatest he.
   during the Army debates at Putney, 29 October 1647

Kathleen Raine 1908–
British poet

21 He has married me with a ring, a ring of bright water.
   'The Marriage of Psyche' (1952)

Walter Ralegh *c.*1552–1618
English explorer and courtier

22 If all the world and love were young,
And truth in every shepherd's tongue,
These pretty pleasures might me move
To live with thee, and be thy love.
   'Answer to Marlow'; see **Donne** 119:7, **Marlowe** 228:15

23 Give me my scallop-shell of quiet,

My staff of faith to walk upon,
My scrip of joy, immortal diet,
My bottle of salvation,
My gown of glory, hope's true gage,
And thus I'll take my pilgrimage.
'The Passionate Man's Pilgrimage' (1604)

1 But true love is a durable fire,
In the mind ever burning.
'Walsinghame'

2 Fain would I climb, yet fear I to fall.
line written on a window-pane, in Thomas
Fuller History of the Worthies of England (1662)
'Devonshire'; see **Elizabeth I** 130:18

3 Even such is Time, which takes in trust
Our youth, our joys, and all we have,
And pays us but with age and dust;
Who in the dark and silent grave,
When we have wandered all our ways,
Shuts up the story of our days:
And from which earth, and grave, and dust,
The Lord shall raise me up, I trust.
written the night before his death, and found in
his Bible at the Gate-house at Westminster

4 O eloquent, just, and mighty Death! . . . thou
hast drawn together all the farstretched
greatness, all the pride, cruelty, and
ambition of man, and covered it all over
with these two narrow words, Hic jacet [Here
lies].
The History of the World (1614) bk. 5, ch. 6

5 'Tis a sharp remedy, but a sure one for all
ills.
on feeling the edge of the axe prior to his execution
D. Hume History of Great Britain (1754) vol. 1,
ch. 4

6 So the heart be right, it is no matter which
way the head lies.
at his execution, on being asked which way he
preferred to lay his head
W. Stebbing Sir Walter Raleigh (1891) ch. 30

Walter Raleigh 1861–1922
English lecturer and critic

7 In examinations those who do not wish to
know ask questions of those who cannot
tell.
Laughter from a Cloud (1923) 'Some Thoughts on
Examinations'

8 I wish I loved the Human Race;
I wish I loved its silly face.
'Wishes of an Elderly Man' (1923)

Srinivasa Ramanujan 1887–1920
Indian mathematician

9 replying to G. H. Hardy's suggestion that the
number of a taxi-cab (1729) was 'dull':
No, it is a very interesting number; it is the
smallest number expressible as a sum of
two cubes in two different ways.
the two ways being 1^3+12^3 and 9^3+10^3
in Proceedings of the London Mathematical Society 26
May 1921

Ayn Rand 1905–82
American writer

10 Civilization is the progress toward a society
of privacy.
The Fountainhead (1947)

John Randolph 1773–1833
American politician

11 Never were abilities so much below
mediocrity so well rewarded; no, not when
Caligula's horse was made Consul.
on the appointment of Richard Rush as US
Secretary of the Treasury
speech, 1 February 1828

12 He is a man of splendid abilities but utterly
corrupt. He shines and stinks like rotten
mackerel by moonlight.
of Edward Livingston
W. Cabell Bruce John Randolph of Roanoke (1923)
vol. 2

Arthur Ransome 1884–1967
English writer

13 BETTER DROWNED THAN DUFFERS IF NOT
DUFFERS WONT DROWN.
Arthur Ransome Swallows and Amazons (1930)
ch. 1

Frederic Raphael 1931–
British novelist and screenwriter

14 Your idea of fidelity is not having more than
one man in bed at the same time.
Darling (1965) ch. 18

Dan Rather 1931–
American journalist

15 I worry that patriotism run amok will
trample the very values that the country
seeks to defend.
in Independent 18 May 2002

Gerald Ratner 1949–
English businessman

16 We even sell a pair of earrings for under £1,
which is cheaper than a prawn sandwich
from Marks & Spencers. But I have to say the
earrings probably won't last as long.
speech to the Institute of Directors, Albert Hall,
23 April 1991

Herbert Read 1893–1968
English art historian

17 Images of flight, of ragged claws 'scuttling
across the floors of silent seas', of excoriated
flesh, frustrated sex, the geometry of fear.
on twentieth-century British sculpture
introduction to catalogue of Venice Biennale,
1952; Richard Calvocoressi British Sculpture in the
Twentieth Century (1981); see **Eliot** 128:32

18 I saw him stab
And stab again
A well-killed Boche.
This is the happy warrior,
This is he . . .
Naked Warriors (1919) 'The Scene of War, 4. The
Happy Warrior'; see **Wordsworth** 364:9

Charles Reade 1814–84
English novelist and dramatist

1 Sow an act, and you reap a habit. Sow a habit and you reap a character. Sow a character, and you reap a destiny.
   attributed; in *Notes and Queries* (9th Series) vol. 12, 17 October 1903

Nancy Reagan 1923–
American actress

2 A woman is like a teabag—only in hot water do you realize how strong she is.
   in *Observer* 29 March 1981

Ronald Reagan 1911–2004
American Republican statesman; 40th President of the US, 1981–9

3 Politics is supposed to be the second oldest profession. I have come to realize that it bears a very close resemblance to the first.
   at a conference in Los Angeles, 2 March 1977

4 I paid for this microphone.
   *in 1980, debating for the Republican nomination against George **Bush**; the moderator had ordered Reagan's microphone turned off when he asked for the participation of other candidates, and the refusal to allow this was held to be very damaging to Bush*
   Lou Cannon *Ronald Reagan* (1982)

5 *President **Carter** had described a proposal for a national health insurance plan*
   JIMMY CARTER: Governor Reagan, again, typically is against such a proposal.
   RONALD REAGAN: There you go again!
   as Republican challenger debating with President Carter in the 1980 presidential campaign; in *Times* 30 October 1980

6 You can tell a lot about a fellow's character by his way of eating jellybeans.
   in *New York Times* 15 January 1981

7 An evil empire.
   of the Soviet Union
   speech to the National Association of Evangelicals, 8 March 1983

8 We will never forget them, nor the last time we saw them this morning, as they prepared for the journey and waved goodbye and 'slipped the surly bonds of earth' to 'touch the face of God.'
   after the loss of the space shuttle Challenger *with all its crew*
   broadcast from the Oval Office, 28 January 1986; see **Magee** 225:2

9 I now begin the journey that will lead me into the sunset of my life.
   statement to the American people revealing that he had Alzheimer's disease
   in *Daily Telegraph* 5 January 1995

Erell Reaves

10 Lady of Spain, I adore you.
   Right from the night I first saw you,
   My heart has been yearning for you,
   What else could any heart do?
   'Lady of Spain' (1913 song)

Red Cloud 1822–1909
Sioux chief

11 You have heard the sound of the white soldier's axe upon the Little Piney. His presence here is . . . an insult to the spirits of our ancestors. Are we then to give up their sacred graves to be ploughed for corn? Dakotas, I am for war!
   speech at council at Fort Laramie, 1866; Charles A. Eastman *Indian Heroes and Great Chieftains* (1918)

Henry Reed 1914–86
English poet and dramatist

12 Today we have naming of parts.
   'Lessons of the War: 1, Naming of Parts' (1946)

13 They call it easing the Spring: it is perfectly easy
   If you have any strength in your thumb: like the bolt,
   And the breech, and the cocking-piece, and the point of balance,
   Which in our case we have not got.
   'Lessons of the War: 1, Naming of Parts' (1946)

John Reed 1887–1920
American journalist and revolutionary

14 Ten days that shook the world.
   title of book (1919)

Joseph Reed 1741–85
American Revolutionary politician

15 I am not worth purchasing, but such as I am, the King of Great Britain is not rich enough to do it.
   replying to an offer from Governor George Johnstone of £10,000, and any office in the Colonies in the King's gift, if he were able successfully to promote a Union between the UK and the US
   reply as recorded in a declaration of Congress, 11 August 1778; the earliest version is:
   My influence is but small, but were it as great as Governor Johnstone would insinuate, the King of Great Britain has nothing within his gift that would tempt me.
   reply to Mrs Elizabeth Ferguson, 21 June 1778; W. B. Read *Life and Correspondence of Joseph Reed* (1847) vol. 1, ch. 18

Max Reger 1873–1916
German composer

16 I am sitting in the smallest room of my house. I have your review before me. In a moment it will be behind me.
   responding to a savage review by Rudolph Louis in Münchener Neueste Nachrichten, *7 February 1906*
   Nicolas Slonimsky *Lexicon of Musical Invective* (1953)

John Reid 1947–
British Labour politician

1 What enjoyment does a single mother of three living in a council estate get? The only enjoyment sometimes is having a cigarette.
in *Sunday Times* 13 June 2004

2 If you have a PhD and a posh accent from a school like yours, you are regarded as a sophisticate . . . You called me an attack dog because I've got a Glasgow accent.
to Jeremy Paxman (see **Paxman** 260:17) on *Newsnight* progamme, 8 March 2005

Keith Reid 1946–
English pop singer and songwriter

3 Her face, at first . . . just ghostly
Turned a whiter shade of pale.
'A Whiter Shade of Pale' (1967 song)

Erich Maria Remarque 1898–1970
German novelist

4 All quiet on the western front.
English title of *Im Westen nichts Neues* (1929 novel); see **Beers** 29:4, **McClellan** 222:11

Montague John Rendall 1862–1950
British governor of the BBC

5 Nation shall speak peace unto nation.
motto of the BBC; see **Bible** 40:5

Jean-François Paul de Gondi, Cardinal de Retz 1613–79
French cardinal

6 There is nothing in the world which does not have its decisive moment, and the masterpiece of good management is to recognize and grasp this moment.
Mémoires (1717) bk. 2

Walter Reuther 1907–70
American labour leader

7 If it looks like a duck, walks like a duck and quacks like a duck, then it just may be a duck.
*as a test, during the **McCarthy** era, of Communist affiliations*
attributed

Paul Revere 1735–1818
American patriot

8 [We agreed] that if the British went out by water, we would show two lanterns in the North Church steeple; and if by land, one as a signal.
*signals to be used if the British troops moved out of Boston; see **Longfellow** 218:6*
arrangements agreed with the Charlestown Committee of Safety on 16 April, 1775

Charles Revson 1906–75
American businessman

9 In the factory we make cosmetics; in the store we sell hope.
A. Tobias *Fire and Ice* (1976)

Joshua Reynolds 1723–92
English painter

10 If you have great talents, industry will improve them: if you have but moderate abilities, industry will supply their deficiency.
Discourses on Art (ed. R. Wark, 1975) no. 2 (11 December 1769)

Malvina Reynolds 1900–78
American songwriter

11 Little boxes on the hillside . . .
And they're all made out of ticky-tacky
And they all look just the same.
on the tract houses in the hills to the south of San Francisco
'Little Boxes' (1962 song)

Cecil Rhodes 1853–1902
South African statesman

12 Ask any man what nationality he would prefer to be, and ninety-nine out of a hundred will tell you that they would prefer to be Englishmen.
Gordon Le Sueur *Cecil Rhodes* (1913)

13 So little done, so much to do.
on the day of his death
Lewis Michell *Life of Rhodes* (1910) vol. 2, ch. 39; see **Tennyson** 333:4

David Ricardo 1772–1823
British economist

14 Rent is that portion of the earth, which is paid to the landlord for the use of the original and indestructible powers of the soil.
On the Principles of Political Economy and Taxation (1817) ch. 2

Alice Caldwell Rice 1870–1942
American humorist

15 Life is made up of desires that seem big and vital one minute and little and absurd the next. I guess we get what's best for us in the end.
A Romance of Billy-Goat Hill (1912) ch. 2

Condoleezza Rice 1954–
American Republican politician

16 When the Founding Fathers said 'we the people', they did not mean me. My ancestors were three-fifths of a man.
in *Independent* 3 April 2004; see **Constitution** 103:6

Grantland Rice 1880–1954
American sports writer

17 For when the One Great Scorer comes to mark against your name,
He writes—not that you won or lost—but how you played the Game.
'Alumnus Football' (1941)

1 Outlined against a blue-grey October sky,
the Four Horsemen rode again.
*report of football match between US Military
Academy at West Point NY and University of
Notre Dame*
   in *New York Tribune* 19 October 1924

Stephen Rice 1637–1715
Irish lawyer

2 I will drive a coach and six horses through
the Act of Settlement.
   W. King *State of the Protestants of Ireland* (1672) ch.
   3, sect. 8

Tim Rice 1944–
English songwriter

3 Prove to me that you're no fool
Walk across my swimming pool.
   Jesus Christ Superstar (1970) 'Herod's Song'; music
   by Andrew Lloyd Webber

Mandy Rice-Davies 1944–
English model and showgirl

4 He would, wouldn't he?
*on hearing that Lord Astor denied her allegations,
concerning himself and his house parties at
Cliveden*
   at the trial of Stephen Ward, 29 June 1963

Adrienne Rich 1923–
American poet and critic

5 The thing I came for:
the wreck and not the story of the wreck
the thing itself and not the myth.
   'Diving into the Wreck' (1973)'

6 Memory says: Want to do right? Don't count
on me.
   'Eastern War Time' (1991)

Ann Richards 1933–
American Democratic politician

7 Poor George, he can't help it—he was born
with a silver foot in his mouth.
   of George **Bush**
      keynote speech at the Democratic convention,
      1988

Frank Richards (Charles Hamilton) 1876–1961
English writer for boys

8 The fat greedy owl of the Remove.
   'Billy Bunter' in the *Magnet* (1909) vol. 3, no. 72
   'The Greyfriars Photographer'

Justin Richardson 1900–75
British poet

9 For years a secret shame destroyed my
   peace—
I'd not read Eliot, Auden or MacNeice.
But then I had a thought that brought me
   hope—
Neither had Chaucer, Shakespeare, Milton,
   Pope.
   'Take Heart, Illiterates' (1966)

Samuel Richardson 1689–1761
English novelist

10 The affair is over. Clarissa lives.
*announcement by Lovelace of his successful
seduction of Clarissa*
   Clarissa (1747–8) vol. 5, letter 22

Cardinal Richelieu 1585–1642
French cleric and statesman

11 If you give me six lines written by the hand
of the most honest of men, I will find
something in them which will hang him.
   attributed

Mordecai Richler 1931–2001
Canadian writer

12 I'm world famous, Dr Parks said, all over
Canada.
   The Incomparable Atuk (1963)

Hans Richter 1843–1916
German conductor

13 Up with your damned nonsense will I put
twice, or perhaps once, but sometimes
always, by God, never.
   attributed

Nicholas Ridley 1929–93
British Conservative politician

14 *of the European community:*
This is all a German racket, designed to take
over the whole of Europe.
   in *Spectator* 14 July 1990

Louis Riel 1844–85
Canadian Métis political leader

15 Every step the Indian takes is based on a
profound step of fairness.
   diary, 6 May 1885

Rig Veda
*a collection of hymns in early Sanskrit, composed
in the 2nd millenium BC*

16 Whence this creation has arisen—perhaps it
formed itself, or perhaps it did not—the
one who looks down on it, in the highest
heaven, only he knows—or perhaps he
does not know.
   Creation Hymn bk. 10, hymn 129, v. 7

17 When they divided the Man, into how many
parts did they apportion him? What did
they call his mouth, his two arms and
thighs and feet?
His mouth became the Brahman; his arms
were made into the Warrior, his thighs
the People, and from his feet the Servants
were born.
   Hymn of Man bk. 10, hymn 190, v. 11

Rainer Maria Rilke 1875–1926
German poet

18 *So leben wir und nehmen immer Abschied.*
We live our lives, for ever taking leave.
   Duineser Elegien (tr. J. B. Leishman and Stephen
   Spender, 1948) no. 8

1 Love consists in this, that two solitudes protect and touch and greet each other.
Letters to a Young Poet (1929) 14 May 1904 (tr. Hugh MacLennan)

2 I hold this to be the highest task for a bond between two people: that each protects the solitude of the other.
letter to Paula Modersohn-Becker, 12 February 1902, in *Gesammelte Briefe* (1904) vol. 1

Arthur Rimbaud 1854–91
French poet

3 . . . *Je me suis baigné dans le Poème De la Mer.*
I have bathed in the Poem of the Sea.
'Le Bâteau ivre' (1883)

4 *Ô saisons, ô châteaux!*
Quelle âme est sans défauts?
O seasons, O castles! What soul is without fault?
'Ô saisons, ô châteaux' (1872)

5 *A l'aurore, armés d'une ardente patience, nous entrerons aux splendides villes.*
At dawn, armed with a burning patience, we shall enter the splendid cities.
'Une Saison en enfer' (1873)

6 *A noir, E blanc, I rouge, U vert, O bleu: voyelles, Je dirais quelque jour vos naissances latentes.*
A black, E white, I red, U green, O blue: vowels, some day I will tell of the births that may be yours.
'Voyelles' (1870)

César Ritz 1850–1918
Swiss hotel proprietor

7 The customer is never wrong.
R. Nevill and C. E. Jerningham *Piccadilly to Pall Mall* (1908)

Antoine de Rivarol 1753–1801
French man of letters

8 *Ce qui n'est pas clair n'est pas français.*
What is not clear is not French.
Discours sur l'Universalité de la Langue Française (1784)

Lord Robbins 1898–1984
British economist

9 Economics is the science which studies human behaviour as a relationship between ends and scarce means which have alternative uses.
Essay on the Nature and Significance of Economic Science (1932) ch. 1, sect. 3

Maximilien Robespierre 1758–94
French revolutionary

10 Any law which violates the inalienable rights of man is essentially unjust and tyrannical; it is not a law at all.
Déclaration des droits de l'homme 24 April 1793, article 6

11 Any institution which does not suppose the people good, and the magistrate corruptible, is evil.
Déclaration des droits de l'homme 24 April 1793, article 25

12 Intimidation without virtue is disastrous; virtue without intimidation is powerless.
J. M. Thompson *The French Revolution* (1943); attributed

Leo Robin 1900–84
American songwriter

13 A kiss on the hand may be quite continental,
But diamonds are a girl's best friend.
'Diamonds are a Girl's Best Friend' (1949 song) from the film *Gentlemen Prefer Blondes*; see **Loos** 218:14

14 Thanks for the memory.
title of song (with Ralph Rainger, 1937)

Elizabeth Robins 1862–1952
American writer

15 To say in print what she thinks is the last thing the woman novelist or journalist is so rash as to attempt . . . Her publishers are not women.
in 1908, as first president of the Women Writers' Suffrage League

Edwin Arlington Robinson 1869–1935
American poet

16 Go to the western gate, Luke Havergal,
There where the vines cling crimson on the wall,
And in the twilight wait for what will come.
'Luke Havergal' (1896)

17 And Richard Cory, one calm summer night,
Went home and put a bullet through his head.
'Richard Cory' (1897)

John Robinson ?1576–1625
English pastor to the Pilgrim Fathers

18 The Lord has more truth yet to break forth out of his holy word.
alleged address to the departing pilgrims, 1620
in *Dictionary of National Biography* (1917–)

19 The Lutherans refuse to advance beyond what Luther saw, while the Calvinists stick fast where they were left by that great man of God, who saw not all things.
regretting the current state of the reformed churches, in the alleged address to the departing pilgrims, 1620
in *Dictionary of National Biography* (1917–)

John Robinson 1919–83
English theologian and bishop

20 Honest to God.
title of book (1963)

Mary Robinson 1944–
Irish Labour stateswoman; President 1990–97

1 Instead of rocking the cradle, they rocked the system.
   in her victory speech, paying tribute to the women of Ireland
      in *The Times* 10 November 1990; see **Wallace** 349:15

Boyle Roche 1743–1807
Irish politician

2 Mr Speaker, I smell a rat; I see him forming in the air and darkening the sky; but I'll nip him in the bud.
   attributed

Lord Rochester 1647–80
English poet

3 'Is there then no more?'
   She cries. 'All this to love and rapture's due;
   Must we not pay a debt to pleasure too?'
   'The Imperfect Enjoyment' (1680)

4 Here lies a great and mighty king
   Whose promise none relies on;
   He never said a foolish thing,
   Nor ever did a wise one.
   of Charles II; an alternative first line reads: 'Here lies our sovereign lord the King'
      John Wilmot, Earl of Rochester 'The King's Epitaph'; see **Charles II** 91:2

5 A merry monarch, scandalous and poor.
   'A Satire on King Charles II' (1697)

John D. Rockefeller 1839–1937
American industrialist and philanthropist

6 The growth of a large business is merely a survival of the fittest ... The American beauty rose can be produced in the splendour and fragrance which bring cheer to its beholder only by sacrificing the early buds which grow up around it.
   W. J. Ghent *Our Benevolent Feudalism* (1902); 'American Beauty Rose' became the title of a 1950 song by Hal David and others; see **Darwin** 110:8, **Spencer** 321:9

Gene Roddenberry 1921–91
American film producer

7 These are the voyages of the starship *Enterprise*. Its five-year mission ... to boldly go where no man has gone before.
   Star Trek (television series, from 1966)

8 Beam us up, Mr Scott.
   often misquoted as, 'Beam me up, Scotty'
      Star Trek (1966 onwards) 'Gamesters of Triskelion'

Anita Roddick 1942–
English businesswoman

9 I think that business practices would improve immeasurably if they were guided by 'feminine' principles—qualities like love and care and intuition.
   Body and Soul (1991)

Theodore Roethke 1908–63
American poet

10 I have known the inexorable sadness of pencils,
   Neat in their boxes, dolour of pad and paper-weight,
   All the misery of manilla folders and mucilage,
   Desolation in immaculate public places.
   'Dolour' (1948)

Samuel Rogers 1763–1855
English poet

11 Think nothing done while aught remains to do.
   'Human Life' (1819) l. 49; see **Lucan** 220:8

12 But there are moments which he calls his own,
   Then, never less alone than when alone,
   Those whom he loved so long and sees no more,
   Loved and still loves—not dead—but gone before,
   He gathers round him.
   'Human Life' (1819) l. 755; see **Cyprian** 109:3, **Norton** 252:5

13 It doesn't much signify whom one marries, for one is sure to find next morning that it was someone else.
   Alexander Dyce (ed.) *Table Talk of Samuel Rogers* (1860)

Will Rogers 1879–1935
American actor and humorist

14 Income Tax has made more Liars out of the American people than Golf.
   The Illiterate Digest (1924) 'Helping the Girls with their Income Taxes'

15 Everything is funny as long as it is happening to Somebody Else.
   The Illiterate Digest (1924) 'Warning to Jokers: lay off the Prince'

16 Well, all I know is what I read in the papers.
   in *New York Times* 30 September 1923

17 You can't say civilization don't advance, however, for in every war they kill you in a new way.
   in *New York Times* 23 December 1929

18 Half our life is spent trying to find something to do with the time we have rushed through life trying to save.
   letter in *New York Times* 29 April 1930

Mme Roland 1754–93
French revolutionary

19 Ô liberté! Ô liberté! que de crimes on commet en ton nom!
   O liberty! O liberty! what crimes are committed in thy name!
   before being guillotined
      A. de Lamartine *Histoire des Girondins* (1847) bk. 51, ch. 8

Richard Rolle de Hampole

*c.*1290–1349
English mystic

1 When Adam dalfe and Eve spane
Go spire if thou may spede,
Where was than the pride of man
That now merres his mede?
*taken in altered form by John Ball as the text of his
revolutionary sermon on the outbreak of the
Peasant's Revolt, 1381: 'When Adam delved and
Eve span, who was then the gentleman?'*
G. G. Perry *Religious Pieces* (Early English Text
Society, Original Series no. 26, revised ed. 1914)

Pierre de Ronsard 1524–85

French poet

2 *Quand vous serez bien vieille, au soir, à la
chandelle,
Assise auprès du feu, dévidant et filant,
Direz, chantant mes vers, en vous émerveillant,
Ronsard me célébrait du temps que j'étais belle.*
When you are very old, and sit in the
candle-light at evening spinning by the fire,
you will say, as you murmur my verses, a
wonder in your eyes, 'Ronsard sang of me in
the days when I was fair.'
Sonnets pour Hélène (1578) bk. 2, no. 42

Eleanor Roosevelt 1884–1962

American humanitarian and diplomat

3 Is there anything we can do for you? For you
are the one in trouble now.
*to Harry **Truman**, who became President on the
death of Franklin D. **Roosevelt***
in conversation, 12 April 1945

4 I cannot believe that war is the best
solution. No one won the last war, and no
one will win the next war.
letter to Harry Truman, 22 March 1948

5 No one can make you feel inferior without
your consent.
in *Catholic Digest* August 1960

Franklin D. Roosevelt 1882–1945

*American Democratic statesman, 32nd President
of the US 1933–45*

6 The forgotten man at the bottom of the
economic pyramid.
radio address, 7 April 1932

7 I pledge you, I pledge myself, to a new deal
for the American people.
speech to the Democratic Convention in
Chicago, 2 July 1932, accepting the presidential
nomination

8 The only thing we have to fear is fear itself.
inaugural address, 4 March 1933

9 We face the arduous days that lie before us
in the warm courage of national unity.
inaugural address, 4 March 1933; see **Bush**
78:17

10 I have seen war . . . I hate war.
speech at Chautauqua, NY, 14 August 1936

11 I see one-third of a nation ill-housed, ill-clad,
ill-nourished.
second inaugural address, 20 January 1937

12 We have always known that heedless self-
interest was bad morals; we know now that
it is bad economics.
second inaugural address, 20 January 1937

13 Your boys are not going to be sent into any
foreign wars.
speech in Boston, 30 October 1940, in *Public
Papers* (1941) vol. 9; see **Johnson** 186:9

14 We must be the great arsenal of democracy.
'Fireside Chat' radio broadcast, 29 December
1940

15 We look forward to a world founded upon
four essential human freedoms. The first is
freedom of speech and
expression—everywhere in the world. The
second is freedom of every person to
worship God in his own way—everywhere
in the world. The third is freedom from
want . . . The fourth is freedom from fear.
message to Congress, 6 January 1941

16 Yesterday, December 7, 1941—a date which
will live in infamy—the United States of
America was suddenly and deliberately
attacked by naval and air forces of the
Empire of Japan.
address to Congress, 8 December 1941

17 Books can not be killed by fire. People die,
but books never die. No man and no force
can abolish memory . . . In this war, we
know, books are weapons. And it is a part of
your dedication always to make them
weapons for man's freedom.
'Message to the Booksellers of America' 6 May
1942, in *Publisher's Weekly* 9 May 1942

18 The work, my friend, is peace. More than an
end of this war—an end to the beginnings of
all wars.
undelivered address for Jefferson Day, 13 April
1945 (the day after Roosevelt died) in *Public
Papers* (1950) vol. 13

Theodore Roosevelt 1858–1919

*American Republican statesman, 26th President
of the US 1901–9*

19 I wish to preach, not the doctrine of ignoble
ease, but the doctrine of the strenuous life.
speech to the Hamilton Club, Chicago, 10 April
1899, in *Works* (Memorial edition, 1923–6) vol.
15

20 I am as strong as a bull moose and you can
use me to the limit.
*'Bull Moose' subsequently became the popular
name of the Progressive Party*
letter to Mark Hanna, 27 June 1900, in *Works*
(Memorial edition, 1923–6) vol. 23

21 Speak softly and carry a big stick; you will
go far.
speech in Chicago, 3 April 1903

1 A man who is good enough to shed his blood for the country is good enough to be given a square deal afterwards.

  speech at the Lincoln Monument, Springfield, Illinois, 4 June 1903

2 The men with the muck-rakes are often indispensable to the well-being of society; but only if they know when to stop raking the muck.

  speech in Washington, 14 April 1906; see **Bunyan** 280:2

3 It is not the critic who counts; not the man who points out how the strong man stumbles, or where the doer of deeds could have done better. The credit belongs to the man who is actually in the arena.

  'Citizenship in a Republic', speech at the Sorbonne, Paris, 23 April 1910

4 We stand at Armageddon, and we battle for the Lord.

  speech at the Republican National Convention, 18 June 1912

5 There is no room in this country for hyphenated Americanism.

  speech in New York, 12 October 1915

6 One of our defects as a nation is a tendency to use what have been called 'weasel words'. When a weasel sucks eggs the meat is sucked out of the egg. If you use a 'weasel word' after another, there is nothing left of the other.

  speech in St Louis, 31 May 1916

7 I have got such a bully pulpit!

  his personal view of the presidency
  in *Outlook* (New York) 27 February 1909

8 To announce that there must be no criticism of the president, or that we are to stand by the president, right or wrong, is not only unpatriotic and servile, but is morally treasonable to the American public.

  in *Kansas City Star* 7 May 1918

Ethel Rosenberg 1916–53
and Julius Rosenberg 1918–53
American husband and wife; convicted of spying for the Russians

9 We are innocent . . . To forsake this truth is to pay too high a price even for the priceless gift of life.

  petition for executive clemency, filed 9 January 1953

Christina Rossetti 1830–94
English poet

10 My heart is like a singing bird
Whose nest is in a watered shoot.
  'A Birthday' (1862)

11 Come to me in the silence of the night;
Come in the speaking silence of a dream.
  'Echo' (1862)

12 For there is no friend like a sister
In calm or stormy weather;
To cheer one on the tedious way,
To fetch one if one goes astray,
To lift one if one totters down,

To strengthen while one stands.
  'Goblin Market' (1862)

13 In the bleak mid-winter
Frosty wind made moan,
Earth stood hard as iron,
Water like a stone;
Snow had fallen, snow on snow,
Snow on snow,
In the bleak mid-winter,
Long ago.
  'Mid-Winter' (1875)

14 Remember me when I am gone away,
Gone far away into the silent land.
  'Remember' (1862)

15 Better by far you should forget and smile
Than that you should remember and be sad.
  'Remember' (1862)

16 Does the road wind up-hill all the way?
Yes, to the very end.
Will the day's journey take the whole long day?
From morn to night, my friend.
  'Up-Hill' (1862)

17 When I am dead, my dearest,
Sing no sad songs for me;
Plant thou no roses at my head,
Nor shady cypress tree:
Be the green grass above me
With showers and dewdrops wet;
And if thou wilt, remember,
And if thou wilt, forget.
  'When I am dead' (1862)

Dante Gabriel Rossetti 1828–82
English poet and painter

18 The blessed damozel leaned out
From the gold bar of Heaven;
Her eyes were deeper than the depth
Of waters stilled at even;
She had three lilies in her hand,
And the stars in her hair were seven.
  'The Blessed Damozel' (1870) st. 1

19 And the souls mounting up to God
Went by her like thin flames.
  'The Blessed Damozel' (1870) st. 7

20 Look in my face; my name is Might-have-been;
I am also called No-more, Too-late, Farewell.
  The House of Life (1881) pt. 2 'A Superscription'

21 Sleepless with cold commemorative eyes.
  The House of Life (1881) pt. 2 'A Superscription'

22 I have been here before,
But when or how I cannot tell:
I know the grass beyond the door,
The sweet keen smell,
The sighing sound, the lights around the shore.
  'Sudden Light' (1870)

Gioacchino Rossini 1792–1868
Italian composer

23 Wagner has lovely moments but awful quarters of an hour.

  to Emile Naumann, April 1867, in E. Naumann *Italienische Tondichter* (1883) vol. 4

Jean Rostand 1894–1977
French biologist

1 The biologist passes, the frog remains.
sometimes quoted as 'Theories pass. The frog remains'
   Inquiétudes d'un biologiste (1967)

2 To be adult is to be alone.
   Pensées d'un biologiste (1954)

3 Kill a man, and you are an assassin. Kill millions of men, and you are a conqueror. Kill everyone, and you are a god.
   Pensées d'un biologiste (1939) p. 116; see **Porteus** 269:7, **Young** 369:24

Leo Rosten 1908–97
American writer and social scientist

4 Any man who hates dogs and babies can't be all bad.
   of W. C. Fields, and often attributed to him
   speech at Masquers' Club dinner, 16 February 1939

Philip Roth 1933–
American novelist

5 Doctor, my doctor, what do you say, LET'S PUT THE ID BACK IN YID!
   Portnoy's Complaint (1967)

Claude-Joseph Rouget de Lisle 1760–1836
French soldier

6 Allons, enfants de la patrie,
   Le jour de gloire est arrivé . . .
   Aux armes, citoyens!
   Formez vos bataillons!
   Come, children of our country, the day of glory has arrived . . . To arms, citizens! Form your battalions!
   'La Marseillaise' (25 April 1792)

Charles Roupell
British lawyer

7 To play billiards well is a sign of an ill-spent youth.
   attributed, in D. Duncan Life of Herbert Spencer (1908) ch. 20

Jean-Jacques Rousseau 1712–78
French philosopher and novelist

8 The social contract.
   title of book, Du contrat social (1762)

9 Man was born free, and everywhere he is in chains.
   Du Contrat social (1762) ch. 1

Martin Joseph Routh 1755–1854
English classicist

10 You will find it a very good practice always to verify your references, sir!
   John William Burgon Lives of Twelve Good Men (1888 ed.) vol. 1

Matthew Rowbottom, Richard Stannard, and The Spice Girls
English songwriters and English pop singers

11 Yo I'll tell you what I want, what I really really want
   so tell me what you want, what you really really want.
   'Wannabe' (1996 song)

Nicholas Rowe 1674–1718
English dramatist

12 Is this that haughty, gallant, gay Lothario?
   The Fair Penitent (1703) act 5, sc. 1

Helen Rowland 1875–1950
American writer

13 A husband is what is left of a lover, after the nerve has been extracted.
   A Guide to Men (1922)

14 Somehow a bachelor never quite gets over the idea that he is a thing of beauty and a boy forever.
   A Guide to Men (1922); see **Keats** 195:10

15 The follies which a man regrets most, in his life, are those which he didn't commit when he had the opportunity.
   A Guide to Men (1922)

Richard Rowland c.1881–1947
American film producer

16 The lunatics have taken charge of the asylum.
   on the take-over of United Artists by Charles Chaplin and others
   Terry Ramsaye A Million and One Nights (1926) vol. 2, ch. 79

Maude Royden 1876–1956
English religious writer

17 The Church should go forward along the path of progress and be no longer satisfied only to represent the Conservative Party at prayer.
   address at Queen's Hall, London, 16 July 1917

Richard Rumbold c.1622–85
English republican conspirator

18 I never could believe that Providence had sent a few men into the world, ready booted and spurred to ride, and millions ready saddled and bridled to be ridden.
   on the scaffold
   T. B. Macaulay History of England vol. 1 (1849) ch. 1

Donald Rumsfeld 1932–
American Republican politician and businessman

19 Learn to say, 'I don't know.' If used when appropriate, it will be often.
   'Rumsfeld's Rules'; interview in Wall Street Journal 29 January 2001

20 If you are not criticized, you may not be doing much.
   'Rumsfeld's Rules'; interview in Wall Street Journal 29 January 2001

1 When they are being moved from place to place, will they be restrained in a way so that they are less likely to be able to kill an American soldier? You bet. Is it inhumane to do that? No. Would it be stupid to do anything else? Yes.

on al-Qaeda prisoners being held in Cuba
in *The Times* 26 January 2002

2 You're thinking of Europe as Germany and France. I don't. I think that's old Europe. If you look at the entire Nato Europe today, the centre of gravity is shifting to the east.

to journalists who asked him about European hostility to a possible war, 22 January 2003
in *Independent* 21 February 2003

3 Stuff happens.

on looting in Iraq
press conference, 11 April 2003

Damon Runyon 1884–1946
American writer

4 Guys and dolls.

title of book (1931)

5 'My boy,' he says, 'always try to rub up against money, for if you rub up against money long enough, some of it may rub off on you.'

in *Cosmopolitan* August 1929, 'A Very Honourable Guy'

6 I long ago come to the conclusion that all life is 6 to 5 against.

in *Collier's* 8 September 1934, 'A Nice Price'

Salman Rushdie 1947–
Indian-born British novelist

7 What is freedom of expression? Without the freedom to offend, it ceases to exist.

in *Weekend Guardian* 10 February 1990

8 One of the things a writer is for is to say the unsayable, speak the unspeakable and ask difficult questions.

in *Independent on Sunday* 10 September 1995 'Quotes of the Week'

9 It means everything—it means freedom.

on the news that the fatwa had effectively been lifted
in *Mail on Sunday* 27 September 1998

Dean Rusk 1909–94
American politician

10 We're eyeball to eyeball, and I think the other fellow just blinked.

on the Cuban missile crisis, 24 October 1962
in *Saturday Evening Post* 8 December 1962

John Ruskin 1819–1900
English art and social critic

11 I have seen, and heard, much of Cockney impudence before now; but never expected to hear a coxcomb ask two hundred guineas for flinging a pot of paint in the public's face.

on Whistler's Nocturne in Black and Gold
Fors Clavigera (1871–84) Letter 79, 18 June 1877; see Whistler 355:23

12 No person who is not a great sculptor or painter can be an architect. If he is not a sculptor or painter, he can only be a *builder*.

Lectures on Architecture and Painting (1854) Lectures 1 and 2 (addenda)

13 Life without industry is guilt, and industry without art is brutality.

Lectures on Art (1870) Lecture 3 'The Relation of Art to Morals' sect. 95

14 All violent feelings . . . produce in us a falseness in all our impressions of external things, which I would generally characterize as the 'Pathetic Fallacy'.

Modern Painters (1856) vol. 3, pt. 4, ch. 12

15 To see clearly is poetry, prophecy, and religion—all in one.

Modern Painters (1856) vol. 3, pt. 4 'Of Modern Landscape'

16 Mountains are the beginning and the end of all natural scenery.

Modern Painters (1856) vol. 4, pt. 5, ch. 20

17 All books are divisible into two classes, the books of the hour, and the books of all time.

Sesame and Lilies (1865) 'Of Kings' Treasuries'

18 When we build, let us think that we build for ever.

Seven Lamps of Architecture (1849) 'The Lamp of Memory' sect. 10

19 Remember that the most beautiful things in the world are the most useless; peacocks and lilies for instance.

Stones of Venice vol. 1 (1851) ch. 2, sect. 17

20 Fine art is that in which the hand, the head, and the heart of man go together.

The Two Paths (1859) Lecture 2

21 There is no wealth but life.

Unto this Last (1862) Essay 4, p. 156

Bertrand Russell 1872–1970
British philosopher and mathematician

22 Men who are unhappy, like men who sleep badly, are always proud of the fact.

The Conquest of Happiness (1930) ch. 1

23 Boredom is . . . a vital problem for the moralist, since half the sins of mankind are caused by the fear of it.

The Conquest of Happiness (1930) ch. 4

24 One of the symptoms of approaching nervous breakdown is the belief that one's work is terribly important, and that to take a holiday would bring all kinds of disaster.

The Conquest of Happiness (1930) ch. 5

25 One should as a rule respect public opinion in so far as is necessary to avoid starvation and to keep out of prison, but anything that goes beyond this is voluntary submission to an unnecessary tyranny.

The Conquest of Happiness (1930) ch. 9

26 A sense of duty is useful in work, but offensive in personal relations. People wish

to be liked, not to be endured with patient resignation.
The Conquest of Happiness (1930) ch. 10

1 Of all forms of caution, caution in love is perhaps the most fatal to true happiness.
The Conquest of Happiness (1930) ch. 12

2 To be able to fill leisure intelligently is the last product of civilization.
The Conquest of Happiness (1930) ch. 14

3 Work is of two kinds: first, altering the position of matter at or near the earth's surface relatively to other such matter; second, telling other people to do so. The first kind is unpleasant and ill paid; the second is pleasant and highly paid.
In Praise of Idleness and Other Essays (1986) title essay (1932)

4 To fear love is to fear life, and those who fear life are already three parts dead.
Marriage and Morals (1929) ch. 19

5 Mathematics may be defined as the subject in which we never know what we are talking about, nor whether what we are saying is true.
Mysticism and Logic (1918) ch. 4

6 The law of causality, I believe, like much that passes muster among philosophers, is a relic of a bygone age, surviving, like the monarchy, only because it is erroneously supposed to do no harm.
Mysticism and Logic (1918) ch. 9

7 Only on the firm foundation of unyielding despair, can the soul's habitation henceforth be safely built.
Philosophical Essays (1910) no. 2

8 Mathematics, rightly viewed, possesses not only truth, but supreme beauty—a beauty cold and austere, like that of sculpture.
Philosophical Essays (1910) no. 4

9 Every man, wherever he goes, is encompassed by a cloud of comforting convictions, which move with him like flies on a summer day.
Sceptical Essays (1928) 'Dreams and Facts'

10 The infliction of cruelty with a good conscience is a delight to moralists. That is why they invented Hell.
Sceptical Essays (1928) 'On the Value of Scepticism'

11 Man is a credulous animal, and must believe *something*; in the absence of good grounds for belief, he will be satisfied with bad ones.
Unpopular Essays (1950) 'An Outline of Intellectual Rubbish'

12 Fear is the main source of superstition, and one of the main sources of cruelty.
Unpopular Essays (1950) 'An Outline of Intellectual Rubbish'

13 'Change' is scientific, 'progress' is ethical; change is indubitable, whereas progress is a matter of controversy.
Unpopular Essays (1950) 'Philosophy and Politics'

Bob Russell
and **Bobby Scott** 1937–90
American songwriters

14 He ain't heavy . . . he's my brother.
title of song (1969)

George William Russell *see* Æ

Lord John Russell 1792–1878
British Whig statesman; Prime Minister 1846–52, 1865–6

15 It is impossible that the whisper of a faction should prevail against the voice of a nation.
reply to an Address from a meeting of 150,000 persons at Birmingham on the defeat of the second Reform Bill, October 1831
S. Walpole *Life of Lord John Russell* (1889) vol. 1, ch. 7

16 If peace cannot be maintained with honour, it is no longer peace.
speech at Greenock, 19 September 1853; see **Chamberlain** 90:5, **Disraeli** 117:16

William Howard Russell
1820–1907
British journalist

17 They dashed on towards that thin red line tipped with steel.
of the Russians charging the British at the battle of Balaclava, 1854
The British Expedition to the Crimea (1877); Russell's original dispatch read, 'That thin red streak topped with a line of steel'

Ernest Rutherford 1871–1937
New Zealand physicist

18 All science is either physics or stamp collecting.
J. B. Birks *Rutherford at Manchester* (1962)

19 If your experiment needs statistics, you ought to have done a better experiment.
Norman T. J. Bailey *The Mathematical Approach to Biology and Medicine* (1967)

20 It was quite the most incredible event that has ever happened to me in my life. It was almost as incredible as if you fired a 15-inch shell at a piece of tissue paper and it came back and hit you.
on the back-scattering effect of metal foil on alpha-particles
E. N. da C. Andrade *Rutherford and the Nature of the Atom* (1964)

21 We haven't got the money, so we've got to think!
in *Bulletin of the Institute of Physics* (1962) vol. 13 (as recalled by R. V. Jones)

Gilbert Ryle 1900–76
English philosopher

22 The dogma of the Ghost in the Machine.
*on the mental-conduct concepts of **Descartes***
The Concept of Mind (1949) ch. 1

Rafael Sabatini 1875–1950
Italian novelist

1 He was born with a gift of laughter and a sense that the world was mad.
Scaramouche (1921) bk. 1, ch. 1

Anwar al-Sadat 1918–81
Egyptian statesman

2 Peace is much more precious than a piece of land.
speech in Cairo, 8 March 1978

Carl Sagan 1934–96
American scientist and writer

3 If you wish to make an apple pie from scratch, you must first invent the universe.
Cosmos (1980) ch. 9

4 To me, it underscores our responsibility to deal more kindly with one another, and to preserve and cherish the pale blue dot, the only home we've ever known.
of Earth as photographed by Voyager 1
Pale Blue Dot (1995)

Françoise Sagan 1935–
French novelist

5 To jealousy, nothing is more frightful than laughter.
La Chamade (1965) ch. 9

Mohammed al-Sahhaf
Iraqi politician

6 There are no American infidels in Baghdad.
press briefing during the war in Iraq
in *Sunday Telegraph* 13 April 2003

7 I now inform you that you are too far from reality.
final briefing to the press in Baghdad
in *Sunday Telegraph* 13 April 2003

Antoine de Saint-Exupéry 1900–44
French novelist

8 Grown-ups never understand anything for themselves, and it is tiresome for children to be always and forever explaining things to them.
Le Petit Prince (1943) ch. 1

9 It is only with the heart that one can see rightly; what is essential is invisible to the eye.
Le Petit Prince (1943) ch. 21

10 Experience shows us that love does not consist in gazing at each other but in looking together in the same direction.
Terre des Hommes (translated as 'Wind, Sand and Stars', 1939) ch. 8

Saki 1870–1916
Scottish writer

11 Waldo is one of those people who would be enormously improved by death.
Beasts and Super-Beasts (1914) 'The Feast of Nemesis'

12 The cook was a good cook, as cooks go; and as cooks go, she went.
Reginald (1904) 'Reginald on Besetting Sins'

13 I always say beauty is only sin deep.
Reginald (1904) 'Reginald's Choir Treat'

14 A little inaccuracy sometimes saves tons of explanation.
The Square Egg (1924) 'Clovis on the Alleged Romance of Business'

J. D. Salinger 1919–
American novelist and short-story writer

15 I keep making up these sex rules for myself, and then I break them right away.
The Catcher in the Rye (1951) ch. 9

16 Take most people, they're crazy about cars ... I'd rather have a goddam horse. A horse is at least *human*, for God's sake.
The Catcher in the Rye (1951) ch. 17

17 I keep picturing all these little kids playing some game in this big field of rye and all ... I mean if they're running and they don't look where they're going I have to come out from somewhere and catch them. That's all I'd do all day. I'd just be the catcher in the rye.
The Catcher in the Rye (1951) ch. 22

Lord Salisbury (3rd Marquess of Salisbury) 1830–1903
British Conservative statesman; Prime Minister 1855–6, 1886–92, 1895–1902

18 Too clever by half.
of Disraeli's amendment on Disestablishment
speech, House of Commons, 30 March 1868; see also **Salisbury** 284:23

19 Never should trust experts. If you believe the doctors, nothing is wholesome: if you believe the theologians, nothing is innocent: if you believe the soldiers, nothing is safe.
letter to Lord Lytton, 15 June 1877; in Lady Gwendolen Cecil *Life of Robert, Marquis of Salisbury* (1921–32) vol. 2

20 We are part of the community of Europe and we must do our duty as such.
speech at Caernarvon, 10 April 1888

21 Horny-handed sons of toil.
in *Quarterly Review* October 1873; later popularized in the US by Denis Kearney (1847–1907); see **Lowell** 220:1

22 By office boys for office boys.
of the Daily Mail
H. Hamilton Fyfe *Northcliffe, an Intimate Biography* (1930) ch. 4

Lord Salisbury (5th Marquess of Salisbury) 1893–1972
British Conservative politician

23 Too clever by half.
of Iain Macleod, Colonial Secretary 'in his relationship to the white communities of Africa'
in the House of Lords, 7 March 1961; see also **Salisbury** 284:18

Lord Samuel 1870–1963
British Liberal politician

1 A library is thought in cold storage.
   A Book of Quotations (1947)

George Sand 1804–76
French novelist

2 We cannot tear out a single page of our life,
but we can throw the book in the fire.
   Mauprat (1837)

3 There is only one happiness in life, to love
and be loved.
   letter to Lina Calamatta, 31 March 1862

Carl Sandburg 1878–1967
American poet

4 Hog Butcher for the World,
Tool Maker, Stacker of Wheat,
Player with Railroads and the Nation's
   Freight Handler;
Stormy, husky, brawling,
City of the Big Shoulders.
   'Chicago' (1916)

5 The fog comes
on little cat feet.
It sits looking
over harbour and city
on silent haunches
and then moves on.
   'Fog' (1916)

6 Pile the bodies high at Austerlitz and
   Waterloo.
Shovel them under and let me work—
I am the grass; I cover all.
   'Grass' (1918)

7 Little girl . . . Sometime they'll give a war
and nobody will come.
   The People, Yes (1936); see **Ginsberg** 151:2

8 I tell you the past is a bucket of ashes.
   'Prairie' (1918)

9 Poetry is the achievement of the synthesis
of hyacinths and biscuits.
   in *Atlantic Monthly* March 1923 'Poetry
   Considered'

10 Slang is a language that rolls up its sleeves,
spits on its hands and goes to work.
   in *New York Times* 13 February 1959

Henry 'Red' Sanders
American football coach

11 Sure, winning isn't everything. It's the only
thing.
   in *Sports Illustrated* 26 December 1955; often
   attributed to Vince Lombardi

George Santayana 1863–1952
Spanish-born philosopher and critic

12 Fanaticism consists in redoubling your
effort when you have forgotten your aim.
   The Life of Reason (1905) vol. 1, introduction

13 Those who cannot remember the past are
condemned to repeat it.
   The Life of Reason (1905) vol. 1, ch. 12

14 There is no cure for birth and death save to
enjoy the interval.
   Soliloquies in England (1922) 'War Shrines'

Sappho
Greek lyric poet of the late 7th century BC

15 Some say an army of cavalry or of infantry
or a fleet of ships is the most beautiful thing
on the black earth. But I say it is whatever
one loves.
   D. L. Page (ed.) *Lyrica Graeca Selecta* (1968) no. 16

16 Just as the sweet-apple reddens on the high
branch, high on the highest, and the apple-
pickers missed it, or rather did not miss it
out, but could not reach it.
   describing a girl before her marriage
   D. L. Page (ed.) *Lyrica Graeca Selecta* (1968) no. 224

John Singer Sargent 1856–1925
American painter

17 Every time I paint a portrait I lose a friend.
   N. Bentley and E. Esar *Treasury of Humorous
   Quotations* (1951)

Leslie Sarony 1897–1985
British songwriter

18 Ain't it grand to be blooming well dead?
   title of song (1932)

Jean-Paul Sartre 1905–80
French philosopher, novelist, dramatist, and critic

19 When the rich wage war it's the poor who
die.
   Le Diable et le bon Dieu (1951) act 1, tableau 1

20 Existence precedes and rules essence.
   L'Être et le néant (1943) pt. 4, ch. 1

21 I am condemned to be free.
   L'Être et le néant (1943) pt. 4, ch. 1

22 Man is a useless passion.
   L'Être et le néant (1943) pt. 4, ch. 2

23 Hell is other people.
   Huis Clos (1944) sc. 5; see **Eliot** 127:27

24 Human life begins on the far side of despair.
   Les Mouches (1943) act 3, sc. 2

25 I hate victims who respect their
executioners.
   Les Séquestrés d'Altona (1960) act 1, sc. 1

Siegfried Sassoon 1886–1967
English poet

26 If I were fierce, and bald, and short of
   breath,
I'd live with scarlet Majors at the Base,
And speed glum heroes up the line to death.
   'Base Details' (1918)

27 Does it matter?—losing your sight? . . .
There's such splendid work for the blind;
And people will always be kind,
As you sit on the terrace remembering
And turning your face to the light.
   'Does it Matter?' (1918)

28 The song was wordless; the singing will
never be done.
   'Everyone Sang' (1919)

1 'He's a cheery old card,' grunted Harry to
  Jack
  As they slogged up to Arras with rifle and
  pack.
  But he did for them both by his plan of
  attack.
  'The General' (1918)

2 Here was the world's worst wound. And
  here with pride
  'Their name liveth for ever' the Gateway
  claims.
  'On Passing the New Menin Gate' (1928); see
  Anonymous 11:6

Ferdinand de Saussure 1857–1913
Swiss linguistics scholar

3 In language there are only differences.
  Course in General Linguistics (1916)

4 Language can . . . be compared with a sheet
  of paper: thought is the front and sound the
  back; one cannot cut the front without
  cutting the back at the same time.
  Course in General Linguistics (1916)

George Savile *see* Lord Halifax

Dorothy L. Sayers 1893–1957
English writer of detective fiction

5 I always have a quotation for everything—it
  saves original thinking.
  Have His Carcase (1932)

Friedrich von Schelling 1775–1854
German philosopher

6 Architecture in general is frozen music.
  Philosophie der Kunst (1809)

Friedrich von Schiller 1759–1805
German dramatist and poet

7 *Freude, schöner Götterfunken,*
  Tochter aus Elysium,
  Wir betreten feuertrunken,
  Himmlische, dein Heiligtum.
  Deine Zauber binden wieder,
  Was die Mode streng geteilt.
  Joy, beautiful radiance of the gods, daughter
  of Elysium, we set foot in your heavenly
  shrine dazzled by your brilliance. Your
  charms re-unite what common use has
  harshly divided.
  'An die Freude' (1785)

8 *Alle Menschen werden Brüder*
  Wo dein sanfter Flügel weilt.
  All men become brothers under your tender
  wing.
  'An die Freude' (1785)

9 The sun does not set in my dominions.
  Philip II
  Don Carlos (1787) act 1, sc. 6; see **North** 251:22

10 With stupidity the gods themselves struggle
   in vain.
   The Maid of Orleans (1801) act 3, sc. 6

11 The world's history is the world's
   judgement.
   'Resignation' (1786) st. 19

Moritz Schlick 1882–1936
German philosopher

12 The meaning of a proposition is the method
   of its verification.
   Philosophical Review (1936) vol. 45

Heinrich Schliemann 1822–90
German archaeologist

13 I have gazed upon the face of Agamemnon.
   on discovering a gold mask at Mycenae, 1876;
   traditional version of his telegram to the minister
   at Athens: 'This one is very like the picture which
   my imagination formed of Agamemnon long ago'
   W. M. Calder and D. A. Traill *Myth, Scandal, and*
   History (1986)

Artur Schnabel 1882–1951
Austrian-born pianist

14 The notes I handle no better than many
   pianists. But the pauses between the
   notes—ah, that is where the art resides!
   in *Chicago Daily News* 11 June 1958

Budd Schulberg 1914–
American writer

15 What makes Sammy run?
   title of book (1941)

E. F. Schumacher 1911–77
German-born economist

16 Small is beautiful. A study of economics as if
   people mattered.
   title of book (1973)

Robert Schumann 1810–56
German composer

17 Hats off, gentlemen—a genius!
   of Chopin
   'An Opus 2' (1831); H. Pleasants (ed.) *Schumann*
   on Music (1965)

Carl Schurz 1829–1906
American soldier and politician

18 My country, right or wrong; if right, to be
   kept right; and if wrong, to be set right!
   speech, US Senate, 29 February 1872; see
   Decatur 111:16

Delmore Schwartz 1913–66
American poet

19 The heavy bear who goes with me,
   A manifold honey to smear his face.
   'The Heavy Bear Who Goes With Me' (1958)

Albert Schweitzer 1875–1965
Franco-German missionary

20 Late on the third day, at the very moment
   when, at sunset, we were making our way
   through a herd of hippopotamuses, there
   flashed upon my mind, unforeseen and
   unsought, the phrase, 'Reverence for Life'.
   Aus meinem Leben und Denken (1933) ch. 13

21 Truth has no special time of its own. Its hour
   is now—always, and indeed then most truly

when it seems most unsuitable to actual circumstances.

Zwischen Wasser und Urwald (On the Edge of the Primeval Forest, 1922) ch. 11

Kurt Schwitters 1887–1948
German painter

1 I am a painter and I nail my pictures together.

R. Hausmann *Am Anfang war Dada* (1972)

C. P. Scott 1846–1932
British journalist

2 Comment is free, but facts are sacred.

in *Manchester Guardian* 5 May 1921; see **Stoppard** 326:11

3 *Television*? The word is half Greek, half Latin. No good can come of it.

Asa Briggs *The BBC: the First Fifty Years* (1985)

Robert Falcon Scott 1868–1912
English polar explorer

4 Great God! this is an awful place.

of the South Pole
diary, 17 January 1912

5 Had we lived, I should have had a tale to tell of the hardihood, endurance, and courage of my companions which would have stirred the heart of every Englishman. These rough notes and our dead bodies must tell the tale.

'Message to the Public' in late editions of *The Times* 11 February 1913, and those of the following day; in *Scott's Last Expedition* (1913) vol. 1, ch. 20

6 For God's sake look after our people.

last diary entry, 29 March 1912

Sir Walter Scott 1771–1832
Scottish novelist and poet

7 But answer came there none.

The Bridal of Triermain (1813) canto 3, st. 10; see **Carroll** 87:4

8 Yet seemed that tone, and gesture bland, Less used to sue than to command.

The Lady of the Lake (1810) canto 1, st. 21; see **Shakespeare** 305:18

9 And the stern joy which warriors feel In foemen worthy of their steel.

The Lady of the Lake (1810) canto 5, st. 10

10 If thou would'st view fair Melrose aright, Go visit it by the pale moonlight.

The Lay of the Last Minstrel (1805) canto 2, st. 1

11 It is the secret sympathy, The silver link, the silken tie, Which heart to heart, and mind to mind, In body and in soul can bind.

The Lay of the Last Minstrel (1805) canto 5, st. 13

12 Breathes there the man, with soul so dead, Who never to himself hath said, This is my own, my native land!

The Lay of the Last Minstrel (1805) canto 6, st. 1

13 Unwept, unhonoured, and unsung.

The Lay of the Last Minstrel (1805) canto 6, st. 1

14 O Caledonia! stern and wild,

Meet nurse for a poetic child!

The Lay of the Last Minstrel (1805) canto 6, st. 2

15 O! many a shaft, at random sent, Finds mark the archer little meant! And many a word, at random spoken, May soothe or wound a heart that's broken.

The Lord of the Isles (1813) canto 5, st. 18

16 And come he slow, or come he fast, It is but Death who comes at last.

Marmion (1808) canto 2, st. 30

17 O, young Lochinvar is come out of the west, Through all the wide Border his steed was the best.

Marmion (1808) canto 5, st. 12 ('Lochinvar' st. 1)

18 So faithful in love, and so dauntless in war, There never was knight like the young Lochinvar.

Marmion (1808) canto 5, st. 12 ('Lochinvar' st. 1)

19 O what a tangled web we weave, When first we practise to deceive!

Marmion (1808) canto 6, st. 17

20 O Woman! in our hours of ease, Uncertain, coy, and hard to please, And variable as the shade By the light quivering aspen made; When pain and anguish wring the brow, A ministering angel thou!

Marmion (1808) canto 6, st. 30; see **Shakespeare** 294:5

21 It's no fish ye're buying—it's men's lives.

The Antiquary (1816) ch. 11

22 Touch not the cat but a glove.

'*but*' = *without*
The Fair Maid of Perth (1828) ch. 34

23 The hour is come, but not the man.

The Heart of Midlothian (1818) ch. 4, title

24 There's a gude time coming.

Rob Roy (1817) ch. 32

25 The play-bill, which is said to have announced the tragedy of Hamlet, the character of the Prince of Denmark being left out.

commonly alluded to as 'Hamlet without the Prince'

The Talisman (1825) introduction; W. J. Parke *Musical Memories* (1830) vol. 1 gives a similar anecdote from 1787

26 We shall never learn to feel and respect our real calling and destiny, unless we have taught ourselves to consider every thing as moonshine, compared with the education of the heart.

to J. G. Lockhart, August 1825, in Lockhart's *Life of Sir Walter Scott* vol. 6 (1837) ch. 2

27 The Big Bow-Wow strain I can do myself like any now going; but the exquisite touch, which renders ordinary commonplace things and characters interesting, from the truth of the description and the sentiment, is denied to me.

on Jane **Austen**

W. E. K. Anderson (ed.) *Journals of Sir Walter Scott* (1972) 14 March 1826; see **Pembroke** 261:10

1 All men who have turned out worth anything have had the chief hand in their own education.

> letter to J. G. Lockhart, *c.*16 June 1830, in H. J. C. Grierson (ed.) *Letters of Sir Walter Scott* vol. 11 (1936)

Scottish Metrical Psalms 1650

2 The Lord's my shepherd, I'll not want.
He makes me down to lie
In pastures green: he leadeth me
the quiet waters by.

> Psalm 23, v. 1; see **Book of Common Prayer** 62:14

3 My head thou dost with oil anoint,
and my cup overflows.

> Psalm 23, v. 1; see **Book of Common Prayer** 62:15

4 I to the hills will lift mine eyes
from whence doth come mine aid.

> Psalm 121, v. 1; see **Book of Common Prayer** 64:20

Edmund Hamilton Sears 1810–76
American minister

5 It came upon the midnight clear,
That glorious song of old,
From Angels bending near the earth
To touch their harps of gold.

> *The Christian Register* (1850) 'That Glorious Song of Old'

John Sedgwick 1813–64
American Union general

6 They couldn't hit an elephant at this distance.

> *comment of a Union general, immediately prior to being killed by enemy fire at the battle of Spotsylvania in the American Civil War*
> Robert Denney *The Civil War Years* (1992)

Alan Seeger 1888–1916
American poet

7 I have a rendezvous with Death
At some disputed barricade.

> 'I Have a Rendezvous with Death' (1916)

Pete Seeger 1919–
American folk singer and songwriter

8 Where have all the flowers gone?

> title of song (1961)

9 Education is when you read the fine print; experience is what you get when you don't.

> L. Botts *Loose Talk* (1980)

John Seeley 1834–95
English historian

10 We [the English] seem, as it were, to have conquered and peopled half the world in a fit of absence of mind.

> *The Expansion of England* (1883) Lecture 1

Erich Segal 1937–

11 Love means not ever having to say you're sorry.

> *Love Story* (1970)

John Selden 1584–1654
English historian and antiquary

12 Old friends are best. King James used to call for his old shoes; they were easiest for his feet.

> *Table Talk* (1689) 'Friends'

13 Ignorance of the law excuses no man; not that all men know the law, but because 'tis an excuse every man will plead, and no man can tell how to confute him.

> *Table Talk* (1689) 'Law'

14 There never was a merry world since the fairies left off dancing, and the Parson left conjuring.

> *Table Talk* (1689) 'Parson'

15 Syllables govern the world.

> *Table Talk* (1689) 'Power: State'

W. C. Sellar 1898–1951
and R. J. Yeatman 1898–1968
British writers

16 For every person who wants to teach there are approximately thirty who don't want to learn—much.

> *And Now All This* (1932) introduction

17 1066 and all That

> title of book (1930)

18 History is not what you thought. *It is what you can remember.*

> *1066 and All That* (1930) 'Compulsory Preface'

19 The Cavaliers (Wrong but Wromantic) and the Roundheads (Right but Repulsive).

> *1066 and All That* (1930) ch. 35

20 AMERICA was thus clearly top nation, and History came to a .

> *1066 and All That* (1930) ch. 62

Seneca ('the Younger') *c.*4 BC–AD 65
Roman philosopher and poet

21 If one does not know to which port one is sailing, no wind is favourable.

> *Epistulae ad Lucilium* no. 71, sect. 3

22 *Homines dum docent discunt.*
Even while they teach, men learn.

> *Epistulae Morales* no. 7, sect. 8

23 Anyone can stop a man's life, but no one his death; a thousand doors open on to it.

> *Phoenissae* l. 152; see **Massinger** 231:3, **Webster** 352:23

Robert W. Service 1874–1958
Canadian poet

24 A promise made is a debt unpaid, and the trail has its own stern code.

> 'The Cremation of Sam McGee' (1907)

25 Ah! the clock is always slow;
It is later than you think.

> 'It Is Later Than You Think' (1921)

26 This is the law of the Yukon, that only the Strong shall thrive;
That surely the Weak shall perish, and only the Fit survive.

> 'The Law of the Yukon' (1907)

1 When we, the Workers, all demand: 'What
are WE fighting for?' . . .
Then, then we'll end that stupid crime, that
devil's madness—War.
'Michael' (1921)

2 Back of the bar, in a solo game, sat
Dangerous Dan McGrew,
And watching his luck was his light-o'-love,
the lady that's known as Lou.
'The Shooting of Dan McGrew' (1907)

Edward Sexby d. 1658
English conspirator

3 Killing no murder briefly discourst in three
questions.
an apology for tyrannicide
title of pamphlet (1657)

Anne Sexton 1928-74
American poet

4 In a dream you are never eighty.
'Old' (1962)

5 But suicides have a special language.
Like carpenters they want to know *which
tools.*
They never ask *why build.*
'Wanting to Die' (1966)

1st Lord Shaftesbury 1621-83
English statesman

6 'Men of sense are really but of one religion.'
. . . 'Pray, my lord, what religion is that
which men of sense agree in?' 'Madam,' says
the earl immediately, 'men of sense never
tell it.'
Bishop Gilbert Burnet *History of My Own Time*
(1724) vol. 1; see **Disraeli** 117:27

3rd Lord Shaftesbury 1671-1713
English statesman and philosopher

7 How comes it to pass, then, that we appear
such cowards in reasoning, and are so afraid
to stand the test of ridicule?
A Letter Concerning Enthusiasm (1708) sect. 2

William Shakespeare 1564-1616
English dramatist
*The line number is given without brackets where
the scene is all verse up to the quotation and the
line number is certain, and in square brackets
where prose makes it variable. All references are
to the Oxford Standard Authors edition in one
volume*

All's Well that Ends Well

8 That I should love a bright particular star
And think to wed it.
All's Well that Ends Well (1603-4) act 1, sc. 1, l. [98]

9 Our remedies oft in ourselves do lie
Which we ascribe to heaven.
All's Well that Ends Well (1603-4) act 1, sc. 1, l.
[232]

10 A young man married is a man that's
marred.
All's Well that Ends Well (1603-4) act 2, sc. 3, l.
[315]

Antony and Cleopatra

11 CLEOPATRA: I'll set a bourn how far to be
beloved.
ANTONY: Then must thou needs find out
new heaven, new earth.
Antony and Cleopatra (1606-7) act 1, sc. 1, l. 16

12 Let Rome in Tiber melt, and the wide arch
Of the ranged empire fall.
Antony and Cleopatra (1606-7) act 1, sc. 1, l. 33

13 A Roman thought hath struck him.
Antony and Cleopatra (1606-7) act 1, sc. 2, l. [91]

14 In time we hate that which we often fear.
Antony and Cleopatra (1606-7) act 1, sc. 3, l. 12

15 Where's my serpent of old Nile?
Antony and Cleopatra (1606-7) act 1, sc. 5, l. 24

16 My salad days,
When I was green in judgment.
Antony and Cleopatra (1606-7) act 1, sc. 5, l. 73

17 The barge she sat in, like a burnished
throne,
Burned on the water.
Antony and Cleopatra (1606-7) act 2, sc. 2, l. [199];
see **Eliot** 129:22

18 For her own person,
It beggared all description.
Antony and Cleopatra (1606-7) act 2, sc. 2, l. [205]

19 Age cannot wither her, nor custom stale
Her infinite variety; other women cloy
The appetites they feed, but she makes
hungry
Where most she satisfies.
Antony and Cleopatra (1606-7) act 2, sc. 2, l. [243]

20 Let's have one other gaudy night.
Antony and Cleopatra (1606-7) act 3, sc. 11, l. 182

21 I am dying, Egypt, dying.
Antony and Cleopatra (1606-7) act 4, sc. 13, l. 18

22 O! withered is the garland of the war,
The soldier's pole is fall'n; young boys and
girls
Are level now with men; the odds is gone,
And there is nothing left remarkable
Beneath the visiting moon.
Antony and Cleopatra (1606-7) act 4, sc. 13, l. 64

23 Let's do it after the high Roman fashion,
And make death proud to take us.
Antony and Cleopatra (1606-7) act 4, sc. 13, l. 87

24 He words me, girls, he words me.
Antony and Cleopatra (1606-7) act 5, sc. 2, l. 190

25 Finish, good lady; the bright day is done,
And we are for the dark.
Antony and Cleopatra (1606-7) act 5, sc. 2, l. 192

26 I shall see
Some squeaking Cleopatra boy my greatness
I' the posture of a whore.
Antony and Cleopatra (1606-7) act 5, sc. 2, l. 218

27 I wish you all joy of the worm.
Antony and Cleopatra (1606-7) act 5, sc. 2, l. [260]

28 Give me my robe, put on my crown; I have
Immortal longings in me.
Antony and Cleopatra (1606-7) act 5, sc. 2, l. [282]

29 I am fire and air; my other elements

I give to baser life.
Antony and Cleopatra (1606–7) act 5, sc. 2, l. [291]

1 Peace! peace!
Dost thou not see my baby at my breast,
That sucks the nurse asleep?
Antony and Cleopatra (1606–7) act 5, sc. 2, l. [309]

As You Like It

2 Fleet the time carelessly, as they did in the
golden world.
As You Like It (1599) act 1, sc. 1, l. [126]

3 Hereafter, in a better world than this,
I shall desire more love and knowledge of
you.
As You Like It (1599) act 1, sc. 2, l. [301]

4 O, how full of briers is this working-day
world!
As You Like It (1599) act 1, sc. 3, l. [12]

5 Sweet are the uses of adversity,
Which like the toad, ugly and venomous,
Wears yet a precious jewel in his head;
And this our life, exempt from public haunt,
Finds tongues in trees, books in the running
brooks,
Sermons in stones, and good in everything.
As You Like It (1599) act 2, sc. 1, l. 12; see **Bernard**
32:11

6 Ay, now am I in Arden; the more fool I.
When I was at home I was in a better place;
but travellers must be content.
As You Like It (1599) act 2, sc. 4, l. [16]

7 Under the greenwood tree
Who loves to lie with me,
And turn his merry note
Unto the sweet bird's throat,
Come hither, come hither, come hither:
Here shall he see
No enemy
But winter and rough weather.
As You Like It (1599) act 2, sc. 5, l. 1

8 I can suck melancholy out of a song as a
weasel sucks eggs.
As You Like It (1599) act 2, sc. 5, l. [12]

9 And so, from hour to hour, we ripe and ripe,
And then from hour to hour, we rot and rot:
And thereby hangs a tale.
As You Like It (1599) act 2, sc. 7, l. 26

10 A worthy fool! Motley's the only wear.
As You Like It (1599) act 2, sc. 7, l. 34

11 All the world's a stage,
And all the men and women merely players:
They have their exits and their entrances;
And one man in his time plays many parts,
His acts being seven ages.
As You Like It (1599) act 2, sc. 7, l. 139

12 At first the infant,
Mewling and puking in the nurse's arms.
And then the whining schoolboy, with his
satchel,
And shining morning face, creeping like
snail
Unwillingly to school.
As You Like It (1599) act 2, sc. 7, l. 143

13 Then a soldier,
Full of strange oaths, and bearded like the
pard,
Jealous in honour, sudden and quick in
quarrel,
Seeking the bubble reputation
Even in the cannon's mouth.
As You Like It (1599) act 2, sc. 7, l. 149

14 The sixth age shifts
Into the lean and slippered pantaloon.
As You Like It (1599) act 2, sc. 7, l. 157

15 Second childishness, and mere oblivion,
Sans teeth, sans eyes, sans taste, sans
everything.
As You Like It (1599) act 2, sc. 7, l. 165

16 Blow, blow, thou winter wind,
Thou art not so unkind
As man's ingratitude.
As You Like It (1599) act 2, sc. 7, l. 174

17 Most friendship is feigning, most loving
mere folly.
As You Like It (1599) act 2, sc. 7, l. 181

18 Run, run, Orlando: carve on every tree
The fair, the chaste, and unexpressive she.
As You Like It (1599) act 3, sc. 2, l. 9

19 O wonderful, wonderful, and most
wonderful wonderful! and yet again
wonderful, and after that, out of all
whooping!
As You Like It (1599) act 3, sc. 2, l. [202]

20 Do you not know I am a woman? when I
think, I must speak.
As You Like It (1599) act 3, sc. 2, l. [265]

21 There was no thought of pleasing you when
she was christened.
As You Like It (1599) act 3, sc. 2, l. [284]

22 Thank heaven, fasting, for a good man's
love.
As You Like It (1599) act 3, sc. 5, l. 58

23 Men are April when they woo, December
when they wed: maids are May when they
are maids, but the sky changes when they
are wives.
As You Like It (1599) act 4, sc. 1, l. [153]

24 Oh! how bitter a thing it is to look into
happiness through another man's eyes.
As You Like It (1599) act 5, sc. 2, l. [48]

25 It was a lover and his lass,
With a hey, and a ho, and a hey nonino,
That o'er the green cornfield did pass,
In the spring time, the only pretty ring time,
When birds do sing, hey ding a ding, ding;
Sweet lovers love the spring.
As You Like It (1599) act 5, sc. 3, l. [18]

26 A poor virgin, sir, an ill-favoured thing, sir,
but mine own.
As You Like It (1599) act 5, sc. 4, l. [60]

27 The retort courteous . . . the quip modest . . .
the reply churlish . . . the reproof valiant . . .
the countercheck quarrelsome . . . the lie
circumstantial . . . the lie direct.
of the degrees of a lie
As You Like It (1599) act 5, sc. 4, l. [96]

1 Your 'if' is the only peace-maker; much virtue in 'if'.
As You Like It (1599) act 5, sc. 4, l. [108]

Coriolanus

2 What is the city but the people?
Coriolanus (1608) act 3, sc. 1, l. 198

3 There is a world elsewhere.
Coriolanus (1608) act 3, sc. 3, l. 133

Cymbeline

4 Boldness be my friend!
Arm me, audacity.
Cymbeline (1609–10) act 1, sc. 6, l. 18

5 Hark! hark! the lark at heaven's gate sings.
Cymbeline (1609–10) act 2, sc. 3, l. [22]

6 Fear no more the heat o' the sun,
Nor the furious winter's rages;
Thou thy worldly task hast done,
Home art gone and ta'en thy wages:
Golden lads and girls all must,
As chimney-sweepers, come to dust.
Cymbeline (1609–10) act 4, sc. 2, l. 258

Hamlet

7 You come most carefully upon your hour.
Hamlet (1601) act 1, sc. 1, l. 6

8 For this relief much thanks.
Hamlet (1601) act 1, sc. 1, l. 8

9 The graves stood tenantless and the sheeted dead
Did squeak and gibber in the Roman streets.
Hamlet (1601) act 1, sc. 1, l. 115

10 And then it started like a guilty thing
Upon a fearful summons.
Hamlet (1601) act 1, sc. 1, l. 148

11 Some say that ever 'gainst that season comes
Wherein our Saviour's birth is celebrated,
The bird of dawning singeth all night long;
And then, they say, no spirit can walk abroad.
Hamlet (1601) act 1, sc. 1, l. 158

12 But, look, the morn, in russet mantle clad,
Walks o'er the dew of yon high eastern hill.
Hamlet (1601) act 1, sc. 1, l. 166

13 A little more than kin, and less than kind.
Hamlet (1601) act 1, sc. 2, l. 65

14 Not so, my lord; I am too much i' the sun.
Hamlet (1601) act 1, sc. 2, l. 67

15 O! that this too too solid flesh would melt,
Thaw, and resolve itself into a dew.
Hamlet (1601) act 1, sc. 2, l. 129

16 How weary, stale, flat, and unprofitable
Seem to me all the uses of this world.
Hamlet (1601) act 1, sc. 2, l. 133

17 So excellent a king; that was, to this,
Hyperion to a satyr.
Hamlet (1601) act 1, sc. 2, l. 139

18 Frailty, thy name is woman!
Hamlet (1601) act 1, sc. 2, l. 146

19 Like Niobe, all tears.
Hamlet (1601) act 1, sc. 2, l. 149

20 No more like my father
Than I to Hercules.
Hamlet (1601) act 1, sc. 2, l. 152

21 It is not, nor it cannot come to good;
But break, my heart, for I must hold my tongue!
Hamlet (1601) act 1, sc. 2, l. 158

22 A truant disposition, good my lord.
Hamlet (1601) act 1, sc. 2, l. 169

23 Thrift, thrift, Horatio! the funeral baked meats
Did coldly furnish forth the marriage tables.
Hamlet (1601) act 1, sc. 2, l. 180

24 In my mind's eye, Horatio.
Hamlet (1601) act 1, sc. 2, l. 185

25 He was a man, take him for all in all,
I shall not look upon his like again.
Hamlet (1601) act 1, sc. 2, l. 187

26 But answer made it none.
Hamlet (1601) act 1, sc. 2, l. 215

27 A countenance more in sorrow than in anger.
Hamlet (1601) act 1, sc. 2, l. 231

28 Himself the primrose path of dalliance treads,
And recks not his own rede.
Hamlet (1601) act 1, sc. 3, l. 50

29 For the apparel oft proclaims the man.
Hamlet (1601) act 1, sc. 3, l. 72

30 Neither a borrower, nor a lender be.
Hamlet (1601) act 1, sc. 3, l. 75

31 This above all: to thine own self be true,
And it must follow, as the night the day,
Thou canst not then be false to any man.
Hamlet (1601) act 1, sc. 3, l. 78; see **Bacon** 23:20

32 Ay, springes to catch woodcocks.
Hamlet (1601) act 1, sc. 3, l. 115

33 It is a nipping and an eager air.
Hamlet (1601) act 1, sc. 4, l. 2

34 But to my mind,—though I am native here,
And to the manner born,—it is a custom
More honoured in the breach than the observance.
Hamlet (1601) act 1, sc. 4, l. 14

35 Angels and ministers of grace defend us!
Hamlet (1601) act 1, sc. 4, l. 39

36 Something is rotten in the state of Denmark.
Hamlet (1601) act 1, sc. 4, l. 90

37 List, list, O, list!
Hamlet (1601) act 1, sc. 5, l. 13

38 I could a tale unfold whose lightest word
Would harrow up thy soul, freeze thy young blood,
Make thy two eyes, like stars, start from their spheres,
Thy knotted and combinèd locks to part,
And each particular hair to stand on end,
Like quills upon the fretful porpentine.
Hamlet (1601) act 1, sc. 5, l. 15

39 Murder most foul, as in the best it is;

But this most foul, strange, and unnatural.
Hamlet (1601) act 1, sc. 5, l. 27

1 O my prophetic soul!
My uncle!
Hamlet (1601) act 1, sc. 5, l. 40

2 O, horrible! O, horrible! most horrible!
Hamlet (1601) act 1, sc. 5, l. 80

3 O villain, villain, smiling, damnèd villain!
My tables,—meet it is I set it down,
That one may smile, and smile, and be a
villain.
Hamlet (1601) act 1, sc. 5, l. 106

4 Well said, old mole! canst work i' the earth
so fast?
Hamlet (1601) act 1, sc. 5, l. 162

5 There are more things in heaven and earth,
Horatio,
Than are dreamt of in your philosophy.
Hamlet (1601) act 1, sc. 5, l. 166; see **Haldane**
159:8

6 To put an antic disposition on.
Hamlet (1601) act 1, sc. 5, l. 172

7 Rest, rest, perturbèd spirit.
Hamlet (1601) act 1, sc. 5, l. 182

8 The time is out of joint; O cursèd spite,
That ever I was born to set it right!
Hamlet (1601) act 1, sc. 5, l. 188

9 By indirections find directions out.
Hamlet (1601) act 2, sc. 1, l. 66

10 Brevity is the soul of wit.
Hamlet (1601) act 2, sc. 2, l. 90

11 More matter with less art.
Hamlet (1601) act 2, sc. 2, l. 95

12 POLONIUS: What do you read, my lord?
HAMLET: Words, words, words.
Hamlet (1601) act 2, sc. 2, l. [195]

13 Though this be madness, yet there is
method in't.
Hamlet (1601) act 2, sc. 2, l. [211]

14 There is nothing either good or bad, but
thinking makes it so.
Hamlet (1601) act 2, sc. 2, l. [259]

15 O God! I could be bounded in a nut-shell,
and count myself a king of infinite space,
were it not that I have bad dreams.
Hamlet (1601) act 2, sc. 2, l. [263]

16 This most excellent canopy, the air, look
you, this brave o'erhanging firmament, this
majestical roof fretted with golden fire,
why, it appears no other thing to me but a
foul and pestilent congregation of vapours.
What a piece of work is a man! How noble
in reason! how infinite in faculty! in form, in
moving, how express and admirable! in
action how like an angel! in apprehension
how like a god! the beauty of the world! the
paragon of animals! And yet, to me, what is
this quintessence of dust? man delights not
me; no, nor woman neither, though, by
your smiling, you seem to say so.
Hamlet (1601) act 2, sc. 2, l. [318]

17 I am but mad north-north-west; when the
wind is southerly, I know a hawk from a
handsaw.
Hamlet (1601) act 2, sc. 2, l. [405]

18 The play, I remember, pleased not the
million; 'twas caviare to the general.
Hamlet (1601) act 2, sc. 2, l. [465]

19 Use every man after his desert, and who
should 'scape whipping?
Hamlet (1601) act 2, sc. 2, l. [561]

20 O, what a rogue and peasant slave am I.
Hamlet (1601) act 2, sc. 2, l. [584]

21 For Hecuba!
What's Hecuba to him or he to Hecuba
That he should weep for her?
Hamlet (1601) act 2, sc. 2, l. [592]

22 The play's the thing
Wherein I'll catch the conscience of the
king.
Hamlet (1601) act 2, sc. 2, l. [641]

23 To be, or not to be: that is the question:
Whether 'tis nobler in the mind to suffer
The slings and arrows of outrageous
fortune,
Or to take arms against a sea of troubles,
And by opposing end them? To die: to sleep;
No more; and, by a sleep to say we end
The heart-ache and the thousand natural
shocks
That flesh is heir to, 'tis a consummation
Devoutly to be wished. To die, to sleep;
To sleep: perchance to dream: ay, there's the
rub;
For in that sleep of death what dreams may
come
When we have shuffled off this mortal coil,
Must give us pause.
Hamlet (1601) act 3, sc. 1, l. 56

24 For who would bear the whips and scorns of
time,
The oppressor's wrong, the proud man's
contumely,
The pangs of disprized love, the law's delay
. . .
When he himself might his quietus make
With a bare bodkin?
Hamlet (1601) act 3, sc. 1, l. 70

25 The undiscovered country from whose
bourn
No traveller returns.
Hamlet (1601) act 3, sc. 1, l. 79

26 Thus conscience doth make cowards of us
all;
And thus the native hue of resolution
Is sicklied o'er with the pale cast of thought.
Hamlet (1601) act 3, sc. 1, l. 83

27 Nymph, in thy orisons
Be all my sins remembered.
Hamlet (1601) act 3, sc. 1, l. 89

28 Get thee to a nunnery.
Hamlet (1601) act 3, sc. 1, l. [124]

29 Be thou as chaste as ice, as pure as snow,
thou shalt not escape calumny.
Hamlet (1601) act 3, sc. 1, l. [142]

1 I say, we will have no more marriages.
Hamlet (1601) act 3, sc. 1, l. [156]

2 O! what a noble mind is here o'erthrown:
The courtier's, soldier's, scholar's, eye,
tongue, sword;
The expectancy and rose of the fair state,
The glass of fashion, and the mould of form,
The observ'd of all observers, quite, quite,
down!
Hamlet (1601) act 3, sc. 1, l. [159]

3 Now see that noble and most sovereign
reason,
Like sweet bells jangled, out of tune and
harsh.
Hamlet (1601) act 3, sc. 1, l. [166]

4 Speak the speech, I pray you, as I
pronounced it to you, trippingly on the
tongue.
Hamlet (1601) act 3, sc. 2, l. 1

5 I would have such a fellow whipped for
o'erdoing Termagant; it out-herods Herod.
Hamlet (1601) act 3, sc. 2, l. 14

6 Suit the action to the word, the word to the
action.
Hamlet (1601) act 3, sc. 2, l. [20]

7 To hold, as 'twere, the mirror up to nature.
Hamlet (1601) act 3, sc. 2, l. [25]

8 Give me that man
That is not passion's slave, and I will wear
him
In my heart's core.
Hamlet (1601) act 3, sc. 2, l. [76]

9 The lady doth protest too much, methinks.
Hamlet (1601) act 3, sc. 2, l. [242]

10 Let the galled jade wince, our withers are
unwrung.
Hamlet (1601) act 3, sc. 2, l. [256]

11 Why, let the stricken deer go weep,
The hart ungallèd play;
For some must watch, while some must
sleep:
So runs the world away.
Hamlet (1601) act 3, sc. 2, l. [287]; see **Cowper**
105:28

12 You would play upon me; you would seem
to know my stops; you would pluck out the
heart of my mystery; you would sound me
from my lowest note to the top of my
compass.
Hamlet (1601) act 3, sc. 2, l. [387]

13 Very like a whale.
Hamlet (1601) act 3, sc. 2, l. [406]

14 They fool me to the top of my bent.
Hamlet (1601) act 3, sc. 2, l. [408]

15 'Tis now the very witching time of night,
When churchyards yawn.
Hamlet (1601) act 3, sc. 2, l. [413]

16 Now might I do it pat, now he is praying.
Hamlet (1601) act 3, sc. 3, l. 73

17 My words fly up, my thoughts remain
below:

Words without thoughts never to heaven
go.
Hamlet (1601) act 3, sc. 3, l. 97

18 How now! a rat? Dead, for a ducat, dead!
Hamlet (1601) act 3, sc. 4, l. 23

19 Thou wretched, rash, intruding fool,
farewell!
I took thee for thy better.
Hamlet (1601) act 3, sc. 4, l. 31

20 A king of shreds and patches.
Hamlet (1601) act 3, sc. 4, l. 102; see **Gilbert**
149:21

21 Assume a virtue, if you have it not.
Hamlet (1601) act 3, sc. 4, l. 160

22 I must be cruel only to be kind.
Hamlet (1601) act 3, sc. 4, l. 178

23 For 'tis the sport to have the enginer
Hoist with his own petar.
Hamlet (1601) act 3, sc. 4, l. 206

24 I'll lug the guts into the neighbour room.
Hamlet (1601) act 3, sc. 4, l. 212

25 Diseases desperate grown,
By desperate appliances are relieved,
Or not at all.
Hamlet (1601) act 4, sc. 2, l. 9; see **Fawkes** 134:14

26 We go to gain a little patch of ground,
That hath in it no profit but the name.
Hamlet (1601) act 4, sc. 4, l. 18

27 How all occasions do inform against me,
And spur my dull revenge!
Hamlet (1601) act 4, sc. 4, l. 32

28 How should I your true love know
From another one?
By his cockle hat and staff,
And his sandal shoon.
Hamlet (1601) act 4, sc. 5, l. [23]

29 Lord! we know what we are, but know not
what we may be.
Hamlet (1601) act 4, sc. 5, l. [43]

30 When sorrows come, they come not single
spies,
But in battalions.
Hamlet (1601) act 4, sc. 5, l. [78]

31 There's such divinity doth hedge a king,
That treason can but peep to what it would.
Hamlet (1601) act 4, sc. 5, l. [123]

32 There's rosemary, that's for remembrance;
pray, love, remember: and there is pansies,
that's for thoughts.
Hamlet (1601) act 4, sc. 5, l. [174]

33 There's rue for you; and here's some for me;
we may call it herb of grace o' Sundays. O!
you must wear your rue with a difference.
There's a daisy; I would give you some
violets, but they withered all when my
father died.
Hamlet (1601) act 4, sc. 5, l. [179]

34 And where the offence is let the great axe
fall.
Hamlet (1601) act 4, sc. 5, l. [218]

35 There is a willow grows aslant a brook,

That shows his hoar leaves in the glassy
stream.
Hamlet (1601) act 4, sc. 7, l. 167

1 There with fantastic garlands did she come,
Of crow-flowers, nettles, daisies, and long
purples,
That liberal shepherds give a grosser name,
But our cold maids do dead men's fingers
call them.
Hamlet (1601) act 4, sc. 7, l. 169

2 There, on the pendent boughs her coronet
weeds
Clambering to hang, an envious sliver
broke,
When down her weedy trophies and herself
Fell in the weeping brook.
Hamlet (1601) act 4, sc. 7, l. 173

3 Alas, poor Yorick. I knew him, Horatio; a
fellow of infinite jest.
Hamlet (1601) act 5, sc. 1, l. [201]

4 Imperious Caesar, dead, and turned to clay,
Might stop a hole to keep the wind away.
Hamlet (1601) act 5, sc. 1, l. [235]

5 A ministering angel shall my sister be,
When thou liest howling.
Hamlet (1601) act 5, sc. 1, l. [263]; see **Scott**
287:20

6 Sweets to the sweet: farewell!
Hamlet (1601) act 5, sc. 1, l. [265]

7 There's a divinity that shapes our ends,
Rough-hew them how we will.
Hamlet (1601) act 5, sc. 2, l. 10

8 Not a whit, we defy augury; there's a special
providence in the fall of a sparrow. If it be
now, 'tis not to come; if it be not to come, it
will be now; if it be not now, yet it will
come: the readiness is all.
Hamlet (1601) act 5, sc. 2, l. [232]

9 A hit, a very palpable hit.
Hamlet (1601) act 5, sc. 2, l. [295]

10 This fell sergeant, death,
Is swift in his arrest.
Hamlet (1601) act 5, sc. 2, l. [350]

11 I am more an antique Roman than a Dane.
Hamlet (1601) act 5, sc. 2, l. [355]

12 Absent thee from felicity awhile,
And in this harsh world draw thy breath in
pain,
To tell my story.
Hamlet (1601) act 5, sc. 2, l. [361]

13 The rest is silence.
Hamlet (1601) act 5, sc. 2, l. [372]

14 Now cracks a noble heart. Good-night, sweet
prince,
And flights of angels sing thee to thy rest!
Hamlet (1601) act 5, sc. 2, l. [373]

15 Rosencrantz and Guildenstern are dead.
Hamlet (1601) act 5, sc. 2, l. [385]

Henry IV, Part 1

16 Let us be Diana's foresters, gentlemen of the
shade, minions of the moon.
Henry IV, Part 1 (1597) act 1, sc. 2, l. [28]

17 If all the year were playing holidays,
To sport would be as tedious as to work;
But when they seldom come, they wished
for come.
Henry IV, Part 1 (1597) act 1, sc. 2, l. [226]

18 Falstaff sweats to death
And lards the lean earth as he walks along.
Henry IV, Part 1 (1597) act 2, sc. 2, l. [119]

19 Out of this nettle, danger, we pluck this
flower, safety.
Henry IV, Part 1 (1597) act 2, sc. 3, l. [11]

20 Nay that's past praying for.
Henry IV, Part 1 (1597) act 2, sc. 4, l. [214]

21 Banish not him thy Harry's company:
banish plump Jack and banish all the world.
Henry IV, Part 1 (1597) act 2, sc. 4, l. [533]

22 O monstrous! but one half-pennyworth of
bread to this intolerable deal of sack!
Henry IV, Part 1 (1597) act 2, sc. 4, l. [598]

23 GLENDOWER: I can call spirits from the vasty
deep.
HOTSPUR: Why, so can I, or so can any man;
But will they come when you do call for
them?
Henry IV, Part 1 (1597) act 3, sc. 1, l. [53]

24 Rebellion lay in his way, and he found it.
Henry IV, Part 1 (1597) act 5, sc. 1, l. 28

25 Thou owest God a death.
Henry IV, Part 1 (1597) act 5, sc. 1, l. [126]; see
Shakespeare 295:6

26 What is honour? A word. What is that word,
honour? Air. A trim reckoning! Who hath it?
He that died o' Wednesday.
Henry IV, Part 1 (1597) act 5, sc. 1, l. [136]

27 Two stars keep not their motion in one
sphere.
Henry IV, Part 1 (1597) act 5, sc. 4, l. 65

28 Poor Jack, farewell!
I could have better spared a better man.
Henry IV, Part 1 (1597) act 5, sc. 4, l. [103]

29 The better part of valour is discretion; in the
which better part, I have saved my life.
Henry IV, Part I (1597) act 5, sc. 4, l. [121]

30 I know thee not, old man: fall to thy
prayers;
How ill white hairs become a fool and jester!
Henry IV, Part 2 (1597) act 5, sc. 5, l. [52]

Henry IV, Part 2

31 Enter Rumour, painted full of tongues.
Henry IV, Part 2 (1597) act 1, sc. 1, stage direction

32 I am not only witty in myself, but the cause
that wit is in other men.
Henry IV, Part 2 (1597) act 1, sc. 2, l. [10]

33 It is the disease of not listening, the malady
of not marking, that I am troubled withal.
Henry IV, Part 2 (1597) act 1, sc. 2, l. [139]

34 I am as poor as Job, my lord, but not so
patient.
Henry IV, Part 2 (1597) act 1, sc. 2, l. [145]

35 CHIEF JUSTICE: God send the prince a better
companion!

FALSTAFF: God send the companion a better prince!

Henry IV, Part 2 (1597) act 1, sc. 2, l. [227]

1 I can get no remedy against this consumption of the purse: borrowing only lingers and lingers it out, but the disease is incurable.

Henry IV, Part 2 (1597) act 1, sc. 2, l. [268]

2 Is it not strange that desire should so many years outlive performance?

Henry IV, Part 2 (1597) act 2, sc. 4, l. [283]

3 Uneasy lies the head that wears a crown.

Henry IV, Part 2 (1597) act 3, sc. 1, l. 31

4 Most forcible Feeble.

Henry IV, Part 2 (1597) act 3, sc. 2, l. [181]

5 We have heard the chimes at midnight.

Henry IV, Part 2 (1597) act 3, sc. 2, l. [231]

6 I care not; a man can die but once; we owe God a death.

Henry IV, Part 2 (1597) act 3, sc. 2, l. [253]; see **Shakespeare** 294:25

7 Thy wish was father, Harry, to that thought.

Henry IV, Part 2 (1597) act 4, sc. 5, l. 91

8 This is the English, not the Turkish court; Not Amurath an Amurath succeeds, But Harry, Harry.

Henry IV, Part 2 (1597) act 5, sc. 2, l. 47

Henry V

9 O! for a Muse of fire, that would ascend The brightest heaven of invention.

Henry V (1599) chorus, l. 1

10 Can this cockpit hold The vasty fields of France? or may we cram Within this wooden O the very casques That did affright the air at Agincourt?

Henry V (1599) chorus, l. 11

11 Consideration like an angel came, And whipped the offending Adam out of him.

Henry V (1599) act 1, sc. 1, l. 28

12 When we have matched our rackets to these balls, We will in France, by God's grace, play a set Shall strike his father's crown into the hazard.

Henry V (1599) act 1, sc. 2, l. 261

13 Now all the youth of England are on fire, And silken dalliance in the wardrobe lies.

Henry V (1599) act 2, chorus, l. 1

14 He's in Arthur's bosom, if ever man went to Arthur's bosom.

Henry V (1599) act 2, sc. 3, l. [9]

15 His nose was as sharp as a pen, and a' babbled of green fields.

Henry V (1599) act 2, sc. 3, l. [17]

16 Once more unto the breach, dear friends, once more; Or close the wall up with our English dead! In peace there's nothing so becomes a man As modest stillness and humility: But when the blast of war blows in our ears, Then imitate the action of the tiger;

Stiffen the sinews, summon up the blood, Disguise fair nature with hard-favoured rage.

Henry V (1599) act 3, sc. 1, l. 1

17 The game's afoot: Follow your spirit; and, upon this charge Cry 'God for Harry! England and Saint George!'

Henry V (1599) act 3, sc. 1, l. 32

18 A little touch of Harry in the night.

Henry V (1599) act 4, chorus, l. 47

19 I think the king is but a man, as I am: the violet smells to him as it doth to me.

Henry V (1599) act 4, sc. 1, l. [106]

20 I am afeard there are few die well that die in a battle; for how can they charitably dispose of any thing when blood is their argument?

Henry V (1599) act 4, sc. 1, l. [149]

21 Every subject's duty is the king's; but every subject's soul is his own.

Henry V (1599) act 4, sc. 1, l. [189]

22 Upon the king! let us our lives, our souls, Our debts, our careful wives, Our children, and our sins lay on the king!

Henry V (1599) act 4, sc. 1, l. [250]

23 And what have kings that privates have not too, Save ceremony, save general ceremony?

Henry V (1599) act 4, sc. 1, l. [258]

24 O God of battles! steel my soldiers' hearts.

Henry V (1599) act 4, sc. 1, l. [309]

25 If we are marked to die, we are enow To do our country loss; and if to live, The fewer men, the greater share of honour.

Henry V (1599) act 4, sc. 3, l. 20

26 He which hath no stomach to this fight, Let him depart.

Henry V (1599) act 4, sc. 3, l. 35

27 This day is called the feast of Crispian: He that outlives this day and comes safe home, Will stand a tip-toe when this day is named, And rouse him at the name of Crispian.

Henry V (1599) act 4, sc. 3, l. 40

28 Then will he strip his sleeve and show his scars, And say, 'These wounds I had on Crispin's day.' Old men forget: yet all shall be forgot, But he'll remember with advantages What feats he did that day.

Henry V (1599) act 4, sc. 3, l. 47

29 We few, we happy few, we band of brothers; For he to-day that sheds his blood with me Shall be my brother; be he ne'er so vile This day shall gentle his condition: And gentlemen in England, now a-bed Shall think themselves accursed they were not here, And hold their manhoods cheap whiles any speaks That fought with us upon Saint Crispin's day.

Henry V (1599) act 4, sc. 3, l. 60

Henry VI, Part 1

1 Expect Saint Martin's summer, halcyon days.
Henry VI, Part 1 (1592) act 1, sc. 2, l. 131

Henry VI, Part 2

2 Thrice is he armed that hath his quarrel just.
Henry VI, Part 2 (1592) act 3, sc. 2, l. 233

3 The first thing we do, let's kill all the lawyers.
Henry VI, Part 2 (1592) act 4, sc. 2, l. [86]

4 And Adam was a gardener.
Henry VI, Part 2 (1592) act 4, sc. 2, l. [146]

5 Away with him! away with him! he speaks Latin.
Henry VI, Part 2 (1592) act 4, sc. 7, l. [62]

Henry VI, Part 3

6 O tiger's heart wrapped in a woman's hide!
Henry VI, Part 3 (1592) act 1, sc. 4, l. 137

7 Suspicion always haunts the guilty mind.
Henry VI, Part 3 (1592) act 5, sc. 6, l. 11

Henry VIII

8 Heat not a furnace for your foe so hot
That it do singe yourself.
Henry VIII (1613) act 1, sc. 1, l. 140; play written with John **Fletcher**

9 Heaven will one day open
The king's eyes, that so long have slept upon
This bold bad man.
Henry VIII (1613) act 2, sc. 2, l. [42]

10 Orpheus with his lute made trees,
And the mountain-tops that freeze,
Bow themselves when he did sing.
Henry VIII (1613) act 3, sc. 1, l. 3

11 I shall fall
Like a bright exhalation in the evening,
And no man see me more.
Henry VIII (1613) act 3, sc. 2, l. 226

12 Farewell! a long farewell, to all my greatness!
Henry VIII (1613) act 3, sc. 2, l. 352

13 When he falls, he falls like Lucifer,
Never to hope again.
Henry VIII (1613) act 3, sc. 2, l. 372

14 Cromwell, I charge thee, fling away ambition:
By that sin fell the angels.
Henry VIII (1613) act 3, sc. 2, l. 441

15 Had I but served my God with half the zeal
I served my king, he would not in mine age
Have left me naked to mine enemies.
Henry VIII (1613) act 3, sc. 2, l. 456; see **Wolsey** 363:13

16 Men's evil manners live in brass; their virtues
We write in water.
Henry VIII (1613) act 4, sc. 2, l. 45; see **Keats** 197:21

Julius Caesar

17 O you hard hearts, you cruel men of Rome,
Knew you not Pompey?
Julius Caesar (1599) act 1, sc. 1, l. [40]

18 Beware the ides of March.
Julius Caesar (1599) act 1, sc. 2, l. 18

19 Why, man, he doth bestride the narrow world
Like a Colossus; and we petty men
Walk under his huge legs, and peep about
To find ourselves dishonourable graves.
Men at some time are masters of their fates:
The fault, dear Brutus, is not in our stars,
But in ourselves, that we are underlings.
Julius Caesar (1599) act 1, sc. 2, l. 134

20 Let me have men about me that are fat;
Sleek-headed men and such as sleep o' nights;
Yond' Cassius has a lean and hungry look;
He thinks too much: such men are dangerous.
Julius Caesar (1599) act 1, sc. 2, l. 191; see **Plutarch** 265:11

21 'Tis very like: he hath the falling sickness.
Julius Caesar (1599) act 1, sc. 2, l. [255]

22 For mine own part, it was Greek to me.
Julius Caesar (1599) act 1, sc. 2, l. [288]

23 It is the bright day that brings forth the adder.
Julius Caesar (1599) act 2, sc. 1, l. 14

24 Let's carve him as a dish fit for the gods,
Not hew him as a carcass fit for hounds.
Julius Caesar (1599) act 2, sc. 1, l. 173

25 When beggars die, there are no comets seen;
The heavens themselves blaze forth the death of princes.
Julius Caesar (1599) act 2, sc. 2, l. 30

26 Cowards die many times before their deaths;
The valiant never taste of death but once.
Julius Caesar (1599) act 2, sc. 2, l. 32

27 But I am constant as the northern star,
Of whose true-fixed and resting quality
There is no fellow in the firmament.
Julius Caesar (1599) act 3, sc. 1, l. 60

28 *Et tu, Brute*? Then fall, Caesar!
Julius Caesar (1599) act 3, sc. 1, l. 77

29 O! pardon me, thou bleeding piece of earth,
That I am meek and gentle with these butchers.
Julius Caesar (1599) act 3, sc. 1, l. 254

30 Cry, 'Havoc!' and let slip the dogs of war.
Julius Caesar (1599) act 3, sc. 1, l. 273

31 Not that I loved Caesar less, but that I loved Rome more.
Julius Caesar (1599) act 3, sc. 2, l. [22]

32 As he was valiant, I honour him: but, as he was ambitious, I slew him.
Julius Caesar (1599) act 3, sc. 2, l. [27]

33 Who is here so base that would be a bondman? If any, speak; for him have I offended . . . I pause for a reply.
Julius Caesar (1599) act 3, sc. 2, l. [31]

1 Friends, Romans, countrymen, lend me your
   ears;
   I come to bury Caesar, not to praise him.
   The evil that men do lives after them,
   The good is oft interrèd with their bones.
   Julius Caesar (1599) act 3, sc. 2, l. [79]

2 For Brutus is an honourable man.
   Julius Caesar (1599) act 3, sc. 2, l. [88]

3 He was my friend, faithful and just to me.
   Julius Caesar (1599) act 3, sc. 2, l. [91]

4 When that the poor have cried, Caesar hath
   wept;
   Ambition should be made of sterner stuff.
   Julius Caesar (1599) act 3, sc. 2, l. [97]

5 If you have tears, prepare to shed them now.
   Julius Caesar (1599) act 3, sc. 2, l. [174]

6 This was the most unkindest cut of all.
   Julius Caesar (1599) act 3, sc. 2, l. [188]

7 O! what a fall was there, my countrymen.
   Julius Caesar (1599) act 3, sc. 2, l. [195]

8 I am no orator, as Brutus is;
   But, as you know me all, a plain, blunt man.
   Julius Caesar (1599) act 3, sc. 2, l. [221]

9 But were I Brutus,
   And Brutus Antony, there were an Antony
   Would ruffle up your spirits, and put a
   tongue
   In every wound of Caesar, that should move
   The stones of Rome to rise and mutiny.
   Julius Caesar (1599) act 3, sc. 2, l. [230]

10 Here was a Caesar! when comes such
   another?
   Julius Caesar (1599) act 3, sc. 2, l. [257]

11 Now let it work; mischief, thou art afoot.
   Julius Caesar (1599) act 3, sc. 2, l. [265]

12 Tear him for his bad verses, tear him for his
   bad verses.
   Julius Caesar (1599) act 3, sc. 3, l. [34]

13 He shall not live; look, with a spot I damn
   him.
   Julius Caesar (1599) act 4, sc. 1, l. 6

14 Let me tell you, Cassius, you yourself
   Are much condemned to have an itching
   palm.
   Julius Caesar (1599) act 4, sc. 3, l. 7

15 There is a tide in the affairs of men,
   Which, taken at the flood, leads on to
   fortune.
   Julius Caesar (1599) act 4, sc. 3, l. 217

16 This was the noblest Roman of them all.
   Julius Caesar (1599) act 5, sc. 5, l. 68

17 His life was gentle, and the elements
   So mixed in him that Nature might stand up
   And say to all the world, 'This was a man!'
   Julius Caesar (1599) act 5, sc. 5, l. 73

King John

18 Grief fills the room up of my absent child,
   Lies in his bed, walks up and down with me.
   King John (1591–8) act 3, sc. 4, l. 93

19 Life is as tedious as a twice-told tale,
   Vexing the dull ear of a drowsy man.
   King John (1591–8) act 3, sc. 4, l. 108

20 To gild refinèd gold, to paint the lily,
   To throw a perfume on the violet,
   To smooth the ice, or add another hue
   Unto the rainbow, or with taper light
   To seek the beauteous eye of heaven to
   garnish,
   Is wasteful and ridiculous excess.
   King John (1591–8) act 4, sc. 2, l. 11

21 Come the three corners of the world in
   arms,
   And we shall shock them: nought shall
   make us rue,
   If England to itself do rest but true.
   King John (1591–8) act 5, sc. 7, l. 116

King Lear

22 Nothing will come of nothing: speak again.
   King Lear (1605–6) act 1, sc. 1, l. [92]

23 LEAR: So young, and so untender?
   CORDELIA: So young, my lord, and true.
   King Lear (1605–6) act 1, sc. 1, l. [108]

24 I want that glib and oily art
   To speak and purpose not.
   King Lear (1605–6) act 1, sc. 1, l. [227]

25 Why bastard? wherefore base?
   When my dimensions are as well compact,
   My mind as generous, and my shape as true,
   As honest madam's issue?
   King Lear (1605–6) act 1, sc. 2, l. 6

26 I grow, I prosper;
   Now, gods, stand up for bastards!
   King Lear (1605–6) act 1, sc. 2, l. 21

27 This is the excellent foppery of the world,
   that, when we are sick in fortune,—often
   the surfeit of our own behaviour,— we
   make guilty of our own disasters the sun,
   the moon, and the stars; as if we were
   villains by necessity, fools by heavenly
   compulsion, knaves, thieves, and treachers
   by spherical predominance, drunkards,
   liars, and adulterers by an enforced
   obedience of planetary influence.
   King Lear (1605–6) act 1, sc. 2, l. [132]

28 Who is it that can tell me who I am?
   King Lear (1605–6) act 1, sc. 4, l. 230

29 How sharper than a serpent's tooth it is
   To have a thankless child!
   King Lear (1605–6) act 1, sc. 4, l. [312]

30 O! let me not be mad, not mad, sweet
   heaven;
   Keep me in temper; I would not be mad!
   King Lear (1605–6) act 1, sc. 5, l. [51]

31 Thou whoreson zed! thou unnecessary
   letter!
   King Lear (1605–6) act 2, sc. 2, l. [68]

32 O, sir! you are old;
   Nature in you stands on the very verge
   Of her confine.
   King Lear (1605–6) act 2, sc. 4, l. [148]

33 O reason not the need! Our basest beggars
   Are in the poorest thing superfluous.
   King Lear (1605–6) act 2, sc. 4, l. 264

1 I will do such things,—
What they are yet I know not,—but they shall be
The terrors of the earth.
King Lear (1605–6) act 2, sc. 4, l. [283]

2 Blow, winds, and crack your cheeks! rage! blow!
You cataracts and hurricanoes, spout
Till you have drenched our steeples, drowned the cocks!
You sulphurous and thought-executing fires,
Vaunt-couriers to oak-cleaving thunderbolts,
Singe my white head!
King Lear (1605–6) act 3, sc. 2, l. 1

3 Rumble thy bellyful! Spit, fire! Spout, rain!
Nor rain, wind, thunder, fire, are my daughters:
I tax not you, you elements, with unkindness.
King Lear (1605–6) act 3, sc. 2, l. 14

4 I am a man
More sinned against than sinning.
King Lear (1605–6) act 3, sc. 2, l. [59]

5 O! that way madness lies; let me shun that.
King Lear (1605–6) act 3, sc. 4, l. 21

6 Take physic, pomp;
Expose thyself to feel what wretches feel.
King Lear (1605–6) act 3, sc. 4, l. 33

7 Thou art the thing itself; unaccommodated man is no more but such a poor, bare, forked animal as thou art.
King Lear (1605–6) act 3, sc. 4, l. [109]

8 This is the foul fiend Flibbertigibbet: he begins at curfew, and walks till the first cock.
King Lear (1605–6) act 3, sc. 4, l. [118]

9 The green mantle of the standing pool.
King Lear (1605–6) act 3, sc. 4, l. [136]

10 The prince of darkness is a gentleman.
King Lear (1605–6) act 3, sc. 4, l. [148]

11 Poor Tom's a-cold.
King Lear (1605–6) act 3, sc. 4, l. [151]

12 Child Roland to the dark tower came,
His word was still, Fie, foh, and fum,
I smell the blood of a British man.
King Lear (1605–6) act 3, sc. 4, l. [185]; see **Browning** 71:26, **Nashe** 248:17

13 Out, vile jelly!
Where is thy lustre now?
King Lear (1605–6) act 3, sc. 7, l. [83]

14 The worst is not,
So long as we can say, 'This is the worst.'
King Lear (1605–6) act 4, sc. 1, l. 27

15 As flies to wanton boys, are we to the gods;
They kill us for their sport.
King Lear (1605–6) act 4, sc. 1, l. 36

16 GLOUCESTER: Is't not the king?
LEAR: Ay, every inch a king.
King Lear (1605–6) act 4, sc. 6, l. [110]

17 Die: die for adultery! No:
The wren goes to't, and the small gilded fly
Does lecher in my sight.
King Lear (1605–6) act 4, sc. 6, l. [115]

18 Get thee glass eyes;
And, like a scurvy politician, seem
To see the things thou dost not.
King Lear (1605–6) act 4, sc. 6, l. [175]

19 When we are born we cry that we are come
To this great stage of fools.
King Lear (1605–6) act 4, sc. 6, l. [187]

20 Thou art a soul in bliss; but I am bound
Upon a wheel of fire.
King Lear (1605–6) act 4, sc. 7, l. 46

21 I am a very foolish, fond old man,
Fourscore and upward, not an hour more or less;
And, to deal plainly,
I fear I am not in my perfect mind.
King Lear (1605–6) act 4, sc. 7, l. 60

22 Men must endure
Their going hence, even as their coming hither:
Ripeness is all.
King Lear (1605–6) act 5, sc. 2, l. 9

23 Come, let's away to prison;
We two alone will sing like birds i' the cage:
When thou dost ask me blessing, I'll kneel down,
And ask of thee forgiveness.
King Lear (1605–6) act 5, sc. 3, l. 8; see **Webster** 353:3

24 The gods are just, and of our pleasant vices
Make instruments to plague us.
King Lear (1605–6) act 5, sc. 3, l. [172]

25 The wheel is come full circle.
King Lear (1605–6) act 5, sc. 3, l. [176]

26 Howl, howl, howl, howl! O! you are men of stones:
Had I your tongue and eyes, I'd use them so
That heaven's vaults should crack. She's gone for ever!
King Lear (1605–6) act 5, sc. 3, l. [259]

27 Her voice was ever soft,
Gentle and low, an excellent thing in woman.
King Lear (1605–6) act 5, sc. 3, l. [274]

28 And my poor fool is hanged! No, no, no life!
Why should a dog, a horse, a rat, have life,
And thou no breath at all? Thou'lt come no more,
Never, never, never, never, never!
King Lear (1605–6) act 5, sc. 3, l. [307]

29 Vex not his ghost: O! let him pass; he hates him
That would upon the rack of this tough world
Stretch him out longer.
King Lear (1605–6) act 5, sc. 3, l. [314]

30 The oldest hath borne most: we that are young,
Shall never see so much, nor live so long.
King Lear (1605–6) act 5, sc. 3, l. [327]

Love's Labour's Lost

31 Cormorant devouring Time.
Love's Labour's Lost (1595) act 1, sc. 1, l. 4

32 From women's eyes this doctrine I derive:

They are the ground, the books, the academes,
From whence doth spring the true Promethean fire.
Love's Labour's Lost (1595) act 4, sc. 3, l. [302]

1 They have been at a great feast of languages, and stolen the scraps.
Love's Labour's Lost (1595) act 5, sc. 1, l. [39]

2 Taffeta phrases, silken terms precise.
Love's Labour's Lost (1595) act 5, sc. 2, l. 407

3 A jest's prosperity lies in the ear
Of him that hears it, never in the tongue
Of him that makes it.
Love's Labour's Lost (1595) act 5, sc. 2, l. [869]

4 When daisies pied and violets blue
And lady-smocks all silver-white
And cuckoo-buds of yellow hue
Do paint the meadows with delight.
Love's Labour's Lost (1595) act 5, sc. 2, l. [902]

5 When icicles hang by the wall,
And Dick the shepherd, blows his nail.
Love's Labour's Lost (1595) act 5, sc. 2, l. [920]

6 The words of Mercury are harsh after the songs of Apollo.
Love's Labour's Lost (1595) act 5, sc. 2, l. [938]

Macbeth

7 FIRST WITCH: When shall we three meet again
In thunder, lightning, or in rain?
SECOND WITCH: When the hurly-burly's done,
When the battle's lost and won.
Macbeth (1606) act 1, sc. 1, l. 1

8 Fair is foul, and foul is fair:
Hover through the fog and filthy air.
Macbeth (1606) act 1, sc. 1, l. 11

9 What bloody man is that?
Macbeth (1606) act 1, sc. 2, l. 1

10 'Aroint thee, witch!' the rump-fed ronyon cries.
Her husband's to Aleppo gone, master o' the Tiger:
But in a sieve I'll thither sail,
And, like a rat without a tail,
I'll do, I'll do, and I'll do.
Macbeth (1606) act 1, sc. 3, l. 7

11 The weird sisters, hand in hand,
Posters of the sea and land,
Thus do go about, about.
Macbeth (1606) act 1, sc. 3, l. 32

12 So foul and fair a day I have not seen.
Macbeth (1606) act 1, sc. 3, l. 38

13 If you can look into the seeds of time,
And say which grain will grow and which will not.
Macbeth (1606) act 1, sc. 3, l. 58

14 Say, from whence
You owe this strange intelligence? or why
Upon this blasted heath you stop our way
With such prophetic greeting?
Macbeth (1606) act 1, sc. 3, l. 72

15 What! can the devil speak true?
Macbeth (1606) act 1, sc. 3, l. 107

16 Two truths are told,
As happy prologues to the swelling act
Of the imperial theme.
Macbeth (1606) act 1, sc. 3, l. 127

17 Present fears
Are less than horrible imaginings.
Macbeth (1606) act 1, sc. 3, l. 137

18 Come what come may,
Time and the hour runs through the roughest day.
Macbeth (1606) act 1, sc. 3, l. 146

19 MALCOLM: Nothing in his life
Became him like the leaving it.
Macbeth (1606) act 1, sc. 4, l. 7

20 There's no art
To find the mind's construction in the face.
Macbeth (1606) act 1, sc. 4, l. 11

21 Glamis thou art, and Cawdor; and shalt be
What thou art promised. Yet I do fear thy nature;
It is too full o' the milk of human kindness
To catch the nearest way; thou wouldst be great,
Art not without ambition; but without
The illness should attend it; what thou wouldst highly,
That thou wouldst holily; wouldst not play false,
And yet wouldst wrongly win.
Macbeth (1606) act 1, sc. 5, l. [16]

22 The raven himself is hoarse
That croaks the fatal entrance of Duncan
Under my battlements.
Macbeth (1606) act 1, sc. 5, l. [38]

23 Unsex me here,
And fill me from the crown to the toe top full
Of direst cruelty.
Macbeth (1606) act 1, sc. 5, l. [38]

24 Come to my woman's breasts,
And take my milk for gall, you murdering ministers.
Macbeth (1606) act 1, sc. 5, l. [47]

25 Your face, my thane, is as a book where men
May read strange matters.
Macbeth (1606) act 1, sc. 5, l. [63]

26 Look like the innocent flower,
But be the serpent under't.
Macbeth (1606) act 1, sc. 5, l. [66]

27 This guest of summer,
The temple-haunting martlet.
Macbeth (1606) act 1, sc. 6, l. 3

28 If it were done when 'tis done, then 'twere well
It were done quickly: if the assassination
Could trammel up the consequence, and catch
With his surcease success; that but this blow
Might be the be-all and the end-all here,
But here, upon this bank and shoal of time,
We'd jump the life to come.
Macbeth (1606) act 1, sc. 7, l. 1

29 Bloody instructions, which, being taught, return,

To plague the inventor.
Macbeth (1606) act 1, sc. 7, l. 9

1 Besides, this Duncan
Hath borne his faculties so meek, hath been
So clear in his great office, that his virtues
Will plead like angels trumpet-tongued,
against
The deep damnation of his taking-off.
Macbeth (1606) act 1, sc. 7, l. 16

2 Pity, like a naked new-born babe.
Macbeth (1606) act 1, sc. 7, l. 21

3 I have no spur
To prick the sides of my intent, but only
Vaulting ambition, which o'erleaps itself,
And falls on the other.
Macbeth (1606) act 1, sc. 7, l. 25

4 He hath honoured me of late; and I have
bought
Golden opinions from all sorts of people.
Macbeth (1606) act 1, sc. 7, l. 32

5 Was the hope drunk,
Wherein you dressed yourself?
Macbeth (1606) act 1, sc. 7, l. 35

6 Letting 'I dare not' wait upon 'I would,'
Like the poor cat i' the adage?
Macbeth (1606) act 1, sc. 7, l. 44

7 I dare do all that may become a man;
Who dares do more is none.
Macbeth (1606) act 1, sc. 7, l. 46

8 LADY MACBETH: I have given suck, and know
How tender 'tis to love the babe that milks
me:
I would, while it was smiling in my face,
Have plucked my nipple from his boneless
gums,
And dash'd the brains out, had I so sworn as
you
Have done to this.
MACBETH: If we should fail,—
LADY MACBETH: We fail!
But screw your courage to the sticking-
place,
And we'll not fail.
Macbeth (1606) act 1, sc. 7, l. 54

9 Bring forth men-children only.
Macbeth (1606) act 1, sc. 7, l. 72

10 False face must hide what the false heart
doth know.
Macbeth (1606) act 1, sc. 7, l. 82

11 There's husbandry in heaven;
Their candles are all out.
Macbeth (1606) act 2, sc. 1, l. 4

12 Is this a dagger which I see before me,
The handle toward my hand? Come, let me
clutch thee:
I have thee not, and yet I see thee still.
Macbeth (1606) act 2, sc. 1, l. 33

13 The bell invites me.
Hear it not, Duncan; for it is a knell
That summons thee to heaven or to hell.
Macbeth (1606) act 2, sc. 1, l. 62

14 It was the owl that shrieked, the fatal
bellman,

Which gives the stern'st good-night.
Macbeth (1606) act 2, sc. 2, l. 4

15 Had he not resembled
My father as he slept I had done't.
Macbeth (1606) act 2, sc. 2, l. 14

16 Methought I heard a voice cry, 'Sleep no
more!
Macbeth does murder sleep,' the innocent
sleep,
Sleep that knits up the ravelled sleave of
care.
Macbeth (1606) act 2, sc. 2, l. 36

17 Glamis hath murdered sleep, and therefore
Cawdor
Shall sleep no more, Macbeth shall sleep no
more!
Macbeth (1606) act 2, sc. 2, l. 43

18 Infirm of purpose!
Give me the daggers. The sleeping and the
dead
Are but as pictures; 'tis the eye of childhood
That fears a painted devil.
Macbeth (1606) act 2, sc. 2, l. 55

19 Will all great Neptune's ocean wash this
blood
Clean from my hand? No, this my hand will
rather
The multitudinous seas incarnadine,
Making the green one red.
Macbeth (1606) act 2, sc. 2, l. 61

20 A little water clears us of this deed.
Macbeth (1606) act 2, sc. 2, l. 68

21 Drink, sir, is a great provoker . . . Lechery,
sir, it provokes, and unprovokes; it
provokes the desire, but it takes away the
performance.
Macbeth (1606) act 2, sc. 3, l. [28]

22 The labour we delight in physics pain.
Macbeth (1606) act 2, sc. 3, l. [56]

23 Confusion now hath made his masterpiece!
Macbeth (1606) act 2, sc. 3, l. [72]

24 Shake off this downy sleep, death's
counterfeit,
And look on death itself!
Macbeth (1606) act 2, sc. 3, l. [83]

25 MACDUFF: Our royal master's murdered!
LADY MACBETH: Woe, alas!
What! in our house?
Macbeth (1606) act 2, sc. 3, l. [95]

26 Had I but died an hour before this chance,
I had lived a blessed time.
Macbeth (1606) act 2, sc. 3, l. [98]

27 There's daggers in men's smiles: the near in
blood,
The nearer bloody.
Macbeth (1606) act 2, sc. 3, l. [147]

28 A falcon, towering in her pride of place,
Was by a mousing owl hawked at and killed.
Macbeth (1606) act 2, sc. 4, l. 12

29 BANQUO: Go not my horse the better,
I must become a borrower of the night
For a dark hour or twain.

MACBETH: Fail not our feast.
Macbeth (1606) act 3, sc. 1, l. 26

1 LADY MACBETH: Things without all remedy
Should be without regard: what's done is
done.
MACBETH: We have scotched the snake, not
killed it.
Macbeth (1606) act 3, sc. 2, l. 11

2 Duncan is in his grave;
After life's fitful fever he sleeps well;
Treason has done his worst: nor steel, nor
poison,
Malice domestic, foreign levy, nothing,
Can touch him further.
Macbeth (1606) act 3, sc. 2, l. 22

3 Come, seeling night,
Scarf up the tender eye of pitiful day,
And with thy bloody and invisible hand,
Cancel and tear to pieces that great bond
Which keeps me pale!
Macbeth (1606) act 3, sc. 2, l. 46

4 Now spurs the lated traveller apace
To gain the timely inn.
Macbeth (1606) act 3, sc. 3, l. 6

5 But now I am cabined, cribbed, confined,
bound in
To saucy doubts and fears.
Macbeth (1606) act 3, sc. 4, l. 24

6 Now good digestion wait on appetite,
And health on both!
Macbeth (1606) act 3, sc. 4, l. 38

7 Thou canst not say I did it: never shake
Thy gory locks at me.
Macbeth (1606) act 3, sc. 4, l. 50

8 Stand not upon the order of your going.
Macbeth (1606) act 3, sc. 4, l. 119

9 It will have blood, they say; blood will have
blood.
Macbeth (1606) act 3, sc. 4, l. 122

10 I am in blood
Stepped in so far that, should I wade no
more,
Returning were as tedious as go o'er.
Macbeth (1606) act 3, sc. 4, l. 136

11 Double, double toil and trouble;
Fire burn and cauldron bubble.
Macbeth (1606) act 4, sc. 1, l. 10

12 Eye of newt, and toe of frog,
Wool of bat, and tongue of dog,
Adder's fork, and blind-worm's sting,
Lizard's leg, and howlet's wing,
For a charm of powerful trouble,
Like a hell-broth boil and bubble.
Macbeth (1606) act 4, sc. 1, l. 14

13 By the pricking of my thumbs,
Something wicked this way comes.
Macbeth (1606) act 4, sc. 1, l. 44

14 MACBETH: How now, you secret, black, and
midnight hags!
What is't you do?
WITCHES: A deed without a name.
Macbeth (1606) act 4, sc. 1, l. 48

15 Be bloody, bold, and resolute.
Macbeth (1606) act 4, sc. 1, l. 79

16 But yet, I'll make assurance double sure,
And take a bond of fate.
Macbeth (1606) act 4, sc. 1, l. 83

17 Macbeth shall never vanquished be until
Great Birnam wood to high Dunsinane hill
Shall come against him.
Macbeth (1606) act 4, sc. 1, l. 92

18 Stands Scotland where it did?
Macbeth (1606) act 4, sc. 3, l. 164

19 Give sorrow words: the grief that does not
speak
Whispers the o'er-fraught heart, and bids it
break.
Macbeth (1606) act 4, sc. 3, l. 209

20 He has no children. All my pretty ones?
Did you say all? O hell-kite! All?
What! all my pretty chickens and their dam,
At one fell swoop?
Macbeth (1606) act 4, sc. 3, l. 216

21 Out, damned spot!
Macbeth (1606) act 5, sc. 1, l. [38]

22 Who would have thought the old man to
have had so much blood in him?
Macbeth (1606) act 5, sc. 1, l. [42]

23 The Thane of Fife had a wife: where is she
now?
Macbeth (1606) act 5, sc. 1, l. [46]

24 All the perfumes of Arabia will not sweeten
this little hand.
Macbeth (1606) act 5, sc. 1, l. [56]

25 What's done cannot be undone.
Macbeth (1606) act 5, sc. 1, l. [74]

26 The devil damn thee black, thou cream-
faced loon!
Where gott'st thou that goose look?
Macbeth (1606) act 5, sc. 3, l. 11

27 I have lived long enough: my way of life
Is fall'n into the sear, the yellow leaf.
Macbeth (1606) act 5, sc. 3, l. 22; see **Byron** 81:15

28 Canst thou not minister to a mind diseased?
Macbeth (1606) act 5, sc. 3, l. 37

29 Throw physic to the dogs; I'll none of it.
Macbeth (1606) act 5, sc. 3, l. 47

30 I have supped full with horrors.
Macbeth (1606) act 5, sc. 5, l. 13

31 She should have died hereafter;
There would have been a time for such a
word,
To-morrow, and to-morrow, and to-morrow,
Creeps in this petty pace from day to day,
To the last syllable of recorded time;
And all our yesterdays have lighted fools
The way to dusty death. Out, out, brief
candle!
Life's but a walking shadow, a poor player,
That struts and frets his hour upon the
stage,
And then is heard no more; it is a tale
Told by an idiot, full of sound and fury,
Signifying nothing.
Macbeth (1606) act 5, sc. 5, l. 16

1   Macduff was from his mother's womb
Untimely ripped.
Macbeth (1606) act 5, sc. 7, l. 44

2   Lay on, Macduff;
And damned be him that first cries, 'Hold,
enough!'
Macbeth (1606) act 5, sc. 7, l. 62

Measure for Measure

3 And liberty plucks justice by the nose.
Measure for Measure (1604) act 1, sc. 3, l. 29

4   O! it is excellent
To have a giant's strength, but it is
tyrannous
To use it like a giant.
Measure for Measure (1604) act 2, sc. 2, l. 107

5   Man, proud man,
Drest in a little brief authority,
Most ignorant of what he's most assured,
His glassy essence, like an angry ape,
Plays such fantastic tricks before high
heaven,
As make the angels weep.
Measure for Measure (1604) act 2, sc. 2, l. 117

6 Be absolute for death; either death or life
Shall thereby be the sweeter.
Measure for Measure (1604) act 3, sc. 1, l. 5

7   If I must die,
I will encounter darkness as a bride,
And hug it in mine arms.
Measure for Measure (1604) act 3, sc. 1, l. 81

8 Ay, but to die, and go we know not where;
To lie in cold obstruction and to rot.
Measure for Measure (1604) act 3, sc. 1, l. 116

9 There, at the moated grange, resides this
dejected Mariana.
Measure for Measure (1604) act 3, sc. 1, l. [279]; see
Tennyson 334:1

The Merchant of Venice

10 God made him, and therefore let him pass
for a man.
The Merchant of Venice (1596–8) act 1, sc. 2, l. [59]

11 I will buy with you, sell with you, talk with
you, walk with you, and so following; but I
will not eat with you, drink with you, nor
pray with you. What news on the Rialto?
The Merchant of Venice (1596–8) act 1, sc. 3, l. [36]

12 If I can catch him once upon the hip,
I will feed fat the ancient grudge I bear him.
The Merchant of Venice (1596–8) act 1, sc. 3, l. [47]

13 The devil can cite Scripture for his purpose.
The Merchant of Venice (1596–8) act 1, sc. 3, l. [99]

14 Still have I borne it with a patient shrug,
For sufferance is the badge of all our tribe.
The Merchant of Venice (1596–8) act 1, sc. 3, l. [110]

15 You call me misbeliever, cut-throat dog,
And spit upon my Jewish gabardine.
The Merchant of Venice (1596–8) act 1, sc. 3, l. [112]

16 It is a wise father that knows his own child.
The Merchant of Venice (1596–8) act 2, sc. 2, l. [83]

17 Truth will come to light; murder cannot be
hid long.
The Merchant of Venice (1596–8) act 2, sc. 2, l. [86]

18 My daughter! O my ducats! O my daughter!
The Merchant of Venice (1596–8) act 2, sc. 8, l. 15

19 The portrait of a blinking idiot.
The Merchant of Venice (1596–8) act 2, sc. 9, l. 54

20 Let him look to his bond.
The Merchant of Venice (1596–8) act 3, sc. 1, l. [51]

21 Hath not a Jew eyes? hath not a Jew hands,
organs, dimensions, senses, affections,
passions?
The Merchant of Venice (1596–8) act 3, sc. 1, l. [63]

22 If you prick us, do we not bleed? if you tickle
us, do we not laugh? if you poison us, do we
not die? and if you wrong us, shall we not
revenge?
The Merchant of Venice (1596–8) act 3, sc. 1, l. [69]

23 The villainy you teach me I will execute, and
it shall go hard but I will better the
instruction.
The Merchant of Venice (1596–8) act 3, sc. 1, l. [76]

24   He makes a swan-like end,
Fading in music.
The Merchant of Venice (1596–8) act 3, sc. 2, l. 44

25 Tell me where is fancy bred.
Or in the heart or in the head?
The Merchant of Venice (1596–8) act 3, sc. 2, l. 63

26 . . . An unlessoned girl, unschooled,
unpractised;
Happy in this, she is not yet so old
But she may learn; happier than this,
She is not bred so dull but she can learn.
The Merchant of Venice (1596–8) act 3, sc. 2, l. 160

27 I pray thee, understand a plain man in his
plain meaning.
The Merchant of Venice (1596–8) act 3, sc. 5, l. [63]

28 I am a tainted wether of the flock,
Meetest for death: the weakest kind of fruit
Drops earliest to the ground.
The Merchant of Venice (1596–8) act 4, sc. 1, l. 114

29 I never knew so young a body with so old a
head.
The Merchant of Venice (1596–8) act 4, sc. 1, l. [163]

30 The quality of mercy is not strained,
It droppeth as the gentle rain from heaven
Upon the place beneath.
The Merchant of Venice (1596–8) act 4, sc. 1, l. [182]

31 Though justice be thy plea, consider this,
That in the course of justice none of us
Should see salvation: we do pray for mercy,
And that same prayer doth teach us all to
render
The deeds of mercy.
The Merchant of Venice (1596–8) act 4, sc. 1, l. [197]

32 Wrest once the law to your authority:
To do a great right, do a little wrong.
The Merchant of Venice (1596–8) act 4, sc. 1, l. [215]

33 A Daniel come to judgement! yea, a Daniel!
The Merchant of Venice (1596–8) act 4, sc. 1, l. [223]

34 The court awards it, and the law doth give it.
The Merchant of Venice (1596–8) act 4, sc. 1, l. [301]

35 He is well paid that is well satisfied.
The Merchant of Venice (1596–8) act 4, sc. 1, l. [416]

1 The moon shines bright: in such a night as
   this . . .
   Troilus methinks mounted the Troyan walls,
   And sighed his soul toward the Grecian
   tents,
   Where Cressid lay that night.
   The Merchant of Venice (1596–8) act 5, sc. 1, l. 1

2 How sweet the moonlight sleeps upon this
   bank!
   Here will we sit, and let the sounds of music
   Creep in our ears; soft stillness and the
   night
   Become the touches of sweet harmony.
   The Merchant of Venice (1596–8) act 5, sc. 1, l. 54

3 Look, how the floor of heaven
   Is thick inlaid with patines of bright gold.
   The Merchant of Venice (1596–8) act 5, sc. 1, l. 58

4 How far that little candle throws his beams!
   So shines a good deed in a naughty world.
   The Merchant of Venice (1596–8) act 5, sc. 1, l. 90

The Merry Wives of Windsor

5 Why, then the world's mine oyster,
   Which I with sword will open.
   The Merry Wives of Windsor (1597) act 2, sc. 2, l. 2

6 There is divinity in odd numbers, either in
   nativity, chance or death.
   The Merry Wives of Windsor (1597) act 5, sc. 1, l. 3

A Midsummer Night's Dream

7 The course of true love never did run
   smooth.
   A Midsummer Night's Dream (1595–6) act 1, sc. 1, l.
   134

8 So quick bright things come to confusion.
   A Midsummer Night's Dream (1595–6) act 1, sc. 1, l.
   149

9 Love looks not with the eyes, but with the
   mind,
   And therefore is winged Cupid painted
   blind.
   A Midsummer Night's Dream (1595–6) act 1, sc. 1, l.
   234

10 The most lamentable comedy, and most
   cruel death of Pyramus and Thisby.
   A Midsummer Night's Dream (1595–6) act 1, sc. 2, l.
   [11]

11 I could play Ercles rarely, or a part to tear a
   cat in, to make all split.
   A Midsummer Night's Dream (1595–6) act 1, sc. 2, l.
   [31]

12 I will roar you as gently as any sucking dove;
   I will roar you as 'twere any nightingale.
   A Midsummer Night's Dream (1595–6) act 1, sc. 2, l.
   [85]

13 Pyramus is a sweet-faced man; a proper
   man, as one shall see in a summer's day.
   A Midsummer Night's Dream (1595–6) act 1, sc. 2, l.
   [89]

14 Over hill, over dale,
   Thorough bush, thorough brier,
   Over park, over pale,
   Thorough flood, thorough fire.
   A Midsummer Night's Dream (1595–6) act 2, sc. 1, l.
   2

15 I must go seek some dew-drops here,
   And hang a pearl in every cowslip's ear.
   A Midsummer Night's Dream (1595–6) act 2, sc. 1, l.
   14

16 The wisest aunt, telling the saddest tale.
   A Midsummer Night's Dream (1595–6) act 2, sc. 1, l.
   51

17 Ill met by moonlight, proud Titania.
   A Midsummer Night's Dream (1595–6) act 2, sc. 1, l.
   60

18 The nine men's morris is filled up with
   mud.
   A Midsummer Night's Dream (1595–6) act 2, sc. 1, l.
   98

19 The seasons alter: hoary-headed frosts
   Fall in the fresh lap of the crimson rose.
   A Midsummer Night's Dream (1595–6) act 2, sc. 1, l.
   107

20 I'll put a girdle round about the earth
   In forty minutes.
   A Midsummer Night's Dream (1595–6) act 2, sc. 1, l.
   175

21 I know a bank whereon the wild thyme
   blows,
   Where oxlips and the nodding violet grows
   Quite over-canopied with luscious
   woodbine,
   With sweet musk-roses, and with eglantine.
   A Midsummer Night's Dream (1595–6) act 2, sc. 1, l.
   249

22 You spotted snakes with double tongue,
   Thorny hedge-hogs, be not seen.
   A Midsummer Night's Dream (1595–6) act 2, sc. 2, l.
   9

23 Weaving spiders come not here;
   Hence you long-legged spinners, hence!
   A Midsummer Night's Dream (1595–6) act 2, sc. 2, l.
   20

24 Look in the almanack; find out moonshine,
   find out moonshine.
   A Midsummer Night's Dream (1595–6) act 3, sc. 1, l.
   [55]

25 What hempen home-spuns have we
   swaggering here,
   So near the cradle of the fairy queen?
   A Midsummer Night's Dream (1595–6) act 3, sc. 1, l.
   [82]

26 Bless thee, Bottom! bless thee! thou art
   translated.
   A Midsummer Night's Dream (1595–6) act 3, sc. 1, l.
   [124]

27 What angel wakes me from my flowery bed?
   A Midsummer Night's Dream (1595–6) act 3, sc. 1, l.
   [135]

28 Lord, what fools these mortals be!
   A Midsummer Night's Dream (1595–6) act 3, sc. 2, l.
   115

29 She was a vixen when she went to school:
   And though she be but little, she is fierce.
   A Midsummer Night's Dream (1595–6) act 3, sc. 2, l.
   324

30 Let us have the tongs and the bones.
   A Midsummer Night's Dream (1595–6) act 4, sc. 1, l.
   [33]

1 The lunatic, the lover, and the poet,
Are of imagination all compact.
A Midsummer Night's Dream (1595–6) act 5, sc. 1, l. 7

2 The poet's eye, in a fine frenzy rolling,
Doth glance from heaven to earth, from earth to heaven;
And, as imagination bodies forth
The forms of things unknown, the poet's pen
Turns them to shapes, and gives to airy nothing
A local habitation and a name.
A Midsummer Night's Dream (1595–6) act 5, sc. 1, l. 12

3 The best in this kind are but shadows, and the worst are no worse, if imagination amend them.
A Midsummer Night's Dream (1595–6) act 5, sc. 1, l. [215]

4 The iron tongue of midnight hath told twelve;
Lovers, to bed; 'tis almost fairy time.
A Midsummer Night's Dream (1595–6) act 5, sc. 1, l. [372]

5 Not a mouse
Shall disturb this hallowed house:
I am sent with broom before,
To sweep the dust behind the door.
A Midsummer Night's Dream (1595–6) act 5, sc. 2, l. 17

Much Ado About Nothing

6 He is a very valiant trencher-man.
Much Ado About Nothing (1598–9) act 1, sc. 1, l. [52]

7 Friendship is constant in all other things
Save in the office and affairs of love.
Much Ado About Nothing (1598–9) act 2, sc. 1, l. [184]

8 There was a star danced, and under that was I born.
Much Ado About Nothing (1598–9) act 2, sc. 1, l. [351]

9 Is it not strange, that sheeps' guts should hale souls out of men's bodies?
Much Ado About Nothing (1598–9) act 2, sc. 3, l. [62]

10 Sigh no more, ladies, sigh no more,
Men were deceivers ever.
Much Ado About Nothing (1598–9) act 2, sc. 3, l. [65]

11 Sits the wind in that corner?
Much Ado About Nothing (1598–9) act 2, sc. 3, l. [108]

12 Well, every one can master a grief but he that has it.
Much Ado About Nothing (1598–9) act 3, sc. 2, l. [28]

13 Comparisons are odorous.
Much Ado About Nothing (1598–9) act 3, sc. 5, l. [18]

14 O! what men dare do! what men may do! what men daily do, not knowing what they do!
Much Ado About Nothing (1598–9) act 4, sc. 1, l. [19]

15 O God, that I were a man! I would eat his heart in the market-place.
Much Ado About Nothing (1598–9) act 4, sc. 1, l. [311]

16 There was never yet philosopher
That could endure the toothache patiently.
Much Ado About Nothing (1598–9) act 5, sc. 1, l. 35

Othello

17 But I will wear my heart upon my sleeve
For daws to peck at: I am not what I am.
Othello (1602–4) act 1, sc. 1, l. 64

18 Even now, now, very now, an old black ram
Is tupping your white ewe.
Othello (1602–4) act 1, sc. 1, l. 88

19 Your daughter and the Moor are now making the beast with two backs.
Othello (1602–4) act 1, sc. 1, l. [117]

20 Keep up your bright swords, for the dew will rust them.
Othello (1602–4) act 1, sc. 2, l. 59

21 I will a round unvarnished tale deliver.
Othello (1602–4) act 1, sc. 3, l. 90

22 And of the Cannibals that each other eat,
The Anthropophagi, and men whose heads
Do grow beneath their shoulders.
Othello (1602–4) act 1, sc. 3, l. 143

23 She loved me for the dangers I had passed,
And I loved her that she did pity them.
Othello (1602–4) act 1, sc. 3, l. 167

24 I do perceive here a divided duty.
Othello (1602–4) act 1, sc. 3, l. 181

25 The robbed that smiles steals something from the thief.
Othello (1602–4) act 1, sc. 3, l. 208

26 Our great captain's captain.
Othello (1602–4) act 2, sc. 1, l. 74

27 To suckle fools and chronicle small beer.
Othello (1602–4) act 2, sc. 1, l. 163

28 If it were now to die,
'Twere now to be most happy.
Othello (1602–4) act 2, sc. 1, l. [192]

29 O! I have lost my reputation. I have lost the immortal part of myself, and what remains is bestial.
Othello (1602–4) act 2, sc. 3, l. [264]

30 Excellent wretch! Perdition catch my soul
But I do love thee! and when I love thee not,
Chaos is come again.
Othello (1602–4) act 3, sc. 3, l. 90

31 Who steals my purse steals trash; 'tis something, nothing;
'Twas mine, 'tis his, and has been slave to thousands;
But he that filches from me my good name
Robs me of that which not enriches him,
And makes me poor indeed.
Othello (1602–4) act 3, sc. 3, l. 157

1 O! beware, my lord, of jealousy;
It is the green-eyed monster which doth mock
The meat it feeds on.
Othello (1602–4) act 3, sc. 3, l. 165

2 If I do prove her haggard,
Though that her jesses were my dear heart-strings,
I'd whistle her off and let her down the wind,
To prey at fortune.
Othello (1602–4) act 3, sc. 3, l. 260

3 I had rather be a toad,
And live upon the vapour of a dungeon,
Than keep a corner in the thing I love
For others' uses.
Othello (1602–4) act 3, sc. 3, l. 270

4 Trifles light as air
Are to the jealous confirmations strong
As proofs of holy writ.
Othello (1602–4) act 3, sc. 3, l. 323

5 Farewell the tranquil mind; farewell content!
Farewell the plumèd troop and the big wars
That make ambition virtue!
Othello (1602–4) act 3, sc. 3, l. 349

6 Pride, pomp, and circumstance of glorious war!
Othello (1602–4) act 3, sc. 3, l. 355

7 Othello's occupation's gone!
Othello (1602–4) act 3, sc. 3, l. 358

8 But yet the pity of it, Iago! O! Iago, the pity of it, Iago!
Othello (1602–4) act 4, sc. 1, l. [205]

9 Those that do teach young babes
Do it with gentle means and easy tasks;
He might have chid me so; for, in good faith,
I am a child to chiding.
Othello (1602–4) act 4, sc. 2, l. 111

10 Sing all a green willow must be my garland.
Othello (1602–4) act 4, sc. 3, l. [49]; see **Heywood** 168:16

11 It is the cause, it is the cause, my soul;
Let me not name it to you, you chaste stars!
It is the cause.
Othello (1602–4) act 5, sc. 2, l. 1

12 Put out the light, and then put out the light.
Othello (1602–4) act 5, sc. 2, l. 7

13 Here is my journey's end, here is my butt,
And very sea-mark of my utmost sail.
Othello (1602–4) act 5, sc. 2, l. 266

14 I have done the state some service, and they know 't;
No more of that. I pray you, in your letters,
When you shall these unlucky deeds relate,
Speak of me as I am; nothing extenuate,
Nor set down aught in malice: then, must you speak
Of one that loved not wisely but too well;
Of one not easily jealous, but, being wrought,
Perplexed in the extreme; of one whose hand,
Like the base Indian, threw a pearl away

Richer than all his tribe.
Othello (1602–4) act 5, sc. 2, l. 338

15 I kissed thee ere I killed thee, no way but this,
Killing myself to die upon a kiss.
Othello (1602–4) act 5, sc. 2, l. 357

Richard II

16 Old John of Gaunt, time-honoured Lancaster.
Richard II (1595) act 1, sc. 1, l. 1

17 The purest treasure mortal times afford
Is spotless reputation; that away,
Men are but gilded loam or painted clay.
Richard II (1595) act 1, sc. 1, l. 177

18 We were not born to sue, but to command.
Richard II (1595) act 1, sc. 1, l. 196; see **Scott** 287:8

19 How long a time lies in one little word!
Four lagging winters and four wanton springs
End in a word; such is the breath of kings.
Richard II (1595) act 1, sc. 3, l. 213

20 There is no virtue like necessity.
Richard II (1595) act 1, sc. 3, l. 278

21 As the last taste of sweets, is sweetest last,
Writ in remembrance more than things long past.
Richard II (1595) act 2, sc. 1, l. 13

22 This royal throne of kings, this sceptered isle,
This earth of majesty, this seat of Mars,
This other Eden, demi-paradise,
This fortress built by Nature for herself
Against infection and the hand of war,
This happy breed of men, this little world,
This precious stone set in the silver sea.
Richard II (1595) act 2, sc. 1, l. 40

23 This blessèd plot, this earth, this realm, this England.
Richard II (1595) act 2, sc. 1, l. 50

24 Grace me no grace, nor uncle me no uncle.
Richard II (1595) act 2, sc. 3, l. 87

25 The caterpillars of the commonwealth.
Richard II (1595) act 2, sc. 3, l. 166

26 Things past redress are now with me past care.
Richard II (1595) act 2, sc. 3, l. 171

27 Not all the water in the rough rude sea
Can wash the balm from an anointed king.
Richard II (1595) act 3, sc. 2, l. 54

28 O! call back yesterday, bid time return.
Richard II (1595) act 3, sc. 2, l. 69

29 Let's talk of graves, of worms, and epitaphs;
Make dust our paper, and with rainy eyes
Write sorrow on the bosom of the earth.
Let's choose executors, and talk of wills.
Richard II (1595) act 3, sc. 2, l. 145

30 For God's sake, let us sit upon the ground
And tell sad stories of the death of kings.
Richard II (1595) act 3, sc. 2, l. 155

31 Within the hollow crown
That rounds the mortal temples of a king

Keeps Death his court.
Richard II (1595) act 3, sc. 2, l. 160

1 Go, bind thou up yon dangling apricocks.
Richard II (1595) act 3, sc. 4, l. 29

2 Here, in this place,
I'll set a bank of rue, sour herb of grace.
Richard II (1595) act 3, sc. 4, l. 104

3 God save the king! Will no man say, amen?
Richard II (1595) act 4, sc. 1, l. 172

4 With mine own tears I wash away my balm,
With mine own hands I give away my
crown.
Richard II (1595) act 4, sc. 1, l. 207

5 How sour sweet music is,
When time is broke, and no proportion
kept!
So is it in the music of men's lives.
Richard II (1595) act 5, sc. 5, l. 42

6 I wasted time, and now doth time waste me.
Richard II (1595) act 5, sc. 5, l. 49

Richard III

7 Now is the winter of our discontent
Made glorious summer by this sun of York.
Richard III (1591) act 1, sc. 1, l. 1

8 This weak piping time of peace.
Richard III (1591) act 1, sc. 1, l. 24

9 No beast so fierce but knows some touch of
pity.
Richard III (1591) act 1, sc. 2, l. 71

10 Was ever woman in this humour wooed?
Was ever woman in this humour won?
Richard III (1591) act 1, sc. 2, l. 229

11 Clarence is come,—false, fleeting, perjured
Clarence.
Richard III (1591) act 1, sc. 4, l. 55

12 Woe to the land that's governed by a child!
Richard III (1591) act 2, sc. 3, l. 11; see **Bible**
39:23

13 So wise so young, they say, do never live
long.
Richard III (1591) act 3, sc. 1, l. 79

14 Talk'st thou to me of 'ifs'? Thou art a traitor:
Off with his head!
Richard III (1591) act 3, sc. 4, l. 74

15 I am not in the giving vein to-day.
Richard III (1591) act 4, sc. 2, l. 115

16 Harp not on that string.
Richard III (1591) act 4, sc. 4, l. 365

17 True hope is swift, and flies with swallow's
wings;
Kings it makes gods, and meaner creatures
kings.
Richard III (1591) act 5, sc. 2, l. 23

18 The king's name is a tower of strength.
Richard III (1591) act 5, sc. 3, l. 12

19 A horse! a horse! my kingdom for a horse!
Richard III (1591) act 5, sc. 4, l. 7

Romeo and Juliet

20 A pair of star-crossed lovers.
Romeo and Juliet (1595) prologue

21 The two hours' traffick of our stage.
Romeo and Juliet (1595) prologue

22 Younger than she are happy mothers made.
Romeo and Juliet (1595) act 1, sc. 2, l. 12

23 O! then, I see, Queen Mab hath been with
you . . .
She is the fairies' midwife, and she comes
In shape no bigger than an agate-stone.
Romeo and Juliet (1595) act 1, sc. 4, l. 53

24 You and I are past our dancing days.
Romeo and Juliet (1595) act 1, sc. 5, l. [35]

25 O! she doth teach the torches to burn bright.
It seems she hangs upon the cheek of night
Like a rich jewel in an Ethiop's ear;
Beauty too rich for use, for earth too dear.
Romeo and Juliet (1595) act 1, sc. 5, l. [48]

26 My only love sprung from my only hate!
Too early seen unknown, and known too
late!
Romeo and Juliet (1595) act 1, sc. 5, l. [142]

27 He jests at scars, that never felt a wound.
But, soft! what light through yonder
window breaks?
It is the east, and Juliet is the sun.
Romeo and Juliet (1595) act 2, sc. 2, l. 1

28 O Romeo, Romeo! wherefore art thou
Romeo?
Romeo and Juliet (1595) act 2, sc. 2, l. 33

29 What's in a name? that which we call a rose
By any other name would smell as sweet.
Romeo and Juliet (1595) act 2, sc. 2, l. 43

30 For stony limits cannot hold love out,
And what love can do that dares love
attempt.
Romeo and Juliet (1595) act 2, sc. 2, l. 67

31 O! swear not by the moon, the inconstant
moon,
That monthly changes in her circled orb,
Lest that thy love prove likewise variable.
Romeo and Juliet (1595) act 2, sc. 2, l. 109

32 It is too rash, too unadvised, too sudden.
Romeo and Juliet (1595) act 2, sc. 2, l. 118

33 Love goes toward love, as schoolboys from
their books;
But love from love, toward school with
heavy looks.
Romeo and Juliet (1595) act 2, sc. 2, l. 156

34 O! for a falconer's voice,
To lure this tassel-gentle back again.
Romeo and Juliet (1595) act 2, sc. 2, l. 158

35 Good-night, good-night! parting is such
sweet sorrow.
Romeo and Juliet (1595) act 2, sc. 2, l. 184

36 I am the very pink of courtesy.
Romeo and Juliet (1595) act 2, sc. 4, l. [63]

37 No, 'tis not so deep as a well, nor so wide as
a church door; but 'tis enough, 'twill serve.
Romeo and Juliet (1595) act 3, sc. 1, l. [100]

38 A plague o' both your houses!
Romeo and Juliet (1595) act 3, sc. 1, l. [112]

39 O! I am Fortune's fool.
Romeo and Juliet (1595) act 3, sc. 1, l. [142]

1 Gallop apace, you fiery-footed steeds,
Towards Phoebus' lodging.
Romeo and Juliet (1595) act 3, sc. 2, l. 1

2 Give me my Romeo: and, when he shall die,
Take him and cut him out in little stars,
And he will make the face of heaven so fine
That all the world will be in love with night,
And pay no worship to the garish sun.
Romeo and Juliet (1595) act 3, sc. 2, l. 21

3 Adversity's sweet milk, philosophy.
Romeo and Juliet (1595) act 3, sc. 3, l. 54

4 It was the nightingale, and not the lark,
That pierced the fearful hollow of thine ear.
Romeo and Juliet (1595) act 3, sc. 5, l. 2

5 Night's candles are burnt out, and jocund day
Stands tiptoe on the misty mountain tops.
Romeo and Juliet (1595) act 3, sc. 5, l. 9

6 I have more care to stay than will to go.
Romeo and Juliet (1595) act 3, sc. 5, l. 23

7 Thank me no thankings, nor proud me no prouds.
Romeo and Juliet (1595) act 3, sc. 5, l. 153

8 Death lies on her like an untimely frost.
Romeo and Juliet (1595) act 4, sc. 5, l. 28

9 Tempt not a desperate man.
Romeo and Juliet (1595) act 5, sc. 3, l. 59

10 How oft when men are at the point of death
Have they been merry! which their keepers call
A lightning before death.
Romeo and Juliet (1595) act 5, sc. 3, l. 88

11   Seal with a righteous kiss
A dateless bargain to engrossing death!
Romeo and Juliet (1595) act 5, sc. 3, l. 114

The Taming of the Shrew

12 Kiss me Kate, we will be married o' Sunday.
The Taming of the Shrew (1592) act 2, sc. 1, l. 318

13 This is the way to kill a wife with kindness.
The Taming of the Shrew (1592) act 4, sc. 1, l. [211]

14 A woman moved is like a fountain troubled,
Muddy, ill-seeming, thick, bereft of beauty.
The Taming of the Shrew (1592) act 5, sc. 2, l. 143

15 Such duty as the subject owes the prince,
Even such a woman oweth to her husband.
The Taming of the Shrew (1592) act 5, sc. 2, l. 156

The Tempest

16 He hath no drowning mark upon him; his complexion is perfect gallows.
The Tempest (1611) act 1, sc. 1, l. [33]

17 Now would I give a thousand furlongs of sea for an acre of barren ground.
The Tempest (1611) act 1, sc. 1, l. [70]

18   What seest thou else
In the dark backward and abysm of time?
The Tempest (1611) act 1, sc. 2, l. 49

19   My library
Was dukedom large enough.
The Tempest (1611) act 1, sc. 2, l. 109

20 The still-vexed Bermoothes.
The Tempest (1611) act 1, sc. 2, l. 229

21 You taught me language; and my profit on't
Is, I know how to curse.
The Tempest (1611) act 1, sc. 2, l. 363

22 Come unto these yellow sands,
And then take hands.
The Tempest (1611) act 1, sc. 2, l. 375

23 Full fathom five thy father lies;
Of his bones are coral made:
Those are pearls that were his eyes:
Nothing of him that doth fade,
But doth suffer a sea-change
Into something rich and strange.
The Tempest (1611) act 1, sc. 2, l. 394

24 What's past is prologue.
The Tempest (1611) act 2, sc. 1, l. [261]

25 A very ancient and fish-like smell.
The Tempest (1611) act 2, sc. 2, l. [27]

26 Misery acquaints a man with strange bedfellows.
The Tempest (1611) act 2, sc. 2, l. [42]

27 Thought is free.
The Tempest (1611) act 3, sc. 2, l. [134]

28 He that dies pays all debts.
The Tempest (1611) act 3, sc. 2, l. [143]

29 Be not afeard: the isle is full of noises,
Sounds and sweet airs, that give delight, and hurt not.
The Tempest (1611) act 3, sc. 2, l. [147]

30 Our revels now are ended. These our actors,
As I foretold you, were all spirits and
Are melted into air, into thin air:
And, like the baseless fabric of this vision,
The cloud-capped towers, the gorgeous palaces,
The solemn temples, the great globe itself,
Yea, all which it inherit, shall dissolve
And, like this insubstantial pageant faded,
Leave not a rack behind. We are such stuff
As dreams are made on, and our little life
Is rounded with a sleep.
The Tempest (1611) act 4, sc. 1, l. 148

31 I do begin to have bloody thoughts.
The Tempest (1611) act 4, sc. 1, l. [221]

32   But this rough magic
I here abjure.
The Tempest (1611) act 5, sc. 1, l. 50

33   I'll break my staff,
Bury it certain fathoms in the earth,
And, deeper than did ever plummet sound,
I'll drown my book.
The Tempest (1611) act 5, sc. 1, l. 54

34 Where the bee sucks, there suck I
In a cowslip's bell I lie;
There I couch when owls do cry.
On the bat's back I do fly
After summer merrily:
Merrily, merrily shall I live now
Under the blossom that hangs on the bough.
The Tempest (1611) act 5, sc. 1, l. 88

35 How beauteous mankind is! O brave new world,
That has such people in't.
The Tempest (1611) act 5, sc. 1, l. 183

Timon of Athens

1 'Tis not enough to help the feeble up,
But to support him after.
*Timon of Athens (c.*1607) act 1, sc. 1, l. 108

2 Men shut their doors against a setting sun.
*Timon of Athens (c.*1607) act 1, sc. 2, l. [152]

3 You fools of fortune, trencher-friends, time's
flies.
*Timon of Athens (c.*1607) act 3, sc. 6, l. [107]

4 We have seen better days.
*Timon of Athens (c.*1607) act 4, sc. 2, l. 27

5 The moon's an arrant thief,
And her pale fire she snatches from the sun.
*Timon of Athens (c.*1607) act 4, sc. 3, l. 437

Titus Andronicus

6 She is a woman, therefore may be wooed;
She is a woman, therefore may be won;
Titus Andronicus (1590) act 2, sc. 1, l. 82

7 Come, and take choice of all my library,
And so beguile thy sorrow.
Titus Andronicus (1590) act 4, sc. 1, l. 34

Troilus and Cressida

8 Things won are done; joy's soul lies in the
doing.
Troilus and Cressida (1602) act 1, sc. 2, l. [311]

9 Take but degree away, untune that string,
And, hark! what discord follows.
Troilus and Cressida (1602) act 1, sc. 3, l. 109

10 To be wise, and love,
Exceeds man's might.
Troilus and Cressida (1602) act 3, sc. 2, l. [163]

11 Time hath, my lord, a wallet at his back,
Wherein he puts alms for oblivion.
Troilus and Cressida (1602) act 3, sc. 3, l. 145

12 Perseverance, dear my lord,
Keeps honour bright.
Troilus and Cressida (1602) act 3, sc. 3, l. 150

13 One touch of nature makes the whole world
kin.
Troilus and Cressida (1602) act 3, sc. 3, l. 175

14 There's language in her eye, her cheek, her
lip,
Nay, her foot speaks; her wanton spirits
look out
At every joint and motive of her body.
Troilus and Cressida (1602) act 4, sc. 5, l. 55

15 The end crowns all,
And that old common arbitrator, Time,
Will one day end it.
Troilus and Cressida (1602) act 4, sc. 5, l. 223

16 Words, words, mere words, no matter from
the heart.
Troilus and Cressida (1602) act 5, sc. 3, l. [109]

Twelfth Night

17 If music be the food of love, play on.
Twelfth Night (1601) act 1, sc. 1, l. 1

18 That strain again! it had a dying fall.
Twelfth Night (1601) act 1, sc. 1, l. 4

19 I am a great eater of beef, and I believe that
does harm to my wit.
Twelfth Night (1601) act 1, sc. 3, l. [92]

20 I would I had bestowed that time in the
tongues that I have in fencing, dancing, and
bear-baiting. O! had I but followed the arts!
Twelfth Night (1601) act 1, sc. 3, l. [99]

21 Many a good hanging prevents a bad
marriage.
Twelfth Night (1601) act 1, sc. 5, l. [20]

22 A plague o' these pickle herring!
Twelfth Night (1601) act 1, sc. 5, l. [127]

23 He is very well-favoured, and he speaks very
shrewishly: one would think his mother's
milk were scarce out of him.
Twelfth Night (1601) act 1, sc. 5, l. [170]

24 Make me a willow cabin at your gate.
Twelfth Night (1601) act 1, sc. 5, l. [289]

25 Halloo your name to the reverberate hills.
Twelfth Night (1601) act 1, sc. 5, l. [293]

26 Not to be a-bed after midnight is to be up
betimes.
Twelfth Night (1601) act 2, sc. 3, l. 1

27 O mistress mine! where are you roaming?
O! stay and hear; your true love's coming,
That can sing both high and low.
Trip no further, pretty sweeting;
Journeys end in lovers meeting,
Every wise man's son doth know.
Twelfth Night (1601) act 2, sc. 3, l. [42]

28 What is love? 'tis not hereafter;
Present mirth hath present laughter;
What's to come is still unsure:
In delay there lies no plenty;
Then come kiss me, sweet and twenty,
Youth's a stuff will not endure.
Twelfth Night (1601) act 2, sc. 3, l. [50]

29 He does it with a better grace, but I do it
more natural.
Twelfth Night (1601) act 2, sc. 3, l. [91]

30 Dost thou think, because thou art virtuous,
there shall be no more cakes and ale?
Twelfth Night (1601) act 2, sc. 3, l. [124]

31 My purpose is, indeed, a horse of that
colour.
Twelfth Night (1601) act 2, sc. 3, l. [184]

32 I was adored once too.
Twelfth Night (1601) act 2, sc. 3, l. [200]

33 Let still the woman take
An elder than herself, so wears she to him,
So sways she level in her husband's heart.
Twelfth Night (1601) act 2, sc. 4, l. 29

34 Come away, come away, death,
And in sad cypress let me be laid.
Twelfth Night (1601) act 2, sc. 4, l. 51

35 Now, the melancholy god protect thee, and
the tailor make thy doublet of changeable
taffeta, for thy mind is a very opal.
Twelfth Night (1601) act 2, sc. 4, l. [74]

36 She never told her love,
But let concealment, like a worm i' the bud,
Feed on her damask cheek: she pined in
thought;

And with a green and yellow melancholy,
She sat like patience on a monument,
Smiling at grief.
Twelfth Night (1601) act 2, sc. 4, l. [112]

1 I am all the daughters of my father's house,
And all the brothers too.
Twelfth Night (1601) act 2, sc. 4, l. [122]

2 But be not afraid of greatness: some men are
born great, some achieve greatness, and
some have greatness thrust upon them.
Twelfth Night (1601) act 2, sc. 5, l. [158]; see
Heller 165:14

3 Remember who commended thy yellow
stockings, and wished to see thee ever cross-
gartered.
Twelfth Night (1601) act 2, sc. 5, l. [168]

4 Love sought is good, but giv'n unsought is
better.
Twelfth Night (1601) act 3, sc. 1, l. [170]

5 In the south suburbs, at the Elephant,
Is best to lodge.
Twelfth Night (1601) act 3, sc. 3, l. 39

6 I think we do know the sweet Roman hand.
Twelfth Night (1601) act 3, sc. 4, l. [31]

7 Why, this is very midsummer madness.
Twelfth Night (1601) act 3, sc. 4, l. [62]

8 If this were played upon a stage now, I could
condemn it as an improbable fiction.
Twelfth Night (1601) act 3, sc. 4, l. [142]

9 More matter for a May morning.
Twelfth Night (1601) act 3, sc. 4, l. [158]

10 Still you keep o' the windy side of the law.
Twelfth Night (1601) act 3, sc. 4, l. [183]

11 Thus the whirligig of time brings in his
revenges.
Twelfth Night (1601) act 5, sc. 1, l. [388]

12 I'll be revenged on the whole pack of you.
Twelfth Night (1601) act 5, sc. 1, l. [390]

13 When that I was and a little tiny boy,
With hey, ho, the wind and the rain;
A foolish thing was but a toy,
For the rain it raineth every day.
Twelfth Night (1601) act 5, sc. 1, l. [401]

The Two Gentlemen of Verona

14 I have no other but a woman's reason:
I think him so, because I think him so.
The Two Gentlemen of Verona (1592–3) act 1, sc. 2,
l. 23

15 O! how this spring of love resembleth
The uncertain glory of an April day.
The Two Gentlemen of Verona (1592–3) act 1, sc. 3,
l. 84

16 Who is Silvia? what is she,
That all our swains commend her?
The Two Gentlemen of Verona (1592–3) act 4, sc. 2,
l. 40

The Winter's Tale

17 A sad tale's best for winter.
I have one of sprites and goblins.
The Winter's Tale (1610–11) act 2, sc. 1, l. 24

18 What's gone and what's past help

Should be past grief.
The Winter's Tale (1610–11) act 3, sc. 2, l. [223]

19 Exit, pursued by a bear.
stage direction
The Winter's Tale (1610–11) act 3, sc. 3

20 When daffodils begin to peer,
With heigh! the doxy, over the dale,
Why, then comes in the sweet o' the year.
The Winter's Tale (1610–11) act 4, sc. 2, l. 1

21 While we lie tumbling in the hay.
The Winter's Tale (1610–11) act 4, sc. 2, l. 12

22 My father named me Autolycus; who being,
as I am, littered under Mercury, was
likewise a snapper-up of unconsidered
trifles.
The Winter's Tale (1610–11) act 4, sc. 2, l. [24]

23 Jog on, jog on the foot-path way,
And merrily hent the stile-a:
A merry heart goes all the day,
Your sad tires in a mile-a.
The Winter's Tale (1610–11) act 4, sc. 2, l. [133]

24 For you there's rosemary and rue; these
keep
Seeming and savour all the winter long.
The Winter's Tale (1610–11) act 4, sc. 3, l. 74

25 The marigold, that goes to bed wi' the sun,
And with him rises weeping.
The Winter's Tale (1610–11) act 4, sc. 3, l. 105

26 Daffodils,
That come before the swallow dares, and
take
The winds of March with beauty.
The Winter's Tale (1610–11) act 4, sc. 3, l. 121

27 Pale prime-roses,
That die unmarried, ere they can behold
Bright Phoebus in his strength,.
The Winter's Tale (1610–11) act 4, sc. 3, l. 122

28 Though I am not naturally honest, I am so
sometimes by chance.
The Winter's Tale (1610–11) act 4, sc. 3, l. [734]

29 Stars, stars!
And all eyes else dead coals.
The Winter's Tale (1610–11) act 5, sc. 1, l. 67

30 O! she's warm.
If this be magic, let it be an art
Lawful as eating.
The Winter's Tale (1610–11) act 5, sc. 3, l. 109

The Passionate Pilgrim (attribution doubtful)

31 Crabbed age and youth cannot live together:
Youth is full of pleasance, age is full of care.
The Passionate Pilgrim (1599) no. 12

32 Age, I do abhor thee, youth, I do adore thee.
The Passionate Pilgrim (1599) no. 12

The Rape of Lucrece

33 Beauty itself doth of itself persuade
The eyes of men without an orator.
The Rape of Lucrece (1594) l. 29

Sonnets

1 To the onlie begetter of these insuing sonnets, Mr. W. H.
also attributed to Thomas Thorpe, the publisher
Sonnets (1609) dedication

2 From fairest creatures we desire increase,
That thereby beauty's rose might never die.
Sonnet 1

3 Shall I compare thee to a summer's day?
Thou art more lovely and more temperate:
Rough winds do shake the darling buds of May,
And summer's lease hath all too short a date.
Sonnet 18

4 But thy eternal summer shall not fade.
Sonnet 18

5 Desiring this man's art, and that man's scope,
With what I most enjoy contented least.
Sonnet 29

6 Haply I think on thee,—and then my state,
Like to the lark at break of day arising
From sullen earth, sings hymns at heaven's gate.
Sonnet 29

7 When to the sessions of sweet silent thought
I summon up remembrance of things past.
Sonnet 30

8 Full many a glorious morning have I seen
Flatter the mountain-tops with sovereign eye.
Sonnet 33

9 Not marble, nor the gilded monuments
Of princes, shall outlive this powerful rhyme.
Sonnet 55

10 Like as the waves make towards the pebbled shore,
So do our minutes hasten to their end.
Sonnet 60

11 Bare ruined choirs, where late the sweet birds sang.
Sonnet 73

12 So all my best is dressing old words new,
Spending again what is already spent.
Sonnet 76

13 Time's thievish progress to eternity.
Sonnet 77

14 Farewell! thou art too dear for my possessing.
Sonnet 87

15 Thus have I had thee, as a dream doth flatter,
In sleep a king, but, waking, no such matter.
Sonnet 87

16 For sweetest things turn sourest by their deeds;
Lilies that fester smell far worse than weeds.
Sonnet 94

17 When in the chronicle of wasted time

I see descriptions of the fairest wights.
Sonnet 106

18 For we, which now behold these present days,
Have eyes to wonder, but lack tongues to praise.
Sonnet 106

19 Alas! 'tis true I have gone here and there,
And made myself a motley to the view,
Sonnet 110

20 My nature is subdued
To what it works in, like the dyer's hand.
Sonnet 111

21 Let me not to the marriage of true minds
Admit impediments. Love is not love
Which alters when it alteration finds.
Sonnet 116

22 Love's not Time's fool.
Sonnet 116

23 Love alters not with his brief hours and weeks,
But bears it out even to the edge of doom.
If this be error, and upon me proved,
I never writ, nor no man ever loved.
Sonnet 116

24 The expense of spirit in a waste of shame
Is lust in action.
Sonnet 129

25 My mistress' eyes are nothing like the sun;
Coral is far more red than her lips' red:
If snow be white, why then her breasts are dun;
If hairs be wires, black wires grow on her head.
Sonnet 130

26 Whoever hath her wish, thou hast thy *Will*,
And *Will* to boot, and *Will* in over-plus.
Sonnet 135

27 When my love swears that she is made of truth,
I do believe her, though I know she lies.
Sonnet 138

28 Two loves I have of comfort and despair,
Which like two spirits do suggest me still:
The better angel is a man right fair,
The worser spirit a woman, coloured ill.
Sonnet 144

29 So shalt thou feed on Death, that feeds on men,
And Death once dead, there's no more dying then.
Sonnet 146

30 For I have sworn thee fair, and thought thee bright,
Who art as black as hell, as dark as night.
Sonnet 147

Venus and Adonis

31 Love is a spirit all compact of fire,
Not gross to sink, but light, and will aspire.
Venus and Adonis (1593) l. 145

32 Love comforteth like sunshine after rain.
Venus and Adonis (1593) l. 799

1 Item, I give unto my wife my second best bed, with the furniture.
  will, 1616; E. K. Chambers William Shakespeare *(1930) vol. 2*

2 Good friend, for Jesu's sake forbear
  To dig the dust enclosed here.
  Blest be the man that spares these stones,
  And curst be he that moves my bones.
  insciption on his grave, Stratford upon Avon, probably composed by himself

Shammai *c.*1st century BC–1st century AD
Jewish scholar and teacher

3 Say little and do much. Receive all men with a cheerful countenance.
  in Talmud *Mishnah 'Pirqei Avot' 1:15*

Bill Shankly 1914–81
Scottish footballer

4 Some people think football is a matter of life and death . . . I can assure them it is much more serious than that.
  in Sunday Times *4 October 1981*

Robert Shapiro 1942–
American lawyer

5 Not only did we play the race card, we played it from the bottom of the deck.
  on the defence team's change of strategy at the trial of O. J. Simpson
  in The Times *5 October 1995; see* **Churchill** 94:17

George Bernard Shaw 1856–1950
Irish dramatist

6 All great truths begin as blasphemies.
  Annajanska *(1919)*

7 One man that has a mind and knows it can always beat ten men who haven't and don't.
  The Apple Cart *(1930) act 1*

8 Oh, you are a very poor soldier—a chocolate cream soldier!
  Arms and the Man *(1898) act 1*

9 Life is not meant to be easy, my child; but take courage: it can be delightful.
  Back to Methuselah *(rev. ed., 1930); see also* **Fraser** 142:8

10 We have no more right to consume happiness without producing it than to consume wealth without producing it.
  Candida *(1898) act 1*

11 I'm only a beer teetotaller, not a champagne teetotaller.
  Candida *(1898) act 3*

12 He [the Briton] is a barbarian, and thinks that the customs of his tribe and island are the laws of nature.
  Caesar and Cleopatra *(1901) act 2*

13 When a stupid man is doing something he is ashamed of, he always declares that it is his duty.
  Caesar and Cleopatra *(1901) act 3*

14 The worst sin towards our fellow creatures is not to hate them, but to be indifferent to them: that's the essence of inhumanity.
  The Devil's Disciple *(1901) act 2*

15 Martyrdom . . . the only way in which a man can become famous without ability.
  The Devil's Disciple *(1901) act 3*

16 SWINDON: What will history say?
  BURGOYNE: History, sir, will tell lies as usual.
  The Devil's Disciple *(1901) act 3*

17 Stimulate the phagocytes.
  The Doctor's Dilemma *(1911) act 1*

18 All professions are conspiracies against the laity.
  The Doctor's Dilemma *(1911) act 1*

19 A government which robs Peter to pay Paul can always depend on the support of Paul.
  Everybody's Political What's What? *(1944) ch. 30*

20 It's all that the young can do for the old, to shock them and keep them up to date.
  Fanny's First Play *(1914) 'Induction'*

21 You have to choose (as a voter) between trusting to the natural stability of gold and the natural stability of the honesty and intelligence of the members of the Government. And, with due respect for these gentlemen, I advise you, as long as the Capitalist system lasts, to vote for gold.
  The Intelligent Woman's Guide to Socialism and Capitalism *(1928) ch. 55*

22 John Bull's other island.
  title of play (1907)

23 What really flatters a man is that you think him worth flattering.
  John Bull's Other Island *(1907) act 4*

24 The greatest of evils and the worst of crimes is poverty.
  Major Barbara *(1907) preface*

25 I am a Millionaire. That is my religion.
  Major Barbara *(1907) act 2*

26 Alcohol is a very necessary article . . . It enables Parliament to do things at eleven at night that no sane person would do at eleven in the morning.
  Major Barbara *(1907) act 2*

27 He knows nothing; and he thinks he knows everything. That points clearly to a political career.
  Major Barbara *(1907) act 3*

28 Nothing is ever done in this world until men are prepared to kill one another if it is not done.
  Major Barbara *(1907) act 3*

29 Like all young men, you greatly exaggerate the difference between one young woman and another.
  Major Barbara *(1907) act 3; see* **Mencken** 232:18

30 But a lifetime of happiness! No man alive could bear it: it would be hell on earth.
  Man and Superman *(1903) act 1*

31 The more things a man is ashamed of, the more respectable he is.
  Man and Superman *(1903) act 1*

1 Hell is full of musical amateurs: music is the brandy of the damned.
Man and Superman (1903) act 3

2 Englishmen never will be slaves: they are free to do whatever the Government and public opinion allow them to do.
Man and Superman (1903) act 3

3 An Englishman thinks he is moral when he is only uncomfortable.
Man and Superman (1903) act 3

4 In the arts of peace Man is a bungler.
Man and Superman (1903) act 3

5 When the military man approaches, the world locks up its spoons and packs off its womankind.
Man and Superman (1903) act 3; see **Emerson** 132:4

6 What is virtue but the Trade Unionism of the married?
Man and Superman (1903) act 3

7 Beauty is all very well at first sight; but who ever looks at it when it has been in the house three days?
Man and Superman (1903) act 4

8 Democracy substitutes election by the incompetent many for appointment by the corrupt few.
Man and Superman (1903) 'Maxims: Democracy'

9 Liberty means responsibility. That is why most men dread it.
Man and Superman (1903) 'Maxims: Liberty and Equality'

10 He who can, does. He who cannot, teaches.
Man and Superman (1903) 'Maxims: Education'

11 Marriage is popular because it combines the maximum of temptation with the maximum of opportunity.
Man and Superman (1903) 'Maxims: Marriage'

12 Titles distinguish the mediocre, embarrass the superior, and are disgraced by the inferior.
Man and Superman (1903) 'Maxims: Titles'

13 If you strike a child take care that you strike it in anger, even at the risk of maiming it for life. A blow in cold blood neither can nor should be forgiven.
Man and Superman (1903) 'Maxims: How to Beat Children'

14 Beware of the man whose god is in the skies.
Man and Superman (1903) 'Maxims: Religion'

15 The reasonable man adapts himself to the world: the unreasonable one persists in trying to adapt the world to himself. Therefore all progress depends on the unreasonable man.
Man and Superman (1903) 'Maxims: Reason'

16 Every man over forty is a scoundrel.
Man and Superman (1903) 'Maxims: Stray Sayings'

17 Youth, which is forgiven everything, forgives itself nothing: age, which forgives itself everything, is forgiven nothing.
Man and Superman (1903) 'Maxims: Stray Sayings'

18 Take care to get what you like or you will be forced to like what you get.
Man and Superman (1903) 'Maxims: Stray Sayings'

19 Self-sacrifice enables us to sacrifice other people without blushing.
Man and Superman (1903) 'Maxims: Self-Sacrifice'

20 You will never find an Englishman in the wrong. He does everything on principle. He ... supports his king on loyal principles and cuts off his king's head on republican principles.
The Man of Destiny (1898)

21 Anarchism is a game at which the police can beat you.
Misalliance (1914)

22 You'll never have a quiet world till you knock the patriotism out of the human race.
O'Flaherty V.C. (1919)

23 The secret of being miserable is to have leisure to bother about whether you are happy or not. The cure for it is occupation.
Parents and Children (1914) 'Children's Happiness'

24 A perpetual holiday is a good working definition of hell.
Parents and Children (1914) 'Children's Happiness'

25 There is only one religion, though there are a hundred versions of it.
Plays Pleasant and Unpleasant (1898) vol. 2, preface

26 It is impossible for an Englishman to open his mouth without making some other Englishman hate or despise him.
Pygmalion (1916) preface

27 I don't want to talk grammar, I want to talk like a lady.
Pygmalion (1916) act 2

28 PICKERING: Have you no morals, man?
DOOLITTLE: Can't afford them, Governor.
Pygmalion (1916) act 2

29 I'm one of the undeserving poor ... up agen middle-class morality all the time ... What is middle-class morality? Just an excuse for never giving me anything.
Pygmalion (1916) act 2

30 Walk! Not bloody likely.
Pygmalion (1916) act 2

31 Must then a Christ perish in torment in every age to save those that have no imagination?
Saint Joan (1924) epilogue

32 Assassination is the extreme form of censorship.
The Showing-Up of Blanco Posnet (1911) 'Limits to Toleration'

1 'Do you know what a pessimist is?' 'A man who thinks everybody is as nasty as himself, and hates them for it.'
An Unsocial Socialist (1887) ch. 5

2 The great advantage of a hotel is that it's a refuge from home life.
You Never Can Tell (1898) act 2

3 The younger generation is knocking at the door, and as I open it there steps spritely in the incomparable Max.
on handing over the theatre review column to Max **Beerbohm**
in *Saturday Review* 21 May 1898 'Valedictory'

4 The trouble, Mr Goldwyn, is that you are only interested in art and I am only interested in money.
telegraphed version of the outcome of a conversation between Shaw and Sam **Goldwyn**
Alva Johnson *The Great Goldwyn* (1937) ch. 3

5 [Dancing is] a perpendicular expression of a horizontal desire.
in *New Statesman* 23 March 1962

6 England and America are two countries divided by a common language.
attributed in this and other forms to George Bernard Shaw, but not found in Shaw's published writings; see **Wilde** 358:2

Hartley Shawcross 1902–2003
British Labour politician

7 'But,' said Alice, 'the question is whether you can make a word mean different things.' 'Not so,' said Humpty-Dumpty, 'the question is which is to be the master. That's all.' We are the masters at the moment, and not only at the moment, but for a very long time to come.
often quoted as, 'We are the masters now'
speech in the House of Commons, 2 April 1946; see **Carroll** 87:11

Patrick Shaw-Stewart 1888–1917

8 Stand in the trench, Achilles,
Flame-capped, and shout for me.
poem (1916)

Mary Shelley 1797–1851
English novelist

9 I beheld the wretch—the miserable monster whom I had created.
Frankenstein (1818) ch. 5

10 Everywhere I see bliss, from which I alone am irrevocably excluded.
Frankenstein (1818) ch. 10

11 Teach him to think for himself? Oh, my God, teach him rather to think like other people!
on her son's education
Matthew Arnold *Essays in Criticism* Second Series (1888) 'Shelley'

Percy Bysshe Shelley 1792–1822
English poet

12 The cemetery is an open space among the ruins, covered in winter with violets and daisies. It might make one in love with death, to think that one should be buried in so sweet a place.
Adonais (1821) preface

13 I weep for Adonais—he is dead!
Adonais (1821) st. 1

14 Winter is come and gone,
But grief returns with the revolving year.
Adonais (1821) st. 18

15 Alas! that all we loved of him should be,
But for our grief, as if it had not been,
And grief itself be mortal!
Adonais (1821) st. 21

16 A pardlike Spirit, beautiful and swift.
Adonais (1821) st. 32

17 He hath awakened from the dream of life.
Adonais (1821) st. 39

18 He has out-soared the shadow of our night.
Adonais (1821) st. 40

19 From the contagion of the world's slow stain
He is secure.
Adonais (1821) st. 40

20 He is a portion of the loveliness
Which once he made more lovely.
Adonais (1821) st. 43

21 Life, like a dome of many-coloured glass,
Stains the white radiance of Eternity.
Adonais (1821) st. 52

22 A widow bird sat mourning for her love
Upon a wintry bough.
Charles the First (1822) sc. 5, l. 9

23 That orbèd maiden, with white fire laden,
Whom mortals call the Moon.
'The Cloud' (1819)

24 I am the daughter of Earth and Water,
And the nursling of the Sky.
I pass through the pores of the ocean and shores;
I change, but I cannot die.
'The Cloud' (1819)

25 I never was attached to that great sect,
Whose doctrine is that each one should select
Out of the crowd a mistress or a friend,
And all the rest, though fair and wise, commend
To cold oblivion.
'Epipsychidion' (1821) l. 149

26 The world's great age begins anew,
The golden years return.
Hellas (1822) l. 1060

27 The awful shadow of some unseen Power
Floats though unseen among us.
'Hymn to Intellectual Beauty' (1816)

28 Thou Paradise of exiles, Italy!
'Julian and Maddalo' (1818) l. 57

29 Most wretched men
Are cradled into poetry by wrong:
They learn in suffering what they teach in song.
'Julian and Maddalo' (1818) l. 544

30 When the lamp is shattered

The light in the dust lies dead—
When the cloud is scattered
The rainbow's glory is shed.
'Lines: When the lamp' (1824)

1 I met Murder on the way—
He had a mask like Castlereagh—
Very smooth he looked, yet grim,
Seven bloodhounds followed him.
'The Mask of Anarchy' (1819) st. 2

2 Nought may endure but Mutability.
'Mutability' (1816)

3 O wild West Wind, thou breath of Autumn's
being,
Thou, from whose unseen presence the
leaves dead
Are driven, like ghosts from an enchanter
fleeing,
Yellow, and black, and pale, and hectic red,
Pestilence-stricken multitudes.
'Ode to the West Wind' (1819) l. 1

4 Destroyer and preserver; hear, oh, hear!
'Ode to the West Wind' (1819) l. 14

5 Oh, lift me as a wave, a leaf, a cloud!
I fall upon the thorns of life! I bleed!
'Ode to the West Wind' (1819) l. 53

6 Make me thy lyre, even as the forest is.
'Ode to the West Wind' (1819) l. 57

7 And, by the incantation of this verse,
Scatter, as from an unextinguished hearth
Ashes and sparks, my words among
mankind!
'Ode to the West Wind' (1819) l. 65

8 If Winter comes, can Spring be far behind?
'Ode to the West Wind' (1819) l. 70

9 I met a traveller from an antique land
Who said: Two vast and trunkless legs of
stone
Stand in the desert.
'Ozymandias' (1819)

10 'My name is Ozymandias, king of kings:
Look on my works, ye Mighty, and despair!'
'Ozymandias' (1819)

11 The hand that mocked them and the heart
that fed.
'Ozymandias' (1819)

12 Hell is a city much like London.
'Peter Bell the Third' (1819) pt. 3, st. 1

13 Ere Babylon was dust,
The Magus Zoroaster, my dead child,
Met his own image walking in the garden.
Prometheus Unbound (1819) act 1, l. 191

14 He gave man speech, and speech created
thought,
Which is the measure of the universe.
Prometheus Unbound (1820) act 2, sc. 4, l. 72

15 My soul is an enchanted boat,
Which, like a sleeping swan, doth float
Upon the silver waves of thy sweet singing.
Prometheus Unbound (1820) act 2, sc. 5, l. 72

16 To suffer woes which Hope thinks infinite;
To forgive wrongs darker than death or
night;
To defy Power, which seems omnipotent;

To love, and bear; to hope till Hope creates
From its own wreck the thing it
contemplates.
Prometheus Unbound (1820) act 4, l. 570

17 How wonderful is Death,
Death and his brother Sleep!
Queen Mab (1813) canto 1, l. 1; see **Daniel** 109:5,
Fletcher 138:13

18 A Sensitive Plant in a garden grew.
'The Sensitive Plant' (1820) pt. 1, l. 1

19 Rarely, rarely, comest thou,
Spirit of Delight!
'Song' (1824); epigraph to **Elgar**'s Second
Symphony

20 Men of England, wherefore plough
For the lords who lay ye low?
'Song to the Men of England' (written 1819)

21 Lift not the painted veil which those who
live
Call Life.
'Sonnet' (1824)

22 An old, mad, blind, despised, and dying
king.
of George III
'Sonnet: England in 1819' (written 1819)

23 Music, when soft voices die,
Vibrates in the memory—
Odours, when sweet violets sicken,
Live within the sense they quicken.
'To—: Music, when soft voices die' (1824)

24 The desire of the moth for the star,
Of the night for the morrow,
The devotion to something afar
From the sphere of our sorrow.
'To—: One word is too often profaned' (1824)

25 Hail to thee, blithe Spirit!
Bird thou never wert.
'To a Skylark' (1819)

26 And singing still dost soar, and soaring ever
singest.
'To a Skylark' (1819)

27 Thou art unseen, but yet I hear thy shrill
delight.
'To a Skylark' (1819)

28 Our sincerest laughter
With some pain is fraught;
Our sweetest songs are those that tell of
saddest thought.
'To a Skylark' (1819)

29 Teach me half the gladness
That thy brain must know,
Such harmonious madness
From my lips would flow
The world should listen then—as I am
listening now.
'To a Skylark' (1819)

30 Swiftly walk o'er the western wave,
Spirit of Night!
'To Night' (1824)

31 Art thou pale for weariness
Of climbing heaven, and gazing on the
earth?
'To the Moon' (1824)

1 And ever changing, like a joyless eye
  That finds no object worth its constancy?
  'To the Moon' (1824)

2 And like a dying lady, lean and pale,
  Who totters forth, wrapped in a gauzy veil.
  'The Waning Moon' (1824)

3 A lovely lady, garmented in light
  From her own beauty.
  'The Witch of Atlas' (written 1820) st. 5

4 The great instrument of moral good is the
  imagination.
  A Defence of Poetry (written 1821)

5 Poetry is the record of the best and happiest
  moments of the happiest and best minds.
  A Defence of Poetry (written 1821)

6 Poets are the unacknowledged legislators of
  the world.
  A Defence of Poetry (written 1821); see **Johnson**
  187:17

William Shenstone 1714–63
English poet and essayist

7 Whoe'er has travelled life's dull round,
  Where'er his stages may have been,
  May sigh to think he still has found
  The warmest welcome, at an inn.
  'Written at an Inn at Henley' (1758); see
  Johnson 189:13

Philip Henry Sheridan 1831–88
*American Union cavalry commander in the Civil
War*

8 The only good Indians I ever saw were dead.
  *in response to the Comanche chief Toch-a-way,
  who described himself as a 'good Indian'*
  at Fort Cobb, January 1869; attributed but
  denied by Sheridan

Richard Brinsley Sheridan
1751–1816
Irish dramatist and Whig politician

9 Illiterate him, I say, quite from your
  memory.
  The Rivals (1775) act 1, sc. 2

10 Madam, a circulating library in a town is as
   an evergreen tree of diabolical knowledge.
   The Rivals (1775) act 1, sc. 2

11 He is the very pineapple of politeness!
   The Rivals (1775) act 3, sc. 3

12 If I reprehend any thing in this world, it is
   the use of my oracular tongue, and a nice
   derangement of epitaphs!
   The Rivals (1775) act 3, sc. 3

13 She's as headstrong as an allegory on the
   banks of the Nile.
   The Rivals (1775) act 3, sc. 3

14 You shall see them on a beautiful quarto
   page where a neat rivulet of text shall
   meander through a meadow of margin.
   The School for Scandal (1777) act 1, sc. 1

15 Here is the whole set! a character dead at
   every word.
   The School for Scandal (1777) act 2, sc. 2; see **Pope**
   268:19

16 Here's to the maiden of bashful fifteen
   Here's to the widow of fifty
   Here's to the flaunting, extravagant quean;
   And here's to the housewife that's thrifty.
   The School for Scandal (1777) act 3, sc. 3

17 An unforgiving eye, and a damned
   disinheriting countenance!
   The School for Scandal (1777) act 4, sc. 1

18 You write with ease, to show your breeding,
   But easy writing's vile hard reading.
   'Clio's Protest' (written 1771, published 1819)

19 A man may surely be allowed to take a glass
   of wine by his own fireside.
   *on being encountered drinking a glass of wine in
   the street, while watching his theatre, the Drury
   Lane, burn down*
   T. Moore Life of Sheridan (1825) vol. 2

20 The Right Honourable gentleman is
   indebted to his memory for his jests, and to
   his imagination for his facts.
   speech in reply to Mr Dundas, in T. Moore Life of
   Sheridan (1825) vol. 2

21 Won't you come into the garden? I would
   like my roses to see you.
   to a young lady; attributed

Sidney Sherman 1805–73
American soldier

22 Remember the Alamo!
   battle cry at San Jacinto, 21 April 1836,
   traditionally attributed to Sherman

William Tecumsah Sherman
1820–91
American Union general

23 Hold out. Relief is coming.
   usually quoted as 'Hold the fort! I am coming!'
   flag signal from Kennesaw Mountain to General
   John Murray Corse at Allatoona Pass, 5 October
   1864; see **Bliss** 58:9

24 [Grant] stood by me when I was crazy, and I
   stood by him when he was drunk; and now
   we stand by each other always.
   *of his relationship with his fellow Union
   commander, Ulysses S.* **Grant**
   in 1864; Geoffrey C. Ward The Civil War (1991)

25 War is the remedy our *enemies* have chosen,
   and I say let us give them all they want.
   in 1864; Geoffrey C. Ward The Civil War (1991)

26 There is many a boy here to-day who looks
   on war as all glory, but, boys, it is all hell.
   speech at Columbus, Ohio, 11 August 1880, in
   Lloyd Lewis Sherman, Fighting Prophet (1932)

27 I will not accept if nominated, and will not
   serve if elected.
   *telegram to General Henderson, on being urged to
   stand as Republican candidate in the 1884 US
   presidential election*
   Memoirs (4th ed., 1891) ch. 27

James Shirley 1596–1666
English dramatist

28 The glories of our blood and state

Are shadows, not substantial things;
There is no armour against fate;
Death lays his icy hand on kings.
The Contention of Ajax and Ulysses (1659) act 1, sc. 3

1 Only the actions of the just
Smell sweet, and blossom in their dust.
The Contention of Ajax and Ulysses (1659) act 1, sc. 3

Mikhail Sholokhov 1905–84
Russian novelist

2 And quiet flows the Don.
title of novel (1934)

Clare Short 1946–
British Labour politician

3 It will be golden elephants next.
suggesting that the government of Montserrat was 'talking mad money' in claiming assistance for evacuating the island
in *Observer* 24 August 1997

4 Reckless with our government; reckless with his own future, position and place in history. It's extraordinarily reckless.
*when asked if she thought that Tony **Blair** was acting recklessly on Iraq*
in an interview on *Westminster Hour* (BBC Radio 4), 9 March 2003

The Shorter Catechism (1647)

5 'What is the chief end of man?'
'To glorify God and to enjoy him for ever'.

The Siddur
Jewish prayer book

6 Hear, O Israel: the Lord our God, the Lord is One.
The Shema; see **Bible** 36:3

7 Blessed are you, O Lord our God and God of our fathers, God of Abraham, God of Isaac, God of Jacob.
The Amidah Benediction 1

8 Blessed are you, O Lord, the Shield of Abraham.
The Amidah Benediction 1

Algernon Sidney 1622–83
English conspirator

9 'Tis not necessary to light a candle to the sun.
Discourses concerning Government (1698) ch. 2, sect. 23; see **Burton** 78:7, **Young** 369:25

10 The law is established, which no passion can disturb. 'Tis void of desire and fear, lust and anger . . . 'Tis deaf, inexorable, inflexible.
Discourses concerning Government (1698) ch. 3, sect. 15

Philip Sidney 1554–86
English soldier, poet, and courtier

11 My true love hath my heart and I have his,
By just exchange one for the other giv'n.
Arcadia ('Old Arcadia', completed 1581) bk. 3

12 Biting my truant pen, beating myself for spite,
'Fool,' said my Muse to me; 'look in thy heart and write.'
Astrophil and Stella (1591) sonnet 1

13 With how sad steps, O Moon, thou climb'st the skies;
How silently, and with how wan a face.
Astrophil and Stella (1591) sonnet 31

14 Poetry . . . A speaking picture, with this end: to teach and delight.
The Defence of Poetry (1595)

15 [The poet] cometh unto you, with a tale which holdeth children from play, and old men from the chimney corner.
The Defence of Poetry (1595)

16 Comedy is an imitation of the common errors of our life.
The Defence of Poetry (1595)

17 Thy necessity is yet greater than mine.
on giving his water-bottle to a dying soldier on the battle-field of Zutphen, 1586; commonly quoted as 'thy need is greater than mine'
Fulke Greville *Life of Sir Philip Sidney* (1652) ch. 12

Emmanuel Joseph Sieyès 1748–1836
French abbot and statesman

18 J'ai vécu.
I survived.
when asked what he had done during the French Revolution
F. A. M. Mignet *Notice historique sur la vie et les travaux de M. le Comte de Sieyès* (1836)

Maurice Sigler 1901–61 and Al Hoffman 1902–60
American songwriters

19 Little man, you've had a busy day.
title of song (1934)

Simone Signoret 1921–85
French actress

20 Chains do not hold a marriage together. It is threads, hundreds of tiny threads which sew people together through the years.
in *Daily Mail* 4 July 1978

Sikh Scriptures
a monotheistic religion founded in the Punjab in the 15th century by Guru Nanak

21 There is neither Hindu nor Muslim.
Mahima Prakas Varatak, tr. W. H. McLeod

Alan Sillitoe 1928–
English writer

22 The loneliness of the long-distance runner.
title of novel (1959)

Georges Simenon 1903–89
Belgian novelist

23 Writing is not a profession but a vocation of unhappiness.
interview in *Paris Review* Summer 1955

Paul Simon 1942–
American singer and songwriter

1 Like a bridge over troubled water
I will lay me down.
'Bridge over Troubled Water' (1970 song)

2 And here's to you, Mrs Robinson
Jesus loves you more than you will know.
'Mrs Robinson' (1967 song, from the film *The Graduate*)

3 People talking without speaking
People hearing without listening . . .
'Fools,' said I, 'You do not know
Silence like a cancer grows.'
'Sound of Silence' (1964 song)

4 Still crazy after all these years.
title of song (1975)

Simonides *c.*556–468 BC
Greek poet

5 Go, tell the Spartans, thou who passest by,
That here obedient to their laws we lie.
epitaph for the 300 Spartans killed at Thermopylae, 480 BC
Herodotus *Histories* bk. 7; attributed

6 Painting is silent poetry, poetry is eloquent painting.
Plutarch *Moralia* 'De Gloria Atheniensium' sect. 3

Konstantin Simonov 1915–79
Russian poet

7 Wait for me and I'll return . . .
Only you and I know how I survived.
It's because you waited as no one else did.
'Wait for Me' (1942)

Harold Simpson

8 Down in the forest something stirred:
It was only the note of a bird.
'Down in the Forest' (1906 song)

Kirke Simpson 1881–1972
American journalist

9 [Warren] Harding of Ohio was chosen by a
group of men in a smoke-filled room early
today as Republican candidate for President.
*often attributed to Harry Daugherty, one of
Harding's supporters, who appears merely to have
concurred with this version of events, when
pressed for comment by Simpson*
news report, filed 12 June 1920; William Safire
New Language of Politics (1968)

George R. Sims 1847–1922
English journalist and dramatist

10 It is Christmas Day in the Workhouse.
'In the Workhouse—Christmas Day' (1879)

Sitting Bull *c.*1831–90
Sioux chief

11 What law have I broken? Is it wrong for me
to love my own? Is it wicked for me because
my skin is red, because I am Sioux, because I

was born where my fathers lived, because I
would die for my people and my country?
to Major Brotherton, recorded July 1881

12 The Black Hills belong to me. If the whites
try to take them, I will fight.
Dee Brown *Bury My Heart at Wounded Knee* (1970)
ch. 12

Edith Sitwell 1887–1964
English poet and critic

13 Still falls the Rain—
Dark as the world of man, black as our
loss—
Blind as the nineteen hundred and forty
nails
Upon the Cross.
'Still Falls the Rain' (1942)

John Skelton *c.*1460–1529
English poet

14 Far may be sought
Erst that ye can find
So courteous, so kind,
As Merry Margaret,
This midsummer flower,
Gentle as falcon
Or hawk of the tower
The Garland of Laurel (1523) 'To Mistress Margaret
Hussey'

B. F. Skinner 1904–90
American psychologist

15 The real question is not whether machines
think but whether men do.
Contingencies of Reinforcement (1969) ch. 9

16 Education is what survives when what has
been learned has been forgotten.
New Scientist 21 May 1964

Christopher Smart 1722–71
English poet

17 For I will consider my Cat Jeoffrey.
For he is the servant of the Living God duly
and daily serving him.
Jubilate Agno (*c.*1758–63) Fragment B, l. 695

18 For he counteracts the powers of darkness
by his electrical skin and glaring eyes.
For he counteracts the Devil, who is death,
by brisking about the life.
Jubilate Agno (*c.*1758–63) Fragment B, l. 721

19 And now the matchless deed's achieved,
Determined, dared, and done.
A Song to David (1763) st. 95

Samuel Smiles 1812–1904
English writer

20 The spirit of self-help is the root of all
genuine growth in the individual.
Self-Help (1859) ch. 1

21 The shortest way to do many things is to do
only one thing at once.
Self-Help (1859) ch. 9

Adam Smith 1723–90
Scottish philosopher and economist

1 It is not from the benevolence of the butcher, the brewer, or the baker, that we expect our dinner, but from their regard to their own interest.
Wealth of Nations (1776) bk. 1, ch. 2

2 People of the same trade seldom meet together, even for merriment and diversion, but the conversation ends in a conspiracy against the public, or in some contrivance to raise prices.
Wealth of Nations (1776) bk. 1, ch. 10, pt. 2

3 The chief enjoyment of riches consists in the parade of riches.
Wealth of Nations (1776) bk. 1, ch. 11

4 Every individual necessarily labours to render the annual revenue of society as great as he can. He generally neither intends to promote the public interest, nor knows how much he is promoting it. He intends only his own gain, and he is, in this, as in many other cases, led by an invisible hand to promote an end which was no part of his intention.
Wealth of Nations (1776) bk. 4, ch. 3; see **Friedman** 142:22

5 To found a great empire for the sole purpose of raising up a people of customers, may at first sight appear a project fit only for a nation of shopkeepers. It is, however, a project altogether unfit for a nation of shopkeepers; but extremely fit for a nation whose government is influenced by shopkeepers.
Wealth of Nations (1776) bk. 4, ch. 7, pt. 3; see **Adams** 2:16, **Napoleon** 248:7

6 Consumption is the sole end and purpose of production; and the interest of the producer ought to be attended to only so far as it may be necessary for promoting that of the consumer.
Wealth of Nations (1776) bk. 4, ch. 8

7 There is no art which one government sooner learns of another than that of draining money from the pockets of the people.
Wealth of Nations (1776) bk. 5, ch. 2

Alfred Emanuel Smith 1873–1944
American politician

8 All the ills of democracy can be cured by more democracy.
speech in Albany, 27 June 1933, in *New York Times* 28 June 1933

Delia Smith
English cook

9 A hen's egg is, quite simply, a work of art, a masterpiece of design and construction with, it has to be said, brilliant packaging.
How To Cook (1998)

Dodie Smith 1896–1990
English novelist and dramatist

10 The family—that dear octopus from whose tentacles we never quite escape.
Dear Octopus (1938)

11 I write this sitting in the kitchen sink.
I Capture the Castle (1948)

Edgar Smith 1857–1938
American songwriter

12 You may tempt the upper classes
With your villainous demi-tasses,
But; Heaven will protect a working-girl!
'Heaven Will Protect the Working-Girl' (1909 song)

F. E. Smith, Lord Birkenhead 1872–1930
British Conservative politician and lawyer

13 The world continues to offer glittering prizes to those who have stout hearts and sharp swords.
rectorial address, Glasgow University, 7 November 1923

14 JUDGE: You are extremely offensive, young man.
SMITH: As a matter of fact, we both are, and the only difference between us is that I am trying to be, and you can't help it.
2nd Earl of Birkenhead *Earl of Birkenhead* (1933) vol. 1, ch. 9

Iain Duncan Smith 1954–
British Conservative politician

15 Do not underestimate the determination of a quiet man.
speech to the Conservative Party Conference, 10 October 2002

Ian Smith 1919–
Rhodesian statesman; Prime Minister of Rhodesia (now Zimbabwe), 1964–79

16 I don't believe in black majority rule in Rhodesia—not in a thousand years.
broadcast speech, 20 March 1976

Logan Pearsall Smith 1865–1946
American-born man of letters

17 The test of a vocation is the love of the drudgery it involves.
Afterthoughts (1931) 'Art and Letters'

18 A best-seller is the gilded tomb of a mediocre talent.
Afterthoughts (1931) 'Art and Letters'

19 People say that life is the thing, but I prefer reading.
Afterthoughts (1931) 'Myself'

20 Thank heavens, the sun has gone in, and I don't have to go out and enjoy it.
Afterthoughts (1931) 'Myself'

21 What I like in a good author is not what he says, but what he whispers.
All Trivia (1933) 'Afterthoughts' pt. 5

Samuel Francis Smith 1808–95
American poet and divine

1 My country, 'tis of thee,
Sweet land of liberty,
Of thee I sing:
Land where my fathers died,
Land of the pilgrims' pride,
From every mountain-side
Let freedom ring.
'America' (1831)

Stevie Smith 1902–71
English poet and novelist

2 A good time was had by all.
title of book (1937)

3 I was much too far out all my life
And not waving but drowning.
'Not Waving but Drowning' (1957)

4 This Englishwoman is so refined
She has no bosom and no behind.
'This Englishwoman' (1937)

Sydney Smith 1771–1845
English clergyman and essayist

5 We shall generally find that the triangular
person has got into the square hole, the
oblong into the triangular, and a square
person has squeezed himself into the round
hole.
Sketches of Moral Philosophy (1849) Lecture 9

6 I have no relish for the country; it is a kind
of healthy grave.
letter to Miss G. Harcourt, 1838

7 Take short views, hope for the best, and
trust in God.
Lady Holland *Memoir* (1855) vol. 1, ch. 6

8 No furniture so charming as books.
Lady Holland *Memoir* (1855) vol. 1, ch. 9; see
Powell 270:8

9 As the French say, there are three
sexes—men, women, and clergymen.
Lady Holland *Memoir* (1855) vol. 1, ch. 9

10 My definition of marriage . . . it resembles a
pair of shears, so joined that they cannot be
separated; often moving in opposite
directions, yet always punishing anyone
who comes between them.
Lady Holland *Memoir* (1855) vol. 1, ch. 11

11 He has occasional flashes of silence, that
make his conversation perfectly delightful.
of **Macaulay**
Lady Holland *Memoir* (1855) vol. 1, ch. 11

12 Let onion atoms lurk within the bowl,
And, scarce-suspected, animate the whole.
Lady Holland *Memoir* (1855) vol. 1, ch. 11
'Receipt for a Salad'

13 Serenely full, the epicure would say,
Fate cannot harm me, I have dined to-day.
Lady Holland *Memoir* (1855) vol. 1, ch. 11
'Receipt for a Salad'; see **Dryden** 122:16

14 I never read a book before reviewing it; it
prejudices a man so.
H. Pearson *The Smith of Smiths* (1934) ch. 3

15 My idea of heaven is, eating *pâté de foie gras*
to the sound of trumpets.
view ascribed by Smith to his friend Henry Luttrell
H. Pearson *The Smith of Smiths* (1934) ch. 10

16 What two ideas are more inseparable than
Beer and Britannia?
H. Pearson *The Smith of Smiths* (1934) ch. 11

Tilly Smith 1994–
British schoolgirl

17 I noticed the sea was all frothy like the top
of a beer. It was bubbling.
*collecting an award from the Marine Society for
helping to save 100 tourists from the tsunami of
December 2004 by remembering her geography
lesson*
in *Sunday Times* 11 September 2005

Walter Chalmers Smith 1824–1908
Scottish clergyman

18 Immortal, invisible, God only wise.
'God, All in All' (1867 hymn)

Tobias Smollett 1721–71
Scottish novelist

19 That great Cham of literature, Samuel
Johnson.
letter to John Wilkes, 16 March 1759

C. P. Snow 1905–80
English novelist and scientist

20 The official world, the corridors of power.
Homecomings (1956) ch. 22

21 The two cultures and the scientific
revolution.
title of The Rede Lecture (1959)

Socrates 469–399 BC
Greek philosopher

22 How many things I can do without!
on looking at a multitude of goods exposed for sale
Diogenes Laertius *Lives of the Philosophers* bk. 2,
ch. 25

23 I know nothing except the fact of my
ignorance.
Diogenes Laertius *Lives of the Philosophers* bk. 2,
sect. 32; see **Milton** 239:19

24 Virtue does not come from money, but from
virtue comes money and all other good
things to man, both to the individual and to
the state.
Plato *Apology* 30b

25 The unexamined life is not worth living.
Plato *Apology* 38a

26 It is never right to do wrong or to requite
wrong with wrong, or when we suffer evil
to defend ourselves by doing evil in return.
Plato *Crito* 49d

27 It is perfectly certain that the soul is
immortal and imperishable, and our souls
will actually exist in another world.
Plato *Phaedo* 107a

1 But, my dearest Agathon, it is truth which you cannot contradict; you can without any difficulty contradict Socrates.
  Plato *Symposium* 201d

2 I am not Athenian or Greek but a citizen of the world.
  Plutarch *Moralia* bk. 7 'On Exile'

3 Crito, we owe a cock to Aesculapius; please pay it and don't forget it.
  last words; Plato *Phaedo* 118

Solon *c.*640–after 556 BC
Greek poet and Athenian statesman

4 I grow old ever learning many things.
  Theodor Bergk (ed.) *Poetae Lyrici Graeci* (1843) no. 18

5 Call no man happy before he dies, he is at best but fortunate.
  Herodotus *Histories* bk. 1, ch. 32; see **Bible** 42:23

Alexander Solzhenitsyn 1918–
Russian novelist

6 You only have power over people as long as you don't take *everything* away from them. But when you've robbed a man of *everything* he's no longer in your power — he's free again.
  The First Circle (1968) ch. 17

7 The Gulag archipelago.
  title of book (1973–5)

William Somerville 1675–1742
English country gentleman

8 The chase, the sport of kings;
Image of war, without its guilt.
  The Chase (1735) bk. 1, l. 14; see **Surtees** 327:20

Anastasio Somoza 1925–80
Nicaraguan dictator

9 You won the elections, but I won the count.
  replying to an accusation of ballot-rigging
  in *Guardian* 17 June 1977; see **Stoppard** 326:9

Stephen Sondheim 1930–
American songwriter

10 I like to be in America!
O.K. by me in America!
Ev'rything free in America
For a small fee in America!
  'America' (1957 song) in *West Side Story*

11 Everything's coming up roses.
  title of song (1959) in *Gypsy*

12 Where are the clowns?
Send in the clowns.
  'Send in the Clowns' (1973 song) in *A Little Night Music*

Susan Sontag 1933–2004
American writer

13 What pornography is really about, ultimately, isn't sex but death.
  in *Partisan Review* Spring 1967

14 The white race *is* the cancer of human history.
  in *Partisan Review* Winter 1967

Sophocles *c.*496–406 BC
Greek dramatist

15 There are many wonderful things, and nothing is more wonderful than man.
  Antigone l. 333

16 Not to be born is, past all prizing, best.
  Oedipus Coloneus l. 1225 (translation by R. C. Jebb); see **Auden** 18:15

Charles Hamilton Sorley
1895–1915
English poet

17 When you see millions of the mouthless dead
Across your dreams in pale battalions go.
  'A Sonnet' (1916)

Robert Southey 1774–1843
English poet and writer

18 Now tell us all about the war,
And what they fought each other for.
  'The Battle of Blenheim' (1800)

19 'But what good came of it at last?'
Quoth little Peterkin.
'Why that I cannot tell,' said he,
'But 'twas a famous victory.'
  'The Battle of Blenheim' (1800)

20 And then they knew the perilous rock,
And blessed the Abbot of Aberbrothock.
  'The Inchcape Rock' (1802)

21 You are old, Father William, the young man cried,
The few locks which are left you are grey;
You are hale, Father William, a hearty old man,
Now tell me the reason, I pray.
  'The Old Man's Comforts' (1799); see **Carroll** 86:7

22 Live as long as you may, the first twenty years are the longest half of your life.
  The Doctor (1812) ch. 130

23 She has made me in love with a cold climate, and frost and snow, with a northern moonlight.
  *on Mary **Wollstonecraft**'s letters from Sweden and Norway*
  letter to his brother Thomas, 28 April 1797; see **Mitford** 241:16

24 Literature cannot be the business of a woman's life: and it ought not to be.
  letter to Charlotte Brontë, 12 March 1837

Robert Southwell *c.*1561–95
English poet and Roman Catholic martyr

25 As I in hoary winter night stood shivering in the snow,
Surprised was I with sudden heat which made my heart to glow;
And lifting up a fearful eye to view what fire was near
A pretty Babe all burning bright did in the air appear.
  'The Burning Babe' (*c.*1590)

Muriel Spark 1918–
British novelist

1 I am putting old heads on your young shoulders . . . all my pupils are the crème de la crème.
The Prime of Miss Jean Brodie (1961) ch. 1

2 Give me a girl at an impressionable age, and she is mine for life.
The Prime of Miss Jean Brodie (1961) ch. 1

3 One's prime is elusive. You little girls, when you grow up, must be on the alert to recognise your prime at whatever time of your life it may occur.
The Prime of Miss Jean Brodie (1961) ch. 1

Herbert Spencer 1820–1903
English philosopher

4 During human progress, every science is evolved out of its corresponding art.
Education (1861) ch. 2

5 Science is organized knowledge.
Education (1861) ch. 2

6 People are beginning to see that the first requisite to success in life is to be a good animal.
Education (1861) ch. 2

7 Absolute morality is the regulation of conduct in such a way that pain shall not be inflicted.
Essays (1891) vol. 3 'Prison Ethics'

8 Evolution . . . is—a change from an indefinite, incoherent homogeneity, to a definite coherent heterogeneity.
First Principles (1862) ch. 16

9 This survival of the fittest which I have here sought to express in mechanical terms, is that which Mr Darwin has called 'natural selection, or the preservation of favoured races in the struggle for life'.
Principles of Biology (1865) pt. 3, ch. 12; see **Darwin** 110:8

10 How often misused words generate misleading thoughts.
Principles of Ethics (1879) bk. 1, pt. 2, ch. 8, sect. 152

11 Progress, therefore, is not an accident, but a necessity . . . It is a part of nature.
Social Statics (1850) pt. 1, ch. 2, sect. 4

12 A clever theft was praiseworthy amongst the Spartans; and it is equally so amongst Christians, provided it be on a sufficiently large scale.
Social Statics (1850) pt. 2, ch. 16, sect. 3

13 Hero-worship is strongest where there is least regard for human freedom.
Social Statics (1850) pt. 4, ch. 30, sect. 6

14 No one can be perfectly free till all are free; no one can be perfectly moral till all are moral; no one can be perfectly happy till all are happy.
Social Statics (1850) pt. 4, ch. 30, sect. 16

Lord Spencer 1964–
English peer

15 Every proprietor and editor of every publication that has paid for intrusive and exploitative photographs of her . . . has blood on their hands today.
*on the death of his sister, **Diana**, Princess of Wales, in a car crash while being pursued by photographers, 31 August 1997*
in *Daily Telegraph* 1 September 1997

16 She needed no royal title to continue to generate her particular brand of magic.
*tribute at the funeral of his sister, **Diana**, Princess of Wales, 7 September 1997*
in *Guardian* 8 September 1997

Raine, Countess Spencer 1929–2004

17 Alas, for our towns and cities. Monstrous carbuncles of concrete have erupted in gentle Georgian Squares.
The Spencers on Spas (1983) p. 14; see **Charles** 91:7

Stephen Spender 1909–95
English poet

18 I think continually of those who were truly great.
'I think continually of those who were truly great' (1933)

19 Born of the sun they travelled a short while towards the sun,
And left the vivid air signed with their honour.
'I think continually of those who were truly great' (1933)

Edmund Spenser c.1552–99
English poet

20 One day I wrote her name upon the strand,
But came the waves and washèd it away:
Again I wrote it with a second hand,
But came the tide, and made my pains his prey.
Amoretti (1595) sonnet 75

21 Open the temple gates unto my love,
Open them wide that she may enter in.
'Epithalamion' (1595) l. 204

22 Ah! when will this long weary day have end,
And lend me leave to come unto my love?
'Epithalamion' (1595) l. 278

23 The general end therefore of all the book is to fashion a gentleman or noble person in virtuous and gentle discipline.
The Faerie Queene (1596) preface

24 A gentle knight was pricking on the plain.
The Faerie Queen (1596) bk. 1, canto 1, st. 1

25 But on his breast a bloody cross he bore,
The dear remembrance of his dying Lord.
The Faerie Queen (1596) bk. 1, canto 1, st. 2

26 Sleep after toil, port after stormy seas,
Ease after war, death after life does greatly please.
The Faerie Queen (1596) bk. 1, canto 9, st. 40

1 And with rich metal loaded every rift.
  The Faerie Queen (1596) bk. 2, canto 7, st. 28; see
  Keats 197:20

2 And all for love, and nothing for reward.
  The Faerie Queen (1596) bk. 2, canto 8, st. 2

3 Be bold, be bold, and everywhere Be bold . . .
  Be not too bold.
  The Faerie Queen (1596) bk. 3, canto 11, st. 54

4 Dan Chaucer, well of English undefiled.
  The Faerie Queen (1596) bk. 4, canto 2, st. 32

5 O sacred hunger of ambitious minds.
  The Faerie Queen (1596) bk. 5, canto 12, st. 1

6 For of the soul the body form doth take;
  For soul is form, and doth the body make.
  'An Hymn in Honour of Beauty' (1596) l. 132

7 Sweet Thames, run softly, till I end my song.
  Prothalamion (1596) l. 54

Baruch Spinoza 1632–77
Dutch philosopher

8 There is no hope without fear, and no fear
  without hope.
  Ethics (1677) pt. 2, para. 178

9 I have striven not to laugh at human
  actions, not to weep at them, nor to hate
  them, but to understand them.
  Tractatus Politicus (1677) ch. 1, sect. 4

Benjamin Spock 1903–98
American paediatrician

10 You know more than you think you do.
   Common Sense Book of Baby and Child Care (1946)

William Archibald Spooner
1844–1930
English clergyman and academic

11 You will find as you grow older that the
   weight of rages will press harder and harder
   upon the employer.
   William Hayter *Spooner* (1977) ch. 6

Cecil Spring-Rice 1859–1918
British diplomat

12 I vow to thee, my country—all earthly
     things above—
   Entire and whole and perfect, the service of
     my love,
   The love that asks no question: the love that
     stands the test,
   That lays upon the altar the dearest and the
     best:
   The love that never falters, the love that
     pays the price,
   The love that makes undaunted the final
     sacrifice.
   'I Vow to Thee, My Country' (written on the eve
   of his departure from Washington, 12 January
   1918)

13 And there's another country, I've heard of
     long ago—
   Most dear to them that love her, most great
     to them that know.
   'I Vow to Thee, My Country' (written 1918)

14 Her ways are ways of gentleness and all her
     paths are Peace.
   'I Vow to Thee, My Country' (written 1918); see
   Bible 38:13

Bruce Springsteen 1949–
American rock singer and songwriter

15 Born in the USA.
   title of song (1984)

16 Born down in a dead man's town
   The first kick I took was when I hit the
     ground.
   'Born in the USA' (1984 song)

17 We gotta get out while we're young,
   'Cause tramps like us, baby, we were born to
     run.
   'Born to Run' (1974 song)

18 Is a dream a lie if it don't come true,
   Or is it something worse?
   'The River' (1980 song)

C. H. Spurgeon 1834–92
English nonconformist preacher

19 If you want truth to go round the world you
   must hire an express train to pull it; but if
   you want a lie to go round the world, it will
   fly: it is as light as a feather, and a breath
   will carry it. It is well said in the old
   proverb, 'a lie will go round the world while
   truth is pulling its boots on'.
   Gems from Spurgeon (1859)

J. C. Squire 1884–1958
English man of letters

20 But I'm not so think as you drunk I am.
   'Ballade of Soporific Absorption' (1931)

21 It did not last: the Devil howling 'Ho!
   Let Einstein be!' restored the status quo.
   'In continuation of Pope on Newton' (1926); see
   Pope 267:4

Mme de Staël 1766–1817
French writer

22 *Tout comprendre rend très indulgent.*
   To be totally understanding makes one very
   indulgent.
   Corinne (1807) bk. 18, ch. 5

Joseph Stalin 1879–1953
Soviet dictator

23 There are various forms of production:
   artillery, automobiles, lorries. You also
   produce 'commodities', 'works', 'products'.
   Such things are highly necessary.
   Engineering things. For people's souls.
   'Products' are highly necessary too.
   'Products' are very important for people's
   souls. You are engineers of human souls.
   speech to writers at **Gorky**'s house, 26 October
   1932; see **Gorky** 154:11

24 The Pope! How many divisions has *he* got?
   on being asked to encourage Catholicism in Russia
   by way of conciliating the Pope, 13 May 1935
   W. S. Churchill *The Gathering Storm* (1948) ch. 8;
   see **Napoleon** 248:5

1 One death is a tragedy, a million deaths a statistic.
  attributed

Henry Morton Stanley 1841–1904
British explorer

2 Dr Livingstone, I presume?
  How I found Livingstone (1872) ch. 11

Charles E. Stanton 1859–1933
American soldier

3 *Lafayette, nous voilà!*
  Lafayette, we are here.
  at the tomb of Lafayette in Paris, 4 July 1917; in
  New York Tribune 6 September 1917

Edwin Mcmasters Stanton
1814–69
American lawyer

4 Now he belongs to the ages.
  of Abraham **Lincoln,** *following his assassination,*
  15 April 1865
  I. M. Tarbell *Life of Abraham Lincoln* (1900) vol. 2

Elizabeth Cady Stanton 1815–1902
American suffragist

5 Woman's degradation is in man's idea of his sexual rights. Our religion, laws, customs, are all founded on the belief that woman was made for man.
  letter to Susan B. Anthony, 14 June 1860

Frank L. Stanton 1857–1927
American journalist and poet

6 Sweetes' li'l' feller,
  Everybody knows;
  Dunno what to call him,
  But he's mighty lak' a rose!
  'Mighty Lak' a Rose' (1901 song)

John Stark 1728–1822
American Revolutionary officer

7 We beat them to-day or Molly Stark's a widow.
  before the Battle of Bennington, 16 August 1777

David Steel 1938–
British Liberal politician

8 I have the good fortune to be the first Liberal leader for over half a century who is able to say to you at the end of our annual assembly: go back to your constituencies and prepare for government.
  speech to the Liberal Party Assembly, 18 September 1981

9 It is the settled will of the majority of people in Scotland that they want not just the symbol, but the substance of the return of democratic control over internal affairs.
  on the announcement that the Stone of Destiny
  would be returned to Scotland
  in *Scotsman* 4 July 1996

Richard Steele 1672–1729
Irish-born essayist and dramatist

10 A woman seldom writes her mind but in her postscript.
  in *The Spectator* no. 79 (31 May 1711); see **Bacon**
  22:18

11 Reading is to the mind what exercise is to the body.
  in *The Tatler* no. 147 (18 March 1710)

Lincoln Steffens 1866–1936
American journalist

12 I have seen the future; and it works.
  following a visit to the Soviet Union in 1919
  letter to Marie Howe, 3 April 1919

Edward Steichen 1879–1973
Luxembourg-born American photographer

13 The mission of photography is to explain man to man and each man to himself.
  Cornell Capa (ed.) *The Concerned Photographer*
  (1972)

Gertrude Stein 1874–1946
American writer

14 Remarks are not literature.
  Autobiography of Alice B. Toklas (1933) ch. 7

15 Pigeons on the grass alas.
  Four Saints in Three Acts (1934) act 3, sc. 2

16 In the United States there is more space where nobody is than where anybody is. That is what makes America what it is.
  The Geographical History of America (1936)

17 Rose is a rose is a rose is a rose, is a rose.
  Sacred Emily (1913)

18 You are all a lost generation.
  of the young who served in the First World War
  subsequently taken by Ernest **Hemingway** as
  his epigraph to *The Sun Also Rises* (1926)

19 'What *is* the answer?' No answer came. She laughed and said, 'In that case what is the question?'
  last words; Donald Sutherland *Gertrude Stein, A*
  Biography of her Work (1951)

John Steinbeck 1902–68
American novelist

20 Man, unlike any other thing organic or inorganic in the universe, grows beyond his work, walks up the stairs of his concepts, emerges ahead of his accomplishments.
  The Grapes of Wrath (1939) ch. 14

21 Okie use' ta mean you was from Oklahoma. Now it means you're a dirty son-of-a-bitch. Okie means you're scum. Don't mean nothing itself, it's the way they say it.
  The Grapes of Wrath (1939) ch. 18

Gloria Steinem 1934–
American journalist

22 We are becoming the men we wanted to marry.
  in *Ms* July/August 1982

1 A woman without a man is like a fish
without a bicycle.
attributed

Stendhal 1783–1842
French novelist

2 Politics in the middle of things that concern
the imagination are like a pistol-shot in the
middle of a concert.
Le Rouge et le noir (1830) bk. 2, ch. 22

J. K. Stephen 1859–92
English journalist and writer of light verse

3 When the Rudyards cease from kipling
And the Haggards ride no more.
'To R.K.' (1891)

James Stephens 1882–1950
Irish poet and nationalist

4 Finality is death. Perfection is finality.
Nothing is perfect. There are lumps in it.
The Crock of Gold (1912) bk. 1, ch. 4

5 I hear a sudden cry of pain!
There is a rabbit in a snare:
Now I hear the cry again,
But I cannot tell from where . . .
Little one! Oh, little one!
I am searching everywhere.
'The Snare' (1915)

Laurence Sterne 1713–68
English novelist

6 They order, said I, this matter better in
France.
A Sentimental Journey (1768) opening words

7 God tempers the wind, said Maria, to the
shorn lamb.
*derived from a French proverb, but familiar in this
form of words*
A Sentimental Journey (1768) 'Maria'

8 I wish either my father or my mother, or
indeed both of them, as they were in duty
both equally bound to it, had minded what
they were about when they begot me.
Tristram Shandy (1759–67) bk. 1, ch. 1

9 'Pray, my dear,' quoth my mother, 'have you
not forgot to wind up the clock?'—'Good
G—!' cried my father, making an
exclamation, but taking care to moderate
his voice at the same time,—'Did ever
woman, since the creation of the world,
interrupt a man with such a silly question?'
Tristram Shandy (1759–67) bk. 1, ch. 1

10 'Tis known by the name of perseverance in
a good cause,—and of obstinacy in a bad
one.
Tristram Shandy (1759–67) bk. 1, ch. 17

11 Writing, when properly managed (as you
may be sure I think mine is) is but a
different name for conversation.
Tristram Shandy (1759–67) bk. 2, ch. 11

12 There is a North-west passage to the
intellectual World.
Tristram Shandy (1759–67) bk. 5, ch. 42

13 L—d! said my mother, what is all this story
about?— A Cock and a Bull, said Yorick.
Tristram Shandy (1759–67) bk. 9, ch. 33

Brooks Stevens 1911–
American industrial designer

14 Our whole economy is based on planned
obsolescence.
Vance Packard *The Waste Makers* (1960) ch. 6

Wallace Stevens 1879–1955
American poet

15 Call the roller of big cigars,
The muscular one, and bid him whip
In kitchen cups concupiscent curds.
'The Emperor of Ice-Cream' (1923)

16 Let be be finale of seem.
The only emperor is the emperor of ice-
cream.
'The Emperor of Ice-Cream' (1923)

17 Poetry is the supreme fiction, madame.
'A High-Toned old Christian Woman' (1923)

18 They said, 'You have a blue guitar,
You do not play things as they are.'
The man replied, 'Things as they are
Are changed upon the blue guitar.'
'The Man with the Blue Guitar' (1937)

19 The palm at the end of the mind,
Beyond the last thought, rises.
'Of Mere Being' (1957)

20 Music is feeling, then, not sound.
'Peter Quince at the Clavier' (1923) pt. 1

21 Beauty is momentary in the mind—
The fitful tracing of a portal;
But in the flesh it is immortal.
The body dies; the body's beauty lives.
'Peter Quince at the Clavier' (1923) pt. 4

22 For the listener, who listens in the snow,
And, nothing himself, beholds
Nothing that is not there and the nothing
that is.
'The Snow Man' (1921)

23 Complacencies of the peignoir, and late
Coffee and oranges in a sunny chair,
And the green freedom of a cockatoo
Upon a rug mingle to dissipate
The holy hush of ancient sacrifice.
'Sunday Morning' (1923) st. 1

24 At evening, casual flocks of pigeons make
Ambiguous undulations as they sink,
Downward to darkness, on extended wings.
'Sunday Morning' (1923) st. 8

25 I do not know which to prefer,
The beauty of inflections
Or the beauty of innuendoes,
The blackbird whistling
Or just after.
'Thirteen Ways of Looking at a Blackbird' (1923)

Adlai Stevenson 1900–65
American Democratic politician

1 If they [the Republicans] will stop telling lies about the Democrats, we will stop telling the truth about them.
  speech during 1952 Presidential campaign; in J. B. Martin *Adlai Stevenson and Illinois* (1976) ch. 8

2 Let's talk sense to the American people. Let's tell them the truth, that there are no gains without pains.
  speech of acceptance at the Democratic National Convention, Chicago, 26 July 1952

3 In America any boy may become President and I suppose it's just one of the risks he takes!
  speech in Indianapolis, 26 September 1952

4 A free society is a society where it is safe to be unpopular.
  speech in Detroit, 7 October 1952; in *Major Campaign Speeches . . . 1952* (1953)

5 The young man who asks you to set him one heart-beat from the Presidency of the United States.
  of Richard Nixon as Vice-Presidential nominee
  speech at Cleveland, Ohio, 23 October 1952

6 We hear the Secretary of State boasting of his brinkmanship—the art of bringing us to the edge of the abyss.
  speech in Hartford, Connecticut, 25 February 1956; see **Dulles** 123:2

7 She would rather light a candle than curse the darkness, and her glow has warmed the world.
  of Eleanor Roosevelt
  in *New York Times* 8 November 1962; see **Benenson** 30:13

Robert Louis Stevenson 1850–94
Scottish novelist

8 Every one lives by selling something.
  Across the Plains (1892) 'Beggars' pt. 3

9 Here lies one who meant well, tried a little, failed much:—surely that may be his epitaph, of which he need not be ashamed.
  Across the Plains (1892) 'A Christmas Sermon' pt. 4

10 Politics is perhaps the only profession for which no preparation is thought necessary.
  Familiar Studies of Men and Books (1882) 'Yoshida-Torajiro'

11 I regard you with an indifference closely bordering on aversion.
  New Arabian Nights (1882) 'The Rajah's Diamond: Story of the Bandbox'

12 The strange case of Dr Jekyll and Mr Hyde.
  title of novel, 1886

13 Man is not truly one, but truly two.
  The Strange Case of Dr Jekyll and Mr Hyde (1886)

14 I travel not to go anywhere, but to go. I travel for travel's sake. The great affair is to move.
  Travels with a Donkey (1879) 'Cheylard and Luc'

15 If landscapes were sold, like the sheets of characters of my boyhood, one penny plain and twopence coloured, I should go the length of twopence every day of my life.
  Travels with a Donkey (1879) 'Father Apollinaris'

16 Fifteen men on the dead man's chest
  Yo-ho-ho, and a bottle of rum!
  Drink and the devil had done for the rest—
  Yo-ho-ho, and a bottle of rum!
  Treasure Island (1883) ch. 1

17 Tip me the black spot.
  Treasure Island (1883) ch. 3

18 Pieces of eight, pieces of eight, pieces of eight!
  Treasure Island (1883) ch. 10

19 Many's the long night I've dreamed of cheese—toasted, mostly.
  Treasure Island (1883) ch. 15

20 There is no duty we so much underrate as the duty of being happy.
  Virginibus Puerisque (1881) 'An Apology for Idlers'

21 To travel hopefully is a better thing than to arrive, and the true success is to labour.
  Virginibus Puerisque (1881) 'El Dorado'

22 Even if we take matrimony at its lowest, even if we regard it as no more than a sort of friendship recognised by the police.
  Virginibus Puerisque (1881) title essay, pt. 1

23 Marriage is like life in this—that it is a field of battle, and not a bed of roses.
  Virginibus Puerisque (1881) title essay, pt. 1

24 The cruellest lies are often told in silence.
  Virginibus Puerisque (1881) title essay, pt. 4

25 If you are going to make a book end badly, it must end badly from the beginning.
  letter to J. M. Barrie, November 1892

26 In winter I get up at night
  And dress by yellow candle-light.
  In summer, quite the other way,—
  I have to go to bed by day.
  A Child's Garden of Verses (1885) 'Bed in Summer'

27 The world is so full of a number of things,
  I'm sure we should all be as happy as kings.
  A Child's Garden of Verses (1885) 'Happy Thought'

28 I was the giant great and still
  That sits upon the pillow-hill,
  And sees before him, dale and plain,
  The pleasant land of counterpane.
  A Child's Garden of Verses (1885) 'The Land of Counterpane'

29 I have a little shadow that goes in and out with me.
  A Child's Garden of Verses (1885) 'My Shadow'

30 A child should always say what's true,
  And speak when he is spoken to,
  And behave mannerly at table:
  At least as far as he is able.
  A Child's Garden of Verses (1885) 'Whole Duty of Children'

31 I will make you brooches and toys for your delight
  Of bird-song at morning and star-shine at night.
  Songs of Travel (1896) 'I will make you brooches and toys for your delight'

1 Sing me a song of a lad that is gone,
Say, could that lad be I?
Merry of soul he sailed on a day
Over the sea to Skye.
  Songs of Travel (1896) 'Sing me a song of a lad
  that is gone'

2 Give to me the life I love,
Let the lave go by me,
Give the jolly heaven above
And the byway nigh me.
  Songs of Travel (1896) 'The Vagabond'

3 All I seek, the heaven above
And the road below me.
  Songs of Travel (1896) 'The Vagabond'

4 Go, little book, and wish to all
Flowers in the garden, meat in the hall.
  Underwoods (1887) 'Envoy'; see **Chaucer** 92:4

5 Under the wide and starry sky
Dig the grave and let me lie.
  Underwoods (1887) 'Requiem'

6 This be the verse you grave for me:
'Here he lies where he longed to be;
Home is the sailor, home from sea,
And the hunter home from the hill.'
  Underwoods (1887) 'Requiem'

Caskie Stinnett 1911–
American writer

7 A diplomat . . . is a person who can tell you
to go to hell in such a way that you actually
look forward to the trip.
  Out of the Red (1960) ch. 4

Samuel John Stone 1839–1900
English clergyman

8 The Church's one foundation
Is Jesus Christ, her Lord;
She is his new creation
By water and the word.
  Lyra Fidelium (1866) 'The Church's one
  foundation'

Tom Stoppard 1937–
British dramatist

9 It's not the voting that's democracy, it's the
counting.
  Jumpers (1972) act 1; see **Somoza** 320:9

10 I'm with you on the free press. It's the
newspapers I can't stand.
  Night and Day (1978) act 1

11 Comment is free but facts are on expenses.
  Night and Day (1978) act 2; see **Scott** 287:2

12 I can do you blood and love without the
rhetoric, and I can do you blood and
rhetoric without the love, and I can do you
all three concurrent or consecutive, but I
can't do you love and rhetoric without the
blood. Blood is compulsory—they're all
blood, you see.
  Rosencrantz and Guildenstern are Dead (1967) act 1

13 Eternity's a terrible thought. I mean,
where's it all going to end?
  Rosencrantz and Guildenstern are Dead (1967) act 2

14 The bad end unhappily, the good unluckily.
That is what tragedy means.
  Rosencrantz and Guildenstern are Dead (1967) act 2;
  see **Wilde** 358:10

15 Life is a gamble at terrible odds—if it was a
bet, you wouldn't take it.
  Rosencrantz and Guildenstern are Dead (1967) act 3

16 War is capitalism with the gloves off.
  Travesties (1975) act 1

William Stoughton 1631–1701
American clergyman

17 God hath sifted a nation that he might send
choice grain into this wilderness.
  sermon in Boston, 29 April 1669

Harriet Beecher Stowe 1811–96
American novelist

18 I s'pect I growed. Don't think nobody never
made me.
Topsy
  Uncle Tom's Cabin (1852) ch. 20

Lytton Strachey 1880–1932
English biographer

19 CHAIRMAN OF MILITARY TRIBUNAL: What
would you do if you saw a German soldier
trying to violate your sister?
STRACHEY: I would try to get between them.
*otherwise rendered as, 'I should interpose my
body'*
  Robert Graves *Good-bye to All That* (1929) ch. 23

20 Discretion is not the better part of
biography.
  Michael Holroyd *Lytton Strachey* vol. 1 (1967)
  preface

21 If this is dying, then I don't think much of it.
on his deathbed
  Michael Holroyd *Lytton Strachey* vol. 2 (1968) pt.
  2, ch. 6

William L. Strauss
and A. J. E. Cave

22 Notwithstanding, if he could be
reincarnated and placed in a New York
subway—provided that he were bathed,
shaved, and dressed in modern clothing—it
is doubtful whether he would attract any
more attention than some of its other
denizens.
of Neanderthal man
  in *Quarterly Review of Biology* Winter 1957

Igor Stravinsky 1882–1971
Russian composer

23 My music is best understood by children
and animals.
  in *Observer* 8 October 1961

Jack Straw 1946–
British Labour politician

24 The divide in the modern world is not the
so-called 'clash of civilizations' between

Islam and the West. The divide is between order and chaos.
in Newsweek 20 January 2003

1 There is no list, and Syria isn't on it.
on the US description of Syria as a rogue state
speech, Qatar; in *Guardian* 15 April 2003 (online edition)

Belinda Stronach 1966–
Canadian Conservative politician

2 The political crisis affecting Canada is too risky and dangerous for blind partnership.
of the Conservative Party's decision to align itself with the separatist Bloc Québécois against the Liberal government of Paul Martin
at a news conference announcing her defection to the Liberals, 17 May 2005

Jan Struther 1901–53
English-born novelist and poet

3 Lord of all hopefulness, Lord of all joy,
Whose trust, ever childlike, no cares could destroy,
Be there at our waking, and give us, we pray,
Your bliss in our hearts, Lord, at the break of the day.
'All Day Hymn' (1931 hymn)

G. A. Studdert Kennedy 1883–1929
British poet

4 When Jesus came to Birmingham they simply passed Him by,
They never hurt a hair of Him, they only let Him die.
Peace Rhymes of a Padre (1921) 'Indifference'

John Suckling 1609–42
English poet and dramatist

5 Why so pale and wan, fond lover?
Prithee, why so pale?
Aglaura (1637) act 4, sc. 1 'Song'

6 Her feet beneath her petticoat,
Like little mice, stole in and out.
'A Ballad upon a Wedding' (1646) st. 8

7 Love is the fart
Of every heart:
It pains a man when 'tis kept close,
And others doth offend, when 'tis let loose.
'Love's Offence' (1646)

8 Out upon it, I have loved
Three whole days together.
'A Poem with the Answer' (1659)

Annie Sullivan 1866–1936
American educator

9 Language grows out of life, out of its needs and experiences . . . *Language* and *knowledge* are indissolubly connected; they are interdependent. Good work in language presupposes and depends on a real knowledge of things
speech to the American Association to Promote the Teaching of Speech to the Deaf, July 1894

Louis Henri Sullivan 1856–1924
American architect

10 Form follows function.
The Tall Office Building Artistically Considered (1896)

Terry Sullivan

11 She sells sea-shells on the sea-shore.
'She Sells Sea-Shells' (1908 song)

Timothy Daniel Sullivan
1827–1914
Irish writer and politician

12 'God save Ireland!' said the heroes;
'God save Ireland', say they all:
Whether on the scaffold high
Or the battlefield we die,
Oh, what matter when for Erin dear we fall.
'God Save Ireland' (1867)

Arthur Hays Sulzberger
1891–1968
American newspaper proprietor

13 We tell the public which way the cat is jumping. The public will take care of the cat.
on journalism
in *Time* 8 May 1950

Edith Summerskill 1901–80
British Labour politician

14 Nagging is the repetition of unpalatable truths.
speech to the Married Women's Association, House of Commons, 14 July 1960

Charles Sumner 1811–74
American politician and orator

15 Where Slavery is, there Liberty cannot be; and where Liberty is, there Slavery cannot be.
'Slavery and the Rebellion'; speech at Cooper Institute 5 November 1864

16 There is the national flag. He must be cold, indeed, who can look upon its folds rippling in the breeze without pride of country.
Are We a Nation? 19 November 1867

Henry Howard, Earl of Surrey
c.1517–47
English poet

17 So cruel prison how could betide, alas,
As proud Windsor?
'So cruel prison' (1557)

18 Wyatt resteth here, that quick could never rest.
'Wyatt resteth here' (1557)

R. S. Surtees 1805–64
English sporting journalist and novelist

19 More people are flattered into virtue than bullied out of vice.
The Analysis of the Hunting Field (1846) ch. 1

20 'Unting is all that's worth living for . . . it's the sport of kings, the image of war without its guilt, and only five-and-twenty per cent of its danger.

Handley Cross (1843) ch. 7; see **Somerville** 320:8

1 Life would be very pleasant if it were not for its enjoyments.

Mr Facey Romford's Hounds (1865) ch. 32; see **Lewis** 214:3

2 There is no secret so close as that between a rider and his horse.

Mr Sponge's Sporting Tour (1853) ch. 31

Italo Svevo 1861–1928
Italian novelist and businessman

3 Last cigarette!!

Zeno's Conscience (1923) ch. 1 and elsewhere

Hannen Swaffer 1879–1962
British journalist

4 Freedom of the press in Britain means freedom to print such of the proprietor's prejudices as the advertisers don't object to.

Tom Driberg *Swaff* (1974) ch. 2

Jonathan Swift 1667–1745
Irish poet and satirist

5 Satire is a sort of glass, wherein beholders do generally discover everybody's face but their own.

The Battle of the Books (1704) preface

6 Instead of dirt and poison we have rather chosen to fill our hives with honey and wax; thus furnishing mankind with the two noblest of things, which are sweetness and light.

The Battle of the Books (1704); see **Arnold** 17:2

7 It is the folly of too many, to mistake the echo of a London coffee-house for the voice of the kingdom.

The Conduct of the Allies (1711)

8 Laws are like cobwebs, which may catch small flies, but let wasps and hornets break through.

A Critical Essay upon the Faculties of the Mind (1709); see **Anacharsis** 6:9

9 I have heard of a man who had a mind to sell his house, and therefore carried a piece of brick in his pocket, which he shewed as a pattern to encourage purchasers.

The Drapier's Letters (1724) no. 2

10 And he gave it for his opinion, that whoever could make two ears of corn or two blades of grass to grow upon a spot of ground where only one grew before, would deserve better of mankind, and do more essential service to his country than the whole race of politicians put together.

Gulliver's Travels (1726) 'A Voyage to Brobdingnag' ch. 7

11 He had been eight years upon a project for extracting sun-beams out of cucumbers, which were to be put into vials hermetically sealed, and let out to warm the air in raw inclement summers.

Gulliver's Travels (1726) 'A Voyage to Laputa, etc.' ch. 5

12 He replied that I must needs be mistaken, or that I *said the thing which was not*. (For they have no word in their language to express lying or falsehood.)

Gulliver's Travels (1726) 'A Voyage to the Houyhnhnms' ch. 3

13 We are so fond of one another, because our ailments are the same.

Journal to Stella (in *Works*, 1768) 1 February 1711

14 Proper words in proper places, make the true definition of a style.

Letter to a Young Gentleman lately entered into Holy Orders (9 January 1720)

15 I have been assured by a very knowing American of my acquaintance in London, that a young healthy child well nursed is at a year old a most delicious, nourishing, and wholesome food, whether stewed, roasted, baked, or boiled, and I make no doubt that it will equally serve in a fricassee, or a ragout.

A Modest Proposal for Preventing the Children of Ireland from being a Burden to their Parents or Country (1729)

16 She wears her clothes, as if they were thrown on her with a pitchfork.

Polite Conversation (1738) Dialogue 1

17 He was a bold man that first eat an oyster.

Polite Conversation (1738) Dialogue 2

18 Last week I saw a woman flayed, and you will hardly believe, how much it altered her person for the worse.

A Tale of a Tub (1704) ch. 9

19 We have just enough religion to make us hate, but not enough to make us love one another.

Thoughts on Various Subjects (1711)

20 When a true genius appears in the world, you may know him by this sign, that the dunces are all in confederacy against him.

Thoughts on Various Subjects (1711)

21 What they do in heaven we are ignorant of; what they do *not* we are told expressly, that they neither marry, nor are given in marriage.

Thoughts on Various Subjects (1711); see **Bible** 45:27

22 The stoical scheme of supplying our wants, by lopping off our desires, is like cutting off our feet when we want shoes.

Thoughts on Various Subjects (1711)

23 Few are qualified to shine in company; but it is in most men's power to be agreeable.

Thoughts on Various Subjects (1727 ed.)

24 Every man desires to live long; but no man would be old.

Thoughts on Various Subjects (1727 ed.)

25 There is nothing in this world constant, but inconstancy.

A Tritical Essay upon the Faculties of the Mind (1709)

26 Then, rising with Aurora's light,
The Muse invoked, sit down to write;
Blot out, correct, insert, refine,
Enlarge, diminish, interline.

'On Poetry' (1733) l. 85

1 So geographers, in Afric-maps,
With savage-pictures fill their gaps;
And o'er unhabitable downs
Place elephants for want of towns.
'On Poetry' (1733) l. 177

2 So, naturalists observe, a flea
Hath smaller fleas that on him prey;
And these have smaller fleas to bite 'em,
And so proceed *ad infinitum*.
'On Poetry' (1733) l. 337

3 Good God! what a genius I had when I wrote
that book.
of A Tale of a Tub
Sir Walter Scott (ed.) *Works of Swift* (1814) vol. 1

4 I shall be like that tree, I shall die at the top.
Sir Walter Scott (ed.) *Works of Swift* (1814) vol. 1

5 A stick and a string, with a fly at one end
and a fool at the other.
*description of angling; the remark has also been
attributed to Samuel* **Johnson**, *in the form 'a stick
and a string, with a worm at one end and a fool
at the other'*
in *The Indicator* 27 October 1819

6 *Ubi saeva indignatio ulterius cor lacerare nequit.*
Where fierce indignation can no longer tear
his heart.
epitaph; Shane Leslie *The Skull of Swift* (1928) ch.
15, see **Yeats** 369:7

Algernon Charles Swinburne
1837–1909
English poet

7 When the hounds of spring are on winter's
traces,
The mother of months in meadow or plain
Fills the shadows and windy places
With lisp of leaves and ripple of rain.
Atalanta in Calydon (1865) chorus 'When the
hounds of spring'

8 And time remembered is grief forgotten,
And frosts are slain and flowers begotten,
And in green underwood and cover
Blossom by blossom the spring begins.
Atalanta in Calydon (1865) chorus 'When the
hounds of spring'

9 Change in a trice
The lilies and languors of virtue
For the raptures and roses of vice.
'Dolores' (1866) st. 9

10 O splendid and sterile Dolores,
Our Lady of Pain.
'Dolores' (1866) st. 9

11 We are not sure of sorrow,
And joy was never sure.
'The Garden of Proserpine' (1866)

12 From too much love of living,
From hope and fear set free,
We thank with brief thanksgiving
Whatever gods may be
That no man lives forever,
That dead men rise up never;
That even the weariest river
Winds somewhere safe to sea.
'The Garden of Proserpine' (1866)

13 Even love, the beloved Republic, that feeds
upon freedom lives.
'Hertha' (1871); see **Forster** 139:19

14 Thou hast conquered, O pale Galilean; the
world has grown grey from Thy breath.
'Hymn to Proserpine' (1866); see **Julian** 193:15

15 If love were what the rose is,
And I were like the leaf,
Our lives would grow together
In sad or singing weather,
Blown fields or flowerful closes,
Green pleasure or grey grief.
'A Match' (1866)

John Millington Synge 1871–1909
Irish dramatist

16 But we do be afraid of the sea, and we do
only be drownded now and again.
The Aran Islands (1907) pt. 2

17 Oh my grief, I've lost him surely. I've lost
the only Playboy of the Western World.
The Playboy of the Western World (1907) act 3

Thomas Szasz 1920–
Hungarian-born psychiatrist

18 Happiness is an imaginary condition,
formerly often attributed by the living to
the dead, now usually attributed by adults
to children, and by children to adults.
The Second Sin (1973) 'Emotions'

19 The stupid neither forgive nor forget; the
naïve forgive and forget; the wise forgive
but do not forget.
The Second Sin (1973) 'Personal Conduct'

20 If you talk to God, you are praying; if God
talks to you, you have schizophrenia. If the
dead talk to you, you are a spiritualist; if
God talks to you, you are a schizophrenic.
The Second Sin (1973) 'Schizophrenia'

21 Formerly, when religion was strong and
science weak, men mistook magic for
medicine; now, when science is strong and
religion weak, men mistake medicine for
magic.
The Second Sin (1973) 'Science and Scientism'

22 Two wrongs don't make a right, but they
make a good excuse.
The Second Sin (1973) 'Social Relations'

Albert von Szent-Györgyi
1893–1986
Hungarian-born biochemist

23 Discovery consists of seeing what everybody
has seen and thinking what nobody has
thought.
Irving Good (ed.) *The Scientist Speculates* (1962)

Tacitus *c.*AD 56–after 117
Roman senator and historian

24 They make a wilderness and call it peace.
Agricola ch. 30

25 *Sine ira et studio.*
With neither anger nor partiality.
Annals bk. 1, ch. 1

1 The more corrupt the state, the more numerous the laws.
> *Annals* bk. 3, ch. 27

2 *Elegantiae arbiter.*
The arbiter of taste.
of Petronius
> *Annals* bk. 16, ch. 18

3 *Deos fortioribus adesse.*
The gods are on the side of the stronger.
> *The Histories* bk. 4, ch. 17; see **Bussy-Rabutin** 78:24

4 *Experientia docuit.*
Experience has taught.
commonly quoted as 'Experientia docet [experience teaches]'
> *The Histories* bk. 5, ch. 6

William Howard Taft 1857–1930
American Republican statesman, 27th President of the US 1909–13

5 Next to the right of liberty, the right of property is the most important individual right guaranteed by the Constitution and the one which, united with that of personal liberty, has contributed more to the growth of civilization than any other institution established by the human race.
> *Popular Government* (1913) ch. 3

Nellie Talbot

6 Jesus wants me for a sunbeam.
> title of hymn (1921) in *CSSM Choruses* No. 1

Charles-Maurice de Talleyrand 1754–1838
French statesman

7 This is the beginning of the end.
on the announcement of Napoleon's Pyrrhic victory at Borodino, 1812
> attributed; Sainte-Beuve *M. de Talleyrand* (1870) ch. 3

8 *Surtout, Messieurs, point de zèle.*
Above all, gentlemen, not the slightest zeal.
> P. Chasles *Voyages d'un critique à travers la vie et les livres* (1868) vol. 2

9 *Ils n'ont rien appris, ni rien oublié.*
They have learnt nothing, and forgotten nothing.
of the Bourbons in exile
> oral tradition, attributed to Talleyrand by the Chevalier de Panat; see **Dumouriez** 123:6

10 That, Sire, is a question of dates.
often quoted as, 'treason is a matter of dates'; replying to the Tsar's criticism of those who 'betrayed the cause of Europe'
> Duff Cooper *Talleyrand* (1932)

The Talmud
compilation of Jewish civil and ceremonial law and legend, dating from the 5th century AD, and comprising the Mishnah and the Gemara. There are two versions of the Talmud, the Babylonian Talmud and the earlier Palestinian or Jerusalem Talmud
see also Hillel, Shammai

Mishnah

11 By three things is the world sustained: by the Law, by the [Temple-]service, and by deeds of loving-kindness.
> *Mishnah* Pirqei Avot 1:2

12 The tradition is a fence around the Law.
> *Mishnah* Pirqei Avot 3:14

13 Beloved is man, for he was created in the image [of God]; still greater was the love in that it was made known to him that he was created in the image of God.
> *Mishnah* Pirqei Avot 3:15

14 Turn it [Torah] and turn it again, for everything is in it.
> *Mishnah* Pirqei Avot 5:22

Gemara

15 Even an iron partition cannot interpose between Israel and their Father in Heaven.
> *Babylonian Talmud* Pesahim 85b

16 *He shall live by them* [the laws of the Torah], but he shall not die because of them.
> *Babylonian Talmud* Yoma 85b

17 If a man divorces his first wife, even the altar sheds tears.
> *Babylonian Talmud* Gittin 90b

Booth Tarkington 1869–1946
American novelist

18 There are two things that will be believed of any man whatsoever, and one of them is that he has taken to drink.
> *Penrod* (1914) ch. 10

Nahum Tate 1652–1715
English dramatist

19 As pants the hart for cooling streams When heated in the chase.
> *New Version of the Psalms* (1696) Psalm 42 (with Nicholas Brady); see **Book of Common Prayer** 62:27

20 Through all the changing scenes of life, In trouble and in joy, The praises of my God shall still My heart and tongue employ.
> *New Version of the Psalms* (1696) Psalm 34 (with Nicholas Brady)

21 While shepherds watched their flocks by night, All seated on the ground, The angel of the Lord came down, And glory shone around.
> *Supplement to the New Version of the Psalms* (1700) 'While Shepherds Watched'

R. H. Tawney 1880–1962
British economic historian

22 Freedom for the pike is death for the minnows.
> *Equality* (ed. 4, rev. ed., 1938) ch. 5, sect. 2

A. J. P. Taylor 1906–90
British historian

23 The First World War had begun—imposed on the statesmen of Europe by railway

timetables. It was an unexpected climax to
the railway age.
The First World War (1963) ch. 1

Ann Taylor 1782–1866
and Jane Taylor 1783–1824
English writers of books for children

1 Who ran to help me when I fell,
And would some pretty story tell,
Or kiss the place to make it well?
My Mother.
Original Poems for Infant Minds (1804) 'My Mother'

2 Twinkle, twinkle, little star,
How I wonder what you are!
Up above the world so high,
Like a diamond in the sky!
Rhymes for the Nursery (1806) 'The Star'; see
Carroll 86:12

Bayard Taylor 1825–78
American traveller and writer

3 Till the sun grows cold,
And the stars are old,
And the leaves of the Judgement Book
unfold.
'Bedouin Song'

Jeremy Taylor 1613–67
English divine

4 This thing . . . that can be understood and
not expressed, may take a neuter
gender;—and every schoolboy knows it.
The Real Presence . . . (1654) sect. 5; see **Macaulay**
221:13

5 As our life is very short, so it is very
miserable, and therefore it is well it is short.
The Rule and Exercise of Holy Dying (1651) ch. 1,
sect. 4

Tom Taylor 1817–80
English dramatist

6 Hawkshaw, the detective.
usually quoted as 'I am Hawkshaw, the detective'
The Ticket-of-leave Man (1863) act 4, sc. 1

Norman Tebbit 1931–
British Conservative politician

7 I grew up in the Thirties with our
unemployed father. He did not riot, he got
on his bike and looked for work.
speech at Conservative Party Conference, 15
October 1981, in *Daily Telegraph* 16 October 1981

8 The cricket test—which side do they cheer
for? . . . Are you still looking back to where
you came from or where you are?
on the loyalties of Britain's immigrant population
interview in *Los Angeles Times*, reported in *Daily
Telegraph* 20 April 1990

Tecumseh 1768–1813
Shawnee chief

9 Where today are the Pequot? Where are the
Narragansett, the Mohican, the Pokanoket,
and many other once powerful tribes of our
people? They have vanished before the
avarice and oppression of the white man, as
snow before the summer sun.
Dee Brown *Bury My Heart at Wounded Knee* (1970)
ch. 1

Pierre Teilhard de Chardin
1881–1955
French Jesuit philosopher and palaeontologist

10 The history of the living world can be
summarised as the elaboration of ever more
perfect eyes within a cosmos in which there
is always something more to be seen.
The Phenomenon of Man (1959)

William Temple 1881–1944
English theologian and archbishop

11 It is a mistake to suppose that God is only, or
even chiefly, concerned with religion.
R. V. C. Bodley *In Search of Serenity* (1955) ch. 12

12 Personally, I have always looked on cricket
as organized loafing.
attributed

John Tenniel 1820–1914
English draughtsman

13 Dropping the pilot.
*on **Bismarck's** departure from office*
cartoon caption, and title of poem, in *Punch* 29
March 1890

Alfred, Lord Tennyson 1809–92
English poet

14 Cleave ever to the sunnier side of doubt.
'The Ancient Sage' (1885) l. 68

15 Break, break, break,
On thy cold grey stones, O Sea!
And I would that my tongue could utter
The thoughts that arise in me.
'Break, Break, Break' (1842)

16 But O for the touch of a vanished hand,
And the sound of a voice that is still!
'Break, Break, Break' (1842)

17 I come from haunts of coot and hern,
I make a sudden sally
And sparkle out among the fern,
To bicker down a valley.
'The Brook' (1855) l. 23

18 For men may come and men may go,
But I go on for ever.
'The Brook' (1855) l. 33

19 Half a league, half a league,
Half a league onward,
All in the valley of Death
Rode the six hundred.
'The Charge of the Light Brigade' (1854)

20 'Forward, the Light Brigade!'
Was there a man dismayed?
Not though the soldier knew
Some one had blundered:
Their's not to make reply,
Their's not to reason why,
Their's but to do and die:
Into the valley of Death

Rode the six hundred.
Cannon to right of them,
Cannon to left of them,
Cannon in front of them
Volleyed and thundered.
'The Charge of the Light Brigade' (1854)

1 Into the jaws of Death,
Into the mouth of Hell.
'The Charge of the Light Brigade' (1854)

2 Sunset and evening star,
And one clear call for me!
And may there be no moaning of the bar,
When I put out to sea.
'Crossing the Bar' (1889)

3 For though from out our bourne of time and
place
The flood may bear me far,
I hope to see my pilot face to face
When I have crossed the bar.
'Crossing the Bar' (1889)

4 A dream of fair women.
title of poem (1832)

5 A daughter of the gods, divinely tall,
And most divinely fair.
'A Dream of Fair Women' (1832) l. 87

6 He clasps the crag with crookèd hands;
Close to the sun in lonely lands,
Ringed with the azure world, he stands.
The wrinkled sea beneath him crawls;
He watches from his mountain walls,
And like a thunderbolt he falls.
'The Eagle' (1851)

7 O Love, O fire! once he drew
With one long kiss my whole soul through
My lips, as sunlight drinketh dew.
'Fatima' (1832) st. 3

8 Closer is He than breathing, and nearer than
hands and feet.
'The Higher Pantheism' (1869)

9 Wearing the white flower of a blameless
life,
Before a thousand peering littlenesses,
In that fierce light which beats upon a
throne,
And blackens every blot.
of Prince **Albert**
Idylls of the King (1862 ed.) dedication l. 24

10 Clothed in white samite, mystic, wonderful.
Idylls of the King 'The Coming of Arthur' (1869) l.
284; 'The Passing of Arthur' (1869) l. 199

11 From the great deep to the great deep he
goes.
Idylls of the King 'The Coming of Arthur' (1869) l.
410

12 Live pure, speak true, right wrong, follow
the King—
Else, wherefore born?
Idylls of the King 'Gareth and Lynette' (1872) l.
117

13 Elaine the fair, Elaine the loveable,
Elaine, the lily maid of Astolat.
Idylls of the King 'Lancelot and Elaine' (1859) l. 1

14 His honour rooted in dishonour stood,

And faith unfaithful kept him falsely true.
Idylls of the King 'Lancelot and Elaine' (1859) l.
871

15 For man is man and master of his fate.
Idylls of the King 'The Marriage of Geraint' (1859)
l. 355

16 It is the little rift within the lute,
That by and by will make the music mute.
Idylls of the King 'Merlin and Vivien' (1859) l. 388

17 And trust me not at all or all in all.
Idylls of the King 'Merlin and Vivien' (1859) l. 396

18 Man dreams of fame while woman wakes to
love.
Idylls of the King 'Merlin and Vivien' (1859) l. 458

19 So all day long the noise of battle rolled
Among the mountains by the winter sea.
Idylls of the King 'The Passing of Arthur' (1869) l.
170

20 Authority forgets a dying king.
Idylls of the King 'The Passing of Arthur' (1869) l.
289

21 The old order changeth, yielding place to
new,
And God fulfils himself in many ways,
Lest one good custom should corrupt the
world.
Idylls of the King 'The Passing of Arthur' (1869) l.
408

22 More things are wrought by prayer
Than this world dreams of.
Idylls of the King 'The Passing of Arthur' (1869) l.
415

23 To the island-valley of Avilion;
Where falls not hail, or rain, or any snow,
Nor ever wind blows loudly; but it lies
Deep-meadowed, happy, fair with orchard
lawns.
Idylls of the King 'The Passing of Arthur' (1869) l.
427

24 Our little systems have their day;
They have their day and cease to be:
They are but broken lights of thee,
And thou, O Lord, art more than they.
In Memoriam (1850) Prologue

25 That men may rise on stepping-stones
Of their dead selves to higher things.
In Memoriam A. H. H. (1850) canto 1

26 Let knowledge grow from more to more,
But more of reverence in us dwell;
That mind and soul, according well,
May make one music as before.
In Memoriam A. H. H. (1850) Prologue

27 For words, like Nature, half reveal
And half conceal the Soul within.
In Memoriam A. H. H. (1850) canto 5

28 The last red leaf is whirled away,
The rooks are blown about the skies.
In Memoriam A. H. H. (1850) canto 15

29 'Tis better to have loved and lost
Than never to have loved at all.
In Memoriam A. H. H. (1850) canto 27; see
Congreve 102:10

30 Oh yet we trust that somehow good

Will be the final goal of ill.
In Memoriam A. H. H. (1850) canto 54

1 But what am I?
An infant crying in the night:
An infant crying for the light:
And with no language but a cry.
In Memoriam A. H. H. (1850) canto 54

2 So careful of the type she seems,
So careless of the single life.
of Nature
In Memoriam A. H. H. (1850) canto 55

3 Nature, red in tooth and claw.
In Memoriam A. H. H. (1850) canto 56

4 So many worlds, so much to do,
So little done, such things to be.
In Memoriam A. H. H. (1850) canto 73; see **Rhodes** 275:13

5 God's finger touched him, and he slept.
In Memoriam A. H. H. (1850) canto 85

6 There lives more faith in honest doubt,
Believe me, than in half the creeds.
In Memoriam A. H. H. (1850) canto 96

7 He seems so near and yet so far.
In Memoriam A. H. H. (1850) canto 97

8 Ring out, wild bells, to the wild sky.
In Memoriam A. H. H. (1850) canto 106

9 Ring out the old, ring in the new,
Ring, happy bells, across the snow:
The year is going, let him go;
Ring out the false, ring in the true.
In Memoriam A. H. H. (1850) canto 106

10 Ring out the thousand wars of old,
Ring in the thousand years of peace.
In Memoriam A. H. H. (1850) canto 106

11 One God, one law, one element,
And one far-off divine event,
To which the whole creation moves.
In Memoriam A. H. H. (1850) canto 131

12 Below the thunders of the upper deep;
Far, far beneath in the abysmal sea,
His ancient, dreamless, uninvaded sleep
The Kraken sleepeth.
'The Kraken' (1830)

13 There hath he lain for ages and will lie
Battening upon huge seaworms in his sleep,
Until the latter fire shall heat the deep.
'The Kraken' (1830)

14 Kind hearts are more than coronets,
And simple faith than Norman blood.
'Lady Clara Vere de Vere' (1842) st. 7

15 On either side the river lie
Long fields of barley and of rye,
That clothe the wold and meet the sky;
And through the field the road runs by
To many-towered Camelot.
'The Lady of Shalott' (1832, revised 1842) pt. 1

16 Willows whiten, aspens quiver,
Little breezes dusk and shiver.
'The Lady of Shalott' (1832, revised 1842) pt. 1

17 'I am half sick of shadows,' said
The Lady of Shalott.
'The Lady of Shalott' (1832, revised 1842) pt. 2

18 'Tirra lirra,' by the river
Sang Sir Lancelot.
'The Lady of Shalott' (1832, revised 1842) pt. 3

19 She left the web, she left the loom,
She made three paces through the room.
'The Lady of Shalott' (1832, revised 1842) pt. 3

20 Out flew the web and floated wide;
The mirror cracked from side to side;
'The curse is come upon me,' cried
The Lady of Shalott.
'The Lady of Shalott' (1832, revised 1842) pt. 3

21 Airy, fairy Lilian.
'Lilian' (1830)

22 In the spring a livelier iris changes on the burnished dove;
In the spring a young man's fancy lightly turns to thoughts of love.
'Locksley Hall' (1842) l. 19

23 But the jingling of the guinea helps the hurt that Honour feels.
'Locksley Hall' (1842) l. 105

24 Men, my brothers, men the workers, ever reaping something new:
That which they have done but earnest of the things that they shall do:
'Locksley Hall' (1842) l. 117

25 For I dipped into the future, far as human eye could see,
Saw the vision of the world, and all the wonder that would be.
'Locksley Hall' (1842) l. 119

26 Pilots of the purple twilight, dropping down with costly bales.
'Locksley Hall' (1842) l. 122

27 Heard the heavens fill with shouting, and there rained a ghastly dew
From the nations' airy navies grappling in the central blue;
'Locksley Hall' (1842) l. 123

28 Till the war-drum throbbed no longer, and the battle-flags were furled
In the Parliament of man, the Federation of the world.
'Locksley Hall' (1842) l. 127

29 Science moves, but slowly slowly, creeping on from point to point.
'Locksley Hall' (1842) l. 134

30 Knowledge comes, but wisdom lingers.
'Locksley Hall' (1842) l. 141

31 I the heir of all the ages, in the foremost files of time.
'Locksley Hall' (1842) l. 178

32 Forward, forward let us range,
Let the great world spin for ever down the ringing grooves of change.
'Locksley Hall' (1842) l. 181

33 Better fifty years of Europe than a cycle of Cathay.
'Locksley Hall' (1842) l. 184

34 Music that gentlier on the spirit lies,
Than tired eyelids upon tired eyes.
'The Lotos-Eaters' (1832) Choric Song, st. 1

35 Death is the end of life; ah, why

Should life all labour be?
'The Lotos-Eaters' (1832) Choric Song, st. 4

1 She only said, 'My life is dreary,
He cometh not,' she said;
She said, 'I am aweary, aweary,
I would that I were dead!'
'Mariana' (1830) st. 1; see **Shakespeare** 302:9

2 I hate that dreadful hollow behind the little
wood.
Maud (1855) pt. 1, sect. 1

3 Faultily faultless, icily regular, splendidly
null,
Dead perfection, no more.
Maud (1855) pt. 1, sect. 2

4 Come into the garden, Maud,
For the black bat, night, has flown,
Come into the garden, Maud,
I am here at the gate alone.
Maud (1855) pt. 1, sect. 22, st. 1

5 Queen rose of the rosebud garden of girls.
Maud (1855) pt. 1, sect. 22, st. 9

6 She is coming, my dove, my dear;
She is coming, my life, my fate;
The red rose cries, 'She is near, she is near;'
And the white rose weeps, 'She is late.'
Maud (1855) pt. 1, sect. 22, st. 10

7 She is coming, my own, my sweet;
Were it ever so airy a tread,
My heart would hear her and beat,
Were it earth in an earthy bed.
Maud (1855) pt. 1, sect. 22, st. 11

8 You must wake and call me early, call me
early, mother dear;
Tomorrow 'ill be the happiest time of all the
glad New-year;
Of all the glad New-year, mother, the
maddest merriest day;
For I'm to be Queen o' the May, mother, I'm
to be Queen o' the May.
'The May Queen' (1832)

9 After it, follow it,
Follow The Gleam.
'Merlin and The Gleam' (1889) st. 9

10 God-gifted organ-voice of England,
Milton, a name to resound for ages.
'Milton: Alcaics' (1863)

11 With prudes for proctors, dowagers for
deans,
And sweet girl-graduates in their golden
hair.
The Princess (1847) 'Prologue' l. 141

12 Sweet and low, sweet and low,
Wind of the western sea.
The Princess (1847) pt. 3, song (added 1850)

13 The splendour falls on castle walls
And snowy summits old in story:
The long light shakes across the lakes,
And the wild cataract leaps in glory.
Blow, bugle, blow, set the wild echoes
flying,
Blow, bugle; answer, echoes, dying, dying,
dying.
The Princess (1847) pt. 4, song (added 1850)

14 O sweet and far from cliff and scar

The horns of Elfland faintly blowing!
The Princess (1847) pt. 4, song (added 1850)

15 Tears, idle tears, I know not what they
mean,
Tears from the depth of some divine despair
Rise in the heart, and gather to the eyes,
In looking on the happy autumn-fields,
And thinking of the days that are no more.
The Princess (1847) pt. 4, l. 21, song (added 1850)

16 Dear as remembered kisses after death.
The Princess (1847) pt. 4, l. 36, song (added 1850)

17 Man is the hunter; woman is his game.
The Princess (1847) pt. 5, l. 147

18 Home they brought her warrior dead.
She nor swooned, nor uttered cry:
All her maidens, watching said,
'She must weep or she will die.'
The Princess (1847) pt. 6, song (added 1850)

19 Rose a nurse of ninety years,
Set his child upon her knee.
The Princess (1847) pt. 6, song (added 1850)

20 Like summer tempest came her tears.
The Princess (1847) pt. 6, song (added 1850)

21 Now sleeps the crimson petal, now the
white;
Nor waves the cypress in the palace walk.
The Princess (1847) pt. 7, l. 161, song (added 1850)

22 Now lies the Earth all Danaë to the stars,
And all thy heart lies open unto me.
The Princess (1847) pt. 7, l. 167, song (added 1850)

23 Now folds the lily all her sweetness up,
And slips into the bosom of the lake:
So fold thyself, my dearest, thou, and slip
Into my bosom and be lost in me.
The Princess (1847) pt. 7, l. 171, song (added 1850)

24 The moan of doves in immemorial elms,
And murmuring of innumerable bees.
The Princess (1847) pt. 7, l. 206, song (added 1850)

25 At Flores in the Azores Sir Richard Grenville
lay.
'The Revenge' (1878) st. 1

26 And the sun went down, and the stars came
out far over the summer sea,
But never a moment ceased the fight of the
one and the fifty-three.
'The Revenge' (1878) st. 9

27 My strength is as the strength of ten,
Because my heart is pure.
'Sir Galahad' (1842)

28 Alone and warming his five wits,
The white owl in the belfry sits.
'Song—The Owl' (1830)

29 The woods decay, the woods decay and fall,
The vapours weep their burthen to the
ground,
Man comes and tills the field and lies
beneath,
And after many a summer dies the swan.
'Tithonus' (1860, revised 1864) l. 1

30 The gods themselves cannot recall their
gifts.
'Tithonus' (1860, revised 1864) l. 52

31 It little profits that an idle king,

By this still hearth, among these barren
crags,
Matched with an agèd wife, I mete and dole
Unequal laws unto a savage race.
'Ulysses' (1842) l. 1

1 I am become a name;
For always roaming with a hungry heart.
'Ulysses' (1842) l. 16

2 Far on the ringing plains of windy Troy.
'Ulysses' (1842) l. 22

3 Yet all experience is an arch wherethrough
Gleams that untravelled world, whose
margin fades
For ever and for ever when I move.
How dull it is to pause, to make an end,
To rust unburnished, not to shine in use!
'Ulysses' (1842) l. 24; see **Adams** 1:19

4 To follow knowledge like a sinking star,
Beyond the utmost bound of human
thought.
'Ulysses' (1842) l. 31

5 This is my son, mine own Telemachus.
'Ulysses' (1842) l. 33

6 Death closes all: but something ere the end,
Some work of noble note, may yet be done,
Not unbecoming men that strove with gods.
'Ulysses' (1842) l. 58

7 It may be that the gulfs will wash us down:
It may be we shall touch the Happy Isles,
And see the great Achilles, whom we knew.
'Ulysses' (1842) l. 69

8 That which we are, we are;
One equal temper of heroic hearts,
Made weak by time and fate, but strong in
will
To strive, to seek, to find, and not to yield.
'Ulysses' (1842) l. 74

9 Every moment dies a man,
Every moment one is born.
'The Vision of Sin' (1842) pt. 4, st. 9; see
Babbage 21:20

10 A louse in the locks of literature.
of Churton Collins
Evan Charteris *Life and Letters of Sir Edmund Gosse*
(1931) ch. 14

Terence *c.*190–159 BC
Roman comic dramatist

11 *Hinc illae lacrimae.*
Hence those tears.
Andria l. 126

12 Nothing has yet been said that's not been
said before.
Eunuchus prologue l. 41

13 I am a man, I count nothing human foreign
to me.
Heauton Timorumenos l. 77

14 *Fortis fortuna adiuvat.*
Fortune assists the brave.
Phormio l. 203; see **Virgil** 347:18

15 *Quot homines tot sententiae: suus cuique mos.*
There are as many opinions as there are
people: each has his own correct way.
Phormio l. 454

Mother Teresa 1910–97
*Roman Catholic nun and missionary, born in what
is now Macedonia of Albanian parentage*

16 We ourselves feel that what we are doing is
just a drop in the ocean. But if that drop was
not in the ocean, I think the ocean would be
less because of that missing drop. I do not
agree with the big way of doing things.
A Gift for God (1975)

17 Now let us do something beautiful for God.
letter to Malcolm Muggeridge before making a
BBC TV programme about the Missionaries of
Charity, 1971; see **Muggeridge** 246:17

18 The biggest disease today is not leprosy or
tuberculosis, but rather the feeling of being
unwanted, uncared for and deserted by
everybody.
in *The Observer* 3 October 1971

19 I see God in every human being. When I
wash the leper's wounds I feel I am nursing
the Lord himself.
in 1977; in obituary, *Guardian* 6 September 1997

20 By blood and origin I am Albanian. My
citizenship is Indian. I am a Catholic nun. As
to my calling, I belong to the whole world.
As to my heart, I belong entirely to the heart
of Jesus.
in *Independent* 6 September 1997; obituary

St Teresa of Ávila 1512–82
Spanish Carmelite nun and mystic
see also **John** 185:14

21 Let nothing trouble you, nothing frighten
you. All things are passing; God never
changes. Patient endurance attains all
things. Whoever possesses God lacks
nothing: God alone suffices.
'St Teresa's Bookmark'; found in her breviary
after her death

22 Our goodness derives not from our capacity
to think but to love.
Book of the Foundations (1610)

23 The important thing is not to think much
but to love much.
The Interior Castle (1588) Mansion 4, ch. 1, para. 7

St Teresa of Lisieux 1873–97
French Carmelite nun

24 I will spend my heaven doing good on earth.
T. N. Taylor (ed.) *Soeur Thérèse of Lisieux* (1912)
epilogue

25 After my death I will let fall a shower of
roses.
T. N. Taylor (ed.) *Soeur Thérèse of Lisieux* (1912)
epilogue

Tertullian c.AD 160–c.225

Roman theologian and Church Father from Carthage

1 'Look,' they say, 'how they [Christians] love one another' (for they themselves hate one another); 'and how they are ready to die for each other' (for they themselves are readier to kill each other).
usually quoted as, 'See how these Christians love one another'
Apologeticus ch. 39, sect. 7

2 As often as we are mown down by you, the more we grow in numbers; the blood of Christians is the seed.
traditionally 'The blood of the martyrs is the seed of the Church'
Apologeticus ch. 50, sect. 13

3 *Certum est quia impossibile est.*
It is certain because it is impossible.
often quoted as 'Credo quia impossibile'
De Carne Christi ch. 5

A. S. J. Tessimond 1902–62

4 Cats, no less liquid than their shadows,
Offer no angles to the wind.
Cats (1934) p. 20

William Makepeace Thackeray 1811–63

English novelist

5 Business first; pleasure afterwards.
The Rose and the Ring (1855) ch. 1

6 If a man's character is to be abused, say what you will, there's nobody like a relation to do the business.
Vanity Fair (1847–8) ch. 19

7 How to live well on nothing a year.
Vanity Fair (1847–8) ch. 36 (title)

8 I think I could be a good woman if I had five thousand a year.
Vanity Fair (1847–8) ch. 36

9 Which of us is happy in this world? Which of us has his desire? or, having it, is satisfied?—Come, children, let us shut up the box and the puppets, for our play is played out.
Vanity Fair (1847–8) ch. 67

10 Werther had a love for Charlotte
Such as words could never utter;
Would you know how first he met her?
She was cutting bread and butter.
'Sorrows of Werther' (1855)

Margaret Thatcher 1925–

British Conservative stateswoman; Prime Minister, 1979–90

11 No woman in my time will be Prime Minister or Chancellor or Foreign Secretary—not the top jobs. Anyway I wouldn't want to be Prime Minister. You have to give yourself 100%.
on her appointment as Shadow Education Spokesman
in *Sunday Telegraph* 26 October 1969

12 In politics if you want anything said, ask a man. If you want anything done, ask a woman.
in *People* (New York) 15 September 1975

13 I stand before you tonight in my red chiffon evening gown, my face softly made up, my fair hair gently waved . . . the Iron Lady of the Western World! Me? A cold war warrior? Well, yes—if that is how they wish to interpret my defence of values and freedoms fundamental to our way of life.
speech at Finchley, 31 January 1976; 'The Iron Lady' was the name given to her by the Soviet defence ministry newspaper *Red Star*, which accused her of trying to revive the cold war

14 No one would remember the Good Samaritan if he'd only had good intentions. He had money as well.
television interview, 6 January 1980

15 To those waiting with bated breath for that favourite media catchphrase, the U-turn, I have only this to say. 'You turn if you want; the lady's not for turning.'
speech at Conservative Party Conference in Brighton, 10 October 1980; see **Fry** 144:6

16 Just rejoice at that news and congratulate our armed forces and the Marines. Rejoice!
on the recapture of South Georgia, usually quoted as, 'Rejoice, rejoice!'
to newsmen outside 10 Downing Street, 25 April 1982

17 It is exciting to have a real crisis on your hands, when you have spent half your political life dealing with humdrum issues like the environment.
on the Falklands campaign, 1982
speech to Scottish Conservative Party conference, 14 May 1982, in Hugo Young *One of Us* (1990) ch. 13

18 I was asked whether I was trying to restore Victorian values. I said straight out I was. And I am.
speech to the British Jewish Community, 21 July 1983, referring to an interview earlier that year

19 Now it must be business as usual.
on the steps of Brighton police station a few hours after the bombing of the Grand Hotel, Brighton; often quoted as 'We shall carry on as usual'
in *The Times* 13 October 1984

20 We can do business together.
of Mikhail **Gorbachev**
in *The Times* 18 December 1984

21 We must try to find ways to starve the terrorist and the hijacker of the oxygen of publicity on which they depend.
speech to American Bar Association in London, 15 July 1985

22 There is no such thing as Society. There are individual men and women, and there are families.
in *Woman's Own* 31 October 1987

23 We have become a grandmother.
in *The Times* 4 March 1989

1 I am naturally very sorry to see you go, but understand . . . your wish to be able to spend more time with your family.
  reply to Norman **Fowler's** *resignation letter*
  in *Guardian* 4 January 1990; see **Fowler** 140:13

2 No! No! No!
  making clear her opposition to a single European currency, and more centralized controls from Brussels
  in the House of Commons, 30 October 1990

3 It's a funny old world.
  on withdrawing from the contest for leadership of the Conservative party
  comment, 22 November 1990

4 Home is where you come to when you have nothing better to do.
  in *Vanity Fair* May 1991

William Roscoe Thayer 1859–1923
American biographer and historian

5 Log-cabin to White House.
  title of biography (1910) of James **Garfield**

Themistocles *c.*528–*c.*462 BC
Greek historian and Athenian statesman

6 The wooden wall is your ships.
  *interpreting the words of the Delphic oracle to the Athenians, before the battle of Salamis in 480 BC,
  'That the wooden wall only shall not fall, but help you and your children'*
  Plutarch *Parallel Lives* 'Themistocles' bk. 2, ch. 1

Thomas à Kempis *c.*1380–1471
German ascetical writer

7 I would far rather feel remorse than know how to define it.
  De Imitatione Christi bk. 1, ch. 1, sect. 3

8 *O quam cito transit gloria mundi.*
  Oh how quickly the glory of the world passes away!
  De Imitatione Christi bk. 1, ch. 3, sect. 6; see **Anonymous** 13:20

9 For man proposes, but God disposes.
  De Imitatione Christi bk. 1, ch. 19, sect. 2

10 Never be completely idle, but either reading, or writing, or praying, or meditating, or at some useful work for the common good.
  De Imitatione Christi bk. 1, ch. 19, sect. 4

11 Today the man is here; tomorrow he is gone. And when he is 'out of sight', quickly also is he out of mind.
  De Imitatione Christi bk. 1, ch. 23, sect. 1

St Thomas Aquinas *c.*1225–74
Italian Dominican friar and Doctor of the Church

12 *Pange, lingua, gloriosi
  Corporis mysterium.*
  Now, my tongue, the mystery telling
  Of the glorious Body sing.
  'Pange Lingua Gloriosi' (Corpus Christi hymn, tr. J. M. Neale, E. Caswall, and others); see **Fortunatus** 139:20

13 *Tantum ergo sacramentum
  Veneremur cernui;
  Et antiquum documentum
  Novo cedat ritui.*
  Therefore we, before him bending,
  This great Sacrament revere;
  Types and shadows have their ending,
  For the newer rite is here.
  'Pange Lingua Gloriosi' (Corpus Christi hymn, tr. J. M. Neale, E. Caswall, and others)

14 Therefore it is necessary to arrive at a prime mover, put in motion by no other; and this everyone understands to be God.
  Summa Theologicae (*c.*1265) pt. 1, qu. 2, art. 3 (tr. English Dominican Fathers)

15 Everything I have written seems like straw by comparison with what I have seen and what has been revealed to me.
  following a mystical experience, after which he did no more teaching or writing
  on 6 December 1273

Brandon Thomas 1856–1914
English dramatist

16 I'm Charley's aunt from Brazil—where the nuts come from.
  Charley's Aunt (1892) act 1

Dylan Thomas 1914–53
Welsh poet

17 Though lovers be lost love shall not;
  And death shall have no dominion.
  'And death shall have no dominion' (1936); see **Bible** 50:3

18 Do not go gentle into that good night,
  Old age should burn and rave at close of day;
  Rage, rage against the dying of the light.
  'Do Not Go Gentle into that Good Night' (1952)

19 Oh as I was young and easy in the mercy of his means,
  Time held me green and dying
  Though I sang in my chains like the sea.
  'Fern Hill' (1946)

20 The force that through the green fuse drives the flower
  Drives my green age.
  'The force that through the green fuse drives the flower' (1934)

21 And I am dumb to tell the crooked rose
  My youth is bent by the same wintry fever.
  'The force that through the green fuse drives the flower' (1934)

22 The hand that signed the paper felled a city;
  Five sovereign fingers taxed the breath,
  Doubled the globe of dead and halved a country;
  These five kings did a king to death.
  'The hand that signed the paper felled a city' (1936)

23 It was my thirtieth year to heaven.
  'Poem in October' (1946)

24 There could I marvel
  My birthday
  Away but the weather turned around.
  'Poem in October' (1946)

1 After the first death, there is no other.
'A Refusal to Mourn the Death, by Fire, of a
Child in London' (1946)

2 I can never remember whether it snowed
for six days and six nights when I was
twelve or whether it snowed for twelve days
and twelve nights when I was six.
A Child's Christmas in Wales (1954)

3 Books that told me everything about the
wasp, except why.
A Child's Christmas in Wales (1954)

4 To begin at the beginning: It is spring,
moonless night in the small town, starless
and bible-black.
Under Milk Wood (1954)

5 The land of my fathers. My fathers can have
it.
of Wales
in *Adam* December 1953; see **James** 182:15

6 A man you don't like who drinks as much as
you do.
definition of an alcoholic
Constantine Fitzgibbon *Life of Dylan Thomas*
(1965) ch. 6

Edward Thomas 1878–1917
English poet

7 Yes; I remember Adlestrop—
The name, because one afternoon
Of heat the express-train drew up there
Unwontedly. It was late June.
'Adlestrop' (1917)

8 The past is the only dead thing that smells
sweet.
'Early one morning in May I set out' (1917)

Elizabeth Thomas 1675–1731
English poet

9 From marrying in haste, and repenting at
leisure;
Not liking the person, yet liking his
treasure:
Libera nos.
'A New Litany, occasioned by an invitation to a
wedding' (1722)

Gwyn Thomas 1913–81
Welsh novelist and dramatist

10 There are still parts of Wales where the only
concession to gaiety is a striped shroud.
in *Punch* 18 June 1958

R. S. Thomas 1913–2000
Welsh poet and clergyman

11 An impotent people,
Sick with inbreeding,
Worrying the carcase of an old song.
'Welsh Landscape' (1955)

Francis Thompson 1859–1907
English poet

12 As the run-stealers flicker to and fro,
To and fro:—
O my Hornby and my Barlow long ago!
'At Lord's' (1913)

13 Nothing begins, and nothing ends,
That is not paid with moan;
For we are born in other's pain,
And perish in our own.
'Daisy' (1913)

14 I fled Him, down the nights and down the
days;
I fled Him, down the arches of the years;
I fled Him, down the labyrinthine ways
Of my own mind; and in the mist of tears
I hid from Him, and under running
laughter.
'The Hound of Heaven' (1913) pt. 1

15 But with unhurrying chase,
And unperturbèd pace,
Deliberate speed, majestic instancy,
They beat—and a Voice beat
More instant than the Feet—
All things betray thee, who betrayest Me.
'The Hound of Heaven' (1913) pt. 1

16 Lo, all things fly thee, for thou fliest Me!'
'The Hound of Heaven' (1913) pt. 5

17 O world invisible, we view thee,
O world intangible, we touch thee,
O world unknowable, we know thee,
Inapprehensible, we clutch thee!
'The Kingdom of God' (1913)

18 'Tis ye, 'tis your estrangèd faces,
That miss the many-splendoured thing.
'The Kingdom of God' (1913)

19 Upon thy so sore loss
Shall shine the traffic of Jacob's ladder
Pitched betwixt Heaven and Charing Cross.
'The Kingdom of God' (1913)

20 And lo, Christ walking on the water
Not of Gennesareth, but Thames!
'The Kingdom of God' (1913)

21 Look for me in the nurseries of heaven.
'To My Godchild Francis M.W.M.' (1913)

Robert Norman Thompson 1914–97
American-born Canadian politician and academic

22 The Americans are our best friends whether
we like it or not.
Peter C. Newman *Home Country: People, Places,
and Power Politics* (1973)

James Thomson 1700–48
Scottish poet

23 When Britain first, at heaven's command,
Arose from out the azure main,
This was the charter of the land,
And guardian angels sung this strain:
'Rule, Britannia, rule the waves;
Britons never will be slaves.'
Alfred: a Masque (1740) act 2

24 Delightful task! to rear the tender thought,
To teach the young idea how to shoot.
The Seasons (1746) 'Spring' l. 1152

25 An elegant sufficiency, content,
Retirement, rural quiet, friendship, books.
The Seasons (1746) 'Spring' l. 1161

1 Sighed and looked unutterable things.
The Seasons (1746) 'Summer' l. 1188

James Thomson 1834–82
Scottish poet

2 The city of dreadful night.
title of poem, written 1870–3

3 Give a man a horse he can ride,
Give a man a boat he can sail.
'Sunday up the River' (written 1865) st. 15

Roy Thomson 1894–1976
Canadian-born British newspaper proprietor

4 Like having your own licence to print money.
on the profitability of commercial television in Britain
R. Braddon *Roy Thomson* (1965) ch. 32

Henry David Thoreau 1817–62
American writer

5 I heartily accept the motto, 'That government is best which governs least' . . . Carried out, it finally amounts to this, which I also believe,— 'That government is best which governs not at all.'
Civil Disobedience (1849); see **O'Sullivan** 255:19

6 Under a government which imprisons any unjustly, the true place for a just man is also a prison.
Civil Disobedience (1849)

7 What does education often do? It makes a straight-cut ditch of a free, meandering brook.
Journal c.November 1850

8 Some circumstantial evidence is very strong, as when you find a trout in the milk.
Journal 11 November 1850

9 Not that the story need be long, but it will take a long while to make it short.
letter to Harrison Blake, 16 November 1857; see **Pascal** 259:16

10 I have travelled a good deal in Concord.
Walden (1854) 'Economy'

11 As if you could kill time without injuring eternity.
Walden (1854) 'Economy'

12 The mass of men lead lives of quiet desperation.
Walden (1854) 'Economy'

13 In any weather, at any hour of the day or night, I have been anxious to improve the nick of time, and notch it on my stick too; to stand on the meeting of two eternities, the past and the future, which is precisely the present moment; to toe that line.
Walden (1854) 'Economy'

14 Beware of all enterprises that require new clothes.
Walden (1854) 'Economy'

15 The three-o'-clock in the morning courage, which Bonaparte thought was the rarest.
Walden (1854) 'Sounds'; see **Napoleon** 248:3

16 Wherever a man goes, men will pursue him and paw him with their dirty institutions, and, if they can, constrain him to belong to their desperate oddfellow society.
Walden (1854) 'The Village'

17 I had three chairs in my house; one for solitude, two for friendship, three for society.
Walden (1854) 'Visitors'

18 I wanted to live deep and suck out all the marrow of life . . . to drive life into a corner, and reduce it to its lowest terms, and, if it proved to be mean, why then to get the whole and genuine meanness of it, and publish its meanness to the world; or if it were sublime, to know it by experience.
Walden (1854) 'Where I lived, and what I lived for'

19 Our life is frittered away by detail . . . Simplify, simplify.
Walden (1854) 'Where I lived, and what I lived for'

20 I once had a sparrow alight upon my shoulder for a moment while I was hoeing in a village garden, and I felt that I was more distinguished by that circumstance than I should have been by any epaulette I could have worn.
Walden (1854) 'Winter Animals'

21 It is not worthwhile to go around the world to count the cats in Zanzibar.
Walden (1854) 'Conclusion'

22 If a man does not keep pace with his companions, perhaps it is because he hears a different drummer. Let him step to the music which he hears, however measured or far away.
Walden (1854) 'Conclusion'

23 It takes two to speak the truth,—one to speak, and another to hear.
A Week on the Concord and Merrimack Rivers (1849) 'Wednesday'

Jeremy Thorpe 1929–
British Liberal politician

24 Greater love hath no man than this, that he lay down his friends for his life.
on Harold **Macmillan**'s *sacking seven of his Cabinet on 13 July 1962*
D. E. Butler and Anthony King *The General Election of 1964* (1965) ch. 1; see **Bible** 49:7

Thucydides c.455–c.400 BC
Greek historian

25 I have written my work, not as an essay which is to win the applause of the moment, but as a possession for all time.
History of the Peloponnesian War bk. 1, ch. 22, sect. 18 (tr. Richard Crawley, 1874)

26 Happiness depends on being free, and freedom depends on being courageous.
History of the Peloponnesian War bk. 2, ch. 4, sect. 43 (tr. Rex Warner)

1 Of the gods we believe, and of men we
know, that by a necessary law of their
nature they rule wherever they can.
History of the Peloponnesian War bk. 5, ch. 105

James Thurber 1894–1961
American humorist

2 Her own mother lived the latter years of her
life in the horrible suspicion that electricity
was dripping invisibly all over the house.
My Life and Hard Times (1933) ch. 2

3 You might as well fall flat on your face as
lean over too far backward.
'The Bear Who Let It Alone' in *New Yorker* 29
April 1939

4 Early to rise and early to bed makes a male
healthy and wealthy and dead.
'The Shrike and the Chipmunks' in *New Yorker*
18 February 1939

5 It's a naïve domestic Burgundy without any
breeding, but I think you'll be amused by its
presumption.
cartoon caption in *New Yorker* 27 March 1937

6 Well, if I called the wrong number, why did
you answer the phone?
cartoon caption in *New Yorker* 5 June 1937

7 Humour is emotional chaos remembered in
tranquillity.
in *New York Post* 29 February 1960; see
Wordsworth 366:19

Edward, Lord Thurlow 1731–1806
English jurist

8 Corporations have neither bodies to be
punished, nor souls to be condemned, they
therefore do as they like.
*usually quoted as 'Did you ever expect a
corporation to have a conscience, when it has no
soul to be damned, and no body to be kicked?'*
John Poynder *Literary Extracts* (1844) vol. 1; see
Coke 99:15

Chidiock Tichborne *c.*1558–86
English Roman Catholic conspirator

9 My prime of youth is but a frost of cares;
My feast of joy is but a dish of pain;
My crop of corn is but a field of tares;
And all my good is but vain hope of gain.
The day is past, and yet I saw no sun;
And now I live, and now my life is done.
'Elegy' (composed in the Tower of London prior
to his execution)

Lionel Tiger 1937–
American anthropologist

10 Male bonding.
Men in Groups (1969)

Paul Tillich 1886–1965
German-born Protestant theologian

11 Neurosis is the way of avoiding non-being by
avoiding being.
The Courage To Be (1952) pt. 2, ch. 3

12 Faith is the state of being ultimately
concerned.
Dynamics of Faith (1957) ch. 1

Tipu Sultan *c.*1750–99

13 In this world I would rather live two days
like a tiger, than two hundred years like a
sheep.
Alexander Beatson *A View of the Origin and
Conduct of the War with Tippoo Sultan* (1800) ch. 10

Titus AD 39–81
Roman emperor from AD 79

14 *Amici, diem perdidi.*
Friends, I have lost a day.
*on reflecting that he had done nothing to help
anybody all day*
Suetonius *Lives of the Caesars* 'Titus' ch. 8, sect. 1

Alexis de Tocqueville 1805–59
French historian and politician

15 History is a gallery of pictures in which
there are few originals and many copies.
L'Ancien régime (1856)

16 Experience shows that the most dangerous
moment for a bad government is generally
that in which it sets about reform.
L'Ancien régime (1856)

17 Their starting point is different, and their
courses are not the same; yet each of them
seems to be marked out by the will of
Heaven to sway the destinies of half the
globe.
referring to Russia and America
De la Démocratie en Amérique (1835–40) vol. 1

Alvin Toffler 1928–
American writer

18 Culture shock is relatively mild in
comparison with a much more serious
malady that might be called 'future shock'.
Future shock is the dizzying disorientation
brought on by the premature arrival of the
future.
in *Horizon* Summer 1965; the book *Future Shock*
was published 1970

J. R. R. Tolkien 1892–1973
British philologist and writer

19 In a hole in the ground there lived a hobbit.
The Hobbit (1937)

20 What has it got in its pocketses?
Gollum trying to solve Bilbo's riddle
The Hobbit (1937) ch. 5

21 Never laugh at live dragons.
The Hobbit (1937) ch. 12

22 One Ring to rule them all, One Ring to find
them
One Ring to bring them all and in the
darkness bind them.
The Lord of the Rings pt. 1 *The Fellowship of the Ring*
(1954) epigraph

1 Do not meddle in the affairs of Wizards, for they are subtle and quick to anger.
The Lord of the Rings pt. 1 *The Fellowship of the Ring* (1954) bk. 1, ch. 3

2 Precious . . . My Precious!
Gollum, referring to the Ring
The Lord of the Rings pt. 3 *The Return of the King* (1955) bk. 6, ch. 3

Leo Tolstoy 1828–1910
Russian novelist

3 All happy families resemble one another, but each unhappy family is unhappy in its own way.
Anna Karenina (1875–7) pt. 1, ch. 1 (tr. A. and L. Maude)

4 Our body is a machine for living. It is organized for that, it is its nature. Let life go on in it unhindered and let it defend itself, it will do more than if you paralyse it by encumbering it with remedies.
War and Peace (1865–9) bk. 10, ch. 29 (tr. A. and L. Maude); see **Le Corbusier** 211:8

5 I sit on a man's back, choking him and making him carry me, and yet assure myself and others that I am very sorry for him and wish to ease his lot by all possible means—except by getting off his back.
What Then Must We Do? (1886) ch. 16 (tr. A. Maude)

6 All newspaper and journalistic activity is an intellectual brothel from which there is no retreat.
letter to Prince V. P. Meshchersky, 22 August 1871

Augustus Montague Toplady 1740–78
English clergyman

7 Rock of Ages, cleft for me,
Let me hide myself in Thee.
Let the water and the blood,
From Thy riven side which flowed,
Be of sin the double cure,
Cleanse me from its guilt and power.
'Rock of Ages, cleft for me' (1776 hymn)

Cyril Tourneur *see* Thomas Middleton

Pete Townshend 1945–
British rock musician and songwriter

8 Hope I die before I get old.
'My Generation' (1965 song)

Arnold Toynbee 1889–1975
English historian

9 Civilization is a movement and not a condition, a voyage and not a harbour.
in *Readers Digest* October 1958

Thomas Traherne *c.*1637–74
English mystic

10 You never enjoy the world aright, till the sea itself floweth in your veins, till you are clothed with the heavens, and crowned with the stars: and perceive yourself to be the sole heir of the whole world.
Centuries of Meditations 'First Century' sect. 29

11 The corn was orient and immortal wheat, which never should be reaped, nor was ever sown. I thought it had stood from everlasting to everlasting.
Centuries of Meditations 'Third Century' sect. 3

Merle Travis 1917–83
American country singer

12 Sixteen tons, what do you get?
Another day older and deeper in debt.
Say brother, don't you call me 'cause I can't go
I owe my soul to the company store.
'Sixteen Tons' (1947 song)

Herbert Beerbohm Tree 1852–1917
English actor-manager

13 He is an old bore. Even the grave yawns for him.
of Israel **Zangwill**
Max Beerbohm *Herbert Beerbohm Tree* (1920) appendix 4

14 Sirs, I have tested your machine. It adds a new terror to life and makes death a long-felt want.
when pressed by a gramophone company for a written testimonial
Hesketh Pearson *Beerbohm Tree* (1956) ch. 19

G. M. Trevelyan 1876–1962
English historian

15 Disinterested intellectual curiosity is the life-blood of real civilization.
English Social History (1942) introduction

16 If the French noblesse had been capable of playing cricket with their peasants, their chateaux would never have been burnt.
English Social History (1942) ch. 8

17 [Education] has produced a vast population able to read but unable to distinguish what is worth reading.
English Social History (1942) ch. 18

David Trimble 1944–
Northern Irish Ulster Unionist politician

18 We are not here to negotiate with them, but to confront them.
on entering the Mitchell talks on Northern Ireland with Sinn Feinn
in *Guardian* 18 September 1997

Tommy Trinder 1909–89
British comedian

19 Overpaid, overfed, oversexed, and over here.
of American troops in Britain during the Second World War
associated with Trinder, but probably not his invention

Anthony Trollope 1815–82
English novelist

1 Three hours a day will produce as much as a man ought to write.
Autobiography (1883) ch. 15

2 Those who have courage to love should have courage to suffer.
The Bertrams (1859) ch. 27

3 Never think that you're not good enough yourself. A man should never think that. My belief is that in life people will take you very much at your own reckoning.
The Small House at Allington (1864) ch. 32

4 Love is like any other luxury. You have no right to it unless you can afford it.
The Way We Live Now (1875) ch. 84

Leon Trotsky 1879–1940
Russian revolutionary

5 Old age is the most unexpected of all things that happen to a man.
Diary in Exile (1959) 8 May 1935

6 You [the Mensheviks] are pitiful isolated individuals; you are bankrupts; your role is played out. Go where you belong from now on — into the dustbin of history!
History of the Russian Revolution (1933) vol. 3, ch. 10; see **Birrell** 55:2

Pierre Trudeau 1919–2000
Canadian Liberal statesman, Prime Minister, 1968–79 and 1980–4

7 The state has no place in the nation's bedrooms.
interview, Ottawa, 22 December 1967

8 Living next to you is in some ways like sleeping with an elephant. No matter how friendly and even-tempered the beast, one is affected by every twitch and grunt.
on relations between Canada and the US
speech at National Press Club, Washington DC, 25 March 1969

Harry S. Truman 1884–1972
American Democratic statesman, 33rd President of the US 1945–53

9 *to reporters the day after his accession to the Presidency on the death of Franklin D. Roosevelt:*
When they told me yesterday what had happened, I felt like the moon, the stars and all the planets had fallen on me.
on 13 April 1945

10 All the President is, is a glorified public relations man who spends his time flattering, kissing and kicking people to get them to do what they are supposed to do anyway.
letter to his sister, 14 November 1947, in *Off the Record* (1980)

11 If you can't stand the heat, get out of the kitchen.
associated with Truman, but attributed by him to Harry Vaughan, his 'military jester'; in *Time* 28 April 1952

12 I never give them [the public] hell. I just tell the truth, and they think it is hell.
in *Look* 3 April 1956

13 A statesman is a politician who's been dead 10 or 15 years.
in *New York World Telegram and Sun* 12 April 1958

14 It's a recession when your neighbour loses his job; it's a depression when you lose yours.
in *Observer* 13 April 1958

15 Wherever you have an efficient government you have a dictatorship.
lecture at Columbia University, 28 April 1959, in *Truman Speaks* (1960)

16 I didn't fire him [General MacArthur] because he was a dumb son of a bitch, although he was, but that's not against the law for generals. If it was, half to three-quarters of them would be in jail.
Merle Miller *Plain Speaking* (1974) ch. 24

17 Always be sincere, even if you don't mean it.
attributed

18 The buck stops here.
unattributed motto on Truman's desk

Donald Trump 1946–
American businessman

19 Deals are my art form. Other people paint beautifully on canvas or write wonderful poetry. I like making deals, preferably big deals. That's how I get my kicks.
Donald Trump and Tony Schwartz *The Art of the Deal* (1987)

Sojourner Truth c.1797–1883
American evangelist and reformer

20 That man . . . says that women need to be helped into carriages, and lifted over ditches . . . Nobody ever helps me into carriages, or over mud puddles, or gives me any best place, and aren't I a woman? . . . I have ploughed, and planted, and gathered into barns, and no man could head me—and aren't I a woman?
speech at Women's Rights Convention, Akron, Ohio, 1851

21 That little man . . . he says women can't have as much rights as men, cause Christ wasn't a woman. Where did your Christ come from? From God and a woman. Man had nothing to do with Him.
speech at Women's Rights Convention, Akron, Ohio, 1851

Sophie Tucker 1884–1966
Russian-born American vaudeville artiste

22 From birth to 18 a girl needs good parents. From 18 to 35, she needs good looks. From 35 to 55, good personality. From 55 on, she needs good cash.
Michael Freedland *Sophie* (1978)

Ivan Turgenev 1818–83
Russian novelist

1 Nature is not a temple, but a workshop, and man's the workman in it.
  Fathers and Sons (1862) ch. 9 (tr. Rosemary Edmonds)

2 Whatever a man prays for, he prays for a miracle. Every prayer reduces itself to this: Great God, grant that twice two be not four.
  Poems in Prose (1881) 'Prayer'

A. R. J. Turgot 1727–81
French economist and statesman

3 *Eripuit coelo fulmen, sceptrumque tyrannis.*
  He snatched the lightning shaft from heaven, and the sceptre from tyrants.
  inscription for a bust of Benjamin **Franklin**, inventor of the lightning conductor; see **Manilius** 227:1

J. M. W. Turner 1775–1851
English landscape painter

4 If I could find anything blacker than black, I'd use it.
  when a friend complained of the blackness of the sails in 'Peace—Burial at Sea' (1844)
  in *Dictionary of National Biography* (1917–)

Walter James Redfern Turner 1889–1946
British writer and critic

5 When I was but thirteen or so
  I went into a golden land,
  Chimborazo, Cotopaxi
  Took me by the hand.
  'Romance' (1916)

Mark Twain 1835–1910
American writer

6 There was things which he stretched, but mainly he told the truth.
  The Adventures of Huckleberry Finn (1884) ch. 1

7 All kings is mostly rapscallions.
  The Adventures of Huckleberry Finn (1884) ch. 23

8 Hain't we got all the fools in town on our side? and ain't that a big enough majority in any town?
  The Adventures of Huckleberry Finn (1884) ch. 26

9 Soap and education are not as sudden as a massacre, but they are more deadly in the long run.
  A Curious Dream (1872) 'Facts concerning the Recent Resignation'

10 Truth is the most valuable thing we have. Let us economize it.
  Following the Equator (1897) ch. 7; see **Armstrong** 16:9

11 It is by the goodness of God that in our country we have those three unspeakably precious things: freedom of speech, freedom of conscience, and the prudence never to practise either of them.
  Following the Equator (1897) ch. 20

12 Man is the Only Animal that Blushes. Or needs to.
  Following the Equator (1897) ch. 27

13 There are several good protections against temptations, but the surest is cowardice.
  Following the Equator (1897) ch. 36

14 It takes your enemy and your friend, working together, to hurt you to the heart: the one to slander you and the other to get the news to you.
  Following the Equator (1897) ch. 45

15 The innocents abroad.
  title of book (1869)

16 They spell it Vinci and pronounce it Vinchy; foreigners always spell better than they pronounce.
  The Innocents Abroad (1869) ch. 19

17 There are laws to protect the freedom of the press's speech, but none that are worth anything to protect the people from the press.
  'License of the Press' (1873)

18 What a good thing Adam had. When he said a good thing he knew nobody had said it before.
  Notebooks (1935)

19 Familiarity breeds contempt—and children.
  Notebooks (1935)

20 Good breeding consists in concealing how much we think of ourselves and how little we think of the other person.
  Notebooks (1935)

21 Adam was but human—this explains it all. He did not want the apple for the apple's sake; he wanted it only because it was forbidden.
  Pudd'nhead Wilson (1894) ch. 2

22 Whoever has lived long enough to find out what life is, knows how deep a debt of gratitude we owe to Adam, the first great benefactor of our race. He brought death into the world.
  Pudd'nhead Wilson (1894) ch. 3

23 Cauliflower is nothing but cabbage with a college education.
  Pudd'nhead Wilson (1894) ch. 5

24 When angry, count four; when very angry, swear.
  Pudd'nhead Wilson (1894) ch. 10

25 As to the Adjective: when in doubt, strike it out.
  Pudd'nhead Wilson (1894) ch. 11

26 Few things are harder to put up with than the annoyance of a good example.
  Pudd'nhead Wilson (1894) ch. 19

27 There is a sumptuous variety about the New England weather that compels the stranger's admiration—and regret. The weather is always doing something there; always attending strictly to business; always

getting up new designs and trying them on the people to see how they will go.

speech to New England Society, 22 December 1876, in *Speeches* (1910)

1 All you need in this life is ignorance and confidence; then success is sure.

letter to Mrs Foote, 2 December 1887, in B. DeCasseres *When Huck Finn Went Highbrow* (1934)

2 The report of my death was an exaggeration.

usually quoted as 'Reports of my death have been greatly exaggerated'
in *New York Journal* 2 June 1897

3 Get your facts first, and then you can distort them as much as you please.

Rudyard Kipling *From Sea to Sea* (1899) letter 37

Kenneth Tynan 1927–80
English theatre critic

4 A critic is a man who knows the way but can't drive the car.

in *New York Times Magazine* 9 January 1966

5 'Sergeant Pepper'—a decisive moment in the history of Western Civilization.

in 1967; Howard Elson *McCartney* (1986)

6 A neurosis is a secret you don't know you're keeping.

Kathleen Tynan *Life of Kenneth Tynan* (1987) ch. 19

William Tyndale c.1494–1536
English translator of the Bible and Protestant martyr

7 If God spare my life, ere many years I will cause a boy that driveth the plough shall know more of the scripture than thou doest!

to an opponent
in *Dictionary of National Biography* (1917–)

8 Lord, open the King of England's eyes!

at the stake
John Foxe *Actes and Monuments* (1570)

Harlan K. Ullman and James P. Wade
American strategic analysts

9 The basis for rapid dominance rests in the ability to affect the will, perception, and understanding of the adversary through imposing sufficient Shock and Awe to achieve the necessary political, strategic, and operational goals of the conflict or crisis that led to the use of force.

Shock and Awe: Achieving Rapid Dominance (1996) ch. 2

Ulpian d. 228
Roman jurist

10 *Nulla iniuria est, quae in volentem fiat.*
No injustice is done to someone who wants that thing done.

usually quoted as 'Volenti non fit iniuria'
Corpus Iuris Civilis Digests bk. 47, ch. 10, sect. 1, subsect. 5

Miguel de Unamuno 1864–1937
Spanish philosopher and writer

11 *La vida es duda,*
y la fe sin la duda es sólo muerte.
Life is doubt,
And faith without doubt is nothing but death.

Poesías (1907) 'Salmo II'

The Upanishads
Hindu sacred treatises written in Sanskrit
c.800–200 BC

12 From delusion lead me to Truth.
From darkness lead me to Light.
from death lead me to immortality.

Brihadāranyaka Upanishad ch. 1, pt. 3, v. 28; see **Kumar** 206:5

13 *Shantih, shantih, shantih.*
Peace! Peace! Peace!

Taittirīya Upanishad ch. 1, pt. 1, mantra; see **Eliot** 130:3

14 Abiding in the midst of ignorance, thinking themselves wise and learned, fools go aimlessly hither and thither, like blind led by the blind.

Katha Upanishad ch. 2, v. 5; see **Bible** 45:6

15 If any man thinks he slays, and if another thinks he is slain, neither knows the ways of truth. The Eternal in man cannot kill: the Eternal in man cannot die.

Katha Upanishad ch. 2, v. 19; see **Bhagavadgita** 33:19, **Emerson** 131:18

John Updike 1932–
American novelist and short-story writer

16 America is a vast conspiracy to make you happy.

Problems (1980) 'How to Love America and Leave it at the Same Time'

17 Celebrity is a mask that eats into the face.

Self-Consciousness: Memoirs (1989)

18 Neutrinos, they are very small
They have no charge and have no mass
And do not interact at all.

'Cosmic Gall ' (1964)

19 The artist brings something into the world that didn't exist before, and . . . he does it without destroying something else.

George Plimpton (ed.) *Writers at Work* (4th series, 1977) ch. 16

Peter Ustinov 1921–2004
Russian-born actor, director, and writer

20 Laughter . . . the most civilized music in the world.

Dear Me (1977) ch. 3

21 I do not believe that friends are necessarily the people you like best, they are merely the people who got there first.

Dear Me (1977) ch. 5

22 At the age of four with paper hats and wooden swords we're all Generals. Only some of us never grow out of it.

Romanoff and Juliet (1956) act 1

Paul Valéry 1871-1945
French poet, critic, and man of letters

1 God created man and, finding him not sufficiently alone, gave him a companion to make him feel his solitude more keenly.
   Tel Quel 1 (1941) 'Moralités'

2 Politics is the art of preventing people from taking part in affairs which properly concern them.
   Tel Quel 2 (1943) 'Rhumbs'

John Vanbrugh 1664-1726
English architect and dramatist

3 BELINDA: Ay, but you know we must return good for evil.
   LADY BRUTE: That may be a mistake in the translation.
   The Provoked Wife (1697) act 1, sc. 1

4 So, now I am in for Hobbes's voyage, a great leap in the dark.
   'Heartfree' on marriage
   The Provoked Wife (1697) act 5, sc. 5; see **Hobbes** 170:23

5 When once a woman has given you her heart, you can never get rid of the rest of her body.
   The Relapse (1696) act 3, sc. 1

Vivian van Damm *c.*1889-1960
British theatre manager

6 We never closed.
   of the Windmill Theatre, London, during the Second World War
   Tonight and Every Night (1952) ch. 18

William Henry Vanderbilt 1821-85
American railway magnate

7 The public be damned!
   on whether the public should be consulted about luxury trains
   letter from A. W. Cole to *New York Times* 25 August 1918

Laurens van der Post 1906-96
South African explorer and writer

8 Human beings are perhaps never more frightening than when they are convinced beyond doubt that they are right.
   Lost World of the Kalahari (1958)

9 I don't think a man who has watched the sun going down could walk away and commit a murder.
   in *Daily Telegraph* 17 December 1996; obituary

Henry Van Dyke 1852-1933
American Presbyterian minister and writer

10 Time is
   Too slow for those who wait,
   Too swift for those who fear,
   Too long for those who grieve,
   Too short for those who rejoice;
   But for those who love,

Time is eternity.
   'Time is too slow for those who wait' (1905), read at the funeral of **Diana**, Princess of Wales; Nigel Rees in 'Quote . . . Unquote' October 1997 notes that the original form of the last line is 'Time is not'

Vincent Van Gogh 1853-90
Dutch painter

11 I cannot help it that my pictures do not sell. Nevertheless the time will come when people will see that they are worth more than the price of the paint.
   letter to his brother Theo, 20 October 1888

Bartolomeo Vanzetti 1888-1927
American anarchist, born in Italy

12 If it had not been for these thing, I might have live out my life talking at street corners to scorning men. I might have die, unmarked, unknown, a failure. Now we are not a failure. This is our career and our triumph.
   statement after being sentenced to death, in M. D. Frankfurter and G. Jackson *Letters of Sacco and Vanzetti* (1928) preface

Michel Vaucaire
French songwriter

13 Non! rien de rien,
   Non! je ne regrette rien.
   No, no regrets,
   No, we will have no regrets.
   'Non, je ne regrette rien' (1960 song); sung by Edith Piaf

Henry Vaughan 1622-95
English poet

14 My soul, there is a country
   Far beyond the stars,
   Where stands a wingèd sentry
   All skilful in the wars.
   Silex Scintillans (1650-5) 'Peace'

15 And in those weaker glories spy
   Some shadows of eternity.
   Silex Scintillans (1650-5) 'The Retreat'

16 But felt through all this fleshly dress
   Bright shoots of everlastingness.
   Silex Scintillans (1650-5) 'The Retreat'

17 They are all gone into the world of light,
   And I alone sit lingering here.
   Silex Scintillans (1650-5) 'They are all gone'

18 Dear, beauteous death! the jewel of the just,
   Shining nowhere but in the dark.
   Silex Scintillans (1650-5) 'They are all gone'

19 I saw Eternity the other night,
   Like a great ring of pure and endless light,
   All calm, as it was bright.
   Silex Scintillans (1650-5) 'The World'

Thorstein Veblen 1857-1929
American economist and social scientist

20 Conspicuous consumption of valuable goods is a means of reputability to the gentleman of leisure.
   Theory of the Leisure Class (1899) ch. 4

Vegetius fl. AD 379–95
Roman military writer

1 *Qui desiderat pacem, praeparet bellum.*
Let him who desires peace, prepare for war.
usually quoted as 'Si vis pacem, para bellum [If
you want peace, prepare for war]'
Epitoma Rei Militaris bk. 3, prologue; see
Aristotle 15:14

Robert Venturi 1925–
American architect

2 Less is a bore.
Complexity and Contradiction in Architecture (1966)
ch. 2

Pierre Vergniaud 1753–93
French revolutionary

3 There was reason to fear that the
Revolution, like Saturn, might devour in
turn each one of her children.
Alphonse de Lamartine *Histoire des Girondins*
(1847) bk. 38, ch. 20

Paul Verlaine 1844–96
French poet

4 *Il pleure dans mon coeur
Comme il pleut sur la ville.*
Tears are shed in my heart like the rain on
the town.
Romances sans paroles (1874) 'Ariettes oubliées'
no. 3

Vespasian AD 9–79
Roman emperor from AD 69

5 *Pecunia non olet.*
Money has no smell.
upon **Titus***'s objecting to his tax on public
lavatories, Vespasian held a coin to Titus's nose;
on being told it didn't smell, he replied,* 'Atque e
lotio est [Yes, that's made from urine]'
traditional summary of Suetonius *Lives of the
Caesars* 'Vespasian' sect. 23

6 *Vae, puto deus fio.*
Woe is me, I think I am becoming a god.
when fatally ill
Suetonius *Lives of the Caesars* 'Vespasian' sect. 23,
subsect. 4

7 An emperor ought to die standing.
last words; Suetonius *Lives of the Caesars*
'Vespasian' sect. 24

Queen Victoria 1819–1901
*British monarch, Queen of the United Kingdom
from 1837*

8 I will be good.
*on being shown a chart of the line of succession, 11
March 1830*
Theodore Martin *The Prince Consort* (1875) vol. 1,
ch. 2

9 He speaks to Me as if I was a public meeting.
of **Gladstone**
G. W. E. Russell *Collections and Recollections* (1898)
ch. 14

10 We are not interested in the possibilities of
defeat; they do not exist.
*on the Boer War during 'Black Week', December
1899*
Lady Gwendolen Cecil *Life of Robert, Marquis of
Salisbury* (1931) vol. 3, ch. 6

11 We are not amused.
attributed, in Caroline Holland *Notebooks of a
Spinster Lady* (1919) ch. 21, 2 January 1900

Gore Vidal 1925–
American novelist and critic

12 Whenever a friend succeeds, a little
something in me dies.
in *Sunday Times Magazine* 16 September 1973

13 *of Truman* **Capote***'s death:*
Good career move.
attributed, 1984

José Antonio Viera Gallo 1943–
Chilean politician

14 Socialism can only arrive by bicycle.
Ivan Illich *Energy and Equity* (1974) epigraph

Gilles Vigneault 1928–
Canadian singer, songwriter, and poet

15 *Mon pays ce n'est pas un pays, c'est l'hiver.*
My country is not a country, it is winter.
'Mon Pays' (1964)

**Philippe-Auguste Villiers de
L'Isle-Adam** 1838–89
French writer

16 Living? The servants will do that for us.
Axël (1890) pt. 4, sect. 2

François Villon *c.*1431– after 63
French poet

17 *Mais où sont les neiges d'antan?*
But where are the snows of yesteryear?
Le Grand Testament (1461) 'Ballade des dames du
temps jadis' (tr. D. G. Rossetti)

St Vincent of Lerins d. *c.*450

18 *Quod ubique, quod semper, quod ab omnibus
creditum est.*
What is everywhere, what is always, what is
by all people believed.
Commonitorium Primum sect. 2

Virgil 70–19 BC
Roman poet

19 *Arma virumque cano, Troiae qui primus ab oris
Italiam fato profugus Laviniaque venit
Litora, multum ille et terris iactatus et alto
Vi superum, saevae memorem Iunonis ob iram.*
I sing of arms and the man who first from
the shores of Troy came destined an exile to
Italy and the Lavinian beaches, a man much
buffeted on land and on the deep by force of
the gods because of fierce Juno's never-
forgetting anger.
Aeneid bk. 1, l. 1; see **Dryden** 122:19

1 *Forsan et haec olim meminisse iuvabit.*
Maybe one day it will be cheering to
remember even these things.
Aeneid bk. 1, l. 203

2 *Dux femina facti.*
The leader of the enterprise a woman.
Aeneid bk. 1, l. 364

3 *Sunt lacrimae rerum et mentem mortalia tangunt.*
There are tears shed for things even here
and mortality touches the heart.
Aeneid bk. 1, l. 462

4 *Equo ne crede, Teucri.*
Quidquid id est, timeo Danaos et dona ferentes.
Do not trust the horse, Trojans. Whatever it
is, I fear the Greeks even when they bring
gifts.
Aeneid bk. 2, l. 48

5 *Dis aliter visum.*
The gods thought otherwise.
Aeneid bk. 2, l. 428

6 *Quid non mortalia pectora cogis,*
Auri sacra fames!
To what do you not drive human hearts,
cursed craving for gold!
Aeneid bk. 3, l. 56

7 *Agnosco veteris vestigia flammae.*
I feel again a spark of that ancient flame.
Aeneid bk. 4, l. 23; see **Dante** 109:14

8 *Varium et mutabile semper*
Femina.
Fickle and changeable always is woman.
Aeneid bk. 4, l. 569

9 *Hos successus alit: possunt, quia posse videntur.*
These success encourages: they can because
they think they can.
Aeneid bk. 5, l. 231

10 *Bella, horrida bella,*
Et Thybrim multo spumantem sanguine cerno.
I see wars, horrible wars, and the Tiber
foaming with much blood.
Aeneid bk. 6, l. 86; see **Powell** 270:12

11 *Facilis descensus Averno:*
Noctes atque dies patet atri ianua Ditis;
Sed revocare gradum superasque evadere ad
auras,
Hoc opus, hic labor est.
Easy is the way down to the Underworld: by
night and by day dark Hades' door stands
open; but to retrace one's steps and to make
a way out to the upper air, that's the task,
that is the labour.
Aeneid bk. 6, l. 126

12 *Stabant orantes primi transmittere cursum*
Tendebantque manus ripae ulterioris amore.
They stood begging to be the first to make
the voyage over and they reached out their
hands in longing for the further shore.
Aeneid bk. 6, l. 313

13 *Spiritus intus alit, totamque infusa per artus*
Mens agitat molem et magno se corpore miscet.
The spirit within nourishes, and mind
instilled throughout the living parts

activates the whole mass and mingles with
the vast frame.
Aeneid bk. 6, l. 726

14 *Tu regere imperio populos, Romane, memento*
(Hae tibi erunt artes), pacique imponere morem,
Parcere subiectis et debellare superbos.
You, Roman, make your task to rule nations
by your government (these shall be your
skills), to impose ordered ways upon a state
of peace, to spare those who have submitted
and to subdue the arrogant.
Aeneid bk. 6, l. 851

15 *Geniumque loci primamque deorum*
Tellurem Nymphasque et adhuc ignota precatur
Flumina.
He prays to the spirit of the place and to
Earth, the first of the gods, and to the
Nymphs and as yet unknown rivers.
Aeneid bk. 7, l. 136; see **Pope** 266:28

16 *Flectere si nequeo superos, Acheronta movebo.*
If I am unable to make the gods above
relent, I shall move Hell.
Aeneid bk. 7, l. 312

17 *Macte nova virtute, puer, sic itur ad astra.*
Blessings on your young courage, boy; that's
the way to the stars.
Aeneid bk. 9, l. 611

18 *Audentis Fortuna iuvat.*
Fortune assists the bold.
often quoted as 'Fortune favours the brave'
Aeneid bk. 10, l. 284; see **Terence** 335:14

19 *Experto credite.*
Trust one who has gone through it.
Aeneid bk. 11, l. 283

20 *Latet anguis in herba.*
There's a snake hidden in the grass.
Eclogues no. 3, l. 93

21 *Ultima Cumaei venit iam carminis aetas;*
Magnus ab integro saeclorum nascitur ordo.
Iam redit et virgo, redeunt Saturnia regna,
Iam nova progenies caelo demittitur alto.
Now has come the last age according to the
oracle at Cumae; the great series of lifetimes
starts anew. Now too the virgin goddess
returns, the golden days of Saturn's reign
return, now a new race is sent down from
high heaven.
Eclogues no. 4, l. 4

22 *Ambo florentes aetatibus, Arcades ambo,*
Et cantare pares et respondere parati.
Both in the flower of their youth, Arcadians
both, and matched and ready alike to start a
song and to respond.
Eclogues no. 7, l. 4

23 *Nunc scio quid sit Amor.*
Now I know what Love is.
Eclogues no. 8, l. 43

24 *Non omnia possumus omnes.*
We can't all do everything.
Eclogues no. 8, l. 63; see **Lucilius** 220:11

25 *Omnia vincit Amor: et nos cedamus Amori.*

Love conquers all things: let us too give in to Love.
Eclogues no. 10, l. 69; see **Chaucer** 91:16

1 *Ultima Thule.*
Farthest Thule.
Georgics no. 1, l. 30

2 *Ter sunt conati imponere Pelio Ossam*
Scilicet atque Ossae frondosum involvere
Olympum;
Ter pater exstructos disiecit fulmine montis.
Three times they endeavoured to pile Ossa on Pelion, no less, and to roll leafy Olympus on top of Ossa; three times our Father broke up the towering mountains with a thunderbolt.
Georgics no. 1, l. 281

3 *Felix qui potuit rerum cognoscere causas.*
Lucky is he who has been able to understand the causes of things.
of **Lucretius**
Georgics no. 2, l. 490

4 *Sed fugit interea, fugit inreparabile tempus.*
But meanwhile it is flying, irretrievable time is flying.
usually quoted as 'tempus fugit [time flies]'
Georgics no. 3, l. 284

Voltaire 1694–1778
French writer and philosopher

5 *Dans ce meilleur des mondes possibles . . . tout est au mieux.*
In this best of possible worlds . . . all is for the best.
usually quoted 'All is for the best in the best of all possible worlds'
Candide (1759) ch. 1

6 If we do not find anything pleasant, at least we shall find something new.
Candide (1759) ch. 17

7 These two nations have been at war over a few acres of snow near Canada, and . . . they are spending on this fine struggle more than Canada itself is worth.
of the struggle between the French and the British for the control of colonial north Canada
Candide (1759) ch. 23

8 *Dans ce pays-ci il est bon de tuer de temps en temps un amiral pour encourager les autres.*
In this country [England] it is thought well to kill an admiral from time to time to encourage the others.
referring to the contentious execution of Admiral Byng (1704–57) for neglect of duty in failing to relieve Minorca
Candide (1759) ch. 23

9 *Il faut cultiver notre jardin.*
We must cultivate our garden.
Candide (1759) ch. 30

10 [Men] use thought only to justify their injustices, and speech only to conceal their thoughts.
Dialogues (1763) 'Le Chapon et la poularde'

11 *Le mieux est l'ennemi du bien.*
The best is the enemy of the good.
Contes (1772) 'La Begueule' l. 2; though often attributed to Voltaire, the notion in fact derives from an Italian proverb quoted in his *Dictionnaire philosophique* (1770 ed.) 'Art Dramatique': 'Le meglio è l'inimico del bene'

12 Common sense is not so common.
Dictionnaire philosophique (1765) 'Sens Commun'

13 Superstition sets the whole world in flames; philosophy quenches them.
Dictionnaire philosophique (1764) 'Superstition'

14 The secret of being a bore . . . is to tell everything.
Discours en vers sur l'homme (1737) 'De la nature de l'homme' l. 172

15 All styles are good except the boring kind.
L'Enfant prodigue (1736) preface

16 *Si Dieu n'existait pas, il faudrait l'inventer.*
If God did not exist, it would be necessary to invent him.
Épîtres no. 96 'A l'Auteur du livre des trois imposteurs'; see **Ovid** 255:24

17 This agglomeration which was called and which still calls itself the Holy Roman Empire was neither holy, nor Roman, nor an empire.
Essai sur l'histoire générale et sur les moeurs et l'esprit des nations (1756) ch. 70

18 History is nothing more than a tableau of crimes and misfortunes.
L'Ingénu (1767) ch. 10; see **Gibbon** 148:14

19 It is one of the superstitions of the human mind to have imagined that virginity could be a virtue.
'The Leningrad Notebooks' (c.1735–50) in T. Besterman (ed.) *Voltaire's Notebooks* (2nd ed., 1968) vol. 2, p. 455

20 Governments need both shepherds and butchers.
'The Piccini Notebooks' (c.1735–50) in T. Besterman (ed.) *Voltaire's Notebooks* (2nd ed., 1968) vol. 2

21 God is on the side not of the heavy battalions, but of the best shots.
'The Piccini Notebooks' (c.1735–50) in T. Besterman (ed.) *Voltaire's Notebooks* (2nd ed., 1968) vol. 2; see **Bussy-Rabutin** 78:24

22 We owe respect to the living; to the dead we owe only truth.
'Première Lettre sur Oedipe' in *Oeuvres* (1785) vol. 1

23 *Quoi que vous fassiez, écrasez l'infâme, et aimez qui vous aime.*
Whatever you do, crush the infamous thing [superstition], and love those who love you.
letter to M. d'Alembert, 28 November 1762, in Voltaire Foundation (ed.) *Complete Works* vol. 25 (1973)

24 It is amusing that a virtue is made of the vice of chastity; and it's a pretty odd sort of chastity at that, which leads men straight

into the sin of Onan, and girls to the waning of their colour.
> letter to M. Mariott, 28 March 1766, in Voltaire Foundation (ed.) *Complete Works* vol. 30 (1973)

1 The art of government is to make two-thirds of a nation pay all it possibly can pay for the benefit of the other third.
> attributed; Walter Bagehot *The English Constitution* (1867) ch. 5

2 The composition of a tragedy requires *testicles.*
> *on being asked why no woman had ever written 'a tolerable tragedy'*
> letter from Byron to John Murray, 2 April 1817

3 I disapprove of what you say, but I will defend to the death your right to say it.
> *to **Helvétius**, following the burning of* De l'esprit *in 1759*
>> attributed to Voltaire, but in fact a later summary of his attitude by S. G. Tallentyre in *The Friends of Voltaire* (1907)

4 This is no time for making new enemies.
> *on being asked to renounce the Devil, on his deathbed*
>> attributed

Derek Walcott 1930–
West Indian poet and dramatist

5 I who have cursed
The drunken officer of British rule, how choose
Between this Africa and the English tongue I love?
> 'A Far Cry From Africa' (1962)

Lech Wałęsa 1943–
Polish trade unionist and statesman, President 1990–95

6 You have riches and freedom here but I feel no sense of faith or direction. You have so many computers, why don't you use them in the search for love?
> in Paris, on his first journey outside the Soviet area, in *Daily Telegraph* 14 December 1988

Alice Walker 1944–
American poet

7 Did this happen to your mother? Did your sister throw up a lot?
> title of poem (1979)

8 Expect nothing. Live frugally on surprise.
> 'Expect nothing' (1973)

9 The quietly pacifist peaceful
always die
to make room for men
who shout.
> 'The QPP' (1973)

10 I think it pisses God off if you walk by the colour purple in a field somewhere and don't notice it.
> *The Colour Purple* (1982)

Felix Walker fl. 1820
American politician

11 I'm talking to Buncombe ['bunkum'].
> *excusing a long, dull, irrelevant speech in the House of Representatives, c.1820 (Buncombe being his constituency)*
> W. Safire *New Language of Politics* (2nd ed., 1972); see **Carlyle** 85:15

George Wallace 1919–98
American Democratic politician

12 Segregation now, segregation tomorrow and segregation forever!
> inaugural speech as Governor of Alabama, January 1963, in *Birmingham World* 19 January 1963

Henry Wallace 1888–1965
American Democratic politician

13 The century on which we are entering—the century which will come out of this war—can be and must be the century of the common man.
> speech, 8 May 1942

William Wallace
American general

14 The enemy we're fighting is a bit different than the one we war-gamed against.
> *of the campaign in Iraq*
> in *New York Times* 28 March 2003

William Ross Wallace d. 1881
American poet

15 For the hand that rocks the cradle
Is the hand that rules the world.
> 'What rules the world' (1865); see **Robinson** 278:1

Graham Wallas 1858–1932
British politicial scientist

16 The little girl had the making of a poet in her who, being told to be sure of her meaning before she spoke, said, 'How can I know what I think till I see what I say?'
> *The Art of Thought* (1926) ch. 4

Edmund Waller 1606–87
English poet

17 Go, lovely rose!
Tell her, that wastes her time and me,
That now she knows,
When I resemble her to thee,
How sweet and fair she seems to be.
> 'Go, lovely rose!' (1645)

Horace Walpole 1717–97
English writer and connoisseur

18 [Strawberry Hill] is a little plaything-house that I got out of Mrs Chenevix's shop, and is the prettiest bauble you ever saw. It is set in enamelled meadows, with filigree hedges.
> letter to Hon. Henry Conway, 8 June 1747

1 The way to ensure summer in England is to have it framed and glazed in a comfortable room.
> letter to Revd William Cole, 28 May 1774

2 The next Augustan age will dawn on the other side of the Atlantic. There will, perhaps, be a Thucydides at Boston, a Xenophon at New York, and, in time, a Virgil at Mexico, and a Newton at Peru. At last, some curious traveller from Lima will visit England and give a description of the ruins of St Paul's, like the editions of Balbec and Palmyra.
> letter to Horace Mann, 24 November 1774; see **Macaulay** 221:14

3 This world is a comedy to those that think, a tragedy to those that feel.
> letter to Anne, Countess of Upper Ossory, 16 August 1776

4 That hyena in petticoats, Mrs Wollstonecraft.
> letter to Hannah More, 26 January 1795

Robert Walpole, Lord Orford
1676–1745
English Whig statesman; first British Prime Minister, 1721–42

5 They now *ring* the bells, but they will soon *wring* their hands.
> *on the declaration of war with Spain, 1739*
> W. Coxe *Memoirs of Sir Robert Walpole* (1798) vol. 1

6 All those men have their price.
> *of fellow parliamentarians*
> W. Coxe *Memoirs of Sir Robert Walpole* (1798) vol. 1

William Walsh 1663–1708
English poet

7 I can endure my own despair,
But not another's hope.
> 'Song: Of All the Torments'

Izaak Walton 1593–1683
English writer

8 Angling may be said to be so like the mathematics, that it can never be fully learnt.
> *The Compleat Angler* (1653) 'Epistle to the Reader'

9 As no man is born an artist, so no man is born an angler.
> *The Compleat Angler* (1653) 'Epistle to the Reader'

10 I am, Sir, a Brother of the Angle.
> *The Compleat Angler* (1653) pt. 1, ch. 1

11 Good company and good discourse are the very sinews of virtue.
> *The Compleat Angler* (1653) pt. 1, ch. 2

12 I love such mirth as does not make friends ashamed to look upon one another next morning.
> *The Compleat Angler* (1653) pt. 1, ch. 5

13 I love any discourse of rivers, and fish and fishing.
> *The Compleat Angler* (1653) pt. 1, ch. 18

14 Look to your health; and if you have it, praise God, and value it next to a good

conscience; for health is the second blessing that we mortals are capable of; a blessing that money cannot buy.
> *The Compleat Angler* (1653) pt. 1, ch. 21

Sam Walton 1919–92
American businessman

15 There is only one boss. The customer. And he can fire everybody in the company from the chairman on down, simply by spending his money somewhere else.
> *Sam Walton: Made in America, My Story*, with J. Huey (1990)

William Warburton 1698–1779
English theologian and bishop

16 Orthodoxy is my doxy; heterodoxy is another man's doxy.
> to Lord Sandwich, in Joseph Priestley *Memoirs* (1807) vol. 1

Artemus Ward 1834–67
American humorist

17 Let us all be happy, and live within our means, even if we have to borrer the money to do it with.
> *Artemus Ward in London* (1867) ch. 7

18 Why is this thus? What is the reason of this thusness?
> *Artemus Ward's Lecture* (1869) 'Heber C. Kimball's Harem'

Barbara Ward 1914–81
British writer and educator

19 We cannot cheat on DNA. We cannot get round photosynthesis. We cannot say I am not going to give a damn about phytoplankton. All these tiny mechanisms provide the preconditions of our planetary life. To say we do not care is to say in the most literal sense that 'we choose death'.
> *Only One Earth* (1972)

Andy Warhol 1927–87
American artist

20 In the future everybody will be world famous for fifteen minutes.
> *Andy Warhol* (1968) (volume released to mark his exhibition in Stockholm, February–March, 1968)

21 Being good in business is the most fascinating kind of art.
> *Philosophy of Andy Warhol (From A to B and Back Again)* (1975)

22 An artist is someone who produces things that people don't need to have but that he—for *some reason*—thinks it would be a good idea to give them.
> *Philosophy of Andy Warhol (From A to B and Back Again)* (1975)

23 Machines have less problems.
> Mike Wrenn *Andy Warhol: In His Own Words* (1991)

Sylvia Townsend Warner
1893–1978
English writer

1 One need not write in a diary what one is to
  remember for ever.
    diary, 22 October 1930

Earl Warren 1891–1974
American Chief Justice

2 In civilized life, law floats in a sea of ethics.
    in *New York Times* 12 November 1962

Booker T. Washington 1856–1915
American educationist and emancipated slave

3 No race can prosper till it learns that there
  is as much dignity in tilling a field as in
  writing a poem.
    Up from Slavery (1901)

4 You can't hold a man down without staying
  down with him.
    attributed

George Washington 1732–99
American statesman, 1st President of the US

5 The fate of unborn millions will now
  depend, under God, on the courage and
  conduct of this army. Our cruel and
  unrelenting enemy leaves us only the choice
  of brave resistance, or the most abject
  submission. We have, therefore, to resolve
  to conquer or die.
    General orders, 2 July 1776, in J. C. Fitzpatrick
    (ed.) *Writings of George Washington* vol. 5 (1932)

6 Few men have virtue to withstand the
  highest bidder.
    letter, 17 August 1779

7 'Tis our true policy to steer clear of
  permanent alliances, with any portion of
  the foreign world.
    President's Address . . . retiring from Public Life 17
    September 1796

8 Let me . . . warn you in the most solemn
  manner against the baneful effects of the
  spirit of party.
    President's Address . . . 17 September 1796

9 The nation which indulges toward another
  an habitual hatred or an habitual fondness
  is in some degree a slave. It is a slave to its
  animosity or to its affection, either of which
  is sufficient to lead it astray from its duty
  and its interest.
    President's Address . . . 17 September 1796

10 I can't tell a lie, Pa; you know I can't tell a
   lie. I did cut it with my hatchet.
    M. L. Weems *Life of George Washington* (10th ed.,
    1810) ch. 2

11 Liberty, when it begins to take root, is a
   plant of rapid growth.
    attributed

Ned Washington 1901–76
American songwriter

12 Hi diddle dee dee (an actor's life for me).
    title of song (1940) from the film *Pinocchio*

13 The night is like a lovely tune,
   Beware my foolish heart!
    'My Foolish Heart' (1949 song)

Thomas Watson Snr. 1874–1956
American businessman

14 You cannot be a success in any business
   without believing that it is the greatest
   business in the world . . . You have to put
   your heart in the business and the business
   in your heart.
    Robert Sobel *IBM: Colossus in Transition* (1981)

William Watson c.1559–1603
English Roman Catholic conspirator

15 *Fiat justitia et ruant coeli.*
   Let justice be done though the heavens fall.
    *A Decacordon of Ten Quodlibeticall Questions
    Concerning Religion and State* (1602), being the
    first citation in an English work of a famous
    maxim; see **Ferdinand** 134:18

William Watson 1858–1936
English poet

16 April, April,
   Laugh thy girlish laughter.
    'April'

17 My hand will miss the insinuated nose,
   Mine eyes the tail that wagged contempt at
   Fate.
    'An Epitaph'

Isaac Watts 1674–1748
English hymn-writer

18 How doth the little busy bee
   Improve each shining hour.
    Divine Songs for Children (1715) 'Against Idleness
    and Mischief'; see **Carroll** 86:5

19 For Satan finds some mischief still
   For idle hands to do.
    Divine Songs for Children (1715) 'Against Idleness
    and Mischief'

20 Let dogs delight to bark and bite,
   For God hath made them so.
    Divine Songs for Children (1715) 'Against
    Quarrelling'

21 Birds in their little nests agree.
    Divine Songs for Children (1715) 'Love between
    Brothers and Sisters'

22 Come, let us join our cheerful songs
   With angels round the throne;
   Ten thousand thousand are their tongues,
   But all their joys are one.
    Hymns and Spiritual Songs (1707) 'Come, let us
    join our cheerful songs'

23 When I survey the wondrous cross
   On which the prince of glory died,
   My richest gain I count but loss,
   And pour contempt on all my pride.
    Hymns and Spiritual Songs (1707) 'Crucifixion to
    the World, by the Cross of Christ'

24 There is a land of pure delight,
   Where saints immortal reign.
    Hymns and Spiritual Songs (1707) 'A Prospect of
    Heaven makes Death easy'

1 Jesus shall reign where'er the sun
Does his successive journeys run;
His kingdom stretch from shore to shore,
Till moons shall wax and wane no more.
The Psalms of David Imitated (1719) Psalm 72

2 Our God, our help in ages past
Our hope for years to come,
Our shelter from the stormy blast,
And our eternal home.
*'Our God' altered to 'O God' by John **Wesley**, 1738*
The Psalms of David Imitated (1719) Psalm 90

3 A thousand ages in Thy sight
Are like an evening gone;
Short as the watch that ends the night
Before the rising sun.
The Psalms of David Imitated (1719) Psalm 90

4 Time, like an ever-rolling stream,
Bears all its sons away.
The Psalms of David Imitated (1719) Psalm 90

Evelyn Waugh 1903–66
English novelist

5 I am not I: thou art not he or she: they are
not they.
Brideshead Revisited (1945) 'Author's Note'

6 Any one who has been to an English public
school will always feel comparatively at
home in prison. It is the people brought up
in the gay intimacy of the slums, Paul
learned, who find prison so soul-destroying.
Decline and Fall (1928) pt. 3, ch. 4

7 Up to a point, Lord Copper.
Scoop (1938) bk. 1, ch. 1

8 'Feather-footed through the plashy fen
passes the questing vole' . . . 'Yes,' said the
Managing Editor. 'That must be good style.'
Scoop (1938) bk. 1, ch. 1

9 News is what a chap who doesn't care much
about anything wants to read. And it's only
news until he's read it. After that it's dead.
Scoop (1938) bk. 1, ch. 5

10 A typical triumph of modern science to find
the only part of Randolph that was not
malignant and remove it.
*on hearing that Randolph Churchill's lung, when
removed, proved non-malignant*
Michael Davie (ed.) *Diaries of Evelyn Waugh* (1976)
'Irregular Notes 1960–65', March 1964

Frederick Weatherly 1848–1929
English songwriter

11 Where are the boys of the old Brigade,
Who fought with us side by side?
'The Old Brigade' (1886 song)

Sidney Webb 1859–1947
English socialist

12 The inevitability of gradualness.
presidential address to the annual conference of
the Labour Party, 26 June 1923

Max Weber 1864–1920
German sociologist

13 The protestant ethic and the spirit of
capitalism.
Archiv für Sozialwissenschaft Sozialpolitik vol. 20
(1904–5) (title of article)

14 In Baxter's view the care for external goods
should only lie on the shoulders of the saint
like 'a light cloak, which can be thrown
aside at any moment.' But fate decreed that
the cloak should become an iron cage.
Gesammelte Aufsätze zur Religionssoziologie (1920)
vol. 1 (tr. T. Parsons, 1930)

15 The concept of the 'official secret' is its
[bureaucracy's] specific invention.
'Politik als Beruf' (1919)

Daniel Webster 1782–1852
American politician

16 It is, Sir, as I have said, a small college. And
yet *there are those who love it!*
argument in the case of the Trustees of
Dartmouth College v. Woodward, 10 March
1818

17 The past, at least, is secure.
second speech in the Senate on Foote's
Resolution, 26 January 1830; *Writings and
Speeches* (1903) vol. 6

18 The people's government, made for the
people, made by the people, and answerable
to the people.
second speech in the Senate on Foote's
Resolution, 26 January 1830; see **Lincoln** 214:20

19 Liberty *and* Union, now and forever, one and
inseparable!
second speech in the Senate on Foote's
Resolution, 26 January 1830

20 I was born an American; I will live an
American; I shall die an American.
speech in the Senate on 'The Compromise Bill',
17 July 1850; *Writings and Speeches* (1903) vol. 10

21 There is always room at the top.
*on being advised against joining the overcrowded
legal profession*
attributed

John Webster c.1580–c.1625
English dramatist

22 I am Duchess of Malfi still.
The Duchess of Malfi (1623) act 4, sc. 2

23 I know death hath ten thousand several
doors
For men to take their exits.
The Duchess of Malfi (1623) act 4, sc. 2; see
Fletcher 138:11, **Massinger** 231:3, **Seneca**
288:23

24 Cover her face; mine eyes dazzle: she died
young.
The Duchess of Malfi (1623) act 4, sc. 2

25 We are merely the stars' tennis-balls, struck
and bandied
Which way please them.
The Duchess of Malfi (1623) act 5, sc. 4

1 'Tis just like a summer birdcage in a garden; the birds that are without despair to get in, and the birds that are within despair, and are in a consumption, for fear they shall never get out.
   The White Devil (1612) act 1, sc. 2

2 Call for the robin-red-breast and the wren, Since o'er shady groves they hover, And with leaves and flowers do cover The friendless bodies of unburied men.
   The White Devil (1612) act 5, sc. 4

3 We think caged birds sing, when indeed they cry.
   The White Devil (1612) act 5, sc. 4; see **Dunbar** 123:7, **Shakespeare** 298:23

Josiah Wedgwood 1730–95
English potter

4 Am I not a man and a brother.
   legend on Wedgwood cameo, depicting a kneeling Negro slave in chains
   reproduced in facsimile in E. Darwin *The Botanic Garden* pt. 1 (1791)

Simone Weil 1909–43
French essayist and philosopher

5 All sins are attempts to fill voids.
   La Pesanteur et la grâce (1948)

6 What a country calls its vital economic interests are not the things which enable its citizens to live, but the things which enable it to make war.
   W. H. Auden *A Certain World* (1971)

Max Weinreich 1894–1969
American Yiddish scholar

7 A language is a dialect with an army and a navy.
   in *Yivo Bleter* January–February 1945

Robert Stanley Weir 1856–1926
Canadian lawyer

8 O Canada! Terre de nos aïeux, Ton front est ceint de fleurons glorieux! Car ton bras sait porter l'épée, Il sait porter la croix!
   O Canada! Our home and native land! True patriot love in all thy sons command. With glowing hearts we see thee rise, The True North strong and free!
   'O Canada' (1908 song); French words written in 1880 by Adolphe-Basile Routhier (1839–1920)

Victor Weisskopf 1908–2002
American physicist

9 It was absolutely marvellous working for Pauli. You could ask him anything. There was no worry that he would think a particular question was stupid, since he thought *all* questions were stupid.
   in *American Journal of Physics* 1977

Johnny Weissmuller 1904–84
American actor

10 Me Tarzan, you Jane.
   summing up his role in Tarzan, the Ape Man (*1932 film*)
   in *Photoplay Magazine* June 1932; the words do not occur in the film or in the original novel by Edgar Rice Burroughs

Chaim Weizmann 1874–1952
Russian-born Israeli statesman, President 1949–52

11 Something had been done for us which, after two thousand years of hope and yearning, would at last give us a resting-place in this terrible world.
   of the Balfour declaration
   speech in Jerusalem, 25 November 1936; see **Balfour** 25:5

Joseph Welch 1890–1960
American lawyer

12 Until this moment, Senator, I think I never really gauged your cruelty or your recklessness . . . Have you no sense of decency, sir? At long last, have you left no sense of decency?
   *to Joseph **McCarthy**, 9 June 1954, defending the US Army against allegations of harbouring subversive activities*
   in *American National Biography* (online edition) 'Joseph McCarthy'

Fay Weldon 1931–
British novelist and scriptwriter

13 There seems to be a general overall pattern in most lives, that nothing happens, and nothing happens, and then all of a sudden everything happens.
   Auto da Fay (2002)

14 The life and loves of a she-devil.
   title of novel (1984)

Orson Welles 1915–85
American actor and film director

15 This is the biggest electric train a boy ever had!
   of the RKO studios
   Roy Fowler *Orson Welles* (1946) ch. 6

16 I hate television. I hate it as much as peanuts. But I can't stop eating peanuts.
   in *New York Herald Tribune* 12 October 1956

17 There are only two emotions in a plane: boredom and terror.
   interview to celebrate his 70th birthday, in *The Times* 6 May 1985

Duke of Wellington 1769–1852
British soldier and statesman

18 As Lord Chesterfield said of the generals of his day, 'I only hope that when the enemy

reads the list of their names, he trembles as I do.'

usually quoted as, 'I don't know what effect these men will have upon the enemy, but, by God, they frighten me'
letter, 29 August 1810, in *Supplementary Despatches . . .* (1860) vol. 6

1 Up Guards and at them!
letter from an officer in the Guards, 22 June 1815, in *The Battle of Waterloo* by a Near Observer [J. Booth] (1815); later denied by Wellington

2 Next to a battle lost, the greatest misery is a battle gained.
in *Diary of Frances, Lady Shelley 1787–1817* (ed. R. Edgcumbe, 1912) vol. 1

3 Publish and be damned.
replying to a blackmail threat prior to the publication of Harriette Wilson's Memoirs (1825)
attributed; Elizabeth Longford *Wellington: The Years of the Sword* (1969) ch. 10

4 I used to say of him that his presence on the field made the difference of forty thousand men.
of Napoleon
Philip Henry Stanhope *Notes of Conversations with the Duke of Wellington* (1888) 2 November 1831

5 Ours is composed of the scum of the earth—the mere scum of the earth.
of the army
Philip Henry Stanhope *Notes of Conversations with the Duke of Wellington* (1888) 4 November 1831

6 I never saw so many shocking bad hats in my life.
on seeing the first Reformed Parliament, 1832
William Fraser *Words on Wellington* (1889)

7 All the business of war, and indeed all the business of life, is to endeavour to find out what you don't know by what you do; that's what I called 'guessing what was at the other side of the hill'.
in *The Croker Papers* (1885) vol. 3 ch. 28

8 The battle of Waterloo was won on the playing fields of Eton.
oral tradition, but probably apocryphal; the earliest reference is a remark said to have been made when revisiting Eton; see Orwell 254:19

9 An extraordinary affair. I gave them their orders and they wanted to stay and discuss them.
of his first Cabinet meeting as Prime Minister
attributed; Peter Hennessy *Whitehall* (1990)

10 If you believe that, you'll believe anything.
to a gentleman who had accosted him in the street saying, 'Mr Jones, I believe?'; George Jones RA (1786–1869), painter of military subjects, bore a striking resemblance to Wellington
Elizabeth Longford *Pillar of State* (1972) ch. 10

H. G. Wells 1866–1946
English novelist

11 Human history becomes more and more a race between education and catastrophe.
The Outline of History (1920) vol. 2, ch. 41, pt. 4

12 The shape of things to come.
title of book (1933)

13 The war that will end war.
title of book (1914); see Lloyd George 216:9

14 Moral indignation is jealousy with a halo.
The Wife of Sir Isaac Harman (1914) ch. 9, sect. 2

15 God damn you all: I told you so.
suggestion for his own epitaph, in conversation with Ernest Barker, 1939
Ernest Barker *Age and Youth* (1953)

Arnold Wesker 1932–
English dramatist

16 Chips with every damn thing. You breed babies and you eat chips with everything.
Chips with Everything (1962) act 1, sc. 2

Charles Wesley 1707–88
English Methodist preacher and hymn-writer

17 Amazing love! How can it be
That thou, my God, shouldst die for me?
'And can it be' (1738 hymn)

18 Hark! how all the welkin rings,
Glory to the King of kings.
Peace on earth and mercy mild,
God and sinners reconciled.
Hymns and Sacred Poems (1739) 'Hymn for Christmas'; the first two lines altered to 'Hark! the herald-angels sing Glory to the new born King' in George Whitefield *Hymns for Social Worship* (1753)

19 Hail, the heaven-born Prince of Peace!
Hail, the Sun of Righteousness!
Hymns and Sacred Poems (1739) 'Hymn for Christmas'; see Bible 42:17

20 O for a thousand tongues to sing.
Hymns and Sacred Poems (1740) 'For the Anniversary Day of one's Conversion'

21 Jesu, lover of my soul,
Let me to thy bosom fly.
Hymns and Sacred Poems (1740) 'In Temptation'

22 Love divine, all loves excelling,
Joy of heav'n, to earth come down,
Fix in us thy humble dwelling,
All thy faithful mercies crown.
Hymns for those that seek . . . Redemption (1747) 'Love divine', based on Dryden; see Dryden 122:6

23 Lo! He comes with clouds descending,
Once for favoured sinners slain.
Hymns of Intercession for all Mankind (1758) 'Lo! He comes'

John Wesley 1703–91
English preacher; founder of Methodism

24 The Gospel of Christ knows of no religion but social; no holiness but social holiness.
Hymns and Sacred Poems (1739) Preface

25 I design plain truth for plain people.
Sermons on Several Occasions (1746)

26 Cleanliness is, indeed, next to godliness.
Sermons on Several Occasions (1788) Sermon 88

1 I went to America to convert the Indians; but oh, who shall convert me?
Journal (ed. N. Curnock) 24 January 1738

2 I felt my heart strangely warmed. I felt I did trust in Christ, Christ alone for salvation; and an assurance was given me that He had taken away *my* sins, even *mine*, and saved *me* from the law of sin and death.
on his conversion
Journal (ed. N. Curnock) 24 May 1738

3 I look upon all the world as my parish.
Journal (ed. N. Curnock) 11 June 1739

4 Though I am always in haste, I am never in a hurry.
letter to Miss March, 10 December 1777, in *Letters* (ed. J. Telford, 1931) vol. 6

Samuel Wesley 1662–1735
English clergyman and poet

5 Style is the dress of thought; a modest dress, Neat, but not gaudy, will true critics please.
'An Epistle to a Friend concerning Poetry' (1700); see **Johnson** 187:8, **Pope** 267:10

Mae West 1892–1980
American film actress

6 I always say, keep a diary and some day it'll keep you.
Every Day's a Holiday (1937 film)

7 Beulah, peel me a grape.
I'm No Angel (1933 film)

8 It's not the men in my life that counts—it's the life in my men.
I'm No Angel (1933 film)

9 'Goodness, what beautiful diamonds!' 'Goodness had nothing to do with it.'
Night After Night (1932 film)

10 Why don't you come up sometime, and see me?
often altered to, 'Why don't you come up and see me sometime?'
She Done Him Wrong (1933 film)

11 Is that a gun in your pocket, or are you just glad to see me?
usually quoted as 'Is that a pistol in your pocket . . .'
Joseph Weintraub *Peel Me a Grape* (1975)

12 I used to be Snow White . . . but I drifted.
Joseph Weintraub *Peel Me a Grape* (1975)

Rebecca West 1892–1983
English novelist and journalist

13 There is no such thing as conversation. It is an illusion. There are intersecting monologues, that is all.
There is No Conversation (1935) 'The Harsh Voice' sect. 1

14 I myself have never been able to find out precisely what feminism is: I only know that people call me a feminist whenever I express sentiments that differentiate me from a doormat or a prostitute.
in *The Clarion* 14 November 1913

15 Journalism—an ability to meet the challenge of filling the space.
in *New York Herald Tribune* 22 April 1956

William C. Westmoreland 1914–
American general

16 Vietnam was the first war ever fought without censorship. Without censorship, things can get terribly confused in the public mind.
attributed, 1982

Edith Wharton 1862–1937
American novelist

17 An unalterable and unquestioned law of the musical world required that the German text of French operas sung by Swedish artists should be translated into Italian for the clearer understanding of English-speaking audiences.
The Age of Innocence (1920) bk. 1, ch. 1

18 Mrs Ballinger is one of the ladies who pursue Culture in bands, as though it were dangerous to meet it alone.
Xingu and Other Stories (1916) 'Xingu'

Richard Whately 1787–1863
English philosopher and theologian

19 Honesty is the best policy; but he who is governed by that maxim is not an honest man.
Apophthegms (1854)

20 It is not that pearls fetch a high price *because* men have dived for them; but on the contrary, men dive for them because they fetch a high price.
Introductory Lectures on Political Economy (1832) p. 253

William Whewell 1794–1866
English philosopher and scientist

21 Hence no force however great can stretch a cord however fine into an horizontal line which is accurately straight: there will always be a bending downwards.
often cited as an example of accidental metre and rhyme, and changed in later editions
Elementary Treatise on Mechanics (1819) ch. 4, problem 2

James McNeill Whistler 1834–1903
American-born painter

22 I am not arguing with you—I am telling you.
The Gentle Art of Making Enemies (1890)

23 I maintain that two and two would continue to make four, in spite of the whine of the amateur for three, or the cry of the critic for five.
Whistler v. Ruskin. Art and Art Critics (1878)

24 No, I ask it for the knowledge of a lifetime.
*in his case against **Ruskin**, replying to the question: 'For two days' labour, you ask two hundred guineas?'*
D. C. Seitz *Whistler Stories* (1913)

1 OSCAR WILDE: How I wish I had said that.
WHISTLER: You will, Oscar, you will.
  R. Ellman *Oscar Wilde* (1987) pt. 2, ch. 5

E. B. White 1899–1985
American humorist

2 Commuter—one who spends his life
In riding to and from his wife;
A man who shaves and takes a train,
And then rides back to shave again.
  'The Commuter' (1982)

3 MOTHER: It's broccoli, dear.
CHILD: I say it's spinach, and I say the hell
with it.
  cartoon caption in *New Yorker* 8 December 1928

4 Democracy is the recurrent suspicion that
more than half of the people are right more
than half of the time.
  in *New Yorker* 3 July 1944

H. Kirke White 1785–1806
English poet

5 Oft in danger, oft in woe,
Onward, Christians, onward go.
  'Oft in danger, oft in woe' (1812 hymn)

Patrick White 1912–90
Australian novelist

6 In all directions stretched the great
Australian Emptiness, in which the mind is
the least of possessions.
  The Vital Decade (1968) 'The Prodigal Son'

T. H. White 1906–64
English novelist

7 Everything not forbidden is compulsory.
  The Sword in the Stone (1938) ch. 13

Theodore H. White 1915–86
American writer and journalist

8 The flood of money that gushes into politics
today is a pollution of democracy.
  in *Time* 19 November 1984

Alfred North Whitehead
1861–1947
English philosopher and mathematician

9 It is more important that a proposition be
interesting than that it be true.
  Adventures of Ideas (1933) pt. 4, ch. 16

10 There are no whole truths; all truths are
half-truths. It is trying to treat them as
whole truths that plays the devil.
  Dialogues (1954) prologue

11 *Ideas won't keep.* Something must be done
about them.
  Dialogues (1954) 28 April 1938

12 Intelligence is quickness to apprehend as
distinct from ability, which is capacity to act
wisely on the thing apprehended.
  Dialogues (1954) 15 December 1939

13 What is morality in any given time or place?
It is what the majority then and there
happen to like, and immorality is what they
dislike.
  Dialogues (1954) 30 August 1941

14 Art is the imposing of a pattern on
experience, and our aesthetic enjoyment is
recognition of the pattern.
  Dialogues (1954) 10 June 1943

15 Civilization advances by extending the
number of important operations which we
can perform without thinking about them.
  Introduction to Mathematics (1911) ch. 5

16 The safest general characterization of the
European philosophical tradition is that it
consists of a series of footnotes to Plato.
  Process and Reality (1929) pt. 2, ch. 1

Katharine Whitehorn 1928–
English journalist

17 An office party is not, as is sometimes
supposed, the Managing Director's chance
to kiss the tea-girl. It is the tea-girl's chance
to kiss the Managing Director.
  Roundabout (1962) 'The Office Party'

George Whiting
American songwriter

18 When you're all dressed up and have no
place to go.
  title of song (1912)

William Whiting 1825–78
English teacher

19 Eternal Father, strong to save,
Whose arm doth bind the restless wave,
Who bidd'st the mighty ocean deep
Its own appointed limits keep:
O hear us when we cry to thee,
For those in peril on the sea.
  'Eternal Father, Strong to Save' (1869 hymn)

Gough Whitlam 1916–
Australian Labor statesman

20 *the Governor-General, Sir John Kerr, had
dismissed the Labor government headed by Gough
Whitlam in November 1975:*
Well may he say 'God Save the Queen'. But
after this nothing will save the Governor-
General . . . Maintain your rage and your
enthusiasm through the campaign for the
election now to be held and until polling
day.
  speech in Canberra, 11 November 1975

Walt Whitman 1819–92
American poet

21 I dreamed in a dream I saw a city invincible
to the attacks of the whole of the rest of
the earth,
I dreamed that was the new city of Friends.
  'I dreamed in a dream' (1867)

22 I sing the body electric.
  title of poem (1855)

23 O Captain! my Captain! our fearful trip is
done,
The ship has weathered every rack, the
prize we sought is won.
  'O Captain! My Captain!' (1871)

24 Exult O shores, and ring O bells! But I with
mournful tread

Walk the deck my Captain lies, Fallen cold
and dead.
'O Captain! My Captain!' (1871)

1 Pioneers! O pioneers!
title of poem (1881)

2 Camerado, this is no book,
Who touches this touches a man.
'So Long!' (1881)

3 I celebrate myself, and sing myself.
'Song of Myself' (written 1855) pt. 1

4 Urge and urge and urge,
Always the procreant urge of the world.
'Song of Myself' (written 1855) pt. 3

5 Has any one supposed it lucky to be born?
I hasten to inform him or her, it is just as
lucky to die and I know it.
'Song of Myself' (written 1855) pt. 7

6 I believe a leaf of grass is no less than the
journey-work of the stars.
'Song of Myself' (written 1855) pt. 31

7 I think I could turn and live with animals,
they are so placid and self-contained,
I stand and look at them long and long.
They do not sweat and whine about their
condition,
They do not lie awake in the dark and weep
for their sins,
They do not make me sick discussing their
duty to God.
'Song of Myself' (written 1855) pt. 32

8 Behold, I do not give lectures or a little
charity,
When I give I give myself.
'Song of Myself' (written 1855) pt. 40

9 Do I contradict myself?
Very well then I contradict myself,
(I am large, I contain multitudes.)
'Song of Myself' (written 1855) pt. 51

10 I sound my barbaric yawp over the roofs of
the world.
'Song of Myself' (written 1855) pt. 52

11 When lilacs last in the dooryard bloomed,
And the great star early drooped in the
western sky in the night,
I mourned, and yet shall mourn with ever-
returning spring.
'When lilacs last in the dooryard bloomed'
(1881) st. 1

12 The United States themselves are essentially
the greatest poem.
Leaves of Grass (1855) preface

John Greenleaf Whittier 1807–92
American poet

13 'Shoot, if you must, this old grey head,
But spare your country's flag,' she said.
'Barbara Frietchie' (1863)

14 Dear Lord and Father of mankind,
Forgive our foolish ways!
Re-clothe us in our rightful mind,
In purer lives thy service find,
In deeper reverence praise.
'The Brewing of Soma' (1872)

15 For of all sad words of tongue or pen,
The saddest are these: 'It might have been!'
'Maud Muller' (1854); see Harte 163:2

16 O brother man! fold to thy heart thy
brother.
'Worship' (1848)

Robert Whittington c.1480–1553?
English grammarian

17 As time requireth, a man of marvellous
mirth and pastimes, and sometime of as sad
gravity, as who say: a man for all seasons.
of Sir Thomas More
Vulgaria (1521) pt. 2 'De constructione
nominum'; Erasmus had applied the idea
earlier in the prefatory letter to In Praise of Folly
(1509), saying that More played 'Omnium
horarum hominem [A man of all hours]'

Charlotte Whitton 1896–1975
Canadian writer and politician

18 Whatever women do they must do twice as
well as men to be thought half as good.
in Canada Month June 1963

William H. Whyte 1917–
American writer

19 The organization man.
title of book (1956)

Ann Widdecombe 1947–
British Conservative politician

20 He has something of the night in him.
of Michael Howard as a contender for the
Conservative leadership
in Sunday Times 11 May 1997 (electronic edition)

Elie Wiesel 1928–
Romanian-born American writer

21 The opposite of love is not hate, it's
indifference. The opposite of art is not
ugliness, it's indifference. The opposite of
faith is not heresy, it's indifference. And the
opposite of life is not death, it's indifference.
in U.S. News and World Report 27 October 1986

22 Take sides. Neutrality helps the oppressor,
never the victim. Silence encourages the
tormentor, never the tormented.
accepting the Nobel Peace Prize
in New York Times 11 December 1986

23 God of forgiveness, do not forgive those
murderers of Jewish children here.
at Auschwitz
in The Times 27 January 1995

Samuel Wilberforce 1805–73
English prelate

24 Was it through his grandfather or his
grandmother that he claimed his descent
from a monkey?
addressed to T. H. Huxley at a meeting of the
British Association for the Advancement of
Science, Oxford, June 1860; see Huxley 179:22

Ella Wheeler Wilcox 1855–1919
American poet

25 Laugh and the world laughs with you;

Weep, and you weep alone.
'Solitude'

1 So many gods, so many creeds,
So many paths that wind and wind,
While just the art of being kind
Is all the sad world needs.
'The World's Need'

Oscar Wilde 1854–1900
Irish dramatist and poet

2 We have really everything in common with
America nowadays except, of course,
language.
The Canterville Ghost (1887)

3 Really, if the lower orders don't set us a
good example, what on earth is the use of
them?
The Importance of Being Earnest (1895) act 1

4 The truth is rarely pure, and never simple.
The Importance of Being Earnest (1895) act 1

5 In married life three is company and two
none.
The Importance of Being Earnest (1895) act 1

6 Ignorance is like a delicate exotic fruit;
touch it and the bloom is gone. The whole
theory of modern education is radically
unsound. Fortunately, in England, at any
rate, education produces no effect
whatsoever.
The Importance of Being Earnest (1895) act 1

7 To lose one parent, Mr Worthing, may be
regarded as a misfortune; to lose both looks
like carelessness.
The Importance of Being Earnest (1895) act 1

8 LADY BRACKNELL: A handbag?
The Importance of Being Earnest (1895) act 1

9 All women become like their mothers. That
is their tragedy. No man does. That's his.
The Importance of Being Earnest (1895) act 1

10 The good ended happily, and the bad
unhappily. That is what fiction means.
The Importance of Being Earnest (1895) act 2; see
Stoppard 326:14

11 I hope you have not been leading a double
life, pretending to be wicked and being
really good all the time. That would be
hypocrisy.
The Importance of Being Earnest (1895) act 2

12 I never travel without my diary. One should
always have something sensational to read
in the train.
The Importance of Being Earnest (1895) act 2

13 Thirty-five is a very attractive age. London
society is full of women of the very highest
birth who have, of their own free choice,
remained thirty-five for years.
The Importance of Being Earnest (1895) act 3

14 Every great man nowadays has his disciples,
and it is always Judas who writes the
biography.
Intentions (1891) 'The Critic as Artist' pt. 1

15 The one duty we owe to history is to rewrite
it.
Intentions (1891) 'The Critic as Artist' pt. 1

16 It is through Art, and through Art only, that
we can realise our perfection; through Art,
and through Art only, that we can shield
ourselves from the sordid perils of actual
existence.
Intentions (1891) 'The Critic as Artist' pt. 2

17 A little sincerity is a dangerous thing, and a
great deal of it is absolutely fatal.
Intentions (1891) 'The Critic as Artist' pt. 2

18 Life imitates Art far more than Art imitates
Life.
Intentions (1891) 'The Decay of Lying'

19 I can resist everything except temptation.
Lady Windermere's Fan (1892) act 1

20 We are all in the gutter, but some of us are
looking at the stars.
Lady Windermere's Fan (1892) act 3

21 A man who knows the price of everything
and the value of nothing.
definition of a cynic
Lady Windermere's Fan (1892) act 3

22 Experience is the name every one gives to
their mistakes.
Lady Windermere's Fan (1892) act 3

23 There is no such thing as a moral or an
immoral book. Books are well written, or
badly written.
The Picture of Dorian Gray (1891) preface

24 The nineteenth century dislike of Realism is
the rage of Caliban seeing his own face in
the glass.
The Picture of Dorian Gray (1891) preface

25 The moral life of man forms part of the
subject matter of the artist, but the morality
of art consists in the perfect use of an
imperfect medium.
The Picture of Dorian Gray (1891) preface

26 There is only one thing in the world worse
than being talked about, and that is not
being talked about.
The Picture of Dorian Gray (1891) ch. 1

27 A man cannot be too careful in the choice of
his enemies.
The Picture of Dorian Gray (1891) ch. 1

28 A cigarette is the perfect type of a perfect
pleasure. It is exquisite, and it leaves one
unsatisfied.
The Picture of Dorian Gray (1891) ch. 6

29 It is better to be beautiful than to be good.
But . . . it is better to be good than to be ugly.
The Picture of Dorian Gray (1891) ch. 17

30 Anybody can be good in the country.
The Picture of Dorian Gray (1891) ch. 19

31 A thing is not necessarily true because a
man dies for it.
The Portrait of Mr W. H. (1901)

32 MRS ALLONBY: They say, Lady Hunstanton,
that when good Americans die they go to
Paris.
LADY HUNSTANTON: Indeed? And when bad
Americans die, where do they go to?
LORD ILLINGWORTH: Oh, they go to America.
A Woman of No Importance (1893) act 1; see
Appleton 14:10

1 The English country gentleman galloping after a fox—the unspeakable in full pursuit of the uneatable.
A Woman of No Importance (1893) act 1

2 One should never trust a woman who tells one her real age. A woman who would tell one that, would tell one anything.
A Woman of No Importance (1893) act 1

3 LORD ILLINGWORTH: The Book of Life begins with a man and a woman in a garden.
MRS ALLONBY: It ends with Revelations.
A Woman of No Importance (1893) act 1

4 Children begin by loving their parents; after a time they judge them; rarely, if ever, do they forgive them.
A Woman of No Importance (1893) act 2

5 You should study the Peerage, Gerald . . . It is the best thing in fiction the English have ever done.
A Woman of No Importance (1893) act 3

6 He did not wear his scarlet coat,
For blood and wine are red,
And blood and wine were on his hands
When they found him with the dead.
The Ballad of Reading Gaol (1898) pt. 1, st. 1

7 I never saw a man who looked
With such a wistful eye
Upon that little tent of blue
Which prisoners call the sky.
The Ballad of Reading Gaol (1898) pt. 1, st. 3

8 Yet each man kills the thing he loves,
By each let this be heard,
Some do it with a bitter look,
Some with a flattering word.
The coward does it with a kiss,
The brave man with a sword!
The Ballad of Reading Gaol (1898) pt. 1, st. 7

9 Something was dead in each of us,
And what was dead was Hope.
The Ballad of Reading Gaol (1898) pt. 3, st. 31

10 For he who lives more lives than one
More deaths than one must die.
The Ballad of Reading Gaol (1898) pt. 3, st. 37

11 And alien tears will fill for him
Pity's long-broken urn,
For his mourners will be outcast men,
And outcasts always mourn.
inscribed on Wilde's tomb in Père Lachaise cemetery
The Ballad of Reading Gaol (1898) pt. 4, st. 23

12 How else but through a broken heart
May Lord Christ enter in?
The Ballad of Reading Gaol (1898) pt. 5, st. 14

13 Democracy means simply the bludgeoning of the people by the people for the people.
in *Fortnightly Review* February 1891 'The Soul of Man under Socialism'; see **Lincoln** 214:20

14 Ah, well, then, I suppose that I shall have to die beyond my means.
at the mention of a huge fee for a surgical operation
R. H. Sherard *Life of Oscar Wilde* (1906) ch. 18

15 Do you want to know the great drama of my life? It's that I have put my genius into my life; all I've put into my works is my talent.
André Gide *Oscar Wilde* (1910) 'In Memoriam'

16 Shaw has not an enemy in the world; and none of his friends like him.
letter from Bernard Shaw to Archibald Henderson, 22 February 1911

17 I have nothing to declare except my genius.
at the New York Custom House
Frank Harris *Oscar Wilde* (1918)

18 Work is the curse of the drinking classes.
H. Pearson *Life of Oscar Wilde* (1946) ch. 12

19 One of us must go.
of the wallpaper in the room where he was dying
attributed, probably apocryphal

Billy Wilder 1906–2002
American screenwriter and director

20 Hindsight is always twenty-twenty.
J. R. Columbo *Wit and Wisdom of the Moviemakers* (1979) ch. 7

Thornton Wilder 1897–1975
American novelist and dramatist

21 Even memory is not necessary for love. There is a land of the living and a land of the dead and the bridge is love, the only survival, the only meaning.
The Bridge of San Luis Rey (1927), closing words

22 Marriage is a bribe to make a housekeeper think she's a householder.
The Merchant of Yonkers (1939) act 1

23 Literature is the orchestration of platitudes.
in *Time* 12 January 1953

Robert Wilensky 1951–
American academic

24 We've all heard that a million monkeys banging on a million typewriters will eventually reproduce the entire works of Shakespeare. Now, thanks to the Internet, we know this is not true.
in *Mail on Sunday* 16 February 1997 'Quotes of the Week'; see **Eddington** 124:21

Wilhelm II ('Kaiser Bill') 1859–1941
German monarch, emperor 1888–1918

25 We have . . . fought for our place in the sun and have won it. It will be my business to see that we retain this place in the sun unchallenged, so that the rays of that sun may exert a fructifying influence upon our foreign trade and traffic.
speech in Hamburg, 18 June 1901; in *The Times* 20 June 1901; see **Bülow** 73:22

John Wilkes 1727–97
English parliamentary reformer

26 EARL OF SANDWICH: 'Pon my soul, Wilkes, I don't know whether you'll die upon the gallows or of the pox.

WILKES: That depends, my Lord, whether I first embrace your Lordship's principles, or your Lordship's mistresses.
> Charles Petrie *The Four Georges* (1935); probably apocryphal

Emma Hart Willard 1787–1870
American pioneer of women's education

1 Rocked in the cradle of the deep.
> title of song (1840), inspired by a prospect of the Bristol Channel

William III (William of Orange)
1650–1702
British monarch, King of Great Britain and Ireland from 1688

2 'Do you not see your country is lost?' asked the Duke of Buckingham. 'There is one way never to see it lost' replied William, 'and that is to die in the last ditch.'
> Bishop Gilbert Burnet *History of My Own Time* (1838 ed.)

3 Every bullet has its billet.
> John Wesley *Journal* (1827) 6 June 1765

Isaac Williams 1802–65
English clergyman

4 Be thou my Guardian and my Guide.
> title of hymn (1842)

Peter Williams

5 Guide me, O thou great Jehovah,
Pilgrim through this barren land;
I am weak, but thou art mighty;
Hold me with thy powerful hand;
Bread of heaven, bread of heaven,
Feed me till I want no more.
first line frequently in the form 'O thou great Redeemer'
> 'Praying for Strength' (1771); translation of 'Arglwydd, arwain trwy'r anialwch' (1745) by William Williams (1717–91)

R. J. P. Williams 1926–
British chemist

6 Biology is the search for the chemistry that works.
> lecture in Oxford, June 1996

Rowan Williams 1950–
British Anglican clergyman

7 I can only ask your prayers as, like Augustine shivering in his shoes on the French coast at the prospect of dealing with the savage English, I stand on the shore wondering what lies ahead.
> in *The Times* 28 September 2002

8 We have to learn to be human alongside all sorts of others, the ones whose company we don't greatly like.
> in *Independent* 1 March 2003

Sarah Williams 1814–68
British writer

9 Though my soul may set in darkness, it will rise in perfect light;

I have loved the stars too fondly to be fearful of the night.
> 'The Old Astronomer to His Pupil' (1920)

Tennessee Williams 1911–83
American dramatist

10 What is the victory of a cat on a hot tin roof?—I wish I knew . . . Just staying on it, I guess, as long as she can.
> *Cat on a Hot Tin Roof* (1955) act 1

11 A vacuum is a hell of a lot better than some of the stuff that nature replaces it with.
> *Cat on a Hot Tin Roof* (1955) act 2

12 Time is the longest distance between two places.
> *The Glass Menagerie* (1945)

13 We're all of us sentenced to solitary confinement inside our own skins, for life!
> *Orpheus Descending* (1958) act 2, sc. 1

14 BLANCHE: I don't want realism.
MITCH: Naw, I guess not.
BLANCHE: I'll tell you what I want. Magic!
> *A Streetcar Named Desire* (1947) sc. 9

15 I have always depended on the kindness of strangers.
> *A Streetcar Named Desire* (1947) sc. 11

William Carlos Williams
1883–1963
American poet

16 so much depends
upon

a red wheel
barrow

glazed with rain
water

beside the white
chickens.
> 'The Red Wheelbarrow' (1923)

Marianne Williamson 1953–
American writer and philanthropist

17 Our deepest fear is not that we are inadequate. Our deepest fear is that we are powerful beyond measure. It is our light, not our darkness, that most frightens us.
> *A Return to Love* (1992) ch. 7

Roy Williamson 1936–90
Scottish folk singer and musician

18 O flower of Scotland, when will we see your like again,
that fought and died for your wee bit hill and glen
and stood against him, proud Edward's army,
and sent him homeward tae think again.
unofficial Scottish Nationalist anthem
> 'O Flower of Scotland' (1968)

Love Maria Willis 1824–1908
American doctor's wife

19 Father, hear the prayer we offer:
Not for ease that prayer shall be.
> 'Father, hear the prayer we offer' (1864 hymn)

Wendell Willkie 1892–1944
American lawyer and politician

1 The constitution does not provide for first and second class citizens.
An American Programme (1944) ch. 2

Angus Wilson 1913–91
English novelist and short-story writer

2 Once a Catholic always a Catholic.
The Wrong Set (1949) p. 168

Charles E. Wilson 1890–1961
American industrialist

3 For years I thought what was good for our country was good for General Motors and vice versa. The difference did not exist. Our company is too big. It goes with the welfare of the country.
testimony to the Senate Armed Services Committee on his proposed nomination for Secretary of Defence, 15 January 1953

Harold Wilson 1916–95
British Labour statesman, Prime Minister 1964–70, 1974–6

4 The Britain that is going to be forged in the white heat of this revolution will be no place for restrictive practices or for outdated methods on either side of industry.
often quoted as, 'the white heat of technology'
speech at the Labour Party Conference, 1 October 1963

5 A week is a long time in politics.
probably first said at the time of the 1964 sterling crisis
Nigel Rees *Sayings of the Century* (1984)

6 From now the pound abroad is worth 14 per cent or so less in terms of other currencies. It does not mean, of course, that the pound here in Britain, in your pocket or purse or in your bank, has been devalued.
often quoted as 'the pound in your pocket'
ministerial broadcast, 19 November 1967

7 Get your tanks off my lawn, Hughie.
to the trade union leader Hugh Scanlon, at Chequers in June 1969
Peter Jenkins *The Battle of Downing Street* (1970)

Harriette Wilson 1789–1846
English courtesan

8 I shall not say why and how I became, at the age of fifteen, the mistress of the Earl of Craven.
Memoirs (1825) opening words

Woodrow Wilson 1856–1924
American Democratic statesman, 28th President of the US 1913–21

9 It is like writing history with lightning. And my only regret is that it is all so terribly true.
on seeing D. W. Griffith's film The Birth of a Nation
at the White House, 18 February 1915

10 No nation is fit to sit in judgement upon any other nation.
speech in New York, 20 April 1915

11 There is such a thing as a man being too proud to fight.
speech in Philadelphia, 10 May 1915

12 We have stood apart, studiously neutral.
speech to Congress, 7 December 1915

13 It must be a peace without victory . . . Only a peace between equals can last.
speech to US Senate, 22 January 1917

14 The world must be made safe for democracy.
speech to Congress, 2 April 1917

15 Once lead this people into war and they will forget there ever was such a thing as tolerance.
John Dos Passos *Mr Wilson's War* (1917) pt. 3, ch. 12

16 Open covenants of peace, openly arrived at.
the first of the 'Fourteen Points'
speech to Congress, 8 January 1918, in *Selected Addresses* (1918)

17 America is the only idealistic nation in the world.
speech at Sioux Falls, South Dakota, 8 September 1919; in *Messages and Papers* (1924) vol. 2

Walter Winchell 1897–1972
American journalist

18 Good evening, Mr and Mrs North America and all the ships at sea. Let's go to press! Flash!
habitual introduction to network radio spot, 1931–56

Anne Finch, Lady Winchilsea 1661–1720
English poet

19 Now the jonquil o'ercomes the feeble brain; We faint beneath the aromatic pain.
'The Spleen' (1701)

Duchess of Windsor (Wallis Simpson) 1896–1986
American-born wife of the former Edward VIII

20 You can never be too rich or too thin.
attributed

Duke of Windsor *see* Edward VIII

Oprah Winfrey 1954–
American talk show host

21 I am grateful for the blessings of wealth, but it hasn't changed who I am. My feet are still on the ground. I'm just wearing better shoes.
in *Independent on Sunday* 18 July 2004

Catherine Winkworth 1827–78
English translator of German hymns

22 Now thank we all our God,

With heart and hands and voices.
Lyra Germanica (1858) 'Now thank we all our God' (translation of Martin Rinkart's 'Nun danket alle Gott', *c.*1636)

1 Praise to the Lord! the Almighty, the King of creation!
title of hymn (1863); translated from the German of Joachim Neander (1650–80)

Robert Winston 1940–
British obstetrician and gynaecologist

2 The kind of child you have depends almost entirely on how you bring it up. Genes and inherited dispositions are pieces of trivia really.
in *Observer* 11 January 2004

John Winthrop 1588–1649
American settler

3 We must consider that we shall be a city upon a hill, the eyes of all people are on us; so that if we shall deal falsely with our God in this work we have undertaken, and so cause Him to withdraw His present help from us, we shall be made a story and a byword through the world.
Christian Charity, A Model Hereof (sermon, 1630)

Robert Charles Winthrop 1809–94
American politician

4 A Star for every State, and a State for every Star.
speech on Boston Common, 27 August 1862, in *Addresses and Speeches* vol. 2 (1867)

Owen Wister 1860–1938
American novelist

5 When you call me that, *smile!*
'that' being 'you son-of-a—'
The Virginian (1902) ch. 2

George Wither 1588–1667
English poet and pamphleteer

6 I loved a lass, a fair one,
As fair as e'er was seen;
She was indeed a rare one,
Another Sheba queen.
A Description of Love (1620) 'I loved a lass, a fair one'

Ludwig Wittgenstein 1889–1951
Austrian-born philosopher

7 Philosophy is a battle against the bewitchment of our intelligence by means of language.
Philosophische Untersuchungen (1953) pt. 1, sect. 109

8 The philosopher's treatment of a question is like the treatment of an illness.
Philosophische Untersuchungen (1953) pt. 1, sect. 255

9 What is your aim in philosophy?—To show the fly the way out of the fly-bottle.
Philosophische Untersuchungen (1953) pt. 1, sect. 309

10 What can be said at all can be said clearly; and whereof one cannot speak thereof one must be silent.
Tractatus Logico-Philosophicus (1922) preface

11 The world is everything that is the case.
Tractatus Logico-Philosophicus (1922)

12 Death is not an event in life: we do not live to experience death.
Tractatus Logico-Philosophicus (1922)

13 The limits of my language mean the limits of my world.
Tractatus Logico-Philosophicus (1922)

14 The world of the happy is quite different from that of the unhappy.
Tractatus Logico-Philosophicus (1922)

15 Tell them I've had a wonderful life.
to his doctor's wife, before losing consciousness, 28 April 1951
Ray Monk *Ludwig Wittgenstein* (1990)

P. G. Wodehouse 1881–1975
English writer; an American citizen from 1955

16 It is never difficult to distinguish between a Scotsman with a grievance and a ray of sunshine.
Blandings Castle and Elsewhere (1935) 'The Custody of the Pumpkin'

17 He spoke with a certain what-is-it in his voice, and I could see that, if not actually disgruntled, he was far from being gruntled.
The Code of the Woosters (1938) ch. 1

18 It is no use telling me that there are bad aunts and good aunts. At the core, they are all alike. Sooner or later, out pops the cloven hoof.
The Code of the Woosters (1938) ch. 2

19 When Aunt is calling to Aunt like mastodons bellowing across primeval swamps.
The Inimitable Jeeves (1923) ch. 16

20 It is a good rule in life never to apologize. The right sort of people do not want apologies, and the wrong sort take a mean advantage of them.
The Man Upstairs (1914) title story; see **Hubbard** 177:7

21 What with excellent browsing and sluicing and cheery conversation and what-not, the afternoon passed quite happily.
My Man Jeeves (1919) 'Jeeves and the Unbidden Guest'

22 Ice formed on the butler's upper slopes.
Pigs Have Wings (1952) ch. 5

23 The Right Hon. was a tubby little chap who looked as if he had been poured into his clothes and had forgotten to say 'When!'
Very Good, Jeeves (1930) 'Jeeves and the Impending Doom'

Charles Wolfe 1791–1823
Irish poet

24 Not a drum was heard, not a funeral note,
As his corse to the rampart we hurried.
'The Burial of Sir John Moore at Corunna' (1817)

1 We buried him darkly at dead of night,
  The sods with our bayonets turning.
  'The Burial of Sir John Moore at Corunna' (1817)

2 We carved not a line, and we raised not a
  stone—
  But we left him alone with his glory.
  'The Burial of Sir John Moore at Corunna' (1817)

Humbert Wolfe 1886–1940
British poet

3 You cannot hope
  to bribe or twist,
  thank God! the
  British journalist.
  But, seeing what
  the man will do
  unbribed, there's
  no occasion to.
  'Over the Fire' (1930)

James Wolfe 1727–59
British general; captor of Quebec

4 The General . . . repeated nearly the whole
  of Gray's Elegy . . . adding, as he concluded,
  that he would prefer being the author of
  that poem to the glory of beating the French
  to-morrow.
  J. Playfair *Biographical Account of J. Robinson* in
  Transactions of the Royal Society of Edinburgh vol. 7
  (1815)

5 Now God be praised, I will die in peace.
  J. Knox *Historical Journal of the Campaigns in North
  America* (ed. A. G. Doughty, 1914) vol. 2

Thomas Wolfe 1900–38
American novelist

6 Which of us has not remained forever
  prison-pent? Which of us is not forever a
  stranger and alone?
  foreword to *Look Homeward, Angel* (1929)

7 You can't go home again.
  title of book, 1940

Tom Wolfe 1931–
American writer

8 The bonfire of the vanities.
  title of novel (1987); deriving from Savonarola's
  'burning of the vanities' in Florence, 1497

9 A liberal is a conservative who has been
  arrested.
  The Bonfire of the Vanities (1987) ch. 24

10 Electric Kool-Aid Acid test.
   title of novel on hippy culture (1968)

Mary Wollstonecraft 1759–97
English feminist

11 To give a sex to mind was not very
   consistent with the principles of a man
   [Rousseau] who argued so warmly, and so
   well, for the immortality of the soul.
   often quoted as, 'Mind has no sex'
   A Vindication of the Rights of Woman (1792) ch. 3

12 I do not wish them [women] to have power
   over men; but over themselves.
   A Vindication of the Rights of Woman (1792) ch. 4

Thomas Wolsey c.1475–1530
English cardinal; Lord Chancellor, 1515–29

13 Had I but served God as diligently as I have
   served the King, he would not have given
   me over in my grey hairs.
   George Cavendish *Negotiations of Thomas Wolsey*
   (1641); see **Shakespeare** 296:15

Kenneth Wolstenholme
English sports commentator

14 They think it's all over—it is now.
   television commentary in closing moments of
   the World Cup Final, 30 July 1966

Mrs Henry Wood 1814–87
English novelist

15 Dead! and . . . never called me mother.
   East Lynne (dramatized by T. A. Palmer, 1874, the
   words do not occur in the novel of 1861)

Thomas Woodrooffe 1899–1978
British naval officer

16 At the present moment, the whole Fleet's lit
   up. When I say 'lit up', I mean lit up by fairy
   lamps.
   *live outside broadcast, Spithead Review, 20 May
   1937*
   Asa Briggs *History of Broadcasting in the UK* (1965)
   vol. 2

Harry Woods

17 Oh we ain't got a barrel of money,
   Maybe we're ragged and funny,
   But we'll travel along
   Singin' a song,
   Side by side.
   'Side by Side' (1927 song)

Virginia Woolf 1882–1941
English novelist

18 Examine for a moment an ordinary mind on
   an ordinary day.
   The Common Reader (1925) 'Modern Fiction'

19 Life is a luminous halo, a semi-transparent
   envelope surrounding us from the
   beginning of consciousness to the end.
   The Common Reader (1925) 'Modern Fiction'

20 On or about December 1910 human nature
   changed.
   'Mr Bennett and Mrs Brown' (1924)

21 A woman must have money and a room of
   her own if she is to write fiction.
   A Room of One's Own (1929) ch. 1

22 Women have served all these centuries as
   looking-glasses possessing the magic and
   delicious power of reflecting the figure of a
   man at twice its natural size.
   A Room of One's Own (1929) ch. 2

23 This is an important book, the critic
   assumes, because it deals with war. This is
   an insignificant book because it deals with
   the feelings of women in a drawing-room.
   A Room of One's Own (1929) ch. 4

24 I have lost friends, some by death . . . others
   through sheer inability to cross the street.
   The Waves (1931)

1 The scratching of pimples on the body of the bootboy at Claridges.

of James Joyce's Ulysses

letter to Lytton Strachey, 24 April 1922

2 I read the book of Job last night. I don't think God comes well out of it.

letter to Lady Robert Cecil, 12 November 1922

3 As an experience, madness is terrific . . . and in its lava I still find most of the things I write about.

letter to Ethel Smyth, 22 June 1930

Alexander Woollcott 1887–1943
American writer

4 She was like a sinking ship firing on the rescuers.

of Mrs Patrick Campbell

While Rome Burns (1944) 'The First Mrs Tanqueray'

5 All the things I really like to do are either illegal, immoral, or fattening.

R. E. Drennan *Wit's End* (1973)

Dorothy Wordsworth 1771–1855
English writer

6 A beautiful evening, very starry, the horned moon.

'Alfoxden Journal' 23 March 1798; see **Coleridge** 100:23

7 I never saw daffodils so beautiful. They grew among the mossy stones about and about them; some rested their heads upon these stones as on a pillow for weariness; and the rest tossed and reeled and danced, and seemed as if they verily laughed with the wind that blew upon them over the lake.

'Grasmere Journal' 15 April 1802; see **Wordsworth** 364:17

Elizabeth Wordsworth 1840–1932
English educationist

8 If all the good people were clever,
And all clever people were good,
The world would be nicer than ever
We thought that it possibly could.
But somehow, 'tis seldom or never
The two hit it off as they should;
The good are so harsh to the clever,
The clever so rude to the good!

'Good and Clever'

William Wordsworth 1770–1850
English poet

9 Who is the happy Warrior? Who is he
Whom every man in arms should wish to be?

'Character of the Happy Warrior' (1807); see **Read** 273:18

10 Earth has not anything to show more fair:
Dull would he be of soul who could pass by
A sight so touching in its majesty:
This City now doth like a garment wear
The beauty of the morning.

'Composed upon Westminster Bridge' (1807)

11 Dear God! the very houses seem asleep;
And all that mighty heart is lying still!

'Composed upon Westminster Bridge' (1807)

12 The light that never was, on sea or land,
The consecration, and the Poet's dream.

on a picture of Peele Castle in a storm

'Elegiac Stanzas' (1807)

13 Bliss was it in that dawn to be alive,
But to be young was very heaven!

'The French Revolution, as it Appeared to Enthusiasts' (1809); also *The Prelude* (1850) bk. 9, l. 108

14 All shod with steel
We hissed along the polished ice.

'Influence of Natural Objects' (1809); also *The Prelude* (1850) bk. 1, l. 414

15 It is a beauteous evening, calm and free.

'It is a beauteous evening, calm and free' (1807)

16 We must be free or die, who speak the tongue
That Shakespeare spake.

'It is not to be thought of that the Flood' (1807)

17 I wandered lonely as a cloud
That floats on high o'er vales and hills,
When all at once I saw a crowd,
A host, of golden daffodils;
Beside the lake, beneath the trees,
Fluttering and dancing in the breeze.

'I wandered lonely as a cloud' (1815 ed.); see **Wordsworth** 364:7

18 For oft, when on my couch I lie
In vacant or in pensive mood,
They flash upon that inward eye
Which is the bliss of solitude;
And then my heart with pleasure fills,
And dances with the daffodils.

'I wandered lonely as a cloud' (1815 ed.)

19 On that best portion of a good man's life,
His little, nameless, unremembered, acts
Of kindness and of love.

'Lines composed a few miles above Tintern Abbey' (1798) l. 40

20 The still, sad music of humanity,
Nor harsh nor grating, though of ample power
To chasten and subdue.

'Lines composed . . . above Tintern Abbey' (1798) l. 91

21 A sense sublime
Of something far more deeply interfused,
Whose dwelling is the light of setting suns,
And the round ocean and the living air,
And the blue sky, and in the mind of man.

'Lines composed . . . above Tintern Abbey' (1798) l. 95

22 And much it grieved my heart to think
What man has made of man.

'Lines Written in Early Spring' (1798)

23 Milton! thou shouldst be living at this hour:
England hath need of thee: she is a fen
Of stagnant waters.

'Milton! thou shouldst be living at this hour' (1807)

24 My heart leaps up when I behold
A rainbow in the sky:

'My heart leaps up when I behold' (1807)

1 The Child is father of the Man.
'My heart leaps up when I behold' (1807); see
Milton 239:16

2 There was a time when meadow, grove, and
stream,
The earth, and every common sight,
To me did seem
Apparelled in celestial light,
The glory and the freshness of a dream.
'Ode. Intimations of Immortality' (1807) st. 1

3 The rainbow comes and goes,
And lovely is the rose.
'Ode. Intimations of Immortality' (1807) st. 2

4 A timely utterance gave that thought relief,
And I again am strong.
'Ode. Intimations of Immortality' (1807) st. 3

5 Whither is fled the visionary gleam?
Where is it now, the glory and the dream?
'Ode. Intimations of Immortality' (1807) st. 4

6 Our birth is but a sleep and a forgetting:
The Soul that rises with us, our life's Star,
Hath had elsewhere its setting,
And cometh from afar:
Not in entire forgetfulness,
And not in utter nakedness,
But trailing clouds of glory do we come
From God, who is our home:
Heaven lies about us in our infancy!
Shades of the prison-house begin to close
Upon the growing boy.
'Ode. Intimations of Immortality' (1807) st. 5

7 And by the vision splendid
Is on his way attended;
At length the man perceives it die away,
And fade into the light of common day.
'Ode. Intimations of Immortality' (1807) st. 5

8 But for those obstinate questionings
Of sense and outward things,
Fallings from us, vanishings;
Blank misgivings of a creature
Moving about in worlds not realised,
High instincts before which our mortal
nature
Did tremble like a guilty thing surprised.
'Ode. Intimations of Immortality' (1807) st. 9

9 Though nothing can bring back the hour
Of splendour in the grass, of glory in the
flower.
'Ode. Intimations of Immortality' (1807) st. 10

10 To me the meanest flower that blows can
give
Thoughts that do often lie too deep for tears.
'Ode. Intimations of Immortality' (1807) st. 11

11 Stern daughter of the voice of God!
'Ode to Duty' (1807)

12 Plain living and high thinking are no more:
The homely beauty of the good old cause
Is gone.
'O friend! I know not which way I must look'
(1807); see **Milton** 240:12

13 Once did she hold the gorgeous East in fee,
And was the safeguard of the West.
'On the Extinction of the Venetian Republic'
(1807)

14 A reasoning, self-sufficing thing,
An intellectual All-in-all!
'A Poet's Epitaph' (1800)

15 In common things that round us lie
Some random truths he can impart,—
The harvest of a quiet eye
That broods and sleeps on his own heart.
'A Poet's Epitaph' (1800)

16 The statue stood
Of Newton, with his prism, and silent face:
The marble index of a mind for ever
Voyaging through strange seas of Thought,
alone.
The Prelude (1850) bk. 3, l. 60

17 A day
Spent in a round of strenuous idleness.
The Prelude (1850) bk. 4, l. 377

18 All things have second birth;
The earthquake is not satisfied at once.
The Prelude (1850) bk. 10, l. 83

19 There is
One great society alone on earth,
The noble Living, and the noble Dead.
The Prelude (1850) bk. 11, l. 393

20 I thought of Chatterton, the marvellous boy,
The sleepless soul that perished in its pride.
'Resolution and Independence' (1807) st. 7

21 We poets in our youth begin in gladness;
But thereof comes in the end despondency
and madness.
'Resolution and Independence' (1807) st. 7

22 Still glides the Stream, and shall for ever
glide;
The Form remains, the Function never dies.
'The River Duddon' (1820) no. 34 'After-
Thought'

23 We feel that we are greater than we know.
'The River Duddon' (1820) no. 34 'After-
Thought'

24 The good old rule
Sufficeth them, the simple plan,
That they should take who have the power,
And they should keep who can.
'Rob Roy's Grave' (1807) l. 37

25 Scorn not the Sonnet; Critic, you have
frowned,
Mindless of its just honours; with this key
Shakespeare unlocked his heart.
'Scorn not the Sonnet' (1827); see **Browning**
72:7

26 She dwelt among the untrodden ways
Beside the springs of Dove,
A maid whom there were none to praise
And very few to love.
'She dwelt among the untrodden ways' (1800)

27 A violet by a mossy stone
Half hidden from the eye!
'She dwelt among the untrodden ways' (1800)

28 She lived unknown, and few could know
When Lucy ceased to be;
But she is in her grave, and, oh,
The difference to me!
'She dwelt among the untrodden ways' (1800)

1 She was a phantom of delight.
  title of poem (1807)

2 And now I see with eye serene
The very pulse of the machine;
A being breathing thoughtful breath.
  'She was a phantom of delight' (1807)

3 A perfect woman; nobly planned,
To warn, to comfort, and command.
  'She was a phantom of delight' (1807)

4 She seemed a thing that could not feel
The touch of earthly years.
  'A slumber did my spirit seal' (1800)

5 Behold her, single in the field,
Yon solitary Highland lass!
  'The Solitary Reaper' (1807)

6 For old, unhappy, far-off things,
And battles long ago.
  'The Solitary Reaper' (1807)

7 What, you are stepping westward?
  'Stepping Westward' (1807)

8 Surprised by joy—impatient as the wind.
  'Surprised by joy—impatient as the wind' (1815)

9 One impulse from a vernal wood
May teach you more of man,
Of moral evil and of good,
Than all the sages can.
  'The Tables Turned' (1798); see **Bernard** 32:11

10 Our meddling intellect
Mis-shapes the beauteous forms of things:—
We murder to dissect.
  'The Tables Turned' (1798)

11 Two Voices are there; one is of the sea,
One of the mountains; each a mighty Voice:
In both from age to age thou didst rejoice,
They were thy chosen music, Liberty!
  'Thought of a Briton on the Subjugation of
  Switzerland' (1807)

12 True to the kindred points of heaven and
home!
  'To a Skylark' (1827)

13 O Cuckoo! Shall I call thee bird,
Or but a wandering voice?
  'To the Cuckoo' (1807)

14 Thy friends are exultations, agonies,
And love, and man's unconquerable mind.
  'To Toussaint L'Ouverture' (1807)

15 A simple child, dear brother Jim,
That lightly draws its breath,
And feels its life in every limb,
What should it know of death?
  'We are Seven' (1798)

16 The world is too much with us; late and
soon,
Getting and spending, we lay waste our
powers.
  'The world is too much with us' (1807)

17 Great God! I'd rather be
A Pagan suckled in a creed outworn;
So might I, standing on this pleasant lea,
Have glimpses that would make me less
forlorn;
Have sight of Proteus rising from the sea;

Or hear old Triton blow his wreathèd horn.
  'The world is too much with us' (1807)

18 It may be safely affirmed, that there neither
is, nor can be, any *essential* difference
between the language of prose and metrical
composition.
  Lyrical Ballads (1800) preface

19 Poetry is the spontaneous overflow of
powerful feelings: it takes its origin from
emotion recollected in tranquillity.
  Lyrical Ballads (2nd ed., 1802) preface

20 Poetry is the breath and finer spirit of all
knowledge; it is the impassioned expression
which is in the countenance of all science.
  Lyrical Ballads (2nd ed., 1802) Preface

21 Never forget what I believe was observed to
you by Coleridge, that every great and
original writer, in proportion as he is great
and original, must himself create the taste
by which he is to be relished.
  letter to Lady Beaumont, 21 May 1807

Henry Wotton 1568–1639
English poet and diplomat

22 This man is freed from servile bands,
Of hope to rise, or fear to fall:—
Lord of himself, though not of lands,
And having nothing, yet hath all.
  'The Character of a Happy Life' (1614)

23 You meaner beauties of the night,
That poorly satisfy our eyes,
More by your number, than your light;
You common people of the skies,
What are you when the moon shall rise?
  'On His Mistress, the Queen of Bohemia' (1624)

24 He first deceased; she for a little tried
To live without him: liked it not, and died.
  'Upon the Death of Sir Albertus Moreton's Wife'
  (1651)

25 Well building hath three conditions.
Commodity, firmness, and delight.
  Elements of Architecture (1624) pt. 1

26 An ambassador is an honest man sent to lie
abroad for the good of his country.
  written in the album of Christopher Fleckmore
  in 1604

Frank Lloyd Wright 1867–1959
American architect

27 The physician can bury his mistakes, but the
architect can only advise his client to plant
vines—so they should go as far as possible
from home to build their first buildings.
  in *New York Times* 4 October 1953, sect. 6

James Wright 1927–80
American poet

28 Suddenly I realize
That if I stepped out of my body I would
break
Into blossom.
  'A Blessing' (1963)

Lady Mary Wroth c.1586–c.1652
English poet

29 Love, a child, is ever crying:

Please him and he straight is flying,
Give him, he the more is craving,
Never satisfied with having.
'Love, a child, is ever crying' (1621)

Thomas Wyatt c.1503–42
English poet

1 They flee from me, that sometime did me
seek
With naked foot, stalking in my chamber.
'They flee from me' (1557)

2 When her loose gown from her shoulders
did fall,
And she me caught in her arms long and
small;
Therewith all sweetly did me kiss,
And softly said, 'Dear heart, how like you
this?'
'They flee from me' (1557)

3 It was no dream: I lay broad waking.
'They flee from me' (1557)

4 There is written her fair neck round about:
'Noli me tangere for Caesar's I am,
And wild for to hold though I seem tame.'
'Whoso list to hunt, I know where is an hind'
(1557)

William Wycherley c.1640–1716
English dramatist

5 And with faint praises one another damn.
of drama critics
The Plain Dealer (1677) prologue; see **Pope** 266:21

Tammy Wynette 1942–98
and **Billy Sherrill** c.1938–

6 Stand by your man.
title of song (1968)

Xenophon c.428–c.354 BC
Greek historian

7 Thalassa, thalassa.
The sea! the sea!
Anabasis bk. 4, ch. 7, sect. 24

Augustin, Marquis de Ximénèz
1726–1817
French poet

8 Attaquons dans ses eaux
La perfide Albion!
Let us attack in her own waters perfidious
Albion!
'L'Ère des Français' (October 1793); see **Bossuet**
66:3

Minoru Yamasaki 1912–88
American architect

9 The World Trade Center should, because of
its importance, become a living
representation of man's belief in humanity,
his need for individual dignity, his belief in
the cooperation of men, and through this
cooperation his ability to find greatness.
Paul Heyer Architects on Architecture (1967)

William Yancey 1814–63
American Confederate politician

10 The man and the hour have met.
*of Jefferson **Davis**, President-elect of the
Confederacy, in 1861*
Shelby Foote The Civil War: Fort Sumter to
Perryville (1991)

W. F. Yeames 1835–1918
British painter

11 And when did you last see your father?
*a Roundhead officer addressing the child of a
Cavalier family*
title of painting (1878), now in the Walker Art
Gallery, Liverpool

W. B. Yeats 1865–1939
Irish poet

12 O body swayed to music, O brightening
glance,
How can we know the dancer from the
dance?
'Among School Children' (1928)

13 A starlit or a moonlit dome disdains
All that man is,
All mere complexities,
The fury and the mire of human veins.
'Byzantium' (1933)

14 That dolphin-torn, that gong-tormented sea.
'Byzantium' (1933)

15 The intellect of man is forced to choose
Perfection of the life, or of the work,
And if it take the second must refuse
A heavenly mansion, raging in the dark.
'The Choice' (1933)

16 I must lie down where all the ladders start,
In the foul rag-and-bone shop of the heart.
'The Circus Animals' Desertion' (1939) pt. 3

17 I made my song a coat
Covered with embroideries
Out of old mythologies.
'A Coat' (1914)

18 For there's more enterprise
In walking naked.
'A Coat' (1914)

19 We were the last romantics.
'Coole Park and Ballylee, 1931' (1933)

20 A woman can be proud and stiff
When on love intent;
But Love has pitched his mansion in
The place of excrement;
For nothing can be sole or whole
That has not been rent.
'Crazy Jane Talks with the Bishop' (1932)

21 Nor dread nor hope attend
A dying animal.
'Death' (1933)

22 He knows death to the bone—
Man has created death.
'Death' (1933)

23 Down by the salley gardens my love and I
did meet;
She passed the salley gardens with little
snow-white feet.

She bid me take love easy, as the leaves
  grow on the tree;
But I, being young and foolish, with her
  would not agree.
'Down by the Salley Gardens' (1889)

1 She bid me take life easy, as the grass grows
  on the weirs;
But I was young and foolish, and now am
  full of tears.
'Down by the Salley Gardens' (1889)

2 I have met them at close of day
Coming with vivid faces
From counter or desk among grey
Eighteenth-century houses.
I have passed with a nod of the head
Or polite meaningless words.
'Easter, 1916' (1921)

3 All changed, changed utterly:
A terrible beauty is born.
'Easter, 1916' (1921)

4 Too long a sacrifice
Can make a stone of the heart.
'Easter, 1916' (1921)

5 I write it out in a verse—
MacDonagh and MacBride
And Connolly and Pearse
Now and in time to be,
Wherever green is worn,
Are changed, changed utterly:
A terrible beauty is born.
'Easter, 1916' (1921)

6 The fascination of what's difficult
Has dried the sap of my veins, and rent
Spontaneous joy and natural content
Out of my heart.
'The Fascination of What's Difficult' (1910)

7 The ghost of Roger Casement
Is beating on the door.
'The Ghost of Roger Casement' (1939)

8 I have spread my dreams under your feet;
Tread softly because you tread on my
  dreams.
'He Wishes for the Cloths of Heaven' (1899)

9 The light of evening, Lissadell,
Great windows open to the south,
Two girls in silk kimonos, both
Beautiful, one a gazelle.
'In Memory of Eva Gore Booth and Con
Markiewicz' (1933)

10 The innocent and the beautiful
Have no enemy but time.
'In Memory of Eva Gore Booth and Con
Markiewicz' (1933)

11 My country is Kiltartan Cross;
My countrymen Kiltartan's poor.
'An Irish Airman Foresees his Death' (1919)

12 Nor law, nor duty bade me fight,
Nor public men, nor cheering crowds.
'An Irish Airman Foresees his Death' (1919)

13 The years to come seemed waste of breath,
A waste of breath the years behind
In balance with this life, this death.
'An Irish Airman Foresees his Death' (1919)

14 I will arise and go now, and go to Innisfree,
And a small cabin build there, of clay and
  wattles made;
Nine bean rows will I have there, a hive for
  the honey-bee,
And live alone in the bee-loud glade.
'The Lake Isle of Innisfree' (1893)

15 I hear lake water lapping with low sounds
  by the shore . . .
I hear it in the deep heart's core.
'The Lake Isle of Innisfree' (1893)

16 A shudder in the loins engenders there
The broken wall, the burning roof and
  tower
And Agamemnon dead.
'Leda and the Swan' (1928)

17 Like a long-legged fly upon the stream
His mind moves upon silence.
'Long-Legged Fly' (1939)

18 Did that play of mine send out
Certain men the English shot?
'The Man and the Echo' (1939)

19 We had fed the heart on fantasies,
The heart's grown brutal from the fare.
'Meditations in Time of Civil War' no. 6 'The
  Stare's Nest by my Window' (1928)

20 Think where man's glory most begins and
  ends,
And say my glory was I had such friends.
'The Municipal Gallery Re-visited' (1939)

21 Why, what could she have done, being what
  she is?
Was there another Troy for her to burn?
'No Second Troy' (1910)

22 I think it better that at times like these
A poet's mouth be silent, for in truth
We have no gift to set a statesman right.
'On being asked for a War Poem' (1919)

23 A pity beyond all telling,
Is hid in the heart of love.
'The Pity of Love' (1893)

24 How but in custom and in ceremony
Are innocence and beauty born?
'A Prayer for My Daughter' (1921)

25 Out of Ireland have we come.
Great hatred, little room,
Maimed us at the start.
I carry from my mother's womb
A fanatic heart.
'Remorse for Intemperate Speech' (1933)

26 That is no country for old men. The young
In one another's arms, birds in the trees
—Those dying generations—at their song,
The salmon-falls, the mackerel-crowded
  seas.
'Sailing to Byzantium' (1928)

27 An aged man is but a paltry thing,
A tattered coat upon a stick, unless
Soul clap its hands and sing, and louder sing
For every tatter in its mortal dress.
'Sailing to Byzantium' (1928)

28 And therefore I have sailed the seas and
  come

To the holy city of Byzantium.
'Sailing to Byzantium' (1928)

1 Things fall apart; the centre cannot hold;
Mere anarchy is loosed upon the world,
The blood-dimmed tide is loosed, and
everywhere
The ceremony of innocence is drowned;
The best lack all conviction, while the worst
Are full of passionate intensity.
'The Second Coming' (1921)

2 And what rough beast, its hour come round
at last,
Slouches towards Bethlehem to be born?
'The Second Coming' (1921)

3 Far-off, most secret and inviolate Rose.
'The Secret Rose' (1899)

4 A woman of so shining loveliness
That men threshed corn at midnight by a
tress,
A little stolen tress.
'The Secret Rose' (1899)

5 Romantic Ireland's dead and gone,
It's with O'Leary in the grave.
'September, 1913' (1914)

6 And pluck till time and times are done
The silver apples of the moon,
The golden apples of the sun.
'Song of Wandering Aengus' (1899)

7 Swift has sailed into his rest;
Savage indignation there
Cannot lacerate his breast.
'Swift's Epitaph' (1933); see **Swift** 329:6

8 But was there ever dog that praised his
fleas?
'To a Poet, Who would have Me Praise certain
bad Poets, Imitators of His and of Mine' (1910)

9 Red Rose, proud Rose, sad Rose of all my
days!
'To the Rose upon the Rood of Time' (1893)

10 Irish poets, learn your trade,
Sing whatever is well made.
'Under Ben Bulben' (1939) pt. 5

11 Cast your mind on other days
That we in coming days may be
Still the indomitable Irishry.
'Under Ben Bulben' (1939) pt. 5

12 Cast a cold eye
On life, on death.
Horseman, pass by!
'Under Ben Bulben' (1939) pt. 6

13 When you are old and grey and full of sleep,
And nodding by the fire, take down this
book,
And slowly read.
'When You Are Old' (1893)

14 Their hearts have not grown old.
'The Wild Swans at Coole' (1919)

15 We make out of the quarrel with others,
rhetoric, but of the quarrel with ourselves,
poetry.
Essays (1924) 'Anima Hominis' sect. 5

16 In dreams begins responsibility.
Responsibilities (1914) epigraph

17 We . . . are no petty people. We are one of
the great stocks of Europe. We are the
people of Burke; we are the people of Swift,
the people of Emmet, the people of Parnell.
of the Anglo-Irish
speech in the Irish Senate, 11 June 1925

18 Think like a wise man but express yourself
like the common people.
Letters on Poetry from W. B. Yeats to Dorothy
Wellesley (1940) 21 December 1935; see **Ascham**
17:15

Boris Yeltsin 1931–
Russian statesman, President 1991–99

19 You can make a throne of bayonets, but you
can't sit on it for long.
*from the top of a tank, during the attempted
military coup against* **Gorbachev**
in *Independent* 24 August 1991; see **Inge** 180:16

20 Today is the last day of an era past.
*at a Berlin ceremony to end the Soviet military
presence*
in *Guardian* 1 September 1994

Andrew Young 1932–
American clergyman and diplomat

21 Nothing is illegal if one hundred well-placed
business men decide to do it.
Morris K. Udall *Too Funny to be President* (1988)

Edward Young 1683–1765
English poet and dramatist

22 Some for renown on scraps of learning dote,
And think they grow immortal as they
quote.
The Love of Fame (1725–8) Satire 1, l. 89

23 Be wise with speed;
A fool at forty is a fool indeed.
The Love of Fame (1725–8) Satire 2, l. 282

24 One to destroy, is murder by the law;
And gibbets keep the lifted hand in awe;
To murder thousands, takes a specious
name,
'War's glorious art', and gives immortal
fame.
The Love of Fame (1725–8) Satire 7, l. 55; see
Porteus 269:7, **Rostand** 281:3

25 How science dwindles, and how volumes
swell,
How commentators each dark passage shun,
And hold their farthing candle to the sun.
The Love of Fame (1725–8) Satire 7, l. 96; see
Burton 78:7, **Sidney** 316:9

26 Tired Nature's sweet restorer, balmy sleep!
Night Thoughts (1742–5) 'Night 1' l. 1

27 Procrastination is the thief of time.
Night Thoughts (1742–5) 'Night 1' l. 393

28 At thirty a man suspects himself a fool;
Knows it at forty, and reforms his plan.
Night Thoughts (1742–5) 'Night 1' l. 417

29 All men think all men mortal, but
themselves.
Night Thoughts (1742–5) 'Night 1' l. 424

1 To know the world, not love her, is thy
point,
She gives but little, nor that little, long.
Night Thoughts (1742–5) 'Night 8' l. 1276; see
Goldsmith 153:12

2 An undevout astronomer is mad.
Night Thoughts (1742–5) 'Night 9' l. 770

3 The course of Nature is the art of God.
Night Thoughts (1742–5) 'Night 9' l. 1267

4 Life is the desert, life the solitude;
Death joins us to the great majority.
The Revenge (1721) act 4; see **Petronius** 262:17

George W. Young 1846–1919

5 The lips that touch liquor must never touch
mine.
title of poem (*c*..1870); also attributed, in a
different form, to Harriet A. Glazebrook, 1874

Neil Young 1945–
and Jeff Blackburn
Canadian singer and songwriter

6 It's better to burn out
Than to fade away.
quoted by Kurt **Cobain** *in his suicide note, 8 April
1994*
'My My, Hey Hey (Out of the Blue)' (1978 song)

Viktor Yushchenko 1954–
Ukrainian statesman

7 We are not on the outskirts of Europe, we
are at the centre of Europe.
in *Independent* 24 January 2005

Israel Zangwill 1864–1926
Jewish spokesman and writer

8 America is God's Crucible, the great
Melting-Pot where all the races of Europe
are melting and re-forming!
The Melting Pot (1908) act 1

Frank Zappa 1940–93
American rock musician and songwriter

9 A drug is neither moral or immoral—it's a
chemical compound. The compound itself is
not a menace to society until a human being
treats it as if consumption bestowed a
temporary licence to act like an asshole.
The Real Frank Zappa Book (1989)

10 Rock journalism is people who can't write
interviewing people who can't talk for
people who can't read.
Linda Botts *Loose Talk* (1980); see **Capp** 84:16

Zeno of Citium c.335–c.263 BC
Greek philosopher, founder of Stoicism

11 The reason why we have two ears and only
one mouth is that we may listen the more
and talk the less.
to a youth who was talking nonsense
Diogenes Laertius *Lives of the Philosophers* 'Zeno'
ch. 7

Zhuangzi *see* Chuang Tzu

Hiller B. Zobel 1932–
American judge

12 Judges must follow their oaths and do their
duty, heedless of editorials, letters,
telegrams, threats, petitions, panellists and
talk shows.
judicial ruling reducing the conviction of Louise
Woodward from murder to manslaughter, 10
November 1997

Zohar
chief text of the Jewish Kabbalah, 13th century

13 He made this world to match the world
above, and whatever exists above has its
counterpart below . . . and all is one.
bk. 2, 20a

Émile Zola 1840–1902
French novelist

14 One forges one's style on the terrible anvil
of daily deadlines.
Le Figaro 1881

15 Truth is on the march, and nothing will stop
it.
on the Dreyfus affair
in *Le Figaro* 25 November 1897

16 J'accuse.
I accuse.
*title of an open letter to the President of the French
Republic, in connection with the Dreyfus affair*
in *L'Aurore* 13 January 1898

Zoroastrian Scriptures
*4th-century texts of a religion of ancient Persia
founded by Zoroaster in the 6th century BC*

17 I profess myself a Mazda-worshipper, a
follower of Zarathustra, opposing the
Daevas, accepting the Ahuric doctrine.
The Gathas The Creed (Fravarane) yasna 12, v. 1,
tr. M. Boyce

18 Truly there are two primal Spirits, twins
renowned to be in conflict. In thought and
word, in act they are two: the better and the
bad.
The Gathas yasna 30, v. 3, tr. M. Boyce

Index

actions a. of the just — SHIR 316:1
a. of two bodies — NEWT 250:13
laugh at human a. — SPIN 322:9
my a. are my ministers' — CHAR 91:2
active a. line on a walk — KLEE 204:4
actor a.'s life for me — WASH 351:12
actors A. are cattle — HITC 170:3
acts desires but a. not — BLAK 56:25
no second a. in American lives — FITZ 137:15
Our a. our angels are — FLET 138:12
actual What is rational is a. — HEGE 165:3
actualité economical with the a. — CLAR 97:3
actum Nil a. credens — LUCA 220:8
ad reminded of that a. — MOND 242:6
adage poor cat i' the a. — SHAK 300:6
Adam A., the goodliest man — MILT 238:23
A. was a gardener — SHAK 296:4
A. was but human — TWAI 343:21
good thing A. had — TWAI 343:18
gratitude we owe to A. — TWAI 343:22
in A. all die — BIBL 50:28
old A. in this Child — BOOK 61:16
riverrun, past Eve and A.'s — JOYC 192:19
When A. delved and Eve span — ROLL 279:1
whipped the offending A. — SHAK 295:11
adamant a. for drift — CHUR 95:3
frame of a. — JOHN 187:25
adazzle sweet, sour; a., dim — HOPK 174:2
added all these things shall be a. — BIBL 44:1
adder brings forth the a. — SHAK 296:23
deaf as an a. — ADAM 2:2
like the deaf a. — BOOK 63:12
addiction a. is bad — JUNG 193:19
prisoners of a. — ILLI 180:13
address non-existent a. — LEWI 213:21
adeste A., fideles — ANON 13:5
adieu Bidding a. — KEAT 196:15
ad infinitum proceed a. — SWIF 329:2
adjective As to the A. — TWAI 343:25
Adlestrop Yes; I remember A. — THOM 338:7
administered Whate'er is best a. — POPE 267:32
administrative a. won't — LYNN 221:1
admiral kill an a. from time to time — VOLT 348:8
admiralty price of a. — KIPL 202:26
admirari Nil a. — HORA 174:25
admire Not to a., is all the art — POPE 268:9
admittance No a. till — CARR 87:16
adolescence a. and obsolescence — LINK 215:11
Adonais I weep for A. — SHEL 313:13
adored I was a. once — SHAK 308:32
adorn a. a tale — JOHN 187:26
adsuitur Purpureus A. pannus — HORA 174:12
adult a. is to be alone — ROST 281:2
not the occupation of an a. — OLIV 253:10
adulteration adultery, but a. — BYRO 81:6
adulteries a. of art — JONS 191:16
adultery call gallantry, and gods a. — BYRO 80:21
committed a. in my heart — CART 88:2
die for a. — SHAK 298:17
Do not a. commit — CLOU 98:18
Not quite a. — BYRO 81:6
Thou shalt not commit a. — BIBL 35:28
woman taken in a. — BIBL 48:32
adults by a. to children — SZAS 329:18
children produce a. — DE V 114:3
advance A. Australia — MCCO 222:14
retrograde if it does not a. — GIBB 149:1
somewhat to a. — POPE 268:7
When we our sails a. — DRAY 121:13
advantage A. rarely comes of it — CLOU 98:18
Japan's a. — HIRO 170:1
take a mean a. of them — WODE 362:20
undertaking of Great A. — ANON 7:18

with equal a. content — CANN 84:6
advent Hark to the a. voice — OAKL 252:14
adventure a. is only an inconvenience — CHES 93:8
awfully big a. — BARR 27:2
most beautiful a. in life — FROH 143:3
pass out into a. — FORS 139:15
to be without an a. — FORE 139:11
adversity a. doth best — BACO 22:10
A.'s sweet milk — SHAK 307:3
bread of a. — BIBL 40:25
fortunes sharpe a. — CHAU 92:3
Sweet are the uses of a. — SHAK 290:5
that will stand a. — CARL 85:17
advertisement soul of an a. — JOHN 187:5
advertisements ideals by its a. — DOUG 120:6
advertisers a. don't object to — SWAF 328:4
advertising A. is the greatest art form — MCLU 224:1
A. may be described — LEAC 210:6
A. the rattling of a stick — ORWE 254:17
lust and calls it a. — LAHR 206:15
money I spend on a. — LEVE 213:11
advice A. is seldom welcome — CHES 92:18
seldom asks a. — ADDI 3:8
advise STREETS FLOODED. PLEASE A. — BENC 30:11
aere Exegi monumentum a. perennius — HORA 175:17
Aesculapius owe a cock to A. — SOCR 320:3
aesthetic a. enjoyment recognition of the pattern — WHIT 356:14
high a. line — GILB 150:12
aetas fugerit invida A. — HORA 175:7
afeared Be not a. — SHAK 307:29
affair a. is over — RICH 276:10
affairs taking part in a. — VALÉ 345:2
tide in the a. — SHAK 297:15
affection A. beaming in one eye — DICK 115:6
affections holiness of the heart's a. — KEAT 197:9
affinities Elective a. — GOET 152:17
affliction bread of a. — BIBL 37:17
mine a. and my misery — BIBL 41:25
waters of a. — BIBL 40:25
affluent a. society — GALB 145:2
afford Can't a. them — SHAW 312:28
unless you can a. it — TROL 342:4
Afghanistan left on A.'s plains — KIPL 203:9
afraid a. of his enemy — PLUT 265:12
a. of the sea — SYNG 329:16
a. of Virginia Woolf — ALBE 4:6
because she was a. of him — MURD 247:6
I, a stranger and a. — HOUS 176:3
in short, I was a. — ELIO 129:1
not that I'm a. to die — ALLE 5:15
taught to be a. — HAMM 160:25
what you are a. to do — EMER 132:7
Afric in A.-maps — SWIF 329:1
Africa A. and her prodigies — BROW 71:11
A. is a scar — BLAI 56:1
A. than my own body — ORTO 254:6
choose between this A. — WALC 349:5
new out of A. — PLIN 265:6
shape of A. — FANO 133:20
sloggin' over A. — KIPL 201:18
Till China and A. meet — AUDE 18:13
African [A.] national consciousness — MACM 224:5
I'm not an A. — GOLD 153:2
struggle of the A. people — MAND 226:16
after A. the first death — THOM 338:1
happily ever a. — ANON 7:9
morning a. — ADE 3:13
one damned thing a. another — HUBB 177:8
Or just a. — STEV 324:25
afternoon At five in the a. — LORC 218:16
lose the war in an a. — CHUR 96:7
summer a. — JAME 183:3

afternoons Winter A.	DICK 116:5	England was too pure an A.	ANON 10:4
Afton Flow gently, sweet A.	BURN 76:18	excellent canopy, the a.	SHAK 292:16
against a. every man	BIBL 34:31	fly through the a.	LEYB 214:7
a. everything	KENN 199:7	I am fire and a.	SHAK 289:29
always vote a.	FIEL 135:21	lands hatless from the a.	BETJ 33:3
life is 6 to 5 a.	RUNY 282:6	music in the a.	ELGA 127:3
not with me is a. me	BIBL 44:35	nipping and an eager a.	SHAK 291:33
somewhat a. thee	BIBL 53:2	**airline** a. ticket to romantic places	MARV 230:1
vote a. somebody	ADAM 1:17	**airplanes** feel about a.	KERR 199:11
who can be a. us	BIBL 50:8	**airy** A., fairy Lilian	TENN 333:21
Agamemnon And A. dead	YEAT 368:16	nations' a. navies	TENN 333:27
face of A.	SCHL 286:13	**Akond** A. of Swat	LEAR 210:8
When A. cried aloud	ELIO 129:16	**Alamo** Remember the A.	SHER 315:22
agate bigger than an a.-stone	SHAK 306:23	**alas** A. but cannot pardon	AUDE 19:21
age A. appears to be best	BACO 22:5	A., poor Yorick	SHAK 294:3
A. cannot wither her	SHAK 289:19	Hugo—a.	GIDE 149:13
a. demanded an image	POUN 269:22	on the grass a.	STEI 323:15
A., I do abhor thee	SHAK 309:32	**albatross** I shot the A.	COLE 100:17
a. is a dream that is dying	O'SH 255:16	**Albert** Went there with young A.	EDGA 125:3
a. of chivalry	BURK 75:18	**Albion** perfidious A.	XIMÉ 367:8
a. of ease	GOLD 153:6	**alcohol** A. a very necessary article	SHAW 311:26
a., which forgives itself	SHAW 312:17	a. doesn't thrill me	PORT 269:2
A. will not be defied	BACO 23:4	a. or morphine	JUNG 193:19
Crabbed a. and youth	SHAK 309:31	taken more out of a.	CHUR 96:1
dawning of the a. of Aquarius	RADO 272:19	**Aldershot** burnish'd by A. sun	BETJ 33:5
days of our a.	BOOK 63:23	**ale** no more cakes and a.	SHAK 308:30
fetch the a. of gold	MILT 237:8	spicy nut-brown a.	MILT 236:23
He was not of an a.	JONS 192:7	**Alexander** gane, like A.	BURN 76:23
if a. could	ESTI 133:3	not A.	ALEX 4:11
invention of a barbarous a.	MILT 237:13	Some talk of A.	ANON 11:1
old a. always fifteen years older	BARU 27:8	**Alexandrine** needless A.	POPE 267:12
Old a. is the most unexpected	TROT 342.5	**algebraic** weaves a. patterns	LOVE 219.8
Soul of the a.	JONS 192:4	**alibi** always has an a.	ELIO 129:9
tells her real a.	WILD 359:2	**Alice** Christopher Robin went down with A.	
very attractive a.	WILD 358:13		MILN 235:13
when Mozart was my a.	LEHR 211:21	**alien** a. people clutching their gods	ELIO 128:27
with a. and dust	RALE 273:3	a. tears will fill for him	WILD 359:11
worth an a. without a name	MORD 244:14	amid the a. corn	KEAT 196:23
aged a. man is but a paltry thing	YEAT 368:27	blame the a.	AESC 3:21
a. thrush	HARD 161:22	damned if I'm an a.	GEOR 148:2
allow this a. man his right	PEEL 261:6	**alike** all places were a. to him	KIPL 203:13
means Certainly a.	BYRO 81:4	**aliter** Dis a. visum	VIRG 347:5
agenda any item of the a.	PARK 259:13	**alive** a. and well	ANON 9:6
agendum quid superessit a.	LUCA 220:8	gets out a.	MORR 245:17
ages belongs to the a.	STAN 323:4	If we can't stay here a.	MONT 243:8
God, our help in a. past	WATT 352:2	man fully a.	IREN 180:23
heir of all the a.	TENN 333:31	noise and tumult when a.	EDWA 125:12
Rock of A.	TOPL 341:7	not just being a.	MART 229:10
aggressors God loves not the a.	KORA 204:21	Not while I'm a.	BEVI 33:18
Agnes St A.' Eve	KEAT 195:11	Officiously to keep a.	CLOU 98:17
agnostic title of 'a.'	HUXL 179:15	still a. at twenty-two	KING 201:11
agnosticism all a. means	DARR 110:1	was dead, and is a.	BIBL 47:33
agnus A. Dei	MISS 240:25	ways of being a.	DAWK 111:7
agonies exultations, a.	WORD 366:14	what keeps you a.	CAST 88:11
agony a. is abated	MACA 222:4	**all** 1066 and a. that	SELL 288:17
am in a.	CATU 89:8	a. for love	SPEN 322:2
agree a. with the book of God	OMAR 253:11	A. for one, one for all	DUMA 123:4
appear to a.	PAIN 257:19	a. hell broke loose	MILT 238:29
colours will a.	BACO 23:18	a. must have prizes	CARR 86:6
agreeable power to be a.	SWIF 328:23	a. shall be well	ELIO 128:18
agreement a. with hell	GARR 146:11	a. shall be well	JULI 193:14
with hell are we at a.	BIBL 40:24	A. that a man hath	BIBL 37:34
a-hunting a. we will go	FIEL 135:9	a. the world is young	KING 201:9
We daren't go a.	ALLI 5:19	a. things to all men	BIBL 50:19
ail Oh, what can a. thee	KEAT 195:23	A. things were made by him	BIBL 48:14
ailments our a. are the same	SWIF 328:13	Jack — I'm a. right	BONE 59:6
aim a. a little above it	LONG 217:10	man for a. seasons	WHIT 357:17
That at which all things a.	ARIS 15:12	or a. in all	TENN 332:17
when you have forgotten your a.	SANT 285:12	we should at a. times	BOOK 61:12
ain't a. necessarily so	HEYW 168:13	**allegiance** a. to the flag	BELL 29:15
Say it a. so	ANON 10:16	**allegory** headstrong as an a.	SHER 315:13
air A. and angels	DONN 119:5	**Allen** love of Barbara A.	BALL 25:8
death of a.	ELIO 128:13	**alley** lives in our a.	CARE 84:21

alley (cont.)
rats' a. ELIO 129:24
alliance A., *n*. In international politics BIER 54:16
alliances clear of permanent a. WASH 351:7
entangling a. with none JEFF 184:7
allies no eternal a. PALM 258:4
alliteration A.'s artful aid CHUR 94:16
allons A., *enfants de la patrie* ROUG 281:6
allow Government and public opinion a. SHAW 312:2
almanack Look in the a. SHAK 303:24
almighty a. dollar IRVI 181:4
A.'s orders to perform ADDI 2:19
A., the King of Creation WINK 362:1
almost A. thou persuadest me BIBL 49:37
alms a. and oblations BOOK 61:6
a. may be in secret BIBL 43:21
puts a. for oblivion SHAK 308:11
alone adult is to be a. ROST 281:2
a. against smiling enemies BOWE 66:14
A. and palely loitering KEAT 195:23
being a. together LA B 206:11
dangerous to meet it a. WHAR 355:18
go home a. JOPL 192:12
I want to be a. GARB 146:1
live, as we dream — a. CONR 102:21
more a. while living CARR 86:2
never less a. ROGE 278:12
never walk a. HAMM 160:24
not sufficiently a. VALÉ 345:1
One is one and all a. ANON 9:2
stranger and a. WOLF 363:6
that the man should be a. BIBL 34:10
We were a. JAME 183:1
who travels a. KIPL 202:14
aloud Angels cry a. BOOK 59:17
Alph A., the sacred river, ran COLE 100:7
Alpha A. and Omega BIBL 53:1
alpine through an A. village LONG 217:12
alps A. on Alps arise POPE 267:7
altar a. with this inscription BIBL 49:30
even the a. sheds tears TALM 330:17
alteram *Audi partem a.* AUGU 20:7
alteration A. though it be HOOK 173:1
alters when it a. finds SHAK 310:21
altered a. her person for the worse SWIF 328:18
alternatives exhausted all other a. EBAN 124:18
ignorance of a. ANGE 7:2
altogether righteous a. BOOK 62:12
alway I am with you a. BIBL 46:21
always a. be an England PARK 259:9
a. in the majority KNOX 204:10
sometimes a. RICH 276:13
Alzheimer he had A.'s disease REAG 274:9
am a.—yet what I am CLAR 96:26
I A. THAT I AM BIBL 35:15
I think, therefore I a. DESC 113:15
Ama *A. et fac quod vis* AUGU 20:8
Amaryllis sport with A. MILT 236:29
amateur whine of the a. for three WHIS 355:23
amaze vainly men themselves a. MARV 229:15
amazing A. grace NEWT 250:18
A. love WESL 354:17
ambassador a. is an honest man WOTT 366:26
amber in a. to observe the forms POPE 266:19
ambiguity Seven types of a. EMPS 132:25
ambition A. can creep BURK 75:28
A. should be made SHAK 297:4
fling away a. SHAK 296:14
make a. virtue SHAK 305:5
Vaulting a. SHAK 300:3
ambitious as he was a., I slew him SHAK 296:32
of a. minds SPEN 322:5
ambo *Arcades a.* VIRG 347:22

Ambree Mary A. BALL 25:13
âme *â. est sans défauts* RIMB 277:4
amen Will no man say, a. SHAK 306:3
America America! A. BATE 27:17
A. is a vast conspiracy UPDI 344:16
A. is God's Crucible ZANG 370:8
A. is now given over HAWT 163:15
A. is the only idealistic WILS 361:17
A.'s present need HARD 161:12
A., thou half-brother BAIL 24:15
A. thus top nation SELL 288:20
Australia looks to A. CURT 108:18
born in A. MALC 226:2
cannot conquer A. PITT 264:5
England and A. divided SHAW 313:6
glorious morning for A. ADAM 2:15
God bless A. BERL 31:20
I like to be in A. SOND 320:10
impresses me most about A. EDWA 125:11
in common with A. WILD 358:2
in the living rooms of A. MCLU 223:19
I, too, sing A. HUGH 177:13
makes A. what it is STEI 323:16
next to god a. CUMM 108:5
O my A. DONN 118:21
to A. to convert the Indians WESL 355:1
United States of A. PAGE 256:20
what A. did you have GINS 151:6
American A. as cherry pie BROW 70:15
A. beauty rose ROCK 278:6
A. families more like BUSH 78:15
A. friends BLAI 55:22
A., this new man CEÈV 166:16
chief business of the A. people COOL 103:14
free man, an A. JOHN 186:5
I am A. bred MILL 234:21
I'm an A. GOLD 153:2
in love with A. names BENÉ 30:14
I shall die an A. WEBS 352:20
Miss A. Pie MCLE 223:15
no A. infidels SAHH 284:6
no second acts in A. lives FITZ 137:15
not a Virginian, but an A. HENR 166:23
oil controlling A. soil DYLA 124:12
send A. boys JOHN 186:9
truth, justice and the A. way ANON 8:5
vacant lands in A. JEFF 184:3
Americanism A. with its sleeves rolled MCCA 222:8
hyphenated A. ROOS 280:5
Americans A. are our best friends THOM 338:22
Good A., when they die APPL 14:10
my fellow A. KENN 199:1
passed to new generation of A. KENN 198:14
when bad A. die WILD 358:32
amicably a. if they can QUIN 272:10
amicus *A. Plato* ARIS 15:23
Amis cocoa for Kingsley A. COPE 104:1
amitti *non a. sed praemitti* CYPR 109:3
ammunition pass the a. FORG 139:12
amo *Non a. te* MART 229:8
Odi et a. CATU 89:8
amok patriotism run a. RATH 273:15
among A. them, but not of them BYRO 80:7
amor *a. che muove il sole* DANT 109:17
A. vincit omnia CHAU 91:16
Nunc scio quid sit A. VIRG 347:23
Omnia vincit a. VIRG 347:25
amorous my a. propensities JOHN 188:4
amour beginning of an A. BEHN 29:9
ampullas *Proicit a.* HORA 174:15
Amurath Not A. an Amurath succeeds SHAK 295:8
amuse talent to a. COWA 105:2
amused a. by its presumption THUR 340:5

We are not a.

amusements but for its a.   LEWI 214:3

analytical A. Engine weaves   LOVE 219:8

anarch Thy hand, great A.   POPE 266:9

anarchism A. is a game   SHAW 312:21

  A. stands for the liberation   GOLD 153:3

anarchist small a. community   BENN 30:22

anarchy Mere a. is loosed   YEAT 369:1

anatomy A. is destiny   FREU 142:16

ancestor If there were an a.   HUXL 179:22

ancestors look backward to their a.   BURK 75:15

ancestral A. voices prophesying war   COLE 100:10

ancestry pride of a.   POWE 270:17

  trace my a.   GILB 149:22

ancient a. and fish-like smell   SHAK 307:25

  A. of days   BIBL 42:8

  A. of Days   GRAN 155:8

  A. times   BACO 22:6

  feet in a. time   BLAK 57:8

  It is an a. Mariner   COLE 100:14

  rivers a. as the world   HUGH 177:14

  signals of the a. flame   DANT 109:14

  spark of that a. flame   VIRG 347:7

and including 'a.'   MCCA 222:10

angel a. from your door   BLAK 57:18

  a. in the house   PATM 260:10

  a. of death   BRIG 68:18

  A. of Death   BYRO 80:19

  a. of the Lord came down   TATE 330:21

  a. of the Lord came upon them   BIBL 47:2

  a. rides in the whirlwind   PAGE 256:19

  ape or an a.   DISR 117:8

  beautiful and ineffectual a.   ARNO 17:5

  better a. is a man   SHAK 310:28

  clip an A.'s wings   KEAT 196:3

  Death's bright a.   PROC 271:5

  for an a. to pass   FIRB 135:23

  Look homeward a.   MILT 237:1

  ministering a.   SHAK 294:5

  ministering a. thou   SCOT 287:20

  What a. wakes me   SHAK 303:27

  White as an a.   BLAK 57:20

  wrote like an a.   GARR 146:7

angeli Non Angli sed A.   GREG 157:7

angels Air and a.   DONN 119:5

  A. and ministers of grace   SHAK 291:35

  A. bending near the earth   SEAR 288:5

  A. cry aloud   BOOK 59:17

  a. fear to tread   POPE 267:18

  a., nor principalities   BIBL 50:9

  behold the a. of God   BIBL 35:2

  better a. of our nature   LINC 214:16

  By that sin fell the a.   SHAK 296:14

  entertained a. unawares   BIBL 52:17

  flights of a.   SHAK 294:14

  Four a. round my head   ANON 9:18

  Hear all ye a.   MILT 238:32

  make the a. weep   SHAK 302:5

  Michael and his a.   BIBL 53:12

  neglect God and his A.   DONN 119:24

  Not Angles but A.   GREG 157:7

  Our acts our a. are   FLET 138:12

  plead like a.   SHAK 300:1

  tongues of men and of a.   BIBL 50:22

  With a. round the throne   WATT 351:22

  women are a.   BYRO 81:23

anger Achilles' cursed a. sing   HOME 172:8

  A. and jealousy   ELIO 127:18

  A. is a short madness   HORA 174:24

  A. is one of the sinews   FULL 144:15

  A. makes dull men   BACO 24:1

  Juno's never-forgetting a.   VIRG 346:19

  Look back in a.   OSBO 255:12

monstrous a. of the guns   OWEN 256:8

more in sorrow than in a.   SHAK 291:27

neither a. nor partiality   TACI 329:25

strike it in a.   SHAW 312:13

angle Brother of the A.   WALT 350:10

angler no man is born an a.   WALT 350:9

angles Not A. but Angels   GREG 157:7

  Offer no a.   TESS 336:4

Angli Non A. sed Angeli   GREG 157:7

angling A. may be said to be   WALT 350:8

Anglo-Saxon A. attitudes   CARR 87:13

angry a. with my friend   BLAK 57:26

  A. young man   PAUL 260:14

  Be ye a.   BIBL 51:17

  when very a., swear   TWAI 343:24

anguis Latet a. in herba   VIRG 347:20

anguish With a. moist   KEAT 195:24

animal attend a dying a.   YEAT 367:21

  Be a good a.   LAWR 209:20

  be a good a.   SPEN 321:6

  every a. is sad   ANON 13:16

  Man is a noble a.   BROW 71:9

  Man is the Only A.   TWAI 343:12

  political a.   ARIS 15:19

  vegetable, a., and mineral   GILB 150:23

animals All a. are equal   ORWE 254:10

  a. are divided   BORG 65:20

  A., whom we have   DARW 110:12

  at its mercy: a.   KUND 206:8

  distinguish us from other a.   BEAU 28:2

  man from a.   OSLE 255:18

  mind of the lower a.   DARW 110:13

  production of the higher a.   DARW 110:9

  turn and live with a.   WHIT 357:7

animate a. the whole   SMIT 319:12

animula A. vagula blandula   HADR 158:13

Anna Here thou, great A.   POPE 268:18

Annabel Lee I and my A.   POE 265:13

annals a. are blank   MONT 243:7

Anne of A. of Cleves   HENR 166:18

  sister A., do you see nothing   PERR 262:6

annihilating A. all that's made   MARV 229:17

anniversaries secret a.   LONG 217:14

annoy a. with what you write   AMIS 6:8

  only does it to a.   CARR 86:9

annoyance a. of a good example   TWAI 343:26

annus a. horribilis   ELIZ 131:2

anointed balm from an a. king   SHAK 305:27

another always a. one walking   ELIO 130:1

  a. fine mess   LAUR 209:16

  in a. country   MARL 228:14

  members one of a.   BIBL 51:16

  not a. thing   BUTL 79:2

  when comes such a.   SHAK 297:10

answer A. a fool   BIBL 38:38

  a. came there none   CARR 87:4

  a. came there none   SCOT 287:7

  a. is blowin' in the wind   DYLA 124:3

  a. made it none   SHAK 291:26

  a. the phone   THUR 340:6

  on the way to a pertinent a.   BRON 69:7

  soft a.   BIBL 38:25

  stay for an a.   BACO 23:16

  what a dusty a.   MERE 233:9

  What is the a.   STEI 323:19

  wisest man can a.   COLT 102:1

answerable a. for what we choose   NEWM 250:8

answered no one a.   DE L 112:15

answering a. that of God   FOX 141:1

ant a.'s a centaur   POUN 270:2

  Go to the a.   BIBL 38:15

antagonist Our a. is our helper   BURK 75:25

Anthropophagi A., and men   SHAK 304:22

antic a. disposition	SHAK 292:6	Aquarius dawning of the age of A.	RADO 272:19
dance an a. hay	MARL 228:10	Aquitaine prince of A.	NERV 249:13
anticipation only in the a. of it	HITC 170:5	Arabia perfumes of A.	SHAK 301:24
anti-destin L'art est un a.	MALR 226:11	Arabs hundred thousand A.	BALF 25:6
antique traveller from an a. land	SHEL 314:9	like the A.	LONG 217:9
antiquity write for A.	LAMB 207:7	Aram Eugene A. walked between	HOOD 172:21
anvil a. of daily deadlines	ZOLA 370:14	Arbeit A. macht frei	ANON 12:20
anxiety A. is love's greatest killer	NIN 251:14	arbiter Elegantiae a.	TACI 330:2
taboo'd by a.	GILB 149:20	arbitrator old common a., Time	SHAK 308:15
any A. old iron	COLL 101:11	arboreal a. in its habits	DARW 110:5
anybody Is there a. there	DE L 112:14	Arcades A. ambo	VIRG 347:22
no one's a.	GILB 149:16	Arcadia Et in A. ego	ANON 13:10
anything A. for a quiet life	MIDD 233:20	Arcadians A. both	VIRG 347:22
A. goes	PORT 268:29	arch all experience is an a.	TENN 335:3
believe in a.	CHES 93:25	experience is an a.	ADAM 1:19
apart have stood a.	WILS 361:12	archer mark the a. little meant	SCOT 287:15
of man's life a thing a.	BYRO 80:24	arches down the a. of the years	THOM 338:14
ape a. for his grandfather	HUXL 179:22	Underneath the A.	FLAN 137:19
Is man an a.	DISR 117:8	archetypes known as a.	JUNG 193:16
naked a.	MORR 245:7	archipelago Gulag a.	SOLZ 320:7
apes a. and peacocks	MASE 230:16	architect a. can only advise	WRIG 366:27
ivory, and a.	BIBL 37:7	A. of the Universe	JEAN 183:16
aphrodisiac Power is the great a.	KISS 204:2	can be an a.	RUSK 282:12
Apollo songs of A.	SHAK 299:6	consent to be the a.	DOST 120:1
swear by A. the physician	HIPP 169:17	architecture A. acts the most slowly	DIMN 116:17
Apollyon his name is A.	BUNY 74:9	A. in general	SCHE 286:6
apologies do not want a.	WODE 362:20	A. is the art	JOHN 186:15
apologize good rule never to a.	WODE 362:20	rise and fall of English a.	BETJ 33:6
Never a.	FISH 136:4	Arden Ay, now am I in A.	SHAK 290:6
apology a. for the Devil	BUTL 79:15	ardet paries cum proximus a.	HORA 175:3
apostles A.: praise thee	BOOK 59:18	ardua a. ad astra	ANON 13:15
I am the least of the a.	BIBL 50:27	are be as they a.	CLEM 98:4
apostolic Catholic and A. Church	BOOK 61:4	we know what we a.	SHAK 293:29
apothecary starved a.	LOCK 217:1	arena actually in the a.	ROOS 280:3
apparel a. oft proclaims the man	SHAK 291:29	argue a. freely	MILT 240:9
apparition Anno 1670, was an a.	AUBR 18:11	arguing not a. with you	WHIS 355:22
appeal a. unto Caesar	BIBL 49:34	will be much a.	MILT 240:8
appear a. considerable	JOHN 189:2	argument All a. is against it	JOHN 189:20
appearance outward a.	BIBL 36:28	a. of the broken window	PANK 258:8
appearing Television is for a. on	COWA 105:12	a. of tyrants	PITT 263:20
appetite good digestion wait on a.	SHAK 301:6	height of this great a.	MILT 237:17
voracious a.	FIEL 135:12	I have found you an a.	JOHN 190:19
appetites carnal lusts and a.	BOOK 61:24	arise A., shine	BIBL 41:16
Our a. as apt to change	DRYD 121:28	aristocracy a. means government by	CHES 93:23
Subdue your a.	DICK 115:10	a. of Great Britain	BRIG 68:19
applause A., n. The echo	BIER 54:17	natural a. among men	JEFF 184:14
apple a. of his eye	BIBL 36:5	aristocratic a. class	ARNO 17:3
a. on the tree	DICK 115:30	Aristotle God of A.	HA-L 159:17
cabbage-leaf to make an a.-pie	FOOT 139:4	arithmetical a. ratio	MALT 226:12
make an a. pie from scratch	SAGA 284:3	ark into the A.	BIBL 34:28
sweet-a. reddens	SAPP 285:16	arm auld moon in her a.	BALL 25:17
want the a. for the apple's sake	TWAI 343:21	did not put your a. around it	BLAC 55:11
apples a., cherries, hops	DICK 115:18	long a. of coincidence	CHAM 90:8
a. of gold	BIBL 38:35	strength with his a.	BIBL 46:33
golden a. of the sun	YEAT 369:6	arma A. virumque cano	VIRG 346:19
Ripe a. drop	MARV 229:16	leges inter a.	CICE 96:23
applied no such things as a. sciences	PAST 260:4	armadas till the great A. come	NEWB 249:16
appointment a. by the corrupt few	SHAW 312:8	Armageddon called in the Hebrew tongue A.	
a. with him in Samarra	MAUG 231:11		BIBL 53:18
approbation A. from Sir Hubert	MORT 246:8	Lincoln County Road or A.	DYLA 124:11
appropriate used when a.	RUMS 281:19	We stand at A.	ROOS 280:4
approve I do not a.	MILL 234:17	armchair like a good a.	MATI 231:6
après A. nous le déluge	POMP 266:4	armed a. conflict	EDEN 125:2
apricocks dangling a.	SHAK 306:1	a. with more than complete steel	ANON 9:3
April A., April, Laugh	WATS 351:16	Armenteers Mademoiselle from A.	ANON 9:17
A. is the cruellest month	ELIO 129:17	armes Aux a., citoyens	ROUG 281:6
bright cold day in A.	ORWE 254:20	armful very nearly an a.	GALT 145:13
glory of an A. day	SHAK 309:15	armies a. clash by night	ARNO 16:13
Men are A. when they woo	SHAK 290:23	stronger than all the a.	ANON 11:8
Now that A.'s there	BROW 72:5	armistice It is an a. for twenty years	FOCH 138:19
Whan that A.	CHAU 91:11	armour a. of God	BIBL 51:20
aprons made themselves a.	BIBL 34:16	a. of light	BIBL 50:12
apt A. Alliteration	CHUR 94:16	a. of light	BOOK 60:19

ashes (*cont.*)
a. to ashes — BOOK 62:6
a. under Uricon — HOUS 176:11
burnt to a. — GRAH 155:1
past is a bucket of a. — SAND 285:8
universe to a. — MISS 241:5
Asia churches which are in A. — BIBL 52:36
not in A. — ARDR 14:18
Asian A. boys ought to be — JOHN 186:9
ask A., and it shall be given — BIBL 44:6
A. me no more — CARE 84:19
a. not what your country — KENN 199:1
could a. him anything — WEIS 353:9
Don't a., don't tell — NUNN 252:12
if you gotta a. — ARMS 16:5
Would this man a. why — AUDE 18:16
asking a. too much — CANN 84:6
time of a. — BOOK 61:22
asleep men were all a. — BRID 68:17
mother was glad to get a. — EMER 132:19
very houses seem a. — WORD 364:11
aspens Willows whiten, a. quiver — TENN 333:16
asphalt only monument the a. road — ELIO 129:13
aspidistra biggest a. in the world — HARP 162:15
Keep the a. flying — ORWE 254:16
ass crowned a. — HENR 166:15
kiss my a. in Macy's window — JOHN 186:10
law is a a. — DICK 115:16
law is such an a. — CHAP 90:19
not covet his a. — BIBL 35:28
with the jawbone of an a. — BIBL 36:18
assassin you are an a. — ROST 281:3
assassination A. has never changed — DISR 117:9
A. is the extreme form — SHAW 312:32
asserted boldly a. — BURR 77:22
asserting a. these rights — LAY 210:3
asses go seek the a. — BIBL 36:24
seeking a. found — MILT 239:17
assume A. a virtue — SHAK 293:21
assurance low on whom a. sits — ELIO 129:28
make a. double sure — SHAK 301:16
Assyrian A. came down — BYRO 80:18
Astolat lily maid of A. — TENN 332:13
astonish A. me — DIAG 114:7
a. the bourgeois — BAUD 27:21
astonished a. at my own moderation — CLIV 98:14
astonishment Your a.'s odd — KNOX 204:11
astra *ardua ad a.* — ANON 13:15
sic itur ad a. — VIRG 347:17
astray like sheep have gone a. — BIBL 41:10
not send their works a. — KORA 205:20
astronomer undevout a. is mad — YOUN 370:2
asunder let no man put a. — BOOK 62:2
let not man put a. — BIBL 45:17
asylum taken charge of the a. — ROWL 281:16
was in an a. — PALM 258:6
atheism inclineth man's mind to a. — BACO 22:12
atheist a. is a man — BUCH 73:15
I am still an a. — BUÑU 74:5
remain a sound a. — LEWI 213:20
sort of a. who does not — ORWE 254:15
atheists no a. in the foxholes — CUMM 108:12
Athenian not A. or Greek — SOCR 320:2
Athens A., the eye of Greece — MILT 239:18
athirst give unto him that is a. — BIBL 53:24
athletes All pro a. are bilingual — HOWE 177:1
Atlantic stormy North A. Ocean — LARD 208:11
atom a. has changed everything — EINS 126:9
carbon a. — JEAN 183:15
grasped the mystery of the a. — BRAD 67:9
atomic primordial a. globule — GILB 149:22
win an a. war — BRAD 67:8
atoms a. and space — DEMO 112:19

a. of Democritus — BLAK 57:10
brain to be composed of a. — HALD 159:9
attach wish to a. — AUST 20:28
attack by his plan of a. — SASS 286:1
called me an a. dog — REID 275:2
Labour's a. dog — PAXM 260:17
lead such dire a. — MACA 222:1
Problems worthy of a. — HEIN 165:5
attacked when a. it defends itself — ANON 12:10
attacking I am a. — FOCH 138:18
attempt that dares love a. — SHAK 306:30
attempted Something a. — LONG 218:10
attendant a. lord, one that will do — ELIO 129:2
attention a. must be paid — MILL 234:23
attic brain a. stocked — DOYL 120:12
furniture in Tolkien's a. — PRAT 270:19
glory of the A. stage — ARNO 16:26
O A. shape — KEAT 196:11
Where the A. bird — MILT 239:18
attire Her rich a. — KEAT 195:13
attitude Fair a. — KEAT 196:11
attitudes Anglo-Saxon a. — CARR 87:13
attraction feels the a. of earth — LONG 217:10
auburn Sweet A., loveliest village — GOLD 153:4
audace *toujours de l'a.* — DANT 109:18
audacity Arm me, a. — SHAK 291:4
aude *sapere a.* — HORA 174:23
audi A. *partem alteram* — AUGU 20:7
audience fit a. find — MILT 238:33
whisks his a. — HORA 174:17
audiences English-speaking a. — WHAR 355:17
auditorem *notas a. rapit* — HORA 174:17
augury we defy a. — SHAK 294:8
August A. is a wicked month — O'BR 252:17
corny as Kansas in A. — HAMM 160:23
recommence in A. — BYRO 81:8
Augustan next A. age — WALP 350:2
auld For a. lang syne — BURN 76:20
aunt A. is calling to Aunt — WODE 362:19
Charley's a. from Brazil — THOM 337:16
aunts bad a. and good aunts — WODE 362:18
his cousins and his a. — GILB 150:17
auream A. *quisquis mediocritatem* — HORA 175:10
auri A. *sacra fames* — VIRG 347:6
Auschwitz write a poem after A. — ADOR 3:18
year spent in A. — LEVI 213:12
austere beauty cold and a. — RUSS 283:8
Austerlitz A. and Waterloo — SAND 285:6
field of A. — KIPL 202:23
Australia Advance A. fair — MCCO 222:14
A. looks to America — CURT 108:18
Australian great A. Emptiness — WHIT 356:6
Austria Don John of A. is going — CHES 93:2
author a. of peace — BOOK 60:2
a. ought to write — FITZ 137:16
Choose an a. — DILL 116:14
expected to see an a. — PASC 259:18
in search of an a. — PIRA 263:16
like in a good a. — SMIT 318:21
authority A. forgets a dying king — TENN 332:20
A. without wisdom — BRAD 67:14
little brief a. — SHAK 302:5
make your peace with a. — MORR 245:21
autobiography a. is an obituary — CRIS 107:4
autocrat a.: that's my trade — CATH 89:1
automobile fix up his a. — CLAR 97:8
autres *encourager les a.* — VOLT 348:8
autumn Early a. — BASH 27:11
happy a. fields — TENN 334:15
mists of the a. mornings — ORWE 254:18
Now it is a. — LAWR 209:24
autumnal one a. face — DONN 118:20
availeth struggle naught a. — CLOU 98:21

avalanche perseverance of a mighty a.   HOUS 176:18
avarice A., the spur   HUME 178:7
  dreams of a.   JOHN 190:7
  dreams of a.   MOOR 243:18
ave a. atque vale   CATU 89:9
  A. Maria   ANON 13:8
avenge a. even a look   BURK 75:17
avenger Time, the a.   BYRO 80:11
averages fugitive from th' law of a.   MAUL 231:13
Averno Facilis descensus A.   VIRG 347:11
aversion bordering on a.   STEV 325:11
Avilion island-valley of A.   TENN 332:23
avis Rara a.   JUVE 194:7
avoiding a. being   TILL 340:11
Avon Sweet Swan of A.   JONS 192:8
awake A., my soul   KEN 198:5
  West's a.   DAVI 111:5
  When you're lying a.   GILB 149:20
awakening O what an a.   MahA 225:11
away a.! for I will fly   KEAT 196:19
  WHEN I'M A.   BONH 59:7
awe Shock and A.   ULLM 344:9
  wonder and a.   KANT 194:19
aweary I am a., aweary   TENN 334:1
awful this is an a. place   SCOT 287:4
awfully a. big adventure   BARR 27:2
awoke a. one morning   BYRO 81:30
  So I a., and behold   BUNY 74:14
  When Gregor Samsa a. one morning   KAFK 194:14
awry leaning all a.   FITZ 136:18
axe a.'s edge did try   MARV 229:18
  a. to the root   PAIN 257:14
  heavy a. without an edge   BRAD 67:14
  let the great a. fall   SHAK 293:34
  Lizzie Borden took an a.   ANON 9:13
axes no a. being ground   BROU 70:12
axis a. of evil   BUSH 78:19
axle fly sat upon the a.-tree   BACO 23:19
Azores Flores in the A.   TENN 334:25
azure slept an a.-lidded sleep   KEAT 195:16

B

babbled b. of green fields   SHAK 295:15
babe love the b.   SHAK 300:8
  naked new-born b.   SHAK 300:2
  pretty B. all burning   SOUT 320:25
babes b. and sucklings   BOOK 62:8
babies b. in the tomatoes   GINS 151:5
  hates dogs and b.   ROST 281:4
  putting milk into b.   CHUR 95:17
baby B. in an ox's stall   BETJ 33:2
  come from, b. dear   MACD 222:18
  first b. laughed   BARR 26:21
  my b. at my breast   SHAK 290:1
  one for my b.   MERC 233:5
Babylon B. in all its desolation   DAVI 111:1
  B. is fallen   BIBL 53:15
  By the waters of B.   BOOK 65:1
  Ere B. was dust   SHEL 314:13
  King in B.   HENL 166:11
  MYSTERY, B. THE GREAT   BIBL 53:19
Bacchus charioted by B.   KEAT 196:19
baccy B. for the Clerk   KIPL 202:24
Bach of J. S. B.   BEEC 29:1
bachelor b. never quite gets over   ROWL 281:14
back at my b. from time to time I hear   ELIO 129:26
  at my b. I always hear   MARV 229:21
  b. in the closet lays   FITZ 136:14
  boys in the b. room   LOES 217:3
  boys in the b. rooms   BEAV 28:5
  counted them all b.   HANR 161:3

looking b.   BIBL 47:12
never turned his b.   BROW 71:21
Not to go b.   POPE 268:7
sit on a man's b.   TOLS 341:5
those before cried 'B.!'   MACA 222:1
time to get b. to basics   MAJO 225:20
wouldn't want them b.   BECK 28:8
backs beast with two b.   SHAK 304:19
  With our b. to the wall   HAIG 159:5
backward B. ran sentences   GIBB 149:7
  look b. to their ancestors   BURK 75:15
bacon b.'s not the only thing   KING 201:12
bad and the b. unhappily   WILD 358:10
  b. aunts and good aunts   WODE 362:18
  b. and unhappily   STOP 326:14
  b. in the best of us   ANON 11:9
  B. laws   BURK 76:5
  b. publicity   BEHA 29:8
  B. women never take the blame   BROO 70:4
  brave b. man   CLAR 97:1
  come to a b. end   BEER 29:3
  Defend the b. against the worse   DAY- 111:11
  either good or b.   SHAK 292:14
  How sad and b.   BROW 71:27
  Mad, and dangerous   LAMB 206:18
  neither good nor b.   BALZ 26:6
  no book so b. that   PLIN 265:8
  shocking b. hats   WELL 354:6
  This bold b. man   SHAK 296:9
  When b. men combine   BURK 75:29
  when she was b.   LONG 218:12
badge red b. of courage   CRAN 106:9
badly end b.   STEV 325:25
  worth doing b.   CHES 93:20
bag b. and baggage   GLAD 151:14
  Lays eggs inside a paper b.   ISHE 181:5
baggage bag and b.   GLAD 151:14
Baghdad B. is determined   HUSS 179:3
  no American infidels in B.   SAHH 284:6
bah 'B.,' said Scrooge   DICK 114:14
Bailey come home Bill B.   CANN 84:12
Bainters hate all Boets and B.   GEOR 147:14
baked b. cookies and had teas   CLIN 98:9
Baker Street B. irregulars   DOYL 121:1
balance art of b.   MATI 231:6
  b. of the Old   CANN 84:10
balances weighed in the b.   BIBL 42:6
bald b., and short of breath   SASS 285:26
  b. and unconvincing   GILB 150:8
  fight between two b. men   BORG 65:23
  Go up, thou b. head   BIBL 37:21
Balfour of the B. declaration   WEIZ 353:11
Balkans damned silly thing in the B.   BISM 55:10
ball b. no question makes   FITZ 136:15
  wind it into a b.   BLAK 56:20
ballads permitted to make all the b.   FLET 138:10
ballot b. is stronger than   LINC 214:12
  ballots peaceful b.   LINC 214:12
balls rackets to these b.   SHAK 295:12
  some of the b. get dropped   BLAI 55:17
balm no b. in Gilead   BIBL 41:21
banality b. of evil   AREN 14:19
band we b. of brothers   SHAK 295:29
bandage wound, not the b.   POTT 269:14
bandaged death b. my eyes   BROW 72:27
Bandar-log What the B. think   KIPL 203:10
bandied struck and b.   WEBS 352:25
bands b. of Orion   BIBL 38:8
Bandusia spring of B.   HORA 175:16
bane Deserve the precious b.   MILT 237:31
baneful b. effects   WASH 351:8
bang Kiss Kiss B. Bang   KAEL 194:13
  no terror in a b.   HITC 170:5

b. with two backs	SHAK 304:19
blond b.	NIET 251:12
fit night out for man or b.	FIEL 135:19
life of his b.	BIBL 38:20
mark, or the name of the b.	BIBL 53:13
marks of the b.	HARD 161:16
more subtil than any b.	BIBL 34:14
No b. so fierce	SHAK 306:9
number of the b.	BIBL 53:14
questing b.	MALO 226:8
serpent subtlest b.	MILT 239:4
What rough b.	YEAT 369:2
who worship the b.	BIBL 53:16
beastie cow'rin', tim'rous b.	BURN 77:19
beastly b. the bourgeois is	LAWR 209:22
b. to the Germans	COWA 105:1
beasts b. at Ephesus	BIBL 50:30
b. of the forest	BOOK 64:4
like brute b.	BOOK 61:24
beat b. generation	KERO 199:9
b. their swords	BIBL 40:5
We b. them today	STAR 323:7
beaten b. path to his door	EMER 132:22
beating glory of b. the French	WOLF 363:4
hearts b.	BROW 72:15
Beatles B.' first LP	LARK 208:14
beatum *ab omni Parte b.*	HORA 175:12
beatus *B. vir qui timet Dominum*	BIBL 53:30
beaut it's a b.	LA G 206:14
beauteous It is a b. evening	WORD 364:15
beauties meaner b. of the night	WOTT 366:23
beautiful All things bright and b.	ALEX 4:14
b. and damned	FITZ 137:7
b. and ineffectual angel	ARNO 17:5
b. and simple	HENR 166:20
b. cannot be the way	COUS 104:17
b. catastrophe	LE C 211:9
B. dreamer	FOST 140:7
b. game	PELÉ 261:8
believe to be b.	MORR 245:14
better to be b.	WILD 358:29
in a b. way	O'KE 253:6
innocent and the b.	YEAT 368:10
most b. thing	SAPP 285:15
most b. things	RUSK 282:19
singing:—'Oh, how b.!'	KIPL 202:6
Small is b.	SCHU 286:16
Something b. for God	MUGG 246:17
something b. for God	TERE 335:17
beauty American b. rose	ROCK 278:6
arrest all b.	CAME 83:3
b. all very well at first sight	SHAW 312:7
b. being only skin-deep	KERR 199:12
b. draws us	POPE 268:16
b. faded	PHIL 263:3
B. in music	IVES 181:8
b. in one's equations	DIRA 117:2
B. is momentary in the mind	STEV 324:21
B. is mysterious	DOST 119:27
B. is no quality	HUME 178:10
b. is only sin deep	SAKI 284:13
b. is past change	HOPK 174:2
B. is the first test	HARD 161:13
B. is truth	KEAT 196:12
B. itself doth of itself	SHAK 309:33
b. of holiness	BOOK 63:28
b. of holiness	MONS 242:12
b. of inflections	STEV 324:25
b. of Israel	BIBL 36:32
B. so ancient	AUGU 20:4
b.'s rose	SHAK 310:2
B. that must die	KEAT 196:15
b. without vanity	BYRO 81:27

body's b. lives	STEV 324:21
dreamed that life was b.	HOOP 173:2
England, home and b.	ARNO 17:10
Exuberance is b.	BLAK 57:5
If you get simple b.	BROW 72:3
imagination seizes as b.	KEAT 197:9
innocence and b. born	YEAT 368:24
looked on B. bare	MILL 234:19
Love built on b.	DONN 118:19
no excellent b.	BACO 22:14
Of its own b.	BYRO 80:10
order and b.	BAUD 27:20
principal b. in building	FULL 144:16
She walks in b.	BYRO 81:17
some b. lies	MILT 236:22
supreme b.	RUSS 283:8
terrible b. is born	YEAT 368:3
thick, bereft of b.	SHAK 307:14
thing of b.	KEAT 195:10
thing of b.	ROWL 281:14
we just b. see	JONS 192:3
winds of March with b.	SHAK 309:26
your b.'s orient deep	CARE 84:19
because B. I do not hope to turn	ELIO 127:24
b. I think him so	SHAK 309:14
B. it's there	MALL 226:6
B. it was he	MONT 242:20
B. We're here	ANON 11:15
becks Nods, and b.	MILT 236:19
become all that may b. a man	SHAK 300:7
becomes that is what he b.	GOET 152:22
bed And so to b.	PEPY 261:15
as little as my b.	KEN 198:6
b. be blest that I lie on	ANON 9:18
found out thy b.	BLAK 58:2
go to b. by day	STEV 325:26
go to b. with me	ALLE 5:14
Lying in b. would be	CHES 93:18
mind is not a b.	AGAT 3:23
(my Love!) in thy cold b.	KING 200:9
my second best b.	SHAK 311:1
not having more than one man in b.	RAPH 273:14
on the lawn I lie in b.	AUDE 19:13
take up thy b., and walk	BIBL 48:29
This b. thy centre is	DONN 119:17
wore in b.	MONR 242:10
bedfellows strange b.	SHAK 307:26
bedroom French widow in every b.	HOFF 171:11
what you do in the b.	CAMP 83:8
bedrooms in the nation's b.	TRUD 342:7
bee b.-loud glade	YEAT 368:14
How doth the little busy b.	WATT 351:18
sting like a b.	ALI 5:7
Where the b. sucks	SHAK 307:34
beef great eater of b.	SHAK 308:19
Roast B., Medium	FERB 134:17
Where's the b.	MOND 242:6
been as if it had not b.	SHEL 313:15
beer B. and Britannia	SMIT 319:16
chronicle small b.	SHAK 304:27
only a b. teetotaller	SHAW 311:11
warm b., invincible suburbs	MAJO 225:19
Beersheba Dan even to B.	BIBL 36:19
bees b. do it	PORT 269:3
innumerable b.	TENN 334:24
beetles special preference for b.	HALD 159:10
before B. we were her people	FROS 143:16
Not lost but gone b.	NORT 252:5
not lost but sent b.	CYPR 109:3
things which are b.	BIBL 51:24
began b. in order	BROW 71:4
begetter To the onlie b.	SHAK 310:1
beggar absent-minded b.	KIPL 201:16

beggar (*cont.*)
b. would enfold himself — KIPL 203:21
beggared b. all description — SHAK 289:18
beggars Our basest b. — SHAK 297:33
When b. die — SHAK 296:25
begged living HOMER b. his bread — ANON 10:19
begging his seed b. their bread — BOOK 62:23
begin B. at the beginning — CARR 86:20
b. at the beginning — THOM 338:4
b. the Beguine — PORT 268:30
b. with certainties — BACO 22:1
But let us b. — KENN 198:18
beginning As it was in the b. — BOOK 59:16
badly from the b. — STEV 325:25
begin at the b. — THOM 338:4
b., a middle — ARIS 15:16
b., a muddle — LARK 209:2
b. is often the end — ELIO 128:16
b. of an Amour — BEHN 29:9
b. of any great matter — DRAK 121:8
b. of the end — TALL 330:7
b. of wisdom — BOOK 64:12
end of the b. — CHUR 95:14
In my b. is my end — ELIO 128:5
In my end is my b. — MARY 230:15
In the b. — BIBL 34:3
In the b. was the Word — BIBL 48:13
Movies should have a b. — GODA 152:3
told you from the b. — BIBL 41:3
beginnings from small b. grow — DRYD 122:1
begins glory most b. and ends — YEAT 368:20
begot when they b. me — STER 324:8
begotten b. by Despair — MARV 229:14
B., not made — BOOK 61:3
only b. of the Father — BIBL 48:19
beguile b. thy sorrow — SHAK 308:7
beguiled serpent b. me — BIBL 34:18
Beguine begin the B. — PORT 268:30
begun b. to fight — JONE 191:9
To have b. is half the job — HORA 174:23
behaviour studies human b. — ROBB 277:9
behind b. your scenes — JOHN 188:4
Get thee b. me, Satan — BIBL 45:10
it will be b. me — REGE 274:16
let them go, B., before — DONN 118:21
no bosom and no b. — SMIT 319:4
things which are b. — BIBL 51:24
those b. cried 'Forward!' — MACA 222:1
with a light b. her — GILB 150:27
behold B. an Israelite — BIBL 48:23
B. the man — BIBL 54:11
being avoiding b. — TILL 340:11
b. comes from non-being — LAO 208:4
darkness of mere b. — JUNG 193:18
have our b. — BIBL 49:31
Lord of all B. — KORA 204:18
not the same thing as b. — PLAT 264:23
unbearable lightness of b. — KUND 206:7
Belfast be kind to B. — CRAI 106:7
belfry while owl in the b. — TENN 334:28
Belial sons Of B., flown with insolence — MILT 237:27
belief all b. is for it — JOHN 189:20
beliefs dust of exploded b. — MADA 224:15
my b. are true — HALD 159:9
believe b. in life — DU B 122:25
b. in miracles — FOX 141:4
b. what they wish — CAES 82:4
b. what we choose — NEWM 250:8
don't b. in fairies — BARR 27:1
fight for what I b. in — CAST 88:11
Firmly I b. — NEWM 250:5
he couldn't b. it — CUMM 108:7
I b. in God the Father — BOOK 59:23

I do b. her — SHAK 310:27
If you b., clap your hands — BARR 27:3
I will not b. — BIBL 49:17
Lord, I b. — BIBL 46:28
must b. *something* — RUSS 283:11
professing to b. — PAIN 257:2
save them that b. — BIBL 50:13
ye will not b. — BIBL 48:28
you'll b. anything — WELL 354:10
believed b. in hope — BIBL 49:42
b. of any man — TARK 330:18
by all people b. — VINC 346:18
Nothing can now be b. — JEFF 184:12
not seen, and yet have b. — BIBL 49:18
believer In a b.'s ear — NEWT 250:20
believers all b. — BOOK 59:19
believes politician never b. what he says — DE G 112:7
believeth He that b. on me — BIBL 48:31
whosoever b. in him — BIBL 48:27
believing stop b. in God — CHES 93:25
Belinda B. smiled — POPE 268:17
bell b. invites me — SHAK 300:13
Cuckoo-echoing, b.-swarmèd — HOPK 173:15
dinner b. — BYRO 81:3
for whom the b. tolls — DONN 119:23
sexton tolled the b. — HOOD 172:22
word is like a b. — KEAT 196:24
bella B., *horrida bella* — VIRG 347:10
Bellamy B.'s veal pies — PITT 264:1
belle *j'étais b.* — RONS 279:2
bellman fatal b. — SHAK 300:14
bells b. of Hell — ANON 9:24
floating many b. down — CUMM 108:4
From the b., bells, bells — POE 265:14
Like sweet b. jangled — SHAK 293:3
now ring the b. — WALP 350:5
Ring out, wild b. — TENN 333:8
ring the b. of Ecstasy — GINS 151:2
ring the b. of Heaven — HODG 171:4
belly God is their b. — BIBL 51:25
bellyful Rumble thy b. — SHAK 298:3
belong b. not to you — GIBR 149:9
don't want to b. to any club — MARX 230:3
man doesn't b. out there — BRAU 68:1
To betray, you must first b. — PHIL 262:20
beloved B. is man — TALM 330:13
Cry, the b. country — PATO 260:11
how far to be b. — SHAK 289:11
man greatly b. — BIBL 42:9
My b. is mine — BIBL 39:34
This is my b. Son — BIBL 43:8
below above, between, b. — DONN 118:21
belt b. without hitting below it — ASQU 18:4
bend right on round the b. — LAUD 209:13
bending always be a b. downwards — WHEW 355:21
beneath married b. me — ASTO 18:6
benedicite B., *omnia opera Domini* — BIBL 54:6
benedictus B. *qui venit* — MISS 240:23
benefactor b. of our race — TWAI 343:22
benefit Every human b. — BURK 75:9
benevolence b. of the butcher — SMIT 318:1
benevolent B. Knowledge — BORG 65:20
benighted B. walks under the midday sun — MILT 236:5
poor b. 'eathen — KIPL 202:3
bent top of my b. — SHAK 293:14
bereft b. Of wet — HOPK 173:20
Berliner *Ich bin ein B.* — KENN 199:3
Bermoothes still-vexed B. — SHAK 307:20
Bermudas remote B. ride — MARV 229:13
berry made a better b. — BUTL 79:19
Bertie Burlington B. — HARG 162:12
beside b. thyself — BIBL 49:36
Christ b. me — PATR 260:13

best bad in the b. of us   ANON 11:9
b. chosen language   AUST 20:26
b. in this kind   SHAK 304:3
b. is like the worst   KIPL 202:16
b. is the enemy of the good   VOLT 348:11
b. is yet to be   BROW 72:28
b. of all possible worlds   BRAD 67:7
b. of all possible worlds   CABE 82:1
b. of all possible worlds   VOLT 348:5
b. rulers   LAO 208:2
b.-seller is the gilded tomb   SMIT 318:18
b. thing God invents   BROW 72:3
b. things in life are free   DE S 113:18
b. when we are boldest   BLAI 56:3
b. when we are boldest   BROW 70:14
b. years are gone   BECK 28:8
get what's b. for us   RICE 275:15
In art the b. is good enough   GOET 152:15
It was the b. of times   DICK 115:23
justest and b.   PLAT 264:20
past all prizing, b.   SOPH 320:16
poetry = the b. words   COLE 101:5
pursuing of the b. ends   HUTC 179:5
record of the b.   SHEL 315:5
Send forth the b.   KIPL 203:8
that is the b.   AUST 21:3
Whate'er is b. administered   POPE 267:32
bestride b. the narrow world   SHAK 296:19
betake b. myself to that course   PEPY 261:20
Bethel O God of B.   DODD 118:15
Bethlehem But thou, B.   BIBL 42:14
little town of B.   BROQ 70:7
Slouches towards B.   YEAT 369:2
betray All things b. thee   THOM 338:15
guts to b. my country   FORS 139:18
To b., you must first belong   PHIL 262:20
betrayed night that he was b.   BOOK 61:14
better All the b. to hear you with   PERR 262:7
appear the b. reason   MILT 238:3
B. by far you should forget   ROSS 280:15
b. man than I am   KIPL 202:8
better spared a b. man   SHAK 294:28
b. than a thousand   BOOK 63:20
b. than it sounds   NYE 252:13
b. the instruction   SHAK 302:23
b. to have loved and lost   TENN 332:29
can only get b.   PETR 262:15
Every day, I am getting b.   COUÉ 104:15
Fail b.   BECK 28:18
far, far b. thing   DICK 115:24
for b. for worse   BOOK 61:27
from worse to b.   HOOK 173:1
from worse to b.   JOHN 186:16
Gad! she'd b.   CARL 85:22
Hereafter, in a b. world   SHAK 290:3
If way to the B. there be   HARD 162:2
I took thee for thy b.   SHAK 293:19
I was in a b. place   SHAK 290:6
make a b. mouse-trap   EMER 132:22
much b. than likely   BRON 69:17
nothing b. to do   THAT 337:4
seemed a little b.   IBSE 180:10
see the b. things   OVID 256:1
We have seen b. days   SHAK 308:4
between 'ouses in b.   BATE 27:16
try to get b. them   STRA 326:19
beware B. my foolish heart   WASH 351:13
b. of the dog   BLIX 58:11
B. of the dog   PETR 262:16
B. the ides of March   SHAK 296:18
bid you b.   KIPL 202:18
bewildered Bewitched, bothered, and b.   HART 162:19
to the utterly b.   CAPP 84:16

bewitched B., bothered, and bewildered   HART 162:19
bewrapt B. past knowing   HARD 162:6
biases critic is a bundle of b.   BALL 26:4
bibendum Nunc est b.   HORA 175:9
Bible B. and the Bible only   CHIL 94:1
English B.   MACA 221:16
have used the B.   KING 201:10
read in de B.   HEYW 168:13
starless and b.-black   THOM 338:4
Bibles B. laid open   HERB 167:22
they had the b.   GEOR 148:5
bicycle arrive by b.   VIER 346:14
fish without a b.   STEI 324:1
so is a b. repair kit   CONN 102:15
bicycling old maids to   MAJO 225:19
bidder withstand the highest b.   WASH 351:6
bien mieux est l'ennemi du b.   VOLT 348:11
big b. enough to take away everything   FORD 139:5
b. squadrons against the small   BUSS 78:24
b. way of doing things   TERE 335:16
b. words for little matters   JOHN 188:19
fall victim to a b. lie   HITL 170:6
shining B.-Sea-Water   LONG 218:3
What b. ears you have   PERR 262:7
bigamy B. is having   ANON 7:14
bigger b. they are   FITZ 137:18
biggest b. aspidistra in the world   HARP 162:15
b. electric train   WELL 353:15
bike got on his b.   TEBB 331:7
bilingual All pro athletes are b.   HOWE 177:1
billabong swagman camped by a b.   PATE 260:9
billboard b. lovely as a tree   NASH 248:15
billet bullet has its b.   WILL 360:3
billiards play b. well   ROUP 281:7
billion b. dollar country   FOST 140:4
billow Fierce was the wild b.   ANAT 6:10
billy B., in one of his sashes   GRAH 155:1
That's the way for B.   HOGG 171:13
till his 'B.' boiled   PATE 260:9
bind b. my hair   HUNT 178:20
b. their kings in chains   BOOK 65:6
b. the sweet influences   BIBL 38:8
b. unto myself today   ALEX 4:17
b. your sons to exile   KIPL 203:8
binds b. to himself a joy   BLAK 57:12
bin Laden having one b.   MUBA 246:14
biographies essence of innumerable b.   CARL 85:4
biography better part of b.   STRA 326:20
B. is about Chaps   BENT 31:9
Judas who writes the b.   WILD 358:14
no history; only b.   EMER 132:8
nothing but b.   DISR 117:24
biologist b. passes   ROST 281:1
biology B. is the search for   WILL 360:6
bird b.-haunted English lawn   ARNO 16:17
b. of dawning   SHAK 291:11
b. on the wing   BOUL 66:9
B. thou never wert   SHEL 314:25
Both man and b.   COLE 100:27
cannot catch the b. of paradise   KHRU 200:3
escaped even as a b.   BOOK 64:24
forgets the dying b.   PAIN 257:13
immortal b.   KEAT 196:22
It's a b.   ANON 8:5
like a singing b.   ROSS 280:10
only the note of a b.   SIMP 317:8
rare b. on this earth   JUVE 194:7
Shall I call thee b.   WORD 366:13
sight of any b.   BIBL 38:11
Stirred for a b.   HOPK 174:10
What b. so sings   LYLY 220:22
why the caged b. sings   DUNB 123:7
birdcage like a summer b.   WEBS 353:1

birds b. are flown · CHAR 90:20
B. build · HOPK 174:8
b. fly through it · HEIS 165:12
b. got to fly · HAMM 160:14
B. in their little nests agree · WATT 351:21
b. of the air have nests · BIBL 44:16
b. that are without despair · WEBS 353:1
late the sweet b. sang · SHAK 310:11
nest of singing b. · JOHN 188:3
no b. sing · KEAT 195:23
singing of b. · BIBL 39:33
sing like b. i' the cage · SHAK 298:23
think caged b. sing · WEBS 353:3
birdsong b. at morning · STEV 325:31
Birmingham B. by way of Beachy Head · CHES 93:4
no great hopes from B. · AUST 20:23
When Jesus came to B. · STUD 327:4
Birnam Great B. wood · SHAK 301:17
birth B., and copulation, and death · ELIO 129:14
b. is but a sleep · WORD 365:6
disqualified by the accident of b. · CHES 93:15
give b. astride of a grave · BECK 28:16
no cure for b. and death · SANT 285:14
one that is coming to b. · O'SH 255:16
present at the b. · ORTO 254:7
Saviour's b. is celebrated · SHAK 291:11
seen b. and death · ELIO 128:26
birthday Happy b. to you · HILL 169:6
marvel my b. away · THOM 337:24
birthright Esau selleth his b. · BIBL 34:34
births b. of time · BACO 22:30
tell of the b. · RIMB 277:6
bis B. dat qui cito dat · PUBL 271:12
biscuits hyacinths and b. · SAND 285:9
bisexuality b. doubles your chances · ALLE 5:17
bishop B. of Rome · BOOK 65:14
make a b. kick a hole · CHAN 90:10
No b., no King · JAME 182:10
bit b. the babies · BROW 72:21
bitch b.-goddess success · JAME 183:9
Gaia is a tough b. · MARG 227:17
old b. gone in the teeth · POUN 270:1
bite b. some of my other generals · GEOR 147:16
man recovered of the b. · GOLD 153:14
bites dead woman b. not · GRAY 156:4
biting b. the hand that lays · GOLD 154:2
bitter be not b. against them · BIBL 51:31
b. herbs · BIBL 35:18
bitterness b. of his soul · BIBL 42:22
bivouac b. of the dead · O'HA 253:4
black art as b. as hell · SHAK 310:30
b. as if bereaved of light · BLAK 57:20
b. as our loss · SITW 317:13
b., but comely · BIBL 39:31
b. dog · JOHN 190:16
blacker than b. · TURN 343:4
B. Hills belong to me · SITT 317:12
B. it stood as night · MILT 238:10
b. majority rule · SMIT 318:16
B. Panther Party · NEWT 250:10
devil damn thee b. · SHAK 301:26
I found some b. people · EQUI 132:30
Just call me b. · GOLD 153:2
looking for a b. hat · BOWE 66:16
not b. and white · BOY 67:4
not have the colour b. · MADI 224:18
old b. magic · MERC 233:6
old b. ram · SHAK 304:18
so long as it is b. · FORD 139:8
Tip me the b. spot · STEV 325:17
Why do you wear b. · CHEK 92:8
with a b. skin · MALC 226:2
young, gifted and b. · HANS 161:4

Young, gifted and b. · IRVI 181:1
blackbird B. has spoken · FARJ 134:3
b. whistling · STEV 324:25
blacker b. than black · TURN 343:4
Blackpool famous seaside place called B. · EDGA 125:3
blame Bad women never take the b. · BROO 70:4
b. at night · POPE 267:15
b. is his who chooses · PLAT 265:2
b. the alien · AESC 3:21
blameless Fearless, b. knight · ANON 12:11
flower of a b. life · TENN 332:9
blaming b. it on you · KIPL 202:9
blanch when counsellors b. · BACO 22:17
blandula Animula vagula b. · HADR 158:13
blank B. cheques · HOLM 172:2
b., my lord · SHAK 308:36
blasphemies truths begin as b. · SHAW 311:6
blasphemy b. against the Holy Ghost · BIBL 44:36
blast b.-beruffled plume · HARD 161:22
b. of war · SHAK 295:16
blasted b. with excess · GRAY 156:21
Upon this b. heath · SHAK 299:14
bleak In the b. mid-winter · ROSS 280:13
bleed do we not b. · SHAK 302:22
thorns of life! I b. · SHEL 314:5
bleeding b., beating fire · JOHN 186:4
b. piece of earth · SHAK 296:29
instead of b., he sings · GARD 146:2
bleeds 'til it b. daylight · COCK 99:4
bless B. 'em all · HUGH 177:12
B. relaxes · BLAK 57:4
B. the Lord · BIBL 54:6
b. ye the Lord · BOOK 59:22
God b. us every one · DICK 114:16
load and b. With fruit · KEAT 197:1
blessed B. are the poor · BIBL 43:13
B. are the pure in heart · KEBL 197:22
B. are you, O Lord · SIDD 316:7
b. art thou among women · BIBL 46:31
B. be he that cometh · BOOK 64:19
b. be the name of the Lord · BIBL 37:33
b. damozel · ROSS 280:18
B. is the man · BOOK 63:19
Judge none b. · BIBL 42:23
more b. to give · BIBL 49:33
This b. plot · SHAK 305:23
blessing b. that money cannot buy · WALT 350:14
national b. · HAMI 160:11
unmixed b. · HORA 175:12
blessings glass of b. · HERB 167:20
blest always to be b. · ARMS 16:2
always To be b. · POPE 267:20
B. pair of Sirens · MILT 236:2
b. that I lie on · ANON 9:18
blight b. man was born for · HOPK 174:5
Blighty back to dear old B. · MILL 235:6
blimp Colonel B. · LOW 219:14
blind accompany my being b. · PEPY 261:20
b. guides · BIBL 45:30
b. lead the blind · BIBL 45:6
b. led by the blind · UPAN 344:14
b. man in a dark room · BOWE 66:16
b. watchmaker · DAWK 111:6
country of the b. · ERAS 133:1
Cupid painted b. · SHAK 303:9
halt, and the b. · BIBL 47:25
old, mad, b. · SHEL 314:22
religion without science is b. · EINS 126:2
right to be b. sometimes · NELS 249:5
splendid work for the b. · SASS 285:27
too dangerous for b. partnership · STRO 327:2
blindness 'eathen in 'is b. · KIPL 201:22
heathen in his b. · HEBE 164:18

Love comes from b. BUSS 78:22
blinds drawing-down of b. OWEN 256:10
blinked other fellow just b. RUSK 282:10
blinking portrait of a b. idiot SHAK 302:19
bliss b. or woe MILT 239:8
B. was it in that dawn WORD 364:13
Everywhere I see b. SHEL 313:10
Of b. on bliss MILT 238:24
soul in b. SHAK 298:20
Where ignorance is b. GRAY 156:18
blithe b. Spirit SHEL 314:25
buxom, b., and debonair MILT 236:18
block old b. itself BURK 76:7
blockhead No man but a b. JOHN 189:14
blond b. beast NIET 251:12
blonde b. to make a bishop kick CHAN 90:10
blondes Gentlemen prefer b. LOOS 218:14
blood b. and ashes PAIN 257:7
b. and iron BISM 55:9
b. and love without STOP 326:12
b. and wine WILD 359:6
b. be the price KIPL 202:26
b. come gargling OWEN 256:11
b. drawn with the lash LINC 215:4
b. is their argument SHAK 295:20
b. of Christians is the seed TERT 336:2
b. Of human sacrifice MILT 237:26
b. of patriots JEFF 184:2
b. on their hands SPEN 321:15
b. on your hands CARL 85:1
B., sweat, and tear-wrung BYRO 80:1
b., toil, tears and sweat CHUR 95:6
b. will have blood SHAK 301:9
but with b. BROW 70:17
by b. Albanian TERE 335:20
Christ's b. streams MARL 228:9
created Man of a b.-clot KORA 205:25
Deliver me from b.-guiltiness BOOK 63:8
enough of b. and tears RABI 272:15
flesh and b. BIBL 51:21
flesh and b. so cheap HOOD 172:27
flow of human b. HUGH 177:14
foaming with much b. POWE 270:12
for cooling the b. FLAN 137:21
glories of our b. and state SHIR 315:28
His b. be on us BIBL 46:18
How much b. must be spilled FATA 134:10
in b. Stepped in SHAK 301:10
innocent of the b. BIBL 46:17
I smell the b. NASH 248:17
I smell the b. SHAK 298:12
Man of B. was there MACA 221:19
mingle my b. BROW 70:16
near in b. SHAK 300:27
on the b. of my men LEE 211:17
pay the b. price BLAI 56:2
rather have b. on my hands GREE 156:23
rivers of b. JEFF 184:18
shall his b. be shed BIBL 34:29
show business with b. BRUN 73:12
so much b. in him SHAK 301:22
summon up the b. SHAK 295:16
thicks man's b. with cold COLE 10:21
Tiber foaming with much b. VIRG 347:10
tincture in the b. DEFO 111:20
waded thro' red b. BALL 25:20
washed in the b. of the Lamb LIND 215:9
wash this b. Clean SHAK 300:19
We be of one b. KIPL 203:11
white in the b. of the Lamb BIBL 53:8
Young b. must have its course KING 201:9
bloodhounds Seven b. followed SHEL 314:1
bloodshed war without b. MAO 227:11

bloody b., bold, and resolute SHAK 301:15
b., but unbowed HENL 166:8
b. cross he bore SPEN 321:25
b. principles and practices FOX 141:2
dark and b. ground O'HA 253:5
have b. thoughts SHAK 307:31
Not b. likely SHAW 312:30
teach B. instructions SHAK 299:29
under the b. past AHER 4:1
What b. man SHAK 299:9
wipe a b. nose GAY 147:4
bloom b. in the spring GILB 150:9
b. is gone WILD 358:6
How can ye b. sae fresh BURN 76:22
hung with b. HOUS 176:6
look at things in b. HOUS 176:7
blooming grand to be b. well dead SARO 285:18
blossom b. as the rose BIBL 40:27
B. by blossom SWIN 329:8
b. in the dust SHIR 316:1
b. soup BASH 27:14
b. that hangs on the bough SHAK 307:34
break Into b. WRIG 366:28
frothiest, blossomiest b. POTT 269:13
hundred flowers b. MAO 227:14
blossoms b., birds, and bowers HERR 168:1
blot art to b. POPE 268:10
b. on the escutcheon GRAY 156:3
B. out, correct SWIF 328:26
blotted b. a thousand JONS 192:10
blow Blow, b., thou winter wind SHAK 290:16
B., bugle, blow TENN 334:13
B. out, you bugles BROO 69:19
B., winds, and crack SHAK 298:2
first b. is half GOLD 153:25
strike the b. BYRO 80:2
when will thou b. ANON 11:18
bloweth wind b. where it listeth BIBL 48:26
blowing answer is b. in the wind DYLA 124:3
I'm forever b. bubbles KENB 198:7
blown flower that once hath b. FITZ 136:12
blows b. so red The rose FITZ 136:10
bludgeoning b. of the people WILD 359:13
blue b.-eyed devil white man FARD 134:2
b. guitar STEV 324:18
b. of the night CROS 107:18
b. remembered hills HOUS 176:13
B., silver-white KEAT 196:26
cherish the pale b. dot SAGA 284:4
in the b. states OBAM 252:16
little tent of b. WILD 359:7
Space is b. HEIS 165:12
bluebell Mary, ma Scotch B. LAUD 209:14
bluebirds b. over the white cliffs BURT 77:27
blues got the Weary B. HUGH 177:15
blunder it is a b. BOUL 66:8
Youth is a b. DISR 117:21
blunt plain, b. man SHAK 297:8
blush born to b. unseen GRAY 156:11
blushed saw its God, and b. CRAS 106:11
blushes Only Animal that B. TWAI 343:12
blushful b. Hippocrene KEAT 196:8
blushing other people without b. SHAW 312:19
board I struck the b. HERB 167:11
There wasn't any B. HERB 167:6
boast For frantic b. KIPL 202:22
Such is the patriot's b. GOLD 153:15
boat b. he can sail THOM 339:3
sank my b. KENN 199:5
boats messing about in b. GRAH 155:3
Boche well-killed B. READ 273:18
Bodhisattva B. who is full of pity MAHĀ 225:8
bodies b. are buried in peace BIBL 42:28

bodies (*cont.*)
B. never lie — DE M 112:18
b. of those — EDWA 125:12
b. of unburied men — WEBS 353:2
One soul inhabiting two b. — ARIS 15:24
our dead b. — SCOT 287:5
Pile the b. high — SAND 285:6
present your b. — BIBL 50:10
souls out of men's b. — SHAK 304:9
bodkin With a bare b. — SHAK 292:24
body Absent in b. — BIBL 50:16
Africa than my own b. — ORTO 254:6
b. continues in its state of rest — NEWT 250:11
b. form doth take — SPEN 322:6
b. is a machine — TOLS 341:4
b., Nature is — POPE 267:24
b. of a weak and feeble woman — ELIZ 130:14
b.'s beauty lives — STEV 324:21
b. swayed to music — YEAT 367:12
commit his b. to the deep — BOOK 65:10
exercise is to the b. — STEE 323:11
gigantic b. — MACA 221:10
Gin a body meet a b. — BURN 76:24
i like my b. — CUMM 108:10
in a sound b. — JUVE 194:12
in mind, b., or estate — BOOK 60:17
interpose my b. — STRA 326:19
John Brown's b. — ANON 9:7
my useless b. — BROW 70:13
no b. to be kicked — THUR 340:8
Of the glorious B. sing — THOM 337:12
out of my b. — HAND 161:1
out of the b. — BIBL 51:9
rid of the rest of her b. — VANB 345:5
sing the b. electric — WHIT 356:22
so young a b. — SHAK 302:29
stepped out of my b. — WRIG 366:28
this is my b. — BIBL 46:11
with my b. I thee worship — BOOK 62:1
Boets hate all B. and Bainters — GEOR 147:14
bog b.-standard comprehensive — CAMP 83:4
Bognor Bugger B. — GEOR 148:3
boil b. at different degrees — EMER 132:18
boilers b. and vats — JOHN 190:7
bois *Nous n'irons plus aux b.* — ANON 12:17
bold Be b., be bold — SPEN 322:3
b. as a hawk — LOVE 219:13
b. as a lion — BIBL 39:1
b. man that first — SWIF 328:17
Fortune assists the b. — VIRG 347:18
let our minds be b. — BRAN 67:15
This b. bad man — SHAK 296:9
boldest best when we are b. — BLAI 56:3
best when we are b. — BROW 70:14
boldly to b. go — RODD 278:7
boldness B., and again boldness — DANT 109:18
B. be my friend — SHAK 291:4
what first? b. — BACO 22:16
bomb atom b. is a paper tiger — MAO 227:13
b. them back into the Stone Age — LEMA 212:5
bombed glad we've been b. — ELIZ 131:5
bomber b. will always get through — BALD 25:3
bombers b. named for girls — JARR 183:12
bombs Come, friendly b. — BETJ 33:4
bond b. between two people — RILK 277:2
look to his b. — SHAK 302:20
take a b. of fate — SHAK 301:16
bondage b. of rhyming — MILT 237:14
house of b. — BIBL 35:24
bonding male b. — TIGE 340:10
bondman b.'s two hundred and fifty years — LINC 215:4
so base that would be a b. — SHAK 296:33
bonds b. of civil society — LOCK 216:20

surly b. of earth — MAGE 225:2
surly b. of earth — REAG 274:8
bondsmen Hereditary b. — BYRO 80:2
bone B. of my bone — MILT 239:8
B. of my bones — BIBL 34:12
hair about the b. — DONN 119:13
knows death to the b. — YEAT 367:22
rag and a b. — KIPL 203:3
boneless b. wonder — CHUR 95:2
bones b. of a single Pomeranian — BISM 55:6
b. of one British Grenadier — HARR 162:16
Can these b. live — BIBL 42:3
conjuring trick with b. — JENK 185:1
dead men lost their b. — ELIO 129:24
he that moves my b. — SHAK 311:2
O ye dry b. — BIBL 42:4
Rattle his b. — NOEL 251:21
tongs and the b. — SHAK 303:30
valley full of b. — BIBL 42:2
bonfire b. of the vanities — WOLF 363:8
bong land where the B.-tree grows — LEAR 210:16
bonjour *B. tristesse* — ÉLUA 131:17
bonny b., bonnie banks — ANON 10:6
saw ye b. Lesley — BURN 76:23
bono *Cui b.* — CICE 96:24
bonum *Summum b.* — CICE 96:18
Boojum Snark *was* a B. — CARR 87:21
book agree with the b. of God — OMAR 253:11
b. a devil's chaplain — DARW 110:11
b. is the precious life-blood — MILT 240:4
b. is the purest essence — CARL 85:21
B. of Life begins — WILD 359:3
b. of nature — GALI 145:7
but his b. — JONS 192:1
Camerado, this is no b. — WHIT 357:2
damned, thick, square b. — GLOU 151:18
destroys a good b. — MILT 240:3
Go, litel b. — CHAU 92:4
Go, little b. — STEV 324:9
great b. — CALL 82:19
I'll drown my b. — SHAK 307:33
leaves of the Judgement B. unfold — TAYL 331:3
make one b. — JOHN 189:8
no b. so bad that — PLIN 265:8
no Frigate like a B. — DICK 115:28
oldest rule in the b. — CARR 86:21
read a b. before reviewing it — SMIT 319:14
sent down to thee the B. — KORA 205:13
this b. I directe To the — CHAU 92:7
throw the b. in the fire — SAND 285:2
throw this b. about — BELL 29:16
to every b. its copy — COLU 102:2
use of a b. — CARR 86:3
when I wrote that b. — SWIF 329:3
writing a b. — BRON 69:17
written a b. — JOWE 192:16
wrote the b. — LINC 215:7
Your face, my thane, is as a b. — SHAK 299:25
books b. are divisible — RUSK 282:17
b. are either dreams or swords — LOWE 219:17
B. are made — FLAU 138:1
b. are to be tasted — BACO 23:12
b. are weapons — ROOS 279:17
B. are well written — WILD 358:23
B. do furnish a room — POWE 270:8
B. must follow sciences — BACO 23:29
B. say: she did this because — BARN 26:16
b., the academes — SHAK 298:32
B. think for me — LAMB 207:3
b. undeservedly forgotten — AUDE 19:25
B. will speak plain — BACO 22:17
borrowers of b. — LAMB 207:1
collection of b. — CARL 85:14

Deep-versed in b.	MILT 239:20	time to be b.	BIBL 39:10
God has written all the b.	BUTL 79:15	took the trouble to be b.	BEAU 28:3
his b. were read	BELL 30:2	to the manner b.	SHAK 291:34
I never read b.	PUNC 271:22	under that was I b.	SHAK 304:8
Keeping b. on charity	PERÓ 262:4	unto us a child is b.	BIBL 40:14
lard their lean b.	BURT 78:1	We were not b. to sue	SHAK 305:18
making many b.	BIBL 39:29	When we are b.	SHAK 298:19
more in woods than b.	BERN 32:11	wherein I was b.	BIBL 37:36
proper study of mankind is b.	HUXL 179:8	borne It is b. in upon me	HARE 162:11
quiet, friendship, b.	THOM 338:25	Still have I b. it	SHAK 302:14
read all the b.	MALL 226:4	borogoves mimsy were the b.	CARR 86:23
read b. *through*	JOHN 189:3	borrow have to b. the money	WARD 350:17
so charming as b.	SMIT 319:8	*men who b.*	LAMB 206:20
spectacles of b.	DRYD 122:21	borrower b., nor a lender be	SHAK 291:30
Wherever b. will be burned	HEIN 165:6	b. of the night	SHAK 300:29
boot b. in the face	PLAT 264:13	**borrowers** b. of books	LAMB 207:1
B., saddle, to horse	BROW 71:23	**borrowing** b. only lingers	SHAK 295:1
b. stamping on a human face	ORWE 255:1	**bosom** b. of a single state	DURH 123:13
bootboy body of the b. at Claridges	WOOL 364:1	Close b.-friend	KEAT 197:1
booted b. and spurred	RUMB 281:18	in Arthur's b.	SHAK 295:14
boots boots—b.—movin'	KIPL 201:18	no b. and no behind	SMIT 319:4
have one's b. on	MONT 242:16	slip Into my b.	TENN 334:23
truth is pulling its b. on	SPUR 322:19	**bosoms** white b.	JOHN 188:4
boozes tell a man who "b."	BURT 77:25	**boss** only one b.	WALT 350:15
bop Playing 'B.'	ELLI 131:8	Boston good old B.	BOSS 66:2
Borden Lizzie B. took an axe	ANON 9:13	**bothered** Bewitched, b., and bewildered	HART 162:19
border B., nor Breed	KIPL 201:17	**botté** *toujours b.*	MONT 242:16
crossing the B.	AUDE 19:11	**bottle** bothers to buy a b.	DWOR 123:16
gaed o'er the b.	BURN 76:23	way out of the b.-bottle	WITT 362:9
bore hero becomes a b.	EMER 132:16	**bottles** new wine into old b.	BIBL 44:21
Less is a b.	VENT 346:2	**bottom** Bless thee, B.	SHAK 303:26
old b.	TREE 341.13	fairies at the b. of our garden	FYLE 144:20
secret of being a b.	VOLT 348:14	forgotten man at the b.	ROOS 279:6
bored *Bores* and B.	BYRO 81:9	**bottomless** Law is a b. pit	ARBU 14:14
Ever to confess you're b.	BERR 32:19	pit that is b.	JAME 182:9
boredom b. and terror	WELL 353:17	**boue** *nostalgie de la b.*	AUGI 19:27
B. a problem for the moralist	RUSS 282:23	**bough** bloom along the b.	HOUS 176:6
Life is first b., then fear	LARK 208:17	bread beneath the b.	FITZ 136:8
bores B. and *Bored*	BYRO 81:9	**boundary** right to fix the b.	PARN 259:15
boring except the b.	VOLT 348:15	**bounded** b. in a nut-shell	SHAK 292:15
born blight man was b. for	HOPK 174:5	**bounden** b. duty	BOOK 61:12
b. again	BIBL 48:25	**bountiful** My Lady b.	FARQ 134:7
b. free	ANON 7:7	**bouquet** b. is better than the taste	POTT 269:16
b. in other's pain	THOM 338:13	**bourgeois** astonish the b.	BAUD 27:21
B. in the USA	SPRI 322:15	beastly the b. is	LAWR 209:22
b. of a woman	BIBL 38:1	b. climb up on them	FLAU 138:1
B. of the sun	SPEN 321:19	**bourn** country from whose b.	SHAK 292:25
B. of the Virgin Mary	BOOK 59:23	set a b. how far	SHAK 289:11
b. out of due time	BIBL 50:27	**bourne** b. of time and place	TENN 332:3
b. out of my due time	MORR 245:11	**Bovary** *Madame B., c'est moi*	FLAU 138:2
b. to run	SPRI 322:17	**bow** B. down before him	MONS 242:12
b. to set it right	SHAK 292:8	b. myself	BIBL 37:24
b. where my fathers lived	SITT 317:11	b. of burning gold	BLAK 57:8
b. with a gift of laughter	SABA 284:1	b. to no man	BRAN 67:18
British subject I was b.	MACD 222:19	drew a b. at a venture	BIBL 37:18
Else, wherefore b.	TENN 332:12	every knee should b.	BIBL 51:22
Every moment one is b.	TENN 335:9	**bowels** in the b. of Christ	CROM 107:9
had not been b.	BIBL 46:10	**bower** lime-tree b. my prison	COLE 100:29
house where I was b.	HOOD 172:23	**bowl** b. we call The Sky	FITZ 136:17
I am not yet b.	MACN 224:11	golden b. be broken	BIBL 39:28
lucky to be b.	WHIT 357:5	lurk within the b.	SMIT 319:12
Man is b. to live	PAST 260:1	Morning in the b. of night	FITZ 136:6
Man is b. unto trouble	BIBL 37:39	**bows** B. down to wood and stone	HEBE 164:18
Man that is b. of a woman	BOOK 62:4	**bow-wow** Big B. strain	SCOT 287:27
Man was b. free	ROUS 281:9	his b. way	PEMB 261:10
Not to be b.	BACO 24:3	**box** b. where sweets lie	HERB 167:25
Not to be b.	SOPH 320:16	**boxes** Little b. on the hillside	REYN 275:11
not to be b. is best	AUDE 18:15	**boxing** B.'s just showbusiness	BRUN 73:12
One is not b. a woman	DE B 111:13	**boy** and a b. forever	ROWL 281:14
powerless to be b.	ARNO 16:24	any b. may become President	STEV 325:3
some men are b. great	SHAK 309:2	Being read to by a b.	ELIO 128:19
sucker b. every minute	BARN 26:19	b. brought in the white sheet	LORC 218:16
those who are to be b.	BURK 75:23	b. my greatness	SHAK 289:26

boy (*cont.*)
b. on the sea-shore — NEWT 250:16
b. stood on the burning deck — HEMA 165:18
b.'s will is the wind's — LONG 217:16
b. will ruin himself — GEOR 148:1
Chatterton, the marvellous b. — WORD 365:20
Let the b. win — EDWA 125:8
little tiny b. — SHAK 309:13
Mad about the b. — COWA 105:3
Minstrel B. to the war — MOOR 244:10
sat the journeying b. — HARD 162:6
schoolrooms for 'the b.' — COOK 103:11
Upon the growing b. — WORD 365:6
boyfriend best way to obtain b. — FIEL 135:7
boys As flies to wanton b. — SHAK 298:15
b. in the back room — LOES 217:3
b. in the back rooms — BEAV 28:5
b. not going to be sent — ROOS 279:13
b. of the old Brigade — WEAT 352:11
Christian b. — ARNO 17:11
for office b. — SALI 284:22
lightfoot b. are laid — HOUS 176:15
send American b. — JOHN 186:9
Till the b. come home — FORD 139:10
bracelet b. of bright hair — DONN 119:13
braces Damn b. — BLAK 57:4
Bradford silk hat on a B. millionaire — ELIO 129:28
braes among thy green b. — BURN 76:18
Ye banks and b. — BURN 76:22
braid b., braid road — BALL 25:19
braids b. of lilies knitting — MILT 236:10
brain Bear of Very Little B. — MILN 235:12
b. attic stocked — DOYL 120:12
b. to be composed of atoms — HALD 159:9
dry b. in a dry season — ELIO 128:21
gleaned my teeming b. — KEAT 197:6
harmful to the b. — JAME 182:9
losing your b. — FOX 141:3
schoolmasters puzzle their b. — GOLD 153:22
brains blow out your b. — KIPL 203:9
b. go to his head — ASQU 18:3
branch b. shall grow — BIBL 40:16
on the high b. — SAPP 285:16
branchy b. between towers — HOPK 173:15
brandy B. for the parson — KIPL 202:24
b. of the damned — SHAW 312:1
drink b. — JOHN 190:1
get me a glass of b. — GEOR 147:18
brass evil manners live in b. — SHAK 296:16
brave b. bad man — CLAR 97:1
Fortune assists the b. — TERE 335:14
Fortune favours the b. — VIRG 347:18
home of the b. — KEY 199:17
How sleep the b. — COLL 101:16
None but the b. — DRYD 121:24
O b. new world — SHAK 307:35
Oh, the b. music — FITZ 136:9
Toll for the b. — COWP 105:21
to-morrow to be b. — ARMS 16:3
braver done one b. thing — DONN 119:19
Brazil Charley's aunt from B. — THOM 337:16
breach More honoured in the b. — SHAK 291:34
Once more unto the b. — SHAK 295:16
bread b. and circuses — JUVE 194:11
b. beneath the bough — FITZ 136:8
b. of adversity — BIBL 40:25
b. of affliction — BIBL 37:17
B. of heaven — WILL 360:5
b. should be so dear — HOOD 172:27
breaking of b. — BIBL 48:12
Cast thy b. upon the waters — BIBL 39:25
cutting b. and butter — THAC 336:10
I am the b. of life — BIBL 48:30

if his son ask b. — BIBL 44:7
live by b. alone — BIBL 43:9
made, like b. — LE G 211:18
one half-pennyworth of b. — SHAK 294:22
our daily b. — BIBL 43:22
Royal slice of b. — MILN 235:15
shalt thou eat b. — BIBL 34:21
taste of another man's b. — DANT 109:16
took B. — BOOK 61:14
took b., and blessed it — BIBL 46:11
took the b. and brake it — ELIZ 130:21
unleavened b. — BIBL 35:18
we did eat b. — BIBL 35:23
break B., break, break — TENN 331:15
b. Into blossom — WRIG 366:28
But b., my heart — SHAK 291:21
if you b. the bloody glass — MACN 224:10
lark at b. of day — SHAK 310:6
Never give a sucker an even b. — FIEL 135:17
shall he not b. — BIBL 41:5
breakdown approaching nervous b. — RUSS 282:24
Madness need not be all b. — LAIN 206:17
breakfast committed b. with it — LEWI 213:22
critical period is b.-time — HERB 167:9
Hope is a good b. — BACO 23:34
impossible things before b. — CARR 87:6
breakfasted b. with you — BRUC 73:9
breaking b. of bread — BIBL 48:12
breast broods with warm b. — HOPK 173:17
parts of the b. — BYRD 79:21
sooth a savage b. — CONG 102:6
weariness May toss him to My b. — HERB 167:21
breastie panic's in thy b. — BURN 77:19
breath Breathe on me, B. of God — HATC 163:6
breathing thoughtful b. — WORD 366:2
call the fleeting b. — GRAY 156:10
every thing that hath b. — BOOK 65:7
feather on the b. of God — HILD 169:1
last b. of Julius Caesar — JEAN 183:14
lightly draws its b. — WORD 366:15
love thee with the b. — BROW 71:18
thou no b. at all — SHAK 298:28
waste of b. — YEAT 368:13
breathe B. on me, Breath of God — HATC 163:6
summer's morn to b. — MILT 239:5
yearning to b. free — LAZA 210:5
breathes B. there the man — SCOT 287:12
breathing Closer is He than b. — TENN 332:8
b. hush in the Close — NEWB 249:18
breathless b. with adoration — WORD 366:... *[illegible]*
bred B. en bawn in a brier-patch — HARR 162:17
Bredon In summertime on B. — HOUS 176:9
breed Border, nor B. — KIPL 201:17
b. of their horses — PENN 261:13
breeding b. consists in concealing — TWAI 343:20
without any b. — THUR 340:5
breeze dancing in the b. — WORD 364:17
breezes b. dusk and shiver — TENN 333:16
breezy B., Sneezy, Freezy — ELLI 131:13
brekekekex B. koax koax — ARIS 15:7
brethren Dearly beloved b. — BOOK 59:11
least of these my b. — BIBL 46:8
brevis Ars longa, vita b. — HIPP 169:15
B. esse laboro — HORA 174:13
brevity B. is the sister — CHEK 92:10
B. is the soul of wit — SHAK 292:10
Its body b. — COLE 100:4
bribe cannot hope to b. or twist — WOLF 363:3
Marriage is a b. — WILD 359:22
brick carried a piece of b. — SWIF 328:9
Follow the yellow b. road — HARB 161:9
Goodbye yellow b. road — JOHN 186:2
inherited it b. — AUGU 20:14
paved with yellow b. — BAUM 27:22

bridal b. of the earth and sky — HERB 167:24
bride encounter darkness as a b. — SHAK 302:7
  Never the blushing b. — LEIG 212:4
  unravished b. of quietness — KEAT 196:5
bridegrooms Of b., brides — HERR 168:1
brides Of bride-grooms, b. — HERR 168:1
bridesmaid always the b. — LEIG 212:4
bridge Beautiful Railway B. — MCGO 223:3
  b. is love — WILD 359:21
  b. over troubled water — SIMO 317:1
  going a b. too far — BROW 71:19
  keep the b. with me — MACA 221:22
brief little b. authority — SHAK 302:5
  strive to be b. — HORA 174:13
brier bawn in a b.-patch — HARR 162:17
briers O, how full of b. — SHAK 290:4
brigade boys of the old B. — WEAT 352:11
bright All things b. and beautiful — ALEX 4:14
  b. day is done — SHAK 289:25
  b. day that brings forth — SHAK 296:23
  b. particular star — SHAK 289:8
  B. the vision — MANT 227:10
  dark and b. — BYRO 81:17
  Death's b. angel — PROC 271:5
  excessive b. — MILT 238:16
  Keep up your b. swords — SHAK 304:20
  look, the land is b. — CLOU 98:23
  quick b. things — SHAK 303:8
  thought thee b. — SHAK 310:30
  torches to burn b. — SHAK 306:25
  Tyger, burning b. — BLAK 58:3
  young lady named B. — BULL 73:21
brightest B. and best — HEBE 164:16
brightness B. falls from the air — NASH 248:18
brilliant dullard's envy of b. men — BEER 29:3
brillig 'Twas b. — CARR 86:23
brim winking at the b. — KEAT 196:18
bring b. home knowledge — JOHN 189:24
  B. me my arrows of desire — BLAK 57:8
brink walked to the b. — DULL 123:2
brinkmanship boasting of his b. — STEV 325:6
brioche mangent de la b. — MARI 227:18
Britain B. a fit country — LLOY 216:10
  B. will still be — MAJO 225:19
  When B. first — THOM 338:23
Britannia Beer and B. — SMIT 319:16
  Rule, B. — THOM 338:23
British as the B. public — MACA 221:12
  blood of a B. man — SHAK 298:12
  bones of one B. Grenadier — HARR 162:16
  B. Grenadier — ANON 11:1
  B. subject I was born — MACD 222:19
  drunken officer of B. rule — WALC 349:5
  so also a B. subject — PALM 258:5
  thank God! the B. journalist — WOLF 363:3
Briton glory in the name of B. — GEOR 147:17
Britons B. never will be slaves — THOM 338:23
broad b. is the way — BIBL 44:9
  how b. and far — JOHN 191:4
  too b. for leaping — HOUS 176:15
broadens travel b. the mind; but — CHES 93:17
broccoli b., dear — WHIT 356:3
  eat any more b. — BUSH 78:13
broken bats have been b. — HOWE 176:21
  Can it be b. — JENK 185:2
  made to be b. — NORT 252:1
  Morning has b. — FARJ 134:3
  not quickly b. — BIBL 39:13
  through a b. heart — WILD 359:12
brokenhearted bind up the b. — BIBL 41:17
broker honest b. — BISM 55:8
bronze monument more lasting than b. — HORA 175:17
brooches b. and toys — STEV 325:31

brood b. of folly — MILT 236:11
broods b. with warm breast — HOPK 173:17
brook free, meandering b. — THOR 339:7
  grows aslant a b. — SHAK 293:35
brooks By b. too broad — HOUS 176:15
broom sent with b. before — SHAK 304:5
brothel intellectual b. — TOLS 341:6
brothels b. with bricks of religion — BLAK 57:1
brother BIG B. IS WATCHING YOU — ORWE 254:21
  B. can you spare a dime — HARB 161:6
  b., hail, and farewell — CATU 89:9
  B. of the Angle — WALT 350:10
  b. sin against me — BIBL 45:16
  B. to Death — DANI 109:5
  closer than a b. — BIBL 38:31
  dear b. here departed — BOOK 62:6
  Death and his b. — SHEL 314:17
  especially Sir B. Sun — FRAN 141:13
  fold to thy heart thy b. — WHIT 357:16
  hateth his b. — BIBL 52:34
  he's my b. — RUSS 283:14
  man and a b. — WEDG 353:4
  my b. is a hairy man — BIBL 34:35
  my b. Jonathan — BIBL 36:35
  my b.'s keeper — BIBL 34:23
  my likeness—my b. — BAUD 27:18
  O b. man — WHIT 357:16
  stick more close than a b. — KIPL 202:27
  want to be the white man's b. — KING 200:18
brotherhood crown thy good with b. — BATE 27:17
  Love the b. — BIBL 52:27
brothers All men become b. — SCHI 286:8
  all the b. too — SHAK 309:1
  live together as b. — KING 200:16
  we band of b. — SHAK 295:29
brow b. of labour — BRYA 73:14
  Your bonny b. was brent — BURN 77:2
brown b. coat — MACA 221:10
  falling on the city b. — BRID 68:17
  Jeanie with the light b. hair — FOST 140:8
  John B.'s body — ANON 9:7
  river Is a strong b. god — ELIO 128:10
Browning God and Robert B. — BROW 73:6
  safety-catch of my B. — JOHS 191:6
brows pallor of girls' b. — OWEN 256:10
browsing b. and sluicing — WODE 362:21
bruise It shall b. thy head — BIBL 34:19
bruised b. in a new place — IRVI 181:3
  b. reed — BIBL 41:5
brush so fine a b. — AUST 21:14
brutal heart's grown b. from the fare — YEAT 368:19
brutality without art is b. — RUSK 282:13
brute Et tu, B.? — SHAK 296:28
  heart of a b. like you — PLAT 264:13
  like b. beasts — BOOK 61:24
brutes Exterminate all the b. — CONR 102:22
  made to live as b. — DANT 109:13
brutish nasty, b., and short — HOBB 170:19
Brutus B. is an honourable man — SHAK 297:2
  You too, B. — CAES 82:9
bubble mostly froth and b. — GORD 154:8
  Seeking the b. reputation — SHAK 290:13
  world's a b. — BACO 24:2
bubbles I'm forever blowing b. — KENB 198:7
  With beaded b. — KEAT 196:18
Bücher wo man B. Verbrennt — HEIN 165:6
buck b. stops here — TRUM 342:18
bucket past is a b. of ashes — SAND 285:8
  stick inside a swill b. — ORWE 254:17
Buckingham Palace changing guard at B. — MILN 235:13
bud be a b. again — KEAT 195:15
  nip him in the b. — ROCH 278:2
Buddha What is the B. — MUMO 247:5

buds darling b. of May — SHAK 310:3
buffalo breath of a b. — CROW 108:1
bugger B. Bognor — GEOR 148:3
bugle Blow, b., blow — TENN 334:13
bugles Blow out, you b. — BROO 69:19
b. calling from sad shires — OWEN 256:9
build Birds b. — HOPK 174:8
easy to b. — IBSE 180:9
Lord b. the house — BOOK 64:26
never ask *why* b. — SEXT 289:5
think we b. for ever — RUSK 282:18
builder can only be a *b.* — RUSK 282:12
building principal beauty in b. — FULL 144:16
very old b. — OSBO 255:10
built Till we have b. Jerusalem — BLAK 57:8
Who b. Thebes — BREC 68:8
bull Cock and a B. — STER 324:13
milk the b. — JOHN 188:16
strong as a b. moose — ROOS 279:20
bullet b. has its billet — WILL 360:3
b. through his head — ROBI 277:17
stronger than the b. — LINC 214:12
bullets bloody b. — LINC 214:12
b. made of platinum — BELL 29:17
bullied b. out of vice — SURT 327:19
bully such a b. pulpit — ROOS 280:7
bulwark floating b. of the island — BLAC 55:14
bum Indicat Motorem B. — GODL 152:4
bump go b. in the night — ANON 8:7
bums corporate welfare b. — LEWI 214:2
Buncombe talking to B. — WALK 349:11
through reporters to B. — CARL 85:15
bungler good nature is a b. — HALI 160:4
Man is a b. — SHAW 312:4
bunk History more or less b. — FORD 139:9
burd b. Helen dropt — BALL 25:9
burden bear any b. — KENN 198:15
borne the b. — BIBL 45:22
b. of them is intolerable — BOOK 61:8
my b. is light — BIBL 44:34
White Man's B. — KIPL 203:8
bureaucracy [b.'s] specific invention — WEBE 352:15
bureaucrats Guidelines for b. — BORE 65:19
burgundy naive domestic B. — THUR 340:5
burial b.-ground God's-Acre — LONG 217:13
buried bodies are b. in peace — BIBL 42:28
b. him darkly — WOLF 363:1
b. in so sweet a place — SHEL 313:12
where some b. Caesar bled — FITZ 136:10
Burlington B. Bertie — HARG 162:12
burn another Troy for her to b. — YEAT 368:21
better to b. out — YOUN 370:6
better to marry than to b. — BIBL 50:18
b. always with this hard, gemlike — PATE 260:8
b. and I am ice — PETR 262:14
sun shall not b. thee — BOOK 64:21
burned B. on the water — SHAK 289:17
b. women — BRAN 67:16
bush b. with fire — BIBL 35:12
men also, in the end, are b. — HEIN 165:6
burning boy stood on the b. deck — HEMA 165:18
b. fiery furnace — BIBL 42:5
b. of the leaves — BINY 55:1
b. patience — RIMB 277:5
b. roof and tower — YEAT 368:16
Is Paris b. — HITL 170:11
Keep the Home-fires b. — FORD 139:10
lady's not for b. — FRY 144:6
out of the b. — BIBL 42:13
pretty Babe all b. — SOUT 320:25
Tyger, b. bright — BLAK 58:3
burnished Furnish'd and b. — BETJ 33:5
like a b. throne — ELIO 129:22

burns candle b. at both ends — MILL 234:18
burnt b.-out ends of smoky days — ELIO 129:10
burps History just b. — BARN 26:17
bury B. my heart at Wounded Knee — BENÉ 30:15
dead b. their dead — BIBL 44:17
good day to b. bad news — MOOR 243:20
physician can b. his mistakes — WRIG 366:27
We will b. you — KHRU 200:2
bus Can it be a Motor B. — GODL 152:4
good design for a b. — HOCK 171:2
missed the b. — CHAM 90:7
not even a b., I'm a tram — HARE 162:11
bush Behold, the b. burned — BIBL 35:12
b. afire with God — BROW 71:14
Thorough b., thorough brier — SHAK 303:14
busier semed b. than he was — CHAU 91:19
business about my Father's b. — BIBL 47:7
Being good in b. — WARH 350:21
b. as usual — THAT 336:19
B. first — THAC 336:5
b. like show business — BERL 32:3
b. practices improve — RODD 278:9
do b. together — THAT 336:20
growth of a large b. — ROCK 278:6
heart in the b. — WATS 351:14
How to succeed in b. — MEAD 231:18
In civil b. — BACO 22:16
it is your b. — HORA 175:3
Liberty is unfinished b. — ANON 9:9
make b. for itself — DICK 114:13
minded their own b. — CARR 86:8
music b. is not — MORR 245:22
occupy their b. — BOOK 64:9
of the American people is b. — COOL 103:14
principal b. of life — BUTL 79:11
settled b. — BACO 23:23
small b. party — BEAZ 28:7
totter on in b. — POPE 267:3
businessmen well-placed b. decide — YOUN 369:21
bust animated b. — GRAY 156:10
busting June is b. out — HAMM 160:17
bustle B. in a House — DICK 115:29
busy be b. — OVID 256:3
b. man has no time — MAUR 231:14
B. old fool — DONN 119:15
had a b. day — SIGL 316:19
how b. I must be — ASTL 18:5
Nowher so b. a man — CHAU 91:19
butcher benevolence of the b. — SMIT 318:1
Hog B. for the World — SAND 285:4
butchered B. to make a Roman holiday — BYRO 80:12
butchers gentle with these b. — SHAK 296:29
shepherds and b. — VOLT 348:20
butler b.'s upper slopes — WODE 362:22
butt here is my b. — SHAK 305:13
knocks you down with the b. — GOLD 153:28
butter b. for the Royal slice of bread — MILN 235:15
cutting bread and b. — THAC 336:10
manage without b. — GOEB 152:5
no money for b. — JOSE 192:15
rather have b. or guns — GOER 152:6
She brought forth b. — BIBL 36:12
buttercups B. and daisies — HOWI 177:3
buttered always on the b. side — PAYN 260:18
butterfly breaks a b. — POPE 266:22
b. dreaming that — CHUA 94:13
flap of a b.'s wings — LORE 218:18
Float like a b. — ALI 5:7
butting B. through the Channel — MASE 230:17
button each b., hook, and lace — LOWE 219:16
little round b. at top — FOOT 139:4
buxom b., blithe, and debonair — MILT 236:18
buy b. it like an honest man — NORT 252:4

b. wine and milk	BIBL 41:12
client will beg to b.	BURR 77:23
Don't b. a single vote more	KENN 198:12
I will b. with you	SHAK 302:11
money can't b. me love	LENN 212:17
no man might b. or sell	BIBL 53:13
buying no fish ye're b.	SCOT 287:21
buys b. everything	MONT 242:14
buzz B.! Buzz! Buzz!	MILN 235:17
stumbling B.	DICK 116:1
by B. and by	MCCO 222:13
bymatter been a b.	BACO 22:18
bypass with a triple b.	HOWA 176:19
byword story and a b.	WINT 362:3
Byzantium holy city of B.	YEAT 368:28

C

ça Ç. ira	ANON 12:9
cabbage c.-leaf to make an apple-pie	FOOT 139:4
c. with a college education	TWAI 343:23
cabbages Of c.—and kings	CARR 87:3
planting my c.	MONT 242:17
cabin Make me a willow c.	SHAK 308:24
cabined c., cribbed, confined	SHAK 301:5
cabinet another to mislead the C.	ASQU 18:1
cable little c. cars climb	CROS 107:19
of c. television	MACK 223:12
Cabots Lowells talk to the C.	BOSS 66:2
cacoethes Scribendi c.	JUVE 194:9
cadence harsh c. of a rugged line	DRYD 122:15
caelum C. non animum mutant	HORA 174:27
Caesar appeal unto C.	BIBL 49:34
Aut C., aut nihil	BORG 65:23
Ave C., morituri te salutant	ANON 13:7
C.'s laurel crown	BLAK 56:11
C.'s wife	CAES 82:5
decree from C. Augustus	BIBL 47:1
for C.'s I am	WYAT 367:4
Hail C.	ANON 13:7
Here was a C.	SHAK 297:10
Imperious C., dead	SHAK 294:4
loved C. less	SHAK 296:31
Render unto C.	BIBL 45:26
unto C. shalt thou go	BIBL 49:35
where some buried C. bled	FITZ 136:10
Caesars C. and Napoleons	HUXL 179:11
cage become an iron c.	WEBE 352:14
Nor iron bars a c.	LOVE 219:9
red breast in a c.	BLAK 56:9
sing like birds i' the c.	SHAK 298:23
caged think c. birds sing	WEBS 353:3
why the c. bird sings	DUNB 123:7
Cain first city C.	COWL 105:13
land God gave to C.	CART 88:6
mark upon C.	BIBL 34:24
cake C. or death	IZZA 181:10
Let them eat c.	MARI 227:18
cakes no more c. and ale	SHAK 308:30
Calais 'C.' lying in my heart	MARY 230:14
calculation c. shining out	DICK 115:6
calculus integral and differential c.	GILB 150:23
Caledonia O C.! stern and wild	SCOT 287:14
calf c. and the young lion	BIBL 40:17
fatted c.	BIBL 47:32
Caliban rage of C.	WILD 358:24
California C. to the New York Island	GUTH 158:11
Caligula C.'s horse was made Consul	RAND 273:11
eyes of C.	MITT 241:18
call c. it a day	COMD 102:4
c. me early, mother dear	TENN 334:8

C. me Ishmael	MELV 232:13
c. of the running tide	MASE 231:1
c. of the wild	LOND 217:5
c. the cattle home	KING 201:7
c. ye upon him	BIBL 41:13
Go, for they c. you	ARNO 16:20
how you c. to me	HARD 162:7
O! c. back yesterday	SHAK 305:28
When you c. me that	WIST 362:5
called c. unto thee, O Lord	BOOK 64:29
many are c.	BIBL 45:25
calling Germany c.	JOYC 193:10
callisthenics c. with words	PARK 259:3
calm c., as it was bright	VAUG 345:19
calumny thou shalt not escape c.	SHAK 292:29
Calvinists C. stick fast	ROBI 277:19
Cambridge C. ladies in furnished souls	CUMM 108:11
came c. first for the Communists	NIEM 251:3
c. unto his own	BIBL 48:18
I c., I saw, I conquered	CAES 82:8
I c. through	MACA 221:6
Tell them I c.	DE L 112:15
camel c. has a single hump	NASH 248:11
c. is a horse	ISSI 181:7
easier for a c.	BIBL 45:19
raiment of c.'s hair	BIBL 43:6
swallow a c.	BIBL 45:30
Take my c., dear	MACA 221:8
Camelot known as C.	LERN 213:5
many-towered C.	TENN 333:15
camera I am a c.	ISHE 181:6
camerado C., this is no book	WHIT 357:2
cammin c. di nostra vita	DANT 109:7
campaign c. in poetry	CUOM 108:14
capital in the c.	BUSH 78:20
campaigns c. for public office	MORE 244:16
can but as we c.	MENA 232:17
C. something, hope	HOPK 173:14
He who c., does	SHAW 312:10
they c. because they think they can	VIRG 347:9
youth replies, I c	EMER 132:1
Canada all over C.	RICH 276:12
C. that shall fill	LAUR 209:17
I see C.	DAVI 110:21
more than C. itself is worth	VOLT 348:7
O C.! Our home	WEIR 353:8
Canadian definition of a C.	BERT 32:20
cancer c. close to the Presidency	DEAN 111:12
Obscene as c.	OWEN 256:11
Silence like a c. grows	SIMO 317:3
white race is the c.	SONT 320:14
candid be c. where we can	POPE 267:19
c. friend	CANN 84:8
candied c. apple, quince	KEAT 195:16
candle better to light a c.	BENE 30:16
c. burned out	JOHN 185:17
c. burns at both ends	MILL 234:18
c. in the wind	JOHN 185:16
c. in the wind	JOHN 186:1
c. of understanding	BIBL 42:19
c. to the sun	SIDN 316:9
c. to the sun	YOUN 369:25
Fire and fleet and c.-lighte	BALL 25:12
light such a c.	LATI 209:12
little c. throws his beams	SHAK 303:4
rather light a c.	STEV 325:7
set a c. in the sun	BURT 78:7
candlelight dress by yellow c.	STEV 325:26
candles c. are all out	SHAK 300:11
Night's c.	SHAK 307:5
wind extinguishes c.	LA R 209:9
candy C. is dandy	NASH 248:14
canem Cave c.	PETR 262:16

cannibal c. uses knife and fork — LEC 211:6
cannibals C. that each other eat — SHAK 304:22
cannon C. to right of them — TENN 331:20
  in the c.'s mouth — SHAK 290:13
cano *Arma virumque c.* — VIRG 346:19
canoe make love in a c. — BERT 32:20
canopy excellent c., the air — SHAK 292:16
Canossa not go to C. — BISM 55:5
can't c. go on — BECK 28:10
cant c. of *Not men* — BURK 75:30
  Clear your mind of c. — JOHN 190:15
cantate *C. Domino canticum novum* — BIBL 53:28
capability Negative C. — KEAT 197:11
capital c. in the campaign — BUSH 78:20
  high c. Of Satan — MILT 238:2
capitalism c. with the gloves off — STOP 326:16
  monopoly stage of c. — LENI 212:6
  spirit of c. — WEBE 352:13
  unacceptable face of c. — HEAT 164:15
captain broken by the team c. — HOWE 176:21
  c. of my soul — HENL 166:9
  my C. lies, Fallen — WHIT 356:24
  O C.! my Captain — WHIT 356:23
  Our great captain's c. — SHAK 304:26
  plain russet-coated c. — CROM 107:7
  ship's c. complaining — POWE 270:14
  train-band c. eke was he — COWP 105:16
captains c. and the kings — KIPL 202:19
  c. courageous — BALL 25:13
  C. of industry — CARL 85:18
  thunder of the c. — BIBL 38:9
captives all prisoners and c. — BOOK 60:15
  proclaim liberty to the c. — BIBL 41:17
car can't drive the c. — TYNA 344:4
  c. could go straight upwards — HOYL 177:6
  c. in every garage — HOOV 173:5
carbon c. atom — JEAN 183:15
carbuncle monstrous c. — CHAR 91:7
carbuncles Monstrous c. — SPEN 321:17
carcase Wheresoever the c. is — BIBL 45:35
card memories are c.-indexes — CONN 102:19
  Orange c. — CHUR 94:17
  play the race c. — SHAP 311:5
cardboard over a c. sea — HARB 161:7
cards c. with a man called Doc — ALGR 5:4
  learned to play at c. — JOHN 188:2
  shuffle the c. — CERV 89:21
  wicked pack of c. — ELIO 129:20
care age is full of c. — SHAK 309:31
  better c. of myself — BLAK 56:7
  Black C. sits behind — HORA 175:13
  don't c. too much for money — LENN 212:17
  Hippocleides doesn't c. — HIPP 169:14
  if, full of c. — DAVI 111:2
  more c. to stay — SHAK 307:6
  Nor c. beyond to-day — GRAY 156:16
  she don't c. — LENN 212:22
  take c. of minutes — CHES 92:17
  Teach us to c. — ELIO 127:25
  Took great C. of his Mother — MILN 235:14
  To say we do not c. — WARD 350:19
  wish I could c. what you do — MITC 241:14
  with me past c. — SHAK 305:26
career C. open to the talents — CARL 85:7
  c. open to the talents — NAPO 248:6
  East is a c. — DISR 118:2
  Good c. move — VIDA 346:13
  our c. and our triumph — VANZ 345:12
careful cannot be too c. — WILD 358:27
  C. now — LINE 215:10
  c. of the type — TENN 333:2
carefully got to be c. taught — HAMM 160:25
  You come most c. — SHAK 291:7

careless c. of the single life — TENN 333:2
  first fine c. rapture — BROW 72:6
  They were c. people — FITZ 137:12
carelessness both looks like c. — WILD 358:7
cares c. that infest the day — LONG 217:9
  Nobody c. — MORT 246:6
  none c. or knows — CLAR 96:26
Carew grave of Mad C. — HAYE 164:2
carnal c. lusts and appetites — BOOK 61:24
caro *verbum c. factum est* — MISS 241:3
carpe *c. diem* — HORA 175:7
carpenter I said to the c. — CART 88:3
carpenters special language like c. — SEXT 289:5
carping each c. tongue — BRAD 67:13
carriage C. held but just Ourselves — DICK 115:26
carried ought to be c. — EPIC 132:27
carrier down from the c.'s cart — LEE 211:14
carrion c. comfort, Despair — HOPK 173:14
carry c. a big stick — ROOS 279:21
  c. knowledge with him — JOHN 189:24
  c. nothing out — BIBL 52:8
  making him c. me — TOLS 341:5
cars c. the great Gothic cathedrals — BART 27:6
  crazy about c. — SALI 284:16
Carthage C. must be destroyed — CATO 89:2
carve Let's c. him — SHAK 296:24
carved c. not a line — WOLF 363:2
  marble not yet c. — MICH 233:18
case c. is concluded — AUGU 20:11
  everything that is the c. — WITT 362:11
  in our c. we have not got — REED 274:13
  lady's in the c. — GAY 147:3
  nothing to do with the c. — GILB 150:9
  would have passed in any c. — BECK 28:15
casements magic c. — KEAT 196:23
cash c. payment — CARL 85:3
  needs good c. — TUCK 342:22
  take the c. in hand — FITZ 136:9
casket seal the hushèd c. — KEAT 196:30
cast C. a cold eye — YEAT 369:12
  c. off the works of darkness — BIBL 50:12
  C. thy bread — BIBL 39:25
  C. your mind on other days — YEAT 369:11
  die is c. — CAES 82:7
  let him first c. a stone — BIBL 48:33
  Satan c. out Satan — BIBL 46:23
castle c. of my skin — LAMM 207:9
  falls on c. walls — TENN 334:13
  house is his c. — COKE 99:14
  rich man in his c. — ALEX 4:15
Castlereagh had a mask like C. — SHEL 314:1
castles C. in the air — IBSE 180:9
casualties c. were low — JARR 183:12
  number of c. — GIUL 151:9
casualty is the first c. — ANON 12:1
cat c. on a hot tin roof — WILL 360:10
  C. that Walked by Himself — KIPL 203:13
  C., the Rat, and Lovell — COLL 101:8
  C. with crimson whiskers — LEAR 210:19
  consider my C. Jeoffrey — SMAR 317:17
  cosmic Cheshire c. — HUXL 179:14
  endow a college, or a c. — POPE 266:26
  Had Tiberius been a c. — ARNO 16:19
  if a c. is black or white — DENG 112:23
  part to tear a c. in — SHAK 303:11
  play with my c. — MONT 243:1
  poor c. i' the adage — SHAK 300:6
  Touch not the c. — SCOT 287:22
  very fine c. — JOHN 190:14
  What c.'s averse to fish — GRAY 156:19
  which way the c. is jumping — SULZ 327:13
catalogue c. of human crime — CHUR 95:7
cataracts You c. and hurricanoes — SHAK 298:2

catastrophe between education and c. WELL 354:11
  drift toward unparalleled c. EINS 126:9
  New York is a c. LE C 211:9
catch catch as c. can FOOT 139:4
  If I can c. him once SHAK 302:12
Catch-22 anything as good as C. HELL 165:15
  only one catch and that was C. HELL 165:13
catcher c. in the rye SALI 284:17
catching poverty's c. BEHN 29:12
categorical imperative is C. KANT 194:22
caterpillars c. of the commonwealth SHAK 305:25
Cathay cycle of C. TENN 333:33
cathedral Heft Of C. Tunes DICK 116:5
cathedrals cars the great Gothic c. BART 27:6
catholic C. and Apostolick Church BOOK 61:4
  C. Faith BOOK 60:9
  lawful for a C. woman MENC 232:22
  Once a C. WILS 361:2
  She [the C. Church] NEWM 250:2
Catholics C. and Communists GREE 156:23
  When Hitler attacked the C. NIEM 251:3
Catiline our patience, C. CICE 96:19
cats C. and monkeys JAME 182:17
  C. look down on us CHUR 96:9
  C., no less liquid TESS 336:4
  count the c. in Zanzibar THOR 339:21
  killed the c. BROW 72:21
  Naming of C. ELIO 129:8
cattle Actors are c. HITC 170:3
  call the c. home KING 201:7
  C. die ANON 14:3
  thousands of great c. BURK 75:22
cauldron Fire burn and c. bubble SHAK 301:11
cauliflower C. is nothing but cabbage TWAI 343:23
causality law of c. RUSS 283:6
causas rerum cognoscere c. VIRG 348:3
cause already in the c. BERG 31:11
  always has some c. ARIS 15:11
  c., or just impediment BOOK 61:22
  c. that wit is SHAK 294:32
  good old C. MILT 240:12
  good old c. WORD 365:12
  great c. of cheering BENN 31:1
  it is the c., my soul SHAK 305:11
  judge thou my c. BIBL 41:26
  Our c. is just DICK 116:8
  perseverance in a good c. STER 324:10
  shew any just c. BOOK 61:25
causes declare the c. JEFF 183:17
  Home of lost c. ARNO 17:4
  knowledge of c. BACO 23:26
  malice, to breed c. JONS 191:19
  Tough on the c. of crime BLAI 55:18
caution c. in love RUSS 283:1
cautiously do c., and look to the end ANON 13:17
cavaliers C. (Wrong but Wromantic) SELL 288:19
cavalry Some say an army of c. SAPP 285:15
cave C. canem PETR 262:16
  vacant interlunar c. MILT 239:23
  wall of the c. PLAT 265:1
caves c. in which we hide FITZ 137:8
  c. of ice COLE 100:9
  dark unfathomed c. of ocean GRAY 156:11
  there will be c. NIET 251:6
caviare c. to the general SHAK 292:18
Cawdor Glamis thou art, and C. SHAK 299:21
cease c. from exploration ELIO 128:15
  c. from mental fight BLAK 57:8
  c. upon the midnight KEAT 196:21
  fears that I may c. to be KEAT 197:6
ceasing Remembering without c. BIBL 52:2
Cecilia Blessed C., appear AUDE 18:12
ceiling draw on the c. CHES 93:18

celebrity C. is a mask UPDI 344:17
  of mathematical c. DOYL 120:18
celestial Apparelled in c. light WORD 365:2
  C. Emporium BORG 65:20
Celia Come, my C. JONS 191:18
celibacy c. has no pleasures JOHN 187:19
cell Each in his narrow c. GRAY 156:8
cells c. and gibbets COOK 103:11
  little grey c. CHRI 94:11
  vast assembly of nerve c. CRIC 107:1
cement grass can grow through c. CHER 92:12
cemetery c. is an open space SHEL 313:12
censor c. of the young HORA 174:18
censorship extreme form of c. SHAW 312:32
  fought without c. WEST 355:16
centaur ant's a c. POUN 270:2
centre at the c. of Europe YUSH 370:7
  c. cannot hold YEAT 369:1
  c. is everywhere ANON 9:22
  My c. is giving way FOCH 138:18
  This bed thy c. is DONN 119:17
centuries All c. but this GILB 150:1
  forty c. look down NAPO 247:21
  Through what wild c. DE L 112:12
century c. of the common man WALL 349:13
  when a new c. begins MANN 227:4
Cerberus C., and blackest Midnight MILT 236:17
ceremony c. of innocence is drowned YEAT 369:1
  general c. SHAK 295:23
  in custom and in c. YEAT 368:24
certain c. because it is impossible TERT 336:3
  c. of nothing KEAT 197:9
  four things c. KIPL 202:7
  lady of a 'c. age' BYRO 81:4
  sure and c. hope BOOK 62:6
  you can be c. KERR 199:14
certainties begin with c. BACO 22:1
  hot for c. MERE 233:9
certainty not the test of c. HOLM 172:5
certified that I may be c. BOOK 62:25
cesspool London, that great c. DOYL 121:2
chaff wheat from the c. HUBB 177:9
chagrin C. d'amour FLOR 138:16
chainless spirit of the c. mind BYRO 81:19
chains better to be in c. KAFK 194:16
  bind their kings in c. BIBL 41:26
  C. do not hold a marriage SIGN 316:20
  deliverance from c. DOUG 120:7
  everywhere he is in c. ROUS 281:9
  lose but their c. MARX 230:13
  sang in my c. THOM 337:19
chainsaw imagination and a c. HIRS 170:2
chair c. est triste MALL 226:4
  C. she sat in ELIO 129:22
chairs three c. in my house THOR 339:17
chaise longue hurly-burly of the c. CAMP 83:7
chalices golden c. JEWE 185:10
Cham great C. of literature SMOL 319:19
chamber stalking in my c. WYAT 367:1
chambermaid arms of a c. JOHN 189:26
champagne get no kick from c. PORT 269:2
  not a c. teetotaller SHAW 311:11
chance All c., direction POPE 267:25
  bludgeonings of c. HENL 166:8
  c. favours only the prepared PAST 260:3
  erring men call c. MILT 236:9
  Give peace a c. LENN 212:19
  in the last c. saloon MELL 232:12
Chancellor C. of the Exchequer LOWE 219:15
chances changes and c. BOOK 61:15
Chanel C. No. 5 MONR 242:10
change C. and decay LYTE 221:3
  c., but I cannot die SHEL 313:24

change (cont.)

C. is constant	DISR 117:10
'C.' is scientific	RUSS 283:13
C. the name	HORA 175:21
c. the past	AGAT 3:24
c. we think we see	FROS 143:10
C. without inconvenience	JOHN 186:16
c. your mind	AURE 20:18
compelled to c. that state	NEWT 250:11
means of some c.	BURK 75:14
more things c.	KARR 195:3
necessary not to c.	FALK 133:19
point is to c. it	MARX 230:8
relief in c.	IRVI 181:3
things will have to c.	LAMP 207:13
torrent of c.	CHES 93:14
wind of c. is blowing	MACM 224:5
wish to c. in the child	JUNG 193:21

changeable c. always is woman — VIRG 347:8

changed changed, c. utterly — YEAT 368:3

changed, c. utterly	YEAT 368:5
c. upon the blue guitar	STEV 324:18
human nature c.	WOOL 363:20
If voting c. anything	LIVI 216:3
we shall all be c.	BIBL 51:3

changes c. and chances — BOOK 61:15

changing c. scenes of life — TATE 330:20

ever c., like a joyless eye	SHEL 315:1
fixed point in a c. age	DOYL 120:16
times they are a-c.	DYLA 124:13

channel Fog in C. — BROC 69:4

chaos C. and darkness — MARR 229:1

C. and old Night	MILT 237:28
C. is come again	SHAK 304:30
C. often breeds life	ADAM 1:21
C. umpire sits	MILT 238:12
dread empire, C.	POPE 266:9
Humour is emotional c.	THUR 340:7
stillness in the midst of c.	BELL 30:7

chapel also build a c. — LUTH 220:18

chaps Biography is about C. — BENT 31:9

chapter c. of accidents — CHES 92:23

repeat a complete c.	JOHN 189:22

character about a fellow's c. — REAG 274:6

by the content of their c.	KING 200:17
c. dead at every word	SHER 315:15
c. in the full current	GOET 152:16
c. is destiny	ELIO 127:21
c. is his fate	HERA 167:4
c. is to be abused	THAC 336:6
Fate and c.	NOVA 252:7
reap a c.	READ 274:1
Sports do not build c.	BROU 70:11
What is c.	JAME 182:20

characters c. and conduct of their rulers — ADAM 2:8

Six c. in search	PIRA 263:16

charge Take thou in c. — MACA 222:2

charging marching, c. feet — JAGG 182:6

Charing Cross existence is at C. — JOHN 189:7

Heaven and C.	THOM 338:19

chariot axle-tree of the c.-wheel — BACO 23:19

c. of fire	BLAK 57:8
Swing low, sweet c.	ANON 11:5
Time's wingèd c.	MARV 229:21

charioted c. by Bacchus — KEAT 196:19

chariots wheels of his c. — BIBL 36:13

charity c. for all — LINC 215:5

C. shall cover	BIBL 52:29
C. suffereth long	BIBL 50:23
have not c.	BIBL 50:22
Keeping books on c.	PERÓ 262:4
lectures or a little c.	WHIT 357:8
not a gesture of c.	MAND 226:19

Charley C.'s aunt from Brazil — THOM 337:16

Charlotte C. has been writing — BRON 69:17

charm What c. can soothe — GOLD 153:27

what c. is	CAMU 83:17

charmed c. it with smiles — CARR 87:20

charmer voice of the c. — BOOK 63:12

Were t'other dear c. away	GAY 147:2

charms Do not all c. fly — KEAT 196:2

endearing young c.	MOOR 244:6
Music has c.	CONG 102:6

Charon C. quit poling — GINS 151:6

charter c. of the land — THOM 338:23

chase have to c. after it — KLEE 204:5

with unhurrying c.	THOM 338:15

chases your picture c. me — RACI 272:18

chaste as c. as ice — SHAK 292:29

c. and fair	JONS 191:14
My English text is c.	GIBB 149:4
Nor ever c.	DONN 118:25

chasten c. and subdue — WORD 364:20

chasteneth he c. — BIBL 52:16

chastised c. you with whips — BIBL 37:8

chastity c. and continency — AUGU 20:1

C.—the most unnatural	HUXL 179:12
'Tis c., my brother	MILT 236:6
vice of c.	VOLT 348:24

chateaux ô c. — RIMB 277:4

Chattanooga C. Choo-choo — GORD 154:9

chatter only idle c. — GILB 150:13

Chatterley Between the end of the C. ban — LARK 208:14

Chatterton C., the marvellous boy — WORD 365:20

cheap flesh and blood so c. — HOOD 172:27

how potent c. music is	COWA 105:9

cheaper c. than a prawn sandwich — RATN 273:16

in the c. seats	LENN 212:15

cheat cannot c. on DNA — WARD 350:19

so lucrative to c.	CLOU 98:19

cheated c. than not to trust — JOHN 187:15

Of being c.	BUTL 79:8
Old men who never c.	BETJ 33:3

cheating period of c. — BIER 54:21

cheats c. with an oath — PLUT 265:12

cheek dancing c.-to-cheek — BERL 31:19

smite thee on thy right c.	BIBL 43:17

cheeks crack your c.! rage! blow — SHAK 298:2

on thy c.	KEAT 195:24

cheer Be of good c. — BIBL 45:4

c. but not inebriate	BERK 31:14
c. but not inebriate	COWP 105:29
Don't c., men	PHIL 263:2
scarce forbear to c.	MACA 222:3
So c. up, my lads	HUGH 177:12
which side do they c. for	TEBB 331:8

cheerful as c. as any man could — PEPY 261:16

c. countenance	BIBL 38:26
c. giver	BIBL 51:7
join our c. songs	WATT 351:22
with a c. countenance	SHAM 311:3

cheerfulness c. was always breaking in — EDWA 125:13

cheering c. us all up — BENN 31:1

cheerio c. my deario — MARQ 228:22

cheers Two c. for Democracy — FORS 139:19

cheese I've dreamed of c. — STEV 325:19

like some valley c.	AUDE 19:20
of c.	FADI 133:18
varieties of c.	DE G 112:6

chemical two c. substances — JUNG 193:20

chemistry c. that works — WILL 360:6

chequerboard c. of nights and days — FITZ 136:14

cheques Blank c. — HOLM 172:2

cherchez C. la femme — DUMA 123:3

Chernobyl cultural C. — MNOU 241:21

cherries apples, c., hops — DICK 115:18

Life is just a bowl of c. BROW 70:18
cherry American as c. pie BROW 70:15
c. hung with snow HOUS 176:7
c. now HOUS 176:6
C. ripe CAMP 83:14
C.-ripe, ripe, ripe HERR 168:2
Under the c. BASH 27:14
cherubim C. and Seraphim HEBE 164:19
Cheshire cosmic C. cat HUXL 179:14
chessboard c. is the world HUXL 179:18
chest on the dead man's c. STEV 325:16
chestnut spreading c. tree LONG 218:9
chevalier c. sans peur et sans reproche ANON 12:11
Chevy Drove my C. to the levee MCLE 223:15
chew can't fart and c. gum JOHN 186:12
chewing gum c. for the eyes ANON 11:2
chicken c. in every pot HOOV 173:5
c. in his pot HENR 166:12
Some c.! Some neck CHUR 95:13
chickens all my pretty c. SHAK 301:20
beside the white c. WILL 360:16
chiding I am a child to c. SHAK 305:9
chief c. end of man SHOR 316:5
Cromwell, our c. of men MILT 240:1
Sinners; of whom I am c. BIBL 52:5
chieftain c. o' the puddin'-race BURN 77:17
child As yet a c. POPE 266:17
C.! do not throw BELL 29:16
C. is father WORD 365:1
c. is not a vase RABE 272:13
c. of Time HALL 160:6
c. should always say what's true STEV 325:30
devoured the infant c. HOUS 176:2
English c. BLAK 57:20
God bless the c. HOLI 171:16
governed by a c. SHAK 306:12
have a thankless c. SHAK 297:29
healthy c. well nursed SWIF 328:15
I am a c. to chiding SHAK 305:9
If you strike a c. SHAW 312:13
I heard one calling, 'C.' HERB 167:13
Is it well with the c. BIBL 37:22
I was a c. POE 265:13
kind of c. you have WINS 362:2
knows his own c. SHAK 302:16
little c. I stand HERR 167:29
Love, a c. WROT 366:29
Magus Zoroaster, my dead c. SHEL 314:13
my absent c. SHAK 297:18
never was a c. so lovely EMER 132:19
On a cloud I saw a c. BLAK 57:15
one c. makes you a parent FROS 143:6
receive one such little c. BIBL 45:13
shocks the mind of a c. PAIN 257:3
simple c. WORD 366:15
spare the rod, and spoil the c. BUTL 79:7
thy king is a c. BIBL 39:23
Train up a c. BIBL 38:33
unto us a c. is born BIBL 40:14
use of a new-born c. FRAN 142:5
When I was a c. BIBL 50:25
wish to change in the c. JUNG 193:21
childbirth Death and taxes and c. MITC 241:13
childhood C. is the kingdom MILL 234:16
c. shows the man MILT 239:16
have you seen my c. JACK 181:15
moment in c. GREE 156:26
childish put away c. things BIBL 50:25
children as c. fear BACO 22:20
become as little c. BIBL 45:12
bring forth c. BIBL 34:20
by c. to adults SZAS 329:18
c. are not your children GIBR 149:9

c. at play MONT 242:19
C. begin by loving WILD 359:4
c. died in the streets AUDE 18:17
C. have never been very good BALD 24:19
c. inter their parents HERO 167:28
c. like the olive-branches BOOK 64:28
c. of a larger growth CHES 92:20
c. of a larger growth DRYD 121:28
c. of light BIBL 47:34
c. produce adults DE V 114:3
C.'s talent to endure ANGE 7:2
c. sweeten labours BACO 23:2
Come, dear c. ARNO 16:15
contempt—and c. TWAI 343:19
draw like these c. PICA 263:7
each one of her c. VERG 346:3
first class, and with c. BENC 30:9
holdeth c. from play SIDN 316:15
How many c. KNIG 204:8
kept from c. and from fools DRYD 122:9
known as the C.'s Hour LONG 217:8
music understood by c. STRA 326:23
Myself and c. three COWP 105:17
not much about having c. LODG 217:2
on us, and on our c. BIBL 46:18
parents obey their c. EDWA 125:11
poor get c. KAHN 194:18
provoke not your c. to wrath BIBL 51:19
raising your c. ONAS 253:12
remember the c. you got BROO 70:5
so are the young c. BOOK 64:27
Suffer the little c. BIBL 46:29
than of their c. PENN 261:13
tiresome for c. SAIN 284:8
upon the c. BIBL 35:25
weeping for her c. BIBL 43:3
wife and c. BACO 22:32
Chile Small earthquake in C. COCK 99:5
chill bitter c. it was KEAT 195:11
chilly c. and grown old BROW 73:5
Chimborazo C., Cotopaxi TURN 343:5
chimes c. at midnight SHAK 295:5
chimney c.-sweepers, come to dust SHAK 291:6
old men from the c. corner SIDN 316:15
chimneys grove of c. MORR 245:5
Your c. I sweep BLAK 57:16
china C. to Peru JOHN 187:24
outer C. 'crost the Bay KIPL 202:15
though c. fall POPE 266:24
Till C. and Africa meet AUDE 18:13
chip c. of the old 'block' BURK 76:7
chips c. with everything WESK 354:16
chivalry age of c. BURK 75:18
chocolate c. cream soldier SHAW 311:8
choice c. of all my library SHAK 308:7
measure and the c. JOHN 187:28
you takes your c. PUNC 271:18
choir in a wailful c. KEAT 197:4
join the c. invisible ELIO 127:23
choirs Bare ruined c. SHAK 310:11
C. and Places BOOK 60:4
c. of wailing shells OWEN 256:9
choisir Gouverner, c'est c. LÉVI 213:15
choked sprang up and c. them BIBL 44:39
choking on a man's back, c. him TOLS 341:5
choo-choo Chattanooga C. GORD 154:9
choose believe what we c. NEWM 250:8
C. an author DILL 116:14
intellect of man is forced to c. YEAT 367:15
not c. not to be HOPK 173:14
to govern is to c. LÉVI 213:15
woman can hardly ever c. ELIO 127:11
chopper cheap and chippy c. GILB 150:4

chord lost c.	PROC 271:4	Stands the C. clock	BROO 69:21
chortled c. in his joy	CARR 86:24	there must be the C.	AMBR 5:22
chosen best c. language	AUST 20:26	**churches** John to the seven c.	BIBL 52:36
c. generation	BIBL 52:26	**churchyards** When c. yawn	SHAK 293:15
few are c.	BIBL 45:25	**cigar** really good 5-cent c.	MARS 229:5
Mary hath c.	BIBL 47:18	**cigarette** c. is the perfect type	WILD 358:28
Christ all at once what C. is	HOPK 174:6	c. that bears a lipstick's traces	MARV 230:1
all things through C.	BIBL 51:29	having a c.	REID 275:1
C. and His saints	ANON 14:2	Last c.	SVEV 328:3
C. being raised from the dead	BIBL 50:3	**cigars** roller of big c.	STEV 324:15
C. beside me	PATR 260:13	**Cinara** C. was my queen	HORA 175:19
C. perish in torment	SHAW 312:31	**Cinarae** bonae Sub regno C.	HORA 175:19
C. receive thy saule	BALL 25:12	**Cincinnatus** C. of the West	BYRO 81:14
C. risen from the dead	BIBL 50:28	**cinders** c., ashes, dust	KEAT 196:1
C.'s blood streams	MARL 228:9	**cinema** c. is truth 24 times per second	GODA 152:1
C. walking on the water	THOM 338:20	**circenses** Panem et c.	JUVE 194:11
C. wasn't a woman	TRUT 342:21	**circle** God is a c.	ANON 9:22
I did trust in C.	WESL 355:2	wheel is come full c.	SHAK 293:16
If Jesus C. were to come	CARL 85:23	**circumference** c. is nowhere	ANON 9:22
Jesus C.	BIBL 52:18	**circumlocution** C. Office	DICK 115:3
Jesus C. his only Son	BOOK 59:23	**circumspectly** walk c.	BIBL 51:18
Lord C. enter in	WILD 359:12	**circumspice** Si monumentum requiris, c.	ANON 13:22
Vision of C.	BLAK 56:16	**circumstance** fell clutch of c.	HENL 166:8
We preach C. crucified	BIBL 50:15	Pride, pomp, and c.	SHAK 305:6
Christe C. eleison	MISS 240:17	**circumstantial** c. evidence	THOR 339:8
christened when she was c.	SHAK 290:21	**circuses** bread and c.	JUVE 194:11
Christian C. boys	ARNO 17:11	**cities** c. we had learned about	JARR 183:12
C. can die	ADDI 3:11	flower of c.	ANON 9:15
C. ideal has not been tried	CHES 93:19	hell to c.	AESC 3:19
C. religion	HUME 178:6	Seven c. warred	HEYW 168:17
Onward, C. soldiers	BARI 26:13	splendid C.	RIMB 277:5
persuadest me to be a C.	BIBL 49:37	streets of a hundred c.	HOOV 173:6
reconstruction of C. life	BONH 59:8	Towered c. please us	MILT 236:24
wonders of the c. religion	MATH 231:4	**citizen** c., first in war	LEE 211:13
you were a C. slave	HENL 166:11	c. of the world	BACO 22:28
Christianity C. better than Truth	COLE 100:30	c. of the world	BOSW 66:4
C. has done a great deal for love	FRAN 141:7	c. of the world	SOCR 320:2
C. is part of the laws	HALE 159:13	c. or the police	AUDE 19:18
His C. was muscular	DISR 117:25	Every c. will make	MORE 244:22
rock 'n' roll or C.	LENN 212:16	I am a Roman c.	CICE 96:21
Christians blood of C. is the seed	TERT 336:2	John Gilpin was a c.	COWP 105:16
C., awake	BYRO 79:22	zealous c.	BURK 75:27
how C. love one another	TERT 336:1	**citizens** first and second class c.	WILL 361:1
Christmas C. Day in the Workhouse	SIMS 317:10	**citizenship** c. Indian	TERE 335:20
C.-morning bells say 'Come!'	BETJ 33:1	**cito** Bis dat qui c. dat	PUBL 271:12
Do they know it's C.	GELD 147:11	**city** big hard-boiled c.	CHAN 90:11
Ghost of C. Past	DICK 114:15	c. is not a concrete jungle	MORR 245:6
insulting C. card	GROS 158:5	C. now doth like a garment wear	WORD 364:10
night before C.	MOOR 243:16	c. of dreadful night	THOM 339:2
turkeys vote for C.	CALL 82:17	C. of God	JOHN 191:4
well that C. should fall	ADDI 3:6	C. of the Big Shoulders	SAND 285:4
white C.	BERL 32:4	c. that is set on an hill	BIBL 43:15
Christopher Robin C. has fallen	MORT 246:6	c. upon a hill	WINT 362:3
C. is saying his prayers	MILN 235:16	first c. Cain	COWL 105:13
chronicle c. of wasted time	SHAK 310:17	Hell is a c.	SHEL 314:12
c. small beer	SHAK 304:27	in populous c. pent	MILT 239:5
chuckles c. of the waves	AESC 3:20	long in c. pent	KEAT 197:5
church Catholick and Apostolick C.	BOOK 61:4	new c. of Friends	WHIT 356:21
Christ's C. militant	BOOK 61:5	no continuing c.	BIBL 52:19
c. for his mother	CYPR 109:2	paper felled a c.	THOM 337:22
C. is 'one generation'	CARE 84:20	rose-red c.	BURG 74:24
C. of [England] should	ROYD 281:17	that great c.	BIBL 53:15
C. shall be free	MAGN 225:4	What is the c. but the people	SHAK 291:2
C.'s one foundation	STON 326:8	Without a c. wall	ALEX 4:18
except in the C.	CYPR 109:4	**civil** c. discord	ADDI 3:3
free c.	CAVO 89:15	In c. business	BACO 22:16
God built a c.	LUTH 220:18	Pray, good people, be c.	GWYN 158:12
Housbondes at c. dore	CHAU 91:20	**civility** C. costs nothing	MONT 242:14
I will build my c.	BIBL 45:9	**civilization** can't say c. don't advance	ROGE 278:17
no salvation outside the c.	AUGU 20:6	C. advances by extending	WHIT 356:15
open the windows of the C.	JOHN 185:13	C. a movement	TOYN 341:9
She [the Catholic C.]	NEWM 250:2	c. has from time to time	ELLI 131:15
some to c. repair	POPE 267:11	C. is the progress	RAND 273:10

Clunton C. and Clunbury	HOUS 176:14
clutching alien people c. their gods	ELIO 128:27
coach c. and six horses	RICE 276:2
indifference and a c. and six	COLM 101:17
rattling of a c.	DONN 119:24
coaches Nine c. waiting	MIDD 233:21
coal island made mainly of c.	BEVA 33:7
coalition rainbow c.	JACK 181:13
coals all eyes else dead c.	SHAK 309:29
c. of fire	BIBL 38:36
coast On the c. of Coromandel	LEAR 210:10
coaster Dirty British c.	MASE 230:17
coat c. of many colours	BIBL 35:6
made my song a c.	YEAT 367:17
stick in his c.	BROW 72:12
tattered c. upon a stick	YEAT 368:27
cobble On c.-stones I lay	FLAN 137:19
Cobbleigh Uncle Tom C.	BALL 26:3
cobwebs Laws are like c.	SWIF 328:8
tickles him the c.	FROS 143:8
cocaine C. habit-forming	BANK 26:7
cock before the c. crow	BIBL 46:12
C. and a Bull	STER 324:13
c. crowing on its own dunghill	ALDI 4:8
c. who thought the sun	ELIO 127:5
owe a c. to Aesculapius	SOCR 320:3
cockatoo green freedom of a c.	STEV 324:23
cockle c. hat and staff	SHAK 293:28
Cockney C. impudence	RUSK 282:11
cockpit Can this c. hold	SHAK 295:10
cocksure c. of anything	MELB 232:7
c. of many things	HOLM 172:5
cocktail weasel under the c. cabinet	PINT 263:15
cocoa c. for Kingsley Amis	COPE 104:1
cod bean and the c.	BOSS 66:2
coeli Rorate, c.	BIBL 54:5
coercion effect of c.	JEFF 184:19
coeur Il pleure dans mon c.	VERL 346:4
coffee C. and oranges	STEV 324:23
c.-house	SWIF 328:7
C., (which makes the politician wise)	POPE 268:21
if this is c.	PUNC 272:1
measured out my life with c. spoons	ELIO 128:31
put poison in your c.	CHUR 96:10
coffin silver plate on a c.	CURR 108:17
cogito C., ergo sum	DESC 113:15
cognoscere rerum c. causas	VIRG 348:3
cohorts his c. were gleaming	BYRO 80:18
coin C., Tiberius	DOBS 118:12
coincidence long arm of c.	CHAM 90:8
coitum Post c.	ANON 13:16
cold Cast a c. eye	YEAT 369:12
c. coming they had of it	ANDR 6:18
c. coming we had of it	ELIO 128:25
c. grave	BALL 26:1
C. in the earth	BRON 69:14
c. relation	BURK 75:27
c. war	BARU 27:7
c. war warrior	THAT 336:13
Fallen c. and dead	WHIT 356:24
in love with a c. climate	SOUT 320:23
lie in c. obstruction	SHAK 302:8
Love in a c. climate	MITF 241:16
neither c. nor hot	BIBL 53:4
offspring of c. hearts	BURK 75:19
Poor Tom's a-c.	SHAK 298:1
spy who came in from the c.	LE C 211:7
thicks man's blood with c.	COLE 100:21
To c. oblivion	SHEL 313:25
Coliseum While stands the C.	BYRO 80:13
You're the C.	PORT 269:6
collections mutilators of c.	LAMB 207:1
collective c. unconscious	JUNG 193:16

college cabbage with a c. education	TWAI 343:23
endow a c.	POPE 266:26
small c.	WEBS 352:16
Collins marry Mr C.	AUST 21:10
colonel C. Blimp	LOW 219:14
C.'s Lady	KIPL 202:13
colossus Like a c.	SHAK 296:19
colour any c. that he wants	FORD 139:8
By convention there is c.	DEMO 112:19
by the c. of their skin	KING 200:17
c., culture or ethnic origin	MACP 224:14
C. has taken hold of me	KLEE 204:5
c. of his hair	HOUS 176:1
c. purple	WALK 349:10
horse of that c.	SHAK 308:31
Life is C.	GREN 157:11
problem of the c. line	DU B 122:26
waning of their c.	VOLT 348:24
coloured penny plain and twopence c.	STEV 325:15
colourless C. green ideas	CHOM 94:6
colours coat of many c.	BIBL 35:6
c. will agree	BACO 23:18
column Fifth c.	MOLA 241:22
comb two bald men over a c.	BORG 65:22
combine When bad men c.	BURK 75:29
come better not c. at all	KEAT 197:13
C. away, come away, death	SHAK 308:34
C., dear children	ARNO 16:15
C., Holy Spirit	LANG 207:19
C. in the speaking silence	ROSS 280:11
C. into the garden	TENN 334:4
C., let us join our cheerful songs	WATT 351:22
c., let us sing	BOOK 63:26
c., Lord Jesus	BIBL 53:26
C. mothers and fathers	DYLA 124:14
C. to me in my dreams	ARNO 16:14
C. to the edge	LOGU 217:4
C. unto me	BIBL 44:33
c. unto my love	SPEN 321:22
C. unto these yellow sands	SHAK 294:8
C. what come may	SHAK 299:18
don't want to c. out	BERR 32:14
he that should c.	BIBL 44:31
King of glory shall c. in	BOOK 62:17
men may c.	TENN 331:18
mine hour is not yet c.	BIBL 48:24
Mr Watson—c. here	BELL 29:14
nobody will c.	SAND 285:7
O c., all ye faithful	ANON 13:5
shape of things to c.	WELL 354:12
Sumer is c. in	ANON 11:4
therefore I cannot c.	BIBL 47:24
'tis not to c.	SHAK 294:8
wheel is c. full circle	SHAK 298:25
when death is c., we are not	EPIC 132:28
where do they all c. from	LENN 212:18
whistle, an' I'll c.	BURN 77:8
Why don't you c. up	WEST 355:10
comeback c. kid	CLIN 98:11
comedy All I need to make a c.	CHAP 90:16
C. is an imitation	SIDN 316:16
C. is tragedy that happens	CART 87:26
c. to those that think	WALP 350:3
most lamentable c.	SHAK 303:10
comely black, but c.	BIBL 39:31
comes conquering hero c.	MORE 244:21
nobody c.	BECK 28:14
comest c. into thy kingdom	BIBL 48:9
cometh Blessed be he that c.	BOOK 64:19
c. unto the Father	BIBL 49:5
He c. not	TENN 334:1
comets no c. seen	SHAK 296:25
comfort carrion c., Despair	HOPK 173:14

c. and despair SHAK 310:28
c. and relieve them BOOK 60:17
c. of feeling safe ANON 10:2
c. ye my people BIBL 40:29
good c., Master Ridley LATI 209:12
great source of c. NIET 251:10
love her, c. her BOOK 61:26
naught for your c. CHES 92:25
to c., and command WORD 366:3
waters of c. BOOK 62:14
comfortable c. estate of widowhood GAY 146:20
c. words BOOK 61:9
comfortably lived c. so long together GAY 146:19
Speak ye c. BIBL 40:29
comforted c. his people BIBL 41:8
they shall be c. BIBL 43:13
would not be c. BIBL 43:3
comforters Miserable c. BIBL 38:2
comforting cloud of c. convictions RUSS 283:9
comical Beautiful c. things HARV 163:4
I often think it's c. GILB 149:18
coming cold c. we had of it ELIO 128:25
C. events cast their shadows CAMP 83:11
c. for us that night BALD 25:1
C. in on a wing and a pray'r ADAM 2:18
C. thro' the rye BURN 76:24
Everything's c. up roses SOND 320:11
good time c. SCOT 287:24
my c. down MORE 244:19
She is c., my dove TENN 334:6
their c. hither SHAK 298:22
Yanks are c. COHA 99:9
comma kiss can be a c. MIST 241:8
command c. success ADDI 2:20
give what you c. AUGU 20:5
not born to sue, but to c. SHAK 305:18
sue than to c. SCOT 287:8
to comfort, and c. WORD 366:3
commandment first and great c. BIBL 45:28
commandments keep his c. BIBL 39:30
commend c. my spirit BIBL 48:11
c. my spirit BOOK 62:20
comment C. is free SCOT 287:2
C. is free STOP 326:11
commentators c. each dark passage YOUN 369:25
commerce In matters of c. CANN 84:6
Peace, c. JEFF 184:7
where c. long prevails GOLD 153:16
commercial put to c. use EDIS 125:4
commit c. his body to the deep BOOK 65:10
committed c. breakfast with it LEWI 213:22
committee C.—a group of men ALLE 5:10
c. is a group of the unwilling ANON 7:16
horse designed by a c. ISSI 181:7
commodity C., firmness, and delight WOTT 366:25
common century of the c. man WALL 349:13
c. law itself COKE 99:13
c. pursuit LEAV 211:3
c. reader JOHN 187:10
c. things that round us WORD 365:15
light of c. day WORD 365:7
like the c. people YEAT 369:18
nor lose the c. touch KIPL 202:10
not already c. LOCK 216:13
nothing c. did or mean MARV 229:18
prefers c.-looking people LINC 215:1
speak as the c. people do ASCH 17:15
trivial round, the c. task KEBL 197:24
commonplace ordinary c. things SCOT 287:27
commons C., faithful to their system MACK 223:13
common sense C. is not VOLT 348:12
C. is nothing more EINS 126:11
C. is the best distributed DESC 113:13

Nothing but c. MORT 246:4
commonwealth caterpillars of the c. SHAK 305:25
commonwealths uniting into c. LOCK 216:21
communicated C. monthly BETJ 33:3
communication c. Of the dead ELIO 128:11
communications Evil c. BIBL 51:1
communion Table, at the C.-time BOOK 60:24
communism caused the fall of c. JOHN 186:3
C. is Soviet power LENI 212:9
spectre of C. MARX 230:11
communist call me a c. CAMA 82:21
I wasn't a C. NIEM 251:3
members of the C. Party MCCA 222:7
What is a c. ELLI 131:11
communists Catholics and C. GREE 156:23
community part of the c. of Europe SALI 284:20
small anarchist c. BENN 30:22
unite into a c. LOCK 216:20
commuter C.—one who spends WHIT 356:2
compact c. which exists GARR 146:11
compacted sweets c. lie HERB 167:25
companion even thou, my c. BOOK 63:10
gave him a c. VALÉ 345:1
send the prince a better c. SHAK 294:35
companions c. for middle age BACO 22:33
company c. and good discourse WALT 350:11
C. for carrying on ANON 7:18
c. he chooses BURT 77:25
c. we don't greatly like WILL 360:8
crowd is not c. BACO 22:33
not good c. AUST 21:3
owe my soul to the c. store TRAV 341:12
shine in c. SWIF 328:23
three is c. WILD 358:5
tone of the c. CHES 92:16
compare not reason and c. BLAK 56:18
Shall I c. thee SHAK 310:3
comparisons C. are odorous SHAK 304:13
compass mariner's needle [c.] BACO 23:33
top of my c. SHAK 293:12
compassed c. me round BOOK 64:16
we also are compassed about BIBL 52:15
compassion friendliness, c. MAHÁ 225:8
sharp c. of the healer's art ELIO 128:9
compassionate Merciful, the C. KORA 204:17
compel c. thee to go a mile BIBL 43:18
competition Approves all forms of c. CLOU 98:20
rigour of c. ANON 7:17
complacencies C. of the peignoir STEV 324:23
complain c. we cannot see BERK 31:16
Never c. and never explain DISR 118:8
complainers c. for the public BURK 75:5
complains Everyone c. of his memory LA R 209:6
complete become c. yourself FRIE 142:21
clad in c. steel MILT 236:6
c. and finished in my mind MOZA 246:13
c. and great CATH 88:18
in herself c. MILT 239:2
complexes feeling-toned c. JUNG 193:16
complexion have a different c. CONR 102:20
complexities All mere c. YEAT 367:13
compliance timely c. FIEL 135:10
complies c. against his will BUTL 79:9
composer requirement for a c. HONE 172:17
compound it's a chemical c. ZAPP 370:9
comprehended darkness c. it not BIBL 48:15
comprehensible universe is c. EINS 126:7
comprehensive bog-standard c. CAMP 83:4
comprendre Tout c. rend très indulgent STAË 322:22
compris Je vous ai c. DE G 112:3
compromise founded upon c. BURK 75:9
compulsion No c. in religion KORA 205:1
Such sweet c. MILT 236:1

compulsory forbidden is c.   WHIT 356:7
computer modern c. hovers   BREN 68:12
computers so many c.   WALĘ 349:6
conceal able to c. it   LA R 209:8
  c. our wants   GOLD 153:19
  should c. it   AUST 20:28
conceit folly and c.   AUST 21:9
  wise in his own c.   BIBL 38:38
conceits accepted for c.   BACO 22:3
conceive virgin shall c.   BIBL 40:12
conceived c. by the Holy Ghost   BOOK 59:23
  my mother c. me   BOOK 63:6
concentrates c. his mind   JOHN 189:18
conception present at the c.   ORTO 254:7
concepts walks up the stairs of his c.   STEI 323:20
concerned being ultimately c.   TILL 340:12
  nobody left to be c.   NIEM 251:3
concert middle of a c.   STEN 324:2
concluded case is c.   AUGU 20:11
concord lover of c.   BOOK 60:2
  travelled a good deal in C.   THOR 339:10
  truth, unity, and c.   BOOK 61:7
concordia C. discors   HORA 175:1
concrete city is not a c. jungle   MORR 245:6
  c. and tyres   LARK 208:18
  c. cloverleaf   MUMF 247:4
concubine c. of a warlord   JUNG 193:22
concupiscent c. curds   STEV 324:15
condemn c. a little more   MAJO 225:18
  Neither do I c. thee   BIBL 48:34
condemned c. to be free   SART 285:21
  you yourself Are much c.   SHAK 297:14
condition c. upon which God   CURR 108:16
  could do in that.   PEPY 261:16
conditions c. of men   BOOK 60:16
conduct c. of their rulers   ADAM 2:8
  c. unbecoming   ANON 7:10
  regulation of c.   SPEN 321:7
  rottenness begins in his c.   JEFF 184:4
cone inverted c.   JOHN 189:22
  sphere, the c.   CÉZA 89:23
cones eat the c. under his pines   FROS 143:20
confederacy dunces are all in c.   SWIF 328:20
conference c. a ready man   BACO 23:13
  naked into the c. chamber   BEVA 33:11
confess c. to almighty God   MISS 240:16
confessions c. of a justified sinner   HOGG 171:14
confidence ignorance and c.   TWAI 344:1
  to inspire c.   CARR 87:22
confident glad c. morning   BROW 72:14
confine verge Of her c.   SHAK 297:32
confined cabined, cribbed, c.   SHAK 301:5
confinement solitary c. inside our own skins
    WILL 360:13
conflict armed c.   EDEN 125:2
  Never in the field of human c.   CHUR 95:11
conflicts all disputes or c.   BRIA 68:14
conforms man c.   ANON 10:17
confounded Confusion worse c.   MILT 238:14
  let me never be c.   BOOK 59:21
confront to c. them   TRIM 341:18
confused anyone who isn't c.   MURR 247:12
confusion come to c.   SHAK 303:8
  C. now hath made   SHAK 300:23
  C. on thy banners wait   GRAY 156:5
  C. worse confounded   MILT 238:14
congeals When love c.   HART 162:20
Congo C. is the trigger   FANO 132:8
congregation c. of vapours   SHAK 292:16
  face of this c.   BOOK 61:23
congress C. makes no progress   LIGN 214:11
conjecture not beyond all c.   BROW 71:6
conjuring c. trick with bones   JENK 185:1

Connaught Hell or C.   CROM 107:15
connect Only c.   FORS 139:16
conquer c. or die   WASH 351:5
  shalt thou c.   CONS 103:5
  we will c.   BEE 28:21
conquered c. and peopled   SEEL 288:10
  I came, I saw, I c.   CAES 82:8
  Thou has c.   SWIN 329:14
conquering c. hero comes   MORE 244:21
  c. one's enemies   GENG 147:13
conqueror you are a c.   ROST 281:3
conquest c. of the earth   CONR 102:20
conquests spread her c.   BURN 76:23
conscience according to c.   MILT 240:9
  c. asks the question   KING 200:19
  C. avaunt   CIBB 96:14
  c. doth make cowards   SHAK 292:26
  c. of the king   SHAK 292:22
  C.: the inner voice   MENC 232:21
  corporation to have a c.   THUR 340:8
  cruelty with a good c.   RUSS 283:10
  cut my c.   HELL 165:16
  freedom of c.   TWAI 343:11
  reason and c.   PRIC 270:21
  scar on the c.   BLAI 56:1
  to C. first   NEWM 250:3
  value next a good c.   WALT 350:14
consciences binding on the c.   JOHN 185:12
consciousness C. . . . is the phenomenon   PENR 261:14
  from the beginning of c.   WOOL 363:19
conscription Not necessarily c.   KING 201:5
consecration c., and the Poet's   WORD 364:12
consent whispering 'I will ne'er c.'   BYRO 80:22
  without his c.   CAMD 83:2
  without your c.   ROOS 279:5
consequences damn the c.   MILN 235:21
  there are c.   INGE 180:18
conservation means of its c.   BURK 75:14
conservatism c. is based upon the idea   CHES 93:14
  What is c.   LINC 214:14
conservative become a c.   AREN 14:21
  c. been arrested   WOLF 363:9
  C. Government   DISR 117:6
  C., n. A statesman   BIER 34:19
  C. Party at prayer   ROYD 281:17
  make me c. when old   FROS 143:22
  makes a man more c.   KEYN 190:8
  Or else a little C.   GILB 149:18
  sound C. government   DISR 117:20
conservatives C. . . . being by the law   MILL 234:5
consider c. her ways, and be wise   BIBL 38:15
  c. how my light is spent   MILT 239:30
  weigh and c.   BACO 23:11
considerable appear c.   JOHN 189:2
considerate C. la vostra semenza   DANT 109:13
consideration C. like an angel came   SHAK 295:11
consistency foolish c.   EMER 132:11
consistent completely c. are the dead   HUXL 179:9
  c. with the laws of nature   FARA 133:21
conspicuous C. consumption   VEBL 345:20
  Vega c. overhead   AUDE 19:13
conspiracies c. against the laity   SHAW 311:18
conspiracy c. against the public   SMIT 318:2
  c. to make you happy   UPDI 344:16
conspiring C. with him   KEAT 197:1
constable c.'s handbook   KING 201:10
constabulary c. duty's to be done   GILB 150:24
constancy no object worth its c.   SHEL 315:1
constant c. as the northern star   SHAK 296:27
  Friendship is c.   SHAK 304:7
  nothing in this world c.   SWIF 328:25
  One here will c. be   BUNY 74:17
constellation bright c.   JEFF 184:8

constituencies go back to your c.   STEE 323:8
constitution c. does not provide   WILL 361:1
  genius of the C.   PITT 264:6
  people made the C.   MARS 229:4
  principle of the English c.   BLAC 55:15
  support its C.   PAGE 256:20
construction mind's c.   SHAK 299:20
consul horse was made C.   RAND 273:11
consult C. the genius   POPE 266:28
consulted right to be c.   BAGE 24:10
consume born to c. resources   HORA 174:22
consumed bush was not c.   BIBL 35:12
consumer c. isn't a moron   OGIL 253:2
  c. society   ILLI 180:13
consumere *fruges c. nati*   HORA 174:22
consumes c. without producing   ORWE 254:8
consummation c. Devoutly to be wished   SHAK 292:23
consummatum *C. est*   BIBL 54:12
consumption Conspicuous c.   VEBL 345:20
  C. is the sole end   SMIT 318:6
  c. of the purse   SHAK 295:1
contact no plan survives first c.   MOLT 242:4
contagion c. of the world's slow stain   SHEL 313:19
contempt c. on all my pride   WATT 351:23
  Familiarity breeds c.   TWAI 343:19
contemptible c. little army   ANON 8:4
  poor c. men   CROM 107:14
content land of lost c.   HOUS 176:13
contented c. least   SHAK 310:5
contest not the victory but the c.   COUB 104:14
continency chastity and c.   AUGU 20:1
continent brought forth upon this c.   LINC 214:20
  C. isolated   BROC 69:4
  overspread the c.   O'SU 255:20
continental may be quite c.   ROBI 277:13
contingency c. for the space shuttle   ANON 7:20
continually think c. of those   SPEN 321:18
continuance c. in well doing   BIBL 49:38
continuation c. of politics   CLAU 97:12
continuing c. unto the end   DRAK 121:6
  no c. city   BIBL 52:19
contraception oral c.   ALLE 5:14
contract C. into a span   HERB 167:20
  from Status to C.   MAIN 225:15
  social c.   ROUS 281:8
  Society is indeed a c.   BURK 75:23
  verbal c. isn't worth   GOLD 154:3
contradict Do I c. myself   WHIT 357:9
  I never c.   DISR 118:7
  Never c.   FISH 136:4
  Read not to c.   BACO 23:11
  truth which you cannot c.   SOCR 320:1
contradictions glaring c.   HUME 178:9
contrariwise 'C.,' continued Tweedledee   CARR 87:2
contrary directed to c. parts   NEWT 250:13
  everythink goes c. with me   DICK 114:17
  On the c.   IBSE 180:10
contribution make his own c.   MORE 244:22
contrite broken and c. heart   ELEA 127:1
control Ground c. to Major Tom   BOWI 67:1
  ought to c. our thoughts   DARW 110:3
controls Who c. the past   ORWE 254:23
controversies forged in c.   FRAN 141:15
convenient c. that there be gods   OVID 255:24
convent C. of the Sacred Heart   ELIO 129:16
convention By c. there is colour   DEMO 112:19
conventional c. truth   NAGA 247:19
  merely c. signs   CARR 87:18
conventionality C. is not morality   BRON 69:9
conversation c. perfectly delightful   SMIT 319:11
  different name for c.   STER 324:11
  no such thing as c.   WEST 355:13
  subject of c.   CHES 92:13

conversations without pictures or c.   CARR 86:3
conversing With thee c.   MILT 238:25
conversion c. of the Jews   MARV 229:20
convert who shall c. me   WESL 355:1
converted Except ye be c.   BIBL 45:12
  have not c. a man   MORL 245:3
convictions cloud of comforting c.   RUSS 283:9
  c. are hills   FITZ 137:8
convince we c. ourselves   JUNI 194:2
convinces man who c. the world   DARW 110:15
convincing less c. than one   HUXL 179:13
cookery c. do   MERE 233:7
cookies baked c. and had teas   CLIN 98:9
cooking c. of the Mediterranean   DAVI 110:17
  'plain' c. cannot be entrusted   MORP 245:4
cooks as c. go   SAKI 284:12
  Devil sends c.   GARR 146:8
cool c. web of language   GRAV 155:16
  in the c. of the day   BIBL 34:16
  rather be dead than c.   COBA 99:1
  Sweet day, so c.   HERB 167:24
cooled C. a long age   KEAT 196:17
cooling for c. the blood   FLAN 137:21
cooperation belief in c.   YAMA 367:9
  partnership and c.   ANON 7:17
coot haunts of c. and hern   TENN 331:17
copies few originals and many c.   TOCQ 340:15
  Make c.   INGR 180:22
copulating skeletons c.   BEEC 28:22
copulation Birth, and c., and death   ELIO 129:14
copy to every book its c.   COLU 102:2
cor *C. ad cor loquitur*   NEWM 250:9
coral C. is far more red   SHAK 310:25
  India's c. strand   HEBE 164:17
corbies twa c.   BALL 25:21
cord silver c. be loosed   BIBL 39:28
  stretch a c. however fine   WHEW 355:21
  threefold c.   BIBL 39:13
corda *Sursum c.*   MISS 240:22
core deep heart's c.   YEAT 368:15
cork c. out of my lunch   FIEL 135:18
corkscrews crooked as c.   AUDE 18:15
cormorant common c. (or shag)   ISHE 181:5
  C. devouring Time   SHAK 298:31
corn amid the alien c.   KEAT 196:23
  c. as high as an elephant's eye   HAMM 160:18
  C. rigs, an' barley rigs   BURN 77:1
  c. was orient   TRAH 341:11
  lower the price of c.   MELB 232:8
  stop raising c.   LEAS 211:2
  there was c. in Egypt   BIBL 35:7
  two ears of c.   SWIF 328:10
corner c. in the thing I love   SHAK 305:3
  c. of a foreign field   BROO 70:2
  drive life into a c.   THOR 339:18
  in a c., some untidy spot   AUDE 19:10
  wind in that c.   SHAK 304:11
corners three c. of the world   SHAK 297:21
Cornish twenty thousand C. men   HAWK 163:10
corny c. as Kansas in August   HAMM 160:23
Coromandel On the coast of C.   LEAR 210:10
coronets more than c.   TENN 333:14
corporate c. welfare bums   LEWI 214:2
corporation c. to have a conscience   THUR 340:8
corporations [c.] cannot commit treason   COKE 99:15
corpore *Mens sana in c. sano*   JUVE 194:12
corpse make a lovely c.   DICK 115:8
correct All present and c.   ANON 7:8
  Blot out, c.   SWIF 328:26
correcteth he c.   BIBL 38:12
correlative objective c.   ELIO 130:5
corridors c. of power   SNOW 319:20
corroborative c. detail   GILB 150:8

corrupt c. good manners BIBL 51:1
more c. the state TACI 330:1
moth and rust doth c. BIBL 43:23
power is apt to c. PITT 264:4
corruption C., the most infallible symptom
GIBB 148:17
corrupts absolute power c. ACTO 1:9
corse c. to the rampart WOLF 362:24
Cortez like stout C. KEAT 196:28
cosmetics we make c. REVS 275:9
cost count the c. IGNA 180:12
Cotopaxi Chimborazo, C. TURN 343:5
cottage Love and a c. COLM 101:17
poorest man may in his c. PITT 264:3
cotton c. is high HEYW 168:14
C. is King CHRI 94:12
c. is king HUGO 178:2
couch when on my c. I lie WORD 364:18
couches banish them to their c. KORA 205:8
counsel c. and might BIBL 40:16
c. that I once heard EMER 132:7
darkeneth c. BIBL 38:7
princely c. in his face MILT 238:5
sometimes c. take POPE 268:18
took sweet c. BOOK 63:10
counsellors when c. blanch BACO 22:17
counsels all good c. BOOK 60:7
count c. the cost IGNA 180:12
Don't c. on me RICH 276:6
if you can c. your money GETT 148:11
I won the c. SOMO 320:9
Let me c. the ways BROW 71:17
let us c. our spoons JOHN 188:15
When angry, c. four TWAI 343:24
counted c. our spoons EMER 132:4
c. them all out HANR 161:3
countenance cheerful c. BIBL 38:26
C. Divine BLAK 57:8
disinheriting c. SHER 315:17
Knight of the Doleful C. CERV 89:19
counter All things c. HOPK 174:2
counterfeit sleep, death's c. SHAK 300:24
counterpane land of c. STEV 325:28
counterpoint Too much c. BEEC 29:1
counterpoints c. to hack post-horses MOZA 246:12
counters Words are wise men's c. HOBB 170:14
counties Forget six c. MORR 245:12
counting it's the c. STOP 326:9
country all their c.'s wishes COLL 101:16
Anyone who loves his c. GARI 146:4
ask not what your c. KENN 199:1
become the clever c. HAWK 163:9
be good in the c. WILD 358:30
betraying my c. FORS 139:18
billion dollar c. FOST 140:4
Britain a fit c. LLOY 216:10
c. be always successful ADAM 2:13
c. has the government MAIS 225:16
C. in the town MART 229:12
c. is lost WILL 360:2
c. is the world PAIN 257:18
c. takes her place EMME 132:23
Cry, the beloved c. PATO 260:11
die for one's c. HORA 175:14
dying for your c. FRAN 141:9
every c. but his own GILB 150:1
fate of this c. DISR 117:14
fight for its King and C. GRAH 154:19
first, best c. GOLD 153:15
for our c.'s good CART 87:27
friend of every c. CANN 84:7
friends of every c. DISR 117:15
God made the c. COWP 105:24

good news from a far c. BIBL 38:37
good of his c. WOTT 366:26
grow up with the c. GREE 156:22
How can you govern a c. DE G 112:6
how I leave my c. PITT 264:1
I love thee still— My c. COWP 105:26
impossible to live in a c. KEAT 197:14
in a c. village AUST 21:13
in another c. MARL 228:14
I pray for the c. HALE 159:12
King and c. need you ANON 12:7
lose for my c. HALE 159:15
love to serve my c. GIBR 149:8
My c. is Kiltartan Cross YEAT 368:11
My c. is not a country VIGN 346:15
My c., right or wrong SCHU 286:18
My c., 'tis of thee SMIT 319:1
My soul, there is a c. VAUG 345:14
no c. for old men YEAT 368:26
no relish for the c. SMIT 319:6
Our c. is the world GARR 146:10
our c., right or wrong DECA 111:16
past is a foreign c. HART 163:3
quarrel in a far away c. CHAM 90:4
serve our c. ADDI 3:1
service of their c. PAIN 257:10
she is my c. still CHUR 94:15
there's another c. SPRI 322:13
to all the c. dear GOLD 153:8
tremble for my c. JEFF 184:20
unmapped c. ELIO 127:8
vow to thee, my c. SPRI 322:12
we can do for our c. HOLM 172:3
what was good for our c. WILS 361:3
While there's a c. lane PARK 259:9
countrymen c. are all mankind GARR 146:10
Friends, Romans, c. SHAK 297:1
hearts of his c. LEE 211:13
rebels are our c. GRAN 155:11
courage C. is the price that Life EARH 124:16
c. never to submit MILT 237:20
C. not simply one of the virtues LEWI 214:1
c. to suffer TROL 342:2
c. without ferocity BYRO 81:27
endurance and c. SCOT 287:5
in the morning c. THOR 339:15
Moral c. is a rarer commodity KENN 199:8
Pathos, piety, c. FORS 139:17
red badge of c. CRAN 106:9
salute your c. GALL 145:9
screw your c. SHAK 300:8
two o'clock in the morning c. NAPO 248:3
warm c. BUSH 78:17
warm c. ROOS 279:9
with a good c. BOOK 62:21
courageous captains c. BALL 25:13
freedom depends on being c. THUC 339:26
course c. of true love SHAK 303:7
finished my c. BIBL 52:11
myself to that c. PEPY 261:20
Of c., of course JAME 183:2
court c. awards it SHAK 302:34
courteous c. to strangers BACO 22:28
courtesy very pink of c. SHAK 306:36
courtmartialled c. in my absence BEHA 29:7
courts Approach with joy his c. KETH 199:16
case is still before the c. HORA 174:14
one day in thy c. BOOK 63:20
courtship C. to marriage CONG 102:8
cousins his c. and his aunts GILB 150:17
covenant c. with death BIBL 40:24
c. with death GARR 146:11
covenanted c. with him BIBL 46:9

covenants Open c. of peace WILS 361:16
cover c. her face WEBS 352:24
I c. all SAND 285:6
covered c. his face BIBL 40:8
covet Thou shalt not c. BIBL 35:28
Thou shalt not c. CLOU 98:20
cow c. is of the bovine ilk NASH 248:12
never saw a Purple C. BURG 74:22
To every c. her calf COLU 102:2
Truth, Sir, is a c. JOHN 188:16
coward No c. soul is mine BRON 69:13
cowardice C. asks the question KING 200:19
surest is c. TWAI 343:13
cowards C. die many times SHAK 296:26
c. in reasoning SHAF 289:7
make c. of us all SHAK 292:26
cowslips c. tall her pensioners be SHAK 303:15
coy Then be not c. HERR 168:6
coyness This c., lady MARV 229:19
crabbed C. age and youth SHAK 309:31
crack C. and sometimes break ELIO 128:4
c. in the tea-cup opens AUDE 18:14
cracked c. from side to side TENN 333:20
crackling c. of thorns BIBL 39:15
cradle c. and the grave DYER 124:1
c. of an infant BURK 75:3
c. of the deep WILL 360:1
c. of the fairy queen SHAK 303:25
c. rocks above an abyss NABO 247:17
from the c. to the grave CHUR 95:16
hand that rocks the c. WALL 349:15
rocking the c. ROBI 278:1
cradling evil c. КОПА 206:2
craft c. so long to lerne CHAU 92:2
cramped won't lie too c. CELA 89:16
crastina Sera nimis vita est c. MART 229:7
craving full as c. too DRYD 121:28
crazy C. like a fox PERE 261:21
c. to fly more missions HELL 165:13
Still c. after all SIMO 317:4
stood by me when I was c. SHER 315:24
cream c.-faced loon SHAK 301:26
c. of the working-class BEAZ 28:6
create c. the taste WORD 366:21
must c. a system BLAK 56:18
What I cannot c. FEYN 135:5
created all men are c. equal ANON 11:14
c. him in his own image DOST 119:28
c. in the image TALM 330:13
c. Man of a blood-clot KORA 205:25
monster whom I had c. SHEL 313:9
Nothing can be c. LUCR 220:13
creation eternal act of c. COLE 101:1
from the first c. LLOY 216:6
I hold C. in my foot HUGH 177:16
present at the C. ALFO 5:2
this c. has arisen RIG 276:16
whole c. moves TENN 333:11
your niche in c. HALL 160:8
creative c. urge BAKU 24:18
creator abide with my C. God CLAR 96:27
C., if He exists HALD 159:10
existence of the C. MAIM 225:14
myself and my C. NEWM 249:20
Remember now thy C. BIBL 39:27
creature God's first C. BACO 23:32
lone lorn c. DICK 114:17
one tiny c. DOST 120:1
creatures c. great and small ALEX 4:14
credit greatly to his c. GILB 150:20
In science the c. goes DARW 110:15
let the c. go FITZ 136:9
people who get the c. MORR 246:1

credite Experto c. VIRG 347:19
credo C. in unum Deum MISS 240:20
C. quia impossibile TERT 336:3
credulous Man is a c. animal RUSS 283:11
creed c. of slaves PITT 263:20
last article of my c. GAND 145:16
creeds live their c. GUES 158:7
so many c. WILC 358:1
than in half the c. TENN 333:6
creep Ambition can c. BURK 75:28
bade me c. past BROW 72:27
make your flesh c. DICK 115:19
creeps c. rustling to her knees KEAT 195:13
crème c. de la crème SPAR 321:1
cribbed cabined, c., confined SHAK 301:5
cricket C.—a game which the English MANC 226:14
c. as organized loafing TEMP 331:12
C. civilizes people MUGA 246:15
c. on the hearth MILT 236:13
c. test TEBB 331:8
c. with their peasants TREV 341:16
When you play Test c. BRAD 67:11
cried when he c. AUDE 18:17
cries on me she c. BALL 25:9
crieth c. in the wilderness BIBL 40:30
crime catalogue of human c. CHUR 95:7
c. of being a young man PITT 264:2
c. you haven't committed POWE 270:10
Napoleon of c. DOYL 120:18
never a c. CORN 104:6
punishment fit the c. GILB 150:6
Tough on c. BLAI 55:18
worse than a c. BOUL 66:8
crimes c. are committed in thy name ROLA 278.18
c., follies, and misfortunes GIBB 148:14
c. of this guilty land BROW 70:17
worst of c. SHAW 311:24
criminal crime and the c. AREN 14:20
ends I think c. KEYN 199:18
while there is a c. element DEBS 111:15
crimson Cat with c. whiskers LEAR 210:19
c. thread of kinship PARK 259:10
Now sleeps the c. petal TENN 334:21
cringe Australian Cultural C. PHIL 263:4
crisis real c. on your hands THAT 336:17
crisp Deep and c. and even NEAL 248:23
Crispian feast of C. SHAK 295:27
crisps like eating c. BOY 67:4
critic c. is a bundle of biases BALL 26:4
c. is a man who knows the way TYNA 344:4
C., you have frowned WORD 365:25
cry of the c. for five WHIS 355:23
important book, the c. assumes WOOL 363:23
not the c. who counts ROOS 280:3
criticism c. of life ARNO 17:6
father of English c. JOHN 187:9
no c. of the president ROOS 280:8
People ask you for c. MAUG 231:9
criticize c. What you can't understand DYLA 124:14
criticized If you are not c. RUMS 281:20
critics c. of the next FITZ 137:16
know who the c. are DISR 117:28
croaks c. the fatal entrance SHAK 299:22
crocodile How doth the little c. CARR 86:5
crocodiles wisdom of the c. BACO 23:22
Cromwell C., I charge thee SHAK 296:14
crook President is a c. NIXO 251:17
crooked crag with c. hands TENN 332:6
c. as corkscrews AUDE 18:15
c. timber of humanity KANT 195:1
set the c. straight MORR 245:11
croppy Hoppy, C., Droppy ELLI 131:13
cross bloody c. he bore SPEN 321:25

cross (*cont.*)
c. of gold — BRYA 73:14
c. of Jesus — BARI 26:13
no c., no crown — PENN 261:11
old rugged c. — BENN 30:18
orgasm has replaced the C. — MUGG 246:18
see thee ever c.-gartered — SHAK 309:3
survey the wondrous c. — WATT 351:23
crossbow With my c. I shot — COLE 100:17
crosses Between the c., row on row — MCCR 222:16
crow before the cock c. — BIBL 46:12
risen to hear him c. — ELIO 127:5
upstart c. — GREE 157:2
crowd c. flowed over London Bridge — ELIO 129:21
c. is not company — BACO 22:23
c. will always save Barabbas — COCT 99:8
Far from the madding c.'s — GRAY 156:14
crowded Across a c. room — HAMM 160:20
c. hour of glorious life — MORD 244:14
crowds talk with c. — KIPL 202:10
crown abdicate the C. — JUAN 193:11
Caesar's laurel c. — BLAK 56:11
c. in possession — PAIN 257:6
c. of life — BIBL 53:3
C. of Thorns — BRON 69:9
c. of thorns — BRYA 73:14
c. of twelve stars — BIBL 53:11
c. thy good with brotherhood — BATE 27:17
glory of my c. — ELIZ 130:16
head that wears a c. — SHAK 295:3
I give away my c. — SHAK 306:4
influence of the C. — DUNN 123:11
no cross, no c. — PENN 261:11
of an earthly c. — MARL 228:18
put on my c. — SHAK 289:28
strike his father's c. — SHAK 295:12
Within the hollow c. — SHAK 305:31
crowned c. with thorns — KELL 198:3
crowning c. mercy — CROM 107:10
crowns Casting down their golden c. — HEBE 164:19
c. are empty things — DEFO 111:23
crucible America is God's C. — ZANG 370:8
crucified c., dead, and buried — BOOK 59:23
when they c. my Lord — ANON 11:16
crucify c. mankind — BRYA 73:14
God they ought to c. — CART 88:3
not even c. him — CARL 85:23
cruel c. and unusual punishment — CONS 103:9
C., but composed — ARNO 16:19
C. necessity — CROM 107:8
c. only to be kind — SHAK 293:22
c. works of nature — DARW 110:11
jealousy is c. as the grave — BIBL 40:2
State business is a c. trade — HALI 160:4
cruellest April is the c. month — ELIO 129:17
c. lies are often told — STEV 325:24
cruelty C. has a human heart — BLAK 58:5
full Of direst c. — SHAK 299:23
infliction of c. — RUSS 283:10
main sources of c. — RUSS 283:12
never really gauged your c. — WELC 353:12
crumbs dogs eat of the c. — BIBL 45:7
fed with the c. — BIBL 48:1
crumpet thinking man's c. — MUIR 247:2
crusade nor is c. — KENN 198:8
this 'c.', this war — BUSH 78:18
cruse oil in a c. — BIBL 37:10
crush c. the infamous thing — VOLT 348:23
cry c. all the way to the bank — LIBE 214:8
c. come unto thee — BOOK 61:21
c. of gulls — ELIO 129:30
C., the beloved country — PATO 260:11
indeed they c. — WEBS 353:3

no language but a c. — TENN 333:1
Truth is the c. — BERK 31:15
we c. that we are come — SHAK 298:19
we still should c. — BACO 24:3
crying child is ever c. — WROT 366:29
c. in the wilderness — BIBL 43:5
cubes sum of two c. — RAMA 273:9
cuckoo C.-echoing, bell-swarmèd — HOPK 173:15
C.! Shall I call thee bird — WORD 366:13
Lhude sing c. — ANON 11:4
weather the c. likes — HARD 162:8
cucumber c. should be well sliced — JOHN 188:1
cucumbers but c. after all — JOHN 190:4
sun-beams out of c. — SWIF 328:11
cui C. bono — CICE 96:24
culpa mea c. — MISS 240:16
O felix c. — MISS 241:7
cult What's a c. — ALTM 5:21
cultivate c. our garden — VOLT 348:9
c. your friendship — JOHN 190:9
cultiver Il faut c. notre jardin — VOLT 348:9
cultural Australian C. Cringe — PHIL 263:4
c. Chernobyl — MNOU 241:21
culture hear the word c. — JOHS 191:6
integral part of c. — GOUL 154:15
man of c. rare — GILB 150:12
pursue C. in bands — WHAR 355:18
stage in moral c. — DARW 110:3
cultures two c. — SNOW 319:21
Cumaei Ultima C. — VIRG 347:21
cumbered c. about much serving — BIBL 47:17
cunning c. men pass for wise — BACO 22:19
right hand forget her c. — BOOK 65:2
silence, exile, and c. — JOYC 193:2
cup Ah, fill the c. — FITZ 136:13
let this c. pass — BIBL 46:13
my c. overflows — SCOT 288:3
tak a c. o' kindness yet — BURN 76:20
Cupid C. painted blind — SHAK 303:9
Cupidinesque Veneres C. — CATU 89:5
cups c., That cheer — COWP 105:29
cura sedet atra C. — HORA 175:13
curantur Similia similibus c. — ANON 13:21
curate like a shabby c. — AUDE 19:24
curb use the snaffle and the c. — CAMP 83:9
cure c. of all diseases — BROW 71:13
C. the disease — BACO 22:25
no c. for birth and death — SANT 285:14
no C. for this Disease — BELL 29:18
cured c. by hanging from a string — KING 201:12
c. by more democracy — SMIT 318:8
C. yesterday of my disease — PRIO 271:1
cures Like c. like — ANON 13:21
curfew c. tolls the knell — GRAY 156:7
curiosity c., freckles, and doubt — PARK 258:12
Disinterested intellectual c. — TREV 341:15
curiouser C. and curiouser — CARR 86:4
curl had a little c. — LONG 218:12
currency Debasing the moral c. — ELIO 127:12
debauch the c. — KEYN 199:19
one c. — NAPO 248:1
curse C. God, and die — BIBL 37:35
c. is come upon me — TENN 333:20
c. of the drinking classes — WILD 359:18
I know how to c. — SHAK 307:21
open foe may prove a c. — GAY 147:5
cursed C. be the heart — BALL 25:9
curst c. be he that moves my bones — SHAK 311:2
curtain Bring down the c. — RABE 272:14
iron c. — CHUR 95:19
kept behind a c. — PAIN 257:17
lets the c. fall — POPE 266:9
curtained C. with cloudy red — MILT 237:9

curtiosity full of 'satiable c.   KIPL 203:15
curtsey C. while you're thinking   CARR 86:25
custodes quis custodiet ipsos C.   JUVE 194:8
custodiet quis c. ipsos Custodes   JUVE 194:8
custom C. is the great guide   HUME 178:4
  c. loathsome to the eye   JAME 182:9
  C. reconciles us   BURK 75:13
  follow the c.   AMBR 6:1
  in c. and in ceremony   YEAT 368:24
  Lest one good c.   TENN 332:21
  unwritten c. supported   CATT 89:4
customer c. is never wrong   RITZ 277:7
  only one boss. The c.   WALT 350:15
customers people of c.   SMIT 318:5
customs c. of his tribe   SHAW 311:12
cut c. him out in little stars   SHAK 307:2
  c. my conscience to fit   HELL 165:16
  most unkindest c. of all   SHAK 297:6
  we are going to c. it off   POWE 270:11
cutting hand the c. edge of the mind   BRON 69:6
cuttlefish like a c.   ORWE 255:3
Cutty-sark Weel done, C.   BURN 77:16
cycle c. of Cathay   TENN 333:33
cylinder in terms of the c.   CÉZA 89:23
cymbal talk but a tinkling c.   BACO 22:23
cymbals well-tuned c.   BOOK 65:7
Cynara faithful to thee, C.   DOWS 120:10
cynic definition of a c.   WILD 358:21
cynosure c. of neighbouring eyes   MILT 236:22
cypress in sad c.   SHAK 308:34

D

dad girls in slacks remember D.   BETJ 33:1
  if the d. is present   ORTO 254:7
  They fuck you up, your mum and d.   LARK 208:21
daffodils d., That come before   SHAK 309:26
  dances with the d.   WORD 364:18
  Fair d., we weep   HERR 168:4
  host, of golden d.   WORD 364:17
  never saw d. so beautiful   WORD 364:7
  what d. were for Wordsworth   LARK 209:3
  When d. begin to peer   SHAK 309:20
dagger Is this a d.   SHAK 300:12
daggers d. in men's smiles   SHAK 300:27
  Give me the d.   SHAK 300:18
daily our d. bread   BIBL 43:22
dairymaid Queen asked the D.   MILN 235:15
daisies Buttercups and d.   HOWI 177:3
  d. pied and violets blue   SHAK 299:4
  Meadows trim with d. pied   MILT 236:21
Dakotas D., I am for war   RED 274:11
dalliance primrose path of d.   SHAK 291:28
dam pretty chickens and their d.   SHAK 301:20
damaged D. people are dangerous   HART 162:18
damages d. his mind   ANON 13:4
dame belle d. sans merci   KEAT 195:26
  nothin' like a d.   HAMM 160:22
damn D. braces   BLAK 57:4
  D. the age   LAMB 207:7
  d. the consequences   MILN 235:21
  D. the torpedoes   FARR 134:9
  D. with faint praise   POPE 266:21
  d. you England   OSBO 255:14
  don't give a d.   MITC 241:14
  one another d.   WYCH 367:5
  with a spot I d. him   SHAK 297:13
damnation d. of his taking-off   SHAK 300:1
damnations Twenty-nine distinct d.   BROW 73:3
damned beautiful and d.   FITZ 137:7
  brandy of the d.   SHAW 312:1

D. from here to Eternity   KIPL 202:4
d. if you don't   DOW 120:9
d. to Fame   POPE 266:6
Faustus must be d.   MARL 228:9
lies, d. lies and statistics   DISR 118:9
public be d.   VAND 345:7
Publish and be d.   WELL 354:3
damnosa D. hereditas   GAIU 145:1
damozel blessed d.   ROSS 280:18
damsel d. with a dulcimer   COLE 100:11
Dan D. even to Beer-sheba   BIBL 36:19
  Dangerous D. McGrew   SERV 289:2
Danaë all D. to the stars   TENN 334:22
Danaos timeo D. et dona ferentes   VIRG 347:4
dance at least before they d.   POPE 268:7
  d. is a measured pace   BACO 22:4
  D. is the hidden language   GRAH 155:2
  d. round in a ring   FROS 143:25
  d. to the music of time   POWE 270:9
  d. wyt me, in irlaunde   ANON 8:18
  know the dancer from the d.   YEAT 367:12
  Let's face the music and d.   BERL 31:21
  Lord of the D.   CART 88:4
  On with the d.   BYRO 80:5
  see me d. the Polka   GROS 158:2
  too far from the d.   POUN 270:4
  will you join the d.   CARR 86:18
danced d. by the light of the moon   LEAR 210:17
  d. in the morning   CART 88:4
  d. with the Prince of Wales   FARJ 134:4
  reeled and d.   WORD 364:7
  There was a star d.   SHAK 304:8
dancer know the d. from the dance   YEAT 367:12
dancers d. are all gone under the hill   ELIO 128:7
  nation of d.   EQUI 132:29
dances d. with the daffodils   WORD 364:18
  it d.   LIGN 214:11
  truest expression in its d.   DE M 112:18
danceth d. without music   HERB 167:27
dancing [D.] a perpendicular expression   SHAW 313:5
  d. cheek-to-cheek   BERL 31:19
  d. is love's proper exercise   DAVI 110:20
  Fluttering and d.   WORD 364:17
  manners of a d. master   JOHN 188:7
  past our d. days   SHAK 306:24
dandy Yankee Doodle D.   COHA 99:10
Dane paying the D.-geld   KIPL 203:5
  Roman than a D.   SHAK 294:11
danger d. from all men   ADAM 2:3
  Oft in d.   WHIT 356:5
  only when in d.   OWEN 256:4
  Out of this nettle, d.   SHAK 294:19
  run into any kind of d.   BOOK 60:3
  so much as to be out of d.   HUXL 179:17
dangerous Damaged people are d.   HART 162:18
  d. to know   LAMB 206:18
  d. to meet it alone   WHAR 355:18
  knowledge is d.   HUXL 179:17
  more d. than an idea   ALAI 4:5
  most d. moment   TOCQ 340:16
  such men are d.   SHAK 296:20
dangers d. of the seas   PARK 259:7
  d. of this night   BOOK 60:8
  d. thou canst make us scorn   BURN 77:14
  No d. fright him   JOHN 187:25
  She loved me for the d.   SHAK 304:23
dangling d. apricocks   SHAK 306:1
Daniel D. come to judgement   SHAK 302:33
Danny hangin' D. Deever   KIPL 201:21
dapple d.-dawn-drawn Falcon   HOPK 174:9
dappled d. things   HOPK 174:1
dare d. to know   HORA 174:23
  I d. not   SHAK 300:6

dare (*cont.*)		than curse the d.	BENE 30:13
none d. call it treason	HARI 162:13	there is d. everywhere	NEHR 249:2
O! what men d. do	SHAK 304:14	Thou makest d.	BOOK 64:4
You who d.	MERE 233:10	two eternities of d.	NABO 247:17
dared d., and done	SMAR 317:19	universal d. buries all	POPE 266:9
dares that d. love attempt	SHAK 306:30	works of d.	BOOK 60:19
Who d. do more is none	SHAK 300:7	**darling** call you d. after sex	BARN 26:18
Who d. wins	ANON 12:2	d. buds of May	SHAK 310:3
Darien Silent, upon a peak in D.	KEAT 196:28	my d. from the lions	BOOK 62:22
daring d. young man	LEYB 214:7	**dart** shook a dreadful d.	MILT 238:10
dark agree in the d.	BACO 23:18	**date** d. which will live in infamy	ROOS 279:16
blind man in a d. room	BOWE 66:16	doubles your chances for a d.	ALLE 5:17
come out of the d.	MANN 227:6	keep them up to d.	SHAW 311:20
comes the d.	COLE 100:22	Standards are always out of d.	BENN 30:25
d. and bloody ground	O'HA 253:5	**dateless** d. bargain	SHAK 307:11
d. and bright	BYRO 81:17	**dates** matter of d.	TALL 330:10
d. and evil days	INGR 180:19	**daughter** d. of debate	ELIZ 130:15
d. and stormy night	BULW 74:1	d. of Earth and Water	SHEL 313:24
d. as night	SHAK 310:30	d. of the gods	TENN 332:5
D. as the world of man	SITW 317:13	Don't put your d. on the stage	COWA 105:5
D. behind it rose the forest	LONG 218:4	ever rear a d.	GAY 146:18
d., dark, dark	MILT 239:22	King's d.	BOOK 63:3
d. is light enough	FRY 144:5	O my ducats! O my d.	SHAK 302:18
d. night of the soul	FITZ 137:13	so is her d.	BIBL 41:27
d. night of the soul	JOHN 185:15	taken his little d.	LONG 218:11
d. Satanic mills	BLAK 57:8	**daughters** d. of my father's house	SHAK 309:1
D. with excessive bright	MILT 238:16	d. of the Philistines	BIBL 36:33
d. world of sin	BICK 54:15	thunder, fire, are my d.	SHAK 298:3
go home in the d.	HENR 166:21	Words are men's d.	MADD 224:16
great leap in the d.	VANB 345:4	words are the d.	JOHN 186:17
hides a d. soul	MILT 236:5	**dauntless** D. the slug-horn	BROW 71:26
In the d. backward	SHAK 307:18	so d. in war	SCOT 287:18
In the nightmare of the d.	AUDE 19:3	**dauphin** kingdom of daylight's d.	HOPK 174:9
leap in the d.	HOBB 170:23	**David** D. his ten thousands	BIBL 36:30
leap into the d.	BROW 71:1	D. wrote the Psalms	NAYL 248:21
O d. dark dark	ELIO 128:8	royal D.'s city	ALEX 4:16
raging in the d.	YEAT 367:15	**dawn** d. comes up like thunder	KIPL 202:15
we are for the d.	SHAK 289:25	D. on our darkness	HEBE 164:16
We work in the d.	JAME 182:18	grey d. is breaking	CRAW 106:13
What in me is d.	MILT 237:17	in that d. to be alive	WORD 364:13
darkeneth d. counsel	BIBL 38:7	Rosy-fingered d.	HOME 172:15
darker I am the d. brother	HUGH 177:13	**dawning** bird of d.	SHAK 291:11
darkies Oh! d., how my heart	FOST 140:10	d. of the age of Aquarius	RADO 272:19
darkling D. I listen	KEAT 196:20	**day** Action this D.	ANON 7:6
d. plain	ARNO 16:13	arrow that flieth by d.	BOOK 63:25
darkly through a glass, d.	BIBL 50:25	bright d. is done	SHAK 289:25
darkness cast off the works of d.	BIBL 50:12	burn thee by d.	BOOK 64:21
Chaos and d.	MARR 229:1	D. by day	BOOK 59:20
counteracts the powers of d.	SMAR 317:18	d. is at hand	BIBL 50:12
curse the d.	STEV 325:7	d. most surely wasted	CHAM 90:9
d. comprehended it not	BIBL 48:15	d. of his death	AUDE 18:21
d. falls at Thy behest	ELLE 131:7	d. of small nations	CHAM 90:2
d. of mere being	JUNG 193:18	d. of vengeance	BIBL 41:17
d. visible	MILT 237:19	d. of wrath	MISS 241:5
d. was upon the face	BIBL 34:3	d. or a brief period	ARIS 15:13
Dawn on our d.	HEBE 164:16	d.'s at the morn	BROW 72:23
Downward to d.	STEV 324:24	d.'s garish eye	MILT 236:15
encounter d. as a bride	SHAK 302:7	d. that I die	MCLE 223:15
even d. and silence	KELL 198:1	d. the music died	MCLE 223:14
Got to kick at the d.	COCK 99:4	d. Thou gavest, Lord	ELLE 131:7
In me there is d.	BONH 59:9	d.-to-day business	LAFO 206:13
in the d. bind them	TOLK 340:22	end of a perfect d.	BOND 59:5
into outer d.	BIBL 44:15	every d. to be lost	JOHN 190:22
Lighten our d.	BOOK 60:8	first d.	BIBL 34:4
light to them that sit in d.	BIBL 46:34	first, last, everlasting d.	DONN 119:6
ocean of d.	FOX 140:15	gold of the d.	CROS 107:18
people that walked in d.	BIBL 40:13	heat of the d.	BIBL 45:22
pestilence that walketh in d.	BOOK 63:25	I have lost a d.	TITU 340:14
prince of the d.	SHAK 298:10	knell of parting d.	GRAY 156:7
rulers of the d.	BIBL 51:21	lark at break of d.	SHAK 310:6
sit in d.	BOOK 64:8	Let the d. perish	BIBL 37:36
sit in d. here	MILT 238:6	long d.'s journey	O'NE 253:14
soul may set in d.	WILL 360:9	met them at close of d.	YEAT 368:2

night and d., brother	BORR 65:24	healthy and wealthy and d.	THUR 340:4
not a second on the d.	COOK 103:10	HOMER d.	ANON 10:19
one d. in thy courts	BOOK 63:20	if the d. rise not	BIBL 50:30
seize the d.	HORA 175:7	If the d. talk to you	SZAS 329:20
sinks the d.-star	MILT 237:2	land of the d.	WILD 359:21
So foul and fair a d.	SHAK 299:12	Lilacs out of the d. land	ELIO 129:17
Sufficient unto the d.	BIBL 44:2	Lycidas is d.	MILT 236:28
They have their d.	TENN 332:24	millions of the mouthless d.	SORL 320:17
through her busy d.	JAGG 182:4	Mistah Kurtz—he d.	CONR 102:24
to a summer's d.	SHAK 310:3	My d. king	JOYC 192:24
tomorrow is another d.	MITC 241:15	not d.—but gone	ROGE 278:12
Until the d. break	BIBL 39:34	not d., but sleepeth	BIBL 44:23
weary d. have end	SPEN 321:22	Not many d.	COCK 99:5
Without all hope of d.	MILT 239:22	Of their d. selves	TENN 332:25
daylight d. in upon magic	BAGE 24:9	on the d. man's chest	STEV 325:16
kingdom of d.'s dauphin	HOPK 174:9	our English d.	SHAK 295:16
'til it bleeds d.	COCK 99:4	past is the only d. thing	THOM 338:8
days behold these present d.	SHAK 310:18	past never d.	FAUL 134:11
burnt-out ends of smoky d.	ELIO 129:10	quick, and the d.	DEWA 114:5
chequerboard of nights and d.	FITZ 136:14	rather be d. than cool	COBA 99:1
D. and months are travellers	BASH 27:15	saying 'Lord Jones D.'	CHES 93:22
d. are evil	BIBL 51:18	sea gave up the d.	BIBL 53:21
d. are in the yellow leaf	BYRO 81:15	Sea shall give up her d.	BOOK 65:10
D. are where we live	LARK 208:16	simplify me when I'm d.	DOUG 120:3
d. grow short	ANDE 6:15	they're a' d.	ANON 8:15
d. of wine and roses	DOWS 120:11	those who are d.	BURK 75:23
d. that are no more	TENN 334:15	told me you were d.	CORY 104:13
E'er half my d.	MILT 239:30	to the d. we owe only truth	VOLT 348:22
first 1,000 d.	KENN 198:18	very d. of winter	ELIO 128:25
in the house three d.	SHAW 312:7	was alive and is d.	ANON 8:14
number of my d.	BOOK 62:25	was d., and is alive	BIBL 47:33
of few d.	BIBL 38:1	ways of being d.	DAWK 111:7
Ten d. that shook the world	REED 274:14	we are all d.	KEYN 199:22
that thy d. may be long	BIBL 35:28	wench is d.	MARL 228:14
Three whole d. together	SUCK 327:8	what was d. was Hope	WILD 359:9
two d. like a tiger	TIPU 340:13	When I am d.	ROSS 280:17
We have seen better d.	SHAK 308:4	without works is d.	BIBL 52:21
dazzle mine eyes d.	WEBS 352:24	you're ten years d.	HAYE 164:1
dead already three parts d.	RUSS 283:4	**deadener** Habit is a great d.	BECK 28:17
and Guildenstern are d.	SHAK 294:15	**deadlines** daily d.	ZOLA 370:14
and the noble D.	WORD 365:19	**deadlock** Holy d.	HERB 167:7
bivouac of the d.	O'HA 253:4	**deadly** more d. in the long run	TWAI 343:9
character d. at every word	SHER 315:15	more d. than the male	KIPL 202:2
cold and pure and very d.	LEWI 214:5	**deaf** d. as an adder	ADAM 2:2
completely consistent are the d.	HUXL 179:9	d., inexorable	SIDN 316:10
composer is to be d.	HONE 172:17	**deal** new d. for the American people	ROOS 279:7
cut in half; he's d.	GRAH 154:20	square d. afterwards	ROOS 280:1
D.! and never called me	WOOD 363:15	**dealing** d. with the modern media	MORR 245:8
d. Body wears	PLAT 264:14	**deals** D. are my art form	TRUM 342:19
d.-born from the press.	HUME 178:11	**deans** dowagers for d.	TENN 334:11
d. bury their dead	BIBL 44:17	**dear** bread should be so d.	HOOD 172:27
d. don't die	LAWR 210:1	D. dead women	BROW 73:5
D., for a ducat	SHAK 293:18	D., dirty Dublin	JOYC 192:18
d. for the duration	ASQU 17:18	d. to them that love her	SPRI 322:13
d. level	ELIO 127:19	Plato is d. to me	ARIS 15:23
d. lion	BIBL 39:19	too d. for my possessing	SHAK 310:14
d. man's town	SPRI 322:16	**deario** cheerio my d.	MARQ 228:22
d. men lost their bones	ELIO 129:24	**dearly** D. beloved brethren	BOOK 59:11
dead Past bury its d.	LONG 217:20	**death** abolish the d. penalty	KARR 195:2
d. shall live	DRYD 122:13	After the first d.	THOM 338:1
d. shall not have died in vain	LINC 214:20	angel of d.	BRIG 68:18
d. sinner	BIER 54:23	Angel of D.	BYRO 80:19
d. woman bites not	GRAY 156:4	any man's d. diminishes me	DONN 119:23
d. writers are remote	ELIO 130:7	at the point of d.	SHAK 307:10
democracy of the d.	CHES 93:13	bargain to engrossing d.	SHAK 307:11
Down among the d.	DYER 124:2	Be absolute for d.	SHAK 302:6
face of the d.	BEER 29:4	before his d.	BIBL 42:23
fortnight d.	ELIO 129:30	Birth, and copulation, and d.	ELIO 129:14
found d. in the woods	KELL 198:2	Brother to D.	DANI 109:5
found, when she was d.	GOLD 153:13	Brother to D.	FLET 138:13
God is d.	FROM 143:5	Brought d. into the world	MILT 237:15
grand to be blooming well d.	SARO 285:18	brought d. into the world	TWAI 343:22
had already been d. a year	LEHR 211:21	build your ship of d.	LAWR 209:24

death (*cont.*)

Cake or d.	IZZA 181:10
Call in thy d.'s-head there	HERB 167:12
Come away, come away, d.	SHAK 308:34
could not stop for D.	DICK 115:26
covenant with d.	BIBL 40:24
covenant with d.	GARR 146:11
day of his d.	AUDE 18:21
Dear, beauteous d.	VAUG 345:18
d. after life	SPEN 321:26
d. a long-felt want	TREE 341:14
D. and his brother	SHEL 314:17
d. and taxes	DEFO 111:17
d. and taxes	FRAN 142:3
D. and taxes and childbirth	MITC 241:13
d. bandaged my eyes	BROW 72:27
D. be not proud	DONN 118:22
D. closes all	TENN 335:6
d. had undone so many	ELIO 129:21
D. has a thousand doors	MASS 231:3
d. hath no more dominion	BIBL 50:3
D. hath so many doors	FLET 138:11
d. hath ten thousand	WEBS 352:23
d. in the pot	BIBL 37:23
D. is a master from Germany	CELA 89:17
[D. is] nature's way	ANON 7:22
D. is not an event in life	WITT 362:12
D. is nothing at all	HOLL 171:18
d. is the cure	BROW 71:13
D. is the end of life	TENN 333:35
D. joins us to	YOUN 370:4
D. lies on her	SHAK 307:8
D. never takes the wise man	LA F 206:12
d., nor life	BIBL 50:9
d. of air	ELIO 128:13
D. of a salesman	MILL 234:22
d. of kings	SHAK 305:30
D.'s bright angel	PROC 271:5
d. shall have no dominion	THOM 337:17
D., the most awful of evils	EPIC 132:28
D. thou shalt die	DONN 118:23
d., where is thy sting	BIBL 51:4
D., where is thy sting-a-ling	ANON 9:24
D. who comes at last	SCOT 287:16
d., who had the soldier singled	DOUG 120:4
D. would eventually take care	JOBS 185:11
disqualified by the accident of d.	CHES 93:15
easeful D.	KEAT 196:20
Even d. is unreliable	BECK 28:19
faithful unto d.	BIBL 53:3
Fear d.	BROW 72:26
feed on D.	SHAK 310:29
Finality is d.	STEP 324:4
forced marches, battles and d.	GARI 146:4
from d. lead me to	UPAN 344:12
Glad to d.'s mystery	HOOD 172:20
his name that sat on him was d.	BIBL 53:7
hour of d.	BOOK 60:14
I am become d.	OPPE 253:17
image of d.	ELIO 127:22
improved by d.	SAKI 284:11
in that sleep of d.	SHAK 292:23
in their d. not divided	BIBL 36:34
in the shadow of d.	BIBL 46:34
in the valley of D.	TENN 331:19
Into the jaws of D.	TENN 332:1
isn't sex but d.	SONT 320:13
just, and mighty D.	RALE 273:4
Keeps D. his court	SHAK 305:31
Lead me from d. to life	KUMA 206:5
liberty, or give me d.	HENR 166:24
life went through with d.	FORT 140:1
living d.	MILT 239:24

Love is strong as d.	BIBL 40:2
love thee better after d.	BROW 71:18
make d. proud	SHAK 289:23
make one in love with d.	SHEL 313:12
Man has created d.	YEAT 367:22
matter of life and d.	SHAN 311:4
Men fear d.	BACO 22:20
Morning after D.	DICK 115:29
much possessed by d.	ELIO 130:4
no cure for birth and d.	SANT 285:14
no one his d.	SENE 288:23
not d., but dying	FIEL 135:8
nothing but d.	UNAM 344:11
only nervousness or d.	LEBO 211:4
owe God a d.	SHAK 295:6
owest God a d.	SHAK 294:25
prepare as though for d.	MANS 227:9
reaction to her d.	ELIZ 131:3
rendezvous with D.	SEEG 288:7
Reports of my d.	TWAI 344:2
Revenge triumphs over d.	BACO 22:21
seen birth and d.	ELIO 128:26
shadow of d.	BOOK 64:8
shall be destroyed is d.	BIBL 50:29
sharpness of d.	BOOK 59:19
sleep, d.'s counterfeit	SHAK 300:24
snares of d.	BOOK 64:16
soul shall taste of d.	KORA 205:6
stroke of d.	JOHN 187:12
sudden d.	BOOK 60:13
swallow up d. in victory	BIBL 40:22
there shall be no more d.	BIBL 53:23
This fell sergeant, d.	SHAK 294:10
Those by d. are few	JEFF 184:10
true to thee till d.	FABE 133:13
up the line to d.	SASS 285:26
valley of the shadow of d.	BOOK 62:15
wages of sin is d.	BIBL 50:4
way to dusty d.	SHAK 301:31
we are in d.	BOOK 62:5
What should it know of d.	WORD 366:15
When d. approached	GIBB 149:5
Why fear d.	FROH 143:3

deaths million d. a statistic
	STAL 323:1
More d. than one must die	WILD 359:10

debasing D. the moral currency — ELIO 127:12

debatable d. line — MACA 221:18

debate daughter of d. — ELIZ 130:15

debonair blithe, and d. — MILT 236:18

debt deeper in d. — TRAV 341:12
national d.	HAMI 160:11
pay a d. to pleasure	ROCH 278:3
we are in d.	MUMF 247:3

debtor d. to his profession — BACO 22:8

debts forgive us our d. — BIBL 43:22
pays all d.	SHAK 307:28

decay Change and d. — LYTE 221:3
D. with imprecision	ELIO 128:4
human things are subject to d.	DRYD 122:7
our love hath no d.	DONN 119:6

decayed sufficiently d. — GILB 150:11

deceased He first d. — WOTT 366:24

deceitful heart is d. — BIBL 41:23

deceits d. of the world — BOOK 60:12

deceive d. ourselves — BIBL 52:31
Oh, don't d. me	ANON 7:25

deceiver d. gay d. — COLM 101:18

deceivers Men were d. ever — SHAK 304:10

deceiving d. elf — KEAT 196:24
nearly d. your friends	CORN 104:10

December D. when they wed — SHAK 290:23
drear nighted D.	KEAT 195:20
May to D.	ANDE 6:15

Decembers fifteen wild D. — BRON 69:14
decency Have you no sense of d. — WELC 353:12
  want of d. — DILL 116:15
decent d. obscurity — GIBB 149:4
decently d. and in order — BIBL 50:26
decide moment to d. — LOWE 220:2
decision make a 'realistic d.' — MCCA 222:9
  will or d. — CHOM 94:7
decisions regard as important the d. — PARK 259:14
decisive d. moment — CART 88:7
  d. moment — RETZ 275:6
deck boy stood on the burning d. — HEMA 165:18
  from the bottom of the d. — SHAP 311:5
  Walk the d. my Captain lies — WHIT 356:24
declaration no d. of war — EDEN 125:2
declare d. the glory of God — BOOK 62:11
  nothing to d. — WILD 359:17
  ye are to d. it — BOOK 61:22
decline writing the d. and fall — GIBB 149:3
decorate painting not made to d. — PICA 263:5
decorum *Dulce et d. est* — HORA 175:14
  Dulce et d. est — OWEN 256:11
decrease d. day after day — LAO 208:7
decree d. from Caesar Augustus — BIBL 47:1
  establish the d. — BIBL 42:7
decrees d. may not change — KING 200:13
deduction d. from the smallest — EINS 126:12
Dee Across the sands of D. — KING 201:7
deed d. is all, the glory nothing — GOET 152:13
  d. without a name — SHAK 301:14
  right d. for the wrong reason — ELIO 129:6
deeds Our d. determine us — ELIO 127:4
deep cradle of the d. — WILL 360:1
  D. and crisp and even — NEAL 248:23
  d. as a well — SHAK 306:37
  D.-versed in books — MILT 239:20
  From the great d. — TENN 332:11
  Out of the d. — BOOK 64:29
  spirits from the vasty d. — SHAK 294:23
  thunders of the upper d. — TENN 333:12
  too d. for tears — WORD 365:10
  wonders in the d. — BOOK 64:9
deepens d. like a coastal shelf — LARK 208:22
deeper In d. reverence praise — WHIT 357:14
deer a-chasing the d. — BURN 77:6
  I was a stricken d. — COWP 105:28
  stricken d. — SHAK 293:11
Deever hangin' Danny D. — KIPL 201:21
défauts *âme est sans d.* — RIMB 277:4
defeat d. is an orphan — CIAN 96:12
  In d.; defiance — CHUR 96:5
  In d. unbeatable — CHUR 96:2
  possibilities of d. — VICT 346:10
  triumph and d. — LONG 217:17
defeated Down with the d. — LIVY 216:4
  history to the d. — AUDE 19:21
defence d. of the indefensible — ORWE 255:4
defend d. ourselves with guns — GOEB 152:5
  d. to the death your right — VOLT 349:3
  d. us from all perils — BOOK 60:8
defended God abandoned, these d. — HOUS 176:4
defends when attacked it d. itself — ANON 12:10
defiance In defeat; d. — CHUR 96:5
defied Age will not be d. — BACO 23:4
defiled shall be d. — BIBL 42:24
define know how to d. it — THOM 337:7
definition d. is the enclosing — BUTL 79:16
  working d. of hell — SHAW 312:24
deformity Art is significant d. — FRY 144:9
dei *D. gloriam* — ANON 13:6
  vox D. — ALCU 4:7
deities some other new d. — PLAT 264:18
déjà d. vu all over again — BERR 32:16

delay deny, or d. — MAGN 225:6
delayed d. till I am indifferent — JOHN 188:8
delegate When in trouble, d. — BORE 65:19
delenda *D. est Carthago* — CATO 89:2
deleted Expletive d. — ANON 8:3
deliberate Where both d. — MARL 228:11
deliberates woman who d. — ADDI 2:21
deliberation D. sat and public care — MILT 238:5
delight born to sweet d. — BLAK 56:14
  Energy is Eternal D. — BLAK 56:21
  ever new d. — MILT 238:30
  firmness, and d. — WOTT 366:25
  hear thy shrill d. — SHEL 314:27
  labour we d. in — SHAK 300:22
  land of pure d. — WATT 351:24
  Let dogs d. — WATT 351:20
  phantom of d. — WORD 366:1
  Spirit of D. — SHEL 314:19
  Studies serve for d. — BACO 23:9
  thing met conceives d. — MILT 239:5
delightful it can be d. — SHAW 311:9
deliver d. us from evil — MISS 240:24
  O d. my soul — BOOK 62:22
deliverance d. from chains — DOUG 120:7
delivered God hath d. him — BIBL 36:31
deluge *Après nous le d.* — POMP 266:4
delusion d., a mockery — DENM 113:1
  under some d. — BURK 76:8
democracies d. against despots — DEMO 112:20
  in d. it is the only sacred — FRAN 141:6
democracy cured by more d. — SMIT 318:8
  D. is the current suspicion — WHIT 356:4
  D. is the name we give — FLER 138:9
  D. is the theory — MENC 232:20
  D. is the worst form — CHUR 95:20
  d. means government — ATTL 18:9
  D. means government by — CHES 93:23
  D. means simply — WILD 359:13
  d. of the dead — CHES 93:13
  D. substitutes election — SHAW 312:8
  d. unbearable — PERE 261:22
  great arsenal of d. — ROOS 279:14
  justice makes d. possible — NIEB 251:2
  less d. to save — ATKI 18:7
  made safe for d. — WILS 361:14
  no d. can afford — BEVE 33:14
  not the voting that's d. — STOP 326:9
  pollution of d. — WHIT 356:8
  Two cheers for D. — FORS 139:19
democrat Senator, and a D. — JOHN 186:5
democrats D. object to men being disqualified — CHES 93:15
demolition d. of a man — LEVI 213:12
demon d.'s that is dreaming — POE 265:21
  wailing for her d.-lover — COLE 100:8
demonstrandum *Quod erat d.* — EUCL 133:4
den d. of thieves — BIBL 45:24
denied Justice d. — MILL 234:20
Denmark in the state of D. — SHAK 291:36
deny d. me thrice — BIBL 46:12
  d., or delay — MAGN 225:6
  d. the being of a devil — MATH 231:5
  I never d. — DISR 118:7
  You must d. yourself — GOET 152:9
Deo *D. gratias* — MISS 240:19
  Jubilate D., omnis terra — BIBL 53:29
depart servant d. in peace — BIBL 47:6
  will not d. — BIBL 38:33
departed glory is d. — BIBL 36:23
departing and at my d. — ANON 8:10
depends d. upon a red wheel barrow — WILL 360:16
deposit greater the d. — LAYT 210:4
depraved suddenly became d. — JUVE 194:6

depression d. when you lose yours TRUM 342:14
deprivation D. is for me LARK 209:3
derangement nice d. of epitaphs SHER 315:12
descending comes with clouds d. WESL 354:23
descensus *Facilis d. Averno* VIRG 347:11
descent d. from a monkey WILB 357:24
description beggared all d. SHAK 289:18
desert d. shall rejoice BIBL 40:27
in a d. land BIBL 36:5
Life is the d. YOUN 370:4
make straight in the d. BIBL 40:30
on the d. air GRAY 156:11
scare myself with my own d. FROS 143:14
Stand in the d. SHEL 314:9
Use every man after his d. SHAK 292:19
deserts D. of vast eternity MARV 229:21
his d. are small MONT 243:11
she d. the night MILT 239:23
deserve and d. to get it MENC 232:20
deserves gets what he d. ANON 12:21
Stonehenge it d. HAWK 163:11
design good d. for a bus HOCK 171:2
designs d. were strictly honourable FIEL 135:13
desipere *Dulce est d.* HORA 175:20
desire by nature d. knowledge ARIS 15:10
d. of power HOBB 170:15
d. of the moth SHEL 314:24
d. should so many years SHAK 295:2
gratified d. BLAK 57:13
Which of us has his d. THAC 336:9
desired I have d. to go HOPK 173:19
More to be d. BOOK 62:12
desires all d. known BOOK 60:25
all holy d. BOOK 60:7
d. but acts not BLAK 56:25
d. of our own hearts BOOK 59:12
d. of the heart AUDE 18:15
d. that seem big RICE 275:15
doing what one d. MILL 234:10
lopping off our d. SWIF 328:22
nurse unacted d. BLAK 57:6
desireth as the hart d. BOOK 62:27
desiring D. this man's art SHAK 310:5
desks Stick close to your d. GILB 150:19
desolation abomination of d. BIBL 45:34
D. in immaculate public places ROET 278:10
Magnificent d. ALDR 4:10
years of d. JEFF 184:18
despair begotten by D. MARV 229:14
carrion comfort, D. HOPK 173:14
comfort and d. SHAK 310:28
Do not d. PUDN 271:14
endure my own d. WALS 350:7
far side of d. SART 285:24
Heaven in Hell's d. BLAK 57:23
some divine d. TENN 334:15
unyielding d. RUSS 283:7
ye Mighty, and d. SHEL 314:10
desperandum *Nil d.* HORA 175:6
desperate Diseases d. grown SHAK 293:25
Tempt not a d. man SHAK 307:9
desperation lives of quiet d. THOR 339:12
despise work for a Government I d. KEYN 199:18
despised d. and rejected BIBL 41:9
despite Hell in Heaven's d. BLAK 57:24
despond slough was D. BUNY 74:7
despondency d. and madness WORD 365:21
despot country governed by a d. JOHN 189:23
despotism d. tempered by epigrams CARL 85:13
despots against d.—suspicion DEMO 112:20
destinies d. of half the globe TOCQ 340:17
destiny Anatomy is d. FREU 142:16
character is d. ELIO 127:21

manifest d. O'SU 255:20
destroy against us to d. us HAGG 158:17
d. the town to save it ANON 9:5
gods wish to d. CONN 102:16
in search of monsters to d. ADAM 2:14
One to d. YOUN 369:24
power to d. MARS 229:3
shall not hurt nor d. BIBL 40:18
Whom the mad would d. LEVI 213:13
winged life d. BLAK 57:12
worms d. this body BIBL 38:4
destroyed Carthage must be d. CATO 89:2
enemy that shall be d. BIBL 50:29
ought to be d. OMAR 253:11
treated generously or d. MACH 223:7
destroyer D. and preserver SHEL 314:4
d. of worlds OPPE 253:17
destroyeth d. in the noon-day BOOK 63:25
destroying without d. something UPDI 344:19
destroys Time which d. all things BHAG 33:20
destruction d. of the whole world HUME 178:13
leadeth to d. BIBL 44:9
Pride goeth before d. BIBL 38:29
to his own d. FRAM 141:5
to their d. draw DONN 119:6
urge for d. BAKU 24:18
whether the mad d. is wrought GAND 145:14
detail corroborative d. GILB 150:8
everything else is d. NAVR 248:20
frittered away by d. THOR 339:19
details God is in the d. MIES 233:23
detective d. story is about JAME 183:5
Hawkshaw, the d. TAYL 331:6
deteriora *D. sequor* OVID 256:1
determination d. of a quiet man SMIT 318:15
d. of incident JAME 182:20
determine we d. our deeds ELIO 127:4
determined D., dared, and done SMAR 317:19
detest d. at leisure BYRO 81:7
deus *puto d. fio* VESP 346:6
Deutschland *D. über alles* HOFF 171:6
deviates d. into sense DRYD 122:8
device with the strange d. LONG 217:12
devices d. and desires BOOK 59:12
man of many d. HOME 172:14
devil apology for the D. BUTL 79:15
blue-eyed d. white man FARD 134:2
can the d. speak true SHAK 299:15
d. and all his works BOOK 61:18
d. can cite Scripture SHAK 302:13
d. damn thee black SHAK 301:26
d. doesn't exist DOST 119:28
D. howling 'Ho' SQUI 322:21
D. sends cooks GARR 146:8
d. should have all HILL 169:7
d.'s madness—War SERV 289:1
d. taketh him up BIBL 43:11
d. would also build LUTH 220:18
face the d. BURN 77:14
fears a painted d. SHAK 300:18
flesh, and the d. BOOK 60:12
God and d. DOST 119:27
laughing d. BYRO 80:17
of the D.'s party BLAK 56:22
reference to the d. CHUR 96:9
there is a D. MATH 231:5
wedlock's the d. BYRO 81:23
white man was *created* a d. MALC 226:1
your adversary the d. BIBL 52:30
Devon If the Dons sight D. NEWB 249:15
devotion object of universal d. IRVI 181:4
devour d. in turn each one VERG 346:3
seeking whom he may d. BIBL 52:30

dies (cont.)
man who d. . . . rich — CARN 85:25
matters not how a man d. — JOHN 188:22
moment d. a man — TENN 335:9
once hath blown for ever d. — FITZ 136:12
something in me d. — VIDA 346:12
diets feel about d. — KERR 199:11
Dieu Si D. n'existait pas — VOLT 348:16
difference d. of forty thousand — WELL 354:4
exaggerate the d. — SHAW 311:29
made all the d. — FROS 143:24
oh, The d. to me — WORD 365:28
wear your rue with a d. — SHAK 293:33
What d. does it make — GAND 145:14
differences in language there are only d. — SAUS 286:3
different boil at d. degrees — EMER 132:18
hears a d. drummer — THOR 339:22
how very d. — ANON 8:17
rich are d. from you and me — FITZ 137:6
thought they were d. — ELIO 128:26
differential integral and d. calculus — GILB 150:23
differently do things d. there — HART 163:3
freedom for the one who thinks d. — LUXE 220:21
difficult d.; and left untried — CHES 93:19
D. do you call it, Sir — JOHN 190:23
d. takes a little time — NANS 247:20
d. to speak — BURK 76:9
d. we do immediately — ANON 7:23
fascination of what's d. — YEAT 368:6
first step that is d. — DU D 122:27
difficulties d. do not make one doubt — NEWM 249:21
difficulty with great d. I am got hither — BUNY 74:18
dig I could not d. — KIPL 202:1
I'll d. with it — HEAN 164:11
digest learn, and inwardly d. — BOOK 60:20
digestion good d. wait on appetite — SHAK 301:6
diggeth He that d. a pit — BIBL 39:22
dignified d. parts — BAGE 24:7
dignitate Cum d. otium — CICE 96:25
dignity d. in tilling a field — WASH 351:3
individual d. — YAMA 367:9
with silent d. — GROS 158:4
dignus non sum d. — MISS 241:1
digressions eloquent d. — HUXL 179:22
dilige D. et quod vis fac — AUGU 20:8
diligence D. is the mother — CERV 89:22
dilly-dally Don't d. on the way — COLL 101:12
dim d. religious light — MILT 236:16
dime Brother can you spare a d. — HARB 161:6
dimensions my d. are as well compact — SHAK 297:25
diminished ought to be d. — DUNN 123:11
dimittis Nunc d. — BIBL 54:8
dine gang and d. — BALL 25:21
dined I have d. today — SMIT 319:13
dinner ask him to d. — CARL 85:23
best number for a d. party — GULB 158:9
d. bell — BYRO 81:3
d. of herbs — BIBL 38:27
good d. and feasting — PEPY 261:18
good d. upon his table — JOHN 191:1
hungry for d. at eight — HART 162:21
we expect our d. — SMIT 318:1
Diogenes would be D. — ALEX 4:11
diplomacy D. is to do and say — GOLD 153:1
diplomat d. . . . is a person — STIN 326:7
diplomats D. tell lies — KRAU 205:26
direct and rule our hearts — BOOK 60:21
direction d., which thou canst not see — POPE 267:25
move in a given d. — HOUS 176:18
directions By indirections find d. out — SHAK 292:9
rode madly off in all d. — LEAC 210:7
directors way with these d. — GOLD 154:2
direful d. in the sound — AUST 20:23

to Greece the d. spring — POPE 268:4
dirt d. doesn't get any worse — CRIS 107:3
D. is only matter — GRAY 156:3
dirty Dear, d. Dublin — JOYC 192:18
Is sex d. — ALLE 5:13
'Jug Jug' to d. ears — ELIO 129:23
dis D. aliter visum — VIRG 347:5
disagree if they d. — OMAR 253:11
when doctors d. — POPE 266:25
disappointed d. by that stroke — JOHN 187:12
disappointing least d. — BARU 27:9
disappointment D. all I endeavour end — HOPK 174:7
d., no matter what — HORN 175:26
disapprove d. of what you say — VOLT 349:3
disaster triumph and d. — KIPL 202:9
disastrous d. and the unpalatable — GALB 145:5
win a war is as d. — CHRI 94:10
disbelief willing suspension of d. — COLE 101:2
discharge d. for loving one — MATL 231:7
no d. in that war — BIBL 39:17
disciples great man has his d. — WILD 358:14
discipline gentle d. — SPEN 321:23
order and military d. — ANON 7:19
discontent winter of d. — CALL 82:16
winter of our d. — SHAK 306:7
discord civil d. — ADDI 3:3
d. doth sow — ELIZ 130:15
hark! what d. follows — SHAK 308:9
discors Concordia d. — HORA 175:1
discouragement There's no d. — BUNY 74:17
discourse company and good d. — WALT 350:11
d. of rivers — WALT 350:13
discover another can d. — DOYL 120:20
discoverers ill d. — BACO 22:2
discovery D. consists of seeing — SZEN 329:23
d. of a new dish — BRIL 69:3
discreet d. diary — CHAN 90:15
discretion D. is not the better part — STRA 326:20
inform their d. — JEFF 184:17
part of valour is d. — SHAK 294:29
discuss stay and d. them — WELL 354:9
discussion government by d. — ATTL 18:9
disease biggest d. today — TERE 335:18
Cured yesterday of my d. — PRIO 271:1
Cure the d. — BACO 22:25
desperate d. — FAWK 134:14
d. at its onset — PERS 262:10
D., Ignorance, and Idleness — BEVE 33:15
D. is an experience — EDDY 125:1
d. is incurable — SHAK 295:1
d. of not listening — SHAK 294:33
incurable d. of writing — JUVE 194:9
Life is an incurable d. — COWL 105:14
no Cure for this D. — BELL 29:18
Progress is a comfortable d. — CUMM 108:8
remedy is worse than the d. — BACO 23:8
suffering from the particular d. — JERO 185:5
this long d., my life — POPE 266:18
diseased mind d. — BYRO 80:10
minister to a mind d. — SHAK 301:28
diseases cure of all d. — BROW 71:13
D. desperate grown — SHAK 293:25
extreme d. — HIPP 169:16
disgrace Intellectual d. Stares — AUDE 19:4
no d. t'be poor — HUBB 177:10
disgraced dies . . . rich dies d. — CARN 85:25
disgruntled if not actually d. — WODE 362:17
disguise better go in d. — BRAT 67:21
D. fair nature — SHAK 295:16
d. which can hide love — LA R 209:5
dish discovery of a new d. — BRIL 69:3
d. fit for the gods — SHAK 296:24
in a lordly d. — BIBL 36:12

dishes who does the d.   FREN 142:14
dishonour rooted in d.   TENN 332:14
disiecti *Etiam d. membra poetae*   HORA 175:24
disinheriting d. countenance   SHER 315:17
disinterested D. intellectual curiosity   TREV 341:15
dislike I, too, d. it   MOOR 244:2
dismal D. Science   CARL 85:16
Disney *of Euro D.*   MNOU 241:21
disobedience man's first d.   MILT 237:15
disorder sweet d. in the dress   HERR 168:3
  with brave d. part   POPE 267:5
displeasing not d. to us   LA R 209:10
disposes God d.   THOM 337:9
disposition antic d.   SHAK 292:6
  truant d.   SHAK 291:22
dispossessed imprisoned or d.   MAGN 225:5
disqualified d. for holding any office   MORE 244:16
disregard Atones for later d.   FROS 143:23
dissatisfied human being d.   MILL 234:15
  I'm d.   MOOR 244:5
dissect murder to d.   WORD 366:10
dissociation d. of sensibility   ELIO 130:8
dissolve d. the people   BREC 68:9
dissolved d. into something   CATH 88:18
dissonance barbarous d.   MILT 236:8
distance d. is nothing   DU D 122:27
  d. lends enchantment   CAMP 83:12
  longest d. between two places   WILL 360:12
distant relation of d. misery   GIBB 148:19
distempered questions the d. part   ELIO 128:9
distillation d. of rumour   CARL 85:11
distinction make no d.   BUSH 78:16
  think that there is no d.   JOHN 188:15
distinctive man's d. mark   BROW 72:1
distinguished d. by that circumstance   THOR 339:20
  d. thing   JAME 183:4
distort then you can d. them   TWAI 344:3
distressed afflicted, or d.   BOOK 60:17
  I am d. for thee   BIBL 36:35
distribute d. as fairly as he can   LOWE 219:15
ditch die in the last d.   WILL 360:2
  fall into the d.   BIBL 45:6
  makes a straight-cut d.   THOR 339:7
dive must d. below   DRYD 121:27
diversity some d.   BARC 26:11
divided d. by a common language   SHAW 313:6
  d. duty   SHAK 304:24
  d. into three parts   CAES 82:3
  d. self   LAIN 206:16
  has harshly d.   SCHI 286:7
  If a house be d.   BIBL 46:24
  in their death not d.   BIBL 36:34
dividing by d. we fall   DICK 116:9
divine d. Majority   DICK 116:3
  human form d.   BLAK 57:17
  one far-off d. event   TENN 333:11
  Right D. of Kings   POPE 266:8
  say that D. providence   JOHN 186:3
  some D. despair   TENN 334:15
  To forgive, is d.   POPE 267:16
divinely most d. fair   TENN 332:5
divinity d. doth hedge a king   SHAK 293:31
  d. in odd numbers   SHAK 303:6
  d. that shapes our ends   SHAK 294:7
divisions How many d. has *he* got   STAL 322:24
divorces d. his first wife   TALM 330:17
dixit *Ipse d.*   CICE 96:17
DNA cannot cheat on D.   WARD 350:19
do can't all d. everything   VIRG 347:24
  damned if you d.   DOW 120:9
  d. not do to your neighbour   HILL 169:10
  d. only one thing   SMIL 317:21
  D. other men   DICK 115:7

  d. what I please   FRED 142:9
  D. what thou wilt   CROW 108:2
  D. what you love   NAVR 248:20
  d. ye even so to them   BIBL 44:8
  George—don't d. that   GREN 157:10
  HOW NOT TO D. IT   DICK 115:3
  I can d. no other   LUTH 220:17
  I'll do, I'll do, and I'll d.   SHAK 299:10
  know not what they d.   BIBL 48:8
  Let's d. it   PORT 269:3
  Let us d.—or die   BURN 77:11
  Love and d. what you will   AUGU 20:8
  not knowing what they d.   SHAK 304:14
  people who d. things   MORR 246:1
  so much to d.   RHOD 275:13
  supposed to d. anyway   TRUM 342:10
  what I d. in any thing   HERB 167:14
  What must I d. to be saved   BIBL 49:27
  what you are afraid to d.   EMER 132:7
Doc cards with a man called D.   ALGR 5:4
docent *dum d. discunt*   SENE 288:22
doctor any other d. whatsoever   HOBB 170:14
  d. found, when she was dead   GOLD 153:13
  God and the d.   OWEN 256:4
doctors believe the d.   SALI 284:19
  when d. disagree   POPE 266:25
doctrine all the winds of d.   MILT 240:10
  d. of ignoble ease   ROOS 279:19
  not for the d.   POPE 267:11
doctrines d. without words   LAO 207:21
dodger artful D.   DICK 115:14
doers be ye d. of the word   BIBL 52:20
dog beaten d. beneath the hail   POUN 270:3
  beware of the d.   BLIX 58:11
  Beware of the d.   PETR 262:16
  black d.   JOHN 190:16
  called me an attack d.   REID 275:2
  d. in the night-time   DOYL 120:19
  d. it was that died   GOLD 153:14
  d. returneth to his vomit   BIBL 38:39
  D. returns to his Vomit   KIPL 202:7
  d.'s walking on his hinder legs   JOHN 188:18
  every d. his day   KING 201:9
  heart to a d. to tear   KIPL 202:18
  Is thy servant a d.   BIBL 37:26
  Labour's attack d.   PAXM 260:17
  living d.   BIBL 39:19
  Lovell our d.   COLL 101:8
  man bites a d.   BOGA 58:16
  over the lazy d.   ANON 10:13
  tongue of d.   SHAK 301:12
  was there ever d.   YEAT 369:8
  whose d. are you   POPE 266:14
  working like a d.   LENN 212:20
  your wife and your d.   HILL 169:3
doggie How much is that d.   MERR 233:12
dogs all things as straw d.   LAO 208:1
  d. eat of the crumbs   BIBL 45:7
  d. go on with their doggy life   AUDE 19:10
  D. look up to us   CHUR 96:9
  d. of Europe bark   AUDE 19:3
  fought the d.   BROW 72:21
  hates d. and babies   ROST 281:4
  Let d. delight   WATT 351:20
  let slip the d. of war   SHAK 296:30
  mad and hungry d.   MCKA 223:10
  Mad d. and Englishmen   COWA 105:4
  Throw physic to the d.   SHAK 301:29
doing continuance in well d.   BIBL 49:38
  joy's soul lies in the d.   SHAK 308:8
  may not be d. much   RUMS 281:20
  not be weary in well d.   BIBL 51:14
  put me to d.   METH 233:16

doing (cont.)
see what she's d. — PUNC 271:21
This is the Lord's d. — BOOK 64:18
doleful Knight of the D. Countenance — CERV 89:19
dollar almighty d. — IRVI 181:4
billion d. country — FOST 140:4
dolore *Nessun maggior d.* — DANT 109:12
Dolores splendid and sterile D. — SWIN 329:10
dolour d. of pad and paper-weight — ROET 278:10
dolphin d.-torn, that gong-tormented — YEAT 367:14
dome d. of many-coloured glass — SHEL 313:21
starlit or a moonlit d. — YEAT 367:13
domestic d. business — MONT 242:21
Malice d. — SHAK 301:2
respectable d. establishment — BENN 30:19
domination against white d. — MAND 226:16
dominations Thrones, d. — MILT 238:32
dominion death hath no more d. — BIBL 50:3
death shall have no d. — THOM 337:17
d. of kings changed — PRIC 270:21
d. of religion — GOLD 153:3
d. of the English — ANON 10:22
Man's d. — BURN 77:20
dominions His Majesty's d. — NORT 251:22
not set in my d. — SCHI 286:9
domino 'falling d.' principle — EISE 126:17
dominus *D. illuminatio mea* — ANON 13:9
D. illuminatio mea — BIBL 53:27
D. vobiscum — MISS 240:14
Nisi D. — BIBL 54:2
Don D. John of Austria is going — CHES 93:2
quiet flows the D. — SHOL 316:2
dona *Requiem aeternam d. eis* — MISS 241:4
done decide that d. can be done — ALLE 5:10
D. because we are too menny — HARD 161:15
d. when 'tis done — SHAK 299:28
he d. her wrong — ANON 8:16
If you want anything d. — THAT 336:12
Inasmuch as ye have d. — BIBL 46:8
Nothing to be d. — BECK 28:11
remained to be d. — LUCA 220:8
something d. — LONG 218:10
Something must be d. — WHIT 356:11
surprised to find it d. — JOHN 188:18
that which is d. — BIBL 39:8
Things won are d. — SHAK 308:8
we have d. those things — BOOK 59:13
What could she have d. — YEAT 368:21
What is to be d. — LENI 212:8
What's d. cannot be undone — SHAK 301:25
what's d. is done — SHAK 301:1
dong D. with a luminous nose — LEAR 210:11
donkeys Lions led by d. — ANON 9:11
Donne John D., Anne Donne — DONN 119:25
Dons If the D. sight Devon — NEWB 249:15
don't about to marry.—'d.' — PUNC 271:17
damned if you d. — DOW 120:9
doodle Yankee D. — ANON 12:6
doom regardless of their d. — GRAY 156:16
to the edge of d. — SHAK 310:23
Doon braes o' bonny D. — BURN 76:22
door angel from your d. — BLAK 57:18
beating on the d. — YEAT 368:7
d. flew open — HOFF 171:8
d. we never opened — ELIO 128:1
I am the d. — BIBL 48:36
knock at the d. — LAMB 207:2
knocking at the d. — SHAW 313:3
lights around the d. — ROSS 280:22
Never open the d. — GRAC 154:18
rapping at my chamber d. — POE 265:17
stand at the d., and knock — BIBL 53:5
Then—shuts the D. — DICK 116:3

through the d. with a gun — CHAN 90:14
when the d. opens — GREE 156:26
whining of a d. — DONN 119:24
wide as a church d. — SHAK 306:37
doorkeeper d. in the house of my God — BOOK 63:20
doormat d. or a prostitute — WEST 355:14
doors close softly the d. — JUST 194:3
Death has a thousand d. — MASS 231:3
Death hath so many d. — FLET 138:11
d. of perception — BLAK 57:7
Men shut their d. — SHAK 308:2
ten thousand several d. — WEBS 352:23
thousand d. open on to it — SENE 288:23
with both d. open — HUGH 177:11
ye everlasting d. — BOOK 62:17
dooryard last in the d. bloomed — WHIT 357:11
dormitat *bonus d. Homerus* — HORA 174:19
dossier draft d. produced — GILL 150:29
dot cherish the pale blue d. — SAGA 284:4
dots damned d. meant — CHUR 94:20
double Double, d. toil and trouble — SHAK 301:11
leading a d. life — WILD 358:11
peace of the d.-bed — CAMP 83:7
doubles d. your chances for a date — ALLE 5:17
doublet tailor make thy d. — SHAK 308:35
doublethink D. means the power — ORWE 254:27
doubt curiosity, freckles, and d. — PARK 258:12
do not make one d. — NEWM 249:21
d. and sorrow — BARI 26:14
in d., strike it out — TWAI 343:25
let us never, never d. — BELL 29:25
Life is d. — UNAM 344:11
more faith in honest d. — TENN 333:6
No possible d. whatever — GILB 149:15
Our d. is our passion — JAME 182:18
philosophy calls all in d. — DONN 118:18
sunnier side of d. — TENN 331:14
wherefore didst thou d. — BIBL 45:5
doubter d. and the doubt — EMER 131:19
doubts end in d. — BACO 22:1
dove on the burnished d. — TENN 333:22
wings like a d. — BOOK 63:9
Dover milestones on the D. Road — DICK 115:4
white cliffs of D. — BURT 77:27
doves harmless as d. — BIBL 44:27
moan of d. — TENN 334:24
dowagers d. for deans — TENN 334:11
down D. among the dead — DYER 124:2
D. and out in Paris — ORWE 254:14
D. in the forest — SIMP 317:8
d. into the darkness — MILL 234:17
D. to Gehenna — KIPL 202:14
fled Him, d. the nights — THOM 338:14
go d. to the sea — BOOK 64:9
He that is d. — BUNY 74:16
kicked d. stairs — HALI 160:5
meet 'em on your way d. — MIZN 241:19
staying d. with him — WASH 351:4
downhearted Are we d. — ANON 7:12
Are we d. — KNIG 204:7
downs in the D. the fleet was moored — GAY 147:7
downwards look no way but d. — BUNY 74:15
dragon d.-green, the luminous — FLEC 138:3
fought against the d. — BIBL 53:12
O to be a d. — MOOR 244:1
dragons laugh at live d. — TOLK 340:21
drains opiate to the d. — KEAT 196:16
Drake D. he's in his hammock — NEWB 249:16
Drang *Sturm und D.* — KAUF 195:7
draw d. like these children — PICA 263:7
d. you to her — DRYD 122:18
drawers d. of water — BIBL 36:8
drawing D. is the true test — INGR 180:21

Dublin Dear, dirty D. — JOYC 192:18
ducat Dead, for a d. — SHAK 293:18
ducats O my d.! O my daughter — SHAK 302:18
duchess chambermaid as of a D. — JOHN 189:26
  I am D. of Malfi still — WEBS 352:22
  That's my last D. — BROW 72:17
duck just forgot to d. — DEMP 112:22
  looks like a d. — REUT 275:7
ducks I turn to d. — HARV 163:4
duffers BETTER DROWNED THAN D. — RANS 273:13
dugs old man with wrinkled d. — ELIO 129:27
duke fully-equipped d. — LLOY 216:8
dukedom d. large enough — SHAK 307:19
dukes drawing room full of d. — AUDE 19:24
dulce D. est desipere — HORA 175:20
  D. et decorum est — HORA 175:14
  D. et decorum est — OWEN 256:11
dulcimer damsel with a d. — COLE 100:11
dull d. in a new way — JOHN 189:6
  d. it is to pause — TENN 335:3
  D. would he be of soul — WORD 364:10
  Sherry is d. — JOHN 188:17
  some d. opiate — KEAT 196:16
  very d., dreary affair — MAUG 231:12
dullard d.'s envy of brilliant men — BEER 29:3
dumb as a sheep is d. — BIBL 41:11
  d. son of a bitch — TRUM 342:16
  d. to tell the crooked rose — THOM 337:21
  So d. he can't fart — JOHN 186:12
Duncan fatal entrance of D. — SHAK 299:22
dunce d. with wits — POPE 266:7
dunces d. are all in confederacy — SWIF 328:20
Dunfermline D. town — BALL 25:15
dungeon Himself is his own d. — MILT 236:5
dungeons Brightest in d., Liberty — BYRO 81:19
dungfork man with a d. — HOPK 174:11
dunghill cock crowing on its own d. — ALDI 4:8
Dunsinane high D. hill — SHAK 301:17
dupes If hopes were d. — CLOU 98:22
durable true love is a d. fire — RALE 273:1
duration d. of the war — ASQU 17:18
dusk each slow d. — OWEN 256:10
  falling of the d. — HEGE 165:4
  forty-three In the d. — GILB 150:27
dust blossom in the d. — SHIR 316:1
  chimney-sweepers, come to d. — SHAK 291:6
  D. hath closed Helen's eye — NASH 248:18
  d. of exploded beliefs — MADA 224:15
  d. thou art — BIBL 34:22
  D. thou art — LONG 217:18
  d. to dust — BOOK 62:6
  Excuse my d. — PARK 259:1
  fear in a handful of d. — ELIO 129:19
  forbear To dig the d. — SHAK 311:2
  Grind them into the d. — BRAD 67:11
  Less than the d. — HOPE 173:13
  not without d. and heat — MILT 240:5
  raised a d. — BERK 31:16
  shake off the d. — BIBL 44:26
  sweep the d. — SHAK 304:5
  what a d. do I raise — BACO 23:19
  Where can the d. alight — HUI- 178:3
  with age and d. — RALE 273:3
dustbin d. of history — TROT 342:6
dustheap d. called 'history' — BIRR 55:2
dusty what a d. answer — MERE 233:9
Dutch fault of the D. — CANN 84:6
duties d. as well as its rights — DRUM 121:16
  d. will be determined — MORE 244:22
  If I had no d. — JOHN 189:17
duty as much a d. as cooperation — GAND 145:17
  daily stage of d. — KEN 198:5
  dare to do our d. — LINC 214:15

declares it is his d. — SHAW 311:13
divided d. — SHAK 304:24
do our d. as such — SALI 284:20
Do your d. — CORN 104:5
d. of an Opposition — DERB 113:11
d. of government — PAIN 257:9
d. we owe to history — WILD 358:15
d. we so much underrate — STEV 325:20
d. we owe to his d. — NELS 249:8
Every subject's d. — SHAK 295:21
I have done my d. — NELS 249:9
life was d. — HOOP 173:2
Nor law, nor d. — YEAT 368:12
performing a public d. — GRAN 155:14
sense of d. useful — RUSS 282:26
Such d. as the subject owes — SHAK 307:15
When D. whispers low — EMER 132:1
whole d. of man — BIBL 39:30
dux D. femina facti — VIRG 347:2
dwarf d. sees farther — COLE 101:3
dwarfish d. whole — COLE 100:4
dwarfs d. on the shoulders — BERN 32:10
  State which d. its men — MILL 234:11
dwell people that on earth do d. — KETH 199:15
dwelling d. is the light — WORD 364:21
dwells She d. with Beauty — KEAT 196:15
dwelt d. among the untrodden ways — WORD 365:26
  d. among us — BIBL 48:19
dwindle d. into a wife — CONG 102:11
dyer like the d.'s hand — SHAK 310:20
dying achieve it through not d. — ALLE 5:18
  attend a d. animal — YEAT 367:21
  bliss of d. — POPE 266:10
  D. a very dull, dreary — MAUG 231:12
  d. breath of Socrates — JEAN 183:14
  D. is an art — PLAT 264:15
  d. of a hundred good symptoms — POPE 268:25
  d. without having laughed — LA B 206:10
  feel that he is d. — CALI 82:13
  groans of love to those of the d. — LOWR 220:7
  he hung, the d. Lord — JACO 182:2
  I am d., Egypt — SHAK 289:21
  If this is d. — STRA 326:21
  like a d. lady — SHEL 315:2
  lips of d. men — ARNO 16:23
  man's d. is more the survivors' affair — MANN 227:7
  mouth of the d. day — AUDE 18:21
  no more d. then — SHAK 310:29
  not death, but d. — FIEL 135:8
  poor devils are d. — PHIL 263:2
  Those d. generations — YEAT 368:26
  Turkey is a d. man — NICH 250:21
  unconscionable time d. — CHAR 91:3
dyke auld fail d. — BALL 25:21

E

E E = mc² — EINS 126:3
each beating each to e. — BROW 72:15
eagle E. has landed — ARMS 16:7
  e. in the air — BIBL 39:4
  Fate is not an e. — BOWE 66:13
  with e. eyes — KEAT 196:28
eagles e. be gathered — BIBL 45:35
  with wings as e. — BIBL 41:4
ear close at the e. of Eve — MILT 238:28
  hath the sow by the right e. — HENR 166:17
  out of your wife's e. — MORT 246:5
  than meets the e. — MILT 236:14
  upon my whorlèd e. — HOPK 173:18
  Vexing the dull e. — SHAK 297:19

earl e. and a knight of the garter	ATTL 18:8
early E. one morning	ANON 7:25
E. to rise	THUR 340:4
had it been e.	JOHN 188:8
Vote e. and vote often	MILE 234:2
earnest I am in e.	GARR 146:9
Life is e.	LONG 217:18
time to be in e.	JOHN 187:6
earrings e. for under £1	RATN 273:16
ears e., and hear not	BOOK 64:15
hath e. to hear	BIBL 46:25
lend me your e.	SHAK 297:1
lets the e. lie back	IVES 181:8
stoppeth her e.	BOOK 63:12
That man's e.	HUGH 177:11
we have two e.	ZENO 370:11
What big e. you have	PERR 262:7
earth bleeding piece of e.	SHAK 296:29
call this planet E.	CLAR 97:6
Cold in the e.	BRON 69:14
conquest of the e.	CONR 102:20
daughter of E. and Water	SHEL 313:24
deep-delvèd e.	KEAT 196:17
E. all Danaë to the stars	TENN 334:22
e. breaks up	BROW 71:24
E. felt the wound	MILT 239:6
E. has not anything to show	WORD 364:10
e. in an earthy bed	TENN 334:7
e. is the Lord's	BIBL 50:20
e. is the Lord's	BOOK 62:16
E.'s crammed with heaven	BROW 71:14
e. shall be full	BIBL 40:18
E.'s the right place for love	FROS 143:9
E. stood hard as iron	ROSS 280:13
famous men have the whole e.	PERI 262:2
feel the e. move	HEMI 166:2
get away from e. awhile	FROS 143:9
giants in the e.	BIBL 34:27
girdle round about the e.	SHAK 303:20
going to and fro in the e.	BIBL 37:32
heaven and the e.	BIBL 34:3
if e. Be but the shadow	MILT 238:31
inherit the e.	BIBL 43:13
It fell to e.	LONG 217:6
lap of E.	GRAY 156:15
Lie heavy on him, E.	EVAN 133:9
move the e.	ARCH 14:17
new heaven and a new e.	BIBL 53:22
new heavens and a new e.	BIBL 41:19
of the e., earthy	BIBL 51:2
on e. peace	BIBL 47:4
On e. there is nothing great	HAMI 160:13
One does not sell the e.	CRAZ 106:14
poetry of e.	KEAT 196:29
salt of the e.	BIBL 43:14
sleepers in that quiet e.	BRON 69:16
surly bonds of e.	MAGE 225:2
surly bonds of e.	REAG 274:8
way of all the e.	BIBL 36:9
work i' the e.	SHAK 292:4
Yours is the E.	KIPL 202:10
earthquake e. is not satisfied	WORD 365:18
Lord was not in the e.	BIBL 37:14
Small e. in Chile	COCK 99:5
earthy of the earth, e.	BIBL 51:2
ease age of e.	GOLD 153:6
for another gives its e.	BLAK 57:23
ignoble e.	ROOS 279:19
Not for e. that prayer	WILL 360:19
take thine e.	BIBL 47:20
True e. in writing	POPE 267:13
easeful e. Death	KEAT 196:20
easer e. of all woes	FLET 138:13

easing e. the Spring	REED 274:13
east E. is a career	DISR 118:2
E. is East	KIPL 201:17
E. of Suez	KIPL 202:16
gorgeous E. in fee	WORD 365:13
It is the e.	SHAK 306:27
look the E. End in the face	ELIZ 131:5
neither from the e.	BOOK 63:16
on the e. of Eden	BIBL 34:25
tried to hustle the E.	KIPL 202:17
wise men from the e.	BIBL 43:1
Easter like an E. Island statue	KEAT 195:8
Eastertide Wearing white for E.	HOUS 176:6
eastward garden e. in Eden	BIBL 34:7
easy e. to take refuge in	IBSE 180:9
e. writing's vile hard reading	SHER 315:18
Life is not meant to be e.	FRAS 142:8
Life is not meant to be e.	SHAW 311:9
normal and e.	JAME 182:22
Summer time an' the livin' is e.	HEYW 168:14
eat e., drink, and be merry	BIBL 47:20
e. the fat of the land	BIBL 35:9
e. to live	MOLI 242:1
e. up and swallow down	MORE 244:15
have meat and cannot e.	BURN 77:3
I did e.	BIBL 34:17
I would e. his heart	SHAK 304:15
Let them e. cake	MARI 227:18
Let us e. and drink	BIBL 40:21
neither should he e.	BIBL 52:4
see what I e.	CARR 86:11
shalt thou e. bread	BIBL 34:21
Take, e.	BIBL 46:11
Take, e., this is my Body	BOOK 61.14
Tell me what you e.	BRIL 69:2
thou shalt not e. of it	BIBL 34:9
to e., and to drink	BIBL 39:18
Ye shall e. it in haste	BIBL 35:19
eaten e. by the bear	HOUS 176:2
eater great e. of beef	SHAK 308:19
Out of the e.	BIBL 36:16
eateth Why e. your Master	BIBL 44:18
eating E. people is wrong	FLAN 137:22
eats Man is what he e.	FEUE 135:3
Ebenezer Pale E. thought it wrong	BELL 30:3
ecce E. homo	BIBL 54:11
ecclesia Ubi Petrus, ibi ergo e.	AMBR 5:22
Ecclesiastes Vanitas vanitatum, dixit E.	BIBL 54:4
echo e. of a platitude	BIER 54:17
Footfalls e. in the memory	ELIO 128:1
sound must seem an e.	POPE 267:14
waiting for the e.	MARQ 228:23
echoes wild e. flying	TENN 334:13
eclipse E. first	O'KE 253:7
total e.	MILT 239:22
eclipsed e. the gaiety	JOHN 187:12
economic vital e. interests	WEIL 353:6
economical e. with the *actualité*	CLAR 97:3
e. with the truth	ARMS 16:9
economics E. is the science	ROBB 277:9
it is bad e.	ROOS 279:12
study of e.	SCHU 286:16
economists e., and calculators	BURK 75:18
economize Let us e. it	TWAI 343:10
economy E. is going without	HOPE 173:8
e. of truth	BURK 76:1
écrasez é. l'*infâme*	VOLT 348:23
ecstasy What wild e.	KEAT 196:6
Eden garden eastward in E.	BIBL 34:7
happier E.	MILT 238:24
loss of E.	MILT 237:15
on the east of E.	BIBL 34:25
other E.	SHAK 305:22

Eden (*cont.*)
Through E. took — MILT 239:14
voice that breathed o'er E. — KEBL 197:25
edge Come to the e. — LOGU 217:4
teeth are set on e. — BIBL 41:28
edged Science is an e. tool — EDDI 124:23
editions e. of Balbec and Palmyra — WALP 350:2
editor E.: a person employed — HUBB 177:9
Edom over E. will I cast out — BOOK 63:13
educated e. and the uneducated — FOST 140:6
government by the badly e. — CHES 93:23
education between e. and catastrophe — WELL 354:11
cabbage with a college e. — TWAI 343:23
discretion by e. — JEFF 184:17
e., education, and education — BLAI 55:19
e. forms the common mind — POPE 266:30
E. has been theirs — AUST 21:4
[E.] has produced — TREV 341:17
E. is what survives — SKIN 317:16
E. is when you read — SEEG 288:9
E. makes a people — BROU 70:10
e. of the heart — SCOT 287:26
e. of the people — DISR 117:14
e. produces no effect — WILD 358:6
e. to Greece — PERI 262:1
in their own e. — SCOT 288:1
liberal e. — BANK 26:9
part of e. — BACO 23:15
Real e. ultimately limited — POUN 270:6
Soap and e. — TWAI 343:9
thank your e. — JONS 191:19
What does e. often do — THOR 339:7
eels e. boil'd in broo — BALL 25:11
effect found in the e. — BERG 31:11
little e. after much labour — AUST 21:14
effective as e. as I should be — MORR 245:8
efficient e. parts — BAGE 24:7
have an e. government — TRUM 342:15
effort redoubling your e. — SANT 285:12
written without e. — JOHN 191:3
effugies *non e.* — CATU 89:10
egg e. boiled very soft — AUST 20:20
e. by pleasure laid — COWP 105:22
e. is, quite simply — SMIT 318:9
e. on our face — BROK 69:5
From the e. — HORA 175:23
got a bad e. — PUNC 271:23
hatched from a swan's e. — ANDE 6:13
eggs all my e. in one bastard — PARK 259:6
as a weasel sucks e. — SHAK 290:8
Lays e. inside a paper bag — ISHE 181:5
roast their e. — BACO 23:21
eglantine with e. — SHAK 303:21
ego *Et in Arcadia e.* — ANON 13:10
egotistical e. sublime — KEAT 197:16
Egypt firstborn in the land of E. — BIBL 35:20
out of the land of E. — BIBL 35:24
there was corn in E. — BIBL 35:7
wonders in the land of E. — BIBL 35:16
Egyptians spoiled the E. — BIBL 35:21
eheu E. *fugaces Labuntur anni* — HORA 175:11
eight Pieces of e. — STEV 325:18
We want e. — ANON 11:17
eighteen before you reach e. — EINS 126:11
eightfold E. Path — PALI 258:3
eighty In a dream you are never e. — SEXT 289:4
Einstein Let E. be — SQUI 322:21
either happy could I be with e. — GAY 147:2
Elaine E., the lily maid — TENN 332:13
élan *é. vital* — BERG 31:12
elder take An e. than herself — SHAK 308:33
elderly e. man of 42 — ASHF 17:16
elect dissolve the people and e. — BREC 68:9

elected will not serve if e. — SHER 315:27
election e. by the incompetent many — SHAW 312:8
e. is coming — ELIO 127:10
elections e. are won — ADAM 1:17
You won the e. — SOMO 320:9
elective E. affinities — GOET 152:17
e. dictatorship — HAIL 159:6
Electra Mourning becomes E. — O'NE 253:15
electric biggest e. train — WELL 353:15
E. Kool-Aid Acid test — WOLF 363:10
sing the body e. — WHIT 356:22
tried to mend the E. Light — BELL 30:1
electrical e. skin and glaring eyes — SMAR 317:18
electricity e. was dripping — THUR 340:2
usefulness of e. — FARA 134:1
electrification e. of the whole country — LENI 212:9
electronic new e. interdependence — MCLU 223:17
elegant e. sufficiency — THOM 338:25
Most intelligent, very e. — BUCK 73:17
so e. — ELIO 129:25
You e. fowl — LEAR 210:16
elegy whole of Gray's E. — WOLF 363:4
eleison *Kyrie e.* — MISS 240:17
elementary E., my dear Watson — DOYL 120:17
'E.,' said he — DOYL 120:17
elements e. So mixed in him — SHAK 297:17
formation of heavier e. — EDDI 124:19
elephant at the E. — SHAK 309:5
corn as high as an e.'s eye — HAMM 160:18
couldn't hit an e. — SEDG 288:6
E.'s Child — KIPL 203:15
masterpiece, an e. — DONN 119:3
sleeping with an e. — TRUD 342:8
elephants e. for want of towns — SWIF 329:1
golden e. next — SHOR 316:3
elf deceiving e. — KEAT 196:24
elfland horns of E. — TENN 334:14
Eli Eli, E., lama sabachthani — BIBL 46:20
Elijah E. passed by him — BIBL 37:15
E. went up by a whirlwind — BIBL 37:19
spirit of E. — BIBL 37:20
eliminated e. the impossible — DOYL 120:21
Elisha rest on E. — BIBL 37:20
elms Behind the e. last night — PRIO 271:2
Beneath those rugged e. — GRAY 156:8
in immemorial e. — TENN 334:24
eloquence e. the soul — MILT 238:8
else happening to Somebody E. — ROGE 278:15
elsewhere There is a world e. — SHAK 291:3
Elysium What E. have ye known — KEAT 196:4
embarras *e. des richesses* — ALLA 5:9
embarrassment e. of riches — ALLA 5:9
embrace do there e. — MARV 229:22
e. your Lordship's principles — WILK 359:26
pity, then e. — POPE 267:29
embroideries Covered with e. — YEAT 367:17
emendation e. wrong — JOHN 187:14
emerald green as e. — COLE 100:16
men, of the E. Isle — DREN 121:14
eminency some e. in ourselves — HOBB 170:12
emotion dependable international e. — ALSO 5:20
e. recollected in tranquillity — WORD 366:19
morality touched by e. — ARNO 17:7
emotional Gluttony an e. escape — DE V 114:1
emotions gamut of the e. — PARK 259:2
only two e. in a plane — WELL 353:17
receptacle for e. — PICA 263:6
emparadised E. in one another's arms — MILT 238:24
emperor belong to the E. — BORG 65:20
E. has nothing on — ANDE 6:12
e. of ice-cream — STEV 324:16
e. to die standing — VESP 346:7
empire All e. is no more — DRYD 121:19

arch Of the ranged e. — SHAK 289:12
course of e. — BERK 31:18
e. walking very slowly — FITZ 137:14
evil e. — REAG 274:7
found a great e. — SMIT 318:5
great e. and little minds — BURK 75:11
great Mother E. — FOST 140:5
idlers of the E. — DOYL 121:2
lost an e. — ACHE 1:6
metropolis of the e. — COBB 99:2
nor Roman, nor an e. — VOLT 348:17
empires day of E. — CHAM 90:2
e. of the future — CHUR 95:18
Hatching vain e. — MILT 238:6
Vaster than e. — MARV 229:20
empirical e. scientific system — POPP 268:26
employed innocently e. — JOHN 189:5
employee In a hierarchy every e. — PETE 262:12
employer harder upon the e. — SPOO 322:11
employment e. to the artisan — BELL 30:1
seek gainful e. — ACHE 1:5
emporium Celestial E. — BORG 65:20
emptiness Form is e. — MAHĀ 225:9
great Australian E. — WHIT 356:6
empty Bring on the e. horses — CURT 109:1
e. spaces Between stars — FROS 143:14
rich he hath sent e. away — BIBL 46:33
singer of an e. day — MORR 245:10
turn down an e. glass — FITZ 137:4
enamelled e. meadows — WALP 349:18
enchanted Enter these e. woods — MERE 233:10
holy and e. — COLE 100:8
Some e. evening — HAMM 160:20
enchantment distance lends e. — CAMP 83:12
enchantments e. of the Middle Age — ARNO 17:4
e. of the Middle Age — BEER 29:2
encircling amid the e. gloom — NEWM 250:7
encounter e. darkness as a bride — SHAK 302:7
encourage right to e. — BAGE 24:10
to e. the others — VOLT 348:8
encourager e. les autres — VOLT 348:8
end beginning of the e. — TALL 330:7
came to an e. all wars — LLOY 216:9
continuing unto the e. — DRAK 121:6
e. badly — STEV 325:25
e. cannot justify the means — HUXL 179:10
e. crowns all — SHAK 308:15
e. in doubts — BACO 22:1
e. is where we start from — ELIO 128:16
e. justifies the means — BUSE 78:9
e., never as means — KANT 194:24
e. of a thousand years of history — GAIT 144:22
e. of history — FUKU 144:11
e. of the beginning — CHUR 95:14
e. to the beginnings of all wars — ROOS 279:18
highest political e. — ACTO 1:8
In my beginning is my e. — ELIO 128:5
In my e. is my beginning — MARY 230:15
let me know mine e. — BOOK 62:25
look to the e. — ANON 13:17
middle, and an e. — ARIS 15:16
muddle, and an e. — LARK 209:2
on to the e. of the road — LAUD 209:13
sans singer, and—sans E. — FITZ 136:11
This was the e. — PLAT 264:20
till you come to the e. — CARR 86:20
unto the e. of the world — BIBL 46:21
Waiting for the e. — EMPS 132:24
war that will e. war — WELL 354:13
where's it all going to e. — STOP 326:13
world will e. in fire — FROS 143:15
world without e. — BOOK 59:16
endearing e. young charms — MOOR 244:6

ended Mass is e. — MISS 241:2
ending way of e. a war — ORWE 255:8
endless born to e. night — BLAK 56:14
in e. night — GRAY 156:21
ends between e. and scarce means — ROBB 277:9
divinity that shapes our e. — SHAK 294:7
pursuing of the best e. — HUTC 179:5
endurance e. and courage — SCOT 287:5
endure Children's talent to e. — ANGE 7:2
e. for a night — BOOK 62:19
e. my own despair — WALS 350:7
e. them — AURE 20:19
e., then pity — POPE 267:29
e. the toothache — SHAK 304:16
human hearts e. — JOHN 187:23
man will not merely e. — FAUL 134:12
stuff will not e. — SHAK 308:28
endured e. with patient resignation — RUSS 282:26
state to be e. — JOHN 187:18
endureth mercy e. for ever — BOOK 64:30
enemies alone against smiling e. — BOWE 66:14
choice of his e. — WILD 358:27
conquering one's e. — GENG 147:13
e. be scattered — BOOK 63:14
e. will not believe — HUBB 177:7
left me naked to mine e. — SHAK 296:15
Love your e. — BIBL 47:9
making new e. — VOLT 349:4
no perpetual e. — PALM 258:4
enemy afraid of his e. — PLUT 265:12
better class of e. — MILL 235:5
e. of good art — CONN 102:17
e. that shall be destroyed — BIBL 50:29
e. to the human race — MILL 235:3
e. we're fighting — WALL 349:14
every man your e. — NELS 249:4
first contact with the e. — MOLT 242:4
I am the e. you killed — OWEN 256:15
If thine e. be hungry — BIBL 38:36
life, its e. — ANOU 14:4
met the e. — PERR 262:9
no e. but time — YEAT 368:10
not an e. in the world — WILD 359:16
one e. — ALI 5:5
sometimes his own worst e. — BEVI 33:18
spoils of the e. — MARC 227:16
vision's greatest e. — BLAK 56:16
will have upon the e. — WELL 353:18
your e. and your friend — TWAI 343:14
energy E. is Eternal Delight — BLAK 56:21
important source of e. — EINS 126:8
enfants e. de la patrie — ROUG 281:6
Les e. terribles — GAVA 146:17
engine be a Really Useful E. — AWDR 21:17
I am An e. — HARE 162:11
two-handed e. — MILT 236:33
engineers age of the e. — HOGB 171:12
e. of human souls — STAL 322:23
e. of the soul — GORK 154:11
not e. of the soul — KENN 199:4
enginer e. Hoist with his own — SHAK 293:23
England ah, faithless E. — BOSS 66:3
always be an E. — PARK 259:9
Be E. what she will — CHUR 94:15
between France and E. — JERR 185:8
damn you E. — OSBO 255:14
E. and America divided — SHAW 313:6
E. and Saint George — SHAK 295:17
E. expects — NELS 249:8
E. has saved herself — PITT 263:21
E. hath need of thee — WORD 364:23
E., home and beauty — ARNO 17:10
E. is a garden — KIPL 202:6

England (*cont.*)

E. is a nation of shopkeepers	NAPO 248:7
E., my England	HENL 166:10
E.'s green and pleasant land	BLAK 57:8
E.'s winding sheet	BLAK 56:13
E., their England	MACD 223:1
E. to be the workshop	DISR 117:5
E. was too pure an Air	ANON 10:4
E. will have her neck wrung	CHUR 95:13
E., with all thy faults	COWP 105:26
ensure summer in E.	WALP 350:1
gentlemen of E.	PARK 259:7
God punish E.	FUNK 144:19
Goodbye, E.'s rose	JOHN 185:18
Gott strafe E.	FUNK 144:19
Heart of E.	DRAY 121:11
History is now and E.	ELIO 128:17
in E. people have	MIKE 233:24
in E.'s song for ever	NEWB 249:17
keep your E.	MUGA 246:16
leads him to E.	JOHN 188:13
Let not E. forget	MILT 240:11
Oh, to be in E.	BROW 72:5
Rule all E.	COLL 101:8
Slaves cannot breathe in E.	COWP 105:25
Speak for E.	AMER 6:2
stately homes of E.	HEMA 166:1
strong arm of E.	PALM 258:5
That is for ever E.	BROO 70:2
that will be E. gone	LARK 208:18
this Realm of E.	BOOK 65:14
this realm, this E.	SHAK 305:23
Wake up, E.	GEOR 147:19
we are the people of E.	CHES 93:6
who only E. know	KIPL 201:23
world where E. is finished	MILL 234:21
youth of E.	SHAK 295:13

Englanders Little E.   ANON 9:12

English bird-haunted E. lawn

	ARNO 16:17
can't think of the E.	CARR 87:1
Certain men the E. shot	YEAT 368:18
Cricket—a game which the E.	MANC 226:14
dominion of the E.	ANON 10:22
E. Bible	MACA 221:16
E. child	BLAK 57:20
E. Church shall be free	MAGN 225:4
E. in taste	MACA 222:5
E., not the Turkish court	SHAK 295:8
E. tongue I love	WALC 349:5
E. unofficial rose	BROO 69:20
E. up with which I will not put	CHUR 95:21
fragments of the E. scene	ORWE 254:18
in the E. language	JAME 183:3
mobilized the E. language	MURR 247:11
rolling E. road	CHES 93:3
Saxon-Danish-Norman E.	DEFO 111:22
seven feet of E. ground	HARO 162:14
well of E. undefiled	SPEN 322:4

Englishman blood of an E.

	NASH 248:17
E., even if he is alone	MIKE 234:1
E. in the wrong	SHAW 312:20
E. thinks he is moral	SHAW 312:3
E. to open his mouth	SHAW 312:16
he is an E.	GILB 150:20
He remains an E.	GILB 150:21
rights of an E.	JUNI 194:1
thing, an E.	DEFO 111:21

Englishmen don't give E. an inch

	BRAD 67:11
E. never will be slaves	SHAW 312:2
first to his E.	MILT 240:7
prefer to be E.	RHOD 275:12
When two E. meet	JOHN 187:3

Englishwoman E. is so refined   SMIT 319:4

enigma e. of the fever chart	ELIO 128:9
mystery inside an e.	CHUR 95:5
enjoy business of life is to e.	BUTL 79:11
e. him for ever	SHOR 316:5
have to go out and e. it	SMIT 318:20
what I most e.	SHAK 310:5
enjoyed little to be e.	JOHN 187:18
still to be e.	KEAT 196:10
enjoyment chief e. of riches	SMIT 318:3
only e. sometimes	REID 275:1
enjoyments if it were not for its e.	SURT 328:1
enlarge E., diminish	SWIF 328:26
enlargement stability or e.	JOHN 186:18
enmity there was e.	KORA 205:18
Enoch E. walked with God	BIBL 34:26
enough e. for everyone's need	BUCH 73:16
e. of blood and tears	RABI 272:15
Hold, e.	SHAK 302:2
Patriotism is not e.	CAVE 89:14
two thousand years is e.	PIUS 264:9
entente long live the E. Cordiale	ELIZ 131:4
enter King of England cannot e.	PITT 264:3
Let no one e.	ANON 13:2
shall not e.	BIBL 45:12
you who e.	DANT 109:8
entered iron e. into his soul	BOOK 64:6
enterprise more e. In walking naked	YEAT 367:18
voyages of the starship E.	RODD 278:7
entertained e. angels unawares	BIBL 52:17
entertainment irrational e.	JOHN 187:11
enthral Except you e. me	DONN 118:25
enthralled but not e.	MILT 236:9
enthusiasm achieved without e.	EMER 132:5
entia E. *non sunt multiplicanda*	OCCA 253:1
entire E. and whole and perfect	SPRI 322:12
envelope semi-transparent e.	WOOL 363:19
environment humdrum issues like the e.	THAT 336:17
envy e., hatred, and malice	BOOK 60:11
moved with e.	BIBL 49:28
prisoners of e.	ILLI 180:13
with e. and revenge	MILT 237:18
épater *é. le bourgeois*	BAUD 27:21
epaulette been by any e.	THOR 339:20
Ephesians Diana of the E.	BIBL 49:32
Ephesus beasts at E.	BIBL 50:30
epicure Serenely full, the e.	SMIT 319:14
epigram Impelled to try an e.	PARK 258:15
What is an E.	COLE 100:4
epigrams despotism tempered by e.	CARL 85:13
episode but the occasional e.	HARD 161:17
epitaph no man write my e.	EMME 132:23
that may be his e.	STEV 325:9
epitaphs nice derangement of e.	SHER 315:12
of worms, and e.	SHAK 305:29
epitome all mankind's e.	DRYD 121:21
eppur E. *si muove*	GALI 145:8
equal all men are created e.	LINC 214:20
consider our e.	DARW 110:12
e. division of unequal earnings	ELLI 131:11
e. in dignity and rights	ANON 7:7
E. Pay for Equal Work	ANTH 14:6
faith shines e.	BRON 69:13
more e. than others	ORWE 254:10
separate and e. station	JEFF 183:17
equality liberty and e.	ARIS 15:22
majestic e. of the law	FRAN 141:8
not e. or fairness	BERL 32:8
equals peace between e.	WILS 361:13
Pigs treat us as e.	CHUR 96:9
equations beauty in one's e.	DIRA 117:2
fire into the e.	HAWK 163:3
equators North Poles and E.	CARR 87:18
equi *currite noctis e.*	MARL 228:9

currite noctis e. OVID 255:23
equivocate I will not e. GARR 146:9
erected least e. spirit MILT 237:30
Erin for E. dear we fall SULL 327:12
eripuit *E. coelo fulmen* TURG 343:3
eripuitque *E. Jovi* MANI 227:1
err Man will e. GOET 152:8
most may e. DRYD 121:22
To e. is human POPE 267:16
erred e., and strayed from thy ways BOOK 59:12
error e. is immense BOLI 59:1
he is in e. LOCK 216:15
limit to infinite e. BREC 68:3
men are liable to e. LOCK 216:16
errors common e. of our life SIDN 316:16
E., like straws DRYD 121:27
reasoned e. HUXL 179:20
Esau E. my brother BIBL 34:35
E. selleth his birthright BIBL 34:34
hands are the hands of E. BIBL 35:1
escalier *esprit de l'e.* DIDE 116:12
escape e. my iambics CATU 89:10
Gluttony an emotional e. DE V 114:1
Let no guilty man e. GRAN 155:14
What struggle to e. KEAT 196:6
escaped e. with the skin of my teeth BIBL 38:3
Our soul is e. BOOK 64:24
escutcheon blot on the e. GRAY 156:3
espoused My fairest, my e. MILT 238:30
my late e. saint MILT 239:32
esprit *e. de l'escalier* DIDE 116:12
essence e. of a human soul CARL 85:21
e. of innumerable biographies CARL 85:4
precedes and rules e. SART 285:20
essenced long e. hair MACA 221:19
essential what is e. SAIN 284:9
estate fourth e. of the realm MACA 221:9
in mind, body, or e. BOOK 60:17
ordered their e. ALEX 4:15
estranging unplumbed, salt, e. sea ARNO 17:1
état *L'É. c'est moi* LOUI 219:1
eternal E. Father, strong to save WHIT 356:19
E. in man cannot kill BHAG 33:19
E. in man cannot kill UPAN 344:15
E. Passion ARNO 16:18
e. rocks beneath BRON 69:15
e. silence PASC 259:20
e. triangle ANON 8:1
Grant them e. rest MISS 241:4
Hope springs e. POPE 267:20
our e. home WATT 352:2
thy e. summer SHAK 310:4
whose e. Word MARR 229:1
eternities meeting of two e. THOR 339:13
eternity Deserts of vast e. MARV 229:21
E. is in love BLAK 56:27
E.'s a terrible thought STOP 326:13
E. shut in a span CRAS 106:12
E.'s sunrise BLAK 57:12
Heads Were toward E. DICK 115:27
pinprick of e. AURE 20:17
progress to e. SHAK 310:13
saw E. the other night VAUG 345:19
shadows of e. VAUG 345:15
Silence is deep as E. CARL 85:6
some conception of e. MANC 226:14
teacher affects e. ADAM 1:22
travellers of e. BASH 27:15
white radiance of E. SHEL 313:21
who love, time is e. VAN 345:10
without injuring e. THOR 339:11
etherized patient e. upon a table ELIO 128:28
ethic protestant e. WEBE 352:13

ethical e. dimension COOK 103:12
nuclear giants and e. infants BRAD 67:10
ethics law floats in a sea of e. WARR 351:2
E. change his skin BIBL 41:22
Eton playing-fields of E. ORWE 254:19
playing fields of E. WELL 354:8
étonne *É.-moi* DIAG 114:7
Etrurian where the E. shades MILT 237:25
Euclid E. alone has looked MILL 234:19
eunuch female e. GREE 157:5
strain, Time's e. HOPK 174:8
eunuchs seraglio of e. FOOT 139:2
euphoric In an e. dream AUDE 19:17
Eureka E.! [I've got it!] ARCH 14:16
Europe another war in E. BISM 55:10
at the centre of E. YUSH 370:7
corrupt as in E. JEFF 184:3
depravations of E. MATH 231:4
dogs of E. bark AUDE 19:3
E. a continent of energetic mongrels FISH 136:2
E. by her example PITT 263:21
E. of nations DE G 112:5
fifty years of E. TENN 333:33
glory of E. BURK 75:18
great stocks of E. YEAT 369:17
lamps are going out all over E. GREY 157:13
map of E. has been changed CHUR 94:22
part of the community of E. SALI 284:20
spectre is haunting E. MARX 230:11
take over the whole of E. RIDL 276:14
that's old E. RUMS 282:2
Whoever speaks of E. BISM 55:7
whole of E. NAPO 248:1
European policy of E. integration KOHL 204:16
eve fairest of her daughters E. MILT 238:23
From far, from e. HOUS 176:12
riverrun, past E. and Adam's JOYC 192:19
When Adam delved and E. span ROLL 279:1
even E. as you and I KIPL 203:3
evening e. and the morning BIBL 34:4
e. is spread out against the sky ELIO 128:28
e. star MILT 239:12
exhalation in the e. SHAK 296:11
It is a beauteous e. WORD 364:15
light of e., Lissadell YEAT 368:9
like an e. gone WATT 352:3
Some enchanted e. HAMM 160:20
event greatest e. it is FOX 140:14
hurries to the main e. HORA 174:17
eventide fast falls the e. LYTE 221:2
events course of human e. JEFF 183:17
E. cast their shadows CAMP 83:11
E., dear boy MACM 224:7
e. have controlled me LINC 215:2
opposition of e. MACM 224:7
ever For e. panting KEAT 196:10
To e. thing BIBL 39:10
evergreen e. tree SHER 315:10
everlasting e. arms BIBL 36:6
e. life BIBL 48:27
e. life BIBL 48:31
e. No CARL 85:20
everlastingness shoots of e. VAUG 345:16
evermore for e. BOOK 64:22
name liveth for e. ANON 11:6
name liveth for e. BIBL 42:28
every E. day, I am getting better COUÉ 104:15
To e. thing BIBL 39:10
everybody E. has won CARR 86:6
everyday science and e. life FRAN 142:6
Everyman E., I will go with thee ANON 8:2
everything against e. KENN 199:7
cannot all do e. LUCI 220:11
can't all do e. VIRG 347:24

everything (*cont.*)

chips with e.	WESK 354:16
E. is fitting	AURE 20:15
e. is in it	TALM 330:14
E. passes	ANON 12:19
e. that is the case	WITT 362:11
E. what it is	BUTL 79:2
Life, the Universe and E.	ADAM 1:13
Macaulay is of e.	MELB 232:7
robbed a man of e.	SOLZ 320:6
sans taste, sans e.	SHAK 290:15
smattering of e.	DICK 115:22

everywhere centre is e. ANON 9:22

Out of the e.	MACD 222:18
Water, water, e.	COLE 100:20

evidence before you have all the e. DOYL 121:3

circumstantial e.	THOR 339:8
e. of things not seen	BIBL 52:14

evil All partial e. POPE 267:25

axis of e.	BUSH 78:19
banality of e.	AREN 14:19
dark and e. days	INGR 180:19
days are e.	BIBL 51:18
deliver us from e.	MISS 240:24
Do e. in return	AUDE 19:16
do e., that good may come	BIBL 49:40
doing e. in return	SOCR 319:26
E., be thou my good	MILT 238:19
E. be to him who evil thinks	ANON 12:12
E. communications	BIBL 51:1
e. cradling	KORA 205:3
e. empire	REAG 274:7
e. is wrought	HOOD 172:24
e. manners live in brass	SHAK 296:16
e. thereof	BIBL 44:2
e. which I would not	BIBL 50:6
face of 'e.'	BURR 77:24
fear nae e.	BURN 77:14
find means of e.	MILT 237:14
for e. to triumph	BURK 76:10
God prepares e.	ANON 13:4
Good and e. shall not be held	KORA 205:18
he that doeth e.	BIBL 52:35
Hypocrisy, the only e.	MILT 238:17
knowing good and e.	BIBL 34:15
like great e.	CALL 82:19
means to fight an e.	DAWS 111:10
meet e.-willers	ELIZ 130:11
necessary e.	BRAD 67:7
necessary e.	PAIN 257:5
non-cooperation with e.	GAND 145:17
on the e. and on the good	BIBL 43:19
open and notorious e. liver	BOOK 60:23
perplexity of radical e.	AREN 14:20
punishment in itself is e.	BENT 31:7
Resist not e.	BIBL 43:17
return good for e.	VANB 345:3
root of all e.	BIBL 52:9
supernatural source of e.	CONR 102:28
unruly e.	BIBL 52:22

evils enamoured of existing e. BIER 54:19

expect new e.	BACO 22:31
greatest of e.	SHAW 311:24
least of e.	GRAC 154:18
make imaginary e.	GOLD 153:20
only by fighting e.	BERL 32:6

evolution E. . . . is—a change SPEN 321:8

Some call it e.	CARR 87:23

ewe one little e. lamb BIBL 36:36

tupping your white e.	SHAK 304:18

Ewig-Weibliche E. zieht uns hinan GOET 152:14

exact not to be e. BURK 75:6

writing an e. man	BACO 23:13

exactitude *L'e. est la politesse* LOUI 219:5

exaggerate e. the difference	SHAW 311:29
exaggerated have been greatly e.	TWAI 344:2
exaggeration e. is a truth	GIBR 149:12

exalted e. among the heathen BOOK 63:5

e. them of low degree	BIBL 46:33
valley shall be e.	BIBL 40:30

exalteth whosoever e. himself BIBL 47:23

examinations E. are formidable COLT 102:1

In e., those who do not wish	RALE 273:7

examine E. for a moment WOOL 363:18

example annoyance of a good e. TWAI 343:26

Europe by her e.	PITT 263:21
E. is always more efficacious	JOHN 187:20
E. is the school	BURK 76:2
set us a good e.	WILD 358:3

examples philosophy from e. DION 117:1

exceed e. his grasp BROW 71:20

excel thou shalt not e. BIBL 35:10

excellence in conformity with e. ARIS 15:13

excellent e. thing in woman SHAK 298:27

excelling all loves e. WESL 354:22

Excelsior strange device E. LONG 217:12

excelsis *Gloria in e.* MISS 240:18

except E. the Lord build BOOK 64:26

exception glad to make an e. MARX 230:4

excess e. of light GRAY 156:21

e. of stupidity	JOHN 188:17
Nothing in e.	ANON 13:3
poverty and e.	PENN 261:12
road of e.	BLAK 56:23

excessive e. bright MILT 238:16

exchange By just e. one for the other SIDN 316:11

excite e. my amorous propensities JOHN 188:4

excitement equal the e. GREE 156:25

excluded irrevocably e. SHEL 313:10

excrement in the place of e. YEAT 367:20

excursion make an e. to hell PRIE 270:22

excuse E. my dust PARK 259:1

make a good e.	SZAS 329:22

excuses Several e. HUXL 179:13

execute zealous Muslims to e. KHOM 199:23

execution stringent e. GRAN 155:13

executioner I am mine own E. DONN 119:21

executioners victims who respect their e. SART 285:25

executive salary of the chief e. GALB 145:3

executors Let's choose e. SHAK 305:29

exercise e. is to the body STEE 323:11

e. of his soul's faculties	ARIS 15:13
for cure, on e. depend	DRYD 122:3
love's proper e.	DAVI 110:20

exertions saved herself by her e. PITT 263:21

exhalation Like a bright e. SHAK 296:11

exile destined as an e. VIRG 346:19

die in e.	GREG 157:8
silence, e., and cunning	JOYC 193:2

exiled outlawed or e. MAGN 225:5

exiles Paradise of e. SHEL 313:28

exist didn't e. before UPDI 344:19

e. in order to save us	DE V 114:2
presumed to e.	OCCA 253:1

existence e. is but a brief crack NABO 247:17

e. of the Creator	MAIM 225:14
e. or when hope	AUST 21:5
E. precedes and rules	SART 285:20
purpose of human e.	JUNG 193:18
Struggle for E.	DARW 110:7
woman's whole e.	BYRO 80:24

existential crude e. malpractice FENT 134:16

existing bother of the e. HAWK 163:12

exists Everything e. FORS 139:17

exit E., pursued by a bear SHAK 309:19

exits men to take their exits WEBS 352:23

ex-parrot THIS IS AN E. — MONT 243:14
expect E. nothing — WALK 349:8
expectations revolution of rising e. — CLEV 98:7
expects England e. — NELS 249:8
Nobody e. — MONT 243:15
expediency be sacrificed to e. — MAUG 231:8
E. asks the question — KING 200:19
expedient e. for us — BIBL 49:1
most e. for them — BOOK 60:6
expedit E. esse deos — OVID 255:24
expelles Naturam e. furca — HORA 174:26
expenditure annual e. nineteen — DICK 114:19
E. rises to meet income — PARK 259:11
expense at the e. of two — CLOU 98:16
e. damnable — CHES 92:24
e. of spirit — SHAK 310:24
sanctifies e. — POPE 266:29
expenses facts are on e. — STOP 326:11
expensive how e. it is to be poor — BALD 24:20
experience all e. is an arch — TENN 335:3
can go beyond his e. — LOCK 216:14
E. has taught — TACI 330:4
e. is an arch — ADAM 1:19
E. is never limited — JAME 182:19
E. is the name — WILD 358:22
e. is what you get — SEEG 288:9
light which e. gives — COLE 101:7
never had much e. — MARQ 228:21
part of e. — BACO 23:15
refuted by e. — POPP 268:26
triumph of hope over e. — JOHN 189:1
trying every e. once — ANON 12:8
we need not e. it — FRIS 143:2
experiences lie the e. of our life — MANN 227:6
experiencing only by e. it — PROU 271:10
experiment e. is the best test — FARA 133:21
e. needs statistics — RUTH 283:19
have them fit e. — DIRA 117:2
never tried an e. — DARW 110:14
social and economic e. — HOOV 173:3
tide of successful e. — JEFF 184:6
experimental e. reasoning — HUME 178:5
expert e. is one who knows more and more — BUTL 79:4
e. is someone who knows — HEIS 165:11
experto E. credite — VIRG 347:19
experts never trust e. — SALI 284:19
explain e. his explanation — BYRO 80:20
e. man to man — STEI 323:13
e. why it didn't happen — CHUR 96:8
Never complain and never e. — DISR 118:8
Never e. — FISH 136:4
Never e. — HUBB 177:7
explained Shut up he e. — LARD 208:12
explaining forever e. things — SAIN 284:8
explanation saves tons of e. — SAKI 284:14
expletive E. deleted — ANON 8:3
exploring end of all our e. — ELIO 128:15
express e. our wants — GOLD 153:19
e. yourself like — YEAT 369:18
Never e. yourself more — BOHR 58:18
expressed ne'er so well e. — POPE 267:9
expression conventional e. — MAHA 225:7
E. is the dress — POPE 267:10
impassioned e. — WORD 366:20
extend attempt to e. their system — MONR 242:8
exterminate E. all the brutes — CONR 102:22
extinction one generation from e. — CARE 84:20
extra add some e., just for you — LARK 208:21
extraordinary e. man — JOHN 190:17
extremism e. in the defence of liberty — GOLD 153:29
exuberance E. is beauty — BLAK 57:5
irrational e. — GREE 157:3
exultations e., agonies — WORD 366:14

eye apple of his e. — BIBL 36:5
beam that is in thine own e. — BIBL 44:4
Cast a cold e. — YEAT 369:12
cast a longing e. — JEFF 184:4
close one e. — DOUG 120:5
custom loathsome to the e. — JAME 182:9
day's garish e. — MILT 236:15
e. for eye — BIBL 35:29
e. of a needle — BIBL 45:19
Green E. — HAYE 164:2
had but one e. — DICK 115:9
harvest of a quiet e. — WORD 365:15
If thine e. offend thee — BIBL 45:14
In my mind's e. — SHAK 291:24
in the twinkling of an e. — BIBL 51:3
language in her e. — SHAK 308:14
like a joyless e. — SHEL 315:1
man a microscopic e. — POPE 267:22
mild and magnificent e. — BROW 72:13
neither e. to see — LENT 213:1
one e. is weeping — FROS 143:8
see e. to eye — BIBL 41:8
soft black e. — MOOR 244:12
to the e. of God — OLIV 253:9
unforgiving e. — SHER 315:17
with his glittering e. — COLE 100:15
with, not through, the e. — BLAK 56:17
eyeball e. to eyeball — RUSK 282:10
eyeless E. in Gaza — MILT 239:21
eyelids tired e. upon tired eyes — TENN 333:34
eyes all e. else dead coals — SHAK 309:29
And her e. were wild — KEAT 195:25
chewing gum for the e. — ANON 11.2
Closed his e. — GRAY 156:21
cold commemorative e. — ROSS 280:21
cynosure of neighbouring e. — MILT 236:22
death bandaged my e. — BROW 72:27
drew his e. along — AUGU 20:2
electrical skin and glaring e. — SMAR 317:18
ever more perfect e. — TEIL 331:10
e. are oddly made — HAMM 160:25
e. have all the seeming — POE 265:21
e. have they, and see not — BOOK 64:15
e. of Caligula — MITT 241:18
e. to wonder — SHAK 310:18
Get thee glass e. — SHAK 298:18
Hath not a Jew e. — SHAK 302:21
King of England's e. — TYND 344:8
Love looks not with the e. — SHAK 303:9
marvellous in our e. — BOOK 64:18
Mine e. have seen — HOWE 177:2
My mistress' e. — SHAK 310:25
night has a thousand e. — BOUR 66:11
Night hath a thousand e. — LYLY 220:23
Smoke gets in your e. — HARB 161:5
Stars scribble on our e. — CRAN 106:8
tempts your wand'ring e. — GRAY 156:20
through another man's e. — SHAK 290:24
why the good Lord made your e. — LEHR 211:19
will lift mine e. — SCOT 288:4
with his half-shut e. — POPE 268:21
with thine e. — JONS 192:2

F

faber F. est suae — CLAU 97:9
Fabians good man fallen among F. — LENI 212:11
fables f. in the legend — BACO 22:11
profane and old wives' f. — BIBL 52:6
fabula F. narratur — HORA 175:21
fac Dilige et quod vis f. — AUGU 20:8

face accustomed to her f. — LERN 213:7
construction in the f. — SHAK 299:20
covered his f. — BIBL 40:8
Cover her f. — WEBS 352:24
f. of Agamemnon — SCHL 286:13
f. of 'evil' — BURR 77:24
f. so pleased my mind — ANON 11:7
fall flat on your f. — THUR 340:3
False f. must hide — SHAK 300:10
garden in her f. — CAMP 83:14
has the f. he deserves — ORWE 255:9
hides a smiling f. — COWP 105:19
honest, sonsie f. — BURN 77:17
I am the family f. — HARD 162:3
in the public's f. — RUSK 282:11
keep your f. — CART 88:9
Look in my f. — ROSS 280:20
Lord make his f. shine — BIBL 35:35
mask that eats into the f. — UPDI 344:17
men stand f. to face — KIPL 201:17
mist in my f. — BROW 72:26
never forget a f. — MARX 230:4
night's starred f. — KEAT 197:7
painted her f. — BIBL 37:28
Pity a human f. — BLAK 57:17
shining morning f. — SHAK 290:12
sing in the robber's f. — JUVE 194:10
socialism would not lose its human f. — DUBČ 122:24
spirit passed before my f. — BIBL 37:38
stamping on a human f. — ORWE 255:1
touched the f. of God — MAGE 225:3
unacceptable f. of capitalism — HEAT 164:15
Was this the f. — MARL 228:7
whole life shows in your f. — BACA 21:21
your f. burns and tickles — FROS 143:8
Your f., my thane — SHAK 299:25
faces Coming with vivid f. — YEAT 368:2
f. are but a gallery — BACO 22:23
grind the f. of the poor — BIBL 40:6
old familiar f. — LAMB 207:5
Private f. in public places — AUDE 19:12
red f., and loose hair — EQUI 132:30
facilis F. descensus Averno — VIRG 347:11
fact irritable reaching after f. — KEAT 197:11
ugly f. — HUXL 179:16
faction Liberty is to f. — MADI 224:19
whisper of a f. — RUSS 283:15
facts built up of f. — POIN 266:1
f. are on expenses — STOP 326:11
f. are sacred — SCOT 287:2
f. when you come to brass tacks — ELIO 129:14
Get your f. first — TWAI 344:3
give you all the f. — AUDE 19:19
imagination for his f. — SHER 315:20
number of empirical f. — EINS 126:12
what I want is, F. — DICK 115:2
faculties exercise of his soul's f. — ARIS 15:13
f. of men — MADI 225:1
fade f. into the light — WORD 365:7
Than to f. away — YOUN 370:6
They simply f. away — FOLE 138:20
faery f. lands forlorn — KEAT 196:23
f.'s child — KEAT 195:25
fail F. better — BECK 28:18
F. not our feast — SHAK 300:29
shall not flag or f. — CHUR 95:9
we'll not f. — SHAK 300:8
failed f. in literature and art — DISR 117:28
f. much — STEV 325:9
fails One sure, if another f. — BROW 73:3
failure f.'s no success at all — DYLA 124:8
Now we are not a f. — VANZ 345:12
political lives end in f. — POWE 270:15

tragic f. — ELIO 127:13
fain F. would I climb — RALE 273:2
faint F., yet pursuing — BIBL 36:14
reap, if we f. not — BIBL 51:14
walk, and not f. — BIBL 41:4
with f. praises — WYCH 367:5
fainted should utterly have f. — BOOK 62:18
fair anything to show more f. — WORD 364:10
British f. play — AITK 4:3
deserves the f. — DRYD 121:24
dream of f. women — TENN 332:4
f. as is the rose — CHAU 92:1
F. is foul — SHAK 299:8
F. stood the wind — DRAY 121:13
f. white linen cloth — BOOK 60:24
I have sworn thee f. — SHAK 310:30
not f. to outward view — COLE 99:19
Sabrina f. — MILT 236:10
she be f. — KEAT 196:8
So foul and f. a day — SHAK 299:12
sweet and f. she seems — WALL 349:17
thou art f., my love — BIBL 39:35
With you f. maid — ANON 9:1
fairest F. Isle — DRYD 122:6
f. of creation — MILT 239:7
From f. creatures — SHAK 310:2
Who is the f. of them all — GRIM 157:15
fairies beginning of f. — BARR 26:21
don't believe in f. — BARR 27:1
Do you believe in f. — BARR 27:3
f. at the bottom of our garden — FYLE 144:20
f. left off dancing — SELD 288:14
f.' midwife — SHAK 306:23
rewards and F. — CORB 104:3
fairness profound step of f. — RIEL 276:15
fairy believes it was a f. — AUBR 18:11
cradle of the f. queen — SHAK 303:25
f. when she's forty — HENL 166:7
Like f. gifts fading — MOOR 244:6
'tis almost f. time — SHAK 304:4
faith Catholic F. — BOOK 60:9
do very little with f. — BUTL 79:18
f. as a grain of mustard seed — BIBL 45:11
f. hath made thee whole — BIBL 44:22
f. is the state — TILL 340:12
F. is the substance — BIBL 52:21
F. of our Fathers — FABE 133:13
f. shines equal — BRON 69:13
f. unfaithful — TENN 332:14
f. without doubt — UNAM 344:11
F. without works — BIBL 52:21
first article of my f. — GAND 145:16
good fight of f. — BIBL 52:10
kept the f. — BIBL 52:11
Let us have f. — LINC 214:15
more f. in honest doubt — TENN 333:6
O thou of little f. — BIBL 45:5
Sea of F. — ARNO 16:11
though I have all f. — BIBL 50:22
What of the f. — HARD 162:5
work of f. — BIBL 52:2
faithful Ever f., ever sure — MILT 236:26
f. and just to me — SHAK 297:3
f. in that which is least — BIBL 47:36
f. to thee, Cynara — DOWS 120:10
f. unto death — BIBL 53:3
good and f. servant — BIBL 46:4
mentally f. to himself — PAIN 257:2
O come, all ye f. — ANON 13:5
So f. in love — SCOT 287:18
faithfulness Great is thy f. — CHIS 94:4
faithless Human on my f. arm — AUDE 19:8
falcon dapple-dawn-drawn F. — HOPK 174:9

f., towering in her pride	SHAK 300:28	**family** f. firm	GEOR 148:4
Gentle as f.	SKEL 317:14	f.—that dear octopus	SMIT 318:10
falconer O! for a f.'s voice	SHAK 306:34	have a young f.	FOWL 140:13
Falklands F. thing was a fight	BORG 65:22	I am the f. face	HARD 162:3
fall and half to f.	POPE 267:28	running of a f.	MONT 242:21
by dividing we f.	DICK 116:9	Selling off the f. silver	MACM 224:6
f. flat on your face	THUR 340:3	spend more time with f.	THAT 337:1
f. in love today	GERS 148:7	**famine** They that die by f.	HENR 166:19
f. into it	BIBL 39:22	**famous** by that time I was too f.	BENC 30:10
f. into the hands	BIBL 52:13	f. for fifteen minutes	WARH 350:20
fear no f.	BUNY 74:16	f. men have the whole earth	PERI 262:2
further they have to f.	FITZ 137:18	f. without ability	SHAW 311:15
hard rain's a gonna f.	DYLA 124:4	found myself f.	BYRO 81:30
it had a dying f.	SHAK 308:18	praise f. men	BIBL 42:27
Life is a horizontal f.	COCT 99:6	'twas a f. victory	SOUT 320:19
O! what a f. was there	SHAK 297:7	world f.	RICH 276:12
Things f. apart	YEAT 369:1	**fan** state of the football f.	HORN 175:26
yet I fear to f.	RALE 273:2	**fanaticism** f. consists in	SANT 285:12
fallacy Pathetic F.	RUSK 282:14	**fanatics** F. have their dreams	KEAT 195:18
fallen Babylon is f.	BIBL 53:15	**fancies** heart of furious f.	ANON 12:5
Christopher Robin has f.	MORT 246:6	**fancy** keep your f. free	HOUS 176:8
F. cold and dead	WHIT 356:24	let the f. roam	KEAT 195:19
f. from grace	BIBL 51:11	where is f. bred	SHAK 302:25
f. from heaven	BIBL 40:19	young man's f.	TENN 333:22
f. into the midst of it	BOOK 63:11	**fantasies** fed the heart on f.	YEAT 368:19
good man f. among Fabians	LENI 212:11	**fantastic** light f. round	MILT 236:4
how are the mighty f.	BIBL 36:32	light f. toe	MILT 236:20
How are the mighty f.	BIBL 36:35	**fantasy** live in a f. world	MURD 247:7
lot is f. unto me	BOOK 62:10	Most modern f.	PRAT 270:19
planets had f. on me	TRUM 342:9	**far** F. and few	LEAR 210:12
falleth where the tree f.	BIBL 39:26	f., far better thing	DICK 115:24
falling catch a f. star	DONN 119:14	F. from the madding crowd's	GRAY 156:14
'f. domino' principle	EISE 126:17	f. side of despair	SART 286:21
t. sickness	SHAK 296:21	going a bridge too f.	BROW 71:19
fallings F. from us, vanishings	WORD 365:8	good news from a f. country	BIBL 38:37
falls F. the Shadow	ELIO 128:23	hills and f. away	GAY 147:1
false bear f. witness	BIBL 35:28	How f. is	KIPL 202:23
Beware of f. prophets	BIBL 44:11	Mexico, so f. from God	DIAZ 114:10
F. face must hide	SHAK 300:10	much too f. out all my life	SMIT 319:3
f., fleeting, perjured	SHAK 306:11	quarrel in a f. away country	CHAM 90:4
f. sincere	POPE 267:1	so near and yet so f.	TENN 333:7
f. to any man	SHAK 291:31	unhappy, f.-off things	WORD 366:6
f. to others	BACO 23:20	**farce** f. is played out	RABE 272:14
philosopher, as equally f.	GIBB 148:13	second as f.	MARX 230:7
Ring out the f.	TENN 333:9	second time as f.	BARN 26:17
falsehood express lying or f.	SWIF 328:12	**farewell** Ae f., and then for ever	BURN 76:17
Let her and F. grapple	MILT 240:10	F.! a long farewell	SHAK 296:12
falsehoods f. which interest dictates	JOHN 187:4	f. content	SHAK 305:5
falseness pleasure in proving their f.	DARW 110:4	f., he is gon	CHAU 91:23
produce in us a f.	RUSK 282:14	F., my friends	DUNC 123:9
Falstaff F. sweats to death	SHAK 294:18	F., rewards	CORB 104:3
falter not the time to f.	BLAI 56:4	Too-late, F.	ROSS 280:20
fame best f. is a writer's fame	LEBO 211:5	**farm** down on the f.	LEWI 214:4
blush to find it f.	POPE 268:12	**farmers** embattled f. stood	EMER 131:20
damned to F.	POPE 266:6	**farrow** old sow that eats her f.	JOYC 192:26
F. is like a river	BACO 23:3	**fart** can't f. and chew gum	JOHN 186:12
F. is the spur	MILT 236:30	forgot the f.	ELIZ 130:20
love and f.	KEAT 197:8	Love is the f.	SUCK 327:7
Man dreams of f.	TENN 332:18	**farthest** F. Thule	VIRG 348:1
nor yet a fool to f.	POPE 266:17	**farthing** f. candle to the sun	YOUN 369:25
Physicians of the Utmost F.	BELL 29:18	**farthings** sold for two f.	BIBL 47:19
to f. unknown	GRAY 156:15	**fascinates** I like work: it f. me	JERO 185:6
fames Aura sacra f.	VIRG 347:6	**fascination** f. frantic	GILB 150:11
familiar f. friend	BOOK 62:26	f. of what's difficult	YEAT 368:6
mine own f. friend	BOOK 63:10	**Fascist** Every woman adores a F.	PLAT 264:13
old f. faces	LAMB 207:5	**fashion** f. a gentleman	SPEN 321:23
familiarity F. breeds contempt	TWAI 343:19	glass of f.	SHAK 293:2
families American f. more like	BUSH 78:15	in my f.	DOWS 120:10
best-regulated f.	DICK 114:23	in my f.	PORT 268:28
f. in a country village	AUST 21:13	**fashioned** F. so slenderly	HOOD 172:18
f. last not three oaks	BROW 71:7	**fashions** fit this year's f.	HELL 165:16
happy f. resemble	TOLS 341:3	**fast** at least twice as f.	CARR 86:26
there are f.	THAT 336:22	come he f.	SCOT 287:16

fast (*cont.*)
grew f. and furious — BURN 77:15
none so f. as stroke — COKE 99:12
Snip! They go so f. — HOFF 171:9
faster F. than a speeding bullet — ANON 8:5
good deal f. — CARR 86:8
fastest travels the f. — KIPL 202:14
fasting die f. — FRAN 141:20
Thank heaven, f. — SHAK 290:22
fat Butter merely makes us f. — GOER 152:6
f. and long-haired — PLUT 265:11
f. friend — BRUM 73:10
f. greedy owl — RICH 276:8
F. is a feminist issue — ORBA 254:1
f. of others' works — BURT 78:1
f. of the land — BIBL 35:9
f. white woman — CORN 104:8
in every f. man — CONN 102:18
men about me that are f. — SHAK 296:20
should himself be f. — JOHN 190:18
thin man inside every f. man — ORWE 254:13
fatal deal of it is absolutely f. — WILD 358:17
f. bellman — SHAK 300:14
f. to true happiness — RUSS 283:1
Our f. shadows — FLET 138:12
fate Art a revolt against f. — MALR 226:11
character is his f. — HERA 167:4
F. and character — NOVA 252:7
F. cannot harm me — SMIT 319:13
F. is not an eagle — BOWE 66:13
f. of a nation — LONG 218:7
f. of this country — DISR 117:14
f. of unborn millions — WASH 351:5
f. wilfully misunderstand me — FROS 143:9
fears his f. too much — MONT 243:11
heart for any f. — LONG 217:22
master of his f. — TENN 332:15
master of my f. — HENL 166:9
no f. that cannot be — CAMU 83:18
smile of f. — DYER 124:1
take a bond of f. — SHAK 301:16
thy f. shall overtake — KING 200:9
when f. summons — DRYD 122:7
father about my F.'s business — BIBL 47:7
cometh unto the f. — BIBL 49:5
Eternal F., strong to save — WHIT 356:19
f. had an accident there — POTT 269:12
F., hear the prayer — WILL 360:19
F.-like, he tends — LYTE 221:5
f. of English criticism — JOHN 187:9
f. of many nations — BIBL 49:42
f. of the Man — WORD 365:1
F. which is in heaven — BIBL 43:20
glad f. — BIBL 38:19
Glory be to the F. — BOOK 59:16
God the F. Almighty — BOOK 61:3
have God for his f. — CYPR 109:2
Honour thy f. and thy mother — BIBL 35:28
In my F.'s house — BIBL 49:4
last see your f. — YEAM 367:10
Lloyd George knew my f. — ANON 9:14
Lord and F. of mankind — WHIT 357:14
Muhammad is not the f. — KORA 205:17
My f. feeds his flocks — HOME 172:7
my f. or my mother — STER 324:8
My f. wept — BLAK 57:25
No more like my f. — SHAK 291:20
O, f. forsaken — JOYC 193:9
only begotten of the f. — BIBL 48:19
Our F. — BIBL 43:22
politique f. — JAME 182:12
resembled My f. as he slept — SHAK 300:15
sash my f. wore — ANON 11:3

shall a man leave his f. — BIBL 34:13
when my f. died — SHAK 293:33
will say unto him, F. — BIBL 47:31
wise f. that knows — SHAK 302:16
wish was f., Harry — SHAK 295:7
without f. bred — MILT 236:11
You are old, F. William — CARR 86:7
fatherly commend to thy f. goodness — BOOK 60:17
fathers because our f. lied — KIPL 201:19
Faith of our F. — FABE 133:13
f., provoke not — BIBL 51:19
Founding F. — RICE 275:16
God of our f. — SIDD 316:7
He f.-forth whose beauty — HOPK 174:2
I am going to my F. — BUNY 74:18
land of my f. — JAME 182:15
My f. can have it — THOM 338:5
sins of the f. — BOOK 60:26
Victory has a hundred f. — CIAN 96:12
years ago our f. brought forth — LINC 214:20
Father William You are old, F. — SOUT 320:21
fathom Full f. five — SHAK 307:23
fathoms fifty f. deep — BALL 25:18
fatted f. calf — BIBL 47:32
fattening illegal, immoral, or f. — WOOL 364:5
fault artist is his own f. — O'HA 253:3
most grievous f. — MISS 240:16
no kind of f. or flaw — GILB 149:17
O happy f. — MISS 241:7
soul is without f. — RIMB 277:4
think it is their f. — BROO 70:4
faultless Faultily f. — TENN 334:3
f. piece to see — POPE 267:8
faults England, with all thy f. — COWP 105:26
f. a little blind — PRIO 270:23
fill you with the f. they had — LARK 208:21
rise to f. — POPE 267:5
With all her f. — CHUR 94:15
faune *après-midi d'un f.* — MALL 226:5
favilla *Solvet saeclum in f.* — MISS 241:5
favour truths being in and out of f. — FROS 143:10
favoured Hail, thou that art highly f. — BIBL 46:31
fay F. *ce que vouldras* — RABE 272:12
fear begins in f. — COLE 101:6
by means of pity and f. — ARIS 15:15
f. and trembling — BIBL 51:23
F. God — BIBL 39:30
F. God — BIBL 52:27
f. in a handful of dust — ELIO 129:19
F. is the foundation — ADAM 2:11
F. is the main source — RUSS 283:12
f. made manifest — EDDY 125:1
f. my name — BIBL 42:17
f. no evil — BOOK 62:15
f. no fall — BUNY 74:16
f. of the Law — JOYC 192:20
f. of the Lord — BIBL 40:16
f. of the Lord — BOOK 64:12
f. those big words — JOYC 193:6
f. to negotiate — KENN 198:17
For f. of finding something worse — BELL 29:19
fourth is freedom from f. — ROOS 279:15
From hope and f. set free — SWIN 329:12
geometry of f. — READ 273:17
grief felt so like f. — LEWI 213:16
hate that which we often f. — SHAK 289:14
Life is first boredom, then f. — LARK 208:17
Men f. death — BACO 22:20
no hope without f. — SPIN 322:8
only thing we have to f. — ROOS 279:8
Our deepest f. is not — WILL 360:17
out of f. — DONN 119:10
robs the mind as f. — BURK 75:12

so long as they f. ACCI 1:3
There is no f. in love BIBL 52:33
those who f. life RUSS 283:4
too much joy or too much f. GRAV 155:16
travel in the direction of our f. BERR 32:18
feared prince to be f. MACH 223:8
fearful f. of the night WILL 360:9
f. symmetry BLAK 58:3
f. thing BIBL 52:13
f. trip is done WHIT 356:23
fearfully f. and wonderfully made BOOK 65:4
fearless F., blameless knight ANON 12:11
fears f. his fate too much MONT 243:11
f. may be liars CLOU 98:22
f. that I may cease to be KEAT 197:6
f. to speak of Ninety-Eight INGR 180:20
from sudden f. BYRO 81:16
griefs and f. BACO 23:1
man who f. the Lord BIBL 53:30
Present f. SHAK 299:17
tie up thy f. HERB 167:12
feast f. of languages SHAK 299:1
f. of reason POPE 268:5
going to a f. JONS 191:15
Paris is a movable f. HEMI 166:3
feasting dinner and f. PEPY 261:18
feather f.-footed through the plashy fen WAUG 352:8
f. in his cap ANON 12:6
f. on the breath of God HILD 169:1
f. to tickle LAMB 207:4
my each f. HUGH 177:16
feathers largest possible amount of f. COLB 99:17
federal Our F. Union JACK 181:11
federation F. of the world TENN 333:28
fee For a small f. in America SOND 320:10
gorgeous East in f. WORD 365:13
feeble help the f. up SHAK 308:1
Most forcible F. SHAK 295:4
o'ercomes the f. brain WINC 361:19
feed f. his flock BIBL 41:2
f. me in a green pasture BOOK 62:14
F. my sheep BIBL 49:19
f. on Death SHAK 310:29
will you still f. me LENN 212:23
feel f. it happen CATU 89:8
f. that he is dying CALI 82:13
f. what wretches feel SHAK 298:6
How does it f. CARL 85:1
making people f. good CHRÉ 94:9
tragedy to those that f. WALP 350:3
feeling formal f. comes DICK 115:25
Music is f., then STEV 324:20
objectification of f. LANG 207:17
feelings overflow of powerful f. WORD 366:19
feeling-toned f. complexes JUNG 193:16
fees answered, as they took their F. BELL 29:18
feet bathe those beauteous f. FLET 138:15
better to die on your f. IBAR 180:2
cutting off our f. SWIF 328:22
dust of your f. BIBL 44:26
f. beneath her petticoat SUCK 327:6
f. have they, and walk not BOOK 64:15
f. in ancient time BLAK 57:8
f. of him that bringeth BIBL 41:7
fog comes on little cat f. SAND 285:5
from his f. the Servants RIG 276:17
marching, charging f. JAGG 182:6
moon under her f. BIBL 53:11
My f. are still on the ground WINF 361:21
palms before my f. CHES 92:27
seven f. of English ground HARO 162:14
shoes from off thy f. BIBL 35:13
slipping underneath our f. FITZ 136:13

felicity Absent thee from f. SHAK 294:12
felix F. qui potuit rerum VIRG 348:3
O f. culpa MISS 241:7
fell At one f. swoop SHAK 301:20
f. among thieves BIBL 47:14
From morn to noon he f. MILT 238:1
It f. by itself JOHN 186:3
feller Sweetes' li'l' f. STAN 323:6
fellow loves his f-men HUNT 178:17
fellowship F. is heaven MORR 245:13
female f. eunuch GREE 157:5
f. heart can gold despise GRAY 156:19
f. of the species KIPL 202:2
male and the f. BIBL 34:28
no f. mind GILM 151:1
no f. Mozart PAGL 257:1
femina Dux f. facti VIRG 347:2
feminine 'f.' principles RODD 278:9
Taste is the f. FITZ 137:5
feminism discussions of f. FREN 142:14
feminist call me a f. WEST 355:14
Fat is a f. issue ORBA 254:1
femme Cherchez la f. DUMA 123:3
fen f. Of stagnant waters WORD 364:23
through the plashy f. WAUG 352:8
fence Don't f. me in PORT 266:11
tradition is a f. TALM 330:12
fences Good f. make good neighbours FROS 143:20
Fenian grave of a dead F. COLL 101:13
left us our F. dead PEAR 261:1
Fermanagh dreary steeples of F. CHUR 94:22
Fermat F.'s last theorem FERM 135:1
ferocious f. in battle COLL 101:14
fertile In such a fix to be so f. NASH 248:10
fester Lilies that f. SHAK 310:16
festina F. lente AUGU 20:13
fetters f. rent in twain DAVI 111:4
Milton wrote in f. BLAK 56:22
fever enigma of the f. chart ELIO 128:9
f. called 'Living' POE 265:16
f. of life is over NEWM 250:4
Février Janvier and F. NICH 251:1
few as grossly as the f. DRYD 121:22
Far and f. LEAR 210:12
f. are chosen BIBL 45:25
fit audience find, though f. MILT 238:33
Gey f. ANON 8:15
so much owed by so many to so f. CHUR 95:11
We few, we happy f. SHAK 295:29
fiat F. justitia FERD 134:18
F. justitia WATS 351:15
f. voluntas MISS 240:24
fickle Whatever is f., freckled HOPK 174:2
fiction best thing in f. WILD 359:5
continuous f. BEVA 33:12
f. is a necessity CHES 93:9
house of f. JAME 182:21
improbable f. SHAK 309:8
Poetry is the supreme f. STEV 324:17
sometimes f. MACA 221:18
Stranger than f. BYRO 81:10
That is what f. means WILD 358:10
fictions f. only and false hair HERB 167:16
fiddle important beyond all this f. MOOR 244:2
Fidele fair F.'s grassy tomb COLL 101:15
fideles Adeste, f. ANON 13:5
fidelity Your idea of f. RAPH 273:14
field comes and tills the f. TENN 334:29
corner of a foreign f. BROO 70:2
lay f. to field BIBL 40:7
lilies of the f. BIBL 43:26
not as simple as to cross a f. PAST 260:2
Not that fair f. Of Enna MILT 238:21

field (cont.)

only inhabitants of the f.	BURK 75:22
presence on the f.	WELL 354:4
single in the f.	WORD 366:5
What though the f. be lost	MILT 237:20
fields plough the f.	CAMP 83:6
fiend f. Flibbertigibbet	SHAK 298:8
f. hid in a cloud	BLAK 57:25
foul F.	BUNY 74:9
frightful f.	COLE 100:26
fierce as I raved and grew more f.	HERB 167:13
but little, she is f.	SHAK 303:29
F. as ten Furies	MILT 238:10
f. light which beats	TENN 332:9
F. was the wild billow	ANAT 6:10
fiery burning f. furnace	BIBL 42:5
throne was like the f. flame	BIBL 42:8
fife Thane of F. had a wife	SHAK 301:23
fifteen At the age of f.	JUNG 193:22
at the age of f.	WILS 361:8
famous for f. minutes	WARH 350:20
F. men on the dead man's chest	STEV 325:16
f. wild Decembers	BRON 69:14
old age always f. years older	BARU 27:8
fifth F. column	MOLA 241:22
fifty At f., everyone	ORWE 255:9
fig sewed f. leaves together	BIBL 34:16
fight begun to f.	JONE 191:9
don't want to f.	HUNT 178:15
f. against the future	GLAD 151:12
f. and fight again	GAIT 144:21
f. and not to heed the wounds	IGNA 180:12
f. for freedom and truth	IBSE 180:6
f. for its King and Country	GRAH 154:19
f. for the living	JONE 191:10
f. for what I believe in	CAST 88:11
f. in the way of God	KORA 204:21
f. in the way of God	KORA 205:9
f. it out on this line	GRAN 155:10
f. no more	JOSE 192:14
f. on the beaches	CHUR 95:9
f. on to the end	HAIG 159:5
F. the good fight	BIBL 52:10
F. the good fight	MONS 242:11
fought a good f.	BIBL 52:11
I will f.	SITT 317:12
never a moment ceased the f.	TENN 334:26
Never give up the f.	MARL 228:4
nor duty bade me f.	YEAT 368:12
no stomach to this f.	SHAK 295:26
peril in the f.	CORN 104:4
those who bade me f.	EWER 133:10
thought it wrong to f.	BELL 30:3
too proud to f.	WILS 361:11
Ulster will f.	CHUR 94:18
fighter f. not a quitter	MAND 226:20
I was ever a f.	BROW 72:27
fighting enemy we're f.	WALL 349:14
first-class f. man	KIPL 202:3
foremost f., fell	BYRO 80:6
What are WE f. for	SERV 289:1
figure f. that thou here seest	JONS 191:21
losing her f. or her face	CART 88:9
figures f. in words only	MURR 247:9
prove anything by f.	CARL 85:2
filigree f. hedges	WALP 349:18
fill Ah, f. the cup	FITZ 136:13
F. me with life anew	HATC 163:6
f. the hour	EMER 132:13
O f. me	MACN 224:11
filling f. the space	WEST 355:15
mind does not require f.	PLUT 265:10
filth identical, and so is f.	FORS 139:17

final f. solution	HEYD 168:12
finality F. is death	STEP 324:4
find do not f. anything pleasant	VOLT 348:6
f. it after many days	BIBL 39:25
returns home to f. it	MOOR 243:19
Run and f. out	KIPL 203:12
strive, to seek, to f.	TENN 335:8
thou shalt f. me	ANON 10:14
findeth f. his life	BIBL 44:30
finds he Who f. himself	ARNO 16:21
fine F. art is that	RUSK 282:20
f. romance with no kisses	FIEL 135:15
F. writing	KEAT 197:18
passage which is particularly f.	JOHN 189:4
very f. cat	JOHN 190:14
fine arts one of the f.	STEI 323:13
finem respice f.	ANON 13:17
finest f. hour	CHUR 95:10
finger God's f. touched him	TENN 333:5
moving f. writes	FITZ 136:16
my f. and my thumb	HEAN 164:11
One f. in the throat	OSLE 255:17
scratching of my f.	HUME 178:13
fingernails indifferent, paring his f.	JOYC 193:1
relatively clean f.	MORT 246:4
fingers cut their own f.	EDDI 124:23
dead men's f.	SHAK 294:1
finish f. the job	CHUR 95:12
Nice guys f. last	DURO 123:14
start together and f.	BEEC 28:23
start to the f.	HORA 175:23
finished f. in the first 100 days	KENN 198:18
f. my course	BIBL 52:11
It is f.	BIBL 49:14
world where England is f.	MILL 234:21
finite f. quantities	BERK 31:13
fire all compact of f.	SHAK 310:31
bound Upon a wheel of f.	SHAK 298:20
bush burned with f.	BIBL 35:12
chariot of f.	BLAK 57:8
coals of f.	BIBL 38:36
don't f. until you see	PUTN 272:4
faith and f. within us	HARD 162:5
Fell in the f.	GRAH 155:1
F. and fleet	BALL 25:12
f. and the rose are one	ELIO 128:18
f. in the head	JOHN 186:4
f. into the equations	HAWK 163:12
f. of my loins	NABO 247:14
f. that's in me now	BECK 28:8
f. to be lit	RABE 272:13
f. when you are ready	DEWE 114:6
gold shines like f.	PIND 263:12
he can f. everybody	WALT 350:15
I am f. and air	SHAK 289:29
kindles f.	LA R 209:9
light my f.	MORR 245:18
Lord was not in the f.	BIBL 37:14
nodding by the f.	YEAT 369:13
O! for a Muse of f.	SHAK 295:9
pale f. she snatches	SHAK 308:5
set a house on f.	BACO 23:21
shouted 'F.'	BELL 29:21
shouting f. in a theatre	HOLM 172:6
soul of f.	JOHN 187:25
spark o' Nature's f.	BURN 76:25
Thorough flood, thorough f.	SHAK 303:14
tongued with f.	ELIO 128:11
tongues like as of f.	BIBL 49:21
true love is a durable f.	RALE 273:1
wabbling back to the F.	KIPL 202:7
wind is to f.	BUSS 78:23
world will end in f.	FROS 143:15

youth of England are on f.   SHAK 295:13
firebrand Ye were as a f.   BIBL 42:13
fired f. the shot   BALL 25:9
firefly f. in the night   CROW 108:1
fires Big f. flare up   FRAN 141:11
fireside at his own f.   SHER 315:19
firm family f.   GEOR 148:4
firmament brave o'erhanging f.   SHAK 292:16
  f. sheweth his handy-work   BOOK 62:11
  spacious f.   ADDI 3:7
  streams in the f.   MARL 228:9
firmly F. I believe   NEWM 250:5
firmness f., and delight   WOTT 366:25
first Eclipse f.   O'KE 253:7
  F. and the Last   KORA 205:24
  f. article of my faith   GAND 145:16
  f. blow is half   GOLD 153:25
  f. fruits of them that slept   BIBL 50:28
  f. in a village   CAES 82:6
  f. in the hearts   LEE 211:13
  f. Kinnock in a thousand   KINN 201:14
  f. man   BIBL 51:2
  f. of human qualities   CHUR 96:3
  f. step that is difficult   DU D 122:27
  f. that ever burst   COLE 100:18
  for the f. time   ELIO 128:15
  last shall be f.   BIBL 45:21
  nothing should be done for the f. time   CORN 104:9
  no truck with f. impulses   MONT 243:10
  people who got there f.   USTI 344:21
  what to put first   PASC 259:17
firstborn smite all the f.   BIBL 35:20
fish f. and fishing   WALT 350:13
  F. are jumpin'   HEYW 168:14
  F. fiddle-de-dee   LEAR 210:18
  F. fuck in it   FIEL 135:20
  F. got to swim   HAMM 160:14
  f. that *talks*   DE L 112:11
  f. without a bicycle   STEI 324:1
  no f. ye're buying   SCOT 287:21
  surrounded by f.   BEVA 33:7
  What cat's averse to f.   GRAY 156:19
fishbone monument sticks like a f.   LOWE 220:4
fishers f. of men   BIBL 43:12
fishlike ancient and f. smell   SHAK 307:25
fit f. audience find   MILT 238:33
fittest Survival of the F.   DARW 110:8
  survival of the f.   SPEN 321:9
five At f. in the afternoon   LORC 218:16
  F. to one   MORR 245:17
  Full fathom f.   SHAK 307:23
  had f. thousand a year   THAC 336:8
  I have wedded f.   CHAU 91:28
  in a f.-pound note   LEAR 210:15
  she hadde f.   CHAU 91:20
  warming his f. wits   TENN 334:28
fix f. up his automobile   CLAR 97:8
fixed f. point in a changing age   DOYL 120:16
  great gulf f.   BIBL 48:2
flag allegiance to the f.   BELL 29:15
  High as a f.   HAMM 160:23
  keep the red f. flying   CONN 102:14
  national f.   SUMN 327:16
  people's f. is deepest red   CONN 102:13
  shall not f. or fail   CHUR 95:9
  spare your country's f.   WHIT 357:13
flame feed his sacred f.   COLE 100:13
  F.-capped, and shout   SHAW 313:8
  f. out like shining   HOPK 173:16
  hard, gemlike f.   PATE 260:8
  signals of the ancient f.   DANT 109:14
  spark of that ancient f.   VIRG 347:7
  tongues of f. are in-folded   ELIO 128:18

When a lovely f. dies   HARB 161:5
flames bursting into f.   MORR 245:16
  by her like thin f.   ROSS 280:19
  Commit it then to the f.   HUME 178:5
  f. in the forehead   MILT 237:2
Flanders brought him a F. mare   HENR 166:18
  In F. fields the poppies blow   MCCR 222:16
flashes f. of silence   SMIT 319:11
flashing His f. eyes   COLE 100:12
flat Very f., Norfolk   COWA 105:8
flats sharps and f.   BROW 72:22
flatter F. the mountain-tops   SHAK 310:8
flattered f. into virtue   SURT 327:19
flattering f., kissing and kicking   TRUM 342:10
  think him worth f.   SHAW 311:23
flattery Everyone likes f.   DISR 118:5
  paid with f.   JOHN 187:2
flaunting f., extravagant quean   SHER 315:16
flaw no kind of fault or f.   GILB 149:17
flaws Psychological f.   ANON 10:12
flax smoking f.   BIBL 41:5
  Three pounds of f.   MUMO 247:5
flayed saw a woman f.   SWIF 328:18
flea literature's performing f.   O'CA 252:19
  louse and a f.   JOHN 190:13
  naturalists observe, a f.   SWIF 329:2
fleas educated f. do it   PORT 269:3
  praised his f.   YEAT 369:8
flectere F. *si nequeo superos*   VIRG 347:16
fled F. is that music   KEAT 196:25
  I f. Him   THOM 338:14
flee f. away, and be at rest   BOOK 63:9
  f. from the wrath to come   BIBL 43:7
  f. when no man pursueth   BIBL 39:1
  They f. from me   WYAT 367:1
fleece f. was white as snow   HALE 159:16
  His forest f.   HOUS 176:10
fleet Fire and f.   BALL 25:12
  F. in which we serve   BOOK 65:8
  F. the time carelessly   SHAK 290:2
  in the Downs the f. was moored   GAY 147:7
  whole F.'s lit up   WOOD 363:16
fleets Ten thousand f.   BYRO 80:15
flesh All f. is grass   BIBL 41:1
  delicate white human f.   FIEL 135:12
  f., alas, is wearied   MALL 226:4
  f. and blood   BIBL 51:21
  f. and blood so cheap   HOOD 172:27
  f., and the devil   BOOK 60:12
  f. is as grass   BIBL 52:25
  f. is weak   BIBL 46:15
  F. of flesh   MILT 239:8
  f. of my flesh   BIBL 34:12
  F. perishes. I live on   HARD 162:3
  in my f. shall I see God   BIBL 38:4
  lusts of the f.   BOOK 61:18
  make your f. creep   DICK 115:19
  my heart and my f.   BOOK 63:18
  they shall be one f.   BIBL 34:13
  this too too solid f.   SHAK 291:15
  thorn in the f.   BIBL 51:10
  Word was made f.   BIBL 48:19
  word was made f.   MISS 241:3
fleshly all this f. dress   VAUG 345:16
flesh pots we sat by the f.   BIBL 35:23
flew and they f.   LOGU 217:4
Flibbertigibbet fiend F.   SHAK 298:8
flicker moment of my greatness f.   ELIO 129:1
flies As f. to wanton boys   SHAK 298:15
  catch small f.   SWIF 328:8
  joy as it f.   BLAK 57:12
fliest for thou f. Me   THOM 338:16
flight not attained by sudden f.   LONG 217:15

fling f. the ringleaders — ARNO 17:13
flirtation innocent f. — BYRO 81:6
float F. like a butterfly — ALI 5:7
floating f. bulwark of the island — BLAC 55:14
  his f. hair — COLE 100:12
floats She f., she hesitates — RACI 272:16
flock feed his f. — BIBL 41:2
  keeping watch over their f. — BIBL 47:2
  tainted wether of the f. — SHAK 302:28
flocks My father feeds his f. — HOME 172:7
  shepherds watched their f. — TATE 330:21
flog f. the rank and file — ARNO 17:13
flood taken at the f. — SHAK 297:15
  ten years before the f. — MARV 229:20
  Thorough f., thorough fire — SHAK 303:14
flooded STREETS F. — BENC 30:11
floods f. drown it — BIBL 40:3
floor fell upon the sanded f. — PAYN 260:18
floors Scuttling across the f. of silent seas — ELIO 128:32
Flora Tasting of F. — KEAT 196:17
Flores F. in the Azores — TENN 334:25
flourisheth f. as a flower — BOOK 64:3
flourishing f. like a green bay-tree — BOOK 62:24
flow blood must yet f. — JEFF 184:18
  F. gently, sweet Afton — BURN 76:18
flower as the f. of the field — BIBL 41:1
  cometh forth like a f. — BIBL 38:1
  drives the f. — THOM 337:20
  flourisheth as a f. — BOOK 64:3
  f. fadeth — BIBL 41:1
  f. of Scotland — WILL 360:18
  f. that once hath blown — FITZ 136:12
  f. thereof falleth — BIBL 52:25
  Full many a f. is born — GRAY 156:11
  Herself a fairer f. — MILT 238:21
  like the innocent f. — SHAK 299:26
  London, thou art the f. — ANON 9:15
  meanest f. that blows — WORD 365:10
  pluck this f., safety — SHAK 294:19
  seize the f. — BURN 77:12
  this same f. that smiles — HERR 168:5
flowerpots your damned f. — BROW 73:2
flowers cool-rooted f. — KEAT 196:26
  Ensnared with f. — MARV 229:16
  f. and fruits of love — BYRO 81:15
  F. in the garden — STEV 326:4
  F. of all hue — MILT 238:20
  f. of the forest — COCK 99:3
  f. of the forest — ELLI 131:9
  f. that bloom in the spring — GILB 150:9
  f. the tenderness of patient minds — OWEN 256:10
  hundred f. blossom — MAO 227:14
  no f., no leaves — HOOD 172:25
  other men's f. — MONT 243:4
  Where have all the f. gone — SEEG 288:8
flowing f. sea — CUNN 108:13
  f. with milk and honey — BIBL 35:14
flown birds are f. — CHAR 90:20
flows Everything f. — HERA 167:2
fluidity solid for f. — CHUR 95:3
flung f. himself from the room — LEAC 210:7
flute soft complaining f. — DRYD 122:12
fluttering F. and dancing — WORD 364:17
fly all things F. thee — THOM 338:16
  f. at one end — SWIF 329:5
  F. envious Time — MILT 237:12
  f. sat upon the axletree — BACO 23:19
  f. through the air — LEYB 214:7
  for I will f. to thee — KEAT 196:19
  long-legged f. upon the stream — YEAT 368:17
  man is not a f. — POPE 267:22
  noise of a f. — DONN 119:24
  said a spider to a f. — HOWI 177:4

show the f. the way out — WITT 362:9
small gilded f. Does lecher — SHAK 298:17
There interposed a F. — DICK 116:1
try to f. by those nets — JOYC 192:25
which way shall I f. — MILT 238:18
flying on the f. trapeze — LEYB 214:7
  time is f. — VIRG 348:4
flying-fishes f. play — KIPL 202:15
foam f. Of perilous seas — KEAT 196:23
  To Noroway o'er the f. — BALL 25:16
foaming f. with much blood — POWE 270:12
foe angry with my f. — BLAK 57:26
  erect and manly f. — CANN 84:8
  f. outstretched — BLAK 58:1
  furnace for your f. — SHAK 296:8
  open f. may prove a curse — GAY 147:5
  willing f. and sea room — ANON 12:4
  wish my deadly f. — BRET 68:13
fog f. and filthy air — SHAK 299:8
  f. comes on little cat feet — SAND 285:5
  F. in Channel — BROC 69:4
  f. in my throat — BROW 72:26
  f. or moonlight — CLAU 97:10
  f. that rubs its back — ELIO 128:30
foil shining from shook f. — HOPK 173:16
fold Do not f. — ANON 7:24
  f. to thy heart thy brother — WHIT 357:16
  like the wolf on the f. — BYRO 80:18
folding f. of the hands — BIBL 38:16
folds f. rippling — SUMN 327:16
folk all music is f. music — ARMS 16:6
  incest and f.-dancing — ANON 12:8
folks O yonge, fresshe f. — CHAU 92:6
  where the old f. stay — FOST 140:9
follies crimes, f., and misfortunes — GIBB 148:14
  f. a man regrets most — ROWL 281:15
follow F. me — BIBL 43:12
  F. The Gleam — TENN 334:9
  F. the van — COLL 101:12
  f. the worse — OVID 256:1
  I really had to f. them — LEDR 211:10
  Pay, pack, and f. — BURT 77:28
folly according to his f. — BIBL 38:38
  brood of f. — MILT 236:11
  f. and conceit — AUST 21:9
  f. of the wise — JOHN 190:24
  fool returneth to his f. — BIBL 38:39
  lovely woman stoops to f. — ELIO 129:29
  lovely woman stoops to f. — GOLD 153:27
  most loving mere f. — SHAK 290:17
  persist in his f. — BLAK 56:28
  shoot F. as it flies — POPE 267:19
  'Tis f. to be wise — GRAY 156:18
  usually ends in f. — COLE 101:6
fond grow too f. of it — LEE 211:16
  so f. of one another — SWIF 328:13
fondly F. do we hope — LINC 215:4
fondness habitual f. — WASH 351:9
fons aquae f. — HORA 175:25
  f. Bandusiae — HORA 175:16
food Continent have good f. — MIKE 233:24
  F. enough for a week — MERR 233:14
  give f. to the poor — CAMA 82:21
  music be the f. of love — SHAK 308:17
  problem is f. — DONL 118:17
  room and f. — MALT 226:13
  wholesome f. — SWIF 328:15
fool Answer a f. — BIBL 38:38
  burnt F.'s bandaged finger — KIPL 202:7
  Busy old f. — DONN 119:15
  every f. is not a poet — POPE 266:15
  f. all the people — LINC 215:8
  f. at forty — YOUN 369:23

f. at the other	SWIF 329:5	**foppery** f. of the world	SHAK 297:27
f. consistent	POPE 267:1	**for** F. ever panting	KEAT 196:10
f. hath said in his heart	BOOK 62:9	who is f. me	HILL 169:12
f. his whole life long	LUTH 220:20	**forasmuch** f. as without thee	BOOK 60:21
f . . . is a man who never tried	DARW 110:14	**forbearance** f. ceases to be a virtue	BURK 75:4
f. is happy	POPE 267:30	**forbid** f. them not	BIBL 46:29
f. lies here	KIPL 202:17	**forbidden** because it was f.	TWAI 343:21
f. returneth to his folly	BIBL 38:39	Everything not f.	WHIT 356:7
'F.,' said my Muse	SIDN 316:12	Of that f. tree	MILT 237:15
f.'s bauble, the mace	CROM 107:12	**force** every living f.	DOST 119:26
f. sees not the same tree	BLAK 56:26	F., and fraud	HOBB 170:20
f. there was	KIPL 203:3	f. that through the green	THOM 337:20
f. would persist	BLAK 56:28	more than our f.	BURK 75:26
greater f. to admire him	BOIL 58:19	motive f. impressed	NEWT 250:12
greatest f. may ask	COLT 102:1	no f. however great	WHEW 355:21
laughter of a f.	BIBL 39:15	Surprised by unjust f.	MILT 236:9
Love's not Time's f.	SHAK 310:22	Who overcomes By f.	MILT 237:29
Prove to me that you're no f.	RICE 276:3	**forces** f. impressed upon it	NEWT 250:11
smarts so little as a f.	POPE 266:16	**forcible** Most f. Feeble	SHAK 295:4
suspects himself a f.	YOUN 369:28	**forcibly** f. if we must	CLAY 97:13
They f. me	SHAK 293:14	**Ford** I am a F., not a Lincoln	FORD 139:6
Thou f.	BIBL 47:21	**forefathers** f. of the hamlet sleep	GRAY 156:8
to manage a f.	KIPL 203:22	Think of your f.	ADAM 2:12
wisest f. in Christendom	HENR 166:14	**forehead** Flames in the f.	MILT 237:2
foolery little f.	OXEN 256:17	**foreign** corner of a f. field	BROO 70:2
foolish Beware my f. heart	WASH 351:13	f. policy	COOK 103:12
f., fond old man	SHAK 298:21	into any f. wars	ROOS 279:13
Forgive our f. ways	WHIT 357:14	Life is a f. language	MORL 245:2
frantic boast and f. word	KIPL 202:22	nothing human f. to me	TERE 335:13
never said a f. thing	ROCH 278:4	past is a f. country	HART 163:3
No man was more f.	JOHN 190:5	portion of the f. world	WASH 351:7
These f. things	MARV 230:1	**foreigners** f. always spell better	TWAI 343:16
young and f.	YEAT 367:23	**Foreign Secretary** F. naked into the conference	
foolishness Mix a little f.	HORA 175:20		BEVA 33:11
unto the Greeks f.	BIBL 50:15	**forelock** occasion's f. watchful	MILT 239:15
fools all the f. in town	TWAI 343:8	**foremost** none who would be f.	MACA 222:1
flannelled f. at the wicket	KIPL 202:12	**forest** beasts of the f.	BOOK 64:4
F. are my theme	BYRO 81:11	behind it rose the f.	LONG 218:4
F.! For I also had my hour	CHES 92:27	Deep in the f.	RACI 272:18
f. go aimlessly	UPAN 344:14	Down in the f.	SIMP 317:8
f. rush in	POPE 267:18	flowers of the f.	COCK 99:3
f. said would happen	MELB 232:10	flowers of the f.	ELLI 131:9
f., the fools, the fools	PEAR 261:1	f. primeval	LONG 217:11
f., who came to scoff	GOLD 153:9	**forests** f. of the night	BLAK 58:3
I am two f.	DONN 119:18	**foretell** ability to f.	CHUR 96:8
kept from children and from f.	DRYD 122:9	**for ever** f. hold his peace	BOOK 61:25
let f. contest	POPE 267:32	mercy endureth f.	BOOK 64:30
millions mostly f.	CARL 85:15	**forget** Better by far you should f.	ROSS 280:15
money of f.	HOBB 170:14	do not thou f. me	ASTL 18:5
one half the world f.	JEFF 184:19	F. six counties	MORR 245:12
perish together as f.	KING 200:18	f. thee, O Jerusalem	BOOK 65:2
scarecrows of f.	HUXL 179:21	f. there ever was such a thing	WILS 361:15
suffer f. gladly	BIBL 51:8	forgive but do not f.	SZAS 329:19
this great stage of f.	SHAK 298:19	if thou wilt, f.	ROSS 280:17
virtue of f.	BACO 22:7	I sometimes f.	DISR 118:7
what f. these mortals be	SHAK 303:28	Lest we f.	KIPL 202:19
foot caught my f. in the mat	GROS 158:4	never f. a face	MARX 230:4
foot—f.—sloggin'	KIPL 201:18	Old men f.	SHAK 295:28
F.-in-the-grave young man	GILB 150:16	**forgetting** consist in merely f.	MAND 226:18
her f. was light	KEAT 195:25	f. is so long	NERU 249:12
I hold Creation in my f.	HUGH 177:16	F. those things	BIBL 51:24
Nay, her f. speaks	SHAK 308:14	memory against f.	KUND 206:6
sets f. upon a worm	COWP 106:3	sleep and a f.	WORD 365:6
silver f. in his mouth	RICH 276:7	world f.	POPE 266:13
football a matter of life and death	SHAN 311:4	**forgive** do not f. those murderers	WIES 357:23
F.? the beautiful game	PELÉ 261:8	do they f. them	WILD 359:4
owe to f.	CAMU 84:3	Father, f. them	BIBL 48:8
state of the f. fan	HORN 175:26	f. him	BIBL 45:16
footfalls F. echo in the memory	ELIO 128:1	F., O Lord, my little jokes	FROS 143:11
footman eternal F. hold my coat	ELIO 129:1	F. our foolish ways	WHIT 357:14
footnotes series of f. to Plato	WHIT 356:16	f. our friends	MEDI 232:2
footpath jog on the f.	SHAK 309:23	f. us our debts	BIBL 43:22
footprints F. on the sands	LONG 217:21	f. us our trespasses	BOOK 59:15

forgive (*cont.*)

f. wrongs darker than death	SHEL 314:16
Lord will f. me	CATH 89:1
to f. a wrong	ELEA 127:1
To f., divine	POPE 267:16
Wilt thou f. that sin	DONN 119:2
wise f. but do not forget	SZAS 329:19
forgiven f. everything	SHAW 312:17
Her sins are f.	BIBL 47:11
restored, f.	LYTE 221:4
forgiveness After such knowledge, what f.	ELIO 128:20
f. is a lovely idea	LEWI 213:17
forgot auld acquaintance be f.	BURN 76:19
by the world f.	POPE 266:13
f. the fart	ELIZ 130:20
just f. to duck	DEMP 112:22
proposed as things f.	POPE 267:17
forgotten been learned has been f.	SKIN 317:16
books undeservedly f.	AUDE 19:25
F. Army	MOUN 246:11
f. man at the bottom	ROOS 279:6
f. nothing and learnt nothing	DUMO 123:6
he himself had f. it	PALM 258:6
injury is much sooner f.	CHES 92:15
learnt nothing and f. nothing	TALL 330:9
not one of them is f.	BIBL 47:19
ruins of f. times	BROW 71:5
things one has f.	CANE 84:5
fork pick up mercury with a f.	LLOY 216:12
forked poor, bare, f. animal	SHAK 298:7
forks pursued it with f.	CARR 87:20
forlorn faery lands f.	KEAT 196:23
F.! the very word	KEAT 196:24
form find a f.	BECK 28:9
F. follows function	SULL 327:10
f. from off my door	POE 265:20
F. is emptiness	MAHĀ 225:9
F. remains	WORD 365:22
human f. divine	BLAK 58:5
formal f. feeling comes	DICK 115:25
formed perhaps it f. itself	RIG 276:16
small, but perfectly f.	COOP 103:17
former f. and the latter	BOOK 60:18
forms f. of government	POPE 267:32
forsaken never the righteous f.	BOOK 62:23
O, father f.	JOYC 193:9
primrose that f. dies	MILT 236:34
why hast thou f. me	BIBL 46:20
forsaking f. all other	BOOK 61:26
fort Hold the f.	BLIS 58:9
Hold the f.	SHER 315:23
fortissimo F. at last	MAHL 225:12
fortnight f. dead	ELIO 129:30
fortuna *Audentis F. iuvat*	VIRG 347:18
fortunate at best but f.	SOLO 320:5
fortune F. assists the brave	TERE 335:14
f.s sharpe adversitee	CHAU 92:3
hostages to f.	BACO 22:32
I am F.'s fool	SHAK 306:39
leads on to f.	SHAK 297:15
mother of good f.	CERV 89:22
possession of a good f.	AUST 21:6
rob a lady of her f.	FIEL 135:13
smith of his own f.	CLAU 97:9
to f. and to fame unknown	GRAY 156:15
You fools of f.	SHAK 308:3
forty at f., the judgement	FRAN 141:19
Every man over f.	SHAW 312:16
fairy when she's f.	HENL 166:7
fool at f.	YOUN 369:23
F. years on	BOWE 66:12
In f. minutes	SHAK 303:20
Knows it at f.	YOUN 369:28

Life begins at f.	PITK 263:19
Men at f.	JUST 194:3
miner, F.-niner	MONT 243:12
forty-three pass for f.	GILB 150:27
forward F., forward let us range	TENN 333:32
from this day f.	BOOK 61:27
look f. to posterity	BURK 75:15
looking f. to the past	OSBO 255:13
marched breast f.	BROW 71:21
nothing to look f. to	FROS 143:12
those behind cried 'F.!'	MACA 222:1
fossil Language is f. poetry	EMER 132:14
foster f.-child of silence	KEAT 196:5
fought f. against Sisera	BIBL 36:11
f. a good fight	BIBL 52:11
f. each other for	SOUT 320:18
to have f. well	COUB 104:14
foul f. Fiend	BUNY 74:9
f. is fair	SHAK 299:8
Murder most f.	SHAK 291:39
So f. and fair a day	SHAK 299:12
found awoke and f. me here	KEAT 195:27
f. a kingdom	MILT 239:17
f. my sheep which was lost	BIBL 47:28
was lost, and is f.	BIBL 47:33
When f., make a note	DICK 114:24
foundation Church's one f.	STON 326:8
f. of most governments	ADAM 2:11
f. of unyielding despair	RUSS 283:7
founded f. the Jewish state	HERZ 168:8
founding f. a bank	BREC 68:7
F. Fathers	RICE 275:16
fount f. whence honour springs	MARL 228:19
fountain f. of all goodness	BOOK 60:5
f. of honour	BACO 22:9
f. of the water of life	BIBL 53:24
f. sealed	BIBL 40:1
like a f. troubled	SHAK 307:14
four At the age of f.	USTI 344:22
F. lagging winters	SHAK 305:19
f.-legged friend	BROO 70:6
F. legs good	ORWE 254:9
say that two plus two make f.	ORWE 254:25
twice two be not f.	TURG 343:2
fourscore come to f. years	BOOK 63:23
fourteen first f. years	GREE 156:25
fourth f. estate of the realm	MACA 221:9
fowler snare of the f.	BOOK 64:24
fowls smale f. maken melodye	CHAU 91:12
fox Crazy like a f.	PERE 261:21
f. knows many things	ARCH 14:15
galloping after a f.	WILD 359:1
prince must be a f.	MACH 223:9
quick brown f.	ANON 10:13
sharp hot stink of f.	HUGH 177:17
foxes f. have a sincere interest	ELIO 127:10
f. have holes	BIBL 44:16
second to the f.	BERL 32:7
foxholes no atheists in the f.	CUMM 108:12
frabjous O f. day	CARR 86:24
fragments These f. I have shored	ELIO 130:2
frailty F., thy name is woman	SHAK 291:18
love's the noblest f.	DRYD 122:4
frame f. of adamant	JOHN 187:25
f. of the world	BERK 31:17
universal f.	BACO 22:11
framed f. and glazed	WALP 350:1
français *n'est pas f.*	RIVA 277:8
France better in F.	STER 324:6
between F. and England	JERR 185:8
F. has lost a battle	DE G 112:2
F. was long a despotism	CARL 85:13
stood the wind for F.	DRAY 121:13

vasty fields of F.   SHAK 295:10
frankincense f., and myrrh   BIBL 43:2
frantic fascination f.   GILB 150:11
frater *f., ave atque vale*   CATU 89:9
fraud Force, and f.   HOBB 170:20
freckled f. like a pard   KEAT 195:28
  Whatever is fickle, f.   HOPK 174:2
freckles curiosity, f., and doubt   PARK 258:12
  In those f.   SHAK 303:15
Fred Here lies F.   ANON 8:14
free as soon write f. verse   FROS 144:3
  be perfectly f.   SPEN 321:14
  best things in life are f.   DE S 113:18
  born f.   ANON 7:7
  but it's f.   KRIS 206:2
  Church shall be f.   MAGN 225:4
  Comment is f.   SCOT 287:2
  condemned to be f.   SART 285:21
  Ev'rything f. in America   SOND 320:10
  favours f. speech   BROU 70:12
  f. again   SOLZ 320:6
  f. agent   AURE 20:18
  f. as nature first made man   DRYD 122:2
  f. church   CAVO 89:15
  freedom to the f.   LINC 214:19
  f. man, an American   JOHN 186:5
  f. society is a society where   STEV 325:4
  Greece might still be f.   BYRO 81:1
  half f.   LINC 214:13
  I am a f. man   MCGO 223:4
  I am not f.   DEBS 111:15
  ignorant and f.   JEFF 184:16
  in chains than to be f.   KAFK 194:16
  land of the f.   KEY 199:17
  Man was born f.   ROUS 281:9
  Mother of the F.   BENS 31:3
  No f. man shall be taken   MAGN 225:5
  protection of f. speech   HOLM 172:6
  should themselves be f.   BROO 69:18
  so far kept us f.   JEFF 184:6
  Teach the f. man   AUDE 19:6
  that moment they are f.   COWP 105:25
  Thou art f.   ARNO 16:22
  Thought is f.   SHAK 307:27
  truth makes men f.   AGAR 3:22
  truth shall make you f.   BIBL 48:35
  Was he f.   AUDE 19:22
  We must be f. or die   WORD 364:16
  Who would be f.   BYRO 80:2
freedom abridging the f. of speech   CONS 103:7
  better organised than f.   PÉGU 261:7
  But what is F.   COLE 99:18
  cause of F.   BOWL 67:2
  depends on f. of the press   JEFF 183:19
  fight for f. and truth   IBSE 180:6
  first is f. of speech   ROOS 279:15
  for human f.   SPEN 321:13
  f. alone that we fight   ANON 10:22
  F. and slavery are mental states   GAND 145:15
  F. and Whisky   BURN 76:21
  f. depends on being courageous   THUC 339:26
  f. for the one who thinks differently   LUXE 220:21
  f. for the pike   TAWN 330:22
  F. hunted   PAIN 257:8
  f. is a noble thing   BARB 26:10
  F. is slavery   ORWE 254:22
  f. is something   BALD 24:21
  F. is the freedom to say   ORWE 254:25
  f. of person   JEFF 184:8
  f. of speech   TWAI 343:11
  F. of the press guaranteed   LIEB 214:9
  F. of the press in Britain   SWAF 328:4
  f. of the press's speech   TWAI 343:17

F.'s just another word   KRIS 206:2
f. to offend   RUSH 282:7
f. to the slave   LINC 214:19
gave my life for f.   EWER 133:10
green f. of a cockatoo   STEV 324:23
it means f.   RUSH 282:9
Let f. ring   SMIT 319:1
no easy walk-over to f.   NEHR 249:3
peace from f.   MALC 226:3
Perfect f. is reserved   COLL 101:10
preserve and enlarge f.   LOCK 216:18
riches and f.   WALE 349:6
road toward f.   MORR 245:20
there can be no f.   LENI 212:7
freedoms four essential human f.   ROOS 279:15
freeing f. some   LINC 214:18
freely F. ye have received   BIBL 44:25
freemen rule o'er f.   BROO 69:18
freeze f. my humanity   MACN 224:11
frei *Arbeit macht f.*   ANON 12:20
French F. are with equal advantage   CANN 84:6
  F. of Parys   CHAU 91:15
  F., or Turk   GILB 150:21
  F. widow in every bedroom   HOFF 171:11
  glory of beating the F.   WOLF 363:4
  If the F. noblesse   TREV 341:16
  not clear is not F.   RIVA 277:8
  not too French F. bean   GILB 150:14
  Speak in F.   CARR 87:1
  to men F.   CHAR 91:5
Frenchman must hate a F.   NELS 249:4
Frenchmen Fifty million F.   ANON 8:6
frenzy Demoniac f.   MILT 239:11
  poet's eye, in a fine f.   SHAK 304:2
frequent f. hearses   POPE 266:11
fresh f. air and fun   EDGA 125:3
  f. as is the month of May   CHAU 91:14
  f. lap of the crimson rose   SHAK 303:19
  O yonge, f. folkes   CHAU 92:6
Freud trouble with F.   DODD 118:14
Freude *F., schöner Götterfunken*   SCHI 286:7
friars f. were singing vespers   GIBB 149:3
fricassee f., or a ragout   SWIF 328:15
friction f. which no man can imagine   CLAU 97:11
Friday My man F.   DEFO 111:19
friend angry with my f.   BLAK 57:26
  as you choose a f.   DILL 116:14
  betraying my f.   FORS 139:18
  Boldness be my f.   SHAK 291:4
  candid f.   CANN 84:8
  diamonds a girl's best f.   ROBI 277:13
  ease some f.   POPE 266:18
  familiar f.   BOOK 62:26
  fat f.   BRUM 73:10
  four-legged f.   BROO 70:6
  F. and associate of this clay   HADR 158:13
  f.-and-relation   MILN 235:10
  F., go up higher   BIBL 47:22
  f. in power   ADAM 1:20
  f. of every country   CANN 84:7
  f. of my better days   HALL 160:9
  f. that sticketh closer   BIBL 38:31
  He was my f.   SHAK 297:3
  I lose a f.   SARG 285:17
  Little F. of all the World   KIPL 203:19
  mine own familiar f.   BOOK 63:10
  no f. like a sister   ROSS 280:12
  only way to have a f.   EMER 132:6
  pretended f. is worse   GAY 147:5
  To find a f.   DOUG 120:5
  What is a f.   ARIS 15:24
  Whenever a f. succeeds   VIDA 346:12
  your enemy and your f.   TWAI 343:14

friendless f. bodies of unburied men WEBS 353:2
friends Americans are our best f. THOM 338:22
  forgive our f. MEDI 232:2
  f. are necessarily USTI 344:21
  f. do not need it HUBB 177:7
  f.' houses JOHN 190:11
  f. of every country DISR 117:15
  F., Romans, countrymen SHAK 297:1
  I had such f. YEAT 368:20
  I have lost f. WOOL 363:24
  in the house of God as f. BOOK 63:10
  lay down his f. for his life THOR 339:24
  life for his f. BIBL 49:7
  love of f. BELL 30:5
  Make to yourselves f. BIBL 47:35
  misfortune of our best f. LA R 209:10
  Money couldn't buy f. MILL 235:5
  my f. pictured within ELGA 127:2
  my list of f. COWP 106:3
  nearly deceiving your f. CORN 104:10
  new city of F. WHIT 356:21
  none of his f. like him WILD 359:16
  no true f. in politics CLAR 97:2
  Old f. are best SELD 288:12
  old f. to trust BACO 22:5
  thousand f. ALI 5:5
  want of f. BRET 68:13
  win f. and influence people CARN 85:26
  with a little help from my f. LENN 212:24
friendship cultivate your f. JOHN 190:9
  F. from knowledge BUSS 78:22
  f. in constant repair JOHN 188:10
  f. is constant SHAK 304:7
  F. is Love BYRO 81:13
  f. recognised by the police STEV 325:22
  f. with all nations JEFF 184:7
  In f. false DRYD 121:18
  Most f. is feigning SHAK 290:17
  two for f. THOR 339:17
frigate no F. like a Book DICK 115:28
frighten by God, they f. me WELL 353:18
  f. the horses CAMP 83:8
frightening never more f. VAN 345:8
frog f. remains ROST 281:1
  leap-splash—a f. BASH 27:12
  toe of f. SHAK 301:12
frogs F. are slightly better MITF 241:17
front F. and back follow LAO 207:21
frontier f. of my Person AUDE 19:15
  new f. KENN 198:13
frost but a f. of cares TICH 340:9
  f. performs its secret ministry COLE 100:5
  like an untimely f. SHAK 307:8
frosts hoary-headed f. SHAK 303:19
froth mostly f. and bubble GORD 154:8
frothy sea was all f. SMIT 319:17
frowning Behind a f. providence COWP 105:19
frozen f. in an out-of-date mould JENK 185:2
  f. music SCHE 286:6
  locked and f. in each eye AUDE 19:4
  sends the f.-ground-swell FROS 143:19
  Your tiny hand is f. GIAC 148:12
fructify [Money should] f. GLAD 151:16
fruges f. consumere nati HORA 174:22
fruit brought forth f. BIBL 44:39
  delicate exotic f. WILD 358:6
  everything is f. AURE 20:15
  f. Of that forbidden tree MILT 237:15
  f. of the Spirit BIBL 51:12
  trees bear strange f. ALLE 5:11
fruitful as the f. vine BOOK 64:28
  Be f., and multiply BIBL 34:6
fruitfulness mellow f. KEAT 197:1

fruition f. of an earthly crown MARL 228:18
fruits By their f. BIBL 44:12
  first f. of them that slept BIBL 50:28
  flowers and f. of love BYRO 81:15
frustra Nisi Dominus f. ANON 13:13
frying-pan talks In the f. DE L 112:11
fuck Fish f. in it FIEL 135:20
  They f. you up, your mum and dad LARK 208:21
  zipless f. JONG 191:12
fudge two-fifths sheer f. LOWE 219:18
fugaces Eheu f. Labuntur anni HORA 175:11
fugit f. inreparabile tempus VIRG 348:4
fugitive f. and cloistered virtue MILT 240:5
  f. from th' law of averages MAUL 231:13
full F. fathom five SHAK 307:23
  F. speed ahead FARR 134:9
  f. tide of human existence JOHN 189:7
fulmen Eripuit coelo f. TURG 343:3
fulness f. thereof BIBL 50:20
fum Fy, fa, f. NASH 248:17
fume black, stinking f. JAME 182:9
fun f. you think they had JONG 191:13
  no reference to f. HERB 167:8
  noted for fresh air and f. EDGA 125:3
function Form follows f. SULL 327:10
  F. never dies WORD 365:22
funeral f. baked meats SHAK 291:23
  F. marches to the grave LONG 217:19
  not a f. note WOLF 362:24
funny Everything is f. ROGE 278:15
  f. old weird THAT 337:3
  F.-peculiar or funny ha-ha HAY 163:17
  Isn't it f. MILN 235:17
  Whatever is f. is subversive ORWE 255:7
furca Naturam expelles f. HORA 174:26
furies Fierce as ten F. MILT 238:10
furious grew fast and f. BURN 77:15
furiously driveth f. BIBL 37:27
  heathen so f. rage BOOK 62:7
furnace burning fiery f. BIBL 42:5
  Heat not a f. SHAK 296:8
furnish Books do f. a room POWE 270:8
  f. all we ought to ask KEBL 197:24
  f. the war HEAR 164:14
furnished Cambridge ladies in f. souls CUMM 108:11
  F. and burnish'd BETJ 33:5
furniture don't trip over the f. COWA 105:11
  No f. so charming SMIT 319:8
  rearranges the f. PRAT 270:19
  stocked with all the f. DOYL 120:12
furor Ira f. brevis est HORA 174:24
further Always a little f. FLEC 138:5
  but no f. PIUS 264:8
  f. one goes LAO 208:6
  f. they have to fall FITZ 137:18
fury Comes the blind F. MILT 236:31
  f. and the mire of human veins YEAT 367:13
  f., like a woman scorned CONG 102:7
  f. of a patient man DRYD 121:23
  sound and f. SHAK 301:31
  War hath no f. MONT 242:15
fuse through the green f. THOM 337:20
fustian f.'s so sublimely bad POPE 266:20
future controls the f. ORWE 254:23
  dipped into the f. TENN 333:25
  empires of the f. CHUR 95:18
  fight against the f. GLAD 151:12
  f. ain't what it used to be BERR 32:13
  F. as a promised land LEWI 213:18
  F. shock TOFF 340:18
  lets the f. in GREE 156:26
  never think of the f. EINS 126:6
  no trust in the f. HORA 175:7

once and f. king · MALO 226:9
past, present and f. · EINS 126:14
perhaps present in time f. · ELIO 127:29
picture of the f. · ORWE 255:1
promise of a bright f. · AHER 4:1
seen the f. and it works · STEF 323:12
Trust no F. · LONG 217:20
fuzzy-wuzzy 'ere's *to* you, F. · KIPL 202:3

G

gabardine my Jewish g. · SHAK 302:15
Gaels great G. of Ireland · CHES 92:26
gag tight g. of place · HEAN 164:13
Gaia G. is a tough bitch · MARG 227:17
gaiety eclipsed the g. · JOHN 187:12
only concession to g. · THOM 338:10
gain g. of a few · POPE 268:22
g. the whole world · BIBL 46:27
gained misery is a battle g. · WELL 354:2
gainful seek g. employment · ACHE 1:5
gains no g. without pains · STEV 325:2
gaiters gas and g. · DICK 115:12
Galatians great text in G. · BROW 73:3
gales cool g. shall fan the glade · POPE 268:14
Galilean O pale G. · SWIN 329:14
You have won, G. · JULI 193:15
Galileo G. in two thousand years · PIUS 264:9
status of G. · GOUL 154:14
gall take my milk for g. · SHAK 299:24
wormwood and the g. · BIBL 41:25
gallantry What men call g. · BYRO 80:21
Gallia G. *est omnis divisa* · CAES 82:3
gallop G. apace · SHAK 307:1
galloped we g. all three · BROW 72:9
gallows die upon the g. · WILK 359:26
nothing but the g. · BURK 75:20
perfect g. · SHAK 307:16
gamble Life is a g. · STOP 326:15
gambler whore and the g. · BLAK 56:13
game Anarchism is a g. · SHAW 312:21
beautiful g. · PELÉ 261:8
g. is about glory · BLAN 58:8
g. of the few · BERK 31:15
g.'s afoot · SHAK 295:17
how you played the G. · RICE 275:17
play the g. · NEWB 249:18
time to win this g. · DRAK 121:9
war's a g. · COWP 105:30
woman is his g. · TENN 334:17
games G. people play · BERN 32:12
g. should be seen · MONT 242:19
gamesmanship theory and practice of g. · POTT 269:17
gamut g. of the emotions · PARK 259:2
gangsters great nations acted like g. · KUBR 206:4
garage to the full g. · HOOV 173:5
Garcia Lorca —and you, G. · GINS 151:5
Garde *La G. meurt* · CAMB 83:1
garden Back to the g. · MITC 241:12
Come into the g. · TENN 334:4
England is a g. · KIPL 202:6
fairies at the bottom of our g. · FYLE 144:20
g. eastward in Eden · BIBL 34:7
g. inclosed · BIBL 40:1
g. in her face · CAMP 83:14
g. is a lovesome thing · BROW 70:19
God the first g. made · COWL 105:13
imperfections of my g. · MONT 242:17
Lord God walking in the g. · BIBL 34:16
man and a woman in a g. · WILD 359:3
nearer God's Heart in a g. · GURN 158:10

planted a g. · BACO 22:26
rosebud g. of girls · TENN 334:5
where a g. should be · HORA 175:25
gardener Adam was a g. · SHAK 296:4
I am but a young g. · JEFF 184:13
gardening g. is but landscape-painting · POPE 268:24
garish day's g. eye · MILT 236:15
garland green willow is my g. · HEYW 168:16
O! withered is the g. · SHAK 289:22
willow must be my g. · SHAK 305:10
garment g. was white as snow · BIBL 42:8
garmented g. in light · SHEL 315:3
garments part my g. · BOOK 62:13
garter knight of the g. · ATTL 18:8
gas g. and gaiters · DICK 115:12
G. smells awful · PARK 258:16
got as far as poison-g. · HARD 161:19
gasp last g. · BIBL 42:29
gate cabin at your g. · SHAK 308:24
how strait the g. · HENL 166:9
lead you in at Heaven's g. · BLAK 56:20
man at the g. of the year · HASK 163:5
Wide is the g. · BIBL 44:9
gates besiege your g. · POPE 266:11
enter then his g. · KETH 199:16
g. of hell · BIBL 45:9
g. to the glorious and unknown · FORS 139:15
Open the temple g. · SPEN 321:21
O ye g. · BOOK 62:17
suicide at its g. · HUSS 179:3
to the g. of Hell · PIUS 264:8
Gath Tell it not in G. · BIBL 36:33
gather G. ye rosebuds · HERR 168:5
gathered g. together in my name · BIBL 45:15
gaudeamus G. *igitur, juvenes dum sumus* · ANON 13:11
gaudy Neat, but not g. · WESL 355:5
one other g. night · SHAK 289:20
Gaul G. as a whole is divided · CAES 82:3
Gaunt Old John of G. · SHAK 305:16
gauzy wrapped in a g. veil · SHEL 315:2
gave Lord g., and the Lord · BIBL 37:33
she g. me of the tree · BIBL 34:17
gay g. deceiver · COLM 101:18
g. Lothario · ROWE 281:12
g. man trapped · BOY 67:3
Gaza Eyeless in G. · MILT 239:21
gazelle nursed a dear g. · MOOR 244:12
one a g. · YEAT 368:9
gazing g. at each other · SAIN 284:10
g. up into heaven · BIBL 49:20
gear not got a reverse g. · BLAI 56:5
geese Like g. about the sky · AUDE 18:13
Gehazi Whence comest thou, G. · BIBL 37:25
Gehenna Down to G. · KIPL 202:14
gem g. of purest ray serene · GRAY 156:11
gemlike hard, g. flame · PATE 260:8
general caviare to the g. · SHAK 292:18
G. notions · MONT 242:13
generalities glittering and sounding g. · CHOA 94:5
Glittering g. · EMER 132:21
General Motors good for G. · WILS 361:3
generals against the law for g. · TRUM 342:16
bite some of my other g. · GEOR 147:16
Russia has two g. · NICH 251:1
we're all G. · USTI 344:22
generation beat g. · KERO 199:9
best minds of my g. · GINS 151:3
g. was stolen · FREE 142:11
G. X · COUP 104:16
in their g. wiser · BIBL 47:34
lost g. · STEI 323:18
O g. of vipers · BIBL 43:7
one g. from extinction · CARE 84:20

generation (cont.)
third and fourth g. — BIBL 35:25
generations g. have trod — HOPK 173:16
g. of men — HOME 172:10
G. pass — BROW 71:7
hungry g. — KEAT 196:22
Those dying g. — YEAT 368:26
generous always g. ones — MONT 243:10
generously treated g. or destroyed — MACH 223:7
genes G. and inherited dispositions — WINS 362:2
go by the name of g. — DAWK 111:9
what males do to g. — JONE 191:11
genetic mechanism for g. material — CRIC 107:2
geniumque G. loci — VIRG 347:15
genius except my g. — WILD 359:17
feminine of g. — FITZ 137:5
g. and art — HAZL 164:5
G. does what it must — MERE 233:11
g. into my life — WILD 359:15
G. is one per cent inspiration — EDIS 125:5
G. is only a greater aptitude — BUFF 73:20
g. of Einstein leads to Hiroshima — PICA 263:10
g. of its scientists — EISE 126:16
g. of the Constitution — PITT 264:6
g. of the place — POPE 266:28
'G.' which means — CARL 85:9
g. would wish to live — ADAM 1:11
gentlemen—a g. — SCHU 286:17
great g. — BEAU 28:3
talent instantly recognizes g. — DOYL 121:5
Three-fifths of him g. — LOWE 219:18
true g. appears — SWIF 328:20
what a g. I had — SWIF 329:3
genteel to the truly g. — HARD 161:16
gentil verray, parfit g. knyght — CHAU 91:13
Gentiles boasting as the G. use — KIPL 202:21
gentle Do not go g. — THOM 337:18
G. as falcon — SKEL 317:14
g. rain from heaven — SHAK 302:30
gentleman definition of a g. — NEWM 250:1
fashion a g. — SPEN 321:23
g. in Whitehall — JAY 183:13
g.'s park — CONS 103:2
mariner with the g. — DRAK 121:8
prince of darkness is a g. — SHAK 298:10
who was then the g. — ROLL 279:1
gentlemanly g. conduct — ARNO 17:12
gentlemen G. go by — KIPL 202:24
g. in England — SHAK 295:29
g. of England — PARK 259:7
G. prefer blondes — LOOS 218:14
G.-rankers — KIPL 202:4
nation of g. — MUGA 246:15
gentleness ways are ways of g. — SPRI 322:14
gently roar you as g. — SHAK 303:12
genuine place for the g. — MOOR 244:2
geographers g., in Afric-maps — SWIF 329:1
geographical g. concept — BISM 55:7
g. expression — METT 233:17
geography G. is about Maps — BENT 31:9
too much g. — KING 201:4
geometrical g. ratio — MALT 226:12
geometry always doing g. — PLAT 265:4
as precise as g. — FLAU 137:24
does not know g. — ANON 13:2
g. of fear — READ 273:17
'royal road' to g. — EUCL 133:6
George G.—don't do that — GREN 157:10
Georgia G. on my mind — GORR 154:12
red hills of G. — KING 200:17
geranium madman shakes a dead g. — ELIO 129:11
German all a G. racket — RIDL 276:14
Germans beastly to the G. — COWA 105:1

G. . . . are going to be squeezed — GEDD 147:10
They're G. Don't mention — CLEE 97:18
Germany at war with G. — CHAM 90:6
Christian life in G. — BONH 59:8
Death is a master from G. — CELA 89:17
G. above all — HOFF 171:6
G. calling — JOYC 193:10
remaining cities of G. — HARR 162:16
Gesang Weib und G. — LUTH 220:20
get G. thee behind me, Satan — BIBL 45:10
g. what you like — SHAW 312:18
getting G. and spending — WORD 366:16
ghastly G. good taste — BETJ 33:6
G., grim and ancient — POE 265:19
ghost G. in the Machine — RYLE 283:22
g. of Roger Casement — YEAT 368:7
g. of the deceased — HOBB 170:22
some old lover's g. — DONN 119:11
ghosties ghoulies and g. — ANON 8:7
ghosts g. of departed quantities — BERK 31:13
ghoulies g. and ghosties — ANON 8:7
giant g. great and still — STEV 325:28
g.'s strength — SHAK 302:4
hand of the g. — BOOK 64:27
like a g. — BOOK 63:17
sees farther than the g. — COLE 101:3
giants for war like precocious g. — PEAR 261:3
g. in the earth — BIBL 34:27
nuclear g. and ethical infants — BRAD 67:10
on the shoulders of g. — NEWT 250:15
shoulders of g. — BERN 32:10
Want one only of five g. — BEVE 33:15
gibber squeak and g. — SHAK 291:9
gibbets cells and g. — COOK 103:11
g. keep the lifted hand in awe — YOUN 369:3
Gibbon Eh! Mr G. — GLOU 151:18
Gibraltar G. may tumble — GERS 148:9
gift last best g. — MILT 238:30
love is the g. of oneself — ANOU 14:5
You have a g. — JONS 191:19
gifted young, g. and black — HANS 161:4
Young, g. and black — IRVI 181:5
giftie g. gie us — BURN 77:18
gifts cannot recall their g. — TENN 334:30
even when they bring g. — VIRG 347:4
presented unto him g. — BIBL 43:2
gigantic g. body — MACA 221:10
gild g. refinèd gold — SHAK 297:20
gilded g. loam — SHAK 305:17
Gilead no balm in G. — BIBL 41:21
Gilpin John G. was a citizen — COWP 105:16
Gipfeln Über allen G. ist Ruh' — GOET 152:18
Gipper Win just one for the G. — GIPP 151:7
girded g. up his loins — BIBL 37:13
girdle g. round about the earth — SHAK 303:20
girl can't get no g. reaction — JAGG 182:5
danced with a g. — FARJ 134:4
diamonds a g.'s best friend — ROBI 277:13
g. at an impressionable age — SPAR 321:2
g. needs good parents — TUCK 342:22
Poor little rich g. — COWA 105:6
pretty g. is like a melody — BERL 32:1
unlessoned g. — SHAK 302:26
was a little g. — LONG 218:12
girlish Laugh thy g. laughter — WATS 351:16
girls bombers named for g. — JARR 183:12
g. in slacks remember Dad — BETJ 33:1
g. that are so smart — CARE 84:21
g. who wear glasses — PARK 258:13
rosebud garden of g. — TENN 334:5
Treaties like g. and roses — DE G 112:8
Gitche Gumee By the shore of G. — LONG 218:3
give freely g. — BIBL 44:25

G., and it shall be given	BIBL 47:10	What a g. morning	ADAM 2:15
g. and not to count	IGNA 180:12	**glory** all things give him g.	HOPK 174:11
G. crowns and pounds	HOUS 176:8	alone with his g.	WOLF 363:2
g. me back my legions	AUGU 20:12	crowned with g. now	KELL 198:3
G. me my Romeo	SHAK 307:2	day of g. has arrived	ROUG 281:6
G. to me the life I love	STEV 326:2	days of our g.	BYRO 81:21
g. to the poor	BIBL 45:18	declare the g. of God	BOOK 62:11
g. what you command	AUGU 20:5	deed is all, the g. nothing	GOET 152:13
more blessed to g.	BIBL 49:33	game is about g.	BLAN 58:8
not as the world giveth, g. I	BIBL 49:6	g. and the dream	WORD 365:5
peace which the world cannot g.	BOOK 60:7	g. and the freshness	WORD 365:2
receive but what we g.	COLE 100:1	g. and the nothing	BYRO 80:16
given I would have g. gladly	JOHN 186:6	g. as of the only begotten	BIBL 48:19
shall be g.	BIBL 46:5	G. be to God	HOPK 174:1
giver cheerful g.	BIBL 51:7	G. be to the Father	BOOK 59:16
gives who g. soon	PUBL 271:12	g. in the name of Briton	GEOR 147:17
giving not in the g. vein	SHAK 306:15	g. in the triumph	CORN 104:4
glad g. confident morning	BROW 72:14	g. is departed	BIBL 36:23
just g. to see me	WEST 355:11	g. is in their shame	BIBL 51:25
too soon made g.	BROW 72:18	g., laud, and honour	NEAL 248:22
gladly g. wolde he lerne	CHAU 91:18	g. never dies	ANON 14:3
I would have given g.	JOHN 186:6	g. of Europe	BURK 75:18
gladness As with g. men of old	DIX 118:11	g. of God	BLAK 57:2
oil of g.	BOOK 63:2	g. of God is a man	IREN 180:23
serve the Lord with g.	BOOK 64:2	g. of man as the flower	BIBL 52:25
Teach me half the g.	SHEL 314:29	g. of my crown	ELIZ 130:16
gladsome Let us with a g. mind	MILT 236:26	g. of the Attic stage	ARNO 16:26
Glamis G. hath murdered sleep	SHAK 300:17	g. of the coming	HOWE 177:2
G. thou art, and Cawdor	SHAK 299:21	g. of the Lord	BIBL 41:16
Glasgow G. Empire on a Saturday night	DODD 118:14	g. of the Lord shone	BIBL 47:2
got a G. accent	REID 275:2	g. of them	BIBL 43:11
glass brighter than g.	HORA 175:16	g. of the world	ANON 13:20
dome of many-coloured g.	SHEL 313:21	g. of this world passes	THOM 337.8
Get thee g. eyes	SHAK 298:18	g. shone around	TATE 330:21
g. of blessings	HERB 167:20	g. that was Greece	POE 265:22
if you break the bloody g.	MACN 224:10	G. to God in the highest	BIBL 47:4
No g. of ours was raised	HEAN 164:12	g. to her	BIBL 50:21
own face in the g.	WILD 358:24	greater g. of God	ANON 13:6
Satire is a sort of g.	SWIF 328:5	greatest g. of a woman	PERI 262:3
take a g. of wine	SHER 315:19	I felt it was g.	BYRO 81:22
through a g., darkly	BIBL 50:25	I go to g.	DUNC 123:9
turn down an empty g.	FITZ 137:4	King of g.	BOOK 62:17
glasses girls who wear g.	PARK 258:13	Land of Hope and G.	BENS 31:3
ladder and some g.	BATE 27:16	looks on war as all g.	SHER 315:26
glassy around the g. sea	HEBE 164:19	name thee Old G.	DRIV 121:15
g., cool, translucent	MILT 236:10	paths of g.	GRAY 156:9
in the g. stream	SHAK 293:35	say my g. was	YEAT 368:20
gleam Follow The G.	TENN 334:9	Solomon in all his g.	BIBL 43:26
glen Down the rushy g.	ALLI 5:19	some desperate g.	OWEN 256:11
glib g. and oily art	SHAK 297:24	There's g. for you	CARR 87:9
glittering g. and sounding generalities	CHOA 94:5	trailing clouds of g.	WORD 365:6
g. prizes	SMIT 318:13	uncertain g.	SHAK 309:15
how that g. taketh me	HERR 168:7	What price g.	ANDE 6:16
with his g. eye	COLE 100:15	yields the true g.	DRAK 121:16
gloaming In the g.	ORRE 254:4	**gloves** capitalism with the g. off	STOP 326:16
Roamin' in the g.	LAUD 209:15	through the fields in g.	CORN 104:8
global g. thinking	LUCE 220:10	with my g. on my hand	HARG 162:12
image of a g. village	MCLU 223:17	**glow** g. has warmed the world	STEV 325:7
globaloney still g.	LUCE 220:10	made my heart to g.	SOUT 320:25
globe destinies of half the g.	TOCQ 340:17	**glow-worm** g. that shines	HAGG 159:2
great g. itself	SHAK 307:30	**glut** g. thy sorrow	KEAT 196:14
hunted round the g.	PAIN 257:8	**gluttony** G. an emotional escape	DE V 114:1
globule primordial atomic g.	GILB 149:22	**gnashing** g. of teeth	BIBL 44:15
gloomy by g. Dis Was gathered	MILT 238:21	**gnat** strain at a g.	BIBL 45:30
gloria G. in excelsis	MISS 240:18	**gnats** small g. mourn	KEAT 197:4
Sic transit g. mundi	ANON 13:20	**go** can't g. on	BECK 28:10
gloriam Dei g.	ANON 13:6	G., and do thou likewise	BIBL 47:16
glories g. of our blood and state	SHIR 315:28	g., and sin no more	BIBL 48:34
in those weaker g. spy	VAUG 345:15	G., and the Lord be with thee	BIBL 36:29
glorious all-g. above	GRAN 155:8	G. anywhere I damn well please	BEVI 33:16
all g. within	BOOK 63:3	G. down, Moses	ANON 11:20
G. things of thee	NEWT 250:19	G., for they call you	ARNO 16:20
Mud! G. mud	FLAN 137:21	G., litel bok	CHAU 92:4

go *(cont.)*

G., little book	STEV 326:4
G., lovely rose	WALL 349:17
g. no more a-roving	BYRO 81:20
G. to jail	ANON 8:12
G. to the ant	BIBL 38:15
G. West, young man	GREE 156:22
G. ye into all the world	BIBL 46:30
I g. on for ever	TENN 331:18
I have a g.	OSBO 255:11
In the name of God, g.	AMER 6:3
In the name of God, g.	CROM 107:11
Let my people g.	BIBL 35:17
no place to g.	BURT 77:26
no place to g.	WHIT 356:18
not g. to Canossa	BISM 55:5
One of us must g.	WILD 359:19
There you g. again	REAG 274:5
thus far shalt thou g.	PARN 259:15
to boldly g.	RODD 278:7
to hell I will g.	MILL 234:6
unto Caesar shalt thou g.	BIBL 49:35
wherever he wants to g.	BRAU 68:1
goal final g. of ill	TENN 332:30
moving freely, without a g.	KLEE 204:4
goals live by positive g.	BERL 32:6
muddied oafs at the g.	KIPL 202:12
goat lust of the g.	BLAK 57:2
with their g. feet	MARL 228:10
goats g. on the left	BIBL 46:6
gobbledygoo your g.	PLAT 264:12
goblins sprites and g.	SHAK 309:17
God acceptable unto G.	BIBL 50:10
Are you there G.	BLUM 58:12
armour of G.	BIBL 51:20
beast or a g.	ARIS 15:20
becoming a g.	VESP 346:6
best thing G. invents	BROW 72:3
burial-ground G.'s-acre	LONG 217:13
bush afire with G.	BROW 71:14
But for the grace of G.	BRAD 67:5
by the hand of G.	MARA 227:15
cause of G.	BOWL 67:2
choose a Jewish G.	BROW 71:3
closer walk with G.	COWP 105:20
conscious water saw its G.	CRAS 106:11
daughter of the voice of G.	WORD 365:11
discussing their duty to G.	WHIT 357:7
don't do G.	CAMP 83:5
don't think G. comes well out of it	WOOL 364:2
Enoch walked with G.	BIBL 34:26
Fear G.	BIBL 39:30
Fear G.	BIBL 52:27
feather on the breath of G.	HILD 169:1
Fellow-citizens: G. reigns	GARF 146:3
For G.'s sake, look after our people	SCOT 287:6
forgotten before G.	BIBL 47:19
gift from G.	ADEN 3:15
glory of G.	BLAK 57:2
G. Almighty first planted	BACO 22:26
G. alone suffices	TERE 335:21
G. and devil	DOST 119:27
G. and I both knew	KLOP 204:6
G. and mammon	BIBL 43:25
G. and Robert Browning	BROW 73:6
G. and the doctor	OWEN 256:4
G. beginning to resemble	HUXL 179:14
G. be in my head	ANON 8:10
G. be merciful	BIBL 48:6
G. be praised	WOLF 363:5
G. be thanked	BROO 70:1
G. bless America	BERL 31:20
G. bless the child	HOLI 171:16
G. bless the Prince	LINL 215:12
G. bless us every one	DICK 114:16
G. cannot alter the past	BUTL 79:10
g. cannot change the past	AGAT 3:24
G. caught his eye	MCCO 222:13
G. disposes	THOM 337:9
G. does not play dice	EINS 126:5
G. has more right	JOHN 185:12
G. has written all the books	BUTL 79:15
G. hath joined together	BIBL 45:17
G. hath made them so	WATT 351:20
G. help the Minister	MELB 232:6
G. in His mercy	CRAI 106:7
G.-intoxicated man	NOVA 252:8
G. is always doing geometry	PLAT 265:4
G. is blameless	PLAT 265:2
G. is dead	FROM 143:5
G. is dead	NIET 251:6
G. is in the details	MIES 233:23
G. is just	JEFF 184:20
G. is love	BIBL 52:32
G. is love, but	LEE 211:11
G. is no respecter	BIBL 49:26
G. is not mocked	BIBL 51:13
G. is on the side	VOLT 348:21
G. is our hope	BOOK 63:4
G. is subtle but not malicious	EINS 126:4
G. is their belly	BIBL 51:25
G. is the Light of the heavens	KORA 205:16
G. is Three	NEWM 250:5
G. is usually on the side	BUSS 78:24
G. is working his purpose out	AING 4:2
G. made me	CATE 88:16
G. made the country	COWP 105:24
G. made the integers	KRON 206:3
G. moves in a mysterious	COWP 105:18
G. must think it exceedingly odd	KNOX 204:11
G. o'erhead	LONG 217:20
G. of Abraham	HA-L 159:17
G. of love	HERB 167:23
G. of our fathers	SIDD 316:7
G. of Things as They are	KIPL 203:6
G. only another artist	PICA 263:9
G., our help in ages past	WATT 352:2
G. prepares evil	ANON 13:4
G. punish England	FUNK 144:19
G. reigned from the wood	FORT 140:2
G. save king Solomon	BIBL 37:4
G. save our gracious king	ANON 8:11
G. save the king	BIBL 36:26
G. save the king	SHAK 306:3
G. save the Queen	WHIT 356:20
G. saw that it was good	BIBL 34:5
G. seems to have left the receiver	KOES 204:15
G.'s finger touched him	TENN 333:5
G.'s first Creature	BACO 23:32
G. shall wipe away	BIBL 53:9
G. shall wipe away	BIBL 53:23
G.'s in his heaven	BROW 72:23
G. so loved the world	BIBL 48:27
G. the Father Almighty	BOOK 59:23
G. the first garden made	COWL 105:13
G. the soul	POPE 267:24
G. they ought to crucify	CART 88:3
G. to be his guide	BUNY 74:16
G., to me, it seems	FULL 144:13
G. took him	BIBL 34:26
G. whom he hath not seen	BIBL 52:34
G. will pardon me	HEIN 165:10
grandeur of G.	HOPK 173:16
greater glory of G.	ANON 13:6
great g. Pan	BROW 71:16
great man of G.	ROBI 277:19

Had G. on his side	DYLA 124:15	suppose that G. is only	TEMP 331:11
Had I but served G.	WOLS 363:13	Teach me, my G. and King	HERB 167:14
hands of the living G.	BIBL 52:13	Thanks to G.	BUÑU 74:5
hath not seen G.	BIBL 52:35	that of G. in every one	FOX 141:1
have G. for his father	CYPR 109:2	them that love G.	BIBL 50:7
He for G. only	MILT 238:22	There is no G.	BOOK 62:9
here is G.'s plenty	DRYD 122:22	thinks little of G.	PLUT 265:12
honest G.	INGE 180:17	three-personed G.	DONN 118:24
Honest to G.	ROBI 277:20	thy God my G.	BIBL 36:21
house of my G.	BOOK 63:20	To glorify G.	SHOR 316:5
How odd Of G.	EWER 133:11	To G. I speak Spanish	CHAR 91:5
If G. be for us	BIBL 50:8	to the eye of G.	OLIV 253:9
if G. did not exist	VOLT 348:16	to the unknown g.	BIBL 49:30
if G. talks to you	SZAS 329:20	touched the face of G.	MAGE 225:3
If only G. would give some sign	ALLE 5:16	touch the face of G.	REAG 274:8
if there be a G.	ANON 10:1	triangles were to make a G.	MONT 243:5
image of G.	TALM 330:13	understands to the G.	THOM 337:14
immortal g. of harmony	BEET 29:6	unto G.	BIBL 45:26
In the name of G., go	AMER 6:3	Very God of very G.	BOOK 61:3
In the name of G., go	CROM 107:11	voice of G.	ALCU 4:7
in the sight of G.	BOOK 61:23	wagering that G. is	PASC 259:21
into the Hand of G.	HASK 163:5	ways of G. to man	POPE 267:19
is the art of G.	YOUN 370:3	What G. abandoned	HOUS 176:4
Just are the ways of G.	MILT 239:25	What hath G. wrought	BIBL 36:1
justify G.'s ways	HOUS 176:16	What hath G. wrought	MORS 246:2
justify the ways of G.	MILT 237:17	When G. at first made man	HERB 167:20
kingdom of G.	BIBL 44:1	where the love of G. goes	LIGH 214:10
kingdom of G.	BIBL 48:25	whom G. hath joined	BOOK 62:2
kingdom of G. is within you	BIBL 48:3	With G. all things are possible	BIBL 45:20
known unto G.	ANON 10:21	Word was with G.	BIBL 48:13
know the mind of G.	HAWK 163:13	you are a g.	ROST 281:3
land G. gave to Cain	CART 00.0	godamm Lhude sing G.	POUN 269:18
like kissing G.	BRUC 73:8	goddess bitch-g. success	JAME 183:9
Lord thy G.	BIBL 35:24	godfathers G. and Godmothers	BOOK 61:17
love the Lord thy G.	BIBL 45:28	godless decent g. people	ELIO 129:13
man sent from G.	BIBL 48:16	godliness next to g.	WESL 354:26
man whose g. is in the skies	SHAW 312:14	godly g., righteous, and sober life	BOOK 59:14
man with G. is always	KNOX 204:10	godmothers Godfathers and G.	BOOK 61:17
Messenger of G.	KORA 205:22	Godot waiting for G.	BECK 28:13
mills of G. grind slowly	LONG 218:1	gods alien people clutching their g.	ELIO 128:27
My God, my G.	BIBL 46:20	By the nine g.	MACA 221:20
Name of G., the Merciful	KORA 204:17	convenient that there be g.	OVID 255:24
nature is the art of G.	BROW 71:12	creates g.	MONT 243:3
nature of G.	ANON 9:22	daughter of the g.	TENN 332:5
Nearer, my G., to thee	ADAM 2:17	dish fit for the g.	SHAK 296:24
neglect G. and his Angels	DONN 119:24	gave birth to the G.	HOLB 171:15
next to g. america	CUMM 108:5	g. are on the side of the stronger	TACI 330:3
Now thank we all our G.	WINK 361:22	g. themselves cannot recall	TENN 334:30
Of all G.'s works	MILT 239:7	g. themselves struggle	SCHI 286:10
of such is the kingdom of G.	BIBL 46:29	g. thought otherwise	VIRG 347:5
O G. of Bethel	DODD 118:15	g. wish to destroy	CONN 102:16
One G., one law	TENN 333:11	in the lap of the g.	HOME 172:13
one G. only	CLOU 98:16	Kings it makes g.	SHAK 306:17
only G. can make a tree	KILM 200:5	loved by the g.	PLAT 264:19
only the Messenger of G.	KORA 205:10	make the g. above relent	VIRG 347:16
others call it G.	CARR 87:23	not recognizing the g.	PLAT 264:18
our G. is still	LUTH 220:19	outcome to the G.	CORN 104:5
Our G.'s forgotten	QUAR 272:8	So many g.	WILC 358:1
out of the mouth of G.	BIBL 43:9	These be thy g., O Israel	BIBL 35:30
owe G. a death	SHAK 295:6	they are called g.	JAME 182:11
peace of G.	JAME 182:13	they first make g.	LEVI 213:13
presume not G. to scan	POPE 267:27	Thou shalt have no other g.	BIBL 35:24
put your trust in G.	BLAC 55:12	What men or g.	KEAT 196:6
respect for the idea of G.	DUHA 123:1	Whom the g. love	MENA 232:16
river Is a strong brown g.	ELIO 128:10	Ye shall be as g.	BIBL 34:15
see G. in every human	TERE 335:19	goest whither thou g., I will go	BIBL 36:21
Sees G. in clouds	POPE 267:21	going At the g. down of the sun	BINY 54:24
shall I see G.	BIBL 38:4	endure Their g. hence	SHAK 298:22
sing My G. and King	HERB 167:10	g. gets tough	KENN 199:6
Something beautiful for G.	MUGG 246:17	g. the way of all the earth	BIBL 36:9
something beautiful for G.	TERE 335:17	g. to a feast	JONS 191:15
Spirit of the Lord G.	BIBL 41:17	g. to and fro in the earth	BIBL 37:32
stop believing in G.	CHES 93:25	not know where he is g.	LIN 215:13

going (cont.)
order of your g. — SHAK 301:8
puck is g. to be — GRET 157:12
to what he was g. — HARD 162:6
gold apples of g. — BIBL 38:35
bringing g., and silver — BIBL 37:7
clothing is of wrought g. — BOOK 63:3
cross of g. — BRYA 73:14
cursed craving for g. — VIRG 347:6
fetch the age of g. — MILT 237:8
gild refinèd g. — SHAK 297:20
g., and frankincense — BIBL 43:2
g. of the day — CROS 107:18
g. shines like fire — PIND 263:12
g., yea, than much fine gold — BOOK 62:12
If g. ruste, what shall iren do — CHAU 91:22
in purple and g. — BYRO 80:18
natural stability of g. — SHAW 311:21
Nor all, that glisters, g. — GRAY 156:20
patines of bright g. — SHAK 303:3
realms of g. — KEAT 196:27
stuffed their mouths with g. — BEVA 33:13
what's become of all the g. — BROW 73:5
golden Casting down their g. crowns — HEBE 164:19
end of a g. string — BLAK 56:20
g. bowl be broken — BIBL 39:28
g. days of Saturn's reign — VIRG 347:21
g. elephants next — SHOR 316:3
G. lads and girls — SHAK 291:6
G. opinions — SHAK 300:4
g. priests — JEWE 185:10
G. Road to Samarkand — FLEC 138:4
G. slumbers kiss your eyes — DEKK 112:10
g. years return — SHEL 313:26
hand that lays the g. egg — GOLD 154:2
His g. locks — PEEL 261:5
in the g. world — SHAK 290:2
in their g. hair — TENN 334:11
Jerusalem the g. — NEAL 248:24
love in a g. bowl — BLAK 56:15
loves the g. mean — HORA 175:10
We are g. — MITC 241:12
went into a g. land — TURN 343:5
Goldengrove G. unleaving — HOPK 174:3
golf made more Liars than G. — ROGE 278:14
thousand lost g. balls — ELIO 129:13
Golgotha in the Hebrew G. — BIBL 49:10
gone All, all are g. — LAMB 207:5
And they are g. — KEAT 195:17
g. altogether beyond — MAHÁ 225:11
g. from original righteousness — BOOK 65:12
g. into the world of light — VAUG 345:10
g. with the wind — DOWS 120:10
not dead—but g. — ROGE 278:12
She's g. for ever — SHAK 298:26
they are g. forever — MANN 227:3
what haste I can to be g. — CROM 107:17
What's g. — SHAK 309:18
when I am g. — ROSS 280:14
gong that g.-tormented sea — YEAT 367:14
gongs Strong g. groaning — CHES 93:2
struck regularly like g. — COWA 105:10
good Address to the unco g. — BURN 76:15
And now g. morrow — DONN 119:10
annoyance of a g. example — TWAI 343:26
any g. thing — BIBL 48:22
anything g. to say — LONG 218:13
be a g. animal — SPEN 321:6
be g. in the country — WILD 358:30
Be g., sweet maid — KING 201:6
being really g. — WILD 358:11
best is the enemy of the g. — VOLT 348:11
better to be g. — WILD 358:29

call no being g. — MILL 234:6
could be a g. woman — THAC 336:8
do evil, that g. may come — BIBL 49:40
Do g. by stealth — POPE 268:12
do g. to them — BIBL 47:9
either g. or bad — SHAK 292:14
Evil, be thou my g. — MILT 238:19
for our country's g. — CART 87:27
For your own g. — FRAM 141:5
go about doing g. — CREI 106:15
God saw that it was g. — BIBL 34:5
g. action by stealth — LAMB 207:8
G. and evil shall not be held — KORA 205:18
g. and faithful servant — BIBL 46:4
G. at which all things aim — ARIS 15:12
g. becomes indistinguishable — DAWS 111:10
g. day to bury bad news — MOOR 243:20
g. ended happily — WILD 358:10
g. fences make good neighbours — FROS 143:20
g. in the worst of us — ANON 11:9
g. man to do nothing — BURK 76:10
g. news from Ghent to Aix — BROW 72:8
G. of man — ARIS 15:13
g. of subjects — DEFO 111:23
g. of the people — CICE 96:16
g. old Cause — MILT 240:12
g. old cause — WORD 365:12
g. people were clever — WORD 364:8
g. that I would I do not — BIBL 50:6
g. time coming — SCOT 287:24
g. time was had by all — SMIT 319:2
g. unluckily — STOP 326:14
g. Will be the final goal — TENN 332:30
g. will toward men — BIBL 47:4
g. without qualification — KANT 194:20
G. women always think — BROO 70:4
had been g. for that man — BIBL 46:10
Hanging is too g. for him — BUNY 74:11
heaven doing g. on earth — TERE 335:24
highest g. — CICE 96:18
His own g. — MILL 234:7
hold fast that which is g. — BIBL 52:3
In art the best is g. enough — GOET 152:15
I will be g. — VICT 346:8
knowing g. and evil — BIBL 34:15
making people feel g. — CHRÉ 94:9
neither g. nor bad — BALZ 26:6
never had it so g. — MACM 224:4
not enough to have a g. mind — DESC 113:14
not g. company — AUST 21:3
of g. report — BIBL 51:28
only g. Indians — SHER 315:8
on the evil and on the g. — BIBL 43:19
or be thought half as g. — WHIT 357:18
out of g. still to find — MILT 237:21
return g. for evil — VANB 345:3
said a g. thing — TWAI 343:18
that you're not g. enough — TROL 342:3
thy g. with brotherhood — BATE 27:17
universal licence to be g. — COLE 99:18
what g. came of it — SOUT 320:19
what was g. for our country — WILS 361:3
When she was g. — LONG 218:12
work together for g. — BIBL 50:7
would be a g. idea — GAND 145:18
would do g. to another — BLAK 56:19
your g. works — BIBL 43:16
goodbye G. to all that — GRAV 155:19
goodly I have a g. heritage — BOOK 62:10
goodness fountain of all g. — BOOK 60:5
g. derives not from — TERE 335:22
G. had nothing to do with it — WEST 355:9
G. is not the same thing — PLAT 264:23

g. of the Lord BOOK 62:18
If g. lead him not HERB 167:21
goodnight G., sweet prince SHAK 294:14
My last G. KING 200:9
goods care for external g. WEBE 352:14
goodwill In peace; g. CHUR 96:5
goose every g. a swan KING 201:9
that g. look SHAK 301:26
gordian She was a g. shape KEAT 195:28
gored you tossed and g. BOSW 66:5
gorgeous g. East in fee WORD 365:13
gory never shake Thy g. locks SHAK 301:7
Welcome to your g. bed BURN 77:10
gospel G. of Christ WESL 354:24
preach the g. BIBL 46:30
got I g. rhythm GERS 148:8
in our case we have not g. REED 274:13
we g. him BREM 68:10
Gothic cars the great G. cathedrals BART 27:6
gotta g. use words when I talk to you ELIO 129:15
gouverner G. c'est choisir LÉVI 213:15
govern g. in prose CUOM 108:14
of Kings to g. wrong POPE 266:8
to g. is to choose LÉVI 213:15
With words we g. men DISR 117:23
governess Be a g. BRON 69:12
government abandon a g. JEFF 184:6
art of g. VOLT 349:1
best g. O'SU 255:19
duty of g. PAIN 257:9
end of g. ADAM 2:10
for a bad g. TOCQ 340:16
forms of g. POPE 267:32
G. and public opinion SHAW 312:2
G. at Washington lives GARF 146:3
g. by discussion ATTL 18:9
g. by the uneducated CHES 93:23
G., even in its best state PAIN 257:5
G. is a contrivance BURK 75:16
g. is best THOR 339:5
g. is influenced by SMIT 318:5
g. it deserves MAIS 225:16
g. of laws ADAM 2:4
G. of laws and not of men FORD 139:7
g. of the people LINC 214:20
g. of the people PAGE 256:20
g. shall be upon his shoulder BIBL 40:14
g. which imprisons THOR 339:6
g. which robs Peter SHAW 311:19
have an efficient g. TRUM 342:15
If the G. is big enough FORD 139:5
members of the G. SHAW 311:21
No G. can be long secure DISR 117:19
one g. sooner learns SMIT 318:7
Peace, order, and good g. ANON 10:7
people's g. WEBS 352:18
prepare for g. STEE 323:8
rule nations by your g. VIRG 347:14
structure of g. HAVE 163:8
support their g. CLEV 98:6
well-ordered g. HALI 160:1
work for a G. I despise KEYN 199:18
worst form of G. CHUR 95:20
governments foundation of most g. ADAM 2:11
g. had better get out of the way EISE 126:18
g. need both shepherds VOLT 348:20
g. of Europe JEFF 183:20
governor save the G.-General WHIT 356:20
governs that which g. least O'SU 255:19
which g. not at all THOR 339:5
gowd man's the g. BURN 76:26
Gower O moral G. CHAU 92:7
grace Amazing g. NEWT 250:18

Angels and ministers of g. SHAK 291:35
But for the g. of God BRAD 67:5
by the g. of God BIBL 50:27
fallen from g. BIBL 51:11
G. me no grace SHAK 305:24
G. under pressure HEMI 166:5
inward and spiritual g. BOOK 61:20
snatch a g. POPE 267:5
speech be alway with g. BIBL 52:1
that g. may abound BIBL 50:1
with a better g. SHAK 308:29
gracious he is g. BOOK 64:30
gradualness inevitability of g. WEBB 352:12
graduates sweet girl-g. TENN 334:11
grain choice g. STOU 326:17
g. of salt PLIN 265:7
world in a g. of sand BLAK 56:8
grammar don't want to talk g. SHAW 312:27
g., and nonsense GOLD 153:22
Heedless of g. BARH 26:12
talking bad g. DISR 117:18
grammatici G. certant HORA 174:14
gramophone g. company TREE 341:14
puts a record on the g. ELIO 129:29
grand down the G. Canyon MARQ 228:23
g. Perhaps BROW 71:22
g. to be blooming well dead SARO 285:18
grandeur charged with the g. HOPK 173:16
g. in this view DARW 110:10
g. that was Rome POE 265:22
grandfather ape for his g. HUXL 179:22
g. or his grandmother WILB 357:24
grandmother grandfather or his g. WILB 357:24
We have become a g. THAT 336:23
grange at the moated g. SHAK 302:9
granites Through g. which titanic wars OWEN 256:13
grant half g. what I wish FROS 143:9
grape peel me a g. WEST 355:7
grapes g. of wrath HOWE 177:2
sour g. BIBL 41:28
grapeshot whiff of g. CARL 85:10
grasp exceed his g. BROW 71:20
G. it like a man of mettle HILL 169:2
grasped haven't g. the situation KERR 199:10
grass All flesh is g. BIBL 41:1
but as g. BOOK 64:3
flesh is as g. BIBL 52:25
g. below CLAR 96:27
g. beyond the door ROSS 280:22
g. can grow through cement CHER 92:12
g. grows on the weirs YEAT 368:1
g. will grow in the streets HOOV 173:6
green g. shorn BACO 22:27
hearing the g. grow ELIO 127:17
I am the g. SAND 285:6
I fall on g. MARV 229:16
leaf of g. is no less WHIT 357:6
Pigeons on the g. STEI 323:15
snake hidden in the g. VIRG 347:20
splendour in the g. WORD 365:9
two blades of g. SWIF 328:10
grasses by short g. PORT 269:8
grasshoppers half a dozen g. BURK 75:22
grassy fair Fidele's g. tomb COLL 101:15
grateful single g. thought LESS 213:10
gratefully O g. sing GRAN 155:8
gratias Deo g. MISS 240:19
gratified g. desire BLAK 57:13
gratitude G., like love ALSO 5:20
g. we owe to Adam TWAI 343:22
grau G. ist alle Theorie GOET 152:10
grave cold g. BALL 26:1
cradle and the g. DYER 124:1

grave (cont.)

Dig the g. and let me lie	STEV 326:5
dread The g. as little	KEN 198:6
Even the g. yawns	TREE 341:13
from the cradle to the g.	CHUR 95:16
Funeral marches to the g.	LONG 217:19
give birth astride of a g.	BECK 28:16
go into my g.	PEPY 261:20
g. is not its goal	LONG 217:18
g. of a dead Fenian	COLL 101:13
g.'s a fine and private	MARV 229:22
g., where is thy victory	BIBL 51:4
g., whither thou goest	BIBL 39:20
into the darkness of the g.	MILL 234:17
jealousy is cruel as the g.	BIBL 40:2
kind of healthy g.	SMIT 319:6
lead but to the g.	GRAY 156:9
pompous in the g.	BROW 71:9
she is in her g.	WORD 365:28
shovel a g. in the air	CELA 89:16
shown Longfellow's g.	MOOR 244:4
stand at my g. and cry	FRYE 144:10
with sorrow to the g.	BIBL 35:8
graved G. inside of it	BROW 72:2
graves g. of their neighbours	EDWA 125:12
g. stood tenantless	SHAK 291:9
Let's talk of g.	SHAK 305:29
greasy grey-green, g., Limpopo	KIPL 203:16
top of the g. pole	DISR 118:6
great both g. and small	COLE 100:27
From the g. deep	TENN 332:11
g. book	CALL 82:19
g. gulf fixed	BIBL 48:2
g. illusion	ANGE 7:1
G. is Diana	BIBL 49:32
g. is truth	BROO 70:8
g. man has his disciples	WILD 358:14
G. Society	JOHN 186:7
g. things from the valley	CHES 93:11
g. to them that know	SPRI 322:13
Lives of g. men	LONG 217:21
many people think him g.	JOHN 189:6
nothing g. but man	HAMI 160:13
Nothing g. was ever achieved	EMER 132:5
some men are born g.	SHAK 309:2
those who were truly g.	SPEN 321:18
To be g. is to be misunderstood	EMER 132:12
with small men no g. thing	MILL 234:11
Great Britain G. has lost an empire	ACHE 1:6
greater G. love hath no man	BIBL 49:7
g. than Solomon	BIBL 44:38
g. than the whole	HESI 168:9
g. than we know	WORD 365:23
thy need is g.	SIDN 316:17
greatest g. event it is	FOX 140:14
g. happiness	HUTC 179:6
g. thing in the world	MONT 242:22
happiness of the g. number	BENT 31:6
I'm the g.	ALI 5:6
life to live as the g. he	RAIN 272:20
greatly g. to his credit	GILB 150:20
greatness farewell, to all my g.	SHAK 296:12
g. thrust upon them	SHAK 309:2
moment of my g. flicker	ELIO 129:1
nature of all g.	BURK 75:6
Greece education to G.	PERI 262:1
glory that was G.	POE 265:22
G. might still be free	BYRO 81:1
isles of G.	BYRO 80:29
To Gaul, to G.	COWP 105:23
greed G. is all right	BOES 58:14
infectious g.	GREE 157:4
not enough for everyone's g.	BUCH 73:16

Greek half G., half Latin	SCOT 287:3
it was G. to me	SHAK 296:22
small Latin, and less G.	JONS 192:6
wife talks G.	JOHN 191:1
Greeks G. had a word	AKIN 4:4
G. seek after wisdom	BIBL 50:14
I fear the G.	VIRG 347:4
unto the G. foolishness	BIBL 50:15
writings of the G.	OMAR 253:11
green bordered by its gardens g.	MORR 245:12
Colourless g. ideas	CHOM 94:6
drives my g. age	THOM 337:20
feed me in a g. pasture	BOOK 62:14
Flora and the country g.	KEAT 196:17
g. and pleasant land	BLAK 57:8
g. as emerald	COLE 100:16
G. Eye	HAYE 164:2
g.-eyed monster	SHAK 305:1
g. grass shorn	BACO 22:27
G. grow the rashes, O	BURN 76:28
G. grow the rushes O	ANON 9:2
g. hill far away	ALEX 4:18
G. how I love you	LORC 218:17
g. in judgment	SHAK 289:16
g. shoots of recovery	LAMO 207:11
How g. was my valley	LLEW 216:5
life springs ever g.	GOET 152:10
Make it a g. peace	DARN 109:21
Making the g. one red	SHAK 300:19
My passport's g.	HEAN 164:12
one g.	BASH 27:11
Their g. felicity	KEAT 195:20
To a g. thought	MARV 229:17
wearin' o' the G.	ANON 9:4
Wherever g. is worn	YEAT 368:5
greenery-yallery g., Grosvenor Gallery	GILB 150:16
greenhouse g. gases	MARG 227:17
Greenland From G.'s icy mountains	HEBE 164:17
Greensleeves G. was all my joy	ANON 8:13
greenwood Under the g. tree	SHAK 290:7
grenadier British G.	ANON 11:1
Pomeranian g.	BISM 55:6
Grenville Richard G. lay	TENN 334:25
grey bring down my g. hairs	BIBL 35:8
Green pleasure or g. grief	SWIN 329:15
g.-green, greasy, Limpopo	KIPL 203:16
hair is g.	BYRO 81:16
in my g. hairs	WOLS 363:13
lend me your g. mare	BALL 26:3
little g. cells	CHRI 94:11
philosophy paints its g.	HEGE 165:4
this old g. head	WHIT 357:13
world has grown g.	SWIN 329:14
you are old and g.	YEAT 369:13
grief acquainted with g.	BIBL 41:9
But g. returns	SHEL 313:14
forethought of g.	BERR 32:17
Green pleasure or grey g.	SWIN 329:15
g. felt so like fear	LEWI 213:16
G. fills the room up	SHAK 297:18
g. forgotten	SWIN 329:8
g. itself be mortal	SHEL 313:15
g. that does not speak	SHAK 301:19
master a g.	SHAK 304:12
pitch of g.	HOPK 173:21
Should be past g.	SHAK 309:18
griefs cutteth g. in halves	BACO 22:24
g. and fears	BACO 23:1
grievance Scotsman with a g.	WODE 362:16
grieved g. my heart to think	WORD 364:22
grieves thing that g. not	MARK 228:1
grieving áre you g.	HOPK 174:3
grievous most g. fault	MISS 240:16

remembrance of them is g. BOOK 61:8
grimace accelerated g. POUN 269:22
grin ending with the g. CARR 86:10
one universal g. FIEL 135:14
grind g. the faces of the poor BIBL 40:6
Laws g. the poor GOLD 153:17
mills of God g. slowly LONG 218:1
grinders incisors and g. BAGE 24:11
groan Condemned alike to g. GRAY 156:17
groans g. of love to those of the dying LOWR 220:7
groined titanic wars had g. OWEN 256:13
grooves moves In determinate g. HARE 162:11
ringing g. of time TENN 333:32
grosser g. name SHAK 294:1
Grosvenor Gallery greenery-yallery, G. GILB 150:16
Groucho of the G. tendency ANON 12:15
ground acre of barren g. SHAK 307:17
as water spilt on the g. BIBL 36:38
fell into good g. BIBL 44:39
gain a little patch of g. SHAK 293:26
G. control to Major Tom BOWI 67:1
holy g. BIBL 35:13
in a fair g. BOOK 62:10
see me cover the g. GROS 158:2
seven feet of English g. HARO 162:14
when I hit the g. SPRI 322:16
grove g. of chimneys MORR 245:5
olive g. of Academe MILT 239:18
groves g. of Academe HORA 175:5
g. of *their* academy BURK 75:20
grow g. up with the country GREE 156:22
They shall g. not old BINY 54:24
growed I s'pect I g. STOW 326:18
growth children of a larger g. CHES 92:20
children of a larger g. DRYD 121:28
root of all genuine g. SMIL 317:20
grudge ancient g. I bear him SHAK 302:12
grumbling rhythmical g. ELIO 130:9
Grundy What will Mrs G. think MORT 246:9
gruntled far from being g. WODE 362:17
guarantees g. all others CHUR 96:3
guard G. us, guide us EDME 125:6
guardian G. and my Guide WILL 360:4
guards G. die CAMB 83:1
Up G. and at them WELL 354:1
who is to guard the g. JUVE 194:8
gude g. time coming SCOT 287:24
guerre *ce n'est pas la g.* BOSQ 66:1
guerrilla g. wins if he does not KISS 204:1
guessing g. what was at the other side WELL 354:7
guest speed the going g. POPE 268:6
Speed the parting g. POPE 268:6
guidance Messenger with the g. KORA 205:21
sent down to be a g. KORA 204:20
guide God to be his g. BUNY 74:16
Guardian and my G. WILL 360:4
g. by the light of reason BRAN 67:15
very g. of life BUTL 79:1
guided g. missiles KING 201:1
guides blind g. BIBL 45:30
Guildenstern Rosencrantz and G. SHAK 294:15
guile in whom is no g. BIBL 48:23
guilt dwell on g. AUST 20:25
Life without industry is g. RUSK 282:13
wash her g. away GOLD 153:27
without its g. SOME 320:8
guilty crimes of this g. land BROW 70:17
G. of dust and sin HERB 167:17
g. thing surprised WORD 365:8
haunts the g. mind SHAK 296:7
Let no g. man escape GRAN 155:14
Saints should be judged g. ORWE 255:6
started like a g. thing SHAK 291:10

ten g. persons escape BLAC 55:16
guinea but the g.'s stamp BURN 76:26
jingling of the g. TENN 333:23
guitar blue g. STEV 324:18
gulag G. archipelago SOLZ 320:7
gulf great g. fixed BIBL 48:2
redwood forest to the G. Stream GUTH 158:11
gulfs g. will wash us down TENN 335:7
whelmed in deeper g. COWP 105:15
gullet g. of New York MILL 235:1
gulls cry of g. ELIO 129:30
gum can't fart and chew g. JOHN 186:12
gun grows out of the barrel of a g. MAO 227:12
Happiness is a warm g. LENN 212:13
Maxim G. BELL 29:24
no g., but I can spit AUDE 19:15
through the door with a g. CHAN 90:14
gunfire towards the sound of g. GRIM 157:17
Gunga Din than I am, G. KIPL 202:8
gunpowder G., Printing CARL 85:8
g. ran out FOOT 139:4
G. Treason and Plot ANON 10:10
Printing, g. BACO 23:33
guns G. aren't lawful PARK 258:16
g. that are hidden FLEI 138:6
hundred men with g. PUZO 272:6
monstrous anger of the g. OWEN 256:8
not found any smoking g. BLIX 58:10
rather have butter or g. GOER 152:6
sell him g. GALL 145:10
They got the g. MORR 245:17
with g. not with butter GOEB 152:5
gusts our g. and storms ELIU 127:8
Gutenberg G. made everybody MCLU 224:2
guts g. of the last priest DIDE 116:11
lug the g. SHAK 293:24
sheeps' g. SHAK 304:9
strangled with the g. MESL 233:15
gutta G. *cavat lapidem* OVID 255:25
gutter We are all in the g. WILD 358:20
guys G. and dolls RUNY 282:4
Nice g. finish last DURO 123:14
gyre Did g. and gimble CARR 86:23
gyves With g. upon his wrist HOOD 172:21

H

ha H., ha BIBL 38:9
habeas corpus protection of *h.* JEFF 184:8
habit Cocaine h.-forming BANK 26:7
Growing old a bad h. MAUR 231:14
H. is a great deadener BECK 28:17
H. with him was all CRAB 106:5
order breeds h. ADAM 1:21
Sow a h. READ 274:1
habitation local h. and a name SHAK 304:2
soul's h. henceforth RUSS 283:7
habitual h. hatred WASH 351:9
nothing is h. but indecision JAME 183:6
hack Do not h. me MONM 242:7
Hackney Marshes You could see to H. BATE 27:16
Hades dark H.' door VIRG 347:11
gates of H. HOME 172:12
haggard prove her h. SHAK 305:2
Haggards H. ride no more STEP 324:3
hags black, and midnight h. SHAK 301:14
hail beaten dog beneath the h. POUN 270:3
H. Mary ANON 13:8
h. the power PERR 262:8
H., thou that art highly favoured BIBL 46:31
H. to thee, blithe Spirit SHEL 314:25

hail (*cont.*)
sharp and sided h.   HOPK 173:19
hair All her h.   BROW 72:25
amber-dropping h.   MILT 236:10
bind my h.   HUNT 178:20
bracelet of bright h.   DONN 119:13
colour of his h.   HOUS 176:1
h. is grey   BYRO 81:16
h. of his head   BIBL 42:8
h. of my flesh stood up   BIBL 37:38
Her h. was long   KEAT 195:25
if a woman have long h.   BIBL 50:21
long essenced h.   MACA 221:19
part my h. behind   ELIO 129:4
raiment of camel's h.   BIBL 43:6
Rapunzel, let down you h.   GRIM 157:16
red faces, and loose h.   EQUI 132:30
right outa my h.   HAMM 160:16
with a single h.   DRYD 122:18
with a single h.   POPE 268:16
with such h.   BROW 73:5
Your ashen h. Shulamith   CELA 89:16
hairs bring down my grey h.   BIBL 35:8
h. of your head   BIBL 44:28
white h.   SHAK 294:30
hairy my brother is a h. man   BIBL 34:35
halcyon h. days   SHAK 296:1
half h.-angel and half-bird   BROW 73:1
h. as old as Time   BURG 74:24
h.-brother of the world   BAIL 24:15
h. is greater   HESI 168:9
h. slave   LINC 214:13
h. that's got my keys   GRAH 154:20
h. was not told me   BIBL 37:6
longest h. of your life   SOUT 320:22
One h. of the world   AUST 20:21
overcome but h. his foe   MILT 237:29
Too clever by h.   SALI 284:18
Too clever by h.   SALI 284:23
hallelujah H. Chorus   HAND 161:1
halloo H. your name   SHAK 308:25
hallow cannot h. this ground   LINC 214:20
hallowed H. be thy name   BIBL 43:22
halls dwelt in marble h.   BUNN 74:4
h. of Montezuma   ANON 8:9
halo jealousy with a h.   WELL 354:14
life is a luminous h.   WOOL 363:19
What after all Is a h.   FRY 144:7
halt h., and the blind   BIBL 47:25
h. ye between two opinions   BIBL 37:11
Hamlet H. without the Prince   SCOT 287:25
not Prince H.   ELIO 129:2
hammock Drake he's in his h.   NEWB 249:16
hand bloody and invisible h.   SHAK 301:3
by the h. of God   MARA 227:15
by the h. of the Lord   BIBL 35:23
gladly shake your h.   BRAN 67:18
h. into the Hand of God   HASK 163:5
h. of Jean Jacques Rousseau   HEIN 165:9
h. that fired   BALL 25:9
h. that lays the golden egg   GOLD 154:2
h. that mocked them   SHEL 314:11
h. that rocks the cradle   WALL 349:15
h. that signed the paper   THOM 337:22
h. that wrote it   CRAN 106:10
h. the cutting edge of the mind   BRON 69:6
h., the head   RUSK 282:20
h. then of the potter   FITZ 136:18
h. to execute   CLAR 96:28
h. to execute   GIBB 148:18
Have still the upper h.   COWA 105:7
Heaving up my either h.   HERR 167:29
His [Ishmael's] h.   BIBL 34:31

into mine h.   BIBL 36:31
invisible h. in politics   FRIE 142:22
kingdom of heaven is at h.   BIBL 43:4
led by an invisible h.   SMIT 318:4
let not thy left h. know   BIBL 43:21
like a man's h.   BIBL 37:12
like the dyer's h.   SHAK 310:20
my h. into his side   BIBL 49:17
one h. clapping   HAKU 159:7
put his h. to the plough   BIBL 47:12
Put out my h. and touched   MAGE 225:3
right h. forget her cunning   BOOK 65:2
sound of the single h.   HAKU 159:7
sweeten this little h.   SHAK 301:24
sweet Roman h.   SHAK 309:6
sword sleep in my h.   BLAK 57:8
They h. in hand   MILT 239:14
Thy h., great Anarch   POPE 266:9
Took me by the h.   TURN 343:5
touch of a vanished h.   TENN 331:16
Whatsoever thy h. findeth   BIBL 39:20
Wouldst hold my h.   HART 163:1
handbag LADY BRACKNELL: A h.   WILD 358:8
handbook constable's h.   KING 201:10
handclasp h.'s a little stronger   CHAP 90:17
handcuffs h. on his wrists   HOUS 176:1
handful fear in a h. of dust   ELIO 129:19
h. of meal   BIBL 37:10
handiwork firmament sheweth his h.   BOOK 62:11
handles Everything has two h.   EPIC 132:27
handmaid nature's h.   DRYD 122:1
handmaiden low estate of his h.   BIBL 46:32
hands blood on their h.   SPEN 321:15
blood on your h.   CARL 85:1
Father, into thy h.   BIBL 48:11
folding of the h.   BIBL 38:16
h., and handle not   BOOK 64:15
h. are the hands of Esau   BIBL 35:1
h. of the living God   BIBL 52:13
h. so deeply inserted   BIER 54:16
hath not a Jew h.   SHAK 302:21
Holding h. at midnight   GERS 148:10
horny h. of toil   LOWE 220:1
house not made with h.   BIBL 51:6
house not made with h.   BROW 71:24
Into thy h.   BOOK 62:20
keep my h. from picking   BOOK 61:19
knit h., and beat the ground   MILT 236:4
License my roving h.   DONN 118:21
Pale h. I loved   HOPE 173:12
reached out their h. in longing   VIRG 347:12
Soul clap its h. and sing   YEAT 368:27
spits on its h.   SAND 285:10
washed his h.   BIBL 46:17
With mine own h.   SHAK 306:4
world's great h.   HUNT 178:18
handsaw know a hawk from a h.   SHAK 292:17
hang all h. together   FRAN 142:1
h. my hat   JERO 185:7
in them which will h. him   RICH 276:11
let him h. there   EHRL 125:15
wretches h.   POPE 268:20
hanged h., drawn, and quartered   PEPY 261:16
h. for stealing horses   HALI 160:2
h. in a fortnight   JOHN 189:18
my poor fool is h.   SHAK 298:28
see him h.   BELL 29:22
hanging cured by h. from a string   KING 201:12
h. Danny Deever   KIPL 201:21
H. is too good for him   BUNY 74:11
Many a good h.   SHAK 308:21
hangs thereby h. a tale   SHAK 290:9
hank bone and a h. of hair   KIPL 203:3

happen can't h. here — LEWI 214:6
fools said would h. — MELB 232:10
h. to your mother — WALK 349:7
poetry makes nothing h. — AUDE 19:2
happens be there when it h. — ALLE 5:15
Nothing h. — BECK 28:14
nothing h. — WELD 353:13
Nothing, like something, h. anywhere — LARK 208:19
Stuff h. — RUMS 282:3
what h. to her — ELIO 127:11
happier seek No h. state — MILT 238:27
happiest h. and best minds — SHEL 315:5
h. women — ELIO 127:20
happily h. ever after — ANON 7:9
happiness brief period of h. — ARIS 15:13
consume h. without producing — SHAW 311:10
enemy to human h. — JOHN 190:10
fatal to true h. — RUSS 283:1
greatest h. — HUTC 179:6
H. depends on being free — THUC 339:26
H. is an imaginary — SZAS 329:18
H. is a warm gun — LENN 212:13
H. is not an ideal — KANT 194:23
h. is produced — JOHN 189:13
H. lies in conquering — GENG 147:13
h. makes up in height — FROS 143:17
h. of society — ADAM 2:10
h. of the greatest number — BENT 31:6
H. was but the occasional — HARD 161:17
lifetime of h. — SHAW 311:30
look into h. — SHAK 290:24
more for human h. — BRIL 69:3
only one h. in life — SAND 285:3
or justice or human h. — BERL 32:8
politics of h. — HUMP 178:14
pursuit of h. — ANON 11:14
pursuit of h. — JEFF 183:18
recipe for h. — AUST 20:24
result h. — DICK 114:19
suited to human h. — DEFO 111:18
that is h. — CATH 88:18
that is h. — EMER 132:13
happy all be as h. as kings — STEV 325:27
Call no man h. — SOLO 320:5
conspiracy to make you h. — UPDI 344:16
duty of being h. — STEV 325:20
had a h. life — HAZL 164:7
H. birthday to you — HILL 169:6
h. could I be with either — GAY 147:2
h. families resemble — TOLS 341:3
H. field or mossy cavern — KEAT 196:4
h. he who crowns in shades — GOLD 153:6
H. in this — SHAK 302:26
H. is the man — BOOK 64:27
H. is the man who fears — BIBL 53:30
h. noise to hear — HOUS 176:9
H. the man — DRYD 122:16
H. the people — MONT 243:7
make a man h. — HORA 174:25
make men h. — POPE 268:9
man would be as h. — JOHN 189:26
must laugh before we are h. — LA B 206:10
one who has been h. — BOET 58:15
policeman's lot is not a h. one — GILB 150:24
remember a h. time — DANT 109:12
someone, somewhere, may be h. — MENC 232:19
splendid and a h. land — GOLD 153:11
This is the h. warrior — READ 273:18
till all are h. — SPEN 321:14
touch the H. Isles — TENN 335:7
'Twere now to be most h. — SHAK 304:28
Was he h. — AUDE 19:22
whether you are h. — MILL 234:3

whether you are h. — SHAW 312:23
Who is the h. Warrior — WORD 364:9
h. world of the h. — WITT 362:14
harbinger Love's h. — MILT 239:12
harbour those who h. them — BUSH 78:16
voyage not a h. — TOYN 341:9
hard h. day's night — LENN 212:20
h. rain's a gonna fall — DYLA 124:4
Long is the way, And h. — MILT 238:7
This is a h. tour — ARMS 16:4
harden h. not your hearts — BOOK 63:27
h. Pharaoh's heart — BIBL 35:16
hardly Johnny, I h. knew ye — BALL 25:10
Hardy Kiss me, H. — NELS 249:10
hare h. sitting up — LAWR 209:21
h. when it is cased — GLAS 151:17
hark H.! the herald-angels — WESL 354:18
harlot h.'s cry — BLAK 56:13
prerogative of the h. — KIPL 203:25
harlots MOTHER OF H. — BIBL 53:19
Harlow silent, as in H. — ASQU 18:2
harm does h. to my wit — SHAK 308:19
do so much h. — CREI 106:15
do the sick no h. — NIGH 251:13
False views do little h. — DARW 110:4
meaning no h. — GREE 156:27
supposed to do no h. — RUSS 283:6
to prevent h. — MILL 234:7
harmless h. as doves — BIBL 44:27
only h. great thing — DONN 119:3
harmonious h. madness — SHEL 314:29
harmony All discord, h. — POPE 267:25
Discordant h. — HORA 175:1
from heavenly h. — DRYD 122:10
herkenyng h. — CHAU 92:5
immortal god of h. — BEET 29:6
harness joints of the h. — BIBL 37:18
harp H. not on that string — SHAK 306:16
h. that once through Tara's halls — MOOR 244:8
wild h. slung behind him — MOOR 244:10
harps touch their h. of gold — SEAR 288:5
harpsichord describing the h. — BEEC 28:22
Harry God for H. — SHAK 295:17
little touch of H. — SHAK 295:18
thy H.'s company — SHAK 294:21
harsh Not h. nor grating — WORD 364:20
so h. to the clever — WORD 364:8
hart As pants the h. — TATE 330:19
as the h. desireth — BOOK 62:27
footed like a h. — MALO 226:8
h. ungallèd — SHAK 293:11
Harvard glass flowers at H. — MOOR 244:4
Yale College and my H. — MELV 232:14
harvest h. is past — BIBL 41:20
h. of a quiet eye — WORD 365:15
h. truly is plenteous — BIBL 44:24
laughs with a h. — JERR 185:9
shine on, h. moon — NORW 252:6
haste always in h. — WESL 355:4
Make h. slowly — AUGU 20:13
maketh h. to be rich — BIBL 39:2
Men love in h. — BYRO 81:7
said in my h. — BOOK 64:17
what h. I can to be gone — CROM 107:17
Without h., but without rest — GOET 152:23
Ye shall eat it in h. — BIBL 35:19
hasten minutes h. to their end — SHAK 310:10
hat hang my h. — JERO 185:7
looking for a black h. — BOWE 66:16
hatched h. from a swan's egg — ANDE 6:13
hatches continually under h. — KEAT 197:14
hatchet cut it with my h. — WASH 351:10
hatching H. vain empires — MILT 238:6

hate h. all Boets and Bainters — GEOR 147:14
h. a song that has sold — BERL 32:5
h. that which we often fear — SHAK 289:14
how much men h. them — GREE 157:6
If h. killed men — BROW 73:2
I h. and I love — CATU 89:8
I h. war — ROOS 279:10
immortal h. — MILT 237:20
letter of h. — OSBO 255:14
Let them h. — ACCI 1:3
make us h. — SWIF 328:19
must h. a Frenchman — NELS 249:4
never bother with people I h. — HART 162:21
not to h. them — SHAW 311:14
of love is not h. — WIES 357:21
People must learn to h. — MAND 226:17
seen much to h. here — MILL 234:21
sprung from my only h. — SHAK 306:26
them also that h. him — BOOK 63:14
them which h. you — BIBL 47:9
time to h. — BIBL 39:12
We can scarcely h. — HAZL 164:6
you h. something in him — HESS 168:10
hateful What is h. to you — HILL 169:10
hates h. dogs and babies — ROST 281:4
h. them for it — SHAW 313:1
hateth h. his brother — BIBL 52:34
hath Unto every one that h. — BIBL 46:5
hating h. all other nations — GASK 146:15
h., my boy, is an art — NASH 248:13
hatless lands h. from the air — BETJ 33:3
hatred common h. for something — CHEK 92:11
envy, h., and malice — BOOK 60:11
Great h., little room — YEAT 368:25
habitual h. — WASH 351:9
h. is by far the longest — BYRO 81:7
h. therewith — BIBL 38:27
love to h. turned — CONG 102:7
public h. — CLAY 97:14
Regulated h. — HARD 161:1
set against the h. — MCEW 223:2
What we need is h. — GENE 147:12
hatreds organization of h. — ADAM 1:18
hats H. off, gentlemen — SCHU 286:17
shocking bad h. — WELL 354:6
haunts h. of coot and hern — TENN 331:17
have haves and the h.-nots — CERV 89:20
h. to take you in — FROS 143:13
I h. thee not — SHAK 300:12
To h. and to hold — BOOK 61:27
Havergal Luke H. — ROBI 277:16
haves and the have-nots — CERV 89:20
havoc Cry, 'H.!' and let slip — SHAK 296:30
hawk h. of the tower — SKEL 317:14
his h., his hound — BALL 25:21
know a h. from a handsaw — SHAK 292:17
Hawkshaw H., the detective — TAYL 331:6
hay lie tumbling in the h. — SHAK 309:21
live on h. — HILL 169:4
hazelnut no bigger than a h. — JULI 193:13
he Art thou h. — BIBL 44:31
H. would, wouldn't he — RICE 276:4
While H. is mine, and I am His — HERB 167:23
head brains go to his h. — ASQU 18:3
dark hole of the h. — HUGH 177:17
God be in my h. — ANON 8:10
Go up, thou bald h. — BIBL 37:21
hairs of your h. — BIBL 44:28
hand, the h. — RUSK 282:20
h. that once was crowned — KELL 198:3
h. that wears a crown — SHAK 295:3
h. thou dust — SCOT 288:3
h. to contrive — CLAR 96:28

h. to contrive — GIBB 148:18
if you can keep your h. — KERR 199:10
If you can keep your h. — KIPL 202:9
It shall bruise thy h. — BIBL 34:19
Johnny-h.-in-air — PUDN 271:14
My h. is bloody, but unbowed — HENL 166:8
My h.'s clear — MACK 223:11
Off with her h. — CARR 86:13
one small h. could carry — GOLD 153:10
Or in the heart or in the h. — SHAK 302:25
shorter by the h. — ELIZ 130:13
should have his h. examined — GOLD 154:4
show my h. to the people — DANT 109:19
so old a h. — SHAK 302:29
where to lay his h. — BIBL 44:16
which way the h. lies — RALE 273:6
headache with a dismal h. — GILB 149:20
heading do you know where we're h. — DYLA 124:11
heads h. Do grow beneath — SHAK 304:22
h. replete with thoughts — COWP 106:1
H. Were toward Eternity — DICK 115:27
Lift up your h. — BOOK 62:17
headstrong h. as an allegory — SHER 315:13
heal Physician, h. thyself — BIBL 47:8
healed h. of a suffering — PROU 271:10
my soul shall be h. — MISS 241:1
ransomed, h. — LYTE 221:4
healer sharp compassion of the h.'s art — ELIO 128:9
healing h. fountain — AUDE 19:6
h. in his wings — BIBL 42:17
H. is a matter of time — HIPP 169:21
h. of the nations — BIBL 53:25
not heroics, but h. — HARD 161:12
health in sickness and in h. — BOOK 61:27
Look to your h. — WALT 350:14
no h. in us — BOOK 59:13
When you have both, it's h. — DONL 118:17
healthful most h. of beverages — PAST 260:5
healthy h. and wealthy and dead — THUR 340:4
h. bones of a single Pomeranian — BISM 55:6
hear All the better to h. you with — PERR 262:7
another to h. — THOR 339:23
hath ears to h. — BIBL 46:25
h. a smile — CROS 107:20
h. in my imagination — MOZA 246:13
H., O Israel — BIBL 36:3
h. our prayers — BOOK 61:21
H. the other side — AUGU 20:7
h. the word of the Lord — BIBL 42:4
h. thy shrill delight — SHEL 314:27
in such wise h. them — BOOK 60:20
make you h. — CONR 102:25
prefer not to h. — AGAR 3:22
you will h. me — DISR 117:4
heard have ye not h. — BIBL 41:3
I will be h. — GARR 146:9
You ain't h. nuttin' yet — JOLS 191:7
hearers not h. only — BIBL 52:20
heareth thy servant h. — BIBL 36:22
hearing People h. without listening — SIMO 317:3
hearses frequent h. — POPE 266:11
heart abundance of the h. — BIBL 44:37
anniversaries of the h. — LONG 217:14
ás the h. grows older — HOPK 174:4
Batter my h. — DONN 118:24
beak from out my h. — POE 265:20
Beware my foolish h. — WASH 351:13
Bury my h. at Wounded Knee — BENÉ 30:15
But break, my h. — SHAK 291:21
committed adultery in my h. — CART 88:2
deep h.'s core — YEAT 368:16
deserts of the h. — AUDE 19:6
desires of the h. — AUDE 18:15

ease a h. like a satin gown	PARK 258:17	Shakespeare unlocked his h.	BROW 72:7
education of the h.	SCOT 287:26	So the h. be right	RALE 273:6
fed my h.	PETR 262:13	squirrel's h. beat	ELIO 127:17
fed the h. on fantasies	YEAT 368:19	Sweeping up the H.	DICK 115:29
Fourteen h. attacks	JOPL 192:11	there will your h. be	BIBL 43:24
from hell's h.	MELV 232:15	time by h.-throbs	BAIL 24:14
gentil h.	CHAU 91:25	true love hath my h.	SIDN 316:11
given you her h.	VANB 345:5	want of h.	HOOD 172:24
grieved my h. to think	WORD 364:22	where my h. is turning ever	FOST 140:9
harden Pharaoh's h.	BIBL 35:16	**heartbeat** h. from the Presidency	STEV 325:5
h. and hands and voices	WINK 361:22	**hearth** By this still h.	TENN 334:31
h. and stomach of a king	ELIZ 130:14	cricket on the h.	MILT 236:13
h. be troubled	BIBL 49:3	from an unextinguished h.	SHEL 314:7
h. for any fate	LONG 217:22	**heartily** let us h. rejoice	BOOK 63:26
h. has its reasons	PASC 259:22	**heartless** restrain the h.	KING 200:13
h.—how shall I say?	BROW 72:18	**hearts** all h. be open	BOOK 60:25
h. in the business	WATS 351:14	all that human h. endure	GOLD 153:18
h. is deceitful	BIBL 41:23	harden not your h.	BOOK 63:27
h. is Highland	GALT 145:12	h. and minds	BIBL 51:27
h. is inditing	BOOK 63:1	h. beating	BROW 72:15
h. is like a singing bird	ROSS 280:10	h. have not grown old	YEAT 369:14
h. is restless	AUGU 19:28	h. of his countrymen	LEE 211:13
h. leaps up	WORD 364:24	heedless h.	GRAY 156:20
H. of England	DRAY 121:11	imagination of their h.	BIBL 46:33
h. of furious fancies	ANON 12:5	Incline our h.	BOOK 61:1
h. of man	DOST 119:27	Kind h. are more than coronets	TENN 333:14
h. of man	HUME 178:9	Lift up your h.	BOOK 61:10
H. of oak	GARR 146:6	offspring of cold h.	BURK 75:19
h.'s a little banged up	MACK 223:11	O you hard h.	SHAK 296:17
h. speaks to heart	FRAN 141:12	Pluck their h. from them	SHAK 295:24
H. speaks to heart	NEWM 250:9	queen in people's h.	DIAN 114:8
h. strangely warmed	WESL 355:2	Two h. that beat as one	HALM 160:10
h. that fed	SHEL 314:11	**heat** can't stand the h.	TRUM 342:11
h. the keener	ANON 14:1	H. not a furnace	SHAK 296:8
h. to a dog to tear	KIPL 202:18	h. of the day	BIBL 45:22
h. to heart	SCOT 287:11	not without dust and h.	MILT 240:5
h. to resolve	GIBB 148:18	white h. of revolution	WILS 361:4
h. upon my sleeve	SHAK 304:17	white h. of technology	WILS 361:4
h. would hear her and beat	TENN 334:7	**heath** Upon this blasted h.	SHAK 299:14
hides one thing in his h.	HOME 172:12	**heathen** exalted among the h.	BOOK 63:5
his little h.	JAME 183:1	h. in his blindness	HEBE 164:18
holiness of the h.'s affections	KEAT 197:9	h. in 'is blindness	KIPL 201:22
If thy h. fails thee	ELIZ 130:18	h. so furiously rage	BOOK 62:7
In my h.'s core	SHAK 293:8	**heather** bonnie bloomin' h.	LAUD 209:14
I would eat his h.	SHAK 304:15	**heaven** All this, and h. too	HENR 167:1
language of the h.	POPE 266:23	all we know of h.	DICK 116:2
left my h. in San Francisco	CROS 107:19	Bread of h.	WILL 360:5
let your h. be strong	LAUD 209:13	by a whirlwind into h.	BIBL 37:19
look in thy h. and write	SIDN 316:12	climbing h., and gazing	SHEL 314:31
lying in my h.	MARY 230:14	climb up into the h.	BOOK 65:3
make a stone of the h.	YEAT 368:4	Earth's crammed with h.	BROW 71:14
Make me a clean h.	BOOK 63:7	face of h. so fine	SHAK 307:2
maketh the h. sick	BIBL 38:22	fallen from h.	BIBL 40:19
man after his own h.	BIBL 36:27	Fellowship is h.	MORR 245:13
may not change the h.	KING 200:13	gazing up into h.	BIBL 49:20
Mercy has a human h.	BLAK 57:17	Give the jolly h. above	STEV 326:2
merry h.	BIBL 38:26	God's in his h.	BROW 72:23
merry h. doeth good	BIBL 38:30	gold bar of H.	ROSS 280:18
My h. aches	KEAT 196:16	great wonder in h.	BIBL 53:11
My h. in hiding	HOPK 174:10	H. and Charing Cross	THOM 338:19
My h. is heavy	GOET 152:12	h. and earth shall pass	BIBL 46:1
my h. is pure	TENN 334:27	h. and the earth	BIBL 34:3
My h.'s in the Highlands	BURN 77:6	h. doing good on earth	TERE 335:24
no longer tear his h.	SWIF 329:6	h. expands	BROW 71:24
no matter from the h.	SHAK 308:16	H. has no rage	CONG 102:7
None but the lonely h.	GOET 152:21	H. in a rage	BLAK 56:9
not your h. away	HOUS 176:8	h. in a wild flower	BLAK 56:8
only with the h.	SAIN 284:9	H. in Hell's despair	BLAK 57:23
Open my h.	BROW 72:2	H. lies about us	WORD 365:6
Or in the h. or in the head	SHAK 302:25	H. sends us good meat	GARR 146:8
O tiger's h.	SHAK 296:6	h.'s vaults should crack	SHAK 298:26
pondered them in her h.	BIBL 47:5	H. what I cannot	DICK 115:30
rag-and-bone shop of the h.	YEAT 367:16	H. will protect	SMIT 318:12

heaven (*cont.*)

h. with their tears	BLAK 58:4
Hell in H.'s despite	BLAK 57:24
house as nigh h.	MORE 244:17
hymns at h.'s gate	SHAK 310:6
idea of h.	SMIT 319:15
Imagine there's no h.	LENN 212:14
into the kingdom of h.	BIBL 45:12
kingdom of h.	BIBL 43:13
kingdom of h.	BIBL 45:1
kingdom of h. is at hand	BIBL 43:4
King of h.	LYTE 221:4
lead you in at H.'s gate	BLAK 56:20
leave to h. the measure	JOHN 187:28
make a h. of hell	MILT 237:22
merrily meet in h.	MORE 244:18
near to h. by sea	GILB 149:14
new h. and a new earth	BIBL 53:22
new h., new earth	SHAK 289:11
Not H. itself	DRYD 122:17
nurseries of h.	THOM 338:21
of h. we have below	ADDI 3:4
open face of h.	KEAT 197:5
open the Kingdom of H.	BOOK 59:19
pennies from h.	BURK 76:11
points of h. and home	WORD 366:12
ring the bells of H.	HODG 171:4
Road to H.	BALL 25:19
silence in h.	BIBL 53:10
sinned against h.	BIBL 47:31
starry h. above me	KANT 194:19
summons thee to h.	SHAK 300:13
that serve in h.	MILT 237:23
things are the sons of h.	JOHN 186:17
things in h. and earth	SHAK 292:5
thirtieth year to h.	THOM 337:23
top of it reached to h.	BIBL 35:2
war in h.	BIBL 53:12
we know the way to h.	ELST 131:16
what's a h. for	BROW 71:20
What they do in h.	SWIF 328:21
which art in h.	BIBL 43:22
Which we ascribe to h.	SHAK 289:9
young was very h.	WORD 364:13

heavenly h. mansion, raging in the dark — YEAT 367:15
heavens behold, I create new h. — BIBL 41:19
H., and all the Powers therein — BOOK 59:17
h. declare the glory — BOOK 62:19
heaventree h. of stars — JOYC 193:8
heaviness H. may endure — BOOK 62:19
heavy He ain't h. — RUSS 283:14
h. bear who goes with me — SCHW 286:19
Hebrew in the H. Golgotha — BIBL 49:10
Hebrides in dreams behold the H. — GALT 145:12
heck doing a h. of a job — BUSH 78:21
Hecuba What's H. to him — SHAK 292:21
hedge divinity doth h. a king — SHAK 293:31
hedgehog h. knows one *big* one — ARCH 14:15
hedgehogs personality belongs to the h. — BERL 32:7
Thorny h., be not seen — SHAK 303:22
hedges into the highways and h. — BIBL 47:26
heedless H. of grammar — BARH 26:12
heel thou shalt bruise his h. — BIBL 34:19
height equal to his h. — LEON 213:3
Happiness makes up in h. — FROS 143:17
heights h. by great men reached — LONG 217:15
heir h. of all the ages — TENN 333:31
h. of the whole world — TRAH 341:10
Helen where H. lies — BALL 25:9
Helena far is St. H. — KIPL 202:23
hell agreement with h. — GARR 146:11
all h. broke loose — MILT 238:29
all we need of h. — DICK 116:2

Better to reign in h.	MILT 237:23
descended into h.	BOOK 59:23
from h.'s heart	MELV 232:15
gates of h.	BIBL 45:9
Heaven in H.'s despair	BLAK 57:23
H. has no terror for me	LARK 208:13
H. in Heaven's despite	BLAK 57:24
H. is a city	SHEL 314:12
H. is oneself	ELIO 127:27
H. is other people	SART 285:23
h. of heaven	MILT 237:22
H. or Connaught	CROM 107:15
H. to ships	AESC 3:19
If Hitler invaded h.	CHUR 96:6
if I go down to h.	BOOK 65:3
Into the mouth of H.	TENN 332:1
I say the h. with it	WHIT 356:3
I shall move H.	VIRG 347:16
it is all h.	SHER 315:26
lack of fellowship is h.	MORR 245:13
made an excursion to h.	PRIE 270:22
myself am h.	MILT 238:18
Nor H. a fury	CONG 102:7
out of h. leads up to light	MILT 238:7
pains of h.	BOOK 64:16
riches grow in h.	MILT 237:31
shout that tore h.'s concave	MILT 237:28
start raising h.	LEAS 211:2
tell you to go to h.	STIN 326:7
there was a way to H.	BUNY 74:13
they think it is h.	TRUM 342:12
this is h.	MARL 228:6
though h. should bar the way	NOYE 252:11
to heaven or to h.	SHAK 300:13
to h. I will go	MILL 234:6
to the gates of H.	PIUS 264:8
walked eye-deep in h.	POUN 269:23
War is h., and all that	HAY 163:16
why they invented H.	RUSS 283:10
with h. are we at agreement	BIBL 40:24
working definition of h.	SHAW 312:24
would be h. on earth	SHAW 311:30

helluva h. town — COMD 102:3
help Can't h. lovin' dat man — HAMM 160:14
God h. me — LUTH 220:17
h. and support of the woman — EDWA 125:10
h. in time of trouble — ANON 7:5
h. the feeble up — SHAK 308:1
look on and h. — LAWR 210:1
make him an h. meet — BIBL 34:10
no h. but Thee — EDME 125:6
scream for h. in dreams — CANE 84:5
Since there's no h. — DRAY 121:10
very present h. in trouble — BOOK 63:4
whence cometh my h. — BOOK 64:20
Who ran to h. me — TAYL 331:1
with a little h. from my friends — LENN 212:24
you can't h. it — SMIT 318:14
your countrymen cannot h. — JOHN 188:12
helper mother's little h. — JAGG 182:4
Our antagonist is our h. — BURK 75:25
helpless H., naked, piping loud — BLAK 57:25
helps Nobody ever h. me — TRUT 342:20
hemisphere portion of this h. — MONR 242:8
hemlock of h. I had drunk — KEAT 196:16
hempen What h. home-spuns — SHAK 303:25
hen better take a wet h. — KHRU 200:3
hence H., loathèd Melancholy — MILT 236:17
H., vain deluding joys — MILT 236:11
Heraclitus They told me, H. — CORY 104:13
herald Hark! the h.-angels — WESL 354:18
herb call it h. of grace — SHAK 293:33
rue, sour h. of grace — SHAK 306:2

herbs bitter h. — BIBL 35:18
bitter h. — HAGG 158:18
dinner of h. — BIBL 38:27
Hercules I to H. — SHAK 291:20
some of H. — ANON 11:1
herd h. wind slowly o'er the lea — GRAY 156:7
Morality is the h.-instinct — NIET 251:7
here can't happen h. — LEWI 214:6
H. am I — BIBL 40:10
H. I am — MACM 224:3
H.'s a how-de-doo — GILB 150:5
H.'s tae us — ANON 8:15
h.'s to you, Mrs Robinson — SIMO 317:2
H. were decent godless people — ELIO 129:13
If we can't stay h. alive — MONT 243:8
I have been h. before — ROSS 280:22
I'm still h. — HOPE 173:11
Mr Watson—come h. — BELL 29:14
We're h. — ANON 11:15
hereafter died h. — SHAK 301:31
h. for ever — BOOK 61:25
world may talk of h. — COLL 101:9
hereditary H. bondsmen — BYRO 80:2
idea of h. legislators — PAIN 257:15
hereditas Damnosa h. — GAIU 145:1
heresies begin as h. — HUXL 179:19
heresy h. signifies no more — HOBB 170:16
heretic oppressor or a h. — CAMU 84:2
heritage I have a goodly h. — BOOK 62:10
hermitage for an h. — LOVE 219:9
hern haunts of coot and h. — TENN 331:17
hero aspires to be a h. — JOHN 190.1
conquering h. comes — MORE 244:21
h. becomes a bore — EMER 132:16
h. to his valet — CORN 104:11
H.-worship is strongest — SPEN 321:13
Millions a h. — PORT 269:7
Show me a h. — FITZ 137:9
Herod for an hour of H. — HOPE 173:9
out-herods H. — SHAK 293:5
heroes fit country for h. — LLOY 216:10
of all the worlds brave h. — ANON 11:1
speed glum h. — SASS 285:26
Thin red line of h. — KIPL 203:1
Unhappy the land that needs h. — BREC 68:4
heroic H. womanhood — LONG 218:2
heroics not h., but healing — HARD 161:12
heroine take a h. — AUST 21:16
herring plague o' these pickle h. — SHAK 308:22
shoals of h. — MACC 222:12
Herz Mein H. ist schwer — GOET 152:12
hesitates She floats, she h. — RACI 272:16
Hesperus H. entreats thy light — JONS 191:14
It was the schooner H. — LONG 218:11
heterodoxy h. is another man's doxy — WARB 350:16
heterogeneity coherent h. — SPEN 321:8
hewers h. of wood — BIBL 36:8
hewn h. out her seven pillars — BIBL 38:17
hey h. for boot and horse — KING 201:9
hic H. jacet — RALE 273:4
hid cannot be h. — BIBL 43:15
I h. from Him — THOM 338:14
Which is, to keep that h. — DONN 119:19
hidden guns that are h. — FLEI 138:6
h. from the eye — WORD 365:27
h. persuaders — PACK 256:18
hide disguise which can h. love — LA R 209:5
he can't h. — LOUI 219:6
h. our own hurts — ELIO 127:14
Let me h. myself — TOPL 341:7
something to h. — LAY 210:3
wrapped in a player's h. — GREE 157:2
hides H. from himself his state — JOHN 187:27

h. one thing in his heart — HOME 172:12
hiding bloody good h. — GRAN 155:7
My heart in h. — HOPK 174:10
Hieronimo H. is mad again — KYD 206:9
high Be ye never so h. — DENN 113:2
corn as h. as an elephant's eye — HAMM 160:18
get h. with a little help — LENN 212:24
h. road — JOHN 188:13
slain upon thy h. places — BIBL 36:32
thing with h.-tech — HOCK 171:3
This h. man — BROW 72:4
wickedness in h. places — BIBL 51:21
ye'll tak' the h. road — ANON 10:6
higher Friend, go up h. — BIBL 47:22
production of the h. animals — DARW 110:9
highest h. good — CICE 96:18
Highland heart is H. — GALT 145:12
solitary H. lass! — WORD 366:5
Highlands My heart's in the H. — BURN 77:6
highness his H.' dog at Kew — POPE 266:14
highway each and ev'ry h. — ANKA 7:4
h. for our God — BIBL 40:30
highwayman h. came riding — NOYE 252:10
highways into the h. and hedges — BIBL 47:26
hill city that is set on an h. — BIBL 43:15
city upon a h. — WINT 362:3
dancers are all gone under the h. — ELIO 128:7
hunter home from h. — STEV 326:6
light on the h. — CHIF 93:26
On a huge h. — DONN 119:4
On the cold h.'s side — KEAT 195:27
hills and the little h. — BOOK 63:15
Black H. belong to me — SITT 317:12
blue remembered h. — HOUS 176:13
convictions are h. — FITZ 137:8
h. are alive — HAMM 160:21
h. like young sheep — BOOK 64:13
H. of the North — OAKL 252:14
H. peep o'er hills — POPE 267:7
I to the h. will lift — SCOT 288:4
mine eyes unto the h. — BOOK 64:20
Over the h. — GAY 147:1
red h. of Georgia — KING 200:17
to the reverberate h. — SHAK 308:25
him cried, 'That's h.!' — BARH 26:12
himself He h. said — CICE 96:17
hinan Ewig-Weibliche zieht uns h. — GOET 152:14
hindsight H. is always twenty-twenty — WILD 359:20
Hindu neither H. nor Muslim — SIKH 316:21
hip once upon the h. — SHAK 302:12
smote them h. and thigh — BIBL 36:17
Hippocrene blushful h. — KEAT 196:18
hippopotamus shoot the H. — BELL 29:17
hire labourer is worthy of his h. — BIBL 47:13
hired They h. the money — COOL 103:15
Hiroshima genius of Einstein leads to H. — PICA 263:10
hiss dismal universal h. — MILT 239:10
hissed h. along the polished ice — WORD 364:14
hissing smallest possible amount of h. — COLB 99:17
historians alter the past, h. can — BUTL 79:10
h. left blanks in their writings — POUN 269:20
h. repeat one another — BROO 70:3
history blank in h.-books — MONT 243:7
Does h. repeat itself — BARN 26:17
dustbin of h. — TROT 342:6
dust-heap called 'h.' — BIRR 55:2
duty we owe to h. — WILD 358:15
end of h. — FUKU 144:11
fair summary of h. — FRAN 141:15
happiest nations, have no h. — ELIO 127:20
H. a distillation — CARL 85:11
H. came to a . — SELL 288:20
H. is a gallery of pictures — TOCQ 340:15

history (cont.)
H. is a nightmare — JOYC 193:7
H. . . . is, indeed, little more — GIBB 148:14
H. is nothing more — VOLT 348:18
H. is not what you thought — SELL 288:18
h. is now and England — ELIO 128:17
h. is on our side — KHRU 200:2
H. is past politics — FREE 142:12
H. is philosophy — DION 117:1
H. is the essence — CARL 85:4
h.-making creature — AUDE 19:23
H. more or less bunk — FORD 139:9
H., *n.* An account — BIER 54:20
h. of class struggles — MARX 230:12
h. of the world — DISR 117:9
H. repeats itself — BROO 70:3
H. teaches us — EBAN 124:18
H. to the defeated — AUDE 19:21
H. will absolve me — CAST 88:13
h. will record — MORS 246:3
hope and h. rhyme — HEAN 164:10
Human h. becomes more — WELL 354:11
learned anything from h. — HEGE 165:1
more worthy than h. — ARIS 15:17
no h.; only biography — EMER 132:8
Read no h. — DISR 117:24
Thames is liquid h. — BURN 76:14
thousand years of h. — GAIT 144:22
too much h. — KING 201:4
War makes good h. — HARD 161:14
what's her h. — SHAK 308:36
What will h. say — SHAW 311:16
world's h. — SCHI 286:11
writing h. with lightning — WILS 361:9
hit very palpable h. — SHAK 294:9
hitch H. your wagon to a star — EMER 132:17
Hitler H. thought he might — CHAM 90:7
If H. invaded hell — CHUR 96:6
When H. attacked the Jews — NIEM 251:3
hitting prove their worth by h. back — HEIN 165:5
without h. below it — ASQU 18:4
hoarse raven himself is h. — SHAK 299:22
Hobbes in for H.'s voyage — VANB 345:4
hobbit there lived a h. — TOLK 340:19
hobgoblin h. of little minds — EMER 132:1
hoe tickle her with a h. — JERR 185:9
hog all England under a h. — COLL 101:8
disadvantage of being a h. — MORT 246:5
Not the whole h. — MILL 235:4
hogamus H., higamous — JAME 183:10
hogs let it not be like h. — MCKA 223:10
hoist H. with his own petar — SHAK 293:23
hold can neither h. him — JEFF 184:16
can't h. a man down — WASH 351:4
gat h. upon me — BOOK 64:16
H., enough — SHAK 302:2
h. fast that which is good — BIBL 52:3
H. the fort — BLIS 58:9
H. the fort — SHER 315:23
To have and to h. — BOOK 61:27
hole dark h. of the head — HUGH 177:17
h. to go out of this world — HOBB 170:23
if you knows of a better 'ole — BAIR 24:16
In a h. in the ground — TOLK 340:19
maketh a h. in the stone — LATI 209:11
holiday Butchered to make a Roman h. — BYRO 80:12
perpetual h. — SHAW 312:24
to take a h. — RUSS 282:24
holidays holiest of all h. — LONG 217:14
playing h. — SHAK 294:17
holier h. than thou — BIBL 41:18
holiest Praise to the H. — NEWM 250:6
holiness beauty of h. — BOOK 63:28

beauty of h. — MONS 242:12
holiness but social h. — WESL 354:24
h. of the heart's affections — KEAT 197:9
hollow hate the dreadful h. — TENN 334:2
We are the h. men — ELIO 128:22
Within the h. crown — SHAK 305:31
Hollywood H. money isn't money — PAHK 259:5
Holy and to the H. Ghost — BOOK 59:16
holy H. deadlock — HERB 167:7
h. ground — BIBL 35:13
H., Holy, Holy — HEBE 164:19
H., holy, holy, Lord — BIBL 53:6
h. simplicity — JERO 185:3
h.-water death — MCGO 223:5
neither h., nor Roman — VOLT 348:17
sabbath day, keep it h. — BIBL 35:27
that which is h. — PLAT 264:19
Holy Ghost blasphemy against the h. — BIBL 44:36
gifts of the H. — BUTL 79:3
H. over the bent World — HOPK 173:17
home can't go h. again — WOLF 363:7
come h. Bill Bailey — CANN 84:12
comes safe h. — SHAK 295:27
England, h. and beauty — ARNO 17:10
feel ashamed of h. — DICK 115:1
for to carry me h. — ANON 11:5
go h. in the dark — HENR 166:21
H. is the place — FROS 143:13
H. is the sailor — STEV 326:6
H. is where you come to — THAT 337:4
H. James — HILL 169:7
h. life of our own dear Queen — ANON 8:17
H. of lost causes — ARNO 17:4
h. of the brave — KEY 199:17
h. sweet home — JERO 185:7
H., sweet home — PAYN 260:19
H. they brought her warrior — TENN 334:18
house is not a h. — ADLE 3:17
hunter h. from hill — STEV 326:6
Keep the H.-fires burning — FORD 139:10
man goeth to his long h. — BIBL 39:28
murder into the h. — HITC 170:4
no place like h. — PAYN 260:20
points of heaven and h. — WORD 366:12
refuge from h. life — SHAW 313:2
Till the boys come h. — FORD 139:10
What's the good of a h. — GROS 158:3
Homer excellent H. nods — HORA 174:19
H. dead — ANON 10:19
H. smote 'is bloomin' lyre — KIPL 203:7
warred for H., being dead — HEYW 168:17
Home Rule morning H. passes — CARS 87:24
homes Stately H. of England — COWA 105:7
stately h. of England — HEMA 166:1
homespuns What hempen h. — SHAK 303:25
homeward Look h. angel — MILT 237:1
homo *Ecce h.* — BIBL 54:11
et h. factus est — MISS 240:21
homogeneity incoherent h. — SPEN 321:8
honest buy it like an h. man — NORT 252:4
few h. men — CROM 107:6
h. broker — BISM 55:8
h. God — INGE 180:17
h. man is laughed at — HALI 160:3
h. man's the noblest work — POPE 268:2
h., sonsie face — BURN 77:17
H. to God — ROBI 277:20
I am not naturally h. — SHAK 309:28
is not an h. man — WHAT 355:19
looking for an h. man — DIOG 116:20
most h. of men — RICH 276:11
poor but she was h. — ANON 10:20
while the nation is h. — DOUG 120:8

honestly If possible h.   HORA 174:21
honesty H. is praised   JUVE 194:5
  H. is the best policy   WHAT 355:19
honey flowing with milk and h.   BIBL 35:14
  hives with h. and wax   SWIF 328:6
  h. still for tea   BROO 69:21
  h. to smear his face   SCHW 286:19
  How a bear likes h.   MILN 235:17
  locusts and wild h.   BIBL 43:6
  sweeter also than h.   BOOK 62:12
  took some h.   LEAR 210:15
  With milk and h. blessed   NEAL 248:24
honeycomb honey, and the h.   BOOK 62:12
honeydew he on h. hath fed   COLE 100:12
honi H. soit qui mal y pense   ANON 12:12
honour As he was valiant, I h. him   SHAK 296:32
  cannot be maintained with h.   RUSS 283:16
  fountain of h.   BACO 22:9
  greater share of h.   SHAK 295:25
  H. all men   BIBL 52:27
  h., and keep her   BOOK 61:26
  h. and life   FRAN 141:10
  H. a physician   BIBL 42:26
  h. rooted in dishonour   TENN 332:14
  h. sinks where commerce   GOLD 153:16
  h. therof   EDWA 125:8
  H. thy father and thy mother   BIBL 35:28
  h. unto the wife   BIBL 52:28
  hurt that H. feels   TENN 333:23
  Keeps h. bright   SHAK 308:12
  Leisure with h.   CICE 96:25
  louder he talked of his h.   EMER 132:4
  Loved I not h. more   LOVE 219:10
  peace I hope with h.   DISR 117:16
  peace with h.   CHAM 90:5
  post of h.   ADDI 3:2
  prophet is not without h.   BIBL 45:3
  roll of h.   CLEV 98:5
  safety, h., and welfare   CHAR 91:1
  signed with their h.   SPEN 321:19
  What is h.   SHAK 294:26
  whence h. springs   MARL 228:19
honourable Brutus is an h. man   SHAK 297:2
  designs were strictly h.   FIEL 135:13
  h. alike in what we give   LINC 214:19
  h. by being necessary   HALE 159:14
honoured h. me of late   SHAK 300:4
honours neither h. nor wages   GARI 146:4
hook with an h.   BIBL 38:10
hope Abandon all h.   DANT 109:8
  All my h. on God   BRID 68:16
  believed in h.   BIBL 49:42
  Can something, h.   HOPK 173:14
  From h. and fear set free   SWIN 329:12
  God is our h.   BOOK 63:4
  He that lives in h.   HERB 167:27
  He that lives upon h.   FRAN 141:20
  h. and history rhyme   HEAN 164:10
  H. deferred   BIBL 38:22
  h. for the best   SMIT 319:7
  h. for years to come   WATT 352:2
  H. is a good breakfast   BACO 23:34
  h. is gone   AUST 21:5
  H. springs eternal   POPE 267:20
  h. till Hope creates   SHEL 314:16
  I can give you no h.   EDDI 124:22
  I fear and h.   PETR 262:14
  in the store we sell h.   REVS 275:9
  Land of H. and Glory   BENS 31:3
  last best h.   LINC 214:19
  look forward to with h.   FROS 143:12
  Never to h. again   SHAK 296:13
  no h. without fear   SPIN 322:8

  Nor dread nor h. attend   YEAT 367:21
  not another's h.   WALS 350:7
  only h. that keeps up   GAY 146:20
  Some blessed H.   HARD 162:1
  sure and certain h.   BOOK 62:6
  triumph of h. over experience   JOHN 189:1
  True h. is swift   SHAK 306:17
  two thousand years of h.   WEIZ 353:11
  Was the h. drunk   SHAK 300:5
  Whatever h. is yours   OWEN 256:14
  what was dead was H.   WILD 359:9
  Where there is despair, h.   FRAN 141:14
hoped things h. for   BIBL 52:14
hopefully travel h. is a better thing   STEV 325:21
hopefulness Lord of all h.   STRU 327:3
hopeless perennially h.   DICK 114:12
hopes h. of its children   EISE 126:16
  If h. were dupes   CLOU 98:22
  no great h. from Birmingham   AUST 20:23
  vanity of human h.   JOHN 187:16
  wholly h. to be   BROW 72:1
hops apples, cherries, h.   DICK 115:18
horizontal h. desire   SHAW 313:5
  Life is a h. fall   COCT 99:6
horn blow his wreathèd h.   WORD 366:17
  h. of the hunter   CRAW 106:13
  won't come out of your h.   PARK 258:10
Hornby H. and my Barlow   THOM 338:12
horned h. moon   WORD 364:6
horns h. of Elfland   TENN 334:14
  memories are hunting h.   APOL 14:7
horny H.-handed sons of toil   SALI 284:21
  h. hands of toil   LOWE 220.1
horribilis annus h.   ELIZ 131:2
horrible h. imaginings   SHAK 299:17
  O, horrible! O, h.   SHAK 292:2
horrid she was h.   LONG 218:12
  very h. thing   BUTL 79:3
  With h. warning   KEAT 195:27
horror h.! The horror   CONR 102:23
  there is no h.   DOYL 121:4
horrors supped full with h.   SHAK 301:30
horse behold a pale h.   BIBL 53:7
  Boot, saddle, to h.   BROW 71:23
  feeds the h. enough oats   GALB 145:4
  h. designed by a committee   ISSI 181:7
  h. he can ride   THOM 339:3
  h. is at least *human*   SALI 284:16
  h. of air   ANON 12:5
  h. of that colour   SHAK 308:31
  h. on the mountain   LORC 218:17
  h. was made Consul   RAND 273:11
  my kingdom for a h.   SHAK 306:19
  never heard no h. sing   ARMS 16:6
  rider and his h.   SURT 328:2
  torturer's h. scratches   AUDE 19:10
  where's the bloody h.   CAMP 83:9
horseback ride On h.   COWP 105:17
horseman H., pass by   YEAT 369:12
  sits behind the h.   HORA 175:13
horsemen Four H. rode again   RICE 276:1
horses breed of their h.   PENN 261:13
  Bring on the empty h.   CURT 109:1
  don't spare the h.   HILL 169:9
  frighten the h.   CAMP 83:8
  generally given to h.   JOHN 187:1
  h. of instruction   BLAK 57:3
  h. of the night   OVID 255:23
  surmised the H. Heads   DICK 115:27
  swap h. when crossing   LINC 215:3
  that h. may not be stolen   HALI 160:2
  They shoot h. don't they   MCCO 222:15
  wild white h. play   ARNO 16:16

horticulture lead a h.   PARK 259:5
hortus *H. ubi et tecto vicinus iugis*   HORA 175:25
hosanna *H. in excelsis*   MISS 240:23
hosannas sweet h. ring   NEAL 248:22
hose out of the turret with a h.   JARR 183:11
hospital first requirement in a H.   NIGH 251:13
host h., of golden daffodils   WORD 364:17
hostages h. to fortune   BACO 22:32
  h. to the fates   LUCA 220:9
hostile universe is not h.   HOLM 171:19
hot h. for certainties   MERE 233:9
  neither cold nor h.   BIBL 53:4
  only in h. water   REAG 274:2
  stars are not h. enough   EDDI 124:19
hotel great advantage of a h.   SHAW 313:2
hound his hawk, his h.   BALL 25:21
hounds h. all join in glorious cry   FIEL 135:9
  h. and his horn in the morning   GRAV 155:15
  h. of spring   SWIN 329:7
hour books of the h.   RUSK 282:17
  fill the h.   EMER 132:13
  finest h.   CHUR 95:10
  for an h. of Herod   HOPE 173:9
  h. is come   SCOT 287:23
  h. of death   BOOK 60:14
  h. of glorious life   MORD 244:14
  I also had my h.   CHES 92:27
  I have had my h.   DRYD 122:17
  Improve each shining h.   WATT 351:18
  its h. come round at last   YEAT 369:2
  Its h. is now   SCHW 286:21
  known as the Children's H.   LONG 217:8
  know not what h.   BIBL 46:3
  man and the h.   YANC 367:10
  matched us with His h.   BROO 70:1
  mine h. is not yet come   BIBL 48:24
  most carefully upon your h.   SHAK 291:7
  Time and the h.   SHAK 299:18
  watch with me one hour   BIBL 44:14
hours h. will take care of themselves   CHES 92:17
  leaden-stepping h.   MILT 237:12
  two golden h.   MANN 227:3
  two h.' traffick   SHAK 306:21
house angel in the h.   PATM 260:10
  beat upon that h.   BIBL 44:13
  heap of stones is a h.   POIN 266:1
  h. as nigh heaven   MORE 244:17
  h. divided   LINC 214:13
  h. is a machine for living in   LE C 211:8
  h. is his castle   COKE 99:14
  h. is much more   MORR 245:5
  h. is not a home   ADLE 3:17
  h. not made with hands   BIBL 51:6
  h. not made with hands   BROW 71:24
  H. of Peers   GILB 149:19
  h. of prayer   BIBL 41:15
  h. of prayer   BIBL 45:24
  h. where I was born   HOOD 172:23
  If a h. be divided   BIBL 46:24
  In my Father's h.   BIBL 49:4
  in the h. of Rimmon   BIBL 37:24
  join house to h.   BIBL 40:7
  little plaything-h.   WALP 349:18
  Lord build the h.   BOOK 64:26
  make a H.   CANN 84:11
  mind to sell his h.   SWIF 328:9
  Set thine h. in order   BIBL 40:28
  so in the way in the h.   GASK 146:13
  sparrow hath found her an h.   BOOK 63:18
  What! in our h.   SHAK 300:25
householder think she's a h.   WILD 359:22
housekeeper make a h. think   WILD 359:22
houses friends' h.   JOHN 190:11

h. are all gone under the sea   ELIO 128:7
h. in between   BATE 27:16
h. thick and sewers   MILT 239:5
nothing in your h.   MORR 245:14
plague o' both your h.   SHAK 306:38
very h. seem asleep   WORD 364:11
housework no need to do any h.   CRIS 107:3
Houston H., we've had a problem   LOVE 219:11
hover H. through the fog   SHAK 299:8
how Here's a h.-de-doo   GILB 150:5
  H. and Where and Who   KIPL 203:17
  H. do I love thee   BROW 71:17
  H. NOT TO DO IT   DICK 115:3
  not say why and h.   WILS 361:8
howl H., howl, howl, howl   SHAK 298:26
Howth H. Castle and Environs   JOYC 192:19
huddled h. masses yearning   LAZA 210:5
Hugo H.—alas   GIDE 149:13
  H. was a madman   COCT 99:7
hum busy h. of men   MILT 236:24
human all h. life is there   JAME 182:17
  full tide of h. existence   JOHN 189:7
  guide of h. life   HUME 178:4
  horse is at least *h.*   SALI 284:16
  h. being dissatisfied   MILL 234:15
  h. condition   MALR 226:10
  h. hearts endure   JOHN 187:23
  H. kind Cannot bear   ELIO 128:2
  h. nature changed   WOOL 363:20
  H. on my faithless arm   AUDE 19:8
  h. speech   FLAU 137:23
  h. things are subject to decay   DRYD 122:7
  h. zoo   MORR 245:6
  knowledge of h. nature   AUST 20:26
  laugh at h. actions   SPIN 322:9
  learn to be h.   WILL 360:8
  milk of h. kindness   SHAK 299:21
  nothing h. foreign to me   TERE 335:13
  Peace, the h. dress   BLAK 57:17
  robot may not injure a h.   ASIM 17:17
  see God in every h.   TERE 335:19
  socialism would not lose its h. face   DUBČ 122:24
  To err is h.   POPE 267:16
  To step aside is h.   BURN 76:16
  wish I loved the H. Race   RALE 273:8
humane Heaven and earth not h.   LAO 208:1
humanity belief in h.   YAMA 367:9
  crooked timber of h.   KANT 195:1
  freeze my h.   MACN 224:11
  h. after Victory   NELS 249:7
  h., reason   BURK 75:8
  Oh, the h.   MORR 245:16
  religion of h.   PAIN 257:11
  sad music of h.   WORD 364:20
  So act as to treat h.   KANT 194:24
  teach governments h.   PAIN 257:14
humble Be it ever so h.   PAYN 260:20
  He that is h.   BUNY 74:16
  never had a h. opinion   BAEZ 24:6
humbleth he that h. himself   BIBL 47:23
humbly walk h. with thy God   BIBL 42:15
humbug 'Bah,' said Scrooge. 'H.!'   DICK 114:14
  h. in a Pickwickian point   DICK 115:17
humiliation Art is born of h.   AUDE 19:26
  valley of H.   BUNY 74:8
humility modest stillness and h.   SHAK 295:16
  pride that apes h.   COLE 100:3
humour Good taste and h.   MUGG 247:1
  H. is emotional chaos   THUR 340:7
  in this h. won   SHAK 306:10
hump camel has a single h.   NASH 248:11
hundred h. flowers blossom   MAO 227:14
  one h. bin Ladens   MUBA 246:14

Six h. threescore and six BIBL 53:14
hunger h. and poverty LARK 208:13
sacred h. SPEN 322:5
shall never h. BIBL 48:30
hungry h. for dinner at eight HART 162:21
h. sheep look up MILT 236:32
If thine enemy be h. BIBL 38:36
lean and h. look SHAK 296:20
Let all who are h. HAGG 158:15
roaming with a h. heart TENN 335:1
Huns H. or Wops MITF 241:17
hunted H. and penned MCKA 223:10
h. round the globe PAIN 257:8
hunter h. home from hill STEV 326:6
Man is the h. TENN 334:17
Nimrod the mighty h. BIBL 34:30
snare of the h. BOOK 63:24
Hunter Dunn Miss J. H. BETJ 33:5
hunting H. is all that's worth SURT 327:20
passion for h. DICK 115:15
weary wi' h. BALL 25:11
huntress Queen and h. JONS 191:14
hurled Swift to be h. HOOD 172:20
hurricane h. on the way FISH 136:1
hurry h., hurry, hurry MIDD 233:21
never in a h. WESL 355:4
old man in a h. CHUR 94:19
hurt h. you to the heart TWAI 343:14
power to h. us BEAU 28:4
shall not h. nor destroy BIBL 40:18
wish to h. BRON 69:8
hurting If the policy isn't h. MAJO 225:17
hurts hide our own h. ELIO 127:14
husband h. what is left of a lover ROWL 281:13
in her h.'s heart SHAK 308:33
left her h. because MURD 247:6
My h. and I ELIZ 131:1
one h. too many ANON 7:14
over hir h. as hir love CHAU 91:30
woman oweth to her h. SHAK 307:15
husbandry h. in heaven SHAK 300:11
husbands Aisles full of h. GINS 151:5
hands of the h. ADAM 1:10
H. at chirche dore CHAU 91:20
H., love your wives BIBL 51:31
hush breathless h. in the Close NEWB 249:18
holy h. of ancient sacrifice STEV 324:23
H., hush MORT 246:6
H.! Hush! Whisper who dares MILN 235:16
hushing H. the latest traffic BRID 68:17
hustle tried to h. the East KIPL 202:17
hut Love in a h. KEAT 196:1
hyacinths h. and biscuits SAND 285:9
Hyde Dr Jekyll and Mr H. STEV 325:12
hyena h. in petticoats WALP 350:4
hygienic most h. of beverages PAST 260:5
hymns h. at heaven's gate SHAK 310:6
Hyperion H. to a satyr SHAK 291:17
hyphenated h. Americanism ROOS 280:5
hypocrisy H. is a tribute LA R 209:7
H., the only evil MILT 238:17
organized h. DISR 117:6
That would be h. WILD 358:11
hypocrite h. in his pleasures JOHN 190:20
h. is really rotten AREN 14:20
H. lecteur,—mon semblable BAUD 27:18
hypocrites other half h. JEFF 184:19
scribes and Pharisees, h. BIBL 45:29
hypotheses do not feign h. NEWT 250:14
smallest number of h. EINS 126:12
hypothesis discard a pet h. LORE 218:19
slaying of a beautiful h. HUXL 179:16

hysteria thin whine of h. DIDI 116:13

I

I I am a camera ISHE 181:6
I am not I WAUG 352:5
I AM THAT I AM BIBL 35:15
I am the State LOUI 219:1
in the infinite I AM COLE 101:1
I plus my surroundings ORTE 254:5
My husband and I ELIZ 131:1
tell me who I am SHAK 297:28
Through which we go Is I DE L 112:16
iambics escape my i. CATU 89:10
ice along the polished i. WORD 364:14
burn and I am i. PETR 262:14
caves of i. COLE 100:9
emperor of i.-cream STEV 324:16
I. formed WODE 362:22
i., mast-high COLE 100:16
skating over thin i. EMER 132:9
Some say in i. FROS 143:15
Iceland Natural History of I. JOHN 189:22
iceman i. cometh O'NE 253:13
Ichabod named the child I. BIBL 36:23
icicles When i. hang by the wall SHAK 299:5
id PUT THE I. BACK IN YID ROTH 281:5
idea forgiveness is a lovely i. LEWI 213:17
i. first occurs DARW 110:15
i. whose time has come ANON 11:8
invasion by an i. HUGO 178:1
more dangerous than an i. ALAI 4:5
only one i. DISR 117:30
pain of a new i. BAGE 24:12
possess but one i. JOHN 188:23
teach the young i. THOM 338:24
wilderness of i. BUTL 79:16
would be a good i. GAND 145:18
ideal i. for which I am prepared MAND 226:16
i. of reason KANT 194:23
idealism morphine or i. JUNG 193:19
idealistic only i. nation WILS 361:17
ideals i. of a nation DOUG 120:6
men without i. CAMU 83:16
ideas Colourless green i. CHOM 94:6
From it our i. are born GENE 147:12
I. won't keep WHIT 356:11
signs of i. JOHN 186:17
identical they exist, but are i. FORS 139:17
Two things are i. LEIB 212:2
ides Beware the i. of March SHAK 296:18
idiot i. who praises GILB 150:1
portrait of a blinking i. SHAK 302:19
tale Told by an i. SHAK 301:31
idle be not i. BURT 78:8
For i. hands to do WATT 351:19
i. as a painted ship COLE 100:19
i. singer of an empty day MORR 245:10
little profits that an i. king TENN 334:31
Never be completely i. THOM 337:10
only i. chatter GILB 150:13
Tears, i. tears TENN 334:15
idleness I. is only the refuge CHES 92:21
round of strenuous i. WORD 365:17
idlers i. of the Empire DOYL 121:2
idling impossible to enjoy i. JERO 185:4
idol one-eyed yellow i. HAYE 164:2
idols i. I have loved FITZ 137:2
if I. it moves, salute it ANON 8:19
i. you can keep your head KERR 199:10
I. you can keep your head KIPL 202:9

if (cont.)
  much virtue in 'i.' — SHAK 291:1
ifs Talk'st thou to me of 'i.' — SHAK 306:14
ignoble i. ease — ROOS 279:19
ignorance Disease, I., and Idleness — BEVE 33:15
  fact of my i. — SOCR 319:23
  i. and confidence — TWAI 344:1
  I. is an evil weed — BEVE 33:14
  I. is like a delicate — WILD 358:6
  i. is never better — FERM 135:2
  I. is not innocence — BROW 72:11
  I. is strength — ORWE 254:22
  i. of nature — HOLB 171:15
  I. of the law — SELD 288:13
  i. or profaneness — MATH 231:5
  no sin but i. — MARL 228:12
  pure i. — JOHN 188:9
  smallest allowance for i. — HUXL 179:18
  Where i. is bliss — GRAY 156:18
  women in a state of i. — KNOX 204:13
ignorant always be i. — AUST 20:28
  i. and free — JEFF 184:15
  many i. men are sure — DARR 110:1
ignores most poetry i. most people — MITC 241:9
ill final goal of i. — TENN 332:30
  ill-clad, i.-nourished — ROOS 279:11
  I. fares the land — GOLD 153:5
  i.-favoured thing, sir — SHAK 290:26
  I. met by moonlight — SHAK 303:17
  one-third of a nation i.-housed — ROOS 279:11
  she's not really i. — JAGG 182:4
  Some think him i.-tempered — LEAR 210:14
  vain, i.-natured — DEFO 111:21
  warn you not to fall i. — KINN 201:13
illegal i., immoral, or fattening — WOOL 364:5
  means that it is not i. — NIXO 251:19
  Nothing is i. if — YOUN 369:21
illegitimate no i. children — GLAD 151:10
illiterate I. him, I say — SHER 315:9
  i. king — HENR 166:15
illness treatment of an i. — WITT 362:8
ills i. of democracy — SMIT 318:8
  i. to come — GRAY 156:16
illuminatio *Dominus i. mea* — ANON 13:9
  Dominus i. mea — BIBL 53:27
illumine What in me is dark, I. — MILT 237:17
illusion great i. — ANGE 7:1
  only an i. — EINS 126:14
  sophistry and i. — HUME 178:5
illusions life's i. I recall — MITC 241:11
illustration i. of character — JAME 182:20
image age demanded an i. — POUN 269:22
  created him in his own i. — DOST 119:28
  i. of death — ELIO 127:22
  i. of God — TALM 330:13
  i. of passion — BART 27:5
  just an i. — GODA 152:2
  kills the i. of God — MILT 240:3
  votre i. me suit — RACI 272:18
imaginary make i. evils — GOLD 153:20
imagination dream of our own i. — BACO 23:24
  ideal of i. — KANT 194:23
  i. amend them — SHAK 304:3
  i. for his facts — SHER 315:20
  I., not invention — CONR 102:27
  i. of their hearts — BIBL 46:33
  i. resembled — MACA 221:17
  of moral good is the i. — SHEL 315:4
  primary i. — COLE 101:1
  save those that have no i. — SHAW 312:31
  shaping spirit of i. — COLE 100:2
  takes a lot of i. — BAIL 24:13
  truth of i. — KEAT 197:9

  Where there is no i. — DOYL 121:4
imagine I. there's no heaven — LENN 212:14
  people i. a vain thing — BOOK 62:7
imaginings horrible i. — SHAK 299:17
imitate i. the action — SHAK 295:16
  Immature poets i. — ELIO 130:6
  never failed to i. them — BALD 24:19
imitation art of I. — LLOY 216:6
imitatores *O i., servum pecus* — HORA 175:4
immanent I. Will — HARD 161:21
Immanuel call his name I. — BIBL 40:12
immemorial in i. elms — TENN 334:24
immense error is i. — BOLI 59:1
immoral illegal, i., or fattening — WOOL 364:5
  moral or an i. book — WILD 358:23
immorality i. is what they dislike — WHIT 356:13
immortal I have I. longings — SHAK 289:28
  i. as they quote — YOUN 369:22
  i. hand or eye — BLAK 58:3
  I., invisible — SMIT 319:18
  i. part of myself — SHAK 304:29
  soul is i. — PLAT 265:3
  soul is i. — SOCR 319:27
immortality belief in i. — DOST 119:26
  i. through my work — ALLE 5:18
  just Ourselves— And I. — DICK 115:26
  lead me to i. — UPAN 344:12
  Milk's leap toward i. — FADI 133:18
  Millions long for i. — ERTZ 133:2
impediment cause, or just i. — BOOK 61:22
imperative i. is Categorical — KANT 194:22
imperfect i. man — JEFF 184:9
  use of an i. medium — WILD 358:25
imperial act Of the i. theme — SHAK 299:16
  our great I. family — ELIZ 130:23
imperialism I. is the monopoly stage — LENI 212:6
  I.'s face — AUDE 19:17
impertinent ask an i. question — BRON 69:7
impious lift an i. hand — BRON 69:9
implacable i. in hate — DRYD 121:18
importance taking decisions of i. — PARK 259:14
important being less i. — MONT 242:21
  i. book, the critic assumes — WOOL 363:23
  same as i. — PRAT 270:18
  trivial and the i. — POTT 269:13
importunate no less i. — MONT 242:21
impossibility Upon I. — MARV 229:14
impossible certain because it is i. — TERT 336:3
  Dream the i. — DARI 109:20
  eliminated the i. — DOYL 120:21
  i. takes a little longer — ANON 7:23
  i. takes a little longer — NANS 247:20
  i.? that will be done — CALO 82:20
  i. to be silent — BURK 76:9
  i. to enjoy idling — JERO 185:4
  six i. things — CARR 87:6
  something is i. — CLAR 97:4
  wish it were i. — JOHN 190:23
impostors treat those two i. — KIPL 202:9
impotent i. people, sick — THOM 338:11
imprecision Decay with i. — ELIO 128:4
impresses i. me most about America — EDWA 125:11
impressionable at an i. age — SPAR 321:2
imprison Take me to you, i. me — DONN 118:25
imprisoned taken or i. — MAGN 225:5
improbability high degree of i. — FISH 136:5
  life is statistical i. — DAWK 111:8
improbable i. possibilities — ARIS 15:18
  whatever remains, *however i.* — DOYL 120:21
improper noun, proper or i. — FULL 144:13
impropriety without i. — GILB 149:20
improve I. each shining hour — WATT 351:18
  i. the nick of time — THOR 339:13

improved i. by death — SAKI 284:11
improvement schemes of political i. — JOHN 188:21
improvements no great i. — MILL 234:4
impulse first i. — CORN 104:6
i. from a vernal wood — WORD 366:9
i. of the moment — AUST 21:8
impulses no truck with first i. — MONT 243:10
impune Nemo me i. lacessit — ANON 13:12
impunity provokes me with i. — ANON 13:12
in going out, and thy coming i. — BOOK 64:22
inability i. to cross the street — WOOL 363:24
inaccuracy i. sometimes saves — SAKI 284:14
inactivity masterly i. — MACK 223:13
inadequate not that we are i. — WILL 360:17
inapprehensible I., we clutch — THOM 338:17
incantation i. of this verse — SHEL 314:7
incapacity courted by I. — BLAK 56:24
incarnadine multitudinous seas i. — SHAK 300:19
incensed I. with indignation — MILT 238:11
incest i. and folk-dancing — ANON 12:8
inch every i. a king — SHAK 298:16
inches die by i. — HENR 166:19
thirty i. from my nose — AUDE 19:15
incident curious i. of the dog — DOYL 120:19
determination of i. — JAME 182:20
incisors i. and grinders — BAGE 24:11
incivility i. and procrastination — DE Q 113:9
inclination just as i. leads him — JOHN 188:14
incline I. our hearts — BOOK 61:1
include i. me out — GOLD 154:1
income Annual i. twenty pounds — DICK 114:19
Expenditure rises to meet i. — PARK 259:11
large i. the best recipe — AUST 20:24
live beyond its i. — BUTL 79:14
moderate i. — DURH 123:12
income tax I. made more liars — ROGE 278:14
incomparable i. Max — SHAW 313:3
incompetence rise to his level of i. — PETE 262:12
incomprehensible most i. fact — EINS 126:7
inconstancy constant, but i. — SWIF 328:25
inconstant i. woman — GAY 147:6
inconvenience Change without i. — JOHN 186:16
i. is only an adventure — CHES 93:8
inconveniences i., and those weighty — HOOK 173:1
incorruptible seagreen I. — CARL 85:12
increase Some races i. — LUCR 220:14
we desire i. — SHAK 310:2
increasing has increased, is i. — DUNN 123:11
incredible i. as if you fired — RUTH 283:20
incurable Life is an i. disease — COWL 105:14
indecision nothing is habitual but i. — JAME 183:6
indefatigability your i. — GALL 145:9
indefensible defence of the i. — ORWE 255:4
independence i. of judges — DENN 113:3
independent easy to be i. — JACK 181:14
indestructible i. Union — CHAS 91:10
indexes memories are card-i. — CONN 102:19
India I.'s coral strand — HEBE 164:17
I. will awake to life — NEHR 249:1
Indian Every step the I. takes — RIEL 276:15
I. in blood and colour — MACA 222:5
I. wilderness — MATH 231:4
Like the base I. — SHAK 305:14
Lo! the poor I. — POPE 267:21
Indians only good I. — SHER 315:8
to convert the I. — WESL 355:1
indifference i. and a coach and six — COLM 101:17
i. closely bordering on — STEV 325:11
it's i. — WIES 357:21
indifferent delayed till I am i. — JOHN 188:8
It is simply i. — HOLM 171:19
to be i. to them — SHAW 311:14
indignation fierce i. — SWIF 329:6

Moral I. is jealousy — WELL 354:14
Savage i. there — YEAT 369:7
indirections By i. find directions out — SHAK 292:9
inditing i. of a good matter — BOOK 63:1
individual i. men and women — THAT 336:22
liberty of the i. — MILL 234:9
individualism system of rugged i. — HOOV 173:4
indivisible Peace is i. — LITV 216:1
indomitable i. Irishry — YEAT 369:11
indulgent makes one very i. — STAË 322:22
industrialists die for the i. — FRAN 141:9
industry Captains of i. — CARL 85:18
i. applies — ANON 10:17
i. will improve them — REYN 275:10
i. without art — RUSK 282:13
national i. of Prussia — MIRA 240:13
not his i. only — BURK 76:4
spur of i. — HUME 178:7
inebriate cheer but not i. — BERK 31:14
cheer but not i. — COWP 105:29
ineffectual beautiful and i. angel — ARNO 17:5
inevitability i. of gradualness — WEBB 352:12
inexactitude terminological i. — CHUR 94:21
inexorable deaf, i. — SIDN 316:10
infâme écrasez l'i. — VOLT 348:23
infamous crush the i. thing — VOLT 348:23
infamy date which will live in i. — ROOS 279:16
infancy about us in our i. — WORD 366:6
infant i. crying in the night — TENN 333:1
i. phenomenon — DICK 115:11
Sooner murder an i. — BLAK 57:6
infectious i. greed — GREE 157:4
inferior disgraced by the i. — SHAW 312:12
make you feel i. — ROOS 279:5
inferiority conscious of an i. — JOHN 189:15
inferno i. of his passions — JUNG 193:17
infidelity I. does not consist — PAIN 257:2
infidels no American i. — SAHH 284:6
infinite door to i. wisdom — BREC 68:3
i.-resource-and-sagacity — KIPL 203:18
I. riches — MARL 228:13
I. spaces — PASC 259:20
I. wrath — MILT 238:18
in the i. I AM — COLE 101:1
number of worlds is i. — ALEX 4:12
infinitive care what a split i. — FOWL 140:12
when I split an i. — CHAN 90:13
infirmity i. of noble mind — MILT 236:30
i. of others — HOBB 170:12
inflation I. one form of taxation — FRIE 143:1
pay to get i. down — LAMO 207:10
inflections beauty of i. — STEV 324:25
influence i. of the Crown — DUNN 123:11
planetary i. — SHAK 297:27
where his i. stops — ADAM 1:22
win friends and i. people — CARN 85:26
influences bind the sweet i. — BIBL 38:8
inform not to i. the reader — ACHE 1:7
occasions do i. against me — SHAK 293:27
information find i. upon it — JOHN 189:10
I only ask for i. — DICK 114:21
knowledge we have lost in i. — ELIO 129:12
little i. — AUST 21:7
unreliability of all i. — CLAU 97:10
ingratitude so unkind As man's i. — SHAK 290:16
inhale didn't i. — CLIN 98:10
inherit i. the earth — BIBL 43:13
inheritance Ruinous i. — GAIU 145:1
inherited Genes and i. dispositions — WINS 362:2
i. it brick — AUGU 20:14
inhumane Is it i. — RUMS 282:1
inhumanity essence of i. — SHAW 311:14
Man's i. to man — BURN 77:4

iniquity hated i. — BOOK 63:2
hated i. — GREG 157:8
i. of oblivion — BROW 71:8
injuries insult to i. — MOOR 243:17
revenge for slight i. — MACH 223:7
injury i. is much sooner forgotten — CHES 92:15
injustice I. anywhere a threat — KING 200:14
i. makes democracy necessary — NIEB 251:2
justice or i. — JOHN 187:29
No i. is done — ULPI 344:10
protect him against i. — PALM 258:5
so finely felt, as i. — DICK 114:28
injustices justify their i. — VOLT 348:10
inlaid thick i. with patines — SHAK 303:3
inn Do you remember an I., Miranda — BELL 30:4
gain the timely i. — SHAK 301:4
no room for them in the i. — BIBL 47:2
tavern or i. — JOHN 189:13
warmest welcome, at an i. — SHEN 315:7
inner have no I. Resources — BERR 32:19
Innisfree go to I. — YEAT 368:14
innocence badge of lost i. — PAIN 257:5
ceremony of i. is drowned — YEAT 369:1
Ignorance is not i. — BROW 72:11
i. and beauty born — YEAT 368:24
i. is like a dumb leper — GREE 156:27
loss of i. — HOWA 176:20
Never such i. again — LARK 208:20
not in i. — ARDR 14:18
innocent heart whose love is i. — BYRO 81:18
i. and the beautiful — YEAT 368:10
i. men, women, and children — JEFF 184:19
i. of the blood — BIBL 46:17
one i. suffer — BLAC 55:16
shall not be i. — BIBL 39:2
We are i. — ROSE 280:9
innocents i. abroad — TWAI 343:15
innovations ill-shapen, so are all i. — BACO 22:30
innovator time is the greatest i. — BACO 22:31
innuendoes beauty of i. — STEV 324:25
inquisition Spanish I. — MONT 243:15
insane Man is quite i. — MONT 243:3
inscription altar with this i. — BIBL 49:30
inscriptions In lapidary i. — JOHN 189:12
insect transformed into a gigantic i. — KAFK 194:14
inseparable one and i. — WEBS 352:19
inside i. the tent pissing out — JOHN 186:11
insignificant i. office — ADAM 2:7
insincerity enemy of clear language i. — ORWE 255:3
insolence flown with i. and wine — MILT 237:27
i. of wealth — JOHN 189:25
supports with i. — JOHN 187:2
inspiration Genius is one per cent i. — EDIS 125:5
instantaneous i. courage — NAPO 248:3
instinct believe upon i. — BRAD 67:6
healthy i. for it — BUTL 79:17
instincts i. and abilities — BALZ 26:6
panders to i. — BENN 30:19
true to your i. — LAWR 209:20
institution i. which does not suppose — ROBE 277:11
It's an i. — HUGH 177:18
institutional i. racism — MACP 224:14
institutions with their dirty i. — THOR 339:16
instruct i. them — AURE 20:19
instruction better the i. — SHAK 302:23
horses of i. — BLAK 57:3
no i. book came with it — FULL 144:14
instrument i. of science — JOHN 186:17
i. of Your peace — FRAN 141:14
insubstantial this i. pageant — SHAK 307:30
insult i. to injuries — MOOR 243:17
sooner forgotten than an i. — CHES 92:15
threatened her with i. — BURK 75:17

insulted never *hope* to get i. — DAVI 111:3
insulting i. Christmas card — GROS 158:5
insurance National compulsory i. — CHUR 95:16
intangible world i., we touch — THOM 338:17
integer *I. vitae* — HORA 175:8
integers God made the i. — KRON 206:3
integral i. and differential calculus — GILB 150:23
integration policy of European i. — KOHL 204:16
integrity I. has no need of rules — CAMU 83:19
i. without knowledge — JOHN 187:21
intellect i. of man is forced to choose — YEAT 367:15
Our meddling i. — WORD 366:10
restless and versatile i. — HUXL 179:22
strengthening one's i. — KEAT 197:19
tickle the i. — LAMB 207:4
intellectual i. ability — ARNO 17:12
i. All-in-all — WORD 365:14
i. bankruptcy — HOLM 172:2
I. disgrace Stares — AUDE 19:4
i. is someone whose mind — CAMU 83:15
to the i. world — STER 324:12
intellectuals treachery of the i. — BEND 30:12
intelligence arresting human i. — LEAC 210:6
bewitchment of our i. — WITT 362:7
I. is quickness to apprehend — WHIT 356:12
intelligent Every i. voter — ADAM 1:15
Most i., very elegant — BUCK 73:17
rule of i. tinkering — EHRL 125:14
so i. — ELIO 129:25
intent first avowed i. — BUNY 74:17
told with bad i. — BLAK 56:10
intentions only had good i. — THAT 336:14
inter children i. their parents — HERO 167:28
interact do not i. at all — UPDI 344:18
interest its duty and its i. — WASH 351:9
passion or i. — LOCK 216:16
regard to their own i. — SMIT 318:1
interested i. in the arts — AYCK 21:18
i. in things — CURI 108:15
only i. in art — SHAW 313:4
interesting proposition be i. — WHIT 356:9
things and characters i. — SCOT 287:27
interests Our i. are eternal — PALM 258:4
interline diminish, i. — SWIF 328:26
international dependable i. emotion — ALSO 5:20
i. wrong — AUDE 19:17
Internet I. is an élite — CHOM 94:8
thanks to the I. — WILE 359:24
interpose i. my body — STRA 326:19
interpretation lost in i. — FROS 144:4
interpreted i. the world — MARX 230:8
interpreters i. between us and the millions — MACA 222:5
intersecting i. monologues — WEST 355:13
interstellar vacant i. spaces — ELIO 128:8
interstices i. between the intersections — JOHN 186:20
intervals lucid i. — BACO 23:25
intimacy determine i. — AUST 21:12
intimidation without i. — ROBE 277:12
intolerable burden of them is i. — BOOK 61:8
intoxicated God-i. man — NOVA 252:8
i. with power — BURK 75:1
intreat I. me not to leave thee — BIBL 36:21
introduce allow me to i. myself — JAGG 182:7
introducing rash, i. — SHAK 293:19
invasion i. by an idea — HUGO 178:1
invent first i. the universe — SAGA 284:3
fitter to i. — BACO 23:23
necessary to i. him — VOLT 348:16
one man can i. — DOYL 120:20
invented Truth exists, lies are i. — BRAQ 67:20
invention brightest heaven of i. — SHAK 295:9
[bureaucracy's] specific i. — WEBE 352:15

Imagination, not i.	CONR 102:27	**is** Whatever I., is RIGHT	POPE 267:26
i. of a barbarous age	MILT 237:13	what the meaning of 'i.' is	CLIN 98:13
i. of a mouse	DISN 117:3	**Ishmael** Call me I.	MELV 232:13
is a happy i.	ANON 13:24	**Islam** another religion than I.	KORA 205:5
It's my own i.	CARR 87:15	I. and the West	STRA 326:24
Marriage a wonderful i.	CONN 102:15	true religion is I.	KORA 205:4
Pure i.	BYRO 81:29	**island** i. made mainly of coal	BEVA 33:7
use of a new i.	FRAN 142:5	i.-valley of Avilion	TENN 332:23
inventions sought out many i.	BIBL 39:16	John Bull's other i.	SHAW 311:22
with their own i.	BOOK 64:7	No man is an I.	DONN 119:22
inventor plague the i.	SHAK 299:29	snug little I.	DIBD 114:11
inverse i. proportion to the sum	PARK 259:13	**isle** Fairest I.	DRYD 122:6
inverted That i. bowl	FITZ 136:17	i. is full of noises	SHAK 307:29
investigation subject of my i.	HUTT 179:7	men, of the Emerald I.	DREN 121:14
invida *fugerit i. Aetas*	HORA 175:7	**isles** i. of Greece	BYRO 80:29
invincible saw a city i.	WHIT 356:21	**isolated** Continent i.	BROC 69:4
inviolate secret and i. Rose	YEAT 369:3	**isolation** splendid i.	FOST 140:5
invisible all things visible and i.	BOOK 61:3	**Israel** between I. and their Father	TALM 330:15
bloody and i. hand	SHAK 301:3	Hear, O I.	SIDD 316:6
Immortal, i.	SMIT 319:18	I. was in Egypt land	ANON 11:20
I., except to God	MILT 238:17	mother in I.	BIBL 36:10
i. hand in politics	FRIE 142:22	sweet psalmist of I.	BIBL 37:3
i., refined out of existence	JOYC 193:1	These be thy gods, O I.	BIBL 35:30
i. to the eye	SAIN 284:9	**Israelite** Behold an I.	BIBL 48:23
join the choir i.	ELIO 127:23	**isst** *Der Mensch ist, was er i.*	FEUE 135:3
led by an i. hand	SMIT 318:4	**ist** *Der Mensch i., was er isst*	FEUE 135:3
no i. means of support	BUCH 73:15	**it** It's just I.	KIPL 203:24
representation of i. things	LEON 213:4	**Italian** to women I.	CHAR 91:5
invisibly Silently, i.	BLAK 57:14	**Italy** has not been in I.	JOHN 189:15
invoking i. the Trinity	PATR 260:12	inside of it, 'I.'	BROW 72:2
inward i. and spiritual grace	BOOK 61:20	I. is a geographical expression	METT 233:17
Outward and the I.	KORA 205:24	Paradise of exiles, I.	SHEL 313:28
ipse *i. dixit*	CICE 96:17	**itch** i. of literature	LOVE 219:12
ira *Ça i.*	ANON 12:9	**itching** have an i. palm	SHAK 297:14
I. furor brevis est	HORA 174:24	**ite** *I. missa est*	MISS 241:2
Sine i. et studio	TACI 329:25	**itur** *sic i. ad astra*	VIRG 347:17
irae *Dies i.*	MISS 241:5	**iudice** *sub i. lis est*	HORA 174:14
Iran has been amputated in I.	EBAD 124:17	**ivory** cargo of i.	MASE 230:16
Iraq president of I.	HUSS 179:4	i., and apes	BIBL 37:7
Ireland daunce wyt me, in i.	ANON 8:18	i. on which I work	AUST 21:14
God save I.	SULL 327:12		
great Gaels of I.	CHES 92:26		
I. hurt you into poetry	AUDE 19:1		
I., Ireland!	GLAD 151:11		
I. is the old sow	JOYC 192:26	# J	
I., long a province	DAVI 111:4	**Jabberwock** Beware the J., my son	CARR 86:23
I. unfree shall never be at peace	PEAR 261:1	**jack** banish plump J.	SHAK 294:21
I. we dreamed of	DE V 113:19	Damn you, J.	BONE 59:6
Out of I. have we come	YEAT 368:25	This J., joke	HOPK 174:6
pacify I.	GLAD 151:13	**jackals** J. piss at their foot	FLAU 138:1
Romantic I.'s dead and gone	YEAT 369:5	**jackknife** j. has Macheath	BREC 68:6
iris livelier i. changes	TENN 333:22	**jacks** calls the knaves, J.	DICK 114:26
Irish I'm I.	MOOR 244:5	**Jackson** J. with his Virginians	BEE 28:21
I. poets, learn your trade	YEAT 369:10	**Jacob** J. served seven years	BIBL 35:4
symbol of I. art	JOYC 193:5	traffic of J.'s ladder	THOM 338:19
Irishry indomitable I.	YEAT 369:11	voice is J.'s voice	BIBL 35:1
iron Any old i.	COLL 101:11	**jade** Let the galled j. wince	SHAK 293:10
become an i. cage	WEBE 352:14	**jail** being in a j.	JOHN 188:11
blood and i.	BISM 55:9	Go to j.	ANON 8:12
Even an i. partition	TALM 330:15	**jam** j. to-morrow	CARR 87:5
he's got i. teeth	GROM 158:1	**James** Home J.	HILL 169:9
If gold ruste, what shall i. do	CHAU 91:22	J. James Morrison Morrison	MILN 235:14
i. curtain	CHUR 95:19	**Jane** you J.	WEIS 353:10
i. entered into his soul	BOOK 64:6	**Janvier** J. and Février	NICH 251:1
i. gates of life	MARV 229:23	**Japan** J.'s advantage	HIRO 170:1
I. Lady	THAT 336:13	**Jarndyce** J. and Jarndyce	DICK 114:12
nobles with links of i.	BOOK 65:6	**jaw** j.-jaw is always better	CHUR 95:23
Nor i. bars a cage	LOVE 219:9	**jawbone** with the j. of an ass	BIBL 36:18
irrational i. entertainment	JOHN 187:11	**jaws** Into the j. of Death	TENN 332:1
i. exuberance	GREE 157:3	j. of power	ADAM 2:9
irrationally I. held truths	HUXL 179:20	**jazz** J. music is to be played	MORT 246:7
irregulars Baker Street i.	DOYL 121:1	**jealous** am a j. God	BIBL 35:25
irrevocabile *volat i. verbum*	HORA 175:2	Art is a j. mistress	EMER 132:3

J. shall be in heaven — BIBL 47:29
j.'s soul lies in the doing — SHAK 308:8
j. was never sure — SWIN 329:11
J., whose hand — KEAT 196:15
let j. be unconfined — BYRO 80:5
Lord of all J. — STRU 327:3
politics of j. — HUMP 178:14
reap in j. — BOOK 64:25
Surprised by j. — WORD 366:8
Where there is sadness, j. — FRAN 141:14
joyful be j. in the Lord — BOOK 64:2
joys All my j. to this are folly — BURT 77:29
j. of parents — BACO 23:1
redoubleth j. — BACO 22:24
vain deluding j. — MILT 236:11
jubilate J. Deo, omnis terra — BIBL 53:29
Judah J.'s seer — MANT 227:10
Judas J. who writes the biography — WILD 358:14
Whether J. Iscariot — DYLA 124:15
judge after a time they j. them — WILD 359:4
Before you j. me — JACK 181:15
decided by the j. — JOHN 187:29
invent than to j. — BACO 23:23
J. none blessed — BIBL 42:23
J. not — BIBL 44:3
j. thou my cause — BIBL 41:26
Justly to j. — BROO 69:18
judgement at forty, the j. — FRAN 141:19
biases the j. — DOYL 121:3
complains of his j. — LA R 209:6
Daniel come to j. — SHAK 302:33
day of j. — BOOK 60:14
fit to sit in j. — WILS 361:10
j. of his peers — MAGN 225:5
leaves of the J. Book unfold — TAYL 331:3
not give his j. rashly — ADDI 3:5
owes you his j. — BURK 76:4
people's j. — DRYD 121:22
world's j. — SCHI 286:11
judgements j. of the Lord — BOOK 62:12
judges independence of j. — DENN 113:3
J. and lawyers are each — EBAD 124:17
j. can tap — MARS 229:6
J. must follow their oaths — ZOBE 370:12
j. soon the sentence sign — POPE 268:20
Judy J. O'Grady — KIPL 202:13
jug j., jug, jug — LYLY 220:22
'J. Jug' to dirty ears — ELIO 129:23
juggling j. a lot of balls — BLAI 55:17
jugular than the j. vein — KORA 205:23
Julia in silks my J. goes — HERR 168:7
my J.'s lips do smile — HERR 168:2
July Born on the fourth of J. — COHA 99:10
on the Fourth of J. — HAMM 160:23
winter—ending in J. — BYRO 81:8
Jumblies where the J. live — LEAR 210:12
June J. is bustin' out — HAMM 160:17
newly sprung in J. — BURN 77:9
When J. is past — CARE 84:19
jungle city is not a concrete j. — MORR 245:6
J. will think — KIPL 203:10
Law of the J. — KIPL 203:23
juniper under a j.-tree — ELIO 127:26
junk J. is the ideal product — BURR 77:23
Juno J.'s never-forgetting anger — VIRG 346:19
jurisdiction j. in this Realm — BOOK 65:14
jury j.-men may dine — POPE 268:20
Trial by j. itself — DENN 113:1
just actions of the j. — SHIR 316:1
all j. works — BOOK 60:7
faithful and j. to me — SHAK 297:3
God is j. — JEFF 184:20
gods are j. — SHAK 298:24

hath his quarrel j. — SHAK 296:2
jewel of the j. — VAUG 345:18
j. an image — GODA 152:2
J. are the ways of God — MILT 239:25
J. as I am — ELLI 131:10
'j.' or 'right' — PLAT 264:21
may not be a j. peace — IZET 181:9
ninety and nine j. persons — BIBL 47:29
on the j. and on the unjust — BIBL 43:19
Our cause is j. — DICK 116:8
place for a j. man — THOR 339:6
rain, it raineth on the j. — BOWE 66:17
Thou art indeed j., Lord — HOPK 174:7
justest wisest and j. — PLAT 264:20
justice act of j. — MAND 226:19
Die he or j. must — MILT 238:15
J. denied — MILL 234:20
J. is in one scale — JEFF 184:16
J. is truth — DISR 117:7
j. makes democracy possible — NIEB 251:2
j. of my quarrel — ANON 9:3
j. or injustice — JOHN 187:29
J. should not only be done — HEWA 168:11
'J.' was done — HARD 161:18
J. with mercy — MILT 239:9
Let j. be done — FERD 134:18
Let j. be done — WATS 351:15
liberty plucks j. — SHAK 302:3
loved j. — GREG 157:8
moderation in the pursuit of j. — GOLD 153:29
more devoted to order than j. — KING 200:15
Poetic J. — POPE 266:5
price of j. — BENN 31:2
reason, and j. — BURK 75:8
Revenge is a kind of wild j. — BACO 23:5
right or j. — MAGN 225:6
Though j. be thy plea — SHAK 302:31
wing of the angel of j. — EBAD 124:17
justifiable j. to men — MILT 239:25
justified confessions of a j. sinner — HOGG 171:14
justifies end j. the means — BUSE 78:9
justify j. God's ways — HOUS 176:16
j. the ways of God — MILT 237:17
justitia Fiat j. — FERD 134:18
justly do j. — BIBL 42:15
juvenes Gaudeamus igitur, J. dum sumus — ANON 13:11

K

Kansas corny as K. in August — HAMM 160:23
K. had better stop raising corn — LEAS 211:2
Kate Kiss me K. — SHAK 307:12
Kathleen Mavourneen K.! the grey dawn — CRAW 106:13
keener edged tool that grows k. — IRVI 181:2
with his k. eye — MARV 229:18
keep honour, and k. her — BOOK 61:26
Ideas won't k. — WHIT 356:11
If you can k. your head — KIPL 202:9
k. the bridge with me — MACA 221:22
k. who can — WORD 365:24
k. your England — MUGA 246:16
some day it'll k. you — WEST 355:6
keeper my brother's k. — BIBL 34:23
Kelly K. from the Isle of Man — MURP 247:8
ken D'ye k. John Peel — GRAV 155:15
kenne k. mich auch nicht — GOET 152:24
Kennedy you're no Jack K. — BENT 31:10
kennst K. du das Land — GOET 152:19
Kensal Green Paradise by way of K. — CHES 93:5
Kent everybody knows K. — DICK 115:18
kept k. the faith — BIBL 52:11

kettle speech is like a cracked k. — FLAU 137:23
Kew Go down to K. — NOYE 252:9
his Highness' dog at K. — POPE 266:14
key out of k. with his time — POUN 269:21
possession of the k. — PAIN 257:6
Turn the k. — KEAT 196:30
With this k. Shakespeare — WORD 365:25
keyboards people want k. — JOBS 185:11
keys half that's got my k. — GRAH 154:20
Khatmandu to the north of K. — HAYE 164:2
kick first k. I took — SPRI 322:16
get no k. from champagne — PORT 269:2
Got to k. at the darkness — COCK 99:4
k. against the pricks — BIBL 49:24
k. to come to the top — KEAT 197:15
kicked k. up stairs — HALI 160:5
no body to be k. — THUR 340:8
kicking flattering, kissing and k. — TRUM 342:10
kid comeback k. — CLIN 98:11
lie down with the k. — BIBL 40:17
kids don't have any k. yourself — LARK 208:22
just a couple of k. — HOLI 171:17
kill able to k. — RUMS 282:1
as k. a good book — MILT 240:3
in every war they k. you in a new way — ROGE 278:17
k. all the lawyers — SHAK 296:3
k. a mockingbird — LEE 211:12
k. a wife with kindness — SHAK 307:13
K. millions of men — ROST 281:3
k. the patient — BACO 22:25
k. us for their sport — SHAK 298:15
k. you if you quote it — BURG 74:23
Licensed to k. — ANON 9:10
Licensed to k. — FLEM 138:8
not to k. anything — JAIN 182:8
Otherwise k. me — MACN 224:12
prepared to k. one another — SHAW 311:28
Thou shalt not k. — BIBL 35:28
Thou shalt not k. — CLOU 98:17
we are going to k. it — POWE 270:11
killed I am the enemy you k. — OWEN 256:15
If hate k. men — BROW 73:2
I'm k., Sire — BROW 72:10
kissed thee ere I k. thee — SHAK 305:15
killer lover and k. are mingled — DOUG 120:4
killeth letter k. — BIBL 51:5
killing K. no murder — SEXB 289:3
medal for k. two men — MATL 231:7
talk of k. time — BOUC 66:7
kills k. all its pupils — BERL 32:9
k. the thing he loves — WILD 359:8
Kiltartan My country is K. Cross — YEAT 368:11
kimonos girls in silk k. — YEAT 368:9
kin little more than k. — SHAK 291:13
makes the whole world k. — SHAK 308:13
kind cruel only to be k. — SHAK 293:22
had been k. — JOHN 188:8
K. hearts are more than coronets — TENN 333:14
less than k. — SHAK 291:13
People will always be k. — SASS 285:27
kindling it only requires k. — PLUT 265:10
kindness breath of k. — ANON 10:2
generates k. — JOHN 188:2
kill a wife with k. — SHAK 307:13
k. and lies are worth — GREE 156:24
milk of human k. — SHAK 299:21
Of k. and of love — WORD 364:19
on the k. of strangers — WILL 360:15
spontaneous k. — JOHN 190:9
tak a cup o' k. yet — BURN 76:20
kindred True to the k. points — WORD 366:12
king authority forgets a dying k. — TENN 332:20
born K. of the Jews — BIBL 43:1

Cotton is K. — CHRI 94:12
cotton is k. — HUGO 178:2
cuts off his k.'s head — SHAW 312:20
despised and dying k. — SHEL 314:22
divinity doth hedge a k. — SHAK 293:31
duty is the k.'s — SHAK 295:21
every inch a k. — SHAK 298:16
fight for its K. and Country — GRAH 154:19
follow the K. — TENN 332:12
God bless.the K. — BYRO 79:24
God save k. Solomon — BIBL 37:4
God save our gracious k. — ANON 8:11
God save the k. — BIBL 36:26
God save the k. — SHAK 306:3
great and mighty k. — ROCH 278:4
have served the K. — WOLS 363:13
Honour the k. — BIBL 52:27
illiterate k. — HENR 166:15
K. and country need you — ANON 12:7
K. asked the Queen — MILN 235:15
k. can do no wrong — BLAC 55:15
K. David and King Solomon — NAYL 248:21
K. enjoys his own again — PARK 259:8
k. in Babylon — HENL 166:11
k. indeed — CHAP 90:18
k. is but a man — SHAK 295:19
k. is truly *parens patriae* — JAME 182:12
k. never dies — BLAC 55:13
K. of England cannot enter — PITT 264:3
K. of England's eyes — TYND 344:8
K. of glory — BOOK 62:17
K. of glory now — NOEL 251:20
K. of Great Britain — REED 274:15
K. of heaven — LYTE 221:4
K. of love — BAKE 24:17
k. of shreds and patches — SHAK 293:20
K. over the Water — ANON 9:8
K.'s daughter — BOOK 63:3
k.'s daughter o' Noroway — BALL 25:16
k. sits in Dunfermline — BALL 25:15
k.'s name — SHAK 306:18
lay on the k. — SHAK 295:22
leave without the k. — ELIZ 131:6
man who would be k. — KIPL 203:20
Moloch, horrid k. — MILT 237:26
My dead k. — JOYC 192:24
neck of the last k. — DIDE 116:11
No bishop, no K. — JAME 182:10
not offended the k. — MORE 244:20
once and future k. — MALO 226:9
Ozymandias, k. of kings — SHEL 314:10
passing brave to be a k. — MARL 228:17
rightwise k. — MALO 226:7
Ruin seize thee, ruthless K. — GRAY 156:5
smote the k. of Israel — BIBL 37:18
speaks ill of your k. — NELS 249:4
stomach of a k. — ELIZ 130:14
thy k. is a child — BIBL 39:23
To be a Pirate K. — GILB 150:22
zeal I served my k. — SHAK 296:15
kingdom comest into thy k. — BIBL 48:9
found a k. — MILT 239:17
into the k. of heaven — BIBL 45:12
k. against kingdom — BIBL 45:33
k. by the sea — POE 265:13
k. of God — BIBL 44:1
k. of God — BIBL 48:25
k. of God is within you — BIBL 48:3
k. of heaven — BIBL 43:13
k. of heaven — BIBL 45:1
k. of heaven is at hand — BIBL 43:4
k. stretch from shore to shore — WATT 352:1
mind to me a k. is — DYER 123:17

my k. for a horse — SHAK 306:19
of such is the k. of God — BIBL 46:29
Thy k. come — BIBL 43:22
voice of the k. — SWIF 328:7
kingdoms all the k. of the world — BIBL 43:11
goodly states and k. — KEAT 196:27
kingly k. crop — DAVI 110:18
kings all be as happy as k. — STEV 325:27
bind their k. in chains — BOOK 65:6
captains and the k. — KIPL 202:19
death of k. — SHAK 305:30
dominion of k. changed — PRIC 270:21
end of k. — DEFO 111:23
five K. left — FARO 134:6
k. are not only God's lieutenants — JAME 182:11
k. haul up the lumps — BREC 68:8
k. is mostly rapscallions — TWAI 343:7
K. will be tyrants — BURK 75:21
K. would not play at — COWP 105:30
last of the k. strangled — MESL 233:15
laws or k. — JOHN 187:23
laws or k. can cause — GOLD 153:18
lays his icy hand on k. — SHIR 315:28
meaner creatures k. — SHAK 306:17
Of cabbages—and k. — CARR 87:3
politeness of k. — LOUI 219:5
Right Divine of K. — POPE 266:8
sport of k. — SOME 320:8
sport of k. — SURT 327:20
walk with K. — KIPL 202:10
War is the trade of k. — DRYD 122:5
kinship crimson thread of k. — PARK 259:10
kinsmen k. die — ANON 14:3
Kipling K. and his views — AUDE 19:5
Rudyards cease from k. — STEP 324:3
kiss Ae fond k. — BURN 76:17
Colder thy k. — BYRO 81:25
k. but in the cup — JONS 192:2
k. can be a comma — MIST 241:8
k. is still a kiss — HUPF 178:21
Kiss K. Bang Bang — KAEL 194:13
K. me, Hardy — NELS 249:10
K. me Kate — SHAK 307:12
k. my ass in Macy's window — JOHN 186:10
k. of the sun for pardon — GURN 158:10
k. on the hand — ROBI 277:13
k. the Managing Director — WHIT 356:17
let us k. and part — DRAY 121:10
sweetly did me k. — WYAT 367:2
With one long k. — TENN 332:7
Wouldst k. me pretty — HART 163:1
kissed k. each other — BOOK 63:21
k. thee ere I killed thee — SHAK 305:15
kisses fine romance with no k. — FIEL 135:15
Give me a thousand k. — CATU 89:7
more than k. — DONN 119:20
remembered k. — TENN 334:16
kissing I wasn't k. her — MARX 230:2
K. don't last — MERE 233:7
k. had to stop — BROW 73:4
k. your hand — LOOS 218:15
like k. God — BRUC 73:8
wonder who's k. her — ADAM 1:14
kit old k.-bag — ANON 11:19
kitchen get out of the k. — TRUM 342:11
send me to eat in the k. — HUGH 177:13
sitting in the k. sink — SMIT 318:11
whip in k. cups — STEV 324:15
knave k. is not punished — HALI 160:3
knaves calls the k., Jacks — DICK 114:26
knee blude to the k. — BALL 25:20
Every k. shall bow — NOEL 251:20
every k. should bow — BIBL 51:22

knees creeps rustling to her k. — KEAT 195:13
live on your k. — IBAR 180:2
knell it is a k. — SHAK 300:13
k. of parting day — GRAY 156:7
like a rising k. — BYRO 80:4
knew Johnny, I hardly k. ye — BALL 25:10
k. it best — BACO 22:15
world k. him not — BIBL 48:18
knife cannibal uses k. and fork — LEC 211:6
my oyster k. — HURS 178:22
smylere with the k. — CHAU 91:26
War to the k. — PALA 257:21
will not use the k. — HIPP 169:19
knight Fearless, blameless k. — ANON 12:11
gentle k. was pricking — SPEN 321:24
k. at arms — KEAT 195:23
k. like the young Lochinvar — SCOT 287:18
K. of the Doleful Countenance — CERV 89:19
new-slain k. — BALL 25:21
that was your k. — PEEL 261:6
verray, parfit gentil k. — CHAU 91:13
knit life to k. me — HOUS 176:12
knits Sleep that k. up — SHAK 300:16
knives night of the long k. — HITL 170:7
knock k., and it shall be opened — BIBL 44:6
k. at the door — LAMB 207:2
k., breathe, shine — DONN 118:24
right to k. him down — JOHN 190:3
stand at the door, and k. — BIBL 53:5
knocked we k. the bastard off — HILL 169:8
knocking K. on the moonlit door — DE L 112:14
knocks k. you down with the butt — GOLD 153:28
knot crowned k. of fire — ELIO 128:18
political k. — BIER 54:18
know all I k. is what I read — ROGE 278:16
all ye need to k. — KEAT 196:12
dare to k. — HORA 174:23
do not pretend to k. — DARR 110:1
don't k. what I'm doing — BRAU 68:2
find out what you don't k. — WELL 354:7
hate any one that we k. — HAZL 164:6
He must k. sumpin' — HAMM 160:19
I do not k. myself — GOET 152:24
I k. nothing — SOCR 319:23
I k. thee not, old man — SHAK 294:30
k. better what is good for people — JAY 183:13
k. Him, love him — CATE 88:16
k. not what they do — BIBL 48:8
k. that I am God — BOOK 63:5
k. that my redeemer liveth — BIBL 38:4
K. then thyself — POPE 267:27
k. the place — ELIO 128:15
k. the world — YOUN 370:1
K. thyself — ANON 13:1
k. to know no more — MILT 238:27
K. what I mean, Harry — BRUN 73:13
k. what I think — WALL 349:16
k. what we are talking about — RUSS 283:5
K. you the land — GOET 152:19
let me k. mine end — BOOK 62:25
master of those who k. — DANT 109:11
no one to k. — ANON 7:18
not k. where he is going — LIN 215:13
say 'I don't k.' — RUMS 281:19
Tell me what you k. — EMER 132:20
things they didn't k. — POUN 269:20
those who do not wish to k. — RALE 273:7
to k. a little — BACO 23:14
To k. this only — MILT 239:19
We must k. — HILB 168:19
What do I k. — MONT 243:2
what should they k. of England — KIPL 201:23
You k. more than you think — SPOC 322:10

know (*cont.*)

you'll never k.	ARMS 16:5
knowed all that there is to be k.	GRAH 155:6
knoweth k. not God	BIBL 52:32
knowing Bewrapt past k.	HARD 162:6
lust of k.	FLEC 138:4
misfortune of k. anything	AUST 20:28
one who INSISTS on k.	POUN 270:6
knowledge After such k., what forgiveness	ELIO 128:20
all k. to be my province	BACO 23:30
All our k. is	POPE 268:3
Benevolent K.	BORG 65:20
bring home k.	JOHN 189:24
by nature desire k.	ARIS 15:10
desire more love and k.	SHAK 290:3
envied kind of k.	ADAM 2:8
follow k. like a sinking star	TENN 335:4
follow virtue and k.	DANT 109:13
Friendship from k.	BUSS 78:22
increaseth k.	BIBL 39:9
K. comes	TENN 333:30
K. dwells In heads	COWP 106:1
k. in mathematics	BACO 24:4
k. in the making	MILT 240:8
k. is dangerous	HUXL 179:17
k. is of two kinds	JOHN 189:10
K. is proud	COWP 106:2
k. itself is power	BACO 23:31
k. of a lifetime	WHIS 355:24
k. of causes	BACO 23:26
k. of good and evil	BIBL 34:8
k. of human nature	AUST 20:26
k. of nature	HOLB 171:15
k. of nothing	DICK 115:22
k. of the Lord	BIBL 40:18
k. of the world	CHES 92:14
k. we have lost in information	ELIO 129:12
k. which they cannot lose	OPPE 253:18
k. without integrity	JOHN 187:21
Language and k.	SULL 327:9
Let k. grow	TENN 332:26
literature of *k.*	DE Q 113:10
make k. available	BLAC 55:11
never better than k.	FERM 135:2
No man's k.	LOCK 216:14
objects of k.	PLAT 264:23
organized k.	SPEN 321:5
province of k. to speak	HOLM 172:1
spirit of k.	BIBL 40:16
tree of diabolical k.	SHER 315:10
tree of the k.	BIBL 34:9
words without k.	BIBL 38:7
known Have ye not k.	BIBL 41:3
k. and the unknown	PINT 263:14
k. too late	SHAK 306:26
k. unto God	ANON 10:21
till I am k.	JOHN 188:8
knows Every schoolboy k.	MACA 221:13
has a mind and k. it	SHAW 311:7
He k. nothing	SHAW 311:27
if you k. of a better 'ole	BAIR 24:16
knows about it all—HE k.	FITZ 136:15
k. what he fights for	CROM 107:7
less one k.	LAO 208:6
sits in the middle and k.	FROS 143:25
who k. does not speak	LAO 208:8
Koran K. was sent down	KORA 204:20
Kraken K. sleepeth	TENN 333:12
Kubla In Xanadu did K. Khan	COLE 100:7
Kurtz Mistah K.—he dead	CONR 102:24
Kyrie K. eleison	MISS 240:17

L

label without a rag of a l.	HUXL 179:15
labour all ye that l.	BIBL 44:33
best when we are L.	BROW 70:14
brow of l.	BRYA 73:14
l. against our own cure	BROW 71:13
l. and not to ask	IGNA 180:12
l. of love	BIBL 52:2
L.'s attack dog	PAXM 260:17
l. we delight in	SHAK 300:22
life all l. be	TENN 333:35
their l. is but lost	BOOK 64:26
youth of l.	GOLD 153:6
labourer l. is worthy of his hire	BIBL 47:13
labourers l. are few	BIBL 44:24
labouring sleep of a l. man	BIBL 39:14
women l. of child	BOOK 60:15
labours Children sweeten l.	BACO 23:2
no l. tire	JOHN 187:25
labyrinthine down the l. ways	THOM 338:14
lacessit *Nemo me impune l.*	ANON 13:12
lack can I l. nothing	BOOK 62:14
lacked questioning, If I l. any thing	HERB 167:17
lacking nothing is l.	LEON 213:2
lacrimae *Hinc illae l.*	TERE 335:11
Sunt l. rerum	VIRG 347:3
lad l. that is gone	STEV 326:1
ladder behold a l.	BIBL 35:2
traffic of Jacob's l.	THOM 338:19
Wiv a l.	BATE 27:16
ladders where all the l. start	YEAT 367:16
laden heavy l.	BIBL 44:33
ladies remember the l.	ADAM 1:10
lady called her his l. fair	KIPL 203:3
I met a l.	KEAT 195:25
l. doth protest too much	SHAK 293:9
l. fair	BALL 25:21
l. of a 'certain age'	BYRO 81:4
L. of Shalott	TENN 333:17
L. of Spain	REAV 274:10
l.'s in the case	GAY 147:3
l.'s not for burning	FRY 144:6
l.'s not for turning	THAT 336:15
l. sweet and kind	ANON 11:7
L. with a Lamp	LONG 218:2
little l. comes by	GAY 147:9
lovely l., garmented	SHEL 315:3
My L. Bountiful	FARQ 134:7
Our L. of Pain	SWIN 329:10
talk like a l.	SHAW 312:27
why the l. is a tramp	HART 162:21
Lafayette *L., nous voilà*	STAN 323:3
laid where they have l. him	BIBL 49:15
lain There hath he l. for ages	TENN 333:13
laisser-faire *L.*	ARGE 15:2
laissez-faire *L.*	ANON 12:16
laity conspiracies against the l.	SHAW 311:18
lake l. water lapping	YEAT 368:15
slips into the bosom of the l.	TENN 334:23
lama Eli, Eli, l. sabachthani	BIBL 46:20
lamb Behold the L. of God	BIBL 48:21
he who made the L.	BLAK 58:4
holy L. of God	BLAK 57:8
l. to the slaughter	BIBL 41:11
Little L. who made thee	BLAK 57:19
Mary had a little l.	HALE 159:16
one little ewe l.	BIBL 36:36
to the shorn l.	STER 324:7
white in the blood of the L.	BIBL 53:8
wolf shall dwell with the l.	BIBL 40:17
lambs gather the l.	BIBL 41:2

lame Science without religion is l.	EINS 126:2
lamp Lady with a L.	LONG 218:2
l. is shattered	SHEL 313:30
Slaves of the L.	ARNO 16:10
lampada vitai l.	LUCR 220:14
lamp post leaning on a l.	GAY 147:9
lamp posts drunken man uses l.	LANG 207:16
lamprey surfeit by eating of a l.	FABY 133:16
lamps l. are going out all over Europe	GREY 157:13
old l. for new	ARAB 14:11
Lancaster time-honoured L.	SHAK 305:16
land by sea as by l.	GILB 149:14
fat of the l.	BIBL 35:9
if by l., one	REVE 275:8
Ill fares the l.	GOLD 153:5
l. flowing with milk	BIBL 35:14
l. God gave to Cain	CART 88:6
l. of counterpane	STEV 325:28
L. of Hope and Glory	BENS 31:3
l. of lost content	HOUS 176:13
l. of my fathers	JAME 182:15
l. of my fathers	THOM 338:5
l. of pure delight	WATT 351:24
l. of the free	KEY 199:17
L. that I love	BERL 31:20
l. was ours before	FROS 143:16
L. where my fathers died	SMIT 319:1
lane to the l. of the dead	AUDE 18:14
more precious than l.	SADA 284:2
one if by l.	LONG 218:6
piece of l.	HORA 175:25
ready by water as by l.	ELST 131:16
seen the promised l.	KING 200:20
splendid and a happy l.	GOLD 153:11
There's the l., or cherry-isle	HERR 168:2
think there is no l.	BACO 22:2
This l. is your land	GUTH 158:11
travel by l. or by water	BOOK 60:15
Unhappy the l. that needs heroes	BREC 68:4
we had the l.	GEOR 148:5
Woe to the l.	SHAK 306:12
landed Eagle has l.	ARMS 16:7
landing fight on the l. grounds	CHUR 95:9
landlord paid to the l.	RICA 275:14
lands take us l. away	DICK 115:28
though not of l.	WOTT 366:22
landscape gardening is but l.-painting	POPE 268:24
landslide pay for a l.	KENN 198:12
lane l. to the land of the dead	AUDE 18:14
lang For auld l. syne	BURN 76:20
language any l. you choose	GILB 149:20
best chosen l.	AUST 20:26
by means of l.	WITT 362:7
cool web of l.	GRAV 155:16
divided by a common l.	SHAW 313:6
enemy of clear l.	ORWE 255:3
enlargement of the l.	JOHN 186:18
entrance into the l.	BACO 23:15
everything else in our l.	MACA 221:16
except, of course, l.	WILD 358:2
hidden l. of the soul	GRAH 155:2
in l. there are only differences	SAUS 286:3
In such lovely l.	LAWR 209:26
l. all nations understand	BEHN 29:13
l. an opera is sung in	APPL 14:9
l. can be compared	SAUS 286:4
L. grows out of life	SULL 327:9
l. in her eye	SHAK 308:14
l. is a dialect with	WEIN 353:7
L. is fossil poetry	EMER 132:14
L. is only the instrument	JOHN 186:17
L. is the dress	JOHN 187:8
l. of priorities	BEVA 33:9
l. of prose	WORD 366:18
l. of the heart	POPE 266:23
l. of the living	ELIO 128:11
l. of the unheard	KING 201:2
L. was not powerful enough	DICK 115:11
Life is a foreign l.	MORL 245:2
limits of my l.	WITT 362:13
mathematical l.	GALI 145:7
merit of l. is clearness	GALE 145:6
mobilized the English l.	MURR 247:11
mystery of l.	KELL 197:27
no l. but a cry	TENN 333:1
obscurity of a learned l.	GIBB 149:4
Political l. . . . is designed	ORWE 255:5
suicides have a special l.	SEXT 289:5
world understands my l.	HAYD 163:18
You taught me l.	SHAK 307:21
languages feast of l.	SHAK 299:1
l. are the pedigree	JOHN 187:30
languors lilies and l.	SWIN 329:9
lantern l. on the stern	COLE 101:7
lanterns show two l.	REVE 275:8
lap in the l. of the gods	HOME 172:13
l. of Earth	GRAY 156:15
lapidary In l. inscriptions	JOHN 189:12
lapping lake water l.	YEAT 368:15
lard l. their lean books	BURT 78:1
lards l. the lean earth	SHAK 294:18
large as l. as life	CARR 87:14
lark bisy l., messager of day	CHAU 91:24
l. ascending	MERE 233:8
l. at break of day	SHAK 310:6
l. at heaven's gate sings	SHAK 291:5
l. now leaves his wat'ry nest	D'AV 110:16
l.'s on the wing	BROW 72:23
larks Four L. and a Wren	LEAR 210:9
What l.	DICK 114:27
larkspur l. listens	TENN 334:6
Lars Porsena L. of Clusium	MACA 221:20
lasciate L. OGNI SPERANZA	DANT 109:8
lash blood drawn with the l.	LINC 215:4
rum, sodomy, prayers, and the l.	CHUR 95:22
lass every l. a queen	KING 201:5
It came with a l.	JAME 182:14
lover and his l.	SHAK 290:25
lassie I love a l.	LAUD 209:14
love she's but a l.	BURN 77:7
last give unto this l.	BIBL 45:23
l. and best	MILT 239:7
l. article of my creed	GAND 145:16
l. best gift	MILT 238:30
l. breath of Julius Caesar	JEAN 183:14
l. day of an era past	YELT 369:20
l. gasp	BIBL 42:29
l. person who has sat on him	HAIG 159:4
l. red leaf	TENN 332:28
l. rose of summer	MOOR 244:11
l. shall be first	BIBL 45:21
l. taste of sweets	SHAK 305:21
l. thing I shall do	PALM 258:7
l. thing one knows	PASC 259:17
l. while they last	DE G 112:8
Look thy l. on all things lovely	DE L 112:13
Nice guys finish l.	DURO 123:14
We were the l. romantics	YEAT 367:19
won the l. war	ROOS 279:4
world's l. night	DONN 119:1
latchet shoe's l.	BIBL 48:20
late l. into the night	BYRO 81:20
not too l. to-morrow	ARMS 16:3
rather l. for me	LARK 208:14
This is a l. parrot	MONT 243:14
Too l. came I	AUGU 20:4

later came l. in life ASQU 17:20
  l. than you think SERV 288:25
latet L. *anguis in herba* VIRG 347:20
Latin half Greek, half L. SCOT 287:3
  he speaks L. SHAK 296:5
  small L. JONS 192:6
latrine mouth had been used as a l. AMIS 6:5
latter former and the l. BOOK 60:18
laudant L. *illa* MART 229:9
laudate l. *et superexaltate eum* BIBL 54:6
laudator l. *temporis acti* HORA 174:18
laugh do we not l. SHAK 302:22
  L., and the world laughs WILC 357:25
  l. at any mortal thing BYRO 81:2
  l. at everything BEAU 28:1
  l. at human actions SPIN 322:9
  l. at live dragons TOLK 340:21
  l. at them AUST 21:11
  L. no man to scorn BIBL 42:22
  L. where we must POPE 267:19
  loud l. that spoke GOLD 153:7
  must l. before we are happy LA B 206:10
  time to l. BIBL 39:11
laughable very l. things JOHN 188:21
laughed first baby l. BARR 26:21
  honest man is l. at HALI 160:3
  one has not l. CHAM 90:9
  when he l. AUDE 18:17
laughing l. devil BYRO 80:17
  l. queen HUNT 178:18
laughs l. with a harvest JERR 185:9
laughter faculty of l. ADDI 3:9
  gift of l. SABA 284:1
  l. and the love BELL 30:5
  L. is nothing else HOBB 170:12
  l. of a fool BIBL 39:15
  L. . . . the most civilized music USTI 344:20
  Laugh thy girlish l. WATS 351:16
  nothing more frightful than l. SAGA 284:5
  Our sincerest l. SHEL 314:28
  present l. SHAK 308:28
launched l. a thousand ships MARL 228:7
laurel Caesar's l. crown BLAK 56:11
laurels l. all are cut ANON 12:17
  Once more, O ye l. MILT 236:27
lauriers l. *sont coupés* ANON 12:17
lava in its l. I still find WOOL 364:3
lave Let the l. go by me STEV 326:2
law according to the l. BIBL 42:7
  against the l. for generals TRUM 342:16
  become a universal l. KANT 194:21
  breaks the l. PLAT 264:18
  built with stones of L. BLAK 57:1
  but by the l. BIBL 50:5
  chief l. CICE 96:16
  end of l. is LOCK 216:18
  fear of the L. JOYC 192:20
  fence around the L. TALM 330:12
  Ignorance of the l. SELD 288:13
  judgement of the l. JACK 181:16
  keep this l. BOOK 61:1
  keystone of the rule of l. DENN 113:3
  l. and the prophets BIBL 44:8
  l. doth give it SHAK 302:34
  l. floats in a sea of ethics WARR 351:2
  l. is a ass DICK 115:16
  L. is a bottomless pit ARBU 14:14
  L. is above you DENN 113:2
  L. is boldly BURR 77:22
  l. is established SIDN 316:10
  l. is such an ass CHAP 90:19
  L. is the true embodiment GILB 149:17
  L. of the Jungle KIPL 203:23

l. of the Yukon SERV 288:26
l. unto themselves BIBL 49:39
lesser breeds without the L. KIPL 202:21
life of the l. COKE 99:13
majestic equality of the l. FRAN 141:8
moral l. within me KANT 194:19
Necessity has no l. PUBL 271:13
Necessity hath no l. CROM 107:13
No brilliance is needed in the l. MORT 246:4
Nor l., nor duty YEAT 368:12
not a l. at all ROBE 277:10
Nothing is l. POWE 270:16
No written l. more binding CATT 89:4
principle of the English l. DICK 114:13
sustained: by the L. TALM 330:11
this is the royal l. CORO 104:12
where no l. is BIBL 49:41
whole of the L. CROW 108:2
Who to himself is l. CHAP 90:18
windy side of the l. SHAK 309:10
Wrest once the l. SHAK 302:32
lawful L. as eating SHAK 309:30
  their l. occasions BOOK 65:9
lawn bird-haunted English l. ARNO 16:17
  Get your tanks off my l. WILS 361:7
  on the l. I lie in bed AUDE 19:13
laws are the l. of nature SHAW 311:12
  Bad l. BURK 76:5
  bad or obnoxious l. GRAN 155:13
  care who should make the l. FLET 138:10
  dole Unequal l. TENN 334:31
  dominion of l. PRIC 270:21
  do with the l. HORS 175:27
  government of l. ADAM 2:4
  Government of l. and not of men FORD 139:7
  l. and learning MANN 227:8
  L. are like cobwebs SWIF 328:8
  L. are silent CICE 96:23
  L. grind the poor GOLD 153:17
  L., like houses BURK 75:31
  l. of Nature HUXL 179:18
  l. or kings JOHN 187:23
  l. or kings can cause GOLD 153:18
  L. were made to be broken NORT 252:1
  more l. and orders LAO 208:9
  more numerous the l. TACI 330:1
  Nature, and Nature's l. POPE 267:4
  neither l. made JOHN 185:12
  part of the l. of England HALE 159:13
  planted thick with l. BOLT 59:2
  sweeps a room as for Thy l. HERB 167:15
  Written l. ANAC 6:9
lawyer l. has no business JOHN 187:29
  l. interprets the truth GIRA 151:8
  l. tells me I may BURK 75:8
  l. with his briefcase PUZO 272:6
lawyers Judges and l. are each EBAD 121:7
  kill all the l. SHAK 296:3
lay I l. me down to sleep ANON 9:23
  l. down his life BIBL 49:7
  L. on, Macduff SHAK 302:2
  L. your sleeping head AUDE 19:8
lays constructing tribal l. KIPL 202:11
Lazarus L. with a triple bypass HOWA 176:19
lazy l. leaden-stepping hours MILT 237:12
lead blind l. the blind BIBL 45:6
  easy to l. BROU 70:10
  l. a horticulture PARK 259:5
  L., kindly Light NEWM 250:7
  L. us, Heavenly Father EDME 125:6
  think we l. BYRO 81:24
leader I am their l. LEDR 211:10
  l. of the enterprise VIRG 347:2

test of a l.	LIPP 215:14
leadership L. means making	CHRÉ 94:9
leaf And I were like the l.	SWIN 329:15
days are in the yellow l.	BYRO 81:15
last red l.	TENN 332:28
yellow l.	SHAK 301:27
league Half a l. onward	TENN 331:19
lean l. and hungry look	SHAK 296:20
l. on one another	BURK 75:31
l. over too far backward	THUR 340:3
leaning l. all awry	FITZ 136:18
leap giant l. for mankind	ARMS 16:8
great l. in the dark	VANB 345:4
l. in the dark	HOBB 170:23
l. into the dark	BROW 71:1
leaped have I l. over a wall	BIBL 37:2
leaping l. from place to place	HARD 162:3
too broad for l.	HOUS 176:15
learn craft so long to l.	CHAU 92:2
don't want to l.	SELL 288:16
l., and inwardly digest	BOOK 60:20
live and l.	POMF 266:3
much desire to l.	MILT 240:8
People must l. to hate	MAND 226:17
while they teach, men l.	SENE 288:22
learned been l. has been forgotten	SKIN 317:16
I've l.	BLAI 56:6
l. anything from history	HEGE 165:1
obscurity of a l. language	GIBB 149:4
privilege of the l.	PEAR 261:2
learning a' the l. I desire	BURN 76:25
enough of l. to misquote	BYRO 81:12
l. many things	SOLO 320:4
little l. is a dangerous thing	POPE 267:6
much l. doth make thee mad	BIBL 49:36
of liberty, and of l.	DISR 117:13
pursuit of l.	LAO 208:7
scraps of l.	YOUN 369:22
Wear your l.	CHES 92:19
will to l.	ASCH 17:14
written for our l.	BOOK 60:20
learnt forgotten nothing and l. nothing	DUMO 123:6
They have l. nothing	TALL 330:9
lease summer's l.	SHAK 310:3
least faithful in that which is l.	BIBL 47:36
l. of these my brethren	BIBL 46:8
leave for ever taking l.	RILK 276:18
Intreat me not to l. thee	BIBL 36:21
l. the outcome	CORN 104:5
l. things alone you leave them	CHES 93:14
l. without the King	ELIZ 131:6
ready to l.	MONT 242:16
shall a man l. his father	BIBL 34:13
leaven l. leaveneth the whole lump	BIBL 50:17
leaves burning of the l.	BINY 55:1
l. of the tree	BIBL 53:25
l. to a tree	KEAT 197:13
Thick as autumnal l.	MILT 237:25
Very like l.	HOME 172:10
leaving like the l. it	SHAK 299:19
lectures l. or a little charity	WHIT 357:8
led we are most l.	BYRO 81:24
left better to be l.	CONG 102:10
goats on the l.	BIBL 46:6
l. thy first love	BIBL 53:2
let not thy l. hand know	BIBL 43:21
other l.	BIBL 46:2
lege Tolle l.	AUGU 20:3
legend before Your l. ever did	JOHN 185:17
before your l. will	JOHN 186:1
fables in the l.	BACO 22:11
Legion My name is L.	BIBL 46:26
legions give me back my l.	AUGU 20:12

legislator l. of mankind	JOHN 187:17
legislators idea of hereditary l.	PAIN 257:15
unacknowledged l.	SHEL 315:6
legs dog's walking on his hinder l.	JOHN 188:18
Four l. good	ORWE 254:9
vast and trunkless l.	SHEL 314:9
legunt sed ista l.	MART 229:9
leisure detest at l.	BYRO 81:7
fill l. intelligently	RUSS 283:2
have l. to bother	SHAW 312:23
increased l.	DISR 117:12
L. with honour	CICE 96:25
When I have l.	HILL 169:13
lemon l.-trees bloom	GOET 152:19
lend l. me your ears	SHAK 297:1
men who l.	LAMB 206:20
lender borrower, nor a l. be	SHAK 291:30
drags its dreary l.	DICK 114:12
drags its slow l.	POPE 267:12
what it lacks in l.	FROS 143:17
Lenore angels name L.	POE 265:18
lente Festina l.	AUGU 20:13
L. currite noctis equi	OVID 255:23
l., lente, currite	MARL 228:9
leopard l. change his spots	BIBL 41:22
l. shall lie down	BIBL 40:17
leopards three white l. sat	ELIO 127:26
leper innocence is like a dumb l.	GREE 156:27
wash the l.'s wounds	TERE 335:19
lerne gladly wolde he l.	CHAU 91:18
Lesbia Let us live, my L.	CATU 89:6
Lesley bonnie L.	BURN 76:23
less L. is a bore	VENT 346:2
L. than the dust	HOPE 173:13
little l.	BROW 71:25
more and more about l. and less	BUTL 79:4
small Latin, and l. Greek	JONS 192:6
lessen l. from day to day	CARR 86:16
lesser l. breeds	KIPL 202:21
lessons l. to be drawn	ELIZ 131:3
reason they're called l.	CARR 86:16
lest L. we forget	KIPL 202:19
let L. my people go	ANON 11:20
L. my people go	BIBL 35:17
L. us with a gladsome mind	MILT 236:26
Lethe go not to L.	KEAT 196:13
waters of L.	GINS 151:6
letter l. killeth	BIBL 51:5
made this [l.] longer	PASC 259:16
my l. to the world	DICK 116:7
scarlet l.	HAWT 163:14
thou unnecessary l.	SHAK 297:31
when he wrote a l.	BACO 22:18
letters L. for the rich	AUDE 19:11
l. get in the wrong places	MILN 235:20
l. mingle souls	DONN 119:20
l. to a non-existent	LEWI 213:21
lettuce eating too much l.	POTT 269:11
levee Drove my Chevy to the l.	MCLE 223:15
level l. of provincial existence	ELIO 127:19
leviathan draw out l.	BIBL 38:10
L., called a commonwealth	HOBB 170:13
L. Hugest of living creatures	MILT 239:1
there is that L.	BOOK 64:5
lewd certain l. fellows	BIBL 49:28
lex suprema est l.	CICE 96:16
lexicographer L. A writer of dictionaries	JOHN 186:19
lexicons We are walking l.	LIVE 216:2
liar answered 'Little L.'	BELL 29:21
best l.	BUTL 79:12
l. should be outlawed	HALI 160:1
liars All men are l.	BOOK 64:17
fears may be l.	CLOU 98:22

liars (cont.)

Income Tax made more L.	ROGE 278:14

liberal as distinguished from the L. — BIER 54:19
damned compact l. majority — IBSE 180:4
either a little L. — GILB 149:18
first L. leader — STEE 323:8
l. education — BANK 26:9
l. is a conservative who — WOLF 363:9
liberals l. can understand — BRUC 73:7
liberation l. of the human mind — GOLD 153:3
liberties give up their l. — BURK 76:8
L. . . . depend on the silence — HOBB 170:21
liberty ardour for l. — PRIC 270:21
Brightest in dungeons, L. — BYRO 81:19
certainly destroys l. — JOHN 190:10
chosen music, L. — WORD 366:11
conceived in all l. — LINC 214:20
dangers to l. lurk — BRAN 67:17
divests himself of natural l. — LOCK 216:20
endanger the public l. — ADAM 2:3
extremism in the defence of l. — GOLD 153:29
given l. to man — CURR 108:16
holy name of l. — GAND 145:14
l. and equality — ARIS 15:22
L. *and* Union — WEBS 352:19
L. cannot be — SUMN 327:15
L. cannot be preserved — ADAM 2:8
l. consists in doing — MILL 234:10
l. depends on freedom — JEFF 183:19
L. is liberty, not — BERL 32:8
l. is precious — LENI 212:12
l. is to faction — MADI 224:19
l. is unfinished business — ANON 9:9
l. means responsibility — SHAW 312:9
L. not a means — ACTO 1:8
l. of the individual — MILL 234:9
l. of the press — JUNI 194:1
l., or give me death — HENR 166:24
l. plucks justice — SHAK 302:3
L.'s in every blow — BURN 77:11
l. to know, to utter — MILT 240:9
L. too must be limited — BURK 75:2
L., when it begins to take root — WASH 351:11
life, and l. — JEFF 183:18
life, l. — ANON 11:14
loudest yelps for l. — JOHN 187:22
love of l. — HAZL 164:4
of l., and of learning — DISR 117:13
O l.! what crimes — ROLA 278:19
proclaim l. to the captives — BIBL 41:17
right of l. — TAFT 330:5
safeguards of l. — FRAN 141:15
survival and the success of l. — KENN 198:15
Sweet land of l. — SMIT 319:1
symptom of constitutional l. — GIBB 148:17
tree of l. — JEFF 184:2
wait for l. — MACA 221:11
when they cry l. — MILT 239:29
Liberty-Hall This is L., gentlemen — GOLD 153:24
library choice of all my l. — SHAK 308:7
circulating l. — SHER 315:10
In his l. — AUST 21:9
l. is thought in cold storage — SAMU 285:1
lumber room of his l. — DOYL 120:12
My l. Was dukedom — SHAK 307:19
public l. — JOHN 187:16
sit in a l. — FITZ 137:10
turn over half a l. — JOHN 189:8
licence L. they mean — MILT 239:29
l. to act like an asshole — ZAPP 370:9
l. to print money — THOM 339:4
universal l. to be good — COLE 99:18
license L. my roving hands — DONN 118:21

licensed L. to kill — ANON 9:10
L. to kill — FLEM 138:8
licentious l. passages — GIBB 149:4
Licht *Mehr L.* — GOET 152:25
lie Bodies never l. — DE M 112:18
can't tell a l. — WASH 351:10
definition of a l. — ANON 7:5
Every word she writes is a l. — MCCA 222:10
fain wald l. down — BALL 25:11
fall victim to a big l. — HITL 170:6
home to a l. — POUN 269:23
Is a dream a l. — SPRI 322:18
isn't told a l. — KIPL 202:25
leads you to believe a l. — BLAK 56:17
L. heavy on him, Earth — EVAN 133:9
l. that makes us realize truth — PICA 263:11
l. will go round the world — SPUR 322:19
mixture of a l. — BACO 23:17
noble l. — PLAT 264:22
no worse l. — JAME 183:8
old L.: Dulce et decorum — OWEN 256:11
possible to l. for the truth — ADLE 3:16
sent to l. abroad — WOTT 366:26
what is a l. — BYRO 81:5
when dead, l. as quietly — EDWA 125:12
lied because our fathers l. — KIPL 201:19
l. to please the mob — KIPL 202:1
lies Beats all the l. — BLAK 56:10
certain, and the rest is l. — FITZ 136:12
History, sir, will tell l. — SHAW 311:16
kindness and l. are worth — GREE 156:24
l. are often told in silence — STEV 325:24
l. beneath your spell — HOPE 173:12
l., damned lies and statistics — DISR 118:9
l. it lives on and propagates — FOSD 140:3
l. of tongue and pen — CHES 92:28
make l. sound truthful — ORWE 255:5
Matilda told such Dreadful L. — BELL 29:20
telling l. about the Democrats — STEV 325:1
though I know she l. — SHAK 310:27
Truth exists, l. are invented — BRAQ 67:20
lieutenants God's l. upon earth — JAME 182:11
life actor's l. for me — WASH 351:12
all human l. is there — JAME 182:17
all part of l.'s rich pageant — MARS 229:2
as large as l. — CARR 87:14
believe in l. — DU B 122:25
Book of L. begins — WILD 359:3
careful of the single l. — TENN 333:2
changing scenes of l. — TATE 330:20
Chaos often breeds l. — ADAM 1:21
criticism of l. — ARNO 17:6
crown of l. — BIBL 53:3
day-to-day business l. is — LAFO 206:13
death after l. — SPEN 321:26
Death is not an event in l. — WITT 362:12
death, nor l. — BIBL 50:9
discovered the secret of l. — CRIC 106:17
Does thy l. destroy — BLAK 58:2
doors to let out l. — FLET 138:11
doors to let out l. — MASS 231:3
drive l. into a corner — THOR 339:18
essence of l. — DAWK 111:8
everlasting l. — BIBL 48:27
everlasting l. — BIBL 48:31
fear love is to fear l. — RUSS 283:4
Fill me with l. anew — HATC 163:6
findeth his l. — BIBL 44:30
forfeit my l. — BROW 70:16
fountain of the water of l. — BIBL 53:24
from the dream of l. — SHEL 313:17
gave my l. for freedom — EWER 133:10
genius into my l. — WILD 359:15

give for his l.	BIBL 37:34	L. without industry is guilt	RUSK 282:13
giveth his l. for the sheep	BIBL 48:37	l. without theory	DISR 117:24
golden tree of actual l.	GOET 152:10	L. would be tolerable	LEWI 214:3
had a happy l.	HAZL 164:7	L. would be very pleasant	SURT 328:1
hath a l. to live	RAIN 272:20	L. would ring the bells	GINS 151:2
honour and l.	FRAN 141:10	live a l. half dead	MILT 239:24
hour of glorious l.	MORD 244:14	live out my l. talking	VANZ 345:12
Human l. is everywhere	JOHN 187:18	long as you have your l.	JAME 182:16
in mourning for my l.	CHEK 92:8	looked at l. from both sides	MITC 241:11
in our l. alone	COLE 100:1	loss of l.	HOWA 176:20
In the midst of l.	BOOK 62:5	Mad from l.'s history	HOOD 172:20
In the midst of l.	MUMF 247:3	matter of l. and death	SHAN 311:4
I've had a wonderful l.	WITT 362:15	measured out my l. with coffee spoons	ELIO 128:31
last of l.	BROW 72:28	my whole l., long or short	ELIZ 130:23
lay down his friends for his l.	THOR 339:24	Night-mare L.-IN-DEATH was she	COLE 100:21
lay down his l.	BIBL 49:7	No, no, no l.	SHAK 298:28
leadeth unto l.	BIBL 44:10	Nothing in his l.	SHAK 299:19
Lead me from death to l.	KUMA 206:5	not the men in my l. that counts	WEST 355:8
l. a glorious cycle of song	PARK 258:11	no wealth but l.	RUSK 282:21
l. all labour be	TENN 333:35	now my l. is done	TICH 340:9
l., and liberty	JEFF 183:18	of man's l. a thing apart	BYRO 80:24
l. and loves of a she-devil	WELD 353:14	O for a l. of sensations	KEAT 197:10
l. and power	FOX 140:16	one l. to lose	HALE 159:15
L. begins at forty	PITK 263:19	only a l. of mistakes	ELIO 127:13
l. beyond life	MILT 240:4	path of our l.	DANT 109:7
l. exists in the universe	JEAN 183:15	Perfection of the l.	YEAT 367:15
L. for life	BIBL 35:29	priceless gift of l.	ROSE 280:9
L. imitates Art	WILD 358:18	Pride of L.	HARD 161:20
l. in the village	LEE 211:14	principal business of l.	BUTL 79:11
l. is 6 to 5 against	RUNY 282:6	really don't know l. at all	MITC 241:11
L. is a foreign language	MORL 245:2	resurrection, and the l.	BIBL 48:38
L. is a gamble	STOP 326:15	Reverence for L.	SCHW 286:20
L. is a great surprise	NABO 247:16	sell the present l.	KORA 205:9
L. is a horizontal fall	COCT 99:6	shilling l. will give you	AUDE 19:19
L. is a luminous halo	WOOL 363:19	single page of our l.	SAND 285:2
L. is an incurable disease	COWL 105:14	slits the thin-spun l.	MILT 236:31
L. is as tedious	SHAK 297:19	spice of l.	COWP 105:27
L. is Colour and Warmth	GREN 157:11	spirit giveth l.	BIBL 51:5
L. is doubt	UNAM 344:11	strenuous l.	ROOS 279:19
L. is first boredom, then fear	LARK 208:17	taking l. by the throat	FROS 144:2
L. is just a bowl of cherries	BROW 70:18	That l. so short	CHAU 92:2
L. is just one damned	HUBB 177:8	this long disease, my l.	POPE 266:18
L. is made up of	RICE 275:15	tired of l.	JOHN 189:19
L. is mostly froth	GORD 154:8	torch of l.	LUCR 220:14
L. is not meant to be easy	FRAS 142:8	tree of l.	BIBL 34:8
L. is not meant to be easy	SHAW 311:9	upon the thorns of l.	SHEL 314:5
L. is real	LONG 217:18	value of l.	MONT 242:18
L. is short, the art long	HIPP 169:15	view of l.	DARW 110:10
L. is the desert	YOUN 370:4	walk in newness of l.	BIBL 50:2
L. is the other way round	LODG 217:2	Was my l. also	OWEN 256:14
l. is the thing	SMIT 318:19	way, the truth, and the l.	BIBL 49:5
L. is too much like a pathless wood	FROS 143:8	well-written L.	CARL 85:5
l. is very short	TAYL 331:5	What is this l.	DAVI 111:2
l. is washed	BARZ 27:10	whole l. shows in your face	BACA 21:21
l., its enemy	ANOU 14:4	Wholesome of l.	HORA 175:8
l., liberty	ANON 11:14	Who saw l. steadily	ARNO 16:26
l., like a dome	SHEL 313:21	Without work, l. goes rotten	CAMU 84:4
l. may perfect be	JONS 192:3	you lived your l.	JOHN 185:16
l. of his beast	BIBL 38:20	life-blood l. of a master spirit	MILT 240:4
l. of the nation secure	DOUG 120:8	lifetime knowledge of a l.	WHIS 355:24
l. of the world	DOST 119:26	. l. of happiness	SHAW 311:30
l. protracted	JOHN 187:27	lift L. her with care	HOOD 172:18
L. says: she did this	BARN 26:16	l. up mine eyes	BOOK 64:20
l.'s dim windows	BLAK 56:17	L. up your heads	BOOK 62:17
l.'s dull round	SHEN 315:7	L. up your hearts	BOOK 61:10
L.'s longing for itself	GIBR 149:3	light armour of l.	BIBL 50:12
L.'s not just being alive	MART 229:10	armour of l.	BOOK 60:19
l. that I have	MARK 228:3	bear witness of that L.	BIBL 48:17
L., the Universe and Everything	ADAM 1:13	brief crack of l.	NABO 247:17
L., to be sure, is nothing much	HOUS 176:5	certain Slant of l.	DICK 116:5
L. too short to stuff a mushroom	CONR 102:29	children of l.	BIBL 47:34
l. was duty	HOOP 173:2	Creature, which was L.	BACO 23:32
l. went through with death	FORT 140:1	crying for the l.	TENN 333:1

light (*cont.*)

dark is l. enough	FRY 144:5
dim religious l.	MILT 236:16
excess of l.	GRAY 156:21
fierce l. which beats	TENN 332:9
From darkness lead me to L.	UPAN 344:12
garmented in l.	SHEL 315:3
gives a lovely l.	MILL 234:18
how my l. is spent	MILT 239:30
infinite ocean of l.	FOX 140:15
into the world of l.	VAUG 345:17
Jeanie with the l. brown hair	FOST 140:8
know what l. is	JOHN 189:16
Lead, kindly L.	NEWM 250:7
Let there be l.	BIBL 34:3
Let there be l.	MARR 229:1
Let your l. so shine	BIBL 43:16
l. at the end of the tunnel	DICK 116:10
l. at the end of the tunnel	LOWE 220:5
l. fantastic round	MILT 236:4
l. fantastic toe	MILT 236:20
l. gleams an instant	BECK 28:16
L. (God's eldest daughter)	FULL 144:16
l. has gone out of our lives	NEHR 249:2
l. in the darkness of mere being	JUNG 193:18
l. in the dust	SHEL 313:30
l. is come	BIBL 41:16
l. my fire	MORR 245:18
l. of common day	WORD 365:7
l. of evening, Lissadell	YEAT 368:9
L. of Light	BOOK 61:3
L. of the heavens	KORA 205:16
l. of the world	BIBL 43:15
l. on the hill	CHIF 93:26
l., shade, and perspective	CONS 103:3
l. shineth in darkness	BIBL 48:15
l. that never was	WORD 364:12
l. to them that sit in darkness	BIBL 46:34
l. within his own clear breast	MILT 236:5
More l.	GOET 152:25
once we lose this l.	JONS 191:17
particles of l.	BLAK 57:10
perpetual l.	MISS 241:4
place of l.	DISR 117:13
progeny of l.	MILT 238:32
pure and endless l.	VAUG 345:19
Put out the l.	SHAK 305:12
seen a great l.	BIBL 40:13
speed far faster than l.	BULL 73:21
sweetness and l.	ARNO 17:2
sweetness and l.	SWIF 328:6
tried to mend the Electric L.	BELL 30:1
Warmth and L.	GREN 157:11
while the l. fails	ELIO 128:17
with a l. behind her	GILB 150:27
with you there is l.	BONH 59:9
lighten L. our darkness	BOOK 60:8
lighter l. than vanity	BUNY 74:10
lightness unbearable l. of being	KUND 206:7
lightning from Jove the l.	MANI 227:1
Shakespeare by flashes of l.	COLE 101;4
snatched the l.	TURG 343:3
writing history with l.	WILS 361:9
lights l. are dim and low	ORRE 254:4
l. around the door	ROSS 280:22
Turn up the l.	HENR 166:21
ligno *Regnavit a l. Deus*	FORT 140:2
like company we don't greatly l.	WILL 360:8
Do what you l.	RABE 272:12
I'd l. to get away	FROS 143:9
L. cures like	ANON 13:21
l. it the least	CHES 92:18
l. this sort of thing	LINC 215:6

l. what you get	SHAW 312:18
look upon his l. again	SHAK 291:25
man you don't l.	THOM 338:6
none of his friends l. him	WILD 359:16
wha's l. us	ANON 8:15
whether we l. it or not	THOM 338:22
will much l.	AUST 21:16
liked l. whate'er She looked on	BROW 72:18
wish to be l.	RUSS 282:26
likely Not bloody l.	SHAW 312:30
likerous l. mouth	CHAU 91:29
likes does what he l. to do	GILL 150:28
likewise Go, and do thou l.	BIBL 47:16
liking Not l. the person	THOM 338:9
lilac Kew in l.-time	NOYE 252:9
lilacs breeding L.	ELIO 129:17
l. last in the dooryard	WHIT 357:11
Lilian Airy, fairy L.	TENN 333:21
lilies braids of l. knitting	MILT 236:10
feedeth among the l.	BIBL 39:34
few l. blow	HOPK 173:19
l. and languors	SWIN 329:9
l. of the field	BIBL 43:26
L. that fester	SHAK 310:16
peacocks and l.	RUSK 282:19
three l. in her hand	ROSS 280:18
lily Elaine, the l. maid	TENN 332:13
folds the l. all her sweetness up	TENN 334:23
l. of the valleys	BIBL 39:32
l. on thy brow	KEAT 195:24
paint the l.	SHAK 297:20
pure as the l.	LAUD 209:14
with a poppy or a l.	GILB 150:15
limbs deck your lower l. in pants	NASH 248:16
l. of a poet	HORA 175:24
lime l.-tree bower my prison	COLE 100:29
limited Liberty too must be l.	BURK 75:2
limits l. of my language	WITT 362:13
stony l.	SHAK 306:30
limousine One perfect l.	PARK 258:14
Limpopo grey-green, greasy, L.	KIPL 203:16
Lincoln I am a Ford, not a L.	FORD 139:6
L. County Road or Armageddon	DYLA 124:11
line active l. on a walk	KLEE 204:4
carved not a l.	WOLF 363:2
direction of the right l.	NEWT 250:12
horizontal l.	WHEW 355:21
l. is length without breadth	EUCL 133:5
l. upon line	BIBL 40:23
lives along the l.	POPE 267:23
problem of the colour l.	DU B 122:26
thin red l.	RUSS 283:17
linen fair white l. cloth	BOOK 60:24
In blanchèd l.	KEAT 195:16
very fine l.	BRUM 73:11
lines Just say the l.	COWA 105:11
l. are fallen unto me	BOOK 62:10
six l. written	RICH 276:11
lingering alone sit l. here	VAUG 345:17
l., with boiling oil	GILB 150:7
lingua *Pange, l.*	FORT 139:20
Pange, l.	THOM 337:12
lining There's a silver l.	FORD 139:10
lion as a roaring l.	BIBL 52:30
bold as a l.	BIBL 39:1
buttocked like a l.	MALO 226:8
calf and the young l.	BIBL 40:17
dead l.	BIBL 39:19
l. to frighten the wolves	MACH 223:9
nation that had l.'s heart	CHUR 95:24
wrath of the l.	BLAK 57:2
lions L. led by donkeys	ANON 9:11
l. roaring	BOOK 64:4

my darling from the l. BOOK 62:22
lips ever at his l. KEAT 196:15
l. of dying men ARNO 16:23
l. that touch liquor YOUN 370:5
my Julia's l. do smile HERR 168:2
My l. are sealed BALD 25:4
people of unclean l. BIBL 40:9
Read my l. BUSH 78:12
saw their starved l. KEAT 195:27
lipstick bears a l.'s traces MARV 230:1
liquefaction l. of her clothes HERR 168:7
liquid Cats, no less l. TESS 336:4
Thames is l. history BURN 76:14
liquor lips that touch l. YOUN 370:5
l. is quicker NASH 248:14
lirra Tirra l. TENN 333:18
lisped I l. in numbers POPE 266:17
list I've got a little l. GILB 149:23
List, list, O, l. SHAK 291:37
There is no l. STRA 327:1
listen Darkling I l. KEAT 196:20
L., my children LONG 218:5
l. the more ZENO 370:11
privilege of wisdom to l. HOLM 172:1
world should l. then SHEL 314:29
listened I've l. BLAI 56:6
listener l., who listens in the snow STEV 324:22
listening disease of not l. SHAK 294:33
People hearing without l. SIMO 317:3
listeth wind bloweth where it l. BIBL 48:26
lit whole Fleet's l. up WOOD 363:16
literary l. productions GIBB 148:15
Never l. attempt HUME 178:11
parole of l. men JOHN 190:8
literature great Cham of l. SMOL 319:19
in l., the oldest BULW 74:3
in the locks of l. TENN 335:10
itch of l. LOVE 219:12
like their l. clear and cold LEWI 214:5
L. cannot be the business SOUT 320:24
L. is a luxury CHES 93:9
l. is my mistress CHEK 92:9
L. is news POUN 270:5
L. mostly about having sex LODG 217:2
l. of *power* DE Q 113:10
l.'s performing flea O'CA 252:19
L. the orchestration of platitudes WILD 359:23
province of l. MACA 221:18
Remarks are not l. STEI 323:14
little big words for l. matters JOHN 188:19
Go, l. bok CHAU 92:4
here a l., and there a little BIBL 40:23
hobgoblin of l. minds EMER 132:11
how l. we think of the other TWAI 343:20
L. boxes on the hillside REYN 275:11
L. drops of water CARN 85:27
L. Englanders ANON 9:12
l. grey cells CHRI 94:11
l. learning is a dangerous thing POPE 267:6
Little man, l. man ELIZ 130:17
L. man, you've had a busy day SIGL 316:19
l. more BROW 71:25
L. one! Oh, little one STEP 324:5
l. people pay taxes HELM 165:17
l. woman who wrote LINC 215:7
Man wants but l. GOLD 153:12
She gives but l. YOUN 370:1
So l. done RHOD 275:13
so l. done TENN 333:4
though she be but l. SHAK 303:29
too l. or too much BARR 26:20
live cannot l. with you MART 229:11
Can these bones l. BIBL 42:3

Come l. with me DONN 119:7
Come l. with me MARL 228:15
Days are where we l. LARK 208:16
desires to l. long SWIF 328:24
enable its citizens to l. WEIL 353:6
he isn't fit to l. KING 200:16
He shall l. by them TALM 330:16
he shall l. in them BIBL 35:33
He shall not l. SHAK 297:13
how long I have to l. BOOK 62:25
If you don't l. it PARK 258:10
in him we l., and move BIBL 49:31
l. all you can JAME 182:16
l. and learn POMF 266:3
l. beyond its income BUTL 79:14
l. in a fantasy world MURD 247:7
l. in peace ARIS 15:14
l. in society ARIS 15:20
l., not as we wish MENA 232:17
l. on your knees IBAR 180:2
l. their creeds GUES 158:7
l. this long BLAK 56:7
l. through someone else FRIE 142:21
l. to do that MART 229:7
l. together as brothers KING 200:18
l., unseen, unknown POPE 268:13
l. well on nothing a year THAC 336:7
l. your life not as simple PAST 260:2
Man is born to l. PAST 260:1
might as well l. PARK 258:16
must l. ARGE 15:3
nations how to l. MILT 240:11
not l. to eat MOLI 242:1
see so much, nor l. so long SHAK 298:30
short time to l. BOOK 62:4
Teach me to l. KEN 198:6
to l. dangerously NIET 251:8
To l. is like to love BUTL 79:17
To l. with thee RALE 272:22
turn and l. with animals WHIT 357:7
wanted to l. deep THOR 339:18
way they have to l. CATH 88:19
We l., as we dream CONR 102:21
We l. our lives RILK 276:18
would you l. for ever FRED 142:10
lived Had we l. SCOT 287:5
I have l. long enough SHAK 301:27
lively l. Oracles of God CORO 104:12
liver open and notorious evil l. BOOK 60:23
lives Clarissa l. RICH 276:10
He that l. upon hope FRAN 141:20
he who l. more lives than one WILD 359:10
how he l. JOHN 188:22
it's men's l. SCOT 287:21
light wind l. or dies KEAT 197:4
l. along the line POPE 267:23
l. of quiet desperation THOR 339:12
make our l. sublime LONG 217:21
ninety l. have been taken MCGO 223:3
pleasant in their l. BIBL 36:34
woman who l. for others LEWI 213:19
liveth know that my redeemer l. BIBL 38:4
name l. for evermore ANON 11:6
name l. for evermore BIBL 42:28
living even for the l. God BOOK 62:27
fever called 'l.' POE 265:16
fight for the l. JONE 191:10
hands of the l. God BIBL 52:13
house is a machine for l. in LE C 211:8
land of the l. WILD 359:21
language of the l. ELIO 128:11
life is not worth l. SOCR 319:25
L. and partly living ELIO 129:5

living (cont.)
l. at this hour   WORD 364:23
l. death   MILT 239:24
l. dog   BIBL 39:19
l. in Philadelphia   FIEL 135:22
l. sacrifice   BIBL 50:10
L.? The servants will do that   VILL 346:16
l. to some purpose   PAIN 257:20
machine for l.   TOLS 341:4
more alone while l.   CARR 86:2
noble L.   WORD 365:19
Plain l. and high thinking   WORD 365:10
respect to the l.   VOLT 348:22
riotous l.   BIBL 47:30
Summer time an' the l. is easy   HEYW 168:14
those who are l.   BURK 75:23
too much love of l.   SWIN 329:12
well and l. in Paris   ANON 9:6
Who, l., had no roof   HEYW 168:17
you'll learn the art of l.   GOET 152:11
Livingstone Dr L., I presume   STAN 323:2
Lloyd George L. knew my father   ANON 9:14
lo L.! He comes   WESL 354:23
L.! the poor Indian   POPE 267:21
load l. and bless With fruit   KEAT 197:1
L. every rift   KEAT 197:20
loaf with a l. of bread   FITZ 136:8
loafing cricket as organized l.   TEMP 331:12
local l., but prized elsewhere   AUDE 19:20
l. habitation and a name   SHAK 304:2
Lochinvar young L. is come   SCOT 287:17
loci Geniumque l.   VIRG 347:15
locks in the l. of literature   TENN 335:10
l. were like the raven   BURN 77:2
never shake Thy gory l.   SHAK 301:7
locust years that the l. hath eaten BIBL 42:11
locusts l. and wild honey   BIBL 43:6
locuta Roma l. est   AUGU 20:11
lodge best to l.   SHAK 309:5
lodged L. with me useless   MILT 239:30
log L.-cabin to White House   THAY 337:5
logic l. of our times   DAY- 111:11
Second L. then   ARIS 15:6
That's l.   CARR 87:2
logical L. consequences   HUXL 179:21
loins girded up his l.   BIBL 37:13
shudder in the l. engenders   YEAT 368:16
loitering Alone and palely l.   KEAT 195:23
Lolita L., light of my life   NABO 247:14
London 1938 in L.   MIDL 233:22
arch of L. Bridge   MACA 221:14
city much like L.   SHEL 314:12
crowd flowed over L. Bridge   ELIO 129:21
L., small and white and clean   MORR 245:12
L., that great cesspool   DOYL 121:2
L., thou art the flower   ANON 9:15
lungs of L.   PITT 264:7
rainy Sunday in L.   DE Q 113:6
tired of L.   JOHN 189:19
lone From the l. shieling   GALT 145:12
l. lorn creetur   DICK 114:17
walking by his wild l.   KIPL 203:14
loneliness l. of the long-distance   SILL 316:22
well of l.   HALL 160:7
lonely All the l. people   LENN 212:18
None but the l. heart   GOET 152:21
Only the l.   ORBI 254:2
lonesome on a l. road   COLE 100:26
long foot and a half l.   HORA 174:15
for such a l. time   MOLI 242:3
How l. a time   SHAK 305:19
how l. I have to live   BOOK 62:25
how l. it takes to succeed   MONT 243:6

if a man have l. hair   BIBL 50:21
In the l. run   KEYN 199:22
live this l.   BLAK 56:7
l. and the short and the tall   HUGH 177:12
l.-distance runner   SILL 316:22
l. in city pent   KEAT 197:5
L. is the way   MILT 238:7
l., long thoughts   LONG 217:16
l., long trail   KING 201:3
l. way to Tipperary   JUDG 193:12
l. week-end   FORS 139:14
Lord, how l.   BIBL 40:11
love me l.   ANON 9:16
man goeth to his l. home   BIBL 39:28
night of the l. knives   HITL 170:7
Nor wants that little l.   GOLD 153:12
story need be l.   THOR 339:9
week is a l. time in politics   WILS 361:5
your way be l.   CAVA 89:11
longa Ars l., vita brevis   HIPP 169:15
longer no l. my own   METH 233:16
longeth l. my soul after thee   BOOK 62:27
longing cast a l. eye   JEFF 184:4
hopeless l.   ARNO 16:14
look do we l. for another   BIBL 44:31
full l. at the worst   HARD 162:2
I l. at the senators   HALE 159:12
l. after our people   SCOT 287:6
l., and pass on   DANT 109:9
L. back in anger   OSBO 255:12
L. for me by moonlight   NOYE 252:11
l. forward to the trip   STIN 326:7
l. in thy heart and write   SIDN 316:12
l. long upon a monkey   CONG 102:12
l. no way but downwards   BUNY 74:15
l. on and help   LAWR 210:1
L., stranger   AUDE 19:7
l. the East End in the face   ELIZ 131:5
L. thy last on all things lovely   DE L 112:13
l. to his bond   SHAK 302:20
L. to it   LINC 214:17
l. to the end   ANON 13:17
l. upon his like again   SHAK 291:25
One cannot l. at this   GOYA 154:16
row one way and l. another   BURT 78:3
sit and l. at it for hours   JERO 185:6
'Tis very sweet to l.   KEAT 197:5
looked more he l. inside   MILN 235:9
looketh man l. on the outward   BIBL 36:28
looking l. back   BIBL 47:12
l. for an honest man   DIOG 116:20
l. one way, and rowing   BUNY 74:12
l. together   SAIN 284:10
someone may be l.   MENC 232:21
stop other people from l.   BLAC 55:11
looking glass cracked l. of a servant JOYC 193:5
looking glasses Women have served as l. WOOL 363:22
looks her l. went everywhere   BROW 72:18
l. like a duck   REUT 275:7
needs good l.   TUCK 342:22
loom she left the l.   TENN 333:19
loon cream-faced l.   SHAK 301:26
loophole l. through which the pervert BRON 69:8
loose all hell broke l.   MILT 238:29
l. the bands of Orion   BIBL 38:8
man who should l. me   LOWE 219:16
loquitur Cor ad cor l.   NEWM 250:9
lord acceptable year of the L.   BIBL 41:17
And I replied, 'My L.'   HERB 167:13
by the hand of the L.   BIBL 35:23
come, L. Jesus   BIBL 53:26
coming of the L.   HOWE 177:2
dwell in the house of the L.   BOOK 62:15

earth is the l.'s	BIBL 50:20	France has not l. the war	DE G 112:2
earth is the L.'s	BOOK 62:16	Home of l. causes	ARNO 17:4
Go, and the L. be with thee	BIBL 36:29	I have l. a day	TITU 340:14
great l.	BEAU 28:3	land of l. content	HOUS 176:13
Great l. of all things	POPE 267:28	l. an empire	ACHE 1:6
L. and Father of mankind	WHIT 357:14	l. chord	PROC 271:4
L. gave, and the Lord	BIBL 37:33	l. generation	STEI 323:18
L. has more truth yet	ROBI 277:18	l. the only Playboy	SYNG 329:17
L., how long	BIBL 40:11	L., yesterday	MANN 227:3
L. in His mercy	CRAI 106:7	Next to a battle l.	WELL 354:2
L. is in this place	BIBL 35:3	Not l. but gone before	NORT 252:5
L. is my shepherd	BOOK 62:14	not l. but sent before	CYPR 109:3
L. is One	SIDD 316:6	not that you won or l.	RICE 275:17
L. looketh on the heart	BIBL 36:28	paradises we have l.	PROU 271:11
L. make his face shine	BIBL 35:35	Though lovers be l.	THOM 337:17
L., now lettest thou	BIBL 47:6	Vietnam was l. in	MCLU 223:19
L. of all hopefulness	STRU 327:3	was l., and is found	BIBL 47:33
L. of himself	WOTT 366:22	what is l. in translation	FROS 144:4
L. of the Dance	CART 88:4	who deliberates is l.	ADDI 2:21
l. of the foul and the brute	COWP 106:4	lot l. is fallen unto me	BOOK 62:10
L. our God is one Lord	BIBL 36:3	policeman's l. is not a happy one	GILB 150:24
L. Randal	BALL 25:11	Remember L.'s wife	BIBL 48:4
L., remember me	BIBL 48:9	Lothario gay L.	ROWE 281:12
L. shall raise me up	RALE 273:3	lots cast l. upon my vesture	BOOK 62:13
L.'s my shepherd	SCOT 288:2	lottery L., with weekly pay-out	ORWE 254:26
L. watch between	BIBL 35:5	Lou lady that's known as L.	SERV 289:2
L., what fools	SHAK 303:28	loud upon the l. cymbals	BOOK 65:7
L., ye know, is God	KETH 199:16	louder l. he talked of his honour	EMER 132:4
Name of the L.	BOOK 64:19	loungers l. and idlers	DOYL 121:2
Praise the L.	FORG 139:12	louse l. and a flea	JOHN 190:13
Rejoice in the L.	BIBL 51:26	l. in the locks of literature	TENN 335:10
remembrance of his dying L.	SPEN 321:25	Louvre You're the L.	PORT 269:6
saying 'L. Jones Dead'	CHES 93:22	love Absence is to l.	BUSS 78:23
Seek ye the L.	BIBL 41:13	Ah, l., let us be true	ARNO 16:12
soul doth magnify the L.	BIBL 46:32	all for l.	SPEN 322:2
taken away my L.	BIBL 49:15	All that matters is l. and work	FREU 142:19
those who love the L.	HUNT 178:16	Amazing!	WESL 354:17
Up to a point, L. Copper	WAUG 352:7	and be my l.	MARL 228:15
way of the L.	BIBL 40:30	and be thy l.	RALE 272:22
we battle for the L.	ROOS 280:4	Anxiety is l.'s greatest killer	NIN 251:14
what hour your L. doth come	BIBL 46:3	Any kiddie in school can l.	NASH 248:13
when they crucified my L.	ANON 11:16	be wise, and l.	SHAK 308:10
Whom the L. loveth	BIBL 52:16	bridge is l.	WILD 359:21
lords l. who lay ye low	SHEL 314:20	but one true l.	BALL 26:1
l. will alway	BARC 26:11	but to l. much	TERE 335:23
wit among L.	JOHN 188:6	came I to l. thee	AUGU 20:4
lore volume of forgotten l.	POE 265:17	caution in l.	RUSS 283:1
lose if you l., you lose nothing	PASC 259:21	come unto my l.	SPEN 321:22
is to l. it	ORWE 255:8	commonly called l.	FIEL 135:12
l. his own soul	BIBL 46:27	corner in the thing I l.	SHAK 305:3
l. one parent	WILD 358:7	could l. thee, Dear	LOVE 219:10
l. the war in an afternoon	CHUR 96:7	courage to l.	TROL 342:2
nothing much to l.	HOUS 176:5	dark secret l.	BLAK 58:2
nothing to l.	MARX 230:13	desire more l. and knowledge	SHAK 290:3
shall l. it	BIBL 44:30	disguise which can hide l.	LA R 209:5
win or l. it all	MONT 243:11	doesn't l. a wall	FROS 143:19
wins if he does not l.	KISS 204:1	done a great deal for l.	FRAN 141:7
losers he shall be among the l.	KORA 205:5	do not l. thee, Dr Fell	BROW 71:2
no winners, but all are l.	CHAM 90:3	Do what you l.	NAVR 248:20
loses l. his misery	ARNO 16:21	Earth's the right place for l.	FROS 143:9
losing l. your brain	FOX 141:3	fall in l. today	GERS 148:7
l. your sight	SASS 285:27	fate of l. is	BARR 26:20
loss do our country l.	SHAK 295:25	fear l. is to fear life	RUSS 283:4
l. of innocence	HOWA 176:20	flowers and fruits of l.	BYRO 81:15
profit and l.	ELIO 129:30	For ever wilt thou l.	KEAT 196:8
lost All is not l.	MILT 237:20	Friendship is L.	BYRO 81:13
all was l.	MILT 239:6	gates unto my l.	SPEN 321:21
and we are l.	PYRR 272:7	God is l., but	LEE 211:11
Are you l. daddy	LARD 208:12	God of l.	HERB 167:23
better to have loved and l.	TENN 332:29	good man's l.	SHAK 290:22
country is l.	WILL 360:2	got l. well weighed up	AMIS 6:6
every day to be l.	JOHN 190:22	Greater l. hath no man	BIBL 49:7
found my sheep which was l.	BIBL 47:28	greater l. hath no man	THOR 339:24

love (*cont.*)

groans of l. to those of the dying	LOWR 220:7
had a l. for Charlotte	THAC 336:10
heart whose l. is innocent	BYRO 81:18
hid in the heart of l.	YEAT 368:23
hold l. out	SHAK 306:30
how can he l. God	BIBL 52:34
how Christians l. one another	TERT 336:1
How do I l. thee	BROW 71:17
how I l. my country	PITT 264:1
How should I your true l. know	SHAK 293:28
hurt us that we l.	BEAU 28:4
I don't l. you	MART 229:8
If I l. you	GOET 152:20
I hate and I l.	CATU 89:8
I knew it was l.	BYRO 81:22
I'll l. you	AUDE 18:13
in l. with a cold climate	SOUT 320:23
in the world is l.	BREN 68:11
King of l.	BAKE 24:17
knew thee but to l. thee	HALL 160:9
know Him, l. him	CATE 88:16
labour of l.	BIBL 52:2
Land that I l.	BERL 31:20
left thy first l.	BIBL 53:2
let me l.	DONN 119:8
let me sow l.	FRAN 141:14
Let's fall in l.	PORT 269:3
let us l.	CATU 89:6
lightly turns to thoughts of l.	TENN 333:22
live with me, and be my l.	DONN 119:7
L., a child	WROT 366:29
L., all alike	DONN 119:16
L. alters not	SHAK 310:23
L. and a cottage	COLM 101:17
L. and do what you will	AUGU 20:8
l. and fame	KEAT 197:8
l. and scandal	FIEL 135:11
l. a thing that can never go wrong	PARK 258:11
L. bade me welcome	HERB 167:17
L. built on beauty	DONN 118:19
l. can find you at every time	CHER 92:12
L. ceases to be a pleasure	BEHN 29:10
L. comes from blindness	BUSS 78:22
L. comforteth like sunshine	SHAK 310:32
L. conquers all things	VIRG 347:25
L. consists in this	RILK 277:1
L., curiosity, freckles, and doubt	PARK 258:12
L. divine	WESL 354:22
l. does not consist	SAIN 284:10
L. doesn't just sit there	LE G 211:18
L. goes toward love	SHAK 306:33
L. has pitched his mansion	YEAT 367:20
l. her, comfort her	BOOK 61:26
l. her till I die	ANON 11:7
L. in a cold climate	MITF 241:16
l. in a golden bowl	BLAK 56:15
L. in a hut	KEAT 196:1
l. in another's soul	LAYT 210:4
L. is a boy	BUTL 79:7
L. is a spirit	SHAK 310:31
L. is a universal migraine	GRAV 155:18
l. is here to stay	GERS 148:9
L. is just a system	BARN 26:18
L. is like any other luxury	TROL 342:4
L. is not love	SHAK 310:21
l. is of a birth as rare	MARV 229:14
l. is slight	MARL 228:11
L. is so short	NERU 249:12
L. is strong as death	BIBL 40:2
L. is the delusion	MENC 232:18
L. is the fart	SUCK 327:7
l. is the gift of oneself	ANOU 14:5

L. is the wisdom of the fool	JOHN 190:24
L. just makes it safer	ICE- 180:11
L. looks not with the eyes	SHAK 303:9
L. means not ever having	SEGA 288:11
L. me little	ANON 9:16
l. of friends	BELL 30:5
l. of liberty	HAZL 164:4
l. of money	BIBL 52:9
l. one another or die	AUDE 19:18
L. seeketh not itself to please	BLAK 57:23
L. seeketh only Self to please	BLAK 57:24
L. set you going	PLAT 264:17
L.'s harbinger	MILT 239:12
l. she's but a lassie	BURN 77:7
l. slights it	BACO 22:21
L.'s like a red, red rose	BURN 77:9
L.'s not Time's fool	SHAK 310:22
L. sought is good	SHAK 309:4
L.'s pleasure lasts but a moment	FLOR 138:16
L.'s proper exercise	DAVI 110:20
l.'s the noblest frailty	DRYD 122:4
l.'s young dream	MOOR 244:9
l. that asks no question	SPRI 322:12
l. that dare not	DOUG 120:2
l. that I have	MARK 228:3
l. that moves the sun	DANT 109:17
L. that never told can be	BLAK 57:14
L. the Beloved Republic	FORS 139:19
l., the beloved Republic	SWIN 329:13
L. the brotherhood	BIBL 52:27
l. thee better after death	BROW 71:18
L., the human form divine	BLAK 57:17
l. the Lord thy God	BIBL 45:28
L. the sinner	AUGU 20:10
l. thy neighbour	BIBL 35:34
l. thy neighbour as thyself	BIBL 45:28
L. to hatred turned	CONG 102:7
L. to the loveless shown	CROS 107:21
l. up groweth	CHAU 92:6
l. were what the rose is	SWIN 329:15
l. . . . whatever that may	CHAR 91:6
l. will yield to business	OVID 256:3
l. without the rhetoric	STOP 326:12
l. wol nat been constreyned	CHAU 91:23
l. you because I need you	FROM 143:4
L. your enemies	BIBL 47:9
L. you ten years before	MARV 229:20
make l. in a canoe	BERT 32:20
making l. all year round	BEAU 28:2
Man's l. is of man's life	BYRO 80:24
Men l. in haste	BYRO 81:7
ministers of L.	COLE 100:13
money can't buy me l.	LENN 212:17
music be the food of l.	SHAK 308:17
my l. and I did meet	YEAT 367:23
My l. for Heathcliff	BRON 69:15
My only l.	SHAK 306:26
My song is l. unknown	CROS 107:21
never l. a stranger	BENS 31:4
not enough to make us l.	SWIF 328:19
Now I know what L. is	VIRG 347:23
office and affairs of l.	SHAK 304:7
Of kindness and of l.	WORD 364:19
O L., O fire	TENN 332:7
O lyric L.	BROW 73:1
Only by l. can men see me	BHAG 34:1
onset and waning of l.	LA B 206:11
Onstage I make l.	JOPL 192:12
opposite of l.	WIES 357:21
our l. hath no decay	DONN 119:6
over hir housbond as hir l.	CHAU 91:30
passing the l. of women	BIBL 36:35
perfect l. casteth out fear	BIBL 52:33

power and effect of l. BURT 78:7
putting l. away DICK 115:29
quick-eyed L., observing HERB 167:17
search for l. WALE 349:6
sports of l. JONS 191:18
support of the woman I l. EDWA 125:10
survive of us is l. LARK 208:15
them that l. God BIBL 50:7
there are those who l. it WEBS 352:16
There is l. of course ANOU 14:4
There is only l. MCEW 223:2
this spring of l. SHAK 309:15
those who l. the Lord HUNT 178:16
thought that l. would last AUDE 18:19
time to l. BIBL 39:12
tired of L. BELL 29:23
To live is like to l. BUTL 79:17
to l. and be loved SAND 285:3
to l. and rapture's due ROCH 278:3
To see her is to l. her BURN 76:23
to think but to l. TERE 335:22
true l. hath my heart SIDN 316:11
true l. is a durable fire RALE 273:1
vegetable l. should grow MARV 229:20
very few to l. WORD 365:26
waters cannot quench l. BIBL 40:3
What is l. SHAK 308:28
When l. congeals HART 162:20
When my l. swears SHAK 310:27
where the l. of God goes LIGH 214:10
Where there is great love CATH 88:17
where, there is no l. BACO 22:23
who l., time is eternity VAN 345:10
Whom the gods l. MENA 232:16
wilder shores of l. BLAN 58:7
woman wakes to l. TENN 332:18
Work is l. made visible GIBR 149:11
world and l. were young RALE 272:22
'You must sit down,' says L. HERB 167:18
loved all we l. of him SHEL 313:15
And the l. one BROW 72:19
better to have l. and lost TENN 332:29
feared than l. MACH 223:8
God so l. the world BIBL 48:27
idols I have l. FITZ 137:2
I have l. SUCK 327:8
I l. a lass WITH 362:6
l. by the gods PLAT 264:19
l. Caesar less SHAK 296:31
l. him so BROW 72:13
l. not at first sight MARL 228:11
l. you, so I drew these tides LAWR 210:2
never to have been l. CONG 102:10
she l. much BIBL 47:11
till we l. DONN 119:9
wish I l. the Human Race RALE 273:8
loveless Love to the l. shown CROS 107:21
loveliness l. I never knew COLE 99:19
portion of the l. SHEL 313:20
woman of shining l. YEAT 369:4
lovely Look thy last on all things l. DE L 112:13
l. and pleasant BIBL 36:34
l. is the rose WORD 365:3
l. woman stoops to folly ELIO 129:29
l. woman stoops to folly GOLD 153:27
more l. and more temperate SHAK 310:3
once he made more l. SHEL 313:20
what a l. war LITT 215:15
whatsoever things are l. BIBL 51:28
woods are l. FROS 143:27
lover l. and his lass SHAK 290:25
l. and killer are mingled DOUG 120:4
l., and the poet SHAK 304:1

l. of my soul WESL 354:21
l.'s quarrel with the world FROS 143:18
sighed as a l. GIBB 149:2
some old l.'s ghost DONN 119:11
what is left of a l. ROWL 281:15
woman loves her l. BYRO 80:27
lovers Journeys end in l. meeting SHAK 308:27
L., to bed SHAK 304:4
star-crossed l. SHAK 306:20
These l. fled away KEAT 195:17
Though l. be lost THOM 337:17
loves all she l. is love BYRO 80:27
because God l. it JULI 193:13
For who l. that MILT 239:29
kills the thing he l. WILD 359:8
life and l. of a she-devil WELD 353:14
our l., must I remember them APOL 14:8
reigned with your l. ELIZ 130:16
lovesome garden is a l. thing BROW 70:19
loveth He that l. not BIBL 52:32
prayeth well, who l. well COLE 100:27
whom the Lord l. BIBL 38:12
Whom the Lord l. BIBL 52:16
loving Can't help l. dat man HAMM 160:14
discharge for l. one MATL 231:7
For l., and for saying so DONN 119:18
heart be still as l. BYRO 81:20
I ain't had no l. NORW 252:6
l. himself better than all COLE 100:30
l. longest AUST 21:5
most l. mere folly SHAK 290:17
loving-kindness deeds of l. TALM 330:11
low l. on whom assurance sits ELIO 129:28
Sweet and l. TENN 334:12
That l. man BROW 72:4
upper station of l. life DEFO 111:18
Lowells L. talk to the Cabots BOSS 66:2
lower l. orders don't set us a good WILD 358:3
l. than vermin BEVA 33:8
While there is a l. class DEBS 111:15
loyalty I want l. JOHN 186:10
L. the Tory's secret weapon KILM 200:6
LSD PC is the L. of the '90s LEAR 210:21
lucid l. intervals BACO 23:25
Lucifer falls like L. SHAK 296:13
L., son of the morning BIBL 40:19
luck watching his l. SERV 289:2
lucky just the l. country HAWK 163:9
l. to be born WHIT 357:5
lucrative so l. to cheat CLOU 98:19
Lucy L. ceased to be WORD 365:28
Luftwaffe With your L. PLAT 264:12
lug l. the guts SHAK 293:24
lugete L., O Veneres CATU 89:5
lugger Once aboard the l. JOHN 191:5
lukewarm thou art l. BIBL 53:4
lullaby Once in a l. HARB 161:8
luminous beating his l. wings ARNO 17:5
with a l. nose LEAR 210:11
lump leaven leaveneth the whole l. BIBL 50:17
lumps l. in it STEP 324:4
lunatic l., the lover SHAK 304:1
lunatics l. have taken charge ROWL 281:16
lunch cork out of my l. FIEL 135:18
unable to l. today PORT 269:4
lungs dangerous to the l. JAME 182:9
from froth-corrupted l. OWEN 256:11
l. of London PITT 264:7
lure l. this tassel-gentle SHAK 306:34
lurk dangers to liberty l. BRAN 67:17
l. outside GRAC 154:18
lurks l. a politician ARIS 15:9
lust l. and calls it advertising LAHR 206:15

lust (*cont.*)
l. of knowing FLEC 138:4
to l. after it LEWI 213:22
lustily sing praises l. unto him BOOK 62:21
lustre Where is thy l. now SHAK 298:13
lusts l. of the flesh BOOK 61:18
lute Apollo's l. MILT 236:7
Orpheus with his l. SHAK 296:10
rift within the l. TENN 332:16
Luther beyond what L. saw ROBI 277:19
lux l. *perpetua* MISS 241:4
luxuries l. of life MOTL 246:10
luxury like any other l. TROL 342:4
Literature is a l. CHES 93:9
l., peace BAUD 27:20
Pessimism is a l. MEIR 232:4
swinish l. of the rich MORR 245:15
Lycidas L. is dead MILT 236:28
lying branch of the art of l. CORN 104:10
express l. or falsehood SWIF 328:12
L. lips are abomination BIBL 38:21
One of you is l. PARK 258:18
smallest amount of l. BUTL 79:12
Lyonnesse When I set out for L. HARD 162:9
lyre Make me thy l. SHEL 314:6
'Omer smote 'is bloomin' l. KIPL 203:7

M

Mab Queen M. hath been with SHAK 306:23
macaroni called it M. ANON 12:6
Macaulay as Tom M. MELB 232:7
Macavity M. WASN'T THERE ELIO 129:9
Macbeth had Lady M. KNIG 204:8
M. does murder sleep SHAK 300:16
M. shall never vanquished be SHAK 301:17
M. shall sleep no more SHAK 300:17
Macduff Lay on, M. SHAK 302:2
M. was from his mother's womb SHAK 302:1
mace fool's bauble, the m. CROM 107:12
Macheath jack-knife has M. BREC 68:6
machine body is a m. TOLS 341:4
Ghost in the M. RYLE 283:22
house is a m. for living in LE C 211:8
m. for turning the red wine DINE 116:18
pulse of the m. WORD 366:2
machines M. have less problems WARH 350:23
their survival m. DAWK 111:9
whether m. think SKIN 317:15
macht *Arbeit m. frei* ANON 12:20
mackerel like rotten m. RAND 273:12
mad All poets are m. BURT 78:4
bad and m. it was BROW 71:27
called me m. LEE 211:15
Hieronimo is m. again KYD 206:9
M. about the boy COWA 105:3
M., bad, and dangerous LAMB 206:18
M. dogs and Englishmen COWA 105:4
m. north-north-west SHAK 292:17
men that God made m. CHES 92:26
much learning doth make thee m. BIBL 49:36
old, m., blind SHEL 314:22
O! let me not be m. SHAK 297:30
pleasure sure, In being m. DRYD 122:14
Whom the m. would destroy LEVI 213:13
world was m. SABA 284:1
madding Far from the m. crowd's GRAY 156:14
made All things were m. by him BIBL 48:14
Begotten, not m. BOOK 61:3
fearfully and wonderfully m. BOOK 65:4
Little Lamb who m. thee BLAK 57:19

m., like bread LE G 211:18
Who m. you CATE 88:16
Madeira M., m'dear FLAN 137:20
madeleine little piece of m. PROU 271:9
mademoiselle M. from Armenteers ANON 9:17
madman m. shakes a dead geranium ELIO 129:11
m. who thought he was COCT 99:7
madmen M. in authority KEYN 199:21
none but m. know DRYD 122:14
madness despondency and m. WORD 365:21
destroyed by m. GINS 151:3
harmonious m. SHEL 314:29
m. is terrific WOOL 364:3
M. need not be all breakdown LAIN 206:17
m. of many POPE 268:22
moment of m. DAVI 110:22
moon-struck m. MILT 239:11
O! that way m. lies SHAK 298:5
Though this be m. SHAK 292:13
to m. near allied DRYD 121:17
very midsummer m. SHAK 309:7
maestro *m. di color che sanno* DANT 109:11
maggot create a m. MONT 243:3
magic daylight in upon m. BAGE 24:9
If this be m. SHAK 309:30
indistinguishable from m. CLAR 97:5
m. casements KEAT 196:23
mistake medicine for m. SZAS 329:21
Ms. Rowling's m. world BYAT 79:20
old black m. MERC 233:6
Parents can plant m. MACN 224:13
rough m. I here abjure SHAK 307:32
secret m. of numbers BROW 71:10
tell you what I want. M. WILL 360:14
magistrate m. corruptible ROBE 277:11
magna M. Charta is such a fellow COKE 99:16
M. est veritas, et praevalet BIBL 54:14
magnanimity M. in politics BURK 75:11
magnanimous M. in victory COLL 101:14
magnificat *M. anima mea Dominum* BIBL 54:7
magnificent M. desolation ALDR 4:10
mild and m. eye BROW 72:13
magnifique *C'est m.* BOSQ 66:1
magnify soul doth m. the Lord BIBL 46:32
we m. thee BOOK 59:20
magpie swollen m. in a fitful sun POUN 270:3
magus M. Zoroaster, my dead child SHEL 314:13
maid m. is mine JOHN 191:5
m. is not dead BIBL 44:23
man with a m. BIBL 39:4
maiden m. of bashful fifteen SHER 315:16
rare and radiant m. POE 265:18
maidens laughter of comely m. DE V 113:19
What m. loth KEAT 196:6
maids Old m. biking ORWE 254:18
Three little m. GILB 150:2
maimed M. us at the start YEAT 368:25
poor, and the m. BIBL 47:25
Maine As M. goes FARL 134:5
maintenance art of motorcycle m. PIRS 263:17
maior *M. erat natu* LUCI 220:11
maistrye constreyned by m. CHAU 91:23
maîtresses *j'aurai des m.* GEOR 147:15
majestic m. equality of the law FRAN 141:8
M. though in ruin MILT 238:5
majesty ride on in m. MILM 235:8
Thy M. how bright FABE 133:14
touching in its m. WORD 364:10
major Ground control to M. Tom BOWI 67:1
modern M.-General GILB 150:23
With M. Major it had been all three HELL 165:14
majority always in the m. KNOX 204:10
big enough m. TWAI 343:8

black m. rule — SMIT 318:16
divine M. — DICK 116:3
gone to join the m. — PETR 262:17
m. are wrong — DEBS 111:14
m. never has right — IBSE 180:5
m. . . . one is enough — DISR 117:26
silent m. — NIXO 251:15
to the great m. — YOUN 370:4
what the m. happen to like — WHIT 356:13
will of the m. — JEFF 184:5
majors live with scarlet M. — SASS 285:26
make does not usually m. anything — PHEL 262:19
M. yourself necessary — EMER 132:2
Scotsman on the m. — BARR 27:4
wrote M. IT NEW — POUN 269:19
maker M. of heaven and earth — BOOK 59:23
M. of heaven and earth — BOOK 61:3
watch must have had a m. — PALE 258:1
malady m. of not marking — SHAK 294:33
male m. and the female — BIBL 34:28
M. bonding — TIGE 340:10
m. of the species — LAWR 209:22
more deadly than the m. — KIPL 202:2
malice envy, hatred, and m. — BOOK 60:1
M. domestic — SHAK 301:2
m., to breed causes — JONS 191:19
m. toward none — LINC 215:5
malicious God is subtle but not m. — EINS 126:4
malignant part of Randolph that was not m. — WAUG 352:10
Malmesey drowned in a barrel of M. — FABY 133:17
malt m. does more than Milton — HOUS 176:16
mama M. may have — HOLI 171:16
mammon God and m. — BIBL 43:25
M. led them on — MILT 237:30
m. of unrighteousness — BIBL 47:35
man against every m. — BIBL 34:31
all that may become a m. — SHAK 300:7
And was made m. — MISS 240:21
arms and the m. — VIRG 346:19
Arms, and the m. I sing — DRYD 122:19
arose as one m. — BIBL 36:20
Both m. and bird — COLE 100:27
by m. shall his blood — BIBL 34:29
century of the common m. — WALL 349:13
chief end of m. — SHOR 316:5
childhood shows the m. — MILT 239:16
come, but not the m. — SCOT 287:23
demolition of a m. — LEVI 213:12
every m. against every man — HOBB 170:17
every m. and nation — LOWE 220:2
Every m. has a right — JOHN 190:3
Every m. over forty — SHAW 312:16
everyone has sat except a m. — CUMM 108:6
extraordinary m. — JOHN 190:17
father of the M. — WORD 365:1
first m. — BIBL 51:2
fit night out for m. or beast — FIEL 135:19
from pig to m. — ORWE 254:11
God has more right than m. — JOHN 185:12
Greater love hath no m. — BIBL 49:7
Happy is the m. — BOOK 64:27
He was a m. — SHAK 291:25
He was her m. — ANON 8:16
I am looking for a m. — DIOG 116:20
in m. there is nothing great — HAMI 160:13
just the m. to do it — BOLT 59:2
last strands of m. — HOPK 173:14
let him pass for a m. — SHAK 302:10
let no m. put asunder — BOOK 62:2
make a m. a woman — PEMB 261:9
m. after his own heart — BIBL 36:27
m. and a brother — WEDG 353:4

m. and the hour — YANC 367:10
m. at the gate of the year — HASK 163:5
M. being . . . by nature all free — LOCK 216:19
m. bites a dog — BOGA 58:16
m. could ease a heart — PARK 258:17
M. dreams of fame — TENN 332:18
m. for all seasons — WHIT 357:17
m. for others — BONH 59:10
m. from animals — OSLE 255:18
M. grows beyond his work — STEI 323:20
M. has created death — YEAT 367:22
M. is a noble animal — BROW 71:9
M. is a tool-using animal — CARL 85:19
M. is a useless passion — SART 285:22
M. is born unto trouble — BIBL 37:39
m. is dead — FROM 143:5
m. is man — TENN 332:15
M. is Nature's sole mistake — GILB 150:25
M. is quite insane — MONT 243:3
m. . . . is so in the way — GASK 146:13
M. is something to be surpassed — NIET 251:4
M. is the hunter — TENN 334:17
M. is the measure — PROT 271:7
M. is the Only Animal — TWAI 343:12
M. is the only creature — ORWE 254:8
m. made the town — COWP 105:24
M. may not marry his Mother — BOOK 65:16
m. not truly one — STEV 325:13
m. of restless intellect — HUXL 179:22
M. owes his entire existence — HEGE 165:2
M. partly is — BROW 72:1
m. proposes — THOM 337:9
M., proud man — SHAK 302:5
m. recovered of the bite — GOLD 153:14
m.'s a man for a' that — BURN 76:27
M.'s dominion — BURN 77:20
m. sent from God — BIBL 48:16
m.'s first disobedience — MILT 237:15
M. shall not live — BIBL 43:9
M.'s inhumanity to man — BURN 77:4
m.'s the gowd — BURN 76:26
M. that is born — BIBL 38:1
M. that is born of a woman — BOOK 62:4
M. wants but little — GOLD 153:12
m. who should loose me — LOWE 219:16
m. who would be king — KIPL 203:20
M. will err — GOET 152:8
m. will not merely endure — FAUL 134:12
m. with a maid — BIBL 39:4
m. write a better book — EMER 132:22
met a m. who wasn't there — MEAR 231:19
more like a m. — LERN 213:6
more wonderful than m. — SOPH 320:15
My m. Friday — DEFO 111:19
new m. may be raised up — BOOK 61:16
nor no m. ever loved — SHAK 310:23
not m. for the sabbath — BIBL 46:22
One m. in a thousand — KIPL 202:27
one small step for a m. — ARMS 16:8
only m. is vile — HEBE 164:18
piece of work is a m. — SHAK 292:16
right m. in the right place — JEFF 184:21
said, ask a m. — THAT 336:12
Stand by your m. — WYNE 367:6
standing by my m. — CLIN 98:8
study of m. is man — CHAR 91:9
Style is the m. — BUFF 73:19
that the m. should be alone — BIBL 34:10
This bold bad m. — SHAK 296:9
this M. and this Woman — BOOK 61:23
This was a m. — SHAK 297:17
Thou art the m. — BIBL 36:37
What bloody m. — SHAK 299:9

man (*cont.*)
what is m.   LENO 212:25
What m. has made of man   WORD 364:22
when a m. should marry   BACO 22:34
When God at first made m.   HERB 167:20
when I became a m.   BIBL 50:25
Whoso would be a m.   EMER 132:10
woman was made for m.   STAN 323:5
woman without a m.   STEI 324:1
You'll be a M., my son   KIPL 202:10
manage m. without butter   GOEB 152:5
managers m. of affairs of women   KORA 205:7
managing kiss the M. Director   WHIT 356:17
Mandalay road to M.   KIPL 202:15
Manderley dreamt I went to M.   DU M 123:5
manger in the rude m. lies   MILT 237:7
laid him in a m.   BIBL 47:2
manhood m. an opportunity   KEIL 197:26
M. a struggle   DISR 117:21
M. taken by the Son   NEWM 250:5
manilla misery of m. folders   ROET 278:10
mankind countrymen are all m.   GARR 146:10
crucify m.   BRYA 73:14
giant leap for m.   ARMS 16:8
legislator of m.   JOHN 187:17
M. must put an end to war   KENN 199:2
M.'s true moral test   KUND 206:8
not in Asia, was m. born   ARDR 14:18
proper study of m.   POPE 267:27
proper study of m. is books   HUXL 179:8
ride m.   EMER 131:21
school of m.   BURK 76:2
slain m. altogether   KORA 205:12
manna his tongue Dropped m.   MILT 238:3
manner after the m. of men   BIBL 50:30
all m. of thing   JULI 193:14
to the m. born   SHAK 291:34
manners corrupt good m.   BIBL 51:1
good table m.   MIKE 233:24
lack of m.   HATH 163:7
m. of a dancing master   JOHN 188:7
Oh, the m.   CICE 96:20
polished m.   COWP 106:3
rectify m.   MILT 240:6
mansion Back to its m.   GRAY 156:10
heavenly m., raging in the dark   YEAT 367:15
Love has pitched his m.   YEAT 367:20
mansions many m.   BIBL 49:4
mantle cast his m. upon him   BIBL 37:15
green m.   SHAK 298:9
in russet m. clad   SHAK 291:12
twitched his m. blue   MILT 237:4
manunkind this busy monster, m.   CUMM 108:8
manure natural m.   JEFF 184:2
manuscript youth's sweet-scented m.   FITZ 137:3
many How m. things   SOCR 319:22
m. are called   BIBL 45:25
m.-headed monster   POPE 268:11
m.-splendoured thing   THOM 338:18
So m. worlds   TENN 333:4
so much owed by so m. to so few   CHUR 95:11
we are m.   BIBL 46:26
map Roll up that m.   PITT 263:22
maps Geography is about M.   BENT 31:9
in Afric-m.   SWIF 329:1
Marathon M. looks on the sea   BYRO 81:1
trivial skirmish fought near M.   GRAV 155:17
marble dwelt in m. halls   BUNN 74:4
Glowed on the m.   ELIO 129:22
left it m.   AUGU 20:14
m. index of a mind   WORD 365:16
m., nor the gilded monuments   SHAK 310:9
m. not yet carved   MICH 233:18

march Beware the ides of M.   SHAK 296:18
boundary of the m. of a nation   PARN 259:15
droghte of M.   CHAU 91:11
mad M. days   MASE 230:17
m. my troops towards   GRIM 157:17
m. towards it   CALL 82:15
Men who m. away   HARD 162:5
take The winds of M.   SHAK 309:26
Truth is on the m.   ZOLA 370:15
marche *congrès ne m. pas*   LIGN 214:11
marched m. breast forward   BROW 71:21
marches Funeral m. to the grave   LONG 217:19
m., charging feet   BARI 26:13
marching M. as to war   JAGG 182:6
soul is m. on   ANON 9:7
truth is m. on   HOWE 177:2
mare brought him a Flanders m.   HENR 166:18
lend me your grey m.   BALL 26:3
qui trans m. currunt   HORA 174:27
Margaret It's me, M.   BLUM 58:12
M. you mourn for   HOPK 174:5
Merry M.   SKEL 317:14
margin m. too narrow   FERM 135:1
Maria *Ave M.*   ANON 13:8
Mariana this dejected M.   SHAK 302:9
Marie I am M. of Roumania   PARK 258:11
Maries Queen had four M.   BALL 25:14
marigold m., that goes to bed   SHAK 309:25
marijuana experimented with m.   CLIN 98:10
mariner It is an ancient M.   COLE 100:14
m. with the gentleman   DRAK 121:8
mark man's distinctive m.   BROW 72:1
m., or the name of the beast   BIBL 53:13
m. upon Cain   BIBL 34:24
no drowning m.   SHAK 307:16
press toward the m.   BIBL 51:24
read, m., learn   BOOK 60:20
would hit the m.   LONG 217:10
market enterprise of the m.   ANON 7:17
gathered in the m.-place   CAVA 89:12
heart in the m.-place   SHAK 304:15
Market Harborough AM IN M.   CHES 93:24
marking malady of not m.   SHAK 294:33
marks m. of the beast   HARD 161:16
marl Over the burning m.   MILT 237:24
marred man that's m.   SHAK 289:10
marriage by way of m.   FIEL 135:13
Chains do not hold a m.   SIGN 316:20
Courtship to m.   CONG 102:8
definition of m.   SMIT 319:10
furnish forth the m. tables   SHAK 291:23
M. a wonderful invention   CONN 102:15
M. has many pains   JOHN 187:19
M. is a bribe   WILD 359:22
M. is like life   STEV 325:23
M. is popular because   SHAW 312:11
m. of true minds   SHAK 310:21
nor are given in m.   SWIF 328:21
prevents a bad m.   SHAK 308:21
three of us in this m.   DIAN 114:9
value of m.   DE V 114:3
marriages have no more m.   SHAK 293:1
married if ever we had been m.   GAY 146:19
imprudently m. the barber   FOOT 139:4
In m. life three is company   WILD 358:5
let us be m.   LEAR 210:16
m. beneath me   ASTO 18:6
m. me with a ring   RAIN 272:21
Reader, I m. him   BRON 69:11
Trade Unionism of the m.   SHAW 312:6
when they got m.   HOLI 171:17
young man m.   SHAK 289:10
marries signify whom one m.   ROGE 278:13

marrow suck out all the m. THOR 339:18
marry better to m. than to burn BIBL 50:18
Can't get away to m. you LEIG 212:3
m. Mr Collins AUST 21:10
m. one another BUTL 79:13
may not m. his Mother BOOK 65:16
men we wanted to m. STEI 323:22
neither m., nor are given BIBL 45:27
persons about to m. PUNC 271:17
they neither m. SWIF 328:21
when a man should m. BACO 22:34
while ye may, go m. HERR 168:6
marrying m. in haste THOM 338:9
Mars Men are from M. GRAY 156:2
marshal m.'s baton LOUI 219:4
Martha M. was cumbered BIBL 47:17
Martin Saint M.'s summer SHAK 296:1
Martini medium Vodka dry M. FLEM 138:7
martlet temple-haunting m. SHAK 299:27
martyr regarded as a m. KHOM 199:23
martyrdom M. is the test JOHN 190:3
m. must run its course AUDE 19:10
M. only way in which a man can SHAW 311:15
martyred shrouded oft our m. dead CONN 102:13
martyrs army of M. BOOK 59:18
marvel m. at nothing HORA 174:25
m. my birthday away THOM 337:24
marvellous Chatterton, the m. boy WORD 365:20
hath done m. things BOOK 64:1
m. demonstration FERM 135:1
m. in our eyes BOOK 64:18
Marxist I am a M. ANON 12:15
I am not a M. MARX 230:10
Marxiste Je suis M. ANON 12:15
Mary Hail M. ANON 13:8
M. Ambree BALL 25:13
M. had a little lamb HALE 159:16
M. hath chosen BIBL 47:18
mask had a m. like Castlereagh SHEL 314:1
m. that eats into the face UPDI 344:17
masochistic m. form of exhibitionism OLIV 253:10
masquerade truth in m. BYRO 81:5
mass activates the whole m. VIRG 347:13
M. is ended MISS 241:2
Paris is well worth a m. HENR 166:13
two thousand years of m. HARD 161:19
Massachusetts denied in M. MILL 234:20
massacre not as sudden as a m. TWAI 343:9
masses huddled m. yearning LAZA 210:5
m. against the classes GLAD 151:15
massy huge m. face MACA 221:10
master Death is a m. from Germany CELA 89:17
m. a grief SHAK 304:12
M.-morality NIET 251:11
m. of his fate TENN 332:15
m. of my fate HENL 166:9
m. of the Party HEAL 164:9
m. of those who know DANT 109:11
slew his m. BIBL 37:29
which is to be m. CARR 87:11
Why eateth your M. BIBL 44:18
masterly m. inactivity MACK 223:13
masterpiece Nature's great m. DONN 119:3
masters never wrong, the Old M. AUDE 19:9
people are the m. BURK 76:6
serve two m. BIBL 43:25
We are not the m. BLAI 55:20
We are the m. now SHAW 313:7
mastery m. of the thing HOPK 174:10
mastiff m.? the right hon. Gentleman's poodle
LLOY 216:7
mastodons like m. bellowing WODE 362:19
masturbation Don't knock m. ALLE 5:12

match lighted m. BROW 72:15
matched m. us with His hour BROO 70:1
matches with that stick of m. MADI 224:17
matchless m. deed's achieved SMAR 317:19
matchwood m., immortal diamond HOPK 174:6
mater Stabat M. dolorosa JACO 182:2
materialism deteriorate into m. MOLT 242:5
mathematical m. language GALI 145:7
of m. celebrity DOYL 120:18
mathematician appear as a pure m. JEAN 183:16
mathematics avoid pregnancy by a resort to m.
MENC 232:22
In m. you don't NEUM 249:14
knowledge in m. BACO 24:4
M. may be defined RUSS 283:5
M., rightly viewed RUSS 283:8
mystical m. BROW 71:4
no place for ugly m. HARD 161:13
so like the m. WALT 350:8
Matilda M. told such Dreadful Lies BELL 29:20
matrimony critical period in m. HERB 167:9
joined together in holy M. BOOK 61:22
m. at its lowest STEV 325:22
matter altering the position of m. RUSS 283:3
between spirit and m. HEIN 165:8
Does it m. SASS 285:27
if it is it doesn't m. GILB 150:26
inditing of a good m. BOOK 63:1
m. out of place GRAY 156:3
More m. with less art SHAK 292:11
root of the m. BIBL 38:5
this m. better in France ETER 324:6
what does that m. GOET 152:20
What is m. PUNC 271:20
wretched m. and lame metre MILT 237:13
matters big words for little m. JOHN 188:19
else you do well m. ONAS 253:12
Nobody that m. MILL 234:16
Matthew M. Mark, Luke, and John ANON 9:18
mattresses through twenty m. ANDE 6:14
mature M. love says FROM 143:4
Maud into the garden, M. TENN 334:4
mausoleum as its m. AMIS 6:5
Max incomparable M. SHAW 313:3
maxim M. Gun BELL 29:24
will that my m. KANT 194:21
maxima mea m. culpa MISS 240:16
may darling buds of M. SHAK 310:3
fressh as is the month of M. CHAU 91:14
I'm to be Queen o' the M. TENN 334:4
matter for a M. morning SHAK 309:9
M. to December ANDE 6:15
merry month of M. BALL 25:8
rose in M. CHAU 92:1
what we m. be SHAK 39:29
maypoles I sing of M. HERR 168:1
Mazda M.-worshipper ZORO 370:17
McCarthyism M. is Americanism with MCCA 222:8
McGregor Mr M.'s garden POTT 269:12
McNamara M.'s War MCNA 224:8
me M. Tarzan WEIS 353:10
save thee and m. OWEN 256:5
meadows M. trim with daisies pied MILT 236:21
meal handful of m. BIBL 37:10
mean Down these m. streets CHAN 90:12
even if you don't m. it TRUM 342:17
Know what I m., Harry BRUN 73:13
loves the golden m. HORA 175:10
nothing common did or m. MARV 229:18
poem should not m. but be MACL 223:16
say what you m. CARR 86:11
whatever that may m. CHAR 91:6
meaner m. beauties of the night WOTT 366:23

hell to m.	AESC 3:19
how much m. hate them	GREE 157:6
I eat m. like air	PLAT 264:16
If m. could get pregnant	KENN 198:10
Measures not m.	CANN 84:9
m. and mountains meet	BLAK 57:11
m. and nations behave wisely	EBAN 124:18
M. are April when they woo	SHAK 290:23
M. are but children	DRYD 121:28
M. are so honest	LERN 213:6
M. at forty	JUST 194:3
m. have got love	AMIS 6:6
M. have had every advantage	AUST 21:4
m. in women do require	BLAK 57:13
m., like satyrs	MARL 228:10
m. may come	TENN 331:18
m. must work	KING 201:8
M., my brothers	TENN 333:24
M. seldom make passes	PARK 258:13
m.'s lack of manners	HATH 163:7
M. were deceivers ever	SHAK 304:10
m. we wanted to marry	STEI 323:22
M. who march away	HARD 162:5
m. who will support me	MELB 232:11
m. with the muck-rakes	ROOS 280:2
Not m., but measures	BURK 75:30
not the m. in my life that counts	WEST 355:8
power over m.	WOLL 363:12
schemes o' mice an' m.	BURN 77:21
think all m. mortal	YOUN 369:29
two strong m.	KIPL 201:17
wealth accumulates, and m. decay	GOLD 152:5
We are the hollow m.	ELIO 128:22
What m. or gods	KEAT 196:6
mend shine, and seek to m.	DONN 118:24
mene M., TEKEL, UPHARSIN	BIBL 42:6
mens M. sana in corpore sano	JUVE 194:12
mental cease from m. fight	BLAK 57:8
Freedom and slavery are m. states	GAND 145:15
mer Poème De la M.	RIMB 277:3
Mercator M.'s North Poles	CARR 87:18
merchant like unto a m. man	BIBL 45:2
m. shall hardly keep himself	BIBL 42:25
merchantman monarchy is a m.	AMES 6:4
mercies For his m. ay endure	MILT 236:26
new m. I see	CHIS 94:4
tender m. of the wicked	BIBL 38:20
merciful God be m.	BIBL 48:6
m. one to another	KORA 205:22
Name of God, the M.	KORA 204:17
these were m. men	BIBL 42:28
mercury m. sank	AUDE 18:21
pick up m. with a fork	LLOY 216:12
words of M.	SHAK 299:6
mercy crowning m.	CROM 107:10
folks over to God's m.	ELIO 127:6
God's gracious m.	BOOK 62:3
Have m. upon us	BOOK 60:10
Justice with m.	MILT 239:9
love m.	BIBL 42:15
M. and truth	BOOK 63:21
m. endureth for ever	BOOK 64:30
M. has a human heart	BLAK 57:17
M. I asked, mercy I found	ANON 7:13
quality of m.	SHAK 302:30
render The deeds of m.	SHAK 302:31
shut the gates of m.	GRAY 156:13
Thy m. on Thy People	KIPL 202:22
wideness in God's m.	FABE 133:15
merde M.	CAMB 83:1
mermaid M. Tavern	KEAT 196:4
mermaids heard the m. singing	ELIO 129:4
hear m. singing	DONN 119:14

merrily m. hent the stile-a	SHAK 309:23
m. meet in heaven	MORE 244:18
Merrily, m. shall I live	SHAK 307:34
merriment m. of parsons	JOHN 190:6
merry all their wars are m.	CHES 92:26
be m.	BIBL 39:18
eat, drink, and be m.	BIBL 47:20
Have they been m.	SHAK 307:10
m. heart	BIBL 38:26
m. heart doeth good	BIBL 38:30
m. heart goes all the day	SHAK 309:23
m. monarch	ROCH 278:5
m. month of May	BALL 25:8
never a m. world	SELD 288:14
mess accommodates the m.	BECK 28:9
Another fine m.	LAUR 209:16
m. of pottage	BIBL 34:34
m. we have made of things	ELIO 127:28
message medium is the m.	MCLU 223:18
messager bisy larke, m. of day	CHAU 91:24
messages m. should be delivered	GOLD 154:5
messenger M. of God	KORA 205:17
M. of God	KORA 205:22
M. with the guidance	KORA 205:21
only the M. of God	KORA 205:10
messing m. about in boats	GRAH 155:3
met Ill m. by moonlight	SHAK 303:17
m. Saddam Hussein	GALL 145:10
m. the enemy	PERR 262:9
m. together	BOOK 63:21
metal with rich m. loaded	SPEN 322:7
metaphysics Explaining m.	BYRO 80:20
M. is the finding	BRAD 67:6
method yet there is m. in't	SHAK 292:13
methods You know my m.	DOYL 120:22
methought M. I saw	MILT 239:32
métier c'est son m.	HEIN 165:10
metre wretched matter and lame m.	MILT 237:13
metrical m. composition	WORD 366:18
metropolis m. of the empire	COBB 99:2
meurt La Garde m.	CAMB 83:1
Mexico M., so far from God	DIAZ 114:10
mezzo Nel m. del cammin	DANT 109:7
mice as long as it catches m.	DENG 112:23
Like little m.	SUCK 327:6
schemes o' m. an' men	BURN 77:21
Michael M. and his angels	BIBL 53:12
Michelangelo Talking of M.	ELIO 128:29
microphone paid for this m.	RFAG 274:4
microscopic man a m. eye	POPE 267:22
middle beginning, a m.	ARIS 15:16
m. way is none at all	ADAM 2:5
mine was the m. state	DEFO 111:18
people in the m. of the road	BEVA 33:10
safely by the m. way	OVID 255:26
Secret sits in the m.	FROS 143:25
middle age enchantments of the M.	BEER 29:2
last enchantments of the M.	ARNO 17:4
M. . . . occurs when you	ADAM 1:16
middle class dregs of the m.	BEAZ 28:6
m. morality	SHAW 312:29
Philistines proper, or m.	ARNO 17:3
midnight a-bed after m.	SHAK 308:26
black, and m. hags	SHAK 301:14
came upon a m. clear	SEAR 288:5
cease upon the m.	KEAT 196:21
Cerberus, and blackest M.	MILT 236:17
chimes at m.	SHAK 295:5
Holding hands at m.	GERS 148:10
iron tongue of m.	SHAK 304:4
m. never come	MARL 228:8
m. ride of Paul Revere	LONG 218:5
M. shakes the memory	ELIO 129:11

midnight (*cont.*)

our m. oil	QUAR 272:9
stroke of the m. hour	NEHR 249:1
'Tis the year's m.	DONN 119:12
upon a m. dreary	POE 265:17
woes at m. rise	LYLY 220:22

midst In the m. of life — BOOK 62:5

there am I in the m. — BIBL 45:15

midsummer very m. madness — SHAK 309:7

midway M. along the path — DANT 109:7

midwife fairies' m. — SHAK 306:23

midwinter In the bleak m. — ROSS 280:13

mieux *m. est l'ennemi du bien* — VOLT 348:11

tout est au m. — VOLT 348:5

might as our m. lessens — ANON 14:1

counsel and m.	BIBL 40:16
do it with thy m.	BIBL 39:20
Exceeds man's m.	SHAK 308:10
It m. have been	HART 163:2
It m. have been	WHIT 357:15
my name is M.-have-been	ROSS 280:20
right makes m.	LINC 214:15
Through the dear m.	MILT 237:3

mightier pen m. than the sword — BULW 74:2

mighty all that m. heart — WORD 364:11

how are the m. fallen	BIBL 36:32
How are the m. fallen	BIBL 36:35
Marlowe's m. line	JONS 192:5
M. lak' a rose	STAN 323:6
m. man is he	LONG 218:9
Nimrod the m. hunter	BIBL 34:30
put down the m.	BIBL 46:33
rushing m. wind	BIBL 49:21

migraine Love is a universal m. — GRAV 155:18

mild m. and magnificent eye — BROW 72:13

mile compel thee to go a m. — BIBL 43:18

miles m. to go before I sleep — FROS 143:27

milestones m. on the Dover Road — DICK 115:4

militant Christ's Church m. — BOOK 61:5

military entrust to m. men — CLEM 98:2

m. divisions	HAVE 163:8
m. man approaches	SHAW 312:5
order and m. discipline	ANON 7:19

milk Adversity's sweet m. — SHAK 307:3

buy wine and m.	BIBL 41:12
drunk the m. of Paradise	COLE 100:12
end is moo, the other, m.	NASH 248:12
flowing with m. and honey	BIBL 35:14
his mother's m.	SHAK 308:23
m. of human kindness	SHAK 299:21
M.'s leap toward immortality	FADI 133:18
m. the bull	JOHN 188:16
putting m. into babies	CHUR 95:17
take my m. for gall	SHAK 299:24
trout in the m.	THOR 339:8
With m. and honey blessed	NEAL 248:24

mill at the m. with slaves — MILT 239:21

old m. by the stream — ARMS 16:1

mille *Da mi basia m.* — CATU 89:7

million Fifty m. Frenchmen — ANON 8:6

m. deaths a statistic	STAL 323:1
want to make a m.	ANON 8:20

millionaire I am a M. — SHAW 311:25

silk hat on a Bradford m. — ELIO 129:28

millions fate of unborn m. — WASH 351:5

I will be m.	PERÓ 262:5
M. long for immortality	ERTZ 133:2
m. of the mouthless dead	SORL 320:17
multiplying m.	O'SU 255:20

mills dark Satanic m. — BLAK 57:8

m. of God grind slowly — LONG 218:1

millstone m. were hanged about his neck — BIBL 45:13

Milton malt does more than M. — HOUS 176:16

M.! thou shouldst be living	WORD 364:23
mute inglorious M.	GRAY 156:12

mimsy m. were the borogoves — CARR 86:23

mince dined on m. — LEAR 210:17

mind absence of m. — SEEL 288:10

at the end of the m.	STEV 324:19
change your m.	AURE 20:18
could not make up his m.	OLIV 253:8
damages his m.	ANON 13:4
empires of the m.	CHUR 95:18
exists merely in the m.	HUME 178:10
frame of m.	HORA 174:27
Georgia on my m.	GORR 154:12
give a sex to m.	WOLL 363:11
hand the cutting edge of the m.	BRON 69:6
has a m. and knows it	SHAW 311:7
human m. in ruins	DAVI 111:1
infirmity of noble m.	MILT 236:30
in m., body, or estate	BOOK 60:17
In my m.'s eye	SHAK 291:24
in the m. of man	WORD 364:21
know the m. of God	HAWK 163:13
liberation of the human m.	GOLD 153:3
losing your m.	FOX 141:3
man's unconquerable m.	WORD 366:14
marble index of a m.	WORD 365:16
m. and soul, according	TENN 332:26
m. at peace	BYRO 81:18
m. be a thoroughfare	KEAT 197:19
m. diseased	BYRO 80:10
m. does not require filling	PLUT 265:10
m. has mountains	HOPK 173:22
M. has no sex	WOLL 363:11
m. is its own place	MILT 237:22
m. is not a bed	AGAT 3:23
m. moves upon silence	YEAT 368:17
m. of the lower animals	DARW 110:13
m.'s construction	SHAK 299:20
m. the least of possessions	WHIT 356:6
m. to me a kingdom is	DYER 123:17
m. watches itself	CAMU 83:15
m. which cannot bear	MENG 233:1
minister to a m. diseased	SHAK 301:28
my m.'s unsworn	EURI 133:7
no female m.	GILM 151:1
not enough to have a good m.	DESC 113:14
nothing great but m.	HAMI 160:13
not in my perfect m.	SHAK 298:21
no way out of the m.	PLAT 264:11
out of m.	THOM 337:11
out of my m.	BELL 30:6
O! what a noble m.	SHAK 293:2
padlock—on her m.	PRIO 270:23
Reading is to the m.	STEE 323:11
robs the m.	BURK 75:12
so-called mortal m.	EDDY 125:1
sound m.	JUVE 194:12
subsistence without a m.	BERK 31:17
travel broadens the m.	CHES 93:17
Until reeled the m.	GIBB 149:7
What is M.	PUNC 271:20
without a m.	BACO 22:11

minds comfortable m. — CUMM 108:11

great empire and little m.	BURK 75:11
hearts and m.	BIBL 51:27
marriage of true m.	SHAK 310:21
M. are like parachutes	DEWA 114:4
M. innocent and quiet	LOVE 219:9
m. of ordinary men	BRON 69:8

mine but m. own — SHAK 290:26

lovin' dat man of m.	HAMM 160:14
m. own familiar friend	BOOK 63:10
she is m. for life	SPAR 321:2

moment decisive m.   RETZ 275:6
  Every m. dies a man   BABB 21:20
  impulse of the m.   AUST 21:8
  m. dies a man   TENN 335:9
  m. in childhood   GREE 156:26
  m. of madness   DAVI 110:22
  m. of my greatness flicker   ELIO 129:1
  one brief shining m.   LERN 213:5
momentary Beauty is m. in the mind   STEV 324:21
  pleasure is m.   CHES 92:24
moments Wagner has lovely m.   ROSS 280:23
monarch merry m.   ROCH 278:5
  m. of all I survey   COWP 106:4
monarchs m. must obey   DRYD 122:7
  righteous m.   BROO 69:18
monarchy absolute M.   PAIN 257:6
  constitutional m.   BAGE 24:10
  m. and succession   PAIN 257:7
  m. is a merchantman   AMES 6:4
  state of m.   JAME 182:11
  universal m. of wit   CARE 84:18
money ain't got a barrel of m.   WOOD 363:17
  bank will lend you m.   HOPE 173:10
  blessing that m. cannot buy   WALT 350:14
  draining m. from the pockets   SMIT 318:7
  getting m.   JOHN 189:5
  haven't got the m.   RUTH 283:21
  have to borrer the m.   WARD 350:17
  He had m. as well   THAT 336:14
  Hollywood m. isn't money   PARK 259:4
  if you can count your m.   GETT 148:11
  licence to print m.   THOM 339:4
  long enough to get m. from   LEAC 210:6
  love of m.   BIBL 52:9
  m. answereth all things   BIBL 39:24
  m. can't buy me love   LENN 212:17
  M. couldn't buy friends   MILL 235:5
  M. doesn't talk, it swears   DYLA 124:5
  M. gives me pleasure   BELL 29:23
  m. gushes into politics   WHIT 356:8
  M. has no smell   VESP 346:5
  M. is like a sixth sense   MAUG 231:10
  M. is like muck   BACO 23:7
  M. . . . is none of the wheels   HUME 178:8
  m. I spend on advertising   LEVE 213:11
  m. of fools   HOBB 170:14
  m. perish with thee   BIBL 49:22
  M. speaks sense   BEHN 29:13
  M. was exactly like sex   BALD 24:22
  not spending m. alone   EISE 126:16
  only interested in m.   SHAW 313:4
  pleasant it is to have m.   CLOU 98:15
  poetry in m.   GRAV 156:1
  poor know that it is m.   BREN 68:11
  retreated back into their m.   FITZ 137:12
  rub up against m.   RUNY 282:5
  somehow, make m.   HORA 174:21
  they have more m.   FITZ 137:6
  They hired the m.   COOL 103:15
  time is m.   FRAN 141:16
  to get all that m.   CHES 93:21
  unlimited m.   CICE 96:22
  use the m. for the poor   PERÓ 262:4
  Virtue does not come from m.   SOCR 319:24
  voice is full of m.   FITZ 137:11
  way the m. goes   MAND 226:15
  When you have m., it's sex   DONL 118:17
  without m. and without price   BIBL 41:12
  wrote, except for m.   JOHN 189:14
  You pays your m.   PUNC 271:18
Mongols M. of our age   HUSS 179:3
mongoose motto of all the m. family   KIPL 203:12
mongrels continent of energetic m.   FISH 136:2

monk m. who shook the world   MONT 243:9
monkey descent from a m.   WILB 357:24
  look long upon a m.   CONG 102:12
  make a m. of a man   BENC 30:8
monkeys Cats and m.   JAME 182:17
  m. banging on typewriters   WILE 359:24
  m. strumming on typewriters   EDDI 124:21
monogamous Woman m.   JAME 183:10
monogamy M. is the same   ANON 7:14
monologues intersecting m.   WEST 355:13
monopoly best of all m. profits   HICK 168:18
  m. stage of capitalism   LENI 212:6
Monroe M. Doctrine   MONR 242:8
  mouth of Marilyn M.   MITT 241:18
monster become a m.   NIET 251:9
  green-eyed m.   SHAK 305:1
  many-headed m.   POPE 268:11
  m. whom I had created   SHEL 313:9
  this busy m., manunkind   CUMM 108:8
monsters in search of m. to destroy   ADAM 2:14
  reason produces m.   GOYA 154:17
monstrous m. carbuncle   CHAR 91:7
  M. carbuncles   SPEN 321:17
  m. regiment of women   KNOX 204:9
montes Parturient m.   HORA 174:16
Montezuma halls of M.   ANON 8:9
  who imprisoned M.   MACA 221:13
month April is the cruellest m.   ELIO 129:17
  fressh as is the m. of May   CHAU 91:14
  m. of tension   LESS 213:9
monument If you seek a m.   ANON 13:22
  m. more lasting than bronze   HORA 175:17
  m. sticks like a fishbone   LOWE 220:4
  only m. the asphalt road   ELIO 129:13
  patience on a m.   SHAK 308:36
monumentum Exegi m. aere perennius   HORA 175:17
  Si m. requiris, circumspice   ANON 13:22
moo One end is m.   NASH 248:12
moocow m. coming down along the road   JOYC 192:23
moon auld m. in her arm   BALL 25:17
  beneath a waning m.   COLE 100:8
  Beneath the visiting m.   SHAK 289:22
  by the light of the m.   LEAR 210:17
  danced in the m.   CART 88:4
  hornèd M.   COLE 100:23
  horned m.   WORD 364:6
  looking at the full m.   GINS 151:4
  minions of the m.   SHAK 294:36
  m. belongs to everyone   DE S 113:18
  m. be still as bright   BYRO 81:20
  m. by night   BOOK 64:21
  m. is in the seventh house   RADO 272:19
  m.'s an arrant thief   SHAK 308:5
  m. shines bright   SHAK 303:1
  m. shone bright on Mrs Porter   ELIO 129:26
  m. the stars   TRUM 342:9
  m. under her feet   BIBL 53:11
  m. walks the night   DE L 112:17
  mortals call the M.   SHEL 313:23
  only a paper m.   HARB 161:7
  sad steps, O M.   SIDN 316:13
  shine on, harvest m.   NORW 252:6
  silent as the m.   MILT 239:23
  Sun and M. should doubt   BLAK 56:12
  voyage to the m.   LARD 208:11
  when the m. shall rise   WOTT 366:23
moonlight How sweet the m. sleeps   SHAK 303:2
  Ill met by m.   SHAK 303:17
  visit it by the pale m.   SCOT 287:10
  Watch for me by m.   NOYE 252:11
moonlit Knocking on the m. door   DE L 112:14
  starlit or a m. dome   YEAT 367:13
moons m. shall wax and wane no more   WATT 352:1

moonshine everything as m.   SCOT 287:26
  find out m.   SHAK 303:24
moonstruck m. madness   MILT 239:11
moose strong as a bull m.   ROOS 279:20
moral Debasing the m. currency   ELIO 127:12
  Englishman thinks he is m.   SHAW 312:3
  Everything's got a m.   CARR 86:14
  instrument of m. good   SHEL 315:4
  Mankind's true m. test   KUND 206:8
  M. courage is a rarer commodity   KENN 199:8
  m. evil and of good   WORD 366:9
  m. flabbiness   JAME 183:9
  m. imperative   DIDI 116:13
  M. indignation is jealousy   WELL 354:14
  m. law within me   KANT 194:19
  m. or an immoral book   WILD 358:23
  O m. Gower   CHAU 92:7
  point a m.   JOHN 187:26
  religious and m. principles   ARNO 17:12
  stage in m. culture   DARW 110:3
  State m. case   JEFF 184:1
  till all are m.   SPEN 321:14
moralist problem for the m.   RUSS 282:23
moralists delight to m.   RUSS 283:10
morality Absolute m.   SPEN 321:7
  fits of m.   MACA 221:12
  know about m.   CAMU 84:3
  may be called M.   KANT 194:22
  middle-class m.   SHAW 312:29
  m. for morality's sake   COUS 104:17
  M. is the herd-instinct   NIET 251:7
  m. of art   WILD 358:25
  m. touched by emotion   ARNO 17:7
  slave-m.   NIET 251:11
  What is m.   WHIT 356:13
morals Have you no m.   SHAW 312:28
  lack of m.   HATH 163:7
  m. of a whore   JOHN 188:7
  self-interest was bad m.   ROOS 279:12
morbo Venienti occurrite m.   PERS 262:10
more For, I have m.   DONN 119:2
  I want some m.   DICK 115:13
  little m.   BROW 71:25
  m. and m. about less and less   BUTL 79:4
  m. equal than others   ORWE 254:10
  m. Piglet wasn't there   MILN 235:9
  M. will mean worse   AMIS 6:7
mores O tempora, O m.   CICE 96:20
mori pro patria m.   HORA 175:8
moriar Non omnis m.   HORA 175:18
morituri Ave Caesar, m. te salutant   ANON 13:7
morn But, look, the m.   SHAK 291:12
  Each m. a thousand roses   FITZ 136:7
  From m. to noon he fell   MILT 238:1
  Salute the happy m.   BYRO 79:22
morning arrested one fine m.   KAFK 194:11
  danced in the m.   CART 88:4
  Early one m.   ANON 7:25
  evening and the m.   BIBL 34:4
  glad confident m.   BROW 72:14
  joy cometh in the m.   BOOK 62:19
  Lucifer, son of the m.   BIBL 40:19
  many a glorious m.   SHAK 310:8
  m. after   ADE 3:13
  m. cometh   BIBL 40:20
  M. has broken   FARJ 134:3
  M. in the bowl of night   FITZ 136:6
  m. rose   KEAT 196:14
  M.'s at seven   BROW 72:23
  m.'s minion   HOPK 174:9
  New every m.   KEBL 197:23
  pay thy m. sacrifice   KEN 198:5
  shining m. face   SHAK 290:12

take you in the m.   BALD 25:1
What a glorious m.   ADAM 2:15
wings of the m.   BOOK 65:3
Morocco we're M. bound   BURK 76:12
moron consumer isn't a m.   OGIL 253:2
See the happy m.   ANON 10:18
morphine m. or idealism   JUNG 193:19
Morris nine men's m.   SHAK 303:18
morrow no thought for the m.   BIBL 44:2
mortal Her last disorder m.   GOLD 153:13
  laugh at any m. thing   BYRO 81:2
  shuffled off this m. coil   SHAK 292:23
  think all men m.   YOUN 369:29
  this m. life   BOOK 61:15
mortality m. touches the heart   VIRG 347:3
  Old m.   BROW 71:5
mortals good that m. know   ADDI 3:4
  not for m.   ARMS 16:2
  not in m.   ADDI 2:20
  what fools these m. be   SHAK 303:28
mortifying m. reflections   CONG 102:12
mortis Timor m. conturbat me   DUNB 123:8
mortuus Passer m. est   CATU 89:5
Moscow M.: those syllables   PUSH 272:3
Moses From M. to Moses   ANON 8:8
  Go down, M.   ANON 11:20
Mosque from the Holy M.   KORA 205:14
mossy Happy field or m. cavern   KEAT 196:4
  violet by a m. stone   WORD 365:27
mote m. that is in thy brother's eye   BIBL 44:4
moth m. and rust doth corrupt   BIBL 43:23
  m. for the star   SHEL 314:24
mother As is the m.   BIBL 41:27
  Behold thy m.   BIBL 49:12
  church for his m.   CYPR 109:2
  gave her m. forty whacks   ANON 9:13
  happen to your m.   WALK 349:7
  heaviness of his m.   BIBL 38:19
  Honour thy father and thy m.   BIBL 35:28
  I arose a m.   BIBL 36:10
  leave his father and his m.   BIBL 34:13
  may not marry his M.   BOOK 65:16
  m. bids me bind   HUNT 178:20
  m. bore me in the southern wild   BLAK 57:20
  M., give me the sun   IBSE 180:7
  m. of all battles   HUSS 179:2
  M. OF HARLOTS   BIBL 53:19
  m. of mankind   MILT 237:18
  m. of Parliaments   BRIG 69:1
  M. of the Free   BENS 31:3
  m.'s little helper   JAGG 182:4
  m. told me as a boy   BERR 32:19
  m. was glad to get asleep   EMER 132:19
  my father or my m.   STER 324:8
  My m. groaned   BLAK 57:25
  never called me m.   WOOD 363:15
  rob his m.   FAUL 134:13
  their Dacian m.   BYRO 80:12
  to make it well? My M.   TAYL 331:1
  Took great care of his M.   MILN 235:14
mothers Come m. and fathers   DYLA 124:14
  happy m. made   SHAK 306:22
  How many m.' hearts   FATA 134:10
  m.-in-law and Wigan Pier   BRID 68:15
  women become like their m.   WILD 358:9
motion alteration of m.   NEWT 250:12
  Devoid of sense and m.   MILT 238:4
  m. of the wheels   HUME 178:8
  poetry in m.   KAUF 195:6
  poetry of m.   GRAH 155:4
  uniform m. in a right line   NEWT 250:11
motions secret m.   BACO 23:26
motives better m. for all the trouble   GREE 157:1

motley made myself a m.	SHAK 310:19
M.'s the only wear	SHAK 290:10
motorcycle art of m. maintenance	PIRS 263:17
mould broke the m.	ARIO 15:4
frozen in an out-of-date m.	JENK 185:2
mouldering many a m. heap	GRAY 156:8
mount m. up with wings	BIBL 41:4
Mount Abora Singing of M.	COLE 100:11
mountain all my holy m.	BIBL 40:18
Climb ev'ry m.	HAMM 160:15
exceeding high m.	BIBL 43:11
Flatter the m.-tops	SHAK 310:8
go up to the m.	KING 200:20
misty m. tops	SHAK 307:5
m. and hill	BIBL 40:30
say unto this m., Remove	BIBL 45:11
Up the airy m.	ALLI 5:19
mountains beautiful upon the m.	BIBL 41:7
men and m. meet	BLAK 57:11
m. also shall bring peace	BOOK 63:15
M. are the beginning	RUSK 282:16
m. by the winter sea	TENN 332:19
m. look on Marathon	BYRO 81:1
M. of Mourne	FREN 142:15
m. skipped like rams	BOOK 64:13
M. will go into labour	HORA 174:16
One of them.	WORD 366:11
river jumps over the m.	AUDE 18:13
so that I could remove m.	BIBL 50:22
mourn Blessed are they that m.	BIBL 43:13
countless thousands m.	BURN 77:4
Margaret you m. for	HOPK 174:5
M., you powers of Charm	CATU 89:5
time to m.	BIBL 39:11
Mourne Mountains of M.	FREN 142:15
mourners let the m. come	AUDE 18:18
mourning in m. for my life	CHEK 92:8
M. becomes Electra	O'NE 253:15
widow bird sat m.	SHEL 313:22
mouse invention of a m.	DISN 117:3
little m. will be born	HORA 174:16
Not a m. Shall disturb	SHAK 304:5
not even a m.	MOOR 243:16
mousetrap make a better m.	EMER 132:22
mouth Englishman to open his m.	SHAW 312:26
m. became the Brahmin	RIG 276:17
m. had been used as a latrine	AMIS 6:5
m. of Marilyn Monroe	MITT 241:18
m. of very babes	BOOK 62:8
m. speaketh	BIBL 44:37
only one m.	ZENO 370:11
out of the m. of God	BIBL 43:9
silver foot in his m.	RICH 276:7
spew thee out of my m.	BIBL 53:4
z is keeping your m. shut	EINS 126:10
mouths m., and speak not	BOOK 64:15
poet's m. be shut	YEAT 368:22
stuffed their m. with gold	BEVA 33:13
moutons Revenons à ces m.	ANON 12:18
movable Paris is a m. feast	HEMI 166:3
move Art has to m. you	HOCK 171:2
But it does m.	GALI 148:8
feel the earth m.	HEMI 166:2
great affair is to m.	STEV 325:14
in him we live, and m.	BIBL 49:31
m. the earth	ARCH 14:17
moved m. about like the wind	GERO 148:6
mover arrive at a prime m.	THOM 337:14
movers m. and shakers	O'SH 255:15
moves If it m., salute it	ANON 8:19
movies M. should have a beginning	GODA 152:3
moving m. finger writes	FITZ 136:16
m. in opposite directions	SMIT 319:10
m. toyshop of their heart	POPE 268:15
plates appear to be m.	PRES 270:20
Mozart no female M.	PAGL 257:1
when M. was my age	LEHR 211:21
MP Being an M.	ABBO 1:1
much how m. we think of ourselves	TWAI 343:20
Sing 'em m.	MELB 232:5
so m. owed by so many to so few	CHUR 95:11
so m. to do	RHOD 275:13
so m. to do	TENN 333:4
muck Money is like m.	BACO 23:7
muckrake m. in his hand	BUNY 74:15
muckrakes men with the m.	ROOS 280:2
mud back in the m.	AUGI 19:27
filled up with m.	SHAK 303:18
M.! Glorious mud	FLAN 137:21
muddle beginning, a m.	LARK 209:2
muddy M., ill-seeming	SHAK 307:14
m. understandings	BURK 75:19
muero Muero porque no m.	JOHN 185:14
Muhammad M. is not the father	KORA 205:17
mule m. of politics	DISR 117:22
mules m. of politics	POWE 270:17
Mulligan plump Buck M.	JOYC 193:3
multiply Be fruitful, and m.	BIBL 34:6
m. my signs and my wonders	BIBL 35:16
multitude m. is in the wrong	DILL 116:16
m. of sins	BIBL 52:29
multitudes I contain m.	WHIT 357:9
mum oafish louts remember M.	BETJ 33:1
They fuck you up, your m. and dad	LARK 208:21
mundi peccata m.	MISS 240:25
Sic transit gloria m.	ANON 13:20
muove amor che m. il sole	DANT 109:17
Eppur si m.	GALI 148:8
murder battle and m.	BOOK 60:13
commit a m.	VAN 345:9
do no m.	BOOK 61:2
I met M. on the way	SHEL 314:1
indulges himself in m.	DE Q 113:9
Killing no m.	SEXB 289:3
m. by the law	YOUN 369:24
m. by the throat	LLOY 216:11
m. cannot be hid long	SHAK 302:17
M. considered	DE Q 113:8
m. into the home	HITC 170:4
M. most foul	SHAK 291:39
m. respectable	ORWE 255:5
m. to dissect	WORD 366:10
M. wol out	CHAU 91:27
One m. made a villain	PORT 269:7
Sooner m. an infant	BLAK 57:6
story is about not m.	JAME 183:5
to m., for the truth	ADLE 3:16
We hear war called m.	MACD 222:20
murdered m. reputations	CONG 102:9
Our royal master's m.	SHAK 300:25
murderer m. for fancy prose style	NABO 247:15
murderers m. of Jewish children	WIES 357:23
m. take the first step	KARR 195:2
murmuring m. of innumerable bees	TENN 334:24
mus nascetur ridiculus m.	HORA 174:16
muscles M. better and nerves more	CUMM 108:10
muscular His Christianity was m.	DISR 117:25
muse M. but served to ease	POPE 266:18
M. invoked	SWIF 328:26
O! for a M. of fire	SHAK 295:9
museum m. inside our heads	LIVE 216:2
mushroom Life too short to stuff a m.	CONR 102:29
music alive with the sound of m.	HAMM 160:21
all m. is folk music	ARMS 16:6
Beauty in m.	IVES 181:8
but the m. there	POPE 267:11

chosen m., liberty | WORD 366:11
compulsion doth in m. lie | MILT 236:1
condition of m. | PATE 260:7
danceth without m. | HERB 167:27
dance to the m. of time | POWE 270:9
day the m. died | MCLE 223:14
essence of m. | MOZA 246:12
Fading in m. | SHAK 302:24
Fled is that m. | KEAT 196:25
frozen m. | SCHE 286:6
how potent cheap m. is | COWA 105:9
How sour sweet m. is | SHAK 306:5
Is there a meaning to m. | COPL 104:2
Let's face the m. and dance | BERL 31:21
make the m. mute | TENN 332:16
May make one m. | TENN 332:26
most civilized m. | USTI 344:20
M. and women | PEPY 261:19
M. begins to atrophy | POUN 270:4
m. be the food of love | SHAK 308:17
m. business is not | MORR 245:22
M. has charms | CONG 102:6
m. in the air | ELGA 127:3
M. is feeling, then | STEV 324:20
M. is your own experience | PARK 258:10
M. shall untune the sky | DRYD 122:13
M. that gentlier on the spirit | TENN 333:34
m. the brandy of the damned | SHAW 312:1
M., the greatest good | ADDI 3:4
M., when soft voices die | SHEL 314:23
My m. is best understood | STRA 326:23
Of m. Dr Johnson used to say | JOHN 191:8
passion cannot M. raise | DRYD 122:11
still, sad m. | WORD 364:20
thou hast thy m. too | KEAT 197:3
uproar's your only m. | KEAT 197:12
We are the m. makers | O'SH 255:15
What then is m. | HEIN 165:8
musical m. as is Apollo's lute | MILT 236:7
musician far below the m. | LEON 213:4
Muslim neither Hindu nor M. | SIKH 316:21
Muslims named you M. | KORA 205:15
zealous M. to execute | KHOM 199:23
Muss *M. es sein* | BEET 29:5
must It m. be | BEET 29:5
Must! Is *m.* a word | ELIZ 130:17
We m. know | HILB 168:19
whispers low, *Thou m.* | EMER 132:1
you m. go on | BECK 28:10
mustard faith as a grain of m. seed | BIBL 45:11
grain of m. seed | BIBL 45:1
mutabile *Varium et m. semper Femina* | VIRG 347:8
mutability Nought may endure but M. | SHEL 314:2
mutant *Caelum non animum m.* | HORA 174:27
mutantur *spatio m.* | LUCR 220:14
mutato *M. nomine de te* | HORA 175:21
mutilate spindle or m. | ANON 7:24
myriad There died a m. | POUN 270:1
myrrh frankincense, and m. | BIBL 43:2
myrtle m. and turkey | AUST 20:24
myrtles Ye m. brown | MILT 236:27
myself I celebrate m. | WHIT 357:3
I do not know m. | GOET 152:24
If I am not for m. | HILL 169:12
Madame Bovary is m. | FLAU 138:2
When I give I give m. | WHIT 357:8
mysterious moves in a m. way | COWP 105:18
mystery grasped the m. of the atom | BRAD 67:9
heart of my m. | SHAK 293:12
I shew you a m. | BIBL 51:3
M., BABYLON THE GREAT | BIBL 53:19
my tongue, the m. telling | THOM 337:12
riddle wrapped in a m. | CHUR 95:5

mystic m. chords of memory | LINC 214:16
m., wonderful | TENN 332:10
mystical m. mathematics | BROW 71:4
m. way of Pythagoras | BROW 71:10
mystify m., mislead, and surprise | JACK 181:17
myth thing itself and not the m. | RICH 276:5
mythologies Out of old m. | YEAT 367:17
myths Science must begin with m. | POPP 268:27

N

nabobs nattering n. | AGNE 3:26
nagging N. is the repetition | SUMM 327:14
nail blows his n. | SHAK 299:5
I n. my pictures together | SCHW 287:1
nails n. bitten and pared | MACA 221:10
nineteen hundred and forty n. | SITW 317:13
print of the n. | BIBL 49:17
naive n. domestic Burgundy | THUR 340:5
n. forgive and forget | SZAS 329:19
naked left me n. to mine enemies | SHAK 296:15
more enterprise In walking n. | YEAT 367:18
N., and ye clothed me | BIBL 46:7
n. ape | MORR 245:7
n. into the conference chamber | BEVA 33:11
stark n. truth | CLEL 98:1
starving hysterical n. | GINS 151:3
With n. foot | WYAT 367:1
nakedness n. of woman | BLAK 57:2
name at the n. of Jesus | BIBL 51:22
At the n. of Jesus | NOEL 251:20
Change the n. | HORA 175:21
dare not speak its n. | DOUG 120:2
deed without a n. | SHAK 301:14
fear my n. | BIBL 42:17
filches from me my good n. | SHAK 304:31
gathered together in my n. | BIBL 45:15
glory in the n. of Briton | GEOR 147:17
Halloo your n. | SHAK 308:25
Hallowed be thy n. | BIBL 43:22
I am become a n. | TENN 335:1
In the n. of God, go | AMER 6:3
In the n. of God, go | CROM 107:11
In the N. of the Father | MISS 240:15
In the N. of thy Lord | KORA 205:25
king's n. | SHAK 306:18
left the n. | JOHN 187:26
Let me not n. it | SHAK 305:11
local habitation and a n. | SHAK 304:2
mark, or the n. of the beast | BIBL 53:13
My n. is Legion | BIBL 46:26
My n. is Ozymandias | SHEL 314:10
n. Achilles assumed | BROW 71:6
n. great in story | BYRO 81:21
n. like yours | CARR 87:7
n. liveth for ever | SASS 286:2
n. liveth for evermore | ANON 11:6
n. liveth for evermore | BIBL 42:28
n. of God in vain | BIBL 35:26
N. of God, the Merciful | KORA 204:17
N. of the Lord | BOOK 64:19
n. upon the strand | SPEN 321:20
n. we give the people | FLER 138:9
no profit but the n. | SHAK 293:26
nothing of a n. | BYRO 80:16
one whose n. was writ | KEAT 197:21
power of Jesus' N. | PERR 262:8
problem that has no n. | FRIE 142:20
unto thy N. give the praise | BOOK 64:14
What's in a n. | SHAK 306:29
Who gave you this N. | BOOK 61:17

name (*cont.*)

worth an age without a n.	MORD 244:14
named N. is the mother	LAO 207:20
n. you Muslims	KORA 205:15
nameless N. here for evermore	POE 265:18
N. is the origin	LAO 207:20
n., unremembered, acts	WORD 364:19
names in love with American n.	BENÉ 30:14
n. of those who love	HUNT 178:16
naming N. of Cats	ELIO 129:8
n. of parts	REED 274:12
Napoleon N. of crime	DOYL 120:18
Napoleons Caesars and N.	HUXL 179:11
narcotic n. be alcohol	JUNG 193:19
Narragansett Where are the N.	TECU 331:9
narrative unconvincing n.	GILB 150:8
narrow n. is the way	BIBL 44:10
nastiest n. thing in the nicest way	GOLD 153:1
nasty as n. as himself	SHAW 313:1
n., brutish, and short	HOBB 170:19
n. party	MAY 231:16
Something n. in the woodshed	GIBB 149:6
nation AMERICA thus top n.	SELL 288:20
boundary of the march of a n.	PARN 259:15
broad mass of a n.	HITL 170:6
every man and n.	LOWE 220:2
fate of a n.	LONG 218:7
n. a le gouvernment	MAIS 225:16
n. expects to be ignorant	JEFF 184:15
n. of dancers	EQUI 132:29
n. of shop-keepers	ADAM 2:16
n. of shopkeepers	NAPO 248:7
n. of shopkeepers	SMIT 318:5
N. once again	DAVI 111:4
n. shall not lift up sword	BIBL 40:5
n. shall rise	BIBL 45:33
N. shall speak peace	REND 275:5
n. talking to itself	MILL 235:2
n. that had lion's heart	CHUR 95:24
n. which indulges toward another	WASH 351:9
new n.	LINC 214:20
No n. is fit	WILS 361:10
no rainbow n.	MADI 224:18
old and haughty n.	MILT 236:3
one-third of a n. ill-housed	ROOS 279:11
terrorize a whole n.	MURR 247:10
voice of a n.	RUSS 283:15
while the n. is honest	DOUG 120:8
national n. debt	HAMI 160:11
n. flag	SUMN 327:16
n. home for the Jewish people	BALF 25:5
nationalism N. is an infantile sickness	EINS 126:15
n. is a silly cock	ALDI 4:8
nationality n., language, religion	JOYC 192:25
what n. he would prefer	RHOD 275:12
nations belong to other n.	GILB 150:21
belong to two different n.	FOST 140:6
day of small n.	CHAM 90:2
Europe of n.	DE G 112:5
father of many n.	BIBL 49:42
fierce contending n.	ADDI 3:3
friendship with all n.	JEFF 184:7
great n. acted like gangsters	KUBR 206:4
hating all other n.	GASK 146:15
healing of the n.	BIBL 53:25
n. how to live	MILT 240:11
pedigree of n.	JOHN 187:30
place among the n.	EMME 132:23
rule n. by your government	VIRG 347:14
Two n.	DISR 117:29
two n. have been at war	VOLT 348:7
two n. warring	DURH 123:13
native by their n. shore	COWP 105:21

in his n. place	JOHN 189:2
my n. land	SCOT 287:12
n. wood-notes wild	MILT 236:25
nattering n. nabobs	AGNE 3:26
natural I do it more n.	SHAK 308:29
N. rights	BENT 31:5
N. Selection	DARW 110:6
N. selection a mechanism	FISH 136:5
twice as n.	CARR 87:14
naturalists n. observe, a flea	SWIF 329:2
nature better angels of our n.	LINC 214:16
body, N. is	POPE 267:24
book of n.	GALI 145:7
by n. desire knowledge	ARIS 15:10
conquered human n.	DICK 115:10
course of N.	YOUN 370:3
cruel works of n.	DARW 110:11
[Death is] n.'s way	ANON 7:22
does N. live	COLE 100:1
drive out n.	HORA 174:26
Eye N.'s walks	POPE 267:19
How N. always does contrive	GILB 149:18
ignorance of n.	HOLB 171:15
In n. there are neither	INGE 180:18
interpreter of n.	JOHN 187:17
It is a part of n.	SPEN 321:11
law of their n.	THUC 340:1
mirror up to n.	SHAK 293:7
My n. is subdued	SHAK 310:20
N. abhors a vacuum	RABE 272:11
N., and Nature's laws	POPE 267:4
n. cannot be fooled	FEYN 135:4
N. cannot be ordered	BACO 23:28
N. does nothing uselessly	ARIS 15:21
N. from her seat	MILT 239:6
N. in awe to him	MILT 237:7
N. in you stands	SHAK 297:32
N. is a temple	BAUD 27:19
n. is but art	POPE 267:25
N. is not a temple	TURG 343:1
n. is the art of God	BROW 71:12
n. made him	ARIO 15:4
n. of war	HOBB 170:18
N., red in tooth and claw	TENN 333:3
N.'s great masterpiece	DONN 119:3
n.'s handmaid art	DRYD 122:1
N.'s social union	BURN 77:20
N.'s sole mistake	GILB 150:25
N.'s sweet restorer	YOUN 369:26
N. to advantage dressed	POPE 267:9
n. to explore	POPE 267:30
N. wears one universal grin	FIEL 135:19
next to N.	LAND 207:14
not n.	CONS 103:2
One touch of n.	SHAK 308:13
paint too much direct from n.	GAUG 146:16
priketh hem n.	CHAU 91:12
read N.	DRYD 122:21
simply follow N.	LAO 208:2
spark o' N.'s fire	BURN 76:25
state that n. hath provided	LOCK 216:17
stuff that n. replaces it with	WILL 360:11
subtlety of n.	BACO 23:27
Treat n. in terms	CÉZA 89:23
violates the order of n.	HERO 167:28
war of n.	DARW 110:9
whatever N. has in store	FERM 135:2
naught n. for your comfort	CHES 92:25
naughty in a n. world	SHAK 303:4
naval N. tradition	CHUR 95:22
navies nations' airy n.	TENN 333:27
navy royal n. of England	BLAC 55:14
Rulers of the Queen's N.	GILB 150:19

upon the n.   CHAR 91:1
nay your n., nay   BIBL 52:24
Nazareth come out of N.   BIBL 48:22
Neaera tangles of N.'s hair   MILT 236:29
Neanderthal of N. man   STRA 326:22
near come not n. to me   BIBL 41:18
so n. and yet so far   TENN 333:7
while he is n.   BIBL 41:13
nearer N., my God, to thee   ADAM 2:17
n. than hands and feet   TENN 332:8
n. to him than the jugular   KORA 205:23
neat N., but not gaudy   WESL 355:5
Still to be n.   JONS 191:15
Nebuchadnezzar N. the king   BIBL 42:5
necessarily ain't n. so   HEYW 168:13
Not n. conscription   KING 201:5
necessary absolutely n.   OCCA 253:1
honourable by being n.   HALE 159:14
if it is deemed n.   BROW 70:16
little visible delight, but n.   BRON 69:15
Make yourself n.   EMER 132:2
n. evil   BRAD 67:7
n. evil   PAIN 257:5
n. not to change   FALK 133:19
n. to salvation   BOOK 65:11
necessities dispense with its n.   MOTL 246:10
n. call out virtues   ADAM 1:11
necessity Cruel is the n.   CROM 107:8
do not see the n.   ARGE 15:3
fiction is a n.   CHES 93:9
N. has no law   PUBL 271:13
N. hath no law   CROM 107:13
N. is the plea   PITT 263:20
N. never made   FRAN 141:18
no virtue like n.   SHAK 305:20
pragmatic n.   DIDI 116:13
neck had but one n.   CALI 82:12
hanged about his n.   BIBL 45:13
Some chicken! Some n.   CHUR 95:13
necklace with our n.   MADI 224:17
nectar comprehend a n.   DICK 116:4
nectarine n., and curious peach   MARV 229:16
need all ye n. to know   KEAT 196:12
face of total n.   BURR 77:24
love you because I n. you   FROM 143:4
n. in this life is ignorance   TWAI 344:1
not enough for everyone's n.   BUCH 73:16
O reason not the n.   SHAK 297:33
People who n. people   MERR 233:13
Requires sorest n.   DICK 116:4
things that people don't n.   WARH 350:22
thy n. is greater   SIDN 316:17
What can I want or n.   HERB 167:23
Will you still n. me   LENN 212:23
needle eye of a n.   BIBL 45:19
needs according to his n.   MARX 230:6
negative N. Capability   KEAT 197:11
prefers a n. peace   KING 200:15
neglect Such sweet n.   JONS 191:16
negotiate n. out of fear   KENN 198:17
not here to n.   TRIM 341:18
negotiating N. with de Valera   LLOY 216:12
Negro N.'s great stumbling block   KING 200:15
places where the average N.   DAVI 111:3
Negroes drivers of n.   JOHN 187:22
neiges où sont les n. d'antan   VILL 346:17
neighbour do not to your n.   HILL 169:10
guts into the n. room   SHAK 293:24
love thy n.   BIBL 35:34
love thy n. as thyself   BIBL 45:28
thy n.'s house   BIBL 35:28
neighbourhood n. of voluntary spies   AUST 21:2
neighbouring cynosure of n. eyes   MILT 236:22

neighbours Good fences make good n.   FROS 143:20
have good n.   ELIZ 130:11
sport for our n.   AUST 21:11
Nell Pretty witty N.   PEPY 261:17
Nellie N. Dean   ARMS 16:1
Nelly Let not poor N. starve   CHAR 91:4
Nelson N. touch   NELS 249:6
Nemo N. me impune lacessit   ANON 13:12
nerve after the n. has been extracted   ROWL 281:13
nerves Muscles better and n. more   CUMM 108:10
nervous approaching n. breakdown   RUSS 282:24
nervousness only n. or death   LEBO 211:4
nest her soft and chilly n.   KEAT 195:14
leaves his wat'ry n.   D'AV 110:16
n. of singing birds   JOHN 188:3
theek our n.   BALL 25:21
nests Birds in their little n. agree   WATT 351:21
built their n. in my beard   LEAR 210:9
net n. is spread   BIBL 38:11
play tennis with the n. down   FROS 144:3
too old to rush up to the n.   ADAM 1:16
nets try to fly by those n.   JOYC 192:25
nettle Out of this n., danger   SHAK 294:19
Tender-handed stroke a n.   HILL 169:2
network N. Anything reticulated   JOHN 186:20
neurosis n. is a secret   TYNA 344:6
N. is a way of avoiding   TILL 340:11
neutral studiously n.   WILS 361:12
neutrality Just for a word 'n.'   BETH 32:21
N. helps the oppressor   WIES 357:22
neutrinos N., they are very small   UPDI 344:18
never come no more, N., never   SHAK 298:28
N. do to-day   PUNC 271:19
N. explain   FISH 136:4
N. explain   HUBB 177:7
n. go to sea   GILB 150:19
n. had it so good   MACM 224:4
N. in the field of human conflict   CHUR 95:11
N. the time   BROW 72:19
n. to have been loved   CONG 102:10
This will n. do   JEFF 184:22
We n. closed   VAN 345:6
nevermore Quoth the Raven, 'N.'   POE 265:20
new beginning of a n. month   MANN 227:4
called the N. World   CANN 84:10
Emperor's n. clothes   ANDE 6:11
find something n.   VOLT 348:6
make a n. acquaintance   JOHN 190:22
make n. acquaintance   JOHN 188:10
making n. enemies   VOLT 349:4
n. and untried   LINC 214:14
n. deal for the American people   ROOS 279:7
N. every morning   KEBL 197:23
n. heaven and a new earth   BIBL 53:22
new heavens and a n. earth   BIBL 41:19
n. man may be raised up   BOOK 61:16
N. opinions are always suspected   LOCK 216:13
n. race is sent down   VIRG 347:21
n. wine into old bottles   BIBL 44:21
n. world order   BUSH 78:14
no n. thing under the sun   BIBL 39:8
O brave n. world   SHAK 307:35
old lamps for n.   ARAB 14:11
require n. clothes   THOR 339:14
shock of the n.   DUNL 123:10
something n. out of Africa   PLIN 265:6
songs for ever n.   KEAT 196:9
so quite n. a thing   CUMM 108:10
unto the Lord a n. song   BOOK 62:21
unto the Lord a n. song   BOOK 64:1
wrote MAKE IT N.   POUN 269:19
newborn use of a n. child   FRAN 142:5
New England N. weather   TWAI 343:27

N.! No! No — THAT 337:2
she said 'n.' — ALLE 5:14
There is n. God — BOOK 62:9
Noah into N.'s ark — COWP 105:23
N. he often said to his wife — CHES 93:7
nobility N. has obligations — LÉVI 213:14
our old n. — MANN 227:8
nobis Non n., Domine — BIBL 54:1
noble Do n. things — KING 201:6
fredome is a n. thing — BARB 26:10
Man is a n. animal — BROW 71:9
n. lie — PLAT 264:22
n. Living — WORD 365:19
n. savage ran — DRYD 122:2
O! what a n. mind — SHAK 293:2
nobles n. with links of iron — BOOK 65:6
noblesse N. oblige — LÉVI 213:14
noblest n. prospect — JOHN 188:13
n. Roman of them all — SHAK 297:16
n. work of God — POPE 268:2
n. work of man — INGE 180:17
nobly n. save — LINC 214:19
nobody N. came — GINS 151:2
n. comes — BECK 28:14
n.'s going to stop 'em — BERR 32:14
n. will come — SAND 285:7
noctis currite n. equi — MARL 228:9
currite n. equi — OVID 255:23
nod dwelt in the land of N. — BIBL 34:25
nods excellent Homer n. — HORA 174:19
N., and becks — MILT 236:19
noise Go placidly amid the n. — FHRM 126:1
happy n. to hear — HOUS 176:9
loud n. at one end — KNOX 204:12
n. of battle rolled — TENN 332:19
those who make the n. — BURK 75:22
noises isle is full of n. — SHAK 307:29
Nokomis wigwam of N. — LONG 218:3
noli N. me tangere — BIBL 54:13
N. me tangere — WYAT 367:4
nominated will not accept if n. — SHER 315:27
nomine In N. Patris — MISS 240:15
non avoiding n.-being — TILL 340:11
comes from n.-being — LAO 208:4
no fury like a n.-combatant — MONT 242:15
n.-cooperation with evil — GAND 145:17
N.-violence is the first article — GAND 145:16
nonconformist man must be a n. — EMER 132:10
none answer came there n. — CARR 87:4
answer came there n. — SCOT 287:7
answer made it n. — SHAK 291:26
malice toward n. — LINC 215:5
nonexistent obsolescent and n. — BREN 68:12
nonsense n., and learning — GOLD 153:22
n. upon stilts — BENT 31:5
your damned n. — RICH 276:13
noon amid the blaze of n. — MILT 239:22
noonday destroyeth in the n. — BOOK 63:25
Norfolk Very flat, N. — COWA 105:8
normal n. and easy — JAME 182:22
normalcy not nostrums but n. — HARD 161:12
Norman simple faith than N. blood — TENN 333:14
Noroway To N. o'er the faem — BALL 25:16
north He was my N., my South — AUDE 18:19
mad n.-north-west — SHAK 292:17
N.-west passage — STER 324:12
True N. strong and free — WEIR 353:8
North America Mr and Mrs N. — WINC 361:18
northern constant as the n. star — SHAK 296:27
N. reticence, the tight gag — HEAN 164:13
Norval My name is N. — HOME 172:7
nose at the end of his n. — LEAR 210:16
Cleopatra's n. been shorter — PASC 259:19

hateful to the n. — JAME 182:9
insinuated n. — WATS 351:17
n. was as sharp as a pen — SHAK 295:15
plucks justice by the n. — SHAK 302:3
thirty inches from my n. — AUDE 19:15
very shiny n. — MARK 228:2
wipe a bloody n. — GAY 147:4
with a luminous n. — LEAR 210:11
noses Athwart men's n. — SHAK 306:23
n. have they, and smell not — BOOK 64:15
slightly flatter n. — CONR 102:20
nostalgie n. de la boue — AUGI 19:27
noster Pater n. — MISS 240:24
nostrums not n. but normalcy — HARD 161:12
not n. I, but the wind — LAWR 209:25
N. unto us, O Lord — BOOK 64:14
said the thing which was n. — SWIF 328:12
Thou shalt n. kill — BIBL 35:28
note living had no n. — GIBB 149:5
longest suicide n. — KAUF 195:5
n. I wanted — JAME 182:22
only the n. of a bird — SIMP 317:8
When found, make a n. — DICK 114:24
notes n. I handle no better — SCHN 286:14
right n. at the right time — BACH 21:22
These rough n. — SCOT 287:5
thick-warbled n. — MILT 239:18
too many n. — JOSE 192:13
nothing brought n. into this world — BIBL 52:8
Caesar or n. — BORG 65:23
Death is n. to us — EPIC 132:28
do n. without it — BUTL 79:18
don't believe in n. — CHES 93:25
Emperor has n. on — ANDE 6:12
forgotten nothing and learnt n. — DUMO 123:6
good man to do n. — BURK 76:10
Goodness had n. to do with it — WEST 355:9
have not charity, I am n. — BIBL 50:22
having n., yet hath all — WOTT 366:22
individually can do n. — ALLE 5:10
live well on n. a year — THAC 336:7
marvel at n. — HORA 174:25
N. — LOUI 219:3
N. ain't worth nothin' — KRIS 206:2
N. begins — THOM 338:13
N. can be created — LUCR 220:13
n. can be sole or whole — YEAT 367:20
n. happens — AURE 20:16
N. happens — BECK 28:14
N. happens — WELD 353:13
N. in excess — ANON 13:3
N. is ever done in this world — SHAW 311:28
N. is here for tears — MILT 239:26
N. is law — POWE 270:16
N. is more dangerous — ALAI 4:5
N., like something, happens anywhere — LARK 208:19
n. of a name — BYRO 80:16
N. should be done for the first time — CORN 104:9
N. to be done — BECK 28:11
N. to do but work — KING 200:8
n. to do with the case — GILB 150:9
n. to look backward to — FROS 143:12
n. to say — CAGE 82:10
n. to say — COLT 101:19
n. to you — BIBL 41:24
N. will come of nothing — SHAK 297:22
not there and the n. that is — STEV 324:22
say n. — HEAN 164:13
that he n. knows — MILT 239:19
Thinking n. done — LUCA 220:8
Think n. done — ROGE 278:11
You ain't heard n. yet — JOLS 191:7
nothingness to n. do sink — KEAT 197:8

O

October O., that ambiguous month · LESS 213:9
octopus dear o. · SMIT 318:10
odd But not so o. · BROW 71:3
  divinity in o. numbers · SHAK 303:6
  God must think it exceedingly o. · KNOX 204:11
  How o. Of God · EWER 133:11
oddfellow desperate o. society · THOR 339:16
odds facing fearful o. · MACA 221:21
oderint O., dum metuant · ACCI 1:3
odi O. et amo · CATU 89:8
odious O.! in woollen · POPE 267:2
odorous Comparisons are o. · SHAK 304:13
odours haste with o. sweet · MILT 237:6
Odyssey thunder of the O. · LANG 207:15
off O. with her head · CARR 86:13
  O. with his head · SHAK 306:14
offence detest th'o. · POPE 266:12
  I was like to give o. · FROS 143:21
  o. inspires less horror · GIBB 148:16
  where the o. is · SHAK 293:34
offend freedom to o. · RUSH 282:7
offended him have I o. · SHAK 296:33
  not o. the king · MORE 244:20
offender love th'o. · POPE 266:12
offenders society o. · GILB 149:23
offensive extremely o. · SMIT 318:14
offer o. he can't refuse · PUZO 272:5
offering o. too little · CANN 84:6
office campaigns for public o. · MORE 244:16
  for o. boys · SALI 284:22
  holding public o. · ACHE 1:5
  in o. but not in power · LAMO 207:12
  insignificant o. · ADAM 2:7
  o. party is not · WHIT 356:17
officer o. and a gentleman · ANON 7:10
official concept of the o. secret · WEBE 352:15
  This high o., all allow · HERB 167:6
oft O. in danger · WHIT 356:5
  o. was thought · POPE 267:9
often Vote early and vote o. · MILE 234:2
oil o. controlling American soil · DYLA 124:12
  o. in a cruse · BIBL 37:10
  o. of gladness · BOOK 63:2
  o. which renders · HUME 178:8
  with boiling o. in it · GILB 150:7
  with o. anoint · SCOT 288:3
oiled in the o. wards · KEAT 196:30
oily glib and o. art · SHAK 297:24
Okie O. means you're scum · STEI 323:21
old adherence to the o. · LINC 214:14
  Any o. iron · COLL 101:11
  As with gladness men of o. · DIX 118:11
  balance of the O. · CANN 84:10
  boys of the o. Brigade · WEAT 352:11
  chilly and grown o. · BROW 73:5
  die before I get o. · TOWN 341:8
  dressing o. words new · SHAK 310:12
  foolish, fond o. man · SHAK 298:21
  good o. Cause · MILT 240:12
  Growing o. a bad habit · MAUR 231:14
  Growing o. is like · POWE 270:10
  Grow o. along with me · BROW 72:28
  hearts have not grown o. · YEAT 369:14
  I grow o. · SOLO 320:4
  I grow o. . . . . I grow old · ELIO 129:3
  instead of o. ones · PEEL 261:4
  make me conservative when o. · FROS 143:22
  man who reviews the o. · CONF 102:5
  Mithridates, he died o. · HOUS 176:17
  name thee O. Glory · DRIV 121:15
  no country for o. men · YEAT 368:26
  no man would be o. · SWIF 328:24
  now am o. · BOOK 62:23

o. Adam in this Child · BOOK 61:16
o. age always fifteen years older · BARU 27:8
O. Age a regret · DISR 117:21
O. age is the most unexpected · TROT 342:5
o. black magic · MERC 233:6
o. familiar faces · LAMB 207:5
O. friends are best · SELD 288:12
o. heads on your young shoulders · SPAR 321:1
o. lamps for new · ARAB 14:11
o. Lie: Dulce et decorum · OWEN 256:11
o., mad, blind · SHEL 314:22
o. man in a dry month · ELIO 128:19
o. man in a hurry · CHUR 94:19
o. man of Thermopylae · LEAR 210:13
O. man river · HAMM 160:19
o. men from the chimney corner · SIDN 316:15
o. men shall dream dreams · BIBL 42:12
o. order changeth · TENN 332:5
O. soldiers never die · FOLE 138:20
o., unhappy, far-off things · WORD 366:6
o. wood best to burn · BACO 22:5
O, sir! you are o. · SHAK 297:32
so o. a head · SHAK 302:29
suppose an o. man decayed · JOHN 190:12
Tell me the o., old story · HANK 161:2
that's o. Europe · RUMS 282:2
They shall grow not o. · BINY 54:24
though an o. man · JEFF 184:13
too o. to rush up to the net · ADAM 1:16
warn you not to grow o. · KINN 201:13
When I am an o. woman · JOSE 192:15
When you are very o. · RONS 279:2
you are o. and grey · YEAT 369:13
You are o., Father William · CARR 86:7
You are o., Father William · SOUT 320:21
young can do for the o. · SHAW 311:20
older Another day o. · TRAV 341:12
  O. men declare war · HOOV 173:7
  o. than the rocks · PATE 260:6
  so much o. then · DYLA 124:10
oldest o. hath borne most · SHAK 298:30
  o. rule in the book · CARR 86:21
olet Pecunia non o. · VESP 346:5
olive children like the o.-branches · BOOK 64:28
Olympus O. on top of Ossa · VIRG 348:2
  Pelion on top of shady O. · HORA 175:15
Omega Alpha and O. · BIBL 53:1
omelette o. all over our suits · BROK 69:5
omnia Amor vincit o. · CHAU 91:16
  non o. possumus omnes · LUCI 220:11
  Non o. possumus omnes · VIRG 347:24
  O. vincit Amor · VIRG 347:25
omnibus man on the Clapham o. · BOWE 66:15
omnipotence proof of God's o. · DE V 114:2
omnis Non o. moriar · HORA 175:18
Onan into the sin of O. · VOLT 348:24
once I was adored o. · SHAK 308:32
  oblation of himself o. offered · BOOK 61:13
  o. and future king · MALO 226:9
  O. in royal David's city · ALEX 4:16
  O. more unto the breach · SHAK 295:16
  O. to every man · LOWE 220:2
  O. upon a time · ANON 10:3
  through this world but o. · GREL 157:9
one All for o., one for all · DUMA 123:4
  all is o. · ZOHA 370:13
  How to be o. up · POTT 269:15
  Lord is O. · SIDD 316:6
  man not truly o. · STEV 325:13
  o. day in thy courts · BOOK 63:20
  o.-eyed man is king · ERAS 133:1
  o. for my baby · MERC 233:5
  o. if by land · LONG 218:6

one (*cont.*)
O. in Three ALEX 4:17
O. man shall have one vote CART 88:10
o. thing at once SMIL 317:21
ought to be Number O. CARR 86:21
square root of minus o. BECK 28:19
Tao produced the O. LAO 208:5
oneself Hell is o. ELIO 127:27
how to be o. MONT 242:22
onion o. atoms lurk SMIT 319:12
only his o. begotten Son BIBL 48:27
It's the o. thing SAND 285:11
o. begotten of the Father BIBL 48:19
O. connect FORS 139:16
O. the lonely ORBI 254:2
To the o. begetter SHAK 310:1
only-begotten o. Son of God BOOK 61:3
onset o. and waning of love LA B 206:11
onstage O. I make love JOPL 192:12
ontogeny o. recapitulates HAEC 158:14
onward O., Christian soldiers BARI 26:13
O. goes the pilgrim band BARI 26:14
open function when they are o. DEWA 114:4
o. and notorious evil liver BOOK 60:23
O. covenants of peace WILS 361:16
O. Sesame ARAB 14:12
o. the Kingdom of Heaven BOOK 59:19
O. the temple gates SPEN 321:21
opera *Benedicite, omnia o. Domini* BIBL 54:6
language an o. is sung in APPL 14:9
O. is when a guy gets stabbed GARD 146:2
operas German text of French o. WHAR 355:17
operations o. which we can perform WHIT 356:15
opiate some dull o. KEAT 196:16
opinion approve a private o. HOBB 170:16
Government and public o. SHAW 312:2
never had a humble o. BAEZ 24:6
of his own o. still BUTL 79:9
O. in good men MILT 240:8
supported by popular o. CATT 89:4
think the last o. right POPE 267:15
vagrant o. BIER 54:22
were of one o. MILL 234:8
whole climate of o. AUDE 18:20
opinions as many o. as people TERE 335:15
Golden o. SHAK 300:4
halt ye between two o. BIBL 37:11
New o. are always suspected LOCK 216:13
Stiff in o. DRYD 121:21
opium o.-dose for keeping beasts KING 201:10
o. of the people MARX 230:5
subtle, and mighty o. DE Q 113:7
opponents o. eventually die PLAN 264:10
opportunities grand o. all around PLUN 265:9
opportunity also a matter of o. HIPP 169:21
maximum of o. SHAW 312:11
meanness of o. ELIO 127:13
o. for achievement KEIL 197:26
o. to keep quiet CHIR 94:3
when he had the c. ROWL 281:15
oppose o. everything DERB 113:11
opposing by o. end them SHAK 292:23
opposition duty of an O. DERB 113:11
formidable O. DISR 117:19
His Majesty's O. HOBH 171:1
oppression violate would be o. JEFF 184:5
oppressor ends as an o. CAMU 84:2
Neutrality helps the o. WIES 357:22
optimist o. is a guy MARQ 228:21
o. proclaims that we live CABE 82:1
oracles lively O. of God CORO 104:12
oracular use of my o. tongue SHER 315:12
oral o. contraception ALLE 5:14

orange clockwork o. BURG 74:21
O. card CHUR 94:17
oranges Coffee and o. STEV 324:23
orator I am no o., as Brutus is SHAK 297:8
without an o. SHAK 309:33
orators play the o. MARL 228:16
oratory first in o. DEMO 112:21
orbed o. maiden SHEL 313:23
orchestra golden rules for an o. BEEC 28:23
orchestration o. of platitudes WILD 359:23
order all is in o. MANS 227:9
began in o. BROW 71:4
best words in the best o. COLE 101:5
decently and in o. BIBL 50:26
more devoted to o. than justice KING 200:15
new world o. BUSH 78:14
not necessarily in that o. GODA 152:3
old o. changeth TENN 332:21
o. and beauty BAUD 27:20
o. breeds habit ADAM 1:21
o. of Melchisedech BOOK 64:11
o. of your going SHAK 301:8
Peace, o., and good government ANON 10:7
prejudice of good o. ANON 7:19
restoration of o. JAME 183:5
Set thine house in o. BIBL 40:28
They o., said I STER 324:6
violates the o. of nature HERO 167:28
ordering o. of the universe ALFO 5:2
orders Almighty's o. to perform ADDI 2:19
don't obey no o. KIPL 201:22
gave them their o. WELL 354:9
ordinary learn to see the o. BAIL 24:13
o. mind WOOL 363:18
warn you not to be o. KINN 201:13
ore Load your subject with o. KEAT 197:20
organ o.-voice of England TENN 334:10
organization o. man WHYT 357:19
o. of forms CART 88:8
o. of hatreds ADAM 1:18
organize Don't waste time mourning—o. HILL 169:5
organized o. hypocrisy DISR 117:6
organizing Only an o. genius BEVA 33:7
orgasm o. has replaced the Cross MUGG 246:18
orient corn was o. TRAH 341:11
original gone from o. righteousness BOOK 65:12
great and o. writer WORD 366:21
great O. frame ADDI 3:7
o. is unfaithful BORG 65:21
saves o. thinking SAYE 286:5
originals few o. and many copies TOCQ 340:15
origins Consider your o. DANT 109:13
Orion bands of O. BIBL 38:8
Orlando Run, run, O. SHAK 290:18
orphan defeat is an o. CIAN 96:12
Orpheus O. with his lute SHAK 296:10
orthodoxy O. is my doxy WARB 350:16
Oscar assume that O. said it PARK 258:15
You will, O. WHIS 356:1
Ossa pile O. on Pelion VIRG 348:2
ostentation use rather than o. GIBB 148:15
ostrich wings of an o. MACA 221:17
Othello O.'s occupation's gone SHAK 305:7
other happens to o. people CART 87:26
I am not as o. men are BIBL 48:5
o. Eden SHAK 305:22
o. men's flowers MONT 243:4
O. voices, other rooms CAPO 84:15
Prudence is the o. woman ANON 10:11
Were t'o. dear charmer away GAY 147:2
wonderful for o. people KERR 199:11
others man for o. BONH 59:10
woman who lives for o. LEWI 213:19

otherwise gods thought o.   VIRG 347:5
Otis Miss O. regrets   PORT 269:4
ought hadn't o. to be   HART 163:2
  o. to have done   BOOK 59:13
our O. Father   BIBL 43:22
ours they are o.   PERR 262:9
ourselves love of o.   HAZL 164:4
  remedies oft in o. do lie   SHAK 289:9
out counted them all o.   HANR 161:3
  get o. and get under   CLAR 97:8
  get o. while we're young   SPRI 322:17
  include me o.   GOLD 154:1
  Mordre wol o.   CHAU 91:27
  O., damned spot   SHAK 301:21
  o.-herods Herod   SHAK 293:5
  o. of the body   BIBL 51:9
  O. of the deep   BOOK 64:29
  preserve thy going o.   BOOK 64:22
outcasts o. always mourn   WILD 359:11
outdated o. methods   WILS 361:4
outdoor system of o. relief   BRIG 68:19
outgrabe mome raths o.   CARR 86:23
outlawed liar should be o.   HALI 160:1
  o. or exiled   MAGN 225:5
outlive o. this powerful rhyme   SHAK 310:9
outlives o. this day   SHAK 295:27
outside just going o.   OATE 252:15
  o. of the text   DERR 113:12
  o. pissing in   JOHN 186:11
outsoared hath o. the shadow   SHEL 313:18
outstretched o. beneath the tree   BLAK 58:1
outvoted they o. me   LEE 211:15
outward man looketh on the o.   BIBL 36:28
  O. and the Inward   KORA 205:24
  o. and visible sign   BOOK 61:20
over ain't o. till it's over   BERR 32:15
  it is all o.   NORT 252:2
  My war is o.   MCGU 223:6
  O. hill, over dale   SHAK 303:14
  oversexed, and o. here   TRIN 341:19
  O. the hills   GAY 147:1
  O. there   COHA 99:9
  They think it's all o.   WOLS 363:14
overcome never o. them   JUNG 193:17
overcomes Who o. By force   MILT 237:29
overlook knowing what to o.   JAME 183:7
overpaid grossly o.   HERB 167:6
  O., overfed, oversexed   TRIN 341:19
overrule threaten to o. him   PAXM 260:16
oversexed o., and over here   TRIN 341:19
ovo Ab o.   HORA 175:23
owe o. God a death   SHAK 295:6
owed so much o. by so many to so few   CHUR 95:11
owest o. God a death   SHAK 294:25
oweth woman o. to her husband   SHAK 307:15
owl fat greedy o.   RICH 276:8
  He respects O.   MILN 235:11
  mousing o.   SHAK 300:28
  O. and the Pussy-Cat   LEAR 210:15
  o., for all his feathers   KEAT 195:11
  o. of Minerva   HEGE 165:4
  o. that shrieked   SHAK 300:14
owls Two O. and a Hen   LEAR 210:9
own but mine o.   SHAK 290:26
  his o. received him not   BIBL 48:18
  money and a room of her o.   WOOL 363:21
  my words are my o.   CHAR 91:2
  only to those who o. one   LIEB 214:9
  To each his o.   ANON 12:21
ownership common o.   ANON 11:13
ox brother to the o.   MARK 228:1
  not covet his o.   BIBL 35:28
  stalled o.   BIBL 38:27

oxen breath of the o.   HAGG 159:2
  Who drives fat o.   JOHN 190:18
Oxenford Clerk there was of O.   CHAU 91:17
Oxford clever men at O.   GRAH 155:6
oxlips o. and the nodding violet   SHAK 303:21
oxygen o. of publicity   THAT 336:21
oyster first eat an o.   SWIF 328:17
  my o. knife   HURS 178:22
  world's mine o.   SHAK 303:5
oysters Poverty and o.   DICK 115:21
Ozymandias My name is O.   SHEL 314:10

P

pace dance is a measured p.   BACO 22:4
  nostra p.   DANT 109:15
  requiescant in p.   MISS 241:6
Pacific stared at the P.   KEAT 196:28
pacifist quietly p. peaceful   WALK 349:9
pacify p. Ireland   GLAD 151:13
pack p. up your troubles   ANON 11:19
  Pay, p., and follow   BURT 77:28
  running with the p.   BUTL 79:6
  whole p. of you   SHAK 309:12
packaging brilliant p.   SMIT 318:9
paddle song my p. sings   JOHN 186:13
paddocks Cold as p.   HERR 167:29
padlock p.—on her mind   PRIO 270:23
pagan P. suckled in a creed outworn   WORD 366:17
page single p. of our life   SAND 285:2
  pageant all part of life's rich p. MARS 229:2
paid attention must be p.   MILL 234:23
  p. for this microphone   REAG 274:4
  we ha' p. in full   KIPL 202:26
  well p. that is well satisfied   SHAK 302:35
pain After great p.   DICK 115:25
  beneath the aromatic p.   WINC 361:19
  born in other's p.   THOM 338:13
  cost Ceres all that p.   MILT 238:21
  Eternal P.   ARNO 16:18
  general drama of p.   HARD 161:17
  intoxication with p.   BRON 69:8
  Joy always came after p.   APOL 14:8
  never inflicts p.   NEWM 250:1
  no greater p.   DANT 109:12
  No p., no palm   PENN 261:11
  Our Lady of P.   SWIN 329:10
  p. of a new idea   BAGE 24:12
  p. shall not be inflicted   SPEN 321:7
  p. to the bear   MACA 221:15
  physics p.   SHAK 300:22
  pleasure after p.   DRYD 121:25
  sure she felt no p.   BROW 72:25
  tender for another's p.   GRAY 156:17
  with no p.   KEAT 196:21
  With some p. is fraught   SHEL 314:28
pains Marriage has many p.   JOHN 187:19
  no gains without p.   STEV 325:2
  p. a man when 'tis kept close   SUCK 327:7
  p. of hell   BOOK 64:16
paint can't pick it up, p. it   ANON 8:19
  flinging a pot of p.   RUSK 282:11
  p. my own reality   KAHL 194:17
  p. objects as I think them   PICA 263:8
  p. the lily   SHAK 297:20
  p. too much direct from nature   GAUG 146:16
  price of the p.   VAN 345:11
  throws aside his p.-pots   HORA 174:15
painted fears a p. devil   SHAK 300:18
  idle as a p. ship   COLE 100:19
  Lift not the p. veil   SHEL 314:21

painted (*cont.*)
p. her face — BIBL 37:28
p. on the wall — BROW 72:17
painter great sculptor or p. — RUSK 282:12
I am a p. — SCHW 287:1
ranks far below the p. — LEON 213:4
scenes made me a p. — CONS 103:1
painting P. became everything — BROW 70:13
P. is silent poetry — SIMO 317:6
p. not made to decorate — PICA 263:5
poem is like a p. — HORA 174:20
pair Sleep on Blest p. — MILT 238:27
palace p. and a prison on each hand — BYRO 80:8
palaces pleasures and p. — PAYN 260:20
pale behold a p. horse — BIBL 53:7
p. fire she snatches — SHAK 308:5
P. grew thy cheek — BYRO 81:25
P. hands I loved — HOPE 173:12
P. prime-roses — SHAK 309:27
whiter shade of p. — REID 275:3
Why so p. and wan — SUCK 327:5
world grew p. — JOHN 187:26
palely Alone and p. loitering — KEAT 195:23
Palestine establishment in P. — BALF 25:5
Palladium P. of all the civil — JUNI 194:1
pallor p. of girls' brows — OWEN 256:10
palls everything p. — ANON 12:19
palm have an itching p. — SHAK 297:14
No pain, no p. — PENN 261:11
p. at the end — STEV 324:19
win the p. — MARV 229:15
palms p. before my feet — CHES 92:27
palpable very p. hit — SHAK 294:9
paltry aged man is but a p. thing — YEAT 368:27
Pan great god P. — BROW 71:16
pancreas adorable p. — KERR 199:12
pandemonium P., the high capital — MILT 238:2
Pandora open that P.'s Box — BEVI 33:17
panem *P. et circenses* — JUVE 194:11
pange *P., lingua* — FORT 139:20
  P., lingua — THOM 337:12
pangs free of any p. — CURT 108:18
panic p.'s in thy breastie — BURN 77:19
Panjandrum grand P. himself — FOOT 139:4
pansies p., that's for thoughts — SHAK 293:32
pantaloon lean and slippered p. — SHAK 290:14
panteth As the hart p. — BOOK 62:27
panther Black P. Party — NEWT 250:10
panting For ever p. — KEAT 196:10
pants As p. the hart — TATE 330:19
deck your lower limbs in p. — NASH 248:16
Panzer P.-man, panzer-man — PLAT 264:12
papa word P., besides — DICK 115:5
papacy p. is not other — HOBB 170:22
paper All reactionaries are p. tigers — MAO 227:13
at a piece of tissue p. — RUTH 283:20
no more personality than a p. cup — CHAN 90:11
only a p. moon — HARB 161:7
p. hats and wooden swords — USTI 344:22
scrap of p. — BETH 32:21
sheet of p. — SAUS 286:4
worth the p. it is written on — GOLD 154:3
papers what I read in the p. — ROGE 278:16
parachutes Minds are like p. — DEWA 114:4
parade p. of riches — SMIT 318:3
paradise cannot catch the bird of p. — KHRU 200:3
drunk the milk of P. — COLE 100:12
keys of P. — DE Q 113:7
P. by way of Kensal Green — CHES 93:5
P. of exiles — SHEL 313:28
p. within thee — MILT 239:13
paved p. — MITC 241:10
weave A p. — KEAT 195:18

wilderness is p. enow — FITZ 136:8
with me in p. — BIBL 48:10
paradises true p. are — PROU 271:11
parallelograms Princess of P. — BYRO 81:28
paranoid Only the p. survive — GROV 158:6
pardlike p. Spirit — SHEL 313:16
pardon Alas but cannot p. — AUDE 19:21
God will p. me — HEIN 165:10
kiss of the sun for p. — GURN 158:10
P. me boy — GORD 154:9
pardons P. him — AUDE 19:5
parens king is truly *p. patriae* — JAME 182:12
parent lose one p. — WILD 358:7
one child makes you a p. — FROS 143:6
parents begin by loving their p. — WILD 359:4
children inter their p. — HERO 167:28
girl needs good p. — TUCK 342:22
joys of p. — BACO 23:1
only illegitimate p. — GLAD 151:10
P. can plant magic — MACN 224:13
p. obey their children — EDWA 125:11
sacrifice and p.' tears — MILT 237:26
stranger to one of your p. — AUST 21:10
parfit verray, p. gentil knyght — CHAU 91:13
paries *p. cum proximus ardet* — HORA 175:3
Paris after they've seen P. — LEWI 214:4
Down and out in P. — ORWE 254:14
go to P. — APPL 14:10
Is P. burning — HITL 170:11
P. is a movable feast — HEMI 166:3
P. is well worth a mass — HENR 166:13
they go to P. — WILD 358:32
parish all the world as my p. — WESL 355:3
park come out to the ball p. — BERR 32:14
gentleman's p. — CONS 103:2
p., a policeman — CHAP 90:16
Poisoning pigeons in the p. — LEHR 211:20
parking put up a p. lot — MITC 241:10
parks p. are the lungs of London — PITT 264:7
parley-voo Hinky, dinky, p. — ANON 9:17
parliament enables P. to do things — SHAW 311:26
p. can do any thing — PEMB 261:9
P. of man — TENN 333:28
P. speaking through reporters — CARL 85:15
Scottish P. — EWIN 133:12
parliamentarian safe pleasure for a p. — CRIT 107:5
parliaments mother of P. — BRIG 69:1
parlour walk into my p. — HOWI 177:4
Parnell Poor P. — JOYC 192:24
parole p. of literary men — JOHN 190:8
paroles *n'emploient les p.* — VOLT 348:10
parrot This is a late p. — MONT 243:14
parson If P. lost his senses — HODG 171:4
P. left off conjuring — SELD 288:14
parsons merriment of p. — JOHN 190:6
part chosen that good p. — BIBL 47:18
let us kiss and p. — DRAY 121:10
p. to tear a cat in — SHAK 303:11
we know in p. — BIBL 50:24
What isn't p. of ourselves — HESS 168:10
parted Mine never shall be p. — MILT 239:8
When we two p. — BYRO 81:25
partiality neither anger nor p. — TACI 329:25
particles p. of light — BLAK 57:10
particular bright p. star — SHAK 289:8
Did nothing in p. — GILB 149:19
particulars in minute p. — BLAK 56:19
parting In every p. — ELIO 127:22
P. is all we know — DICK 116:2
p. is such sweet sorrow — SHAK 306:35
p. of the ways — BIBL 42:1
Speed the p. guest — POPE 268:6
partly Living and p. living — ELIO 129:5

partnership too dangerous for blind p.	STRO 327:2
parts above its p.	ARIS 15:11
dignified p.	BAGE 24:7
naming of p.	REED 274:12
P. of it are excellent	PUNC 271:23
p. of one stupendous whole	POPE 267:24
save all the p.	EHRL 125:14
sum of the p.	ANON 12:3
parturient *P. montes*	HORA 174:16
party master of the P.	HEAL 164:9
nasty p.	MAY 231:16
none was for a p.	MACA 221:23
Not a select p.	KEAT 197:19
office p. is not	WHIT 356:17
p.'s over	COMD 102:4
P.-spirit, which at best is	POPE 268:22
save the P. we love	GAIT 144:21
sooner every p. breaks up	AUST 20:22
spirit of p.	WASH 351:8
Stick to your p.	DISR 118:4
stupidest p.	MILL 234:5
three-p. politics	KENN 198:9
voted at my p.'s call	GILB 150:18
pasarán *No p.*	IBAR 180:3
pass Do not p. go	ANON 8:12
let him p. for a man	SHAK 302:10
let this cup p.	BIBL 46:13
look, and p. on	DANT 109:9
my words shall not p.	BIBL 46:1
O! let him p.	SHAK 298:29
p., and turn again	EMER 131:18
p. for forty-three	GILB 150:27
p. in the night	LONG 218:8
p. the ammunition	FORG 139:12
p. through this world	GREL 157:9
They shall not p.	ANON 12:14
They shall not p.	IBAR 180:3
passage North-west p.	STER 324:12
p. which is particularly fine	JOHN 189:4
passed p. by on the other side	BIBL 47:15
p. the time	BECK 28:15
passer *P. mortuus est*	CATU 89:5
passeront *Ils ne p. pas*	ANON 12:14
passes Everything p.	ANON 12:19
Men seldom make p.	PARK 258:13
p. the glory of the world	ANON 13:20
passeth p. all understanding	BIBL 51:27
passing did but see her p. by	ANON 11:7
p.-bells for these who die	OWEN 256:8
p. brave to be a king	MARL 228:17
p. the love of women	BIBL 36:35
passion all p. spent	MILT 239:27
Eternal P.	ARNO 16:18
image of p.	BART 27:5
In her first p.	BYRO 80:27
Man is a useless p.	SART 285:22
no good if a p. is in you	BLAK 56:12
No p. so effectually	BURK 75:12
p. cannot Music raise	DRYD 122:11
p. for hunting	DICK 115:15
P. makes the world go	ICE- 180:11
p. or interest	LOCK 216:16
p.'s slave	SHAK 293:8
prose and the p.	FORS 139:16
ruling p. conquers	POPE 266:27
Search then the Ruling P.	POPE 267:1
vows his p. is infinite	PARK 258:18
passions diminishes commonplace p.	LA R 209:9
inferno of his p.	JUNG 193:17
slave of the p.	HUME 178:12
Passover come to our P. feast	HAGG 158:15
it is the Lord's p.	BIBL 35:19
passport My p.'s green	HEAN 164:12

past cannot remember the p.	SANT 285:13
change the p.	AGAT 3:24
dead P. bury its dead	LONG 217:20
Ghost of Christmas P.	DICK 114:15
God cannot alter the p.	BUTL 79:10
last day of an era p.	YELT 369:20
looking forward to the p.	OSBO 255:13
neither repeat his p.	AUDE 19:23
nothing but the p.	KEYN 199:20
nothing more than the p.	BERG 31:11
p. as a watch	BOOK 63:22
P. is a bucket of ashes	SAND 285:8
p. is a foreign country	HART 163:3
p. is secure	WEBS 352:17
p. is the only dead thing	THOM 338:8
p. never dead	FAUL 134:11
P. our dancing days	SHAK 306:24
p., present and future	EINS 126:14
remembrance of things p.	SHAK 310:7
things long p.	SHAK 305:21
Things p. redress	SHAK 305:26
Time present and time p.	ELIO 127:29
under the bloody p.	AHER 4:1
upon the p. has power	DRYD 122:17
What's p. is prologue	SHAK 307:24
Who controls the p.	ORWE 256:3
pastime take his p. therein	BOOK 64:5
pasture feed me in a green p.	BOOK 62:14
pastures fresh woods, and p. new	MILT 237:4
In p. green	SCOT 288:2
pat Now might I do it p.	SHAK 293:16
patch poor potsherd, p.	HOPK 174:6
patches king of shreds and p.	SHAK 293:20
pâté de foie gras eating p.	SMIT 319:15
pater *P. noster*	MISS 240:24
paternalism lessons of p.	CLEV 98:6
path beaten p. to his door	EMER 132:22
Eightfold P.	PALI 258:3
in the straight p.	KORA 204:19
pathetic P. Fallacy	RUSK 282:14
That's what it is. P.	MILN 235:18
pathless pleasure in the p. woods	BYRO 80:14
too much like a p. wood	FROS 143:8
Truth is a p. land	KRIS 206:1
pathos P., piety, courage	FORS 139:17
paths all her p. are peace	BIBL 38:13
all her p. are Peace	SPRI 322:14
p. of glory	GRAY 156:9
So many p.	WILC 358:1
patience abuse our p.	CICE 96:19
aptitude for p.	BUFF 73:20
burning p.	RIMB 277:5
my p. is now at an end	HITL 170:10
p., and shuffle the cards	CERV 89:21
p. of Job	BIBL 52:23
p. on a monument	SHAK 308:36
p. will achieve	BURK 75:26
patient fury of a p. man	DRYD 121:23
kill the p.	BACO 22:25
not so p.	SHAK 294:34
P. continuance	BIBL 49:38
P. endurance attains all	TERE 335:21
p. etherized upon a table	ELIO 128:28
patines p. of bright gold	SHAK 303:3
patria Died some, pro p.	POUN 269:23
pro p. mori	HORA 175:14
patrie *enfants de la p.*	ROUG 281:6
patries *Europe des p.*	DE G 112:5
patriot honest p., in the full tide	JEFF 184:6
p. of the world	CANN 84:7
Such is the p.'s boast	GOLD 153:15
patriotism knock the p. out of the human race	
	SHAW 312:22

p. fetch a high price — WHAT 355:20
p. that were his eyes — SHAK 307:23
Pearse Tom P. — BALL 26:3
peasant rogue and p. slave — SHAK 292:20
peasants cricket with their p. — TREV 341:16
pebble smoother p. — NEWT 250:16
peccata p. *mundi* — MISS 240:25
peccavi p. *nimis cogitatione* — MISS 240:16
pectora *non mortalia p. cogis* — VIRG 347:6
peculiar Funny-p. or funny ha-ha — HAY 163:17
  p. people — BIBL 52:26
pecunia P. *non olet* — VESP 346:5
pedant apothegmatical P. — NASH 248:17
pede *nunc p. libero* — HORA 175:9
pedestrians two classes of p. — DEWA 114:5
pedigree languages are the p. — JOHN 187:30
peel p. me a grape — WEST 355:7
peepers where you get them p. — MERC 233:4
peeping sun Came p. in at morn — HOOD 172:23
peer hath not left his p. — MILT 236:28
peerage should study the P. — WILD 359:5
  When I want a p. — NORT 252:4
peers House of P. — GILB 149:19
  judgement of his p. — MAGN 225:5
peignoir Complacencies of the p. — STEV 324:23
peine *joie venait toujours après la p.* — APOL 14:8
pelican bird is the p. — MERR 233:14
Pelion P. *imposuisse Olympo* — HORA 175:15
  pile Ossa on P. — VIRG 348:2
pen Before my p. has gleaned — KEAT 197:6
  Biting my truant p. — SIDN 316:12
  mightier than the p. — HOGB 171:12
  My tongue is the p. — BOOK 63:1
  nose was as sharp as a p. — SHAK 295:15
  p. has been in their hands — AUST 21:4
  p. in his hand — JOHN 190:5
  p. is worse than the sword — BURT 78:5
  p. mightier than the sword — BULW 74:2
  scratching of a p. — LOVE 219:12
  squat p. rests — HEAN 164:11
pence Take care of the p. — LOWN 220:6
pencil coloured p. long enough — CHES 93:18
pencils sadness of p. — ROET 278:10
pennies p. from heaven — BURK 76:11
penny Not a p. off the pay — COOK 103:10
  p. plain and twopence coloured — STEV 325:15
pens Let other p. dwell — AUST 20:25
pension p. list of the republic — CLEV 98:5
pensive Come, p. nun — MILT 236:12
people All p. that on earth do dwell — KETH 199:15
  as if p. mattered — SCHU 286:16
  as many opinions as p. — TERE 335:15
  Before we were her p. — FROS 143:16
  bludgeoning of the p. — WILD 359:13
  by the p. — PAGE 256:20
  die for the p. — BIBL 49:1
  dissolve the p. — BREC 68:9
  fiery, impulsive p. — HOUS 176:18
  fool all the p. — LINC 215:8
  good of the p. — CICE 96:16
  Let my p. go — ANON 11:20
  Let my p. go — BIBL 35:17
  look after our p. — SCOT 287:6
  made for the p. — WEBS 352:18
  more than half the p. are right — WHIT 356:4
  Most p. ignore most poetry — MITC 241:9
  no petty p. — YEAT 369:17
  opium of the p. — MARX 230:5
  p. are the masters — BLAI 55:20
  p. are the masters — BURK 76:6
  p. arose as one — BIBL 36:20
  p. as base as itself — PULI 271:16
  P. die, but books never die — ROOS 279:17

p. don't do such things — IBSE 180:8
p. imagine a vain thing — BOOK 62:7
p. is grass — BIBL 41:1
p. made the Constitution — MARS 229:4
P.'s Princess — BLAI 55:21
p. that walked in darkness — BIBL 40:13
p. who got there first — USTI 344:21
People who need p. — MERR 233:13
save the p. — ELLI 131:12
support of the p. — CLEV 98:6
suppose the p. good — ROBE 277:11
thy p. shall be my people — BIBL 36:21
understanded of the p. — BOOK 65:13
voice of the p. — ALCU 4:7
What is the city but the p. — SHAK 291:2
peopled conquered and p. — SEEL 288:10
pepper Sergeant P. — TYNA 344:5
percentage reasonable p. — BECK 28:12
perception Agent of all human P. — COLE 101:1
  doors of p. — BLAK 57:7
  no p., appellation — MAHA 225:7
perdition P. catch my soul — SHAK 304:30
perennius *Exegi monumentum aere p.* — HORA 175:17
perestroika restructuring [p.] — GORB 154:7
perfect Be ye therefore p. — BIBL 43:20
  end of a p. day — BOND 59:5
  ever more p. eyes — TEIL 331:10
  If thou wilt be p. — BIBL 45:18
  life may p. be — JONS 192:3
  Nothing is p. — STEP 324:4
  One p. rose — PARK 258:14
  p. use of an imperfect medium — WILD 358:25
  p. woman; nobly planned — WORD 366:3
  service is p. freedom — BOOK 60:2
perfected p. your religion — KORA 205:11
  woman is p. — PLAT 264:14
perfection Dead p., no more — TENN 334:3
  P. is the child — HALL 160:6
  P. of the life — YEAT 367:15
  Pictures of p. — AUST 21:15
  pursuit of p. — ARNO 17:2
  realise our p. — WILD 358:16
  Trifles make p. — MICH 233:19
  very pink of p. — GOLD 153:23
perfectly P. pure and good — BROW 72:24
  small, but p. formed — COOP 103:17
perfide *ah, la p. Angleterre* — BOSS 66:3
perfidious p. Albion — XIMÉ 367:8
  p. friends — MEDI 232:2
perform Almighty's orders to p. — ADDI 2:19
  p. without thinking — WHIT 356:15
  zeal will p. this — BIBL 40:15
performance so many years outlive p. — SHAK 295:2
  takes away the p. — SHAK 300:21
performing aroma of p. seals — HART 162:20
perfume curious p. — AUBR 18:11
perfumes No p. — BRUM 73:11
  p. of Arabia — SHAK 301:24
perhaps grand P. — BROW 71:22
  seek a great p. — RABE 272:14
peril p. in the fight — CORN 104:4
  those in p. on the sea — WHIT 356:19
perils defend us from all p. — BOOK 60:8
perish if I p., I perish — BIBL 37:31
  Let the day p. — BIBL 37:36
  money p. with thee — BIBL 49:22
  people p. — BIBL 39:3
  P. the thought — CIBB 96:13
  p. together as fools — KING 200:18
  p. with the sword — BIBL 46:16
  should not p. — BIBL 48:27
perished p., each alone — COWP 105:15
perjured p. Clarence — SHAK 306:11

permitted p. to make all the ballads — FLET 138:10
perpendicular p. expression of horizontal — SHAW 313:5
perpetua *lux p.* — MISS 241:4
perpetual p. light — MISS 241:4
  p. night — JONS 191:17
persecuted I p. the church of God — BIBL 50:27
  merely because he is p. — GOUL 154:14
persecutest Saul, why p. thou me — BIBL 49:23
persecution P. is not an original feature — PAIN 257:16
Persepolis through P. — MARL 228:17
perseverance P., dear my lord — SHAK 308:12
  p. in a good cause — STER 324:10
Persians Medes and P. — BIBL 42:7
  Truth-loving P. — GRAV 155:17
persistence take the place of p. — COOL 103:16
person most superior p. — ANON 9:21
  no more than a p. — AUDE 18:20
  p. on business from Porlock — COLE 100:6
personal No p. consideration — GRAN 155:14
  P. isn't the same — PRAT 270:18
  warm p. gesture — GALB 145:3
personalities meeting of two p. — JUNG 193:20
personality From 35 to 55, good p. — TUCK 342:22
  no more p. than a paper cup — CHAN 90:11
persons no respecter of p. — BIBL 49:26
  things, not in p. — CURI 108:15
perspective light, shade, and p. — CONS 103:3
perspiration ninety-nine per cent p. — EDIS 125:5
persuaders hidden p. — PACK 256:18
persuadest Almost thou p. me — BIBL 49:37
persuading By p. others — JUNI 194:2
persuasive p. argument — FRAM 141:5
perturbed rest, p. spirit — SHAK 292:7
Peru China to P. — JOHN 187:24
perversions of all the sexual p. — HUXL 179:12
pervert loophole through which the p. — BRON 69:8
pessimism p. is a luxury — MEIR 232:4
pessimist know what a p. is — SHAW 313:1
  p. fears this is true — CABE 82:1
  p. waiting for rain — COHE 99:11
pestilence breeds p. — BLAK 56:25
  p. and war — MILT 238:11
  p. that walketh in darkness — BOOK 63:25
  plague and p. — NASH 248:19
petal dropping a rose p. — MARQ 228:23
  Now sleeps the crimson p. — TENN 334:21
petar Hoist with his own p. — SHAK 293:23
Peter government which robs P. — SHAW 311:19
  Shock-headed P. — HOFF 171:10
  Thou art P. — BIBL 45:9
  Where P. is — AMBR 5:22
petticoat feet beneath her p. — SUCK 327:6
petticoats hyena in p. — WALP 350:4
petty no p. people — YEAT 369:17
phagocytes Stimulate the p. — SHAW 311:17
phantom p. of delight — WORD 366:1
Pharisee face of the P. — BRON 69:9
Pharisees drowns in the P.' hypocrisy — PAST 260:2
  scribes and P., hypocrites — BIBL 45:29
phenomena p. of the universe — HUXL 179:18
phenomenon infant p. — DICK 115:11
Philadelphia living in P. — FIEL 135:22
Philip from P. drunk — ANON 7:11
Philistines daughters of the P. — BIBL 36:33
  P. proper — ARNO 17:3
philologists P., who chase — COWP 105:23
philosopher in my time to be a p. — EDWA 125:13
  p.'s treatment — WITT 362:8
  some p. has said it — CICE 96:15
philosophers p. and scholars — PASC 259:24
philosophical European p. tradition — WHIT 356:16
  poetry is something more p. — ARIS 15:17
philosophy divine p. — MILT 236:7

dreamt of in your p. — SHAK 292:5
  false p. — MILT 238:9
  History is p. — DION 117:1
  mere touch of cold p. — KEAT 196:2
  p. calls all in doubt — DONN 118:18
  p. inclineth man's mind — BACO 22:12
  P. is a battle — WITT 362:7
  p. paints its grey — HEGE 165:4
  p. quenches them — VOLT 348:13
  P. will clip — KEAT 196:3
  superstition to enslave a p. — INGE 180:14
  sweet milk, p. — SHAK 307:3
Phlebas P. the Phoenician — ELIO 129:30
Phoenician Phlebas the P. — ELIO 129:30
phone answer the p. — THUR 340:6
  never even made a p. call — CHOM 94:8
photograph p. is a secret — ARBU 14:13
photographer be a good p. — BAIL 24:13
photography mission of p. — STEI 323:13
  p. is the simultaneous — CART 88:8
  P. is truth — GODA 152:1
phrase ancient Saxon p. — LONG 217:13
phrases Taffeta p. — SHAK 299:2
phylogeny recapitulates p. — HAEC 158:14
physic Take p., pomp — SHAK 298:6
  Throw p. to the dogs — SHAK 301:29
physical p. illustration — MAXW 231:15
physician died last night of my p. — PRIO 271:1
  Honour a p. — BIBL 42:26
  need not a p. — BIBL 44:19
  p. can bury his mistakes — WRIG 366:27
  P., heal thyself — BIBL 47:8
  swear by Apollo the p. — HIPP 169:17
physicians P. of the Utmost Fame — BELL 29:18
physicists p. have known sin — OPPE 253:18
physics p. or stamp collecting — RUTH 283:18
  p. pain — SHAK 300:22
pianist shoot the p. — ANON 10:9
pianists no better than many p. — SCHN 286:14
Piccadilly Goodbye, P. — JUDG 193:12
  walk down P. — GILB 150:15
picket p.'s off duty forever — BEER 29:4
picking keep my hands from p. — BOOK 61:19
pickle weaned on a p. — ANON 11:12
Pickwickian P. sense — DICK 115:17
picnic Teddy Bears have their P. — BRAT 67:21
pictura *Ut p. poesis* — HORA 174:20
picture look Not on his p. — JONS 192:1
  One p. is worth ten thousand — BARN 26:15
  speaking p., with this end — SIDN 316:14
  your p. chases me — RACI 272:18
pictured my friends p. within — ELGA 127:2
pictures cutting all the p. out — BELL 29:16
  furnish the p. — HEAR 164:14
  P. are for entertainment — GOLD 154:5
  p. aren't good enough — CAPA 84:14
  p. do not sell — VAN 345:11
  P. of perfection — AUST 21:15
  without p. or conversations — CARR 86:3
pie Miss American P. — MCLE 223:15
  p. in the sky — HILL 169:4
  put into a p. — POTT 269:12
pieces P. of eight — STEV 325:18
  thirty p. of silver — BIBL 46:9
Pierian taste not the P. spring — POPE 267:6
piety nor all thy p. nor wit — FITZ 136:16
  p. more prone — ALEX 5:1
pig from p. to man — ORWE 254:11
  p. got up and slowly walked away — BURT 77:25
  p. satisfied — MILL 234:15
pigeons casual flocks of p. — STEV 324:24
  P. on the grass — STEI 323:15

Poisoning p. LEHR 211:20
pigs P. treat us as equals CHUR 96:9
whether p. have wings CARR 87:3
pike freedom for the p. TAWN 330:22
Pilate jesting P. BACO 23:16
P. saith unto him BIBL 49:8
Suffered under Pontius P. BOOK 59:23
water like P. GREE 156:23
pile p. Ossa on Pelion VIRG 348:2
P. the bodies high SAND 285:6
piled p. in large cities JEFF 184:3
pilgrim Onward goes the p. band BARI 26:14
To be a p. BUNY 74:17
pilgrimage I'll take my p. RALE 272:23
succeed me in my p. BUNY 74:18
pilgrimages longen folk to goon on p. CHAU 91:12
pilgrims land of the p. CUMM 108:5
Land of the p.' pride SMIT 319:1
We are the P., master FLEC 138:5
pill little yellow p. JAGG 182:4
pillar became a p. of salt BIBL 34:32
p. of a cloud BIBL 35:22
seemed A p. of state MILT 238:5
pillars hewn out her seven p. BIBL 38:17
pillow like the feather p. HAIG 159:4
upon the p.-hill STEV 325:28
pillows P. his chin MILT 237:9
pilot Dropping the p. TENN 331:13
See my p. face to face TENN 332:3
pilots P. of the purple twilight TENN 333:26
Pimpernel demmed, elusive P. ORCZ 254:3
pimples scratching of p. on the body WOOL 364:1
pineapple p. of politeness SHER 315:11
pink very p. of courtesy SHAK 306:36
very p. of perfection GOLD 153:23
pinprick p. of eternity AURE 20:17
pinstripe come in a p. suit FEIN 134:15
pint p. of plain O'BR 252:18
p.—that's very nearly GALT 145:13
pioneers P.! O pioneers WHIT 357:1
pipes open the p. BYRD 79:21
What p. and timbrels KEAT 196:6
piping For ever p. songs KEAT 196:9
Helpless, naked, p. loud BLAK 57:25
P. songs of pleasant glee BLAK 57:15
weak p. time SHAK 306:8
pips until the p. squeak GEDD 147:10
pirate To be a P. King GILB 150:22
piss pitcher of warm p. GARN 146:5
pissing inside the tent p. out JOHN 186:11
pistol I reach for my p. JOHS 191:6
p. in your pocket WEST 355:11
p.-shot in the middle STEN 324:2
pun is a p. LAMB 207:4
when his p. misses fire GOLD 153:28
pit digged a p. before me BOOK 63:11
He that diggeth a p. BIBL 39:22
Law is a bottomless p. ARBU 14:14
monster of the p. POPE 268:11
pitch He that toucheth p. BIBL 42:24
p. of grief HOPK 173:21
pitcher p. be broken at the fountain BIBL 39:28
pitchfork drive out nature with a p. HORA 174:26
thrown on her with a p. SWIF 328:16
use my wit as a p. LARK 209:1
pitiful God be p. BROW 71:15
pity by means of p. and fear ARIS 15:15
cherish p. BLAK 57:18
endure, then p. POPE 267:29
full of p. and concerned MAHÀ 225:8
P. a human face BLAK 57:17
p. beyond all telling YEAT 368:23
P., like a naked new-born SHAK 300:2

p. renneth soone CHAU 91:25
p. this busy monster CUMM 108:8
Poetry is in the p. OWEN 256:6
seas of p. lie AUDE 19:4
she did p. them SHAK 304:23
some touch of p. SHAK 306:9
yet the p. of it, Iago SHAK 305:8
place all other things give p. GAY 147:3
and the p. thereof BOOK 64:3
genius of the p. POPE 266:28
Get p. and wealth POPE 268:8
In p. of strife CAST 88:12
keep in the same p. CARR 86:26
know the p. ELIO 128:15
Lord is in this p. BIBL 35:3
no p. to go WHIT 356:18
p. in the sun BÚLO 73:22
p. in the sun WILH 359:25
p. within the meaning ANON 10:8
prepare a p. for you BIBL 49:4
right man in the right p. JEFF 184:21
rising to great p. BACO 22:29
spirit of the p. VIRG 347:15
till there be no p. BIBL 40:7
time and the p. BROW 72:19
Time, P. DRYD 122:20
places all p. were alike to him KIPL 203:13
longest distance between two p. WILL 360:12
P. where they sing BOOK 60:4
Proper words in proper p. SWIF 328:14
quietest p. HOUS 176:14
placidly Go p. amid the noise EHRM 126:1
plagiarism from one author, it's p. MIZN 241:20
plagiarize P.! Let no one else's work LEHR 211:19
plague instruments to p. us SHAK 298:24
p. and pestilence NASH 248:19
p. o' both your houses SHAK 306:38
p. the inventor SHAK 299:29
plain best p. set BACO 22:13
Books will speak p. BACO 22:17
darkling p. ARNO 16:13
make it p. upon tables BIBL 42:16
penny p. and twopence coloured STEV 325:15
pint of p. O'BR 252:18
p., blunt man SHAK 297:8
'p.' cooking cannot be entrusted MORP 245:4
P. living and high thinking WORD 365:12
p. meaning SHAK 302:27
pricking on the p. SPEN 321:24
truth for p. people WESL 354:25
plainness Manifest p. LAO 208:3
plains p. of windy Troy TENN 335:2
plaisir P. d'amour FLOR 138:16
plan by his p. of attack SASS 286:1
no p. of operations reaches MOLT 242:4
rest on its original p. BURK 75:3
plane only two emotions in a p. WELL 353:17
planet new p. swims into his ken KEAT 196:28
planetary p. influence SHAK 297:27
planets stars and all the p. TRUM 342:9
planned p. obsolescence STEV 324:14
planning p. is indispensable EISE 126:19
plans p. are useless EISE 126:19
plant p. of rapid growth WASH 351:11
Sensitive P. SHEL 314:18
time to p. BIBL 39:10
What is a weed? A p. EMER 132:15
planting p. my cabbages MONT 242:17
plants forced p. JOHN 190:4
He that p. trees FULL 144:17
talk to the p. CHAR 91:8
plasters p., pills, and ointment LOCK 217:1
plates p. appear to be moving PRES 270:20

platinum bullets made of p.   BELL 29:17
platitude echo of a p.   BIER 54:17
  p. is simply a truth repeated   BALD 25:2
platitudes orchestration of p.   WILD 359:23
Plato attachment à la P.   GILB 150:14
  P. is dear to me   ARIS 15:23
  P.'s retirement   MILT 239:18
  p. told him: he couldn't   CUMM 108:7
  series of footnotes to P.   WHIT 356:16
plaudits p. of the throng   LONG 217:17
plausible neat, p., and wrong   MENC 232:23
plausibly p. maintained   BURR 77:22
play children at p.   MONT 242:19
  Did that p. of mine send out   YEAT 368:18
  Games people p.   BERN 32:12
  holdeth children from p.   SIDN 316:15
  I could p. Ercles rarely   SHAK 303:11
  Kings would not p. at   COWP 105:30
  little victims p.   GRAY 156:16
  our p. is played out   THAC 336:9
  p.'s the thing   SHAK 292:22
  p. the game   NEWB 249:18
  p. things as they are   STEV 324:18
  p. with my cat   MONT 243:1
  very dull p.   CONG 102:8
  y is p.   EINS 126:10
playboy lost the only P.   SYNG 329:17
player as strikes the p.   FITZ 136:15
  p. on the other side   HUXL 179:18
  wrapped in a p.'s hide   GREE 157:2
players men and women merely p.   SHAK 290:11
playing won on the p. fields   WELL 354:8
plaything little p.-house   WALP 349:18
plea Though justice be thy p.   SHAK 302:31
  without one p.   ELLI 131:10
pleasance Youth is full of p.   SHAK 309:31
pleasant do not find anything p.   VOLT 348:6
  green and p. land   BLAK 57:8
  in p. places   BOOK 62:10
  Life would be very p.   SURT 328:1
  p. it is to have money   CLOU 98:15
  P. to know Mr Lear   LEAR 210:14
pleasantness ways are ways of p.   BIBL 38:13
please do what I p.   FRED 142:9
  Nothing can p. many   JOHN 187:13
  only Self to p.   BLAK 57:24
  To tax and to p.   BURK 75:7
pleased in whom I am well p.   BIBL 43:8
  p. not the million   SHAK 292:18
pleases every prospect p.   HEBE 164:18
pleasure doth ever add p.   BACO 23:17
  egg by p. laid   COWP 105:22
  greatest p. I know   LAMB 207:8
  harmless p.   JOHN 187:12
  heart with p. fills   WORD 364:18
  Love ceases to be a p.   BEHN 29:10
  pay a debt to p.   ROCH 278:3
  p. after pain   DRYD 121:25
  p. afterwards   THAC 336:5
  P. at the helm   GRAY 156:6
  P. in the pathless woods   BYRO 80:14
  p. is momentary   CHES 92:24
  P. never is at home   KEAT 195:19
  P.'s a sin   BYRO 80:23
  p. sure, In being mad   DRYD 122:14
  p. to the spectators   MACA 221:15
  read without p.   JOHN 191:3
  soul of p.   BEHN 29:11
  stately p.-dome decree   COLE 100:7
  type of a perfect p.   WILD 358:28
  Youth and P. meet   BYRO 80:5
pleasures all the p. prove   MARL 228:15
  celibacy has no p.   JOHN 187:19

hypocrite in his p.   JOHN 190:20
  p. and palaces   PAYN 260:20
  p. are like poppies   BURN 77:12
  purest of human p.   BACO 22:26
  some new p. prove   DONN 119:7
  tear our p.   MARV 229:23
  understand the p.   AUST 20:21
plebiscite justice by p.   ZOBE 370:12
pledge I will p. with mine   JONS 192:2
  p. allegiance   BELL 29:15
Pleiades influences of P.   BIBL 38:8
pleni P. sunt coeli   MISS 240:23
plenty here is God's p.   DRYD 122:22
pleut il p. sa ville   VERL 346:4
plot Gunpowder Treason and P.   ANON 10:10
  now the p. thickens   BUCK 73:18
  This blessèd p.   SHAK 305:23
plough boy that driveth the p.   TYND 344:7
  p. the fields   CAMP 83:6
  put his hand to the p.   BIBL 47:12
  wherefore p.   SHEL 314:20
ploughman p. and professor   JEFF 184:1
  p. homeward plods   GRAY 156:7
ploughshares swords into p.   BIBL 40:5
pluck p. it out   BIBL 45:14
  p. till time and times are done   YEAT 369:6
plumage pities the p.   PAIN 257:13
plumber choose to be a p.   EINS 126:13
plume blast-beruffled p.   HARD 161:22
plummet did ever p. sound   SHAK 307:33
plures Abiit ad p.   PETR 262:17
plus Il n'y a p. de Pyrénées   LOUI 219:2
  P. ça change   KARR 195:3
Plutonian Night's P. shore   POE 265:19
Pobble P. who has no toes   LEAR 210:18
pocket gun in your p.   WEST 355:11
  in Britain, in your p.   WILS 361:6
  in each other's p.   BIER 54:16
  not scruple to pick a p.   DENN 113:4
pockets in the p. of the people   GLAD 151:16
pocketses got in its p.   TOLK 340:20
poem being the author of that p.   WOLF 363:4
  essentially the greatest p.   WHIT 357:12
  p. is like a painting   HORA 174:20
  p. lovely as a tree   KILM 200:4
  P. of the Sea   RIMB 277:3
  p. should not mean but be   MACL 223:16
  write a p. after Auschwitz   ADOR 3:18
poems P. are made by fools like me   KILM 200:5
poesis Ut pictura p.   HORA 174:20
poet All a p. can do is warn   OWEN 256:7
  and the P.'s dream   WORD 364:12
  every fool is not a p.   POPE 266:15
  found no sacred p.   ELIO 127:13
  limbs of a p.   HORA 175:24
  lover, and the p.   SHAK 304:1
  never be a p.   DRYD 122:23
  No p. ever interpreted   GIRA 151:8
  p. ranks far below the painter   LEON 213:4
  p.'s eye, in a fine frenzy   SHAK 304:2
  p.'s hope: to be   AUDE 19:20
  p.'s mouth be shut   YEAT 368:22
  starved p.   LOCK 217:1
  was a true P.   BLAK 56:22
poetae Etiam disiecti membra p.   HORA 175:24
poetic constitutes p. faith   COLE 101:2
  nurse for a p. child   SCOT 287:14
  P. Justice   POPE 266:5
poetry best piece of p.   JONS 191:20
  campaign in p.   CUOM 108:14
  cradled into p. by wrong   SHEL 313:29
  dead art Of p.   POUN 269:21
  If p. comes not   KEAT 197:13

Ireland hurt you into p.	AUDE 19:1	p. will	LYNN 221:1
It is not p.	POPE 266:20	schemes of p. improvement	JOHN 188:21
Language is fossil p.	EMER 132:14	**politician** like a scurvy p.	SHAK 298:18
most p. ignores most people	MITC 241:9	lurks a p.	ARIS 15:9
p. begins to atrophy	POUN 270:4	makes the p. wise	POPE 268:21
p. in money	GRAV 156:1	p. is an arse upon	CUMM 108:6
p. in motion	KAUF 195:6	p. never believes what he says	DE G 112:7
P. is a subject as precise	FLAU 137:24	P.'s corpse	BELL 29:22
P. is at bottom	ARNO 17:6	p. to complain about	POWE 270:14
P. is a way	FROS 144:2	p. who steals	PLUN 265:9
p. is eloquent painting	SIMO 317:6	popular p.	ARIS 15:8
P. is in the pity	OWEN 256:6	statesman is a p.	TRUM 342:13
p. is more philosophical	ARIS 15:17	**politicians** Old p. chew	POPE 267:3
P. is the achievement	SAND 285:9	too serious to be left to p.	DE G 112:4
P. is the breath	WORD 366:20	whole race of p.	SWIF 328:10
P. is the record of the best	SHEL 315:5	**politics** continuation of p.	CLAU 97:12
P. is the spontaneous overflow	WORD 366:19	From p., it was an easy step	AUST 21:1
P. is the supreme fiction	STEV 324:17	In p., if you want anything	THAT 336:12
P. is what is lost	FROS 144:4	in p. the middle way	ADAM 2:5
p. makes nothing happen	AUDE 19:2	In p., what begins in fear	COLE 101:6
P. must be *as well written*	POUN 270:7	invisible hand in p.	FRIE 142:22
p. of earth	KEAT 196:29	Magnanimity in p.	BURK 75:11
p. of motion	GRAH 155:4	mule of p.	DISR 117:22
p., prophecy, and religion	RUSK 282:15	no true friends in p.	CLAR 97:2
P.'s a mere drug	FARQ 134:8	P. and the fate	CAMU 83:16
p. = the *best* words	COLE 101:5	P. are now nothing more	JOHN 189:11
quarrel with ourselves, p.	YEAT 369:15	P., as a practice	ADAM 1:18
saying it and that is p.	CAGE 82:10	P. in the middle	STEN 324:2
saying so In whining p.	DONN 119:18	P. is not the art	GALB 145:5
Sir, what is p.	JOHN 189:16	p. is present history	FREE 142:12
Writing a book of p.	MARQ 228:23	P. is the art of preventing	VALÉ 345:2
poets All p. are mad	BURT 78:4	P. is the Art of the Possible	BUTL 79:5
Irish p., learn your trade	YEAT 369:10	P. is the only profession	STEV 325:10
mature p. steal	ELIO 130:6	P. is war without bloodshed	MAO 227:11
P. are the unacknowledged	SHEL 315:6	p. of happiness	HUMP 178:14
Souls of p. dead	KEAT 196:4	p. of the left	JENK 185:2
We p. in our youth	WORD 365:21	P. supposed to be	REAG 274:3
point from p. to point	TENN 333:29	P. too serious a matter	DE G 112:4
p. a moral	JOHN 187:26	secret of p.	BISM 55:3
still p. of the turning world	ELIO 128:3	three-party p.	KENN 198:9
Up to a p., Lord Copper	WAUG 352:7	week is a long time in p.	WILS 361:5
poison administer a p. to anybody	HIPP 169:18	zeal in p.	JUNI 194:2
got as far as p.-gas	HARD 161:19	**politique** p. father	JAME 182:12
put p. in your coffee	CHUR 96:10	**Polka** see me dance the P.	GROS 158:2
strongest p. ever known	BLAK 56:11	**pollution** p. of democracy	WHIT 356:8
poisoning P. pigeons	LEHR 211:20	**Polly** Our P. is a sad slut	GAY 146:18
poisonous for its p. wine	KEAT 196:13	**polygamous** Man is p.	JAME 183:10
pole from pole to p.	COLE 100:25	**Pomeranian** P. grenadier	BISM 55:6
top of the greasy p.	DISR 118:6	**pomp** p. of yesterday	KIPL 202:20
polecat semi-house-trained p.	FOOT 139:3	Pride, p., and circumstance	SHAK 305:6
police citizen or the p.	AUDE 19:18	Take physic, p.	SHAK 298:6
friendship recognised by the p.	STEV 325:22	**Pompey** Knew you not P.	SHAK 296:17
p. can beat you	SHAW 312:21	**pompous** p. in the grave	BROW 71:9
p. were to blame	GRAN 155:7	**pomps** p. and vanity	BOOK 61:18
policeman p. and a pretty girl	CHAP 90:16	**pond** Old p., leap-splash	BASH 27:12
p.'s lot	GILB 150:24	**pondered** them in her heart	BIBL 47:5
terrorist and the p.	CONR 102:26	**ponies** Five and twenty p.	KIPL 202:24
policy foreign p.	COOK 103:12	**poodle** right hon. Gentleman's p.	LLOY 216:7
Honesty is the best p.	WHAT 355:19	**pool** Walk across my swimming p.	RICE 276:3
If the p. isn't hurting	MAJO 225:17	**pools** p. are filled with water	BOOK 63:19
My [foreign] p.	BEVI 33:16	Where the p. are bright	HOGG 171:13
national p.	BRIA 68:14	**poop** O p.-poop	GRAH 155:5
polite p. meaningless words	YEAT 368:2	**poor** Blessed are the p.	BIBL 43:13
politeness pineapple of p.	SHER 315:11	bring in hither the p.	BIBL 47:25
p. of kings	LOUI 219:5	give food to the p.	CAMA 82:21
political half your p. life	THAT 336:17	give to the p.	BIBL 45:18
highest p. end	ACTO 1:8	grind the faces of the p.	BIBL 40:6
points to a p. career	SHAW 311:27	help the many who are p.	KENN 198:16
p. animal	ARIS 15:19	how expensive it is to be p.	BALD 24:20
P. language . . . is designed	ORWE 255:5	Laws grind the p.	GOLD 153:17
p. lives end in failure	POWE 270:15	My countrymen Kiltartan's p.	YEAT 368:11
p. power of another	LOCK 216:19	no disgrace t'be p.	HUBB 177:10
p. speech and writing	ORWE 255:4	no peasant in my kingdom so p.	HENR 166:12

poor (cont.)

p. always ye have — BIBL 49:2
p. but she was honest — ANON 10:20
p. get children — KAHN 194:18
p. know that it is money — BREN 68:11
P. little rich girl — COWA 105:6
p. man at his gate — ALEX 4:15
p. man had nothing — BIBL 36:36
p. who die — SART 285:19
Resolve not to be p. — JOHN 190:10
RICH AND THE P. — DISR 117:29
rich on the p. — JEFF 183:20
undeserving p. — SHAW 312:29
your tired, your p. — LAZA 210:5
poorer for richer for p. — BOOK 61:27
poorest p. he that is in England — RAIN 272:20
p. man may in his cottage — PITT 264:3
pop P. goes the weasel — MAND 226:15
pope P.! How many divisions — STAL 322:24
to the P. afterwards — NEWM 250:3
poppies In Flanders fields the p. blow — MCCR 222:16
pleasures are like p. — BURN 77:12
poppy with a p. or a lily — GILB 150:15
populace clamours of the p. — ADAM 2:2
popular p. politician — ARIS 15:8
population p., when unchecked — MALT 226:12
populi Salus p. — CICE 96:16
Vox p. — ALCU 4:7
Porlock on business from P. — COLE 100:6
pornography p. is really about — SONT 320:13
P. the attempt to insult sex — LAWR 209:18
porpentine quills upon the fretful p. — SHAK 291:38
port In ev'ry p. a mistress — GAY 147:8
p., for men — JOHN 190:1
to which p. one is sailing — SENE 288:21
portal fitful tracing of a p. — STEV 324:21
Porter moon shone bright on Mrs P. — ELIO 129:26
portion p. of a good man's life — WORD 364:19
portmanteau like a p. — CARR 87:12
portrait Every time I paint a p. — SARG 285:17
p. of a blinking idiot — SHAK 302:19
p. of the artist — JOYC 192:22
position altering the p. of matter — RUSS 283:3
only p. for women — CARM 85:24
p. ridiculous — CHES 92:24
positive ac-cent-tchu-ate the p. — MERC 233:3
power of p. thinking — PEAL 260:21
possessed in order to be p. — BURK 75:2
much p. by death — ELIO 130:4
possessing too dear for my p. — SHAK 310:14
possession Man's best p. — EURI 133:8
p. for all time — THUC 339:25
possessions All my p. — ELIZ 130:22
least of p. — WHIT 356:6
possibilities improbable p. — ARIS 15:18
possibility deny the p. of anything — HUXL 180:1
possible all things p. — BACO 23:26
art of the p. — BISM 55:4
Art of the P. — BUTL 79:5
art of the p. — GALB 145:5
best of all p. worlds — BRAD 67:7
if a thing is p. — CALO 82:20
p. you may be mistaken — CROM 107:9
something is p. — CLAR 97:4
With God all things are p. — BIBL 45:20
possumus Non omnia p. omnes — VIRG 347:24
possunt p., quia posse videntur — VIRG 347:9
post driving briskly in a p.-chaise — JOHN 189:17
P. coitum — ANON 13:16
p. of honour — ADDI 3:2
posted p. presence of the watcher — JAME 182:21
posterity go down to p. — DISR 117:18
hope of p. — POWE 270:17

look forward to p. — BURK 75:15
P. do something for us — ADDI 3:10
Think of your p. — ADAM 2:12
trustees of P. — DISR 118:1
write for p. — ADE 3:12
posters P. of the sea and land — SHAK 299:11
postman p. always rings twice — CAIN 82:11
postscript but in her p. — STEE 323:10
most material in the p. — BACO 22:18
pot chicken in every p. — HOOV 173:5
chicken in his p. — HENR 166:12
death in the p. — BIBL 37:23
flinging a p. of paint — RUSK 282:11
under a p. — BIBL 39:15
who the p. — FITZ 137:1
potato bashful young p. — GILB 150:14
potent how p. cheap music is — COWA 105:9
Potomac All quiet along the P. — BEER 29:4
quiet along the P. — MCCL 222:11
potsherd poor p., patch — HOPK 174:6
pottage mess of p. — BIBL 34:34
potter hand then of the p. — FITZ 136:18
Who is the p., pray — FITZ 137:1
poultry lives of the p. — ELIO 127:10
pound p. here in Britain — WILS 361:6
pounds Give crowns and p. — HOUS 176:8
p. will take care — LOWN 220:6
poured p. into his clothes — WODE 362:23
poverty hunger and p. — LARK 208:13
Overcoming p. is not — MAND 226:19
p. and excess — PENN 261:12
P. and oysters — DICK 115:21
P. is a great enemy — JOHN 190:10
p.'s catching — BEHN 29:11
struggled with p. — BALD 24:20
worst of crimes is p. — SHAW 311:24
powder keep your p. dry — BLAC 55:12
when your p.'s runnin' low — NEWB 249:15
powdered Still to be p. — JONS 191:15
power because we had p. — BENÉ 30:16
corridors of p. — SNOW 319:20
defy P. — SHEL 314:16
desire of p. — HOBB 170:15
desires to have—P. — BOUL 66:10
friend in p. — ADAM 1:20
greater the p. — BURK 76:3
his p. and his love — GRAN 155:8
in office but not in p. — LAMO 207:12
intoxicated with p. — BURK 75:1
jaws of p. — ADAM 2:9
knowledge itself is p. — BACO 23:31
life and p. — FOX 140:16
literature of p. — DE Q 113:10
live without a common p. — HOBB 170:17
love of p. — HAZL 164:4
only have p. over people — SOLZ 320:6
O wad some P. — BURN 77:18
political p. of another — LOCK 216:19
p. can be rightfully exercised — MILL 234:7
p. grows out of the barrel of a gun — MAO 227:12
p. in trust — DRYD 121:19
p. is a trust — DISR 118:3
P. is not a means — ORWE 254:28
P. is the great aphrodisiac — KISS 204:2
p. of Jesus' Name — PERR 262:8
p. of suppress — NORT 252:3
p. of the written word — CONR 102:25
p. over men — WOLL 363:12
P. tends to corrupt — ACTO 1:9
p. to endanger — ADAM 2:3
p. to tax — MARS 229:3
p. Which erring men call chance — MILT 236:9
P. without responsibility — KIPL 203:25

shadow of some unseen P.	SHEL 313:27	woman's p.	JOHN 188:18
source of p.	MARS 229:6	precedency point of p.	JOHN 190:13
struggle of man against p.	KUND 206:6	precedent is a dangerous p.	CORN 104:9
take who have the p.	WORD 365:24	precept more efficacious than p.	JOHN 187:20
Unlimited p.	PITT 264:4	p. must be upon precept	BIBL 40:23
upon the past has p.	DRYD 122:17	precious Deserve the p. bane	MILT 237:31
What p. have you got	BENN 30:17	My P.	TOLK 341:2
powerful fear is that we are p.	WILL 360:17	so p. it must be rationed	LENI 212:12
powerless p. to be born	ARNO 16:24	This p. stone	SHAK 305:22
powers against p.	BIBL 51:21	**predicament** It is a p.	BENN 30:23
high contracting p.	BRIA 68:14	**preference** special p. for beetles	HALD 159:10
principalities, nor p.	BIBL 50:9	**pregnancy** avoid p. by a resort to mathematics	
principalities, or p.	BIBL 51:30		MENC 232:22
real separation of p.	DENN 113:3	**pregnant** If men could get p.	KENN 198:10
ultimate p. of the society	JEFF 184:17	**prejudice** P., n. A vagrant opinion	BIER 54:22
virtues, p.	MILT 238:32	p. runs in favour of two	DICK 115:9
we lay waste our p.	WORD 366:16	PRIDE AND P.	BURN 76:13
pox or of the p.	WILK 359:26	religious p.	HUXL 179:22
practices bloody principles and p.	FOX 141:2	**prejudices** deposit of p.	EINS 126:11
practise never to p. either	TWAI 343:11	it p. a man so	SMIT 319:14
praevalet Magna est veritas, et p.	BIBL 54:14	proprietor's p.	SWAF 328:4
praise Apostles: p. thee	BOOK 59:18	**preparation** no p. is thought necessary	STEV 325:10
as is p.	ASCH 17:14	**prepare** not to p. for life	PAST 260:1
Damn with faint p.	POPE 266:21	p. a place for you	BIBL 49:4
how to p.	AUDE 19:6	p. to shed them now	SHAK 297:5
is p. indeed	MORT 246:8	P. ye the way	BIBL 40:30
lack tongues to p.	SHAK 310:18	P. ye the way of the Lord	BIBL 43:5
named thee but to p.	HALL 160:9	**prepared** BE P.	BADE 24:5
p. at morning	POPE 267:15	favours only the p.	PAST 260:3
P. belongs to God	KORA 204:18	world not yet p.	DOYL 120:15
p. famous men	BIBL 42:27	**prerogative** p. of the harlot	KIPL 203:25
P. my soul	LYTE 221:4	**presbyter** New P. is but old Priest	MILT 237:11
P. the Lord	FORG 139:12	**presence** before his p. with a song	BOOK 64:2
P. the Lord, for he is kind	MILT 236:26	posted p. of the watcher	JAME 182:21
p. those works	MART 229:9	p. on the field	WELL 354:4
P. to the Holiest	NEWM 250:6	**present** Act in the living P.	LONG 217:20
P. to the Lord	WINK 362:1	All p. and correct	ANON 7:8
they only want p.	MAUG 231:9	know nothing but the p.	KEYN 199:20
unto thy Name give the p.	BOOK 64:14	No time like the p.	MANL 227:2
We p. thee, O God	BOOK 59:17	past, p. and future	EINS 126:14
praised God be p.	BROW 71:15	p. contains nothing more	BERG 31:11
p. his fleas	YEAT 369:8	p. in spirit	BIBL 50:16
praiser p. of past times	HORA 174:18	p. laughter	SHAK 308:28
praises with faint p.	WYCH 367:5	p., past, and future, sees	BLAK 57:21
pram p. in the hall	CONN 102:17	Time p. and time past	ELIO 127:29
pray came to scoff, remained to p.	GOLD 153:9	un-birthday p.	CARR 87:8
fervently do we p.	LINC 215:4	very p. help in trouble	BOOK 63:4
I p. for the country	HALE 159:12	What if this p.	DONN 119:1
Often when I p.	LEWI 213:21	who controls the p.	ORWE 254:23
P. for the dead	JONE 191:10	**presents** P., I often say, endear Absents	LAMB 206:19
p. you, master Lieutenant	MORE 244:19	**preservation** p. of their property	LOCK 216:21
Watch and p.	BIBL 46:15	**preserve** do not p. myself	ORTE 254:5
Work and p.	HILL 169:4	p. and enlarge freedom	LOCK 216:18
prayer Conservative Party at p.	ROYD 281:17	p. thy going out	BOOK 64:22
Father, hear the p.	WILL 360:19	**preserved** need not be p.	OMAR 253:11
house of p.	BIBL 41:15	Union: it must be p.	JACK 181:11
house of p.	BIBL 45:24	**preserver** Destroyer and p.	SHEL 314:4
lift up the hands in p.	HOPK 174:11	**presidency** cancer close to the P.	DEAN 111:12
on a wing and a p.	ADAM 2:18	heart-beat from the P.	STEV 325:5
perfect p.	LESS 213:10	vice-p. isn't worth a pitcher	GARN 146:5
p. reduces itself	TURG 343:2	**president** All the P. is	TRUM 342:10
things are wrought by p.	TENN 332:22	anybody could become P.	DARR 110:2
prayers among my p.	HORA 175:25	any boy may become P.	STEV 325:3
ask your p.	WILL 360:7	I'm P.	BUSH 78:13
Christopher Robin is saying his p.	MILN 235:16	no criticism of the p.	ROOS 280:8
hear our p.	BOOK 61:21	P. is a crook	NIXO 251:17
prayeth p. well, who loveth well	COLE 100:27	p. of Iraq	HUSS 179:4
praying now he is p.	SHAK 293:16	P. of the Immortals	HARD 161:18
past p. for	SHAK 294:20	P.'s spouse	BUSH 78:10
writing, or p.	THOM 337:10	rather be right than be P.	CLAY 97:5
preach p. the gospel	BIBL 46:30	used to be the next p.	GORE 154:10
preachers best of all p.	GUES 158:7	When the P. does it	NIXO 251:19
preaching foolishness of p.	BIBL 50:13	**press** be named P.-men	ARNO 16:10

p. station	ADDI 3:2	**Promethean** true P. fire	SHAK 298:32
sphere of p. life	MELB 232:9	**promise** P., large promise	JOHN 187:5
privilege p. I claim	AUST 21:5	p. made is a debt unpaid	SERV 288:24
prize lawful p.	GRAY 156:20	**promised** O Jesus, I have p.	BODE 58:13
prized local, but p. elsewhere	AUDE 19:20	P. from eternal years	CASW 88:15
prizes all must have p.	CARR 86:6	reach the p. land	CALL 82:15
glittering p.	SMIT 318:13	seen the p. land	KING 200:20
winners of the big p.	ORWE 254:26	**promises** have p. to keep	FROS 143:27
probability increasing p.	FISH 136:5	Vote for the man who p. least	BARU 27:9
p. is the very guide	BUTL 79:1	young man of p.	BALF 25:7
probable P. impossibilities	ARIS 15:18	**promising** first call p.	CONN 102:16
problem can't see the p.	CHES 93:16	**promontory** See one p.	BURT 78:6
Houston, we've had a p.	LOVE 219:11	Stretched like a p.	MILT 239:1
p. of the colour line	DU B 122:26	**promotion** p. cometh neither from	BOOK 63:16
p. that has no name	FRIE 142:20	You'll get no p.	HUGH 177:12
p. to be overcome	KEIL 197:26	**prone** position for women is p.	CARM 85:24
refused to work at any p.	EDIS 125:4	**pronounce** better than they p.	TWAI 343:16
three-pipe p.	DOYL 120:13	could not frame to p. it	BIBL 36:15
you're part of the p.	CLEA 97:17	**proofs** p. of holy writ	SHAK 305:4
problems Machines have less p.	WARH 350:23	**propaganda** on p.	CORN 104:10
P. worthy of attack	HEIN 165:5	**proper** noun, p. or improper	FULL 144:13
proceed just works do p.	BOOK 60:7	p. man	SHAK 303:13
procession torchlight p.	O'SU 255:21	P. words in proper places	SWIF 328:14
proclaims apparel oft p. the man	SHAK 291:29	**properly** never did anything p.	LEAR 210:13
procrastination incivility and p.	DE Q 113:9	**property** degrees and kinds of p.	MADI 225:1
p. is the art of	MARQ 228:20	makes it his p.	LOCK 216:17
P. is the thief	YOUN 369:27	preservation of their p.	LOCK 216:21
procreant Always the p. urge	WHIT 357:4	P. has its duties	DRUM 121:16
proctors prudes for p.	TENN 334:11	P. is theft	PROU 271:8
prodigies Africa and her p.	BROW 71:11	public p.	JEFF 184:11
producing consumes without p.	ORWE 254:8	right of p.	TAFT 330:5
production means of p.	ANON 11:13	Thieves respect p.	CHES 93:12
purpose of p.	SMIT 318:6	**prophecy** poetry, p., and religion	RUSK 282:15
productions literary p.	GIBB 148:15	p. is the most gratuitous	ELIO 127:15
p. of time	BLAK 56:27	**prophesy** sons and daughters shall p.	BIBL 42:12
profane p. and old wives' fables	BIBL 52:6	**prophet** arise among you a p.	BIBL 36:4
profanity speak English and p.	HOWE 177:1	p. is not without honour	BIBL 45:3
profession debtor to his p.	BACO 22:8	**prophetic** O my p. soul	SHAK 292:1
in the course of my p.	HIPP 169:20	p. greeting	SHAK 299:14
second oldest p.	REAG 274:3	**prophets** Beware of false p.	BIBL 44:11
professions p. are conspiracies	SHAW 311:18	fellowship of the P.	BOOK 59:18
professor ploughman and p.	JEFF 184:1	Is Saul also among the p.	BIBL 36:25
profit no p. but the name	SHAK 293:26	law and the p.	BIBL 44:8
p. and loss	ELIO 129:30	**proportion** strangeness in the p.	BACO 22:14
To whose p.	CICE 96:24	**proposes** man p.	THOM 337:9
what shall it p. a man	BIBL 46:27	**proposition** accept the p.	AYER 21:19
profits best of all monopoly p.	HICK 168:18	meaning of a p.	SCHL 286:12
little p. that an idle king	TENN 334:31	**proprietor** p.'s prejudices	SWAF 328:4
nothing p. more	MILT 239:3	**prose** as well written as p.	POUN 270:7
profundis De p. clamavi	BIBL 54:3	but p. run mad	POPE 266:20
progress Congress makes no p.	LIGN 214:11	Good p. like a window-pane	ORWE 254:12
no summer p.	ANDR 6:18	govern in p.	CUOM 108:14
principle of all social p.	FOUR 140:11	in p. or rhyme	MILT 237:16
p. depends on unreasonable man	SHAW 312:15	language of p.	WORD 366:18
p. if a cannibal uses	LEC 211:6	p. and the passion	FORS 139:16
P. is a comfortable disease	CUMM 108:8	P. = words in their best order	COLE 101:5
p. is based upon	BUTL 79:14	shut me up in p.	DICK 116:6
'p.' is ethical	RUSS 283:13	speaking p. without knowing it	MOLI 242:2
P. is not an accident	SPEN 321:11	**Proserpine** P. gathering flowers	MILT 238:21
P., man's distinctive mark	BROW 71:1	**prospect** every p. pleases	HEBE 164:18
Social P. began	KIPL 202:7	noblest p.	JOHN 188:13
Time's thievish p.	SHAK 310:13	**prosper** I grow, I p.	SHAK 297:26
What we call 'p.'	ELLI 131:14	sinners' ways p.	HOPK 174:7
progression Nothing in p. can rest	BURK 75:3	Treason doth never p.	HARI 162:13
progressive in a p. country	DISR 117:10	**prosperity** jest's p.	SHAK 299:3
p. societies	MAIN 225:15	man to han ben in p.	CHAU 92:3
prohibition enacting P.	HOOV 173:3	man who can stand p.	CARL 85:17
proie à sa p. attachée	RACI 272:17	P. doth best	BACO 22:10
projects fitter for new p.	BACO 23:23	**prostitute** doormat or a p.	WEST 355:14
proletariat dictatorship of the p.	MARX 230:9	**prostitutes** small nations like p.	KUBR 206:4
prologue very witty p.	CONG 102:8	**protect** p. a working-girl	SMIT 318:12
What's past is p.	SHAK 307:24	p. the writer	ACHE 1:7
prologues happy p.	SHAK 299:16	two solitudes p.	RILK 277:1

protection calls mutely for p.   GREE 156:27
  mercy and p.   BOOK 62:3
protest lady doth p. too much   SHAK 293:9
Protestant Hitler attacked the P. church   NIEM 251:3
  I am the P. whore   GWYN 158:12
  P. counterpoint   BEEC 29:1
  p. ethic   WEBE 352:13
  P. Province of Ulster   CARS 87:24
  P. Religion   CARL 85:8
Protestants religion of P.   CHIL 94:1
Proteus sight of P. rising   WORD 366:17
protoplasmal p. primordial globule   GILB 149:22
protracted p. woe   JOHN 187:27
proud all the p. and mighty have   DYER 124:1
  Death be not p.   DONN 118:22
  make death p.   SHAK 289:23
  p. in arms   MILT 236:3
  p. me no prouds   SHAK 307:7
  p. of the fact   RUSS 282:22
  scattered the p.   BIBL 46:33
  too p. to fight   WILS 361:11
prove P. all things   BIBL 52:3
  p. anything by figures   CARL 85:2
  p. our chance   DRAY 121:13
proverbs Solomon wrote the P.   NAYL 248:21
providence assert eternal p.   MILT 237:17
  Behind a frowning p.   COWP 105:19
  P. had sent a few men   RUMB 281:18
  P. their guide   MILT 239:14
  way that P. dictates   HITL 170:8
province all knowledge to be my p.   BACO 23:30
  p. they have desolated   GLAD 151:14
provincial level of p. existence   ELIO 127:19
proving pleasure in p. their falseness   DARW 110:4
provocation as in the p.   BOOK 63:27
provoke fathers, p. not   BIBL 51:19
provoker Drink, sir, is a great p.   SHAK 300:21
provokes No one p. me   ANON 13:12
proximus paries cum p. ardet   HORA 175:3
prudence P. is a rich, ugly   BLAK 56:24
  P. is the other woman   ANON 10:11
prudent every p. act   BURK 75:9
prudes p. for proctors   TENN 334:11
prunes p. and prism   DICK 115:5
pruninghooks spears into p.   BIBL 40:5
Prussia national industry of P.   MIRA 240:13
psalmist sweet p. of Israel   BIBL 37:3
psalms David wrote the P.   NAYL 248:21
psychiatrist man who goes to a p.   GOLD 154:4
psychological P. flaws   ANON 10:12
public as if I was a p. meeting   VICT 346:9
  assumes a p. trust   JEFF 184:11
  complainers for the p.   BURK 75:5
  Desolation in immaculate p. places   ROET 278:10
  English p. school   WAUG 352:6
  excites the p. odium   CLAY 97:14
  glorified p. relations man   TRUM 342:10
  I and the p. know   AUDE 19:16
  one to mislead the p.   ASQU 18:1
  precedence over p. relations   FEYN 135:4
  Private faces in p. places   AUDE 19:12
  p. be damned   VAND 345:7
  respect p. opinion   RUSS 282:25
  sound Of p. scorn   MILT 239:10
  tell the p. which way   SULZ 327:13
  wider p. life   ELIO 127:9
publicans p. and sinners   BIBL 44:18
publicity bad p.   BEHA 29:8
  eternal p.   BENN 31:2
  oxygen of p.   THAT 336:21
publish P. and be damned   WELL 354:3
  p. it not   BIBL 36:33
  p., right or wrong   BYRO 81:11

publisher Barabbas was a p.   CAMP 83:13
  makes everybody a p.   MCLU 224:2
publishers numerous p.   ADE 3:12
  p. are not women   ROBI 277:15
publishing p. faster than you think   PAUL 260:15
puck p. is going to be   GRET 157:12
pudding chieftain o' the p.-race   BURN 77:17
pull P. down thy VANITY   POUN 270:3
pulls p. a lady through   MARQ 228:22
pulpit such a bully p.   ROOS 280:7
pulsanda P. tellus   HORA 175:9
pulse My P., like a soft drum   KING 200:11
  p. of the machine   WORD 366:2
pumpkins early p. blow   LEAR 210:10
pun make so vile a p.   DENN 113:4
  p. is a pistol   LAMB 207:4
punctuality P. is the politeness   LOUI 219:5
punish God p. England   FUNK 144:19
punishing p. anyone who comes between   SMIT 319:10
punishment cruel and unusual p.   CONS 103:9
  less horror than the p.   GIBB 148:16
  p. fit the crime   GILB 150:6
  p. is mischief   BENT 31:7
  p. is not for revenge   FRY 144:8
  suffer first p.   CRAN 106:10
punishments charged with p.   HENL 166:9
  sanguinary p.   PAIN 257:14
pupils kills all its p.   BERL 32:9
puppets shut up the box and the p.   THAC 336:9
purchasing not worth p.   REED 274:15
pure as p. as snow   SHAK 292:29
  Blessed are the p. in heart   KEBL 197:22
  Live p., speak true   TENN 332:12
  my heart is p.   TENN 334:27
  Perfectly p. and good   BROW 72:24
  p. as the driven slush   BANK 26:8
  p. as the lily   LAUD 209:14
  truth is rarely p.   WILD 358:4
  Unto the p.   BIBL 52:12
  whatsoever things are p.   BIBL 51:28
purgation p. of such emotions   ARIS 15:15
purify p. the dialect of the tribe   ELIO 128:14
puritan P. hated bear-baiting   MACA 221:15
puritanism P. The haunting fear   MENC 232:19
purple colour p.   WALK 349:10
  deep p. falls   PARI 258:9
  in p. and gold   BYRO 80:18
  in the p. of Emperors   KIPL 203:21
  I shall wear p.   JOSE 192:15
  never saw a P. Cow   BURG 74:22
  p. patch or two   HORA 174:12
purpose any p. perverts art   CONS 103:4
  fits thy p.   AURE 20:15
  Infirm of p.   SHAK 300:18
  My p. is, indeed   SHAK 308:31
  politics of p.   HUMP 178:14
  p. of human existence   JUNG 193:18
  time to every p.   BIBL 39:10
  working his p. out   AING 4:2
purpureus P. Adsuitur pannus   HORA 174:12
purse consumption of the p.   SHAK 295:1
  empty p.   BRET 68:13
  steals my p.   SHAK 304:31
pursueth flee when no man p.   BIBL 39:1
pursuing Faint, yet p.   BIBL 36:14
  still p.   LONG 217:22
pursuit common p.   LEAV 211:3
  p. of happiness   ANON 11:14
  p. of happiness   JEFF 183:18
  p. of perfection   ARNO 17:2
  p. of the uneatable   WILD 359:1
  What mad p.   KEAT 196:6
purus scelerisque p.   HORA 175:8

pushed and he p. — LOGU 217:4
pussy Owl and the P-Cat — LEAR 210:15
put P. me to what you will — METH 233:16
p. not your trust — BOOK 65:5
P. out the light — SHAK 305:12
up with which I will not p. — CHUR 95:21
puzzles Nothing p. me more — LAMB 207:6
pyramid bottom of the economic p. — ROOS 279:6
pyramids not like children but like p. — FLAU 138:1
summit of these p. — NAPO 247:21
Pyramus P. and Thisby — SHAK 303:10
Pyrenees P. are no more — LOUI 219:2
Pythagoras mystical way of P. — BROW 71:10

Q

quad No one about in the Q. — KNOX 204:11
quadruped hairy q. — DARW 110:5
quaint and curious war is — HARD 162:4
qualis Non sum q. eram — HORA 175:19
qualities such as would wear well — GOLD 153:26
quality q. of mercy — SHAK 302:30
q. which guarantees all — CHUR 96:3
quanta O q. qualia — ABEL 1:2
quantities ghosts of departed q. — BERK 31:13
quarks Three q. for Muster Mark — JOYC 192:21
quarrel hath his q. just — SHAK 296:2
justice of my q. — ANON 9:3
lover's q. with the world — FROS 143:18
no q. with the Viet Cong — ALI 5:8
q. in a far away country — CHAM 90:4
q. with ourselves, poetry — YEAT 369:15
takes one to make a q. — INGE 180:15
quarrels who in q. interpose — GAY 147:4
quarters awful q. of an hour — ROSS 280:23
quarto beautiful q. page — SHER 315:14
quean flaunting, extravagant q. — SHER 315:16
Quebec Long Live Free Q. — DE G 112:9
queen Cinara was my q. — HORA 175:19
cold q. of England — CHES 93:1
home life of our own dear Q. — ANON 8:17
I'm to be Q. o' the May — TENN 334:8
laughing Q. — HUNT 178:18
Q. and huntress — JONS 191:14
Q. had four Maries — BALL 25:14
q. in people's hearts — DIAN 114:8
q. of Scots — ELIZ 130:10
q. of Sheba — BIBL 37:5
Q. rose of the rosebud garden — TENN 334:5
Rulers of the Q.'s Navee — GILB 150:19
To toast The Q. — HEAN 164:12
queens Q. have died young — NASH 248:18
queer All the world is q. — OWEN 256:5
queerer universe q. than we suppose — HALD 159:8
quench shall he not q. — BIBL 41:5
waters cannot q. love — BIBL 40:3
questing passes the q. vole — WAUG 352:8
q. beast — MALO 226:8
question Answer to the Great Q. — ADAM 1:13
ask an impertinent q. — BRON 69:7
asked any clear q. — CAMU 83:17
Others abide our q. — ARNO 16:22
q. is — CARR 87:11
q. is absurd — AUDE 19:22
q. why we died — KIPL 201:19
such a silly q. — STER 324:9
that is the q. — SHAK 292:23
what is the q. — STEI 323:19
questionings for those obstinate q. — WORD 365:8
questions all q. were stupid — WEIS 353:9
ask q. of those who cannot tell — RALE 273:7

puzzling q. — BROW 71:6
q. the distempered part — ELIO 128:9
Them that asks no q. — KIPL 202:25
queue orderly q. of one — MIKE 234:1
quick Come! q. as you can — DE L 112:11
q., and the dead — DEWA 114:5
q. could never rest — SURR 327:18
q. to blame — AESC 3:21
quickly It were done q. — SHAK 299:28
Quicunque Q. vult — BOOK 60:9
quiet All q. along the Potomac — BEER 29:4
alone with the q. day — JAME 183:1
Anything for a q. life — MIDD 233:20
determination of a q. man — SMIT 318:15
harvest of a q. eye — WORD 365:15
lives of q. desperation — THOR 339:12
never have a q. world — SHAW 312:22
opportunity to keep q. — CHIR 94:3
q. along the Potomac — MCCL 222:11
q. flows the Don — SHOL 316:2
q. life — HICK 168:18
q. on the western front — REMA 275:4
sleepers in that q. earth — BRON 69:16
quietest q. places — HOUS 176:14
quietly q. pacifist peaceful — WALK 349:9
quietness unravished bride of q. — KEAT 196:5
quietus q. make With a bare bodkin — SHAK 292:24
quills q. upon the fretful porpentine — SHAK 291:38
quince slices of q. — LEAR 210:17
quinquireme Q. of Nineveh — MASE 230:16
quintessence q. of dust — SHAK 292:16
quip q. modest — SHAK 290:27
quires Q. and Places — BOOK 60:4
quis q. custodiet ipsos Custodes — JUVE 194:8
quitter fighter not a q. — MAND 226:20
quiver hath his q. full — BIBL 54:10
quo Q. vadis — BIBL 54:10
quotation always have a q. — SAYE 286:5
Every q. contributes — JOHN 186:18
quotations I hate q. — EMER 132:20
read books of q. — CHUR 96:4
swathed himself in q. — KIPL 203:21
quote immortal as they q. — YOUN 369:22
kill you if you q. it — BURG 74:23
man is to q. him — BENC 30:8

R

rabbit r. in a snare — STEP 324:5
race melted into a new r. — CEEV 106:16
No r. can prosper — WASH 351:3
play the r. card — SHAP 311:5
r. between education — WELL 354:11
r. is not to the swift — BIBL 39:21
r. is to the swift — DAVI 110:19
r. that is set before us — BIBL 52:15
run out thy r. — MILT 237:12
white r. is the cancer — SONT 320:14
racer melodist to a fine r. — MOZA 246:12
races darker to the lighter r. — DU B 122:26
Some r. increase — LUCR 220:14
two distinct r. — LAMB 206:20
Rachel R. weeping — BIBL 43:3
served seven years for R. — BIBL 35:4
racism institutional r. — MACP 224:14
rack r. of this tough world — SHAK 298:29
racket all a German r. — RIDL 276:14
rackets r. to these balls — SHAK 295:12
radical never dared be r. when young — FROS 143:22
radio had the r. on — MONR 242:9
rag foul r.-and-bone shop — YEAT 367:16

rag (*cont.*)
r. and a bone | KIPL 203:3
Shakespeherian R. | ELIO 129:25
rage hard-favoured r. | SHAK 295:16
heathen so furiously r. | BOOK 62:7
Heaven has no r. | CONG 102:7
Heaven in a r. | BLAK 56:9
r. against the dying of the light | THOM 337:18
r. of Caliban | WILD 358:24
rages weight of r. | SPOO 322:11
ragged pair of r. claws | ELIO 128:32
raging r. in the dark | YEAT 367:15
strong drink is r. | BIBL 38:32
ragout fricassee, or a r. | SWIF 328:15
rags r. of time | DONN 119:16
railway by r. timetables | TAYL 330:23
R. termini | FORS 139:15
with a r.-share | CARR 87:20
rain drop of r. maketh a hole | LATI 209:11
gentle r. from heaven | SHAK 302:30
glazed with r. water | WILL 360:16
hard r.'s a gonna fall | DYLA 124:4
latter r. | BOOK 60:18
like sunshine after r. | SHAK 310:32
r. in Spain | LERN 213:8
r. it raineth every day | SHAK 309:13
r., it raineth on the just | BOWE 66:17
R.! Rain! Rain | KEAT 197:14
sendeth r. | BIBL 43:19
small drops of r. | BALL 26:1
small r. down can rain | ANON 11:18
Still falls the r. | SITW 317:13
waiting for it to r. | COHE 99:11
waiting for r. | ELIO 128:19
rainbow no r. nation | MADI 224:18
r. coalition | JACK 181:13
r. comes and goes | WORD 365:3
r.'s glory is shed | SHEL 313:30
Somewhere over the r. | HARB 161:8
when I behold A r. | WORD 364:24
raineth R. drop and staineth slop | POUN 269:18
rains r. pennies from heaven | BURK 76:11
rainy R. days | BASH 27:13
r. Sunday in London | DE Q 113:6
raise Lord shall r. me up | RALE 273:3
raised r. not a stone | WOLF 363:2
raising stop r. corn | LEAS 211:2
ram r. caught in a thicket | BIBL 34:33
Rama In R. was there a voice | BIBL 43:3
Ramadan month of R. | KORA 204:20
rampart corse to the r. | WOLF 362:24
rams mountains skipped like r. | BOOK 64:13
Ramsbottom Mr and Mrs R. | EDGA 125:3
ran Who r. to help me | TAYL 331:1
Randal Lord R. | BALL 25:11
random word, at r. spoken | SCOT 287:15
rank r. is but the guinea's stamp | BURN 76:26
r. me with whom you will | METH 233:16
rankers Gentlemen-r. | KIPL 202:4
ranks In the r. of death | MOOR 244:10
r. of Tuscany | MACA 222:3
ransomed R., healed | LYTE 221:4
rape you r. it | DEGA 112:1
Raphael draw like R. | PICA 263:7
rapid r., unintelligible patter | GILB 150:26
rapist r. bothers to buy a bottle | DWOR 123:16
rapists all men are r. | FREN 142:13
rapping r. at my chamber door | POE 265:17
rapscallions kings is mostly r. | TWAI 343:7
rapture first fine careless r. | BROW 72:6
Modified r. | GILB 150:3
Rapunzel R., let down your hair | GRIM 157:16
rara R. *avis* | JUVE 194:7

rare man of culture r. | GILB 150:12
O r. Ben Jonson | ANON 10:5
was indeed a r. one | WITH 362:6
rarely R., rarely, comest thou | SHEL 314:19
rascals R., would you live | FRED 142:10
rash too r., too unadvised | SHAK 306:32
rat Anyone can r. | CHUR 95:1
Cat, the R., and Lovell | COLL 101:8
creeps like a r. | BOWE 66:13
giant r. of Sumatra | DOYL 120:15
How now! a r. | SHAK 293:18
r. without a tail | SHAK 299:10
smell a r. | ROCH 278:2
rathe r. primrose that forsaken dies | MILT 236:34
ratio geometrical r. | MALT 226:12
rational What is r. is actual | HEGE 165:3
rationed so precious it must be r. | LENI 212:12
rats r.' alley | ELIO 129:24
R.! They fought the dogs | BROW 72:21
rattle Pleased with a r. | POPE 267:31
R. his bones | NOEL 251:21
raved as I r. and grew more fierce | HERB 167:13
raven grim and ancient r. | POE 265:19
Poe with this r. | LOWE 219:18
r. himself is hoarse | SHAK 299:22
ravening r. wolves | BIBL 44:11
ravish except you r. me | DONN 118:25
ravished would have r. her | FIEL 135:10
ravishing dear r. thing | BEHN 29:9
ray r. of sunshine | WODE 362:16
razor arse full of r. blades | KEAT 195:8
mirror and a r. | JOYC 193:3
Occam's R. | OCCA 253:1
reach could not r. it | SAPP 285:16
I r. for my pistol | JOHS 191:6
man's r. should exceed | BROW 71:20
r. the promised land | CALL 82:15
reaching r. forth | BIBL 51:24
reaction can't get no girl r. | JAGG 182:5
if there is any r. | JUNG 193:20
opposed an equal r. | NEWT 250:13
reactionaries All r. are paper tigers | MAO 227:13
read Being r. to by a boy | ELIO 128:19
but r. these | MART 229:9
In science, r. | BULW 74:3
man ought to r. | JOHN 188:14
not r. Eliot, Auden | RICH 276:9
only news until he's r. it | WAUG 352:9
people who can't r. | ZAPP 370:10
r. a book before reviewing it | SMIT 319:14
r. books *through* | JOHN 189:3
r. in the train | WILD 358:12
r., mark, learn | BOOK 60:20
r., much of the night | ELIO 129:18
R. my lips | BUSH 78:12
R. not to contradict | BACO 23:11
r. strange matters | SHAK 299:25
r. without pleasure | JOHN 191:3
Take up and r. | AUGU 20:3
want to r. a novel | DISR 118:10
What do you r. | SHAK 292:12
what I r. in the papers | ROGE 278:16
reader common r. | JOHN 187:10
Hypocrite r. | BAUD 27:18
no tears in the r. | FROS 144:1
R., I married him | BRON 69:11
readeth he may run that r. it | BIBL 42:16
readiness r. is all | SHAK 294:8
reading careful of his r. | LEWI 213:20
get nowadays from r. | GREE 156:25
he was r. | AUGU 20:2
Peace is poor r. | HARD 161:14
prefer r. | SMIT 318:19

r. is right — JOHN 187:14
R. is to the mind — STEE 323:11
R. maketh a full man — BACO 23:13
r., or writing — THOM 337:10
vile hard r. — SHER 315:18
what is worth r. — TREV 341:17
ready always r. to go — LA F 206:12
conference a r. man — BACO 23:13
fire when you are r. — DEWE 114:6
necessity of being r. — LINC 214:17
of a r. writer — BOOK 63:1
real Life is r. — LONG 217:18
r. Simon Pure — CENT 89:18
speechless r. — BARZ 27:10
realism dislike of R. — WILD 358:24
I don't want r. — WILL 360:14
realistic make a 'r. decision' — MCCA 222:9
reality bear very much r. — ELIO 128:2
find r. — MURD 247:7
in r. there are atoms — DEMO 112:19
paint my own r. — KAHL 194:17
r. take precedence — FEYN 135:4
too far from r. — SAHH 284:7
really as in itself it r. is — ARNO 17:8
be a R. Useful Engine — AWDR 21:17
what I r. really want — ROWB 281:11
realms r. of gold — KEAT 196:27
whom three r. obey — POPE 268:18
reap r. a character — READ 274:1
r., if we faint not — BIBL 51:14
r. in joy — BOOK 64:25
r. the whirlwind — BIBL 42:10
that shall he also r. — BIBL 51:13
reaping ever r. something new — TENN 333:24
No, r. — BOTT 66:6
rear r. the tender thought — THOM 338:24
reason appear the better r. — MILT 238:3
Blotting out r. — GRAV 155:18
Can they r. — BENT 31:8
conquers r. still — POPE 266:27
erring R.'s spite — POPE 267:26
feast of r. — POPE 268:5
guide by the light of r. — BRAN 67:15
ideal of r. — KANT 194:23
kills r. itself — MILT 240:3
most sovereign r. — SHAK 293:3
Nothing without a r. — LEIB 212:1
not r. and compare — BLAK 56:18
O r. not the need — SHAK 297:33
R. always means — GASK 146:14
r. and conscience — PRIC 270:21
r., and justice — BURK 75:8
r. is against it — BUTL 79:17
R. is, and ought to be — HUME 178:12
R. is the life of the law — COKE 99:13
r. knows nothing of — PASC 259:22
r. produces monsters — GOYA 154:17
r. why I cannot tell — BROW 71:2
right deed for the wrong r. — ELIO 129:6
that is not r. — POWE 270:16
Their's not to r. why — TENN 331:20
triumph of human r. — HAWK 163:13
woman's r. — SHAK 309:14
reasonable r. man adapts — SHAW 312:15
will must be r. — JEFF 184:5
reasoning abstract r. — HUME 178:5
cowards in r. — SHAF 289:7
r., self-sufficing thing — WORD 365:14
reasons finding of bad r. — BRAD 67:6
five r. — ALDR 4:9
heart has its r. — PASC 259:22
rebel die like a true-blue r. — HILL 169:5
What is a r. — CAMU 83:21

rebellion little r. now and then — JEFF 183:21
R. lay in his way — SHAK 294:24
R. to tyrants — BRAD 67:12
rum, Romanism, and r. — BURC 74:20
rebels r. are our countrymen — GRAN 155:11
subjects are r. — BURK 75:21
recall cannot r. their gifts — TENN 334:30
takes wing beyond r. — HORA 175:2
recapitulates ontogeny r. — HAEC 158:14
receive r. but what we give — COLE 100:1
r. one such little child — BIBL 45:13
than to r. — BIBL 49:33
received Freely ye have r. — BIBL 44:25
his own r. him not — BIBL 48:18
receiver have left the r. off the hook — KOES 204:15
receptacle r. for emotions — PICA 263:6
recession r. when your neighbour — TRUM 342:14
spend way out of a r. — CALL 82:14
recirculation commodious vicus of r. — JOYC 192:19
reckless r. with our government — SHOR 316:4
reckoning at your own r. — TROL 342:3
reconciles feasting r. everybody — PEPY 261:18
reconciliation True r. does not — MAND 226:18
reconstruction r. of Christian life — BONH 59:8
reconvened hereby r. — EWIN 133:12
rectangular proceedings are quite r. — BYRO 81:28
recte Si possis r. — HORA 174:21
rectum one in the r. — OSLE 255:17
recurret usque r. — HORA 174:26
red blows so r. The rose — FITZ 136:10
her lips' r. — SHAK 310:25
in the r. states — OBAM 252:16
keep the r. flag flying — CONN 102:14
Luve's like a r., red rose — BURN 77:9
Making the green one r. — SHAK 300:19
my skin is r. — SITT 317:11
people's flag is deepest r. — CONN 102:13
r. in tooth and claw — TENN 333:3
r. wheel barrow — WILL 360:16
rise with my r. hair — PLAT 264:16
thin r. line — RUSS 283:17
Thin r. line of 'eroes — KIPL 203:1
wine when it is r. — BIBL 38:34
reddens sweet-apple r. — SAPP 285:16
redeemed r. Jerusalem — BIBL 41:8
redeemer know that my r. liveth — BIBL 38:4
O thou great R. — WILL 360:5
such a mighty R. — MISS 241:7
To thee, R. — NEAL 248:22
redeeming R. the time — BIBL 51:18
redemptorem meruit habere R. — MISS 241:7
redress Things past r. — SHAK 305:26
redwood r. forest to the Gulf Stream — GUTH 158:11
reed bruised r. — BIBL 41:5
he is a thinking r. — PASC 259:23
r. shaken with the wind — BIBL 44:32
reeds in the r. by the river — BROW 71:16
reel They r. to and fro — BOOK 64:10
reeled Until r. the mind — GIBB 149:7
referee having two you are a r. — FROS 143:6
reference within my terms of r. — HUTT 179:7
references verify your r. — ROUT 281:10
refine insert, r. — SWIF 328:26
refined Englishwoman is so r. — SMIT 319:4
reform Peace, retrenchment, and r. — BRIG 68:20
r. the criminal — FRY 144:8
sets about r. — TOCQ 340:16
refreshed r. with wine — BOOK 63:17
refuge easy to take r. in — IBSE 180:9
God is thy r. — BIBL 36:6
Patriotism is the last r. — JOHN 189:9
r. from home life — SHAW 313:2
refusal great r. — DANT 109:10

refuse offer he can't r. — PUZO 272:5
refute I r. it *thus* — JOHN 188:20
  r. a sneer — PALE 258:2
regard least r. for — SPEN 321:13
regardless r. of their doom — GRAY 156:16
regiment r. of women — KNOX 204:9
register r. of the crimes, follies — GIBB 148:14
regnavit *R. a ligno Deus* — FORT 140:2
regnum *adveniat r. tuum* — MISS 240:24
regret Old Age a r. — DISR 117:21
regrets Miss Otis r. — PORT 269:4
  no r. — VAUC 345:13
regrette *je ne r. rien* — VAUC 345:13
regular icily r. — TENN 334:3
regulate r. printing — MILT 240:6
regulated R. hatred — HARD 161:11
reign Better to r. in hell — MILT 237:23
  Long to r. over us — ANON 8:11
  r. of Chaos and old Night — MILT 237:28
reigned r. with your loves — ELIZ 130:16
reindeer Red-Nosed R. — MARK 228:2
rejected despised and r. — BIBL 41:9
rejoice let us heartily r. — BOOK 63:26
  Let us then r. — ANON 13:1
  Philistines r. — BIBL 36:33
  r. at that news — THAT 336:16
  R. in the Lord — BIBL 51:26
rejoiced spirit hath r. — BIBL 46:32
relation cold r. — BURK 75:27
  nobody like a r. — THAC 336:6
relations in personal r. — RUSS 282:26
  not have sexual r. — CLIN 98:12
relative Success is r. — ELIO 127:28
relaxes Bless r. — BLAK 57:4
relent make him once r. — BUNY 74:17
  make the gods above r. — VIRG 347:16
relief For this r. much thanks — SHAK 291:8
  gave that thought r. — WORD 365:4
  system of outdoor r. — BRIG 68:19
relieve comfort and r. them — BOOK 60:17
relieved By desperate appliances are r. — SHAK 293:25
religio *Tantum r. potuit* — LUCR 220:12
religion all of the same r. — DISR 117:27
  another r. than Islam — KORA 205:5
  As to r. — PAIN 257:9
  become a popular r. — INGE 180:14
  brothels with bricks of r. — BLAK 57:1
  but of one r. — SHAF 289:6
  concerned with r. — TEMP 331:11
  dominion of r. — GOLD 153:3
  establishment of r. — CONS 103:7
  feature of *any* r. — PAIN 257:16
  Freedom of r. — JEFF 184:8
  just enough r. — SWIF 328:19
  men's minds to r. — BACO 22:12
  much wrong could r. induce — LUCR 220:12
  No compulsion in r. — KORA 205:1
  no r. but social — WESL 354:24
  only one r. — SHAW 312:25
  perfected your r. — KORA 205:11
  poetry, prophecy, and r. — RUSK 282:15
  politics as well as in r. — JUNI 194:2
  r. but a childish toy — MARL 228:12
  r. for religion's sake — COUS 104:17
  r. into after-dinner toasts — NEWM 250:3
  r. is allowed to invade — MELB 232:9
  R. is by no means — CHES 92:13
  R. is the sigh — MARX 230:5
  r. is to do good — PAIN 257:18
  r. of feeble minds — BURK 75:24
  r. of humanity — PAIN 257:11
  r. of Socialism — BEVA 33:9
  r. to me has always been — POTT 269:14

r. weak — SZAS 329:21
r. without science is blind — EINS 126:2
reproach to r. — PENN 261:12
rum and true r. — BYRO 80:25
start your own r. — ANON 8:20
system of r. — PAIN 257:3
That is my r. — SHAW 311:25
true meaning of r. — ARNO 17:7
true r. is Islam — KORA 205:4
religions sixty different r. — CARA 84:17
religious dim r. light — MILT 236:16
  r. and moral principles — ARNO 17:12
  r. prejudice — HUXL 179:22
relished by which he is to be r. — WORD 366:21
rem *quocumque modo r.* — HORA 174:21
  R. tene — CATO 89:3
remain things have been, things r. — CLOU 98:21
remains aught r. to do — ROGE 278:11
remarkable nothing left r. — SHAK 289:22
remarks R. are not literature — STEI 323:14
  said our r. before us — DONA 118:16
remedies Extreme r. — HIPP 169:16
  r. oft in ourselves do lie — SHAK 289:9
  will not apply new r. — BACO 22:31
remedy dangerous r. — FAWK 134:14
  r. is worse than the disease — BACO 23:8
  r. our *enemies* have chosen — SHER 315:25
  Things without all r. — SHAK 301:1
  'Tis a sharp r. — RALE 273:5
remember cannot r. the past — SANT 285:13
  Do you r. an Inn, Miranda — BELL 30:4
  if thou wilt, r. — ROSS 280:17
  I r., I remember — HOOD 172:23
  Lord, r. me — BIBL 48:9
  r. a happy time — DANT 109:12
  r. and be sad — ROSS 280:15
  r. even these things — VIRG 347:1
  r. for ever — WARN 351:1
  R. me — ROSS 280:14
  R. me when I am dead — DOUG 120:3
  R. now thy Creator — BIBL 39:27
  R. the Alamo — SHER 315:22
  r. the children you got — BROO 70:5
  r. the Fifth of November — ANON 10:10
  R. the sabbath day — BIBL 35:27
  r., whan it passed is — CHAU 92:3
  We will r. them — BINY 54:24
  what you can r. — SELL 288:18
  Yes; I r. Adlestrop — THOM 338:7
  You must r. this — HUPF 178:21
remembered blue r. hills — HOUS 176:13
  r. around the world — DISN 117:3
  r. for a very long time — MCGO 223:3
  r. kisses — TENN 334:16
remembering R. without ceasing — BIBL 52:2
remembrance Do this in r. of me — BOOK 61:14
  r. of his dying Lord — SPEN 321:25
  r. of them is grievous — BOOK 61:8
  r. of things past — SHAK 310:7
  rosemary, that's for r. — SHAK 293:32
  Writ in r. more — SHAK 305:21
remind R. me of you — MARV 230:1
remorse rather feel r. — THOM 337:7
  R., the fatal egg — COWP 105:22
remove owl of the R. — RICH 276:8
  say unto this mountain, R. — BIBL 45:11
render R. unto Caesar — BIBL 45:26
rendezvous r. with Death — SEEG 288:7
renew r. a right spirit — BOOK 63:7
renounce I r. war — FOSD 140:3
  r. the devil — BOOK 61:18
renown r. on scraps of learning — YOUN 369:22
rent R. is that portion — RICA 275:14

r. we pay for our room — CLAY 97:16
repair friendship in constant r. — JOHN 188:10
repay I will r. — BIBL 50:11
repeal r. of bad or obnoxious laws — GRAN 155:13
repeat condemned to r. it — SANT 285:13
neither r. his past — AUDE 19:23
repeated mistake shall not be r. — ANON 10:15
simply a truth r. — BALD 25:2
repeats History r. itself — BROO 70:3
repent R. ye — BIBL 43:4
repentance sinners to r. — BIBL 44:20
repente *Nemo r. fuit turpissimus* — JUVE 194:6
repented strove, and much r. — BYRO 80:22
repenteth sinner that r. — BIBL 47:29
repetition r. of unpalatable truths — SUMM 327:14
reply I pause for a r. — SHAK 296:33
r. churlish — SHAK 290:27
Their's not to make r. — TENN 331:20
report of good r. — BIBL 51:28
reporters speaking through r. — CARL 85:15
reports R. of my death — TWAI 344:2
repose earned a night's r. — LONG 218:10
representation Taxation and r. — CAMD 83:2
Taxation without r. — OTIS 255:22
representations r. of general nature — JOHN 187:13
representative Your r. owes you — BURK 76:4
repression result of forced r. — MILL 234:13
reproche *Chevalier sans peur et sans r.* — ANON 12:11
reproof r. valiant — SHAK 290:27
republic Love the Beloved R. — FORS 139:19
love, the beloved R. — SWIN 329:13
Our R. and its press — PULI 271:15
r. is a raft — AMES 6:4
republican on r. principles — SHAW 312:20
Republicans We are R. — BURC 74:20
repugnant r. to the Word of God — BOOK 65:13
reputation O! I have lost my r. — SHAK 304:29
r. and the favour — JEFF 184:9
r. dies — POPE 268:19
Seeking the bubble r. — SHAK 290:13
sold my r. for a song — FITZ 137:2
spotless r. — SHAK 305:17
reputations murdered r. — CONG 102:9
requiem *R. aeternam dona eis* — MISS 241:4
requiescant *r. in pace* — MISS 241:6
require thought 'e might r. — KIPL 203:7
required soul shall be r. of thee — BIBL 47:21
re-rat ingenuity to r. — CHUR 95:1
res *in medias r.* — HORA 174:17
rescuers firing on the r. — WOOL 364:4
research Basic r. is what — BRAU 68:2
r. the art of the soluble — MEDA 232:1
steal from many, it's r. — MIZN 241:20
resign Few die and none r. — JEFF 184:10
resignation by r. none — JEFF 184:10
resigned I am not r. — MILL 234:17
more r. to — CATH 88:19
resist r. everything except temptation — WILD 358:19
resistance no length of r. — BONA 59:4
resistible r. rise of Arturo Ui — BREC 68:5
resolute bloody, bold, and r. — SHAK 301:15
resolution native hue of r. — SHAK 292:26
resolve R. not to be poor — JOHN 190:10
R. to be thyself — ARNO 16:21
resource r.-and-sagacity — KIPL 203:18
resources born to consume r. — HORA 174:22
Have no Inner R. — BERR 32:19
respect r. for the idea of God — DUHA 123:1
r. of the people — MARS 229:6
r. to the living — VOLT 348:22
respectable more r. he is — SHAW 311:31
respecter no r. of persons — BIBL 49:26
respice *r. finem* — ANON 13:17

responsibility In dreams begins r. — YEAT 369:16
Liberty means r. — SHAW 312:9
no sense of r. — KNOX 204:12
Power without r. — KIPL 203:25
responsible r. for such an absurd world — DUHA 123:1
rest choose Their place of r. — MILT 239:14
far, far better r. — DICK 115:24
flee away, and be at r. — BOOK 63:9
Grant them eternal r. — MISS 241:4
holy r. — NEWM 250:4
I will give you r. — BIBL 44:33
no r. day or night — BIBL 53:16
R. in soft peace — JONS 191:20
r. is silence — SHAK 294:13
R., rest, perturbèd spirit — SHAK 292:7
Swift has sailed into his r. — YEAT 369:7
talk about the r. of us — ANON 11:9
weary be at r. — BIBL 37:37
Without haste, but without r. — GOET 152:23
restaurant table at a good r. — LEBO 211:5
resteth Wyatt r. here — SURR 327:18
resting give us a r-place — WEIZ 353:11
restless heart is r. — AUGU 19:28
restoration not revolution, but r. — HARD 161:12
restored r., forgiven — LYTE 227:4
restorer Nature's sweet r. — YOUN 369:26
restraint r. with which they write — CAMP 83:9
restructuring r. [perestroika] — GORB 154:7
rests until it r. in you — AUGU 19:28
result r. happiness — DICK 114:19
resurrection in the r. — BIBL 45:27
on the Day of R. — KORA 205:6
r., and the life — BIBL 48:38
R. to eternal life — BOOK 62:6
retaliate r. for a soul slain — KORA 205:12
reticence Northern r., the tight gag — HEAN 164:13
reticulated *Network*. Anything r. — JOHN 186:20
retire r. from this station — JEFF 184:9
retort r. courteous — SHAK 290:27
retreating Have you seen yourself r. — NASH 248:16
my right is r. — FOCH 138:18
retrenchment Peace, r., and reform — BRIG 68:20
retrograde r. if it does not advance — GIBB 149:1
return I shall r. — MACA 221:6
I will r. — PERÓ 262:5
r. of democratic control — STEE 323:9
Should I never r. — MANS 227:9
unto dust shalt thou r. — BIBL 34:22
returning R. were as tedious — SHAK 301:10
reveal like Nature, half r. — TENN 332:27
r. Himself — MILT 240:7
revealed what has been r. — THOM 337:15
revelation except by r. — KORA 205:19
revelations ends with R. — WILD 359:3
extraordinary r. — BUTL 79:3
offers stupendous r. — HOFF 171:11
revelry r. by night — BYRO 80:3
revels Our r. now are ended — SHAK 307:30
revenge man that studieth r. — BACO 23:6
Punishment is not for r. — FRY 144:8
r. for slight injuries — MACH 223:7
r. is a kind of wild justice — BACO 23:5
r.! Timotheus cries — DRYD 121:26
R. triumphs over death — BACO 22:21
spur my dull r. — SHAK 293:27
study of r. — MILT 237:20
with envy and r. — MILT 237:18
revenged I'll be r. — SHAK 309:12
revenges brings in his r. — SHAK 309:11
revenons *R. à ces moutons* — ANON 12:18
reverence In deeper r. praise — WHIT 357:14
R. for Life — SCHW 286:20
reverse not got a r. gear — BLAI 56:5

review your r. before me — REGE 274:16
reviewing read a book before r. it — SMIT 319:14
revolt r., disorder — MORR 245:20
revolution after the r. — AREN 14:21
age of r. — JEFF 184:8
crust over a volcano of r. — ELLI 131:15
not r., but restoration — HARD 161:12
R., like Saturn — VERG 346:3
r. of rising expectations — CLEV 98:7
safeguard a r. — ORWE 254:28
revolutionary Every r. ends — CAMU 84:2
forge his r. spirit — GUEV 158:8
revolutions All modern r. — CAMU 84:1
share in two r. — PAIN 257:20
revolver resembles a r. — FANO 133:20
revolving with the r. year — SHEL 313:14
reward nothing for r. — SPEN 322:2
not to ask for any r. — IGNA 180:12
only r. of virtue — EMER 132:6
rewards r. and Fairies — CORB 104:3
rewrite is to r. it — WILD 358:15
rex r. quondam — MALO 226:9
rhetoric aimless r. — HUXL 179:22
love without the r. — STOP 326:12
quarrel with others, r. — YEAT 369:15
rhetorician sophistical r. — DISR 117:17
Rhodesia black majority rule in R. — SMIT 318:16
rhyme hope and history r. — HEAN 164:10
in prose or r. — MILT 237:16
outlive this powerful r. — SHAK 310:9
R. being . . . but the invention — MILT 237:13
still more tired of R. — BELL 29:23
rhyming bondage of r. — MILT 237:14
rhythm I got r. — GERS 148:8
sweet, soft, plenty r. — MORT 246:7
rhythmical r. grumbling — ELIO 130:9
Rialto What news on the R. — SHAK 302:11
rib r., which the Lord God — BIBL 34:11
riband Just for a r. — BROW 72:12
ribbon road was a r. of moonlight — NOYE 252:10
rice r. field, ocean — BASH 27:11
rich fell from the r. man's table — BIBL 48:1
maketh haste to be r. — BIBL 39:2
man who dies . . . r. — CARN 85:25
neither r. nor rare — POPE 266:19
never be too r. or too thin — WIND 361:20
not really a r. man — GETT 148:11
not r. enough — REED 274:15
Poor little r. girl — COWA 105:6
potentiality of growing r. — JOHN 190:7
R. AND THE POOR — DISR 117:29
r. are different from you and me — FITZ 137:6
r. are the scum of the earth — CHES 93:10
r. beyond the dreams — MOOR 243:18
r. get rich — KAHN 194:18
r. he hath sent empty away — BIBL 46:33
r. man in his castle — ALEX 4:15
r. on the poor — JEFF 183:20
r. wage war — SART 285:19
r. with forty pounds a year — GOLD 153:8
r. wot gets the gravy — ANON 10:20
save the few who are r. — KENN 198:16
sincerely want to be r. — CORN 104:7
swinish luxury of the r. — MORR 245:15
Richard R.'s himself again — CIBB 96:14
richer for r. for poorer — BOOK 61:27
R. than all his tribe — SHAK 305:14
riches embarrassment of r. — ALLA 5:9
Infinite r. — MARL 228:13
parade of r. — SMIT 318:3
R. are for spending — BACO 22:22
r. grow in hell — MILT 237:31
unsearchable r. of Christ — BIBL 51:15

world's r., which dispersed lie — HERB 167:20
riddle r. of the sands — CHIL 93:27
r. of the world — POPE 267:28
r. wrapped in a mystery — CHUR 95:5
ride r. in triumph — MARL 228:17
r. of Paul Revere — LONG 218:5
R. on! ride on in majesty — MILM 235:8
She's got a ticket to r. — LENN 212:22
rider r. and his horse — SURT 328:2
ridicule r. is the best test — CHES 92:22
stand the test of r. — SHAF 289:7
ridiculous no spectacle so r. — MACA 221:12
position r. — CHES 92:24
step above the r. — PAIN 257:4
sublime to the r. — NAPO 248:2
ridiculus nascetur r. mus — HORA 174:16
riding highwayman came r. — NOYE 252:10
r. that night — LONG 218:7
Ridley good comfort, Master R. — LATI 209:12
rien Ils n'ont r. appris — TALL 330:9
je ne regrette r. — VAUC 345:13
R. — LOUI 219:3
rifle r. all the breathing spring — COLL 101:15
roll to your r. — KIPL 203:9
rift loaded every r. — SPEN 322:1
Load every r. — KEAT 197:20
r. within the lute — TENN 332:16
right All's r. with the world — BROW 72:23
convinced that they are r. — VAN 345:8
defend to the death your r. — VOLT 349:3
firmness in the r. — LINC 215:5
grounded on just and r. — MILT 239:3
if r., to be kept right — SCHU 286:18
I had rather be r. — CLAY 97:15
individual r. — TAFT 330:5
is it r. — KING 200:19
It must be r. — CRAB 106:5
Jack — I'm all r. — BONE 59:6
'just' or 'r.' — PLAT 264:21
majority never has r. — IBSE 180:5
more than half the people are r. — WHIT 356:4
my r. is retreating — FOCH 138:18
never r. to do wrong — SOCR 319:26
no more r. to consume — SHAW 311:10
of—them—is—r. — KIPL 202:11
our country, r. or wrong — DECA 111:16
renew a r. spirit — BOOK 63:7
r., and our bounden duty — BOOK 61:12
r. deed for the wrong reason — ELIO 129:6
R. Divine of Kings — POPE 266:8
r. little, tight little Island — DIBD 114:11
r. makes might — LINC 214:15
r. man in the right place — JEFF 184:21
r. notes at the right time — BACH 21:22
r. there is none to dispute — COWP 106:4
r. thought — PALI 258:3
r. to be consulted — BAGE 24:10
r. to be obeyed — JOHN 185:12
r. wrong — TENN 332:12
sheep on his r. hand — BIBL 46:6
To do a great r. — SHAK 302:32
Two wrongs don't make a r. — SZAS 329:22
Want to do r. — RICH 276:6
Whatever IS, is R. — POPE 267:26
righteous godly, r., and sober life — BOOK 59:14
never the r. forsaken — BOOK 62:23
not come to call the r. — BIBL 44:20
r. are bold — BIBL 39:1
r. man — BIBL 38:20
souls of the r. — BIBL 42:20
righteousness clouds rain down r. — BIBL 54:5
loved r., and hated iniquity — BOOK 63:2
pursue r. — PLAT 265:3

r. and peace	BOOK 63:21	Follow the yellow brick r.	HARB 161:9
r. hath not been forgotten	BIBL 42:28	Golden R. to Samarkand	FLEC 138:4
Sun of R.	BIBL 42:17	Goodbye yellow brick r.	JOHN 186:2
Sun of R.	WESL 354:19	high r.	JOHN 188:13
rightful will to be r.	JEFF 184:5	on a lonesome r.	COLE 100:26
rights as much r. as men	TRUT 342:21	one more for the r.	MERC 233:5
asserting these r.	LAY 210:3	on to the end of the r.	LAUD 209:15
duties as well as its r.	DRUM 121:16	people in the middle of the r.	BEVA 33:10
extension of women's r.	FOUR 140:11	r. of excess	BLAK 56:23
inalienable r.	ROBE 277:10	R. to Heaven	BALL 25:19
Natural r.	BENT 31:5	r. to the City of Emeralds	BAUM 27:22
r. are disregarded	BROW 70:16	r. toward freedom	MORR 245:20
r. of an Englishman	JUNI 194:1	r. up and the road down	HERA 167:5
Stand up for your r.	MARL 228:4	r. was a ribbon of moonlight	NOYE 252:10
unalienable r.	ANON 11:14	r. wind up-hill	ROSS 280:16
rigid decisions that are r.	PROD 271:6	rolling English r.	CHES 93:3
rigs Corn r., an' barley rigs	BURN 77:1	shut the r. through the woods	KIPL 203:4
rime r. was on the spray	HARD 162:9	up the white r.	ELIO 130:1
Rimmon in the house of R.	BIBL 37:24	ye'll tak' the high r.	ANON 10:6
ring Like a great r.	VAUG 345:19	**roads** How many r.	DYLA 124:3
now r. the bells	WALP 350:5	Two r. diverged	FROS 143:24
One R. to rule them all	TOLK 340:22	**roam** Everywhere I r.	FOST 140:10
only pretty r. time	SHAK 290:25	**roaming** R. in the gloamin'	LAUD 209:15
r. at the end of his nose	LEAR 210:16	r. with a hungry heart	TENN 335:1
r. is worn away	OVID 255:25	where are you r.	SHAK 308:27
r. of bright water	RAIN 272:21	**roar** called upon to give the r.	CHUR 95:24
R. out, wild bells	TENN 333:8	die of that r.	ELIO 127:17
r. the bells of Heaven	HODG 171:4	r. you as gently	SHAK 303:12
What shall we do for a r.	LEAR 210:16	**roareth** What is this that r. thus	GODL 152:4
With this R. I thee wed	BOOK 62:1	**roast** R. Beef, Medium	FERB 134:17
ringleaders fling the r.	ARNO 17:13	r. their eggs	BACO 23:21
rings postman always r. twice	CAIN 82:11	**rob** r. a lady of her fortune	FIEL 135:13
riot r. is at bottom	KING 201:2	r. his mother	FAUL 134:13
riotous r. living	BIBL 47:30	**robbed** We was r.	JACO 182:1
ripe Cherry r.	CAMP 83:14	**robber** Barabbas was a r.	BIBL 49:9
we r. and ripe	SHAK 290:9	**robbing** from r. he comes next	DE Q 113:9
ripeness R. is all	SHAK 298:22	r. a bank	BREC 68:7
ripper no female Jack the R.	PAGL 257:1	**robe** Give me my r.	SHAK 289:28
rise Created half to r.	POPE 267:28	**robes** washed their r.	BIBL 53:8
Early to r.	THUR 340:4	**robin** Call for the r.-red-breast	WEBS 353:2
resistible r. of Arturo Ui	BREC 68:5	r. red breast	BLAK 56:9
r. against nation	BIBL 45:33	**Robinson** here's to you, Mrs R.	SIMO 317:2
r. at ten thirty	HARG 162:12	**robot** r. may not injure a human	ASIM 17:17
r. on stepping-stones	TENN 332:25	**robotics** Rules of R.	ASIM 17:17
still, like air, I'll r.	ANGE 7:3	**robs** government which r. Peter	SHAW 311:19
risen r. up against us to destroy	HAGG 158:17	**rock** founded upon a r.	BIBL 44:13
rises sun also r.	HEMI 166:4	from the Tarpeian r.	ARNO 17:13
rising means of r.	JOHN 189:11	knew the perilous r.	SOUT 320:20
revolution of r. expectations	CLEV 98:7	R. journalism is people	ZAPP 370:10
r. to great place	BACO 22:29	R. of Ages	TOPL 341:7
risks just one of the r. he takes	STEV 325:3	Sex and drugs and r. and roll	DURY 123:15
risky too r. and dangerous	STRO 327:2	upon this r.	BIBL 45:9
ritui Novo cedat r.	THOM 337:13	**rocked** R. in the cradle of the deep	WILL 360:1
river Among the r. sallows	KEAT 197:4	r. the system	ROBI 278:1
black flowing r.	HOOD 172:19	**rocket** rose like a r.	PAIN 257:12
either side the r. lie	TENN 333:15	**Rockies** R. may crumble	GERS 148:9
Fame is like a r.	BACO 23:3	**rocking** r. a grown man	BURK 75:3
in the reeds by the r.	BROW 71:16	**rocks** eternal r. beneath	BRON 69:15
Let us cross over the r.	JACK 181:18	hand that r. the cradle	WALL 349:15
Ol' man r.	HAMM 160:19	older than the r.	PATE 260:6
r. Is a strong brown god	ELIO 128:10	**rod** shall come forth a r.	BIBL 40:16
r. jumps over the mountains	AUDE 18:13	spare the r., and spoil the child	BUTL 79:7
r. of crystal light	FIEL 135:6	spareth his r.	BIBL 38:24
twice into the same r.	HERA 167:3	thy r. and thy staff	BOOK 62:15
riverrun r., past Eve and Adam's	JOYC 192:19	**rode** r. madly off	LEAC 210:7
rivers discourse of r.	WALT 350:13	**rogue** r. and peasant slave	SHAK 292:20
I've known r.	HUGH 177:14	**roi** que le r.	ANON 12:13
R. and mountain-spring	OAKL 252:14	**Roland** Childe R. to the Dark Tower	BROW 71:26
r. of blood	JEFF 184:18	Child R. to the dark tower	SHAK 298:12
r. run into the sea	BIBL 39:7	**roll** drugs and rock and r.	DURY 123:15
rivulet neat r. of text	SHER 315:14	r. all our strength	MARV 229:23
road And the r. below me	STEV 326:3	R. on, thou deep	BYRO 80:15
braid, braid r.	BALL 25:19	R. up that map	PITT 263:22

rolled bottoms of my trousers r. — ELIO 129:3
rolling jus' keeps r. along — HAMM 160:19
Like a r. stone — DYLA 124:7
r. English road — CHES 93:3
Roman deceased R. Empire — HOBB 170:22
high R. fashion — SHAK 289:23
I am a R. citizen — CICE 96:21
make a R. holiday — BYRO 80:12
more an antique R. — SHAK 294:11
neither holy, nor R. — VOLT 348:17
noblest R. of them all — SHAK 297:16
R. and his trouble — HOUS 176:11
R., make your task to rule — VIRG 347:14
R. people — CALI 82:12
R.-Saxon-Danish-Norman — DEFO 111:22
R.'s life — MACA 222:2
R. thought hath struck him — SHAK 289:13
sweet R. hand — SHAK 309:6
Roman Catholic R. Church — MACA 221:14
romance fine r. with no kisses — FIEL 135:15
symbols of a high r. — KEAT 197:7
Romanism rum, R., and rebellion — BURC 74:20
Romans Friends, R., countrymen — SHAK 297:1
romantic airline ticket to r. places — MARV 230:1
R. Ireland's dead and gone — YEAT 369:5
ruin that's r. — GILB 150:11
Wrong but R. — SELL 288:19
romantics We were the last r. — YEAT 367:19
Romanus Civis R. sum — CICE 96:21
Civis R. sum — PALM 258:5
Rome Bishop of R. — BOOK 65:14
cruel men of R. — SHAK 296:17
grandeur that was R. — POE 265:22
Let R. in Tiber melt — SHAK 289:12
loved R. more — SHAK 296:31
Men, I'm getting out of R. — GARI 146:4
Oh R.! my country — BYRO 80:9
R. has spoken — AUGU 20:11
R. shall stand — BYRO 80:13
second at R. — CAES 82:6
When I go to R. — AMBR 6:1
Romeo wherefore art thou R. — SHAK 306:28
romping r. of sturdy children — DE V 113:19
Ronsard R. me célébrait — RONS 279:2
roof cat on a hot tin r. — WILL 360:10
come under my r. — BIBL 44:14
enter under my r. — MISS 241:1
Who, living, had no r. — HEYW 168:17
rooks r. are blown — TENN 332:28
room always r. at the top — WEBS 352:21
Books do furnish a r. — POWE 270:8
boys in the back r. — LOES 217:3
Great hatred, little r. — YEAT 368:25
into the next r. — HOLL 171:18
money and a r. of her own — WOOL 363:21
no r. for them in the inn — BIBL 47:2
riches in a little r. — MARL 228:13
smallest r. of my house — REGE 274:16
smoke-filled r. — SIMP 317:9
struggle for r. — MALT 226:13
rooms boys in the back r. — BEAV 28:5
Other voices, other r. — CAPO 84:15
root axe to the r. — PAIN 257:14
begins to take r. — WASH 351:11
perced to the r. — CHAU 91:11
r. of all evil — BIBL 52:9
r. of the matter — BIBL 38:5
rope refuse to set his hand to a r. — DRAK 121:8
rorate R., coeli — BIBL 54:5
rose American beauty r. — ROCK 278:6
beauty's r. — SHAK 310:2
blossom as the r. — BIBL 40:27
blows so red The r. — FITZ 136:10
dumb to tell the crooked r. — THOM 337:21
English unofficial r. — BROO 69:20
expectancy and r. — SHAK 293:2
fading r. — CARE 84:19
fayr as is the r. — CHAU 92:1
fire and the r. are one — ELIO 128:18
Go, lovely r. — WALL 349:17
Goodbye, England's r. — JOHN 185:18
Into the r.-garden — ELIO 128:1
last r. of summer — MOOR 244:11
lovely is the r. — WORD 365:3
love were what the r. is — SWIN 329:15
Luve's like a red, red r. — BURN 77:9
Mighty lak' a r. — STAN 323:6
morning r. — KEAT 196:14
One perfect r. — PARK 258:14
Queen r. of the rosebud garden — TENN 334:5
r. By any other name — SHAK 306:29
r. in dark and evil days — INGR 180:19
R. is a rose — STEI 323:17
R. of all my days — YEAT 369:9
r. of Sharon — BIBL 39:32
r. of yesterday — FITZ 136:7
r.-red city — BURG 74:24
r. should shut — KEAT 195:15
R., thou art sick — BLAK 58:2
R., were you not — PRIO 271:2
Roves back the r. — DE L 112:12
secret and inviolate R. — YEAT 369:3
vanish with the r. — FITZ 137:3
white r. of Scotland — MACD 222:17
white r. weeps — TENN 334:6
without thorn the r. — MILT 238:20
rosebuds Gather ye r. — HERR 168:5
rosemary r. and rue — SHAK 309:24
r., that's for remembrance — SHAK 293:32
Rosencrantz R. and Guildenstern — SHAK 294:15
roses ash the burnt r. leave — ELIO 128:12
days of wine and r. — DOWS 120:11
Each morn a thousand r. — FITZ 136:7
Everything's coming up r. — SOND 320:11
let fall a shower of r. — TERE 335:25
like my r. to see you — SHER 315:21
not a bed of r. — STEV 325:23
Plant thou no r. — ROSS 280:17
roses, r., all the way — BROW 72:20
scent of the r. — MOOR 244:7
smells like r. — JOHN 186:10
Treaties like girls and r. — DE G 114:8
rosy R.-fingered dawn — HOME 172:15
rot in cold obstruction and to r. — SHAK 302:8
we r. and rot — SHAK 290:9
rotten hypocrite is really r. — AREN 14:20
like r. mackerel — RAND 273:12
Something is r. — SHAK 291:36
rottenness r. begins in his conduct — JEFF 184:4
rough R.-hew them how we will — SHAK 294:7
r. magic I here abjure — SHAK 307:32
R. winds do shake — SHAK 310:3
round into the r. hole — SMIT 319:5
r. as a ball — JULI 193:13
R. both the shires — HOUS 176:9
r. unvarnished tale — SHAK 304:21
Roundheads R. (Right but Repulsive) — SELL 288:19
roving go no more a-r. — BYRO 81:20
row r. one way and look another — BURT 78:3
rowed All r. fast — COKE 99:12
rowing looking one way, and r. — BUNY 74:12
royal needed no r. title — SPEN 321:16
r. banners forward go — FORT 140:1
r. priesthood — BIBL 52:26
'r. road' to geometry — EUCL 133:6
r. road to the unconscious — FREU 142:17

this is the r. Law CORO 104:12
royalist more of a r. ANON 12:13
royaliste *plus r.* ANON 12:13
royalty r. is to be reverenced BAGE 24:9
 when you come to R. DISR 118:5
rub ay, there's the r. SHAK 292:23
 r. up against money RUNY 282:5
rubies above r. BIBL 38:6
 price is far above r. BIBL 39:5
rubs fog that r. its back ELIO 128:30
rude so r. to the good WORD 364:8
 You have been very r. CHIR 94:2
Rudolph R., the Red-Nosed MARK 228:2
rue rosemary and r. SHAK 309:24
 set a bank of r. SHAK 306:2
 There's r. for you SHAK 293:33
ruffle r. up your spirits SHAK 297:9
rugged harsh cadence of a r. line DRYD 122:15
 old r. cross BENN 30:18
 system of r. individualism HOOV 173:4
rugs like a million bloody r. FITZ 137:14
Ruh *Meine R.' ist hin* GOET 152:12
 Über allen Gipfeln Ist R.' GOET 152:18
Ruhm *Tat ist alles, nichts der R.* GOET 152:13
ruin Majestic though in r. MILT 238:5
 Resolved to r. DRYD 121:18
 r. himself in twelve months GEOR 148:1
 R. seize thee GRAY 156:5
 r. that's romantic GILB 150:11
 r. upon ruin MILT 238:14
ruinous R. inheritance GAIU 145:1
ruins human mind in r. DAVI 111:1
 shored against my r. ELIO 130.2
rule good old r. WORD 365:24
 oldest r. in the book CARR 86:21
 One Ring to r. them all TOLK 340:22
 R., Britannia THOM 338:23
 r. o'er freemen BROO 69:18
 r. the state DRYD 121:18
 r. wherever they can THUC 340:1
ruler r. in Israel BIBL 42:14
rulers best r. LAO 208:2
 conduct of their r. ADAM 2:8
 r., mostly knaves BIER 54:20
 r. of the darkness BIBL 51:21
 R. of the Queen's Navee GILB 150:19
rules hand that r. the world WALL 349:15
 Integrity has no need of r. CAMU 83:19
 keep making up these sex r. SALI 284:15
 R. and models HAZL 164:5
 R. of Robotics ASIM 17:17
 r. of the game HUXL 179:18
 wouldn't obey the r. BENN 30:22
ruling r. passion conquers POPE 266:27
 Search then the R. Passion POPE 267:1
rum r. and true religion BYRO 80:25
 r., Romanism, and rebellion BURC 74:20
 r., sodomy, prayers, and the lash CHUR 95:22
rumble r. of a distant drum FITZ 136:9
 R. thy bellyful SHAK 298:3
rumour distillation of r. CARL 85:11
 Enter R., painted SHAK 294:31
rumours wars and r. of wars BIBL 45:32
run born to r. SPRI 322:17
 enabled him to r. MACA 221:17
 He can r. LOUI 219:6
 he may r. that readeth it BIBL 42:16
 In the long r. KEYN 199:22
 never did r. smooth SHAK 303:7
 R. and find out KIPL 203:12
 R., run, Orlando SHAK 290:18
 r.-stealers flicker THOM 338:12
 r. with patience BIBL 52:15

shine, and r. to and fro BIBL 42:21
 They get r. down BEVA 33:10
 we will make him r. MARV 229:23
 What makes Sammy r. SCHU 286:15
runcible ate with a r. spoon LEAR 210:17
 R. Cat with crimson whiskers LEAR 210:19
runnable r. stag DAVI 110:18
runner long-distance r. SILL 316:22
running all the r. *you* can do CARR 86:26
 r. over BIBL 47:10
 r. with the pack BUTL 79:6
Rupert R. of the Rhine MACA 221:19
rural Retirement, r. quiet THOM 338:25
rus *R. in urbe* MART 229:12
rush fools r. in POPE 267:18
rushed r. into the field BYRO 80:6
rushes *Green grow the r. O* ANON 9:2
 Green grow the r., O BURN 76:28
rushing r. mighty wind BIBL 49:21
russet plain r.-coated captain CROM 107:7
Russia forecast the action of R. CHUR 95:5
 R. has two generals NICH 251:1
Russian he might have been a R. GILB 150:21
 tumult in the R. heart PUSH 272:3
rust moth and r. doth corrupt BIBL 43:23
 r. unburnished, not to shine TENN 335:3
 wear out than to r. out CUMB 108:3
Ruth sad heart of R. KEAT 196:23
ruthless Ruin seize thee, r. King! GRAY 156:5
rye catcher in the r. SALI 284:17
 Comin thro' the r. BURN 76:24
 fields of barley and of r. TENN 333:15

S

sabachthani Eli, Eli, lama s. BIBL 46:20
sabbath Remember the s. day BIBL 35:27
 s. was made for man BIBL 46:22
sabbaths endless S. ABEL 1:2
Sabidi *Non amo te, S.* MART 229:8
sable S.-vested Night MILT 238:13
Sabrina S. fair MILT 236:10
sack intolerable deal of s. SHAK 294:22
 S. the lot FISH 136:3
sacrament abortion would be a s. KENN 198:10
 great S. revere THOM 337:13
sacred feed his s. flame COLE 100:13
 only s. thing FRAN 141:6
sacrifice approaching s. MILM 235:8
 blood Of human s. MILT 237:26
 highest s. is ELEA 127:1
 holy hush of ancient s. STEV 324:23
 living s. BIBL 50:10
 Passover s. HAGG 158:18
 pay thy morning s. KEN 198:5
 s. other people SHAW 312:19
 sufficient s. BOOK 61:13
 Thine ancient S. KIPL 202:19
 Too long a s. YEAT 368:4
sacrificed be s. to expediency MAUG 231:8
sad all their songs are s. CHES 92:26
 How s. and bad BROW 71:27
 of all s. words WHIT 357:15
 remember and be s. ROSS 280:15
 s. steps, O Moon SIDN 316:13
 s. tires in a mile-a SHAK 309:23
 world is s. and dreary FOST 140:10
Saddam I am S. Hussein HUSS 179:4
 met S. Hussein GALL 145:10
sadder s. and a wiser man COLE 100:28
saddest telling the s. tale SHAK 303:16

saddest (cont.)
tell of s. thought — SHEL 314:28
saddle Boot, s., to horse — BROW 71:23
Things are in the s. — EMER 131:21
saddled s. and bridled — RUMB 281:18
saeclum Solvet s. in favilla — MISS 241:5
safe feeling s. with a person — ANON 10:2
made s. for democracy — WILS 361:14
s. lodging — NEWM 250:4
s. to be unpopular — STEV 325:4
see me s. up — MORE 244:19
safeguard s. of the West — WORD 365:13
safer Love just makes it s. — ICE- 180:11
s. for a prince — MACH 223:8
safety s., honour, and welfare — CHAR 91:1
s. is in our speed — EMER 132:9
strike against public s. — COOL 103:13
sagacity resource-and-s. — KIPL 203:18
sagas frosty s. — CRAN 106:8
sages all the s. can — WORD 366:9
said fool hath s. in his heart — BOOK 62:9
He himself s. — CICE 96:17
if you want anything s. — THAT 336:12
nobody had s. it before — TWAI 343:18
not been s. before — TERE 335:12
s. on both sides — ADDI 3:5
s. our remarks before us — DONA 118:16
sail s. on, O Ship of State — LONG 217:7
sea-mark of my utmost s. — SHAK 305:13
sailed I have s. the seas — YEAT 368:28
sailing S. over a cardboard sea — HARB 161:7
to which port one is s. — SENE 288:21
sailor Home is the s. — STEV 326:6
No man will be a s. — JOHN 188:11
sailors tell thee, s., when away — GAY 147:3
saint call me a s. — CAMA 82:21
my late espousèd s. — MILT 239:32
S. Martin's summer — SHAK 296:1
s., n. A dead sinner — BIER 54:23
saints Christ and His s. — ANON 14:2
s. immortal reign — WATT 351:24
S. should be judged guilty — ORWE 255:6
saisons Ô s. — RIMB 277:4
sake Art for art's s. — CONS 103:4
loseth his life for my s. — BIBL 44:30
Saki him, O S. — FITZ 137:4
salad s. days — SHAK 289:16
salary s. of the chief executive — GALB 145:3
salesman Death of a s. — MILL 234:22
s. is got to dream — MILL 234:24
salley by the s. gardens — YEAT 367:23
Sally none like pretty S. — CARE 84:21
salmon s. sing in the street — AUDE 18:13
saloon in the last chance s. — MELL 232:12
salt became a pillar of s. — BIBL 34:32
grain of s. — PLIN 265:7
how s. is the taste — DANT 109:16
s. of the earth — BIBL 43:14
seasoned with s. — BIBL 52:1
unplumbed, s., estranging sea — ARNO 17:1
Salteena S. was an elderly man — ASHF 17:16
salus S. populi — CICE 96:16
salutant Ave Caesar, morituri te s. — ANON 13:7
salute If it moves, s. it — ANON 8:19
S. the happy morn — BYRO 79:22
s. your courage — GALL 145:9
those about to die s. you — ANON 13:7
salvation bottle of s. — RALE 272:23
cannot be s. — CYPR 109:4
necessary to s. — BOOK 65:11
no s. outside the church — AUGU 20:6
strength of our s. — BOOK 63:26
Work out your own s. — BIBL 51:23

Samaritan remember the Good S. — THAT 336:14
Samarkand Golden Road to S. — FLEC 138:4
Samarra appointment with him in S. — MAUG 231:11
same all say the s. — MELB 232:8
Ever the s. — ANON 13:18
more they are the s. — KARR 195:3
s. yesterday, and to day — BIBL 52:18
you are the s. — MART 229:11
samite Clothed in white s. — TENN 332:10
Sammy What makes S. run — SCHU 286:15
sancta s. simplicitas — JERO 185:3
sanctus S., sanctus, sanctus — MISS 240:23
sand Little grains of s. — CARN 85:27
on the edge of the s. — LEAR 210:17
s. against the wind — BLAK 57:9
world in a grain of s. — BLAK 56:8
sandal s. shoon — SHAK 293:28
sands Across the s. of Dee — KING 201:7
Come unto these yellow s. — SHAK 307:22
Footprints on the s. — LONG 217:21
riddle of the s. — CHIL 93:27
s. upon the Red sea shore — BLAK 57:10
sandwich cheaper than a prawn s. — RATN 273:16
taste again that raw-onion s. — BARN 26:17
sane if he was s. he had to fly — HELL 165:13
San Francisco left my heart in S. — CROS 107:19
sang s. in my chains — THOM 337:19
sank s. my boat — KENN 199:5
Sighted sub, s. same — MASO 231:2
sano Mens sana in corpore s. — JUVE 194:12
sans sans singer, and—s. End — FITZ 136:11
S. teeth, sans eyes — SHAK 290:15
Santa Claus there is a S. — CHUR 94:14
sap dried the s. of my veins — YEAT 368:6
sapere s. aude — HORA 174:23
sapienti Dictum s. — PLAU 265:5
Sappho Where burning S. loved — BYRO 80:29
sardines s. will be thrown — CANT 84:13
sash s. my father wore — ANON 11:3
sashes one of his nice new s. — GRAH 155:1
sat everyone has s. except a man — CUMM 108:6
s. too long here — CROM 107:11
we s. down and wept — BOOK 65:1
Satan Get thee behind me, S. — BIBL 45:10
high capital Of S. — MILT 238:2
Lord said unto S. — BIBL 37:32
S. cast out Satan — BIBL 46:23
S. finds some mischief still — WATT 351:19
S. stood Unterrified — MILT 238:11
Satanic dark S. mills — BLAK 57:8
satiable full of s. curtiosity — KIPL 203:15
satin ease a heart like a s. gown — PARK 258:17
satire hard not to write s. — JUVE 194:4
let s. be my song — BYRO 81:11
S. is a sort of glass — SWIF 328:5
S. is what closes Saturday — KAUF 195:4
S. or sense — POPE 266:22
satisfaction can't get no s. — JAGG 182:5
satisfied can't be s. — HUGH 177:15
fool s. — MILL 234:15
well paid that is well s. — SHAK 302:35
satisfy poorly s. our eyes — WOTT 366:23
satisfying s. a voracious appetite — FIEL 135:12
Saturday closes S. night — KAUF 195:4
Glasgow Empire on a S. night — DODD 118:14
Saturn Revolution, like S. — VERG 346:3
Saturnia redeunt S. regna — VIRG 347:21
satyr Hyperion to a s. — SHAK 291:17
satyrs men, like s. — MARL 228:10
sauce only one s. — CARA 84:17
Saul Is S. also among the prophets — BIBL 36:25
S. and Jonathan — BIBL 36:34
S. hath slain his thousands — BIBL 36:30

S., why persecutest thou me — BIBL 49:23
savage dealing with the s. English — WILL 360:7
  laws unto a s. race — TENN 334:31
  noble s. ran — DRYD 122:2
  sooth a s. breast — CONG 102:6
savaged s. by a dead sheep — HEAL 164:8
save destroy the town to s. it — ANON 9:5
  exist in order to s. us — DE V 114:2
  God s. king Solomon — BIBL 37:4
  himself he cannot s. — BIBL 46:19
  rushed through life trying to s. — ROGE 278:18
  s. his soul — BIBL 41:29
  Save me, oh, s. me — CANN 84:8
  s. the Governor-General — WHIT 356:20
  s. the people — ELLI 131:12
  s. the Union — LINC 214:18
  s. those that have no imagination — SHAW 312:31
  To s. your world — AUDE 18:16
saved He s. others — BIBL 46:19
  we are not s. — BIBL 41:20
  What must I do to be s. — BIBL 49:27
  Whosoever will be s. — BOOK 60:9
saviour S.'s birth is celebrated — SHAK 291:11
  s. spring to life — BIBL 54:5
savour keep Seeming and s. — SHAK 309:24
  salt have lost his s. — BIBL 43:14
saw I came, I s., I conquered — CAES 82:8
Saxon ancient S. phrase — LONG 217:13
say all s. *the same* — MELB 232:8
  anything good to s. — LONG 218:13
  don't s. nothin' — HAMM 160:19
  Have something to s. — ARNO 17:9
  Lat thame s. — ANON 11.10
  nothing to s. — CAGE 82:10
  nothing to s. — COLT 101:19
  not s. why and how — WILS 361:8
  S. it ain't so — ANON 10:16
  S. little and do much — SHAM 311:3
  s. only the word — MISS 241:1
  s. something — GOOD 154:6
  s. what they please — FRED 142:9
  s. what you mean — CARR 86:11
  see what I s. — WALL 349:16
  someone else has got to s. — GASK 146:14
  whatever you s. — HEAN 164:13
  wink wink, s. no more — MONT 243:13
saying For loving, and for s. so — DONN 119:18
  were s. yesterday — LUIS 220:15
says not what he s. — SMIT 318:21
scaffold forever on the s. — LOWE 220:3
scale sufficiently large s. — SPEN 321:12
  with her lifted s. — POPE 266:5
scallop s.-shell of quiet — RALE 272:23
scan gently s. your brother man — BURN 76:16
scandal Love and s. — FIEL 135:11
scandalous s. and poor — ROCH 278:5
scapegoat Let him go for a s. — BIBL 35:32
scar s. on the conscience — BLAI 56:1
scare myself with my own desert — FROS 143:14
scarecrows s. of fools — HUXL 179:21
scared always been s. of *you* — PLAT 264:12
scarf S. up the tender eye — SHAK 301:3
scarlet His sins were s. — BELL 30:2
  raise the s. standard — CONN 102:14
  s. letter — HAWT 163:14
  s. soldiers — AUDE 19:14
  sins be as s. — BIBL 40:4
  wear his s. coat — WILD 359:6
scars He jests at s. — SHAK 306:27
  show his s. — SHAK 295:28
scattered enemies be s. — BOOK 63:14
  s. the proud — BIBL 46:33
  s. verses — PETR 262:13

scelerisque *s. purus* — HORA 175:8
scenery among savage s. — HOFF 171:11
  end of all natural s. — RUSK 282:16
scenes behind your s. — JOHN 188:4
scent s. of the roses — MOOR 244:7
sceptered s. isle — SHAK 305:22
sceptic too much of a s. — HUXL 180:1
schemes s. of political improvement — JOHN 188:21
  s. o' mice an' men — BURN 77:21
schizophrenic you are a s. — SZAS 329:20
Schleswig-Holstein S. question — PALM 258:6
scholars philosophers and s. — PASC 259:24
  S. dispute — HORA 174:14
school every s. knows it — TAYL 331:4
  goeth to s. — BACO 23:15
  learned about in s. — JARR 183:12
  s. of mankind — BURK 76:2
  s. of Stratford atte Bowe — CHAU 91:15
schoolboy Every s. knows — MACA 221:13
  whining s., with his satchel — SHAK 290:12
schoolboys s. from their books — SHAK 306:33
schoolchildren What all s. learn — AUDE 19:16
schoolgirl priggish s. — GRIG 157:14
schoolman no s.'s subtle art — POPE 266:23
schoolmaster s. is abroad — BROU 70:9
schoolmasters s. puzzle their brain — GOLD 153:22
schoolrooms s. for 'the boy' — COOK 103:11
schools hundred s. of thought contend — MAO 227:14
schooner It was the s. Hesperus — LONG 218:11
science aim of s. — BREC 68:3
  All s. physics or stamp collecting — RUTH 283:18
  applications of s. — PAST 260:4
  countenance of all s. — WORD 366:20
  Dismal S. — CARL 85:16
  essence of s. — BRON 69:7
  grand aim of all s. — EINS 126:12
  How s. dwindles — YOUN 369:25
  In s., read — BULW 74:3
  In s. the credit goes — DARW 110:15
  In s., we must be — CURI 108:15
  instrument of s. — JOHN 186:17
  it is not s. — KELV 198:4
  s. and everyday life — FRAN 142:6
  S. finds — ANON 10:17
  S. is an edged tool — EDDI 124:23
  s. is at a loss — CHOM 94:7
  S. is built up of facts — POIN 266:1
  S. is organized knowledge — SPEN 321:5
  S. is part of culture — GOUL 154:15
  s. is strong — SZAS 329:21
  S. moves, but slowly — TENN 333:29
  S. must begin with myths — POPP 268:27
  s. reassures — BRAQ 67:19
  S. without religion is lame — EINS 126:2
  tragedy of S. — HUXL 179:16
  triumph of modern s. — WAUG 352:10
  true s. and study — CHAR 91:9
sciences Books must follow s. — BACO 23:29
scientific empirical s. system — POPP 268:26
  new s. truth — PLAN 264:10
  plunges into s. questions — HUXL 179:22
  s. power has outrun — KING 201:1
  S. truth — MAXW 231:15
scientist elderly s. states — CLAR 97:4
  exercise for a research s. — LORE 218:19
  not try to become a s. — EINS 126:13
scientists company of s. — AUDE 19:24
scissor long, red-legged s.-man — HOFF 171:8
scissors end up using s. — HOCK 171:3
scoff fools, who came to s. — GOLD 153:9
scope that man's s. — SHAK 310:5
score no matter what the s. — HORN 175:26
scorer One Great S. — RICE 275:17

scorn Laugh no man to s.	BIBL 42:22	Over the s. to Skye	STEV 326:1
S. not the Sonnet	WORD 365:25	over the summer s.	TENN 334:26
sound Of public s.	MILT 239:10	Poem of the S.	RIMB 277:3
surmounted by s.	CAMU 83:18	sailed the wintry s.	LONG 218:11
think foul s.	ELIZ 130:14	s. gave up the dead	BIBL 53:21
scorned fury, like a woman s.	CONG 102:7	s. is not full	BIBL 39:7
scorpions chastise you with s.	BIBL 37:8	s. itself floweth in your veins	TRAH 341:10
Scotch as a S. banker	DAVI 110:21	s.-mark of my utmost sail	SHAK 305:13
Mary, ma S. Bluebell	LAUD 209:14	S. of Faith	ARNO 16:11
scotched s. the snake	SHAK 301:1	S. shall give up her dead	BOOK 65:10
Scotchman S. ever sees	JOHN 188:13	s.! the sea!	XENO 367:7
Scotland flower of S.	WILL 360:18	s. to shining sea	BATE 27:17
I do indeed come from S.	JOHN 188:12	s. was all frothy	SMIT 319:17
in S. supports the people	JOHN 187:1	see nothing but s.	BACO 22:2
Stands S.	SHAK 301:18	serpent-haunted s.	FLEC 138:3
white rose of S.	MACD 222:17	set in the silver s.	SHAK 305:22
Scots S. lords at his feet	BALL 25:18	snotgreen s.	JOYC 193:4
S., wha hae wi' Wallace bled	BURN 77:10	suffer a s.-change	SHAK 307:23
Scotsman S. on the make	BARR 27:4	there was no more s.	BIBL 53:22
S. with a grievance	WODE 362:16	those in peril on the s.	WHIT 356:19
Scottish S. Parliament	EWIN 133:12	thousand furlongs of s.	SHAK 307:17
Scotty Beam me up, S.	RODD 278:8	to the s. in ships	BOOK 64:9
scoundrel over forty is a s.	SHAW 312:16	two if by s.	LONG 218:6
refuge of a s.	JOHN 189:9	unplumbed, salt, estranging s.	ARNO 17:1
scouts s.' motto	BADE 24:5	uttermost parts of the s.	BOOK 65:3
scrabble s. with all the vowels	ELLI 131:8	water in the rough rude s.	SHAK 305:27
scrap s. of paper	BETH 32:21	waves of the s.	AESC 3:20
scraps stolen the s.	SHAK 299:1	went to s.	LEAR 210:15
scratch quick sharp s.	BROW 72:15	who rush across the s.	HORA 174:27
scratching s. of a pen	LOVE 219:12	why the s. is boiling hot	CARR 87:3
s. of my finger	HUME 178:13	willing foe and s. room	ANON 12:4
s. of pimples on the body	WOOL 364:1	wine-dark s.	HOME 172:16
screw s. your courage	SHAK 300:8	wrinkled s. beneath him	TENN 332:6
turn of the s.	JAME 182:23	**seagreen** s. Incorruptible	CARL 85:12
scribble Always s., scribble, scribble	GLOU 151:18	**seagulls** When s. follow a trawler	CANT 84:13
scribbling mob of s. women	HAWT 163:15	**seal** opened the seventh s.	BIBL 53:10
scribendi S. cacoethes	JUVE 194:9	S. of the Prophets	KORA 205:17
scribes s. and Pharisees, hypocrites	BIBL 45:29	**sealed** My lips are s.	BALD 25:4
scrip My s. of joy	RALE 272:23	**sealing wax** ships—and s.	CARR 87:3
scripture devil can cite S.	SHAK 302:13	**sear** fall'n into the s.	SHAK 301:27
Holy S. containeth	BOOK 65:11	**search** in s. of an author	PIRA 263:16
know more of the s.	TYND 344:7	travels the world in s.	MOOR 243:19
S. moveth us	BOOK 59:11	**seas** dangers of the s.	PARK 259:7
scriptures all holy S.	BOOK 60:20	foam Of perilous s.	KEAT 196:23
scroll charged with punishments the s.	HENL 166:9	Scuttling across the floors of silent s.	ELIO 128:32
scrotumtightening s. sea	JOYC 193:4	strange s. of thought	WORD 365:16
sculptor great s. or painter	RUSK 282:12	such as pass on the s.	BOOK 65:9
sculpture like that of s.	RUSS 283:8	**seashells** She sells s.	SULL 327:11
scum Okie means you're s.	STEI 323:21	**seashore** boy on the s.	NEWT 250:16
rich are the s. of the earth	CHES 93:10	**season** dry brain in a dry s.	ELIO 128:21
s. of the earth	WELL 354:5	In a summer s.	LANG 207:18
scuttling S. across the floors of silent seas	ELIO 128:32	man has every s.	FOND 139:1
sea around the glassy s.	HEBE 164:19	no s. knows, nor clime	DONN 119:16
as the waters cover the s.	BIBL 40:18	S. of mists	KEAT 197:1
beneath a rougher s.	COWP 105:15	there is a s.	BIBL 39:10
best thing is—the s.	JERR 185:8	word spoken in due s.	BIBL 38:28
burst Into that silent s.	COLE 100:18	**seasoned** Like s. timber	HERB 167:26
cloud out of the s.	BIBL 37:12	s. with salt	BIBL 52:1
cold grey stones, O S.	TENN 331:15	**seasons** lovers' s. run	DONN 119:15
complaining about the s.	POWE 270:14	man for all s.	WHIT 357:17
dominion of the s.	COVE 104:18	O s., O castles	RIMB 277:4
down to the s. again	MASE 230:18	s. alter	SHAK 303:19
flowing s.	CUNN 108:13	**seaworms** Battening upon huge s.	TENN 333:13
having been at s.	JOHN 189:21	**second** my s. best bed	SHAK 311:1
home from s.	STEV 326:6	no s. acts	FITZ 137:15
houses are all gone under the s.	ELIO 128:7	no s. spring	PHIL 263:3
In a solitude of the s.	HARD 161:20	not a s. on the day	COOK 103:10
in my chains like the s.	THOM 337:19	s. at Rome	CAES 82:6
in the abysmal s.	TENN 333:12	s. oldest profession	REAG 274:3
Into a s. of dew	FIEL 135:6	things have s. birth	WORD 365:18
near to heaven by s.	GILB 149:14	truth 24 times per s.	GODA 152:1
never go to s.	GILB 150:19	when you come s.	HILL 169:3
one is of the s.	WORD 366:11	**secrecy** S. the human dress	BLAK 58:5

secret alms may be in s.   BIBL 43:21
  ceases to be a s.   BEHN 29:10
  concept of the official s.   WEBE 352:15
  discovered the s. of life   CRIC 106:17
  joys of parents are s.   BACO 23:1
  neurosis is a s.   TYNA 344:6
  no s. so close   SURT 328:2
  photograph is a s.   ARBU 14:13
  s. and inviolate Rose   YEAT 369:3
  s. anniversaries   LONG 217:14
  s., black, and midnight hags   SHAK 301:14
  s. magic of numbers   BROW 71:10
  s. of politics   BISM 55:3
  s. of the Lord   KEBL 197:22
  S. sits in the middle   FROS 143:25
secrets no s. are hid   BOOK 60:25
  s. are edged tools   DRYD 122:9
  such things to be holy s.   HIPP 169:20
sect attached to that great s.   SHEL 313:25
  loving his own s.   COLE 100:30
  paradise for a s.   KEAT 195:18
secure He is s.   SHEL 313:19
  past is s.   WEBS 352:17
sedge s. has withered   KEAT 195:23
seduction In s., the rapist   DWOR 123:16
see All that we s.   POE 265:15
  complain we cannot s.   BERK 31:16
  In all things Thee to s.   HERB 167:14
  into the wilderness to s.   BIBL 44:32
  I shall never s.   KILM 200:4
  last s. your father   YEAM 367:11
  like my roses to s. you   SHER 315:21
  make you s.   CONR 103:26
  never s. so much   SHAK 298:30
  no man s. me more   SHAK 296:11
  not worth going to s.   JOHN 190:2
  one can s. rightly   SAIN 284:9
  rather s. than be one   BURG 74:22
  s. me dance the Polka   GROS 158:2
  s. me sometime   WEST 355:10
  S. one promontory   BURT 78:6
  s. oursels as others see us   BURN 77:18
  s. the goodness   BOOK 62:18
  s. the object   ARNO 17:8
  s. the things thou dost not   SHAK 298:18
  s. what I eat   CARR 86:11
  s. what I say   WALL 349:16
  s. with, not through, the eye   BLAK 56:17
  they shall s. our God   KEBL 197:22
  To s. her is to love her   BURN 76:23
  wait and s.   ASQU 17:19
  yet I s. thee still   SHAK 300:12
  You s., but you do not observe   DOYL 120:14
seed blood of Christians is the s.   TERT 336:2
  good s. on the land   CAMP 83:6
seeds into the s. of time   SHAK 299:13
seeing s. what everybody has seen   SZEN 329:23
seek All I s., the heaven above   STEV 326:3
  go s. the asses   BIBL 36:24
  If you s. a monument   ANON 13:22
  s., and ye shall find   BIBL 44:6
  S. ye first the kingdom   BIBL 44:1
  S. ye the Lord   BIBL 41:13
  sometime did me s.   WYAT 367:1
  strive, to s., to find   TENN 335:8
  We s. him here   ORCZ 254:3
seeking s. asses found   MILT 239:17
seeming keep S. and savour   SHAK 309:24
seems s. too little or   BARR 26:20
seen anybody here is s. Kelly   MURP 247:8
  evidence of things not s.   BIBL 52:14
  God whom he hath not s.   BIBL 52:34
  I have s. war   ROOS 279:10

not s., and yet have believed   BIBL 49:18
s. one city slum   AGNE 3:25
should be s. to be done   HEWA 168:11
Too early s. unknown   SHAK 306:26
what I have s.   THOM 337:15
Who hath not s. thee   KEAT 197:2
segregation S. now   WALL 349:12
Seine flows the S.   APOL 14:8
seize s. the day   HORA 175:7
  s. the flow'r   BURN 77:12
select each one should s.   SHEL 313:25
  Not a s. party   KEAT 197:19
selection Natural S.   DARW 110:6
  Natural s. a mechanism   FISH 136:5
self divided s.   LAIN 206:16
  only S. to please   BLAK 57:24
  to thine own s. be true   SHAK 291:31
self-consumer s. of my woes   CLAR 96:26
self-defence it was in s.   MARL 228:5
self-esteem s., grounded on just   MILT 239:3
self-evident s. beings   NEWM 249:20
  truths to be s.   ANON 11:14
self-help spirit of s.   SMIL 317:20
self-interest heedless s.   ROOS 279:12
selfishness Reduce s.   LAO 208:3
self-love s. and social   POPE 268:1
self-preservation s. in the other   JEFF 184:16
self-righteousness S. is not religion   BRON 69:9
self-sacrifice S. enables us   SHAW 312:19
self-sufficing reasoning, s. thing   WORD 365:14
sell dreams to us   BEDD 28:20
  I s. here, Sir   BOUL 66:10
  mind to s. his house   SWIF 328:9
  no man might buy or s.   BIBL 53:13
  One does not s. the earth   CRAZ 106:14
  s., or deny, or delay   MAGN 225:6
  s. that thou hast   BIBL 45:18
  s. the present life   KORA 205:9
selling lives by s. something   STEV 325:8
  S. off the family silver   MACM 224:6
semblable Hypocrite lecteur,—mon s.   BAUD 27:18
semi s.-house-trained polecat   FOOT 139:3
semper Quod ubique, quod s.   VINC 346:18
  S. aliquid novi   PLIN 265:6
  S. eadem   ANON 13:18
  Sic s. tyrannis   ANON 13:19
senator S., and a Democrat   JOHN 186:5
senators I look at the s.   HALE 159:12
  s. burst with laughter   AUDE 18:17
send S. in the clowns   SOND 320:12
  s. me   BIBL 40:10
sensational s. to read in the train   WILD 358:12
sensations O for a life of s.   KEAT 197:10
sense Common s. is not   VOLT 348:12
  deviates into s.   DRYD 122:8
  Devoid of s. and motion   MILT 238:4
  echo to the s.   POPE 267:14
  Have you no s. of decency   WELC 353:12
  men of s. never tell   SHAF 289:6
  Money is like a sixth s.   MAUG 231:10
  Satire or s.   POPE 266:22
  Take care of the s.   CARR 86:15
  talk s. to the American people   STEV 325:2
  want of s.   DILL 116:15
senses subtlety of the s.   BACO 23:27
sensibility dissociation of s.   ELIO 130:8
  it is an immense s.   JAME 182:19
sensible S. men   DISR 117:27
sensitive S. Plant   SHEL 314:18
sensual s. pleasure without vice   JOHN 191:2
sent man s. from God   BIBL 48:16
sentence No! No! S. first   CARR 86:22
  s. is enough   PLAU 265:5

sentence (*cont.*)
s. is factually significant — AYER 21:19
sentenced s. to death in my absence — BEHA 29:7
sentences Backward ran s. — GIBB 149:7
sentry stands a wingèd s. — VAUG 345:14
separate can't s. peace — MALC 226:3
s. and equal station — JEFF 183:17
separated they cannot be s. — SMIT 319:10
separately all hang s. — FRAN 142:1
separation impel them to the s. — JEFF 183:17
prepare for a s. — QUIN 272:10
real s. of powers — DENN 113:3
September days hath S. — ANON 11:11
When you reach S. — ANDE 6:15
sepulchres s. — BIBL 45:31
seraglio s. of eunuchs — FOOT 139:2
seraphims Above it stood the s. — BIBL 40:8
serfdom abolish s. — ALEX 4:13
sergeant S. Pepper — TYNA 344:5
This fell s., death — SHAK 294:10
serial obituary in s. form — CRIS 107:4
serious s.-minded activity — MONT 242:19
War is too s. — CLEM 98:2
sermon rejected the S. on the Mount — BRAD 67:9
sermons S. and soda-water — BYRO 80:26
S. in stones — SHAK 290:5
serpent be the s. under't — SHAK 299:26
infernal s. — MILT 237:18
my s. of old Nile — SHAK 289:15
Now the s. was more subtil — BIBL 34:14
s. beguiled me — BIBL 34:18
s.-haunted sea — FLEC 138:3
s. subtlest beast — MILT 239:4
s. upon a rock — BIBL 39:4
sharper than a s.'s tooth — SHAK 297:29
serpents wise as s. — BIBL 44:27
servant carried His s. by night — KORA 205:10
cracked lookingglass of a s. — JOYC 193:5
good and faithful s. — BIBL 46:4
Is thy s. a dog — BIBL 37:26
s. depart in peace — BIBL 47:6
s. of the Living God — SMAR 317:17
s. with this clause — HERB 167:15
thy s. heareth — BIBL 36:22
Your s.'s cut in half — GRAH 154:20
servants Between them and s. — BARC 26:11
s. will do that for us — VILL 346:16
serve Fleet in which we s. — BOOK 65:8
love to s. my country — GIBR 149:8
s. Him in this world — CATE 88:16
s. in the wars — BOOK 65:15
s. the Lord with gladness — BOOK 64:2
s. two masters — BIBL 43:25
s. your captives' need — KIPL 203:8
than s. in heaven — MILT 237:23
They also s. — MILT 239:31
will not s. if elected — SHER 315:27
service devoted to your s. — ELIZ 130:23
done the state some s. — SHAK 305:14
Every kind of s. — HALE 159:14
Pressed into s. — FROS 143:26
s. is perfect freedom — BOOK 60:2
s.? The rent we pay — CLAY 97:16
servile freed from s. bands — WOTT 366:22
serving cumbered about much s. — BIBL 47:17
six honest s.-men — KIPL 203:17
servitude base laws of s. — DRYD 122:2
servum *O imitatores, s. pecus* — HORA 175:4
sesame Open S. — ARAB 14:12
sesquipedalia s. *verba* — HORA 174:15
sessions s. of sweet silent thought — SHAK 310:7
set s. himself doggedly to it — JOHN 188:5
S. thine house in order — BIBL 40:28

sets sun never s. — NORT 251:22
setting against a s. sun — SHAK 308:2
settled s. will — STEE 323:9
settlement through the Act of S. — RICE 276:2
seven acts being s. ages — SHAK 290:11
hewn out her s. pillars — BIBL 38:17
Jacob served s. years — BIBL 35:4
s. days are more than enough — AUST 21:12
s. feet of English ground — HARO 162:14
S. types of ambiguity — EMPS 132:25
Until seventy times s. — BIBL 45:16
seventh moon is in the s. house — RADO 272:19
opened the s. seal — BIBL 53:10
seventy At s.-seven it is time — JOHN 187:6
s. years young — HOLM 172:4
Until s. times seven — BIBL 45:16
sever kiss, and then we s. — BURN 76:17
several S. excuses — HUXL 179:13
sewers houses thick and s. — MILT 239:5
sex attempt to insult s. — LAWR 209:18
call you darling after s. — BARN 26:18
dies from lack of s. — ATWO 18:10
for my own s. — AUST 21:5
give a s. to mind — WOLL 363:11
isn't s. but death — SONT 320:13
Is s. dirty — ALLE 5:13
keep making up these s. rules — SALI 284:15
Mind has no s. — WOLL 363:11
Money was exactly like s. — BALD 24:22
mostly about having s. — LODG 217:2
only unnatural s. act — KINS 201:15
practically conceal its s. — NASH 248:10
S. and drugs and rock and roll — DURY 123:15
S. and taxes — JONE 191:11
S. never an obsession — BOY 67:4
s. with someone I love — ALLE 5:12
subordination of one s. — MILL 234:12
weaker s. — ALEX 5:1
When you have money, it's s. — DONL 118:17
sexes there are three s. — SMIT 319:9
sexier make it s. — GILL 150:29
sexton s. tolled the bell — HOOD 172:22
sexual man's idea of his s. rights — STAN 323:5
not have s. relations — CLIN 98:12
of all the s. perversions — HUXL 179:12
S. intercourse began — LARK 208:14
shabby tamed and s. tigers — HODG 171:4
shade gentlemen of the s. — SHAK 294:16
in a green s. — MARV 229:17
light, s., and perspective — CONS 103:3
sitting in the s. — KIPL 202:6
whiter s. of pale — REID 275:3
shades S. of the prison-house — WORD 365:6
till the s. lengthen — NEWM 250:4
shadow but the s. of heaven — MILT 238:31
dream of a s. — PIND 263:13
Falls the S. — ELIO 128:23
fleeth also as a s. — BIBL 38:1
in the s. of death — BIBL 46:34
little s. that goes — STEV 325:29
little s. that runs — CROW 108:1
little s. that runs — HAGG 159:2
s. of death — BIBL 40:13
s. of death — BOOK 64:8
s. of our night — SHEL 313:18
s. of some unseen Power — SHEL 313:27
s. of the Valois — CHES 93:1
s. will be shown — NIET 251:6
valley of the s. of death — BOOK 62:15
shadows but s. — SHAK 304:3
events cast their s. — CAMP 83:11
half sick of s. — TENN 333:17
less liquid than their s. — TESS 336:4

long s. on county grounds | MAJO 225:19
Our fatal s. | FLET 138:12
see only their own s. | PLAT 265:1
s. flee away | BIBL 39:34
Types and s. | THOM 337:13
shaft s., at random sent | SCOT 287:15
shag common cormorant (or s.) | ISHE 181:5
shake Earth must s. | HORA 175:9
only S.-scene in a country | GREE 157:2
s. off the dust | BIBL 44:26
shaken S. and not stirred | FLEM 138:7
shakers movers and s. | O'SH 255:15
Shakespeare less S. he | BROW 72:7
Our sweetest S. | MILT 236:25
reproduce works of S. | WILE 359:24
S. by flashes of lightning | COLE 101:4
S. unlocked his heart | WORD 365:25
S.—the nearest thing | OLIV 253:9
When I read S. | LAWR 209:26
Shakespearean That S. rag | BUCK 73:17
Shakespeherian S. Rag | ELIO 129:25
Shalimar loved beside the S. | HOPE 173:12
shallow s. in himself | MILT 239:20
Shalott Lady of S. | TENN 333:17
shalt Thou s. have no other gods | BIBL 35:24
shame glory is in their s. | BIBL 51:25
secret s. destroyed | RICH 276:9
s. unto him | BIBL 50:21
waste of s. | SHAK 310:24
shantih S., shantih | ELIO 130:3
shape might be any s. | CARR 87:7
pressed out of s. | FROS 143:26
s. of things to come | WELL 354:12
shapen s. in wickedness | BOOK 63:6
shaping s. spirit of imagination | COLE 100:2
share all persons alike s. | ARIS 15:22
shark s. has pretty teeth | BREC 68:6
sharks s. circling, and waiting | CLAR 97:2
Sharon rose of S. | BIBL 39:32
sharp 'Tis a s. remedy | RALE 273:5
sharpening s. my oyster knife | HURS 178:22
sharper s. than a serpent's tooth | SHAK 297:29
sharpness s. of death | BOOK 59:19
sharps s. and flats | BROW 72:22
shatter s. the vase | MOOR 244:7
shaves and s. and takes a train | WHIT 356:2
she chaste, and unexpressive s. | SHAK 290:18
life and loves of a s.-devil | WELD 353:14
S. sells sea-shells | SULL 327:11
S. who must be obeyed | HAGG 159:3
shearers sheep before her s. | BIBL 41:11
shears resembles a pair of s. | SMIT 319:10
with th' abhorrèd s. | MILT 236:31
sheaves bring his s. with him | BOOK 64:25
Sheba Another S. queen | WITH 362:6
queen of S. | BIBL 37:5
shed Burke under a s. | JOHN 190:17
prepare to s. them now | SHAK 297:5
shall his blood be s. | BIBL 34:29
sheep ensample to his s. | CHAU 91:21
Feed my s. | BIBL 49:19
found my s. which was lost | BIBL 47:28
get back to these s. | ANON 12:18
giveth his life for the s. | BIBL 48:37
hills like young s. | BOOK 64:13
hungry s. look up | MILT 236:32
in s.'s clothing | BIBL 44:11
like lost s. | BOOK 59:12
like s. have gone astray | BIBL 41:10
mere s.-herding | POUN 270:6
savaged by a dead s. | HEAL 164:8
s. before her shearers | BIBL 41:11
s. in sheep's clothing | CHUR 96:11

s. on his right hand | BIBL 46:6
s. that have not a shepherd | BIBL 37:16
s., that were wont to be | MORE 244:15
s. to pass resolutions | INGE 180:15
two hundred years like a s. | TIPU 340:13
sheeps s.' guts | SHAK 304:9
sheet brought in the white s. | LORC 218:16
England's winding s. | BLAK 56:13
wet s. | CUNN 108:13
shell fired a 15-inch s. | RUTH 283:20
prettier s. | NEWT 250:16
Shelley did you once see S. | BROW 72:16
shells choirs of wailing s. | OWEN 256:9
shelter s. from the stormy blast | WATT 352:2
shelves symmetry of s. | LAMB 207:1
shepherd call you, S. | ARNO 16:20
Dick the s. | SHAK 299:5
God of love my S. is | HERB 167:23
good s. | BIBL 48:37
Lord is my s. | BOOK 62:14
Lord's my s. | SCOT 288:2
my s. is | BAKE 24:17
sheep that have not a s. | BIBL 37:16
shepherds s. abiding in the field | BIBL 47:2
s. and butchers | VOLT 348:20
s. give a grosser name | SHAK 294:1
s. watched their flocks | TATE 330:21
sheriff I shot the s. | MARL 228:5
Sherman general (yes mam) s. | CUMM 108:7
shibboleth Say now S. | BIBL 36:15
shield Our S. and Defender | GRAN 155:8
S. of Abraham | SIDD 316:8
s. of British fair play | AITK 4:3
trusty s. | LUTH 220:19
shieling From the lone s. | GALT 145:12
shift let me s. for myself | MORE 244:19
shilling s. life will give you | AUDE 19:19
shine Arise, s. | BIBL 41:16
Boy you can gimme a s. | GORD 154:9
Let your light so s. | BIBL 43:16
Lord make his face s. | BIBL 35:35
s., and run to and fro | BIBL 42:21
s. in company | SWIF 328:23
s. on, harvest moon | NORW 252:6
shines s. and stinks | RAND 273:12
shining s. from shook foil | HOPK 173:16
s. morning face | SHAK 290:12
S. nowhere but in the dark | VAUG 345:18
woman of s. loveliness | YEAT 369:4
ship all I ask is a tall s. | MASE 230:18
being in a s. | JOHN 188:11
build your s. of death | LAWR 209:24
idle as a painted s. | COLE 100:19
infantry or a fleet of s. | SAPP 285:15
like a sinking s. | WOOL 364:4
O S. of State | LONG 217:7
s. has weathered every rack | WHIT 356:23
S. me somewheres | KIPL 202:16
s. on the sea | LORC 218:17
ships all the s. at sea | WINC 361:18
Hell to s. | AESC 3:19
launched a thousand s. | MARL 228:7
Of shoes—and s. | CARR 87:3
S. that pass in the night | LONG 218:8
something wrong with our bloody s. | BEAT 27:23
There go the s. | BOOK 64:5
to the sea in s. | BOOK 64:9
we've got the s. | HUNT 178:15
wooden wall is your s. | THEM 337:6
shire That s. which we may call | DRAY 121:11
shires bugles calling from sad s. | OWEN 256:9
Round both the s. | HOUS 176:9

shirt Song of the S.	HOOD 172:26	on the s. of giants	NEWT 250:15
shit s. in a silk stocking	NAPO 248:9	on your young s.	SPAR 321:1
shock-proof s. detector	HEMI 166:6	s. held the sky suspended	HOUS 176:4
shiver praised and left to s.	JUVE 194:5	s. of giants	BERN 32:10
tremble and s.	HOOD 172:19	**shout** shouted with a great s.	BIBL 36:7
shivering like Augustine s.	WILL 360:7	s. that tore hell's concave	MILT 237:28
shoal bank and s. of time	SHAK 299:28	S. with the largest	DICK 115:20
shoals s. of herring	MACC 222:12	**shouting** thunder and the s.	BIBL 38:9
shock characterized by s.	FRAN 142:7	tumult and the s.	KIPL 202:19
Future s.	TOFF 340:18	**show** business like s. business	BERL 32:3
S. and Awe	ULLM 344:9	s. any just cause	BOOK 61:25
S.-headed Peter	HOFF 171:10	s. business with blood	BRUN 73:12
s. of the new	DUNL 123:10	s. that you have one	CHES 92:19
s. them and keep them up to date	SHAW 311:20	**showers** with his s. soote	CHAU 91:11
short, sharp s.	GILB 150:4	**showery** S., Flowery, Bowery	ELLI 131:13
we shall s. them	SHAK 297:21	**showing** worth s.	DANT 109:19
shocked s. by this subject	BOHR 58:17	**shreds** king of s. and patches	SHAK 293:20
shocking looked on as something s.	PORT 268:29	thing of s. and patches	GILB 149:21
shocks s. the mind of a child	PAIN 257:3	**shrewishly** speaks very s.	SHAK 308:23
shoe cast out my s.	BOOK 63:13	**shrieking** s. and squeaking	BROW 72:22
s.'s latchet	BIBL 48:20	**shrimp** s. learns to whistle	KHRU 200:1
shoes call for his old s.	SELD 288:12	**shrink** all the boards did s.	COLE 100:20
I'm just wearing better s.	WINF 361:21	**shroud** stain the stiff dishonoured s.	ELIO 129:16
Of s.—and ships	CARR 87:3	striped s.	THOM 338:10
Put off thy s.	BIBL 35:13	**shrug** with a patient s.	SHAK 302:14
shoeshine riding on a smile and a s.	MILL 234:24	**shudder** s. in the loins engenders	YEAT 368:16
shook monk who s. the world	MONT 243:9	**shuffle** s. the cards	CERV 89:21
more it's s. it shines	HAMI 160:12	**shuffled** s. off this mortal coil	SHAK 292:23
Ten days that s. the world	REED 274:14	**shun** let me s. that	SHAK 298:5
shoot S., if you must	WHIT 357:13	**shut** Men s. their doors	SHAK 308:2
s. me in my absence	BEHA 29:7	S. up he explained	LARD 208:12
s. the Hippopotamus	BELL 29:17	**shutter** click the s.	EISE 126:20
s. the pianist	ANON 10:9	**shuttle** contingency for the space s.	ANON 7:20
They s. horses don't they	MCCO 222:15	**si** S. possis recte	HORA 174:21
young idea how to s.	THOM 338:24	**Sibyllam** Nam S. quidem Cumis	PETR 262:18
You s. a fellow down	HARD 162:4	**sick** do not make me s.	WHIT 357:7
shooting war minus the s.	ORWE 255:2	do the s. no harm	NIGH 251:13
shoots green s. of recovery	LAMO 207:11	extremely s.	PRIO 271:2
shop back to the s.	LOCK 217:1	half s. of shadows	TENN 333:17
foul rag-and-bone s.	YEAT 367:16	I am s., I must die	NASH 248:18
shopkeepers nation of s.	ADAM 2:16	Rose, thou art s.	BLAK 58:2
nation of s.	NAPO 248:7	s. and wicked	AUST 21:15
shore for the further s.	SMIT 318:5	s., and ye visited me	BIBL 46:7
s. Of the wide world	VIRG 347:12	s. for home	KEAT 196:23
sounds by the s.	KEAT 197:8	they that are s.	BIBL 44:19
stretch from s. to shore	YEAT 368:15	treatment to help the s.	HIPP 169:18
shored s. against my ruins	WATT 352:1	when he is s.	JOHN 190:11
shores wilder s. of love	ELIO 130:2	**sickness** falling s.	SHAK 296:21
shorn green grass s.	BLAN 58:7	in s. and in health	BOOK 61:27
short Anger is a s. madness	BACO 22:27	s. that destroyeth	BOOK 63:25
by s. grasses	HORA 174:24	**side** Hear the other s.	AUGU 20:7
it is well it is s.	PORT 269:8	my hand into his s.	BIBL 49:17
long and the s. and the tall	TAYL 331:5	on the other s.	BUNY 74:19
nasty, brutish, and s.	HUGH 177:12	other s. of the hill	WELL 354:7
s., sharp shock	HOBB 170:19	passed by on the other s.	BIBL 47:15
s. time to live	GILB 150:4	S. by side	WOOD 363:17
Take s. views	BOOK 62:4	Who is on my s.	BIBL 37:30
That lyf so s.	SMIT 319:7	**sides** looked at life from both s.	MITC 241:11
while to make it s.	CHAU 92:2	said on both s.	ADDI 3:5
shorter s. by the head	THOR 339:9	**sidestreets** down the s.	GINS 151:4
time to make it s.	ELIZ 130:13	**Siegfried** washing on the S. Line	KENN 198:11
shot be s. at	PASC 259:16	**sieve** in a s. I'll thither sail	SHAK 299:10
Certain men the English s.	HARD 162:10	went to sea in a S.	LEAR 210:12
fired the s.	YEAT 368:18	**sifted** s. a nation	STOU 326:17
I s. the sheriff	BALL 25:9	**sigh** s. no more, ladies	SHAK 304:10
s. heard round the world	MARL 228:5	**sighed** S. and looked	THOM 339:1
shots of the best s.	EMER 131:20	s. as a lover	GIBB 149:2
shoulder giant's s. to mount on	VOLT 348:21	s. his soul	SHAK 303:1
stand s. to shoulder	COLE 101:3	**sighs** on the Bridge of S.	BYRO 80:8
shoulders City of the Big S.	BLAI 55:22	sound of s.	PETR 262:13
from her s. did fall	SAND 285:4	**sight** all very well at first s.	SHAW 312:7
grow beneath their s.	WYAT 367:2	in the s. of God	BOOK 61:23
	SHAK 304:22	out of s.	THOM 337:11

thousand years in thy s.	BOOK 63:22	s., snarling trumpets	KEAT 195:12
sights few more impressive s.	BARR 27:4	There's a s. lining	FORD 139:10
sign If only God would give some s.	ALLE 5:16	thirty pieces of s.	BIBL 46:9
In this s. shalt thou conquer	CONS 103:5	time hath to s. turned	PEEL 261:5
Jews require a s.	BIBL 50:14	s. snarling trumpets	SHAK 309:16
outward and visible s.	BOOK 61:20	**similia** S. similibus curantur	ANON 13:21
signal do not see the s.	NELS 249:5	**Simon** real S. Pure	CENT 89:18
signals s. of the ancient flame	DANT 109:14	**simple** and never s.	WILD 358:4
signed hand that s. the paper	THOM 337:22	beautiful and s.	HENR 166:20
significance s. of an event	CART 88:8	Everything is very s. in war	CLAU 97:11
signo In hoc s. vinces	CONS 103:5	**simplicitas** O sancta s.	HUSS 179:1
signs merely conventional s.	CARR 87:18	**simplicity** Embrace s.	LAO 208:3
multiply my s. and my wonders	BIBL 35:16	holy s.	JERO 185:3
s. and wonders	BIBL 48:28	O holy s.	HUSS 179:1
s. of the times	BIBL 45:8	**simplify** s. me when I'm dead	DOUG 120:3
words are but the s.	JOHN 186:17	S., simplify	THOR 339:19
silence easy step to s.	AUST 21:1	**Simpsons** less like the S.	BUSH 78:15
eternal s.	PASC 259:20	**sin** beauty is only s. deep	SAKI 284:13
even darkness and s.	KELL 198:1	brother s. against me	BIBL 45:16
flashes of s.	SMIT 319:11	by making a s. of it	FRAN 141:7
foster-child of s.	KEAT 196:5	dark world of s.	BICK 54:15
Go to where the s. is	GOOD 154:6	fall into no s.	BOOK 60:3
lies are often told in s.	STEV 325:24	go, and s. no more	BIBL 48:34
mind moves upon s.	YEAT 368:17	hate the s.	AUGU 20:10
other side of s.	ELIO 127:17	He that is without s.	BIBL 48:33
rest is s.	SHAK 294:13	I had not known s.	BIBL 50:5
s., exile, and cunning	JOYC 193:2	in s. hath my mother	BOOK 63:6
s. in heaven	BIBL 53:10	lose the s.	POPE 266:12
S. is deep as Eternity	CARL 85:6	My s., my soul	NABO 247:14
S. is the virtue	BACO 22:7	no s. but ignorance	MARL 228:12
s. of a dream	ROSS 280:11	not innocence but s.	BROW 72:11
s. of the law	HOBB 170:21	physicists have known s.	OPPE 253:18
S., sing to me	HOPK 173:18	Shall we continue in s.	BIBL 50:1
Sound of S.	SIMO 317:3	single venial s.	NEWM 250:2
With s. and tears	BYRO 81:26	S. is behovely	JULI 193:14
silenced because you have s. him	MORL 245:3	s. not	BIBL 51:17
silencing justified in s.	MILL 234:8	s.'s a pleasure	BYRO 80:23
silent impossible to be s.	BURK 76:9	taketh away the s.	BIBL 48:21
into the s. land	ROSS 280:14	wages of s. is death	BIBL 50:4
Laws are s.	CICE 96:23	we have no s.	BIBL 52:31
mornings are strangely s.	CARS 87:25	Which is my s.	DONN 119:2
one must be s.	WITT 362:10	worst s. towards our fellow	SHAW 311:14
s. majority	NIXO 251:15	your s. will find you out	BIBL 36:2
S., upon a peak in Darien	KEAT 196:28	**sincere** Always be s.	TRUM 342:17
t is s.	ASQU 18:2	**sincerely** s. want to be rich	CORN 104:7
unlocked her s. throat	GIBB 149:5	**sincerity** s. is a dangerous thing	WILD 358:17
silk make a s. purse	MORT 246:5	**sinews** s. of the soul	FULL 144:15
shit in a s. stocking	NAPO 248:9	s. of war	CICE 96:22
s. hat on a Bradford millionaire	ELIO 129:28	Stiffen the s.	SHAK 295:16
s. makes the difference	FULL 144:18	very s. of virtue	WALT 350:11
s. stockings	JOHN 188:4	**sing** celebrate myself, and s. myself	WHIT 357:3
soft as s. remains	HILL 169:2	come, let us s.	BOOK 63:26
silken s. terms precise	SHAK 299:2	I'll s. you twelve O	ANON 9:2
s. tie	SCOT 287:11	I s. of brooks	HERR 168:1
silks in s. my Julia goes	HERR 168:7	I, too, s. America	HUGH 177:13
silkworm of s. size or immense	MOOR 244:1	never heard no horse s.	ARMS 16:6
silkworms s. droop	BASH 27:13	Places where they s.	BOOK 60:4
silliest s. woman can manage a clever man	KIPL 203:22	Silence, s. to me	HOPK 173:18
silly it's good to be s.	HORA 175:20	S. 'em muck	MELB 232:5
such a s. question	STER 324:9	s. in the robber's face	JUVE 194:10
You were s. like us	AUDE 19:1	s. like birds i' the cage	SHAK 298:23
silvae paulum s. super his	HORA 175:25	S. me a song	STEV 326:1
silvas inter s. Academi	HORA 175:5	S., my tongue	FORT 139:20
silver all the Georgian s.	MACM 224:6	S. no sad songs	ROSS 280:17
bringing gold, and s.	BIBL 37:7	s. the ancient ways	YEAT 369:9
for a handful of s.	BROW 72:12	s. the body electric	WHIT 356:22
in her s. shoon	DE L 112:17	S. unto the Lord	BOOK 62:21
Selling off the family s.	MACM 224:6	S. unto the Lord	BOOK 64:1
s. apples of the moon	YEAT 369:6	Soul clap its hands and s.	YEAT 368:27
s. cord be loosed	BIBL 39:28	think that they will s. to me	ELIO 129:4
s. foot in his mouth	RICH 276:7	thousand tongues to s.	WESL 354:20
s. link	SCOT 287:11	Who would not sing for S.	MILT 236:18
s. plate on a coffin	CURR 108:17	world in ev'ry corner s.	HERB 167:10

singe it do s. yourself	SHAK 296:8	s. honest serving-men	KIPL 203:17
singeing s. of the King of Spain's Beard	DRAK 121:7	S. hundred threescore and six	BIBL 53:14
singer sans s., and—sans End	FITZ 136:11	snowed for s. days	THOM 338:2
s. of an empty day	MORR 245:10	**sixty** rate of s. minutes an hour	LEWI 213:18
singing exercise of s.	BYRD 79:21	When I'm s. four	LENN 212:23
hear mermaids s.	DONN 119:14	**skate** I s. to where	GRET 157:12
like a s. bird	ROSS 280:10	**skating** s. over thin ice	EMER 132:9
nest of s. birds	JOHN 188:3	**skeletons** s. copulating	BEEC 28:22
s. of birds	BIBL 39:33	**skies** danced the s.	MAGE 225:2
s. still dost soar	SHEL 314:26	man whose god is in the s.	SHAW 312:14
s. will never be done	SASS 285:28	thou climb'st the s.	SIDN 316:13
waves of thy sweet s.	SHEL 314:15	watcher of the s.	KEAT 196:28
single but a s. thought	HALM 160:10	**skin** beauty being only s.-deep	KERR 199:12
come not s. spies	SHAK 293:30	Can the Ethiopian change his s.	BIBL 41:22
s. in the field	WORD 366:5	castle of my s.	LAMM 207:9
s. man in possession	AUST 21:6	my s. is red	SITT 317:11
with a s. hair	DRYD 122:18	s. is a different shade	HAMM 160:25
single-handedly perhaps be won s.	LULA 220:16	s. of my teeth	BIBL 38:3
sings instead of bleeding, he s.	GARD 146:2	skull beneath the s.	ELIO 130:4
song my paddle s.	JOHN 186:13	thick s. is a gift	ADEN 3:15
why the caged bird s.	DUNB 123:7	**skins** sisters under their s.	KIPL 202:13
sinister strange and s.	JAME 182:22	**skipped** mountains s. like rams	BOOK 64:13
sink sitting in the kitchen s.	SMIT 318:11	**skipper** s. had taken his little daughter	LONG 218:11
sinking like a s. ship	WOOL 364:4	**skirmish** trivial s. fought near Marathon	GRAV 155:17
sinned More s. against than sinning	SHAK 298:4	**skull** place of a s.	BIBL 49:10
s. against heaven	BIBL 47:31	s. beneath the skin	ELIO 130:4
s. exceedingly	MISS 240:16	**sky** above, the vaulted s.	CLAR 96:27
sinner confessions of a justified s.	HOGG 171:14	And the blue s.	WORD 364:21
dead s.	BIER 54:23	bowl we call The S.	FITZ 136:17
Love the s.	AUGU 20:10	clean the s.	ELIO 129:7
s. that repenteth	BIBL 47:29	diamond in the s.	TAYL 331:2
to me a s.	BIBL 48:6	ethereal s.	ADDI 3:7
who is that young s.	HOUS 176:1	evening is spread out against the s.	ELIO 128:28
sinners favoured the s. slain	WESL 354:23	Music shall untune the s.	DRYD 122:13
God and s. reconciled	WESL 354:18	pie in the s.	HILL 169:4
miserable s.	BOOK 60:10	prisoners call the s.	WILD 359:7
publicans and s.	BIBL 44:18	shoulders held the s. suspended	HOUS 176:4
S.; of whom I am chief	BIBL 52:5	wide and starry s.	STEV 326:5
s. to repentance	BIBL 44:20	yon twelve-winded s.	HOUS 176:12
s.' ways prosper	HOPK 174:7	**Skye** Over the sea to S.	BOUL 66:9
sinning More sinned against than s.	SHAK 298:4	Over the sea to S.	STEV 326:1
sins Be all my s. remembered	SHAK 292:27	**slain** new-s. knight	BALL 25:21
half the s. of mankind	RUSS 282:23	s. a thousand men	BIBL 36:18
Her s. are forgiven	BIBL 47:11	s. his thousands	BIBL 36:30
His s. were scarlet	BELL 30:2	s. in the way of God	KORA 205:20
manifold s. and wickedness	BOOK 59:11	s. think he is slain	EMER 131:18
multitude of s.	BIBL 52:29	**slander** one to s. you	TWAI 343:14
s. are attempts to fill	WEIL 353:5	**slang** S. is a language	SAND 285:10
s. be as scarlet	BIBL 40:4	**slanged** sneered and s.	BELL 29:22
s. of the fathers	BOOK 60:26	**slant** certain S. of light	DICK 116:5
sint S. *ut sunt*	CLEM 98:4	**slaughter** lamb to the s.	BIBL 41:11
Sion remembered thee, O S.	BOOK 65:1	through s. to a throne	GRAY 156:13
sirens Blest pair of S.	MILT 236:2	**slave** Better be a s.	BRON 69:12
Sisera fought against S.	BIBL 36:11	freedom to the s.	LINC 214:19
sister my s., my spouse	BIBL 40:1	freeing any s.	LINC 214:18
no friend like a s.	ROSS 280:12	half s.	LINC 214:13
s. and my sister's child	COWP 105:17	moment the s. resolves	GAND 145:15
s. throw up a lot	WALK 349:7	No s. is a slave to the same lengths	MILL 234:14
trying to violate your s.	STRA 326:19	passion's s.	SHAK 293:8
sisterhood S. is powerful	MORG 245:1	s.-morality	NIET 251:11
sisters And so do his s.	GILB 150:17	s. of the passions	HUME 178:12
harmonious s.	MILT 236:2	s. to its animosity	WASH 351:9
s. under their skins	KIPL 202:13	you were a Christian s.	HENL 166:11
weird s.	SHAK 299:11	**slavery** S. is	SUMN 327:15
Sisyphus imagine that S. is happy	CAMU 83:20	S. they can have	BURK 75:10
sit So I did s. and eat	HERB 167:18	sold off into s.	TRUT 342:20
Teach us to s. still	ELIO 127:25	state of s.	GILL 150:28
Though I s. down now	DISR 117:4	testimony against s.	DOUG 120:7
sits I s. and thinks	PUNC 272:2	wise and good in s.	MACA 221:11
sitting s. in the kitchen sink	SMIT 318:11	**slaves** Air for S. to breathe	ANON 10:4
stay s. down	CART 88:9	at the mill with s.	MILT 239:21
situation s. excellent	FOCH 138:18	Britons never will be s.	THOM 338:23
six Rode the s. hundred	TENN 331:19	creed of s.	PITT 263:20

Englishmen never will be s.   SHAW 312:2
have made our s.   DARW 110:12
Now we are s.   HAGG 158:16
S. cannot breathe in England   COWP 105:25
S. of the Lamp   ARNO 16:10
sons of former s.   KING 200:17
slavish O imitators, you s. herd   HORA 175:4
slayer s. think he slays   EMER 131:18
slays If any man thinks he s.   UPAN 344:15
man thinks he s.   BHAG 33:19
slayer think he s.   EMER 131:18
Whoso s. a soul   KORA 205:12
sleekit Wee, s., cow'rin'   BURN 77:19
sleep balmy s.   YOUN 369:26
Care-charmer S.   DANI 109:5
Care-charming S.   FLET 138:13
Death and his brother S.   SHEL 314:17
do I wake or s.   KEAT 196:25
grey and full of s.   YEAT 369:13
How s. the brave   COLL 101:16
I lay me down to s.   ANON 9:23
In s. a king   SHAK 310:15
in soot I s.   BLAK 57:16
Let us s. now   OWEN 256:16
little s.   BIBL 38:16
Macbeth does murder s.   SHAK 300:16
Macbeth shall s. no more   SHAK 300:17
men who s. badly   RUSS 282:22
miles to go before I s.   FROS 143:27
One short s. past   DONN 118:23
Shake off this downy s.   SHAK 300:24
S. after toil   SPEN 321:26
s. and a forgetting   WORD 365:6
S.! it is a gentle thing   COLE 100:25
S. no more   SHAK 300:16
s. of a labouring man   BIBL 39:14
S. on Blest pair   MILT 238:27
S. on (my Love!)   KING 200:9
slept an azure-lidded s.   KEAT 195:16
some must s.   SHAK 293:11
uninvaded s.   TENN 333:12
We shall not all s.   BIBL 51:3
sleepers seven s. den   DONN 119:9
s. in that quiet earth   BRON 69:16
sleepeth not dead, but s.   BIBL 44:23
sleeping Lay your s. head   AUDE 19:8
s. with an elephant   TRUD 342:8
sleepless s. soul that perished   WORD 365:20
s. with cold commemorative   ROSS 280:21
sleeps Now s. the crimson petal   TENN 334:21
while the world s.   NEHR 249:1
sleepwalker assurance of a s.   HITL 170:8
sleeve Ash on an old man's s.   ELIO 128:12
heart upon my s.   SHAK 304:17
sleeves Americanism with its s. rolled   MCCA 222:8
language that rolls up its s.   SAND 285:10
slepen s. al the nyght with open ye   CHAU 91:12
slept His saints s.   ANON 14:2
slew s. his master   BIBL 37:16
slimy thousand s. things   COLE 100:24
slings s. and arrows   SHAK 292:23
slip s., slide, perish   ELIO 128:4
slippered lean and s. pantaloon   SHAK 290:14
slit S. your girl's   KING 201:11
slits s. the thin-spun life   MILT 236:31
slitty all be s.-eyed   PHIL 263:1
sliver envious s. broke   SHAK 294:2
slop woman with a s.-pail   HOPK 174:11
slopes butler's upper s.   WODE 362:22
sloth Shake off dull s.   KEN 198:5
time in studies is s.   BACO 23:10
slouches S. towards Bethlehem   YEAT 369:2
slough friendly bombs, fall on S.   BETJ 33:4

s. was Despond   BUNY 74:7
slow come he s.   SCOT 287:16
telling you to s. down   ANON 7:22
Time is too s.   VAN 345:10
slowly angel to pass, flying s.   FIRB 135:23
Architecture acts the most s.   DIMN 116:17
Make haste s.   AUGU 20:13
mills of God grind s.   LONG 218:1
Run s.   OVID 255:23
Science moves, but s.   TENN 333:29
twist s. in the wind   EHRL 125:15
sluggard thou s.   BIBL 38:15
slughorn Dauntless the s.   BROW 71:26
sluicing browsing and s.   WODE 362:21
slum seen one city s.   AGNE 3:25
slumber little s.   BIBL 38:16
S.'s chain has bound me   MOOR 244:13
slumbers Golden s. kiss your eyes   DEKK 112:10
slums gay intimacy of the s.   WAUG 352:6
slush pure as the driven s.   BANK 26:8
small big squadrons against the s.   BUSS 78:24
both great and s.   COLE 100:27
day of s. nations   CHAM 90:2
grind exceeding s.   LONG 218:1
In s. proportions   JONS 192:3
s. business party   BEAZ 28:7
s., but perfectly formed   COOP 103:17
s. college   WEBS 352:16
S. is beautiful   SCHU 286:16
s. Latin   JONS 192:6
still s. voice   BIBL 37:14
they are very s.   UPDI 344:10
with s. men no great thing   MILL 234:11
smaller s. fleas to bite 'em   SWIF 329:2
smallest s. amount of lying   BUTL 79:12
s. room of my house   REGE 274:16
smart girls that are so s.   CARE 84:21
smashed s. up things and creatures   FITZ 137:12
smattering s. of everything   DICK 115:22
smell ancient and fish-like s.   SHAK 307:25
I s. the blood   SHAK 298:12
Money has no s.   VESP 346:5
s. and hideous hum   GODL 152:4
s. a rat   ROCH 278:2
sweet keen s.   ROSS 280:22
smelleth s. the battle afar off   BIBL 38:9
smells s. like roses   JOHN 186:10
smile call me that, s.   WIST 362:5
has a nice s.   GROM 158:1
hear a s.   CROS 107:20
my Julia's lips do s.   HERR 168:2
riding on a s. and a shoeshine   MILL 234:24
s., and be a villain   SHAK 292:3
S. at us, pay us   CHES 93:6
s. dwells a little longer   CHAP 90:17
s. of accomplishment   PLAT 264:14
s. of cosmic Cheshire cat   HUXL 179:14
s., smile, smile   ANON 11:19
smiler s. with the knyf   CHAU 91:26
smiles charmed it with s.   CARR 87:20
daggers in men's s.   SHAK 300:27
robbed that s.   SHAK 304:25
smiling hides a s. face   COWP 105:19
s., damnèd villain   SHAK 292:3
S. through her tears   HOME 172:11
smite ready to s. once   MILT 236:33
s. all the firstborn   BIBL 35:20
s. thee on thy right cheek   BIBL 43:17
smith s., a mighty man is he   LONG 218:9
s. of his own fortune   CLAU 97:9
smithy village s. stands   LONG 218:9
smoke can't see their s.   FLEI 138:6
s.-filled room   SIMP 317:9

smoke (*cont.*)
S. gets in your eyes   HARB 161:5
s. of their torment   BIBL 53:16
Stygian s.   JAME 182:9
smoking not found any s. guns   BLIX 58:10
s. flax   BIBL 41:5
smoky burnt-out ends of s. days   ELIO 129:10
smooth I am a s. man   BIBL 34:35
never did run s.   SHAK 303:7
smote s. the king of Israel   BIBL 37:18
s. them hip and thigh   BIBL 36:17
snail creeping like s.   SHAK 290:12
said a whiting to a s.   CARR 86:17
s.'s on the thorn   BROW 72:23
snake like a wounded s.   POPE 267:12
scotched the s.   SHAK 301:1
s. hidden in the grass   VIRG 347:20
snakes no s. to be met with   JOHN 189:22
You spotted s.   SHAK 303:22
snapper s.-up of unconsidered trifles   SHAK 309:22
snare mockery, and a s.   DENM 113:1
rabbit in a s.   STEP 324:5
s. of the fowler   BOOK 64:24
s. of the hunter   BOOK 63:24
snares s. of death   BOOK 64:16
Snark S. *was* a Boojum   CARR 87:21
snatch s. me away   FROS 143:9
snatched s. from Jove   MANI 227:1
s. the lightning   TURG 343:3
sneer devil in his s.   BYRO 80:17
refute a s.   PALE 258:2
teach the rest to s.   POPE 266:21
They s. at me   FITZ 136:18
sneering I was born s.   GILB 149:22
snicker hold my coat, and s.   ELIO 129:1
snip S.! Snap! Snip   HOFF 171:9
snobbery S. with Violence   BENN 30:21
snorted Or s. we   DONN 119:9
snotgreen s. sea   JOYC 193:4
snow amid the winter's s.   CASW 88:15
congealed s.   PARK 259:4
few acres of s.   VOLT 348:7
I, this incessant s.   DE L 112:16
listens in the s.   STEV 324:22
shivering in the s.   SOUT 320:25
s. before the summer sun   TECU 331:9
s. came flying   BRID 68:17
s. falling faintly   JOYC 192:17
S. on snow   ROSS 280:13
used to be S. White   WEST 355:12
white as s.   BIBL 40:4
snowed s. for six days   THOM 338:2
snows s. of yesteryear   VILL 346:17
snowy S., Flowy, Blowy   ELLI 131:13
snug s. little Island   DIBD 114:11
so And s. do I   HARD 162:8
if it was s., it might be   CARR 87:2
soaked s. to the skin   COHE 99:11
soap smiles and s.   CARR 87:20
S. and education   TWAI 343:9
What! no s.   FOOT 139:4
soar creep as well as s.   BURK 75:28
not to s.   MACA 221:17
soaring s. ever singest   SHEL 314:26
sober Be s., be vigilant   BIBL 52:30
godly, righteous, and s. life   BOOK 59:14
s. me up   FITZ 137:10
S., steadfast, and demure   MILT 236:12
to Philip s.   ANON 7:11
social no religion but s.   WESL 354:24
self-love and s.   POPE 268:1
s. and economic experiment   HOOV 173:3
s. contract   ROUS 281:8

socialism religion of S.   BEVA 33:9
S. can only arrive   VIER 346:14
s. would not lose its human face   DUBČ 122:24
socialists We are all s. now   HARC 161:10
society affluent s.   GALB 145:2
bonds of civil s.   LOCK 216:20
consolidates s.   JOHN 188:2
desperate oddfellow s.   THOR 339:16
Great S.   JOHN 186:7
happiness of s.   ADAM 2:10
live in s.   ARIS 15:20
no such thing as S.   THAT 336:22
One great s.   WORD 365:19
selects her own S.   DICK 116:3
S. is indeed a contract   BURK 75:23
S. is now one polished horde   BYRO 81:9
S. needs to condemn   MAJO 225:18
s. of privacy   RAND 273:10
s. where it is safe to be   STEV 325:4
three for s.   THOR 339:17
sock Jonson's learnèd s.   MILT 236:25
Socrates contradict S.   SOCR 320:1
soda Sermons and s.-water   BYRO 80:26
sodomy rum, s., prayers, and the lash   CHUR 95:22
sods s. with our bayonets turning   WOLF 363:1
soft her s. and chilly nest   KEAT 195:14
s. answer   BIBL 38:25
s. as the dawn   LOVE 219:13
s. under-belly of Europe   CHUR 95:15
s. was the sun   LANG 207:18
softly s. and suddenly vanish   CARR 87:19
S. come and softly go   ORRE 254:4
Tread s.   YEAT 368:8
softness s. of my body will be guarded   LOWE 219:16
soil grows in every s.   BURK 75:10
powers of the s.   RICA 275:14
sold s. all that he had   BIBL 45:2
s. my reputation   FITZ 137:2
soldier chocolate cream s.   SHAW 311:8
death, who had the s. singled   DOUG 120:4
go to your Gawd like a s.   KIPL 203:9
having been a s.   JOHN 189:21
s. of the Great War   ANON 10:21
s.'s life is terrible hard   MILN 235:13
s.'s pride   BROW 72:10
soldiers believe the s.   SALI 284:19
Old s. never die   FOLE 138:20
Onward, Christian s.   BARI 26:13
our s. slighted   QUAR 272:8
scarlet s.   AUDE 19:14
s., mostly fools   BIER 54:20
S., this solitude   DE L 112:16
steel my s.' hearts   SHAK 295:24
sole *amor che muove il s.*   DANT 109:17
solid s. for fluidity   CHUR 95:3
solitary Be not s.   BURT 78:8
s. confinement inside our own skins   WILL 360:13
s. Highland lass!   WORD 366:5
Their s. way   MILT 239:14
till I am s.   JOHN 188:8
solitude each protects the s.   RILK 277:2
feel his s. more keenly   VALÉ 345:1
one for s.   THOR 339:17
s. of the sea   HARD 161:20
s. Through which we go   DE L 112:16
solitudes two s. protect   RILK 277:1
solitudinem S. *faciunt pacem*   TACI 329:24
Solomon all S.'s wisdom   BIBL 37:5
anointed S.   BIBL 37:4
greater than S.   BIBL 44:38
S. in all his glory   BIBL 43:26
S. wrote the Proverbs   NAYL 248:21
soluble art of the s.   MEDA 232:1

solution always a well-known s.   MENC 232:23
  can't see the s.   CHES 93:16
  either part of the s.   CLEA 97:17
  final s.   HEYD 168:12
  kind of s.   CAVA 89:13
  total s.   GOER 152:7
some fool s. of the people   LINC 215:8
somebody When every one is s.   GILB 149:16
someone it was s. else   ROGE 278:13
  necessary to s.   EMER 132:2
  s., somewhere, may be happy   MENC 232:19
something s. for Posterity   ADDI 3:10
  S. must be done   EDWA 125:9
  s. of the night   WIDD 357:20
  S. should be done   EDWA 125:9
  s. to forgive   LEWI 213:17
  Time for a little s.   MILN 235:19
sometime see me s.   WEST 355:10
  woman is a s. thing   HEYW 168:15
sometimes s. always   RICH 276:13
somewhat s. against thee   BIBL 53:2
somewhere get s. else   CARR 86:26
  S. over the rainbow   HARB 161:8
son bear a s.   BIBL 40:12
  be called thy s.   BIBL 47:31
  brought forth her firstborn s.   BIBL 47:2
  Forgive your s.   JOYC 193:9
  hateth his s.   BIBL 38:24
  his only begotten S.   BIBL 48:27
  if his s. ask bread   BIBL 44:7
  leichter of a fair s.   ELIZ 130:10
  my s. was dead   BIBL 47:33
  O Absalom, my s., my son   BIBL 37:1
  S. of man   BIBL 44:16
  This is my beloved S.   BIBL 43:8
  This is my s.   TENN 335:5
  unto us a s. is given   BIBL 40:14
  wise s.   BIBL 38:19
  Woman, behold thy s.   BIBL 49:12
song before his presence with a s.   BOOK 64:2
  carcase of an old s.   THOM 338:11
  glorious s. of old   SEAR 288:5
  hate a s. that has sold   BERL 32:5
  let satire be my s.   BYRO 81:11
  made my s. a coat   YEAT 367:17
  My s. is love unknown   CROS 107:21
  On wings of s.   HEIN 165:7
  play a s. for me   DYLA 124:9
  Sans wine, sans s.   FITZ 136:11
  sold my reputation for a s.   FITZ 137:2
  s. charms the sense   MILT 238:8
  s. is ended   BERL 32:2
  s. my paddle sings   JOHN 186:13
  s. of praise be sung   POTT 269:9
  S. of the Shirt   HOOD 172:26
  s. that found a path   KEAT 196:23
  s. that never ends   GOET 152:9
  s. the Syrens sang   BROW 71:6
  s. was wordless   SASS 285:28
  start a s.   VIRG 347:22
  till I end my s.   SPEN 322:7
  Time is our tedious s.   MILT 237:10
  unto the Lord a new s.   BOOK 62:21
  unto the Lord a new s.   BOOK 64:1
  what they teach in s.   SHEL 313:29
  wine and s.   LUTH 220:20
songs all their s. are sad   CHES 92:26
  For ever piping s.   KEAT 196:9
  Sing no sad s.   ROSS 280:17
  s. of Apollo   SHAK 299:6
  s. of pleasant glee   BLAK 57:15
  s. of Spring   KEAT 197:3
  sweetest s. are those   SHEL 314:28

sonnet Scorn not the S.   WORD 365:25
sonnets written s. all his life   BYRO 80:28
sons Bears all its s. away   WATT 352:4
  God's s. are things   MADD 224:16
  My s. ought to study mathematics   ADAM 2:6
  s. and daughters of Life   GIBR 149:9
  s. and daughters shall prophesy   BIBL 42:12
  s. Of Belial, flown with insolence   MILT 237:27
  S. of the dark and bloody ground   O'HA 253:5
  s. of the morning   HEBE 164:16
sooner s. every party breaks up   AUST 20:22
soot in s. I sleep   BLAK 57:16
sophistry s. and illusion   HUME 178:5
soporific lettuce is 's.'   POTT 269:11
sorrow any sorrow like unto my s.   BIBL 41:24
  beguile thy s.   SHAK 308:7
  doubt and s.   BARI 26:14
  Give s. words   SHAK 301:19
  glut thy s.   KEAT 196:14
  increaseth s.   BIBL 39:9
  In s. thou shalt bring forth   BIBL 34:20
  Love's s. lasts all through life   FLOR 138:16
  more in s. than in anger   SHAK 291:27
  not sure of s.   SWIN 329:11
  sphere of our s.   SHEL 314:24
  such sweet s.   SHAK 306:35
  with s. to the grave   BIBL 35:8
sorrows man of s.   BIBL 41:9
  When s. come   SHAK 293:30
sorry having to say you're s.   SEGA 288:11
  heartily s.   BOOK 61:8
  I'm s., now, I wrote it   BURG 74:23
  S. for itself   LAWR 209:23
sorts all s. and conditions   BOOK 60:16
Sosostris Madame S.   ELIO 129:20
soteriological In s. terms   FENT 134:16
sought Love s. is good   SHAK 309:4
  s. it with thimbles   CARR 87:20
soul bitterness of his s.   BIBL 42:22
  captain of my s.   HENL 166:9
  casket of my s.   KEAT 196:30
  city of the s.   BYRO 80:9
  dark night of the s.   FITZ 137:13
  dark night of the s.   JOHN 185:15
  engineers of the s.   GORK 154:11
  essence of a human s.   CARL 85:21
  every subject's s.   SHAK 295:21
  flow of s.   POPE 268:5
  give his own s.   BOLT 59:3
  half conceal the S. within   TENN 332:27
  hidden language of the s.   GRAH 155:2
  if I have a s.   ANON 10:1
  iron entered into his s.   BOOK 64:6
  longeth my s. after thee   BOOK 62:27
  lose his own s.   BIBL 46:27
  love in another's s.   LAYT 210:4
  lover of my s.   WESL 354:21
  Medicine for the s.   ANON 9:19
  mind and s., according   TENN 332:26
  my s. is white   BLAK 57:20
  My s., there is a country   VAUG 345:14
  my unconquerable s.   HENL 166:8
  my whole s. through My lips   TENN 332:7
  No coward s. is mine   BRON 69:13
  no s. to be damned   THUR 340:8
  not engineers of the s.   KENN 199:4
  One s. inhabiting two bodies   ARIS 15:24
  owe my s. to the company store   TRAV 341:12
  Perdition catch my s.   SHAK 304:30
  pray the Lord my s. to take   ANON 9:23
  save his s.   BIBL 41:29
  sighed his s.   SHAK 303:1
  sinews of the s.   FULL 144:15

soul (*cont.*)
s., a spirit — FAUL 134:12
S. clap its hands and sing — YEAT 368:27
s. doth magnify the Lord — BIBL 46:32
s. in bliss — SHAK 298:20
s. is an enchanted boat — SHEL 314:15
s. is Christ's abode — KEBL 197:22
s. is form — SPEN 322:6
s. is immortal — PLAT 265:3
s. is immortal — SOCR 319:27
s. is marching on — ANON 9:7
s. of a man is born — JOYC 192:25
s. of fire — JOHN 187:25
s. of our dear brother — BOOK 62:6
s. of pleasure — BEHN 29:11
S. of the Age — JONS 192:4
S. selects her own — DICK 116:3
s. shall be required of thee — BIBL 47:21
s. swooned slowly — JOYC 192:17
S., thou hast much goods — BIBL 47:20
sweet and virtuous S. — HERB 167:26
than that one s. — NEWM 250:2
two to bear my s. away — ANON 9:18
vale of s.-making — KEAT 197:17
windows of the s. — BLAK 56:17
with s. so dead — SCOT 287:12
soulless when work is s. — CAMU 84:4
souls engineers of human s. — STAL 322:23
letters mingle s. — DONN 119:20
open windows into men's s. — ELIZ 130:19
our waking s. — DONN 119:10
s. mounting up to God — ROSS 280:19
S. of poets dead — KEAT 196:4
s. of the righteous — BIBL 42:20
s. out of men's bodies — SHAK 304:9
they have no s. — COKE 99:15
times that try men's s. — PAIN 257:10
Two s. — HALM 160:10
sound alive with the s. of music — HAMM 160:21
deep s. strikes — BYRO 80:4
feeling, then, not s. — STEV 324:20
in a s. body — JUVE 194:12
s. and fury — SHAK 301:31
s. must seem an echo — POPE 267:14
S. of Silence — SIMO 317:3
s. of surprise — BALL 26:5
s. the back — SAUS 286:4
what is that s. — AUDE 19:14
sounds better than it s. — NYE 252:13
S. and sweet airs — SHAK 307:29
s. will take care — CARR 86:15
soup blossom s. — BASH 27:14
S. of the evening — CARR 86:19
sour How s. sweet music is — SHAK 306:5
s. grapes — BIBL 41:28
source s. of little visible delight — BRON 69:15
sourest sweetest things turn s. — SHAK 310:16
south full of the warm S. — KEAT 196:18
go s. in the winter — ELIO 129:18
nor yet from the s. — BOOK 63:16
S. is avenged — BOOT 65:17
southern bore me in the s. wild — BLAK 57:20
S. trees bear strange — ALLE 5:11
souvenirs s. sont cors de chasse — APOL 14:7
sovereign Here lies our s. lord — ROCH 278:4
he will have no s. — COKE 99:16
S. has — BAGE 24:10
s. Nation — PAGE 256:20
subject and a s. — CHAR 90:21
to be a S. — ELIZ 130:11
sovereignty s. is an artificial soul — HOBB 170:13
sovereynetee Wommen desiren to have s. — CHAU 91:30
soviet Communism is S. power — LENI 212:9

sow hath the s. by the right ear — HENR 166:17
old s. that eats her farrow — JOYC 192:26
s. in tears — BOOK 64:25
S. returns to her Mire — KIPL 202:7
soweth whatsoever a man s. — BIBL 51:13
sown s. the wind — BIBL 42:10
space art of how to waste s. — JOHN 186:15
contingency for the s. shuttle — ANON 7:20
Filling a s. — O'KE 253:6
filling the s. — WEST 355:15
more s. where nobody is — STEI 323:16
S. is blue — HEIS 165:12
S. isn't remote — HOYL 177:6
time and s. — LAMB 207:6
untrespassed sanctity of s. — MAGE 225:3
spaces empty s. Between stars — FROS 143:14
s. in your togetherness — GIBR 149:10
vacant interstellar s. — ELIO 128:8
spaceship regarding S. Earth — FULL 144:14
spade call a s. a spade — BURT 78:2
Spain Lady of S. — REAV 274:10
leave S. — JUAN 193:11
rain in S. — LERN 213:8
span Contract into a s. — HERB 167:20
Eternity shut in a s. — CRAS 106:12
Less than a s. — BACO 24:2
Spaniards thrash the S. too — DRAK 121:9
Spanish To God I speak S. — CHAR 91:5
spare Brother can you s. a dime — HARB 161:6
do in his s. time — GILL 150:28
s. the beechen tree — CAMP 83:10
s. your country's flag — WHIT 357:13
Woodman, s. that tree — MORR 245:9
spared better s. a better man — SHAK 294:28
spareth s. his rod — BIBL 38:24
spark s.-gap is mightier — HOGB 171:12
s. of that ancient flame — VIRG 347:7
s. o' Nature's fire — BURN 76:25
Vital s. — POPE 266:10
sparks Ashes and s. — SHEL 314:7
as the s. fly upward — BIBL 37:39
s. among the stubble — BIBL 42:21
sparrow fall of a s. — SHAK 294:8
My lady's s. is dead — CATU 89:5
s. alight upon my shoulder — THOR 339:20
s. hath found her an house — BOOK 63:18
sparrows five s. sold — BIBL 47:19
pass through for the s. — GALB 145:4
two s. sold — BIBL 44:28
Spartans Go, tell the S. — SIMO 317:5
speak Books will s. plain — BACO 22:17
dare not s. its name — DOUG 120:2
didn't s. up — NIEM 251:3
difficult to s. — BURK 76:9
fears to s. of Ninety-Eight — INGR 180:20
grief that does not s. — SHAK 301:19
let him now s. — BOOK 61:25
Let us not s. of them — DANT 109:9
neither s. they — BOOK 64:15
one to s. — THOR 339:23
province of knowledge to s. — HOLM 172:1
s. as the common people do — ASCH 17:15
S. for England — AMER 6:2
S., Lord — BIBL 36:22
S. softly — ROOS 279:21
S. the speech — SHAK 293:4
s. when he is spoken to — STEV 325:30
S. ye comfortably — BIBL 40:29
when I think, I must s. — SHAK 290:20
whereof one cannot s. — WITT 362:10
speaking People talking without s. — SIMO 317:3
s. picture, with this end — SIDN 316:14
speaks He s. to Me — VICT 346:9

hides one thing and s. another | HOME 172:12
who s. does not know | LAO 208:8
spear Bring me my s. | BLAK 57:8
With a burning s. | ANON 12:5
spears s. into pruninghooks | BIBL 40:5
stars threw down their s. | BLAK 58:4
spectacle no s. so ridiculous | MACA 221:12
spectacles s. of books | DRYD 122:21
spectre s. of Communism | MARX 230:11
speech abridging the freedom of s. | CONS 103:7
freedom of s. | TWAI 343:11
freedom of the press's s. | TWAI 343:17
function of s. to free | BRAN 67:16
Speak the s. | SHAK 293:4
s. be alway with grace | BIBL 52:1
s. created thought | SHEL 314:14
S. impelled us | ELIO 128:14
S. is civilization itself | MANN 227:5
s. is like a cracked kettle | FLAU 137:23
s. is shallow as Time | CARL 85:6
s. only to conceal | VOLT 348:10
true use of s. | GOLD 153:19
verse is a measured s. | BACO 22:4
speechless s. real | BARZ 27:10
speed safety is in our s. | EMER 132:9
S., bonnie boat | BOUL 66:9
s. far faster than light | BULL 73:21
s. glum heroes | SASS 285:26
s. the going guest | POPE 268:6
S. the parting guest | POPE 268:6
Unsafe at any s. | NADE 247:18
spell foreigners always s. better | TWAI 343:16
lies beneath your s. | HOPE 173:12
s. of great knowledge | MAHA 225:10
s. TUESDAY | MILN 235:11
spelling s. is Wobbly | MILN 235:20
spend I intend to s. it | BUSH 78:20
s. more time with my family | FOWL 140:13
s. your way out | CALL 82:14
whatever you have, s. less | JOHN 190:10
spending Getting and s. | WORD 366:16
Riches are for s. | BACO 22:22
S. again | SHAK 310:12
spent all passion s. | MILT 239:27
speranza LASCIATE OGNI S. | DANT 109:8
spew s. thee out of my mouth | BIBL 53:4
sphere motion in one s. | SHAK 294:27
s., the cone | CÉZA 89:23
these walls thy s. | DONN 119:17
spice s. of life | COWP 105:27
spices land of s. | HERB 167:19
spicy s. nut-brown ale | MILT 236:23
spider kind of huge s.-web | JAME 182:19
said a s. to a fly | HOWI 177:4
s.'s touch, how exquisitely fine | POPE 267:23
spiders like s.' webs | ANAC 6:9
Weaving s. come not | SHAK 303:23
spies come not single s. | SHAK 293:30
voluntary s. | AUST 21:2
spill let them not s. me | MACN 224:12
spilt as water s. on the ground | BIBL 36:38
spin great world s. for ever | TENN 333:32
neither do they s. | BIBL 43:26
spinach I say it's s. | WHIT 356:3
spindle s. or mutilate | ANON 7:24
spinners long-legged s. | SHAK 303:23
spinning at evening s. | RONS 279:2
spires dreaming s. | ARNO 16:25
three steeple-house s. | FOX 140:17
spirit between s. and matter | HEIN 165:8
blithe S. | SHEL 314:25
Come, Holy S. | LANG 207:19
commend my s. | BIBL 48:11

commend my s. | BOOK 62:20
every pure and wise s. | EMER 132:12
forge his s. spirit | GUEV 158:8
fruit of the S. | BIBL 51:12
Love is a s. | SHAK 310:31
no more s. in her | BIBL 37:5
no s. can walk abroad | SHAK 291:11
pardlike S. | SHEL 313:16
poor in s. | BIBL 43:13
present in s. | BIBL 50:16
renew a right s. | BOOK 63:7
shaping s. of imagination | COLE 100:2
s. capable of compassion | FAUL 134:12
s. giveth life | BIBL 51:5
s. hath rejoiced | BIBL 46:32
s. indeed is willing | BIBL 46:15
s. of all knowledge | WORD 366:20
S. of Delight | SHEL 314:19
S. of Elijah | BIBL 37:20
S. of God | BIBL 34:3
s. of party | WASH 351:8
s. of the chainless mind | BYRO 81:19
s. of the Lord | BIBL 40:16
S. of the Lord God | BIBL 41:17
s. of the place | VIRG 347:15
s. passed before my face | BIBL 37:38
s. within nourishes | VIRG 347:13
spirits insult to the s. | RED 274:11
ruffle up your s. | SHAK 297:9
s. from the vasty deep | SHAK 294:23
two primal S. | ZORO 370:18
spiritu Et cum s. tuo | MISS 240:14
spiritual inward and s. grace | BOOK 61:20
Millions of s. creatures | MILT 238:26
Music is s. | MORR 245:22
not being a s. people | MANC 226:14
outrun our s. power | KING 201:1
spiritualist you are a s. | SZAS 329:20
spiritus Sancte S. | LANG 207:19
S. intus alit | VIRG 347:13
spit no gun, but I can s. | AUDE 19:15
s. upon my Jewish gabardine | SHAK 302:15
splash Old pond, leap-s. | BASH 27:12
splendeat late qui s. | HORA 174:12
splendid by the vision s. | WORD 365:7
s. and a happy land | GOLD 153:11
s. isolation | FOST 140:5
splendour s. falls on castle walls | TENN 334:13
s. in the grass | WORD 365:9
Stung by the s. | BROW 71:28
splendoured many-s. thing | THOM 338:18
split care what a s. infinitive | FOWL 140:12
make all s. | SHAK 303:11
when I s. an infinitive | CHAN 90:13
spoiled the Egyptians | BIBL 35:21
spoils belong the s. | MARC 227:16
spoken never been s. to like this | CHIR 94:2
never have s. yet | CHES 93:6
Rome has s. | AUGU 20:11
spoon ate with a runcible s. | LEAR 210:17
spoons counted our s. | EMER 132:4
let us count our s. | JOHN 188:15
world locks up its s. | SHAW 312:5
sport ended his s. with Tess | HARD 161:18
kill us for their s. | SHAK 298:15
owe to s. | CAMU 84:3
Serious s. | ORWE 255:2
s. for our neighbours | AUST 21:11
s. of kings | SOME 320:8
s. of kings | SURT 327:20
s. with Amaryllis | MILT 236:29
s. would be as tedious | SHAK 294:17
sports S. do not build character | BROU 70:11

sports (cont.)
s. of love — JONS 191:18
spot Out, damned s. — SHAK 301:21
Tip me the black s. — STEV 325:17
with a s. I damn him — SHAK 297:13
spots leopard change his s. — BIBL 41:22
spotted You s. snakes — SHAK 303:22
spouse my sister, my s. — BIBL 40:1
President's s. — BUSH 78:10
sprang s. to the stirrup — BROW 72:9
spread except it be s. — BACO 23:7
s. my dreams under your feet — YEAT 368:8
spring Alas, that s. should vanish — FITZ 137:3
bloom in the s. — GILB 150:9
Blossom by blossom the s. — SWIN 329:8
can S. be far behind — SHEL 314:8
easing the S. — REED 274:13
hounds of s. — SWIN 329:7
In the s. a young man's fancy — TENN 333:22
no second s. — PHIL 263:3
No s., nor summer beauty — DONN 118:20
only the right to s. — FOND 139:1
Pierian s. — DRAY 121:12
rifle all the breathing s. — COLL 101:15
songs of S. — KEAT 197:3
s. now comes unheralded — CARS 87:25
s. shut up, a fountain sealed — BIBL 40:1
Sweet lovers love the s. — SHAK 290:25
Sweet s., full of sweet days — HERB 167:25
this s. of love — SHAK 309:15
year's at the s. — BROW 72:23
springes s. to catch woodcocks — SHAK 291:32
springs Fifty s. — HOUS 176:7
Where s. not fail — HOPK 173:19
sprite fleeting, wav'ring s. — HADR 158:13
sprites s. and goblins — SHAK 309:17
spur Fame is the s. — MILT 236:30
I have no s. — SHAK 300:3
spurs this day to wynne his s. — EDWA 125:8
win his s. — EDWA 125:8
spy s. who came in from the cold — LE C 211:7
squadrons big s. against the small — BUSS 78:24
wingèd s. of the sky — MILM 235:8
square S. deal afterwards — ROOS 280:1
s. person has squeezed himself — SMIT 319:5
squat s. like a toad — MILT 238:28
s. pen rests — HEAN 164:11
squawking seven stars go s. — AUDE 18:13
squeak s. and gibber — SHAK 291:9
until the pips s. — GEDD 147:10
squeaking shrieking and s. — BROW 72:22
s. Cleopatra — SHAK 289:26
stab do I s. at thee — MELV 232:15
saw him s. — READ 273:18
stabat S. Mater dolorosa — JACO 182:2
stability natural s. of gold — SHAW 311:21
s. or enlargement — JOHN 186:18
s. pact is stupid — PROD 271:6
stable nothing s. in the world — KEAT 197:12
staff cockle hat and s. — SHAK 293:28
s. of faith to walk upon — RALE 272:23
thy rod and thy s. — BOOK 62:15
stag runnable s. — DAVI 110:18
stage All the world's a s. — SHAK 290:11
Don't put your daughter on the s. — COWA 105:5
played upon a s. — SHAK 309:8
this great s. of fools — SHAK 298:19
traffick of our s. — SHAK 306:21
wonder of our s. — JONS 192:4
stages four s. of man — LINK 215:11
stagger s. like a drunken man — BOOK 64:10
stagnant fen Of s. waters — WORD 364:23
stain bright s. on the vision — GRAV 155:18

stained kick a hole in a s. glass window — CHAN 90:10
s. with their own works — BOOK 64:7
stair by a winding s. — BACO 22:29
stairs another man's s. — DANT 109:16
stale How weary, s., flat — SHAK 291:16
stalking s. in my chamber — WYAT 367:1
stall Baby in an ox's s. — BETJ 33:2
stamp but the guinea's s. — BURN 76:26
physics or s. collecting — RUTH 283:18
stand By uniting we s. — DICK 116:9
can't s. the heat — TRUM 342:11
firm spot on which to s. — ARCH 14:17
Get up, s. up — MARL 228:4
Here s. I — LUTH 220:17
no time to s. and stare — DAVI 111:2
s. and look at them — WHIT 357:7
s. at the door, and knock — BIBL 53:5
S. by thyself — BIBL 41:18
S. by your man — WYNE 367:6
s. on either hand — MACA 221:22
s. out of my sun — DIOG 116:19
S. still — MARL 228:8
s. up for bastards — SHAK 297:26
s. up for Jesus — DUFF 122:28
who only s. and wait — MILT 239:31
standard raise the scarlet s. — CONN 102:14
standards S. are always out of date — BENN 30:20
standing mantle of the s. pool — SHAK 298:9
ought to die s. — VESP 346:7
s. by my man — CLIN 98:8
stands S. Scotland — SHAK 301:18
S. the Church clock — BROO 69:21
sun now s. — JOSE 192:14
star Being a s. has made it possible — DAVI 111:3
bright Occidental s. — BIBL 34:2
bright particular s. — SHAK 289:8
Bright s. — KEAT 195:9
catch a falling s. — DONN 119:14
constant as the northern s. — SHAK 296:27
evening s. — MILT 239:12
guests s.-scattered — FITZ 137:4
guiding s. behold — DIX 118:11
Hitch your wagon to a s. — EMER 132:17
like a falling s. — MILT 238:1
moth for the s. — SHEL 314:24
s.-crossed lovers — SHAK 306:20
S. for every State — WINT 362:4
s.-led wizards — MILT 237:6
s.-spangled banner — KEY 199:17
s. to steer her by — MASE 230:18
Sunset and evening s. — TENN 332:2
There was a s. danced — SHAK 304:8
twinkle, little s. — TAYL 331:2
we have seen his s. — BIBL 43:1
with one bright s. — COLE 100:23
stardust We are s. — MITC 241:12
stare no time to stand and s. — DAVI 111:2
Stark Molly S.'s a widow — STAR 323:7
starless s. and bible-black — THOM 338:4
starlight S. and dewdrop — FOST 140:7
s. lit my lonesomeness — HARD 162:9
starlit s. or a moonlit dome — YEAT 367:13
starred No memory of having s. — FROS 143:23
starry beautiful evening, very s. — WORD 364:6
wide and s. sky — STEV 326:5
stars all Danaë to the s. — TENN 334:22
climb half-way to the s. — CROS 107:19
crowned with the s. — TRAH 341:10
crown of twelve s. — BIBL 53:11
cut him out in little s. — SHAK 307:2
day-blind s. — BERR 32:17
erratik s. — CHAU 92:5
Far beyond the s. — VAUG 345:14

heaventree of s.	JOYC 193:8
journey-work of the s.	WHIT 357:6
looking at the s.	WILD 358:20
loved the s. too fondly	WILL 360:9
not in our s.	SHAK 296:19
puts the s. to flight	FITZ 136:6
seven s. go squawking	AUDE 18:13
s. are not hot enough	EDDI 124:19
s. are old	TAYL 331:3
s. came out	TENN 334:26
s. in her hair	ROSS 280:18
s. in their courses	BIBL 36:11
s. keep not their motion	SHAK 294:27
s. rush out	COLE 100:22
S. scribble on our eyes	CRAN 106:8
Stars, s.	SHAK 309:29
s.' tennis-balls	WEBS 352:25
s. threw down their spears	BLAK 58:4
s. where no human race is	FROS 143:14
struggle to the s.	ANON 13:15
sun and the other s.	DANT 109:17
way to the s.	VIRG 347:17
you chaste s.	SHAK 305:11
starshine s. at night	STEV 325:31
starship voyages of the s. *Enterprise*	RODD 278:7
start end is where we s. from	ELIO 128:16
s. together and finish	BEEC 28:23
s. to the finish	HORA 175:23
started arrive where we s.	ELIO 128:15
s. like a guilty thing	SHAK 291:10
starter few thought he was a s.	ATTL 18:8
startle come down and s.	AUDE 18:12
starts everything by s.	DRYD 121:21
starve Let not poor Nelly s.	CHAR 91:4
starved s. poet	LOCK 217:1
state all were for the s.	MACA 221:23
bosom of a single s.	DURH 123:13
done the s. some service	SHAK 305:14
glories of our blood and s.	SHIR 315:28
I am the S.	LOUI 219:1
in a free s.	CAVO 89:15
mine was the middle s.	DEFO 111:18
no such thing as the S.	AUDE 19:18
Only in the s.	HEGE 165:2
O Ship of S.	LONG 217:7
reinforcement of the S.	CAMU 84:1
rule the s.	DRYD 121:18
S. business is a cruel trade	HALI 160:4
S. for every Star	WINT 362:4
s. has no place	TRUD 342:7
S. is not 'abolished'	ENGE 132:26
s. to be endured	JOHN 187:18
S. which dwarfs its men	MILL 234:11
s. without the means	BURK 75:14
While the S. exists	LENI 212:7
stately S. Homes of England	COWA 105:7
s. homes of England	HEMA 166:1
S., plump Buck Mulligan	JOYC 193:3
states goodly s. and kingdoms	KEAT 196:27
indestructible S.	CHAS 91:10
many sovereign S.	PAGE 256:20
statesman set a s. right	YEAT 368:22
s. is a politician	TRUM 342:13
station antique s.	BEER 29:2
her s. keeping	JACO 182:2
private s.	ADDI 3:2
statistic million deaths a s.	STAL 323:1
statistical life is s. improbability	DAWK 111:8
statistics experiment needs s.	RUTH 283:19
give plenty of s.	CARR 87:22
lies, damned lies and s.	DISR 118:9
uses s. as a drunken man	LANG 207:16
We are just s.	HORA 174:22

status *from S. to Contract*	MAIN 225:15
status quo restored the s.	SQUI 322:21
statutes keep my s.	BIBL 35:33
stay here I s.	MACM 224:3
If we can't s. here alive	MONT 243:8
love is here to s.	GERS 148:9
more care to s.	SHAK 307:6
S. for me there	KING 200:10
things to s. as they are	LAMP 207:13
stays nothing s.	HERA 167:2
steadfast s. as thou art	KEAT 195:9
steady S., boys, steady	GARR 146:6
steal silently s. away	LONG 217:9
s. from many, it's research	MIZN 241:20
S. from the world	POPE 268:13
s. more than a hundred men	PUZO 272:6
s. my Basil-pot	KEAT 195:21
s. my thunder	DENN 113:5
thieves break through and s.	BIBL 43:23
Thou shalt not s.	BIBL 35:28
Thou shalt not s.	CLOU 98:19
stealing hanged for s. horses	HALI 160:2
picking and s.	BOOK 61:19
steals politician who s.	PLUN 265:9
s. my purse	SHAK 304:31
s. something	SHAK 304:25
stealth Do good by s.	POPE 268:12
good action by s.	LAMB 207:8
steam employ s. navigation	LARD 208:11
steamers little holiday s.	PRIE 270:22
steed his s. was the best	SCOT 287:17
steel All shod with s.	WORD 364:14
clad in complete s.	MILT 236:6
Give them the cold s.	ARMI 15:25
more than complete s.	ANON 9:3
with a line of s.	RUSS 283:17
worthy of their s.	SCOT 287:9
wounded surgeon plies the s.	ELIO 128:9
steeple North Church s.	REVE 275:8
three s.-house spires	FOX 140:17
steeples dreary S. of Fermanagh	CHUR 94:22
s. far and near	HOUS 176:9
stelle *muove il sole e l'altre s.*	DANT 109:17
stem s. of Jesse	BIBL 40:16
step first s. that is difficult	DU D 122:27
One more s. along	CART 88:5
one small s. for a man	ARMS 16:8
To s. aside is human	BURN 76:16
stepped in blood S. in	SHAK 301:10
stepping rise on s.-stones	TENN 332:25
s. westward	WORD 366:7
steps sad s., O Moon	SIDN 316:13
uneasy s. Over the burning marl	MILT 237:24
wandering s. and slow	MILT 239:14
stern S. daughter of the voice of God	WORD 365:11
s. made of s. stuff	SHAK 297:4
sterner commended the unjust s.	BIBL 47:34
steward commended the unjust s.	BIBL 47:34
stick carry a big s.	ROOS 279:21
fell like the s.	PAIN 257:12
rattling of a s. inside	ORWE 254:17
s. and a string	SWIF 329:5
S. close to your desks	GILB 150:19
s. more close than a brother	KIPL 202:27
tattered coat upon a s.	YEAT 368:27
sticketh friend that s. closer	BIBL 38:31
stiff woman can be proud and s.	YEAT 367:20
stiffnecked thou art a s. people	BIBL 35:31
still Because they liked me 's.'	DICK 116:6
beside the s. waters	BOOK 62:14
Be s. then, and know	BOOK 63:5
heart is lying s.	WORD 364:11
I'm s. here	HOPE 173:11
S. crazy after all	SIMO 317:4

still (*cont.*)
S. falls the rain — SITW 317:13
S. glides the Stream — WORD 365:22
s., like air, I'll rise — ANGE 7:3
s. point of the turning world — ELIO 128:3
s., sad music — WORD 364:20
s. small voice — BIBL 37:14
s. they gazed — GOLD 153:10
s.-vexed Bermoothes — SHAK 307:20
stillness modest s. and humility — SHAK 295:16
s. in the midst of chaos — BELL 30:7
stilly Oft, in the s. night — MOOR 244:13
stilts nonsense upon s. — BENT 31:5
stimulate S. the phagocytes — SHAW 311:17
stimulation unnatural s. — MILL 234:13
sting death, where is thy s. — BIBL 51:4
s. like a bee — ALI 5:7
where is thy s.-a-ling-a-ling — ANON 9:24
stings s. you for your pains — HILL 169:2
stir S. up, we beseech thee — BOOK 60:22
stirbt er s. ab — ENGE 132:26
stirred Shaken and not s. — FLEM 138:7
something s. — SIMP 317:8
stirrup sprang to the s. — BROW 72:9
s. and the ground — ANON 7:13
stirs Will that s. and urges — HARD 161:21
stitch S.! stitch! stitch — HOOD 172:26
stocking glimpse of s. — PORT 268:29
stockings thy yellow s. — SHAK 309:3
stoical s. scheme of supplying — SWIF 328:22
stolen generation was s. — FREE 142:11
s. the scraps — SHAK 299:1
S. waters are sweet — BIBL 38:18
stolid S. and stunned — MARK 228:1
stomach army marches on its s. — NAPO 248:4
for thy s.'s sake — BIBL 52:7
no s. to this fight — SHAK 295:26
s. of a king — ELIZ 130:14
stone bomb them back into the S. Age — LEMA 212:5
flung the s. — FITZ 136:6
give him a s. — BIBL 44:7
hollows out a s. — OVID 255:25
let him first cast a s. — BIBL 48:33
Let them not make me a s. — MACN 224:12
Like a rolling s. — DYLA 124:7
like a s. wall — BEE 28:21
make a s. of the heart — YEAT 368:4
not a s. Tell where I lie — POPE 268:13
on sufferers from s. — HIPP 169:19
Raise the s. — ANON 10:14
S. walls do not a prison make — LOVE 219:9
s. which the builders refused — BOOK 64:18
sword out of this s. — MALO 226:7
This precious s. — SHAK 305:22
Under every s. — ARIS 15:9
Virtue is like a rich s. — BACO 22:13
Stonehenge S. it deserves — HAWK 163:11
stones Sermons in s. — SHAK 290:5
s. will teach you — BERN 32:11
stony s. limits — SHAK 306:30
stood s. by me when I was crazy — SHER 315:24
stop come to the end: then s. — CARR 86:20
could not s. for Death — DICK 115:26
kissing had to s. — BROW 73:4
Might s. a hole — SHAK 294:4
nobody's going to s. 'em — BERR 32:14
nothing will s. it — ZOLA 370:15
S. all the clocks — AUDE 18:18
S. the world — NEWL 249:19
stoppeth s. one of three — COLE 100:14
stops buck s. here — TRUM 342:18
know my s. — SHAK 293:12
storage thought in cold s. — SAMU 285:1

store amid thy s. — KEAT 197:2
in the s. we sell hope — REVS 275:9
stories tell sad s. — SHAK 305:30
storm coming s. — GLAD 151:11
directs the s. — ADDI 2:19
directs this s. — PAGE 256:19
fled away into the s. — KEAT 195:17
S. and stress — KAUF 195:7
stormy dark and s. night — BULW 74:1
S. weather — KOEH 204:14
story about you, that s. — HORA 175:21
name great in s. — BYRO 81:21
novel tells a s. — FORS 139:13
s. and a byword — WINT 362:3
s. need be long — THOR 339:9
s. of our days — RALE 273:3
tell my s. — SHAK 294:12
St Paul's ruins of S. — MACA 221:14
ruins of S. — WALP 350:2
straight in the path s. — KORA 204:19
line which is accurately s. — WHEW 355:21
makes a s.-cut ditch — THOR 339:7
no s. thing — KANT 195:1
street which is called S. — BIBL 49:25
strain s. at a gnat — BIBL 45:30
s., Time's eunuch — HOPK 174:8
That s. again — SHAK 308:18
Words s. — ELIO 128:4
strait S. is the gate — BIBL 44:10
strand name upon the s. — SPEN 321:20
walk down the S. — HARG 162:12
strands last s. of man — HOPK 173:14
strange s. and sinister — JAME 182:22
s., and unnatural — SHAK 291:39
stranger in a s. land — BIBL 35:11
strangeness s. in the proportion — BACO 22:14
stranger I, a s. and afraid — HOUS 176:3
Look, s. — AUDE 19:7
never love a s. — BENS 31:4
s. and alone — WOLF 363:6
s., and ye took me in — BIBL 46:7
s. in a strange land — BIBL 35:11
S. than fiction — BYRO 81:10
s. to one of your parents — AUST 21:10
You may see a s. — HAMM 160:20
strangers courteous to s. — BACO 22:28
entertain s. — BIBL 52:17
on the kindness of s. — WILL 360:15
strangled And s. her — BROW 72:25
s. with the guts — MESL 233:15
Stratford atte Bowe scole of S. — CHAU 91:15
straw all things as s. dogs — LAO 208:1
seems like s. — THOM 337:15
strawberry of the s. — BUTL 79:19
S. fields forever — LENN 212:21
Strawberry Hill [S.] is — WALP 349:18
stray If with me you'd fondly s. — GAY 147:1
strayed erred, and s. from thy ways — BOOK 59:12
streak thin red s. — RUSS 283:17
stream like an ever-rolling s. — WATT 352:4
long-legged fly upon the s. — YEAT 368:17
old mill by the s. — ARMS 16:1
Still glides the S. — WORD 365:22
streamers s. waving in the wind — GAY 147:7
streams hart for cooling s. — TATE 330:19
s. in the firmament — MARL 228:9
street don't do it in the s. — CAMP 83:8
inability to cross the s. — WOOL 363:24
jostling in the s. — BLAK 57:11
s. which is called Straight — BIBL 49:25
sunny side of the s. — FIEL 135:16
talking at s. corners — VANZ 345:12
streets children died in the s. — AUDE 18:17

Down these mean s. — CHAN 90:12
grass will grow in the s. — HOOV 173:6
s. FLOODED — BENC 30:11
strength as the s. of ten — TENN 334:27
from s. to strength — BOOK 63:19
giant's s. — SHAK 302:4
ordained s. — BOOK 62:8
our hope and s. — BOOK 63:4
roll all our s. — MARV 229:23
s. with his arm — BIBL 46:33
s. without insolence — BYRO 81:27
tower of s. — SHAK 306:18
strengthen s. while one stands — ROSS 280:12
strengtheneth Christ which s. me — BIBL 51:29
strengthens s. our nerves — BURK 75:25
strenuous round of s. idleness — WORD 365:17
s. life — ROOS 279:19
stress Storm and s. — KAUF 195:7
stretch S. him out longer — SHAK 298:29
stretched things he s. — TWAI 343:6
stricken I was a s. deer — COWP 105:28
s. deer — SHAK 293:11
stride At one s. comes the dark — COLE 100:22
strife In place of s. — CAST 88:12
none was worth my s. — LAND 207:14
s. is o'er — POTT 269:9
strike in doubt, s. it out — TWAI 343:25
s. against public safety — COOL 103:13
S. him — CALI 82:13
s. it in anger — SHAW 312:13
s. it out — JOHN 189:4
yet afraid to s. — POPE 266:21
strikes as s. the player — FITZ 136:15
string end of a golden s. — BLAK 56:20
one long yellow s. — BROW 72:25
s. that ties them — MONT 243:4
untune that s. — SHAK 308:9
stringent s. execution — GRAN 155:13
strip s. his sleeve — SHAK 295:28
striped s. like a zebra — KEAT 195:28
s. shroud — THOM 338:10
strive need'st not s. — CLOU 98:17
s., to seek, to find — TENN 335:8
strives err while yet he s. — GOET 152:8
striving s. evermore for these — GREN 157:11
stroke none so fast as s. — COKE 99:12
strong all s. enough — LA R 209:4
battle to the s. — BIBL 39:21
battle to the s. — DAVI 110:19
men be so s. — BOOK 63:23
only the S. shall thrive — SERV 288:26
out of the s. — BIBL 36:16
realize how s. she is — REAG 274:2
s. name of the Trinity — ALEX 4:17
weak overcomes the s. — LAO 208:10
stronger interest of the s. — PLAT 264:21
on the side of the s. — TACI 330:3
stronghold safe s. — LUTH 220:19
strove s., and much repented — BYRO 80:22
s. with none — LAND 207:14
struck I s. the board — HERB 167:11
s. regularly like gongs — COWA 105:10
they s. at my life — FOX 140:17
structure good s. in a winding stair — HERB 167:16
struggle class s. — MARX 230:9
gods themselves s. — SCHI 286:10
Manhood a s. — DISR 117:21
S. for Existence — DARW 110:7
s. for room — MALT 226:13
s. itself towards the heights — CAMU 83:20
s. naught availeth — CLOU 98:21
s. of man against power — KUND 206:6
What s. to escape — KEAT 196:6

struggles history of class s. — MARX 230:12
stubble sparks among the s. — BIBL 42:21
studies Fred's s. — ELIO 127:16
S. serve for delight — BACO 23:9
too much time in s. — BACO 23:10
studieth man that s. revenge — BACO 23:6
studio *Sine ira et s.* — TACI 329:25
studiously s. neutral — WILS 361:12
study I must s. politics and war — ADAM 2:6
leisure, I will s. — HILL 169:13
much s. is a weariness — BIBL 39:29
previous s. — AUST 21:8
proper s. of mankind — POPE 267:27
proper s. of mankind is books — HUXL 179:8
s. of man is man — CHAR 91:9
stuff Life too short to s. a mushroom — CONR 102:29
made of sterner s. — SHAK 297:4
S. happens — RUMS 282:3
s. of life — HOUS 176:12
stumbles how the strong man s. — ROOS 280:3
stumbling-block unto the Jews a s. — BIBL 50:15
stung S. by the splendour — BROW 71:28
stupid all questions were s. — WEIS 353:9
stability pact is s. — PROD 271:6
s. enough to want it — CHES 93:21
s. is doing something — SHAW 311:13
s. neither forgive nor — SZAS 329:19
Would it be s. — RUMS 282:1
stupidest s. party — MILL 234:5
stupidity excess of s. — JOHN 188:17
With s. the gods themselves — SCHI 286:10
Sturm *S. und Drang* — KAUF 195:7
Stygian In S. cave forlorn — MILT 236:17
S. smoke — JAME 182:9
style definition of a s. — SWIF 328:14
forges one's s. — ZOLA 370:14
has no real s. — PICA 263:9
murderer for fancy prose s. — NABO 247:15
only secret of s. — ARNO 17:9
see a natural s. — PASC 259:18
S. is the dress of thought — WESL 355:5
S. is the man — BUFF 73:19
styles All s. are good — VOLT 348:15
sub Sighted s., sank same — MASO 231:2
subdue chasten and s. — WORD 364:20
s. the arrogant — VIRG 347:14
subdued My nature is s. — SHAK 310:20
subject British s. I was born — MACD 222:19
Every s.'s duty — SHAK 295:21
Grasp the s. — CATO 89:3
shocked by this s. — BOHR 58:17
s. and a sovereign — CHAR 90:21
s. of conversation — CHES 92:13
We know a s. ourselves — JOHN 189:10
what it is to be a s. — ELIZ 130:11
subjects good of s. — DEFO 111:23
s. are rebels — BURK 75:21
sublime egotistical s. — KEAT 197:16
My object all s. — GILB 150:6
step above the s. — PAIN 257:4
s. to the ridiculous — NAPO 248:2
submerged s. tenth — BOOT 65:18
subordination s. of one sex — MILL 234:12
subsistence S. only increases — MALT 226:12
s. without a mind — BERK 31:17
substance wasted his s. — BIBL 47:30
substitute no s. for victory — MACA 221:7
subtle God is s. but not malicious — EINS 126:4
Now the serpent was more s. — BIBL 34:14
subtlest serpent s. beast — MILT 239:4
subtlety s. of nature — BACO 23:27
suburb new s. beyond the runway — BETJ 33:3
suburbs In the south s. — SHAK 309:5

subversive Whatever is funny is s. ORWE 255:7
subway in a New York s. STRA 326:22
succeed how long it takes to s. MONT 243:6
  How to s. in business MEAD 231:18
succeeds Whenever a friend s. VIDA 346:12
success bitch-goddess s. JAME 183:9
  command s. ADDI 2:20
  first requisite to s. SPEN 321:6
  If A is a s. in life EINS 126:10
  no s. like failure DYLA 124:8
  s. depends on MONT 243:6
  S. is counted sweetest DICK 116:4
  S. is relative ELIO 127:28
  s. is sure TWAI 344:1
  this ecstasy, is s. PATE 260:8
successful whether s. or otherwise ADAM 2:13
succession monarchy and s. PAIN 257:7
successively hear the parts s. MOZA 246:13
successus Hos s. alit VIRG 347:9
such of s. is the kingdom of God BIBL 46:29
sucker Never give a s. an even break FIEL 135:17
  s. born every minute BARN 26:19
sucking any s. dove SHAK 303:12
suckle s. fools SHAK 304:27
sucklings babes and s. BOOK 62:8
sucks as a weasel s. eggs SHAK 290:8
Sudan your 'ome in the S. KIPL 202:3
sudden s. glory arising HOBB 170:12
  s. thought BROW 71:28
  too unadvised, too s. SHAK 306:32
suddenly s. became depraved JUVE 194:6
Sudeten problem of the S. Germans HITL 170:10
sue Less used to s. SCOT 287:8
Suez East of S. KIPL 202:16
suffer Can they s. BENT 31:8
  courage to s. TROL 342:2
  Knows what I s. GOET 152:21
  s. fools gladly BIBL 51:8
  S. the little children BIBL 46:29
sufferance s. is the badge SHAK 302:14
suffered S. under Pontius Pilate BOOK 59:23
suffereth Charity s. long BIBL 50:23
suffering About s. they were never wrong AUDE 19:9
  healed of a s. PROU 271:10
  put me to s. METH 233:16
  s. from the particular disease JERO 185:5
sufferings To each his s. GRAY 156:17
suffices God alone s. TERE 335:21
sufficiency elegant s. THOM 338:25
sufficient s. sacrifice BOOK 61:13
  S. unto the day BIBL 44:2
suicide it is s. MACD 222:20
  longest s. note KAUF 195:5
  thought of s. NIET 251:10
suicides s. have a special language SEXT 289:5
suis J'y s. MACM 224:3
suitable s. case for treatment MERC 233:2
suits omelette all over our s. BROK 69:5
sulk s. about having no boyfriend FIEL 135:7
sultry where the climate's s. BYRO 80:21
sum Cogito, ergo s. DESC 113:15
  s. of them all ARIS 15:11
  s. of the parts ANON 12:3
Sumatra giant rat of S. DOYL 120:15
summer After many a s. TENN 334:29
  ensure s. in England WALP 350:1
  Eternal s. gilds them yet BYRO 80:29
  guest of s. SHAK 299:27
  if it takes all s. GRAN 155:10
  In a s. season LANG 207:18
  In s., quite the other way STEV 325:26
  last rose of s. MOOR 244:11
  like a s. birdcage WEBS 353:1

Like s. tempest TENN 334:20
No spring, nor s. beauty DONN 118:20
no s. progress ANDR 6:18
over the s. sea TENN 334:26
Saint Martin's s. SHAK 296:1
see in a s.'s day SHAK 303:13
s. afternoon JAME 183:3
s. is ended BIBL 41:20
S. is icumen in ANON 11:4
s.'s lease SHAK 310:3
S. time and the livin' is easy HEYW 168:14
thy eternal s. SHAK 310:4
to a s.'s day SHAK 310:3
summertime In s. on Bredon HOUS 176:9
summons Upon a fearful s. SHAK 291:10
summum S. bonum CICE 96:18
sun against a setting s. SHAK 308:2
  all, except their s., is set BYRO 80:29
  At the going down of the s. BINY 54:24
  Born of the s. SPEN 321:19
  candle to the s. SIDN 316:9
  candle to the s. YOUN 369:25
  cannot make our s. Stand MARV 229:23
  especially Sir Brother S. FRAN 141:13
  golden apples of the s. YEAT 369:6
  I am too much i' the s. SHAK 291:14
  Juliet is the s. SHAK 306:27
  love that moves the s. DANT 109:17
  maketh his sun to rise BIBL 43:19
  maturing s. KEAT 197:1
  Mother, give me the s. IBSE 180:7
  no new thing under the s. BIBL 39:8
  nothing like the s. SHAK 310:25
  old fool, unruly s. DONN 119:15
  out in the midday s. COWA 105:4
  place in the s. BÜLO 73:22
  place in the s. WILH 359:25
  places Under the s. HOUS 176:14
  ran the s. down with talk CALL 82:18
  reign where'er the s. WATT 352:1
  soft was the s. LANG 207:18
  stand out of my s. DIOG 116:19
  s. also rises HEMI 166:4
  S. and Moon should doubt BLAK 56:22
  s. does not set SCHI 286:9
  s. go down upon your wrath BIBL 51:17
  s. grows cold TAYL 331:3
  s. has gone in SMIT 318:20
  s. never sets NORT 251:22
  s. now stands JOSE 192:14
  S. of righteousness BIBL 42:17
  S. of Righteousness WESL 354:19
  s. of York SHAK 306:7
  s. shall not burn thee BOOK 64:21
  S.'s rim dips COLE 100:22
  s. to me is dark MILT 239:23
  tired the s. with talking CORY 104:13
  under the midday s. MILT 236:5
  watched the s. going down VAN 345:9
  when the s. in bed MILT 237:9
  woman clothed with the s. BIBL 53:11
sunbeam Jesus wants me for a s. TALB 330:6
sunbeams s. out of cucumbers SWIF 328:11
Sunday Here of a S. morning HOUS 176:9
  rainy S. afternoon ERTZ 133:2
  rainy S. in London DE Q 113:6
  She was the S. CLAR 97:7
  working week and S. best AUDE 18:19
sunflower S.! weary of time BLAK 57:22
sunk s. beneath the wave COWP 105:21
sunnier s. side of doubt TENN 331:14
sunny s. pleasure-dome COLE 100:9
  s. side of the street FIEL 135:16

sunrise Eternity's s.	BLAK 57:12	their s. machines	DAWK 111:9
suns light of setting s.	WORD 364:21	without victory, there is no s.	CHUR 95:8
S., that set	JONS 191:17	survive know they can s.	HART 162:18
sunset make a fine s.	MADA 224:15	Only the paranoid s.	GROV 158:6
S. and evening star	TENN 332:2	s. of us is love	LARK 208:15
s. breezes shiver	NEWB 249:17	survived I s.	SIEY 316:18
s. of my life	REAG 274:9	know how I s.	SIMO 317:7
sunshine like s. after rain	SHAK 310:32	survivors more the s.' affair	MANN 227:7
ray of s.	WODE 362:16	Susan black-eyed S. came aboard	GAY 147:7
sunt Sint ut s.	CLEM 98:4	suspect makes a man s. much	BACO 23:14
sup s. with my Lord Jesus Christ	BRUC 73:9	suspected New opinions are always s.	LOCK 216:13
superfluity barren s. of words	GART 146:12	suspension willing s. of disbelief	COLE 101:2
superfluous in the poorest thing s.	SHAK 297:33	suspicion above s.	CAES 82:5
nothing is s.	LEON 213:2	against despots—s.	DEMO 112:20
s. in me	ADAM 1:12	S. always haunts	SHAK 296:7
superior embarrass the s.	SHAW 312:12	s. that more than half	WHIT 356:4
most s. person	ANON 9:21	swaddling wrapped him in s. clothes	BIBL 47:2
S. people never make long visits	MOOR 244:4	swagman Once a jolly s.	PATE 260:9
superman I teach you the s.	NIET 251:4	swains all our s. commend her	SHAK 309:16
It's S.	ANON 8:5	swallow and the s. a nest	BOOK 63:18
supernatural s. source of evil	CONR 102:28	before the s. dares	SHAK 309:26
superstition main source of s.	RUSS 283:12	s. a camel	BIBL 45:30
S. is the religion	BURK 75:24	swamps across primeval s.	WODE 362:19
s. sets the whole world	VOLT 348:13	swan hatched from a s.'s egg	ANDE 6:13
s. to enslave a philosophy	INGE 180:14	like a sleeping s.	SHEL 314:15
superstitions end as s.	HUXL 179:19	many a summer dies the s.	TENN 334:29
s. of the human mind	VOLT 348:19	silver s.	GIBB 149:5
superwoman I am not S.	BLAI 55:17	so much as a black s.	JUVE 194:7
supped s. full with horrors	SHAK 301:30	Sweet S. of Avon	JONS 192:8
supper S. of the Lord	BOOK 61:20	Swanee down upon the S. River	FOST 140:9
supplications make our common s.	BOOK 60:6	swanlike He makes a s. end	SHAK 302:24
support depend on the s. of Paul	SHAW 311:19	swap s. horses when crossing	LINC 215:3
help and s. of the woman	EDWA 125:10	swear s. by Apollo the physician	HIPP 169:17
no invisible means of s.	BUCH 73:15	s. not by the moon	SHAK 306:31
s. him after	SHAK 308:1	when very angry, s.	TWAI 343:24
s. me when I am in the wrong	MELB 232:11	swears Money doesn't talk, it s.	DYLA 124:5
s. of the people	CLEV 98:6	sweat Blood, s., and tear-wrung	BYRO 80:1
s. us all the day long	NEWM 250:4	blood, toil, tears and s.	CHUR 95:6
swears that he will s. it	JACK 181:12	In the s. of thy face	BIBL 34:21
visible means of s.	BIER 54:22	spend our midday s.	QUAR 272:9
without the s. of all	LULA 220:16	s. of its labourers	EISE 126:16
supports s. with insolence	JOHN 187:2	sweats Falstaff s. to death	SHAK 294:18
suppose universe queerer than we s.	HALD 159:8	sweep Mountains of Mourne s. down	FREN 142:15
suppress power of s.	NORT 252:3	s. the dust	SHAK 304:5
surcease catch With his s. success	SHAK 299:28	Your chimneys I s.	BLAK 57:16
sure joy was never s.	SWIN 329:11	sweeping S. up the Heart	DICK 115:29
What nobody is s. about	BELL 29:25	sweeps s. a room as for Thy laws	HERB 167:15
surface looks dingy on the s.	PIRS 263:18	sweet dead thing that smells s.	THOM 338:8
surfeit s. by eating of a lamprey	FABY 133:16	Home, s. home	PAYN 260:19
surfing We are s. food	MACK 223:12	how it was s.	BROW 71:27
surge s. and thunder	LANG 207:15	How s. the moonlight sleeps	SHAK 303:2
surgeon wounded s. plies the steel	ELIO 128:9	if TO-DAY be s.	FITZ 136:13
surmise with a wild s.	KEAT 196:28	kiss me, s. and twenty	SHAK 308:28
surprise Life is a great s.	NABO 247:16	Life is very s.	BORR 65:24
Live frugally on s.	WALK 349:8	Pyramus is a s.-faced man	SHAK 303:13
mystify, mislead, and s.	JACK 181:17	Stolen waters are s.	BIBL 38:18
No s. for the writer	FROS 144:1	such s. sorrow	SHAK 306:35
sound of s.	BALL 26:5	S. and low	TENN 334:12
wise man by s.	LA F 206:12	S. are the uses of adversity	SHAK 290:5
surprised guilty thing s.	WORD 365:8	S. day, so cool	HERB 167:24
S. by joy	WORD 366:8	s. o' the year	SHAK 309:20
S. by unjust force	MILT 236:9	s. peas, on tip-toe	KEAT 195:22
surprises millions of s.	HERB 167:22	S., soft, plenty rhythm	MORT 246:7
surrender die but do not s.	CAMB 83:1	s. the name of Jesus	NEWT 250:20
I s. to you	GERO 148:6	technically s.	OPPE 253:19
unconditional and immediate s.	GRAN 155:9	took s. counsel	BOOK 63:10
we shall never s.	CHUR 95:9	sweeteners s. of tea	FIEL 135:11
surroundings I plus my s.	ORTE 254:5	sweeter s. also than honey	BOOK 62:12
sursum S. corda	MISS 240:22	those unheard Are s.	KEAT 196:7
survey monarch of all I s.	COWP 106:4	sweetest Success is counted s.	DICK 116:4
s. the wondrous cross	WATT 351:23	sweetness came forth s.	BIBL 36:16
survival S. of the Fittest	DARW 110:8	s. and light	ARNO 17:2
s. of the fittest	SPEN 321:9	s. and light	SWIF 328:6

T

stop people t.	ATTL 18:9	sweeteners of t.	FIEL 135:11
tired the sun with t.	CORY 104:13	T. and sympathy	ANDE 6:17
tall all I ask is a t. ship	MASE 230:18	t. for two	CAES 82:2
divinely t.	TENN 332:5	**teabag** woman is like a t.	REAG 274:2
don't look t.	PORT 269:8	**teach** Even while they t.	SENE 288:22
for this the clay grew t.	OWEN 256:12	gladly t.	CHAU 91:18
long and the short and the t.	HUGH 177:12	qualified to t. others	CONF 102:5
taller t. than other men	HARO 162:14	t. him rather to think	SHEL 313:11
tambourine Mr T. Man	DYLA 124:9	T. me, my God and King	HERB 167:14
tame tongue can no man t.	BIBL 52:22	T. me to live	KEN 198:6
tangere *Noli me t.*	BIBL 54:13	T. the free man	AUDE 19:6
tangled t. web we weave	SCOT 287:19	t. the torches	SHAK 306:25
tangles t. of Neaera's hair	MILT 236:29	t. the young idea	THOM 338:24
tango Takes two to t.	HOFF 171:5	T. us to care	ELIO 127:25
tanks Get your t. off my lawn	WILS 361:7	t. young babes	SHAK 305:9
tantum *T. ergo sacramentum*	THOM 337:13	to t. and delight	SIDN 316:14
T. religio potuit	LUCR 220:12	wants to t.	SELL 288:16
Tao not the eternal T.	LAO 207:20	**teacher** t. affects eternity	ADAM 1:22
tapping suddenly there came a t.	POE 265:17	Time is a great t.	BERL 32:9
tar T. water	BERK 31:14	**teaches** experience t.	TACI 330:4
Tara through T.'s halls	MOOR 244:8	He who cannot, t.	SHAW 312:10
tarnished neither t. nor afraid	CHAN 90:12	**teaching** t. nations how to live	MILT 240:11
Tarquin great house of T.	MACA 221:20	**teacup** crack in the t. opens	AUDE 18:14
tarry Why t. the wheels	BIBL 36:13	**tear** T. him for his bad verses	SHAK 297:12
You may for ever t.	HERR 168:6	**tears** bitter t. to shed	CORY 104:13
Tarzan Me T.	WEIS 353:10	blood, toil, t. and sweat	CHUR 95:6
task what he reads as a t.	JOHN 188:14	brought me t.	CALL 82:18
tassel lure this t.-gentle	SHAK 306:34	came her t.	TENN 334:20
tassie fill it in a silver t.	BURN 77:5	crocodiles, that shed t.	BACO 23:22
taste arbiter of t.	TACI 330:2	Drop, drop, slow t.	FLET 138:15
bouquet is better than the t.	POTT 269:16	enough of blood and t.	RABI 272:15
create the t.	WORD 366:21	even the altar sheds t.	TALM 330:17
difference of t. in jokes	ELIO 127:7	God will wipe away t.	BIBL 40:22
ghastly good t.	BETJ 33:6	Hence those t.	TERE 335:11
Good t. and humour	MUGG 247:1	How many t. shall we cry	FATA 134:10
last t. of sweets	SHAK 305:21	If you have t.	SHAK 297:5
never t. who always drink	PRIO 271:3	Like Niobe, all t.	SHAK 291:19
T. is the feminine	FITZ 137:5	No t. in the writer	FROS 144:1
t. my meat	HERB 167:18	Nothing is here for t.	MILT 239:26
tasted books are to be t.	BACO 23:12	now am full of t.	YEAT 368:1
tasting T. of Flora	KEAT 196:17	Smiling through her t.	HOME 172:11
Tat *T. ist alles, nichts der Ruhm*	GOET 152:13	sow in t.	BOOK 64:25
tattered t. coat upon a stick	YEAT 368:27	t. I cannot hide	HARB 161:5
taught afterward he t.	CHAU 91:21	T., idle tears	TENN 334:15
as if you t. them not	POPE 267:17	t. shed for things	VIRG 347:3
got to be carefully t.	HAMM 160:25	too deep for t.	WORD 365:10
what we have t. her	GAY 146:18	wipe away all t.	BIBL 53:9
You t. me language	SHAK 307:21	wipe away all t.	BIBL 53:23
tavern t. or inn	JOHN 189:13	With mine own t.	SHAK 306:4
tax power to t.	MARS 229:3	With silence and t.	BYRO 81:26
soon be able to t. it	FARA 134:1	**tearsday** moanday, t., wailsday	JOYC 192:20
To t. and to please	BURK 75:7	**teases** Because he knows it t.	CARR 86:9
taxation art of t. consists	COLB 99:17	**tea tray** t. in the sky	CARR 86:12
Inflation one form of t.	FRIE 143:1	**technically** t. sweet	OPPE 253:19
T. and representation	CAMD 83:2	**technology** advanced t. is	CLAR 97:5
T. without representation	OTIS 255:22	T. . . . the knack of so arranging	FRIS 143:2
taxed world should be t.	BIBL 47:1	white heat of t.	WILS 361:4
taxes as true . . . as t.	DICK 114:22	**tecum** *Nec t. possum vivere*	MART 229:11
death and t.	DEFO 111:17	**Teddy** T. Bears have their Picnic	BRAT 67:21
death and t.	FRAN 142:3	**tedious** t. as a twice-told tale	SHAK 297:19
Death and t. and childbirth	MITC 241:13	**teeming** gleaned my t. brain	KEAT 197:6
little people pay t.	HELM 165:17	**teeth** gnashing of t.	BIBL 44:15
no new t.	BUSH 78:12	he's got iron t.	GROM 158:1
Sex and t.	JONE 191:11	old bitch gone in the t.	POUN 270:1
t. shall be apportioned	CONS 103:6	shark has pretty t.	BREC 68:6
taxi-cab look like a t.	HUGH 177:11	skin of my t.	BIBL 38:3
taxing t. machine	LOWE 219:15	t. are set on edge	BIBL 41:28
Tay Bridge of the Silv'ry T.	MCGO 223:3	untying with the t.	BIER 54:18
tayl likerous t.	CHAU 91:29	**teetotaller** only a beer t.	SHAW 311:11
tea and sometimes t.	POPE 268:18	**tekel** MENE, T., UPHARSIN	BIBL 42:6
honey still for t.	BROO 69:21	**Telemachus** mine own T.	TENN 335:5
if this is t.	PUNC 272:1	**television** I hate t.	WELL 353:16
shameless t.-drinker	JOHN 187:7	T. brought brutality	MCLU 223:19

more t. and bandits	LAO 208:9	t. makes it so	SHAK 292:14
One of the t.	BECK 28:12	t. man's crumpet	MUIR 247:2
t. break through and steal	BIBL 43:23	t. what nobody has thought	SZEN 329:23
T. respect property	CHES 93:12	**thinks** If any man t. he slays	UPAN 344:15
thievish Time's t. progress	SHAK 310:13	I sits and t.	PUNC 272:2
thigh smote them hip and t.	BIBL 36:17	man t. he slays	BHAG 33:19
thighs his t. the People	RIG 276:17	t. he knows everything	SHAW 311:27
thimbles sought it with t.	CARR 87:20	what she t.	ROBI 277:15
thin never be too rich or too t.	WIND 361:20	**third** t. who walks always	ELIO 130:1
pale and t. ones	PLUT 265:11	**thirst** I t.	BIBL 49:13
t. man inside every fat man	ORWE 254:13	shall never t.	BIBL 48:30
t. one wildly signalling	CONN 102:18	soul is a t. for God	BOOK 62:27
t. red line	RUSS 283:17	**thirsty** cold waters to a t. soul	BIBL 38:37
T. red line of 'eroes	KIPL 203:1	Drinking when we are not t.	BEAU 28:2
thine Not my will, but t., be done	BIBL 48:7	**thirteen** clocks were striking t.	ORWE 254:20
thing draw the T. as he sees It	KIPL 203:6	**thirtieth** t. year to heaven	THOM 337:23
ill-favoured t., sir	SHAK 290:26	**thirty** At t. a man suspects	YOUN 369:28
one damned t. after another	HUBB 177:8	remained t.-five for years	WILD 358:13
one t. at once	SMIL 317:21	T. days hath	ANON 11:11
play's the t.	SHAK 292:22	t. pieces of silver	BIBL 46:9
sort of t. they like	LINC 215:6	**this** T. was a man	SHAK 297:17
t. itself and not the myth	RICH 276:5	**thorn** Oak, and Ash, and T.	KIPL 203:2
t. of beauty	KEAT 195:10	snail's on the t.	BROW 72:23
thingish Thing which seemed very T.	MILN 235:12	t. in the flesh	BIBL 51:10
things all t. through Christ	BIBL 51:29	without t. the rose	MILT 238:20
all t. to all men	BIBL 50:19	**thorns** crackling of t.	BIBL 39:15
God's sons are t.	MADD 224:16	crown of t.	BRYA 73:14
people don't do such t.	IBSE 180:8	some fell among t.	BIBL 44:39
quick bright t.	SHAK 303:8	upon the t. of life	SHEL 314:5
tears shed for t.	VIRG 347:3	**thoroughfare** t. for all thoughts	KEAT 197:19
T. ain't what they used to be	PERS 262:11	**thou** t. art not he or she	WAUG 352:5
T. are in the saddle	EMER 131:21	T. art the man	BIBL 36:37
t. are the sons of heaven	JOHN 186:17	t. shalt have no other gods	BIBL 35:24
t. are wrought by prayer	TENN 332:22	T. swell! Thou witty	HART 163:1
T. can only get better	PETR 262:15	**thought** beautiful clean t.	LAWR 209:21
T. fall apart	YEAT 369:1	Beyond the last t.	STEV 324:19
t. they didn't know	POUN 269:20	bound of human t.	TENN 335:4
think because I t. him so	SHAK 309:14	dress of t.	JOHN 187:8
can't make her t.	PARK 259:5	dress of t.	POPE 267:10
capacity to t.	TERE 335:22	father, Harry, to that t.	SHAK 295:7
comedy to those that t.	WALP 350:3	forced into a state of t.	GALS 145:11
don't t. I'll fall in love	GERS 148:7	form Of every t.	MICH 233:18
don't t. much of it	STRA 326:21	gave that t. relief	WORD 365:4
easier to act than to t.	AREN 15:1	modes of t.	MILL 234:4
fun you t. they had	JONG 191:13	no t. for the morrow	BIBL 44:2
Haply I t. on thee	SHAK 310:6	oft was t.	POPE 267:9
I can't t. for you	DYLA 124:15	pale cast of t.	SHAK 292:26
impulse to t. independently	PLUT 265:10	Perish the t.	CIBB 96:13
I t., therefore I am	DESC 113:15	put t. in a concentration camp	ROOS 279:17
know what I t.	WALL 349:16	rear the tender t.	THOM 338:24
more clearly than you t.	BOHR 58:18	right t.	PALI 258:3
not so t. as you drunk	SQUI 322:20	Roman t. hath struck him	SHAK 289:13
not to t. much but	TERE 335:23	single grateful t.	LESS 213:10
paint objects as I t. them	PICA 263:8	speech created t.	SHEL 314:14
publishing faster than you t.	PAUL 260:15	strange seas of t.	WORD 365:16
t. alike who think at all	PAIN 257:19	sudden t.	BROW 71:28
t. as wise men do	ASCH 17:15	sweet silent t.	SHAK 310:7
T. like a wise man	YEAT 369:18	t. in cold storage	SAMU 285:1
t. like other people	SHEL 313:11	T. is free	SHAK 307:27
T. of your forefathers	ADAM 2:12	t. is the front	SAUS 286:4
t. too little	DRYD 121:20	t. is viscous	ADAM 2:1
we've got to t.	RUTH 283:21	T. shall be the harder	ANON 14:1
What the Bandar-log t.	KIPL 203:10	thought the t.	BALL 25:9
when I t., I must speak	SHAK 290:20	t., word, and deed	MISS 240:16
whether machines t.	SKIN 317:15	To a green t.	MARV 229:17
who never t.	PRIO 271:3	very t. of Thee	CASW 88:14
You know more than you t.	SPOC 322:10	want of t.	HOOD 172:24
thinking Every t. man	ADAM 1:15	**thoughtcrime** t. literally impossible	ORWE 254:24
he is a t. reed	PASC 259:23	**thoughts** conceal their t.	VOLT 348:10
our modes of t.	EINS 126:9	have bloody t.	SHAK 307:31
Plain living and high t.	WORD 365:12	in a shroud Of t.	BYRO 80:7
power of positive t.	PEAL 260:21	long, long t.	LONG 217:16
saves original t.	SAYE 286:5	misleading t.	SPEN 321:10

thoughts (*cont.*)
my t. are not your thoughts — BIBL 41:14
ought to control our t. — DARW 110:3
pansies, that's for t. — SHAK 293:32
rather than of t. — KEAT 197:10
thoroughfare for all t. — KEAT 197:19
t. of other men — COWP 106:1
T. that do often lie — WORD 365:10
Words without t. — SHAK 293:17
thousand better than a t. — BOOK 63:20
blotted a t. — JONS 192:10
Death has a t. doors — MASS 231:3
Empire lasts for a t. years — CHUR 95:10
first t. days — KENN 198:18
Give me a t. kisses — CATU 89:7
had five t. a year — THAC 336:8
night has a t. eyes — BOUR 66:11
Night hath a t. eyes — LYLY 220:23
not in a t. years — SMIT 318:16
ten t. things — LAO 208:5
t. ages in Thy sight — WATT 352:3
t. doors open on to it — SENE 288:23
t. thousand slimy things — COLE 100:24
t. tongues to sing — WESL 354:20
t. years in thy sight — BOOK 63:22
t. years of history — GAIT 144:22
thrall Thee hath in t. — KEAT 195:26
thread crimson t. of kinship — PARK 259:10
threads hundreds of tiny t. — SIGN 316:20
threaten t. to overrule him — PAXM 260:16
threatened t. its life — CARR 87:20
three confessing the T. — PATR 260:12
divided into t. parts — CAES 82:3
give him t. sides — MONT 243:5
tell you t. times — CARR 87:17
Though he was only t. — MILN 235:14
t. fifths of all other persons — CONS 103:6
t.-fifths of a man — RICE 275:16
T. hours a day — TROL 342:1
T. in One — ALEX 4:17
t. is company — WILD 358:5
T. little maids — GILB 150:2
t. o'clock in the morning — FITZ 137:13
t.-o-clock in the morning — THOR 339:15
t. of us in this marriage — DIAN 114:9
t.-party politics — KENN 198:9
t.-pipe problem — DOYL 120:13
T. whole days together — SUCK 327:8
When shall we t. meet — SHAK 299:7
where two or t. — BIBL 45:15
threefold t. cord — BIBL 39:13
threescore t. years and ten — BOOK 63:23
thrice deny me t. — BIBL 46:12
T. is he armed — SHAK 296:2
thrift Thrift, t., Horatio — SHAK 291:23
thrills t. the ear — AUDE 19:14
throat fog in my t. — BROW 72:26
her little t. around — BROW 72:25
if your t. 'tis hard to slit — KING 201:11
in the city's t. — LOWE 220:4
murder by the t. — LLOY 216:11
taking life by the t. — FROS 144:2
unlocked her silent t. — GIBB 149:5
throne beats upon a t. — TENN 332:9
Bust outlasts the t. — DOBS 118:12
I saw a great white t. — BIBL 53:20
like a burnished t. — ELIO 129:22
like a burnished t. — SHAK 289:17
Lord sitting upon a t. — BIBL 40:8
t. of bayonets — INGE 180:16
t. of bayonets — YELT 369:19
t. was like the fiery flame — BIBL 42:8
through slaughter to a t. — GRAY 156:13

up to the T. — KIPL 202:14
thrones Not t. and crowns, but men — ELLI 131:12
T., dominations — MILT 238:32
t., or dominions — BIBL 51:30
through live t. someone else — FRIE 142:21
one who has gone t. it — VIRG 347:19
read books t. — JOHN 189:3
t. you but not from you — GIBR 149:9
throw sister t. up a lot — WALK 349:7
thrown t. out, as good for nothing — JOHN 188:1
thrush aged t. — HARD 161:22
That's the wise t. — BROW 72:6
Thule *Ultima T.* — VIRG 348:1
thumbs both his t. are off — HOFF 171:9
By the pricking of my t. — SHAK 301:13
thunder dawn comes up like t. — KIPL 202:15
steal my t. — DENN 113:5
surge and t. — LANG 207:15
t. of the captains — BIBL 38:9
voice like t. — DAVI 111:5
thunderbolt like a t. he falls — TENN 332:6
thus T. have I had thee — SHAK 310:15
thusness reason of this t. — WARD 350:18
thyme whereon the wild t. blows — SHAK 303:21
thyself beside t. — BIBL 49:36
Tiber River T. foaming — POWE 270:12
T.! father Tiber — MACA 222:2
T. foaming with much blood — VIRG 347:10
Tiberius Coin, T. — DOBS 118:12
Had T. been a cat — ARNO 16:19
ticket She's got a t. to ride — LENN 212:22
take a t. at Victoria — BEVI 33:16
tickle if you t. us — SHAK 302:22
t. her with a hoe — JERR 185:9
tickled t. with a straw — POPE 267:31
tide But came the t. — SPEN 321:20
call of the running t. — MASE 231:1
full t. of human existence — JOHN 189:7
tether time or t. — BURN 77:13
t. in the affairs — SHAK 297:15
tides drew these t. of men — LAWR 210:2
tidings bringeth good t. — BIBL 41:7
good t. of great joy — BIBL 47:3
ties string that t. them — MONT 243:4
tiger action of the t. — SHAK 295:16
atom bomb is a paper t. — MAO 227:13
O t.'s heart — SHAK 296:6
t.'s heart wrapped — GREE 157:2
T., Tyger — BLAK 58:3
two days like a t. — TIPU 340:13
tigers tamed and shabby t. — HODG 171:4
t. of wrath — BLAK 57:9
t. which they dare not dismount — CHUR 95:4
tight t. gag of place — HEAN 164:13
timber crooked t. of humanity — KANT 195:1
Like seasoned t. — HERB 167:26
time abysm of t. — SHAK 307:18
As t. goes by — HUPF 178:21
bid t. return — SHAK 305:28
births of t. — BACO 22:30
born out of due t. — BIBL 50:27
but for all t. — JONS 192:7
child of T. — HALL 160:6
chronicle of wasted t. — SHAK 310:17
Cormorant devouring T. — SHAK 298:31
dance to the music of t. — POWE 270:9
devote more t. — FOWL 140:13
Even such is T. — RALE 273:3
find something to do with the t. — ROGE 278:18
Fleet the t. carelessly — SHAK 290:2
Fly envious T. — MILT 237:12
for a moment of t. — ELIZ 130:22
good t. was had by all — SMIT 319:2

half as old as T.	BURG 74:24	t. to win this game	DRAK 121:9
Healing is a matter of t.	HIPP 169:21	T. which destroys all things	BHAG 33:20
How t. is slipping	FITZ 136:13	t. will come	DISR 117:4
idea whose t. has come	ANON 11:8	T. will run back	MILT 237:8
I forget all t.	MILT 238:25	T., you thief	HUNT 178:19
if you could kill t.	THOR 339:11	to fill the t. available	PARK 259:12
improve the nick of t.	THOR 339:13	trencher-friends, t.'s flies	SHAK 308:3
instant of t.	AURE 20:17	unconscionable t. dying	CHAR 91:3
into the seeds of t.	SHAK 299:13	use your t.	HERR 168:6
It saves t.	CARR 86:25	very good t. it was	JOYC 192:23
Love's not T.'s fool	SHAK 310:22	When t. is broke	SHAK 306:5
may be some t.	OATE 252:15	whips and scorns of t.	SHAK 292:24
no enemy but t.	YEAT 368:10	whirligig of t.	SHAK 309:11
No t. like the present	MANL 227:2	womb of t.	HEIN 165:9
not the t. to falter	BLAI 56:4	world enough, and t.	MARV 229:19
now doth t. waste me	SHAK 306:6	**timely** t. compliance	FIEL 135:10
old common arbitrator, T.	SHAK 308:15	t. utterance	WORD 365:4
Once upon a t.	ANON 10:3	**timeo** t. *Danaos et dona ferentes*	VIRG 347:4
on the sands of t.	LONG 217:21	**times** It was the best of t.	DICK 115:23
O t. too swift	PEEL 261:5	Oh, the t.	CICE 96:20
passed the t.	BECK 28:15	praiser of past t.	HORA 174:18
peace for our t.	CHAM 90:5	signs of the t.	BIBL 45:8
peace in our t.	BOOK 60:1	T. has made many ministries	BAGE 24:8
possession for all t.	THUC 339:25	t. in which a genius	ADAM 1:11
productions of t.	BLAK 56:27	t. that try men's souls	PAIN 257:10
puzzles me more than t.	LAMB 207:6	t. they are a-changin'	DYLA 124:13
rags of t.	DONN 119:16	t. will not mend	PARK 259:8
Redeeming the t.	BIBL 51:18	**timetables** by railway t.	TAYL 330:23
ringing grooves of t.	TENN 333:32	**timor** T. *mortis conturbat me*	DUNB 123:8
speech is shallow as T.	CARL 85:6	**tin** cat on a hot t. roof	WILL 360:10
spend more t. with family	THAT 337:1	cheap t. trays	MASE 230:17
strain, T.'s eunuch	HOPK 174:8	corrugated t. roof	BEEC 28:22
Sun-flower! weary of t.	BLAK 57:22	**tincture** t. in the blood	DEFO 111:20
talk of killing t.	BOUC 66:7	**tinkering** rule of intelligent t.	EHRL 125:14
tether t. or tide	BURN 77:13	**tintinnabulation** To the t.	POE 265:14
thief of t.	YOUN 369:27	**tiny** Your t. hand is frozen	GIAC 148:12
T. and the hour	SHAK 299:18	**tip** Within the nether t.	COLE 100:23
t. and the place	BROW 72:19	**Tipperary** long way to T.	JUDG 193:12
t. and times are done	YEAT 369:6	**tiptoe** jocund day Stands t.	SHAK 307:5
t. by heart-throbs	BAIL 24:14	sweet peas, on t.	KEAT 195:22
T. for a little something	MILN 235:19	**tired** Give me your t., your poor	LAZA 210:5
t. has come	CARR 87:3	t. her head	BIBL 37:28
T. has no divisions	MANN 227:4	t. of Bath	AUST 20:27
T. hath, my lord, a wallet	SHAK 308:11	t. of London	JOHN 189:19
T. held me green	THOM 337:19	t. of Love	BELL 29:23
T. is a great teacher	BERL 32:9	t. the sun with talking	CORY 104:13
t. is fleeing	HORA 175:7	**Tiresias** T., old man with wrinkled dugs	ELIO 129:27
T. is fleeting	LONG 217:19	**tirra** T. lirra	TENN 333:18
t. is flying	VIRG 348:4	**titanic** t. wars had groined	OWEN 256:13
t. is money	FRAN 141:16	**title** needed no royal t.	SPEN 321:16
t. is money	HUGO 178:2	**titles** T. are shadows	DEFO 111:23
T. is on our side	GLAD 151:12	T. distinguish the mediocre	SHAW 312:12
T. is our tedious song	MILT 237:10	**titwillow** Willow, t.	GILB 150:10
t. is out of joint	SHAK 292:8	**toad** let the t. work	LARK 209:1
t. is running out	KOES 204:15	like the t., ugly	SHAK 290:5
t. is the greatest innovator	BACO 22:31	rather be a t.	SHAK 305:3
T. is too slow	VAN 345:10	squat like a t.	MILT 238:28
T., like an ever-rolling stream	WATT 352:4	**toads** imaginary gardens with real t.	MOOR 244:3
t. of asking	BOOK 61:22	**toast** My t. would be	ADAM 2:13
T., Place	DRYD 122:20	never had a piece of t.	PAYN 260:18
T., present and time past	ELIO 127:29	**toasted** cheese—t., mostly	STEV 325:19
t. remembered	SWIN 329:8	**tocsin** t. of the soul	BYRO 81:3
t.'s arrow	EDDI 124:20	**today** if T. be sweet	FITZ 136:13
T. spent on any item	PARK 259:13	I have lived t.	DRYD 122:16
T. stays, *we* go	DOBS 118:13	let us do something t.	COLL 101:9
T.'s thievish progress	SHAK 310:13	live t.	MART 229:7
T.'s wingèd chariot	MARV 229:21	never jam t.	CARR 87:5
T., the avenger	BYRO 80:11	standing here t.	JOHN 186:6
T. the devourer	OVID 256:2	T. if ye will hear	BOOK 63:27
T. the longest distance	WILL 360:12	T. is the last day	YELT 369:20
T. the subtle thief	MILT 239:28	T. shalt thou be with me	BIBL 48:10
t. to be in earnest	JOHN 187:6	T. we have naming of parts	REED 274:12
t. to every purpose	BIBL 39:10	we gave our t.	EDMO 125:7

toe light fantastic t. — MILT 236:20
toes Pobble who has no t. — LEAR 210:18
toff Saunter along like a t. — HARG 162:12
together lived comfortably so long t. — GAY 146:19
togetherness spaces in your t. — GIBR 149:10
toil bleared, smeared with t. — HOPK 173:16
blood, t., tears and sweat — CHUR 95:6
day in t. — QUAR 272:9
Double, double t. and trouble — SHAK 301:11
Horny-handed sons of t. — SALI 284:21
horny hands of t. — LOWE 220:1
they t. not — BIBL 43:26
unrequited t. — LINC 215:4
toiling t. upward in the night — LONG 217:15
tokens Words are the t. — BACO 22:3
told half was not t. me — BIBL 37:6
I t. you so — WELL 354:15
plato t. him: he couldn't — CUMM 108:7
t. my wrath — BLAK 57:26
t. you from the beginning — BIBL 41:3
tolerable Life would be t. — LEWI 214:3
tolerance such a thing as t. — WILS 361:15
toll T. for the brave — COWP 105:21
t. me back from thee — KEAT 196:24
tolle T. lege — AUGU 20:3
tollis t. peccata mundi — MISS 240:25
tolls for whom the bell t. — DONN 119:23
Tom Ground control to Major T. — BOWI 67:1
Poor T.'s a-cold — SHAK 298:11
tomatoes babies in the t. — GINS 151:5
tomb fair Fidele's grassy t. — COLL 101:15
t. of a mediocre talent — SMIT 318:18
Tommy T. this, an' Tommy that — KIPL 203:1
tomorrow For your t. we gave — EDMO 125:7
jam t. — CARR 87:5
put off till t. — PUNC 271:19
This, no t. hath — DONN 119:6
T., and to-morrow — SHAK 301:31
T. do thy worst — DRYD 122:16
t. is another day — MITC 241:15
t.'s life's too late — MART 229:7
t. to be brave — ARMS 16:3
t. we shall die — BIBL 40:21
Unborn t. — FITZ 136:13
tomtit little t. Sang — GILB 150:10
tone t. of the company — CHES 92:16
tongs t. and the bones — SHAK 303:30
tongue his t. Dropped manna — MILT 238:3
hold your t. — DONN 119:8
I must hold my t. — SHAK 291:21
iron t. of midnight — SHAK 304:4
lies of t. and pen — CHES 92:28
my t. could utter — TENN 331:15
My t. is the pen — BOOK 63:1
My t. swore — EURI 133:7
my t. the mystery telling — THOM 337:12
nor t. to speak — LENT 213:1
sharp t. — IRVI 181:2
Sing, my t. — FORT 139:20
tip of the t. taking — NABO 247:14
t. can no man tame — BIBL 52:22
t. In every wound — SHAK 297:9
t. not understood — BOOK 65:13
t. That Shakespeare spake — WORD 364:16
t. to persuade — CLAR 96:28
use of my oracular t. — SHER 315:12
voice and t. — AUGU 20:2
yield to the t. — BIER 54:18
tongued t. with fire — ELIO 128:11
tongues lack t. to praise — SHAK 310:18
painted full of t. — SHAK 294:31
thousand t. to sing — WESL 354:20
time in the t. — SHAK 308:20

t. like as of fire — BIBL 49:21
t. of men and of angels — BIBL 50:22
tonight Not t., Josephine — NAPO 248:8
tons Sixteen t. — TRAV 341:12
too we are t. menny — HARD 161:15
took 'E went an' t. — KIPL 203:7
tool edged t. that grows keener — IRVI 181:2
Man is a t.-making animal — FRAN 142:4
Man is a t.-using animal — CARL 85:19
Science is an edged t. — EDDI 124:23
tools Give us the t. — CHUR 95:12
secrets are edged t. — DRYD 122:9
t. to him that can handle them — CARL 85:7
tooth red in t. and claw — TENN 333:3
sharper than a serpent's t. — SHAK 297:29
t. for tooth — BIBL 35:29
toothache endure the t. — SHAK 304:16
toothpaste t. is out of the tube — HALD 159:11
top always room at the t. — WEBS 352:21
I shall die at the t. — SWIF 329:4
t. if it reached to heaven — BIBL 35:2
t. thing in the world — KEAT 197:18
You're the t. — PORT 269:6
Torah found in the T. — ELEA 127:1
Turn it [T.] — TALM 330:14
torch t. of life — LUCR 220:14
t. passed to a new generation — KENN 198:14
Truth, like a t. — HAMI 160:12
torches teach the t. — SHAK 306:25
torchlight t. procession — O'SU 255:21
torment smoke of their t. — BIBL 53:16
tornado set off a t. in Texas — LORE 218:18
torpedoes Damn the t. — FARR 134:9
torture t. to death — DOST 120:1
torturer t.'s horse scratches — AUDE 19:10
Tory deep burning hatred for the T. Party — BEVA 33:8
Loyalty the T.'s secret weapon — KILM 200:6
T. men and Whig measures — DISR 117:20
tossed you t. and gored — BOSW 66:5
total t. solution — GOER 152:7
totalitarianism under the name of t. — GAND 145:14
totters Who t. forth — SHEL 315:2
touch little t. of Harry — SHAK 295:18
Nelson t. — NELS 249:6
nothing, Can t. him further — SHAK 301:2
One t. of nature — SHAK 308:13
puts it not unto the t. — MONT 243:11
T. me not — BIBL 49:16
T. not the cat — SCOT 287:22
t. of earthly years — WORD 366:4
touches Who t. this touches a man — WHIT 357:2
toucheth He that t. pitch — BIBL 42:24
tough t. get going — KENN 199:6
T. on crime — BLAI 55:18
toughness T. doesn't have to come — FEIN 134:15
tour This is a hard t. — ARMS 16:4
tourist loathsome is the British t. — KILV 200:7
whisper to the t. — BEER 29:2
tout T. passe — ANON 12:19
toves slithy t. — CARR 86:23
tower Child Roland to the dark t. — SHAK 298:12
prisoner in the T. — FABY 133:17
to the Dark T. came — BROW 71:26
t. of strength — SHAK 306:18
with the blasted t. — NERV 249:13
towered t. cities please us — MILT 236:24
towers branchy between t. — HOPK 173:15
Whispering from her t. — ARNO 17:4
towery T. city — HOPK 173:15
town Country in the t. — MART 229:12
destroy the t. to save it — ANON 9:5
little t. of Bethlehem — BROO 70:7
lived in a pretty how t. — CUMM 108:4

man made the t.	COWP 105:24	**traps** recognize the t.	MACH 223:9
never go down to the end of the t.	MILN 235:14	**trash** steals t.	SHAK 304:31
towns Seven wealthy t.	ANON 10:19	**travel** real way to t.	GRAH 155:4
toys brooches and t.	STEV 325:31	t. broadens the mind; but	CHES 93:17
toyshop moving t. of their heart	POPE 268:15	t. by land or by water	BOOK 60:15
traces on winter's t.	SWIN 329:7	t. for travel's sake	STEV 325:14
tracing fitful t. of a portal	STEV 324:21	t. hopefully is a better thing	STEV 325:21
track T. twenty nine	GORD 154:9	t. in the direction of our fear	BERR 32:18
trade all is seared with t.	HOPK 173:16	T., in the younger sort	BACO 23:15
autocrat: that's my t.	CATH 89:1	T. light	JUVE 194:10
from the vulgar t.	MARL 228:13	two classes of t.	BENC 30:9
great t.	BURK 75:6	**travelled** took the one less t.	FROS 143:24
Irish poets, learn your t.	YEAT 369:10	t. a good deal in Concord	THOR 339:10
It is his t.	HEIN 165:10	**traveller** good t. is one	LIN 215:13
People of the same t.	SMIT 318:2	No t. returns	SHAK 292:25
There isn't any T.	HERB 167:6	said the T.	DE L 112:14
War is the t. of kings	DRYD 122:5	spurs the lated t.	SHAK 301:4
wheels of t.	HUME 178:8	t. from an antique land	SHEL 314:9
trade unionism t. of the married	SHAW 312:6	**travellers** t. of eternity	BASH 27:15
trading t. on the blood	LEE 211:17	**travels** t. the fastest	KIPL 202:14
tradition t. Approves	CLOU 98:20	t. the world in search	MOOR 243:19
t. is a fence	TALM 330:12	**trawler** When seagulls follow a t.	CANT 84:13
T. means giving votes to	CHES 93:13	**treachery** t. of the intellectuals	BEND 30:12
t. objects to their being disqualified	CHES 93:15	**tread** Doth close behind him t.	COLE 100:26
traduced t. Joseph K.	KAFK 194:15	so airy a tread	TENN 334:7
traffic Hushing the latest t.	BRID 68:17	T. softly	YEAT 368:8
means of t.	MARL 228:13	**treason** [corporations] cannot commit t.	COKE 99:15
t. of Jacob's ladder	THOM 338:19	Gunpowder T. and Plot	ANON 10:10
two hours' t.	SHAK 306:21	In trust I have found t.	ELIZ 130:12
trafficking permitted t.	KORA 205:2	last temptation is the greatest t.	ELIO 129:6
tragedy comedy is t. that happens	CART 87:26	love the t.	DANI 109:6
composition of a t.	VOLT 349:2	none dare call it t.	HARI 162:13
first time as t.	BARN 26:17	t. a matter	TALL 330:10
first time as t.	MARX 230:7	T. has done his worst	SHAK 301:2
go, litel myn t.	CHAU 92:4	t., make the most of it	HENR 166:22
I will write you a t.	FITZ 137:9	**treasure** liking his t.	THOM 338:9
That is their t.	WILD 358:9	purest t. mortal times afford	SHAK 305:17
t. is thus a representation	ARIS 15:15	t. in heaven	BIBL 45:18
t. of a man	OLIV 253:8	Where your t. is	BIBL 43:24
t. of Science	HUXL 179:16	**treasures** t. upon earth	BIBL 43:23
t. to those that feel	WALP 350:3	**treat** t. them as if they were	GOET 152:22
what t. means	STOP 326:14	**treaties** T. like girls and roses	DE G 112:8
tragic t. failure	ELIO 127:13	**treatise** T. of Human Nature	HUME 178:11
trahison t. des clercs	BEND 30:12	**treatment** suitable case for t.	MERC 233:2
trail long, long t.	KING 201:3	t. of a question	WITT 362:8
t. has its own stern code	SERV 288:24	**treaty** not a peace t.	FOCH 138:19
train biggest electric t.	WELL 353:15	t. with Russia	BISM 55:3
express-t. drew up there	THOM 338:7	**tree** apple on the t.	DICK 115:30
headlight of an oncoming t.	DICK 116:10	billboard lovely as a t.	NASH 248:15
light of the oncoming t.	LOWE 220:5	finds that this t.	KNOX 204:11
read in the t.	WILD 358:12	fool sees not the same t.	BLAK 56:26
shaves and takes a t.	WHIT 356:2	golden t. of actual life	GOET 152:10
T. up a child	BIBL 38:33	happy, happy t.	KEAT 195:20
traitor hate the t.	DANI 109:6	leaves of the t.	BIBL 53:25
tram not even a bus, I'm a t.	HARE 162:11	Of that forbidden t.	MILT 237:15
tramp why the lady is a t.	HART 162:21	only God can make a t.	KILM 200:5
trample t. the very values	RATH 273:15	outstretched beneath the t.	BLAK 58:1
tranquil Farewell to the t. mind	SHAK 305:5	poem lovely as a t.	KILM 200:4
tranquillity chaos remembered in t.	THUR 340:7	shall be like that t.	SWIF 329:4
recollected in t.	WORD 366:19	she gave me of the t.	BIBL 34:17
T. Base here	ARMS 16:7	spare the beechen t.	CAMP 83:10
transcendental of a t. kind	GILB 150:13	to my mind than a t.	MORR 245:5
transgression there is no t.	BIBL 49:41	t. of knowledge	BIBL 34:8
transgressions wounded for our t.	BIBL 41:10	t. of liberty	JEFF 184:2
transgressors way of t.	BIBL 38:23	t. of life	BIBL 34:8
transit O quam cito t. gloria mundi	THOM 337:8	t. of the knowledge	BIBL 34:9
Sic t. gloria mundi	ANON 13:20	t.'s inclined	POPE 266:30
translated bless thee! thou art t.	SHAK 303:26	Under the greenwood t.	SHAK 290:7
t. into Italian	WHAR 355:17	where the t. falleth	BIBL 39:26
translation mistake in the t.	VANB 345:3	Woodman, spare that t.	MORR 245:9
unfaithful to the t.	BORG 65:21	**treen** t. priests	JEWE 185:10
what is lost in t.	FROS 144:4	**trees** all the t. are green	KING 201:9
trapeze on the flying t.	LEYB 214:7	apple t. will never get across	FROS 143:20

trees (*cont.*)
He that plants t.   FULL 144:17
I like t.   CATH 88:19
Loveliest of t.   HOUS 176:6
shade of the t.   JACK 181:18
T. and stones will teach   BERN 32:11
t., And the mountain-tops   SHAK 296:10
t. bear strange fruit   ALLE 5:11
t. that grow so fair   KIPL 203:2
while some t. stand   BROW 71:7
Trelawny And shall T. die   HAWK 163:10
tremble t. for my country   JEFF 184:20
trembles t. as I do   WELL 353:18
trembling fear and t.   BIBL 51:23
T., hoping   POPE 266:10
T. in her soft   KEAT 195:14
trencher t.-friends, time's flies   SHAK 308:3
trencherman very valiant t.   SHAK 304:6
trespasses forgive us our t.   BOOK 59:15
tresses Fair t. man's imperial race   POPE 268:16
trial t. by juries   JEFF 184:8
T. by jury itself   DENM 113:1
triangle eternal t.   ANON 8:1
triangles t. were to make a God   MONT 243:5
tribal constructing t. lays   KIPL 202:11
tribe purify the dialect of the t.   ELIO 128:14
tribes two mighty t.   BYRO 81:9
tribute Hypocrisy is a t.   LA R 209:7
trick conjuring t. with bones   JENK 185:1
win the t.   HOYL 177:5
trickle T.-down theory   GALB 145:4
tried Christian ideal has not been t.   CHES 93:19
she for a little t.   WOTT 366:24
t. a little   STEV 325:9
trifles T. light as air   SHAK 305:4
T. make perfection   MICH 233:19
unconsidered t.   SHAK 309:22
trinity invoking the T.   PATR 260:12
name of the T.   ALEX 4:17
trip don't t. over the furniture   COWA 105:11
forward to the t.   STIN 326:7
t. it as ye go   MILT 236:20
triple with a t. bypass   HOWA 176:19
trippingly t. on the tongue   SHAK 293:4
tristesse *Adieu t.*   ÉLUA 131:17
Triton T. blow his wreathèd horn   WORD 366:17
triumph for evil to t.   BURK 76:10
glory in the t.   CORN 104:4
our career and our t.   VANZ 345:12
t. and defeat   LONG 217:17
t. and disaster   KIPL 202:9
t. of hope over experience   JOHN 189:1
t. of modern science   WAUG 352:10
Victor's t. won   POTT 269:9
trivial such t. people   LAWR 209:26
t. and the important   POTT 269:13
t. round, the common task   KEBL 197:24
Trojan what T. 'orses will jump out   BEVI 33:17
troops t. towards the sound   GRIM 157:17
trophies her weedy t.   SHAK 294:2
trouble better motives for all the t.   GREE 157:1
capacity of taking t.   CARL 85:9
Double, double toil and t.   SHAK 301:11
full of t.   BIBL 38:1
help in time of t.   ANON 7:5
In t. and in joy   TATE 330:20
Let nothing t. you   TERE 335:21
Man is born unto t.   BIBL 37:39
Roman and his t.   HOUS 176:11
There may be t. ahead   BERL 31:21
there's t. brewing   KNIG 204:7
took the t. to be born   BEAU 28:3
When in t., delegate   BORE 65:19

wood's in t.   HOUS 176:10
you are the one in t.   ROOS 279:3
troubled bridge over t. water   SIMO 317:1
heart be t.   BIBL 49:3
I am t.   MOOR 244:5
troubles against a sea of t.   SHAK 292:23
From t. of the world   HARV 163:4
pack up your t.   ANON 11:19
troubling wicked cease from t.   BIBL 37:37
trousers bottoms of my t. rolled   ELIO 129:3
cloud in t.   MAYA 231:17
have your best t. on   IBSE 180:6
trout t. in the milk   THOR 339:8
Where the gray t. lies   HOGG 171:13
trovato *è molto ben t.*   ANON 13:24
trowel lay it on with a t.   DISR 118:5
Troy another T. for her to burn   YEAT 368:21
from the shores of T.   VIRG 346:19
plains of windy T.   TENN 335:2
sacked T.'s sacred city   HOME 172:14
truant t. disposition   SHAK 291:22
trucks learn about t.   AWDR 21:17
true Ah, love, let us be t.   ARNO 16:12
always say what's t.   STEV 325:30
always t. to you, darlin'   PORT 268:28
And is it t.   BETJ 33:2
as t. . . . as taxes   DICK 114:22
by the people as equally t.   GIBB 148:13
can the devil speak t.   SHAK 299:15
course of t. love   SHAK 303:7
If it is not t.   ANON 13:24
Live pure, speak t.   TENN 332:12
not necessarily t.   WILD 358:31
Ring in the t.   TENN 333:9
than that it be t.   WHIT 356:9
three times is t.   CARR 87:17
too wonderful to be t.   FARA 133:21
to thine own self be t.   SHAK 291:31
t. love hath my heart   SIDN 316:11
t. to thyself   BACO 23:20
Whatsoever things are t.   BIBL 51:28
what we are saying is t.   RUSS 283:5
trumpet sound of the t.   BIBL 36:7
t. shall be heard on high   DRYD 122:13
trumpets saith among the t.   BIBL 38:9
silver, snarling t.   KEAT 195:12
to the sound of t.   SMIT 319:15
t. sounded for him   BUNY 74:19
trunkless vast and t. legs   SHEL 314:9
trust assumes a public t.   JEFF 184:11
cheated than not to t.   JOHN 187:15
I did t. in Christ   WESL 355:2
In t. I have found treason   ELIZ 130:12
Just t. yourself   GOET 152:11
Never t. the artist   LAWR 209:19
no t. in the future   HORA 175:7
power in t.   DRYD 121:19
power is in a t.   DISR 118:5
put your t. in God   BLAC 55:12
t. in God   SMIT 319:7
t. in princes   BOOK 65:5
t. me not at all   TENN 332:17
T. one who has gone through it   VIRG 347:10
trusted friend, whom I t.   BOOK 62:26
in thee have I t.   BOOK 59:21
truth Art is not t.   PICA 263:11
Beauty is t.   KEAT 196:12
best test of t.   CHES 92:22
Christianity better than T.   COLE 100:30
cinema is t. 24 times per second   GODA 152:1
dearer still is t.   ARIS 15:23
diminution of the love of t.   JOHN 187:4
economical with the t.   ARMS 16:9

two (*cont.*)

There went in t. and two	BIBL 34:28
twice t. be not four	TURG 343:2
T. and two only	NEWM 249:20
t. and two would continue to make	WHIS 355:23
t. cultures	SNOW 319:21
t. ears of corn	SWIF 328:10
t.-handed engine	MILT 236:33
t. hours' traffick	SHAK 306:21
t. hundred thousand men	NAPO 248:5
T. nations	DISR 117:29
t. o'clock in the morning	NAPO 248:3
t. or three are gathered	BOOK 60:6
t. people miserable	BUTL 79:13
t. primal Spirits	ZORO 370:18
t. things that will be believed	TARK 330:18
where t. or three	BIBL 45:15
twopence penny plain and t. coloured	STEV 325:15
tyger T., Tyger	BLAK 58:3
tygers t. of wrath	BLAK 57:3
type careful of the t.	TENN 333:2
people couldn't t.	JOBS 185:11
types Seven t. of ambiguity	EMPS 132:25
T. and shadows	THOM 337:13
typewriters banging on million t.	WILE 359:24
monkeys strumming on t.	EDDI 124:21
tyrannis *Sic semper t.*	ANON 13:19
Sic semper t.	BOOT 65:17
tyrannous t. To use it like a giant	SHAK 302:4
tyranny conditions of t.	AREN 15:1
T. is always better organized	PÉGU 261:7
unnecessary t.	RUSS 282:25
wage war against a monstrous t.	CHUR 95:7
without representation is t.	OTIS 255:22
worst sort of t.	BURK 76:5
tyrants all men would be t.	DEFO 111:20
argument of t.	PITT 263:20
Kings will be t.	BURK 75:21
men would be t.	ADAM 1:10
patriots and t.	JEFF 184:2
Rebellion to t.	BRAD 67:12
sceptre from t.	TURG 343:3
Tyre Nineveh and T.	KIPL 202:20
tyres concrete and t.	LARK 208:18
Tyrian budded T.	KEAT 196:26

U

ubi *U. Petrus, ibi ergo ecclesia*	AMBR 5:22
ubique *Quod u., quod semper*	VINC 346:18
ubiquities blazing u.	EMER 132:21
ugly never saw an u. thing	CONS 103:3
no place for u. mathematics	HARD 161:13
than to be u.	WILD 358:29
Ulster Protestant Province of U.	CARS 87:24
to which U. will not go	BONA 59:4
U. will fight	CHUR 94:18
ulterioris *ripae u. amore*	VIRG 347:12
ultima *U. Thule*	VIRG 348:1
ultimate u. truth	NAGA 247:19
umble so very 'u.	DICK 114:20
umbrella steals the just's u.	BOWE 66:17
umpire Chaos u. sits	MILT 238:12
unacceptable u. face of capitalism	HEAT 164:15
unacknowledged u. legislators	SHEL 315:6
unattempted u. yet in prose or rhyme	MILT 237:16
unaware And I was u.	HARD 162:1
unbearable in victory u.	CHUR 96:2
u. lightness of being	KUND 206:7
unbeatable In defeat u.	CHUR 96:2

unbeautiful u. and have comfortable minds	CUMM 108:11
unbecoming u. the character	ANON 7:10
unbelief help thou mine u.	BIBL 46:28
unbelievers hard against the u.	KORA 205:22
unbirthday u. present	CARR 87:8
unbowed bloody, but u.	HENL 166:8
unburied bodies of u. men	WEBS 353:2
uncharitableness from all u.	BOOK 60:11
uncle My u.	SHAK 292:1
u. me no uncle	SHAK 305:24
U. Tom Cobbleigh	BALL 26:3
unclean people of u. lips	BIBL 40:9
unco Address to the u. guid	BURN 76:15
uncomfortable when he is only u.	SHAW 312:3
unconditional u. and immediate surrender	GRAN 155:9
unconquerable man's u. mind	WORD 366:14
u. will	MILT 237:20
unconscionable u. time dying	CHAR 91:3
unconscious knowledge of the u.	FREU 142:17
royal road to the u.	FREU 142:17
unconsidered u. trifles	SHAK 309:22
unconvincing bald and u.	GILB 150:8
uncreating U. word	POPE 266:9
undefiled well of English u.	SPEN 322:4
under get out and get u.	CLAR 97:8
underbelly soft u. of Europe	CHUR 95:15
u. of the Axis	CHUR 95:15
underground Johnny u.	PUDN 271:14
underlings ourselves, that we are u.	SHAK 296:19
underneath U. the Arches	FLAN 137:19
understand criticize What you can't u.	DYLA 124:14
doesn't u. the situation	MURR 247:12
don't u. things	NEUM 249:14
failed to u.	BOHR 58:17
Grown-ups never u. anything	SAIN 284:8
I do not u.	FEYN 135:5
liberals can u.	BRUC 73:7
to u. them	SPIN 322:9
u. a little less	MAJO 225:18
understanded tongue not u.	BOOK 65:13
understanding candle of u.	BIBL 42:19
find you an u.	JOHN 190:19
pass all u.	JAME 182:13
passeth all u.	BIBL 51:27
To be totally u.	STAÊ 322:22
wisdom and u.	BIBL 40:16
with all thy getting get u.	BIBL 38:14
understandings muddy u.	BURK 75:19
understands as he u. it	JACK 181:12
world u. my language	HAYD 163:18
understood I have u. you	DE G 112:3
music u. by children	STRA 326:23
u. by others	JACK 181:12
undertaking no such u. has been received	CHAM 90:6
undeservedly books u. forgotten	AUDE 19:25
undeserving u. poor	SHAW 312:29
undevout u. astronomer is mad	YOUN 370:2
undiscovered u. country	SHAK 292:25
undone death had u. so many	ELIO 129:21
I am u.	BIBL 40:9
John Donne, Anne Donne, U.	DONN 119:25
We have left u.	BOOK 59:13
What's done cannot be u.	SHAK 301:25
uneasy U. lies the head	SHAK 295:3
uneatable pursuit of the u.	WILD 359:1
uneducated government by the u.	CHES 93:23
u. man to read books	CHUR 96:4
unemployment rising u.	LAMO 207:10
unequal equal division of u. earnings	ELLI 131:11
unespied In the ocean's bosom u.	MARV 229:13
unexamined u. life is not worth	SOCR 319:25

unexpected Old age is the most u. TROT 342:5
unexplained you're u. as yet HALL 160:8
unfaithful faith u. TENN 332:14
  original is u. BORG 65:21
unfamiliar u. terms GALE 145:6
unfeeling u. for his own GRAY 156:17
unfinished Liberty is u. business ANON 9:9
unforgiving u. eye SHER 315:17
unfortunate u. man BOET 58:15
ungodliness tents of u. BOOK 63:20
ungodly u. in great power BOOK 62:24
unhappily bad end u. STOP 326:14
unhappiness vocation of u. SIME 316:23
unhappy each u. family TOLS 341:3
  I'm u. CHEK 92:8
  Men who are u. RUSS 282:22
  that of the u. WITT 362:14
  u., far-off things WORD 366:6
  U. the land that needs heroes BREC 68:4
unheard language of the u. KING 201:2
  those u. Are sweeter KEAT 196:7
unholy sights u. MILT 236:17
unhonoured Unwept, u. SCOT 287:13
uninspiring may be u. GEOR 148:2
unintelligible rapid, u. patter GILB 150:26
union determined to preserve this U. HOUS 176:18
  indestructible U. CHAS 91:10
  Join the u., girls ANTH 14:6
  Liberty and U. WEBS 352:19
  O U., strong and great LONG 217:7
  Our Federal U. JACK 181:11
  our u. is perfect DICK 116:8
  save the U. LINC 214:18
unions when Hitler attacked the u. NIEM 251:3
unite Workers of the world, u. MARX 230:13
United States believe in the U. PAGE 256:20
  close to the U. DIAZ 114:10
  U. themselves WHIT 357:12
unities Three U. DRYD 122:20
uniting By u. we stand DICK 116:9
unity national u. BUSH 78:11
  national u. ROOS 279:9
  truth, u., and concord BOOK 61:7
universal become a u. law KANT 194:21
  one u. grin FIEL 135:14
  u. frame BACO 22:11
  u. good POPE 267:25
  u. monarchy of wit CARE 84:18
universe Architect of the U. JEAN 183:16
  fact about the u. EINS 126:7
  first invent the u. SAGA 284:3
  hell of a good u. next door CUMM 108:9
  Life, the U. and Everything ADAM 1:13
  measure of the u. SHEL 314:14
  ordering of the u. ALFO 5:2
  Put back Thy u. JONE 191:8
  u. go to all the bother HAWK 163:12
  u. is not hostile HOLM 171:19
  u. queerer than we suppose HALD 159:8
  u.'s existence is made known PENR 261:14
  we and the u. exist HAWK 163:13
university able to get to a u. KINN 201:14
  U. of these days CARL 85:14
  U. should be DISR 117:13
unjust commended the u. steward BIBL 47:34
  on the just and on the u. BIBL 43:19
  u. steals BOWE 66:17
unjustly teach to talk u. ARIS 15:6
unkindest most u. cut of all SHAK 297:6
unknowable world u., we know THOM 338:17
unknowing cloud of u. ANON 7:15
unknown gates to the glorious and u. FORS 139:15
  known and the u. PINT 263:14

live, unseen, u. POPE 268:13
  My song is love u. CROS 107:21
  She lived u. WORD 365:28
  things u. POPE 267:17
  to the u. god BIBL 49:30
unleavened u. bread BIBL 35:18
  u. bread HAGG 158:18
unleaving Goldengrove u. HOPK 174:3
unlessoned u. girl SHAK 302:26
unloose not worthy to u. BIBL 48:20
unluckily good u. STOP 326:14
unmapped u. country ELIO 127:8
unmarried prime-roses, That die u. SHAK 309:27
unmixed u. blessing HORA 175:12
unnatural only u. sex act KINS 201:15
unnecessary thou u. letter SHAK 297:31
unofficial English u. rose BROO 69:20
unpalatable disastrous and the u. GALB 145:5
unpatriotic u. and servile ROOS 280:8
unplumbed u., salt, estranging sea ARNO 17:1
unpopular safe to be u. STEV 325:4
unprincipled sold by the u. CAPP 84:16
unprofitable flat, and u. SHAK 291:16
unreasonable progress depends on u. man
                                    SHAW 312:15
unreliable Even death is u. BECK 28:19
unremembered nameless, u., acts WORD 364:19
unrighteousness mammon of u. BIBL 47:35
unruly old fool, u. sun DONN 119:15
  u. evil BIBL 52:22
unsafe U. at any speed NADE 247:18
unsatisfied leaves one u. WILD 358:28
unsayable say the u. RUSH 282:8
unsearchable u. riches of Christ BIBL 51:15
unseen born to blush u. GRAY 156:11
  Thou art u. SHEL 314:27
  u. among us SHEL 313:27
  walk the earth U. MILT 238:26
unsex U. me here SHAK 299:23
unspeakable speak the u. RUSH 282:8
  u. in full pursuit WILD 359:1
unstable U. as water BIBL 35:10
unsung unhonoured, and u. SCOT 287:13
untalented product of the u. CAPP 84:16
untender So young, and so u. SHAK 297:23
unterrified Satan stood U. MILT 238:11
untimely U. ripped SHAK 302:1
unto give u. this last BIBL 45:23
  u. us a child is born BIBL 40:14
untravelled Gleams that u. world TENN 335:3
untried difficult; and left u. CHES 93:19
  new and u. LINC 214:14
untrodden among the u. ways WORD 365:26
untroubled u. where I lie CLAR 96:27
untune Music shall u. the sky DRYD 122:13
unusual cruel and u. punishment CONS 103:9
unutterable looked u. things THOM 339:1
unvarnished round u. tale SHAK 304:21
unwanted feeling of being u. TERE 335:18
unwept U., unhonoured SCOT 287:13
unwholesome not u. AUST 20:20
unwilling committee is a group of the u. ANON 7:16
up be u. betimes SHAK 308:26
  nice to people on your way u. MIZN 241:19
  U. Guards and at them WELL 354:1
  u.-hill all the way ROSS 280:16
  U. to a point, Lord Copper WAUG 352:7
  U. with your damned nonsense RICH 276:13
upharsin MENE, TEKEL, U. BIBL 42:6
upper butler's u. slopes WODE 362:22
  prove the u. classes COWA 105:7
  u. station of low life DEFO 111:18
upright God hath made man u. BIBL 39:16

verbal v. contract isn't worth	GOLD 154:3
verbo *sed tantum dic v.*	MISS 241:1
verbosa *v. rusticitas*	JERO 185:3
verbosity crude v.	JERO 185:3
exuberance of his own v.	DISR 117:17
verbrennt *wo man Bücher V.*	HEIN 165:6
verbum V. caro factum est	MISS 241:3
V. sapienti	PLAU 265:5
volat irrevocabile v.	HORA 175:2
verdict v. afterwards	CARR 86:22
verge get to the v.	DULL 123:2
verifiability criterion of v.	AYER 21:19
verification method of its v.	SCHL 286:12
verify v. your references	ROUT 281:10
verily v., I say unto you	BIBL 48:31
verisimilitude artistic v.	GILB 150:8
veritas *magis amica v.*	ARIS 15:23
Magna est v., et praevalet	BIBL 54:14
vermilion V.-spotted, golden	KEAT 195:28
vermin lower than v.	BEVA 33:8
Vermont so goes V.	FARL 134:5
vernal from a v. wood	WORD 366:9
vero *Se non è v.*	ANON 13:24
verse as soon write free v.	FROS 144:3
incantation of this v.	SHEL 314:7
No subject for immortal v.	DAY- 111:11
v. is a measured speech	BACO 22:4
Voice, and V.	MILT 236:2
write it out in a v.	YEAT 368:5
verses scattered v.	PETR 262:13
Tear him for his bad v.	SHAK 297:12
versions hundred v. of it	SHAW 312.25
verum *quaerere v.*	HORA 175:5
very V. God of very God	BOOK 61:3
vespers friars were singing v.	GIBB 149:3
vessel gilded v. goes	GRAY 156:6
unto the weaker v.	BIBL 52:28
Vestal blameless V.'s lost	POPE 266:13
vesture cast lots upon my v.	BOOK 62:13
Vexilla *Vexilla regis prodeunt*	FORT 140:1
vexing V. the dull ear	SHAK 297:19
vibrates V. in the memory	SHEL 314:23
vibration brave v. each way free	HERR 168:7
vice Art is v.	DEGA 112:1
best discover v.	BACO 22:10
bullied out of v.	SURT 327:19
defence of liberty is no v.	GOLD 153:29
raptures and roses of v.	SWIN 329:9
sensual pleasure without v.	JOHN 191:2
V. is a monster	POPE 267:29
v. of chastity	VOLT 348:24
v. pays to virtue	LA R 209:7
virtue and v.	JOHN 188:15
vice-presidency of the v.	ADAM 2:7
vices our pleasant v.	SHAK 298:24
vicisti V., *Galilae*	JULI 193:15
victim It marks its v.	CLAY 97:14
oppressor, never the v.	WIES 357:22
v. must be found	GILB 149:23
victims little v. play	GRAY 156:16
v. who respect their executioners	SART 285:25
victis *Vae v.*	LIVY 216:4
victor to the v. belong	MARC 227:16
Victoria take a ticket at V.	BEVI 33:16
Victorian V. values	THAT 336:18
victories Peace hath her v.	MILT 240:2
proper use of v.	POLY 266:2
victory grave, where is thy v.	BIBL 51:4
humanity after V.	NELS 249:7
In v.; magnanimity	CHUR 96:5
in v. unbearable	CHUR 96:2
magnanimous in v.	COLL 101:14
no substitute for v.	MACA 221:7

not the v. but the contest	COUB 104:14
One more such v.	PYRR 272:7
peace without v.	WILS 361:13
swallow up death in v.	BIBL 40:22
'twas a famous v.	SOUT 320:19
V. has a hundred fathers	CIAN 96:12
v. in spite of all terror	CHUR 95:8
vidi *Veni, v., vici*	CAES 82:8
vie v. humaine commence	SART 285:24
vieillesse *si v. pouvait*	ESTI 133:3
Viet Cong no quarrel with the V.	ALI 5:8
Vietnam last man to die in V.	KERR 199:13
V. was lost in	MCLU 223:19
V. was the first	WEST 355:16
view lends enchantment to the v.	CAMP 83:12
motley to the v.	SHAK 310:19
views Kipling and his v.	AUDE 19:5
vigilance eternal v.	CURR 108:16
vigilant Be sober, be v.	BIBL 52:30
vile only man is v.	HEBE 164:18
village first in a v.	CAES 82:6
image of a global v.	MCLU 223:17
in a country v.	AUST 21:13
life in the v.	LEE 211:14
Sweet Auburn, loveliest v.	GOLD 153:4
villages pleasant v. and farms	MILT 239:5
villain One murder made a v.	PORT 269:7
smiling, damnèd v.	SHAK 292:3
villainy v. you teach me	SHAK 302:23
vinces *In hoc signo v.*	CONS 103:5
Vinci spell it V.	TWAI 343:16
vincit *Omnia v. Amor*	VIRG 347:25
vindicate v. the ways of God	POPE 267:19
vine as the fruitful v.	BOOK 64:28
clusters of the v.	MARV 229:16
vines advise his client to plant v.	WRIG 366:27
bless With fruit the v.	KEAT 197:1
vintage O, for a draught of v.	KEAT 196:17
trampling out the v.	HOWE 177:2
violence Snobbery with V.	BENN 30:21
v. is necessary	BROW 70:15
violent All v. feelings	RUSK 282:14
violently v. if they must	QUIN 272:10
violet v. by a mossy stone	WORD 365:27
v. smells to him	SHAK 295:19
violets I would give you some v.	SHAK 293:33
vipers O generation of v.	BIBL 43:7
vir *Beatus v. qui timet Dominum*	BIBL 53:30
Virgil V. at Mexico	WALP 350:2
virgin v. goddess returns	VIRG 347:21
v. shall conceive	BIBL 40:12
Virginian I am not a V.	HENR 166:23
virginity for my v.	PRIO 271:2
v. could be a virtue	VOLT 348:19
virtue Assume a v.	SHAK 293:21
best discover v.	BACO 22:10
excellence or v.	ARIS 15:13
Few men have v. to withstand	WASH 351:6
flattered into v.	SURT 327:19
follow v. and knowledge	DANT 109:13
form of every v. at the testing point	LEWI 214:1
lilies and languors of v.	SWIN 329:9
no v. like necessity	SHAK 305:20
only reward of v.	EMER 132:6
very sinews of v.	WALT 350:11
vice pays to v.	LA R 209:7
virginity could be a v.	VOLT 348:19
v. and talents	JEFF 184:14
v. and vice	JOHN 188:15
V. does not come from money	SOCR 319:24
V. is like a rich stone	BACO 22:13
v. is made of the vice	VOLT 348:24
V. is the fount	MARL 228:19

W

we w. eternally	DONN 118:23
wakening Our w. and uprising	KEBL 197:23
wakes Hock-carts, wassails, w.	HERR 168:1
What angel w. me	SHAK 303:27
waking I lay broad w.	WYAT 367:3
w., no such matter	SHAK 310:15
Wales bless the Prince of W.	LINL 215:12
still parts of W.	THOM 338:10
whole world . . . But for W.	BOLT 59:3
walk closer w. with God	COWP 105:20
men must w.	POPE 268:7
never w. alone	HAMM 160:24
no easy w.-over to freedom	NEHR 249:3
take up thy bed, and w.	BIBL 48:29
taking a w. that day	BRON 69:10
upon which the people w.	CRAZ 106:14
W. across my swimming pool	RICE 276:3
w. a little faster	CARR 86:17
W. cheerfully over the world	FOX 141:1
w. circumspectly	BIBL 51:18
w. humbly with thy God	BIBL 42:15
w. in fear and dread	COLE 100:26
w. in newness of life	BIBL 50:2
w. o'er the western wave	SHEL 314:30
w. on the wild side	ALGR 5:3
W. upon England's mountains green	BLAK 57:8
w. ye	BIBL 40:26
Where'er you w.	POPE 268:14
Yea, though I w.	BOOK 62:15
walked He w. by himself	KIPL 203:13
slowly w. away	BURT 77:25
w. through the wilderness	BUNY 74:6
walking empire w. very slowly	FITZ 137:14
Lord God w. in the garden	BIBL 34:16
w. up and down	BIBL 37:32
walks She w. in beauty	BYRO 81:17
w. always beside you	ELIO 130:1
wall close the w. up	SHAK 295:16
doesn't love a w.	FROS 143:19
have I leaped over a w.	BIBL 37:2
like a stone w.	BEE 28:21
w. fell down flat	BIBL 36:7
w. next door catches fire	HORA 175:3
Watch the w., my darling	KIPL 202:24
With our backs to the w.	HAIG 159:5
Without a city w.	ALEX 4:18
wooden w. is your ships	THEM 337:6
Wallace hae wi' W. bled	BURN 77:10
wallet Time hath, my lord, a w.	SHAK 308:11
walling What I was w. in	FROS 143:21
walls Stone w. do not a prison make	LOVE 219:9
these w. thy sphere	DONN 119:17
wooden w. are the best	COVE 104:18
Waltons more like the W.	BUSH 78:15
waltzing You'll come a-w., Matilda	PATE 260:9
waly w., waly, up the bank	BALL 26:2
wan Why so pale and w.	SUCK 327:5
wandered w. far and wide	HOME 172:14
w. lonely as a cloud	WORD 364:17
wandering but a w. voice	WORD 366:13
W. between two worlds	ARNO 16:24
w. minstrel I	GILB 149:21
waning onset and w. of love	LA B 206:11
want don't w. him	MILN 235:10
in w. of a wife	AUST 21:6
I shall not w.	BOOK 62:14
I w. some more	DICK 115:13
probably won't w.	HOPE 173:8
that people know what they w.	MENC 232:20
third is freedom from w.	ROOS 279:15
w. it the most	CHES 92:18
w. of decency	DILL 116:15
W. one only of five giants	BEVE 33:15

we w. it now	MORR 245:19
What can I w. or need	HERB 167:23
What does a woman w.	FREU 142:18
what I really really w.	ROWB 281:11
wanting found w.	BIBL 42:6
wantonly unadvisedly, lightly, or w.	BOOK 61:24
wantonness in clothes a w.	HERR 168:3
wants Man w. but little	GOLD 153:12
provide for human w.	BURK 75:16
wanwood worlds of w. leafmeal	HOPK 174:4
war After each w.	ATKI 18:7
Ancestral voices prophesying w.	COLE 100:10
another w. in Europe	BISM 55:10
at w. with Germany	CHAM 90:6
better than to w.-war	CHUR 95:23
blast of w.	SHAK 295:16
business of w.	WELL 354:7
but it is not w.	BOSQ 66:1
calamities of w.	JOHN 187:4
cold w.	BARU 27:7
cold w. warrior	THAT 336:13
condition which is called w.	HOBB 170:17
cruellest and most terrible w.	LLOY 216:9
desolation of w.	GEOR 147:20
Don't mention the w.	CLEE 97:18
easier to make w.	CLEM 98:3
Either w. is obsolete or men are	FULL 144:12
enable it to make w.	WEIL 353:6
endless w. still breed	MILT 237:5
Everything is very simple in w.	CLAU 97:11
first w. fought without	WEST 355:16
First World W. had begun	TAYL 330:23
France has not lost the w.	DE G 112:2
furnish the w.	HEAR 164:14
I am for w.	RED 274:11
if someone gave a w.	GINS 151:2
I hate w.	ROOS 279:10
I have seen w.	ROOS 279:10
Image of w.	SOME 320:8
I must study politics and w.	ADAM 2:6
in every w. they kill you in a new way	ROGE 278:17
In w., no winners	CHAM 90:3
In w.; resolution	CHUR 96:5
in w. the two cardinal virtues	HOBB 170:20
I renounce w.	FOSD 140:3
lead this people into w.	WILS 361:15
let slip the dogs of w.	SHAK 296:30
liking for w.	BENN 30:19
looks on w. as all glory	SHER 315:26
lose the w. in an afternoon	CHUR 96:7
made this great w.	LINC 215:7
make w. that we may live	ARIS 15:14
Mankind must put an end to w.	KENN 199:2
McNamara's W.	MCNA 224:8
My w. is over	MCGU 223:6
nature of w.	HOBB 170:18
neither shall they learn w.	BIBL 40:5
never was a good w.	FRAN 142:2
no declaration of w.	EDEN 125:2
no discharge in that w.	BIBL 39:17
Older men declare w.	HOOV 173:7
pattern called a w.	LOWE 219:16
pestilence and w.	MILT 238:11
prepare for w.	VEGE 346:1
provoke a new civil w.	JUAN 193:11
quaint and curious w. is	HARD 162:4
recourse to w.	BRIA 68:14
rich wage w.	SART 285:19
seek no wider w.	JOHN 186:8
silent in time of w.	CICE 96:23
sinews of w.	CICE 96:22
special problem in w.	CLAU 97:10
subject is W.	OWEN 256:6

war (cont.)

tell us all about the w.	SOUT 320:18
tempered by w.	KENN 198:14
they'll give a w.	SAND 285:7
this is w.	ADAM 1:12
this w. on terrorism	BUSH 78:18
time of w.	BIBL 39:12
to the w. is gone	MOOR 244:10
two nations have been at w.	VOLT 348:7
wage w. against a monstrous tyranny	CHUR 95:7
w. and peace in 21st century	KOHL 204:16
w.-gamed against	WALL 349:14
W. hath no fury	MONT 242:15
w. in heaven	BIBL 53:12
w. is a necessary part	MOLT 242:5
W. is capitalism with	STOP 326:16
W. is continuation of politics	CLAU 97:12
W. is hell, and all that	HAY 163:16
W. is not the word	KENN 198:8
w. is over	GRAN 155:11
W. is peace	ORWE 254:22
w. is politics with bloodshed	MAO 227:11
w. is so terrible	LEE 211:16
W. is the national industry	MIRA 240:13
W. is the remedy	SHER 315:25
W. is the trade of kings	DRYD 122:5
W. is too serious	CLEM 98:2
W. makes good history	HARD 161:14
w. minus the shooting	ORWE 255:2
w. of nature	DARW 110:9
w.'s a game	COWP 105:30
w. situation	HIRO 170:1
w. that will end war	WELL 354:13
W. to the knife	PALA 257:21
way of ending a w.	ORWE 255:8
We hear w. called murder	MACD 222:20
we prepare for w.	PEAR 261:3
what a lovely w.	LITT 215:15
When w. is declared	ANON 12:1
win an atomic w.	BRAD 67:8
win a w. is as disastrous	CHRI 94:10
won the last w.	ROOS 279:4
warfare w. is accomplished	BIBL 40:29
warlord concubine of a w.	JUNG 193:22
warm For ever w.	KEAT 196:10
O! she's w.	SHAK 309:30
w. courage	BUSH 78:17
w. courage	ROOS 279:9
warmed heart strangely w.	WESL 355:2
warmth W. and Light	GREN 157:11
warn All a poet can do is w.	OWEN 256:7
right to w.	BAGE 24:10
w., to comfort, and command	WORD 366:3
w. you not to be ordinary	KINN 201:13
warning With horrid w.	KEAT 195:27
warrant not a sufficient w.	MILL 234:7
warring two nations w.	DURH 123:13
warrior cold war w.	THAT 336:13
Home they brought her w.	TENN 334:18
This is the happy w.	READ 273:18
Who is the happy W.	WORD 364:9
wars all their w. are merry	CHES 92:26
came to an end all w.	LLOY 216:9
end to the beginnings of all w.	ROOS 279:18
how do w. start	KRAU 205:26
into any foreign w.	ROOS 279:13
occasion of all w.	FOX 140:16
serve in the w.	BOOK 65:15
thousand w. of old	TENN 333:10
w. and rumours of wars	BIBL 45:32
w., horrible wars	VIRG 347:10
warts w. and all	CROM 107:16
was Thinks what ne'er w.	POPE 267:8

wash Moab is my w.-pot	BOOK 63:13
w. that man right outa	HAMM 160:16
w. the wind	ELIO 129:7
washed w. his hands	BIBL 46:17
w. in the blood of the Lamb	LIND 215:9
washing country w.	BRUM 73:11
w. on the Siegfried Line	KENN 198:11
Washington Government at W. lives	GARF 146:3
wasp everything about the w.	THOM 338:3
wasps w. and hornets break through	SWIF 328:8
wassails Hock-carts, w., wakes	HERR 168:1
waste art of how to w. space	JOHN 186:15
now doth time w. me	SHAK 306:6
w. howling wilderness	BIBL 36:5
w. of breath	YEAT 368:13
w. of shame	SHAK 310:24
w. places of Jerusalem	BIBL 41:8
we lay w. our powers	WORD 366:16
wasted day most surely w.	CHAM 90:9
spend on advertising is w.	LEVE 213:11
w. his substance	BIBL 47:30
wasteful clumsy, w., blundering	DARW 110:11
watch could ye not watch with me	BIBL 46:14
keeping w. over their flock	BIBL 47:2
learning, like your w.	CHES 92:19
like a fat gold w.	PLAT 264:17
some must w.	SHAK 293:11
W. and pray	BIBL 46:15
w. between me and thee	BIBL 35:5
w. in the night	BOOK 63:22
w. must have had a maker	PALE 258:1
w. not one another	DONN 119:10
W. therefore	BIBL 46:3
watcher posted presence of the w.	JAME 182:21
w. of the skies	KEAT 196:28
watchful occasion's forelock w.	MILT 239:15
watching BIG BROTHER IS W. YOU	ORWE 254:21
watchmaker blind w.	DAWK 111:6
watchman W., what of the night	BIBL 40:20
water as w. spilt on the ground	BIBL 36:38
bridge over troubled w.	SIMO 317:1
conscious w. saw its God	CRAS 106:11
daughter of Earth and W.	SHEL 313:24
desireth the w.-brooks	BOOK 62:27
drawers of w.	BIBL 36:8
fountain of the w. of life	BIBL 53:24
if I were under w.	KEAT 197:15
King over the W.	ANON 9:8
Little drops of w.	CARN 85:27
little w. clears us	SHAK 300:20
name was writ in w.	KEAT 197:21
presence of still w.	BERR 32:17
ready by w. as by land	ELST 131:16
ring of bright w.	RAIN 272:21
shining Big-Sea-W.	LONG 218:4
spring of ever-flowing w.	HORA 175:25
Tar w.	BERK 31:14
travel by land or by w.	BOOK 60:15
Unstable as w.	BIBL 35:10
virtues We write in w.	SHAK 296:16
walking on the w.	THOM 338:20
w. and a crust	KEAT 196:1
w. hollows out	OVID 255:25
w. in the rough rude sea	SHAK 305:27
W. is best	PIND 263:12
w. like Pilate	GREE 156:23
'w.' meant the wonderful	KELL 197:27
w. of affliction	BIBL 37:17
W., water, everywhere	COLE 100:20
weaker than w.	LAO 208:10
where the w. goes	CHES 93:7
watered w. heaven with their tears	BLAK 58:4
Waterloo Austerlitz and W.	SAND 285:6

battle of W. WELL 354:8
battle of W. won ORWE 254:19
waterman great-grandfather was but a w. BUNY 74:12
watermelons down by the w. GINS 151:5
watermen w., that row one way BURT 78:3
waters as the w. cover the sea BIBL 40:18
beside the still w. BOOK 62:14
By the w. of Babylon BOOK 65:1
Cast thy bread upon the w. BIBL 39:25
cold w. to a thirsty soul BIBL 38:37
face of the w. BIBL 34:3
in great w. BOOK 64:9
quiet w. by SCOT 288:2
Stolen w. are sweet BIBL 38:18
w. cannot quench love BIBL 40:3
w. of affliction BIBL 40:25
w. of comfort BOOK 62:14
Watson Elementary, my dear W. DOYL 120:17
Mr W.—come here BELL 29:14
wave bind the restless w. WHIT 356:19
cool, translucent w. MILT 236:10
lift me as a w. SHEL 314:5
upon an orient w. MILT 237:9
waves chuckles of the w. AESC 3:20
Him that walked the w. MILT 237:3
Like as the w. SHAK 310:10
w. and washèd it away SPEN 321:20
w. were always saying DICK 114:25
When the w. turn the minutes LIGH 214:10
wild w. saying CARP 86:1
waving not w. but drowning SMIT 319:3
wax hives with honey and w SWIF 328:6
way broad is the w. BIBL 44:9
by w. of Beachy Head CHES 93:4
every one to his own w. BIBL 41:10
going the w. of all the earth BIBL 36:9
I did it my w. ANKA 7:4
If w. to the Better there be HARD 162:2
long w. to Tipperary JUDG 193:12
no w. out of the mind PLAT 264:11
Prepare ye the w. of the Lord BIBL 43:5
there was a w. to Hell BUNY 74:13
This is the w. BIBL 40:26
W. down upon the Swanee FOST 140:9
w. of a man with a maid BIBL 39:4
w. of taking life FROS 144:2
w. of the Lord BIBL 40:30
w. of transgressors BIBL 38:23
W. that can be told of LAO 207:20
w., the truth, and the life BIBL 49:5
w. to the stars VIRG 347:17
your w. be long CAVA 89:11
ways in whose heart are thy w. BOOK 63:19
justify the w. of God MILT 237:17
Let me count the w. BROW 71:17
neither are your w. my ways BIBL 41:14
parting of the w. BIBL 42:1
vindicate the w. of God POPE 267:19
w. are ways of pleasantness BIBL 38:13
w. be unconfined PRIO 270:23
we W.'re here ANON 11:15
weak flesh is w. BIBL 46:15
refuge of w. minds CHES 92:21
w. overcomes the strong LAO 208:10
w. piping time SHAK 306:8
weaker unto the w. vessel BIBL 52:28
w. sex ALEX 5:1
wealth consume w. without producing SHAW 311:10
get w. and place POPE 268:8
grateful for the blessings of w. WINF 361:21
I'm a man of w. JAGG 182:7
insolence of w. JOHN 189:25
no w. but life RUSK 282:21

w. accumulates, and men decay GOLD 153:5
w. and commerce MANN 227:8
w. is a sacred thing FRAN 141:6
wealthy business of the w. man BELL 30:1
weaned w. on a pickle ANON 11:12
weapon art is not a w. KENN 199:4
Loyalty the Tory's secret w. KILM 200:6
offensive and dangerous w. PICA 263:5
shield and w. LUTH 220:19
weapons books are w. ROOS 279:17
fightings with outward w. FOX 141:2
wear w. BOOK 65:15
wear better to w. out CUMB 108:3
qualities as would w. well GOLD 153:26
w. him In my heart's core SHAK 293:8
w. of winning BELL 30:5
weariness much study is a w. BIBL 39:29
pale for w. SHEL 314:31
w. May toss him to My breast HERB 167:21
wearing w. o' the Green ANON 9:4
weary got the W. Blues HUGH 177:15
How w., stale, flat SHAK 291:16
not be w. in well doing BIBL 51:14
run, and not be w. BIBL 41:4
w. be at rest BIBL 37:37
weasel as a w. sucks eggs SHAK 290:8
Pop goes the w. MAND 226:15
w. under the cocktail cabinet PINT 263:15
w. word ROOS 280:6
weather first talk is of the w. JOHN 187:3
Some are w.-wise FRAN 141:17
Stormy w. KOEH 204:14
w. is always doing something TWAI 343:27
w. the cuckoo likes HARD 162:8
w. turned around THOM 337:24
winter and rough w. SHAK 290:7
you won't hold up the w. MACN 224:10
weave tangled web we w. SCOT 287:19
web cool w. of language GRAV 155:16
She left the w. TENN 333:19
tangled w. we weave SCOT 287:19
webs like spiders' w. ANAC 6:9
Webster Like W.'s Dictionary BURK 76:12
wed With this Ring I thee w. BOOK 62:1
wedded I have w. fyve CHAU 91:28
wedding as she did her w. gown GOLD 153:26
earliest w.-day KEBL 197:25
w. clothes ADDI 3:8
wedlock w.'s the devil BYRO 81:23
wee W., sleekit, cow'rin' BURN 77:19
weed Ignorance is an evil w. BEVE 33:14
w. that grows BURK 75:10
What is a w.? A plant EMER 132:15
weeds coronet w. SHAK 294:2
smell far worse than w. SHAK 310:16
week die in my w. JOPL 192:11
Sunday In every w. CLAR 97:7
w. after next CARR 87:16
w. a long time in politics WILS 361:5
weekend long w. FORS 139:14
weep fear of having to w. BEAU 28:1
I may not w. BYRO 81:2
I w. for Adonais SHEL 313:13
That he should w. for her SHAK 292:21
time to w. BIBL 39:11
w. and know why HOPK 174:4
W., and you weep alone WILC 357:25
w. or she will die TENN 334:18
women must w. KING 201:8
weeping w. and gnashing BIBL 44:15
w. for her children BIBL 43:3
Weib W. und Gesang LUTH 220:20
weigh w. and consider BACO 23:11

weighed w. in the balances — BIBL 42:6
weight w. of rages — SPOO 322:11
Wein W., Weib und Gesang — LUTH 220:20
weird w. sisters — SHAK 299:11
welcome Advice is seldom w. — CHES 92:18
Love bade me w. — HERB 167:17
warmest w., at an inn — SHEN 315:7
W., all wonders — CRAS 106:12
W. the coming — POPE 268:6
W. the sixte — CHAU 91:28
W. to your gory bed — BURN 77:10
welfare anxious for its w. — BURK 75:5
concerned with the w. — MAHÀ 225:8
corporate w. bums — LEWI 214:2
w. of this realm — CHAR 91:1
well alive and w. — ANON 9:6
all shall be w. — ELIO 128:18
all shall be w. — JULI 193:14
being w. — MART 229:10
deep as a w. — SHAK 306:37
Is it w. with the child — BIBL 37:22
It is not done w. — JOHN 188:18
not wisely but too w. — SHAK 305:14
one who meant w. — STEV 325:9
rare as a w.-spent one — CARL 85:5
shall be w. again — ARNO 16:14
use it for a w. — BOOK 63:19
W. done — BIBL 46:4
w.-informed mind — AUST 20:28
w. of English undefiled — SPEN 322:4
w. of loneliness — HALL 160:7
w.-tuned cymbals — BOOK 65:7
w.-written Life — CARL 85:5
wen great w. of all — COBB 99:2
Wenceslas Good King W. — NEAL 248:23
wench w. is dead — MARL 228:14
Wenlock On W. Edge — HOUS 176:10
wept Jesus w. — BIBL 48:39
we sat down and w. — BOOK 65:1
Werther W. had a love for Charlotte — THAC 336:10
west Cincinnatus of the W. — BYRO 81:14
come out of the w. — SCOT 287:17
Go W., young man — GREE 156:22
Islam and the W. — STRA 326:24
nor from the w. — BOOK 63:16
O wild W. Wind — SHEL 314:3
safeguard of the W. — WORD 365:13
W. is West — KIPL 201:17
W.'s awake — DAVI 111:5
where the W. begins — CHAP 90:17
western delivered by W. Union — GOLD 154:5
Go to the w. gate — ROBI 277:16
o'er the w. wave — SHEL 314:30
Playboy of the W. World — SYNG 329:17
quiet on the w. front — REMA 275:4
Wind of the w. sea — TENN 334:12
westward stepping w. — WORD 366:7
w., look, the land — CLOU 98:23
W. the course of empire — BERK 31:18
wet w. and wildness — HOPK 173:20
w. sheet — CUNN 108:13
wether tainted w. of the flock — SHAK 302:28
whacks gave her mother forty w. — ANON 9:13
whale unconquering w. — MELV 232:15
Very like a w. — SHAK 293:13
whaleship w. was my Yale College — MELV 232:14
what for my own self w. am I — HILL 169:14
W. and Why and When — KIPL 203:17
W. is to be done — LENI 212:8
why, or which, or w. — LEAR 210:8
wheat orient and immortal w. — TRAH 341:11
w. from the chaff — HUBB 177:9
wheel beneath thy Chariot w. — HOPE 173:13

butterfly upon a w. — POPE 266:22
red w. barrow — WILL 360:16
wheels w. of trade — HUME 178:8
Why tarry the w. — BIBL 36:13
when forgotten to say 'W.!' — WODE 362:23
If not now w. — HILL 169:12
w. a man should marry — BACO 22:34
w. did you last see — YEAM 367:11
W. you call me that — WIST 362:5
whence W. comest thou — BIBL 37:25
w. cometh my help — BOOK 64:20
w. did he whence — LENO 212:25
w. it cometh — BIBL 48:26
where fixed the w. and when — HAWK 163:10
I knew not w. — LONG 217:6
W. are you going — BIBL 54:10
W. did you come from — MACD 222:18
w. do they all come from — LENN 212:18
W. OUGHT I TO BE — CHES 93:24
wherefore w. art thou Romeo — SHAK 306:28
W. does he why — LENO 212:25
whereof w. one cannot speak — WITT 362:10
whetstone no such w. — ASCH 17:14
whiff w. of grapeshot — CARL 85:10
Whig Tory men and W. measures — DISR 117:25
whimper Not with a bang but a w. — ELIO 128:24
whine thin w. of hysteria — DIDI 116:13
whip Do not forget the w. — NIET 251:5
W.'s duty — CANN 84:11
whipped w. the offending Adam — SHAK 295:11
whipping who should 'scape w. — SHAK 292:19
whips chastised you with w. — BIBL 37:8
w. and scorns of time — SHAK 292:24
whirligig w. of time — SHAK 309:11
whirlwind angel rides in the w. — PAGE 256:19
Elijah went up by a w. — BIBL 37:19
reap the w. — BIBL 42:10
Rides in the w. — ADDI 2:19
whiskers Cat with crimson w. — LEAR 210:19
whisky Freedom and W. — BURN 76:21
good old boys drinkin' w. — MCLE 223:15
whisper w. of a faction — RUSS 283:15
w. to the tourist — BEER 29:2
W. who dares — MILN 235:16
whispering just w. in her mouth — MARX 230:2
whispers what he w. — SMIT 318:21
whistle I'd w. her off — SHAK 305:2
shrimp learns to w. — KHRU 200:1
W. and she'll come — FLET 138:14
w., an' I'll come — BURN 77:8
white blue-eyed devil w. man — FARD 134:2
fat w. woman — CORN 104:8
garment was w. as snow — BIBL 42:8
see the w. of their eyes — PUTN 272:4
tupping your w. ewe — SHAK 304:18
up the w. road — ELIO 130:1
want to be the w. man's brother — KING 200:12
When the w. man came — GEOR 148:5
W. as an angel — BLAK 57:20
w. as snow — BIBL 40:4
w. Christmas — BERL 32:4
w. cliffs of Dover — BURT 77:27
w. hairs — SHAK 294:30
w. heat of technology — WILS 361:4
w. In a single night — BYRO 81:16
w. in the blood of the Lamb — BIBL 53:8
W. Man's Burden — KIPL 203:8
w. man was created a devil — MALC 226:1
w. men with horrible looks — EQUI 132:30
w. owl in the belfry — TENN 334:28
w. race is the cancer — SONT 320:14
wild w. horses play — ARNO 16:16
whited w. sepulchres — BIBL 45:31

how little w. OXEN 256:17
price of w. BIBL 38:6
privilege of w. to listen HOLM 172:1
quintessence of w. JAIN 182:8
righteousness with w. PLAT 265:3
to the palace of w. BLAK 56:23
we had w. BENÉ 30:16
w. and understanding BIBL 40:16
w. be put in a silver rod BLAK 56:15
W. denotes the pursuing HUTC 179:5
W. hath builded her house BIBL 38:17
W. in minds attentive COWP 106:1
W. is humble COWP 106:2
W. is the principal thing BIBL 38:14
w. lingers TENN 333:30
w. of the crocodiles BACO 23:22
w. of the fool JOHN 190:24
w. we have lost in knowledge ELIO 129:12
wise art of being w. JAME 183:7
beacons of w. men HUXL 179:21
be w., and love SHAK 308:10
Be w. with speed YOUN 369:23
consider her ways, and be w. BIBL 38:15
cunning men pass for w. BACO 22:19
enough for the w. PLAU 265:5
more w. when he had JOHN 190:5
Nor ever did a w. one ROCH 278:4
So w. so young SHAK 306:13
that a w. man sees BLAK 56:26
think as w. men do ASCH 17:15
'Tis folly to be w. GRAY 156:18
What all the w. men promised MELB 232:10
w. as serpents BIBL 44:27
w. father that knows SHAK 302:16
w., for cure DRYD 122:3
w. forgive but do not forget SZAS 329:19
w. in his own conceit BIBL 38:38
w. men from the east BIBL 43:1
w. son BIBL 38:19
wisecracking w. is simply callisthenics PARK 259:3
wisely nations behave w. EBAN 124:18
not w. but too well SHAK 305:14
wiser he is w. today POPE 268:23
in their generation w. BIBL 47:34
not the w. grow POMF 266:3
sadder and a w. man COLE 100:28
wisest first and w. of them MILT 239:19
w. and justest PLAT 264:20
w. fool in Christendom HENR 166:14
w. man can answer COLT 102:1
wish believe what they w. CAES 82:4
live, not as we w. MENA 232:17
Whoever hath her w. SHAK 310:26
w. I loved the Human Race RALE 273:8
w. was father, Harry SHAK 295:7
wit at thirty, the w. FRAN 141:19
Brevity is the soul of w. SHAK 292:10
nor all thy piety nor w. FITZ 136:16
sharpen a good w. ASCH 17:14
Staircase w. DIDE 116:12
True w. is Nature POPE 267:9
universal monarchy of w. CARE 84:18
use my w. as a pitchfork LARK 209:1
w. among Lords JOHN 188:6
w. and humour AUST 20:26
W. has truth in it PARK 259:3
w. its soul COLE 100:4
W. will shine DRYD 122:15
w. with dunces POPE 266:7
witch Aroint thee, w. SHAK 299:10
witches Men feared w. BRAN 67:16
witching w. time of night SHAK 293:15
with He that is not w. me BIBL 44:35

I am w. you alway BIBL 46:21
withdrawing long, w. roar ARNO 16:11
wither Age cannot w. her SHAK 289:19
withered are w. away COCK 99:3
O! w. is the garland SHAK 289:22
withereth grass w. BIBL 52:25
rose Fast w. too KEAT 195:24
withers it w. away ENGE 132:26
our w. are unwrung SHAK 293:10
within kingdom of God is w. you BIBL 48:3
without forasmuch as w. thee BOOK 60:21
I can do w. SOCR 319:22
with you—or w. you MART 229:11
witness bear false w. BIBL 35:28
bear w. of that Light BIBL 48:17
witnesses cloud of w. BIBL 52:15
w. against mankind KORA 205:15
w. to the desolation of war GEOR 147:20
wits Great w. DRYD 121:17
Great w. sometimes may POPE 267:5
warming his five w. TENN 334:28
witty dull men w. BACO 24:1
Thou swell! Thou w. HART 163:1
w. in myself SHAK 294:32
wives Husbands, love your w. BIBL 51:31
profane and old w.' fables BIBL 52:6
W. are young men's mistresses BACO 22:33
wizards affairs of W. TOLK 341:1
star-led w. MILT 237:6
wobbly spelling is W. MILN 235:20
woe discover sights of w. MILT 237:19
gave signs of w. MILT 239:6
oft in w. WHIT 356:5
protracted w. JOHN 187:27
W. is me BIBL 40:9
W. to thee, O land BIBL 39:23
W. to the land SHAK 306:12
w. unto them BIBL 40:7
woes Of w. unnumbered POPE 268:4
self-consumer of my w. CLAR 96:26
w. which Hope thinks infinite SHEL 314:16
wolf like the w. on the fold BYRO 80:18
w. by the ears JEFF 184:16
w. of a different opinion INGE 180:15
w. shall dwell with the lamb BIBL 40:17
W. that shall keep it KIPL 203:23
wolfsbane twist W., tight-rooted KEAT 196:13
wolves frighten the w. MACH 223:9
ravening w. BIBL 44:11
woman aren't I a w. TRUT 342:20
body of a weak and feeble w. ELIZ 130:14
born of a w. BIBL 38:1
business of a w.'s life SOUT 320:24
changeable always is w. VIRG 347:8
Christ wasn't a w. TRUT 342:21
Come to my w.'s breasts SHAK 299:24
could be a good w. THAC 336:8
dead w. bites not GRAY 156:4
done, ask a w. THAT 336:12
Do you not know I am a w. SHAK 290:20
Eternal W. draws us upward GOET 152:14
Every w. adores a Fascist PLAT 264:20
excellent thing in w. SHAK 298:27
fat white w. CORN 104:8
Frailty, thy name is w. SHAK 291:18
fury, like a w. scorned CONG 102:7
greatest glory of a w. PERI 262:3
if a w. have long hair BIBL 50:21
in a w.'s hide SHAK 296:6
inconstant w. GAY 147:6
just like a w. DYLA 124:6
leader of the enterprise a w. VIRG 347:2
Let us look for the w. DUMA 123:3

woman (*cont.*)

little w. who wrote	LINC 215:7
lovely w. stoops to folly	GOLD 153:27
made he a w.	BIBL 34:11
make a man a w.	PEMB 261:9
Man that is born of a w.	BOOK 62:4
nakedness of w.	BLAK 57:2
never trust a w.	WILD 359:2
no, nor w. neither	SHAK 292:16
No w. will be Prime Minister	THAT 336:11
One is not born a w.	DE B 111:13
one young w. and another	SHAW 311:29
perfect w.; nobly planned	WORD 366:3
post-chaise with a pretty w.	JOHN 189:17
Prudence is the other w.	ANON 10:11
she's a w.	RACI 272:16
takes a very clever w.	KIPL 203:22
that one w. differs from another	MENC 232:18
this Man and this W.	BOOK 61:23
trapped in a w.'s body	BOY 67:3
virtuous w.	BIBL 39:5
What does a w. want	FREU 142:18
Why can't a w. be	LERN 213:6
wisest w. in Europe	ELIO 129:20
W., behold thy son	BIBL 49:12
w. can be proud and stiff	YEAT 367:20
w. can hardly ever choose	ELIO 127:11
w. clothed with the sun	BIBL 53:11
w. especially	AUST 20:28
w. has given you her heart	VANB 345:5
W.! in our hours of ease	SCOT 287:20
w. in this humour	SHAK 306:10
w. is a sometime thing	HEYW 168:15
w. is his game	TENN 334:17
w. is like a teabag	REAG 274:2
w. loves her lover	BYRO 80:27
w. moved	SHAK 307:14
W. much missed	HARD 162:7
w. must have money	WOOL 363:21
w. of mean understanding	AUST 21:7
w. of shining loveliness	YEAT 369:4
w. only the right to spring	FOND 139:1
W.'s degradation	STAN 323:5
w. seldom asks advice	ADDI 3:8
w. seldom writes her mind	STEE 323:10
w.'s preaching	JOHN 188:18
w.'s reason	SHAK 309:14
w.'s whole existence	BYRO 80:24
w. take An elder	SHAK 308:33
w. taken in adultery	BIBL 48:32
W. the nigger of the world	ONO 253:16
w. wakes to love	TENN 332:18
W., what have I to do	BIBL 48:24
w. who deliberates	ADDI 2:21
w. who did not care	KIPL 203:3
w. who lives for others	LEWI 213:19
w. whom thou gavest	BIBL 34:17
w., wine and song	LUTH 220:20
w. with a slop-pail	HOPK 174:11
w. without a man	STEI 324:1
womanhood Heroic w.	LONG 218:2
womankind packs off its w.	SHAW 312:5
womb from his mother's w.	SHAK 302:1
w. of time	HEIN 165:9
w. of uncreated night	MILT 238:4
women blessed art thou among w.	BIBL 46:31
Certain w. should be struck	COWA 105:10
dream of fair w.	TENN 332:4
extension of w.'s rights	FOUR 140:11
feelings of w. in a drawing-room	WOOL 363:23
going to w.	NIET 251:5
Good w. always think	BROO 70:4
happiest w.	ELIO 127:20

have wine and w.	BYRO 80:26
hops, and w.	DICK 115:18
managers of affairs of w.	KORA 205:7
mob of scribbling w.	HAWT 163:15
Music and w.	PEPY 261:19
now called the nature of w.	MILL 234:13
passing the love of w.	BIBL 36:35
position for w. is prone	CARM 85:24
publishers are not w.	ROBI 277:15
regiment of w.	KNOX 204:9
Righteous w. are obedient	KORA 205:8
Some w.'ll stay in a man's memory	KIPL 203:24
to w. Italian	CHAR 91:5
Whatever w. do	WHIT 357:18
w. are from Venus	GRAY 156:2
W. are only children	CHES 92:20
w. become like their mothers	WILD 358:29
w. come and go	ELIO 128:29
W. desiren to have sovereynetee	CHAU 91:30
W. don't seem to think	AMIS 6:6
W. have served as looking-glasses	WOOL 363:22
W. have very little idea	GREE 157:6
w. in a state of ignorance	KNOX 204:13
w. in men require	BLAK 57:13
w. labouring of child	BOOK 60:15
w. must weep	KING 201:8
w. need to be helped	TRUT 342:20
won EVERYBODY has w.	CARR 86:6
in this humour w.	SHAK 306:10
I w. the count	SOMO 320:9
No one w.	ROOS 279:4
not that you w. or lost	RICE 275:17
not to have w.	COUB 104:14
Things w. are done	SHAK 308:8
woman, therefore may be w.	SHAK 308:6
wonder boneless w.	CHUR 95:2
great w. in heaven	BIBL 53:11
I w. any man alive	GAY 146:18
I w. by my troth	DONN 119:9
state of w.	GOUL 154:13
still the w. grew	GOLD 153:10
w. of our stage	JONS 192:4
w. that would be	TENN 333:25
w. who's kissing her	ADAM 1:14
wonderful God, how w. Thou art	FABE 133:14
I've had a w. life	WITT 362:15
many w. things	SOPH 320:15
most w. wonderful	SHAK 290:19
too w. to be true	FARA 133:21
Yes, w. things	CART 88:1
wonderfully fearfully and w. made	BOOK 65:4
wonders Everything has its w.	KELL 198:1
His w. to perform	COWP 105:18
multiply my signs and my w.	BIBL 35:16
signs and w.	BIBL 48:28
Welcome, all w.	CRAS 106:12
w. in the deep	BOOK 64:9
w. we seek without us	BROW 71:11
wondrous survey the w. cross	WATT 351:23
won't administrative w.	LYNN 221:1
wood behind the little w.	TENN 334:2
Bows down to w. and stone	HEBE 164:18
bows down to w. and stone	KIPL 201:22
cleave the w.	ANON 10:14
hewers of w.	BIBL 36:8
native w.-notes wild	MILT 236:25
old w. best to burn	BACO 22:5
w.'s in trouble	HOUS 176:10
woodcocks springes to catch w.	SHAK 291:32
wooden Sailed off in a w. shoe	FIEL 135:6
Within this w. O	SHAK 295:10
w. wall is your ships	THEM 337:6
w. walls are best	COVE 104:18

works (*cont.*)

your good w.	BIBL 43:16
workshop nation may be its w.	CHAM 90:1
not a temple but a w.	TURG 343:1
w. of the world	DISR 117:5
world All's right with the w.	BROW 72:23
all the kingdoms of the w.	BIBL 43:11
all the sad w. needs	WILC 358:1
All the w. is sad	FOST 140:10
all the w. is young	KING 201:9
All the w.'s a stage	SHAK 290:11
all the w. was gay	POPE 268:17
along the W. I go	CART 88:5
bestride the narrow w.	SHAK 296:19
brought nothing into this w.	BIBL 52:8
citizen of the w.	BOSW 66:4
citizen of the w.	SOCR 320:2
country is the w.	PAIN 257:18
dark w. of sin	BICK 54:15
deceits of the w.	BOOK 60:12
destruction of the whole w.	HUME 178:13
enjoy the w. aright	TRAH 341:10
foppery of the w.	SHAK 297:27
frame of the w.	BERK 31:17
funny old w.	THAT 337:3
gain the whole w.	BIBL 46:27
glory of the w.	ANON 13:20
glory of this w. passes	THOM 337:8
God so loved the w.	BIBL 48:27
go out of this w.	HOBB 170:23
governs the whole w.	OXEN 256:17
great w. spin for ever	TENN 333:32
half-brother of the w.	BAIL 24:15
Hog Butcher for the W.	SAND 285:4
in a naughty w.	SHAK 303:1
In a w. I never made	HOUS 176:3
interpreted the w.	MARX 230:8
into the w. alone	CARR 86:2
knowledge of the w.	CHES 92:14
know the w.	YOUN 370:1
light of the w.	BIBL 43:15
limits of my w.	WITT 362:13
Little Friend of all the W.	KIPL 203:19
makes the whole w. kin	SHAK 308:13
monk who shook the w.	MONT 243:9
my letter to the w.	DICK 116:7
new w. order	BUSH 78:14
not as the w. giveth, give I	BIBL 49:6
O brave new w.	SHAK 307:35
Our country is the w.	GARR 146:10
peace which the w. cannot give	BOOK 60:7
rack of this tough w.	SHAK 298:29
still point of the turning w.	ELIO 128:3
Stop the w.	NEWL 249:19
Syllables govern the w.	SELD 288:15
symphony like the w.	MAHL 225:13
Ten days that shook the w.	REED 274:14
Than this w. dreams of	TENN 332:22
There is a w. elsewhere	SHAK 291:3
this dark w. and wide	MILT 239:30
though the w. perish	FERD 134:18
three corners of the w.	SHAK 297:21
through this w. but once	GREL 157:9
unto the end of the w.	BIBL 46:21
way the w. ends	ELIO 128:24
We want the w.	MORR 245:19
What is the w.	DE L 112:16
What would the w. be	HOPK 173:20
wilderness of this w.	BUNY 74:6
workshop of the w.	DISR 117:5
w. and love were young	RALE 272:22
w. empty of people	LAWR 209:21
w. enough, and time	MARV 229:19

w. famous	RICH 276:12
w. forgetting	POPE 266:13
w. grew pale	JOHN 187:26
w. in a grain of sand	BLAK 56:8
w. invisible	THOM 338:17
w. is a comedy	WALP 350:3
w. is charged	HOPK 173:16
w. is everything that is the case	WITT 362:11
w. is so full	STEV 325:27
w. is too much with us	WORD 366:16
w. knew him not	BIBL 48:18
w. must be made safe	WILS 361:14
w. of the happy	WITT 362:14
w.'s a bubble	BACO 24:2
w.'s great age begins anew	SHEL 313:26
w.'s history	SCHI 286:11
w. should be taxed	BIBL 47:1
w.'s last night	DONN 119:1
w.'s mine oyster	SHAK 303:5
w.'s worst wound	SASS 286:2
w. upside down	BIBL 49:29
w. was all before them	MILT 239:14
w. will end in fire	FROS 143:15
w. without end	BOOK 59:16
w. would go round	CARR 86:8
youth of the w.	BACO 22:6
worlds best of all possible w.	CABE 82:1
best of all possible w.	VOLT 348:5
destroyer of w.	OPPE 253:17
number of w. is infinite	ALEX 4:12
Wandering between two w.	ARNO 16:24
what w. away	BROW 71:25
w. of wanwood leafmeal	HOPK 174:4
worm invisible w.	BLAK 58:2
joy of the w.	SHAK 289:27
sets foot upon a w.	COWP 106:3
w. i' the bud	SHAK 308:36
w., the canker, and the grief	BYRO 81:15
worms diet of w.	FENT 134:16
w. destroy this body	BIBL 38:4
wormwood w. and the gall	BIBL 41:25
worrying What's the use of w.	ANON 11:19
worse Defend the bad against the w.	DAY- 111:11
follow the w.	OVID 256:1
for better for w.	BOOK 61:27
For fear of finding something w.	BELL 29:19
from w. to better	HOOK 173:1
from w. to better	JOHN 186:16
is it something w.	SPRI 322:18
make the w. appear	MILT 238:3
mean the W. one	ARIS 15:6
More will mean w.	AMIS 6:7
We make them w.	GOET 152:22
w. than a crime	BOUL 66:8
worst are no w.	SHAK 304:3
worship earth doth w. thee	BOOK 59:17
O w. the King	GRAN 155:8
O w. the Lord	BOOK 63:28
second is freedom to w.	ROOS 279:15
various modes of w.	GIBB 148:13
we w. thy Name	BOOK 59:20
who w. the beast	BIBL 53:16
with my body I thee w.	BOOK 62:1
w. the Lord	MONS 242:12
worst full look at the w.	HARD 162:2
good in the w. of us	ANON 11:9
it was the w. of times	DICK 115:23
knew the w. too young	KIPL 202:5
No w., there is none	HOPK 173:21
This is the w.	SHAK 298:14
To-morrow do thy w.	DRYD 122:16
world's w. wound	SASS 286:2
w. form of Government	CHUR 95:20

X

X Generation X   COUP 104:16
Xanadu In X. did Kubla Khan   COLE 100:7
Xerox X. makes everybody   MCLU 224:2

Y

Yale whaleship was my Y. College   MELV 232:14
yang embrace the y.   LAO 208:5
Yankee Y. Doodle   ANON 12:6
  Y. Doodle Dandy   COHA 99:10
Yanks Y. are coming   COHA 99:9
yawns Even the grave y.   TREE 341:13
yawp sound my barbaric y.   WHIT 357:10
yea Let your y. be yea   BIBL 52:24
year acceptable y. of the Lord   BIBL 41:17
  man at the gate of the y.   HASK 163:5
  Next y. in Jerusalem   HAGG 159:1
  thirtieth y. to heaven   THOM 337:23
  'Tis the y.'s midnight   DONN 119:12
  y. is dying   TENN 333:9
  y.'s at the spring   BROW 72:23
years after all these y.   SIMO 317:4
  Forty y. on   BOWE 66:12
  Jacob served seven y.   BIBL 35:4
  more than a hundred y.   FROS 143:16
  thousand y. in thy sight   BOOK 63:22
  threescore y. and ten   BOOK 63:23
  touch of earthly y.   WORD 366:4
  two hundred y. like a sheep   TIPU 340:13
  two thousand y. of hope   WEIZ 353:11
  y. are slipping by   HORA 175:11
  y. of desolation   JEFF 184:18
  y. that the locust hath eaten   BIBL 42:11
  y. to come   YEAT 368:13
yellow Come unto these y. sands   SHAK 307:22
  Follow the y. brick road   HARB 161:9
  Goodbye y. brick road   JOHN 186:2
  one long y. string   BROW 72:25
  paved with y. brick   BAUM 27:22
  thy y. stockings   SHAK 309:3
  Y., and black, and pale   SHEL 314:3
  Y. God forever gazes   HAYE 164:2
  y. leaf   SHAK 301:27
yelps loudest y. for liberty   JOHN 187:22
yes getting the answer y.   CAMU 83:17
  Y., Virginia   CHUR 94:14
yesterday but as y.   BOOK 63:22
  dead y.   FITZ 136:13
  give me y.   JONE 191:8
  keeping up with y.   MARQ 228:20
  O! call back y.   SHAK 305:28
  rose of y.   FITZ 136:7
  same y., and to day   BIBL 52:18
  were saying y.   LUIS 220:15
yesterdays all our y.   SHAK 301:31
yesteryear snows of y.   VILL 346:17
yet but not y.   AUGU 20:1
yid PUT THE ID BACK IN Y.   ROTH 281:5
yield and not to y.   TENN 335:8
yin take the y.   LAO 208:5
yo-ho-ho Y., and a bottle of rum   STEV 325:16
yoke my y. is easy   BIBL 44:34
Yonghy-Bonghy-Bó Lived the Y.   LEAR 210:10
Yorick Alas, poor Y.   SHAK 294:3
you cannot live with y.   MART 229:11
  Y.'ll never walk   HAMM 160:24
  Y. too, Brutus   CAES 82:9
  'Y.' your joys and sorrows   CRIC 107:1
young artist as a y. man   JOYC 192:22

censor of the y.   HORA 174:18
crime of being a y. man   PITT 264:2
defrauded y.   KIPL 202:1
dies y.   MENA 232:16
for ever y.   KEAT 196:10
get out while we're y.   SPRI 322:17
I have been y.   BOOK 62:23
I'll die y.   BRUC 73:8
knew the worst too y.   KIPL 202:5
y. dream   MOOR 244:9
on your y. shoulders   SPAR 321:1
O y., fresshe folkes   CHAU 92:6
seventy years y.   HOLM 172:4
So wise so y.   SHAK 306:13
so y. a body   SHAK 302:29
So y., and so untender   SHAK 297:23
what the world would call y. men   PEEL 261:4
While we are y.   ANON 13:11
y. and foolish   YEAT 367:23
Y. blood must have its course   KING 201:9
y. can do for the old   SHAW 311:20
y., gifted and black   HANS 161:4
Y., gifted and black   IRVI 181:1
y. man married   SHAK 289:10
Y. men are fitter   BACO 23:23
y. men shall see visions   BIBL 42:12
y. men think it is   HOUS 176:5
y. was very heaven   WORD 364:13
younger Y. than she   SHAK 306:22
  y. than that now   DYLA 124:10
yours y. and yours   MARK 228:3
youth Crabbed age and y.   SHAK 309:31
  days of our y.   BYRO 81:21
  days of thy y.   BIBL 39:27
  flower of their y.   VIRG 347:22
  If y. knew   ESTI 133:3
  it is y. who must fight   HOOV 173:7
  My prime of y.   TICH 340:9
  red sweet wine of y.   BROO 69:19
  sign of an ill-spent y.   ROUP 281:7
  subtle thief of y.   MILT 239:28
  thoughts of y. are long   LONG 217:16
  Y. and Pleasure meet   BYRO 80:5
  y., I do adore thee   SHAK 309:32
  Y. is a blunder   DISR 117:21
  Y. of a Nation   DISR 118:1
  y. of England   SHAK 295:13
  y. of his generation   FITZ 137:16
  y. of labour   GOLD 153:6
  y. of the world   BACO 22:6
  Y. on the prow   GRAY 156:6
  y. replies, I can   EMER 132:1
  Y.'s a stuff   SHAK 308:28
  y.'s sweet-scented manuscript   FITZ 137:3
  y. to fortune   GRAY 156:15
  Y., which is forgiven   SHAW 312:17
  Y. would be an ideal state   ASQU 17:20

Z

Zadok Z. the priest   BIBL 37:4
Zanzibar count the cats in Z.   THOR 339:21
Zarathustra follower of Z.   ZORO 370:17
Zauber Deine Z. binden wieder   SCHI 286:7
zeal by men of Z.   BRAN 67:17
  holy mistaken z.   JUNI 194:2
  not the slightest z.   TALL 330:8
  z. of the Lord   BIBL 40:15
zealous z. citizen   BURK 75:27
zed Thou whoreson z.   SHAK 297:31

Zen Z. and the art   PIRS 263:17
zenith from the z. like a falling star   MILT 238:1
Zimbabwe keep my Z.   MUGA 246:16
Zion Z., city of our God   NEWT 250:19

Zionism Z., be it right or wrong   BALF 25:6
zipless z. fuck   JONG 191:12
Zitronen *Land, wo die Z. blühn*   GOET 152:19
zoo human z.   MORR 245:6

Sayings and Slogans

Advertising slogans

1 Access—your flexible friend.
  Access credit card, 1981 onwards

2 An ace caff with quite a nice museum attached.
  the Victoria and Albert Museum, February 1989

3 All human life is there.
  the *News of the World*; used by Maurice Smelt in the late 1950s

4 All the news that's fit to print.
  motto of the *New York Times*, from 1896; coined by its proprietor Adolph S. Ochs

5 American Express? . . . That'll do nicely, sir.
  American Express credit card, 1970s

6 And all because the lady loves Milk Tray.
  Cadbury's Milk Tray chocolates, 1968 onwards

7 Australians wouldn't give a XXXX for anything else.
  Castlemaine lager, 1986 onwards

8 Beanz meanz Heinz.
  Heinz baked beans, c.1967; coined by Maurice Drake

9 Beauty is power.
  Helena Rubinstein's Valaze Skin Food, 1904

10 Because I'm worth it.
  advertising slogan for L'Oreal, from mid 1980s

11 Bovril . . . Prevents that sinking feeling.
  Bovril, 1920; coined by H. H. Harris

12 . . . But I know a man who can.
  Automobile Association, 1980s

13 Can you tell Stork from butter?
  Stork margarine, from c.1956

14 Cool as a mountain stream.
  Consulate menthol cigarettes, early 1960s onwards

15 A diamond is forever.
  De Beers Consolidated Mines, 1940s onwards

16 Does she . . . or doesn't she?
  Clairol hair colouring, 1950s

17 Don't be vague, ask for Haig.
  Haig whisky, c.1936

18 Don't forget the fruit gums, Mum.
  Rowntree's Fruit gums, 1958–61

19 Drinka Pinta Milka Day.
  National Dairy Council, 1958; coined by Bertrand Whitehead

20 Even your closest friends won't tell you.
  Listerine mouthwash, US, 1923

21 Every picture tells a story.
  advertisement for Doan's Backache Kidney Pills (early 1900s)

22 Full of Eastern promise.
  Fry's Turkish Delight, 1950s onwards

23 The future's bright, the future's Orange.
  slogan for Orange telecom company, mid 1990s

24 Go to work on an egg.
  British Egg Marketing Board, from 1957; perhaps written by Fay Weldon or Mary Gowing

25 Guinness is good for you.
  reply universally given to researchers asking people why they drank Guinness
  adopted by Oswald Greene, c.1929

26 Happiness is a cigar called Hamlet.
  Hamlet cigars, UK

27 Have a break, have a Kit-Kat.
  Rowntree's Kit-Kat, from c.1955

28 Heineken refreshes the parts other beers cannot reach.
  Heineken lager, 1975 onwards

29 High o'er the fence leaps Sunny Jim 'Force' is the food that raises him.
  breakfast cereal (1903)

30 Horlicks guards against night starvation.
  Horlicks malted milk drink, 1930s

31 If you want to get ahead, get a hat.
  the Hat Council, 1965

32 I liked it so much, I bought the company!
  Remington Shavers, 1980; spoken by the company's new owner Victor Kiam (1926–2001)

33 I'm only here for the beer.
  Double Diamond beer, 1971 onwards

34 It beats as it sweeps as it cleans.
  Hoover vacuum cleaners, 1919

35 It could be you.
  British national lottery, from 1994

36 It's finger lickin' good.
  Kentucky fried chicken, from 1958

37 It's good to talk.
  British Telecom, from 1994

38 It's tingling fresh. It's fresh as ice.
  Gibbs toothpaste; the first advertising slogan heard on British television, 22 September 1955

39 I was a seven-stone weakling.
  Charles Atlas body-building, originally in US

40 Keep that schoolgirl complexion.
  Palmolive soap, from 1917

41 Kills all known germs.
  Domestos bleach, 1959

42 Let the train take the strain.
  British Rail, 1970 onwards

43 Let your fingers do the walking.
  Bell system Telephone Directory Yellow Pages, 1960s

44 The man you love to hate.
  billing for Erich von Stroheim in the film *The Heart of Humanity* (1918)

45 A Mars a day helps you work, rest and play.
  Mars bar, c.1960 onwards

46 The mint with the hole.
  Life-Savers, US, 1920; and for Rowntree's Polo mints, UK from 1947

1 My Goodness, My Guinness.
Guinness stout, 1935

2 Never knowingly undersold.
motto of the John Lewis Partnership, from
c.1920

3 Nice one, Cyril.
taken up by supporters of Cyril Knowles,
Tottenham Hotspur footballer; the Spurs team
later made a record featuring the line
Wonderloaf, 1972

4 No manager ever got fired for buying IBM.
IBM

5 Oxo gives a meal man-appeal.
Oxo beef extract, c.1960

6 Persil washes whiter—and it shows.
Persil washing powder, 1970s

7 Put a tiger in your tank.
Esso petrol, 1964

8 Say it with flowers.
Society of American Florists, 1917, coined by
Patrick O'Keefe

9 Sch . . . you know who.
Schweppes mineral drinks, 1960s

10 Someone, somewhere, wants a letter from
you.
British Post Office, 1960s

11 Stop me and buy one.
Wall's ice cream, from spring 1922; coined by
Cecil Rodd

12 Tell Sid.
privatization of British Gas, 1986

13 They come as a boon and a blessing to men,
The Pickwick, the Owl, and the Waverley
pen.
advertisement by MacNiven and H. Cameron
Ltd., current by 1879

14 Things go better with Coke.
Coca-Cola, 1963

15 Top people take The Times.
The Times newspaper, from January 1959

16 Vorsprung durch Technik.
Progress through technology.
Audi motors (advertising slogan, from 1986)

17 We are the Ovaltineys,
Little [or Happy] girls and boys.
'We are the Ovaltineys' (song from c.1935);
Ovaltine drink

18 We're number two. We try harder.
Avis car rentals

19 We won't make a drama out of a crisis.
Commercial Union insurance

20 Where's the beef?
Wendy's Hamburgers, from January 1984

21 Worth a guinea a box.
Beecham's pills, from c.1859, from the chance
remark of a lady purchaser

22 You press the button, we do the rest.
advertising slogan to launch Kodak camera
1888, coined by George Eastman (1854–1932)

23 You're never alone with a Strand.
Strand cigarettes, 1960

Cartoon captions

24 Fog in Channel—Continent isolated.
newspaper placard in cartoon, Round the Bend
with Brockbank (1948) by the British cartoonist
Russell Brockbank (1913–); the phrase
'Continent isolated' was quoted as already
current by John Gunther Inside Europe (1938)

25 I feel like a fugitive from th' law of averages.
showing Willie and Joe, American GIs, under fire
caption in Up Front (1945), by Bill Mauldin
(1921–)

26 It's a naive domestic Burgundy without any
breeding, but I think you'll be amused by its
presumption.
caption in New Yorker 27 March 1937, by James
Thurber

27 MOTHER: It's broccoli, dear.
CHILD: I say it's spinach, and I say the hell
with it.
caption in New Yorker 8 December 1928, by E. B.
White

28 The man who . . .
illustrating social gaffes resulting from snobbery
opening words of the caption for a series of
cartoons (first appearing in 1912) by H. M.
Bateman (1887–1970)

29 No son—they're not the same—devolution
takes longer.
father to his son, who is reading a book on
evolution
caption in Scots Independent January 1978, by
Ewen Bain (1925–89)

30 On the Internet, nobody knows you're a
dog.
a large dog at a desk, paw on keyboard,
enlightening a smaller friend
caption in New Yorker, July 1993, by the
American cartoonist Peter Steiner

31 The price of petrol has been raised by a
penny. Official.
a torpedoed sailor with oil-stained face lying on a
raft; the message was intended to be a warning
against wasting petrol, but it was taken by some
as suggesting that lives were being put at risk for
profit
caption in Daily Mirror 3 March 1942; cartoon by
Philip Zec (1909–83) and caption by 'Cassandra'
(William Connor, 1909–67).

32 We have met the enemy and he is us.
the cartoon-strip character, Pogo the opossum,
looking at litter under a tree; used as an Earth
Day poster in 1971
Pogo cartoon, 1970, by the American cartoonist
Walt Kelly (1913–73); the comment is a
modification of the message in which
Commodore Perry (1785–1819) reported his
victory over the British in the battle of Lake
Erie, 1813, 'We have met the enemy, and they
are ours'

33 Well, if I called the wrong number, why did
you answer the phone?
in New Yorker 5 June 1937, by James Thurber

1 Well, if you knows of a better 'ole, go to it.
Old Bill and a friend in a shellhole under fire
caption in *Fragments from France* (1915), by the
British cartoonist Bruce Bairnsfather
(1888–1959)

Catchphrases

2 CECIL: After you, Claude.
CLAUDE: No, after you, Cecil.
ITMA (BBC radio programme, 1939–49), written
by Ted Kavanagh

3 And now for something completely
different.
Monty Python's Flying Circus (BBC TV programme,
1969–74)

4 Anyone for tennis?
said to be typical of drawing-room comedies;
perhaps from George Bernard Shaw 'Anybody
on for a game of tennis?' *Misalliance* (1914)

5 Are you sitting comfortably? Then I'll begin.
Listen with Mother (BBC radio programme for
children, 1950–82)

6 Can I do you now, sir?
spoken by 'Mrs Mopp'
ITMA (BBC radio programme, 1939–49), written
by Ted Kavanagh

7 Can you hear me, mother?
used by Sandy Powell

8 Come on! Come on!
habitual adjuration by Jeremy Paxman to
contestants on *University Challenge* on BBC2
(1994–)

9 The day war broke out.
*customary preamble to radio monologues in the
role of a Home Guard*
used by Robb Wilton from *c.*1940

10 Didn't she [*or* he *or* they] do well?
used by Bruce Forsyth in 'The Generation
Game' on BBC Television, 1973 onwards

11 Does my bum look big in this?
used by Arabella Weir in *The Fast Show* on BBC
Television 1994–97

12 Don't forget the diver.
ITMA (BBC radio programme, 1939–49), written
by Ted Kavanagh

13 Don't have nightmares. Do sleep well.
habitual closing words for BBC1's *Crimewatch*
(1984–), spoken by Nick Ross

14 Eat my shorts!
The Simpsons (American TV series, 1990–),
created by Matt Groening

15 Ee, it was agony, Ivy.
Ray's a Laugh (BBC radio programme, 1949–61),
written by Ted Ray

16 Evening, all.
opening words spoken by Jack Warner as
Sergeant Dixon in *Dixon of Dock Green* (BBC
television series, 1956–76), written by Ted
Willis

17 Everybody wants to get inta the act!
used by Jimmy Durante

18 An everyday story of country folk.
introduction to *The Archers* (BBC radio serial,
1950 onwards), written by Geoffrey Webb and
Edward J. Mason

19 George—don't do that.
used by Joyce Grenfell as a recurring line in
monologues about a nursery school, from the
1950s

20 Give him the money, Barney.
Have a Go! (BBC radio quiz programme,
1946–67), used by Wilfred Pickles

21 A good idea—son.
Educating Archie, 1950–3 BBC radio comedy
series, written by Eric Sykes and Max Bygraves

22 Good morning, sir—was there something?
used by Sam Costa in radio comedy series *Much-
Binding-in-the-Marsh*, written by Richard
Murdoch and Kenneth Horne, started 2 January
1947

23 Goodnight, children . . . everywhere.
*closing words normally spoken by 'Uncle Mac' in
the 1930s and 1940s*
on *Children's Hour* (BBC Radio programme);
written by Derek McCulloch

24 Have you read any good books lately?
used by Richard Murdoch in radio comedy
series *Much-Binding-in-the-Marsh*, written by
Richard Murdoch and Kenneth Horne, started 2
January 1947

25 Hello, good evening, and welcome.
used by David Frost in 'The Frost Programme'
on BBC Television, 1966 onwards

26 Here come de judge.
from the song-title 'Here comes the judge'
(1968); written by Dewey 'Pigmeat' Markham,
Dick Alen, Bob Astor, and Sarah Harvey

27 Here's one I made earlier.
*culmination to directions for making a model out
of empty yoghurt pots, coat-hangers, and similar
domestic items*
children's BBC television programme *Blue Peter*,
1963 onwards

28 He shoots! He scores!
used by Foster William Hewitt (1902–85),
Canadian broadcaster, at ice-hockey games; first
said over the radio 4 April 1933 at the game
between the Toronto Maple Leafs and the
Boston Bruins

29 I didn't get where I am today without . . . .
used by the manager C. J. in BBC television
series *The Fall and Rise of Reginald Perrin*
(1976–80); based on David Nobbs *The Death of
Reginald Perrin* (1975)

30 I don't like this game, let's play another
game—let's play doctor and nurses.
phrase first used by Bluebottle in 'The Phantom
Head-Shaver' in *The Goon Show* (BBC radio series)
15 October 1954, written by Spike Milligan; the
catchphrase was often 'I do not like this game'

31 I don't mind if I do.
spoken by 'Colonel Chinstrap'
ITMA (BBC radio programme, 1939–49), written
by Ted Kavanagh

1 I go—I come back.
spoken by 'Ali Oop'
ITMA (BBC radio programme, 1939–49), written by Ted Kavanagh

2 I have a cunning plan.
Baldrick's habitual overoptimistic promise in *Blackadder II* (1987 television series), written by Richard Curtis and Ben Elton

3 I'm Bart Simpson: who the hell are you?
The Simpsons (American TV series, 1990–), created by Matt Groening

4 I'm in charge.
used by Bruce Forsyth in 'Sunday Night at the London Palladium' on ITV, 1958 onwards

5 I'm worried about Jim.
frequent line in *Mrs Dale's Diary*, BBC radio series 1948–69

6 It all depends what you mean by . . .
habitually used by C. E. M. Joad when replying to questions on 'The Brains Trust' (formerly 'Any Questions'), BBC radio (1941–8)

7 It's a good thing.
customary form of approbation in the areas of home decorating and cooking from US businesswoman Martha Stewart (1941–)

8 It's being so cheerful as keeps me going.
spoken by 'Mona Lott'
ITMA (BBC radio programme, 1939–49), written by Ted Kavanagh

9 I've arrived and to prove it I'm here!
Educating Archie, 1950–3 BBC radio comedy series, written by Eric Sykes and Max Bygraves

10 I've started so I'll finish.
said when a contestant's time runs out while a question is being put
Magnus Magnusson on *Mastermind*, BBC television (1972–97)

11 Just like that!
used by Tommy Cooper

12 Keep on truckin'.
used by Robert Crumb in cartoons from *c*.1972

13 Left hand down a bit!
The Navy Lark (BBC radio series, 1959–77), written by Laurie Wyman

14 Let's be careful out there.
Hill Street Blues (television series, 1981 onwards), written by Steven Bochco and Michael Kozoll

15 Meredith, we're in!
originating in a stage sketch by Fred Kitchen, *The Bailiff* (1907); J. P. Gallagher *Fred Karno* (1971) ch. 9

16 Mind my bike!
used by Jack Warner in the BBC radio series *Garrison Theatre*, 1939 onwards

17 Nice to see you—to see you, nice.
used by Bruce Forsyth in 'The Generation Game' on BBC Television, 1973 onwards

18 Oh, calamity!
used by Robertson Hare

19 Ohhh, I don't *believe* it!
Victor Meldrew in *One Foot in the Grave* (BBC television series, 1989–), written by David Renwick

20 Once again we stop the mighty roar of London's traffic.
In Town Tonight (BBC radio series, 1933–60) preamble

21 Pass the sick bag, Alice.
used by John Junor; in *Sunday Express* and elsewhere, from 1980 or earlier

22 Phone a friend.
advice to contestants by Chris Tarrant, host of the ITV quiz show *Who Wants to be a Millionaire* (1998–)

23 Seriously, though, he's doing a grand job!
popularized by David Frost in 'That Was The Week That Was', on BBC Television, 1962-3; originally deriving from a sketch written for Roy Kinnear

24 Shome mishtake, shurely?
in *Private Eye* magazine, 1980s

25 So farewell then . . .
frequent opening of poems by 'E. J. Thribb' in Private Eye *magazine, usually as an obituary* 1970s onwards

26 Take me to your leader.
from science-fiction stories

27 The truth is out there.
The X Files (American television series, 1993–), created by Chris Carter

28 Very interesting . . . but stupid.
Rowan and Martin's Laugh-In (American television series, 1967–73), written by Dan Rowan and Dick Martin

29 The weekend starts here.
Ready, Steady, Go, British television series, *c*.1963

30 We have ways of making you talk.
perhaps originating in the line 'We have ways of making men talk' in *Lives of a Bengal Lancer* (1935 film), written by Waldemar Young et al.

31 What's up, Doc?
Bugs Bunny cartoons, written by Tex Avery from *c*.1940

32 Who loves ya, baby?
used by Telly Savalas in American TV series *Kojak* (1973-8)

33 Without hesitation, deviation, or repetition.
instruction for contestants' monologues on the panel show *Just a Minute* (BBC Radio, 1967–)

34 You are the weakest link . . . goodbye.
used by Anne Robinson on the television game-show *The Weakest Link* (2000–)

35 You bet your sweet bippy.
Rowan and Martin's Laugh-In (American television series, 1967–73), written by Dan Rowan and Dick Martin

36 You might very well think that. I couldn't possibly comment.
the Chief Whip's habitual response to questioning House of Cards *(televised 1990); written by Michael Dobbs*

37 You're going to like this . . . not a lot . . . but you'll like it!
used by Paul Daniels in his conjuring act, especially on television from 1981 onwards

1 You rotten swines. I told you I'd be deaded.

phrase first used by Bluebottle in 'Hastings Flyer' in *The Goon Show* (BBC radio series) 3 January 1956, written by Spike Milligan

2 Your starter for ten.

phrase often used by Bamber Gascoigne in *University Challenge* (ITV quiz series, 1962–87)

3 You silly twisted boy.

phrase first used in 'The Dreaded Batter Pudding Hurler' in *The Goon Show* (BBC radio series) 12 October 1954, written by Spike Milligan

Film lines

4 Anyway, Ma, I made it . . . Top of the world!

White Heat (1949 film) written by Ivan Goff and Ben Roberts; last lines—spoken by James Cagney

5 Cancel the kitchen scraps for lepers and orphans. No more merciful beheadings. And call off Christmas!

Robin Hood, Prince of Thieves (1991 film), written by Pen Densham and John Watson; spoken by Alan Rickman

6 Don't let's ask for the moon! We have the stars!

Now, Voyager (1942 film), from the novel (1941) by Olive Higgins Prouty; spoken by Bette Davis

7 Either he's dead, or my watch has stopped.

A Day at the Races (1937 film) written by Robert Pirosh, George Seaton, and George Oppenheimer; spoken by Groucho Marx

8 E.T. phone home.

E.T. (1982 film) written by Melissa Mathison

9 Fasten your seat-belts, it's going to be a bumpy night.

All About Eve (1950 film) written by Joseph L. Mankiewicz; spoken by Bette Davis

10 Frankly, my dear, I don't give a damn!

Gone with the Wind (1939 film) written by Sidney Howard and based on the novel by Margaret Mitchell; spoken by Clark Gable

11 Go ahead, make my day.

Sudden Impact (1983 film) written by Joseph C. Stinson; spoken by Clint Eastwood

12 Greed—for lack of a better word—is good. Greed is right. Greed works.

Wall Street (1987 film) written by Stanley Weiser and Oliver Stone; spoken by Michael Douglas

13 Here's looking at you, kid.

Casablanca (1942 film) written by Julius J. Epstein, Philip G. Epstein, and Howard Koch; spoken by Humphrey Bogart to Ingrid Bergman

14 I ate his liver with some fava beans and a nice chianti.

The Silence of the Lambs (1991 film, based on the novel by Thomas Harris), written by Thomas Harris (1940–) and Ted Tally (1952–); spoken by Anthony Hopkins as Hannibal Lecter

15 I could have had class. I could have been a contender.

On the Waterfront (1954 film) written by Budd Schulberg; spoken by Marlon Brando

16 I fear all we have done is awaken a sleeping giant and fill him with a terrible resolve.

Tora! Tora! Tora! (1970 film), written by Larry Forrester, Hideo Oguni, and Ryuzo Kikushima; said by the Japanese admiral Isoroku Yamamoto, referring to Pearl Harbor, although there is no evidence that Yamamoto used these words

17 If she can stand it, I can. Play it!

usually quoted as 'Play it again, Sam'

Casablanca (1942 film) written by Julius J. Epstein, Philip G. Epstein, and Howard Koch; spoken by Humphrey Bogart

18 If you can't leave in a taxi you can leave in a huff. If that's too soon, you can leave in a minute and a huff.

Duck Soup (1933 film) written by Bert Kalmar, Harry Ruby, Arthur Sheekman, and Nat Perrin; spoken by Groucho Marx

19 If you carry a 00 number it means you're licensed to kill, not get killed.

Dr No (1962 film), written by Richard Maibaum, Johanna Harwood, and Berkely Mather, and based on the novel by Ian Fleming; spoken by Bernard Lee as 'M'

20 I'll be back.

The Terminator (1984 film) written by James Cameron (1954–) and Gale Anne Hurd; spoken by Arnold Schwarzenegger

21 I'll have what she's having.

woman to waiter, seeing Sally acting an orgasm

When Harry Met Sally (1989 film) written by Nora Ephron

22 I love the smell of napalm in the morning. It smells like victory.

Apocalypse Now (1979 film) written by John Milius and Francis Ford Coppola; spoken by Robert Duvall

23 In Italy for thirty years under the Borgias they had warfare, terror, murder, bloodshed—they produced Michelangelo, Leonardo da Vinci and the Renaissance. In Switzerland they had brotherly love, five hundred years of democracy and peace and what did that produce . . . ? The cuckoo clock.

The Third Man (1949 film); words added by Orson Welles to Graham Greene's screenplay

24 I see dead people.

The Sixth Sense (1999 film, written by Manoj Night Shyamalan), spoken by Haley Joel Osment

25 It's a funny old world—a man's lucky if he gets out of it alive.

You're Telling Me (1934 film), written by Walter de Leon and Paul M. Jones; spoken by W. C. Fields

26 DRIFTWOOD (Groucho Marx): It's all right. That's—that's in every contract. That's—that's what they call a sanity clause.
FIORELLO (Chico Marx): You can't fool me. There ain't no Sanity Claus.

Night at the Opera (1935 film) written by George S. Kaufman and Morrie Ryskind

1 Let's get out of these wet clothes and into a dry Martini.
line coined in the 1920s by Robert Benchley's press agent and adopted by Mae West in *Every Day's a Holiday* (1937 film)

2 Let's go to work.
Reservoir Dogs (1992 film) written and directed by Quentin Tarantino; spoken by Lawrence Tierney

3 Lunch is for wimps.
Wall Street (1987 film) written by Stanley Weiser and Oliver Stone (1946–)

4 Madness! Madness!
The Bridge on the River Kwai (1957 film of the novel by Pierre Boulle) written by Carl Foreman, closing line

5 Major Strasser has been shot. Round up the usual suspects.
Casablanca (1942 film) written by Julius J. Epstein, Philip G. Epstein, and Howard Koch; spoken by Claude Rains

6 Man your ships, and may the force be with you.
Star Wars (1977 film) written by George Lucas

7 Marriage isn't a word . . . it's a *sentence*!
The Crowd (1928 film) written by King Vidor

8 Maybe just whistle. You know how to whistle, don't you, Steve? You just put your lips together and blow.
To Have and Have Not (1944 film) written by Jules Furthman and William Faulkner; spoken by Lauren Bacall

9 EUNICE GRAYSON: Mr—?
SEAN CONNERY: Bond. James Bond.
Dr No (1962 film), written by Richard Maibaum, Johanna Harwood, and Berkely Mather, and based on the novel by Ian Fleming

10 Mr Kane was a man who got everything he wanted, and then lost it. Maybe Rosebud was something he couldn't get or something he lost. Anyway, it wouldn't have explained anything. I don't think any word can explain a man's life. No, I guess Rosebud is just a piece in a jigsaw puzzle, a missing piece.
Citizen Kane (1941 film) written by Herman J. Mankiewicz and Orson Welles

11 My momma always said life was like a box of chocolates . . . you never know what you're gonna get.
Forrest Gump (1994 film), written by Eric Ross, based on the novel (1986) by Winston Groom; spoken by Tom Hanks

12 Nature, Mr Allnutt, is what we are put into this world to rise above.
The African Queen (1951 film) written by James Agee; spoken by Katharine Hepburn; not in the novel by C. S. Forester

13 Of all the gin joints in all the towns in all the world, she walks into mine.
Casablanca (1942 film) written by Julius J. Epstein, Philip G. Epstein, and Howard Koch; spoken by Humphrey Bogart

14 Oh no, it wasn't the aeroplanes. It was Beauty killed the Beast.
King Kong (1933 film) written by James Creelman and Ruth Rose, final words

15 The pellet with the poison's in the vessel with the pestle. The chalice from the palace has the brew that is true.
The Court Jester (1955 film) written by Norman Panama and Melvin Frank; spoken by Danny Kaye

16 Remember, you're fighting for this woman's honour . . . which is probably more than she ever did.
Duck Soup (1933 film) written by Bert Kalmar, Harry Ruby, Arthur Sheekman, and Nat Perrin; spoken by Groucho Marx

17 The son of a bitch stole my watch!
The Front Page (1931 film), from the play (1928) by Charles MacArthur and Ben Hecht

18 That was a little bit more information than I needed to know.
Pulp Fiction (1994 film) written by Quentin Tarantino (1963–); spoken by Uma Thurman

19 To infinity and beyond.
Toy Story (1995) written by Joel Cohen, et al.; spoken by Buzz Lightyear

20 Toto, I've a feeling we're not in Kansas any more.
The Wizard of Oz (1939 film) written by Noel Langley (1911–), Florence Ryerson, and Edgar Allan Wolfe; spoken by Judy Garland

21 GERRY: We can't get married at all . . . I'm a man.
OSGOOD: Well, nobody's perfect.
Some Like It Hot (1959 film) written by Billy Wilder and I. A. L. Diamond; closing words spoken by Jack Lemmon and Joe E. Brown

22 What a dump!
Beyond the Forest (1949 film) written by Lenore Coffee; line spoken by Bette Davis, entering a room

23 What have the Romans ever done for us?
Monty Python's Life of Brian (1983 film) written by John Cleese, Graham Chapman, Eric Idle, Michael Palin, Terry Gilliam, and Terry Jones

24 When the legend becomes fact, print the legend.
The Man who Shot Liberty Valance (1962 film) written by Willis Goldbeck and James Warner Bellah

25 Why, a four-year-old child could understand this report. Run out and find me a four-year-old child. I can't make head or tail of it.
Duck Soup (1933 film) written by Bert Kalmar, Harry Ruby, Arthur Sheekman, and Nat Perrin; spoken by Groucho Marx

26 NINOTCHKA: Why should you carry other people's bags?
PORTER: Well, that's my business, Madame.
NINOTCHKA: That's no business. That's social injustice.
PORTER: That depends on the tip.
Ninotchka (1939 film) written by Charles Brackett, Billy Wilder, and Walter Reisch

1 You finally, really did it—you maniacs! You blew it up! Damn you! Damn you all to hell!
Planet of the Apes (1968 film, written by Michael Wilson and Rod Serling); spoken by Charlton Heston

2 You're going out a youngster but you've *got* to come back a star.
42nd Street (1933 film) written by James Seymour and Rian James

3 You're here to stay until the rustle in your dying throat relieves you!
Beau Hunks (1931 film; re-named *Beau Chumps* for British audiences) written by H. M. Walker; addressed to Laurel and Hardy

4 JOE GILLIS: You used to be in pictures. You used to be big.
NORMA DESMOND: I am big. It's the pictures that got small.
Sunset Boulevard (1950 film) written by Charles Brackett, Billy Wilder, and D. M. Marshman Jr

Last words

5 *Adieu, mes amis. Je vais à la gloire.*
Farewell, my friends. I go to glory.
Isadora Duncan (1878–1927), before her scarf caught in a car wheel, breaking her neck
Mary Desti *Isadora Duncan's End* (1929) ch. 25

6 All my possessions for a moment of time.
Queen Elizabeth I (1533–1603)
attributed, but almost certainly apocryphal

7 Be of good comfort Master Ridley, and play the man. We shall this day light such a candle by God's grace in England, as (I trust) shall never be put out.
Hugh Latimer (c.1485–1555), prior to being burned for heresy, 16 October 1555
John Foxe *Actes and Monuments* (1570 ed.)

8 Bugger Bognor.
King George V (1865–1936) on his deathbed in 1936, when someone remarked 'Cheer up, your Majesty, you will soon be at Bognor again'; alternatively, a comment made in 1929, when it was proposed that the town be named Bognor Regis on account of the king's convalescence there after a serious illness
probably apocryphal; Kenneth Rose *King George V* (1983) ch. 9

9 Come closer, boys. It will be easier for you.
Erskine Childers (1870–1922) to the firing squad at his execution
Burke Wilkinson *The Zeal of the Convert* (1976) ch. 26

10 Crito, we owe a cock to Aesculapius; please pay it and don't forget it.
Socrates (469–399 BC)
Plato *Phaedo* 118

11 Die, my dear Doctor, that's the last thing I shall do!
Lord Palmerston (1784–1865)
E. Latham *Famous Sayings and their Authors* (1904)

12 *Dieu me pardonnera, c'est son métier.*
God will pardon me, it is His trade.
Heinrich Heine (1797–1856), on his deathbed
Alfred Meissner *Heinrich Heine. Erinnerungen* (1856) ch. 5

13 *Dilexi iustitiam et odi iniquitatem, propterea morior in exilio.*
I have loved justice and hated iniquity: therefore I die in exile.
Pope Gregory VII (c.1020–85) at Salerno, following his conflict with the Emperor Henry IV
J. W. Bowden *The Life and Pontificate of Gregory VII* (1840) vol. 2, bk. 3, ch. 20

14 Don't let the awkward squad fire over me.
said by Robert Burns (1759–96) shortly before his death
A. Cunningham *The Works of Robert Burns; with his Life* vol. 1 (1834)

15 An emperor ought to die standing.
Vespasian (AD 9–79)
Suetonius *Lives of the Caesars* 'Vespasian' sect. 24

16 For God's sake look after our people.
Robert Falcon Scott (1868–1912)
last diary entry, 29 March 1912, in *Scott's Last Expedition* (1913) vol. 1, ch. 20

17 For my name and memory, I leave it to men's charitable speeches, and to foreign nations, and the next ages.
will of Francis Bacon (1561–1626), 19 December 1625
J. Spedding (ed.) *The Letters and Life of Francis Bacon* vol. 7 (1874)

18 Give Dayrolles a chair.
Lord Chesterfield (1694–1773) to his godson Dayrolles
W. H. Craig *Life of Lord Chesterfield* (1907)

19 God save Ireland!
called out from the dock by the Manchester Martyrs, William Allen (d. 1867), Michael Larkin (d. 1867), and William O'Brien (d. 1867)
Robert Kee *The Bold Fenian Men* (1989)

20 Greetings, we win!
dying words of Pheidippides (or Philippides) (d. 490 BC), having run back to Athens from Marathon with news of victory over the Persians
Lucian bk. 3, ch. 64 'Pro Lapsu inter salutandum' para. 3

21 How's the Empire?
said by King George V (1865–1936) to his private secretary on the morning of his death
letter from Lord Wigram, 31 January 1936, in J. E. Wrench *Geoffrey Dawson and Our Times* (1955) ch. 28

22 I am about to take my last voyage, a great leap in the dark.
Thomas Hobbes (1588–1679)
attributed, but with no authoritative source; a contemporary version is:
On his death bed he should say that he was 91 years finding out a hole to go out of this world, and at length found it.
Anthony Wood diary, 10 December 1679, in Andrew Clark (ed.) *The Life and Times of Anthony Wood* vol. 2 (1892)

1 *Je vais quérir un grand peut-être . . . Tirez le
rideau, la farce est jouée.*
I am going to seek a great perhaps . . . Bring
down the curtain, the farce is played out.
François Rabelais (c.1494–c.1553)
> attributed, probably apocryphal; Jean Fleury
> *Rabelais et ses oeuvres* (1877) vol. 1, ch. 3, pt. 15

2 I am just going outside and may be some
time.
Captain Lawrence Oates (1880–1912)
> Robert Falcon Scott diary entry, 16–17 March
> 1912 in *Scott's Last Expedition* (1913) ch. 20

3 I die happy.
Charles James Fox (1749–1806)
> Lord John Russell *Life and Times of C. J. Fox* vol. 3
> (1860) ch. 69

4 I find, then, I am but a bad anatomist.
*Wolfe Tone (1763–98), who in trying to cut his
throat in prison severed his windpipe instead of
his jugular, and lingered for several days*
> Oliver Knox *Rebels and Informers* (1998)

5 If this is dying, then I don't think much of it.
Lytton Strachey (1880–1932), on his deathbed
> Michael Holroyd *Lytton Strachey* vol. 2 (1968) pt.
> 2, ch. 6

6 I have lived as a philosopher and I die as a
Christian.
*Giovanni Jacopo Casanova (1725–98), Italian
adventurer*
> *The Memoirs of Casanova* (1937) p. 492

7 I hope for a happy exit and I hope never to
come back.
Frida Kahlo (1907–54)
> last diary entry; Martha Zamora *Frida Kahlo: the
> Brush of Anguish* (1990)

8 I lived uncertain, I die doubtful: O thou
Being of beings, have mercy upon me!
Aristotle (384–322 BC)
> attributed, probably apocryphal; a Latin version
> was current in the early 17th century

9 I'm stuck in this building . . . I just wanted
you to know that I love you. Bye bye.
*final recorded message for her husband from
Melissa Hughes in the World Trade Center, 11
September 2001; 'I love you' was the final
telephone message from many of those trapped in
the buildings and planes involved in the day's
terrorist attacks*
> in *Guardian* 14 September 2001

10 I'm tired, and I have to go to sleep.
*Allen Ginsberg (1912–97), before lapsing into a
final coma*
> in *Athens News* 9 April 1997

11 In this life there's nothing new in dying,
But nor, of course, is living any newer.
*Sergei Yesenin (1895–1925); his final poem,
written in his own blood the day before he hanged
himself in his Leningrad hotel room, 28 December
1925*
> 'Goodbye, my Friend, Goodbye' (translated by
> Gordon McVay)

12 I only regret that I have but one life to lose
for my country.
*Nathan Hale (1755–76), prior to his execution by
the British for spying, 22 September 1776*
> Henry Phelps Johnston *Nathan Hale, 1776* (1914)
> ch. 7

13 It is a bad cause which cannot bear the
words of a dying man.
*Sir Henry Vane (1613–62) as drums and trumpets
were ordered to sound at his execution to drown
anything he might say*
> Charles Dickens *A Child's History of England*
> (1853) ch. 35

14 It is dark for writing but I will try to by
touch. It looks as though there is no chance.
*final written message from Dmitry Kolesnikov, one
of those lost in the Russian nuclear submarine
Kursk*
> in *Daily Telegraph* 3 November 2000

15 It's been so long since I've had champagne.
*Anton Chekhov (1860–1904), after which, he
slowly drank the glass and died*
> Henri Troyat *Chekhov* (1984)

16 I've got the bows up . . . I'm going . . . I'm on
my back . . . I've gone. Oh.
*last recorded words of Donald Campbell
(1921-67), killed while trying to break his own
water speed record; the wreckage of his boat
Bluebird, with Campbell's body, was found and
raised in March 2001*
> in *Times* 9 March 2001

17 I will die like a true-blue rebel. Don't waste
any time in mourning—organize.
*Joe Hill (1879–1915) before his death by firing
squad*
> farewell telegram to Bill Haywood, 18
> November 1915, in *Salt Lake (Utah) Tribune* 19
> November 1915

18 June 3, Cold Harbor. I was killed.
*the diary entry of a Unionist soldier, found in his
pocket after the failed attack on Cold Harbor, 3
June 1864*
> attributed, perhaps apocryphal

19 Let not poor Nelly starve.
*Charles II (1630–85), referring to Nell Gwyn, his
mistress*
> Bishop Gilbert Burnet *History of My Own Time*
> (1724) vol. 1, bk. 3

20 Let's do it!
*Gary Gilmore (1941–77) to the firing squad at his
execution; after his conviction for murder, Gilmore
had refused to appeal, and petitioned the Supreme
Court that the execution should be carried out*
> Norman Mailer *The Executioner's Song* (1979)

21 Let's roll.
Todd Beamer, 11 September 2001
> heard by telephone operator as Beamer and
> other passengers were planning to storm the
> cockpit of the hijacked United Airlines Flight
> 93; the plane crashed in Pennsylvania minutes
> later; in *Washington Post* 17 September 2001

1 Let us cross over the river and rest under the shade of the trees.
Thomas Jonathan 'Stonewall' Jackson (1824–63)
M. Miner and H. Rawson *American Heritage Dictionary of American Quotations* (1997)

2 Lord have mercy on my poor country that is so barbarously oppressed.
Andrew Fletcher of Saltoun (1655–1716), Scottish patriot and anti-Unionist
September 1716

3 Lord, open the King of England's eyes!
William Tyndale (c.1494–1536), at the stake
John Foxe *Actes and Monuments* (1570)

4 Lord take my soul, but the struggle continues.
Ken Saro-Wiwa (1941–95), just before he was hanged
in *Daily Telegraph* 13 November 1995

5 The love boat has crashed against the everyday. You and I, we are quits, and there is no point in listing mutual pains, sorrows, and hurts.
from an unfinished poem found among Mayakovsky's papers, a variant of which he quoted in his suicide letter
Vladimir Mayakovsky (1893–1930) letter 12 April 1930

6 Love? What is it? Most natural painkiller. What there is . . . LOVE.
final entry in the journal of William S. Burroughs, 1 August 1997, the day before he died
in *New Yorker* 18 August 1997

7 *Mehr Licht!*
More light!
Johann Wolfgang von Goethe (1749–1832); abbreviated version of 'Macht doch den zweiten Fensterladen auch auf, damit mehr Licht hereinkomme [Open the second shutter, so that more light can come in]'
K. W. Müller *Goethes letze literarische Thätigkeit* (1832)

8 My design is to make what haste I can to be gone.
Oliver Cromwell (1599–1658)
John Morley *Oliver Cromwell* (1900) bk. 5, ch. 10

9 Now God be praised, I will die in peace.
James Wolfe (1727–59)
J. Knox *Historical Journal of the Campaigns in North America* (ed. A. G. Doughty, 1914) vol. 2

10 Now I'll have eine kleine Pause.
last words of Kathleen Ferrier (1912–53)
Gerald Moore *Am I Too Loud?* (1962)

11 Oh, my country! how I leave my country!
William Pitt (1759–1806); also variously reported as 'How I love my country'; *and* 'My country! oh, my country!'
Earl Stanhope *Life of the Rt. Hon. William Pitt* vol. 3 (1879) ch. 43; Earl Stanhope *Life of the Rt. Hon. William Pitt* (1st ed.), vol. 4 (1862) ch. 43; and G. Rose *Diaries and Correspondence* (1860) vol. 2, 23 January 1806; oral tradition reports:
I think I could eat one of Bellamy's veal pies.
attributed

12 *Ô liberté! Ô liberté! que de crimes on commet en ton nom!*
O liberty! O liberty! what crimes are committed in thy name!
Mme Roland (1754–93), before being guillotined
A. de Lamartine *Histoire des Girondins* (1847) bk. 51, ch. 8

13 One of us must go.
Oscar Wilde (1854–1900), of the wallpaper in the room where he was dying
attributed, probably apocryphal

14 On, on, on.
Tom Simpson (1937–67), British cyclist, after collapsing on Mont Ventoux in the Tour de France; usually quoted as, 'Put me back on my bike'
William Fotheringham *Put Me Back on My Bike* (2002) ch. 2

15 On the contrary.
Henrik Ibsen (1828–1906), after a nurse had said that he 'seemed to be a little better'
Michael Meyer *Ibsen* (1967)

16 *Qualis artifex pereo!*
What an artist dies with me!
Nero (AD 37–68)
Suetonius *Lives of the Caesars* 'Nero' sect. 49

17 Remember—.
Charles I (1600–49), giving his George (insignia of the Order of the Garter) to Bishop Juxon
speech on the scaffold, 30 January 1649

18 See in what peace a Christian can die.
Joseph Addison (1672–1719), dying words to his stepson Lord Warwick
Edward Young *Conjectures on Original Composition* (1759)

19 So little done, so much to do.
Cecil Rhodes (1853–1902), on the day of his death
Lewis Michell *Life of Rhodes* (1910) vol. 2, ch. 39

20 Strike the tent.
Robert E. Lee (1807–70), 12 October 1870
attributed

21 Such is life.
Ned Kelly (1855–80), Australian outlaw, before being hanged, 11 November 1880
Frank Clune *The Kelly Hunters* (1955)

22 Tell them I've had a wonderful life.
Ludwig Wittgenstein (1889–1951) to his doctor's wife, before losing consciousness, 28 April 1951
Ray Monk *Ludwig Wittgenstein* (1990)

23 Tell them to stand up for Jesus.
American evangelist, Dudley Atkins Tyng (d. 1858), to George Duffield, inspiring him to write the hymn
Ian Bradley (ed.) *The Penguin Book of Hymns* (1989)

24 Thank God, I have done my duty.
Horatio, Lord Nelson (1758–1805) at the battle of Trafalgar, 21 October 1805
Robert Southey *Life of Nelson* (1813) ch. 9

25 That would really have been the last cigarette.
Italo Svevo (1861–1928), when refused a cigarette as he lay dying after a car accident
Livia Veneziani Svevo *Memoir of Italo Svevo* (1950)

1 They couldn't hit an elephant at this distance.
John Sedgwick (d. 1864), Union general, immediately prior to being killed by enemy fire at the battle of Spotsylvania in the American Civil War
Robert Denney *The Civil War Years* (1992)

2 This hath not offended the king.
Thomas More (1478–1535), lifting his beard aside after laying his head on the block
Francis Bacon *Apophthegms New and Old* (1625) no. 22

3 This is a beautiful country!
John Brown (1800–59) as he rode to the gallows, seated on his coffin
at his execution on 2 December 1859

4 This is the Fourth?
Thomas Jefferson (1743–1826)
on 4 July 1826

5 This, this is the end of earth. I am content.
John Quincy Adams (1767–1848) on collapsing in the Senate, 21 February 1848 (he died two days later)
William H. Seward *Eulogy of John Quincy Adams to Legislature of New York* 1848

6 Thomas—Jefferson—still surv—
John Adams (1735–1826), on 4 July 1826; Jefferson died on the same day

7 Turn up the lights; I don't want to go home in the dark.
O. Henry (1862–1910), quoting a song
Charles Alphonso Smith *O. Henry Biography* (1916) ch. 9
I'm afraid to come home in the dark.
Harry Williams (1874–1924) title of song (1907)

8 Useless! Useless!
John Wilkes Booth (1838–65)
Philip van Doren Stern *The Man Who Killed Lincoln* (1939)

9 *Vicisti, Galilaee.*
You have won, Galilean.
supposed dying words of the Roman emperor Julian the Apostate (AD c.332–363)
a late embellishment of Theodoret *Ecclesiastical History* (AD c.450) bk. 3, ch. 25

10 We are all going to Heaven, and Vandyke is of the company.
Thomas Gainsborough (1727–88)
attributed, in William B. Boulton *Thomas Gainsborough* (1905) ch. 9

11 We are putting passengers off in small boats ... Engine room getting flooded ... CQ.
CQD was the original SOS call for shipping
last signals sent from the *Titanic*, 15 April 1912

12 Well, I've had a happy life.
William Hazlitt (1778–1830)
W. C. Hazlitt *Memoirs of William Hazlitt* (1867)

13 'What is the answer?' No answer came. She laughed and said, 'In that case what is the question?'
Gertrude Stein (1874–1946)
Donald Sutherland *Gertrude Stein, A Biography of her Work* (1951)

14 Why fear death? It is the most beautiful adventure in life.
Charles Frohman (1860–1915), before drowning in the Lusitania, 7 May 1915
I. F. Marcosson and D. Frohman *Charles Frohman* (1916) ch. 19

15 Why not? Why not? Why not? Yeah.
Timothy Leary (1920–96)
in *Independent* 1 June 1996

16 Would to God this wound had been for Ireland.
Patrick Sarsfield (c.1655–93) on being mortally wounded at the battle of Landen, 19 August 1693, while fighting for France
attributed

Misquotations

17 Beam me up, Scotty.
supposedly the form in which Captain Kirk habitually requested to be returned from a planet to the Starship *Enterprise*; in fact the nearest equivalent found is
Beam us up, Mr Scott.
Gene Roddenberry *Star Trek* (1966 onwards) 'Gamesters of Triskelion'

18 The budget should be balanced, the treasury should be refilled, public debt should be reduced, the arrogance of officialdom should be tempered and controlled, assistance to foreign lands should be curtailed lest Rome should become bankrupt, the mobs should be forced to work and not depend on government for subsistence.
attributed to Cicero in *Congressional Record* 25 April 1968, but not traced in his works

19 The capitalists will sell us the rope with which to hang them.
attributed to Lenin, but not found in his published works; I. U. Annenkov, in 'Remembrances of Lenin' includes a manuscript note attributed to Lenin:
They [capitalists] will furnish credits which will serve us for the support of the Communist Party in their countries and, by supplying us materials and technical equipment which we lack, will restore our military industry necessary for our future attacks against our suppliers. To put it in other words, they will work on the preparation of their own suicide.
in *Novyi Zhurnal/New Review* September 1961

20 Come with me to the Casbah.
often attributed to Charles Boyer (1898–1978) in the film Algiers *(1938), but the line does not in fact occur*
L. Swindell *Charles Boyer* (1983)

21 Crisis? What crisis?
in *Sun* headline, 11 January 1979; summarizing James Callaghan's remark
I don't think other people in the world would share the view there is mounting chaos.
interview at London Airport, 10 January 1979

1 Dark forces at work.

popular summary of comment attributed to Queen Elizabeth II by former royal butler Paul Burrell, reported in the *Daily Mirror* as:

There are powers at work in this country about which we have no knowledge.

in *The Times* 7 November 2002

2 Dreams are the royal road to the unconscious.

popular summary of Sigmund Freud's view

The interpretation of dreams is the royal road to a knowledge of the unconscious activities of the mind.

The Interpretation of Dreams (2nd ed., 1909)

3 The dying breath of Socrates.

usual formulation of the proposition set out by James Jeans

If we assume that the last breath of, say, Julius Caesar has by now become thoroughly scattered through the atmosphere, then the chances are that each of us inhales one molecule of it with every breath we take.

An Introduction to the Kinetic Theory of Gases (1940)

4 Elementary, my dear Watson, elementary.

remark attributed to Sherlock Holmes, but not found in this form in any book by Arthur Conan Doyle, first found in P.G. Wodehouse Psmith Journalist *(1915)*

attributed

5 The good Christian should beware of mathematicians, and all those who make empty prophecies. The danger already exists that mathematicians have made a covenant with the Devil to darken the spirit and to confine man in the bonds of Hell.

mistranslation of St Augustine's *De Genesi ad Litteram*; the Latin word 'mathematicus' means both 'mathematician' and 'astrologer'

6 A good day to bury bad news.

popular misquotation of Jo Moore's email of 11 September 2001

It is now a very good day to get out anything we want to bury.

email sent in the aftermath of the terrorist action in America, 11 September 2001

in *Daily Telegraph* 10 October 2001

7 The green shoots of recovery.

popular misquotation of the Chancellor's upbeat assessment of the economic situation

The green shoots of economic spring are appearing once again.

Norman Lamont, speech at Conservative Party Conference, 9 October 1991

8 I paint with my prick.

attributed to Pierre Auguste Renoir (1841–1919); possibly an inversion of

It's with my brush I make love.

A. André *Renoir* (1919)

9 It's life, Jim, but not as we know it.

late 20th century saying associated with the television series *Star Trek* (1966–), created by Gene Roddenberry; the saying does not occur in

the series but derives from the 1987 song 'Star Trekkin' ' sung by The Firm

10 *when asked what jazz is:*

Man, if you gotta ask you'll never know.

frequently quoted version of Louis Armstrong's response

If you still have to ask . . . shame on you.

Max Jones et al. *Salute to Satchmo* (1970)

11 Me Tarzan, you Jane.

Johnny Weissmuller summing up his role in Tarzan, the Ape Man *(1932 film); the words occur neither in the film nor the original, by Edgar Rice Burroughs*

in *Photoplay Magazine* June 1932

12 My lips are sealed.

misquotation from Stanley Baldwin's speech on the Abyssinian crisis

I shall be but a short time tonight. I have seldom spoken with greater regret, for my lips are not yet unsealed. Were these troubles over I would make a case, and I guarantee that not a man would go into the lobby against us.

speech in the House of Commons, 10 December 1935

13 Play it again, Sam.

in the film Casablanca, *written by Julius J. Epstein et al., Humphrey Bogart says, 'If she can stand it, I can. Play it!'; earlier in the film Ingrid Bergman says, 'Play it, Sam. Play* As Time Goes By.'

Casablanca (1942 film)

14 Put me back on my bike.

commonly quoted as the last words of Tom Simpson (1937–67), British cyclist, after collapsing on Mont Ventoux in the Tour de France; his actual words were 'On, on, on'

William Fotheringham *Put Me Back on My Bike* (2002) ch. 2

15 Selling off the family silver.

summary of Harold Macmillan's attack on privatization

First of all the Georgian silver goes, and then all that nice furniture that used to be in the saloon. Then the Canalettos go.

speech to the Tory Reform Group, 8 November 1985

16 Shouting fire in a crowded theatre.

popular summary of Oliver Wendell Holmes Jr.'s definition of the limits of free speech; see below

The most stringent protection of free speech would not protect a man falsely shouting fire in a theatre and causing a panic.

in *Schenck v. United States* (1919)

17 The soft under-belly of Europe.

popular version of Winston Churchill's phrase

We make this wide encircling movement in the Mediterranean, having for its primary object the recovery of the command of that vital sea, but also having for its object the exposure of the underbelly of the Axis, especially Italy, to heavy attack.

speech in the House of Commons, 11 November 1942

1 Something must be done.

popular summary of King Edward VIII's words at the derelict Dowlais Iron and Steel Works, 18 November 1936

These works brought all these people here. Something should be done to get them at work again.

in *Western Mail* 19 November 1936

2 We are the masters now.

from Hartley Shawcross's assertion of Labour's strength after winning the 1945 election, "But," said Alice, "the question is whether you can make a word mean different things." "Not so," said Humpty-Dumpty, "the question is which is to be master. That's all." We are the masters at the moment, and not only at the moment, but for a very long time to come.'

in the House of Commons, 2 April 1946; see below

'The question is,' said Humpty Dumpty, 'which is to be master—that's all.'

Lewis Carroll (1832–98) *Through the Looking-Glass* (1872)

3 We trained hard . . . but it seemed that every time we were beginning to form up into teams we would be reorganized. I was to learn later in life that we tend to meet any new situation by reorganizing; and a wonderful method it can be for creating the illusion of progress while producing confusion, inefficiency, and demoralization.

late 20th century saying, frequently attributed to Petronius Arbiter (d. AD 65), but not found in his works

4 The white heat of technology.

phrase deriving from Harold Wilson's speech

The Britain that is going to be forged in the white heat of this revolution will be no place for restrictive practices or for outdated methods on either side of industry.

speech at the Labour Party Conference, 1 October 1963

5 Why don't you come up and see me sometime?

alteration of Mae West's invitation

Why don't you come up sometime, and see me?

She Done Him Wrong (1933 film)

6 You dirty rat!

associated with James Cagney (1899–1986), but not used by him in any film; in a speech at the American Film Institute banquet, 13 March 1974, Cagney said, 'I never said "Mmm, you dirty rat!"'

Cagney by Cagney (1976)

Modern sayings and slogans

7 Been there, done that, got the T-shirt.

'been there, done that' recorded from 1980s, expanded form from 1990s

8 Burn your bra.

feminist slogan, 1970s

9 Close your eyes and think of England.

said to derive from a 1912 entry in the journal of Lady Hillingdon, but the journal has never been traced

10 Crime doesn't pay.

a slogan of the FBI and the cartoon detective Dick Tracy

11 Daddy, what did you do in the Great War?

daughter to father in First World War recruiting poster

12 [Death is] nature's way of telling you to slow down.

life insurance proverb; in *Newsweek* 25 April 1960

13 A dog is for life, not just for Christmas.

slogan of the National Canine Defence League

14 Do not fold, spindle or mutilate.

instruction on punched cards (1950s, and in differing forms from the 1930s)

15 Don't get mad, get even.

late twentieth century saying

16 The family that prays together stays together.

motto devised by Al Scalpone for the Roman Catholic Family Rosary Crusade, 1947

17 Garbage in, garbage out.

in computing, incorrect or faulty input will always cause poor output; origin of the acronym GIGO

18 Give me a child for the first seven years, and you may do what you like with him afterwards.

attributed as a Jesuit maxim, in *Lean's Collectanea* vol. 3 (1903)

19 If anything can go wrong, it will.

commonly known as Murphy's Law

mid twentieth century saying; said to have been invented by George Nichols in 1949, based on a remark by his colleague Captain E. Murphy

20 If it ain't broke, don't fix it.

Bert Lance in *Nation's Business* May 1977

21 If you can't beat them, join them.

beat is usually replaced by lick in the US

mid twentieth century saying

22 If you pay peanuts, you get monkeys.

mid twentieth century saying

23 If you're not part of the solution, you're part of the problem.

late twentieth century saying

24 I married my husband for life, not for lunch.

origin unknown

25 I'm backing Britain.

slogan coined by workers at the Colt factory, Surbiton, Surrey in 1968, and subsequently used in a national campaign

26 It takes 40 dumb animals to make a fur coat, but only one to wear it.

slogan of an anti-fur campaign poster, 1980s

1 Let's run it up the flagpole and see if anyone salutes it.
recorded as an established advertising expression in the 1960s

2 Life is a sexually transmitted disease.
graffito found on the London Underground, in D. J. Enright (ed.) *The Faber Book of Fevers and Frets* (1989)

3 Make love not war.
student slogan, 1960s

4 *Nil carborundum illegitimi.*
Don't let the bastards grind you down.
cod Latin saying in circulation during the Second World War, though possibly of earlier origin

5 Nostalgia isn't what it used to be.
graffito; taken as title of book by Simone Signoret, 1978

6 The opera ain't over 'til the fat lady sings.
Dan Cook, in *Washington Post* 3 June 1978

7 Pile it high, sell it cheap.
slogan coined by John Cohen, founder of Tesco

8 There's no such thing as a free lunch.
colloquial axiom in US economics from the 1960s, much associated with Milton Friedman; recorded in form 'there ain't no such thing as a free lunch' from 1938, which gave rise to the acronym TANSTAAFL

9 Think globally, act locally.
Friends of the Earth slogan, *c*.1985

10 To err is human but to really foul things up requires a computer.
Farmers' Almanac for 1978 'Capsules of Wisdom'

11 What goes around comes around.
late twentieth century saying

12 What you see is what you get.
a computing expression, from which the acronym wysiwyg *derives*
late twentieth century saying

Newspaper headlines and leaders

13 Believe it or not.
title of syndicated newspaper feature (from 1918), written by Robert L. Ripley

14 Bush Wins It.
original headline in the Miami Herald *for 8 November 2000; changed in final edition to 'It's Not Over Yet'*
in *Daily Telegraph* 9 November 2000

15 Crisis? What crisis?
summarizing James Callaghan's response in an interview at London airport, 'I don't think other people in the world would share the view there is mounting chaos'
headline in *Sun*, 11 January 1979

16 Dewey defeats Truman.
anticipating the result of the Presidential election, which Harry Truman won against expectation
in *Chicago Tribune* 3 November 1948

17 Downing Street's dodgy dossier of 'intelligence' about Iraq.
referring to a briefing document on Iraqi weaponry which was later withdrawn
leading article, *Observer* 9 February 2003

18 Egghead weds hourglass.
on the marriage of Arthur Miller and Marilyn Monroe
headline in *Variety* 1956; attributed

19 The filth and the fury.
following a notorious interview with the Sex Pistols broadcast live on Thames Television
headline in *Daily Mirror*, 2 December 1976

20 45 Minutes from Attack.
Evening Standard 24 September 2002

21 Freddie Starr ate my hamster.
headline in *Sun* 13 March 1986

22 GOTCHA!
on the sinking of the General Belgrano
headline in *Sun* 4 May 1982

23 Go West, young man, go West!
editorial in *Terre Haute* [Indiana] *Express* (1851), by John L. B. Soule

24 Is THIS the most dangerous man in Britain?
headline beside a picture of Tony Blair, attacking his perceived sympathy for the euro
in *Sun* 25 June 1998

25 It *is* a moral issue.
leader following the resignation of John Profumo
in *The Times* 11 June 1963

26 It's that man again . . . ! At the head of a cavalcade of seven black motor cars Hitler swept out of his Berlin Chancellery last night on a mystery journey.
headline in *Daily Express* 2 May 1939; the acronym ITMA became the title of a BBC radio show, from September 1939

27 It's The Sun wot won it.
following the 1992 general election
headline in *Sun* 11 April 1992

28 King's Moll Reno'd in Wolsey's home town.
US newspaper headline on the divorce proceedings of Wallis Simpson (later Duchess of Windsor) in Ipswich
Frances Donaldson *Edward VIII* (1974) ch. 7

29 Sawdust Caesars: Mods v. Rockers battles flare again.
Daily Express 19 May 1964

30 Splendid isolation.
headline in *The Times* 22 January 1896, referring to
In these somewhat troublesome days when the great Mother Empire stands splendidly isolated in Europe.
speech by George Foster, 16 January 1896, in *Official Report of the Debates of the House of Commons of the Dominion of Canada* (1896) vol. 41

31 Sticks nix hick pix.
front-page headline on the lack of enthusiasm for farm dramas among rural populations
in *Variety* 17 July 1935

1 Unless the people—the people everywhere—come forward and petition, ay, thunder for reform.

leader on the Reform Bill, possibly written by Edward Sterling, resulting in the nickname 'The Thunderer'

in *The Times* 29 January 1831; the phrase 'we thundered out' had been used earlier, 11 February 1829

2 Wall St. lays an egg.

crash headline, *Variety* 30 October 1929

3 We shall not pretend that there is nothing in his long career which those who respect and admire him would wish otherwise.

on Edward VII's accession to the throne

in *The Times* 23 January 1901, leading article

4 Who breaks a butterfly on a wheel?

defending Mick Jagger after his arrest for cannabis possession

leader in *The Times* 1 June 1967, written by William Rees-Mogg, and quoting Alexander Pope's 'Who breaks a butterfly upon a wheel?'

5 Whose finger do you want on the trigger?

referring to the atom bomb

headline in *Daily Mirror* 21 September 1951

6 Winter of discontent.

headline in *Sun* 30 April 1979

7 Yes, Virginia, there is a Santa Claus.

replying to a letter from eight-year-old Virginia O'Hanlon

editorial by Francis Pharcellus Church (1839–1906) in New York *Sun*, 21 September 1897

Official advice

8 Careless talk costs lives.

Second World War security slogan (popularly inverted as 'careless lives cost talk')

9 Clunk, click, every trip.

road safety campaign promoting the use of seat-belts, 1971

10 Coughs and sneezes spread diseases. Trap the germs in your handkerchief.

Second World War health slogan (1942)

11 Dig for Victory.

Second World War slogan; see below:

Let 'Dig for Victory' be the motto of every one with a garden and of every able-bodied man and woman capable of digging an allotment in their spare time. Reginald Dorman-Smith radio broadcast, 3 October 1939

12 Don't ask a man to drink and drive.

UK road safety slogan, from 1964

13 Don't die of ignorance.

Aids publicity campaign, 1987

14 Duck and cover.

US advice in the event of a missile attack, *c.*1950; associated particularly with children's cartoon character 'Bert the Turtle'

15 Is your journey *really* necessary?

slogan coined to discourage Civil Servants from going home for Christmas, 1939

16 Just say no.

motto of the Nancy Reagan Drug Abuse Fund, founded 1985

17 Keep Britain tidy.

issued by the Central Office of Information, 1950s

18 Make do and mend.

wartime slogan, 1940s

19 Slip, slop, slap.

sun protection slogan, meaning slip on a T-shirt, slop on some suncream, slap on a hat

Australian health education programme, 1980s

20 Smoking can seriously damage your health.

government health warning now required by British law to be printed on cigarette packets

from early 1970s, in form 'Smoking can damage your health'

21 Stop-look-and-listen.

road safety slogan, current in the US from 1912

22 *Taisez-vous! Méfiez-vous! Les oreilles ennemies vous écoutent.*

Keep your mouth shut! Be on your guard! Enemy ears are listening to you.

official notice in France, 1915

23 Tradition dictates that we have a lawn—but do we really need one? Why not increase the size of your borders or replace lawned areas with paving stones or gravel?

Severn Trent Water 'The Gardener's Water Code' (1996)

Political sayings and slogans

24 All power to the Soviets.

workers in Petrograd, 1917

25 All the way with LBJ.

US Democratic Party campaign slogan, 1960

26 Are you now, or have you ever been, a member of the Communist Party?

from 1947, the question habitually put by the House Un-American Activities Committee (HUAC) to those appearing before it, now particularly associated with the McCarthy period of the 1950s

27 Are you thinking what we're thinking?

Conservative Party, 2005

28 As Maine goes, so goes the nation.

American political saying, *c.*1840

29 Ban the bomb.

US anti-nuclear slogan, adopted by the Campaign for Nuclear Disarmament, 1953 onwards

30 A bayonet is a weapon with a worker at each end.

British pacifist slogan (1940)

31 Better red than dead.

slogan of nuclear disarmament campaigners, late 1950s

32 A bigger bang for a buck.

Charles E. Wilson's defence policy, in *Newsweek* 22 March 1954

33 Black is beautiful.

slogan of American civil rights campaigners, mid-1960s

1 Burn, baby, burn.
Black extremist slogan in use during the Los Angeles riots, August 1965

2 Can't pay, won't pay.
anti-Poll Tax slogan, c.1990

3 *Ein Reich, ein Volk, ein Führer.*
One realm, one people, one leader.
Nazi Party slogan, early 1930s

4 Fair shares for all, is Labour's call.
slogan for the North Battersea by-election, 1946, coined by Douglas Jay
Douglas Jay *Change and Fortune* (1980) ch. 7

5 Fifty-four forty, or fight!
slogan of expansionist Democrats in the US presidential campaign of 1844, in which the Oregon boundary definition was an issue (in 1846 the new Democratic president, James K. Polk, compromised on the 49th parallel with Great Britain)

6 Hey, hey, LBJ, how many kids did you kill today?
anti-Vietnam marching slogan, 1960s

7 I like Ike.
used when General Eisenhower was first seen as a potential presidential nominee
US button badge, 1947; coined by Henry D. Spalding

8 It'll play in Peoria.
catchphrase of the Nixon administration (early 1970s) meaning 'it will be acceptable to middle America', but originating in a standard music hall joke of the 1930s

9 It's morning again in America.
slogan for Ronald Reagan's election campaign, 1984; coined by Hal Riney; in *Newsweek* 6 August 1984

10 It's the economy, stupid.
on a sign put up at the 1992 Clinton presidential campaign headquarters by campaign manager James Carville

11 Keep the bastards honest.
coined by the Australian politician Don Chipp (1925–), on leaving the Liberal Party to form the Australian Democrats

12 *Kraft durch Freude.*
Strength through joy.
German Labour Front slogan, from 1933; coined by Robert Ley

13 Labour isn't working.
on poster showing a long queue outside an unemployment office
Conservative Party slogan 1978–9

14 Labour's double whammy.
Conservative Party election slogan 1992

15 *Liberté! Égalité! Fraternité!*
Freedom! Equality! Brotherhood!
motto of the French Revolution, but of earlier origin
the Club des Cordeliers passed a motion, 30 June 1793, 'that owners should be urged to paint on the front of their houses, in large letters, the words: Unity, indivisibility of the Republic, Liberty, Equality, Fraternity or death';

in *Journal de Paris* no. 182 (from 1795 the words 'or death' were dropped)

16 Life's better with the Conservatives. Don't let Labour ruin it.
Conservative Party election slogan, 1959

17 New Labour, new danger.
Conservative slogan, 1996

18 No surrender!
the defenders of the besieged city of Derry to the Jacobite army of James II, April 1689, adopted as a slogan of Protestant Ulster
Jonathan Bardon *A History of Ulster* (1992)

19 Not in my name.
protesters against the war in Iraq, 2003

20 The personal is political.
1970s feminist slogan, attributed to Carol Hanisch (1945–)

21 Power to the people.
slogan of the Black Panther movement, from c.1968 onwards

22 Save the pound.
slogan for those opposed to the single currency, used particularly in the Conservative campaign for the 2001 British General Election

23 Things can only get better.
Labour campaign slogan, 1997, from the song by Jamie Petrie and Peter Cunnah
Things can only get better.
title of song (1994)

24 Thirteen years of Tory misrule.
unofficial Labour party election slogan, also in the form 'Thirteen wasted years', 1964

25 Three acres and a cow.
regarded as the requirement for self-sufficiency; associated with the radical politician Jesse Collings and his land reform campaign begun in 1885
Jesse Collings in the House of Commons, 26 January 1886, although used earlier by Joseph Chamberlain in a speech at Evesham (in *The Times* 17 November 1885), by which time it was already proverbial

26 Tippecanoe and Tyler, too.
presidential campaign song for William Henry Harrison, 1840
attributed to A. C. Ross (fl. 1840)

27 Votes for women.
adopted when it proved impossible to use a banner with the longer slogan 'Will the Liberal Party Give Votes for Women?' made by Emmeline Pankhurst, Christabel Pankhurst, and Annie Kenney
slogan of the women's suffrage movement, from 13 October 1905; Emmeline Pankhurst *My Own Story* (1914)

28 War will cease when men refuse to fight.
pacifist slogan, from c.1936 (often quoted as, 'Wars will cease . . . ')

29 We shall not be moved.
title of labour and civil rights song (1931) adapted from an earlier gospel hymn

30 We shall overcome.
title of song, originating from before the American Civil War, adapted as a Baptist hymn ('I'll Overcome Some Day', 1901) by C. Albert

Tindley; revived in 1946 as a protest song by black tobacco workers, and in 1963 during the black Civil Rights Campaign

1 Would you buy a used car from this man?
campaign slogan directed against Richard Nixon, 1968

2 Yes it hurt, yes it worked.
Conservative Party slogan, 1996, alluding to John Major's comment as Chancellor, 'If it isn't hurting, it isn't working'

3 Yesterday's men (they failed before!).
Labour Party slogan, referring to the Conservatives, 1970; coined by David Kingsley, Dennis Lyons, and Peter Lovell-Davis

Taglines for films

4 Be afraid. Be very afraid.
The Fly (1986 film), written by David Cronenberg

5 Being the adventures of a young man whose principal interests are rape, ultra-violence and Beethoven.
A Clockwork Orange (1972 film)

6 Garbo talks.
Anna Christie (1930 film), her first talkie

7 He said 'I'll be back!' . . . and he meant it!
Terminator 2: Judgment Day (1991 film)

8 In space no one can hear you scream.
Alien (1979 film)

9 Just when you thought it was safe to go back in the water.
publicity for *Jaws 2* (1978 film)

10 A long time ago in a galaxy far, far away . . .
Star Wars (1977)

11 Love means never having to say you're sorry.
Love Story (1970 film); from the novel (1970) by Erich Segal (1937–)

12 The man you love to hate.
anonymous billing for Erich von Stroheim in the film *The Heart of Humanity* (1918)

13 Mean, Moody and Magnificent!
The Outlaw (1946 film) starring Jane Russell

14 Please don't tell the ending. It's the only one we have.
Psycho (1960 film)

15 Somewhere in the universe, there must be something better than Man.
Planet of the Apes (1968 film)

16 They're young . . . they're in love . . . and they kill people.
Bonnie and Clyde (1967 film)

17 We are not alone.
Close Encounters of the Third Kind (1977 film)

18 Where were you in '62?
American Graffiti (1973 film)

Telegrams

19 AM IN MARKET HARBOROUGH. WHERE OUGHT I TO BE?
sent by G. K. Chesterton to his wife in London
G. K. Chesterton *Autobiography* (1936)

20 BETTER DROWNED THAN DUFFERS IF NOT DUFFERS WONT DROWN.
Arthur Ransome *Swallows and Amazons* (1930)

21 GOOD WORK, MARY. WE ALL KNEW YOU HAD IT IN YOU.
from Dorothy Parker to Mrs Sherwood on the arrival of her baby
Alexander Woollcott *While Rome Burns* (1934) 'Our Mrs Parker'

22 HOW DARE YOU BECOME PRIME MINISTER WHEN I'M AWAY GREAT LOVE CONSTANT THOUGHT VIOLET.
from Violet Bonham Carter (1887–1969) to her father, H. H. Asquith, 7 April 1908
Mark Bonham Carter and Mark Pottle (eds.) *Lantern Slides* (1996)

23 NURSE UNUPBLOWN.
Evelyn Waugh's terse response to the cable request 'Require earliest name life story photograph American nurse upblown Adowa.'
Waugh in Abyssinia (1936)

24 *in response to a telegraphic enquiry,* HOW OLD CARY GRANT?:
OLD CARY GRANT FINE. HOW YOU?
from Cary Grant (1904–86)
R. Schickel *Cary Grant* (1983)

25 STREETS FLOODED. PLEASE ADVISE.
message sent by Robert Benchley on arriving in Venice
R. E. Drennan (ed.) *Wits End* (1973)

26 UNABLE OBTAIN BIDET. SUGGEST HANDSTAND IN SHOWER.
from Billy Wilder to his wife, who had asked him to send her a bidet from Paris
Leslie Halliwell *Filmgoer's Book of Quotes* (1973)

27 WELCOME STORIES EX-CHICAGO NOT UNDULY EMPHASISING CRIME.
authorizing the young Times *correspondent in America, Claud Cockburn, to report a murder in Al Capone's Chicago*
Claud Cockburn *In Time of Trouble* (1956)

Oxford Paperback Reference

The Concise Oxford Dictionary of Quotations
Edited by Elizabeth Knowles

Based on the highly acclaimed *Oxford Dictionary of Quotations*, this paperback edition maintains its extensive coverage of literary and historical quotations, and contains completely up-to-date material. A fascinating read and an essential reference tool.

The Oxford Dictionary of Humorous Quotations
Edited by Ned Sherrin

From the sharply witty to the downright hilarious, this sparkling collection will appeal to all senses of humour.

Quotations by Subject
Edited by Susan Ratcliffe

A collection of over 7,000 quotations, arranged thematically for easy look-up. Covers an enormous range of nearly 600 themes from 'The Internet' to 'Parliament'.

The Concise Oxford Dictionary of Phrase and Fable
Edited by Elizabeth Knowles

Provides a wealth of fascinating and informative detail for over 10,000 phrases and allusions used in English today. Find out about anything from the 'Trojan horse' to 'ground zero'.

OXFORD

Oxford Paperback Reference

The Concise Oxford Companion to English Literature
Margaret Drabble and Jenny Stringer

Based on the best-selling *Oxford Companion to English Literature*, this is an indispensable guide to all aspects of English literature.

Review of the parent volume
'a magisterial and monumental achievement'

Literary Review

The Concise Oxford Companion to Irish Literature
Robert Welch

From the ogam alphabet developed in the 4th century to Roddy Doyle, this is a comprehensive guide to writers, works, topics, folklore, and historical and cultural events.

Review of the parent volume
'Heroic volume ... It surpasses previous exercises of similar nature in the richness of its detail and the ecumenism of its approach.'

Times Literary Supplement

A Dictionary of Shakespeare
Stanley Wells

Compiled by one of the best-known international authorities on the playwright's works, this dictionary offers up-to-date information on all aspects of Shakespeare, both in his own time and in later ages.

OXFORD